SEVENTH EDITION

INTRODUCTION TO PSYCHOLOGY

SEVENTH EDITION

INTRODUCTION TO

PSYCHOLOGY

ERNEST R. HILGARD
Stanford University

RITA L. ATKINSON

RICHARD C. ATKINSON
Stanford University

Harcourt Brace Jovanovich, Inc.
New York   San Diego   Chicago   San Francisco   Atlanta

INTRODUCTION TO PSYCHOLOGY, SEVENTH EDITION
Hilgard/Atkinson/Atkinson

ISBN: 0-15-543668-6
Library of Congress Catalog Card Number: 78-71165

Printed in the United States of America

Acknowledgments and Copyrights

Cover: details from Morris Louis, *Aleph Series I:* 1960,
Private Collection. Photograph courtesy André Emmerich Gallery.
Part and chapter opening art: Elizabeth Wiener
New technical art: Craven Graphics

Text
page 172 Benson, H., Kotch, J. B., Crasweller, K. D., and Greenwood, M. M., "Historical and clinical considerations of the relaxation response," *American scientist* 65 (July 1977): 441–43. **209** Köhler, W., *The mentality of apes* Reprinted by permission of Routledge & Kegan Paul, Ltd. **501–02** Snyder, W. U., and others, *Casebook of nondirective counseling* Copyright © 1947 by Houghton Mifflin Co. Reprinted by permission of Houghton Mifflin Co. **532** Luchins, A., "Primacy-recency in impression formation," in C. I. Hovland (ed.), *The order of presentation in persuasion.* New Haven, Conn.: Yale University Press, 1957, pp. 34–35.

continued on page 639, which constitutes a continuation of the copyright page

Preface

Students take introductory psychology for a variety of reasons, but few of them are motivated primarily by the desire to know what psychologists are doing. They want to know what is relevant to their lives, their futures, and the problems confronting society. They want the subject matter to be pertinent to their own interests as well as to pressing social issues that require intelligent decisions. As in previous editions, we have attempted to write for the student, but in a manner that will satisfy the critical psychologist as well. Our goal has been to be responsive to student interests without sacrificing scientific rigor or scholarship.

To accomplish this goal, we have relied on consultation and feedback from three sources—students, instructors, and specialists in various areas of psychology. To make certain our subject matter was readily comprehensible to students and pertinent to the human issues with which they are concerned, we asked a number of students to comment on each section of the text in terms of interest value, clarity, and level of difficulty. We found their responses helpful and enlightening.

Several college instructors who specialize in teaching the introductory course read the manuscript as it evolved, commenting on its suitability for their students and on any problems they foresaw in teaching the material to beginning psychology students. We also benefited greatly from the many detailed comments and suggestions we received from users of the sixth edition.

To keep abreast of developments in psychological theory and research, we asked experts in the appropriate area to review each chapter. Typically, three or more specialists, outstanding in their field, commented on each chapter in the early stages of revision and in its final form. By such extensive consultation we sought to ensure that the material presented in this book represents accurately the current state of knowledge in psychology.

Users of the sixth edition will recognize that the organization of the book remains essentially the same, with two exceptions. The central elements in the chapter on optimizing learning have been updated and integrated into Chapter 7, "Conditioning and Learning," and Chapter 8, "Remembering and Forgetting." The order of the two chapters in Part Six, "Personality and Individuality," has been reversed, so that intelligence and ability testing are now treated before personality and personality assessment. Although the overall organization is largely unchanged, each chapter has been carefully revised, and a number of them are entirely new.

The idea that psychological problems can be studied from different viewpoints, explicitly introduced in the last edition, has been further elaborated in this edition. Chapter 1 introduces five approaches to the study of psychology—neurobiological, behavioral, cognitive, psychoanalytic, and phenomenological/humanistic. These approaches reappear in later chapters whenever a particular topic can be examined from several viewpoints. A consideration of alternative approaches provides a cohesive framework for examining a wide array of different phenomena and the theories that have been proposed to explain them.

The chapters written by Professor Daryl J. Bem of Cornell University for the last edition—"Social Psychology" and "Psychology and Society"—received high praise for their interest and clarity. His revisions of these chapters for this edition include provocative and lively new material on such topics as social influence, race prejudice, the mass media, and environmental psychology.

Professor Edward E. Smith of Stanford University has contributed two new chapters in his area of expertise. Chapter 8, "Remembering and Forgetting," is a remarkably well integrated presentation of current theories and research on the three stages of memory—encoding, storage, and retrieval—as they relate to both short- and long-term memory. It also includes material on improving memory, as well as a section on the way we use inferences, stereotypes, and schemata to "construct" memories of complex events. Chapter 9, "Language and Thought," provides a clear and interesting account of the way people form concepts and use them to communicate and to solve problems.

Professors Bem and Smith have had outstanding research careers and are both known as brilliant teachers of the introductory psychology course. We are extremely pleased that they are contributing to this book.

We have tried to cover contemporary psychology in a textbook of reasonable length. But each instructor must design his or her course according to course objectives, type of students, and available time. Even if not all chapters are assigned, students will at least have them for reference. For a short course we believe that it is better to treat a reduced number of chapters fully than to attempt to cover the entire text. Two possible 14-chapter courses are proposed below, one for a course with an experimental-biological emphasis, the other for a course with a personal-social emphasis. These outlines only illustrate possible combinations.

	EXPERIMENTAL-BIOLOGICAL EMPHASIS	PERSONAL-SOCIAL EMPHASIS	CHAPTER
Part One	1	1	The Nature of Psychology
Part Two	2	—	Biological Basis of Behavior
	3	3	Psychological Development
Part Three	4	—	Sensory Processes
	5	5	Perception
	6	6	Consciousness and Control
Part Four	7	7	Conditioning and Learning
	8	8	Remembering and Forgetting
	9	—	Language and Thought
Part Five	10	—	Basic Drives and Motives
	—	11	Human Motivation and Emotion
Part Six	12	12	Mental Abilities and Their Measurement

The order of topics can be changed. For example, some instructors feel that student interest can be better aroused by beginning the course with material on personality, abnormal, and social psychology, leaving more difficult topics such as learning, perception, and physiological psychology until later. The authors have experimented with such a scheme in their own teaching and have not found it satisfactory. Beginning with the more personally relevant and intriguing topics may get the course off to a fast start, but it often gives the students a distorted idea of what psychology is about. In addition, many students are ill prepared for, and disgruntled by, the more difficult material when it is sprung on them later in the course. Our preferred approach is to cover the chapter on developmental psychology early in the course, thereby exposing the student to a range of provocative topics in psychology. Then we turn to some of the more technical areas like perception, learning, and motivation, and end the course with personality, abnormal, and social psychology. But each instructor must choose the order of topics he or she finds congenial; the book has been written so that a variety of arrangements is possible.

The many decisions that must be made in teaching the introductory psychology course are skillfully discussed by Professor John C. Ruch of Mills College in the *Instructor's Handbook*. Instructors are urged to obtain a copy of this handbook, which provides valuable information for both the beginning and the experienced instructor, as well as for teaching assistants. As further instructional aids, we have again provided a thoroughly revised *Study Guide with Programmed Units and Learning Objectives*, a *Mastery Study Guide*, which can be used as a self-paced course, a *Mastery Instructor's Guide*, and a new, expanded set of test items.

Our debts of gratitude to those who have helped with the preparation of the book continue to mount. Among the individuals acknowledged on pages viii–ix, we owe special thanks to John C. Ruch, whose advice at every stage of this revision was invaluable.

We are also indebted to Carolyn Young for the dedication with which she undertook the monumental task of typing the manuscript, compiling the references, and checking for errors. Her skill at all of these tasks is unsurpassed. We are thankful too for the patience, skill, and efficiency of our publisher's staff.

Richard Atkinson is currently on leave of absence from Stanford University, serving as Director of the National Science Foundation, Washington, D.C. Since the responsibilities of this position required a total commitment of his time and energy, he did not participate in the preparation of the current edition. He plans to return to research and teaching when his term as Director of the Foundation is completed and to contribute to future revisions of the book.

Rita L. Atkinson
Ernest R. Hilgard

Acknowledgments

Over the years we have been helped immeasurably by countless people who have shared with us their scholarly and pedagogical expertise. It is impossible to thank them all individually, but they have our continuing gratitude.

A number of professors teaching introductory psychology offered us invaluable, detailed, chapter-by-chapter comments on the sixth edition as inputs for our planning of the seventh edition:

H. S. Bertilson, Concordia College, Moorhead, Minnesota

Nancy S. Breland, Trenton State College

Charles I. Brooks, King's College

Benjamin Burack, Roosevelt University

Thomas Burgess, Franklin College

Gerald E. Burson, Northern Oklahoma College

David Campbell, University of Kansas

Bernard Casella, Bergen Community College

Frank Costin, University of Illinois

Norman L. Culbertson, Yakima Valley College

Michael E. Doherty, Bowling Green State University

David C. Edwards, Iowa State University

Louis L. Elloie, Jr., San Diego Mesa College

Helen L. Field, Holyoke Community College

W. B. Ghiselli, University of Missouri—Kansas City

R. W. Giroux, Tacoma Community College

David C. Glossner, Monroe Community College

Jon Gosser, Delta College

Gordon Hammerle, Adrian College

David P. Hanson, James Madison University

Margaret L. Healey, University of North Carolina at Chapel Hill

James T. Henderson, Wingate College

Annette R. Hiedemann, West Virginia Wesleyan College

Winfred F. Hill, Northwestern University

Sam Hollingsworth, West Virginia Wesleyan College

Floyd S. Holm, Southern Utah State College

Joan R. Humphries, Miami-Dade Community College, North Campus

D. Robert Jacobs, Indiana University of Pennsylvania

Lawrence L. Jesky, Seton Hill College

David A. Johnson, Sweet Briar College

James J. Johnston, University of Wisconsin—Stevens Point

Norman William Katz, University of New Mexico

B. L. Kintz, Western Washington State College

Allan B. Laidlaw, Dixie College

Tim Lehmann, Valencia Community College

Velma Elaine Marshburn, Prairie State College

Glen Martin, Patrick Henry Community College

Robert C. Mathews, Louisiana State University

John Stewart McGovern, St. Lawrence University

Fred McKinney, University of Missouri—Columbia

Richard H. McKinstry, Pennsylvania State University: Hazleton Campus

Sister Maurice McManama, Seton Hill College

Ronald W. Mosher, Anchorage Community College

Robert Numan, University of Santa Clara

Howard B. Orenstein, Western Maryland College

Richard P. Pentz, Indian River Community College

Gregory Pezzetti, Chapman College
Peggy Pittas, Lynchburg College
Carol Raye, Barnard College
Duane Reeder, Glendale Community
College
Karen Salley, Lycoming College
David J. Schneider, University of Texas
at San Antonio
Frederick W. Schwartz, East Los Angeles
College
William G. Siemens, Anchorage
Community College
Lora S. Simon, Holyoke Community
College
Audrey M. Skaife, University of
Wisconsin—Oshkosh
Kay H. Smith, Brigham Young University
George R. Soika, University of
Wisconsin—Oshkosh

John W. Somervill, University of
Northern Iowa
Sibyl M. Strain, Los Angeles Southwest
College
Charles T. Sullivan, Ursinus College
Paul A. Susen, Morris Harvey College
Elizabeth Decker Tanke, University of
Santa Clara
Jack G. Thompson, Centre College of
Kentucky
Allen A. Turnbull, Carleton University
Jerry R. Venn, Mary Baldwin College
Robert T. Wiater, Bergen Community
College
D. Louis Wood, University of Arkansas
at Little Rock
M. L. Zanich, Indiana University of
Pennsylvania: Armstrong County
Rudolph L. Zlody, Holy Cross College

Professors Ruth Cline (Los Angeles Valley College), Ronald H. Forgus (Lake Forest College), Ruth Lyell (San Jose State University), Eugene Raxten (Los Angeles Valley College), and Edward E. Smith (Stanford University) have our renewed thanks for their advice on the previous edition.

Critical post-publication reviews of sixth edition chapters or of revised chapters (or both) were generously provided by the following people:

Irwin Altman, University of Utah
John Altrocchi, University of Nevada:
Reno
Richard D. Ashmore, Rutgers University
—Livingston College
Joan S. Baizer, School of Medicine, State
University of New York at Buffalo
Allen E. Bergin, Brigham Young
University
Ellen Berscheid, University of Minnesota
Randolph Blake, Northwestern University
Thomas J. Bouchard, Jr., University of
Minnesota
Robert M. Boynton, University of
California, San Diego
Isidor Chein, New York University
Eve V. Clark, Stanford University
Herbert H. Clark, Stanford University
Charles Clifton, University of
Massachusetts
Robert Crowder, Yale University
Richard J. Davidson, State University of
New York at Purchase
Richard T. Day, Manchester Community
College
Jerome E. Doppelt, Psychological
Corporation
Ebbe B. Ebbesen, University of
California, San Diego
Norman S. Endler, York University
Mitchell Glickstein, Brown University
Charles G. Gross, Princeton University
Willard W. Hartup, University of
Minnesota
William Hazelett, University of Pittsburgh
Julian Hochberg, Columbia University

Robert R. Holt, New York University
Lloyd Kaufman, New York University
Ellen M. Markman, Stanford University
Gerald M. Murch, Portland State
University
Barbara M. Newman, Ohio State
University
Philip R. Newman
Terry Powley, Yale University
Howard Rachlin, State University of New
York at Stony Brook
Judith Rodin, Yale University
Nicholas L. Rohrman, Colby College
John C. Ruch, Mills College
Carol M. Santa, Rutgers University—
Douglass College
Sandra Scarr, Yale University
Barry Schwartz, Swarthmore College
Jerome L. Singer, Yale University
Arlene Skolnick, University of California,
Berkeley
Richard E. Snow, Stanford University
Solomon H. Snyder, The Johns Hopkins
School of Medicine
J. E. R. Staddon, Duke University
Albert J. Stunkard, University of
Pennsylvania
Chris Swoyer, University of Oklahoma
Irving B. Weiner, Case Western Reserve
University
Jerry S. Wiggins, University of British
Columbia
Lauren Wispé, University of Oklahoma
Philip B. Young, Towson State
University
Mark Zanna, University of Waterloo

Contents

2 | PART ONE
Psychology as a
Scientific and
Humanistic Endeavor

28 | PART TWO
Biological and
Developmental
Processes

**PART FIVE
Motivation and
Emotion**

**PART SIX
Personality and
Individuality**

PART ONE

Psychology as a Scientific and Humanistic Endeavor

1 The Nature of Psychology

1
The Nature
of Psychology

P sychology touches almost every aspect of our lives. As society has
become more complex, psychology has assumed an increasingly important role in solving human problems. Psychologists are concerned with
an astonishing variety of problems. Some are of broad concern. What child-
rearing methods produce happy and effective adults? How can mental illness be
prevented? What can be done to eliminate race prejudice? What family and
social conditions contribute to alienation, aggression, and crime?

Other problems are more specific. What is the best treatment for drug
addiction or obesity? How should a survey be designed and administered to
measure public opinion accurately? How can people be persuaded to give up
smoking? What is the most effective method for teaching children to read?
How should the dials on the instrument panel of a jet aircraft be arranged to
minimize perceptual errors? Can a blind person be given artificial sight by
electrical stimulation of small wires implanted in the brain? Psychologists are
working on these and many other problems.

Psychology also affects our lives through its influence on laws and public
policy. Laws concerning discrimination, capital punishment, pornography,
sexual behavior, and the conditions under which individuals may be held legally
responsible for their actions are influenced by psychological theories of human
nature. For example, laws pertaining to sexual deviancy have changed markedly in the past 25 years as research has shown that many sexual acts, previously classed as perversions, are quite "normal" in the sense that most people
engage in them.

The effect of TV violence on children is of concern to parents and psychologists. Only after studies provided evidence of the harmful effects of such
programs has it been possible to modify TV programming policies. More brutal
TV fare is gradually being replaced with shows like *Sesame Street* and *The
Electric Company,* which represent concerted efforts by psychologists and
educators to make learning interesting, fun, and effective.

Because psychology affects so many aspects of our lives it is important,
even for those who do not intend to specialize in the field, to know something
about its basic facts and research methods. An introductory course in psychology should give you a better understanding of why people behave as they
do and should provide insights into your own attitudes and reactions. It should
also help you evaluate the many claims made in the name of psychology.
Headlines like the following appear every day in the newspapers:

Experiences during infancy determine adult intelligence
New drug discovered to improve memory
Anxiety controlled by self-regulation of brain waves
Proof of mental telepathy found
Psychologist devises method for curing impotency
Violent crimes related to defective genes
Emotional stability and family size closely related
Homosexuality linked to parental attitudes

How can you judge the validity of such claims? In part, by knowing what psychological facts have been firmly established and by being familiar with the kind of evidence necessary to give credence to a new "discovery." This book reviews the current state of knowledge in psychology. It also examines the nature of research—how a psychologist formulates a hypothesis and devises methods to prove or disprove it.

Psychology is relatively young compared to other scientific disciplines, and recent years have seen a virtual explosion in psychological research. As a result, psychological theories and concepts have been continuously evolving and changing. For this reason, it is difficult to give a precise definition of psychology. Basically, psychologists are interested in finding out "why people act as they do." But there are different ways of explaining human actions. Before we provide a formal definition of psychology, it will be useful to consider alternative approaches to explaining psychological phenomena.

Conceptual Approaches to Psychology

Any action a person takes can be explained from several different points of view. Suppose, for example, you walk across the street. This act can be described in terms of the firing of the nerves that activate the muscles that move the legs that transport you across the street. It can also be described without reference to anything within the body: the green light is a stimulus to which you respond by crossing the street. Or your action might be explained in terms of its ultimate purpose or goal: you plan to visit a friend, and crossing the street is one of many acts involved in carrying out the plan.

Just as there are different ways of describing such a simple act as crossing the street, there are also different approaches to psychology. The following discussion describes five approaches to psychology. Other schemes or categories are possible, but the ones presented here provide an insight into the major conceptions of modern psychology. Because these diverse viewpoints will appear repeatedly throughout the book, we will provide only a brief description of some main points.

One should bear in mind that these approaches are not mutually exclusive; rather, they tend to focus on different aspects of a complex problem. There is no "right" or "wrong" approach to the study of human behavior. Most psychologists take an eclectic approach, using a synthesis of several viewpoints in explaining different psychological phenomena.

Neurobiological Approach

The human brain, with its 12 billion nerve cells and almost infinite number of interconnections and pathways, may well be the most complex structure in the

Fig. 1-1 Social behavior controlled by brain stimulation
Electrodes surgically implanted in the brain of these chimpanzees can be stimulated by remote radio control. Depending on how the animals' brains are stimulated, the experimenter can make one dominant and the other submissive in their social interactions.

universe. In principle, all psychological events are represented in some manner by the activity of the brain and nervous system in conjunction with the other body systems. One approach to the study of human beings attempts to relate their actions to events taking place inside the body, particularly within the brain and nervous system. This approach seeks to specify the neurobiological processes that underlie behavior and mental events. For example, a psychologist studying learning from the neurobiological approach is interested in the changes that take place in the nervous system as the result of learning a new task. Visual perception can be studied by recording the activity of nerve cells in the brain as the eye is exposed to simple patterns of lines.

Recent discoveries have made it dramatically clear that there is an intimate relationship between brain activity and behavior and experience. Emotional reactions, such as fear and rage, have been produced in animals and humans by mild electrical stimulation of specific areas deep in the brain (see Figure 1-1). Electrical stimulation of certain areas in the human brain will produce sensations of pleasure and pain and even vivid memories of past events (see Figure 1-2).

Ultimately, it may be possible to specify the neurobiological mechanisms underlying even the most complex human actions. However, a comprehensive neurobiological theory of behavior is at present only a remote possibility.

Because of the complexity of the brain and the fact that live human brains are seldom available for study, tremendous gaps exist in our knowledge of neural functioning. A psychological conception of ourselves based solely on neurobiology would be inadequate indeed. For this reason, other methods are used to investigate psychological phenomena. In many instances, it is more practical to study antecedent conditions and their consequences without worrying about what goes on inside the organism.

Behavioral Approach

A person eats breakfast, rides a bicycle, talks, blushes, laughs, and cries. All these are forms of *behavior*, those activities of an organism that can be observed. With the behavioral approach, a psychologist studies individuals by looking at their *behavior* rather than at their internal workings. The view that behavior should be the sole subject matter of psychology was first advanced by the American psychologist John B. Watson in the early 1900s. Before that, psychology had been defined as the study of mental experiences or activities, and its data were largely self-observations in the form of *introspection*. Introspection refers to a very careful observing and recording of one's own perceptions and feelings. The early psychologists trained themselves to analyze their own reactions in minute detail, hoping to unravel the mysteries of the mind. Watson felt that introspection was a futile approach. He argued that if psychology were to be a science, its data must be observable and measurable. Only you can observe your perceptions and feelings, but someone else can observe your actions. Watson maintained that only by studying what people do—their behavior—is an objective science of psychology possible.

Behaviorism, as Watson's position came to be called, helped shape the course of psychology during the first half of this century, and its outgrowth, stimulus-response psychology, is still influential in America, particularly because of the work of Harvard psychologist B. F. Skinner. Stimulus-response psychology (or S-R psychology for short) studies the stimuli that elicit behavioral responses, the rewards and punishments that maintain these responses, and the modifications in behavior obtained by changing the patterns of rewards

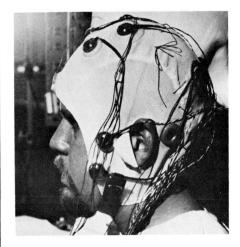

Fig. 1-2 A brain wired for pleasure
Microelectrodes implanted in specific areas deep in the brain of this young man produce a sensation of pleasure when stimulated by mild current. He had previously been driven to the brink of suicide by spells of deep depression. When the wired cap is attached to the microelectrodes, the man can produce pleasurable sensations by pressing a button on a control box. Brain stimulation studies with microelectrodes in animals are helping psychologists understand emotion-producing centers of the brain. Diagnostic procedures with humans, such as the one depicted here, are employed only in extreme cases, when other methods have failed to relieve suffering.

John B. Watson

B. F. Skinner

and punishments. Stimulus-response psychology is *not* concerned with what goes on inside the organism; for this reason it has been called the "black box" approach. S-R psychologists maintain that although the brain and nervous system carry on activities that the psychologist cannot see (inside the black box), a science of psychology can be based strictly on what goes into the box and what comes out, without worrying about what takes place inside. Thus, a theory of learning can be developed by observing how learned behavior varies with environmental conditions—for example, what stimulus conditions and patterns of reward and punishment lead to the fastest learning with the fewest errors. The theory need not specify the changes that learning produces in the nervous system in order to be valuable. In science and engineering, such an approach to the study of mechanical or biological systems is sometimes referred to as an *input-output analysis*.

A strict S-R approach does not consider the individual's *conscious experiences.* Conscious experiences are simply those events the experiencing person is fully aware of. You may be aware of the various thoughts and hypotheses that go through your mind as you solve a difficult problem. You know what it feels like to be angry or frightened or excited. An observer may judge from your actions the kind of emotion you are experiencing, but the conscious process —the actual awareness of the emotion—is yours alone. A psychologist can record what a person *says* about his or her conscious experiences (the verbal report) and from this objective data can make *inferences* about the person's mental activity. But, by and large, S-R psychologists have not chosen to study the mental processes that intervene between the stimulus and the observable response.

Today, few psychologists would regard themselves as strict behaviorists. Nevertheless, as we shall see, several important modern developments—such as social learning theory—have evolved from the earlier work in behavioral psychology.

Cognitive Approach

Cognitive psychologists argue that we are not merely passive receptors of stimuli; the mind actively processes the information it receives and transforms it into new forms and categories (see Figure 1-3). What you are looking at on this page is an arrangement of ink particles. At least, that is the physical stimulus. But the sensory input to the visual system is a pattern of light rays reflected from the page to the eye. These inputs initiate neural processes that transmit information to the brain and eventually result in seeing, reading, and (perhaps) remembering. Numerous transformations occur between the stimulus and your experience of seeing and reading. These involve not only transformations of the light rays into some kind of visual image, but also processes that compare that image with others stored in memory. (What if you had never seen a book or the printed word before? Your response to the stimulus, which is the array of ink particles that forms the words on this page, would be quite different. What you perceive depends on past experience.)

Cognition refers to those mental processes that transform the sensory input in various ways, code it, store it in memory, and retrieve it for later use. Perception, imagery, problem solving, remembering, and thinking are terms that describe hypothetical stages of cognition. These are all stages that can intervene between a stimulus and a response. As we shall see, one can theorize about these stages and how they work without resorting to neurobiological explanations (Neisser, 1976).[1]

The cognitive approach to the study of psychology developed partly in reaction to the narrowness of the S-R view. To conceive of human actions solely in terms of stimulus input and response output may be adequate for the study of very simple forms of behavior, but this approach neglects too many interesting areas of human functioning. People can think, plan, make decisions on the basis of remembered information, and selectively choose among those environmental stimuli that require attention.

Behaviorism rejected the subjective study of "mental life" in order to make psychology a science. It provided a valuable service by making psychologists aware of the need for objectivity and measurement. Cognitive psychology attempts to investigate internal mental processes, but—as later chapters will show—in an objective and scientific manner.

An analogy has sometimes been made between a strict S-R psychology and a telephone switchboard; the stimulus goes in and, after a series of cross connections and circuits through the brain, the response comes out. Cognitive psychology can be considered analogous to a modern computer—or what in its most general sense is now called an "information processing system." Incoming information is processed in various ways—selected, compared and combined with other information already in memory, transformed, rearranged, and so on. The response output depends on the nature of these internal processes and their state at that moment in time.

Kenneth Craik, a British psychologist and one of the early advocates of cognitive psychology, proposed that the brain is like a computer capable of modeling or paralleling external events. "If," he said, "the organism carries a 'small-scale model' of external reality and of its own possible actions within its head, it is able to try out various alternatives, conclude which is the best of them, react to future situations before they arise, utilize the knowledge of past events in dealing with the future, and in every way to react in a much fuller, safer and more competent manner to the emergencies which face it" (Craik, 1952). The notion of a "mental model of reality" is central to a cognitive approach to psychology.

Psychoanalytic Approach

The psychoanalytic conception of human behavior was developed by Sigmund Freud in Europe at about the same time that behaviorism was evolving in the United States. Unlike the ideas discussed thus far, psychoanalytic concepts are based on extensive case studies of individual patients rather than on experimental studies. Psychoanalytic ideas have had a profound influence on psychological thinking. The basic assumption of Freud's theory is that much of our behavior stems from processes that are unconscious. By *unconscious processes* Freud meant thoughts, fears, and wishes a person is unaware of, but which still influence behavior. He believed that many of the impulses that are forbidden or punished by parents and society during childhood are derived from innate instincts. Because these impulses are innate, they exert a pervasive influence that must be dealt with in some manner. Forbidding them merely drives them out of awareness into the unconscious, where they remain to affect

[1]Throughout this book the reader will find references, cited by author and date, that document or expand the statements made here. Detailed publishing information on these studies appears in the reference list at the end of the book. The reference list also serves as an index to the pages on which the citations appear.

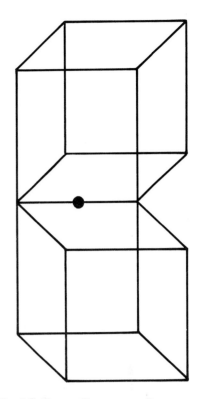

Fig. 1-3 Perception as an active process
We continually extract patterns from objects we see, trying to match them with something meaningful. Stare at the dot in the center between the cubes to establish for yourself the fluctuating nature of perception. Your brain performs all sorts of transformations, seeking out the different patterns inherent in the cubes.

Sigmund Freud

behavior. According to Freud, unconscious impulses find expression in dreams, slips of speech, mannerisms, and symptoms of neurotic illness, as well as through such socially approved behavior as artistic, literary, or scientific activity.

Most psychologists do not completely accept Freud's view of the unconscious. They would probably agree that individuals are not fully aware of some aspects of their personality. But they prefer to speak of degrees of awareness rather than assume that a sharp distinction exists between conscious and unconscious thoughts.

Freud's theories of personality and the psychoanalytic method for treating mental illness will be discussed in later chapters. At this point we will note only that Freud believed that all of our actions have a cause, but the cause is often some unconscious motive rather than the rational reason we may give for our behavior. Freud's view of human nature was essentially negative. We are driven by the same basic instincts as animals (primarily sex and aggression) and are continually struggling against a society that stresses the control of these impulses. Because Freud believed that aggression was a basic instinct, he was pessimistic about the possibility of people ever living together peacefully.

Phenomenological or Humanistic Approach

The phenomenological approach focuses on *subjective experience.* It is concerned with the individual's own perception and interpretation of events—the individual's *phenomenology.* This approach seeks to understand events, or phenomena, as they are experienced by the individual and to do so without imposing any preconceptions or theoretical ideas. Phenomenological psychologists believe that we can learn more about human nature by studying people's perceptions of themselves and of their world than we can by observing their actions. Two people might behave quite differently in response to the same situation; only by asking how each interprets the situation can we fully understand their behavior.

To some extent this approach represents a reaction against the "mechanistic" nature of both behaviorism and psychoanalysis. Rather then viewing people as controlled by external stimuli or by unconscious instincts, phenomenological psychologists prefer to believe that we are responsible for our actions. We are not "acted on" by forces outside our control, but are "actors" capable of controlling our own destiny. The issue here is one of *determinism* versus *free will.* The other approaches we have discussed emphasize the scientific method; they attempt to identify the relevant psychological variables and use them to predict and control behavior. Phenomenological psychologists, in contrast, are not concerned with prediction and control. Their emphasis is on understanding the individual's inner life and experiences. They believe that, although animal behavior may be predictable and under environmental control, human behavior depends primarily on how the individual perceives the world in general and the immediate situation in particular.

Some phenomenological theories are also called *humanistic,* because they emphasize those qualities that distinguish people from animals—primarily their free will and their drive toward *self-actualization.* According to humanistic theories, an individual's main motivational force is a tendency toward growth and self-actualization. Each of us has a basic need to develop our potential to the fullest, to progress beyond where we are now. Although we may be blocked by all kinds of environmental and cultural obstacles, our natural tendency is toward actualization of our potential.

With its emphasis on developing one's potential, humanistic psychology has been closely associated with encounter groups and various types of "consciousness-expanding" and mystical experiences. It is more aligned with literature and the humanities than with science. In fact, some humanists would even reject scientific psychology, claiming that its methods can contribute nothing worthwhile to an understanding of human nature.

As a warning that psychology needs to focus its attention on solving problems relevant to human welfare rather than studying isolated bits of behavior in the laboratory, the humanistic view makes a valuable point. But to assume that the difficult problems in today's highly complicated society can be solved by discarding all that we have learned about the scientific methods of investigation is fallacious indeed. To quote one psychologist concerned with this issue, "We can no more afford a psychology that is humanistic at the expense of being scientific than we can afford one that is 'scientific' at the expense of human relevance" (Smith, 1973).

Application of Different Conceptions

The details of each of these different psychological conceptions will become clearer as we encounter them in subsequent chapters. Any given area of study in psychology may be approached from several viewpoints. For example, in studying aggression, the physiological psychologist would be interested in investigating the brain mechanisms responsible for such behavior. As we shall see in Chapter 11, aggressive behavior in animals has been provoked and controlled by electrical and chemical stimulation of specific areas deep in the brain. An S-R psychologist might be interested in determining the kinds of learning experiences that make one person more aggressive than another. He or she might also study the specific stimuli that provoke hostile acts in a particular situation. A cognitive psychologist might focus on how individuals perceive certain events (in terms of their anger-arousing characteristics) and how these perceptions can be modified by providing the person with different types of information. A psychoanalyst might want to find out what childhood experiences foster the control of aggression or its channeling into socially

Fig. 1-4 Viewpoints in psychology
The analysis of psychological phenomena can be approached from several viewpoints. Each offers a somewhat different explanation of why individuals act as they do, and each makes a contribution to our conception of the total person. The Greek letter psi, ψ, is sometimes used as an abbreviation for psychology.

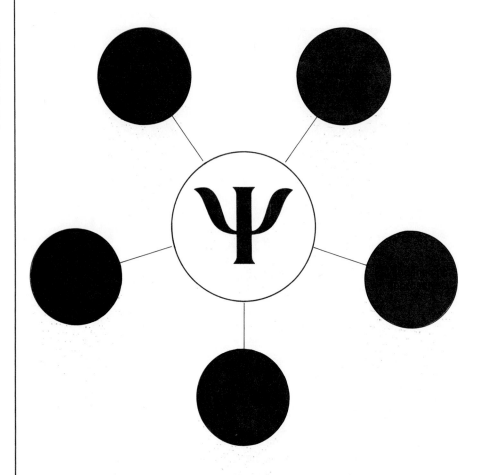

acceptable forms. The humanistic psychologist might focus on those aspects of society that promote aggression by blocking the individual's progress toward self-actualization.

Each approach suggests a somewhat different way to modify or change an individual's behavior. For example, the neurobiologist would look for a drug or some other biological means, such as surgery, for controlling aggression. The behaviorist would try to modify the environmental conditions to provide new learning experiences that reward nonaggressive types of behavior. Cognitive psychologists would use an approach similar to that of the behaviorists, although they might focus more on the individual's perceptions and thought processes in anger-arousing situations. The psychoanalyst might probe the individual's unconscious to discover why the hostility is directed toward certain people or situations and then try to redirect it into more acceptable channels. The humanistic psychologist would probably be concerned with changing society's priorities to place more emphasis on improving interpersonal relationships and providing conditions that promote the development of our potential for constructive and cooperative actions.

In making these distinctions we have probably overstated the case. While some psychologists might consider themselves strict behaviorists and others might hold a firm psychoanalytic view of human nature, many are fairly eclectic. They feel free to select from several approaches the concepts that seem most appropriate for the problem with which they are working. Put another way, all of these approaches have something important to say about human nature, and few psychologists would insist that only one of them contains the "whole truth."

Developmental and Interactive Explanations of Behavior

We have discussed five conceptual approaches to the study of psychology. Regardless of the particular approach, however, two modes of explanation will recur as we look at various topics throughout the book. One of them is *developmental;* the other, *interactive.* A developmental explanation stresses the historical roots of present behavior; it focuses on the individual's genetic endowment, cultural environment, and past learning experiences. An interactive explanation deals with the current influences acting on the individual to arouse or control behavior; these include motives and needs that are currently active, the stimuli that are perceived, and the possibilities for action that are available.

Suppose for example, you ask why Greg started a fist fight with a classmate. A developmental explanation of this behavior might include facts such as the following: his inherited size and strength made it easy for him as a toddler to get his way by aggressive actions; his parents never punished him for fighting; the classmate unconsciously reminds Greg of his own older

*Critical discussions are introduced from time to time to point up controversial issues or to treat a topic in more detail. They may be omitted at the discretion of the instructor.

brother with whom he has a long-standing rivalry. An interactive explanation might point to the following facts: it was a hot day; the school bus had been late; Greg was reprimanded by the teacher for his tardiness; and, to top it off, he had forgotten his lunch bag.

Both modes of explanation, developmental and interactive, belong together, because development always provides the potential that is capitalized on in the present. If Greg's background had not included factors that predisposed him to act aggressively, he might have responded differently in the current frustrating situation; for example, he might have withdrawn to a corner and sulked instead of fighting with his classmate. At some points in the text we will find that explanations of behavior are largely developmental; at other points, interactive explanations are stressed. But the one explanation never excludes the other.

Psychoanalysis, with its emphasis on early childhood experiences, favors developmental explanations. Behaviorism, which stresses learning, is also largely a developmental psychology. In contrast, phenomenological theories and some cognitive theories are primarily interactive, because they focus on the individual's current perception

and interpretation of events. But all psychological theories must be concerned with present influences on behavior as well as residues from the past.

It is important to keep both modes of explanation in mind in order to avoid explaining too much according to the past or too much according to the present. For example, if we discover that teen-age boys with alcoholic fathers are more apt to get into trouble with the law than boys whose fathers are not alcoholics, we should not be tempted to adopt the developmental explanation that a particular boy is delinquent *because* he has an alcoholic father. His delinquency reflects the fact that he is having problems *at the present time*—in relation to specific temptations, friends, lack of other opportunities, and so on.

It is the current problems that must be understood if they are to be corrected. Yet it may help us in the long run to deal with juvenile crime if we know the kind of early history that contributes to delinquency as well as the kinds of neighborhood problems and social problems that encourage delinquent behavior. It is not illogical to accept both a developmental and an interactive explanation at the same time.

Scope of Contemporary Psychology

Throughout its brief history, psychology has been defined in many different ways (see Table 1-1). The early psychologists defined their field as "the study of mental activity." With the development of behaviorism at the beginning of this century and its concern for studying only those phenomena that could be objectively measured, psychology was redefined as "the study of behavior." This definition usually included the investigation of animal as well as human behavior on the assumptions that (1) information from experiments with subhuman species could be generalized to the human organism and (2) animal behavior was of interest in its own right. From the 1930s through the 1960s, most psychology textbooks used this definition. The cycle has come around

TABLE 1-1
Changing definitions of psychology

Psychology is the Science of Mental Life, both of its phenomena and of their conditions. . . . The phenomena are such things as we call feelings, desires, cognitions, reasonings, decisions, and the like.   William James, 1890

All consciousness everywhere, normal or abnormal, human or animal, is the subject matter which the psychologist attempts to describe or explain; and no definition of his science is wholly acceptable which designates more or less than just this.
James Angell, 1910

For the behaviorist, psychology is that division of natural science which takes human behavior—the doings and sayings, both learned and unlearned—as its subject matter.   John B. Watson, 1919

As a provisional definition of psychology, we may say that its problem is the scientific study of the behavior of living creatures in their contact with the outer world.   Kurt Koffka, 1925

Conceived broadly, psychology seeks to discover the general laws which explain the behavior of living organisms. It attempts to identify, describe, and classify the several types of activity of which the animal, human or other, is capable.
Arthur Gates, 1931

What is man? To this question psychology seeks an answer.
Edwin Boring, 1939

Today, psychology is most commonly defined as "the science of behavior." Interestingly enough, however, the meaning of "behavior" has itself expanded so that it now takes in a good bit of what was formerly dealt with as experience . . . such private (subjective) processes as thinking are now dealt with as "internal behavior."
Norman Munn, 1951

Psychology is usually defined as the scientific study of behavior. Its subject matter includes behavioral processes that are observable, such as gestures, speech, and physiological changes, and processes that can only be inferred as thoughts and dreams.   Kenneth Clark and George Miller, 1970

again with the development of cognitive and phenomenological psychology; most current definitions of psychology include references to both behavior and mental processes.

For our purposes, we will define psychology as *the science that studies behavior and mental processes*. This definition reflects psychology's concern with an objective study of observable behavior and still recognizes the importance of understanding mental processes that cannot be directly observed but must be inferred from behavioral and physiological data. But we need not dwell on a definition. From a practical viewpoint, we can get a better idea of what psychology *is* from looking at what psychologists *do*.

Fields of Psychology

About half the people who have advanced degrees in psychology work in colleges and universities, although teaching is not always their primary activity. They may devote much of their time to research or counseling. Others work in the public schools, in hospitals or clinics, in government agencies, or in business and industry. Those in private practice, who offer their services to the public for a fee, represent a relatively small but growing fraction of the field. Psychologists do a variety of things in a variety of locations. Table 1-2 gives an estimate of the proportion of psychologists engaged in different fields of activity.

EXPERIMENTAL AND PHYSIOLOGICAL PSYCHOLOGY   The term "experimental" is really a misnomer, because psychologists in other areas of specialization carry out experiments too. But this category usually consists of those psychologists who use experimental methods to study how people react to sensory stimuli, perceive the world around them, learn and remember, respond emotionally, and are motivated to action, whether by hunger or the desire to succeed in life. *Experimental psychologists* also work with animals. Sometimes they attempt to relate animal and human behavior; sometimes they study animals in order to compare the behavior of different species (comparative psychology). Whatever their interest, experimental psychologists are concerned with developing precise methods of measurement and control.

An area of research closely related to both experimental psychology and biology is physiological psychology. *Physiological psychologists* seek to discover the relationship between biological processes and behavior. How do sex hormones influence behavior? What area of the brain controls speech? How do drugs like marijuana and LSD affect coordination and memory? Two rapidly developing areas of interdisciplinary research are the *neurosciences* (concerned with all aspects of the nervous system, including the relationship between brain function and behavior) and *psychopharmacology* (the study of drugs and behavior).

DEVELOPMENTAL, SOCIAL, AND PERSONALITY PSYCHOLOGY   The categories of developmental psychology, social psychology, and personality psychology overlap. *Developmental psychologists* are concerned with human growth and the factors that shape behavior from birth to old age. They might study a specific ability, such as how language develops and changes in the growing child, or a particular period of life, such as infancy, the preschool years, or adolescence.

Because human development takes place in the context of other persons—parents, siblings, playmates, and school companions—a large part of development is social. *Social psychologists* are interested in the ways that interactions with other people influence attitudes and behavior. They are concerned also with the behavior of groups. Social psychologists are perhaps best known for their work in public opinion and attitude surveys and in market research. Surveys are now widely used by newspapers, magazines, radio and TV networks, as well as by government agencies, such as the Bureau of the Census.

Social psychologists investigate such topics as propaganda and persuasion, conformity, and intergroup conflict. At present a significant part of their research effort is directed toward identifying the factors that contribute to prejudice and to aggression.

To the extent that personality is both a developmental and social product, the province of personality psychology overlaps both of the other categories. *Personality psychologists* focus on differences between individuals. They are interested in ways of classifying individuals for useful purposes as well as in studying each individual's unique qualities.

CLINICAL AND COUNSELING PSYCHOLOGY   The greatest number of psychologists are engaged in clinical psychology, the application of psychological principles to the diagnosis and treatment of emotional and behavioral problems—mental illness, juvenile delinquency, criminal behavior, drug addiction, mental retardation, marital and family conflict, and other less serious

TABLE 1-2
Fields of psychology
The primary specialties of individuals holding a doctorate degree in psychology

FIELD	PERCENTAGE OF INDIVIDUALS
Experimental and physiological	14
Developmental, social, and personality	17
Clinical and counseling	41
School and educational	14
Industrial and engineering	9
Others	5
	100

A school psychologist administering a test

adjustment problems. *Clinical psychologists* may work in mental hospitals, juvenile courts or probation offices, mental health clinics, institutions for the mentally retarded, prisons, or university medical schools. They may also practice privately, often in association with other professionals; their affiliations with the medical profession, especially psychiatry, are close.

Counseling psychologists serve many of the same functions, although they usually deal with less serious problems. They often work with high school or university students, providing help with problems of social adjustment and vocational and educational goals. Together, clinical and counseling psychologists account for about 41 percent of all psychologists in the United States.

SCHOOL AND EDUCATIONAL PSYCHOLOGY The public schools provide a wide range of opportunities for psychologists. Because the beginnings of serious emotional problems often appear in the early grades, many elementary schools employ psychologists whose training combines courses in child development, education, and clinical psychology. These *school psychologists* work with individual children to evaluate learning and emotional problems; administering and interpreting intelligence, achievement, and personality tests is part of their job. In consultation with parents and teachers they plan ways of helping the child both in the classroom and in the home. They also provide a valuable resource for teachers, offering suggestions for coping with classroom problems.

Educational psychologists are specialists in learning and teaching. They may work in the public school system, but more often are employed by a university's school of education, where they do research on teaching methods and help train teachers and school psychologists.

INDUSTRIAL AND ENGINEERING PSYCHOLOGY *Industrial psychologists* (sometimes called *organizational psychologists*) may work for a particular company or as consultants for a number of business organizations. They are concerned with such problems as selecting people most suitable for a particular job, developing job training programs, and participating in management decisions that involve the morale and welfare of employees.

Engineering psychologists seek to make the relationship between people and machines as satisfactory as possible—to design machines so that human errors are minimized. For example, engineering psychologists were involved in developing space capsules in which astronauts could live and function efficiently. Designing underwater habitats for oceanographic research or developing artificial limbs and other prosthetic devices for handicapped individuals are other examples of their work.

Along with social psychologists and other scientists, engineering psychologists are concerned with environmental issues—problems of noise, air and water pollution, overcrowding, and toxic agents—that must be solved in planning for the future. A new term for this area of research, which is becoming increasingly active, is *environmental psychology*.

EMERGING SPECIALITIES In addition to the areas we have mentioned are some newer career possibilities in psychology. *Forensic psychologists* work within the legal, judicial, and correctional systems in a variety of ways—for example, consulting with police departments and probation officers to increase their understanding of the human problems with which they must deal, working with prison inmates and their families, participating in decisions about whether an accused person is mentally competent to stand trial, and preparing psychological reports to help judges decide on the most appropriate course of action for a convicted criminal.

Psychologists who specialize in *computer science* may plan the design and data analysis of experiments that require the kind of complex calculations that can only be done with a computer. Or they may work in the area of *artificial intelligence,* which uses computers to perform the kind of intellectual tasks that are considered characteristic of human thought (see Chapter 9).

Because of their expertise in experimental design—the procedures for gathering and analyzing data—psychologists also work in the area of *evaluation research.* Many of the federal and local programs designed to solve social problems involve large expenditures of money and personnel. Consequently, it is essential to determine whether such programs—aimed, for example, at early education for underprivileged children, preventing drug abuse among high school students, or providing job training for unemployed youths—are effective. Psychologists are becoming increasingly active in the evaluation of public programs in such areas as education, health, and employment.

Basic and Applied Research

Research in psychology, as in all fields of science, has two focuses of interest —basic research and applied research. *Basic research* is concerned with the quest for knowledge, regardless of whether it has immediate practical value. Psychologists who study learning in the laboratory may not be concerned with improving teaching methods, although their findings may eventually have applications in education. They want to satisfy their curiosity about the laws that govern learning. The results may have practical consequences, but that is not their chief concern.

Applied research seeks to improve the human condition by discovering something that can be put to practical use. A psychologist trying out two different methods for teaching algebra in a school classroom is concerned with finding the most effective way of teaching mathematics. The results may have implications for a more basic or fundamental understanding of learning, but the goal is a practical one of improving teaching methods. Of course, the methods that the psychologist wants to test in the classroom may be suggested by the basic research of the laboratory scientist.

Some fields of psychology are concerned largely with applied research and applications—for example, clinical and counseling psychology. Other fields focus primarily on basic research, such as experimental and physiological psychology. But most fields of psychology involve a mix of basic and applied research as well as applications.

All sciences have their basic and applied aspects: botany and agriculture, physics and engineering, physiology and medicine, biochemistry and pharmacology, to name a few. Although the applied-basic distinction is meaningful, it is somewhat artificial, because research often serves both scientific curiosity and practical goals at the same time. A clinical psychologist may gather data in the treatment of patients that are pertinent to basic theories about the cause of mental disorders.

Behavioral and Social Sciences

A study of human activity should go beyond what happens to an isolated individual and consider the institutional arrangements in which individuals live: the family, the community, and the larger society, with their complex interrelationships. Because these arrangements are much too varied to be understood from any single standpoint, a number of fields of inquiry have developed: anthropology, economics, geography, linguistics, political science, sociology, and other specialties. Taken together, these are known as the *behavioral* or *social sciences.* The term "social science" used to be the more inclusive one, with behavioral science restricted to those fields that focused more particularly on individual behavior (psychology, anthropology, and linguistics). As all fields have grown to appreciate that individual and social behavior cannot be understood one without the other, the terms "behavioral science" and "social science" have come to be used somewhat interchangeably.

A subfield of psychology like social psychology would tend to be viewed as part of the social sciences, because it focuses on social phenomena. Physiological psychology, on the other hand, would be thought of as a behavioral science, because it studies the biological basis of the behavior of individual organisms. Educational psychology, when studying how an individual child learns to read or do arithmetic, would be labeled as a behavioral science; but in its study of group interactions in the classroom it would be a social science. Thus, psychology may be referred to as a behavioral science when the discussion emphasizes the individual and as a social science when the emphasis is on groups of individuals in interaction.

Research Methods

The aim of science is to provide new and useful information in the form of verifiable data: data obtained under conditions such that other qualified people can make similar observations and obtain the same results. This task calls for orderliness and precision in uncovering relationships and in communicating them to others. The scientific ideal is not always achieved, but as a science becomes better established it rests on an increasing number of relationships that can be taken for granted because they have been validated so often.

Experimental Method

The experimental method can be used outside the laboratory as well as inside. Thus, it is possible in an experiment in economics to investigate the effects of different taxation methods by trying these methods out on separate but similar communities. The experimental method is a matter of logic, not of location. Even so, most experimentation takes place in special laboratories, chiefly because the control of conditions commonly requires special equipment that is best housed and used in one place. The laboratory is generally located in a university or in a research institute of some kind, where it is accessible to scientists who work on a variety of topics.

The distinguishing characteristic of a laboratory is that it is a place where the experimenter can carefully control conditions and take measurements in order to discover *relationships among variables.* A *variable* is something that can occur with different values. For example, in an experiment seeking to discover the relationship between learning ability and age, both learning ability and age can have different values—learning being either slow or fast and the learner being either young or old. To the extent that learning ability changes systematically with increasing age, we can discover an orderly relationship between them.

Measuring pulse rate and strength of grip in a laboratory study

The ability to exercise precise control over variables distinguishes the experimental method from other methods of observation. If the experimenter seeks to discover whether learning ability depends on the amount of sleep a person has had, the amount of sleep can be controlled by arranging to have several groups of subjects spend the night in the laboratory. One group might be allowed to go to sleep at 11:00 P.M., another at 1:00 A.M., and the third group might be kept awake until 4:00 A.M. By waking all the subjects at the same time and giving each the same learning task, the experimenter can determine whether the subjects with more sleep master the task more quickly than those with less sleep.

In this study, the different amounts of sleep are the antecedent conditions; the learning performances are the results of these conditions. We call the antecedent condition the *independent variable*, because it is independent of what the subject does. The variable affected by changes in the antecedent conditions is called the *dependent variable;* in psychological research the dependent variable is usually some measure of the subject's behavior. The phrase *is a function of* is used to express the dependency of one variable on another. Thus, for the experiment above, we could say that the subjects' ability to learn a new task is a function of the amount of sleep they had.

An experiment concerned with the effect of marijuana on memory may make the distinction between independent and dependent variables clearer. Male subjects were assigned to four groups comparable in age and educational level. When a subject arrived at the laboratory he was given an oral dose of marijuana in the form of a "brownie cookie." All subjects were given the same type of cookie and the same instructions. But the dosage level of the marijuana was different for each group: 5, 10, 15, or 20 milligrams of THC, the active ingredient in marijuana.

After consuming the marijuana the subject engaged in a series of tasks, one of which was to memorize 10 lists of words. Each list contained 20 unrelated words, so the memorization task was quite difficult. One week later the subject was brought back to the laboratory and asked to recall as many words as possible from all of the lists. Figure 1-5 shows the percentage of words recalled for each of the four groups. Note that recall decreases as a function of the amount of marijuana taken at the time the subject studied the lists. (There was more to the experiment, but this description is sufficient for our purposes.)

The experimenters had worked out a careful *plan* before bringing the subjects to the laboratory. Except for the dosage of marijuana, they held all conditions constant: the general setting for the experiment, the instructions to the subjects, the material to be memorized, the time allowed for memorization, and the conditions under which recall was tested. The only factor permitted to vary across the four groups was the dosage of marijuana—the *independent variable*. The *dependent variable* was the amount of material recalled one week later. The marijuana dosage was measured in milligrams of THC; memory was measured by the percentage of words recalled a week later. The experimenters could plot the relationship between the independent and dependent variables as shown in Figure 1-5. Finally, the experimenters used enough subjects (20 per group) so that they could count on similar results if the experiment were repeated with a different sample of subjects. The letter N is generally used to denote the number of subjects in each group; in this study, $N = 20$.

The degree of control possible in the laboratory makes a laboratory experiment the preferred scientific method when it can be used appropriately. Precision instruments are usually necessary to control stimuli and to obtain exact data. The experimenter may need to produce colors of known wavelengths in

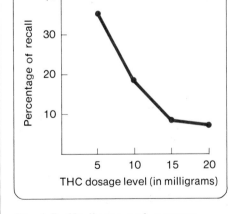

Fig. 1-5 Marijuana and memory
Subjects memorized word lists after taking varying dosages of THC (the active ingredient in marijuana). Recall tests administered a week later measured how much of the memorized material was retained. The figure shows the relationship between dosage level (independent variable) and recall score (dependent variable). (After Darley and others, 1973)

vision studies or sounds of known frequency in audition studies. It may be necessary to expose a visual display for a precisely timed fraction of a second in a memory experiment. With precision instruments time can be measured in thousandths of a second, and physiological activity can be studied by means of very slight electrical currents amplified from the brain. Thus, the psychological laboratory has audiometers, photometers, oscilloscopes, electronic timers, electroencephalographs, and computers.

The value of an experiment is not determined, however, by the amount of apparatus used. If the logic of experimentation requires precision apparatus, then such apparatus should be used; if it does not, good experimentation can be carried out with pencil-and-paper procedures.

Moreover, for psychology to develop as a science it is not essential that all its problems be brought into the laboratory. Some sciences, such as geology and astronomy, are experimental only to a very limited extent. Now that we have seen the value of the laboratory approach, without establishing its claims as exclusive, we turn to other methods used in psychological investigations.

Observational Method

The early stages of a science necessitate exploration to become familiar with the relationships that later will be the object of more precise study. Careful observation of animal and human behavior (including the study of our own conscious processes) is the starting point of psychology. Observation of primates in their native environment of Africa may tell us things about their social organization that will help us conduct our laboratory investigations (see Figure 1-6). Study of preliterate tribes reveals the ranges of variation in human institutions, which would go unrecognized if we confined our study to men and women of our own culture. Motion pictures of newborn babies reveal the details of movement patterns shortly after birth and the types of stimuli to which babies are responsive.

In making observations of naturally occurring behavior, however, there is a risk that anecdotes may be substituted for genuine observation, or interpretations for descriptions. We may be tempted, for example, to say that an animal known to have been without food for a long time is "looking for food" when all we observe is heightened activity. Investigators must be trained to observe and record accurately in order to avoid projecting their own wishes or biases onto what they report.

Observational methods have also been brought into the laboratory. In their extensive study of the physiological aspects of human sexuality, Masters and Johnson (1966) developed techniques that permitted direct observation of sexual responses in the laboratory. The intimate nature of the research required careful planning to devise procedures for making the subjects feel at ease in the laboratory and to develop appropriate methods for observing and recording their responses. The data included (1) observations of behavior, (2) recordings of physiological changes, and (3) responses to questions asked about the subject's sensations before, during, and after sexual stimulation.

Masters and Johnson would be the first to agree that human sexuality has many dimensions in addition to the biological one. But, as they point out, we need to know the basic anatomical and physiological facts of sexual response before we can understand the psychological aspects. Their research has shown that some of the psychological hypotheses regarding sex (for example, the nature of the female orgasm and factors that contribute to sexual adequacy) are based on false biological assumptions. We will return to this topic in a later chapter.

Fig. 1-6 Baboons observed in their natural habitat
Such naturalistic studies tell more about social behavior than strictly experimental studies can. For example, grooming behavior, as shown in the picture, is a common form of social contact among baboons in the wild.

Survey Method

Some problems that are difficult to study by direct observation may be studied through the use of questionnaires or interviews. For example, prior to the Masters and Johnson research on sexual response, most of the information on how people behave sexually (as opposed to how laws, religion, or society said they should behave) came from extensive surveys conducted by the late Alfred Kinsey and his associates some 30 years ago. Information from thousands of individual interviews was analyzed to form the basis of *Sexual Behavior in the Human Male* (Kinsey and others, 1948) and *Sexual Behavior in the Human Female* (Kinsey and others, 1953).

Surveys have also been used to obtain information on political opinions, consumer preferences, health care needs, and many other topics. The Gallup poll and the United States Census are probably the most familiar surveys. An adequate survey requires a carefully pretested questionnaire, a group of interviewers trained in its use, a sample carefully selected to ensure that the respondents are representative of the population to be studied, and appropriate methods of data analysis, so that the results are properly interpreted.

Test Method

The test is an important research instrument in contemporary psychology. It is used to measure all kinds of abilities, interests, attitudes, and accomplishments. Tests enable the psychologist to obtain large quantities of data from people with a minimum disturbance of their daily routines and without elaborate laboratory equipment. A test essentially presents a uniform situation to a group of people who vary in aspects relevant to the situation (such as intelligence, manual dexterity, anxiety, or perceptual skills). An analysis of the results then relates variations in test scores to variations among people.

Test construction and use are, however, not simple matters. They involve many steps in item preparation, scaling, and establishing norms. Later chapters will explore the problems of testing in some detail.

Case Histories

Scientific biographies, known as case histories, are important sources of data for psychologists studying individuals. There can, of course, be case histories of institutions or groups of people as well.

Most case histories are prepared by *reconstructing the biography* of a person on the basis of remembered events and records. Reconstruction is necessary because the individual's earlier history often does not become a matter of interest until that person develops some sort of problem; at such time, knowledge of the past is thought to be important for understanding present behavior. The retrospective method may result in distortions of events or oversights, but it is often the only method available.

Case histories may also be based on a *longitudinal study.* This type of study follows an individual or group of individuals over an extended period of time, with measurements made at periodic intervals. Thus, the case history is constructed from actual observations made by the investigator according to a plan. The advantage of a longitudinal study is that it does not depend on the memories of those interviewed at a later date. The disadvantage is that in most studies a large amount of data has to be collected from many individuals in the hope that some of the data will eventually show the characteristics of interest to the investigator—perhaps unusual creative abilities or some forms of mental disturbance.

"How would you like me to answer that question? As a member of my ethnic group, educational class, income group, or religious category?"

Drawing by D. Fradon © 1969 The New Yorker Magazine, Inc.

Measurement in Psychology

Whatever methods psychologists use, sooner or later they find it necessary to make statements about *amounts,* or *quantities.* Variables have to be assessed in some objective manner, so that investigations can be repeated and confirmed by others. Occasionally a variable can be sorted into *classes,* or *categories,* as when boys and girls are separated for the study of sex differences. Sometimes the variables are subject to ordinary *physical measurement:* for example, hours of sleep deprivation, dosage level of a drug, or time required to press a brake pedal when a light flashes. Sometimes variables have to be *scaled* in a manner that places them in some sort of order. For example, in rating a patient's feelings of insecurity, a psychotherapist might use a five-point scale ranging from never through rarely, sometimes, often, and always. Usually, for purposes of precise communication, *numbers* are assigned to variables. The term *measurement* can be used whenever numerical values are assigned to independent and dependent variables, or indeed to any variable.[2]

Experimental Design

An investigator must plan all the details of an experiment. He or she must specify the procedure to be used in the collection of data, how the data will be analyzed, and the inferences that can reasonably be drawn from such data and their analyses. The expression *experimental design* is used to describe the procedures used in planning an experiment.

The simplest experimental designs are those in which the investigator manipulates one variable (the independent variable) and studies its effects on another variable (the dependent variable). The ideal is to hold everything constant except the independent variable, in order to obtain an assertion of the form, "With everything else constant, when X increases, Y also increases." Or, in other cases, "When X increases, Y decreases." Note that almost any content can fit into this kind of statement—the subjective experience of loudness related to the physical energy of the sound source, rate of learning related to age of the learner, or fear of snakes related to prior experience with snakes.

The method of *graphical representation* is a convenient one, with the independent variable plotted on the horizontal axis (the abscissa) and the dependent variable plotted on the vertical axis (the ordinate), as shown in Figure 1-5. We shall see later that psychological theories often attempt to predict what form such a curve will take. The orderly relation between the variables can be stated more precisely by fitting a mathematical equation to the relationship. In other words, we are interested in more than the fact that when X increases, Y also increases; we want to know what the precise relationship is.

Sometimes an experiment focuses only on the influence of a single condition, which can be either present or absent. (Such a condition is simply a variable with only two values, one representing its presence, the other its absence.) In this case, the experimental design commonly calls for an *experimental group* with the condition present and a *control group* with the condition absent. The results of such an experiment are presented in Figure 1-7. Inspecting the figure, we see that the experimental group, which received computer-assisted learning, scored higher on reading achievement tests than the control group, which did not receive such instruction.

"I'm suffering a real identity crisis . . . I keep getting assigned to the control group."

[2]This discussion of measurement and statistics is designed to give the student a general introduction to the problems involved in order to facilitate understanding of the tables and charts in later chapters. A more thorough discussion of statistics is provided in the Appendix.

In some instances it is necessary to investigate the simultaneous effects of several variables. Suppose, for example, that you are studying the effects of moisture, temperature, and illumination on plant growth. You could hold two of these variables constant and study the effect of the third. A little reflection will show how limited this design would be. Unless *favorable* levels of the other variables were chosen, the plant would not live, and the experiment could not be performed at all; but *how* favorable the other variables must be cannot be determined in advance. A better procedure would be to vary moisture, temperature, and illumination in different combinations. Then the effect of one variable would be studied not against a *constant* value of other variables, but against an *array* of other values. Many behavioral science problems have this multivariable character. School performance, for example, is affected by the child's native ability, diet, family background, the school facilities, the teacher's skill, and so on. The statistical problems of such a *multivariate design* are more complex than those of a design involving changes in only one independent variable at a time, but the yield in information is often greater for the same amount of experimental effort.

Interpreting Statistical Statements

Because descriptions of the results of psychological studies usually include statistical statements, it is well to be familiar with the most common of these, so that the reports will appear less baffling.

The most common statistic is the *mean,* or arithmetic average, which is the sum of the measures divided by the number of these measures. In experiments with a control group there are often two means to be compared: a mean for the sample of subjects in the experimental group and a mean for the sample of subjects in the control group. The difference between these two means is, of course, what interests us. If the difference is large, we may accept it at face value. But what if the difference is small? What if our measures are somewhat crude and subject to error? What if a few extreme cases are producing the difference? Statisticians solve these problems by producing tests of the *significance of a difference.* A psychologist who says that the difference between the experimental and the control group is "statistically significant" means that certain statistical tests have been applied to the data and that the observed difference is *trustworthy.* The psychologist is not commenting on the importance or practical significance of the results but is telling us that the statistical tests indicate that the difference observed is likely to occur again if the experiment is repeated. Many chance factors can influence the results of an experiment. By using statistical tests, psychologists can judge the likelihood that the observed difference is, in fact, due to the effect of the independent variable rather than an unhappy accident of chance factors.

Correlation as an Alternative to Experimentation

Sometimes strict experimental control is not possible. For example, the experimenter interested in the human brain is not free to surgically remove portions at will, as can be done with those of lower animals. But when brain damage occurs through disease or injury the experimenter can study how parts of the brain are related to behavior. For instance, a relationship may be found between the extent of damage at the back of the brain and the amount of difficulty in vision. This method of analyzing correspondences, without experimental control over them, is known as *correlation.*

When large masses of data are available, correlation is often the best

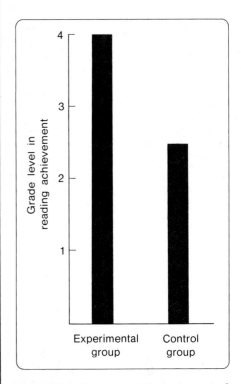

Fig. 1-7 Experimental and control groups
Each day grade school children in the experimental group participated in a computer-assisted learning (CAL) program in reading. The computer presented the instructional materials to the children and then tested them on how much they had learned. CAL has the advantage of working with each student in a highly individualized way, concentrating on those areas in which the student is having the most difficulty. The control group had no supplementary CAL in reading. At the end of the third grade all students in both groups were given a standardized reading test. It was administered by testers who had no knowledge of which students had received CAL and which had not. As the figure indicates, students in the experimental group scored higher on the test than students in the control group, suggesting that CAL has been beneficial. In this experiment, the independent variable is the presence or absence of CAL; the dependent variable is the student's score on the reading test. (After Atkinson, 1976)

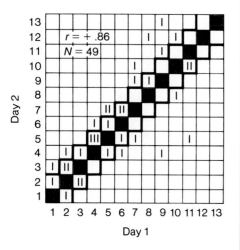

Fig. 1-8 A scatter diagram illustrating correlation
Each tally indicates the combined scores of one subject on two separate days of testing hypnotic susceptibility. Tallies in the colored area indicate identical scores on both tests; those between the solid lines indicate a difference of no more than one point between the two scores. The correlation of $r = +.86$ means that the performances were fairly consistent on the two days. There were 49 subjects in this study; thus $N = 49$. (After Hilgard, 1961)

available method for discovering relationships. Suppose we have records of the high school grades of students entering college. The best way to find out the relation between high school grades and freshman grades in college is to *correlate* them—that is, to find out if those who did well in high school generally do well in college, and vice versa. Measurement in correlation studies is provided by the *coefficient of correlation,* symbolized by the letter *r,* which expresses the degree of relationship.

COEFFICIENT OF CORRELATION The relationships expressed by a coefficient of correlation are made clearer by a diagram of actual test results (see Figure 1-8). Forty-nine subjects were given a test of their susceptibility to hypnosis on two separate days. Each tally in the diagram represents the *combined* score of one subject on the two tests. Thus, two subjects made scores of 1 on both days, and two other subjects made scores of 13 on both days. But one subject (see the lower right-hand portion of the diagram) made a score of 11 on the first test but only 5 on the second one.

If all subjects had repeated their original scores on the second day, all the tallies would have fallen in the diagonal colored squares, and the correlation would have been $r = +1.00$. Enough tallies fall to either side, however, so that in this case the correlation drops to $r = +.86$. The method for calculating the coefficient of correlation is described in the Appendix to this book; at this point we will only set forth some rules of thumb that will help you interpret correlation coefficients when you encounter them in later chapters.

1 A correlation of $r = +1.00$ means a perfect *positive* relationship between two variables. If weight corresponded exactly to height, so that you could state precisely a person's weight if you knew his or her height, then height and weight would be perfectly correlated. When the correlation is positive, the plus sign is often omitted.

2 A correlation of $r = -1.00$ means a perfect *negative* relationship. For example, if the price of a used car decreased as its age increased, so that one could precisely specify the price if the age were known, then the relation between the car's age and price would be expressed by a correlation of $r = -1.00$.

3 A correlation of $r = .00$ signifies no relation. Thus, one would expect a zero correlation between the number of freckles on people's faces and their scores on an intelligence test. Knowing the value of one variable in no way helps predict the value of the other variable.

4 A correlation between $r = .00$ and either $+1.00$ or -1.00 indicates an imperfect relationship. The *degree of relationship* is specified by the extent to which the value of the correlation approaches 1.00, plus or minus.

5 A correlation is *not* a percentage, so a correlation of $r = .25$ cannot be interpreted as being half as great as one of $r = .50$. The degree of relationship expressed by a correlation coefficient varies more nearly with its *square.* Thus, a correlation of $r = .70$ expresses nearly double the relationship of $r = .50$; that is, $.70^2 = .49$ is nearly double $.50^2 = .25$.

6 It helps to have some idea of the sizes of correlations commonly reported: (a) a correlation of $r = .50$ between the height of a parent and the adult height of the child; (b) correlations of about $r = .40$ between scholastic aptitude tests and freshman grades in college; (c) correlations of about $r = .75$ between grades in the first semester of the freshman year and those in the second semester.

7 The sign of a correlation is often arbitrary. For example, if the number of classes missed correlated $-.50$ with the course grade, then the correlation

between number of classes attended and the course grade would be +.50. The change of sign would not change the interpretation of the findings.

8 Some supplementary information is needed to indicate whether or not a given correlation is *statistically significant.* This is the same problem encountered in determining whether a difference between two means is significant. For example, if too few cases have been studied, a few extreme cases might produce a high correlation, although no correlation exists in the total population. Hence statistical methods have been developed for determining the significance of a correlation; the most dependable correlations are based on a large number of cases.

CAUSE AND EFFECT RELATIONSHIPS Before concluding this section, we should emphasize an important distinction between experimental and correlational studies. In an experimental study, one variable (the independent variable) is systematically manipulated to determine its effect on some other variable (the dependent variable). Similar cause-effect relationships cannot always be inferred from correlational studies. The fallacy of interpreting correlations as implying cause and effect is best illustrated with a few examples. The softness of the asphalt in the streets of a city may correlate with the number of sunstroke cases, but this does not mean that soft asphalt gives off some kind of poison that sends people to hospitals. We understand the cause in this example—a hot sun both softens the asphalt and produces sunstroke. Another common example is the high positive correlation obtained for the number of storks seen nesting in French villages and the number of childbirths recorded in the same communities. We shall leave it to the reader's ingenuity to figure out possible reasons for such a correlation without postulating a cause-effect relation between babies and storks. These examples provide sufficient warning against giving a causal interpretation to a correlation. When two variables are correlated, variation in one may *possibly* be the cause of variation in the other, but in the absence of other evidence, no such conclusion is justified.

Overview of the Book

Psychologists today are in the process of investigating thousands of different problems ranging from microelectrode studies of how individual brain cells change during learning to studies of the effects of population density and overcrowding on social behavior. Deciding how to classify these problems into topics and how to present the topics in the most meaningful order is difficult. In older sciences, such as physics and chemistry, where facts and theories are fairly well established, most introductory textbooks arrange their topics in approximately the same order—starting with basic concepts and proceeding to the more complex. In a science as young as psychology, however, where theories are still very preliminary and so much remains unknown, the natural order of topics is not always clear. If you examine a number of introductory psychology texts you will find considerable variation in the grouping and ordering of topics. Should we know how people perceive the world around them in order to understand how they learn new things? Or does learning determine how we perceive our environment? Should we discuss what motivates a person to action so that we can understand his or her personality? Or can motivation be better understood if we look first at the way personality develops as a function of basic needs? Despite such unresolved questions we have tried to arrange the topics in this book so that the understanding of the issues in each chapter will provide a background for the study of problems in the next.

To understand how people interact with their environment, we need to know something about their biological equipment. In Part Two (Biological and Developmental Processes), the first chapter describes how the nervous and endocrine systems function to integrate and control behavior. Since behavior also depends on the interaction between inherited characteristics and environmental conditions, this chapter includes, in addition, a discussion of how inherited characteristics are transmitted and studied.

The second chapter in Part Two provides an overview of the individual's development from infancy through adolescence and adulthood. By noting how abilities, attitudes, and personality develop, and the problems that must be faced at different stages of life, we can appreciate more fully the kinds of questions to which psychology seeks answers.

We know the world around us through our senses. To understand how individuals react to their world we should know how the sense organs mediate the sensations of light, sound, touch, and taste; how the organism interprets and reacts to patterns of stimuli; and the characteristics of human consciousness under both normal and altered states of awareness. These topics are the substance of Part Three (Perception and Consciousness).

Part Four (Learning, Remembering, and Thinking) is concerned with the processes by which we acquire skills and knowledge, remember them, and use them for purposes of communication, problem solving, and thinking.

Part Five (Motivation and Emotion) deals with the forces that energize and direct behavior; these include biological needs as well as psychological motives and emotions.

The ways in which individuals differ from one another, both in personal characteristics and abilities, is the substance of Part Six (Personality and Individuality). How we cope with stress, and the development and treatment of abnormal behavior, provide the topics for Part Seven (Conflict, Adjustment, and Mental Health).

Part Eight (Social Behavior) is concerned with our social interactions—how we influence others and are influenced by them and how we function in groups.

SUMMARY

1   The study of psychology can be approached from several viewpoints. The *neurobiological approach* attempts to relate our actions to events taking place inside the body, particularly in the brain and nervous system. The *behavioral approach* focuses on those external activities of the organism that can be observed and measured. *Cognitive psychology* is concerned with the way the brain actively processes incoming information by transforming it internally in various ways. The *psychoanalytic approach* emphasizes unconscious motives stemming from sexual and aggressive impulses repressed in childhood. *Phenomenological* and *humanistic* approaches focus on the person's subjective experiences, freedom of choice, and motivation toward self-actualization. A particular area of psychological investigation can be approached from several of these viewpoints.

2   Psychology is defined as the *science that studies behavior and mental processes*. Its numerous areas of specialization include experimental and physiological psychology; developmental, social, and personality psychology; clinical and counseling psychology; school and educational psychology; industrial and engineering psychology. Some fields of psychology focus

largely on *basic research* and others on *applied research* and its applications. Psychology is one of the *behavioral,* or *social, sciences.*

3　When applicable, the *experimental method* is preferred for studying problems, because it seeks to control all *variables,* except the one being studied, and provides for precise measurement of the *independent* and *dependent variables.* The independent variable is the one manipulated by the experimenter; the dependent variable, usually some measure of the subject's behavior, is affected by changes in the independent variable.

4　Other methods for investigating psychological problems include the *observational method,* the *survey method,* the *test method,* and *case histories.*

5　Measurement in psychology requires arranging observations so that numerical values can be assigned to the resulting data. One approach is through *experimental design,* in which experiments are so arranged that changes in the dependent variable can be studied in relation to changes in the independent variable (or to several variables at once). If the independent variable is something that is either present or absent, the *control group* method is appropriate; then the experimenter compares what happens in a given setting when the variable is present and when it is absent. Any differences in *means* can be tested for *significance* by appropriate statistical tests.

6　Another approach to research is by way of *correlation.* When the experimenter does not have control of the independent variable, he or she can make widely ranging observations and then study how one variable changes as another one changes. This method often is used with scores from psychological tests. A correlation between X and Y tells how a change in X is related to a change in Y. If the relation is one-to-one, then the *coefficient of correlation* is either $r = +1.00$ or $r = -1.00$; correlations between 0 and ± 1.00 represent imperfect relationships.

FURTHER READING

The topical interests and theories of any contemporary science can often be understood best according to their history. Several useful books are Murphy and Kovach, *Historical introduction to modern psychology* (3rd ed., 1972), Schultz, *A history of modern psychology* (2nd ed., 1975), and Watson, *The great psychologists: From Aristotle to Freud* (1978), in paperback.

The various conceptual approaches to psychology are discussed in Hall and Lindzey, *Theories of personality* (3rd ed., 1978). Nordby and Hall, *A guide to psychologists and their concepts* (1974) provides brief accounts of major psychologists and their contributions. The methods of psychological research are presented in Wood, *Fundamentals of psychological research* (2nd ed., 1977), Johnson and Solso, *An introduction to experimental design in psychology: A case approach* (2nd ed., 1978), and Meyers and Grossen, *Behavioral research: Theory, procedure, and design* (2nd ed., 1978).

The relation of psychology to the other behavioral or social sciences is considered in Clark and Miller (eds.), *Psychology: Behavioral and social sciences survey committee* (1970). The *Annual review of psychology,* published in book form each year, selects 15 to 20 areas of psychology for a review of recent literature; these reviews are quite technical but provide a useful access to the world literature in psychology.

To find out more about career opportunities in psychology and the training required to become a psychologist, write to the American Psychological Association (1200 Seventeenth Street N.W., Washington, D.C. 20036) for a copy of their booklet, *A career in psychology.*

PART TWO

Biological and Developmental Processes

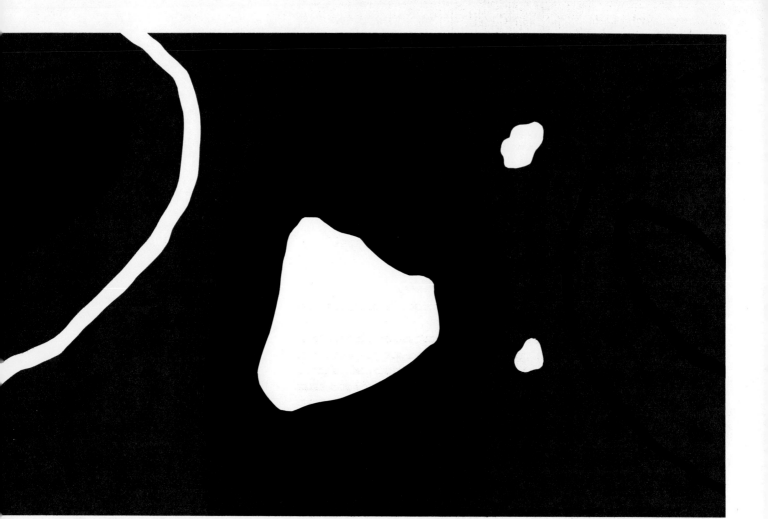

2
Biological Basis
of Behavior

Behavior, from blinking an eyelid to driving a car or solving a mathematical equation, depends on the integration of numerous processes within the body. This integration is provided by the nervous system with the help of the endocrine glands.

Consider, for example, all the processes that must coordinate effectively for you to stop your car at a red light. First of all, you must see the light; this means that the light must attract the attention of one of your sense organs, your eye. Neural impulses from your eye are relayed to your brain, where various features of the stimulus are analyzed and compared with information about past events stored in your memory. (You recognize that a red light in a certain context means "stop.") The process of pressing the brake pedal begins when the motor area of the brain signals the muscles of your leg and foot to respond. In order to do so, the brain must know where your foot *is* as well as where you want it to go. The brain must have some sort of register of the position of body parts relative to one another, which is used to plan directed movements. You do not stop the car with one sudden movement of your leg, however. A specialized part of your brain receives continual *feedback* from leg and foot muscles so that you are aware of how much pressure is being exerted and can alter your movements accordingly. At the same time, your eyes and some of your other body senses tell you how effectively the car is stopping. If the light turned red as you were speeding toward the intersection, some of your endocrine glands would also be activated, leading to increased heart rate, more rapid respiration, and other metabolic changes associated with fear; these processes would speed your reactions in an emergency. Your stopping at a red light may seem quick and automatic, but it involves numerous complex messages and adjustments. The information for these activities is transmitted by individual nerve cells, or neurons.

In fact, many aspects of human behavior and mental functioning cannot be fully understood without some knowledge of the underlying biological processes. Our nervous system, sense organs, muscles, and glands enable us to be aware of and adjust to our environment. Our perception of events depends on how our sense organs detect stimuli and how our brain interprets information coming from the senses. Much of our behavior is motivated by such needs as

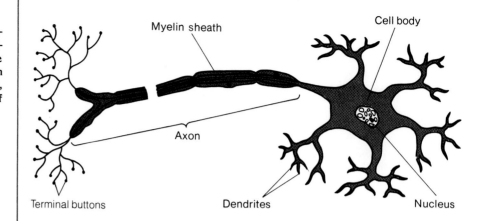

Myelin sheath

Cell body

Axon

Terminal buttons

Dendrites

Nucleus

hunger, thirst, and the avoidance of fatigue or pain. Our ability to use language, to think, and to solve problems depends on a brain structure that is incredibly complex compared to that of lower animals. And these unique abilities can easily be influenced by any number of physiological changes.

Some of the research relating specific psychological events to biological processes will be discussed when we talk, for example, about perception or motivation and emotion. This chapter provides a brief overview of the nervous system. Students with a background in biology will find most of the material familiar.

Basic Units of the Nervous System

The human brain is composed of some 10 to 12 billion specialized cells called *neurons*, the basic units of the nervous system. It is important to understand neurons, for they undoubtedly hold the secrets of learning and mental functioning. We know their role in the transmission and coordination of nervous impulses, and we know how some types of neural circuits work, but we are just beginning to unravel their more complex functioning in learning, emotion, and thought.

Neurons and Nerves

Although nerve cells differ markedly in size and appearance, depending on the specialized job they perform, they have certain common characteristics (see Figure 2-1). Projecting from the *cell body* are a number of short fibers called *dendrites* (from the Greek word *dendron*, meaning "tree"). The dendrites and the membrane covering the cell body receive messages from adjacent neurons. These messages are transmitted to other neurons (or to muscles and glands) by a long, slender tube called an *axon*. If an axon is stimulated, it will conduct impulses in either direction (that is, toward the cell body or away from it). However, nervous impulses can cross the junctions between neurons, called *synapses*, only in one direction—from the axon of one neuron to the cell body or dendrites of another neuron.

A synapse is not a direct connection; there is a slight physical separation across which the impulse is transmitted by means of chemicals contained in the *terminal buttons* at the end of the axon. The axons from a great many neurons

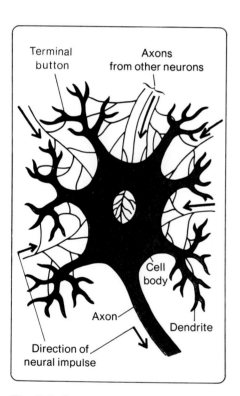

Terminal button

Axons from other neurons

Cell body

Axon

Dendrite

Direction of neural impulse

Fig. 2-2 Synapses at the cell body of a neuron
Many different axons, each of which branches repeatedly, synapse on the dendrites and cell body of a single neuron. Each branch of an axon ends in a swelling called a terminal button, which contains the chemical that transmits the nerve impulse across the synapse to the dendrites or cell body of the next cell.

(perhaps about 1,000) may synapse with the dendrites and cell body of a single neuron (see Figure 2-2).

While all neurons have these general features, they vary greatly in size and shape. A neuron in the spinal cord may have an axon two to three feet long, running from the tip of the spine to the big toe; a neuron in the brain may cover only a few thousandths of an inch with all its parts. Neurons that carry messages to the brain or spinal cord about what is going on in the environment or within the body are called *afferent neurons.* Afferent neurons receive their input from *receptors,* which are specialized cells in the sense organs, muscles, skin, and joints. Receptors detect physical or chemical changes and translate these events into impulses that travel along afferent neurons to the brain or spinal cord. As we will see in Chapter 4, different receptors respond to different forms of energy; receptors in the eye respond to electromagnetic energy; those in the ear, to changes in air pressure; those in the nose, to the shape of certain molecules; and so on. The receptors translate these stimuli into a form that can be transmitted by the nerve cells. In addition to carrying messages from the sense organs, afferent neurons convey to the brain information about the position of our muscles and joints.

Efferent neurons convey outgoing signals from the brain or spinal cord to the muscles that control our movement as well as to those that control the functioning of the digestive organs, heart, bladder, and iris of the eye. They also control the hormonal secretion of many glands. It may help to remember that *efferent* neurons carry information to the *effector* organs—the muscles and glands.

A *nerve* is a bundle of elongated axons belonging to hundreds or thousands of neurons. A single nerve may contain both afferent and efferent neurons. Closely interwoven among the neurons are a large number of *glial cells* (from the Greek word *glia,* meaning "glue"). Until recently, researchers thought that their chief function was to hold the neurons in place and provide them with nutrients. However, new evidence indicates that the glial cells engage in complex chemical interactions with neighboring nerve cells and may play an important role in nerve conduction.

Transmission of Neural Impulses

The movement of a neural impulse along a nerve is quite different from the flow of electric current through a wire. Electricity travels at the speed of light (186,300 miles per second), whereas a nerve impulse in the human body may travel at anywhere from 2 to 200 miles per hour, depending on the diameter of the axon and other factors. The analogy of a fuse has sometimes been used: when a fuse is lighted, one part of the fuse lights the next part, the impulse being regenerated along the way. However, the details of neural transmission are much more complex than this. The process is *electrochemical.* The thin membrane that holds together the protoplasm of the cell is not equally permeable to the different types of electrically charged ions that normally float in the protoplasm of the cell and in the liquid surrounding the cell. In its resting state, the cell membrane keeps out positively charged sodium ions (Na^+) and allows in potassium ions (K^+) and chloride ions (Cl^-). As a result, there is a small electrical potential, or difference, across the membrane. The inside of a nerve cell is slightly more negative than the outside; this is its *resting potential.*

When the axon of a nerve cell is stimulated, the electric potential across the membrane is reduced at the point of stimulation. If the reduction in potential is large enough, the permeability of the cell membrane suddenly changes, allow-

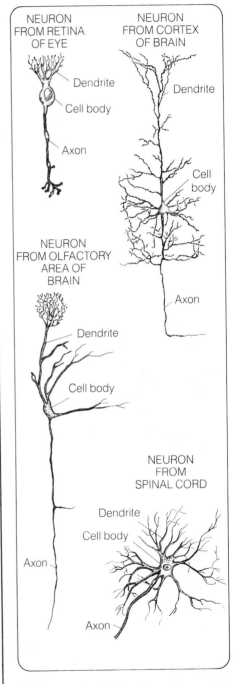

Shapes and relative sizes of neurons

ing the sodium ions to enter the cell. This process is called *depolarization;* now the outside of the cell membrane is *negative* with respect to the inside. This change affects the adjacent portion of the axon, causing its membrane to permit the inflow of sodium ions. This process, repeating itself down the length of the axon, is the nerve impulse. The nerve impulse is also known as the *action potential,* in contrast to the resting potential, of the neuron. Because the nerve impulse is generated anew at each stage along the axon, it does not diminish in size during transmission.

The axons of most neurons are covered by a thin sheath, the *myelin sheath,* which serves to insulate them from each other; such fibers are known as *myelinated* fibers. If the myelin sheath were continuous, it would prevent conduction, but it is interrupted approximately every two millimeters by constrictions called *nodes,* where the myelin is very thin or absent. Because conduction jumps along the axon from node to node, it is much more rapid in myelinated fibers than in nonmyelinated fibers. The myelin sheath was a late development in evolution and is characteristic of the nervous systems of higher animals. The fact that the formation of the myelin sheath of many nerve fibers in the brain is not completed until some time after birth suggests that the maturation of some of the infant's sensory and motor abilities may be related to the gradual process of myelination.

Synaptic Transmission

The synaptic junction between neurons is of tremendous importance because it is there that nerve cells transfer signals; depending on the way groups of neurons interact, some messages may get through and others may not. A single neuron transmits an impulse, or "fires," when the stimulation reaching it exceeds a certain threshold level. Because its axon does not transmit at all prior to this, the neuron is said to follow an *all-or-none* principle of action. The neuron fires in a single, brief burst and is then temporarily inactive (in what is called a *refractory phase*) for a few thousandths of a second. During the refractory phase the cell returns to its resting potential. The size of the action potential is constant, and once started it travels all the way down the axon to the synapses. But whether the neuron fires or not depends on *graded potentials* (potentials that are not all-or-none but can be any size) in the dendrites or cell body. These graded potentials are induced by stimulation at the synapses by other neurons, and their size varies with the amount and kind of incoming activity. When the sum of the graded potentials becomes sufficiently large, enough depolarization is generated to trigger the all-or-none action potential. If the graded potentials do not reach the discharge threshold of the action potential, no activity occurs.

Since the size of the action potential is constant—that is, it does not vary with the strength of the stimulus—how is information concerning stimulus intensity conveyed? The answer is that a strong stimulus will (1) cause the individual neuron to fire more frequently and (2) fire more neurons than a weaker stimulus. For example, the neurons in a nerve that is responding to the stretching of a muscle will fire at a rate proportional to the amount of stretch, and the greater the stretch, the more neurons will fire.

An interesting new area of research studies the relationships between neuron activity and behavior. The electrical activity of a single neuron can be recorded by a microelectrode that is less than $1/50,000$ of an inch in diameter at the tip. Microelectrodes implanted in different areas of an animal's brain make it possible to determine which nerve cells respond to a particular stimulus (such

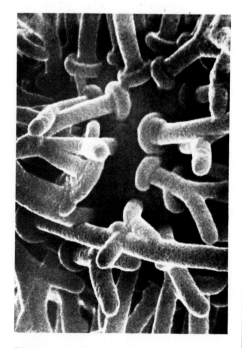

Photograph of nerve fibers and terminal buttons

as touching a certain spot on the animal's body) or how the pattern of neuron firing changes as the animal becomes more proficient in learning to perform a new task. Also, by examining nerve tissue with an electron microscope, it is possible to count and measure synapses. Recent studies have shown that synapses change in number, size, and excitability as the result of an animal's early experience.

Although still in the pioneering stage, this research may provide the key to understanding the changes that occur in the brain as the result of learning. It may well be that anatomical changes in the number and structure of synapses account for our ability to remember things over long periods of time.

NEUROTRANSMITTERS   As we have said, the nerve cells do not connect directly at the synapse; there is a slight gap across which the signal must be transmitted (see Figure 2-3). Although in a few areas of the nervous system the electrical activity in one neuron can stimulate another neuron directly, in most instances a chemical serves as the transmitter agent. When a neural impulse reaches the end of the axon, the chemical—which is stored in tiny vesicles in the terminal button—is released into the synaptic gap, or cleft. This chemical *neurotransmitter* acts on the membrane of the receiving cell to change its permeability in the direction of depolarization. If depolarization becomes large enough to exceed the threshold point, the cell fires an all-or-none action potential down its own axon to influence other neurons. The greater the number of synapses releasing neurotransmitters onto the receiving cell, the more likely it is that the cell will fire.

This process occurs at an *excitatory synapse*. But there are also *inhibitory synapses* that work in an analogous but opposite manner. The neurotransmitter released at an inhibitory synapse produces a shift in the cell membrane potential of the receiving neuron that is *opposite* in direction to the action potential. That is, at an inhibitory synapse the neurotransmitter tends to keep the membrane potential of the receiving cell *below* threshold. During this brief period, it is considerably more difficult for excitatory synapses to fire the neuron. Remember that any one neuron receives synapses from many other nerve cells. Some of these synapses may be excitatory and some inhibitory. The constant interplay of excitation and inhibition determines the likelihood that a given neuron will fire an all-or-none action potential at any given moment.

A number of neurotransmitters have been identified, and many others probably exist. Acetylcholine (ACh) is the chemical transmitter at every synapse where a nerve axon terminates at a skeletal muscle fiber and hence is responsible for muscle contraction. Certain drugs that block the release of ACh from the terminal buttons can cause fatal muscular paralysis. For example, *botulinus toxin*, which can form in improperly canned foods, can cause death when the muscles involved in breathing become paralyzed. *Curare*, a poison once used by South American Indians to tip their arrows, occupies the receptor site in the receiving cell, thus preventing ACh from acting, and resulting in temporary paralysis. Death from curare also results from an inability to expand the chest to breathe. But if the victim is artificially respirated until the effects of the drug wear off, there is no permanent damage. Some of the nerve gases developed for warfare cause paralysis by destroying an enzyme that normally inactivates ACh once a nerve has fired. This produces a buildup of ACh to a point at which further synaptic transmission is impossible.

Some of the mood-altering drugs (such as tranquilizers and LSD) probably create their effects by changing activity at the synapses. The tranquilizer

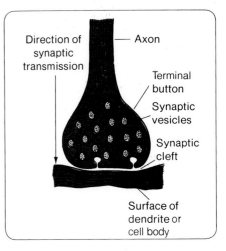

Fig. 2-3 Synaptic junction
When a nerve impulse reaches the end of an axon it stimulates the synaptic vesicles to discharge their chemical contents into the synaptic cleft. This transmitter chemical changes the membrane permeability of the receiving cell, making it either more likely to fire (excitatory synapse) or less likely to fire (inhibitory synapse).

Neurotransmitters and Human Memory

It seems reasonable to assume that if neural transmission could be made more efficient, there might be a resulting increase in the efficiency with which we learn and remember information. And, indeed, recent research suggests that this may be the case. Acetylcholine (ACh), in addition to its role in muscle action, is the chemical transmitter for many of the synapses in the brain. Studies show that a drug called *physostigmine*, which increases the availability of ACh at neuron synapses, improves learning and memory in human subjects. (Physostigmine inhibits the action of an enzyme that destroys ACh.)

In one experiment, subjects were asked to memorize a list of 20 unrelated words. They then wrote down as many words as they could remember and, at the end of the trial, were told the words they had forgotten. The test was repeated six times. In the experimental condition the subjects were given an injection of physostigmine; in the control condition they were injected with a saline solution (which has no physiological effect). Figure 2-4 shows the number of words recalled under each condition for the six learn-

Fig. 2-4 Effects of physostigmine on memory
Total number of words recalled from a list of 20 words on each of six learning trials. In the experimental condition (red) the subjects were given an injection of physostigmine; in the control condition (black) they were injected with a neutral (saline) solution. (After Davis and others, 1978)

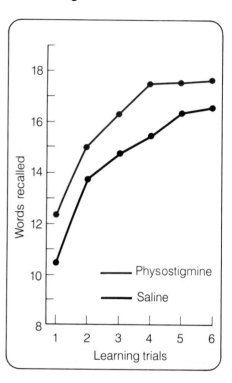

ing trials. Performance was significantly better following the injection of physostigmine.

Related experiments with humans and animals support the possibility that memory can be improved by increasing the activity of nerve cells that use ACh as a transmitter (e.g., Sitaram and others, 1978). In addition, autopsies of individuals who suffered from *senile dementia* (a mental deterioration that may occur with old age) show a loss of nerve cells that contain ACh. Drugs that reduce the activity of these neurons can produce a memory disorder similar to senile dementia, even in young children.

At present it is not clear whether physostigmine affects only memory or whether it also affects higher-order mental functions. Since research in this area is still at an early stage, we should not conclude that there will soon be "memory pills" on the market that we can take to sharpen our cognitive abilities.

chlorpromazine blocks the release of the neurotransmitter norepinephrine and thus allows fewer messages to get through. LSD is similar in composition to the neurotransmitter serotonin, which affects emotions. Evidence shows that LSD accumulates in certain brain cells, where it may act like serotonin and overstimulate the cells.

Much research remains to be done on the mysteries of synaptic transmission. The answers to many problems ranging from memory to mental illness may become clearer as we discover more about the intricacies of neural communication.

Organization of the Nervous System

Nerves, groups of axons bundled together, spread out to every part of the body—to sense receptors, skin, muscles, and internal organs. The neuron cell bodies are not part of the long nerves but are grouped together into *nuclei* (in the brain or spinal cord) and *ganglia* (lying outside the spinal cord or close to some of the internal organs).

Divisions of the Nervous System

All parts of the nervous system are interrelated. However, for purposes of anatomical discussion, the nervous system can be separated into the following divisions and subdivisions:

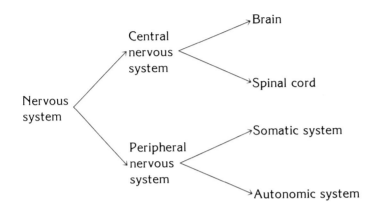

The *central nervous system* includes all the nerves in the brain and spinal cord, and it contains the majority of the body's neurons. The *peripheral nervous system* consists of the nerves leading from the brain and spinal cord to the other parts of the body. The peripheral nervous system is further subdivided into the *somatic system* and the *autonomic system*.

The nerves of the somatic system transmit information about external stimulation from the skin, muscles, and joints to the central nervous system; they make us aware of pain, pressure, and temperature variations. Nerves of the somatic system also carry impulses from the central nervous system back to the body parts, where they initiate action. All the muscles we use in making voluntary movements, as well as involuntary adjustments in posture and balance, are controlled by these nerves.

The nerves of the autonomic system run to and from the internal organs, regulating such processes as respiration, heart rate, and digestion. The autonomic system, which plays a major role in emotion, will be discussed later in this chapter.

Spinal Cord

The nerve fibers running from various parts of the body to and from the brain are gathered together in the spinal cord, where they are protected by the bony spinal vertebrae. Some of the very simplest stimulus-response reflexes are carried out within the spinal cord. One example is the knee jerk, the extension of the leg in response to a tap on the tendon that runs in front of the knee cap. Frequently a doctor uses this test to determine the efficiency of the spinal reflexes. The natural function of this reflex is to ensure that the leg will extend when the knee is bent by the force of gravity so that the organism remains standing. When the knee tendon is tapped, the attached muscle stretches, and a message from sensory cells embedded in the muscle is transmitted through

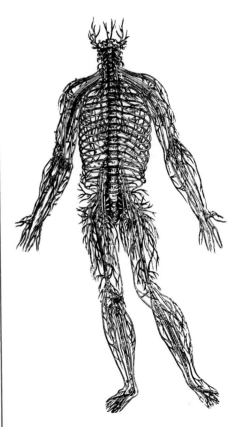

A woodcut showing the delineation of the spinal nerves done in 1543 by Andreas Vesalius.

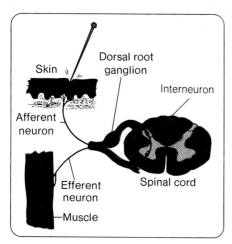

Fig. 2-5 Three-neuron reflex arc
Diagram illustrates how nerve impulses from a sense organ in the skin reach a skeletal muscle by a three-neuron arc at the level of entrance to the spinal cord. Awareness of this automatic reflex occurs because impulses also reach the cerebral hemisphere by way of an ascending tract. The H-shaped portion is gray matter at the center of the spinal cord, consisting largely of cell bodies and their interconnections.

afferent neurons to the spinal cord. There the afferent neurons synapse directly with many efferent neurons, whose axons run back to the same muscle, causing it to contract and the leg to extend.

Although this response *can* occur solely in the spinal cord without any assistance from the brain, it normally is modulated by messages from the higher nervous centers. If you grip your hands together just before the knee is tapped, the extension movement is exaggerated. And if you want to consciously inhibit the reflex just before the doctor taps the tendon, you can do so. The basic mechanism is built into the spinal cord, but it is under the control of the brain.

The simplest reflex may involve only afferent and efferent neurons, but most reflexes also involve one or more *interneurons* in the spinal cord, which mediate between incoming and outgoing neurons. The interneurons increase the possibility of more complex reflex activity. Figure 2-5 shows a basic three-neuron reflex arc.

Some reflexes are controlled at the level of the spinal cord by arcs of this type. For example, if the spinal cord is severed from the brain (as in the case of a paraplegic accident victim), reflexes such as the knee jerk and erection of the penis still function—even though there is neither voluntary movement nor sensation below the point of injury. But most activity involves transmission of nerve impulses to the brain, where complex interactions with other neurons occur. These interactions may involve only the lower, more primitive sections of the brain (as in walking), or they may require numerous complicated circuits through the higher sections of the brain (as in thinking and problem solving).

Hierarchical Structure of the Brain

As the spinal cord enters the bony skull it enlarges into the *brain stem,* which contains all the ascending and descending nerve fibers that link the body with the higher brain structures as well as some important nuclei (clusters of nerve cell bodies). From an evolutionary viewpoint, the brain stem is the oldest part of the brain. It includes structures (found in all vertebrates) that regulate the complex reflexes—for example, respiration, heart rate, and temperature—necessary for the maintenance of life. The activity controlled by the brain stem is much more complex than that controlled by the spinal cord, but it is still fairly reflexive in nature. That is, the neural connections within the brain stem are largely fixed and automatic.

The *cerebral hemispheres* (known collectively as the *cerebrum*) constitute most of the brain. They are attached to a small part of the brain stem and balloon out from it on all sides, surrounding and concealing most of it from view. In order to see the structures of the brain stem, it is necessary to slice through the middle of the brain to get the view shown in Figure 2-6. The cerebrum, which developed later than the brain stem in the evolutionary process, is the center for nonreflexive mental processes.

Some brain structures are clearly demarcated; others gradually merge into each other, and this causes considerable debate about their exact boundaries and the neural functions they control. For our purposes it will be helpful to think of the human brain as composed of three concentric layers that developed at different stages in evolution: (1) a primitive central core, (2) the limbic

CEREBRUM
(Surface: cerebral cortex)
Sense perception; voluntary
movements; learning, remembering,
thinking; emotion; consciousness

THALAMUS
Sensory relay station
on the way to the
cerebral cortex

CORPUS CALLOSUM
Fibers connecting the
two cerebral hemispheres

HYPOTHALAMUS
Control of visceral
and somatic functions,
such as temperature,
metabolism, and
endocrine balance

RETICULAR SYSTEM
Arousal system that
activates wide regions
of the cerebral cortex

CEREBELLUM
Muscle tone; body
balance; coordination
of voluntary movement

PITUITARY GLAND
An endocrine gland

MEDULLA
Controls breathing,
swallowing, digestion,
and heartbeat

SPINAL CORD
Conduction paths for
motor and sensory
impulses; local reflexes
(for example, knee jerk)

Fig. 2-6 The human brain
This schematic drawing shows the main subdivisions of the human central nervous system and their functions. (Only the upper portion of the spinal cord, which is also part of the central nervous system, is shown here.)

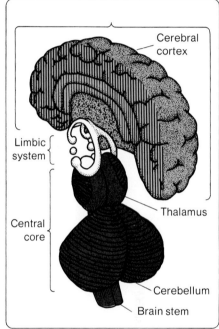

Cerebral cortex

Limbic system

Thalamus

Central core

Cerebellum

Brain stem

Fig. 2-7 Three concentric layers of the human brain
The central core and the limbic system are shown in their entirety, but the left cerebral hemisphere has been removed. The cerebellum of the central core controls balance and muscular coordination; the thalamus serves as a switchboard for messages coming from the sense organs; the hypothalamus (not shown, but located below the thalamus) regulates endocrine activity and such life-maintaining processes as metabolism and temperature control. The limbic system is concerned with actions that satisfy basic needs and with emotion. The cerebral cortex, an outer layer of cells covering the cerebrum, is the center of higher mental processes, where sensations are registered, voluntary actions initiated, decisions made, and memories stored.

system, which later evolved upon this core, and (3) the cerebrum, which is the center for higher mental processes. Figure 2-7 shows how these layers fit together and are closely interconnected. The three concentric layers may be compared with the more detailed cross section of the human brain in Figure 2-6.

Central Core

The central core includes most of the brain stem. The first slight enlargement of the spinal cord as it enters the skull is the *medulla*, a narrow structure (about an inch and a half long) that controls breathing and some reflexes that help the organism maintain an upright posture. At this point, also, the major nerve tracts coming up from the spinal cord and descending from the brain cross over so that the right side of the brain receives sensory impulses from and controls the left side of the body, and the left side of the brain receives sensory impulses from and controls the right side of the body. We will have more to say about the significance of this crossover later.

CEREBELLUM Attached to the rear of the brain stem, slightly above the medulla, is a convoluted structure, the *cerebellum*. The cerebellum is concerned primarily with the regulation of motor coordination, and its structure is much the same in lower vertebrates (such as snakes and fish) as in mammals, including humans. Specific movements are initiated at higher levels, but their coordination and adjustment in relation to the environment depend on the cerebellum. The cerebellum regulates muscle tone and controls all the intricate movements involved in the swimming of a fish, the flight of a bird, or the playing of a musical instrument by a human being. Damage to the cerebellum results in jerky, uncoordinated movements; often the person can no longer automatically perform even simple movements (such as walking), but must concentrate on each step involved in the total action.

THALAMUS AND HYPOTHALAMUS Located just above the brain stem inside the cerebral hemispheres are two egg-shaped groups of nerve cell nuclei that make up the *thalamus*. One region of the thalamus acts as a relay station and directs incoming information to the cerebrum from the sense receptors for vision, hearing, touch, taste, and smell. Another region of the thalamus plays an important role in the control of sleep and wakefulness and is considered part of the *limbic system*.

The *hypothalamus* is a much smaller structure, located just below the thalamus. Despite its size, the hypothalamus plays an extremely important role in many different kinds of motivation. Centers in the hypothalamus govern eating, drinking, sexual behavior, and temperature control. The hypothalamus regulates endocrine activity and maintains *homeostasis*. Homeostasis refers to the general level of functioning characteristic of the healthy organism, such as normal body temperature, heart rate, and blood pressure. Under stress, the usual equilibrium is disturbed, and processes are set into motion to correct the disequilibrium and return the body to its normal level of functioning. For example, if we are too warm we perspire, and if we are too cool we shiver. Both these processes tend to restore normal temperature and are controlled by the hypothalamus. The hypothalamus appears to contain control mechanisms that detect changes in body systems and correct the imbalance.

The hypothalamus also plays an important role in emotion. We noted in Chapter 1 that mild electrical stimulation of certain areas in the hypothalamus produces feelings of pleasure, while stimulation in adjacent regions produces sensations that appear to be unpleasant or painful. By its influence on the pituitary gland, which lies just below it (see Figure 2-6), the hypothalamus controls reactions to fear and stress.

RETICULAR SYSTEM A network of neural circuits that extends from the lower brain stem up to the thalamus, traversing through some of the other central core structures, is the *reticular* ("network") *system*. The reticular system plays an important role in controlling our state of arousal or awareness. When an electric current of a certain voltage is sent through electrodes implanted in the reticular system of a cat or dog, the animal goes to sleep; stimulation by a current with a more rapidly changing wave form awakens the sleeping animal. If lesions are made in the reticular system, the animal often becomes permanently stuporous or goes into a coma.

The reticular system is not the only brain region that controls sleep and waking; other areas of the brain stem are involved, as are the thalamus and parts of the cerebral cortex. The reticular system may function to integrate signals from the various areas concerned with arousal.

The reticular system also appears to play a role in our ability to selectively focus attention. All of the sense receptors have nerve fibers that feed into the reticular system; and there is some evidence that the system may act as a filter, allowing some sensory messages to pass to the cerebral cortex (to conscious awareness) while blocking or toning down others. Thus, in a moment of intense concentration you may be unaware of the noises around you or a pain that was previously quite noticeable.

Limbic System

Around the central core of the brain, lying along the innermost edge of the cerebral hemispheres, are a number of structures that grouped together are called the *limbic system*. From an evolutionary view, the limbic system is more recent than the central core; it is not found in organisms below mammals on the phylogenetic scale. This system is closely interconnected with the hypothalamus and appears to impose additional controls over some of the "instinctive" behaviors regulated by the hypothalamus and brain stem. Animals that have no limbic system (for example, fish and reptiles) carry out activities such as feeding, attacking, fleeing from danger, and mating by means of very stereotyped behaviors. In mammals, the limbic system seems to inhibit some of the instinctive behavior patterns, allowing the organism to be more responsive to changes in the environment.

One part of the limbic system, the *hippocampus*, appears to play a special role in memory. Individuals with damage to this area are apparently unable to store new information in memory. They can remember skills and information learned prior to the injury but cannot remember anything new (Milner, 1964).

The limbic system is also involved in emotional behavior. Monkeys with lesions in some regions of the limbic system show rage reactions at the slightest provocation—suggesting that the destroyed area was exerting an inhibiting influence. Monkeys with lesions in other areas of the limbic system no longer express aggressive behavior and show no hostility when attacked. They simply ignore the attacker and act as if nothing had happened.

Treating the brain as three concentric structures—a central core, the limbic system, and the cerebrum—must not lead us to think of these interrelated structures as independent. We might use the analogy of a bank of interrelated computers. Each has specialized functions, but they still work together to produce the most effective result. Similarly, the analysis of information coming from the senses requires one kind of computation and decision process (for which the cerebrum is well adapted) differing from that which controls a reflexive sequence of activities (the limbic system). The finer adjustments of the muscles (as in writing or playing a musical instrument) require another kind of control system, in this case mediated by the cerebellum. All these activities are ordered into complex subordinate and superordinate systems that maintain the integrity of the organism.

Both playing (photo at left) and fighting (photo at right) appear to be controlled by the limbic system.

How the Brain

The brain is a very complex structure, and great ingenuity is required to discover how it operates. How can we tell whether a particular part of the brain is associated with a particular behavior? Historically, the question of *localization of brain function*—whether certain brain areas control specific acts or functions—has been a topic of debate. Some early investigators sought to construct a detailed "map" of the brain, locating the neural centers that control such specific functions as speaking, recognizing spoken words, recognizing printed words, and so forth (Broca, 1861; Fritsch and Hitzig, 1870). Some even went so far as to specify one brain area for reading English and a separate area for reading French (Hinshelwood, 1900). Others proposed that the brain acts as a total mass with few localized functions—all areas were assumed to be "equipotential." They based their conclusions on experiments with rats in which varying amounts and locations of brain tissue were destroyed surgically. The *amount* of tissue destruction appeared to be much more important to the animal's behavior than the specific area involved (Lashley, 1929).

Technological advances in recent years have made it possible to study the brain more precisely than ever before. It is now well established that some functions are localized in fairly circumscribed brain areas; speech, recognition of spoken words, and the production of motor responses are examples. All areas of the human brain are not equipotential. On the other hand, many different brain regions are involved in such higher mental processes as reasoning and problem solving. In addition, many functions are duplicated in more than one brain area. Thus, if one part of the brain is damaged by concussion or stroke, other areas can often take over its functions.

The following four methods are the ones used most often by physiological

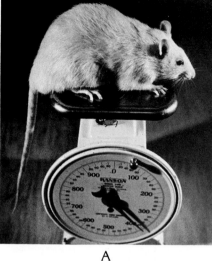

A

Fig. 2-8 Electrodes implanted in the brain
A. Rat being weighed before operation to determine the proper dose of anaesthetic. **B.** Anaesthetized rat under the stereotaxic instrument, which implants the electrodes through tiny holes in the skull. **C.** Insertion of screws that help to anchor dental cement to skull. **D.** Electrodes are cemented and connected to pins that project from the cement. **E.** Rat with electrodes implanted.

B

D

psychologists and neurophysiologists in studying the brain.

1 *Injury or surgical ablation.* Noting the kinds of symptoms produced when tumors or injuries damage certain parts of the brain may give clues about functions controlled by the area. Early observations that injury to the left side of the brain usually resulted in speech defects, whereas damage to the right side did not, led to localization of a speech center in the left cerebral hemisphere. Improved methods of locating the area of injury and assessing the kind of language func-

tions disturbed have specified more exactly the areas involved in different linguistic abilities.

In experiments with animals it is possible to remove systematically parts of the brain (or destroy the tissue electrically) and observe the kinds of defects that result. Sometimes ablation operations are performed on human patients when the removal of abnormal brain tissue is essential to their well-being (for example, to remove tumors or control epilepsy). Such patients are carefully studied to assess the effects of the operation on their abilities.

2 *Electrical or chemical stimulation.*

Is Studied

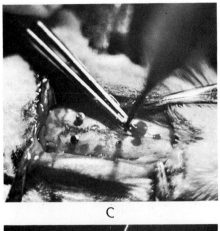

C

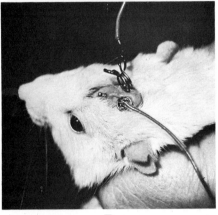

E

Stimulating parts of the brain with mild electrical currents produces effects on behavior. Brain surgery on human patients is often done under local anaesthesia so the surgeon can tell (by the patient's responses when different points are stimulated electrically) which area to remove. From patient reports of sensations during stimulation, fairly accurate maps of the cortex have been obtained.

Experimenters have used permanently implanted electrodes in animals to produce repeated stimulation of a local part of the brain (see Figure 2-8). Studies with such electrodes help determine where sensory effects occur and where various types of muscular activity are controlled.

Chemical stimulation has also been used to affect behavior. A small tube is inserted into the animal's brain so that its end touches the area of interest. A minute amount of some chemical, often one that resembles a neurotransmitter, is delivered through the tube and the behavioral effects are observed.

3 *Electrical effects of neural activity.* When neural action occurs, slight electrical currents are produced. By inserting at appropriate places electrodes connected to measuring devices, the experimenter can detect whether impulses starting at, say, the ear reach the part of the brain where the electrodes are inserted.

The brain as a whole also produces rhythmical electrical discharges. The record of these total brain discharges, known as an *electroencephalogram* (EEG), plays its part in the study of central nervous system activity. For example, if a particular kind of stimulation changes the rhythmic discharges picked up from one part of the brain and does not affect the discharges from another part, we can assume that the stimulation affected that particular region (see Figure 2-9).

4 *Single neuron activity.* The development of extremely refined microelectrodes (about one thousandth of a millimeter in size) has made it possible to record the nerve impulse from a single neuron. This technique, which permits the investigator to study the activity of a single nerve cell while the organism is being exposed to different stimuli, yields information that cannot be obtained by recording massed electrical discharges (the EEG).

These methods are noted here; later chapters will give examples of how results obtained by these methods further our psychological understanding.

Fig. 2-9 Electrical action of the brain Through electrodes attached to the outside of the skull, the electroencephalograph measures the pattern of electrical activity within the brain. When the brain is at rest, the basic pattern is a large-amplitude "alpha" wave of about 10 cycles per second, as shown in the extreme left of A and in the first six seconds of B and C. When the brain responds to sensory inputs, such as vision or touch, or when it is engaged by a mental problem, the alpha waves give way to irregular waves that are higher in frequency and lower in amplitude. (After Eccles, 1958)

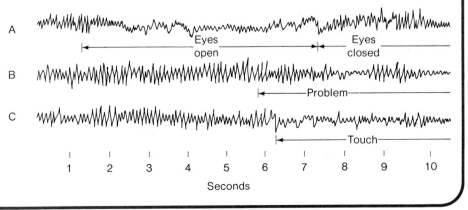

Cerebral Cortex

Structure of the Cerebral Cortex

The cerebrum is more highly developed in human beings than in any other organism. The *cerebral cortex* is the thick layer of nerve cell bodies covering the cerebrum; in Latin, *cortex* means "bark." If you look at a preserved brain, the cortical layer appears gray, because it consists largely of nerve cell bodies and unmyelinated fibers—hence the term "gray matter." The inside of the cerebrum, beneath the cortex, is composed mostly of myelinated axons and appears white. (A live brain appears slightly pinkish, because of the blood supply.) It is in the cerebral cortex that all complex mental activity takes place.

The cerebral cortex of a lower mammal, such as the rat, is small and relatively smooth. As we ascend the phylogenetic scale toward the higher mammals, the amount of cortex relative to the amount of total brain tissue increases accordingly, and the cortex becomes progressively more wrinkled and convoluted, so that its actual surface area is far greater than it would be if it were a smooth covering over the surface of the cerebrum. There is a general correlation between the cortical development of a species, its position on the phylogenetic scale, and the complexity of its behavior.

There are indications that the development of the cerebral cortex can be influenced by the organism's early experience. A rat raised in an "enriched" environment (in a large cage with playmates and all kinds of equipment to climb on and investigate) develops a heavier and thicker cerebral cortex than a rat raised alone in a bare cage; and the rat in an enriched environment will learn more readily (Rosenzweig and Bennett, 1976).

All of the sensory systems (for example, vision, audition, and touch) project information to the cortex, each system to a specific region. The motor systems, which control the muscles and glands, originate in an area known as the *motor cortex*. The rest of the cortex, which is neither sensory nor motor, is called the *association cortex*. This is the area concerned with more complex aspects of behavior—memory, thought, and language—and it is by far the largest area of the cortex in human brains.

Before discussing some of these areas, we need a few landmarks to use in describing areas of the *cerebral hemispheres*. The two hemispheres are symmetrical, one on the right and one on the left, with a deep division between them, running from front to rear. So our first classification is the division into *right* and *left hemispheres*. For the most part, functions of the right side of the body are controlled by the left hemisphere and functions of the left side, by the right hemisphere. Each hemisphere is divided into four *lobes:* the *frontal, parietal, occipital,* and *temporal*. The divisions between these lobes are shown in Figure 2-10. The frontal lobe is separated from the parietal lobe by the *central fissure,* running down from the part of the cerebrum near the top of the head sideways toward the ears. The division between the parietal lobe and the occipital lobe is not as clear-cut; for our purpose, it suffices to know that the parietal lobe is at the top of the brain, behind the central fissure, while the occipital lobe is at the rear of the brain. The temporal lobe is set off by a deep fissure at the side of the brain, the *lateral fissure*.

Cortical Areas and Their Functions

MOTOR AREA The *motor area,* which controls all movements of the body, lies just in front of the central fissure, half of the body being represented by

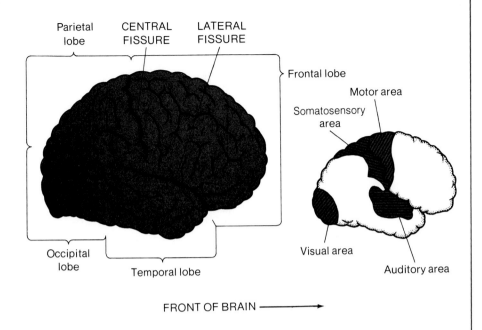

Parietal lobe   CENTRAL FISSURE   LATERAL FISSURE

Frontal lobe

Occipital lobe

Temporal lobe

FRONT OF BRAIN →

Motor area

Somatosensory area

Visual area

Auditory area

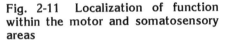

Fig. 2-10 Localization of function in the human cortex
Left: the lobes of the cerebral hemispheres and the divisions separating them. Right: the somatosensory, motor, visual, and auditory areas.

each side. When stimulated electrically, parts of the motor area cause movements in the extremities; when these parts are injured, movement of the same extremities is impaired. The body is represented in approximately upside-down form, movement of the toes being mediated by the part near the top of the head, and tongue and mouth movements by the part near the bottom of the area (see Figure 2-11). Movements on the right side of the body originate through stimulation of the motor area of the left hemisphere; movements on the left side, through stimulation of the right hemisphere.

SOMATOSENSORY AREA In the parietal lobe, separated from the motor area by the central fissure, lies an area that if stimulated electrically produces

Fig. 2-11 Localization of function within the motor and somatosensory areas
Two cross sections through the cerebrum are indicated: one for the motor cortex (in red) and the other for the somatosensory cortex (in gray). The various functions are represented in mirror image in both hemispheres, but in the figure only one side is labeled. (After Penfield and Rasmussen, 1950)

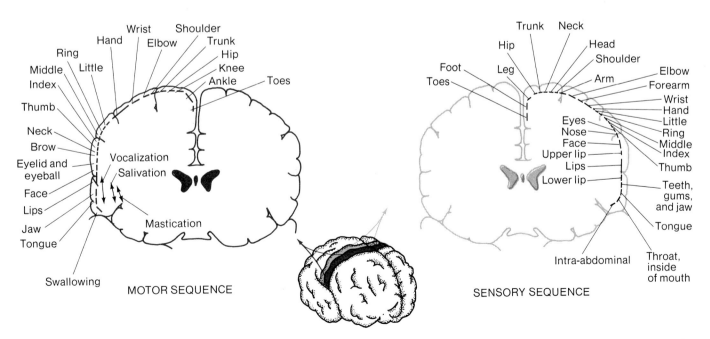

sensory experiences, as though a part of the body were being touched or moved. This is called the *somatosensory* (body-sense) *area.* Heat, cold, touch, pain, and the sense of body movement are all represented here. The lower extremities of the body are represented high on the area of the opposite hemisphere; the face, low.

It seems to be a general rule that the amount of cortex corresponding to a particular region of the body surface is directly related to the sensitivity and use of that region. Figure 2-11 shows that the area devoted to the hands and fingers, for example, is much larger than that devoted to the feet and toes. (This is true for both sensation and movement.) Among four-footed mammals, the dog has only a small amount of cortical tissue representing the forepaws, whereas the raccoon, which makes extensive use of its forepaws in exploring and manipulating its environment, has a much larger representative cortical area, including regions for the separate fingers of the forepaw (Welker, Johnson, and Pubols, 1964). The rat, which learns a great deal about its environment by means of its sensitive whiskers, has a separate cortical area for each whisker (Van der Loos and Woolsey, 1973).

VISUAL AREA At the back of each occipital lobe is an area important in vision, known as the *visual cortex* (see Figure 2-10). As we will see in Chapter 5, investigators have gained detailed knowledge of this area through studies of the electrical responses of single cells in the visual cortex of cats and monkeys.

When the visual cortex of human beings is stimulated electrically during the course of brain surgery, the patient (who is under local anaesthetic) reports seeing flashes or spots of light. This phenomenon forms the basis for research that may eventually provide "artificial vision" for blind people. An array of electrodes were implanted in the visual cortex of two blind subjects (see Figure 2-12). When different groups of these electrodes were stimulated electrically, the blind subjects experienced patterns of visual sensations. Although these sensations were a crude approximation of real sight, further research may provide a practical device that will enable blind persons to perceive objects and to read.

AUDITORY AREA The *auditory area* is found on the surface of the temporal lobe at the side of each hemisphere. There is some spatial distribution, one part being sensitive to high tones and a different part sensitive to low tones. Both

Fig. 2-12 Artificial vision
The figure on the left below shows the experimental setup. A thin strip of Teflon with 64 electrode contacts is inserted against the visual cortex. Wires from each electrode connect to a computer. By stimulating pairs of electrodes at a time, it is possible to map on a TV screen (with the aid of a computer) the relative position of each stimulated light spot, or phosphene, in the subject's visual cortex. Once the phosphene makeup of the subject's visual field is known, the experimenters stimulate the electrodes to present patterns and letters to the visual field. The subject draws on a pad what he or she "sees." A potential artificial vision device is shown on the right. (After Dobelle and others, 1976)

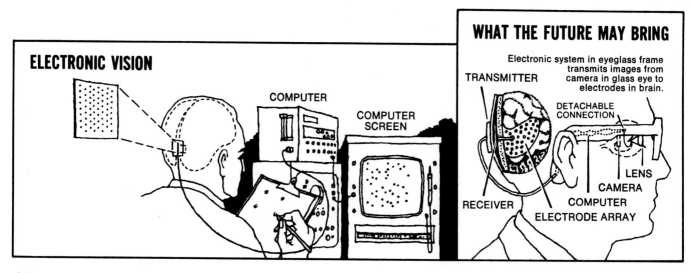

ELECTRONIC VISION

COMPUTER

COMPUTER SCREEN

WHAT THE FUTURE MAY BRING

Electronic system in eyeglass frame transmits images from camera in glass eye to electrodes in brain.

TRANSMITTER

DETACHABLE CONNECTION

LENS

CAMERA

COMPUTER

ELECTRODE ARRAY

RECEIVER

ears are represented in the auditory areas on both sides, so that the loss of one temporal lobe has very little effect on hearing.

The relation between the auditory area and behavior is illustrated by an experiment in which monkeys with electrodes implanted in their auditory cortex were trained to press a key in response to a tone. When the tone was turned on, the animal required approximately 200 milliseconds to respond. When, however, direct electrical stimulation of the auditory cortex was substituted for the tone, the response time was 185 milliseconds. The 15-millisecond difference between responses to acoustic and cortical stimulation presumably reflects the time required for the nerve impulse to reach the auditory cortex. The fact that recordings of action potentials in the auditory cortex also show a 15-millisecond delay following onset of the tone supports this assumption (Miller, Moody, and Stebbins, 1969).

ASSOCIATION AREAS   The many large areas of the cerebral cortex that are not directly concerned with sensory or motor processes are called *association areas*. They integrate inputs from more than one sensory channel and also function in learning, memory, language, and thinking.

The *frontal association areas* (those parts of the frontal lobes anterior to the motor area) appear to play an important role in the thought processes required for problem solving. In monkeys, for example, lesions in the frontal lobes destroy the ability to solve a delayed-response problem. In this kind of problem, food is placed in one of two cups while the monkey watches, and the cups are covered with identical objects. An opaque screen is then placed between the monkey and the cups; after a specified time (from 5 to 60 seconds) the screen is removed and the monkey is allowed to choose one of the cups. Normal monkeys can "remember" the correct cup after delays of several minutes, but monkeys with frontal lobe lesions cannot solve the problem if the delay is more than a second or so (French and Harlow, 1962). This delayed-response deficit following brain lesions is unique to the frontal cortex; it does not occur if lesions are made in other cortical regions.

Human beings who have suffered damage to the frontal lobes can perform many intellectual tasks normally, including delayed-response problems. Their ability to use language probably enables them to remember the correct response. They do have difficulty, however, when it is necessary to shift frequently from one method of working on a problem to another method (Milner, 1964).

The *posterior association areas* are located among the various primary sensory areas and appear to consist of subareas, each serving a particular sense. For example, the lower portion of the temporal lobe is related to visual perception. Lesions in this area produce deficits in the ability to recognize and discriminate different forms. The lesion does not cause loss of visual acuity as would be true of a lesion in the primary visual area of the occipital lobe; the individual "sees" the forms (and can trace the outline with his or her finger) but cannot identify the shape or distinguish it from a different form.

A Divided Brain

So far we have treated the cerebral hemispheres as if they were identical, save for the fact that the left hemisphere controls the right side of the body and the right hemisphere controls the left. And, indeed, to the naked eye the two halves of the human brain do look like mirror images of each other. But closer examination reveals certain asymmetries; when brains are carefully measured during autopsies, one hemisphere, usually the left, is almost always larger than the other—this is true even for fetal brains (Galaburda and others, 1978). These anatomical differences are related to differences in function between the two hemispheres: the left cerebral hemisphere is specialized for the use of language, while the right hemisphere is specialized for mental imagery and the understanding of spatial relationships.

As early as 1861, the anthropologist Paul Broca examined the brain of a patient with speech loss and found damage in an area of the left hemisphere just above the lateral fissure in the frontal lobe. This region, known as *Broca's area*, is involved in the production of speech sounds—that is, in the control of the tongue and jaws in speaking. Destruction of the equivalent region in the right hemisphere usually does not result in speech impairment. The brain areas involved in understanding speech and in the ability to write and understand written words are also usually located in the left hemisphere. Thus, a person who suffers a stroke that damages the left hemisphere is more likely to show language impairment than one whose damage is confined to the right hemisphere. This is usually true for right-handed individuals because their left hemisphere is almost always dominant. (Remember that the left hemisphere controls the motor functions of the right side of the body.) Some left-handed people have speech centers located in the right hemisphere or divided between the two; but about 60 percent have language functions in the left hemisphere (the same as right-handed individuals).

While the left hemisphere's role in language has been known for some time—largely through studies of the effects of brain damage—only recently has it been possible to actually investigate what each hemisphere can do on its own. In the normal individual, the brain functions as an integrated whole; information in one hemisphere is immediately transferred to the other by way of a broad band of connecting nerve fibers called the *corpus callosum*. This connecting bridge can cause a problem in some forms of epilepsy, because a seizure starting in one hemisphere may cross over and trigger a massive discharge of neurons in the other. In an effort to prevent such generalized seizures in some severe epileptics, the corpus callosum was severed surgically. The operation was successful. There was a significant decrease in seizures in both hemispheres, apparently because they reciprocally excite each other. In addition, there appeared to be no undesirable aftereffects; the patients seemed to function as well as individuals whose hemispheres were still connected. It took some very special tests to demonstrate the differences between the two hemispheres and the effect that separating them has on the individuals' mental processes. A little more background information is needed to understand the experiments we are about to describe.

We have seen that the major motor nerves cross over as they leave the brain, so that the left cerebral hemisphere controls the right side of the body and the right hemisphere, the left. We noted also that the area for the production of speech (Broca's area) is located in the left hemisphere. Remember that when the eyes are fixated directly ahead, images to the left of the fixation point go through both eyes to the right side of the brain and images to the right of the fixation point go to the left side of the brain (see Figure 2-13). Thus each hemisphere has a view of that half of the visual field in which "its" hand normally functions; that is, the left hemisphere sees the right hand in the right visual field. In the normal brain, stimuli entering one hemisphere are rapidly communicated, by way of the corpus callosum, to the other, so that our brain functions as a unit. We will see what happens when the corpus callosum is severed—called a *split brain*—so that the two hemispheres cannot communicate.

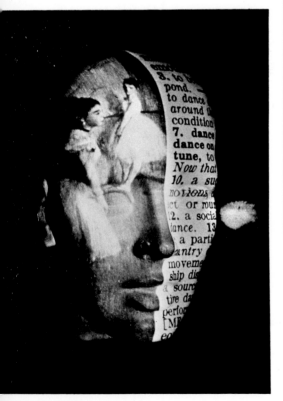

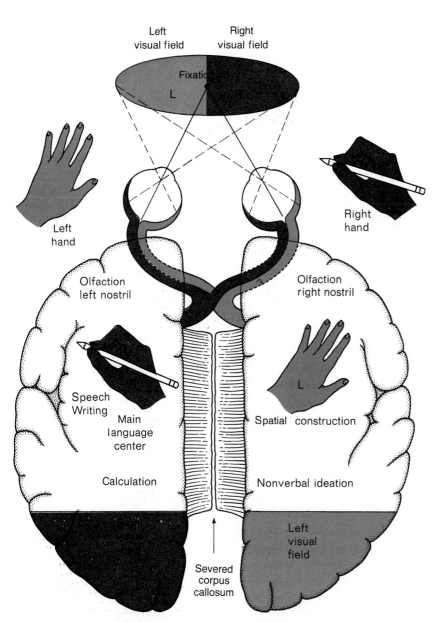

Left visual field Right visual field

Fixation point

L

Left hand

Right hand

Olfaction left nostril

Olfaction right nostril

Speech Writing

Main language center

Spatial construction

Calculation

Nonverbal ideation

L

Right visual field

Left visual field

Severed corpus callosum

Fig. 2-13 Sensory inputs to the two hemispheres

With the eyes fixated straight ahead, stimuli to the left of the fixation point go to the right cerebral hemisphere and stimuli to the right go to the left hemisphere. The left hemisphere controls movements of the right hand, and the right hemisphere controls the left hand. Hearing is largely crossed in its input, but some sound representation goes to the same hemisphere as the ear. Olfaction is received on the same side as the nostril. The left hemisphere is dominant for most people; it controls written and spoken language and mathematical calculations. The minor, right hemisphere can understand only simple language. Its main ability seems to involve spatial construction and pattern sense.

Experiments with Split-Brain Subjects

In one test situation, a male subject with a split brain is seated in front of a screen that hides his hands from view (see Figure 2-14A). His gaze is fixed at a spot on the center of the screen and the word *nut* is flashed very briefly (for one-tenth of a second) on the left side of the screen. Remember that this visual image goes to the right side of the brain, which controls the left side of the body. With his left hand the subject can easily pick out the nut from a pile of objects hidden from view. But he cannot tell the experimenter what word flashed on the screen, because language depends on the left hemisphere and the visual image of *nut* was not transmitted to the left side. When questioned, the split-brain subject seems unaware of what his left hand is doing! Since the sensory input from the left hand goes to the right hemisphere, the left hemisphere receives no information about what the left hand is feeling or doing. All information is fed back to the right hemisphere, which received the original visual input of the word *nut*.

It is important that the word be flashed on the screen for no more than

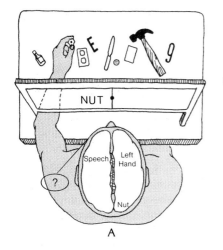 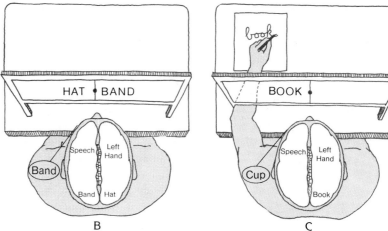

A   B   C

Fig. 2-14 Testing the abilities of the two hemispheres
A. The split-brain subject correctly retrieves an object by touch with the left hand when its name is flashed to the right hemisphere, but he cannot name the object or describe what he has done. B. The word *hatband* is flashed so that *hat* goes to the right cerebral hemisphere and *band* goes to the left hemisphere. The subject reports that he sees the word *band* but has no idea what kind of band. C. A list of common objects (including *book* and *cup*) is initially shown to both hemispheres. One word from the list (*book*) is then projected to the right hemisphere. When given the command to do so, the left hand begins writing the word *book*, but when questioned the subject doesn't know what his left hand has written and guesses "cup." (After Sperry, 1970; and Nebes and Sperry, 1971)

one-tenth of a second. If it remains longer the subject can move his eyes so that the word is also projected to the left hemisphere. If the split-brain subject can move his eyes freely, information goes to both cerebral hemispheres; this is one reason why the deficiencies caused by severing the corpus callosum are not readily apparent in a person's daily activities.

Further experiments support the idea that the split-brain subject is only aware of what is going on in the left hemisphere because it is that hemisphere alone that can communicate through language. Figure 2-14B shows another test situation. The word *hatband* is flashed on the screen so that *hat* goes to the right hemisphere and *band* to the left. When asked what word he saw, the subject replies, "band." When asked what kind of band, he makes all sorts of guesses—"rubber band," "rock band," "band of robbers," and so forth, and only hits on "hatband" by chance. Tests with other word combinations (such as *keycase* and *suitcase*), split so that half is projected to each hemisphere, show similar results. What is perceived by the right hemisphere does not transfer over to the left into the conscious awareness of the split-brain subject. With the corpus callosum severed, each hemisphere seems oblivious of the experiences of the other.

If the split-brain subject is blindfolded and a familiar object (such as a comb, toothbrush, or keycase) is placed in his left hand, he appears to know what it is. For example, he can demonstrate its use by appropriate gestures; but he cannot express this knowledge in speech. If asked what is going on while he is manipulating the object, he has no idea. This is true as long as any sensory input from the object to the left (talking) hemisphere is blocked. But if the subject's right hand inadvertently touches the object or if it makes a characteristic sound (like the jingling of a keycase), then the speaking hemisphere immediately gives the right answer.

Although the right hemisphere cannot speak, it does have some linguistic capabilities. It recognized the meaning of the word *nut*, as we saw in our first example, and it can write a little. In the experiment illustrated in Figure 2-14C the split-brain subject is first shown a list of common objects such as cup, knife, book, and glass. This list is displayed long enough for the words to be projected to both hemispheres. Next, the list is removed and one of the words, for example, *book*, is flashed briefly on the left side of the screen so that it goes to the right hemisphere. If the subject is asked to write what he saw, his left hand will begin writing the word *book*. If asked what his left hand has written, he has no idea and will guess at any of the words on the original list. The subject knows he has written something, because he feels the writing movements through his body. But because there is no communication between the right hemisphere that saw and wrote the word and the left hemisphere that controls speech, the subject has no awareness of what he wrote.

Major and Minor Hemispheres

Studies with split-brain subjects have made clear the striking differences between the functions of the two hemispheres. The major, left hemisphere governs our ability to express ourselves in language. It can perform many complicated sequential and analytic activities and is skilled in mathematical computations. The minor, right hemisphere can comprehend very simple language. It can respond to simple nouns by selecting objects such as a nut or comb, and it can even respond to associations of these objects. For example, if the right hemisphere is asked to retrieve from a group of objects the one used "for lighting fire," it will instruct the left hand to select a match. But it cannot comprehend more abstract linguistic forms. If the right hemisphere is presented with such simple commands as "wink," "nod," "shake head," or "smile," it seldom responds. The right hemisphere can add simple two-digit numbers, but can do little beyond this in the way of calculation.

Although the right hemisphere may deserve the term "minor," it is not without special abilities of its own. The right hemisphere appears to have a highly developed spatial and pattern sense. It is superior to the left hemisphere in constructing geometric and perspective drawings (see Figure 2-15). It can

Design	Left hand	Right hand

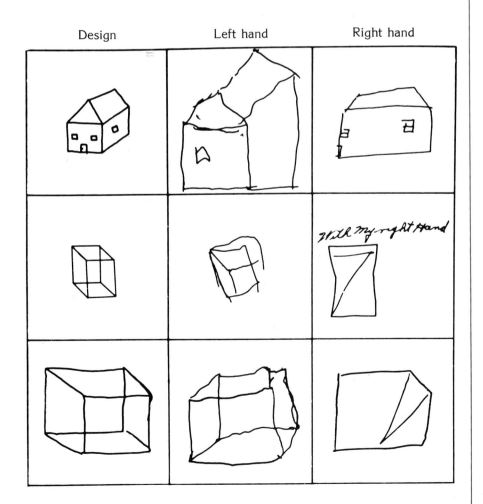

Fig. 2-15 Spatial drawing by split-brain subject
The left hand, guided by the right hemisphere, can copy three-dimensional designs (although somewhat crudely because the subject is right-handed). The right hand, guided by the dominant left hemisphere, is unable to reproduce the geometric designs (although it can write words with ease). (After Gazzaniga, 1970)

assemble colored blocks to match a complex design much more effectively than the left hemisphere. When split-brain subjects are asked to use their right hand to assemble the blocks according to a picture design, they make numerous mistakes. Sometimes they have trouble keeping their left hand from automatically correcting the mistakes being made by the right hand.

Studies with normal individuals tend to confirm the different specializations of the two hemispheres. For example, when information is flashed briefly to the right hemisphere and either a verbal or nonverbal response is required, the nonverbal response comes more quickly than the verbal response. A verbal response apparently requires that the information be sent across the corpus callosum to the left hemisphere, which takes time (Gazzaniga, 1972). And studies of the electrical impulses given off by the brain (EEG) suggest that during a verbal task activity increases in the left hemisphere, whereas during a spatial task activity increases in the right (Ornstein, 1977).

Some researchers believe that the minor hemisphere plays a special role in musical and artistic abilities, emotions, and dreaming. They would separate the analytical scientist or mathematician from the creative artist on the basis of the relative dominance of their cerebral hemispheres (see Figure 2-16). More evidence is needed, however, to substantiate such claims.

The specialization of the two hemispheres appears to develop along with language development. If the left hemisphere of a young child is damaged, the right one can take over the language functions without too much difficulty. Left-hemisphere damage in an adult, however, almost invariably produces language disability. The fact that right-handedness is the norm for human beings is probably related to the fact that the left hemisphere controls speech.

There is some evidence that children who have a special reading problem called *dyslexia* (they tend to read words backwards or to confuse *d*'s with *b*'s and *p*'s) may have spatial abilities that are represented in both hemispheres rather than primarily in the right, as is the usual case. Bilateral representation of spatial functions might overload the linguistic hemisphere (the left) and interfere with its functioning (Whitelson, 1977).

Fig. 2-16 How the brain divides its work
Research with both split-brain and normal subjects indicates that different functions are specialized in either the left or right hemisphere. This figure presents a very speculative attempt to summarize the research findings; the cerebral locations for some of these abilities have not been firmly established by research.

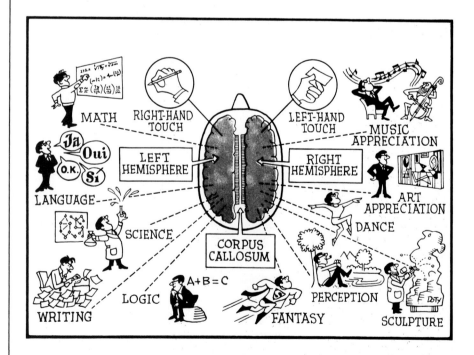

Autonomic Nervous System

We noted earlier that the peripheral nervous system, which includes those nerves connecting the brain and spinal cord with the outlying regions of the body, consists of two divisions. The somatic system controls the skeletal muscles and receives information from the skin, muscles, and various sensory receptors. The autonomic system controls the glands and the smooth muscles that comprise the heart, blood vessels, and the lining of the stomach and intestines. (These muscles are called "smooth" because microscopic examination shows that they lack the striated appearance characteristic of skeletal muscles.) The somatic system then controls the striated muscles; the autonomic system controls the smooth muscles. The autonomic nervous system derives its name from the fact that many of the activities it controls are autonomous, or self-regulating—such as digestion and circulation, which continue even when a person is asleep or unconscious.

The autonomic nervous system has two divisions—the *sympathetic* and the *parasympathetic*—which are often antagonistic in their actions.

Sympathetic Division

On either side of the spinal column lie chains of nerve fibers and masses of cell bodies (ganglia) from which fibers extend to the various visceral organs. These chains are known as the *sympathetic chains*. The fibers coming from the spinal cord to the sympathetic chains originate in the thoracic and lumbar portions of the spine, between the cervical (neck) and the sacral (lower spine) regions. All the fibers and ganglia together constitute the sympathetic division of the autonomic system (see Figure 2-17).

The sympathetic division tends to act as a unit. During emotional excitement it simultaneously speeds up the heart, dilates the arteries of the skeletal muscles and heart, and constricts the arteries of the skin and digestive organs; its action also leads to perspiration and to secretion of certain hormones that increase emotional arousal.

Parasympathetic Division

The parasympathetic division has two parts, some of its fibers originating in the cranial region (above those of the sympathetic system) and others originating in the sacral region (below those of the sympathetic system).

Unlike the sympathetic system, the parasympathetic division tends to affect one organ at a time. If the sympathetic system is thought of as dominant during violent and excited activity, the parasympathetic system may be thought of as dominant during quiescence. It participates in digestion and, in general, it maintains the functions that conserve and protect bodily resources.

Interaction Between the Divisions

When both sympathetic and parasympathetic fibers are connected to the same muscle or gland, they usually act in opposite manners. Thus, the sympathetic system speeds the heart rate, the parasympathetic system slows it; the sympathetic system inhibits digestive processes, the parasympathetic system.

Fig. 2-17 The autonomic nervous system

Neurons of the sympathetic division originate in the thoracic and lumbar regions of the spinal cord; they form synaptic junctions with ganglia lying just outside the cord. Neurons of the parasympathetic division exit from the medulla region of the brain stem and from the lower (sacral) end of the spinal cord; they connect with ganglia near the organs stimulated. Most, but not all, internal organs are innervated by both divisions, which function in opposition to each other. The normal state of the body, somewhere between extreme excitement and vegetative placidity, results from the interplay of these two systems.

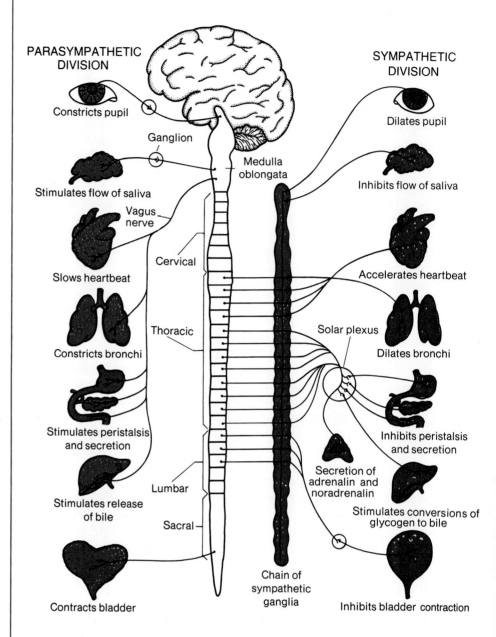

PARASYMPATHETIC DIVISION

SYMPATHETIC DIVISION

Constricts pupil

Dilates pupil

Ganglion

Medulla oblongata

Stimulates flow of saliva

Inhibits flow of saliva

Vagus nerve

Slows heartbeat

Cervical

Accelerates heartbeat

Solar plexus

Constricts bronchi

Thoracic

Dilates bronchi

Stimulates peristalsis and secretion

Inhibits peristalsis and secretion

Secretion of adrenalin and noradrenalin

Stimulates release of bile

Lumbar

Stimulates conversions of glycogen to bile

Sacral

Contracts bladder

Chain of sympathetic ganglia

Inhibits bladder contraction

facilitates them; the sympathetic system dilates the pupils of the eyes, the parasympathetic system constricts them. Both systems are usually exerting some influence (that is, both are usually "on"), but one temporarily dominates the other.

There are some exceptions to the principle that the two systems are antagonistic. Although the sympathetic system is usually dominant during fear and excitement, a not uncommon parasympathetic symptom during extreme emotion is the involuntary discharge of the bladder or bowels. Another example is the complete sex act in the male, which requires erection (parasympathetic) followed by ejaculation (sympathetic). Thus, while the two divisions are often antagonistic, they interact in complex ways, and their interaction is not fully understood.

Endocrine System

Many of the bodily reactions that result from activity of the autonomic nervous system are produced by the action of that system on the endocrine glands. The endocrine glands secrete *hormones*, special chemical messengers, that are carried throughout the body by the bloodstream.[1] These chemicals are as essential as the nervous system to the integration of the organism's activities and to the maintenance of homeostasis. Indeed, the functioning of the nervous system depends on them. For example, some neurons use a hormone, norepinephrine, as their chemical transmitter. Other hormones modify the excitability of neurons. The endocrine glands play an important role in growth, sexual and maternal behavior, the individual's characteristic level of energy and mood, and reaction to stress. Some endocrine glands are controlled by the nervous system, whereas others respond to the internal state of the body.

Pituitary Gland

One of the major endocrine glands, the pituitary, is partly an outgrowth of the brain and is joined to it just below the hypothalamus (refer back to Figure 2-6). The pituitary gland has been called the "master gland," because it produces the largest number of different hormones and controls the secretion of several other endocrine glands. The pituitary has two independently functioning parts.

The *posterior pituitary* is a direct extension of the nervous system. Two hormones produced in the hypothalamus are transported along nerve axons for release by the posterior pituitary. One hormone influences the contraction of the uterus during childbirth and the reflexive ejection of milk from the mammary glands; the other regulates the amount of water in the body cells and indirectly controls blood pressure.

The *anterior pituitary* is also controlled by the hypothalamus, but in a different way. Certain hormones released by the hypothalamus are carried to the anterior pituitary by a system of tiny blood vessels. They stimulate the anterior pituitary to release its own hormones.

One of the anterior pituitary hormones has the crucial job of controlling the timing and amount of body growth. Too little of this hormone can create a dwarf, while oversecretion can produce a giant. A number of other hormones released by the anterior pituitary trigger the action of other endocrine glands—the thyroid; the sex glands, or gonads; and one part of the adrenal glands. Courtship, mating, and reproductive behavior in many animals involve a complex interaction between the activity of the nervous system and the influence of the anterior pituitary on the sex glands.

Adrenal Glands

The adrenal glands, located just above the kidneys, play an extremely important role in neural functioning and in the ability of the body to cope with stress. Each adrenal gland has two parts, an inner core and an outer layer. The inner core secretes *epinephrine* (also known as adrenalin) and *norepinephrine* (noradrenalin). Epinephrine acts in a number of ways to prepare the organism

---

[1]Endocrine glands are distinguished from the other glands by the fact that they secrete directly into the bloodstream. Glands such as the salivary and tear glands have ducts that enable them to secrete fluids directly onto the body surface or into body cavities; their influence is thus less widespread.

for an emergency; it is closely involved with the action of the sympathetic division of the autonomic nervous system. Epinephrine, for example, acts on the smooth muscles and the sweat glands in a way similar to that of the sympathetic system. It causes nervous perspiration, constriction of the blood vessels in the stomach and intestines, and makes the heart beat faster (as anyone who has ever had a shot of adrenalin knows). It also acts on part of the reticular system, which excites the sympathetic system, which in turn stimulates the adrenals to secrete more epinephrine. Hence, a closed circuit maintaining emotional arousal is formed. Such a closed system is one reason why it takes a while for strong emotional excitement to subside even after the disturbing cause is removed. When captured, some wild animals suffer such an intense stress reaction that their physiological system never returns to a state of homeostasis; they go into shock and die.

Norepinephrine also prepares the organism for emergency action. As it reaches the pituitary in its travels through the bloodstream, it stimulates the pituitary to release a hormone that acts on the outer layer of the adrenal glands, stimulating the release of a group of hormones called *steroids*. Steroids cause the liver to release stored sugar so the body has energy for quick action. They also help to maintain the normal metabolic processes of the body. One of the adrenal steroids is *cortisol*, a synthetic form of which—cortisone—is used in the treatment of allergic reactions, arthritis, and shock. Patients treated with cortisone sometimes develop mental symptoms—for example, severe depression. Cortisol and some other steroids may play a role in mental illness.

This description of the complex action of the pituitary and adrenal glands and their interaction with the nervous system indicates the crucial role of the endocrine system in the integration of bodily responses.

Genetic Influences on Behavior

To understand the biological foundations of behavior we need to know something about hereditary influences. The field of *behavior genetics* combines the methods of genetics and psychology to study the inheritance of behavioral characteristics. We know that many physical characteristics, such as height, bone structure, and hair and eye color, are inherited. Behavioral geneticists are interested in the degree to which psychological characteristics, such as ability, temperament, and emotional stability, are transmitted from parent to offspring.

All behavior depends on the *interaction* between heredity and environment. The old heredity *versus* environment issue is no longer a meaningful question. Instead, researchers ask how heredity limits the individual's potential and to what degree favorable or unfavorable environmental conditions can modify the inherited potential.

Chromosomes and Genes

The hereditary units we receive from our parents and transmit to our offspring are carried by microscopic particles, known as *chromosomes*, found in the nucleus of each cell in the body. Most body cells contain 46 chromosomes. At conception, the human being receives 23 chromosomes from the father's sperm and 23 chromosomes from the mother's ovum. These 46 chromosomes form 23 pairs, which are duplicated as the cells divide and are thus found in every cell of the body (see Figure 2-18). Each chromosome is composed of many individual hereditary units called *genes*, which also occur in pairs—one gene of each pair comes from the sperm chromosomes and one gene from the ovum chromosomes.[2] Thus, a child receives only half of each parent's total genes. We have no exact way of counting genes, for, unlike the chromosomes, they do not show up under the microscope as separate particles. The total number of genes in each human chromosome is around 1,000—perhaps higher. Because the number of genes is so high, it is extremely unlikely that two human beings would have the same heredity, even with the same parents. One exception is *identical twins*, who, having developed from the same fertilized egg, have exactly the same chromosomes and genes.

An important attribute of some genes is *dominance* or *recessiveness*. If both members of a gene pair are dominant, the individual will manifest the trait determined by the genes. If one gene is dominant and the other recessive, the individual will show the form of the trait determined by the dominant gene but will also carry the recessive gene, which may be expressed in a different way as a trait in offspring. A recessive form of the trait will be expressed only if the genes contributed by both parents are recessive. The genes determining eye color, for example, act in a pattern of dominance and recessiveness. Blue eyes are recessive. Thus for a child to be blue-eyed both parents must be blue-eyed, or if one parent is brown-eyed that parent must carry a recessive gene for blue eyes. Two brown-eyed parents can produce a blue-eyed child only if both carry a gene for blue eyes.

Some of the characteristics that are carried by recessive genes are baldness, albinism, hemophilia, and a susceptibility to poison ivy. Not all gene pairs follow the dominant-recessive pattern, and—as we shall see later—most human characteristics are determined by many genes acting together rather than by a single gene pair.

SEX-LINKED GENES Male and female chromosomes appear the same when examined under the microscope, except for pair number 23, the so-called sex chromosomes. Pair 23 determines the sex of the individual and carries genes for certain traits that are called "sex-linked." A normal female has two similar-looking chromosomes in pair 23, called "X chromosomes." A normal male has one X chromosome in pair 23 and one that looks slightly different, called a "Y chromosome" (see Figure 2-18). Thus, the normal female chromosome pair 23 is represented by the symbol XX and the normal male pair, by XY.

When most body cells reproduce the resulting cells have the same number of chromosomes (46) as the parent cell. However, when sperm and egg cells reproduce the chromosome pairs separate and half go to each "daughter" cell. Thus, egg and sperm cells have only 23 chromosomes and do not survive more than a few days unless they join to complete the 46 chromosomes necessary for proper cell functioning.

Each egg cell has an X chromosome and each sperm cell has either an X or a Y chromosome. If an X-type sperm is the first to enter an egg cell, the fertilized ovum will have an XX chromosome pair, and the child will be a female. If a Y-type sperm fertilizes the egg, the twenty-third chromosome will be of the XY-type, and the child will be a male. The adult male usually produces an equal

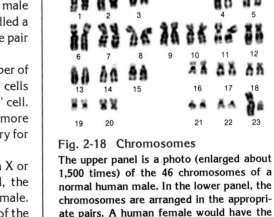

Fig. 2-18 Chromosomes
The upper panel is a photo (enlarged about 1,500 times) of the 46 chromosomes of a normal human male. In the lower panel, the chromosomes are arranged in the appropriate pairs. A human female would have the same pairs 1 through 22, but pair 23 would be XX rather than XY. Each chromosome appears double here because the preparation was made at a stage during mitosis, in which each chromosome has duplicated itself and is about to split apart.

[2] The actual carrier of hereditary information within the genes is a complex nucleic acid called DNA (deoxyribonucleic acid). The discovery in 1953 of the molecular structure of DNA and the method by which this molecule duplicates itself during cell division and transfers its genetic code from the fertilized egg to direct the development of other body cells was a major scientific breakthrough.

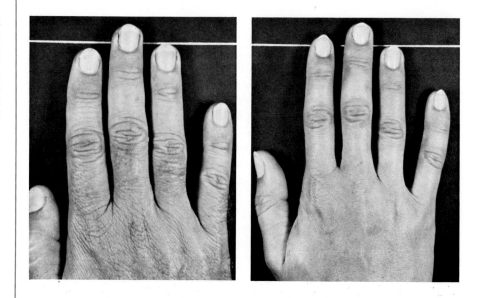

A sex-influenced gene seems to be related to the relative length of the index finger as compared to the other fingers. A gene that causes the index finger to be shorter than the fourth finger appears to be dominant in males and recessive in females. The male index finger, on the left, is shorter than the fourth finger, but the female index finger on the right is longer than the fourth finger. (Courtesy A. M. Winchester)

number of X- and Y-type sperm, so that the chances of his producing male or female children are essentially equal. The female inherits one X chromosome from the mother, one from the father; the male inherits his X chromosome from the mother, his Y chromosome from the father. Thus, it is the father's chromosome contribution that determines a child's sex.

The X chromosome may carry either dominant or recessive genes; the Y chromosome carries a few genes dominant for male sexual characteristics but otherwise acts in heredity as though it carries only recessive genes. Thus, most recessive characteristics carried by a man's X chromosome will be expressed, since they are not blocked by dominant genes. For example, colorblindness is a recessive sex-linked characteristic. A man will be colorblind if he inherits a colorblind gene on the X chromosome he receives from his mother. Females are less often colorblind, because to be so they would have to have both a colorblind father and a mother who is either colorblind or carries a recessive gene for colorblindness. A number of genetically determined disorders are linked to abnormalities of, or recessive genes carried by, the twenty-third chromosome pair. These are called sex-linked disorders.

Chromosomal Abnormalities

Sometimes part of a chromosome may be lost during cell division. The loss of an entire chromosome usually results in death for the developing organism, but there are exceptions. On rare occasions a female may be born with only one X chromosome instead of the usual XX. Females with this condition (known as *Turner's syndrome*) fail to develop sexually at puberty. Although usually of normal intelligence, they show some specific cognitive defects: they do poorly in arithmetic and on tests of visual form perception and spatial organization.

Sometimes when the twenty-third chromosome fails to divide properly, the developing organism ends up with an extra X or Y chromosome. An individual with an XXY twenty-third chromosome is physically a male, with penis and testicles, but with marked feminine characteristics. His breasts are enlarged and his testes are small and do not produce sperm. This condition (known as *Klinefelter's syndrome*) is surprisingly common—about 1 in every 400 births. Some of the Russian "female" athletes, whose physical abilities were superior to those of normal females, were found to be XXY when a chromosome test was required.

Another sex chromosome abnormality in males has received considerable publicity. Men with an extra Y chromosome (type XYY) are taller than average and are reported to be unusually aggressive. Early studies suggested that the incidence of XYY males among prison inmates—particularly those convicted of violent crimes—was much higher than in the population at large. Newspaper accounts exaggerated these findings, portraying the XYY male as an individual genetically predisposed toward aggression and violence. Several XYY men were even acquitted of criminal charges on the grounds that they were helpless victims of their inheritance and, thus, could not be held responsible for their acts.

More recent studies seriously question whether there is any link between the presence of an extra Y chromosome and aggression. They find that XYY males in the general population (about 1 in every 1,000 births) are no more aggressive than normal males (Owen, 1972; Hook, 1973). Nevertheless, survey data indicate that males with this genetic makeup *are* more likely than normal males to be inmates of prisons or mental hospitals. We don't know why this is so; at this point little is known about the effects of the XYY chromosomal type on personality and behavior.

Deviations from the usual number of chromosomes in pairs other than the sex chromosomes have also been linked to specific disorders. For example, an extra chromosome on pair 21 results in a form of mental deficiency commonly called *Down's syndrome,* which is discussed in Chapter 12.

Genetic Studies of Behavior

A few disorders result from chromosomal abnormalities, and some traits are determined by single genes. But most human characteristics are determined by many sets of genes; they are *polygenic.* Traits such as intelligence, height, and

"You can't talk to that crowd—they've all got extra Y chromosomes."

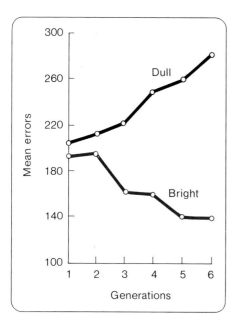

Fig. 2-19 Inheritance of maze learning in rats
Mean error scores of "bright" and "dull" rats selectively bred for maze-running ability. (After Thompson, 1954)

emotionality do not fall into distinct categories, but show continuous variation. People are not either dull or bright; intelligence is distributed over a broad range, with most individuals located near the middle. Sometimes a specific genetic defect can result in mental retardation, but in most instances a person's intellectual potential is determined by a number of genes that influence the factors underlying different abilities. And, of course, what happens to this genetic potential depends on environmental conditions.

SELECTIVE BREEDING One method of studying the heritability of traits in animals is by selective breeding. Animals that are high in a certain trait or low in a certain trait are mated with each other. For example, to study the inheritance of learning ability in rats, the females that do poorly in learning to run a maze are mated with males that do poorly; the females that do well are mated with the males that do well. The offspring of these matings are tested on the same maze. On the basis of performance, the brightest are mated with the brightest and the dullest, with the dullest. (To ensure that environmental conditions are kept constant, the offspring of "dull" mothers are sometimes given to "bright" mothers to raise, so that genetic endowment rather than adequacy of maternal care is being tested.) After a few rodent generations, a "bright" and a "dull" strain of rats can be produced (see Figure 2-19). When tested a year later the descendents of the maze-bright rats are still superior to the descendents of the maze-dull rats in learning several different types of mazes (Rosenzweig, 1969).

Selective breeding has been used to show the inheritance of a number of behavioral characteristics. Dogs have been bred to be excitable or lethargic; chickens, to be aggressive and sexually active; and fruit flies, to be more or less attracted to light (Scott and Fuller, 1965; McClearn and DeFries, 1973). It has even been possible to breed a strain of mice that prefers alcohol and a strain that does not; the preference may be based on genetic differences in the level of a liver enzyme that aids in the metabolic breakdown of alcohol (Eriksson, 1972).

If a trait is influenced by heredity, then it should be possible to change it by selective breeding. If selective breeding does not alter a trait, then we assume that trait is primarily dependent on environmental factors and is not differentially influenced by the genes.

TWIN STUDIES Since carefully controlled breeding experiments cannot be carried out with human beings, the behavior geneticist has had to look instead at similarities and differences in behavior among individuals who are related genetically. Family pedigrees often show that certain traits run in families. The problem, however, is that families are not only linked genetically, but also share the same environment over a period of time. Thus, if musical talent runs in the family, is it because of genetic potential or the importance parents place on music and the training they provide? Do children of alcoholics become alcoholics because of genetic tendencies or environmental conditions? To overcome the problem, behavioral geneticists prefer to study genetic influences on behavior in twins.

Identical twins develop from a single fertilized egg and thus share the same heredity. (They are called *monozygotic*, since they result from a single zygote, or fertilized ovum.) Fraternal twins develop from different egg cells and are no more alike genetically than are ordinary siblings. (They are called *dizygotic*, or two-egged.) Studies comparing identical and fraternal twins help to sort out the influence of environment and heredity. Identical twins are found to be much more similar in intelligence than fraternal twins, even when they are separated at birth and reared in different homes (see Chapter 12). Identical twins are also more similar than fraternal twins in some personality characteristics and in susceptibility to the mental disorder of *schizophrenia* (see Chapter 15). Twin studies have proved to be a useful method of investigating genetic influences on human behavior.

Environmental Influences on Gene Action

The hereditary potential with which an individual enters the world is very much influenced by the environment that he or she encounters. This interaction will be made clear in the following chapters. At this point, two examples will suffice to illustrate the point. The tendency to develop diabetes is hereditary, although the exact method of transmission is unknown. Diabetes is manifested as an elevation of the blood-sugar level. The assumption is that the genes determine the production of insulin, which, in turn, affects the metabolism of carbohydrates and, hence, the level of sugar in the blood. But people who carry the genetic potential for diabetes do not always develop the disease. A study of identical twins (one or the other of whom had diabetes) found that in 15 percent of the pairs only one twin developed the disease. The unafflicted twin clearly carried the genes for diabetes, but apparently was spared because his or her diet made fewer demands for carbohydrate metabolism. Thus, diabetes is caused neither by heredity alone nor by environment alone, but by the interaction of the two.

A similar situation is found in the case of the mental illness called *schizophrenia*. As we shall see in Chapter 15, substantial evidence indicates a heredity component to the disorder. If one identical twin is schizophrenic, chances are high that the other twin will exhibit some signs of mental disturbance. But whether or not the other twin develops the full-blown disease will depend on a number of environmental factors. The genes may predispose, but the environment decides.

This chapter has focused on the biological determinants of behavior—the action of the nervous and endocrine systems and the way in which individual characteristics are inherited. Subsequent chapters will examine how these biological factors interact with environmental conditions to determine behavior in many areas of human functioning.

SUMMARY

1 The nervous system is composed of cells called *neurons*, which receive stimulation by way of their *dendrites* and *cell bodies* and transmit impulses via their *axons*. *Afferent neurons* carry messages from the sense *receptors* to the brain and spinal cord; *efferent neurons* transmit signals from the brain and spinal cord to the *effector organs*, the muscles and glands. Axon fibers group together to form *nerves;* neuron cell bodies are grouped together into *nuclei* and *ganglia.*

2 Two types of transmission of the nerve impulse are important: along nerve fibers and across the synaptic junction between the neurons. Transmission along fibers is via an electrochemical process involving the interchange of sodium and potassium ions through the cell membrane, which generates the *action potential;* the conduction is much more rapid for *myelinated fibers.* Chemical intermediaries, called *neurotransmitters*, also activate a neuron across a *synapse.* The neurotransmitters act on the dendrites and cell body of the receiving neuron to change its membrane permeability either toward

the firing threshold (at an *excitatory synapse*) or away from the threshold (at an *inhibitory synapse*). The combination of excitatory and inhibitory activity at its many synapses determines whether or not a neuron will fire.

3 The nervous system is divided into the *central nervous system* (all the nerves in the brain and spinal cord) and the *peripheral nervous system* (the nerves leading from the brain and spinal cord to other parts of the body). Subdivisions of the peripheral nervous system are the *somatic system,* whose nerves carry messages to and from the sense receptors, muscles, and body surface, and the *autonomic system,* whose nerves connect with the internal organs.

4 Simple reflexes, such as the knee jerk, are carried out within the spinal cord by a three-neuron arc consisting of afferent and efferent neurons and *interneurons.*

5 The human brain is composed of three concentric layers: a *central core;* the *limbic system,* which evolved from this core; and an outer layer, the *cerebrum,* which is the most recent evolutionary development and constitutes the center for higher mental processes.

a The central core includes the *medulla,* responsible for respiration and postural reflexes; the *cerebellum,* concerned with motor coordination; the *thalamus,* a relay station for incoming sensory information; and the *hypothalamus,* important in emotion and in maintaining homeostasis. The *reticular system,* which crosses through several of the above structures, controls the organism's state of arousal.

b The *limbic system* controls some of the "instinctive" activities—feeding, attacking, fleeing from danger, mating—regulated by the hypothalamus; it also plays an important role in emotion and memory.

c The *cerebrum* is divided into two *cerebral hemispheres.* The convoluted surface of these hemispheres, the *cerebral cortex,* controls discrimination, choice, learning, and thinking—the "higher mental processes," which are the most flexible and least stereotyped aspects of behavior. Certain areas of the cortex represent centers for specific sensory inputs or for control of specific movements. The remainder of the cortex consists of *association areas.*

6 When the *corpus callosum* (the band of nerve fibers connecting the two cerebral hemispheres) is severed, significant differences in the functioning of the cerebral hemispheres can be observed. The left, *major hemisphere* is skilled in language and mathematical abilities. The right, *minor hemisphere* can understand some language but cannot communicate through speech; it has a highly developed spatial and pattern sense.

7 The *autonomic nervous system* is made up of two parts, a *sympathetic* and a *parasympathetic* division. Because its fibers mediate the action of the smooth muscles and of the glands, the autonomic system is particularly important in emotional reactions. The sympathetic division is usually involved in excited action and the parasympathetic, in quiescent states. But the antagonism between the two divisions is not universal; they do cooperate in complex ways.

8 The *endocrine glands* secrete hormones into the bloodstream that are important for emotional and motivational behavior and for some aspects of personality. They are an essential partner to the nervous system in integrating behavior, and their action is closely tied to the activity of the hypothalamus and the autonomic nervous system. The *pituitary* and the *adrenal glands* are two of the most important endocrine glands.

9 An individual's hereditary potential, carried by the *chromosomes* and *genes*, will influence psychological as well as physical characteristics. Some genes are *dominant*, some *recessive*, and some *sex-linked*. Most human characteristics are *polygenic*—that is, determined by many sets of genes.

10 *Selective breeding*—mating animals that are high in a certain trait or low in a certain trait—is one method of studying the influence of heredity. Another method for sorting out the effects of environment and heredity is *twin studies*, in which the characteristics of identical, or *monozygotic*, twins (who share the same heredity) are compared with those of fraternal, or *dizygotic*, twins (who are no more alike genetically than ordinary siblings).

11 All behavior depends on the *interaction* between heredity and environment; the genes set the limits of the individual's potential, but what happens to this potential depends on the environment.

FURTHER READING

Good introductions to physiological psychology are Thompson, *Introduction to physiological psychology* (1975), Carlson, *Physiology of behavior* (1977), Hassett, *A primer of psychophysiology* (1978), and Schwartz, *Physiological psychology* (2nd ed., 1978). Blakemore's *Mechanics of the mind* (1977) and Kuffler and Nicholls, *From neuron to brain* (1976) are excellent sources in paperback.

A survey of genetic influences on behavior is provided by McClearn and DeFries, *Introduction to behavioral genetics* (1973) and Fuller and Thompson, *Foundations of behavior genetics* (1978).

For a survey of research on the function of the two cerebral hemispheres, see Chall and Mirskey (eds.), *Education and the brain* (1978).

3
Psychological Development

O f all mammals, human beings are the most immature at birth and require the longest period of development before they are capable of all the activities and skills characteristic of their species. In general, the higher on the phylogenetic scale the organism is, the more complex its nervous system and the longer the time required to reach maturity. For example, the lemur, a primitive primate, can move about on its own shortly after birth and is soon able to eat adult food and fend for itself. The newborn monkey is dependent for several months; the infant baboon remains with its mother for several years. The human offspring is dependent for many years and requires a long period of learning and interaction with others before becoming self-sufficient.

Adult behavior and personality characteristics are influenced by events that occur during the early years of life. The saying "the child is father of the man" reflects this continuity between childhood and adulthood. Thus, to understand the psychological processes of human adults—their perceptions, patterns of thinking, motives, emotions, conflicts, and ways of coping with conflicts—we need to know how these processes originate and change over time.

Psychologists may study the average or "typical" rate of development. At what age does the average child begin to speak? How rapidly does vocabulary increase with age? Such data, in addition to having intrinsic interest, are important in solving problems of education.

Developmental psychologists are concerned also with how certain behaviors develop and why they appear when they do. Why do most children not walk or utter their first word until they are about a year old? What behaviors precede these accomplishments? Can normal development be accelerated? What factors produce abnormal development, such as mental illness or retardation?

From a practical standpoint, knowing how early experiences mold an individual may make us wiser in the way we raise our children. Many problems that confront society—aggression, alienation, suicide, and mental illness—could perhaps be averted if we better understood how parental behavior and attitudes affect children, how some of these problems originate, and how they might be dealt with at an early age.

Mother gibbon and child

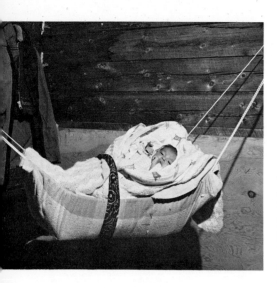

A typical baby hammock used by the Vanta Kuchin Indians of Canada

In this chapter, we will discuss several general principles of development as well as some behavior and attitude changes that occur as the individual matures from infancy to adulthood. Our purpose is to provide an overview of psychological development. The development of certain specific abilities, such as language and perception, will be considered later in the chapters devoted to these topics.

Factors Governing Development

Human development is determined by a continuous interaction between heredity and environment. At the moment of conception a remarkable number of personal characteristics are already determined by the genetic structure of the fertilized ovum. Our genes program our growing cells so that we develop into a person, rather than a fish, a bird, or a monkey. They decide our skin and hair color, general body size, sex, and (to some extent) our intelligence and emotional temperament. The *biological predispositions* present at birth interact with the *experiences* encountered in the course of growing up to determine individual development.

Our experiences depend on the specific culture, social group, and family in which we are raised. Cultures differ in their methods of child-rearing. For example, among the Utku Eskimos of Hudson Bay, aggression is regarded as an undesirable characteristic. When the child is about two or three years old, Utku parents begin to discourage expressions of anger and aggression by means of the "silent treatment"—that is, by ignoring the child whenever such behaviors occur. This method seems to be fairly effective; one rarely sees aggressive behavior among Utku children over four or five years of age (Briggs, 1970). In the United States, the amount of aggression a child shows depends partly on the social group and partly on the family in which the child is raised. Children from very poor families tend, *on the average,* to be more aggressive than children from middle- or upper-class homes (Langner and others, 1977). But a child's tendency to fight or show other forms of aggression also depends on the particular family in which he or she is raised—the kind of behavior modeled by the parents and the way they reward or punish aggressive acts. A child is exposed to many different conditions—some are shared with other children in the culture, some are common to the child's social group, and some are unique to his or her family.

The question as to whether heredity ("nature") or environment ("nurture") is more important in determining the course of human development has long been a topic of debate. But it seems clear that the two are inseparable. The development of the newborn infant depends on the interaction between biological predispositions and the experiences provided by the environment. For example, all human infants are born with the ability to learn a spoken language—other species are not. In the normal course of development all human beings learn to speak. But they are not able to talk before they have attained a certain level of neurological development—no infant less than a year old speaks in sentences. Children raised in a stimulating environment where people talk to them and reward them for making speech-like sounds will talk earlier than children without such attention. And the language they speak will be that of their own culture. Thus, learning to speak has both biological and environmental components. Most aspects of human development are similar, in the sense that the end result depends on the interaction between biological predispositions and environmental experiences.

"Grantz is charting his life based on genetic vs. environmental factors."

Maturation

Genetic determinants are expressed through the process of *maturation*. Maturation refers to innately determined sequences of growth or bodily changes that are *relatively* independent of environmental events. We say "relatively" because such changes occur over a wide range of environmental conditions; if the environment is decidedly atypical or inadequate in some way, maturational processes will be affected. While maturation is most apparent during childhood, it continues into adult life. Some of the changes that occur at adolescence, as well as some of the changes that occur with aging, are regulated by a biologically determined time schedule.

Maturation is demonstrated clearly by fetal development. The human fetus develops within the mother's body according to a fairly fixed time schedule, and fetal behavior (such as turning and kicking) also follows an orderly sequence that depends on the stage of growth. Premature infants who are kept alive in an incubator develop at much the same rate as infants who remain in the uterus full term. The regularity of development before birth illustrates what we mean by maturation. If the uterine environment is seriously abnormal in some way, however, maturational processes can be disrupted. For example, if the mother contracts German measles during the first three months of pregnancy (when the basic organ systems are developing according to an innately programmed schedule), the infant may be born deaf, blind, or brain-damaged—the type of defect depending on which organ system was in a critical stage of development at the time of infection. Maternal malnutrition, alcohol,

Fig. 3-1 Babies develop at different rates
Although development is orderly, some infants reach each stage ahead of others. The left end of the bar indicates the age by which 25 percent of infants have achieved the stated performance, whereas the right end gives the age by which 90 percent have accomplished the behavior. The vertical mark on each bar gives the age by which 50 percent have achieved it. (After Frankenburg and Dodds, 1967)

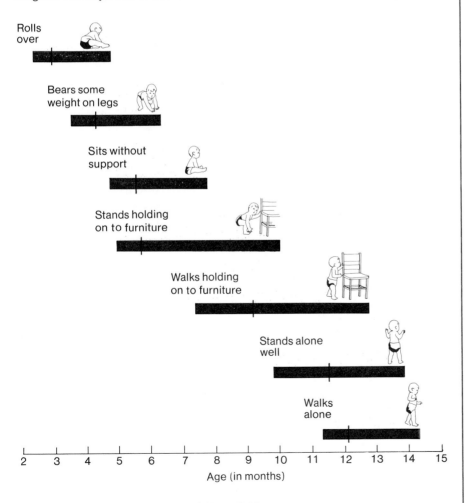

Rolls over

Bears some weight on legs

Sits without support

Stands holding on to furniture

Walks holding on to furniture

Stands alone well

Walks alone

2 3 4 5 6 7 8 9 10 11 12 13 14 15

Age (in months)

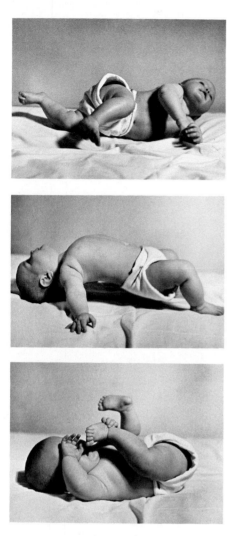

A six-month-old baby discovers how to roll over

and certain drugs are among the other factors that can affect the normal maturation of the fetus.

Motor development after birth—using the hands and fingers, standing, walking—also follows a regular sequence. For example, such activities as rolling over, crawling, and pulling up to a standing position occur in the same order in most children. Unless we believe that all parents subject their offspring to the same training regime (an unlikely possibility), we must assume that growth processes determine the order of behavior. As Figure 3-1 shows, not all children go through the sequence at the same rate; some infants are more than four or five months ahead of others in standing alone or walking. But the *order* in which they go from one stage to the next is generally the same in all infants.

Because the child's mastery of the movements necessary for sitting, standing, walking, and using hands and fingers follows such an orderly sequence and because children in all cultures accomplish these skills at *roughly* the same age, motor development appears to be primarily a maturational process little influenced by the environment in which the child is reared.

Sequences and Stages in Development

Many behaviors follow a natural sequence of development. Infants reach for an object before they are able to pick it up. We learn to walk before we run; we learn to speak words before sentences; we learn to count by rote before we understand the concept of numbers. Sequences in development usually proceed from simple behaviors to those that are more differentiated and complex. For example, newborn infants can clasp and unclasp their fingers and wave their arms about—occasionally managing to connect the thumb with the mouth. As infants mature these simple actions become differentiated into more complex behaviors—patting an object, grasping it, picking it up, moving it toward the mouth, or throwing it.

Psychologists generally agree that there are orderly sequences in development that depend on the maturation of the organism as it interacts with its environment. In explaining developmental sequences, some psychologists prefer to interpret them as a *continuous process,* in which biological factors interplay with learning to produce a smooth and continuous change in behavior. Other psychologists agree on the sequential character of development but are less impressed by the continuity of the process and see it more as a series of steps. For this reason, they have introduced the concept of *stages.*

We identify rather broad stages when we divide the life span into successive periods of infancy, childhood, adolescence, and adulthood. Parents use the term *stage* when they refer to their two-year-old as going through a "negative stage" (saying "no" to every request) or their adolescent as being in a "rebellious stage" (challenging parental authority). When psychologists refer to developmental stages they have a more precise concept in mind: the concept of stages implies that (1) behaviors at a given stage are organized around a *dominant theme,* (2) behaviors at one stage are *qualitatively different* from behaviors that appear at earlier or later stages, and (3) all children go through the same stages *in the same order.* Environmental factors may speed up or slow down development, but the order of stages is invariant; a child cannot achieve a later stage without going through an earlier one.

Later in this chapter we will look at several stage theories; one focuses on stages of cognitive development, another on stages of moral development, and the third on stages of social development. While some psychologists believe that stage theories are a useful way of describing development, others believe that development is better interpreted as a continuous process of acquiring new behaviors through experience. They do not accept the qualitative shifts in behavior that stage theories imply. We will examine the evidence for both viewpoints as we go along.

Early Years

Newborn infants appear to be fairly unresponsive creatures who spend most of their time sleeping, feeding, or crying. However, new experimental techniques tell us that they are much more responsive to their environment than was previously supposed. For example, infants as young as one or two days old can discriminate differences in taste. They much prefer sweet-tasting liquids to those that are salty, bitter, or bland; and they can even discriminate degrees of sweetness. Infants normally suck in bursts (short groups of sucks) with rest pauses in between. When a sweet fluid is delivered through the nipple, they engage in more sucks per minute, suck more deeply, and take fewer rest pauses than they do with plain water or less sweet fluids. As the sugar concentration doubles, there is a doubling of tongue pressure on the nipple (Nowlis and Kessen, 1976). It is a little discouraging to find that even infants have a "sweet tooth"! Given the choice between human breast milk and a sweeter formula of cow's milk, however, infants clearly prefer the breast milk (MacFarlane, 1977).

A newborn's sense of smell has been tested by presenting different smells on cotton swabs and noting head turning as well as changes in heart rate and respiration (see Figure 3-2). When a sweet smell is presented, infants turn their heads toward it and heart and respiration are slowed down—presumably a measure of interest and attention. A sour or acid smell causes infants to turn their heads away, and heart rate and respiration accelerate, indicating distress. Infants are even able to discriminate subtle differences in smells. After only a few days of nursing experience, infants will consistently turn their heads toward a pad saturated with their mother's milk in preference to one saturated with another mother's milk (MacFarlane, 1977). These innate taste and smell reactions have a clear adaptive value—helping the infant to avoid noxious substances.

The sucking response has also been used to test hearing. A normal infant will stop sucking and pause to listen to a new sound. After a few repetitions the infant will no longer pay attention; if a slightly different sound is introduced, the infant will pause to attend again.

Newborn infants can follow a moving object with their eyes shortly after birth, but their lenses do not focus for about a month; until then they can see an object clearly only when it is about a foot in front of them.

Effects of Early Experience

The development from an alert but fairly helpless newborn to a walking and talking two-year-old progresses at an astonishing rate. Indeed, changes occur more rapidly during the first two years of life than at any other period, except for the nine months before birth. As we noted earlier, the achievement of such physical skills as sitting, reaching for objects, crawling, and walking depends on the maturation of the muscles, nervous system, and other body parts. All babies achieve these skills without any special training. But psychologists have

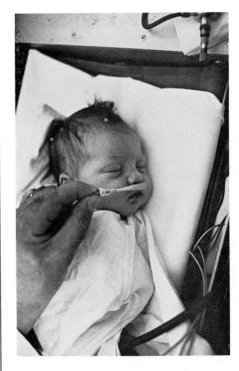

Fig. 3-2 Testing the newborn's sense of smell
Head turning and measures of heart rate and respiration are used to determine a two-day-old infant's reaction to various odors.

long been interested in whether environmental conditions can accelerate or retard maturational processes.

RESTRICTED ENVIRONMENTS   Although no special training is required for a child to walk at the appropriate time, a certain amount of environmental stimulation appears to be necessary. Children raised in institutions who are handled infrequently and given little opportunity to move about will sit, stand, and walk much later than normal. One study of an orphanage in Iran found that only 42 percent of the children were able to sit alone at two years, and only 15 percent could walk alone at age four (Dennis, 1960). Contrast these percentages with the norms given for home-reared children in Figure 3-1. It should be emphasized that this particular orphanage provided a more impoverished environment than most. The caretakers were low in intelligence and had little education. They provided for the physical needs of the children but made no effort to play with or talk to them. Infants remained in their cribs all day except when being fed or changed. Older children were placed in a playpen for part of the day, but there were few toys or other objects to play with.

INCREASED STIMULATION   To determine whether increased stimulation and the opportunity to move about improves the development of motor skills, two psychologists tested 30 of the Iranian orphan infants on a scale measuring various aspects of infant development and then divided them into two groups. One group remained in their cribs as before. The other babies were taken to a playroom for an hour each day, propped into a sitting position, and allowed to play with a variety of toys and objects. When the two groups were tested again a month later, the infants in the experimental group showed a marked gain in development compared with those who had remained in their cribs.

Although motor development is largely dependent on maturation, the experiences of being able to move about freely and reach for interesting objects are also necessary.

A related study shows the effect of early stimulation on *visually directed reaching*—a visual-motor response that develops in clearly specified maturational steps. A month-old baby lying on his or her back will stare at an attractive object held above but will make no attempt to reach for it. By two months, the baby will swipe at it accurately but with a closed fist. By four months the baby will alternate glances between his or her raised open hand and the object, gradually narrowing the gap. By five months the baby will accurately reach and successfully grasp the object.

Although the universality of this response sequence indicates a large degree of maturational dependence, the rate of development can be accelerated. The environment of a group of month-old infants in a state hospital was enriched by:

1 Increasing the amount of handling.
2 Placing the infants on their stomachs and removing the crib liners for several periods each day so they could observe the activities around them.
3 Replacing white crib sheets and liners with patterned ones.
4 Hanging elaborate ornaments over the cribs featuring contrasting colors and forms for the infants to look at and explore with their hands.

Infants who received this kind of treatment succeeded in visually directed reaching at an average age of three and a half months, as contrasted with five months for a control group reared in the relatively unstimulating conditions of normal hospital routine. Interestingly enough, the enriched-environment infants were delayed in one aspect of their development: they did not begin visually studying their hands until about two months, as contrasted with a month and a half for the control infants. With virtually nothing else to look at, the control infants discovered their hands earlier than the experimental group.

Note, however, that increased stimulation will not result in accelerated development unless infants are maturationally ready. In fact, too much stimulation too soon may be upsetting. During the first five weeks of the above experiment, infants in the enriched group spent less time looking at their surroundings (seeming to ignore the ornaments and patterned crib liners) and engaged in much more crying than did the control infants. It may be that month-old infants are actually distressed by being surrounded by more stimulation than they are able to respond to. A subsequent study found that providing infants with only a simple but colorful object mounted on the crib rails for the first two months of life and then introducing more complex ornaments during the third month seemed to produce optimal development. These infants showed no signs of unusual distress, were consistently attentive to their surroundings, and achieved visually directed reaching at *less* than three months. Thus, we see the importance of providing stimulation appropriate to the level of maturation (White, 1971).

Early Experiences and Later Development

How permanent are the effects of early stimulation or deprivation? As far as motor skills are concerned, early experiences probably do not have a lasting effect. Stimulation accelerated the development of visually directed reaching by a few months, but it is doubtful whether the experimental and control infants differed much in manual dexterity by the time they were a year old. Children from the Iranian orphanage who were adopted before the age of two quickly attained, and thereafter maintained, normal development (Dennis, 1973).

Infants in an isolated Indian village in Guatemala are kept inside the family's windowless hut for the first year of life in the belief that sunshine and air will cause sickness. They have little opportunity to crawl about, and their parents seldom play with them. When these children are allowed to leave the hut, they are behind United States children in physical skills. But they catch up and by the age of three are as well-coordinated as other children (Kagan and Klein, 1973).

As far as other areas of development are concerned—language ability, intellectual skills, and emotional development—early deprivation does appear to have lasting effects. Children whose learning opportunities are restricted during the first two or three years of life—who are not talked to, read to, or encouraged to explore their environment—are seriously behind in language and intellectual skills by the time they enter school and may never catch up.[1]

The importance of a stimulating environment in the early years for later intellectual development is illustrated by a classic study by Skeels and Dye (1939). A group of orphaned children (whose development at the age of 19 months was so retarded that adoption was out of the question) was transferred to an institution for the mentally retarded. In this institution, in contrast to the overcrowded orphanage, each child was placed in the care of an older, mildly retarded girl who served as a surrogate mother, spending great amounts of time playing with, talking to, and informally training the child. In addition, the living quarters were spacious and well equipped with toys. As soon as the

[1]See Chapter 12 for a discussion of Headstart programs for culturally disadvantaged children.

children could walk, they began to attend a nursery school where additional play materials and stimulation were provided. After a period of four years, this experimental group showed an average gain in intelligence of 32 IQ points; a control group that remained in the orphanage showed a loss of 21 points. A follow-up study over 20 years later found the experimental group to be still superior to the control group (Skeels, 1966). Most of the experimental group had completed high school (one-third had gone to college), were self-supporting, and had married and produced children of normal intelligence. Most of the control group, on the other hand, had not progressed beyond third grade and either remained institutionalized or did not earn enough to be self-supporting.

Although the number of subjects in this study was small and the possibility of some innate intellectual differences between the experimental and control groups cannot be completely ruled out, the results are sufficiently impressive to indicate the importance of a stimulating early environment for later intellectual development.

As we shall see later in this chapter, the lack of a close and caring relationship with an adult during the early years can have a profound effect on later emotional and social development.

Cognitive Development

As adults we take many aspects of our world for granted. We know, for example, that our arm is part of our body and that the table it is resting on is not. We recognize our hat as the same object whether it is lying on the table or on the closet shelf. We know that if we leave our house to walk across the street, we have to turn around to get back home. We know that a lead ball weighs more than a plastic ball, and we adjust our muscles accordingly when we pick up one or the other. But these facts, taken for granted by us, are a matter of learning for infants. From their encounters with objects and people, children learn to make sense out of their world. They proceed with remarkable speed from the elementary knowledge gained by manipulating objects to the kind of abstract thinking characteristic of adults.

Although most parents are aware of the intellectual changes that accompany their children's physical growth, they would have difficulty describing the nature of these changes. The Swiss psychologist Jean Piaget has made the most intensive study of children's cognitive development. After many years of careful observation, Piaget has developed a theory of how cognition develops through a series of stages as children mature (see Table 3-1).

Sensorimotor Stage

Noting the close interplay between motor activity and perception in infants, Piaget designated the first two years as a *sensorimotor stage.* During this period, infants are busy discovering the relationships between sensations and motor behavior. They learn, for example, how far they have to reach to grasp an object, what happens when they push their food dish to the edge of the table, and that their hand is part of their body and the crib rail is not. Through countless "experiments," infants begin to develop a concept of themselves as separate from the external world. An important discovery during this stage is the concept of *object permanence*—an awareness that an object continues to exist even when it is not present to the senses. If a cloth is placed over a toy for

Jean Piaget

TABLE 3-1
Piaget's stages of intellectual development
The ages given are averages. They may vary considerably depending on intelligence, cultural background, and socioeconomic factors, but the order of progression is assumed to be the same for all children. Piaget has described more detailed phases within each stage; only a very general characterization of each stage is given here.

STAGE	APPROXIMATE AGES	CHARACTERIZATION
1 Sensorimotor	Birth–2 years	Infant differentiates him or herself from objects; gradually becomes aware of the relationship between own actions and their effects on the environment so that he or she can act intentionally and make interesting events last longer (if the infant shakes a rattle it will make a noise); learns that objects continue to exist even though no longer visible (object permanence).
2 Preoperational	2–7 years	Uses language and can represent objects by images and words; is still *egocentric*, the world revolves around the infant and he or she has difficulty taking the viewpoint of others; classifies objects by single salient features: if A is like B in one respect, must be like B in other respects; toward the end of this stage begins to use numbers and develop conservation concepts.
3 Concrete operational	7–12 years	Becomes capable of logical thought; achieves conservation concepts in this order: number (age 6), mass (age 7), weight (age 9); can classify objects, order them in series along a dimension (such as size), and understand relational terms (A is longer than B).
4 Formal operational	12 years and up	Can think in abstract terms, follow logical propositions, and reason by hypothesis; isolates the elements of a problem and systematically explores all possible solutions; becomes concerned with the hypothetical, the future, and ideological problems.

Fig. 3-3 Object permanence
When the toy is hidden by a screen, the infant acts as if it no longer exists. The infant does not yet have the concept of object permanence.

which an eight-month-old is reaching, the infant immediately stops and appears to lose interest. He or she seems neither surprised nor upset, makes no attempt to search for the toy, and acts as if it ceased to exist (see Figure 3-3). In contrast, a 10-month-old will actively search for an object that has been hidden under a cloth or behind a screen. The older baby seems to realize that the object exists even though it is out of sight. He or she has attained the concept of object permanence. But even at this age search is limited; if the infant has had repeated success in retrieving a toy hidden in one place, he or she will continue to look for it in that spot even after having watched while it was being concealed in a new location. Not until about one year of age will a child consistently look for an object where it was last seen to disappear regardless of what has happened on previous trials.

Preoperational Stage

By about one-and-a-half to two years of age, children have begun to use language. Words, as symbols, can represent things or groups of things. And one object can represent (symbolize) another. Thus, in play a three-year-old may treat a stick as if it were a horse and ride it around the room; a block of wood can become a car; one doll can become a mother and the other a baby.

Although three- and four-year-olds can think in symbolic terms, their words and images are not yet organized in a very logical way. Piaget calls the two-to-seven-years stage of cognitive development *preoperational,* because the child does not yet comprehend certain rules or *operations.* An operation is a mental routine for transposing information, and it is reversible; every operation has its logical opposite. Cutting a circle into four equal pie-shaped wedges is part of an operation because we can reverse the procedure and put the pieces back to form a whole. The rule that we square the number 3 to get 9 is part of an operation because we can reverse the operation and take the square root of 9 to get 3. In the preoperational stage of cognitive development, a child's understanding of such rules is absent or weak. Piaget illustrates this deficit by some experiments on the development of what he calls *conservation.*

As adults we take conservation principles for granted: the amount (mass) of a substance is not changed when its shape is changed or when it is divided into parts; the total weight of a set of objects will remain the same no matter how they are packaged together; and liquids do not change in amount when they are poured from a container of one shape to that of another. For children, however, attainment of these concepts is an aspect of intellectual growth that requires several years.

In a study of the conservation of mass, a child is given some clay to make into a ball equal to another ball of the same material; the child declares them to be "the same." Now, leaving one for reference, the other is rolled out into a long sausage shape while the child watches. If the child is about four years old, he or she no longer considers the two objects to contain the same amount of clay: the longer one contains more (see Figure 3-4). Not until the age of seven do the majority of children reach the stage where the clay in the longer object is perceived to be equal in amount to that in the reference ball.

The same kind of experiment can be used to study the conservation of weight. For example, children who know that equal things will balance on a scale (they can test this with the two balls to begin with) are asked whether the sausage-shaped form will keep the scale arm balanced as did the original ball.

Fig. 3-4 Concept of conservation
A four-year-old acknowledges that the two balls of clay are the same size. But when one ball is rolled into a long thin shape, he says that it has more clay. Not until he is several years older will he state that the two different shapes contain the same amount of clay.

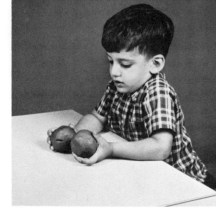

Conservation of weight is a more difficult concept to conceive than conservation of mass, and it comes a year or so later in development.

Children younger than seven have difficulty with conservation concepts because their thinking is still dominated by visual impressions. A change in the perceptual quality of the clay mass means more to them than subtle qualities, such as the volume the clay occupies regardless of its shape. The young child's reliance on visual impressions is made clear by a somewhat different conservation experiment. If a row of black checkers is matched one for one against an equal row of red checkers, the five- or six-year-old will say there are the same number of each. If the black checkers are brought closer together to form a cluster, the five-year-old says there are now more red ones—even though no checkers have been removed (see Figure 3-5). The impression of the length of the row of red checkers overrides the numerical equality that was obvious when the objects were matched. In contrast, seven-year-olds assume that if the number of objects was equal before, it must remain equal. At this age, numerical equality is more significant than visual impression.

Operational Stages

Between the ages of 7 and 12, the *concrete operational stage,* children master the various conservation concepts and begin to perform still other logical manipulations. For example, they can order objects on the basis of a dimension, such as height or weight. They can also form a mental representation of a series of actions. Five-year-olds can find their way to a friend's house but cannot direct you there or trace the route with paper and pencil. They can find the way because they know they have to turn at certain places, but they have no overall picture of the route. In contrast, eight-year-olds can readily draw a map of the route.

Piaget calls this period the concrete operational stage: although children are using abstract terms, they are doing so only in relation to concrete objects. Not until the final stage of cognitive development, the *formal operational stage,* which begins around age 11 or 12, are youngsters able to reason in purely symbolic terms.

In one test for formal operational thinking, the subject tries to discover what determines the period of oscillation of a simple pendulum. The subject is presented with a length of string suspended from a hook and several weights that can be attached to the lower end. He or she can vary the length of the string, change the attached weight, and alter the height from which the bob is released.

Children still in the concrete operational stage will experiment changing some of the variables, but not in a systematic way. Adolescents of even average ability will set up a series of hypotheses and proceed to systematically test each one. They reason that if a particular variable (weight) affects the period of oscillation, then the effect will appear only if they change one variable and hold all others constant. If this variable seems to have no effect on the time of swing, they rule it out and try another. Considering all the possibilities, working out the consequences for each hypothesis, and confirming or denying these consequences is the essence of what Piaget calls formal operational thought.

This ability to conceive of possibilities beyond what is present in reality—to think of alternatives to the way things are—permeates adolescent thinking and is tied in with adolescents' tendency to be concerned with metaphysical and ideological problems and to question the way in which adults run the world.

Fig. 3-5 Conservation experiment
When the two rows of seven checkers are evenly spaced, most children report that they contain the same amount. When one row is then clustered into a smaller space, children under six or seven will say the original row contains more.

Development

The possibility that children's views on moral issues change with age according to predictable stages has been the subject of extensive research by Lawrence Kohlberg at Harvard University. Using as a background Piaget's work on moral reasoning (*The Moral Judgment of the Child*, 1932), Kohlberg sought to determine whether there are universal stages in the development of moral judgments. He presented stories such as the following to children and adults of various ages and cultural backgrounds.

> In Europe, a lady was dying because she was very sick. There was one drug that the doctors said might save her. This medicine was discovered by a man living in the same town. It cost him $200 to make it, but he charged $2,000 for just a little of it. The sick lady's husband, Heinz, tried to borrow enough money to buy the drug. He went to everyone he knew to borrow the money. But he could borrow only half of what he needed. He told the man who made the drug that his wife was dying, and asked him to sell the medicine cheaper or let him pay later. But the man said, "No, I made the drug and I'm going to make money from it." So Heinz broke into the store and stole the drug.

The subject is asked, "Should Heinz have done that? Was it actually wrong or right? Why?" By analyzing the an-

TABLE 3-2
Stages in the development of moral reasoning

LEVELS AND STAGES	ILLUSTRATIVE BEHAVIOR
Level I Premoral	
1 Punishment and obedience orientation	Obeys rules in order to avoid punishment
2 Naive instrumental hedonism	Conforms to obtain rewards, to have favors returned
Level II Morality of conventional role-conformity	
3 "Good-boy" morality of maintaining good relations, approval of others	Conforms to avoid disapproval, dislike by others
4 Authority-maintaining morality	Conforms to avoid censure by legitimate authorities, with resultant guilt
Level III Morality of self-accepted moral principles	
5 Morality of contract, of individual rights, and of democratically accepted law	Conforms to maintain the respect of the impartial spectator judging in terms of community welfare
6 Morality of individual principles of conscience	Conforms to avoid self-condemnation

Source: Kohlberg (1967)

swers to a series of stories of this type—each portraying a moral dilemma—Kohlberg arrived at six developmental stages of moral judgment grouped into three broad levels (see Table 3-2). The answers are stage-assigned, not on the basis of whether the action is judged right or wrong, but on the reasons given for the decision. For example, agreeing that Heinz should have stolen the drug because "If you let your wife die, you'll get in trouble" or condemning him for his actions because "If you steal the drug you'll be caught and sent to jail" are both scored at stage 1. In both instances the man's actions are evaluated as right or wrong on the basis of anticipated punishment.

Kohlberg's studies indicate that the moral judgments of children who are seven years old and younger are predominantly at level I—actions are

Evaluation of Piaget's Theory

Research with children of different ages and backgrounds supports Piaget's observations of the *sequences* in cognitive development. However, the *ages* at which children reach the different levels vary considerably, depending on many factors. A very bright 10-year-old child might be skillful at systematically analyzing a problem and testing hypotheses, whereas some adults never achieve formal operational thinking. Children from middle-income homes

# of Moral Reasoning

evaluated in terms of whether they avoid punishment or lead to rewards. By age 13, a majority of the moral dilemmas are resolved at level II—actions are evaluated in terms of maintaining a good image in the eyes of other people. This is the level of conventional morality. In the first stage at this level (stage 3), one seeks approval by being "nice"; this orientation expands in the next stage (stage 4) to include "doing one's duty," showing respect for authority, and conforming to the social order in which one is raised.

According to Kohlberg, many individuals never progress beyond level II. He sees the stages of moral development as closely tied to Piaget's stages of cognitive development, and only those who have achieved the later stages of formal operational thought are capable of the kind of abstract thinking necessary for postconventional morality at level III. The highest stage of moral development (level III, stage 6) requires formulating abstract ethical principles and conforming to them to avoid self-condemnation. Kohlberg reports that less than 10 percent of his subjects over age 16 show the kind of "clear-principled" stage 6 thinking exemplified by the following response of a 16-year-old to Heinz's dilemma: "By the law of society he was wrong but by the law of nature or of God the druggist was wrong and the husband was justified. Human life is above financial gain. Regardless of who was dying, if it was a total stranger, man has a duty to save him from dying" (Kohlberg, 1969, p. 244).

Kohlberg describes children as "moral philosophers" who develop moral standards of their own; these standards do not necessarily come from parents or peers but emerge from the cognitive interaction of children with their social environment. Movement from one stage to the next involves an internal cognitive reorganization rather than a simple acquisition of the moral concepts prevalent in their culture (Kohlberg, 1973).

Other psychologists disagree, pointing out that the development of conscience is not simply a function of maturing cognitive abilities; children's identification with their parents and the way in which they are rewarded or punished for behavior in specific situations will influence their moral views. So also will the moral standards espoused by the children's peers and the way in which TV characters resolve their dilemmas. Studies have shown that moral judgments can be modified by exposure to models; when children watch adults who are reinforced for expressing a moral viewpoint based on principles different from their own, they may change their judgments up or down a level, depending on the particular model they watched (Bandura and McDonald, 1963).

Kohlberg's critics have argued, in addition, that individuals at a given age often express judgments that span several levels—that is, are not confined to one stage; their opinions vary depending on the particular circumstances portrayed in the dilemma (Fishkin, Keniston, and MacKinnon, 1973).

Thus, although there are obviously age trends in the way children think about moral issues, these often can be explained more simply by looking at what parents teach and reinforce in children at different ages than by proposing a set sequence of stages. Very young children may need the threat of punishment to keep them from doing something hazardous—"If you hit little sister, I will spank you." As children mature in their ability to understand language, social sanctions may replace physical ones—"If you hit little sister, I will be very angry; good children don't do such things."

A separate issue concerns how well moral reasoning—as measured by verbal responses to moral dilemmas—correlates with moral behavior. Kohlberg claims that moral thought and moral action are closely related. Other investigators, however, are not convinced that the correspondence between what people say and what they do is quite so close (Kurtines and Greif, 1974). And some believe that the specific situation is an important determiner of moral behavior; people cheat in some situations and not in others (Mischel and Mischel, 1974).

Moral conduct undoubtedly depends on a number of factors. One of them is the ability to reason about moral dilemmas. Another equally important factor is the ability to empathize with other people (that is, to put oneself in their place), to consider the long-range consequences of one's actions rather than the immediate gain, and to regulate or control one's behavior.

master conservation concepts at an earlier age than those from poor homes; and urban children earlier than rural children.

These differences raise the question of whether special training can accelerate progress through the cognitive stages. Different techniques have been used to try to speed up the transition from one stage to the next, with most of the studies focusing on conservation concepts. The usual procedure is to test a group of children on a conservation problem (for example, conservation of amount, using either water or clay), divide those who are nonconservers into experimental and control groups, provide the experimental group with special training, and retest both groups to see whether the performance of children in the trained group differs from the performance of those who received no training. The training may involve direct teaching of conservation principles—for example, showing the children that different shapes of clay weigh the same on a scale. Or it may be indirectly related to conservation—for example, drawing attention to the fact that objects simultaneously possess a number of characteristics by having the children practice naming the characteristics of objects and noting the ways in which they are similar or different.

Studies on the training of conservation principles have had conflicting results. Some report no success; others claim that the concept can be taught. Probably the safest conclusion is that instruction can yield some acceleration in cognitive development; however, progress from one stage to the next depends on maturational changes, so that training is most effective if it occurs when the child is ready (Glaser and Resnick, 1972).

Personality and Social Development

An infant's first social contacts are with the person who cares for him or her, usually the mother. The manner in which the caretaker responds to the infant's needs—patiently with warmth and concern, or brusquely with little sensitivity to discomfort—will influence the child's attitudes toward other people. Some psychologists believe that a person's basic feelings of trust in others are determined by experiences during the first years of life (Bowlby, 1973; Erikson, 1963, 1976).

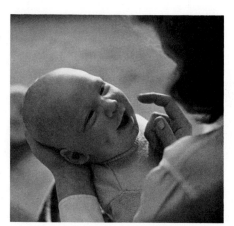

Early Social Responses

By two months of age the average child will smile at the sight of the mother's face. Most mothers, delighted with this response, will go to great lengths to encourage repetition. Indeed, the infant's ability to smile at such an early age may play an important role in strengthening the mother-child bond. The first smiles tell the caretaker that the infant "recognizes (loves) me"—which is not true in any personal sense as yet—and encourages the caretaker to be even more affectionate and stimulating in response. The infant smiles and coos at the mother; she pats, smiles, and vocalizes in return, thereby stimulating an even more enthusiastic response from her infant. Each reinforces social responses in the other.

Infants all over the world begin to smile at about the same age, whether raised in a remote African village or a middle-class American home. This suggests that maturation is more important in determining the onset of smiling than conditions of rearing. The fact that blind babies smile at about the same age as sighted infants (in response to their parents' voices rather than faces) adds support to this conclusion (Eibl-Eibesfeldt, 1970).

Even though smiling may be an innately programmed response, its development depends on environmental conditions. Babies raised in orphanages where their caretakers provide physical care but little social interaction gradually decrease their frequency of smiling. If institutionalized infants are given daily periods of special attention—if they are picked up, carried, talked to, and played with—they smile as often as home-reared infants (Brackbill, 1958).

In their early smiling responses infants are not very selective; they will smile at anything that vaguely resembles the human face, even flat cardboard masks with the features scrambled or distorted. The eyes and mouth elicit the most frequent smiles, regardless of how they are arranged on the face. With increasing age infants begin to prefer human faces to masks and will smile more readily to a smiling face than to one that is scowling. At about eight months of age the appearance of a strange face will often fail to elicit a smile and may produce signs of wariness or distress. By this time infants have begun to distinguish familiar faces from strange ones.

Attachment

In addition to smiling, infants make other social responses to their mothers (or caretakers). They coo and vocalize, snuggle closely when held, and scan the face of the person holding them. As soon as infants can crawl, they try to follow their mothers as they move from room to room.

The infant's tendency to seek closeness to particular people and to feel more secure in their presence is called *attachment.* The young of other species show attachment to their mother in different ways. Infant monkeys cling to their mother's chest as she moves about; puppies climb over each other in their attempts to reach the warm belly of their mother; ducklings and baby chicks follow their mother about, making sounds to which she responds and going to her when they are frightened. These early, unlearned responses to the mother have a clear adaptive value—preventing the organism from wandering away from the source of care and getting lost.

Psychologists at first theorized that attachment to the mother developed because she, as a source of food, satisfied one of the infant's most basic needs. But some facts did not fit. For example, ducklings and baby chicks feed themselves from birth, yet they still follow their mothers about and spend a great deal of time in contact with them. The comfort they derive from the mother's presence cannot come from her role in feeding. A series of well-known experiments with monkeys showed that there was more to mother-infant attachment than nutritional needs (Harlow and Suomi, 1970).

ATTACHMENT IN MONKEYS Infant monkeys were separated from their mothers shortly after birth and placed with two artificial "mothers" constructed of wire mesh with wooden heads; the torso of one of the "mothers" was bare wire; the other was covered with foam rubber and terry cloth, making it more "cuddly" and easy to cling to (see Figure 3-6). Either "mother" could be equipped to provide milk by means of a bottle attached to its "chest."

The experiment sought to determine whether the "mother" that was always the source of food would be the one to which the young monkey would cling. The results were clear-cut: no matter which mother provided food, the infant monkey spent its time clinging to the terry cloth, "cuddly" mother. This purely passive but soft-contact mother was a source of security. For example, the obvious fear of the infant monkey placed in a strange environment was allayed if the infant could make contact with the cloth mother. While holding on to the cloth mother with one hand or foot, the monkey was willing to explore objects that were otherwise too terrifying to approach. Similar responses can be observed in one- to two-year-old children who are willing to explore strange territory as long as their mother is only a few feet away.

Fig. 3-6 A monkey's response to an artificial mother
Although fed via the wire mother, the infant spends more time with the terry cloth mother. The terry cloth mother provides security and a safe base from which to explore strange objects.

Further studies revealed some additional features that infant monkeys seek in their mothers. They prefer an artificial mother that "rocks" to an immobile one, and they prefer a warm mother to a cold one. Given a cloth mother and a wire mother of the same temperature, the infant monkey always preferred the cloth mother. But if the wire mother was heated, the newborn chose it over a cool cloth mother for the first two weeks of life. After that, the infant monkeys spent more and more time with the cloth mother.

The infant monkey's attachment to its mother is thus an innate response to certain stimuli provided by her. Warmth, rocking, and food are important, but *contact comfort*—the opportunity to cling to and rub against something soft—seems to be the most important attribute for monkeys.

Although contact with a cuddly, artificial mother provides an important aspect of "mothering," it is not enough for satisfactory development. Infant monkeys raised with artificial mothers and isolated from other monkeys during the first six months of life showed various types of bizarre behavior in adulthood. They rarely engaged in normal interaction with other monkeys later on (either cowering in fear or showing abnormally aggressive behavior), and their sexual responses were inappropriate. When female monkeys who had been deprived of early social contact were successfully mated (after considerable effort), they made very poor mothers, tending to neglect or abuse their infants. For monkeys, interaction with other members of their species during the first six months of life appears to be crucial for normal social development.

ATTACHMENT IN HUMAN INFANTS Although we should be careful in generalizing from experimental work on monkeys to human development, there is evidence that the human infant's attachment to the mother (or primary caretaker) serves the same important functions—it provides the security necessary for the child to explore the environment, and it forms the basis for interpersonal relationships in later years. Young children are much more willing to investigate strange surroundings when mother is nearby. The failure to form an attachment to one or a few primary persons in the early years has been related to an inability to develop close personal relationships in adulthood (Bowlby, 1973).

Normally, attachment to the mother—as measured by seeking to remain near her and crying when separated—reaches a peak at about age two; from then on the child becomes progressively more willing to be separated from the mother. By about age three, the child is sufficiently secure in the mother's absence to be able to interact with other children or adults (see Figure 3-7).

A series of studies designed to investigate attachment in young children has revealed some interesting differences in the quality of the mother-child relationship. The laboratory setup, called the "strange situation," involves the following episodes:

1 The mother brings the child into the experimental room, places the child on a small chair surrounded by toys, and then goes to sit at the opposite end of the room.
2 After a few minutes a stranger enters the room, sits quietly for a while, and then attempts to engage the child in play with a toy.
3 The mother leaves the room.
4 The mother returns and engages the child in play while the stranger slips out.
5 The mother leaves and the child is left alone for three minutes.
6 The stranger returns.
7 The mother returns.

The child is observed through a one-way mirror during the entire sequence, and any number of different measures can be recorded—child's activity level and play involvement, crying or other distress signs, proximity to and attempts to gain attention of mother, proximity to and willingness to interact with the stranger, and so on.

Fig. 3-7 Mother attachment and age The "strange situation" was used to study age changes in attachment behavior. The child was observed through a one-way mirror and the frequency of crying recorded during the sequence of episodes noted along the base line. The episodes are described more fully in the text; no data was reported for episodes 4 and 7. Note that crying in response to being left with a stranger or left alone decreases from ages two to three, indicating that the child is more willing to be separated from the mother. (After Maccoby and Feldman, 1972)

One study using the "strange situation" with one-year-olds found that some of the most significant individual differences showed up in the baby's reaction to the mother when she returned. Almost all the babies were uneasy during the mother's absence, whether left with the stranger or completely alone; signs of distress ranged from fussing and visually searching for the mother to loud crying. On the mother's return, more than half of the babies immediately sought close contact with her and showed a need for closeness for a while thereafter. But some babies conspicuously ignored the mother on her return; and some displayed seemingly ambivalent behavior—for example, they would cry to be picked up and then squirm angrily to get down.

Observation of the same babies in the home revealed that those babies who sought contact with the mother on reunion were much more secure (cried less often, were more responsive to their mother's verbal commands, and were less upset by their mother's coming and going) than babies who were either avoidant or ambivalent on reunion in the strange situation.

The investigator concluded, on the basis of these and other data, that all babies become attached to the mother by the time they are one year old, but the quality of the attachment differs depending on the mother's responsiveness to the baby's needs. Most babies show *secure attachment*, but some show *anxious attachment.* The avoidant or ambivalent behavior shown by anxiously attached babies on reunion with the mother is assumed to be a defense against the anxiety occasioned by a mother who cannot be depended on. It is a mild form of the more extreme kind of detachment observed in young children who have had to endure long separations from the parents. Such children often appear indifferent to their parents when they are first reunited (Ainsworth, 1973).

Anxious attachment is associated with insensitive or unresponsive mothering during the first year. The mothers of babies who show anxious attachment tend to respond more on the basis of their own wishes or moods than to signals from the baby. For example, they will respond to the baby's cries for attention when they feel like cuddling the baby, but will ignore such cries at other times. Such insensitivity produces feelings of insecurity in the infant (Stayton, 1973).

Interaction with Siblings and Peers

While a close relationship with a warm and responsive adult is essential for a child's emotional development, interaction with other children plays an important role, too.

As we saw before, infant monkeys who are raised with only their mothers and have no opportunity to play with other young monkeys do not develop normal patterns of behavior. When introduced to other monkeys later on, they may be abnormally fearful of contact—screaming in fright at the approach of another monkey—or overly aggressive; they also show inappropriate sexual responses (Suomi, 1977).

In the normal course of development, an infant monkey spends the first eight weeks of life exclusively with its mother. From then on the young monkey spends more and more time swinging, chasing, and wrestling with its mates. From these early play activities the young monkey learns to enjoy physical contact, to control aggression, and to develop the grasping and mounting responses that will lead to adult sexual behavior.

Human children also learn many of their social skills in interaction with each other. They learn to give and take, to share in cooperative ventures, to enjoy each other's actions, and to understand how another person feels. Peers

Group Versus Family Care:

More and more women today are working outside of the home. There are some five million working mothers in the United States with children under five years of age, and the number appears to be increasing. In view of the research on infant attachment, it is important to consider the effects that this trend will have on future generations. Will the development of children who spend most of their waking hours in a day-care center differ from those who remain at home with their mother?

A number of countries have a longer history of communal child-rearing than we do. In China, Russia, and Israel, mothers are encouraged to work while their children are cared for in state-run institutions. In China, for example, mothers can leave their infants in a nursery at their place of work as soon as the infants are two months old. The mother leaves her job at intervals to nurse the infant. By the time the baby is two or three years old, he or she is usually dropped off at a day-care center near the home in the morning and picked up when the parents return from work in the evening.

On the collective farms, or *kibbutzim*, of Israel the children are cared for from early infancy by professional caretakers, called *metapelets*, in houses separate from those of the parents. Practices differ somewhat from one kibbutz to another, but the following

Chinese infants in a factory "feeding station"
The infants' mothers, working nearby, will nurse them during breaks in the work shift.

arrangement is typical. During the first year of life, the mother provides the major portion of the feeding and care of her infant, although the infant is still housed in the communal nursery. After the first year, the mother works full time and the parents see their child mainly during the evening and on Saturdays.

Information about the effects of communal care on children's develop-

ment in China and Russia is limited, but there have been a number of studies of kibbutz children. For example, one study found that kibbutz children were equal in physical and mental skills to Israeli children raised in private homes, and both groups were superior to Israeli children reared in orphanages (Kohen-Raz, 1968). Because earlier studies had shown that children raised in orphanages were retarded in social

become models to imitate as well as important dispensers of rewards and punishments. By watching the actions of peers, children may learn a new skill (how to build a bridge with blocks) or the consequences of certain behaviors (aggression gets other children into trouble).

A number of experiments have shown the influence of peer models on children's behavior. For example, four- and five-year-olds who watched one of their classmates being very generous in sharing some prizes were much more generous when their turn came to share than children who had not watched the generous model (Hartup and Coates, 1967). As we will see in Chapter 11, if a child watches a model being rewarded for certain behaviors, the child is more likely to imitate those behaviors than if he or she sees the model being punished.

What Happens When Mother Works?

and intellectual development, those responsible for setting up the kibbutz child-care centers were especially concerned with providing a warm relationship with a mother-substitute as well as sufficient intellectual stimulation. They realized that adequate physical care was not enough to produce a healthy child. Consequently, the metapelets received special training in all areas of child development.

Because they spend more time with their peers, kibbutz-raised children develop some social characteristics earlier than children raised at home. For example, they develop a feeling of group concern and identification while very young; they also acquire early the ability to understand how another child feels (Rabkin and Rabkin, 1969; Nahir and Yussen, 1977).

Interestingly enough, being separated from the mother for most of the day does not appear to weaken the mother-child attachment. When kibbutz children were observed in the strange situation at age two and a half, they were just as concerned over separation fom the mother as were United States children raised at home (Maccoby and Feldman, 1972). When kibbutz children were left with mother and a stranger, they appeared more secure than when left with the metapelet and a stranger—as evidenced by the amount of time spent playing, as opposed to

Nursery at a kibbutz

hovering near the metapelet (Fox, 1975).

Similar results have been found when day-care children in the United States are compared with home-reared children. There seems to be little difference between the two groups either in the amount of protest shown when left by the mother in an unfamiliar room or in the tendency to seek closeness to the mother when tired or upset (Kagan and others, 1978). Children form attachments to a number of people (father, grandparent, nursery school teacher), but the attachment to the mother appears to be a special bond that is unrelated to the number of hours per day the child spends with her.

Any attempt to evaluate the effects of home care versus group care obviously depends on the quality of the child-care facility and the nature of the home. A survey of studies concerned with the effects of day care in the United States concluded that there are no negative effects on the children, provided the centers are run by trained personnel in charge of small numbers of children (Bee, 1974).

The mother's attitude toward her role is equally important. If the mother is satisfied with what she is doing—at home or at work—the child is better off emotionally (Hoffman and Nye, 1974). If the mother feels isolated and confined at home, then both mother and child might be happier if the child spends some part of the day at a good child-care center or with a parent substitute. Single parents who have recently been divorced probably have the greatest need for help in child rearing, since the first year following divorce is very stressful for most families—the household tends to be disorganized, discipline is inconsistent, and angry interactions between mother and child are frequent (Hetherington, 1978).

The way other children respond to a child's behavior is an important modifying influence. Selfishness that may have been accepted by doting parents may not be tolerated by the child's peers. Children reinforce certain actions in their playmates—by approval and attention—and punish others.

Child-Rearing Practices and Later Behavior

Methods of child-rearing vary considerably from country to country and from one social group to another. Even within middle-income homes in the United States, attitudes have tended to fluctuate in cycles on such matters as toilet training, feeding schedules, bottle versus breast feeding, and permissiveness versus firm control.

During the first third of this century, child-rearing practices were fairly strict. Parents were advised not to spoil their babies by picking them up every time they cried, to feed them according to a fixed schedule (whether hungry or not), and to toilet train within the first year. Thumb sucking and handling the genitals were to be vigorously discouraged. This quite rigid approach was partly the result of the influence of behaviorism; the goal was to build "good" habits and extinguish bad ones—and the earlier the parents started, the better. The following quotation from John B. Watson, the father of behaviorism, carries to a ridiculous extreme the notion of a controlled, objective, unemotional way of handling children.

> There is a sensible way of treating children. Treat them as though they were young adults. Dress them, bathe them with care and circumspection. Let your behavior always be objective and kindly firm. Never hug and kiss them, never let them sit on your lap. If you must, kiss them once on the forehead when they say goodnight. Shake hands with them in the morning. Give them a pat on the head if they have made an extraordinarily good job of a difficult task. Try it out. In a week's time you will find how easy it is to be perfectly objective with your child and at the same time kindly. You will be utterly ashamed of the mawkish, sentimental way you have been handling it. (Watson, 1928)

It is doubtful whether many parents followed such a rigid program, but this was the advice of the "experts" at the time.

During the 1940s, the trend shifted toward more permissive and flexible child-care methods. Views on child development were being influenced by psychoanalytic theory, which stressed the importance of the child's emotional security and the damage that might result from harsh control of natural impulses. Under the guidance of Dr. Benjamin Spock, parents were advised to follow their own inclinations and adapt schedules to fit both the child's and their own needs. Toilet training should be delayed until the child was old enough to understand its purpose (not before the middle of the second year), and neither thumb sucking nor genital touching was to be considered a matter of great concern.

Interestingly enough, the pendulum appears to be swinging back. Parents today seem to feel that permissiveness is not the answer. Their approach to child-rearing includes a moderate degree of control, firm discipline, and punishment when necessary (Walters and Grusec, 1977).

That children flourish under a wide variety of rearing methods is a tribute to their adaptability and probably an indication that specific methods are less important than the basic attitude of the parents.

Attempts to relate specific child-rearing techniques—type of feeding schedule, age of weaning or toilet training—to later personality characteristics have not been very successful. The inconsistent results obtained probably are due to several factors. For one thing, parents' reports of how they handled their children may be fairly inaccurate, particularly when memory for the children's early days is required. Parents tend to report what they *think they should do* in handling their offspring, rather than what they actually do. There are also numerous ways of applying any specific child-rearing method. For example, two children may be toilet trained at the same early age; one mother is firm but patient, while the other is firm and impatient, expressing disappointment when the child fails. Both mothers toilet train "early" but communicate quite different attitudes to the child.

Although specific techniques may not be very predictive of later personality traits, we do have some evidence of the kind of parent-child relationships that produce competent and self-confident youngsters. In a series of studies, three- and four-year-old children were observed at home and in nursery school and rated on five measures of competency: (1) self-control, (2) the tendency to approach new or unexpected situations with curiosity and enthusiasm, (3) vitality, (4) self-reliance, and (5) the ability to express warmth toward playmates. On the basis of ratings on these characteristics, three groups of children were selected for further study. Children in group I were the most mature and competent, scoring high on all five characteristics. Group II children were moderately self-reliant and self-controlled but rather apprehensive in new situations and not much interested in interacting with other children. Group III children were the most immature; they were much less self-reliant and self-controlled than the children in the other two groups, highly dependent on adults for help, and apt to retreat from new situations.

The investigator next looked at the child-rearing practices of all the parents by interviewing them and by observing how they interacted with their children in the home. The investigator focused on four dimensions of the parent-child relationship: (1) *control*—how much the parents tried to influence the child's activities and modify the expression of dependent or aggressive behavior in line with their own standards; (2) *maturity demands*—the amount of pressure on the child to perform at his or her level of ability; (3) *clarity of parent-child communication*—how well the parents explained their reasons when they wanted the child to obey and the extent to which they took the child's opinions and feelings into consideration; (4) *parental nurturance*—the warmth and compassion the parents showed toward the child and their pleasure in his or her accomplishments.

As Figure 3-8 shows, the parents of the mature and competent children (group I) are high on all four dimensions. They are warm, loving, and communicate well with their children. While they respect their children's opinions, they are generally firm and clear about the behavior they consider appropriate. The parents of the children who were moderately self-controlled and self-reliant but somewhat withdrawn and distrustful (group II) tend to be fairly controlling but not very warm and affectionate toward their children or concerned with their opinions. The parents of the most immature children (group III) are affectionate toward their children but not very controlling or demanding. These parents tend to be ineffective and disorganized in running their households and lax in setting guidelines for behavior and disciplining or rewarding their children.

In subsequent studies, the investigator proceeded in the reverse direction— that is, selecting parents that fitted the above descriptions and then looking at the behaviors of their preschool children. Although the results are too detailed to describe here, we can draw some general conclusions. Parents who are fairly firm and consistent in their expectations of how their children should behave but who are also warm and affectionate and respect their children's opinions tend to produce competent and self-reliant preschoolers. When the parents are very controlling and more concerned with their own needs than with those of their children, their offspring may be fairly self-controlled but not very secure or confident in their approach to new situations or other people. Very permissive parents, who neither reward responsible behavior nor discourage immature behavior, produce youngsters with the least self-reliance and self-control. In summary, competence and self-confidence in young children seem best fostered by a warm and nurturant home where parents reward responsible behavior but also encourage independent actions and decision making (Baumrind, 1972).

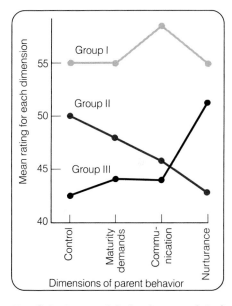

Fig. 3-8 Parental behavior as related to child behavior
Nursery school children were evaluated in terms of competency and maturity; group I are the most competent children; group III are the most immature and dependent. The figure shows how the parents of each group were rated on four dimensions: control of the child's activities, pressure demands for mature behavior, clarity of parent-child communication, and nurturance or warmth. (Baumrind, 1967)

Identification

As children develop, they acquire many attitudes and behavior patterns that are similar to those of their parents. Sometimes the resemblance between a youngster and a parent in such characteristics as manner of walking, gestures, and voice inflection is striking. The child is said to *identify* with the parent (see Figure 3-9).

The concept of identification comes from psychoanalysis and played an important role in Freud's theorizing. In psychoanalytic theory, identification refers to the unconscious process by which an individual takes on the characteristics (attitudes, patterns of behavior, emotions) of another person. Young children, by duplicating the attitudes and attributes of their parents, come to feel that they have absorbed some of the parents' strength and adequacy.

Identification, according to the psychoanalytic view, involves more than simply imitating parental behavior; the child responds as if he or she *were* the parent. Thus, a young girl who identifies with her mother feels proud when her mother receives an award or honor—as if she herself had been the recipient. She feels sad when her mother suffers a disappointment. Through the process of identification, the child acquires the diverse behaviors involved in developing self-control, a conscience, and the appropriate sex role. The child's conscience, for example, is formed by incorporating parental standards of conduct so that the child acts in accordance with these standards even when the parent is absent and experiences guilt when he or she violates them.

Fig. 3-9 A child identifies with the parent

Some psychologists question the psychoanalytic view of identification as an unconscious, unitary process. They point out that not all children identify with their parents in all respects. A girl, for example, may emulate her mother's social skills and sense of humor but not her moral values. They view identification as a form of learning; children imitate certain parental behaviors because they are rewarded for doing so. Peers, teachers, and TV heroes are other models who serve as sources of imitation or identification. According to this view, identification is a continuous process in which new responses are acquired as a function of both direct and vicarious experiences with parents and other models.

Most psychologists—regardless of how they define it—view identification as the basic process in the socialization of children. By modeling behavior after the important people in their environment, children acquire the attitudes and behaviors expected of adults in their society. Parents, because they are children's earliest and most frequent associates, serve as the primary source of identification. The parent of the opposite sex usually serves as the model for sex-typed behavior.

Sex Roles

Each culture sets certain approved ways in which men and women are expected to behave; these are the *sex-role standards* for that culture. The standards for masculine and feminine behavior vary from culture to culture and may change over time within a culture. Certainly our view of what is appropriate behavior today is radically different from what it was 50 years ago. Women are no longer expected to be dependent, submissive, and noncompetitive; men are not criticized for enjoying such domestic activities as cooking and sewing or for expressing artistic and tender feelings. Standards of dress and appearances

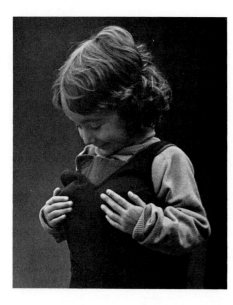

have changed markedly, too. Within each culture the roles of men and women still differ, however, and these roles are transmitted in large part by the parents. The man a boy knows best is usually his father and a girl's first exposure to the woman's role is through her mother. Parental attitudes toward themselves and one another are major influences on the child's view of masculine and feminine roles.

SEX TYPING Even before they are old enough to realize that there are two sexes, children may be treated differently depending on their sex. A female infant is often dressed in so-called feminine colors, such as pink, and may be handled more delicately by her parents than a male. A male infant may be dressed in blue and played with more vigorously by his father than a female. Parents may, without meaning to, reinforce dependency in girls and achievement and assertiveness in boys. By providing "sex-appropriate" toys and encouraging "sex-appropriate" play activities, parents can instill sex-role stereotypes at an early age.

One method of measuring sex-typed behavior is to have the child choose between various toys and activities. Doll carriages and dishes are arbitrarily classified as feminine, dump trucks and tools as masculine. Examples of neutral toys (appropriate to either sex) are wading pools and roller skates. Studies using this method indicate that boys as young as three prefer sex-appropriate toys. Many girls show an early preference for masculine toys and games; in kindergarten more girls show a preference for masculine toys than boys do for feminine toys. With increasing age, both girls and boys make increasingly more sex-appropriate choices, but boys consistently make more of them than do girls (see Figure 3-10).

How do we account for these differences? For one thing, there is an unfortunate tendency for both sexes to view "masculine" activities as superior to "feminine" ones. And in our culture the taboos against effeminate behavior for boys are stronger than those against masculine behavior for girls. Learning how to be masculine seems to be largely a matter of avoiding any behavior regarded as "sissyish." When kindergarten boys were individually permitted to play with a group of attractive feminine toys and unattractive neutral toys, most of them avoided the feminine toys, spending their time with the unattractive and dilapidated neutral toys. The presence of an adult increased avoidance of the feminine toys, whereas observation of another boy playing with the feminine toys reduced avoidance. Observing a girl play with the feminine toys brought no change in behavior (Kobasigawa, Arakaki, and Awiguni, 1966).

Current attempts to prevent sex-role stereotyping by encouraging children to engage in a wide range of activities, without implying that any activity is either masculine or feminine, may change the results in future studies of this kind. While there may be some innate sex differences in abilities and interests, sex-role standards are primarily culturally determined.

Factors Influencing Identification

Many personal qualities are not strongly sex typed. For example, enthusiasm, sense of humor, friendliness, and integrity are characteristics shared by both men and women. A child may learn such traits from *either* parent without violating the cultural sex standards. When college students were interviewed about their behavioral similarities to their parents in temperament and inter-

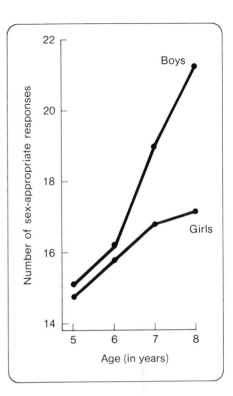

Fig. 3-10 Sex-typing in young children When a choice is given between two toys (one masculine and the other feminine), the number of sex-appropriate responses increases with age for both boys and girls. Note that boys consistently make more of these responses than do girls, although the difference is very small at ages five and six. (Data from DeLucia, 1963)

Sex Differences

"Girls are more fluent verbally; boys are better at math." "Girls can memorize well, but boys are superior in abstract thinking." "Girls tend to be passive and to seek approval; boys are aggressive and independent." You have probably heard these and other claims about psychological differences between the sexes. What is the evidence? Do males and females differ consistently in abilities and personality traits? And, if so, are these differences the result of biology or of social learning? A careful review of more than 2,000 books and research articles concludes that many common assumptions about sex differences are myths with no foundation in fact; but there appear to be some real and interesting psychological differences between males and females (Maccoby and Jacklin, 1974).

Tests of overall intelligence show no consistent sex differences—in part because the tests are designed not to. In constructing intelligence tests, care is taken either to eliminate items on which the sexes are believed to differ or to balance items on which females have an advantage with those that give males an advantage. Tests of specific intellectual abilities, however, do show some sex differences. These differences, which are absent or negligible during childhood, begin to appear in

early adolescence. For example, beginning at about 10 or 11 years of age, girls, *on the average,* outscore boys on many measures of *verbal ability*—vocabulary size, comprehension of difficult written material, and verbal fluency.

While adolescent males may lag behind in verbal skills, they tend, *on the average,* to be superior to females on tests of *visual-spatial ability.* Visual-spatial skills are involved in such tasks as conceptualizing how an object in space would look from a different perspective, aiming at targets, map reading, or finding a simple geometric form embedded in a more complex figure (see Figure 3-11). The mathematical skills of boys also appear to increase faster than those of girls after age 13, but the differences are not as consistent as those for spatial ability. Girls are about equal to boys when mathematical problems are given in verbal form; boys excel in dealing with numbers or geometric forms.

In talking about sex differences in verbal or spatial abilities, it is important to remember that we are referring to *average* differences over large groups of youngsters; some girls are better at spatial tasks than most boys, and some boys are more verbally fluent than most girls.

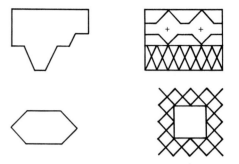

Fig. 3-11 **Embedded-figures test**
The subject must identify the simple figures in the more complex ones.

Because sex differences in these abilities do not emerge until adolescence, it seems reasonable to conclude that they reflect differences in training and social expectations. After all, girls are usually encouraged to develop interests in poetry, literature, and drama; boys are expected to be more concerned with science, engineering, and mechanics. This is undoubtedly part of the story, but it is also possible that sex differences in ability may be based on biological differences that do not appear until the nervous system reaches a certain level of maturation—namely, puberty. This possibility seems most likely for spatial abilities. In a study of youngsters aged 10 to 16

ests, a fourth of the men believed that they resembled their mothers in these respects and a similar proportion of girls thought they resembled their fathers; many reported resemblances to both parents (Hilgard, 1970).

Experiments give us some clues as to the kinds of variables that influence identification. For example, several studies have shown that adults who are warm and nurturant are more likely to be imitated than those who are not. Boys who score high on masculinity tests tend to have warmer, more affectionate relationships with their fathers than boys who score low. Girls who are rated as quite feminine also have a warmer, closer relationship with their mothers than girls evaluated as less feminine (Mussen and Rutherford, 1963).

The adult's power in controlling the child's environment also affects the tendency to identify. When the mother is dominant, girls tend to identify much more with her than with the father, and boys may have difficulty developing the

in Behavior

years, late maturers were found to be better at visual-spatial tasks than early maturers, regardless of sex; and the older the youngster at the onset of puberty, the better his or her performance on spatial, relative to verbal, tasks (Waber, 1977). Since females, on the average, mature earlier than males, rate of physical maturation may be an important determinant of sex differences in spatial ability.

In terms of personality traits, most studies have found surprisingly few differences between the sexes, particularly during the early years. Little girls are *not* more dependent than little boys, as is commonly believed, nor are they more sociable. Toddlers of both sexes seek to be close to their parents, especially when they are under stress; and they seem equally willing to leave their parents to explore a new environment (Maccoby and Jacklin, 1974). Differences in sociability show up only to the extent that boys during the elementary grades tend to play in "gangs," whereas girls are more apt to get together in groups of two or three.

The one area in which observed sex differences are consistent with popular beliefs is aggression. Boys *are* more aggressive than girls starting at about age two—when children first begin to interact in social play. This is true in a wide range of settings and for almost every culture that has been studied. Boys are not only more physically aggressive than girls, but also more verbally aggressive; they are more likely than girls to exchange verbal taunts and insults—often as a prelude to physical aggression.

Clearly, social learning has a lot to do with the expression of aggression. Many parents believe that a boy should be able to fight for his rights, and a boy has all kinds of aggressive models (in books, television, and movies) to show him how. Girls, on the other hand, are expected to get their way by more subtle means. In view of such social conditioning, it seems reasonable to assume that girls have the same potential for aggression as boys but inhibit its expression for fear of punishment. Some psychologists believe that this is the case (Feshbach and Feshbach, 1973). Others believe that, although social expectations and role models influence the expression of aggression, females are by their biological nature less aggressive (Maccoby and Jacklin, 1974). They point to the fact that girls show less fantasy aggression than boys. If girls are suppressing hostile impulses because of fear of punishment, such impulses might be expected to occur in fantasy or in "safe" situations. But even in an experimental situation where aggression is expected and encouraged—the subject is instructed to administer electric shocks to a "learner" whenever the learner makes a mistake—males tend to administer longer and stronger shocks to their victims than females (Titley and Viney, 1969). These findings do not suggest that females have a lot of "bottled-up" aggression waiting for a safe outlet.

In their survey of sex differences, Maccoby and Jacklin discovered that males and females are alike in more respects than is commonly supposed. Among the differences found, some may be the result of social learning and others may reflect biological predispositions. But even those differences that have a biological base can be modified by learning. For example, girls who initially score lower than boys on tests of visual-spatial ability can equal the boys' scores with practice. And certainly girls can be taught to be more aggressive, while boys can learn to modify their aggressive responses.

In rearing their young, societies can accentuate what they believe to be innate differences, or they can choose to encourage in both sexes the characteristics most useful for their particular society.

masculine sex role. In father-dominant homes, girls are more similar to their fathers than in mother-dominant homes, but they still identify to a large degree with the mother. For girls, the mother's warmth and self-confidence seem to be more important than her powerfulness (Hetherington and Frankie, 1967).

A third factor that influences identification is the perception of similarities between oneself and the model. To the extent that a child has some objective basis for perceiving him or herself as similar to the parent, the child will tend to identify with that parent. A girl who is tall and large-boned with facial features similar to those of her father may have more difficulty identifying with her petite mother than a younger sister who is similar to the mother in build.

To the extent that both parents are seen as nurturant, powerful, and competent, the child will identify with both, although the stronger identification generally will be with the parent of the same sex.

Drawing by Opie; © 1978 The New Yorker Magazine, Inc.

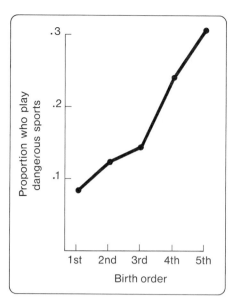

Fig. 3-12 Birth order and participation in dangerous sports
The graph shows the proportion of male undergraduates who play dangerous sports (football, rugby, soccer) in relation to their birth order. Note that the first-born is less likely to engage in a dangerous sport than later-borns. The study found no relationship between birth order and participation in nondangerous sports, such as baseball or crew. (Data from Nisbett, 1968a)

Identification with Siblings

Although parents are the primary identification figures, siblings play an important role, too. The sex of the other siblings influences the child's interests and behavior; girls with older brothers are likely to be more masculine (tomboyish) and competitive than girls with older sisters. Similarly, boys with older sisters tend to be less aggressive than boys with older brothers.

Birth order also affects the child's relationships within the family. One study of large families identified three personality roles that were related to birth order: the responsible child (often the first-born), the sociable, well-liked child (often the second), and the spoiled child (often the youngest) (Bossard and Ball, 1955).

First-born or only children occupy a unique position in the family for several reasons. Parents have more time and attention to devote to their first child and are apt to be more cautious, indulgent, and protective. The first-born does not have to compete with older siblings; and for a while, he or she has only adult models to copy and adult standards of conduct to emulate, while later-borns have siblings with whom to identify.

Research indicates that these factors do have an effect. First-born or only children are more likely to score at the upper extremes on intelligence tests, do well in college, and achieve eminence. Among finalists for the National Merit Scholarship from two-children families, there are twice as many first-borns as second-borns. Among finalists from three-child families, there are as many first-borns as second- and third-borns combined (Nichols, 1968). First-born or only children have also been found to be more conscientious, cooperative, and cautious than later-born children (Altus, 1966); and, as Figure 3-12 shows, they are less likely to engage in dangerous sports. We should stress the fact that these are only *trends;* many famous achievers were later-born children (Benjamin Franklin, for example, was the fifteenth of seventeen children), and many first-born children do not possess any of the characteristics just noted.

The more conscientious and cooperative nature of first-borns probably reflects an attempt to maintain their "privileged" status with the parents in the face of possible displacement by the newly arrived sibling. The later-born may feel less competent than the older sibling (not realizing that his or her inadequacies are a function of age) and may try to excel in other ways—for example, by being more physically daring.

While competition with younger siblings may partially account for the higher achievement of first-borns, it does not explain the equally high achievement of only children. The most likely explanation is that parents have more time and energy to devote to an only child and, thus, may provide a richer, more stimulating environment. As the family becomes larger, the parents may pay increasingly less attention to each child.

Adolescence

Adolescence refers to the period of transition from childhood to adulthood. Its age limits are not clearly specified, but it extends roughly from age 12 to the late teens, when physical growth is nearly complete. During this period, the young person develops to sexual maturity, establishes an identity as an individual apart from the family, and faces the task of deciding how to earn a living.

A few generations ago, adolescence as we know it today was nonexistent. Many teen-agers worked 14 hours a day and moved from childhood into the responsibilities of adulthood with little time for transition. With a decrease in the need for unskilled workers and an increase in the length of apprenticeship required to enter a profession, the interval between physical maturity and adult status has lengthened. Such symbols of maturity as financial independence from parents and completion of school are accomplished at later ages. Young people are not given many adult privileges until late in their teens; in most states they cannot work full time, sign legal documents, drink alcoholic beverages, marry, or vote.

A gradual transition to adult status has some advantages. It gives the young person a longer period in which to develop skills and prepare for the future, but it tends to produce a period of conflict and vacillation between dependence and independence. It is difficult to feel completely self-sufficient while living at home or receiving financial support from one's parents.

Sexual Development

At the onset of adolescence, most youngsters experience a period of very rapid physical growth (the *adolescent growth spurt*) accompanied by the gradual development of reproductive organs and *secondary sex characteristics* (breast development in girls, beard growth in boys, and the appearance of pubic hair in both sexes). These changes occur over a period of about two years and culminate in *puberty*, marked by menstruation in girls and by the appearance of live sperm cells in the urine of boys.

There is wide variation in the ages at which puberty is reached. Some girls may menstruate as early as 11, others as late as 17—the average age being 12 years 9 months. Boys show a similar range in the ages at which they reach sexual maturity; but on the average, boys experience their growth spurt and mature two years later than girls (see Figure 3-13). Boys and girls average the same height and weight until about 11, when the girls suddenly spurt ahead in both dimensions. Girls maintain this difference for about two years, at which point the boys forge ahead and remain there for the rest of their lives. This difference in rate of physical development is striking in seventh- or eighth-grade classrooms, where one can find quite mature young women seated alongside a group of immature boys.

Although girls on the average mature earlier than boys, there are large individual differences. Some girls will mature *later* than some boys. Numerous studies have investigated whether there are personality differences between early- and late-maturing children. How does a late-maturing boy feel when he is shorter than most of his classmates? How does an early-maturing girl feel when she towers over most of the boys in her class?

Late-maturing boys face a particularly difficult adjustment because of the importance of strength and physical prowess in their peer activities. During the period when they are shorter and less sturdy than their classmates, they may lose out on practice of game skills and may never catch up with the early maturers, who take the lead in physical activities. Studies indicate that boys who mature late tend to be less popular than their classmates, have poorer self-concepts, and engage in more immature attention-seeking behavior. They feel rejected and dominated by their peers. The early maturers, on the other hand, tend to be more self-confident and independent. A few of these personality differences between early and late maturers persist into adulthood, long after the physical differences have disappeared (Mussen and Jones, 1958).

The effects of rate of maturation on personality are less striking for girls. Some early-maturing girls may be at a disadvantage because they are more

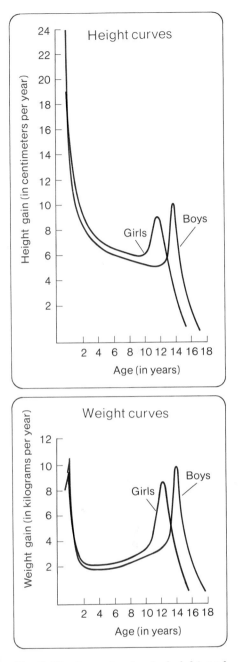

Fig. 3-13 Annual gains in height and weight
Note that the peak period comes earlier for girls than for boys. (After Tanner, Whitehouse, and Takaishi, 1966)

ADOLESCENCE

89

grown-up than their peers in the late elementary grades; but by the junior high-school years, the early maturers tend to have more prestige among classmates and to take leadership in school activities. At this stage, the late-maturing girls, like the boys, may have less adequate self-concepts and poorer relations with their parents and peers (Weatherly, 1964).

Sexual Standards and Behavior

The bodily changes that accompany sexual maturing are a source of both pride and embarrassment. How comfortable the adolescent feels with his or her new physique and the urges that accompany it depends to a large extent on the attitudes toward sexual development conveyed by parents and peers. Parental attitudes of secrecy or taboos concerning sex generate feelings of anxiety, which may be overcome only gradually by the more matter-of-fact views of the young person's peers.

The last 15 years have witnessed an almost revolutionary change in attitudes toward sexual activity. Views regarding premarital sex, homosexuality, extramarital sex, and specific sexual acts are probably more open and permissive today than they have been at any time in recent history. Young people are exposed to sexual stimuli in magazines, television, and the movies to a greater extent than ever before. Satisfactory birth control methods and the availability of abortions have lessened fear of pregnancy. All of these changes give the newly matured individual more freedom today. These changes may produce more conflict, too, since guidelines for "appropriate" behavior are less clear than they were in the past. In some families, the divergence between adolescent and parental standards of sexual morality may be great.

Have more permissive attitudes toward sex been accompanied by changes in actual behavior? Some experts maintain that young people today are simply more open about activities their predecessors carried on in secret. But the data beginning to accumulate indicate definite changes in adolescent sexual behavior. A nationwide survey that interviewed 13- to 19-year-olds found that 59 percent of the boys and 45 percent of the girls reported having experienced sexual intercourse. And a sizable proportion of these nonvirgins had become so before they were 16 (see Table 3-3).

While strictly comparable data from earlier periods are not available, the studies conducted by Alfred Kinsey about 30 years ago found that only about 20 percent of the females and 40 percent of the males reported experiencing sexual intercourse by the time they were 20 years old. Today's adolescents appear to be engaging in sexual activity at an earlier age than did their parents.

The change in sex standards does not seem to be in the direction of greater promiscuity. While some of the boys said they had experienced intercourse with several partners, most of the girls reported they had limited their sexual relations to one boy with whom they were "in love" at the time. These young people feel that sex is a part of love and of intimate relationships and that it need not necessarily be restricted to the context of marriage.

Today's adolescents tend to reject the "double standard," whereby men are allowed more sexual freedom than women. In the study referred to in Table 3-3, a majority of both boys and girls felt that what was moral for one sex was moral for the other. The majority of the adolescents in this study also felt that their sexual standards were quite different from their parents' and that, although they had a close relationship with their parents in many respects, sex was the area in which they were less likely to communicate. Many of today's parents

VIRGINS (All adolescents who have not had sexual intercourse)	ALL TEEN-AGERS	BY SEX		BY AGE	
		BOYS	GIRLS	13–15	16–19
Sexually inexperienced (Virgins with no beginning sexual activities)	22%	20%	25%	39%	9%
Sexual beginners (Virgins who have actively or passively experienced sexual petting)	17	14	19	12	21
Unclassified virgins (Virgins who for whatever reason could not be classified in the above groups)	9	7	11	12	6
Total	**48%**	**41%**	**55%**	**63%**	**36%**
NONVIRGINS (All adolescents who have had sexual intercourse one or more times)					
Serial monogamists (Nonvirgins having a sexual relationship with one person)	21%	15%	28%	9%	31%
Sexual adventurers (Nonvirgins freely moving from one sexual-intercourse partner to another)	15	24	6	10	18
Inactive nonvirgins (Nonvirgins who have not had sexual intercourse for more than one year)	12	13	10	15	10
Unclassified nonvirgins (Nonvirgins who for whatever reason could not be classified in the above groups)	4	7	1	3	5
Total	**52%**	**59%**	**45%**	**37%**	**64%**

Source: After Sorenson (1973)

TABLE 3-3
Adolescent sexual experience
These data are from interviews with 400 individuals, ages 13 to 19. The sample was selected on the basis of the 1970 United States Census to represent the adolescent population in terms of such variables as race, geographical location, family income and size, and urban-rural residence. The results are similar to those of several studies using larger but less representative samples.

seem willing to allow their offspring sexual freedom (as long as they are not directly confronted by the facts) but unwilling to discuss the topic with them.

Search for Identity

A major task confronting the adolescent is to develop a sense of individual *identity*—to find answers to the questions "Who am I?" and "Where am I going?" The search for personal identity involves deciding what is important or worth doing and formulating standards of conduct for evaluating one's own behavior as well as the behavior of others. It also involves feelings about one's own worth and competence.

Adolescents' sense of identity develops gradually out of the various identifications of childhood. Young children's values and moral standards are largely those of their parents; their feelings of self-esteem stem primarily from the parents' view of them. As youngsters move into the wider world of high school, the values of the peer group become increasingly important—as do the appraisals of teachers and other adults. Adolescents try to synthesize these values and appraisals into a consistent picture. To the extent that parents, teachers, and peers project consistent values, the search for identity becomes easier.

Role Confusion

When parental views and values differ markedly from those of peers and other important figures, the possibility for conflict is great and the adolescent may experience what has been called *role confusion*—the adolescent tries one role after another and has difficulty synthesizing the different roles into a single identity. As one teen-age girl put it:

> I'm fairly prim and proper at home because my parents have firm views about how a young girl should behave. At school I toe the line too, although I don't hesitate to express my opinions. When I'm with my girl friends, I relax and act fairly silly; I'm usually the first to suggest smoking pot or doing something crazy. On a date I tend to act helpless and docile. Who am I really?

In a simple society where identification models are few and social roles are limited, the task of forming an identity is relatively easy. In a society as complex and rapidly changing as ours, it is a difficult and lengthy task for many adolescents. They are faced with an almost infinite array of possibilities in terms of how to behave and what to do in life.

One way to delay forming a personal identity is to form a kind of adolescent group identity by wearing special clothes, devising a special language, listening to certain records. Each generation of teen-agers has its own fads and trends. But an adolescent group identity only postpones the problem of forming an adult identity.

One way of approaching the identity problem is to try out various roles and ways of behaving. Many experts believe that adolescence should be a period of role experimentation in which the youngster can explore different ideologies and interests. They are concerned that today's academic competition and career pressures are depriving many adolescents of the opportunity to explore. As a result, some are "dropping out" temporarily to have time to think about what they want to do in life and to experiment with various identities. The Peace Corps, communes, and such religious groups as the Jesus movement and the Hare Krishna sect often provide temporary commitments to an alternative life style; they give the young person a group to identify with and time to formulate a more permanent set of beliefs.

The search for identity can be resolved in a number of ways. Some young people, after a period of experimentation and soul searching, commit themselves to a life goal and proceed toward it. For some, the "identity crisis" may not occur at all; these are adolescents who accept their parents' values without question and who proceed toward a career consistent with their parents' views. In a sense, their identity "crystallized" early in life.

Still other young people adopt a *deviant identity*—one that is at odds with the values of the society. For example, a young man who has been pressured all his life to go to law school and then join the family firm may rebel and decide to become a bum. Some ghetto adolescents, rather than risk failure in attempting to rise above their social conditions, may adopt a deviant identity and take pride in being "nothing."

Other adolescents may go through a prolonged period of identity confusion and have great difficulty "finding themselves." In some cases, an identity definition may ultimately be worked out after much trial and error. In others, the person may never have a strong sense of personal identity even as an adult. This is the individual who never develops commitments or loyalties.

A study of college students who were in a state of identity confusion found that many of them were dissatisfied with their parents' way of life, yet could not get very involved in fashioning one of their own. In the words of one subject:

> Let's say I'm a Psych. major. I have no idea what I will do with it. I try not to plan more than a week in advance. My parents would like me to settle down and get married. That seems pretty far off right now. Mother would love it if I stayed right at home. . . . I have plans to go to Africa this summer, go to Europe by myself next fall. After that I don't know. (Waterman and Waterman, 1974)

This same study found that a large proportion of college freshmen were still struggling with problems of identity formation, but by the senior year many had been resolved.

One's personal identity, once formed, is not necessarily static. Even in their later years, some adults acquire new interests and skills; they may even embark on a totally different career. These changes will modify their sense of who they are.

Generation Gap

According to some views, our society has been changing so rapidly that the values of today's parents are inappropriate to the problems and conditions faced by their teen-age children. Drugs, the birth control pill, and a climate of increased sexual permissiveness create problems for young people that their parents did not have to face. Rapid scientific and technological advances have tended to make parental knowledge obsolete with reference to what their children are expected to know. These and other factors have led some experts to conclude that there is an almost unsurmountable gap between the values of today's parents and those of their adolescent sons and daughters. They view with alarm the lack of understanding and communication between the two generations.

Recent research, however, leads to a much less pessimistic view. There is some distance between the attitudes of the two generations, to be sure, but it is not nearly as great as the mass media would have us believe. Survey studies indicate that the values of parents and their offspring are quite similar.

Table 3-4 shows the results of a study on parent-adolescent values in the United States and Denmark. There is a close correspondence between mothers

TABLE 3-4
Responses to the question, "What is the best way to get ahead in life?" Note that mothers and adolescents hold similar values but there are national differences in the emphasis on hard work versus a pleasant personality.

	UNITED STATES		DENMARK	
	ADOLES-CENTS	MOTHERS	ADOLES-CENTS	MOTHERS
Work hard	52%	56%	13%	9%
Have a pleasant personality	22	17	43	50
Know the right people	4	2	12	10
Save your money	1	2	5	3
Get a higher education	18	22	23	27
Have a special talent	3	1	4	1
Total	100%	100%	100%	100%

Source: Kandel and Lesser (1972)

TABLE 3-5
Adolescent and parent values in two
countries

VALUES	PERCENTAGE OF INDIVIDUALS WHO RANK EACH OF THE VALUES LISTED AT LEFT AS "EXTREMELY IMPORTANT"			
	UNITED STATES		DENMARK	
	ADOLES-CENTS	MOTHERS	ADOLES-CENTS	MOTHERS
FAMILY				
1 Doing things with the family	42	65	17	42
2 Helping at home	30	43	23	31
3 Respecting one's parents	87	96	60	76
4 Living up to one's religious ideals	9	15	2	4
5 Pleasing one's parents	34	11	52	20
PEER GROUP				
6 Being a leader in activities	20	11	4	1
7 Participating in sports	31	14	37	18
8 Going out on dates	40	6	35	2
9 Being popular in school	46	19	45	28
10 Earning money	56	36	30	17
11 Being accepted by other students	18	5	15	11
12 Being well liked	54	44	32	27
13 Having a good reputation	78	93	53	71
SCHOOL				
14 Preferred school image:				
Brilliant student	33	74	55	64
Athlete or leader in activities	34	21	10	7
Most popular	33	5	35	29
15 Learning much in school	39	69	31	64
16 Working hard on studies	54	83	32	54
17 Doing serious reading	28	54	21	51
18 Planning for the future	78	80	38	44

Source: Kandel and Lesser (1972)

and their youngsters regarding the activities and personal qualities rated as most important. The differences between the two countries are greater than those between parent and teen-ager. Americans emphasize hard work and achievement; the Danes stress a pleasant personality and the ability to get along with others (see Table 3-5).

Survey studies indicate that most adolescents have a generally close and warm relationship with their parents. In one nationwide survey, the majority of 13- to 19-year-olds interviewed said they respected their parents (88 percent) and their parents' opinions (80 percent); they enjoyed being with them (73 percent) and felt their relationship was warm and affectionate (78 percent). The area where there was least communality of viewpoint was sex; only about one-third of the adolescents felt they shared common attitudes with their parents on sexual values (Sorenson, 1973).

Development as a Lifelong Process

Development does not end with the attainment of physical maturity. It is a continuous process extending from birth through adulthood to old age. Bodily changes occur throughout life, affecting the individual's attitudes, cognitive processes, and behavior. The kinds of problems people must cope with change throughout the life span, too.

Erik Erikson has proposed a series of eight stages to characterize development from the cradle to the grave. He calls them *psychosocial stages*, because he believes that the psychological development of individuals depends on the social relations established at various points in life. At each stage, there are special problems or "crises" to be confronted. Erickson's stages of psychosocial development are shown in Table 3-6. Although these stages are not based on scientific evidence, they call attention to the kinds of problems people encounter during their life.

We touched on some of these problems earlier in the chapter. We noted that the infant's feelings of trust in other people depends to a large extent on the way early needs are handled by the mother. During the second year of life (when children begin to move about on their own), they want to explore, investigate, and do things for themselves. To the extent that parents encourage such activities, children begin to develop a sense of independence or autonomy. They learn to control some of their impulses and to feel pride in their accomplishments. Overprotection—restricting what the child is permitted to do—or ridiculing unsuccessful attempts may cause the child to doubt his or her abilities.

During the preschool years (ages three through five) children progress from simple self-control to an ability to initiate activities and carry them out. Again, parental attitudes—encouraging or discouraging—can make children feel inadequate (or guilty, if they initiate an activity that the adult views as shameful).

During the elementary school years, children learn the skills valued by society. These include not only reading and writing, but physical skills and the ability to share responsibility and get along with other people. To the extent

TABLE 3-6
Erikson's eight stages of psychosocial development

STAGES	PSYCHOSOCIAL CRISES	SIGNIFICANT SOCIAL RELATIONS	FAVORABLE OUTCOME
1 First year of life	Trust versus mistrust	Mother or mother substitute	Trust and optimism
2 Second year	Autonomy versus doubt	Parents	Sense of self-control and adequacy
3 Third through fifth years	Initiative versus guilt	Basic family	Purpose and direction; ability to initiate one's own activities
4 Sixth year to puberty	Industry versus inferiority	Neighborhood; school	Competence in intellectual, social, and physical skills
5 Adolescence	Identity versus confusion	Peer groups and outgroups; models of leadership	An integrated image of oneself as a unique person
6 Early adulthood	Intimacy versus isolation	Partners in friendship; sex, competition, cooperation	Ability to form close and lasting relationships; to make career commitments
7 Middle adulthood	Generativity versus self-absorption	Divided labor and shared household	Concern for family, society, and future generations
8 The aging years	Integrity versus despair	"Mankind"; "My Kind"	A sense of fulfillment and satisfaction with one's life; willingness to face death

Source: Erikson (1963), modified from original

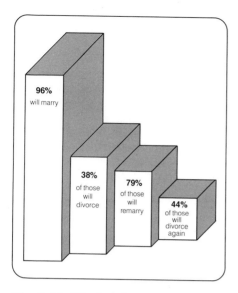

Fig. 3-14 The marriage odds
Percentages are for United States adults during 1978.

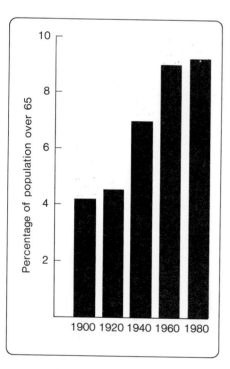

Fig. 3-15 The aged in the United States
The percentage of the total population aged 65 or over has more than doubled in the last half-century, though the trend shows signs of slackening. (United States Bureau of the Census)

that efforts in these areas are successful, children develop feelings of competence; unsuccessful efforts result in feelings of inferiority.

Finding one's personal identity, as we noted in the last section, is the major psychosocial crisis of adolescence.

Early Adulthood

During the early adult years, people commit themselves to an occupation, and many will marry or form other types of intimate relationships. Intimacy means an ability to care about others and to share experiences with them. People who cannot commit themselves to a loving relationship—because they fear being hurt or are unable to share—risk being isolated.

Approximately 96 percent of Americans do marry, and most of them do so during the early adult years. Individuals tend to look for marriage partners whose ethnic, social, and religious backgrounds match their own. Contrary to popular opinion, women appear to be *less* romantic in their approach to mate selection than men. Men tend to fall in love more quickly than women and to be satisfied with the qualities of their prospective mate. Women, on the other hand, are more practical and cautious in deciding whom to marry (Rubin, 1973).

This finding is not surprising when we consider that marriage traditionally requires a greater change in life style for women than for men. A married man continues in his career, whereas a woman may be required to give up the relative independence of single life for the demands and responsibilities of wife and mother. Whom she marries may determine where and how well she lives, as well as what her role in life will be.

Once married, both partners must learn to adapt to new demands and responsibilities. The arrival of children requires even greater adjustment. That such adjustments are not easy in a society as complex as ours is indicated by the high divorce rate. More than 38 percent of all *first* marriages in the United States end in divorce. Taking into account remarriages and divorces, about 44 percent of *all* marriages end in divorce (see Figure 3-14). Interestingly enough, second marriages are generally as happy as those first marriages that endure (Kimmel, 1974).

Much debate centers on whether happy marriages are based on similarity of interests and temperament ("like attracts like") or on the fact that the two partners complement rather than replicate one another ("opposites attract"). There are studies that support each viewpoint, so no conclusive answer can be given. It is clear that many different patterns of marital relations function satisfactorily, but the following elements seem to be common to the various patterns: (1) mutual respect—each partner finds some important quality or ability to respect in the other; the greater the number of areas of respect, the more satisfactory the marriage; (2) tolerance—the ability to accept one another's shortcomings; and (3) the ability to agree on common goals and to work toward such goals.

Middle Adulthood

The middle years of adulthood, roughly ages 40 to 60, are, for many people, the most productive period. Men in their forties are usually at the peak of their careers. Women have less responsibility at home now that the children are growing older and can devote more time to career or civic activities. This is the age group that essentially runs society, in terms of both power and responsibility.

What Erikson means by *generativity* in middle adulthood is a concern with guiding and providing for the next generation. Feelings of satisfaction at this stage in life come from helping one's own teen-age children become adults, providing for others that need help, and seeing one's contributions to society as valuable. Feelings of despair may come from the realization that one has not achieved the goals set as a young adult or that what one is doing is not important.

As people approach their fifties, their view of the life span tends to change. Instead of looking at life in terms of time-since-birth, as younger people do, they begin to think in terms of years-left-to-live. Having faced the aging or death of their parents, they begin to realize the inevitability of their own death. At this point, many people restructure their lives in terms of priorities, deciding what is important to do in the years remaining. A man who has spent his years building a successful company may leave it to join the Peace Corps or return to school. A woman who has raised her family may develop a new career or become active in politics. A couple may leave their jobs in the city to purchase a small farm.

The Aging Years

The years after 65 bring new problems. Declining physical strength limits the older person's activities; a debilitating illness can make the individual feel demoralizingly helpless. Retirement, which brings idle hours to be filled, may lessen feelings of worth and self-esteem. The death of one's spouse, siblings, and friends can make life unbearably lonely, particularly for those whose children live far away. Since the proportion of older people in the population is progressively increasing (see Figure 3-15), such problems require renewed attention and research. Retirement villages and programs that actively involve older people in community life—as teacher aids, library assistants, guards at school crossings—have proved to be a step in the right direction. But much more needs to be done.

Despite the obvious problems of aging, a study of 70- to 79-year-olds suggests that growing old is not so bad. Seventy-five percent reported that they were satisfied with their lives after retirement. Most were fairly active and not lonely; and few showed signs of senility or mental illness (Neugarten, 1971).

Erikson's last psychosocial crisis, *integrity versus despair,* is concerned with the way one faces the end of life. Old age is a time of reflection, of looking back on the events of a lifetime. To the extent that one has successfully coped with the problems posed at each of the earlier stages of life, one has a sense of wholeness and integrity—of a life well lived. If the elderly person looks back on life with regret, seeing it as a series of missed opportunities and failures, then the final years will be ones of despair.

SUMMARY

1 Human development involves a *continuous interaction* between *heredity* (biological predispositions determined by one's genes) and *environment* (the experiences encountered while growing up in a particular family and culture). Genetic determinants express themselves through the process of *maturation*—innately determined sequences of growth or bodily changes that are relatively independent of the environment. Motor development, for example, is largely a maturational process, because all children master skills

such as crawling, standing, and walking in the same sequence and at roughly the same age.

2 Development proceeds in *orderly sequences* from simple behaviors to those that are more differentiated and complex. An unresolved question, however, is whether development should be viewed as a *continuous process* of acquiring new behaviors through experience or a series of successive *stages* that are qualitatively different from each other.

3 Although the development of physical skills depends largely on maturation, restricted environments can delay motor development, and increased stimulation can accelerate it—provided the child is maturationally ready. While early deprivation or stimulation do not appear to have a lasting effect on motor skills, development in other areas—language, intelligence, personality—may be permanently affected by early experiences.

4 Piaget's theory describes stages in *cognitive*, or *intellectual*, *growth*, proceeding from the *sensorimotor stage* (where an important discovery is *object permanence*), through the *preoperational stage* (symbols begin to be used), and the *concrete operational stage* (*conservation concepts* develop), to the *formal operational stage* (hypotheses are tested systematically in problem solving).

5 Early social attachments form the basis for close interpersonal relations in adulthood. Insensitive mothering or repeated separations may undermine the child's trust and produce *anxious attachment*. Interactions with siblings and peers are also important for normal development. Although no consistent relationships have been found between specific child-rearing techniques and later personality traits, a child's competency and self-confidence are best fostered by a warm and nurturant home where parents reward responsible behavior but also encourage independent actions and decision making.

6 Children acquire the attitudes and behaviors expected by society—self-control, a conscience, and the appropriate sex role—largely through the process of *identification. Sex typing*, the tendency to view certain activities as appropriate only for one sex, develops through parental and cultural influences. Children are most apt to identify with adults who are warm, nurturant, powerful, and are viewed as similar to them in some way.

7 The age at which adolescents reach *puberty*, or sexual maturity, varies greatly, although girls, on the average, mature two years earlier than boys. Late maturers of either sex tend to have poorer self-concepts than early maturers. Survey data indicate that adolescents today are experiencing sexual intercourse at an earlier age than their parents did and are rejecting the double standard of sexual behavior.

8 In their search for personal *identity*, adolescents try to synthesize the values and views of people important to them (parents, teachers, and peers) into a cohesive self-picture. When these values are not consistent, adolescents may experience *role confusion*—trying out one social role after another before finding a sense of individual identity. Although adolescence is a period of reexamining beliefs and challenging the values of parents and society, most adolescents end up with values very similar to those of their parents—at least on the important issues.

9 Development is a life-long process: individuals change both physically and psychologically, and they encounter new adjustment problems throughout life. Erikson's *psychosocial stages* describe problems, or crises, in social relations that must be confronted at various points in life. These range from

"trust versus mistrust" during the first year of life, through "intimacy versus isolation" in early adulthood, to "integrity versus despair" as individuals face death.

Comprehensive textbooks on child development include Mussen, Conger, and Kagan, *Child development and personality* (4th ed., 1974), Elkind and Weiner, *Development of the child* (1978), and Bee, *The developing child* (2nd ed., 1978). *Child development: An introduction* (1976) by Biehler includes some interesting background material in the form of "on the spot" visits to the laboratories of well-known child psychologists (past and present) as they investigate and theorize about children's behavior.

A two-volume overview of the major theories and research in child development may be found in Mussen (ed.), *Carmichael's manual of child psychology* (3rd ed., 1970).

Cognitive development (1977) by Flavell presents a thorough introduction to this topic. For a brief introduction to Piaget's theory, see Phillips, *The origins of intellect: Piaget's theory* (2nd ed., 1975).

The problems of adolescence are dealt with in Conger, *Adolescence and youth: Psychological development in a changing world* (2nd ed., 1977) and Jersild, Brook, and Brook, *The psychology of adolescence* (3rd ed., 1978). For the later years, see Kennedy, *Human development: The adult years and aging* (1978).

PART THREE

Perception and Consciousness

4
Sensory Processes

All information about the world comes to us by way of our senses. They warn us of impending danger and furnish the information we need to interpret events and anticipate the future. They also provide pleasure and pain. How do we distinguish colors, judge the quality of a vintage wine, or interpret the rhythm of music? We need answers to these questions, since they form the basis for examining more complex psychological phenomena.

To understand perception we need to know something of how the sensory mechanisms are constructed and how they mediate the sensations of light, sound, touch, taste, and the like. But perception involves more than the discrimination of individual stimuli; the human organism must be able to interpret and react to patterns of stimuli. It must be able to extract information from the changing array of stimulation provided by the environment. In this chapter, we will consider the role of the specific sense organs in perceiving. In the next chapter, we will discuss the perception of complex objects and events.

There are two different, but closely related, approaches to the study of sensory processes: basic research and applied research. Basic research attempts to discover what aspects of the environment the sense organs respond to, how they register this information, and how it is conveyed to the brain. Such knowledge is sought with no concern for specific applications; it is a first step in understanding the higher-order cognitive processes.

As our technology becomes increasingly complex, it depends more and more on accurate perceptual discriminations by human beings. Here is the need for applied research. The radar operator must be able to distinguish the visual blips on the radar screen that indicate the approach of aircraft. The sonar operator must discriminate between the echoes returning from a school of fish and those from a submarine. The pilot monitors an elaborate panel of instruments and makes necessary adjustments. The astronaut must make countless complex discriminations under conditions of weightlessness and acceleration that alter normal functioning. Through applied research on sensory processes, scientists seek to determine our ability to discriminate and interpret sensory stimuli so that our capabilities can be matched to the task requirements. Both the basic and the applied approach have contributed to our understanding of sensory phenomena.

Some General Properties of the Senses

Absolute Thresholds

A spot of light in a dark room must reach some measurable intensity before it can be distinguished from darkness. A sound emitted in an otherwise sound-

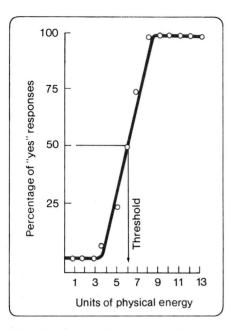

Fig. 4-1 Psychophysical function
Plotted on the ordinate is the percentage of times the subject responds, "Yes, I detect the stimulus"; on the abscissa is the measure of the physical energy of the stimulus. Psychophysical functions can be obtained for any sensory modality; when vision is involved, the function is sometimes called the "frequency-of-seeing curve."

proof room must reach a certain intensity level before it can be heard. That is, a certain minimum stimulation of sense organs is required before there will be any sensory experience. The minimum physical energy necessary to activate a given sensory system is known as the *absolute threshold.* The absolute threshold can be determined by presenting the subject with a stimulus of given intensity and asking whether or not it is detectable; on the next trial, a different stimulus intensity is used, and so on, through a wide range of intensities. The term "absolute threshold" is somewhat inappropriate, however, because the investigator does not arrive at a *single* intensity value below which the stimulus is never detected and above which it is always detected. We find, instead, a range of intensities over which the physical energy of the stimulus gradually moves from having no effect to having a partial effect (sometimes detected and sometimes not) to having a complete effect.

This region of partial effect is illustrated in Figure 4-1. The curve in the figure is called a *psychophysical function,* because it expresses the relationship between a *psychological variable* (the experience of perceiving the stimulus) and a *physical variable* (the physical intensity of the stimulus). It plots the percentage of times the subject says, "Yes, I detect a stimulus," against a measure of the physical energy of the stimulus. In this example, the subject almost never reports the presence of a stimulus below an energy level of three units and almost always reports one above nine units. In the figure, the frequency of reporting the presence of a stimulus gradually increases between three and nine units.

How do we define a threshold when performance can be characterized by a psychophysical function like that in Figure 4-1? Is it the point at which the subject's curve first appears to break away from zero (in this case at about three physical units) or the point at which it finally appears to reach 100-percent responding (in this case at about nine units)? Obviously, the definition of a threshold must be somewhat arbitrary. For various reasons, psychologists have agreed to define the *absolute threshold* as that value at which the stimulus is perceived 50 percent of the time. Thus, for the data displayed in Figure 4-1, the absolute threshold would be six units.

Table 4-1 lists some estimates of absolute thresholds for various senses in terms that are readily familiar. Of course, the absolute threshold varies considerably from one individual to the next. The threshold for a particular individual will also vary from time to time, depending on the person's physical condition and motivational state.

TABLE 4-1
Some approximate values for absolute thresholds

SENSE	THRESHOLD
Vision	A candle flame seen at 30 miles on a dark, clear night
Hearing	The tick of a watch under quiet conditions at 20 feet
Taste	One teaspoon of sugar in two gallons of water
Smell	One drop of perfume diffused into the entire volume of a six-room apartment
Touch	The wing of a fly falling on your cheek from a distance of one centimeter

Source: Galanter (1962)

SENSE	WEBER'S CONSTANT
Pitch of a tone (frequency)	$\frac{1}{333}$
Visual brightness	$\frac{1}{60}$
Lifted weights	$\frac{1}{50}$
Loudness of a tone	$\frac{1}{10}$
Pressure on skin surface	$\frac{1}{7}$
Taste for saline solution	$\frac{1}{5}$

Source: Data are approximate, from various determinations

TABLE 4-2
Weber's constant
Approximate values of Weber's constant for various sensory discriminations. The smaller the fraction, the smaller the amount of additional stimulation needed to produce a j.n.d.

Difference Thresholds

Just as there must be a certain minimum amount of stimulation before we can perceive a stimulus, so there must also be a certain magnitude of difference between two stimuli before we can distinguish one from the other. The minimum amount of stimulation necessary to tell two stimuli apart is known as the *difference threshold*. Two lights of red appearance must differ in wavelength by some finite amount before they can be discriminated from each other; two tones must differ in intensity by a measurable amount before one can be heard as louder than the other. Thus, thresholds are identified at the transitions between no experience and some experience (the absolute threshold) and between no difference and some difference (the difference threshold).

Like the absolute threshold, the difference threshold is defined as a statistically reliable quantity. It is the amount of change in physical energy necessary for a subject to detect reliably a difference between two stimuli. Psychologists frequently use the term *just noticeable difference* (j.n.d.) to refer to this amount of change.

One remarkable feature of the human organism and, for that matter, of most animals is that the difference threshold tends to be a constant fraction of the stimulus intensity. To illustrate, suppose we estimate the difference threshold for a subject judging weights. If the subject is given a 100-gram weight, we note that the difference threshold is 2 grams; that is, the 100-gram weight must be compared to a weight of at least 102 grams in order for the subject to reliably detect a j.n.d. If the subject is given a 200-gram weight, the difference threshold is 4 grams. For a 400-gram weight, the difference threshold is 8 grams; for an 800-gram weight, the difference threshold is 16 grams. Note that the difference threshold relative to the weight being judged is constant:

$$\frac{2}{100} = \frac{4}{200} = \frac{8}{400} = \frac{16}{800} = .02$$

This relationship is known as *Weber's law*, named after Ernst Weber, who pointed it out over a century ago. Stated mathematically, if I is the amount of stimulation taken as a referent, and ΔI is the increase in stimulation necessary for a j.n.d., then

$$\frac{\Delta I}{I} = k$$

where k is a constant that does not depend on I. The quantity k is called *Weber's constant*. In our example, $k = .02$.

Table 4-2 presents values of Weber's constant for various senses. The

ROC Curves

The problem of establishing thresholds involves some complications that can be illustrated by the following experiment. Suppose we wanted to determine the likelihood that a subject will detect a particular weak auditory signal. An experiment could be set up involving a series of trials, each initiated with a warning light followed by the auditory signal. The subject would be asked to indicate on each trial whether he or she heard the signal. Suppose that on 100 such trials the subject reported hearing the signal 62 times. How should this result be interpreted? On each trial, precisely the same signal is presented, and the responses presumably tell us something about the subject's ability to detect it. But if the subject knows the same tone will be presented on each trial, what prevents him or her from always saying "yes"? Obviously nothing, but we assume that the subject is honest and is trying to do as good a job as possible. The task of detecting very weak signals is difficult, however, and even a conscientious subject will often be uncertain whether to respond "yes" or "no" on a given trial. Further, motives and expectations can influence our judgments; even the most reliable subject may unconsciously tend toward "yes" answers to impress the experimenter with his or her acuity.

To deal with this problem, *catch trials*, on which there is no signal, can be introduced to see what the subject will do. The following results are typical of a subject's performance in an experiment involving several hundred trials, 10 percent of which are randomly selected as catch trials.

Each entry in the table represents the proportion of times the subject answered "yes" or "no" when the signal was or was not presented. For example, in 89 percent of the trials on which a signal was presented, the subject said, "yes, there was a signal." We refer to these correct responses as *hits*. When the subject says "yes, there was a signal" on a trial when the signal was not presented, the response is called a *false alarm*. In the example, the probability of a hit was .89 and the probability of a false alarm was .52.

How can we interpret the fact that the subject falsely reported hearing the signal on 52 percent of the catch trials? We might conclude that the subject is careless or inattentive, except for the fact that these results are typical of data obtained with dedicated, highly trained subjects. Even under the best conditions, subjects make false alarms. The answer to the question of how to interpret false alarms appears when some additional observations are made. Suppose that the subject is

tested for several days with the same signal but with the percentage of catch trials varied from day to day. Results from such an experiment, in which the number of catch trials ranged from 10 percent to 90 percent, are given in the table in Figure 4-2. These data show that hits and false alarms both change as the proportion of catch trials is manipulated. As the proportion of catch trials increases, the subject becomes aware of this fact (either consciously or unconsciously) and biases his or her judgments in favor of more "no" responses. Put another way, the subject's *expectation* of a large number of catch trials inhibits "yes" responses, which leads to a decrease in both hits and false alarms.

Obviously, there is no fixed probability that the subject will detect a given intensity signal; the probability varies as the proportion of catch trials is manipulated. At first glance, this is a discouraging picture, and one may question whether a simple measure can be devised to describe the subject's sensitivity level for a particular signal. Fortunately, recent developments have provided a clever answer. It involves plotting the hit and false alarm probabilities, as is done in the top graph in Figure 4-2. Note, for example, that the point farthest to the right is for data obtained when 10 percent of the trials were catch trials; referring to the table, the hit rate plotted on the ordinate is .89, and the false alarm rate on the

tremendous range in values reflects the fact that some sensory systems are much more responsive to change than others.

We can see approximations of Weber's law operating in our everyday experience. For example, consider the brightness given off by a three-way light bulb (50-100-150 watts): the change in brightness from 50 to 100 watts is very noticeable, that from 100 to 150 much less so. A 10-minute increase in air-travel time from Los Angeles to San Francisco may be detected as a just noticeable difference, but a similar increase in travel time from San Francisco to London is not. An increase of five dollars in the cost of a skirt is quite noticeable, whereas a similar increase in the cost of a new car is of little concern.

Many theories have been proposed about the structure of the sensory system that make Weber's law hold. Research initiated by these theories has

abscissa is .52. When all five points are plotted, an orderly picture emerges. The points fall on a symmetric bow-shaped curve. If we ran still other experiments with the same signal but different percentages of catch trials, the hit and false alarm probabilities would differ from those in the table but would fall somewhere on the curve. This curve is called the *receiver-operating-characteristic curve*—or more simply, the ROC curve. The term "ROC" describes the fact that the curve measures the operating, or sensitivity, characteristics of a person receiving signals.

The points that are plotted in the top figure are for a fixed signal intensity. When a stronger signal is used, the ROC curve arches higher; when the signal is weaker, the ROC curve is closer to the diagonal line. Thus, the degree of bowedness of the ROC curve is determined by the intensity of the signal. The measure used to define the bowedness of the ROC curve is called d'. The bottom graph in Figure 4-2 gives several ROC curves for d', ranging from zero through three.

Thus, hit and false alarm rates can be converted into a d' value that is a psychological dimension measuring the subject's sensitivity level for a particular signal. Manipulating the percentage of catch trials (or any of a number of other variables) will affect hits and false alarms for a fixed signal, but the proportions will always fall on an ROC

Fig. 4-2 ROC Curves

The table presents data on the relationship between hits and false alarms as the percentage of catch trials is increased. The top figure plots these same data in the form of an ROC curve. The bottom figure presents ROC curves for several different values of d'. The more intense the signal, the higher the value of d'; the d' value for the data in the table is 1.18.

Percentage of catch trials	Probability of a hit	Probability of a false alarm
10	.89	.52
30	.83	.41
50	.76	.32
70	.62	.19
90	.28	.04

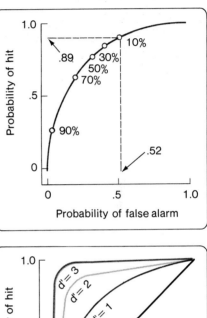

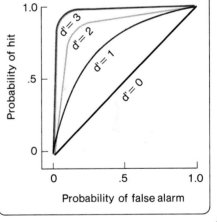

curve defined by a particular d' value. Theoretical work based on this method for measuring sensitivity is called *signal detectability theory* (Green and Birdsall, 1978). Even in a simple task like signal detection, performance is not just a function of the signal intensity but depends on the experience, motives, and expectations of the subject. Signal detectability theory permits one to separate out these factors and obtain a relatively pure measure of the sensory process. This measure, d', characterizes the sensory capacities of a subject, independent of nonsensory variables that influence his or her judgments. For an account of signal detectability theory, see Egan (1975) and Ludel (1978).

made it clear that the sensory system is more complex than Weber's law indicates. Weber's law holds fairly well in the middle range of sensory experiences but not at the extremes, particularly at very low levels of stimulation.

Although Weber's law was formulated for difference thresholds, Fechner (1860) soon extended it to develop psychological scales for measuring the full range of sensory experiences. Fechner's method involved calculating successive j.n.d.'s, starting at the lowest possible energy level, and continuing to some arbitrarily chosen maximum energy level. This scale indicated, for example, how far a given stimulus (in number of j.n.d.'s) was above the absolute threshold or what the judged difference was between two stimuli of different magnitude (difference in number of j.n.d.'s between the two stimuli). For Fechner, such a scale provided an insight into the relationship between the physical magnitude of a stimulus and its perceived, or psychological, magnitude. After considering scales for several different senses derived in this manner, Fechner noted that the perceived magnitude of many stimuli increased arithmetically as the physical magnitude increased logarithmically. This relationship is known as the *Weber-Fechner law.*

This logarithmic equation, although approximately correct, has been modified by modern workers to fit results from a wide variety of experiments. Equations relating sensory experience to the intensity of the physical stimulus have proved extremely helpful to engineers designing telephones, video displays, tape recorders, and other types of communication equipment. They tell the designer how intense a signal must be in order that it may be perceived accurately under varying conditions.

The Visual Sense

Each sense organ responds to a particular type of physical energy. The eye is sensitive to that portion of electromagnetic energy that we call light. It is convenient to think of electromagnetic energy as traveling in waves, with wavelengths (the distance from one crest of a wave to the next) varying tremendously from the shortest cosmic rays (10-trillionths of an inch) to long radio waves that may measure many miles. The wavelengths that the human eye perceives as light extend only from about 380 nanometers (nm) to about 780 nm. Since a nanometer is one-billionth of a meter, it is clear that visible energy is but a very small section of the total electromagnetic spectrum.

More than 300 years ago, Sir Isaac Newton discovered that sunlight passing through a prism breaks into a band of varicolored light (called a *spectrum*), such as we see in a rainbow. The colors correspond to wavelengths—the red end of the spectrum is produced by the longer waves and the violet end by the short waves. The prism spreads the light waves out by bending the short wavelengths more than the long ones (see Figure 4-9).

Visual experience may occur by stimulation other than light waves. Pressure on the eyeball or electrical stimulation of certain areas of the brain will produce the sensation of light. These observations indicate that the experience of light is a quality produced in the visual system. The visible portion of the electro-

Fig. 4-3 Top view of right eye
A light ray entering the eye on its way to the retina passes through the following parts: *cornea*—a tough transparent membrane; *aqueous humor*—a watery fluid; *lens*—a transparent body whose shape can be changed by the ciliary muscles, thereby focusing near or distant objects on the retina; and *vitreous humor*—a transparent jelly filling the interior of the eye. The amount of light entering the eye is regulated by the size of the *pupil,* a small hole in the front of the eye formed by the *iris.* The iris consists of a ring of muscles that can contract or expand, thereby controlling pupil size. The iris gives the eyes their characteristic color (blue, brown, and so forth).

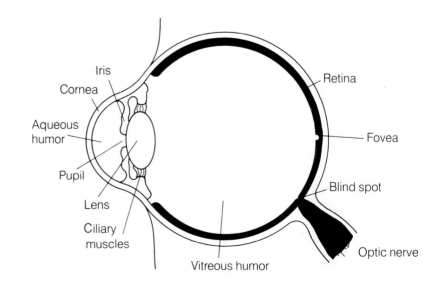

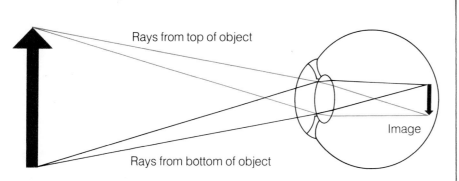

Rays from top of object

Image

Rays from bottom of object

An object as an array of points
Each point on an object sends out light rays in *all* directions, but only some of these rays actually enter the eye. Light rays from the same point on an object pass through different places on the lens. If the eye is to see the object, these different rays have to come back together (converge) at a single point on the retina. For each point on an object, there will be matching points on the retinal image. Note that the retinal image is inverted and is much smaller than the actual object. This figure shows only two rays of light from a point at the top of the arrow and two from a point at the bottom. Remember that light rays go out in every direction from each point on the object. The two lines in our figure are a schematic way of showing boundaries on the collection of rays from a point on the object that enter the eye and converge to a single point on the retina.

magnetic spectrum is called *light* because it is what usually produces sensation in the visual system.

The Human Eye

The main parts of the human eye are shown in Figure 4-3. Light enters the eye through the transparent *cornea.* The amount of light entering the eye is regulated by the diameter of the *pupil;* the *lens* then focuses the light on the sensitive surface, the *retina.* This function of the lens is similar to the way a camera is made to focus images of objects at various distances by moving the lens toward or away from the plane of the film. Constriction and dilation of the pupil are controlled by the autonomic nervous system (Chapter 2): the para-sympathetic division controls the change in pupil size as a function of change in illumination (in much the same way that we increase the shutter opening of a camera to admit more light on a dark day and decrease the opening under bright conditions). The sympathetic division dilates the pupil under conditions of strong emotion, either pleasant or unpleasant. Even conditions of mild emotional arousal or interest will result in systematic changes in pupil size (see Figure 4-4).

The retina, the light-sensitive surface at the back of the eye, has three main layers: (1) the *rods* and *cones*—the photosensitive cells (or photoreceptors) that convert light energy into neural signals; (2) the *bipolar cells,* which make synaptic connections with the rods and cones; and (3) the *ganglion cells,* the fibers of which form the *optic nerve* (see Figure 4-5). Strangely enough, the rods and cones form the *rear* layer of the retina. The light waves not only have to pass through the lens and liquids that fill the eyeball (none of which is a perfect transmitter of light) but also have to penetrate the network of blood vessels and the bipolar and ganglion cells that lie on the inside of the eye before reaching the photoreceptors. Note "direction of light" arrows at the top of Figure 4-5.

If you stare at a homogeneous field, such as a blue sky, you can see the movement of blood through the retinal blood vessels that lie in front of the

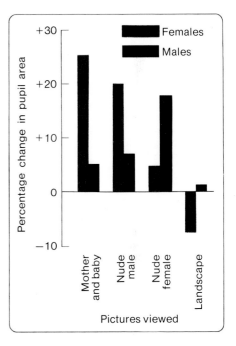

Fig. 4-4 Changes in pupil size as a response to pictures
Changes in pupil size were recorded on film and later measured. The figure shows the percentage of increase or decrease in pupil area in response to various pictures for both male and female subjects. The amount of light entering the eye was constant for all pictures. The sexes differ quite markedly with regard to the interest value of these particular pictures. A later study showed that the homosexual male could be distinguished from the heterosexual male on the basis of pupillary responses to pictures of female pinups. (Data from Hess and Polt, 1960)

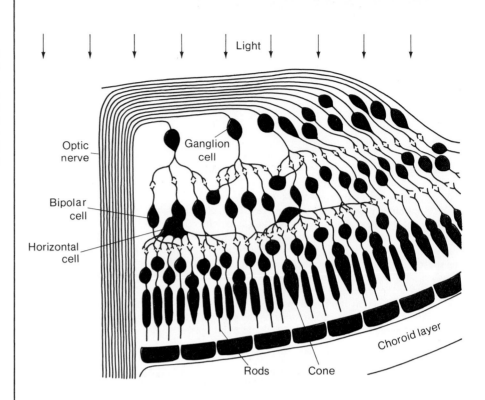

Fig. 4-5 Layers of the retina
Shown here are the main layers of the retina: rods and cones, bipolar cells, and ganglion cells. The bipolar cells receive signals from one or more rods or cones and transmit them to the nerve fibers, whose cell bodies are shown as the ganglion cells. Integration across the retina is accomplished by horizontal cells that connect rods and cones and by internal association cells at the ganglion cell level.

rods and cones. The blood vessel walls can be seen as pairs of narrow lines in the periphery of our vision, and the disk-shaped objects that appear to move between these lines are the red blood cells flowing through the vessels.

The most sensitive portion of the eye (in normal daylight vision) is a part of the retina called the *fovea.* This area plays a major role in perception, and yet it is so small that the projection (or image) of a thumbnail viewed at arm's length will cover it. Not far from the fovea is an insensitive area, called the *blind spot,* where the nerve fibers from the ganglion cells of the retina come together to form the optic nerve. Although we are not normally aware of the blind spot, we can easily demonstrate its existence. Follow the instructions given in Figure 4-6.

Figure 4-7 shows the optic nerve fibers leading from each eye to the *occipital lobes* of the brain, where vision is represented. Notice that some of the fibers go from the right eye to the right cerebral hemisphere and from the left eye to the left hemisphere, whereas other fibers cross over at a junction called the *optic chiasma* and go to the opposite hemisphere. Fibers from the right sides of both eyes go to the right hemisphere of the brain, and fibers from

Fig. 4-6 Locating the blind spot
A. With your right eye closed, stare at the cross in the upper right-hand corner. Move the book back and forth at about one foot from the eye. When the black circle on the left disappears, it is projected onto the blind spot.
B. Without moving the book and with your right eye still closed, stare at the cross in the lower right-hand corner. When the white space falls in the blind spot, the black line appears to be continuous. This phenomenon helps us to understand why we are not ordinarily aware of the blind spot. In effect, the brain "fills in" parts of the visual field to which we are not sensitive.

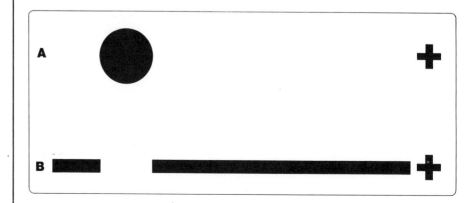

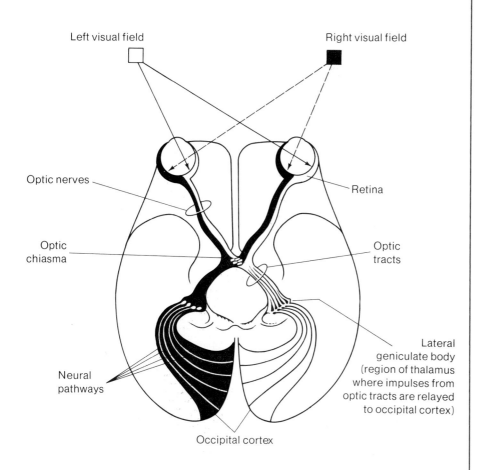

Left visual field

Right visual field

Optic nerves

Retina

Optic chiasma

Optic tracts

Neural pathways

Lateral geniculate body (region of thalamus where impulses from optic tracts are relayed to occipital cortex)

Occipital cortex

Fig. 4-7 Visual pathways
Light waves from objects in the right visual field fall on the left half of each retina; light waves from the left visual field fall on the right half of each retina. The optic nerve bundles from each eye meet at the optic chiasma, where the nerve fibers from the inner, or nasal, half of the retina cross over and go to opposite sides of the brain. Thus stimuli falling on the right side of each retina are transmitted to the occipital cortex of the right cerebral hemisphere, and stimuli impinging on the left side of each retina are transmitted to the left cerebral hemisphere. In terms of the visual field, this means that objects in the right visual field are projected to the left cerebral hemisphere, while objects in the left visual field are projected to the right hemisphere.

the left sides of both eyes go to the left hemisphere. Consequently, damage to the occipital lobe of one hemisphere (say, the left) will result in blind areas in the left sides of *both* eyes. This fact is sometimes helpful in pinpointing the location of a brain tumor or injury.

Rods and Cones

The retinal cells of special interest are the photoreceptors: the cylindrical rods and the more bulbous cones. The cones, active only in daylight vision, permit us to see both *achromatic colors* (white, black, and the intermediate grays) and *chromatic colors* (red, green, blue, and so forth). The rods function mainly under reduced illumination (at twilight or night) and permit us to see only achromatic colors. The two types of photoreceptors differ in much the same way that color film differs from black-and-white film. Black-and-white film (rods) is more sensitive than color film and can produce a picture even under conditions of dim illumination. Color film (cones) requires much more intense light to produce a clear image.

More than 6 million cones and 100 million rods are distributed, somewhat unevenly, throughout the retina. The fovea contains only cones—some 50,000 of them packed together in an area smaller than a square millimeter. The area outside the fovea contains both rods and cones, with the cones decreasing in number from the center of the retina to the periphery. The rods are connected in groups to bipolar and ganglion cells, and each group has one neuron running to the optic nerve. The cones in the periphery of the retina are grouped together in units along with the rods, but each of the cones in the fovea has

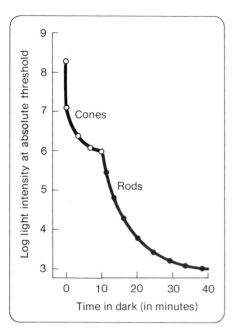

Fig. 4-8 The course of dark adaptation Subjects look at a bright light until the retina has become light adapted. When the subjects are then placed in darkness, they become increasingly sensitive to fainter test flashes as the retina gradually becomes dark adapted. The curve shows the minimum light intensity for the test flash to be seen. The unfilled data points indicate at which points the color of the test flash was clearly visible; the filled data points indicate when the test flash appeared colorless. Note the sharp break in the curve at about 10 minutes, which is called the rod-cone break. By changing the color of the light flash or the area of the retina tested, it can be shown that the first part of the curve describes adaptation of the cones and the second, adaptation of the rods. (Data are approximate, from various determinations)

virtually its own "private wire" to the brain (see Figure 4-5). Our vision is more acute when light waves strike the fovea, because the nonconverging "private wires" do not mix signals. For this reason, when we want to see an object clearly we turn our head to look directly at it, so that the image falls on our fovea. Under dim illumination, however, when the cones are not operative, we can more easily detect a faint stimulus, such as a dim star, if we do not look directly at it but let its image fall just outside the foveal region, where rod density is the greatest.

Although the rods will respond to a much dimmer stimulus than will the cones, the image they give is less clear. At night, objects have indistinct outlines and lack much of the detail seen in daylight. Knowing that groups of rods are connected to a single neuron, we realize why this would be so. Because signals from many rods converge on a single optic nerve fiber, interpretation by the brain is less accurate than it would be for the "private wire" cone cells in the fovea.

DARK ADAPTATION Most motorists find driving at dusk hazardous. This is because the transition from day to night vision takes place gradually as daylight diminishes. And at twilight, both the cones and rods are operating, but neither with full effectiveness. A sudden change from conditions of light to dark, or vice versa, is even more difficult to adjust to. It takes several minutes for the eye to shift from dim light to brightness and even longer to adjust from bright light to darkness. We have all experienced the difficulty of finding our way to an empty seat when entering a dark theater. After a few minutes our eyes become accustomed to the dark, and we are able to see people around us even though the lighting has not changed. We have undergone *dark adaptation.*

The course of dark adaptation provides further evidence for the difference in action between the rods and cones (see Figure 4-8). The first part of the curve shows that the cones become increasingly sensitive to fainter lights, but after five minutes in the dark their sensitivity has increased as much as it will. The rods, however, continue to adapt and do not reach their maximum sensitivity for about a half-hour.

The dark-adapted eye is much more sensitive to lights with wavelengths in the blue-green region than to the longer wavelengths in the red region. This difference has an important practical implication for the individual who must work in a darkened room or shift quickly from conditions of light to dark, such as a photographer or a ship's navigator on night duty. Wearing red goggles (or working in a room illuminated by red light) greatly reduces the time required for dark adaptation. Since red light stimulates the cones but not the rods, the rods remain in a state of dark adaptation. Under conditions of red light, the person can see well enough to work and still be almost completely dark adapted when it becomes necessary to go into the dark.

Color Vision

For the human subject, the color spectrum fades into invisibility at the extreme ends, red and violet (see Figure 4-9).[1] Some vivid colors that we see are not in the spectrum at all. They do not correspond to any single wavelength of light but are produced by mixing lights of different wavelengths. These are the "nonspectral" purples that do look like a mixture of red and blue. Another

---

[1] A useful mnemonic for remembering the order of colors on the spectrum involves the coined name "ROY G. BIV," formed from the first letters of the colors: red, orange, yellow, green, blue, indigo, and violet.

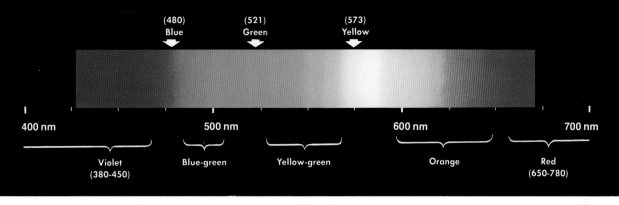

Fig. 4-9   The solar spectrum
The colors are in the order of the rainbow, as they are seen when sunlight is sent through a prism.
The numbers give the wavelength of the various colors in nanometers (nm); a nanometer is one-billionth of a meter.

Fig. 4-10   A color circle showing complementary colors
The colors opposite each other, if in proper proportions, will mix on a color wheel to yield the neutral gray at the center. Wavelengths are indicated around the circle in nanometers (nm). Note that the spectral colors lie in their natural order on the circle, but their spacing is not uniform by wavelength. The circle also includes the nonspectral reds and purples.

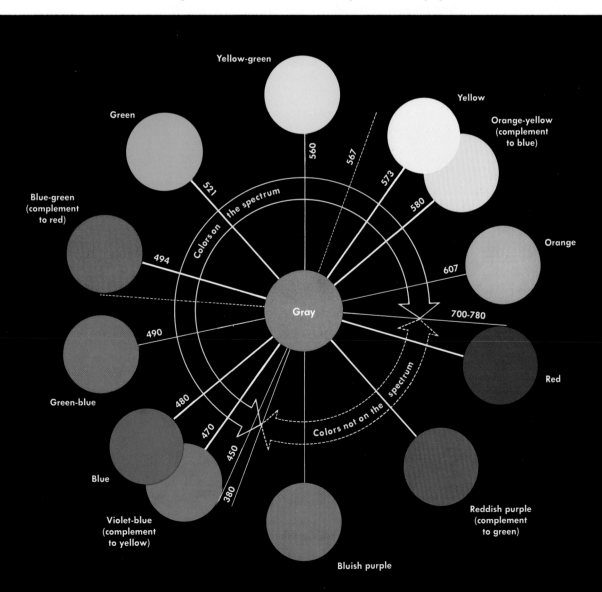

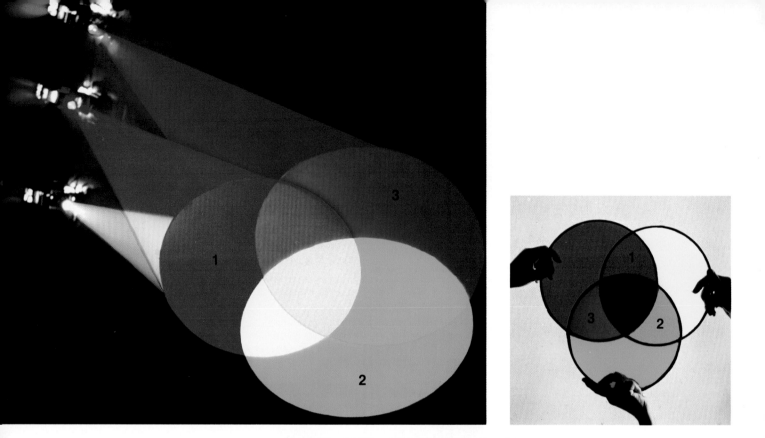

Fig. 4-11 Additive and subtractive color mixtures

Additive color mixture (illustrated by the figure at the left) takes place when lights are mixed. Red and green lights combine to give yellow, green and bluish purple to give blue, and so on. The three colors overlap in the center to give white. Mixture of any two of the colors produces the complement of the third, as shown in the triangular portions.

Subtractive color mixture (illustrated by the figure at the right) takes place when pigments are mixed or when light is transmitted through colored filters placed one over another. Usually blue-green and yellow will mix to give green and complementary colors will reduce to black, as in the example given. Unlike an additive mixture, one cannot always tell from the color of the components what color will result. For example, blue and green will commonly yield blue-green by subtractive mixture, but with some filters they may yield red. Note that in the photograph to the right the numbered triangular portions are the original complementary colors used in the additive mixture, but here they appear as a result of subtractive mixture.

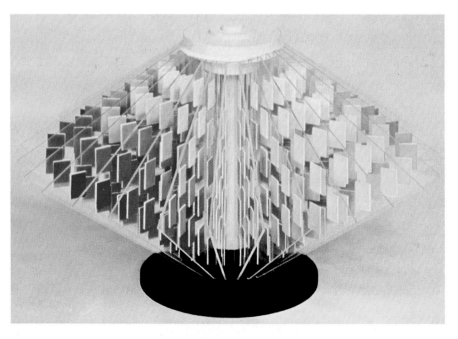

Fig. 4-12 The color solid

The three dimensions of color can be represented on a double cone: hue is represented by points around the circumference, saturation by points along the radius, and brightness by points on the vertical axis. A vertical slice taken from the color solid will show differences in saturation and brightness of a single hue.

Purkinje shift

The Purkinje shift illustrates the difference between rod and cone vision. In daylight or normal conditions of illumination, the two flowers above are seen with cone vision and are equally visible, the red appearing brighter than the blue. If you look at them for about five minutes in very dim light, however, the red flower will no longer be visible. If the light is dim enough, only rod vision will be involved. You can hasten the effect by staring at the center of the red flower. This causes the red to fall on the area of the retina with increased density of cones and the blue to fall on the area with greater density of rods.

Fig. 4-13   Tests for colorblindness

Two plates used in colorblindness tests. In the left plate, individuals with certain kinds of red-green blindness see only the number 5; others see only the 7; still others, no number at all. Those with normal vision see 57. Similarly, in the right plate, people with normal vision see the number 15, whereas those with red-green blindness see no number at all.

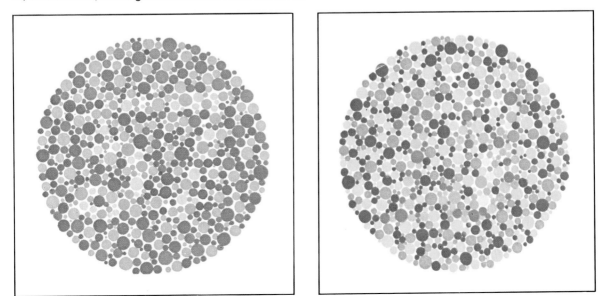

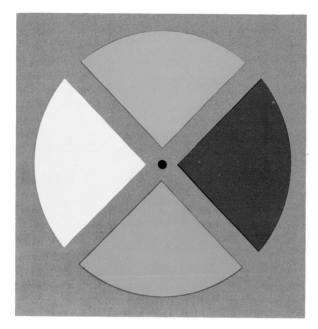

Fig. 4-14 Negative afterimages
Look steadily for about a minute at the dot in the center of the colors; then transfer your gaze to the dot in the gray field on the right. You should see patches that are the complementary colors of the original—the blue, red, green, and yellow will be replaced by yellow, green, red, and blue.

Negative afterimages are also illustrated in this contemporary work of art by Jasper Johns. Stare at the dot in the middle of the upper square for about a minute and then shift your eyes to the dot in the middle of the white field. (*Targets*, litho from nine stones and two aluminum plates, 1967–1968)

nonspectral color is a range of red that looks like the "purest" red to most observers but is actually obtained by a particular mixture of wavelengths.

An interesting relationship exists among colors. If the spectral colors are wrapped around the circumference of a circle, allowing room between the red and violet ends of the spectrum for the purples and reds not found on it, the colors opposite each other on the circle will be *complementary*. That is, if lights of these colors are mixed in proper proportions, they disappear into a neutral gray. Figure 4-10 presents such a *color circle*. For convenience in remembering the positions, we usually name the main complementary pairs as blue-yellow and red-green, although the yellow complementary to blue is slightly orange, and the green complementary to red is really a blue-green.

Those familiar with painting may argue that yellow and blue are not complementaries, because those pigments when mixed give green, not gray. But we are talking here about mixing *lights*, not pigments. The principles of mixture in the two cases are not contradictory. The mixture of lights is an *additive* mixture, whereas the mixture of pigments is a *subtractive* mixture—because of the way in which pigments selectively absorb some of the light. Light is the source of all color, and pigments are simply reflectors and absorbers of light. They achieve their color by absorbing certain parts of the spectrum and reflecting the parts that remain. For example, the pigment in the chlorophyll of plants absorbs most of the purple, blue, and red wavelengths of light; the green that remains is reflected back to the eye, so we see most vegetation as various shades of green. Black pigment absorbs all wavelengths and reflects very little light. White pigment reflects equally all the colors of light but in much greater amounts than black pigment. For more information on additive and subtractive color, see Figure 4-11.

Some of the colors on the color circle appear more elementary than others; that is, they appear to be composed of a single hue. These elementary colors are called *psychological primaries*, and usually four primary colors are named—red, yellow, green, and blue. Between them are "secondary" colors, in which the primary components are still identifiable: orange between red and yellow, yellow-greens between yellow and green, blue-greens between green and blue, and purples (indigos) and violets between blue and red. Another set of primaries is called *color-mixture primaries*. Any three widely spaced colors on the spectrum can be used to produce all the other colors by additive mixture. The three colors usually chosen are a red, a green, and a blue. Thus, colors between red and green on the color circle can be produced by additively mixing a pure red and pure green; the exact color obtained will depend on the respective energy levels of the red and green light sources. Similarly, colors between green and blue on the color circle can be obtained by their additive mixtures, and the same holds for blue and red. With additive mixing, almost the entire color circle can be produced with just three colors.

Color television provides a common example of additive color mixture. Examination of the television screen with a magnifying glass will reveal that there are tiny dots of only three colors (red, green, and blue). Addition occurs because the dots are so close together that the eye cannot separate them, so their retinal images overlap. The "pointillist" painters hit on this idea 75 years or so ago.

PSYCHOLOGICAL DIMENSIONS OF COLOR How do you describe a color? Light waves can be described physically through the measurement of wavelengths and amplitude (the height of the wave). But when we try to describe what we see, we must resort to three psychological dimensions: hue, brightness, and saturation. *Hue* refers to what we ordinarily think of as the "name" of the color—for example, red, green, and so forth. The circumference of the color circle provides the scale along which the hues can be placed in order.

Another dimension of color is *brightness.* The physical basis of brightness is primarily the energy of the light source, which corresponds to the amplitude of the wave. But brightness also depends to some extent on wavelength. Yellow, for example, appears somewhat brighter than red and blue wavelengths, even when all three have equal amplitudes.

A third dimension is *saturation,* which refers to the apparent purity of the color. Highly saturated colors appear to be pure hues, without any gray; colors of low saturation appear close to gray. Saturation is determined primarily by the complexity of the light wave. A light wave composed of only one wavelength will produce the most highly saturated color. Light waves with many components result in colors of low saturation. However, as colors of a single wavelength become brighter (merge into white) or darker (merge into black) they begin to lose the apparent purity of their hues; the change in brightness is accompanied by a reduction in saturation.

The relationship between hue, brightness, and saturation will become clearer if we look at the *color solid* (see Figure 4-12), which represents all three simultaneously. The dimension of hue is represented by points around the circumference; saturation, by points along the radius, going from a pure or highly saturated color on the outside to a gray or unsaturated color in the center; and brightness, by points along the vertical axis, going toward black at the bottom and white at the top. On any vertical half-slice taken through the center of the solid, all the colors are the same hue (wavelength) but vary in brightness and saturation.

COLORBLINDNESS To understand colorblindness, we may think of the normal eye as discriminating three systems of color: light-dark, yellow-blue, and red-green. All other combinations can be derived from these. Colorblindness results from a deficiency in one or two of these systems, the light-dark system remaining intact if the person can see at all. The person with normal vision is called a *trichromat.* A person who lacks one system but has use of the other two is called a *dichromat,* and is partially colorblind. Finally, the person with only the light-dark system is a *monochromat* and is totally colorblind.

By far, the most common form of colorblindness is red-green blindness, with the blue-yellow and light-dark systems intact. Total colorblindness, in which the person sees merely black, white, and gray, is extremely rare; yellow-blue blindness, in which red-green discrimination is preserved, is rarer still.

Many colorblind persons are unaware of their defect because they are able to make such skillful use of their remaining color discrimination, combining it with the learned colors and color names of familiar objects. Because our color vocabulary is not clear for unsaturated colors, the colorblind person can make some mistakes on these troublesome colors without being noticed.

There are many tests available for the detection of colorblindness. They usually require the subject to read a figure composed of colored dots on a background of other colored dots (see Figure 4-13). The colors are chosen to confuse subjects who have the various forms of color deficiency.

NEGATIVE AFTERIMAGES If you stare at a *red* circle and then look at a plain gray surface, you are likely to see a *green* circle on it; that is, you experience a *negative afterimage.* It is called a negative afterimage because green is the complementary color of red on the color circle. Not all afterimages are in the

Theories of Color Vision

Exactly how do the photoreceptors of the retina manage to send a different message to the brain for each of the many colors in the spectrum? Each attempt to explain how the eye sees color has taken as its starting point one of the three sets of facts about color that we have just discussed: color mixture, negative afterimages, and colorblindness.

One of the earliest theories of color vision—proposed by the English physicist Thomas Young in 1802 and modified by the German physiologist Hermann von Helmholtz a half-century later—was based on the fact that three colors are sufficient to produce all the colors in the spectrum. The *Young-Helmholtz theory* proposes three different kinds of color receptors, each maximally sensitive to a different wavelength (one sensitive to red wavelengths, one to blue, and one to green). All other colors are produced by a combined stimulation of these receptors. Yellow is produced when red and green receptors are stimulated simultaneously. White is produced when all three receptors are stimulated simultaneously. The modern form of the Young-Helmholtz theory attempts to link three kinds of cones (or three kinds of cone substances) with the three colors.

However, the Young-Helmholtz theory has not been able to explain some of the facts of colorblindness. If yellow is produced by activity in red and green receptors, how is it that a person with red-green colorblindness has no difficulty seeing yellow? Another color theory, formulated by Ewald Hering in 1870, attempted to solve this problem. Hering felt that the Young-Helmholtz theory did not adequately reflect visual experience. He based his theory of color vision on the *psychological primaries* rather than on the color-mixing primaries and argued that yellow is as basic a color as red, blue, or green. It does not appear to be a mixture of other colors, as orange appears to be a mixture of red and yellow or purple a mixture of red and blue.

Hering was impressed with the facts of *afterimages*, by the appearance of red-green and blue-yellow as pairs in so many circumstances. He proposed that there were three types of cones: one that responded to degrees of brightness, the black-white continuum; and two color cones, one provided the basis for red-green perception and the other for blue-yellow. Each receptor was assumed to function in two ways. One color of the pair was produced when the receptor was in a building-up phase (*anabolic*), and the other appeared when the receptor was in a tearing-down phase (*catabolic*). The two phases cannot occur at the same time in a given receptor; when a yellow-blue cone is stimulated it responds with either yellow or blue. It cannot react both ways simultaneously. That is why, according to the theory, we never see a red-green or a blue-yellow, whereas it is possible to see a reddish blue or greenish yellow. When stimulation is withdrawn, as in the negative afterimage experiment, the contrasting color appears because the anabolic-catabolic process is reversed. When we look at a blue circle and then transfer our gaze to a white sheet of paper, a yellow circle appears when the catabolic process takes over (see Figure 4-14). Hering's theory has become known as the *opponent-process theory*. In its modern form, this theory assumes that the opponent processes take place not in the cones but in coding mechanisms closer to the brain in the optic system.

Recent developments suggest that both theories may be partially correct. Using a procedure called *microspectrophotometry*, it is possible to direct different wavelengths of light through single cones in the human retina and analyze the energy transmitted by means of a computer. Three kinds of light-sensitive pigments in the cones have been identified using this technique: one type primarily sensitive to wavelengths in the blue band, one sensitive to green, and a third sensitive to yellow. Although the third cone type had its peak sensitivity at 577 nm (which is yellow), these cones were also sensitive to the longer wavelengths (up to 650 nm) of the yellowish red part of the spectrum. These measurements appear to support the Young-Helmholtz theory, although it is not clear whether the three cone types should be called blue, green, and yellow, or blue, green, and red.

At the same time, recordings taken with microelectrodes give evidence of an "on" and "off" type of process in bipolar cells and in cells of the lateral geniculate body—that portion of the thalamus where visual impulses are relayed to the visual cortex (see Figure 4-7). Some cells respond with a burst of impulses when stimulated by short wavelengths but are inhibited (respond as "off" cells) during illumination with long wavelengths, showing a burst of firing when stimulation ceases. Other cells are active when stimulated by long wavelengths and inhibited by short wavelengths. These results indicate an opponent-process operating not in the cones themselves, but farther along in the pathway from the eye to the brain.

At this point of scientific development it appears that color vision is a two-stage process: the retina contains pigments that respond differentially to the lights of three different colors; these responses are encoded into two-color, on-off signals by cells farther along in the optic system for transmission to the higher visual centers. A final theory of color vision will probably be a modification of this two-stage theory. The interesting feature is that two theories, those of Hering and Young-Helmholtz, proposed over a century ago, have had to wait until recent technological developments (microspectrophotometry and single-neuron recording) could provide verification of their propositions (Hurvich, 1978).

complementary color, however. After staring at a very bright light, you are likely to see a whole succession of colors, but seeing the complementary color is very common. Afterimages are illustrated in Figure 4-14. The phenomena of color mixing, colorblindness, and negative afterimages have played an important role in theorizing about color vision.

Neural Processing of Visual Information

Research on neural activity during visual stimulation suggests that much of the information transmitted to the brain is concerned with differences and changes in the environment. Because the rods and cones of the human eye are so minute and difficult to isolate for study, this research has been done primarily with lower organisms. The horseshoe crab is a particularly good subject, because each of its eyes contains about 800 individual receptor cells, each with its own lens and nerve fiber going directly to the brain. An electrode can be placed on a single nerve fiber and its response to light stimulation measured. These experiments have shown that different light intensities cause the fiber to fire at different frequencies, indicating that intensity information is conveyed to the brain by the rate of nerve firings.

If a light is projected onto a single receptor, causing its fiber to begin firing, and a neighboring receptor is then stimulated, the original fiber will begin to fire at a slower rate. The activation of the second receptor inhibits the first. This inhibitory effect is exerted mutually among the receptors so that each inhibits, and is inhibited by, its neighbor. The impulse from each receptor flows out of its optic nerve, but part of the impulse is diverted into horizontal nerve cells and flows to neighboring receptors and inhibits them. This mechanism, called *recurrent inhibition,* has interesting consequences. Suppose that both receptor units A and B are stimulated with a light. Now if we also stimulate C, it will inhibit B; B will fire less frequently and consequently will have less of an inhibitory effect on A. Thus, even though the light intensity on B is the same, B will have less of an inhibitory effect on A if B itself is more inhibited by C. We can extend this process to show that a system with recurrent inhibition will display a burst of neural impulses in the optic nerve when a light is first turned on; but after the light has been on for a while inhibition will gradually build up, and the nerve activity will drop back approximately to its resting level. When the light is turned off, the receptors will fire less rapidly, but the inhibitory effects still remain for a brief period; thus, the neural activity in the optic fibers will drop far below the resting level and then gradually return to it as the inhibitory effects dissipate. In general, any change in intensity—either up or down—will have an effect on the activity of the fibers. An increase in intensity will result in a temporary increase in neural activity, after which it returns almost to its resting level; a decrease in intensity causes a temporary decrease in activity and a subsequent return to the resting level.

A system with recurrent inhibition has the ability to transmit information about changes in the environment while suppressing information about parts of the environment that are steady and unchanging. Such a system has adaptive value for the organism; attention to changing aspects of its surroundings is important for survival. Recurrent inhibition in the human visual system is demonstrated in Figure 4-15.

STABILIZED IMAGES The concept of recurrent inhibition implies that retinal receptors are particularly sensitive to changes in the environment; steady, unchanging stimulation tends to be ignored. Why, then, doesn't something

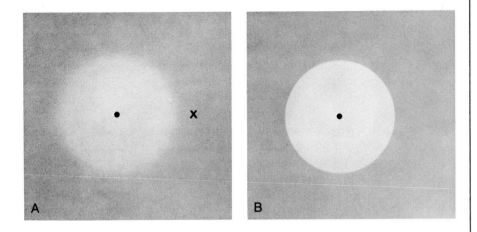

A   B

Fig. 4-15 Recurrent inhibition

With one eye closed, stare at the dot in the middle of A. You will notice that the blurred, light-colored disk soon fades and disappears. Close the seeing eye for a few seconds and then open it; the disk will reappear and then fade again. If you stare at the dot until the disk fades and then shift your gaze to the X, you will find that the disk reappears, and it will reappear each time you shift your eyes between the dot and the X.

If you try doing the same thing with B, the disk will not disappear. Although you think you are staring at the dot steadily, your eyes are constantly making little oscillating movements. These minute oscillations, which we are unaware of even though they occur continually, cause light from the stimulus to strike different retinal receptors from one moment to the next. When you are looking at the edge of something and your eye shifts from one side of the edge to the other, the receptors perceive a change in intensity. The intensity changes that occur with eye oscillations allow the receptors to continue firing at a high rate, and the disk remains visible. The same thing happens when you stare at the dot in A; but because the gradient of intensity of the blurred disk is more gradual, the eye movements produce a smaller change in intensity on the receptors viewing the edge of the blurred disk. The changes in intensity are so small that little neural excitation occurs in the receptors, and the disk fades out. Closing and opening your eye causes marked changes in intensity and so does moving your eye to stare at the X. (After Cornsweet, 1970)

disappear if we stare at it over a period of time? The reason is that the eyes continually make minute oscillatory movements that cause light from the stimulus to strike different retinal receptors from one moment to the next. What would happen if we could immobilize the eye so that these normal oscillations did not occur? It is impossible to hold the eye steady, but several devices have been developed to eliminate the movement of the image on the retina. One device is a tiny slide projector mounted on a contact lens attached to the cornea (diagramed in Figure 4-16). The slide is projected onto a screen, and the eye with the contact lens looks at the image. Since the lens and projector move with the eye, the image presented to the retina is stabilized; that is, the retinal image impinges on the same retinal receptors regardless of eye movements. When the projector is first turned on, the subject sees the projected figure with normal visual acuity. Within a few seconds, however, the image begins to fade; and within a minute, it disappears altogether. This phenomenon is not caused by the attachment of the projector to the eye, because if the image that has disappeared is flickered or moved on the retina it immediately reappears.

From the research on recurrent inhibition and stabilized retinal images we can conclude that changes in the illumination on receptors are necessary for us to see things. Without changes in intensity, everything disappears. Our ability to see stationary objects depends on a visual system that responds to changes in illumination and on an eye that transforms a fixed image into changing stimulation on the retina.

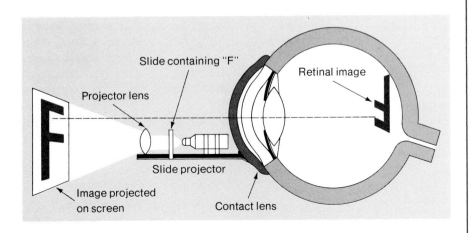

Fig. 4-16 Stabilized image

A device to demonstrate that without movement of the eye in relation to a scene, the scene disappears. A tiny projector mounted on a contact lens is worn over the subject's cornea. With each movement of the eyeball, the lens and projector also move so that the projected image always falls on the same area of the retina. After a few seconds the image will fade and then disappear. (After Cornsweet, 1970)

Fig. 4-17 Sound wave
As the tuning fork vibrates, it produces successive waves of compression and expansion
of the air. If the tuning fork makes 100 vibrations per second, it produces a sound
wave with 100 compressions per second
(that is, 100 Hz).

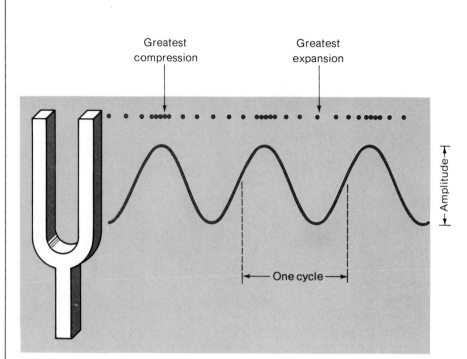

Fig. 4-17 Sound wave
As the tuning fork vibrates, it produces successive waves of compression and expansion
of the air. If the tuning fork makes 100 vibrations per second, it produces a sound
wave with 100 compressions per second
(that is, 100 Hz).

The Auditory Sense

While the eye responds to electromagnetic energy, the ear is sensitive to
mechanical energy—to *pressure changes* among the molecules in the atmosphere. A vibrating object, such as a tuning fork, causes successive waves of
compression and expansion among the air molecules surrounding it. The sound
waves generated by the vibration of molecules (in air, water, or some other
medium) are the stimuli for hearing. Unlike light, sound must travel through a
medium; a ringing bell suspended in a vacuum jar cannot be heard when the air
is pumped out.

Simple sound waves can be graphically represented, as in Figure 4-17, where
the cycles of the wave represent the successive compression and expansion of
the air as the sound wave moves along. The two main characteristics of such a
wave are its frequency and its amplitude. *Frequency* is measured in number of

Viewing a sound signal
Using an electronic instrument called an oscilloscope, we can produce pictures of sound
waves. Vibrations of the air molecules in a
sound wave are picked up by a microphone.
These movements are converted by the microphone into an electric current. The oscilloscope changes the current into a moving
picture on a screen. The oscilloscope picture
is a graph of how pressure changes with
time.

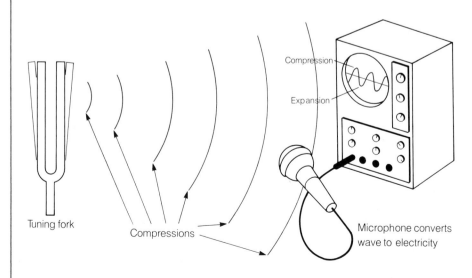

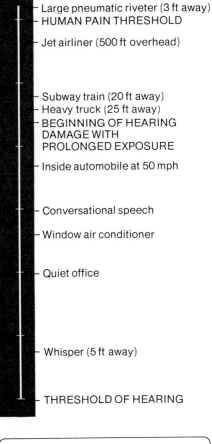

Fig. 4-18 Decibel scale
The loudness of various common sounds scaled in decibels. The takeoff blast of the Saturn V moon rocket, measured at the launching pad, is approximately 180 db. For laboratory rats, prolonged exposure to 150 db causes death.

Large pneumatic riveter (3 ft away)
HUMAN PAIN THRESHOLD

Jet airliner (500 ft overhead)

Subway train (20 ft away)
Heavy truck (25 ft away)
BEGINNING OF HEARING DAMAGE WITH PROLONGED EXPOSURE

Inside automobile at 50 mph

Conversational speech

Window air conditioner

Quiet office

Whisper (5 ft away)

THRESHOLD OF HEARING

vibrations per second; that is, the number of times per second that the complete cycle of the sound wave is repeated. The unit Hertz (abbreviated Hz) is used to denote *cycles per second;* that is, one cycle per second is one Hz.[2] *Amplitude* refers to the amount of compression and expansion of air, as represented by the height of the wave from base to crest.

Pitch and Loudness

The frequency of a sound wave determines what we experience as *pitch.* However, the pitch of a tone can be somewhat affected by the intensity of the stimulus. So even pitch is not simply related to a single physical attribute of the stimulus. Similarly, loudness is most strongly related to the amplitude of the sound wave, or energy of the sound. However, a low-frequency sound wave having the same amplitude as a high-frequency sound wave may not sound equally loud.

Human beings can hear frequencies that range from about 20 to 20,000 Hz. A familiar reference on this range is provided by the piano, which produces frequencies from roughly 27 to 4,200 Hz. All organisms cannot hear the same range of frequencies; for example, dog-calling whistles make use of tones that are too high in frequency for humans to hear.

We all know the difference between a loud and a soft sound, but assigning scale values to intensity is not so easy. Scientists from the Bell Telephone Laboratories have formulated a convenient unit for converting the physical pressures at the eardrum into an understandable scale. The unit is called a *decibel* (one-tenth of a *bel,* named in honor of Alexander Graham Bell, and abbreviated db). A rough idea of what the decibel measures is provided by the scale of familiar sounds shown in Figure 4-18. Zero decibels is arbitrarily set as the absolute threshold for hearing a 1,000 Hz tone. At about 120 db, sound intensity becomes painful; the loudness of normal conversation is about midway between these extremes, at 60 db. Exposure to sound intensities of 90 db or above for extended periods of time can result in permanent deafness. Some rock musicians, for example, have suffered serious hearing loss. Airport runway crews and pneumatic drill operators wear ear mufflers to guard against possible damage.

The absolute threshold for hearing varies with the frequency of the stimulus (see Figure 4-19). Tones in the range of 800 to 6,000 Hz require less than 10 db to reach threshold, whereas tones less than 100 Hz or greater than 15,000 Hz require 40 db or more to reach threshold.

Complex Tones and Noise

Just as the colors we see are seldom pure hues produced by a single wavelength of light, so the sounds we hear are seldom pure tones represented by a sound wave of a single frequency. Even the musical note produced by striking middle C on the piano has (in addition to its fundamental tone of 262 Hz)

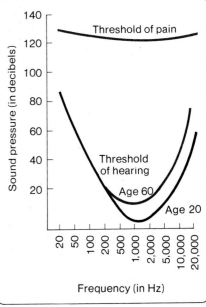

Fig. 4-19 Threshold of hearing
The top curve is the threshold of pain. The convex curves below are the thresholds of hearing for ages 20 and 60. With increase in age, hearing is affected primarily in the range of frequencies above 500 Hz. (Data are approximate, from various determinations)

---

[2] The unit of frequency is named in honor of the German physicist Heinrich Hertz (1857–1894). Note that light waves are conventionally specified in terms of the length of the wave, whereas sound waves are described on the basis of the number of waves per unit of time. There is nothing fundamental about this; either can be described either way.

THE AUDITORY SENSE

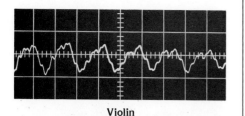

Violin

Clarinet

Fig. 4-20 Oscilloscope pictures of the same note played on two different instruments

Louis Armstrong blows one of the notes that made him the world's most famous trumpeter. The curve is an oscilloscope picture showing pressure changes when a pure note is played on a trumpet.

overtones, which are multiples of that frequency. The overtones occur because at the same time the piano wire vibrates as a whole, producing a *fundamental tone* of 262 Hz, it also vibrates in halves, thirds, quarters, fifths, and so on, with each partial vibration producing its own frequency.

Why do the same notes sound different on the piano and the trumpet? The sounds of one musical instrument differ from those of another in the number of overtones produced. They also differ because the construction of the instrument enhances certain overtones—parts of the instrument vibrate in step (resonate) with some overtones more than with others. This characteristic quality of a musical tone is called *timbre.* It is the timbre of a tone that tells us whether it is being produced by a piano or a clarinet. If all overtones are eliminated by the use of sound filters, it is impossible to determine what instrument is being played. Instead of the regular sound wave pictured in Figure 4-17, a tone from a musical instrument has a complex wave form, preserving only the peaks and troughs that define the fundamental pitch; the high and low points are the same but the wave is jagged or irregular rather than smooth (see Figure 4-20).

If we compare the psychological dimensions of color with those of tone, the following correspondences hold approximately:

Hue ⟷ Pitch
Brightness ⟷ Loudness
Saturation ⟷ Timbre

Hue and pitch are functions of wave frequency; brightness and loudness are functions of amplitude; saturation is a result of mixture, just as timbre is. But these are only analogies and are limited, as all analogies are.

What happens when two tones are sounded together? They do not lose their identity as colors do when mixed, but they may lead to a fusion that is heard as *consonant* (pleasant) or as *dissonant* (unpleasant). The two tones create a third tone based on the difference in their frequencies. This *difference* tone may or may not harmonize with the fundamental tones sounded; for this reason some combinations of tones are preferred to others. Musical harmony depends in part on the interaction between fundamental tones, overtones, and difference tones, which combine to make up the complex tonal stimulus.

A *noise* is a sound composed of many frequencies not in harmonious relation to one another. Acoustical experts sometimes speak of *white noise* when referring to a noise composed of all frequencies in the sound spectrum at roughly the same energy level, or loudness. White noise is analogous to white light, which is composed of all frequencies in the light spectrum. The sound of an empty TV channel or a bathroom shower approximates the sound of white noise.

A noise with energy concentrated in certain frequency bands may have a characteristic pitch. For example, we may legitimately use the musical term "bass" to characterize the sound of a drum, even though a drum is more noisy than tonal. Speech sounds make simultaneous use of tonal qualities and noise qualities: *vowels* are tonal, and *consonants* are noisy.

The Human Ear

The *external ear* connects with the *auditory canal,* leading to the *eardrum,* a movable diaphragm activated by sound waves entering the ear (see Figure 4-21). On the inner side of the diaphragm is a cavity housing the bony transmitters of the *middle ear* (three small bones called the *hammer, anvil,* and

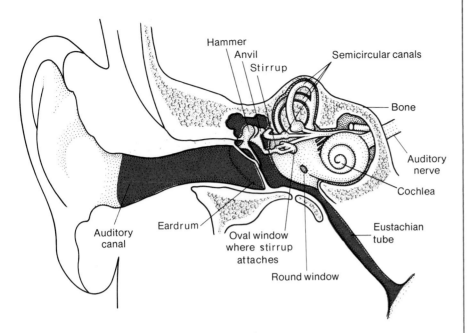

Fig. 4-21 A cross section of the ear
This drawing shows the general structure of
the ear. For the detailed structure of the
cochlea, see Fig. 4-22.

stirrup). The hammer is attached firmly to the eardrum and the stirrup to another membrane, the *oval window*. The oval window conducts the sounds to the *cochlea*, the auditory portion of the *inner ear*. Because the oval window is much smaller than the eardrum, small movements at the eardrum are condensed into a magnified pressure on the oval window.

Pressure at the oval window sets into motion the fluid inside the cochlea (see Figure 4-22). Pressure changes in the fluid displace the *basilar membrane*

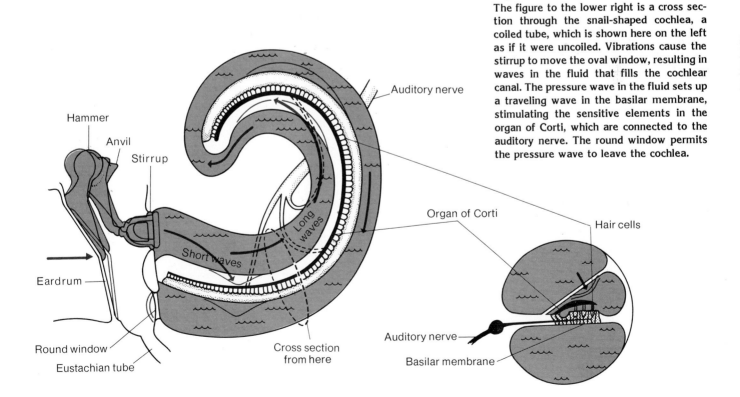

Fig. 4-22 Receptors for hearing
The figure to the lower right is a cross section through the snail-shaped cochlea, a coiled tube, which is shown here on the left as if it were uncoiled. Vibrations cause the stirrup to move the oval window, resulting in waves in the fluid that fills the cochlear canal. The pressure wave in the fluid sets up a traveling wave in the basilar membrane, stimulating the sensitive elements in the organ of Corti, which are connected to the auditory nerve. The round window permits the pressure wave to leave the cochlea.

THE AUDITORY SENSE

Theories of Hearing

As we have noted, sound waves traveling through the fluid of the cochlea cause the basilar membrane to be displaced, thus activating the hair cells of the organ of Corti, which are connected to fibers of the auditory nerve. But how does a structure as small as the organ of Corti (less than the size of a pea) enable us to differentiate thousands of different tones? What are the mechanisms that provide for discriminations in pitch and loudness?

Loudness appears to be determined by the total number of nerve fibers firing and by the activation of certain high threshold fibers—that is, nerve fibers that require considerable bending of the hair cells in order to be stimulated. Pitch is a more complicated matter. The two major theories of pitch discrimination are the place theory and the frequency theory. The *place theory* assumes that the frequency of a tone is indicated by the region of the basilar membrane that is maximally displaced by the sound wave. Von Békésy tested this theory in a series of experiments for which he was awarded the Nobel Prize in 1961. He cut tiny holes in the cochlea of guinea pigs and observed the basilar membrane with a microscope as the ear was being stimulated by tones of different frequencies. He discovered that high frequency tones maximally displaced the narrow end of the basilar membrane near the oval window; tones of intermediate frequency caused displacement further toward the other end of the basilar membrane. Unfortunately for the consistency of the theory, however, low tones activated the entire membrane with roughly equal

displacement. This result and the fact that tones of intermediate frequency displace a fairly broad area of the membrane make it unlikely that differential displacement of the basilar membrane is sufficient to fully explain our ability to discriminate pitch at low frequencies.

This leads us to the *frequency theory*, which assumes that the cochlea acts like a microphone and the auditory nerve like a telephone wire. According to this theory, pitch is determined by the frequency of impulses traveling up the auditory nerve. The greater the frequency, the higher the pitch. Studies have shown that for tones of up to about 4,000 Hz the electrical response of the auditory nerve does track the frequency of the tone. Thus a tone of 500 Hz produces 500 evoked responses per second in the nerve; a tone of 2,000 Hz produces 2,000 responses; and so on. Since an individual neuron can conduct only about 1,000 impulses per second, the ability of the auditory nerve to track frequencies above this point up to 4,000 Hz has to be explained in terms of a *volley principle.* This principle assumes that the different groups of fibers fire in turn, in a sort of squad system. Different squads fire at each compression of the sound wave. One group may fire at the first compression, remain in a refractory phase while another group discharges, and then be ready to fire again at the third compression. Thus, although no one fiber responds at each compression, all respond synchronously with the frequency of the sound wave. For a 2,000 Hz tone, there would be a spurt of activity in the auditory nerve every

half of a millisecond, with different groups of neurons firing each time. Pitch at intermediate frequencies depends on the firing frequency of the volleys, not on that of the individual nerve fibers.

As was the case with theories of color vision, an ultimate explanation of pitch discrimination will probably include some aspects of both theories. Both the *place* of excitation on the basilar membrane and the *frequency* of nerve response appear to be involved in transmitting information about the frequency of a tone. Place seems to be important for high frequencies (above 4,000 Hz), whereas synchronous discharge in nerve fibers is important for the lower frequencies.

Additional coding of auditory information takes place in the auditory pathways closer to the brain and in the auditory cortex itself. An auditory nerve fiber makes synaptic connections with at least four other neurons on its way to the auditory cortex. At each of these levels, neurons can be found that fire at the onset of a tone, or decrease their firing when a tone is turned on, or discharge continuously to a maintained tone, or discharge only when a sound is presented to both ears. In addition, as we ascend from the auditory nerve to the auditory cortex, the range of frequencies to which a particular cell will respond becomes increasingly narrow. Thus, coding of information becomes more precise as the cortex is approached. A general theory of hearing will also have to take into account neural codes based on different types of response patterns at each synaptic level of the auditory system.

in the cochlea, on which the *organ of Corti* rests. This displacement stimulates the sensitive elements in the *hair cells* of the organ of Corti, which are connected with the auditory nerve.

The pathways of the auditory nerves resemble those of the optic nerves in that nerve fibers from each ear travel to both cerebral hemispheres (terminating in the temporal lobes). Thus, destruction of one temporal lobe will not cause complete deafness in either ear.

The Other Senses

Senses other than vision and audition are important for survival, but they lack the richness of patterning and organization that have led us to call sight and hearing the "higher senses." Our symbolic experiences are expressed largely in visual and auditory terms. Our spoken language is to be *heard*; our written language is to be *seen*. Musical notation permits music to be read or played on an instrument. Except for Braille (the raised form of printing that permits the blind to read), we do not have any comparable symbolic coding of odors, tastes, or touches.

Smell

From an evolutionary viewpoint, smell is one of the most primitive and most important of the senses. The sense organ for smell has a position of prominence in the head appropriate to a sense intended to guide behavior. Smell has a more direct route to the brain than any other sense. The receptors high in the nose, in the *olfactory epithelium* of each nasal cavity, are connected without synapse directly to the olfactory bulbs of the brain, which lie just below the frontal lobes. The olfactory bulbs are in turn connected with the olfactory cortex on the inside of the temporal lobes and extend to the neighboring cortex; the exact neural connections are still unknown. In fish, the olfactory cortex makes up the entire cerebral hemispheres. In dogs, the olfactory cortex represents about one-third of the area of the side of the brain; in humans, it represents only one-twentieth of this area. For this reason, both the United States Postal Service and the Bureau of Customs have dogs trained to check unopened packages for heroin and marijuana, and specially trained police dogs have sniffed out hidden explosives.

A dog at work for the Postal Service

Taste

The primary taste qualities are *sweet, sour, salty,* and *bitter.* Other taste experiences are composed of fusions of these qualities with each other along with the other senses. Smell, texture, temperature, and, sometimes, pain (judging from the pleasure some diners derive from highly spiced food) all contribute to the sensations we experience when we taste a food. When we drink a cup of coffee we enjoy its aroma and its warmth by means of senses other than taste; the taste sense provides only for the sweet-sour-salty-bitter components.

The taste receptors are found in the *taste buds,* on the edges and toward the back of the tongue; a few are located elsewhere in the soft palate, the pharynx, and the larynx. It is known that the number of taste buds decreases with age, so older people are less sensitive to taste than children. Some taste buds at the tip of the tongue react only to sweet, salty, or sour; others react to some or all of these in combination. In general, sensitivity to sweet is greatest at the tip of the tongue, to salty on the tip and the sides, to sour on the sides, and to bitter on the back.

Each of the approximately 10,000 taste buds in the human adult has 15 to 20 taste cells arranged in bud-like form on its tip, much like the segments of an orange. These taste cells are continuously reproducing themselves at the rate of a complete turnover for each taste bud every seven days. Consequently, the taste cells we kill when we scald our tongue with a cup of hot coffee provide no cause for concern; they are quickly replenished. Recordings from microelectrodes implanted in single cells show that even the individual cells vary in their

Taste discrimination by experts

This electronic system enables a blind woman to "see" by skin sensation. The TV camera on her right converts the image of the telephone into the pattern of dots shown on the TV monitor behind her. Then, hundreds of tiny cones vibrate against her back, allowing her to feel the dot pattern (shown here by fluorescent paint) and perceive the image of the phone.

response to the four basic taste stimuli; that is, some cells may respond only to sugar and salt while others on the same taste bud may respond only to salt and acids, and so forth.

Measurement of impulses from the taste nerve fibers and behavioral evidence show that other animals differ from humans in the receptivity of their taste buds. Cats and chickens, for example, appear to have no taste receptors that respond to sweet, whereas dogs, rats, pigs, and most other vertebrates do. This helps explain the observation by pet owners that dogs are usually fond of desserts, while cats generally ignore them (Dethier, 1978).

The Skin Sensations

The familiar sense of touch is not a single sense, but includes at least four: *pressure, pain, warm,* and *cold*—all of which are felt through distinct kinds of sensitive spots on the skin surface. All other skin sensations that we commonly describe, such as itch, tickle, quick-pricking pain, or dull, long-lasting pain, are variations of these four basic sensations. An itching sensation, for example, can be produced by stimulating pain spots with a gentle, repeated needle prick; tickle is experienced when adjacent pressure spots on the skin are touched lightly in rapid succession.

The precise receptors for the various skin sensations have been the subject of much study and dispute. At one time, scientists identified a number of quite different nerve-end structures in the skin, each of which was thought to be the specific receptor for one of the four sensations. Subsequent studies, however, failed to substantiate such claims: when investigators "mapped" cold, warm, pressure, and pain spots on their own skin, excised the underlying tissue, and examined it microscopically, there was no consistent relationship between the type of sensation experienced and the type of underlying nerve-end structures. Only two things can be stated with some degree of certainty:

1 Nerve fibers at the base of hair follicles serve as receptors for light pressure (but they are not the only such receptors, since the lips—which are hairless—are quite sensitive to pressure).
2 Free nerve-endings that terminate in the epidermis are involved in pain reception.

If there are only warm and cold sensitive spots on the skin's surface, how can we experience the feeling of "hot"? The answer is that "hot" results from the *simultaneous* stimulation of warm and cold spots. This is demonstrated with a device that allows two streams of water to be passed through intertwined coils (see Figure 4-23). If cold water passes through both coils, they of course feel cold when grasped with one hand. If warm water passes through both, they feel warm. But when cold water circulates through one set of coils and warm water through the other, the coils feel *hot.* Although this is not the way the experience of "hot" is usually produced, it is the way the receptors respond. Cold spots have two thresholds. They respond to stimuli of low temperature, do not respond to stimuli of intermediate temperature, but respond again to stimuli of high temperature. High temperatures, then, activate *both* warm and cold spots, and the felt experience of "hot" depends on this simultaneous effect.

Kinesthesis and Equilibratory Senses

Our ordinary vocabulary lacks a word for the sensory system that informs us of the position and movement of parts of the body. In technical language, it is *kinesthesis*—the muscle, tendon, and joint sense. Sense organs in the joints and tendons detect position and movement; sense organs in the muscles serve to automatically modulate muscle contraction or expansion but give little information that we are directly aware of.

Without kinesthesis we would have great difficulty in maintaining posture, and in walking, climbing, and controlling voluntary movements such as reaching, grasping, and manipulating. Whenever we act, we first make somewhat tentative movements and then adjust them according to their environmental effects. If something turns out to be heavier than expected, we brace ourselves and lift with greater effort. If we slip or stumble as we walk, we promptly make corrective movements. The kinesthetic sense gives us a feedback from the environment that keeps telling us how things are going. We take this sense for granted until a foot "goes to sleep" and we realize how strange it is to walk without any information as to the foot's contact with the floor.

Cooperating with kinesthesis are the *equilibratory senses*, which deal with total body position in relation to gravity and with motion of the body as a whole. The relation of bodily parts to one another and to external objects is the responsibility of kinesthesis; the orientation of the body in space is the responsibility of the equilibratory senses.

The sense organs for equilibrium, located in the inner ear, are a series of cavities extending from the cochlea. There are two systems: the *semicircular canals* and the *vestibular sacs*.

The three semicircular canals, each roughly perpendicular to the others, lie in three planes, so that bodily rotation in any one of the planes will have maximum effect on one of the canals and rotation at any angle to the planes will affect more than one. The canals are filled with a fluid that moves when the head rotates and exerts pressure on hair cells similar to those of the organ of Corti. Displacement of these hair cells by the movement of the fluid stimulates a nonauditory branch of the auditory nerve. When rotation is slow and of moderate amount, the chief consequence is information that we are moving. When it is more extreme, we experience dizziness and nausea.

The vestibular sacs, located between the base of the semicircular canals and the cochlea, provide for our perception of bodily position when the body is at

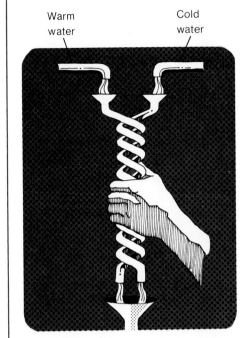

Fig. 4-23 "Hot" as simultaneous stimulation of warm and cold spots When cold water (0–5°C) is circulated through one coil and warm water (40–44°C) through another intertwining coil, the subject experiences a hot, burning sensation on grasping the coils. This experiment demonstrates that the sensation of "hot" is produced by the simultaneous stimulation of warm and cold spots in the skin.

rest. They respond to the tilt or position of the head and do not require rotation to be stimulated. The receptors, again, are hair cells that protrude into a gelatinous mass containing small crystals called *otoliths* (literally, "ear stones"). The normal pressure of the otoliths on the hair cells gives us the sense of upright position, and any distortion tells us that the head is tilted.

The equilibratory senses also signal accelerated motion in a straight line, but sometimes they produce illusions that distort the true path of motion. These illusions occur in flying, because of changes in speed and the banking and climbing of the plane. For example, when a plane is increasing its speed gradually, a blindfolded subject may feel sure that the plane is climbing; if its speed is decreasing gradually, the subject may feel equally sure that it is diving. Thus, under conditions of poor visibility, pilots do better to trust their instruments than their equilibratory senses.

SUMMARY

1 All sense experiences have an *absolute threshold* and *difference thresholds* (j.n.d.'s). According to *Weber's law*, difference thresholds tend to be a constant fraction of the stimulus intensity. A *psychophysical function* expresses the relationship between a psychological variable (the experience of perceiving the stimulus) and the physical variable (the intensity of the stimulus).

2 The eye receives light waves by way of the *cornea, pupil, lens*, and *retina*. The actual receptors are the *rods* and *cones* of the retina. The cones, scattered throughout the retina but concentrated in the *fovea*, are receptors for both black and white and hue (*chromatic* colors). The rods, in the periphery of the eye, allow us to see only black and white (the *achromatic* colors), and function mainly under reduced illumination. In night vision, only the rods function.

3 The distinctive roles of the rods and cones can be inferred from *dark adaptation*, in which the cones reach their maximum sensitivity in about five minutes, while the rods continue to become increasingly sensitive for about a half-hour.

4 The *chromatic colors* can be arranged around a color circle (following the order of wavelengths) with space allowed for the nonspectral purples and reds. When properly spaced, the colors opposite each other are *complementaries*. When complementary colors are mixed as lights (*additive* mixture), they cancel each other and result in a neutral gray. Although four *psychological primaries* can be identified (red, yellow, green, and blue), three *color primaries* (red, green, and blue) are enough to produce the range of hues by additive mixture. The chief dimensions of color are *hue, brightness*, and *saturation*.

5 Most people discriminate three color systems; a colorblind individual is deficient in either the red-green or yellow-blue system (a *dichromat*) or both (a *monochromat*). *Negative afterimages* emphasize the pairing of colors, for the withdrawal of stimulation of one hue usually produces the complementary hue.

6 Research on *recurrent inhibition* and *stabilized retinal images* indicates that only changes in illumination are seen. Without change in the intensity of light, everything disappears.

7 The chief dimensions of auditory experience are *pitch*, determined by the *frequency* of vibration of the sound waves, and *loudness*, determined by the *amplitude* of these waves. The absolute threshold for hearing depends on

the frequency of the tone; very low- or very high-pitched tones must be more intense than tones in the middle range of frequencies to be heard.

8 Most tones are not pure; that is, they are not composed of only a single frequency. Musical instruments may be differentiated by the *timbre* of their tones, a quality that depends on the *overtones* and on other characteristics differing from one instrument to another. Complex sounds composed of many frequencies not in harmonious relation to one another are called *noise*.

9 The auditory apparatus consists of the *external ear*, leading by way of the auditory canal to the *eardrum*, which is next to the *middle ear*. The bones of the middle ear transmit the sound waves to the *oval window*, leading to the *inner ear*. The *cochlea* houses the receptors of the inner ear—sensitive *hair cells* in the *organ of Corti*, which is located on the *basilar membrane*. Wave motion in the fluid of the inner ear agitates these hair cells, which in turn activate the auditory nerve.

10 The other senses, important as they are, do not enter as much into our symbolic behavior, so they are thought of as "lower senses." They include *smell, taste,* the four *skin sensations* (pressure, pain, warm, cold), *kinesthesis* (muscle, tendon, and joint sense), and the *equilibratory senses.*

FURTHER READING

For a general introduction to the various senses, see Lindsay and Norman, *Human information processing* (2nd ed., 1977). Also see Kaufman, *Perception* (1979), Ludel, *Introduction to sensory processes* (1978), Schiffman, *Sensation and perception* (1976), and Rock, *An introduction to perception* (1975). *Experimental psychology* (3rd ed., 1971), edited by Kling and Riggs, is a useful reference book, with a number of chapters on sensory psychology. The multiple-volume *Handbook of perception* (1975–1979), edited by Carterette and Friedman, covers all aspects of perception.

For mathematical theories of sensory psychology, see Krantz, Atkinson, Luce, and Suppes (eds.), *Contemporary developments in mathematical psychology* (1974) and Egan, *Signal detection theory and ROC analysis* (1975).

5
Perception

W e live in a world of objects and people—a world that constantly bombards our senses with stimuli. Only under the most unusual circumstances are we aware of a single stimulus, such as a point of light in a dark room or a pure tone in a soundproof chamber. We see pictures instead of spots of light and hear words or music instead of pure tones. We react to patterns of stimuli, usually with little awareness of the parts composing the pattern. When we put together a jigsaw puzzle, the colors and sizes of the many individual pieces look different from the way they look when the puzzle is completed. A detail of an oil painting may appear to be a meaningless collection of daubs of paint. The total impression from organized stimuli has properties not predictable from the parts in isolation. Perception is the process by which we organize and interpret the patterns of stimuli in our environment.

The theoretical significance of the "pattern of stimuli" in producing a perceptual experience was recognized early by proponents of *Gestalt psychology*, a school of psychology that developed in Germany toward the end of the nineteenth century. *Gestalt* is a German word that has no exact English translation, though "form," "configuration," or "pattern" comes close. The word helps to emphasize that the whole affects the way in which the parts are perceived; perception acts to draw the sensory data together into a wholistic pattern, or *Gestalten*. For this reason, it is sometimes said that "the whole is different from the sum of its parts"—a favorite phrase of Gestalt psychologists.

The perception of objects and events takes place within a framework of space and time. Vision and audition provide the most complex patterns of these perceptual experiences. Vision is our preferred spatial sense, giving us variegated patterns of form and color in three dimensions. But it also provides a sense of time, because we see succession, movement, and change. Audition is a spatial sense too; we can be aware simultaneously of many sounds coming from different locations. But spatial patterns in audition are more limited than those of vision. Audition is primarily a time sense; its main patterns are those of succession, change, and rhythm. Because vision is so important as a spatial sense, our discussion of perception will focus on visual processes.

At the top is the painting *La Parade* by the French artist Georges Seurat. An enlargement of one part of the picture (shown below) illustrates how it is composed of separate daubs of paint. The total impression is more than the sum of its parts.

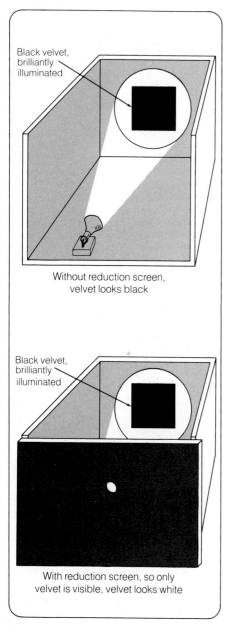

Black velvet, brilliantly illuminated

Without reduction screen, velvet looks black

Black velvet, brilliantly illuminated

With reduction screen, so only velvet is visible, velvet looks white

Fig. 5-1 Effects of surroundings on brightness constancy
Even though the square of velvet is brilliantly illuminated, it still looks black, provided the illuminated white background is also visible. However, when only the velvet is visible through the reduction screen, it looks white, even though the illumination on it is the same.

Object Perception and Perceptual Constancies

If you look around the room and ask yourself what you see, the answer is likely to be, "a room full of objects," or "a room full of people and objects." Or you may pick out specific people or objects. But you are not likely to report that you see a mosaic of light and shadow. We tend to perceive *things* rather than the *sensory features* that describe them. Detached sensory features ("blueness," "squareness," or "softness") can be perceived, but they are usually perceived as the qualities of objects. You are aware of the blue flowers or the square box or the soft pillow—not "blueness," "squareness," or "softness."

Our perceptual experiences are not isolated; they build a world of identifiable things. Objects endure, so that we meet the same object over and over again. When you turn your head away, you think of objects as remaining where you saw them. We perceive a familiar object as permanent and stable regardless of light conditions, the position from which we see it, or its distance from us. The tendency to see a familiar object as having normal brightness and color regardless of the light conditions is called *brightness constancy* and *color constancy*. The tendency to see an object's shape as unchanging regardless of the viewing angle is called *shape constancy*. The tendency to see an object as the same size regardless of distance is called *size constancy*. Finally, the fact that an object appears to retain its "same" position, even as we move about, is known as *location constancy*. The word *constancy* is an exaggeration, but it dramatizes our relatively stable perception of objects.

Brightness and Color Constancy

Black velvet looks just as black to us in sunlight as in shadow, even though it reflects more light in the sunlight. We refer to this fact as *brightness constancy*. Although this effect holds under ordinary circumstances, a change in the surroundings can destroy it. Attach the black velvet to a white board and throw a bright light on both it and the board. It still looks black. Now place an opaque screen between you and the velvet, with a small opening in the screen, so that you can see only a small patch of the velvet (see Figure 5-1). This screen is called a *reduction screen*—it reduces what you see to the actual light reflected from a surface, independent of the surroundings. Now the velvet looks *white*, because the light coming through the reduction screen is brighter than the reduction screen itself. When we perceive objects in natural settings, we somehow take into account the total illumination and are thereby able to maintain brightness constancy.

Similar considerations apply for *color constancy*. Familiar objects appear to retain their color under a variety of lighting conditions. The owner of a blue car sees it as blue, whether looking at it in bright sunlight, in dim illumination, or under a yellow street light. The car owner is relying on memory of the car's color, which contributes to color constancy. Information about the nature of the illumination and about the color of surrounding objects are also clues to color constancy. When we do not have these clues, color constancy diminishes or disappears. If you look at a ripe tomato through a narrow tube that obscures the nature of the object, the tomato will appear to be blue or brown or any of a number of other colors, depending on the wavelengths of the light being reflected from it. Without color constancy clues we see the color of objects according to the wavelengths of light being reflected to the eye.

Shape and Size Constancy

When a door swings open toward us, its shape (projected on the retina) goes through a series of changes. The door's rectangular shape becomes a trapezoid, with the edge toward us looking wider than the hinged edge; then the trapezoid grows thinner, until all that is projected on the retina is a vertical line the thickness of the door. We can readily distinguish these changes, but our psychological experience is of an unchanging door swinging on its hinges. The fact that the door's shape does not seem to change is an example of *shape constancy*. We see the top of a cup as "circular," whether we view it from the side or from the top.

As an object is moved farther away, we tend to see it as more or less unchanging in size. This is referred to as *size constancy*. Hold a quarter a foot in front of your eyes and then move it out to arm's length. Does it appear to get smaller? Not noticeably so. Yet the retinal image of the quarter when it is 12 inches away is twice the size of the image of the quarter when it is 24 inches from the eye (see Figure 5-2). We certainly do not perceive it as becoming half its size as we move it to arm's length.

When we look at a distant object, we can judge its size in one of three ways:

1 *Retinal size.* We might judge it according to the retinal image, seeing it as smaller the farther away it is. The retinal projection of an object at 20 feet is half the retinal projection at 10 feet.
2 *Object size.* We might judge an object by its true size and hence see it as remaining constant in size regardless of its distance.
3 *Compromise between retinal size and object size.* We might compromise and see the object as smaller at a distance, but not as much smaller as the size of the retinal image indicates.

The last of the three alternatives is what usually occurs. Our size perceptions represent compromises between retinal size and object size. How well size constancy operates depends on distance cues and *on our familiarity with the object.* The more information available about the distance of the object, the more the perceived size approaches the actual size. The fewer distance clues we have, the more the perceived size approaches the size of the retinal image, unless the object is very familiar. Familiarity with an object enables us to judge its appropriate size, even in the absence of distance cues.

Size constancy develops largely as the result of experience. Figure 5-3 shows the results of an experiment comparing the performance of eight-year-olds and adults in judging the size of objects at different distances. At a

Fig. 5-2 Object size and retinal image
This figure illustrates the geometric relationship between the physical size of an object and the size of its projection on the retina. Arrow A and arrow B represent objects of the same size, but one is twice as far from the eye's lens as the other. As a result, the image projected on the retina by A is approximately half as large as that projected by B. The object represented by arrow C is smaller than A but closer to the eye; note that arrows A and C produce retinal images of the same size.

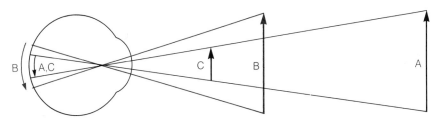

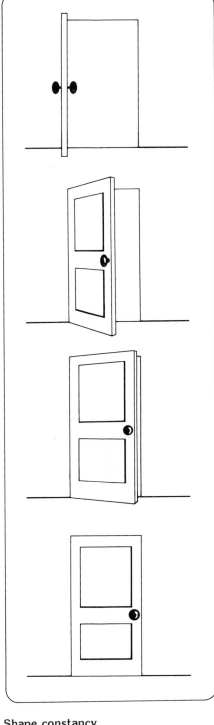

Shape constancy
The various retinal images from an opening door are quite different, and yet we perceive a rectangular door.

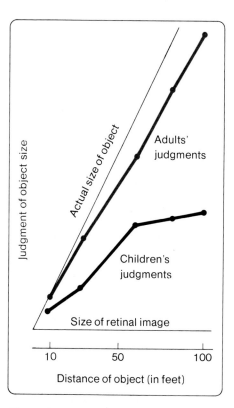

Fig. 5-3 Size perception and age
Adults and eight-year-old children viewed objects at distances ranging from 10 to 100 feet. The physical sizes of the objects were adjusted at the various distances so that the image projected on the retina was always the same size. The horizontal line indicates the size of the retinal image (which is constant for all distances), and the diagonal line indicates the size of the physical object (which increases with distance). Note that adults make fairly accurate size judgments no matter how distant the object. The judgments of children, however, appear to be increasingly influenced by the size of the retinal image as the object is placed farther away. (Data from Zeigler and Leibowitz, 1957)

distance of 10 feet, both children and adults show close to perfect size constancy—their judgment of size agrees with the physical size of the object. At increasing distances, the children show increasingly less size constancy (their size estimates are closely related to the size of the retinal image), while the adults' judgments remain quite accurate. These experimental results are consistent with observed actions of young children. A three-year-old watching cars from a lookout point high above a roadway may see the cars as miniatures and even beg to have them as toys.

The effect of limited experience on the development of size constancy is further illustrated by an incident concerning a Pygmy who was taken for the first time from his home in the forest (where distance viewing is naturally obstructed by trees and foliage) into open country. When he spotted a herd of buffalo grazing several miles away, he thought they were "insects." He refused to believe that they were buffalo and actually larger in size than the forest buffalo with which he was familiar. As he approached the animals, he became alarmed, because they appeared to be growing in size; he suspected that he was the victim of some sort of magic. Later, when he saw a boat with several men in it sailing some distance from the shore, he perceived it as a scrap of wood floating on the water. Just as a small child's limited experience causes errors in perceptions, the Pygmy's inexperience with distance viewing created similar misperceptions (Turnbull, 1961).

Location Constancy

Despite the fact that a myriad of changing impressions strike the retina as we move about, we perceive objects in a setting that remains essentially fixed—*location constancy*. We take location constancy for granted, but unusual conditions show that it, too, depends on past experience.

Experiments that use special glasses to rearrange the visual environment demonstrate the role of learning in location constancy. In a classic study conducted more than 75 years ago, Stratton fitted himself with lenses that not only inverted the visual field, so that he saw the world upside down, but also reversed it, so that objects perceived on the left were actually on the right, and vice versa. Stratton reports that at first the world seemed to lose its stability:

> When I moved my head or body so that my sight swept over the scene, the movement was not felt to be solely in the observer, as in normal vision, but was referred both to the observer and to objects beyond . . . I did not feel as if I were visually ranging over a set of motionless objects, but the whole field of things swept and swung before my eyes. (Stratton, 1897, p. 342)

After a few days he began to regain some location constancy, and the swirling sensation decreased. Another sign of restored location constancy was that he was again able to hear a fire crackle in the fireplace where he saw it, a harmony of location that at first he had lost, because only his eyes—and not his ears—were perceiving in reverse. Although the distortion provided by the lenses made even the simplest task difficult, Stratton adjusted as the experiment progressed. He bumped into objects less frequently and was able to perform such tasks as washing and eating, which initially had been very difficult. When he finally removed the glasses, he again needed time to adjust before he regained his old visual-motor habits. Since then, similar experiments have been conducted with comparable results. Human subjects show a remarkable ability to regain location constancy in a visually rearranged world (Welch, 1978).

132

Adjusting to a Visually Distorted World

How do people adjust when wearing distorting lenses? Do they learn to see the world differently? Or do their visual perceptions remain unchanged while they learn to *respond* differently to them?

An experiment by Rock and Harris helps answer these questions. The subjects were asked to point under a table to one of five targets at the other end of the table (see Figure 5-4). During the first part of the experiment, the glass surface of the table was covered with a black cloth so that the sub-

jects could see the targets but not their hand beneath the glass. Even so, they were able to point to the targets accurately. These data provided a base line with which to compare later responses. During the next phase, the subjects wore prism goggles that displaced vision so that objects appeared to be four inches to the right of their actual location. The cloth was removed, and the subjects practiced pointing to the center target. At first the prisms caused them to miss the target, but they quickly became quite accurate. In

the third part of the experiment, the goggles were removed and the subjects were tested both with the adapted hand (the one they had used to practice pointing at the targets while wearing the goggles) and with the other hand. On tests with the adapted hand, the subjects showed a shift in pointing that was consistent with the extent of visual displacement provided by the goggles. With the other hand, however, they made little or no shift. It appears that adaptation to the visual distortion involved a change in the position sense of the adapted arm rather than a change in visual perception. If subjects had learned to see the target in a new location, we would have expected them to point to that place with either hand.

It is not clear to what extent these results can be generalized to apply to Stratton's experiments, which involved more radical visual distortion and in which the subject could move about more freely. Nevertheless, it seems likely that the adaptation that occurred as Stratton learned to coordinate his movements with the rearranged visual world was in part due to a change in the position sense of his limbs.

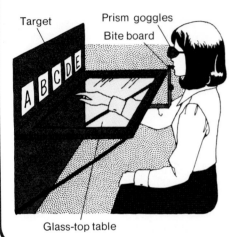

Fig. 5-4 Visual displacement
An apparatus for testing displaced vision. There are five targets, and the goggles are selected so that the visual field is displaced to the right by about four inches (the same as the distance between adjacent targets). A cover can be placed over the table top when desired, to prevent subjects from seeing where they are pointing. The bite board ensures that the head remains steady throughout the experiment. The experimenter instructs subjects to point to targets one at a time and then measures the discrepancy between where the finger is pointing and the target. (After Rock and Harris, 1967)

Organization and Perception

The perceptual constancies imply that the perceptual process "organizes" diverse arrays of stimuli into meaningful percepts. We can identify some principles of perception that help to explain how objects and events are organized and perceived.

Figure and Ground

Geometrical patterns are always perceived as figures against a background and thus appear to be like objects, with contours and boundaries. Organizing stimuli into *figure* and *ground* is basic to stimulus patterning. Patterns do not have to contain identifiable objects to be structured as figure and ground. Patterns of black and white and many wallpaper designs are perceived as figure-ground relationships, even though the figure and ground may reverse from one moment to the next. Note that in Figure 5-5 the part that you see as *figure* seems more solid and well defined and appears in front of the back-

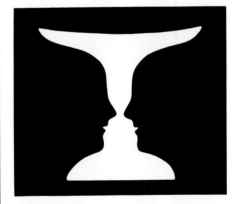

Fig. 5-5 Reversible figure and ground
The reversible goblet is a demonstration of a figure-ground reversal. Note that either the light portion (the goblet) or the dark portion (two profiles) can be perceived as a figure against a background.

Fig. 5-6 Artistic use of reversible figure and ground
Circle Limit IV (Heaven and Hell), a woodcut by M. C. Escher. The angels and devils alternate, but neither seems to dominate the other.

Fig. 5-7 *The Slave Market with Disappearing Bust of Voltaire* by Salvador Dali
In the center of this painting is a reversible figure. Two nuns standing in an archway reverse to form a bust of Voltaire.

Fig. 5-8 Ambiguous figure-ground effects
An ambiguous drawing that can be seen either as a pretty young woman or as an unattractive old woman.

ground, even though you know it is printed on the surface of the page. You seem to look through the spaces in and around the figure to a uniform background, whether the background is the light or the dark color. Figures 5-6, 5-7, and 5-8 show somewhat different kinds of reversible figure-ground effects.

Studies of what people blind from birth see when their sight is restored through surgery indicate that they first perceive figure-ground relationships. Adults who see for the first time have no difficulty seeing *something* as a figure on a background, although they are unable to identify objects by sight that are very familiar by touch.

We can perceive figure-ground relationships through senses other than vision. For example, we may hear the song of a bird against a background of outdoor noises or the melody played by a violin against the harmonies of the rest of the orchestra. Some of the factors that determine what is perceived as figure against ground will be considered later, in the discussion of selective attention.

Perceptual Grouping and Patterning

Even simple patterns of lines and dots fall into ordered relationships when we look at them. In the top part of Figure 5-9, we tend to see three *pairs* of lines, with an *extra* line at the right. But notice that we could have seen three pairs beginning at the right with an extra line at the left. The slight modification in the lines in the lower part of the figure causes us to do just that. This tendency to *structure* what we see is very compelling; what we see in figures seems to be forced on us by the patterns of stimulation. The properties of wholes affect the ways in which parts are perceived. This illustrates the idea of Gestalt psychology that the whole is different from the sum of its parts.

Visual Illusions

For the most part, our perceptions serve us very well. Most of the time, seeing is believing. However, our perceptions do fail at times, and such failures provide important clues about how the perceptual process works. Hence, in the study of perception, psychologists have turned to illusions, in which perceptions are misleading, in order to better understand the process.

Psychologists have studied geometrical illusions for many years but still do not totally agree on their explanations. Some illusions are based on relative size in contrast with surroundings (see Figure 5-10A). Others may be understood if we suppose the figures to be projected in the third dimension (see Figures 5-10B through E). If the horizontal lines in B were actually drawn on the surface of a solid double cone or if those in C were placed on a system of wires meeting at the horizon, they would have to be curved in order to be seen as parallel. But because we tend to view these figures as though they were perspective (three-dimensional) drawings, we see the parallel lines as curved. Similarly, the backgrounds in illusions D and E can be viewed as three-dimensional (either concave or convex), thereby distorting the square and circle superimposed on them.

Figure 5-10F, the Ponzo illusion, can be better understood if we look at the photograph in Figure 5-11. The illusion in Figure 5-10F can be thought of as a flat projection of three-dimensional space, with the vertical lines converging in the distance, as in the picture of the railroad tracks. We know from experience that the distant railroad ties are the same size as the near ones, even though the retinal image they give is much smaller. If real objects were lying between the tracks, the upper colored rectangle in the picture would be perceived as more distant. Because the brain tries to compensate for the expected shrinkage of images with distance (even though in this case there is no shrinkage for which to compensate), we see the upper rectangle as larger.

The fact that the Ponzo illusion becomes greater from childhood to adult-

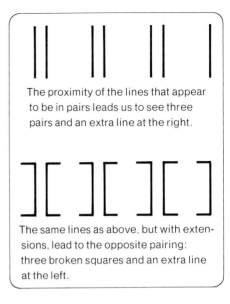

The proximity of the lines that appear to be in pairs leads us to see three pairs and an extra line at the right.

The same lines as above, but with extensions, lead to the opposite pairing: three broken squares and an extra line at the left.

Fig. 5-9 Patterning and perceptual grouping

Fig. 5-11 An illusion involving perspective
The two rectangles superimposed on the photograph are precisely the same size. However, because we know that the railroad ties are all the same length, the rectangle that is farther away is unconsciously enlarged. In fact, if the rectangles were real objects lying between the tracks, we would correctly judge the more distant one to be larger.

Fig. 5-10 Illusions
A. Illusion based on relative size. The center circles are the same size, but the one to the left looks larger. B,C,D,E. Illusions based on intersecting lines. The horizontal lines in B and C are parallel. The inscribed figures in D and E are perfectly symmetrical. F. Ponzo illusion. The two horizontal lines are the same length, but the upper one appears longer.

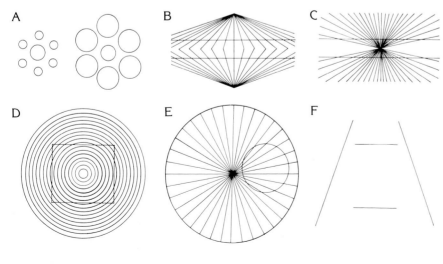

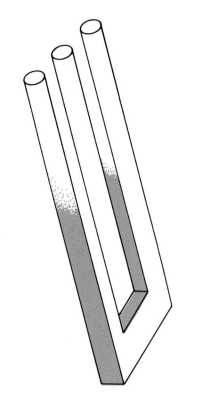

Fig. 5-12 An impossible figure
This drawing appears as a U at the bottom, but has three prongs at the top. The effect is a product of incompatible figure-ground relations. The object is seen in three dimensions, with the "ground" for the lower part forming the "figure" for the central prong at the top.

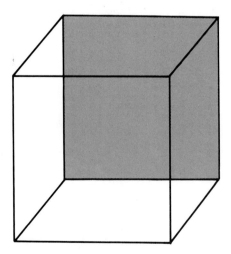

Fig. 5-13 Necker cube
An illusion devised in 1832 by the Swiss naturalist L. A. Necker. Note that the tinted surface can appear as either the front or the rear surface of a transparent cube.

hood suggests that the illusion depends on learning to use perspective cues in two-dimensional drawings (Parrish, Lundy, and Leibowitz, 1968). Some of the problems of seeing three-dimensional forms on a two-dimensional surface are illustrated by the "impossible figure" (see Figure 5-12). Incompatible information is given to the eye, and the brain cannot decide how to interpret it.

Perceptual Hypotheses

Figure 5-13 shows a classic example of a reversible figure, the Necker cube. As you study the figure, you will see that your perception of it changes. You will find that the tinted surface sometimes appears as the front of the figure and sometimes as the back. Once you have observed the cube change perspective, it will jump back and forth between the two perspectives without any effort on your part. In fact, you will probably find it impossible to maintain a steady fixation on only one aspect.

Hypothesis Testing

Reversible figures like the Necker cube indicate that our perceptions are not a static mirroring of visual stimuli. Perceiving can be thought of as a search for the best interpretation of sensory information, based on our knowledge of the characteristics of objects. From a cognitive viewpoint, a perceived object is a *hypothesis* suggested by the sensory data. The pattern of the Necker cube contains no clue as to which of two alternative hypotheses is correct, so the perceptual system entertains, or tests, first one and then the other hypothesis and never settles on an answer. The problem arises because the Necker cube is a three-dimensional object represented on a two-dimensional surface. If we were to see it in three-dimensional form, there would be many cues to tell us which hypothesis to choose (Gregory, 1970).

The notion of *hypothesis testing* emphasizes the active nature of perception. The perceptual system does not passively sense inputs, but searches for the percept that is most consistent with the sensory data. In most situations there is only one reasonable interpretation of the sensory data, and the search for the correct percept proceeds so quickly and automatically that we are unaware of it. Only under unusual conditions, as when we view ambiguous figures, does the hypothesis-testing nature of perception become apparent.

Context and Experience

The hypotheses tested and the percepts formed depend not only on the features of the object, but also on the *context* within which the object is viewed. Figure 5-14 illustrates the role of context in perception. The center of the figure can be seen either as the letter B or the number 13, depending on the context in which it appears. Similarly, *past experience* influences the perceptual hypotheses we form when we see something for the first time. Look again at the ambiguous drawing of the young woman–old woman in Figure 5-8. On first viewing, about 65 percent of the people report seeing an attractive young woman, and 35 percent see an old woman. But if we first show a group of subjects a set of unambiguous pictures all depicting young women and then show them the ambiguous picture, they almost always see it as a young woman. The reverse can be demonstrated by first showing subjects a set of pictures all showing old women. Textbooks on perception are filled with examples demonstrating that the same stimulus can give rise to different percepts, depending on the context in which it is observed and the past experience of the observer.

Analysis-by-Synthesis

A theory that views perception as an active, hypothesis-testing process—influenced by context and past experience—has been called *analysis-by-synthesis* (Neisser, 1976). According to this theory, the perceiver uses *features* of the object, its context, and past experiences to make a "best guess" about what is seen. The term "analysis-by-synthesis" implies that the perceiver "analyzes" the object into features and then uses these features to "synthesize" (or construct) a percept that best fits all of the information—the sensory input, the context, and past experience.

Analysis-by-synthesis can be compared with what paleontologists do when reconstructing a dinosaur skeleton. What is found at a dig is a mass of bone fragments, rocks, roots, and other debris. The scientists do not take all of the rubble and try to form it into an object. Rather, they pick and choose—selecting some fragments, discarding others, making new parts with plaster, and trying different combinations until they have a complete skeleton that represents their best guess based on the fragments found at the dig.

Analysis-by-synthesis is a useful theory for emphasizing the cognitive nature of perceptions. But it is not the full story. Some aspects of perception are innate; they are determined by the structure of the nervous system. The history of perceptual theory has involved a debate between extreme positions. One position views perception as an active cognitive process, while the other sees it as a mechanistic system fixed by the inherent structure of the nervous system. As more and more evidence accumulates, it becomes apparent that neither theory alone can explain the range of perceptual phenomena. Modern research is not concerned with defending or attacking either of these positions, but rather with building a theory that incorporates the best of both. We shall return to this point later, when we discuss the role of learning in perception.

Movement Perception

Events are organized in time as well as in space. The pattern of a melody is an organization in time, just as a geometrical figure is an organization in space. When you perceive movement, you sense action in space taking place over time.

Previously it was thought that the cues for the perception of movement were caused by the successive stimulation of rods and cones as the image of the object moved across the retinal surface. Most psychologists, however, now favor the theory of motion perception proposed by Gibson (1968). He points out that the eyes are constantly in motion, so that the visual field (whether fixed or in motion) is always stimulating different cells in the retina. In fact, as noted earlier, such eye movements are necessary to prevent the retinal receptors from adapting and causing the image to disappear (see p. 117).

According to Gibson, the cues for motion perception are present in the environment. We see an object in motion because as it moves it successively covers and uncovers portions of the immobile background. Also, we see

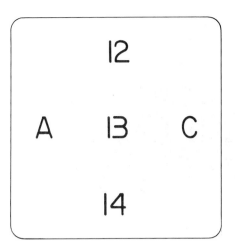

Fig. 5-14 **Effect of context on perception**
The figure in the center is ambiguous, and the way we see it depends on whether we look from left to right or from top to bottom.

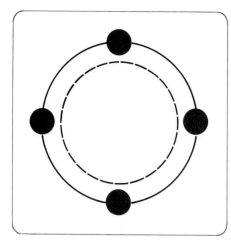

Fig. 5-15 The phi phenomenon
In a dark room, if one of these four lights blinks on and off, followed shortly by another, there is the illusion of a single light moving from the first position to the second. When all four lights flash on and off in rapid sequence, it appears that a single light is traveling in a circle, but the perceived size of the circle is smaller (indicated by the dashed lines) than would be the case if the lights were actually rotating.

objects in motion as changing in space; we see new portions while other portions disappear from view. Thus, it does not matter whether we track the moving object or look at the background. Both cases will produce a sensation of object movement. An interesting special case occurs when the entire visual field is in motion. Such a situation produces ambiguous cues that often lead to a false perception. Thus, it is difficult to tell whether your car is rolling backward or is stationary when a truck or bus beside you (which fills the window of your car) pulls forward.

Apparent Motion

It is also possible to perceive motion without a moving pattern of stimulation. We will now consider some examples of this kind of *apparent motion.*

AUTOKINETIC EFFECT If you stare for a few seconds at a single spot of light in a completely dark room, the light will appear to move about in an erratic manner—sometimes oscillating back and forth, sometimes swooping off in one direction or another. This apparent movement of a stationary light, known as the *autokinetic effect,* has been studied in many experiments, but there is still no certain explanation for it. It is clear, however, that the autokinetic effect occurs only in a visually impoverished environment, where there is no frame of reference that can be used to determine that the light spot is stationary. When the room is lightened so that walls and furniture provide a context and background, the effect disappears. Pilots flying at night are susceptible to the autokinetic phenomenon. To minimize the effect, they will line up a distant beacon with the edge of a windshield or some other frame of reference.

STROBOSCOPIC MOTION Another kind of apparent motion, familiar to us as the basis for films, is known as *stroboscopic motion.* This illusion of motion is created when separated stimuli, not in motion, are presented in succession. Each frame of a film is slightly different from the preceding one, but if the frames are presented rapidly, the pictures blend into smooth motion.

A simpler form of stroboscopic motion, known as the *phi phenomenon,* has been studied extensively in the laboratory. One arrangement is diagramed in Figure 5-15. The four lights can be turned on and off in any order. When one light blinks on and off, followed shortly by another, there is the illusion of a single light moving from the position of the first to the position of the second. The apparent movement is seen as occurring through the empty space between the two lights. When the four lights flash on and off in a clockwise sequence, you see a rotating circle, but the apparent diameter of the circle is less than that of a circle that would actually pass through the four lights. Whatever "attracts" the light to the position of the next light operates also to "attract" it toward the center of the circle, thereby making the circle smaller. The two tendencies result in the compromise that is seen as a circle too small to pass through the actual position of the lights. Even though the phi phenomenon is illusory, it causes us to perceive the same structure we would perceive in real motion. For example, in Figure 5-16A the perceived motion is through an arc, but in the plane of the paper; in Figure 5-16B, the motion is seen in the third dimension, the figure turning over as it moves across.

Real Motion

The examples of apparent motion demonstrate that the perception of motion does not depend *solely* on real physical movement of stimuli in the environment. We can see apparent motion when there is no real motion at all. The perception of real motion is even more complex; it depends on relations between objects within the visual field—and the interpretation we place on these relationships. Whenever there is movement, the perceptual system must decide what is moving and what is stationary with respect to some frame of reference.

Experiments have shown that when the only information we have about movement is visual, we tend to assume that large objects are stationary and smaller objects are moving. If a subject views a spot of light within a frame and the frame is moved while the spot remains stationary, the subject will perceive the spot as moving. Regardless of which is moved, the spot or the frame, the subject will report that it is the spot that is moving against the background. We experience this type of *induced movement* when we view the moon through a thin cover of moving clouds. In a clear sky, the moon appears to be stationary. When framed by the moving clouds, the moon will appear to race across the sky, while the clouds appear stationary.

When we are walking or running, the decision about what aspect of our surroundings is moving is less of a problem, because sensations from our limbs inform us of our motion along the ground. When we are moving in a car or plane, our principal source of information is visual. Under these conditions, we are more susceptible to illusions of induced movement. We are not always certain whether it is our car that is moving or the one next to us. Illusions of this kind are so frequent in air travel (particularly during night flights, when it is difficult to establish a frame of reference) that pilots learn to trust their instruments rather than their perceptions. Astronauts faced an even greater problem when attempting to land a spacecraft on the moon. In the unfamiliar conditions of space, the size, distance, and velocity of objects may be misjudged when evaluated on the basis of perceptual experiences on earth.

Depth Perception

Our study of perception would be incomplete without considering the problems of perceiving the third dimension—that is, distance and depth. The retina is essentially a two-dimensional surface. How, then, is it possible to perceive things as filling a space of three dimensions?

Binocular Cues to Depth

Many aspects of vision can be studied by considering phenomena that can be registered with one eye only. Individuals with vision in only one eye have most of the visual experiences of individuals using two eyes. They see colors, forms, and space relationships, including third-dimensional configurations. We might suppose that two eyes have evolved merely to provide a "spare" in case of injury, just as there are two kidneys although one is enough.

People with vision in both eyes, however, do have advantages over those with vision in one eye: their total visual field is larger, so that more can be seen at once, and they have the benefit of stereoscopic vision. In *stereoscopic vision*, the two eyes cooperate so that we experience depth and distance. A *stereoscope* is a device that demonstrates that the experience of depth and distance does indeed depend on the cooperation of the two eyes. Two normal photographs, each taken from a slightly different angle, are used in the stereoscope. The two photographs, presented one before each eye, combine to form a

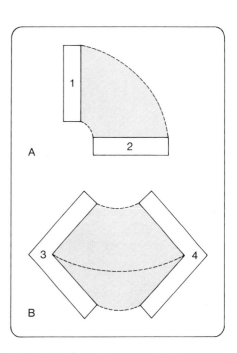

Fig. 5-16 Special cases of phi movement
If a light is flashed on and off behind opening 1 in a screen and a moment later behind opening 2, then it appears as though a single bar of light is moving in an arc between the two positions in the plane of the paper. If a light is flashed on and off behind opening 3 and an instant later behind opening 4, then the motion is seen in the third dimension, as if the figure were flipping over (like turning a page in a book) as it moves across.

"Excuse me for shouting—I thought you were farther away."

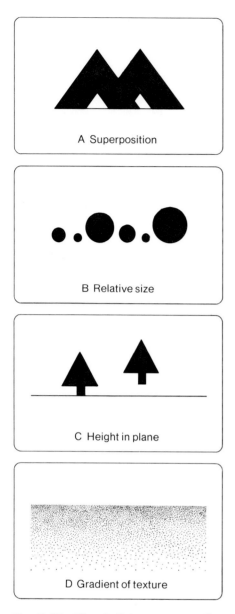

A Superposition

B Relative size

C Height in plane

D Gradient of texture

Fig. 5-17 Visual distance perception
Several types of cues used in the perception of distance are shown here.

Fig. 5-18 Deliberate misuse of depth cues
Engraving entitled *Satire on False Perspective* after William Hogarth (1754). At first glance, the picture appears sensible, but closer inspection indicates that the scene could not appear as depicted. Note the many ways in which the artist has misused depth cues to achieve unusual effects.

picture with depth very different from that of a single photograph. The depth appears real, as though the objects pictured were set up exactly on a stage in their true relations of depth and distance.

Stereoscopic experience differs from the experience of the third dimension in single, flat pictures because of *binocular disparity.* Since our eyes are separated in our head, the left eye does not get exactly the same view as the right eye; the stereoscopic effect results from the combination of these slightly different pictures into one view. You can easily demonstrate binocular disparity for yourself. With one eye closed, hold a pencil about a foot in front of you and line it up with some vertical edge on the opposite wall. Open that eye and close the other. The pencil will appear to have moved a considerable distance from its original alignment. If you line up the pencil with both eyes open and then close each eye alternately, you can determine which is your dominant eye; if the pencil shifts when you close the right eye, your right eye is dominant (which is usually the case with right-handed individuals).

The facts of stereoscopic vision are clear enough, but just how the process works is not so clear. Because of the way in which the nerve fibers from the eyes are separated in passing to the brain (see Figure 4-7), the combination cannot take place in the eyes. Information from the two eyes must somehow be combined in the brain, probably at the level of the visual cortex (Kaufman, 1979).

Monocular Cues to Depth

Although two eyes help us to perceive depth and distance, we are by no means restricted to binocular effects for depth and distance perception. Closing one eye causes the loss of some precision, but there is much left to go on. Artists

Fig. 5-19 Paradox of depth
Engraving by the Dutch artist M. C. Escher, *Waterfall* (1961). The artist's "false use" of depth cues makes the water appear to move uphill through a series of "level" channels.

are able to give depth to a picture because they can make use of the many *monocular cues* that tell us the distance of objects.

Figure 5-17 illustrates four types of cues that are used in depth perception. If one object appears to cut off the view of another, we usually perceive the first object as nearer (see Figure 5-17A). If there is an array of like objects of different sizes, the smaller ones are perceived as being in the distance. Even a series of scattered circles of different sizes may be viewed as spheres of the same size at varying distances (see Figure 5-17B). Another cue of perspective is height in the horizontal plane. As we look along a flat plane, objects farther away appear to be higher, so that we can create the impression of depth for objects of the same size by placing them at different heights (see Figure 5-17C). Even for irregular surfaces, such as a rocky desert or the waving surface of the ocean, there is a gradient of texture with distance, so that the "grain" becomes finer as distance becomes greater (see Figure 5-17D).

Just as artists can make a picture appear to have depth, so also can they distort distance cues. The engraving in Figure 5-18 is such an example; the various cues for depth perception have been deliberately misused to produce an absurd figure. Another example is Figure 5-19, which shows a waterfall where the water at the top is supplied from the bottom by a series of "level" channels.

Visual Coding and Pattern Recognition

Experiments using microelectrodes to record neural activity in the visual cortex have helped explain the complexities of perception. In the typical

Pattern

If the nervous system has *feature detectors*, then these detectors can be used for pattern recognition. How this might be done is illustrated by a model for recognizing hand-printed letters of the alphabet (Selfridge and Neisser, 1960). The model has been implemented on a computer and used with success in recognizing letters printed by different people and under different conditions. Although we would not claim that the model simulates the actual processes that a human uses in recognizing letters, it suggests how the perceptual system might work.

Recognizing hand-printed letters is not a trivial task when one considers the tremendous variations in width, height, slant, and so forth that may occur from one printing to the next (see Figure 5-20). The model assumes that letters can be described in terms of a *feature list.* For example, the letter H consists of two lines that are more vertical than horizontal and one line that is more horizontal than vertical; it also has a concavity (open space) at the top and at the bottom. These features taken together specify the letter H, but any of these features alone would not be enough to specify it. For example, A also has two more or less vertical lines,

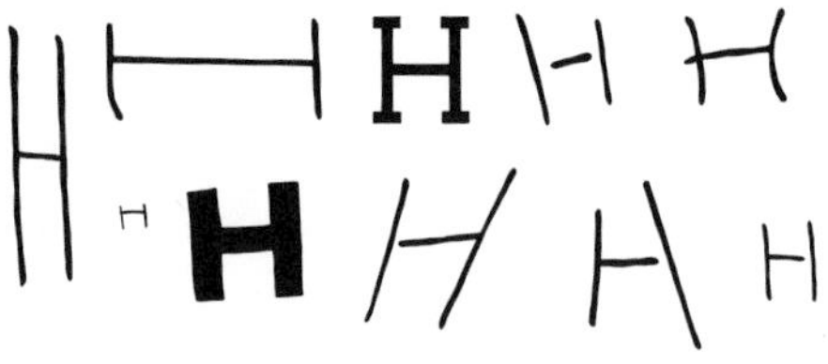

Fig. 5-20 Pattern recognition
An array of stimuli that are dissimilar in many respects but should all be classified as the letter H. The recognition of hand-printed letters is a problem that has received a great deal of attention from psychologists and computer scientists, both for practical and theoretical reasons.

one horizontal line, and a concavity at the bottom; but it does not have a concavity at the top, and that feature distinguishes it from H.

A feature list is stored in the computer's memory for each letter in the alphabet. When a test letter is presented, its features are extracted and compared with each of the feature lists in memory until a match occurs. To illustrate the process, we will consider a highly simplified program to distinguish among the letters A, H, V, and Y. With such a small set of letters, the pattern recognition process can rely on

experiment, a microelectrode is implanted in the visual cortex of a cat or a monkey. The microelectrode is extremely small and is placed in such a way that recordings can be obtained from a single nerve cell while the animal's eyes are being stimulated by visual forms projected on a screen (see Figure 5-22). Unlike neurons in the retina and optic nerve, most cells in the visual cortex do not respond when the eye is stimulated by large or diffuse spots of light. Instead, these cortical cells are highly specific in terms of the stimuli to which they respond.

Feature Detectors

Hubel and Wiesel (1968), pioneers in microelectrode studies of the brain, identified two types of neurons in the visual cortex—called *simple* and *complex cells.* Simple cells become active when the eye is exposed to a line stimulus, like a bar of light or a straight edge (a straight line boundary between light and dark regions). Whether or not a particular simple cell responds depends on the

Recognition Models

the presence or absence of just three features: a concavity at the top of the letter, a cross bar, and a vertical line. When a test letter is presented, the computer first asks: "Is there a concavity at the top?" If the answer is "no," then the test letter is classified as an A. If "yes," the computer would next ask: "Is there a cross bar?" If "yes," the letter is H. If "no," the next question would be "Is there a vertical line?" If "yes," the letter is Y; if "no," the letter is V. The scheme for checking features is illustrated in Figure 5-21. It is called a *sorting tree,* for as we move through the tree we sort inputs into appropriate output categories.

This program is extremely simple. Far more complex ones are now in operation that are accurate in discriminating both hand-printed and handwritten letters. Although most of these programs are still in an experimental stage, several have reached technological maturity. The Post Office, for example, has installed several Zip Code–readers that can discriminate hand-printed or typed digits. What is important for our purposes is to show how a set of feature detectors in conjunction with a sorting tree can recognize complex patterns. The human perceptual

Fig. 5-21 Sorting tree
A pattern recognition program that employs three test features to categorize the hand-printed letters A, H, V, and Y. The tests are applied in order, with each outcome determining the next step. Each diamond indicates a decision point in the process that requires a "yes" or "no" answer.

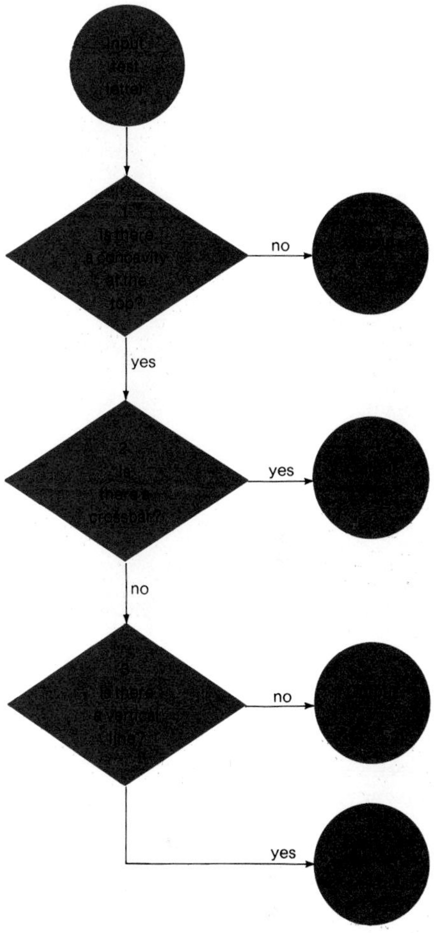

system may operate in a similar manner. Stored in your memory would be a feature list for "Aunt Sara"; it might include the width of her mouth, the slant of her nose, the color of her eyes, and so forth. When you encounter someone, the feature detectors are activated, and if the extracted features match the list in your memory associated with Aunt Sara, then you know who it is.

How we recognize complex patterns, a problem many psychologists are now studying, is just beginning to be understood. In wrestling with the problem, the psychologist's approach ranges from a concern with neurophysiological data to testing complex models by simulating them on a computer. It is just such diversity that gives promise of significant advances in the field.

orientations of the bar of light and its location in the animal's visual field. A bar shown vertically on the screen may activate a given cortical cell, whereas the same cell will fail to respond (but others will respond) if the bar is displaced to one side or moved appreciably out of the vertical. Apparently, some neurons respond only to a particular stimulus with specific orientation and location. A complex cell also responds to a line segment with a particular orientation (for example, vertical), but it responds no matter where in an area of the visual field the line segment appears. Moreover, complex cells respond with sustained firing as the line segment moves across the visual field, so long as it maintains its proper orientation.

From what is now known, it appears that a complex cell receives inputs from a large number of simple cells, all with the same field orientation. Thus, a complex cell that responds to a vertical bar receives nerve fibers from those simple cells that respond to vertical bars. Each simple cell is activated only if the bar is at a particular location in the receptive field; the complex cell, on the other hand, is activated by any vertical bar, no matter where it appears.

Fig. 5-22 Recording cortical activity
A partially anaesthetized monkey is placed in a device that holds its head in a fixed position. A moving bar of light, which varies in direction and speed, is projected onto the screen. A microelectrode implanted in the visual cortex of the monkey monitors activity from a single neuron, and this activity is amplified and displayed on an oscilloscope.

Hierarchical Feature Analyzers

This converging of a set of simple cells on one complex cell can be illustrated at a still higher level in the nervous system. Hubel and Wiesel recorded neural activity in the visual cortex by cells they named *hypercomplex cells.* These cells are active only if the stimulus line is in a particular orientation and of a specific length and width. The hypercomplex cell appears to be connected to an array of complex cells; the excitatory and inhibitory activities of each of the complex cells are such that the hypercomplex cell is activated only if the line segment is of a specific length.

Thus, we see that a stimulus can be coded in a hierarchical manner, with higher centers using the information coded at lower centers. When a straight line of a particular length is moved across the visual field, it will activate a succession of simple cells, each responding to the particular orientation and location of the line. These simple cells then activate a smaller set of complex cells that preserve the orientation information and add information about the movement of the line. Finally, the complex cells converge on a hypercomplex cell that specifies the exact length of the line and preserves information about its orientation and motion.

At present, we do not know how far a hierarchical analysis of this sort can be carried, but it is known that there are still other cells in the visual cortex that respond to specific patterns, like curves and angles. And there is evidence that in monkeys there are some cells so finely tuned that they respond only to particular shapes of objects. Since everything we see is reducible to a series of minute lines at angles to each other, it may well be that these various types of cells (which act to detect particular features of a visual display) are the building blocks out of which complex perceptions are formed.

Role of Learning in Perception

The phenomena of perceptual organization, movement and depth perception, and the various perceptual constancies are easily and convincingly demonstrated, so that by now there is general agreement over what is perceived. Disagreements remain, however, over how to *explain* what happens. One of the traditional questions about visual perception has been whether our abilities to perceive the spatial aspects of the environment are learned or innate—the familiar nature-nurture problem. Its investigation with relation to perception goes back to the philosophers of the seventeenth and eighteenth centuries.

Nativist and Empiricist Viewpoints

One group, the *nativists* (including Descartes and Kant), argued that we are born with the ability to perceive the way we do. In contrast, the *empiricists* (including Berkeley and Locke) maintained that we learn our ways of perceiving through experience with objects in the world about us. As noted earlier in this chapter, contemporary psychologists believe that a fruitful integration of these two viewpoints is possible. No one today really doubts that practice and experience affect perception. The question is whether we are born with some ability to perceive objects and space in our environment or whether these abilities are entirely learned. There are several areas of research that yield information on the role of learning in perception.

Effects of Restored Vision

As far back as the seventeenth century, Locke quoted a letter he received from a colleague, in which the problem was posed:

> Suppose a man *born* blind, and now adult, taught by his *touch* to distinguish between a cube and a sphere of the same metal, and nighly of the same bigness, so as to tell, when he felt one and the other, which is the cube, which the sphere. Suppose that the cube and the sphere placed on a table, and the blind man be made to see . . . [could he] now distinguish and tell which is the globe, which the cube? (Locke, 1690)

Locke, supporting the empiricist viewpoint, concluded that he could not.

A partial answer to this question is provided by studies of individuals who were blind from birth with cataracts on both eyes and whose vision was restored by surgery when they were adults (Senden, 1960). When the eye bandages were removed for the first time, the patients were confused by the bewildering array of visual stimuli. They were, however, able to distinguish figure from ground (apparently perceiving figure-ground relationships in much the same way as normally sighted people do), to fixate figures, scan them, and to follow moving figures with their eyes. These abilities then appear to be innate. Patients could not identify by sight alone objects familiar by touch—such as faces, knives, and keys. They could not distinguish a triangle from a square without counting the number of corners or tracing the outline with a finger. They also could not tell which of two uneven sticks was longer without feeling them, although they might report that the two sticks looked somehow different. It took several weeks of training for such patients to learn to identify simple objects by sight; and even after identification had been learned in a specific situation, the patients showed little evidence of generalization of perceptual constancy. A white triangle might not be recognized when viewed with colored light or when turned upside down. The poor performance cannot be attributed to difficulty in discriminating colors; the restored-vision patients could distinguish between colors (although they did not at first know which name to attach to which color) long before they could distinguish between shapes.

These studies of previously blind adults suggest that our perceptions develop gradually from primitive visual experiences in which figure-ground relationships and color predominate, becoming more accurate and more detailed with learning. They cannot, however, be taken as conclusive evidence of the innate visual ability of the infant. We do not know what deteriorative changes may have occurred over the years the adult subjects were blind, nor do we know what compensating skills these adults may have developed to overcome their handicap.

Effects of Visual Deprivation

In an attempt to provide a more controlled situation, similar to restored vision in humans, animals have been raised in various degrees of darkness and then tested for visual ability. Investigators who reared infant chimpanzees in total darkness until they were 16 months old found that the animals had serious perceptual deficiencies when they were tested upon first exposure to light. But it was discovered later that these chimpanzees had suffered neuronal deterioration in various parts of the visual system. Apparently a certain amount of light stimulation is necessary for normal neural development of the visual system. Without any light stimulation, nerve cells in the retina and the visual cortex begin to atrophy. This fact is interesting in itself, but it does not tell us much about the role of learning in perceptual development.

Later studies made use of translucent goggles, so that the animals received light stimulation, but diffuse and unpatterned. Studies with monkeys, chimpanzees, and kittens wearing translucent goggles from birth to anywhere from one to three months of age show that although some simple perceptual abilities were unimpaired, more complex visual activity was seriously affected. The visually deprived animals did almost as well as normal animals in distinguishing differences in color, brightness, and size. But they could not follow a moving object with their eyes, discriminate forms (a circle from a square), or perceive depth (Riesen, 1965).

These findings are supported by research recording single-cell activity in the visual cortex. In one experiment, kittens were raised in an environment where they were exposed only to bright dots; they were never shown straight lines, contours, or edges. When these animals were subsequently tested using a procedure like the one shown in Figure 5-22, their visual cortex contained neurons of an abnormal type that responded well to small spots of light and showed little of the customary preference for lines and edges. Even at the level of individual cells in the visual cortex, the effects of prior experience are evident (Blakemore, 1974; Barlow, 1975). Similar studies have been done with kittens raised in a visual environment consisting solely of vertical or horizontal stripes. These animals behave as though they are blind to diagonal lines, and no neurons in their visual cortex appear to be tuned to this orientation (Mitchell, 1977).

The same, it seems, may hold true for humans. Euro-Canadians raised in a "carpentered" environment, with its vertical and horizontal contours (straight sidewalks and rectangular buildings), were tested against Cree Indians from a more diverse environment. The Cree life style, for example, alternates between a summer cook tent and a winter lodge—both structures have line contours of virtually all orientations (see Figure 5-23). Visual acuity was tested by presenting parallel lines in various orientations; the subject had to judge whether the lines were fused or separated. The Euro-Canadians exhibited a higher acuity for vertical and horizontal orientations than for diagonal orientations. The Crees, however, showed no differences; they were equally good at all orientations. There is no evidence to suggest genetically determined differences in the visual system of the two groups. Rather, the acuity of the Crees may be the result of their visual experience (Annis and Frost, 1973).

Perception in Infants

If human infants could tell us what their world looks like, many of our questions concerning the development of perception might be answered. Since they cannot, experimenters have had to stretch their ingenuity to try to measure the visual abilities of infants.

Several investigators have studied the infant's perception of height (a special case of depth perception), using the "visual cliff" shown in Figure 5-24. They have tested human and various animal infants in attempts to determine whether the ability to perceive and avoid a brink is innate or must be learned by the experience of falling off and getting hurt. Most parents, mindful of the caution they exercise to keep their offspring from falling out of the crib or down the stairs, would assume that the ability to appreciate height is something the child must learn. But observation of human infants' susceptibility to

Fig. 5-23 An environment of diagonal lines
A Cree Indian summer cook tent, or *meechwop*, at Wemindji, a small Indian village on the east coast of James Bay, Quebec. These structures, along with the Cree winter lodges, or *matoocan*, have contours in virtually all orientations.

146

such accidents does not tell us whether they are unable to discriminate depth or can indeed respond to depth cues but lack the motor control to keep from falling.

Gibson and Walk (1960) tested the response of infants, ranging in age from 6 to 14 months, when placed on the center board of the visual cliff. The mother called to the child from the cliff side and from the shallow side successively. Almost all the infants crawled off onto the shallow side but refused to crawl onto the deep side. Their dependence on vision was demonstrated by the fact that they frequently peered through the glass on the deep side and then backed away. Some of the infants patted the glass with their hands but still remained unassured that it was solid and refused to cross.

Since the infants could not be tested until they were old enough to crawl, the experiment does not prove that depth perception is present at birth. The results of studies with other organisms, however, indicate that depth perception is present at least as soon as the animal is able to move about. Chickens tested when less than 24 hours old never made a mistake by stepping off onto the deep side. Goats and lambs placed on the center board as soon as they could stand (some only one day old) always chose the shallow side. When placed on the deep side, such animals characteristically froze in a state of immobility.

Experiments designed to isolate the specific visual depth cues to which the organism responds on the visual cliff have yielded contradictory results; it seems, however, that monocular cues are sufficient. Infants who wore eye patches on one eye discriminated as well as those with binocular vision (Walk, 1968).

Attention and Perception

Our perceptions are selective. We do not react equally to all the stimuli impinging upon us; instead, we focus on a few. This perceptual focusing is called *attention.* Through attentive processes, we keep selected stimuli in focus and resist distracting stimuli.

As you sit reading, stop for a moment, close your eyes, and attend to the various stimuli affecting you. Notice, for example, the tightness of your left shoe, the pressure of clothing on your shoulders, the sounds coming from outside the room. We are constantly bombarded by stimuli to which we do not attend. In fact, our brains would be hopelessly overloaded if we had to attend to every stimulus present in our environment. Somehow, our brains select those stimuli that are pertinent and ignore the others, until a change in a particular stimulus makes it important for us to notice it.

Selective Attention

There is evidence, however, that even though we are not actively attending to certain stimuli, they still register in some form in our perceptual system—although we may not recognize them at the time. Consider what takes place during a cocktail party. Out of the complex mixture of sounds generated by the many voices taken together, you are able to listen to one voice. Although you may think you are not attending to the other voices, let someone in the far corner of the room mention your name and you are immediately aware of it.

Fig. 5-24 The "visual cliff"
Infants and young animals show an ability to perceive depth as soon as they can move about. The visual cliff consists of two surfaces, both displaying the same pattern, which are covered by a sheet of thick glass. One surface is directly under the glass; the other is dropped several feet. When placed on the center board (the area between the deep and the shallow sides), the infant refuses to cross to the deep side but will readily move off the board onto the shallow side. (After Gibson and Walk, 1960)

A young goat cautiously approaching the deep side of a visual cliff

Apparently the nervous system monitors the other voices for relevant stimuli without your being aware of such activity.

The cocktail party situation raises two interesting questions: (1) How are we able to focus attention on one conversation out of the many that surround us? (2) How much do we register of the conversations to which we are not attending?

Some of the cues that enable us to concentrate on one voice in a babel of many are the directions of sound, lip movements of the speaker, and the particular voice characteristics of the speaker (whether the voice is male or female, its speed, and its intonation). Even if all these cues are eliminated (by recording two messages spoken by the same speaker and playing them simultaneously), it is still possible to distinguish the messages. The task is a difficult one requiring intense concentration, but most subjects can separate the two messages, apparently by relying on the grammatical and semantic content of the spoken material for cues. In the absence of appropriate grammatical cues, however, the task of separating two simultaneous messages by the same speaker becomes impossible.

Information about how much we register from conversations to which we are not attending is provided by an experimental situation similar to the cocktail party. Two different spoken messages are presented to the subject by means of earphones, one to the right ear and the other to the left. The subject has no difficulty in listening to either message at will; he or she can reject the unwanted one or switch attention back and forth from one speech to the other. If asked to repeat aloud the speech presented to one ear, the subject can do it fairly well even though the message is continuous. The subject's words are slightly delayed behind those of the message being repeated, and the voice tends to have a monotonous noninflective quality. At the end of the passage, the subject may have little idea of what it was all about, particularly if the material is difficult. What about the message to which the subject was not attending? How much information is assimilated via the unattended ear? The answer depends on a number of factors, including the difficulty of the two messages. If the attended message is a familiar nursery rhyme, the subject will recall a fair amount of the message to the unattended ear. With more difficult material, however, the subject usually can recall nothing of the verbal content of the unattended message. The subject is aware of certain general characteristics: whether the message was speech rather than a pure tone, whether the voice was male or female, and whether his or her own name was mentioned in the message.

If the subject is interrupted while repeating the message to the attending ear and asked quickly what was just presented to the other ear, there does appear to be some temporary memory for the message not attended to. This is similar to the situation in which someone to whom you are not listening asks you a question; your immediate response is "What did you say?"—but before the question is repeated, you suddenly realize what was asked.

Determiners of Stimulus Selection

Studies of this kind have led to the conclusion that the nervous system must have some kind of register where incoming sensory information is temporarily stored in a rather crude and unanalyzed form. Of all the stimuli that bombard our senses, only those that our higher mental processes tell us are relevant at the moment will be selected for attention. Some sort of attention mechanism selects for further processing those sensory inputs that seem most important or pertinent. Certain classes of sensory inputs, such as the sound of one's name, can be expected to have a permanently high level of pertinence, but most will fluctuate, depending on ongoing events (Norman, 1976).

What factors determine which of many competing stimuli will be selected for attention? The physical characteristics of the stimulus are important, as are our own internal needs, expectancies, and past experience. Advertisers are concerned with discovering these factors, so that they can direct attention to their products. Some physical properties of the stimulus that are important in gaining attention are *intensity, size, contrast,* and *movement.*

Certain internal variables, such as motives and expectations, are also important in determining which stimulus attracts attention. The advertiser counts on an appeal to the male sex drives when pictures of scantily clad females are used to advertise anything from carpets to automobile tires. In those countries where hunger is a more generally unsatisfied drive than sex, pictures of food prove to be powerful attention-getters.

Because of habitual or momentary interests, individuals vary in their responses to the same stimuli. The naturalist will hear sounds in the woods that the ordinary picnicker would miss. A mother will hear her baby's cry above the conversation in a room full of people. These two illustrations represent abiding interests. Sometimes momentary interest controls attention. When you leaf through a book looking for a particular diagram, only pages with illustrations cause you to hesitate; others you ignore. Emotional states, especially moods, may also affect our attention. When we are in a hostile mood, we notice personal comments that we might not pay attention to when we are in a more friendly mood.

Physiological Correlates of Attention

When a stimulus attracts our attention, we usually perform certain body movements that enhance reception. If it is a visual stimulus, we turn our head in the proper direction—our eyes turn so that the image falls on the fovea, our pupils dilate momentarily to allow more light to enter the eye, and the lens muscles work to bring the image clearly into focus. If the stimulus is a faint auditory signal, we may cup our hands behind our ears or turn one ear in the direction of the sound, keeping the rest of our body very still so as to enhance reception. These body movements are accompanied by certain physiological changes. The physiological reactions that occur in response to stimulus changes in the environment form such a consistent pattern that they have been called the *orienting reflex,* and they have been studied extensively by psychologists.

The orienting reflex occurs in both humans and animals in response to even minimal changes in the stimulus environment. The physiological accompaniments of attention (in addition to the body movements mentioned above) include dilation of the blood vessels in the head, constriction of the peripheral blood vessels, certain changes in the gross electrical responses of the brain (EEG), and changes in muscle tone, heart rate, and respiration. These responses serve two functions: (1) they facilitate the reception of stimulation, and (2) they prepare the organism for a quick response, in case action is needed. We can see why such a reflex is valuable for self-preservation.

The facilitating effect of the orienting reflex on sensory reception can be demonstrated in the laboratory. The arousal of the reflex by a loud tone will increase visual sensitivity, making it possible for the subject to see a light that was too faint to be detected before the arousal. The orienting reflex habituates over time, however. With repeated presentation of the sound, the reflex gradually diminishes; the visual threshold returns to its original level, and the same light intensity no longer evokes a response. Any change in the tone, or the introduction of a new stimulus, will reactivate the orienting reflex to its original strength (Sokolov, 1976).

Extrasensory Perception

If there are so many influences on perception other than those coming from the presented stimuli, are there perhaps perceptions that require no sense organ stimulation whatsoever? The answer to this question is the source of a continuing controversy within psychology over the status of *extrasensory perception* (ESP). Although some psychologists believe that the evidence for the existence of certain forms of ESP is now incontrovertible, most remain unconvinced.

The phenomena under discussion (sometimes called *parapsychological phenomena*) are of two main kinds:

1 Extrasensory perception (ESP).
   a Telepathy, or thought transference from one person to another.
   b Clairvoyance, or the perception of objects or events not influencing the senses (such as stating the number and suit of a playing card that is in a sealed envelope).
   c Precognition, or the perception of a future event.
2 Psychokinesis (PK), or mentally manipulating objects without touching them (for example, "willing" that a particular number come up in the throw of dice).

ESP Experiments

Experimenters investigating these phenomena work in accordance with the usual rules of science and generally disavow any connection between their work and spiritualism, supernaturalism, and other occult doctrines. Yet the phenomena with which they deal are so extraordinary and so similar to superstitious beliefs that many scientists reject even the legitimacy of their inquiries. Such a priori judgments are out of place in science; the real question is whether the empirical evidence is acceptable by ordinary scientific standards. Many psychologists who are not convinced are nevertheless ready to accept evidence that they find satisfactory. For example, the possibility of some sort of influence from one brain to another, other than by way of the sense organs, would not be inconceivable within the present framework of science. Some of the other phenomena, such as precognition, are more difficult to find believable—but if the experiments were reproducible, previous beliefs would have to yield to the facts.

Much of the early research on ESP was done by Rhine (1942), using a card "guessing" procedure. The typical ESP pack consists of 25 cards with five different symbols—so that by guessing alone, one should average five hits per pack (see Figure 5-25). Even very successful subjects seldom score as many as seven hits on a regular basis, but they may score above five often enough to meet accepted standards for statistical significance. In the typical experiment,

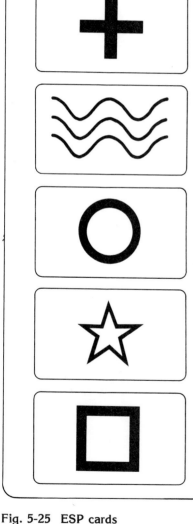

Fig. 5-25 ESP cards
Each card in the ESP pack bears one of the five symbols (cross, wave, circle, star, rectangle).

the cards are shuffled and placed out of the subject's view; the subject then identifies the cards one at a time. If the experimenter, or "sender," looks at each card before the subject responds, the study is concerned with telepathy. If the experimenter does not look at the card (it is face down on the pack), then the study is concerned with clairvoyance.

The card-guessing procedure may seem artificial and not conducive to good psychic performance, but it has several advantages: (1) the experiment can be carefully controlled, so that there is no possibility of cheating; (2) the experiment can be repeated with the same subject at different times, or with different groups of subjects; and (3) the statistical significance of an experimental outcome (number of correct matches) can be evaluated using standard statistical techniques.

The kind of evidence used in support of the nonchance nature of the findings can be illustrated by the successive runs of one "sensitive" subject, Mrs. Gloria Stewart, who was studied in England over a long period (see Table 5-1). If the evidence is viewed in the same spirit as that from any other experiment, it would be clear that Mrs. Stewart responded above chance on the telepathy trials but not on the clairvoyance ones. These results meet certain objections about card arrangements sometimes voiced against such experiments; her chance performance on the clairvoyance trials shows that above-chance scores are not an inevitable result possibly related to the method of shuffling the cards.

TABLE 5-1
Results of telepathy and clairvoyance trials with one subject

YEAR OF SUCCESSIVE BLOCKS OF 200 TRIALS	HITS PER 200 TRIALS (EXPECTED = 40)	
	TELEPATHY TRIALS	CLAIRVOYANCE TRIALS
1945	65 58 62 58 60	51 42 29 47 38
1947	54 55 65	35 36 31
1948	39 56	38 43
1949	49 51 33	40 37 42
Total hits Expected hits Difference Hits per 25 trials	707 520 +187 6.8	509 520 −11 4.9

Source: Soal and Bateman (1954)

Issues in Evaluating ESP

In the following discussion, we will expand on the objections that psychologists have to the ESP and PK experiments and to *psi*, the special ability attributed to the "sensitive" subject.

1   *General skepticism about extraordinary phenomena.* Throughout history, there have always been reports of strange happenings, ghosts, poltergeists (noisy spirits who engage in throwing things about), and dreams foretelling the future. The continuing appearance of these stories does not make them true. The much publicized Israeli "psychic" Uri Geller is an example. Geller claims that he is able to read people's minds, cause metal objects to "magically" bend, and perform a number of other supernatural feats. Some scientists who have observed Geller's performances are convinced of his psychic powers. On several occasions, however, Geller has been caught—even filmed—in acts of deception, and his tricks exposed (Randi, 1978). Despite this evidence, some believers continue to maintain that his powers are genuine.

This case is not unique. Almost every year, strong claims are made for the powers of some newly discovered psychic. Careful examination reveals that the individual is using trickery and that the psychic feats can be duplicated by a skilled magician. Yet some researchers in parapsychology are so messianic about their field that they either do not see through the obvious trickery or they conclude that, while the individuals may occasionally cheat, they still have paranormal powers. When those most convinced about ESP are also convinced about al-

ready disproven phenomena, their testimony carries less weight than if they were more critical.

2   *Failure of improved methods to increase the yield.* In most scientific fields, the assay from the ore becomes richer as the experimental methods become more refined. But the reverse trend is found in ESP experiments; it is almost a truism in research in the fields of telepathy and clairvoyance that the poorer the conditions, the better the results. In the early days of Rhine's experiments at Duke University, subjects who had high ESP scores were rather common. As the experiments became better controlled, however, the number of high-scoring subjects diminished. A similar decrease in significant results with improved experimental control has been found in PK studies (Hyman, 1977).

3   *Lack of consistency in the phenomena.* Sensitive subjects in Rhine's experiments appear to be equally successful at clairvoyance and telepathy, but subjects in a British laboratory appear to be good at telepathy and not at clairvoyance. Other peculiarities emerge. In a famous series of experiments in England, one subject gave no evidence of either telepathy or clairvoyance when scored in the usual way against the target card. Instead, he was shown to be successful in *precognition telepathy*—that is, in guessing what was going to be on the experimenter's mind on the next trial (Soal and Bateman, 1954). Why, the skeptic asks, does the direct telepathy fail with this subject in favor of something far more mysterious than the telepathic success of Mrs. Stewart?

Because *psi* ability appears to lack consistency, explanations of it can be produced with the greatest of freedom. It need not be affected in any ordinary way by space or time, so that success over great distances is accepted as a sign of its extraordinary power rather than something to cause a search for artifacts. Similarly, the precognition experiments are merely evidence to the ESP proponents that it is as easy to read what is *about* to be on someone else's mind as what is on it now. The PK effects, which require the subject to produce certain outcomes in dice rolling by mental effort ("mind over matter"), are said to occur without any transfer of physical energy—thus presumably violating the conservation of energy. But in any experimental work, *some* aspects of time and space have to be respected. Unless some restraint is shown, one might invent any number of hypotheses: the subject was perceiving the cards in reverse order, in a place-skipping order, and so on. With an unlimited number of hypotheses no test is possible (Diaconis, 1978).

Believers in *psi* are impatient with this kind of criticism. They say that more is asked of them than of other experimenters. And in fact, we do ask more of them. To demonstrate something highly implausible requires better evidence than to demonstrate something plausible. Supporting evidence for the plausible finding comes from many directions, whereas the implausible finding must hang on a slender thread of evidence until systematic relationships are found that tie it firmly to what is known.

Skepticism About ESP

One of the chief reasons for skepticism about ESP is that no method has been found for reliably demonstrating the phenomena. Procedures that produce significant results for one experimenter do not do so for another. Even the same experimenter testing the same individuals over a period of time may obtain significant results on one occasion and yet be unable to repeat the results later. Lack of replicability is a serious problem. In other scientific fields, an experimental finding is not considered established until the experiment has been repeated by several researchers with the same results. Until ESP experiments can be shown to be replicable, the authenticity of the phenomena is open to question.

A second complaint about ESP research is that the results do not vary systematically with the introduction of different experimental manipulations. This objection, however, is not entirely fair. Some results are reported where subjects are more successful on early trials than later ones, and there is evidence that subjects with a favorable attitude to ESP produce positive results, while an unfavorable attitude leads to below-chance scores. It has also been reported that the emotional states of the sender and receiver are important; when the sender is emotionally aroused and the receiver is reclining in a relaxed state, ESP is maximal. Finally, there are a number of studies that find ESP to be better when the receiver is dreaming or in a hypnotic state rather than in a normal, waking state. For a review of these studies, see Wolman and others (1977).

Empirical findings that meet ordinary statistical standards are offered in support of ESP and PK. Why, then, do the results not become a part of established psychological science? The arguments used against ESP and PK can be summarized as follows:

1 Many claims of extraordinary phenomena in the past have turned out to be false when carefully investigated.
2 Improved experimental methods have failed to yield larger and/or more reliable effects than crude methods.
3 There is a general lack of consistency in the phenomena, without which formal theorizing cannot replace the current vague speculations about what may be taking place.

These criticisms are not decisive. It is desirable to keep an open mind about issues that permit empirical demonstration, as some ESP phenomena do. At the same time, it should be clear that the reservations of the majority of psychologists are based on more than stubborn prejudice.

SUMMARY

1 We mainly perceive objects, rather than their *sensory features,* and we perceive these objects as stable and enduring. This stability depends on the various *constancies* of *brightness, color, shape, size,* and *location.* Size perception usually represents a compromise between retinal size and object size. The greater the number of distance cues available and the more familiar the object, the more the perceived size approaches object size. As environmental cues are reduced, perception approaches retinal size (that is, it corresponds to the size indicated by the retinal image).
2 A basic organizing principle of visual perception is *figure* and *ground.* We recognize patterns as figures against a background whether or not the patterns are familiar. Reversible figures illustrate the fact that perception involves an active search for the best interpretation of sensory information rather than a static mirroring of visual stimuli.
3 Visual illusions are incorrect perceptual hypotheses. Some are based on *size contrasts* with the surroundings, whereas others are created when we try to interpret figures on a two-dimensional surface as if they were three dimensional.

4 From a cognitive viewpoint, a percept is a hypothesis suggested by the sensory data. *Hypothesis testing* emphasizes the active nature of perception and depends on *context* and *past experience*. *Analysis-by-synthesis* is a theory of perception based on the concept of hypothesis testing.

5 Early theories of motion perception assumed that the cues for movement were the successive stimulation of rods and cones as the image of an object moved across the retina. Most psychologists, however, now believe that the cues to motion are in the environment; for example, we see an object in motion because as it moves it successively covers and uncovers portions of the immobile background.

6 Under some conditions it is possible to perceive motion without a moving pattern of stimulation. Examples of such *apparent motion* are the *autokinetic effect, phi phenomenon,* and *stroboscopic motion.* The perception of motion, whether real or apparent, depends on the relations between objects within the visual field—and the interpretation we place on these relationships based on prior experience.

7 Visual depth is perceived binocularly with the help of *stereoscopic vision,* the fusion of the slightly different images of the two eyes. Depth is perceived monocularly with the aid of a number of cues: superposition of objects, relative size, height in the horizontal plane, and gradients of texture.

8 Studies based on recordings from the visual cortex of animals indicate that there are cells in the brain tuned to detect highly specific *features,* such as straight lines and edges. Feature detectors in a hierarchical arrangement may provide the basis for the recognition of complex stimulus patterns.

9 Both learning and innate factors contribute to our abilities to perceive aspects of our environment. Perception of figure-ground relationships, color, and depth appears to be largely innate. Form perception, although based on an innate organization of cortical cells that respond selectively to specific features of the stimulus, must be mastered through experience.

10 Perception is *selective.* At any moment in time we *attend* to only part of the influx of sensory stimulation. Stimuli to which we are not actively attending may be registered temporarily in the nervous system, but they are not selected for attention unless deemed pertinent. Factors that favor attention to one stimulus in preference to another reside in its physical properties (intensity, size, contrast, and movement), the individual's internal needs and expectancies, as well as the momentary interests of the individual.

11 The *orienting reflex* is a pattern of physiological reactions that correlates with attention. These reactions facilitate the reception of stimuli and prepare the organism for action.

12 *Extrasensory perception* (ESP) in its various forms (telepathy, clairvoyance, precognition) and *psychokinesis* (PK), the influencing of physical events by mental operations, are areas of controversy in psychology. There are many reasons for reserving judgment on these phenomena, but an a priori condemnation of the experiments is unjustified. The experiments raise interesting issues about the criteria by which scientific credibility is established.

FURTHER READING

Textbooks covering the topics dealt with in this chapter are Kaufman, *Perception* (1979), Hochberg, *Perception* (2nd ed., 1978), Schiffman, *Sensation and perception* (1976), Lindsay and Norman, *Human information processing* (2nd ed., 1977), and Rock, *An introduction to perception* (1975). More detailed coverage may be found in the multiple-volume, *Handbook of perception* (1975–1979), edited by Carterette and Friedman.

Problems of attention, perceptual coding, pattern recognition, and visual search are discussed in Neisser, *Cognition and reality* (1976), Reed, *Psychological processes in pattern recognition* (1973), Norman, *Memory and attention: An introduction to human information processing* (2nd ed., 1976), and Boden, *Artificial intelligence and natural man* (1977).

For a review of extrasensory perception, see Wolman, Dale, Schmeidler, and Ullman (eds.), *Handbook of parapsychology* (1977).

6
Consciousness and Control

I n the 1960s many young people, followed by their elders, began to experiment with psychedelic ("mind-expanding") drugs, meditation, eastern religions, extrasensory perception (ESP), and occultism. Dissatisfied with the materialism of contemporary society and the emphasis on technology, they turned inward to discover the range of human potential. Their goal, broadly defined, was to heighten awareness—to enlarge the boundaries of consciousness (Stone, 1976). Traditional ways of seeking knowledge were rejected or set aside.

As often happens, stirrings in the community at large awakened interest among laboratory scientists. Neglected topics, such as sleep and dreams, the effects of drugs, and hypnosis, began to attract researchers. The study of altered forms of consciousness acquired a new respectability. Thus, what began as an essentially anti-intellectual movement in the counterculture created a shift of interest in the academic and scientific culture as well. As a result, psychologists have had to rethink the role of consciousness in human behavior.

Consciousness: What It Is and What It Does

To be conscious is to be alert and active, as you are when you awake from sleep; it means to know oneself and to be aware of one's surroundings. Many chapters of this book have direct bearing on the study of consciousness. Our knowledge of the world comes by way of the senses, and, despite occasional illusions, our senses are remarkably accurate in guiding us about. (Sensation and perception are discussed in detail in Chapters 4 and 5). Still, we would be helpless without information stored in memory (see Chapter 8). In asking how we store data in memory and recover it to serve our purposes, psychologists are essentially asking questions about consciousness. Memories and present perceptions, in the context of planning, lead to thinking, mulling things over, reflecting, and creative imagination—which are often expressed in language (see Chapter 9). Of course, much thought can be expressed as idle daydreaming, which is part of conscious activity. Night dreaming also belongs in this category. When a dream is remembered, it is a conscious product, no matter how mysterious its production may be. All of these conscious processes take place against a background of emotions, hopes, and needs (see Chapters 10 and 11), and of the appreciation of beauty and other human values.

The goal of this chapter is to provide a background for the various threads that are considered throughout the other chapters, where the context of consciousness is more or less taken for granted. We will consider various mental processes from the viewpoint of the individual as the observer, initiator, and controller of his or her own thoughts, fantasies, and experiences.

Nonconscious, Preconscious, and Unconscious

That things drift in and out of consciousness is a common experience. We not only remember and forget, we shift our attention from one thing to another, perform habitual acts absent-mindedly, and so on. Hence it is useful to distinguish among degrees of awareness.

NONCONSCIOUS PROCESSES Some activities never become conscious. Changes in the secretion of body hormones or in the concentration of salt in the blood are examples of *nonconscious* activities. Sometimes there are conscious effects that are connected with what is happening at the nonconscious level—for example, in the diabetic person who learns to detect the consequences of too much sugar in the blood. In essence, however, the underlying processes themselves are never conscious and therefore may be described as nonconscious.

PRECONSCIOUS PROCESSES Freud termed *preconscious* those memories that are available to consciousness but are not conscious at a given moment. I may not be conscious now of my vacation trip last summer, but the memory is accessible if I wish to call it forth; then the events become a vivid part of my consciousness. These processes are so familiar that they are often simply classified as *available memories*—although they may not be instantly available. For example, we sometimes experience the "tip-of-the-tongue" phenomenon, when we know something, such as someone's name, and know we know it, but it does not readily come to consciousness.

UNCONSCIOUS PROCESSES The experiences described as *unconscious* are less available to awareness than preconscious experiences. Yet they differ from nonconscious experiences in the way they influence our memories, motives, and emotions. Unconscious processes are inferred to explain certain behaviors—for example, forgotten memories or emotions that we do not understand. Occasionally, something from the unconscious may intrude into consciousness. Perhaps we reveal an unconscious wish by calling someone by the wrong name or by inserting a negative in a sentence intended to express something positive. This unintentionally revealed "secret," if truly unconscious, is a secret to the person whose statements are unintentionally distorted. Freud was one of the first to recognize that conscious acts or experiences might reveal the unconscious, for example, in dreams, mannerisms, or even symptoms of illness. Freud thought we could learn about the unconscious by interpreting these signs. Just because we can infer what happens at the unconscious level does not mean that we have made the unconscious conscious.

Sometimes the terms *subconscious* and *unconscious* are used synonymously to describe these processes. We can, however, make some distinctions between them.

Subconscious experiences operate very much as conscious ones do, except that they are so far toward the outer margins of consciousness that we are unaware of them. For example, you may not be conscious of hearing a clock strike the hour until, after a few strokes, you become alert. Then you can count the strokes that you did not know you heard; they influenced you subconsciously. The field of investigation in psychology known as *subliminal perception* deals with the types of sensory stimulation too faint to be consciously detected (hence "subliminal," or below threshold). Such stimuli may be registered by our sense organs and show residual influences, even though the perception is subconscious. For example, something perceived in this way may later show an influence on imagination or on something "guessed" (Dixon, 1971). The use of the term "subliminal" for such perception is unfortunate, however. To go undetected a stimulus does not have to be so weak as to be below some physiological threshold. It simply may not be attended to, as in the example of the clock striking the hour.

In contrast to this explanation of the subconscious, Freud attached a special meaning to the unconscious. According to his psychoanalytic theory, the unconscious is made up of active mental processes that are much like conscious mental activities but go on without our awareness. For emotional or motivational reasons, consciously experienced events are driven out of consciousness and lost to memory; that is, these memories are *repressed* to the unconscious, where they remain active in some form. This dynamic unconscious is responsible for producing the various signs of unconscious activity described earlier. The unconscious cannot be detected directly, but is inferred from apparently irrational behavior and dreams. Carl Jung, an early disciple of Freud, expanded Freud's notion of the unconscious to include a collective, or racial, unconscious, which is inherited and shared by all.

Repression to the unconscious may not explain all mental activities that become unavailable to consciousness, however. Perhaps thoughts that might be conscious are merely set aside, split off from the available thoughts that are conscious. In this they may be more like memories in the preconscious or subconscious, because they can become fully available to consciousness at a later time. Unlike thoughts in the deep unconscious, which have to be inferred, subconscious ideas may make their way into consciousness and can then be seen for what they are. This, in essence, was Pierre Janet's concept of *dissociation* (1889). The distinction is important in those techniques of psychotherapy that try to bring concealed memories to consciousness (see Chapter 16). It makes a difference if the hidden material becomes available directly or has to be inferred from the signs or symptoms derived from it. Either interpretation may be valid in certain instances, so that the concepts of experiences alongside each other (as in subconscious experiences) or some of them lying more deeply buried (as in repressed unconscious) are supplementary rather than contradictory.

Consciousness Itself

The term *consciousness* refers to a wide range of mental phenomena. Among these, we can identify two basic modes of consciousness: *passive*, receptive states (as when we lie back and listen to music) and *active*, productive mental activities (as when we make plans).

PASSIVE MODE Receiving information from the environment is the main function of the body's sensory systems, leading to awareness of what is going on in our surroundings as well as within our own bodies. Sensory experiences are blended in complex ways with memories, fantasies, dreams, and hopes, all of which are represented in consciousness. As we reflect on our experiences we are aware of pleasures and pains, likes and dislikes. Aesthetic sensitivity supplements mere receptivity to stimuli. We seek experiences we find intrinsically satisfying and savor these moments. Because there is a continuity to our experiences, we know and value ourselves in a way no one else can. For these many reasons, a search of consciousness gives individuals who feel at odds with society the hope of some sort of restoration or reconciliation. The counterculture of the 1960s demonstrated this. It emphasized the passive mode of consciousness, assigning supreme value to sensitivity to the present moment, detached from all concern for either the past or the future. For example, the final stage in the practice of yoga is said to be *samadhi,* in which individuality is given up through merging with an object of meditation, producing a state of tranquility and bliss. However, receptivity or sensitivity is only part of consciousness.

ACTIVE MODE Planning is a major part of mental life, whether the plan is simple and readily completed (like mailing a letter at the corner box) or long range (like planning for a career in medicine) (Miller, Galanter, and Pribram, 1960). Events that have not yet occurred are represented in consciousness as future possibilities; alternative "scenarios" may be envisioned, choices made, and appropriate activities initiated. For example, the creative artist, scientist, or inventor begins with an image of something novel and valuable—a vague intent—and then does the hard work to refine a product in line with his or her intentions. Consciousness plays an active role as the person looks ahead, tests the product against an ideal, and presses on against discouragement. The active role of consciousness in initiating and monitoring what is done—in producing ideas and in guiding behavior—contrasts with the passive receptive role of consciousness.

Consciousness as an Agent of Control

It is relatively easy, on paper, to distinguish among passive and active consciousness, the nonconscious, preconscious, and unconscious. However, in reality—in experience—the boundaries are blurred. This becomes clear when we look at the question of control. As did many others, the American psychologist William James equated consciousness ("mentality") with voluntary control. In his classic *Principles of Psychology,* James wrote,

> *The pursuance of future ends and the choice of means for their attainment are thus the mark and criterion of the presence of mentality* in a phenomenon. . . . We impute no mentality to sticks and stones because they never seem to move for *the sake of anything,* but always when pushed, and then indifferently and with no signs of choice. So we unhesitatingly call them senseless. (James, 1890, vol. I, p. 8)

For James, to be conscious was to be in control.

Certainly, control is one function of consciousness. However, not all controls are voluntary, or conscious. Voluntary and involuntary processes illustrate what we mean by alternate control processes—some conscious, some not conscious. Obviously all processes that have to be regulated require a control mechanism of some sort.

The Behaviorist's Rejection of Consciousness

Psychology began as a study of consciousness, and its method was self-observation by way of introspection. Soon uneasiness about introspection as a scientific method led to attacks on consciousness itself, culminating in the behaviorism of John B. Watson (1913), who rejected consciousness as the subject matter for scientific psychology and introspection as a method (see Chapter 1).

Watson's reasons for rejecting consciousness were good ones—otherwise he would not have attracted so many followers for so many years. Some psychologists still consider themselves to be behaviorists (e.g., Skinner, 1974); others believe that, although psychology has benefited from behaviorism, the approach is now too restrictive.

Watson saw clearly that if psychology studied only consciousness, with introspection its method, then it would exclude the study of animals, infants, and mentally disturbed people, since they were either incapable of introspection or their introspections could not be trusted. He noted also that if psychology was to be like other sciences its observations should be re-peatable by others, preferably yielding data that could be recorded by instruments. This would lead to the *objectivity* of other sciences in contrast with the subjectivity of introspection. In other words, if psychology dealt with actual behavior, it would be dealing with *public* events, instead of *private* events, which are observable only by the experiencing person.

Behaviorism did not require as radical a change as its pronouncements seemed to imply, for there were already many moves toward objectivity. Much psychological data already consisted of records of successful and unsuccessful performances, of time measurements of physiological indicators—such as changes in respiration—with a minimum of reports of private experience.

The behaviorists themselves dealt with private events when their investigations required them to. They accepted *verbal responses* as a substitute for introspection when the subject's own experiences were studied. What the subject said was objective, regardless of the uncertainties about the underlying subjective conditions. Still, many psychologists continued to be-lieve, regardless of the behaviorists, that when subjects said they saw a series of colored afterimages after staring at a bright light, they probably did see colors in succession. That is, their words were not the whole story: the words referred to something of additional psychological interest.

There are clearly other mental events, such as aroused memories, that intervene between a presented stimulus and a response to it. While behaviorists could deal with many aspects of such events in terms of verbal behavior, their preoccupation with observable behavior caused them to neglect interesting psychological problems, such as dreams and hallucinations, because the prominence of subjective aspects made the topics distasteful to them.

Beginning about 1950, psychologists began to recognize that the facts of consciousness are too pervasive and important to be neglected. This does not mean that psychology must again be defined exclusively as the study of consciousness; it means only that a complete psychology cannot afford to neglect the facts of consciousness.

Let us begin with conscious controls. In general, the more voluntary a process, the more conscious it is. The very meaning of voluntary is that it is something deliberately chosen and planned, and carried out with some goal or purpose in mind.

What about the controls of involuntary processes? The body is a marvelous self-regulating mechanism, with controls provided by the integrating mechanisms of the nervous system with the help of the endocrine glands (see Chapter 2). The homeostatic processes of the body illustrate how well controls can operate at a nonconscious level.

Some controls that were once fully conscious may become *habitual,* so that they are less conscious and the activities become more automatic. This does not mean that the activities are no longer under control. The control at some level may be much the same as it was when the activity was conscious. One interpretation, which we return to later, is that the control is essentially the same as before but has been *dissociated* from consciousness. Learning to ride a bicycle at first requires intense concentration but soon becomes as natural as walking—which also had to be learned at one time. Hence, some control is like switching to automatic pilot on an airplane, freeing the human pilot for other duties. The decision to initiate such an activity may be deliberate and

CONSCIOUSNESS: WHAT IT IS AND WHAT IT DOES

voluntary, but once the activity is set in motion, it runs its course by habit. The control is no longer conscious. Another example is that of a pianist who carries on a conversation with a bystander while performing a familiar piece. The pianist is exercising control over two activities—playing and talking—but does not think about the music unless a wrong key is hit and alerts his or her attention to it, temporarily disrupting the conversation. Dreams are very largely beyond conscious control. However, I know that a dream I remember is my dream and that I must in some sense have been the playwright and producer of the drama that unfolded within it.

We have recognized voluntary controls that are vividly conscious, voluntary controls that have become less conscious as the activities have become habitual, and nonconscious controls. It is evident that different controls may operate simultaneously (in parallel) or in alternation.

To the extent that unconscious processes (as distinct from nonconscious ones) exert control, we are confronted with problems of *divided consciousness*, because unconscious processes have so many characteristics of consciousness.

It has long been believed that consciousness must represent something unified, because the "I" or "me" is the same today as it was yesterday. This is something of an illusion sustained by the continuity of memories. I recognize myself as the same person today that I was yesterday, because even after a period of unconsciousness—while asleep or anaesthetized—I can pick up my old memories as a way of knowing who I am. The gap of unconsciousness is closed and the feeling of continuity and unity restored. In fact, however, the various control systems, of which now one and now another may be dominant, tell us that whatever unity we do experience is unstable, and some divisions of consciousness may be the rule.

Divided Consciousness

To illustrate how consciousness may be divided, we will discuss a laboratory study of a familiar type of selective attention and a case study of extreme divisions of the personality.

Divided Attention

Like a spotlight in the dark, our awareness can shift from what is going on in our bodies to what is happening outside or to events we remember or imagine. Even an ordinary conversation involves a variety of simultaneous activities. We can pay close attention to the speaker yet have enough surplus attention to plan our responses and carry on internal conversations at the same time. When two people talk, they appear to be taking turns, but much more is going on. Person A, while listening to person B, is simultaneously planning a reply. While replying, person A may monitor how effective the remarks are by watching the facial expression of person B, perhaps changing the direction of the argument if it is not producing the desired effect. At the same time, person A may be thinking to him or herself that the conversation has continued long enough and some way should be found to end it. Thus several streams of conscious activity (listening, talking, criticizing, planning) appear to go on simultaneously or in rapid succession.

In other situations, the person directs attention to one thing but ignores

another that might become conscious. In one experiment, two videotaped games were shown to the subjects simultaneously, one overlapping the other. One game consisted of attempting to slap the hand of the opponent before the opponent had the chance to withdraw it; the other consisted of tossing a ball among three players (see Figure 6-1). Subjects were asked to attend to one of the games, ignoring the other, and to press a key whenever the target event (either a throw or an attempt at hand-slapping) occurred in the game being watched. The targets appeared at a rate of about 40 per minute. There was practically no interference between the two games: errors did not exceed 3 percent. Performance deteriorated, however, if subjects attempted to monitor both games at once. It seems that information from the unattended game can be "registered" visually but still not be "seen."

How can we account for the divisions of consciousness that permit us to disregard one set of stimuli in favor of another? One view is that we can only really attend to one thing at a time. Rapid shifts from one information source to another account for an occasional illusion of attending to two things at once. These shifts between information sources are known as *serial* (or *intermittent*) *processing.* Alternatively, attention may be divided between two things. If the two attentive processes are indeed simultaneous, they represent *parallel processing.*

In an alternate form of parallel processing, part of the attentive effort and planning may continue without any awareness of it at all. Information from one source is processed consciously, the other subconsciously. The concealed part of the total ongoing thought and action may be described as *dissociated* from the conscious experience of the person.

Multiple Personalities

The divisions of consciousness that permit us to do more than one thing at a time (such as humming a tune while reading) do not seem very remarkable, because we can shift our attention from one task to the other if we choose to do so. On occasion, however, individuals lose control of the systems that regulate what they do and experience. An extreme example, *multiple personalities*, illustrates the complexities of consciousness that are possible.

In cases of multiple or alternating personalities, the individual has more than one organization of his or her subpersonalities. In one personality, the individual may be happy and carefree; in another, anxious and sullen. The personalities shift back and forth, but each retains its separate identity. Some amnesia is characteristic, so personality A is unaware of personality B, although in some instances, personality B may be fully aware of personality A.

In earlier centuries these changes were commonly attributed to the invasion of the body by an outside spirit, or possession. Today they are viewed naturalistically as a split, or dissociation, within the personality. Clear-cut cases are uncommon, but several have appeared in recent years. Among the best known are those of Eve White, with her alternate personalities, known as Eve Black and Jane (Thigpen and Cleckley, 1957), and more recently, Evelyn, with the three personalities of Gina, Mary, and Evelyn (Osgood and others, 1976).

The case of Jonah, a 27-year-old man who came to a hospital with complaints of severe headaches that were often followed by memory loss, has been carefully studied. Hospital attendants noticed striking changes in his personality on different days, and the psychiatrist in charge detected three distinct secondary personalities. The relatively stable personality structures that emerged are diagrammed in Figure 6-2 and can be characterized as follows:

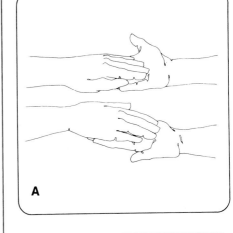

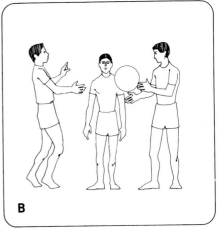

Fig. 6-1 The selective looking experiment
The hand-slapping game (A) and the ball-tossing game (B) were presented simultaneously, one overlapping the other (C). Subjects were successful in watching one game and neglecting the other. (Neisser and Becklen, 1975)

DIVIDED CONSCIOUSNESS

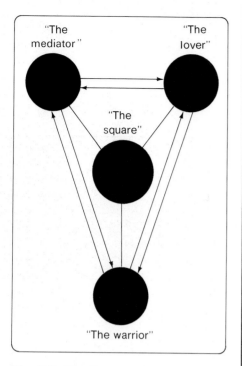

Fig. 6-2 The four component personalities, with their degrees of awareness of each other

The three personalities on the periphery have superficial knowledge of each other but are intimately familiar with Jonah, who is totally unaware of them. Another temporarily emerging personality, De Nova, is not shown. (From Ludwig and others, 1972)

Jonah. The primary personality. Shy, retiring, polite, passive, and highly conventional, he is designated "the square." Sometimes frightened and confused during interviews, Jonah is unaware of the other personalities.

Sammy. He has the most intact memories. He can coexist with Jonah or set Jonah aside and take over. He claims to be ready when Jonah needs legal advice or is in trouble. He is designated "the mediator." Sammy remembers emerging at age six, when Jonah's mother stabbed his stepfather and Sammy persuaded the parents never to fight again in front of the children.

King Young. He emerged when Jonah was six or seven years old to straighten out Jonah's sexual identity after his mother occasionally dressed him in girls' clothing at home and Jonah became confused about boys' and girls' names at school. King Young has looked after Jonah's sexual interests ever since; hence he is designated "the lover." He is only dimly aware of the other personalities.

Usoffa Abdulla. A cold, belligerent, and angry person. Usoffa is capable of ignoring pain. It is his sworn duty to watch over and protect Jonah; hence he is designated "the warrior." He emerged at age 9 or 10, when a gang of white boys beat up Jonah, who is black, without provocation. Jonah was helpless; but Usoffa emerged, he fought viciously and vehemently against the attackers. He, too, is only dimly aware of the other personalities.

The differences among these personalities are evident in their self-portraits (see Figure 6-3). The four personalities tested very differently on all measures having to do with emotionally laden topics, but scored essentially alike on tests relatively free of emotion or interpersonal conflict, such as intelligence or vocabulary tests.

The outcome of the treatment, in which the four personalities were to be

Fig. 6-3 Self-portraits of Jonah's four personalities
(From Ludwig and others, 1972)

fused into one through hypnosis, has not been reported. However, some early indications were that Jonah seemed "sicker" with all the strands of his personality in the open than with the secondary personalities in abeyance except when needed. The authors of the study conjectured that, for Jonah, four heads were perhaps better than one!

Thus, consciousness may indeed be divided, sometimes so sharply that several personalities seem to be living in one body. It is easy to see how, in an era of less psychological understanding, these personalities might be viewed as alien spirits who had invaded the body.

Sleep and Dreams

Conscious activities may take place in different contexts from those of normal waking conditions. These conditions can be described as *altered states of consciousness*. They are distinguishable from the conditions described as divided consciousness in that they are general states producing a context for modified consciousness. For example, a person drunk on alcohol may react very differently in a social situation from that same person when sober. Hence, drunkenness may be conceived as a state within which conscious activities can be studied to find, for example, how judgment is affected, how emotions are aroused, and so on. In this section on sleep and dreams and in the following ones on meditation, drugs, and hypnosis, the problem of altered states of consciousness is central—especially the effect that the altered context has on the conscious processes occurring within it.

The most familiar change of state is that between waking and sleeping. Were sleep an entirely unconscious state it would not be considered an altered state of consciousness. However sleep, like drunkenness, is a context in which a different kind of thinking goes on, especially as reflected in dreams.

Biologically, sleep is partly a restorative state. However, it is more complex than that, for whatever the condition of the body, a person can choose either to sleep or to remain awake. Sleep is not altogether unconscious, for upon waking, we can recall dreams. It is not entirely quiescent, because some people walk in their sleep. Nor is it entirely insensitive, because a mother can be awakened by the cry of her baby. It is not altogether planless, because some people can decide to wake up at a given time and do so. Still, sleep is the most obvious change in the conscious state; most of us experience the transitions between the two states (sleep and waking) at least twice a day.

Sleep

Three aspects of sleep illustrate some of the problems associated with an understanding of sleep: sleep schedules (the characteristic times between periods of sleeping and periods of waking), depth of sleep, and voluntary and involuntary controls that affect sleep.

SLEEP SCHEDULES The newborn baby tends to alternate frequently between sleeping and waking. Eventually the night-day rhythm is established. The total sleeping time drops from 16 hours per day to 13 hours per day within the first six months of life. Adults report an average night's sleep of seven and a half hours, but this varies greatly; some manage very well on as little as three hours per night (Jones and Oswald, 1968). One elderly woman averaged only 45

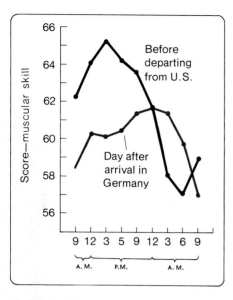

Fig. 6-4 Change in circadian rhythm after travel to a new time zone
Average results for eight subjects flying from the United States to Germany, with a six-hour time difference. The black line represents the scores on a test taken more than three days prior to departure; the red line represents corresponding scores on the day after arrival in Germany. (After Klein, Wegmann, and Hunt, 1972)

minutes of sleep per night (Meddis, Pearson, and Langford, 1973). Then there are "larks," who go to bed early and rise early, and "owls," who go to bed late and rise late (Webb, 1975).

Humans share a natural rhythm of biological processes with other mammals, a biological clock known as the *circadian rhythm* that closely follows the night-and-day periodicity of the world we live in. In free conditions, the human cycle tends to have a natural period of 25 hours, but external events modify the natural rhythm in favor of a 24-hour period (Aschoff, 1965). Because of their circadian rhythms, some travelers find it hard to adapt to the new time cycles that jet travel can produce in a few hours. "Jet lag" may persist for several days. In one study, American students who traveled from the United States to Germany took 12 days to recover from the outward flight and 10 days to recover from the homeward flight, as indicated by a test of precision of muscular skill. Apparently it is easier to return to an old cycle than to establish a new one. Figure 6-4 shows the change in rhythm the day after their arrival in Europe. Related experiments indicate that jet lag is due to interference with the normal rhythm rather than to loss of sleep (Webb, Agnew, and Williams, 1971).

DEPTH OF SLEEP Some people are readily aroused from sleep, and others, the "deep sleepers," are hard to awaken. Research begun in the 1930s (Loomis, Harvey, and Hobart, 1937) has produced sophisticated techniques for measuring the depth of sleep as well as for determining when dreams are occurring (Dement and Kleitman, 1957). Figure 6-5 illustrates these techniques.

We now know that sleep involves five stages—four stages of depth, and a fifth stage known as rapid-eye-movement (REM) sleep, in which dreams commonly occur (see Figure 6-6). When a person who is awake closes his or her eyes and relaxes, the brain waves characteristically show a regular pattern of 8 to 13 vibrations (Hz) per second (known as *alpha waves*). As the individual drifts into stage 1 sleep, the brain waves become less regular and are reduced in amplitude, with little or no alpha. Stage 2 is characterized by the appearance of spindles—short runs of rhythmical responses of 13 to 16 Hz, slightly higher than alpha—and occasional rises and falls in the amplitude of the EEG. The still-deeper stages, 3 and 4, are characterized by slow waves (known as *delta waves*). It becomes more and more difficult to awaken the person during these stages. (However, something personal, such as a familiar name, can often arouse a person from a deep stage while a more impersonal stimulus, such as a loud sound, may not.)

After the person has been asleep for an hour or so, another change occurs. The EEG record goes back to stage 1, but the subject does not wake up. Instead, eye movements appear on the record, as indicated at the bottom of Figure 6-6. This stage is known as REM; the others are known as non-REM (or NREM). When aroused from the REM stage, the subject commonly reports a dream. Even though sleep at this stage is apparently light and the person is dreaming, it is as difficult to arouse the sleeper from the REM stage as from stage 2.

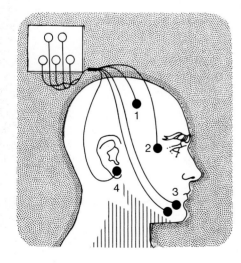

Fig. 6-5 Arrangements of electrodes for recording electrophysiology of sleep
Dream researchers use electrodes to record (1) electrical changes from the scalp, the electroencephalogram, or EEG; (2) rapid eye movements, or REMs; and (3) electrical impulses from the muscles of the chin—the electromyogram, or EMG. A neutral electrode on the ear (4) completes the circuit through the amplifiers that produce the graphical records. Although measured from the scalp, the EEG provides evidence of spontaneous activity of the brain underlying the electrodes.

STAGES OF SLEEP

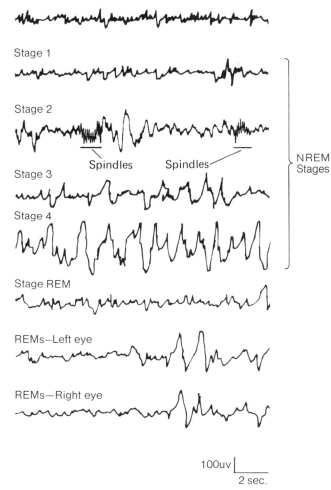

Stage 0 (awake)

Stage 1

Stage 2

Spindles   Spindles

Stage 3

Stage 4

} NREM Stages

Stage REM

REMs—Left eye

REMs—Right eye

100uv |
         | 2 sec.

Fig. 6-6 Stages of sleep

Fig. 6-6 Stages of sleep
Changes in EEG from waking through the stages of sleep are shown at the top of the chart, followed by the REM stage. During the REM stage the EEG is similar to that of stage 1, but rapid eye movements (REMs), essentially absent during the other stages, appear. The bottom lines show the REMs recorded from each eye.

The stages vary throughout the night, and there are great individual differences. However, there is a general pattern of going through the first four stages during the initial hour of sleep before REM occurs. The deeper stages (3 and 4) tend to disappear in the second half of the night as REM becomes more prominent (see Figure 6-7).

VOLUNTARY AND INVOLUNTARY CONTROL OF SLEEP People suffering from *insomnia* have great difficulty falling asleep or remaining asleep throughout the night. In a large-sample survey of adults, 6 percent of the males and 14 percent of the females reported insomnia "fairly often" or "often" (Kripke and Simons, 1976). However, those who report insomnia may have a false conception of how little they sleep, because they remember only the time when they were awake and have no recollection of the period of sleep. One study that monitored self-professed "insomniacs" found that only about half of them were actually awake as much as 30 minutes during the night (Carskadon, Mitler, and Dement, 1974).

Ordinarily we have a great deal of voluntary control in deciding when to sleep and when to stay awake. Most college students can go to sleep at any

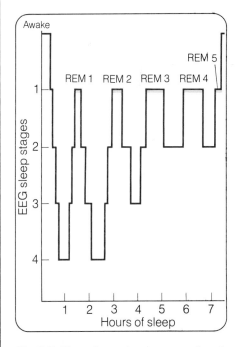

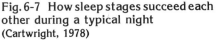

Fig. 6-7 How sleep stages succeed each other during a typical night
(Cartwright, 1978)

time of day, provided the conditions are right and they choose to do so, whether or not they are accustomed to napping. One study found that 60 percent of 430 students occasionally took naps in the daytime—some every day, some only occasionally. The remaining 40 percent reported that they never napped (Evans and others, 1977). Of the nappers, 22 percent napped because they enjoyed it, for reasons other than the need for sleep. The remaining 78 percent took naps only when they had lost sleep—either the night before, or cumulatively over several days—and needed to make up for lost sleep.

SLEEP DISORDERS   There are some disorders of sleep that are more severe than the familiar complaints of insomnia—for example, *narcolepsy* and *apnea.*

Narcolepsy is an uncontrollable tendency to fall asleep, whether one is sitting at a desk, driving a car, or carrying on a conversation. If a student falls asleep while the professor is lecturing, this is perfectly normal, but if the professor falls asleep while lecturing, that is narcolepsy. In a study of 190 patients who complained that they could not stay awake in the daytime, 65 percent were diagnosed as suffering from narcolepsy (Guilleminault and others, 1975). Such patients often engage in automatic behavior they later forget. For example, some patients experienced temporary "blackouts" in which they drove a car satisfactorily for some miles and then found themselves registering at a hotel, forgetting how they got there or why they were there. Some 300,000 persons in the United States suffer from narcolepsy. Emotional excitement may trigger one form of narcolepsy, known as *cataplexy*, in which the person suddenly collapses because of muscular relaxation and loss of postural control. There may be a hereditary component; for example, dogs have been bred that show the tendency in extreme form, collapsing in the midst of their play (Mitler and Dement, 1977). Comparison with normal sleep suggests that in cataplexy the person may pass directly into REM sleep, with its attendant muscular relaxation, without going through the usual sleep stages.

In the study referred to above, another 22 percent suffered from *apnea*, a condition in which the individual cannot breathe while asleep. The person must awaken repeatedly throughout the night in order to survive, because during the short periods of sleep the windpipe is closed off. These disturbances of sleep, and sleep-like interferences of waking states, show the complexity of control systems, both involuntary and voluntary.

Dreams

Dreams are products of the imagination in which memories or fantasies are temporarily confused with external reality. Dreams have a spontaneous, non-voluntary quality that distinguishes them from ordered rational thinking. The processes that control dreaming are hidden. For this reason dreams represent a familiar form of divided consciousness, or dissociation.

DREAM THEORIES   Because of their spontaneity, we tend to think of dreams as trying to tell us something. It is no wonder dream interpretation has a long history, going back as far as Joseph's interpretations of Pharoah's dreams. Of modern interpreters of dreams, Freud (1900) was undoubtedly the most influential. Freud felt that dreams were influenced by wishes (or by drives, in more modern terms); in the dream, forbidden desires were acted out in disguised form. Hence, the dream had a *manifest content*—the actually experienced dream—and a *latent content*—the deeper motives that the dream disguised. The purpose of the dream was, in part, to protect sleep by preventing the emergence of thoughts that would otherwise disturb the sleeper. Freud recognized, however, that the dream sometimes fails in its work—for instance, when the dreamer awakens frightened because of the anxiety aroused within the dream (Freud, 1933).

Jung (1968) developed his own theory of dreams. Basic to Jung's interpretation of dreams is the conception of *archetypes*—fundamental notions such as God, Mother, Wise Old Man—which he believed to exist in a collective unconscious shared by each individual. In dreams, these archetypes emerge in interaction between the conscious and unconscious parts of the personality. The archetypes often appear in symbolic quaternary form in the dream (four people, representing parts of the personality, or various aspects of masculinity and femininity, good and evil, and so forth).

Other investigators see dreams as a form of problem solving, in which metaphors and associations help the dreamer to deal with ongoing personal problems (French and Fromm, 1963; Hall, 1966).

WHAT RESEARCH SAYS ABOUT FREUD'S THEORY   When awakened during REM sleep, subjects commonly report a dream—if awakened during NREM sleep, they may also report mental activity, but they are likely to describe it as "just thoughts" rather than as a dream (Monroe and others, 1965). The fact that it is more difficult to awaken a person from REM than from stage 1 (the EEG background for REM) provides some initial support for Freud's idea that dreams protect sleep. An additional partial test of the Freudian theory is to deprive subjects of REM sleep, thus depriving them of dreams. If subjects are awakened every time there is an onset of REM, they have a night's sleep without dreams. Early experiments indicated that after such deprivation there was more REM sleep the following night, indicating that there is a kind of quota for REM; and when there is less one night, more will be required the next. Indirectly, this would support the Freudian theory of dreams as a protector of sleep.

However, other findings of sleep and dream studies contradict the interpretation of REM as a protector of sleep. In the first place, REM is prominent in infants (even in the prematurely born), when meaningful dreams are unlikely to occur, and also in lower mammals. The study of the dreams of older children shows that their dreams reflect the realistic activities of their waking lives and that emotional disturbances occur in their dreams when there are emotional disturbances in their waking lives (Foulkes, 1971).

The only conclusion to be drawn is that the psychophysiological studies of dreams have given little support to the Freudian theory that the purpose of dreams is to protect sleep.

SOME BASIC QUESTIONS   Even though investigators do not yet completely understand dreams, modern methods of study have answered a great many questions about them. Here are some representative questions that have been answered.

Does everyone dream? Although many people do not recall dreams in the morning, "recallers" and "nonrecallers" appear to dream equally often, if we accept the REM-sleep evidence (Goodenough and others, 1959).

Two hypotheses have been proposed to account for the differences in recall of dreams. One is that nonrecallers have an inherent difficulty in recalling dreams (Lewis and others, 1966). The other hypothesis is that some people awaken more readily in the midst of REM sleep, and thus report more dreams. In other words, the reason we remember dreaming is that we happened to wake

"Greetings. You are now entering the Rapid Eye Movement phase of your sleep cycle."

Drawing by Ed Fisher. Reprinted by permission of the Chicago Tribune. New York News Syndicate

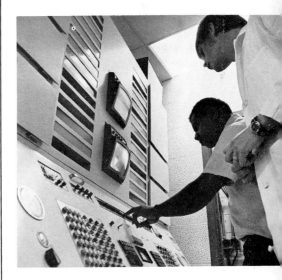

Monitoring a laboratory sleeper
The physiological indicators produced by a sleeping person in an adjacent room are recorded throughout the night.

Effects of REM Deprivation

REM deprivation studies are of interest in connection with topics other than dream theory. It now appears that REM deprivation produces more variations in waking performances than NREM deprivation.

One study compared a group of subjects who frequently engaged in waking fantasies with another group who did not. If REM ordinarily provides for fantasy experiences during the night and if there is a daily "quota," those who fantasize a good deal in the daytime may not need as much nighttime REM. This was found to be the case after REM deprivation in the first half of the night: only those who did not fantasize in the daytime increased their REMs during the second half of the deprivation night. Interestingly, after several nights of total REM deprivation, the daytime fantasizers showed little change in their waking fantasy, but the other group, those who did not fantasize in the daytime, increased their waking fantasy and even enriched their fantasy experiences (Cartwright and Ratzel, 1972).

It appears that people who engage in daytime pictorial fantasies enrich their appreciation of reality and therefore may achieve a better intellectual and emotional balance. In connection with this interpretation, studies indicate that REM deprivation may improve the waking moods for otherwise depressed persons (Vogel, 1975).

up while we were dreaming (Webb and Kersey, 1967). Regardless of the fate of these hypotheses, the evidence is that everyone dreams.

How long do dreams last? Occasionally it seems that dreams are almost instantaneous. The alarm clock rings and we awaken from a complex dream of a fire breaking out and fire engines roaring up with their sirens blaring. However, when subjects are asked to describe or pantomime a dream, the time it takes for them to do so is directly proportional to the length of time they were in REM sleep before being awakened (Dement and Wolpert, 1958). In some instances, a rich memory may be tapped by a single cue or reminder while dreaming. The ringing alarm clock, for example, reinstates a complete scene of fire and fire engines from earlier memories. Although the instigation of the dream may be brief, what is revived as a dream may be complex when we recall or recount the dream on awakening.

Do we incorporate external stimuli into our dreams? Often a sleeper delays awakening by "translating" the sound of the alarm clock into another sound—for example, a fire engine siren. To create a similar situation, Dement and Wolpert (1958) sprayed cold water on subjects who had been in REM sleep for several minutes. They were allowed to sleep several minutes more, then awakened and asked to recall their dream. In a number of cases, the water had been incorporated into the dreams. For example, one subject was following a woman when she suddenly collapsed and he noticed water dripping on her head from a hole in the ceiling. He was rescuing her when the experimenters woke him up. In another study, names spoken by the experimenter during REM sleep were incorporated into subjects' dreams (Berger, 1963).

When do sleeptalking and sleepwalking take place? Careful laboratory studies have been made of known sleeptalkers. A total of 206 speeches recorded during the night from 13 subjects (averaging 3.9 speeches per subject per night) showed that 75 to 80 percent occurred during NREM sleep, while 20 to 25 percent occurred during REM sleep (Arkin and others, 1970). Sleepwalking is also associated with NREM sleep. Subjects usually forget what they did while sleepwalking, and the dreams they remember bear no resemblance to what they did while walking about (Jacobson and Kales, 1967).

Do people know when they are dreaming? The purpose of this discussion has been to illustrate divided consciousness—in particular, instances when more than one control system appear to be operating. Such divided controls are evident when the dream flows on, as if autonomously, at the same time the person is aware of dreaming. One test is to have the subject hold a switch in one hand while sleeping, with instructions to close it while dreaming (Salamy, 1970). Subjects can apparently be trained within one night to discriminate between periods of dreaming and nondreaming (Brown and Cartwright, 1978).

Meditation

Unlike sleep and dreams, which are natural changes of state, *meditation* is an effort to produce a desired state of consciousness by following prescribed exercises.

Because we can think and dream, we can transcend the everyday world and contemplate visions of ideal, imaginary worlds. In past ages, people have isolated themselves on mountain tops, fasted, performed special rituals, or in other ways sought experiences of novelty and depth. Often this quest has been invested with religious significance. In recent years, many westerners have adopted eastern practices such as Zen Buddhism, yoga, and similar disciplines for spiritual reasons, or simply to relax and increase their self-awareness.

Transcendental Meditation

A somewhat commercialized and secular form of meditation has been widely promoted in the United States (and elsewhere) by Maharishi Mahesh Yoga, under the name of Transcendental Meditation, or TM (Forem, 1973).

The technique, while simple, is learned from a qualified instructor. A *mantra* is chosen for each subject at the time of instruction. This is a special sound that is repeated over and over to produce the deep rest and refined awareness that is said to characterize TM. "Because individuals differ in the quality of the vibrations which constitute their individual personalities, the right selection of a thought for a particular individual is of vital importance" (Maharishi, 1963, p. 56).

A formalized and ritualized set of claims of this kind, without evidence for the beliefs, is commonly called a *cult*, and many meditation and relaxation cults have developed in the United States. When enthusiasm begins to wane, the claims often become more extreme, as indeed they have for TM. In 1977, the Maharishi trained his teachers to believe that they could lead the followers to the *siddhis*, or supernatural powers, which would enable them to walk through walls and hover in midair through levitation (*Time*, August 8, 1977).

Meditation for Relaxation

A former supporter of Transcendental Meditation taught subjects how to meditate in the laboratory and found that mystical associations are quite unnecessary (Benson, 1975; Benson and others, 1977). Benson's relaxation

Meditation

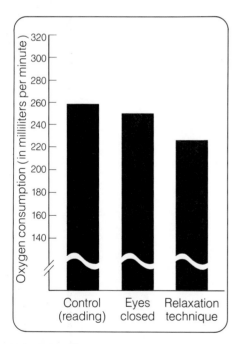

Fig. 6-8 Effect of relaxation technique on oxygen consumption
Oxygen consumption decreased significantly from both the control and eyes-closed period with use of the relaxation technique. There was no significant change between the eyes-closed and the control periods. (Benson and others, 1977)

technique through meditation includes the following steps:

1 Sit quietly in a comfortable position and close your eyes.
2 Deeply relax all your muscles, beginning at your feet and progressing up to your face. Keep them deeply relaxed.
3 Breathe through your nose. Become aware of your breathing. As you breathe out, say the word *one* silently to yourself. For example, breathe in . . . out, *one;* in . . . out, *one*, etc. Continue for 20 minutes. You may open your eyes to check the time, but do not use an alarm. When you finish, sit quietly for several minutes at first with closed eyes and later with opened eyes.
4 Do not worry about whether you are successful in achieving a deep level of relaxation. Maintain a passive attitude and permit relaxation to occur at its own pace. Expect other thoughts. When these distracting thoughts occur, ignore them by thinking "Oh well" and continue repeating "one." With practice the response should come with little effort.
5 Practice the technique once or twice daily, but not within two hours after any meal, since the digestive processes seem to interfere with the subjective changes. (Benson and others, 1977, p. 442)

Subjects who learned this technique decreased their oxygen consumption, carbon dioxide elimination, and respiration rate (all of which are associated with relaxation). In Figure 6-8 the reduction in respiratory rate is compared with respiratory rate while reading silently and while sitting with eyes closed. The subjects reported feelings quite similar to those reported as a consequence of other meditative practices: peace of mind, a feeling of being at ease with the world, and a sense of well-being. Some even described the state as ecstatic and beautiful (Dean, 1970).

There is no assurance that these experiences are a direct result of physiological relaxation through meditation. Subjective changes associated with relaxation are cognitive and may be produced by running around the block as well as by sitting passively. Benson has stated: "Regardless of the subjective feelings described by our subjects, we found that the physiologic changes such as decreased oxygen consumption are taking place" (Benson, 1975, p. 164). We are therefore uncertain as to what features of the meditation technique produce the subjective changes.

Effects of Psychoactive Drugs on Consciousness

Since ancient times drugs have been used to poison, cure, relieve pain, and produce sleep or hallucinations. Familiar drugs, such as caffeine, tobacco, and alcohol, have become so accepted in western cultures that we scarcely think of them as drugs. Others, such as opium derivatives, thought to lead to socially undesirable or dangerous behavior, have been subject to severe legal restrictions. Because many of these drugs produce subjective effects, they are known as *psychoactive.* Drug addiction (or drug dependency) as a personal and social problem is dealt with in Chapter 15. Our concern here is the psychological effects—the changes in consciousness, in feelings of well-being or depression. Of the drugs most widely used for their psychological effects—caffeine, tobacco, and alcohol—we shall consider only alcohol, because it is representative of depressant drugs. We shall also discuss another depressant, heroin; two stimulants, amphetamines and cocaine; and two hallucinogens, LSD and marijuana.

Depressants

ALCOHOL In small quantities alcohol appears to be a stimulant. In reality, it is a depressant that inhibits some of the restraints on social behavior. The initial relaxation may turn to anger and aggression; later, the depressing effects cause drowsiness and sleep. At concentrations of .03 to .05 percent in the blood, alcohol produces lightheadedness, relaxation, and release of inhibitions. At a concentration of .1 percent (say, after three cocktails or three bottles of beer), most sensory and motor functions become severely impaired. The drinker is seriously incapacitated at a level of .2 percent, and a level above .4 percent may cause death. The legal definition of intoxication is usually a concentration of .10 to .15 percent.

Consumption of alcohol leads to intoxication as an altered state, as noted earlier, with consequent effects on conscious experiences. Among these are experiences that illustrate dissociation. Occasionally when intoxicated persons become sober, they have amnesia for what occurred while they were drunk. When next intoxicated, however, the memory of the previous drunken episode may return (Overton, 1972). This is described as *state-dependent learning:* something is learned in state A, forgotten in state B, and recalled again in state A. Drugs like alcohol that characteristically produce state-dependent learning are classified as dissociative drugs. (Ho, Chute, and Richards, 1977).

The hallucinations associated with excessive use of alcohol occur in two main forms. *Delirium tremens* (in which visual hallucinations of snakes, turkey gobblers, or other animal forms terrify the patient) is a symptom of alcoholic poisoning that sets in when alcohol is withdrawn. Many other drugs also produce corresponding withdrawal symptoms once addiction has occurred. Delirium tremens is serious and may cause death. In *alcoholic hallucinosis,* the person experiences auditory hallucinations (perhaps hearing voices while under the influence of alcohol) but otherwise is not disoriented. The symptoms correspond in some respects to those of schizophrenia (see Chapter 15), and there may be underlying personality problems that produce the condition. In most cases, however, drugs produce visual rather than auditory hallucinations (Zikmund, 1972).

HEROIN Opium and its derivatives—collectively known as *opiates* and classified as *narcotics*—are widely used both medically and illegally. Opium, which comes from the juice of the opium poppy, has *morphine* and *codeine* as its active ingredients. Codeine is mild; morphine is stronger; and *heroin,* derived from morphine, is even more potent. When administered by the same method as morphine, heroin is about three times as potent. Because of its impurities, however, street heroin is less powerful than morphine by weight. Addicts smoke or swallow opium, inject morphine intravenously, and either sniff or inject heroin. Hence, considerations of strength must also take into account the method by which the drug enters the body.

The motives for using heroin, like any human motives, are complex. At first heroin produces a positive sense of well-being. Experienced adult users report a special "thrill," or "rush," within a minute or two after an intravenous injection, which some describe as intensely pleasurable, similar to an orgasm.

Youths who sniff heroin report that they forget everything that troubles them (Chein and others, 1964). Following this, the user feels "fixed," or gratified, with no hunger, pain, or sexual urges. He or she may "go on the nod," alternately waking and drowsing while comfortably watching television or reading a book. Unlike the alcoholic, the heroin user can readily produce skilled responses to agility and intellectual tests and seldom becomes aggressive or assaultive. The changes in consciousness produced by heroin use are not very striking; there are no exciting visual experiences or feelings of being transported elsewhere. Rather, heroin produces changes in mood or self-confidence, or reduces anxiety (the user either feels more comfortable with people or escapes from them). Such motives lead to addiction to a dangerous drug, with a disregard for the consequences.

Stimulants

AMPHETAMINES Amphetamines are powerful stimulants, sold under such trade names as Methedrine, Dexedrine, and Benzedrine, and known colloquially by such names as "speed," "uppers," and "bennies." The immediate effects are an increase in alertness, wakefulness, and decreased feelings of fatigue or boredom. Strenuous activities that require effort and endurance may become easier when amphetamines are taken (Weiss and Laties, 1962). As with other drugs, the positive effects suffice as motivation for their use. There are also medical applications, as in weight reduction through loss of appetite and in the treatment of hyperactive children. Unless used cautiously, the drug may do more harm than good.

We may distinguish three patterns of amphetamine use, initially serving somewhat different motives, but all affecting consciousness in one way or another (Tinklenberg, 1972).

First, low doses are taken for limited periods to overcome fatigue, for example, during such activities as long nighttime driving, military maneuvers, or cramming for examinations. Were there no escalation in use, the effects might prove more beneficial than harmful, although there is some danger of impaired judgment and postamphetamine depression.

The second pattern—sustained oral doses, gradually increasing in amount—occurs when people use amphetamines to control their weight or prevent fatigue and depression over long periods of time. Eventually undesirable consequences may result, including unfounded suspiciousness, hostility, and persecutory delusions (Snyder, 1973).

The third, extreme pattern—large intravenous amounts—commonly ends in a "run," in which the person injects the drug every few hours over a period of several days. There is an immediate pleasant experience, termed a "flash," or "rush," followed by irritability and discomfort, which require an additional injection, and so on. The episode ends in a "crash," a deep sleep followed by a period of lethargy and depression. The amphetamine user may seek relief from this discomfort by turning to a sedative, such as heroin.

COCAINE Because the use of cocaine ("coke") has become more widespread in the last decade, its psychological effects are also of interest. Until recently, the study of the specific psychological effects of cocaine has been neglected, despite the existence of one of the earliest careful studies of the psychopharmacological effects of any drug by Sigmund Freud (1885; reproduced in

Freud, 1974). His account of his own use of cocaine was at first highly favorable to the drug and encouraged its use. He noted

> the exhilaration and lasting euphoria, which in no way differs from the normal euphoria of the healthy person. . . . You perceive an increase of self-control and possess more vitality and capacity for work. . . . In other words, you are simply normal, and it is so hard to believe that you are under the influence of any drug. . . . Long intensive mental or physical work is performed without any fatigue. . . . This result is enjoyed without any of the unpleasant after-effects that follow exhilaration brought about by alcohol. . . . Absolutely no craving for the further use of cocaine appears after the first, or even repeated taking of the drug; one feels rather a curious aversion to it. (Freud, 1974, p. 9)

Freud soon withdrew this unreserved support, however, for he treated a friend, with disastrous results. The friend developed a severe addiction to cocaine, demanded far greater dosages of the drug than Freud ever recommended, and was debilitated by the drug until his death.

Recent investigations have considered both the dose and the mode of administration—that is, sniffing or intravenous injection. One study found that sniffing produced immediate acute effects, described as "highs," which peaked in 10 minutes and (except in the case of large doses) disappeared within 30 minutes. Intravenous injections added "speeding" effects and reduced hunger; no specific effects on the user's strength were detected (Resnick, Kestenbaum, and Schwartz, 1977). With small doses by either method, the effects were generally pleasant, although some depressed persons indicated unpleasant reactions. With large doses, users experienced unpleasantly rapid heart rates and severe loss of appetite.

Because the reactions to cocaine and amphetamines are almost indistinguishable, some of the cocaine on the market is adulterated with an amphetamine, a cheaper and more readily available drug, but also more dangerous at usual dosages. Both cocaine and amphetamines decrease appetite and produce euphoria. Both may cause acute paranoia, which can be indistinguishable from paranoid schizophrenia.

Hallucinogens

Unlike the drugs previously considered, there are a number that are used for the hallucinations or visions they produce—for example, mescaline, derived from cactus, and psilocybin, derived from mushrooms. These represent a subclass of hallucinogens and are known as *psychedelic* drugs because their most prominent reactions are perceptual alterations and changes in the state of consciousness. LSD (lysergic acid diethylamide), DMT (dimethyltriptamine), DOM (dimethoxy-methyl-amphetamine—also known as STP, for "serenity-tranquility-peace"), and many others belong in this class. Various psychedelics differ in the duration of their acute action. For example, DMT acts only for an hour, while LSD and mescaline last from 8 to 12 hours.

Other drugs that produce hallucinations have other effects as well and should be distinguished from the psychedelics. A dangerous drug that became well known recently is phencyclidine (PCP), known as "angel dust." It occasionally produces hallucinations, but has many unpredictable side-effects, such as irrational or violent behavior.

We will discuss the hallucinogens LSD and marijuana because popular and scientific interest has endured long enough for their psychological effects to be well known.

LSD Although LSD, or "acid," was once the most popular psychedelic drug, the widespread knowledge of its dangers has reduced its use. One problem with LSD is that its effects are highly individual and unpredictable. Some users have vivid hallucinatory experiences of colors and sounds, whereas others have mystical or semireligious experiences. Any user may have an adverse reaction (or "bad trip"), even those who have had many pleasant LSD experiences. Since the disturbances are often severe enough to cause the user to seek professional help, psychiatrists and clinical psychologists have now had considerable experience with adverse LSD reactions.

A disturbing delayed consequence of the use of LSD is the so-called "flashback," in which visual hallucinations suddenly appear days, weeks, or months after the last use of the drug. The individual may experience illusions (the apparent movement of an object in a fixed position or misinterpretations of images) or even hallucinations similar to those experienced when using the drug. LSD is almost completely eliminated from the body within 24 hours after it is taken, so that the flashback effect must be some sort of restoration of memories that were stored from the prior experience (Stanton, Mintz, and Franklin, 1976).

More threatening to the LSD user is the loss of reality orientation in the mystical states associated with the drug. This may lead to highly irrational and disoriented behavior and, occasionally, to a panic state in which the subject feels he or she is not in control. There have been reports of people jumping from high places when in this state.

MARIJUANA The most popular of all the illicit drugs, marijuana (*cannabis*), commonly known as "pot" or "grass," is derived from the hemp plant. Users smoke or eat the leaves of the marijuana plant to induce a general excitement or euphoria.

In the 1960s and 1970s, many young people in the United States used marijuana as other generations used alcohol; the legal restrictions today appear to be no more inhibiting than those outlawing alcohol were during Prohibition.

The active ingredient in marijuana is THC (tetrahydrocannabinol). Taken orally in small doses (5 to 10 milligrams), THC produces a mild "high"; larger doses (30 to 70 milligrams) produce severe and longer-lasting reactions, resembling those of other hallucinogenic drugs. As with alcohol, the reaction often has two stages: a period of stimulation and euphoria, followed by a period of tranquility and, with higher doses, sleep. Although reactions to alcohol and marijuana are similar, especially with mild doses, one peculiarity of marijuana is that it may distort the time sense.

The subjective experiences of marijuana users have been carefully studied by Tart (1971). He interviewed 150 subjects, all of whom had used marijuana at least a dozen times prior to the study and most of whom used it once a week or more during the months of the study. The subjects reported many sensory and perceptual changes: some distortions of space and time, changes in social perception and experience, and a number of "out-of-body" experiences. Some users believed that they were able to communicate by telepathy, and many reported a general euphoria and sense of well-being. The characteristic reports are summarized in Table 6-1.

In concluding this discussion, several aspects of drugs and their effects on

TABLE 6-1
Characteristic effects at various levels
of marijuana intoxication*

LEVEL OF MARIJUANA INTOXICATION	BEHAVIORAL AND EXPERIMENTAL EFFECTS
Mild	Less noisy at parties than when "tipsy" or drunk New, subtle quality to sounds
Fair	Taste sensations have new qualities Easy to get to sleep at bedtime Enjoy eating a lot (Hard to play ordinary social games) (Less need to feel in control of things) (Invariably feel good from turning on) (Understand words of songs better)
Fair to strong	Time passes more slowly Distance in walking changed More childlike, open to experience Physically relaxed (See patterns in normally ambiguous material) (Difficult to read) (Touch more exciting, sensual) (Greater spatial separation between musical instruments) (Visual imagery more intense)
Strong	(Easily sidetracked)
Strong to very strong	(Forget start of conversation)

Source: After Tart (1971, p. 245)
*The effects in parentheses are less common.

consciousness are worth noting. First, the range of subjective experiences following the use of drugs is very wide, both in response to a particular drug and in the same person's response to different drugs. Some experiences are highly pleasurable, while others represent frightening dissociations. Second, the objective changes in behavior, such as the effects on fatigue or aggression, are also highly variable, dependent on dosage, and in many instances unpredictable. Finally, the social setting in which the drug is taken may influence the user's experiences and behavior. That the results may endure—and reappear as flashbacks—shows that the influences on brain processes may be profound. What is most evident is that, in resorting to drugs, individuals relinquish some of their normal controls by assigning control to a chemical agent.

Hypnotically Produced Changes in Consciousness

Of all states of divided or altered consciousness and control, none raises more questions than *hypnosis*. Once associated with the bizarre and occult, hypnosis has now become the subject of rigorous scientific investigation. As in all fields of psychological investigation, uncertainties remain, but by now there are many firmly established facts.

The Hypnotic Experience

In order to hypnotize a willing and cooperative subject (the only kind who can be hypnotized under most circumstances), the hypnotist uses a number of methods to lead the person to relinquish some control to the hypnotist and to accept some reality distortion. Often the hypnotist will ask the subject to stare at some small target (such as a thumbtack on the wall), concentrate all thoughts on the target, and gradually become relaxed or sleepy. The suggestion of sleep is a convenient one, because it suggests being in a relaxed state, out of touch with ordinary environmental demands. But it is only a metaphor. The subject is told that he or she will not really go to sleep and continues to listen to the hypnotist.

It is possible to achieve the same results by other methods. For example, a hyperalert hypnotic trance, characterized by increased tension and alertness, can also be produced. Subjects riding a stationary laboratory bicycle after receiving suggestions of strength and alertness feel less than normal fatigue and are still as responsive to hypnotic suggestions as those who have had a conventional relaxation induction (Banyai and Hilgard, 1976).

The modern hypnotist does not use authoritarian commands. Indeed, with a little training, subjects can hypnotize themselves (Ruch, 1975). The subject enters the hypnotic state when the conditions are right; the hypnotist merely helps set these conditions.

The following changes are characteristic of the subject's condition in hypnosis:

1 *The subject ceases to make plans.* When deeply hypnotized, the subject does not like to initiate activity and would rather wait for the hypnotist to suggest what to do.
2 *Attention is redistributed.* Under hypnosis, attention becomes more selective than usual. If the subject is told to listen only to the hypnotist's voice, the subject will ignore any other voices in the room.
3 *Reality testing is reduced and reality distortion accepted.* Ordinarily people check to see that they are awake, oriented in space and time, not suffering from illusions, and so on. Under hypnosis the subject may uncritically accept hallucinated experiences (for example, petting an imaginary rabbit).
4 *Suggestibility is increased.* One has to accept suggestions in order to be hypnotized at all. Whether normal suggestibility is increased under hypnosis is a matter of some dispute, but careful studies find an increase in suggestibility following hypnotic induction, though perhaps less than is commonly supposed (Ruch, Morgan, and Hilgard, 1973).
5 *The hypnotized subject readily enacts unusual roles.* When told to adopt a role, such as reenacting one's behavior at a much younger age, the hypnotized subject commonly will do so and carry out complex activities related to that role. There may be something of an actor in each of us, and the permissiveness of the hypnotic situation, in which ordinary restraints on behavior are set aside, makes this role behavior congenial. Sarbin and Coe (1972) have hypothesized that those who can be hypnotized have a strong ability for acting to begin with and have appropriate attitudes toward adopting new roles.
6 *Posthypnotic amnesia is often present.* When instructed to do so, highly responsive hypnotic subjects forget all or most of what transpired during the hypnotic session. When a prearranged release signal is given, the memories are restored.

Involuntary movement of the arms, or paralysis of movement, may be produced readily by hypnotic suggestion.

Responsiveness to suggestions is only part of hypnosis. When subjects are encouraged to go deeper into hypnosis, they eventually reach a state in which they are unresponsive to the hypnotist's suggestions (except when a prearranged signal returns them to a level at which they can communicate). In describing this state, subjects often use terms similar to those used to describe mystical experiences, such as a separation of mind from body, a feeling of oneness with the universe, a sense of gaining knowledge, but of a kind that is not communicable (Tart, 1972).

Not all people are equally responsive to hypnotic procedures, although special training can bring about some modifications. A retest 10 years later of subjects who had been tested for responsiveness as undergraduates showed a correlation of .60 between earlier and later scores (Morgan, Johnson, and Hilgard, 1974). Furthermore, the greater similarity of scores for identical (monozygotic) twins compared with fraternal (dizygotic) twins suggests that the ability to be hypnotized may have a hereditary component (Morgan, 1973).

Interviews with hundreds of subjects, before and after hypnosis, indicate that early childhood experiences may either generate or maintain susceptibility to hypnosis (J. R. Hilgard, 1970, 1974). A capacity to become deeply involved in imaginative experiences, including hypnosis, may derive from parents who are themselves deeply involved in such areas as reading, music, religion, or the aesthetic appreciation of nature. Alternatively, a child whose parents are caring but very strict may develop a tendency to escape harassment by moving off into a realm of imagination. The child thus practices the kind of dissociations that are later to be used in hypnosis.

How are the changes that are brought about within hypnosis related to divided consciousness? To answer this question, we will consider the results of the study of several topics within hypnosis.

Posthypnotic Amnesia

Posthypnotic amnesia is a recoverable amnesia; events are "forgotten" but stored in memory and remembered again when the amnesia is reversed at a signal from the hypnotist. Figure 6-9 shows the individual differences in amnesia following a single hypnotic session, when a total of 10 items could be forgotten. To be sure that we are dealing with true amnesia, not ordinary forgetting, we reverse the amnesia to see how many items are then remembered. This procedure establishes the genuineness of hypnotic amnesia; for after "recovering" from the effects of amnesia the hypnotic amnesic's memories are as good as the memories of those who do not respond to suggestions of amnesia (Nace, Orne, and Hammer, 1974). The ability to search for a particular memory in the memory store is a feature of conscious control; the search can be interrupted by hypnosis, without affecting the stored memory (Kihlstrom and Evans, 1976).

Posthypnotic Suggestions

Amnesia is only one form of *posthypnotic suggestion*. For example, while hypnotized, the subject may be told that soon after hypnosis is ended he or she will cough three times but will forget that the hypnotist had said anything about coughing. Dehypnotized, the subject behaves normally, except for the brief coughing spell. Questioned about it, the subject's reply is likely to be, "My throat was dry after sitting so quietly" (or, "my throat tickled"), "but now

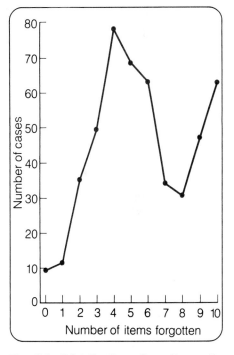

Fig. 6-9 Distribution of posthypnotic amnesia in college students
The scores are plotted according to items forgotten after a posthypnotic amnesia suggestion was given within a single session of hypnosis. The sample consisted of 491 college students. A total of 10 items could be forgotten. The plot shows how many students forgot none at all (0), at one extreme, and how many forgot all of the items (10), at the other extreme. (From Cooper, 1979)

it feels all right." Assigning an acceptable reason to behavior that may be carried out for reasons that are unknown to the person is called *rationalization* (see Chapter 14). Such behavior, in its various forms, provides instances of the subconscious control of voluntary action.

Posthypnotic suggestions are not invariably acted on, however. There is no evidence that an unscrupulous hypnotist can persuade a hypnotized subject to commit a crime he or she would not otherwise commit (Barber, 1961; Orne, 1965). Because people can be persuaded to commit crimes when hypnosis is not involved, there are bound to be a few cases in which hypnosis *appears* to be successful in inducing criminal behavior (Coe, 1977).

Age Regression

While hypnotized, a subject may be asked to relive an experience of his or her earlier life, such as a birthday at age 10. Here, one of several kinds of division of consciousness may occur. For example, the early experience may be pictured as if it were on a TV screen, with visual and auditory hallucinations. The hypnotized person is conscious of being present as the viewer but does not feel he or she is producing the scene. Another type of experience is the actual reliving, as if one were a child having the experiences. The "child" may describe the clothing being worn; may run a hand through his or her hair, describing its length (as different from its present length); may recognize classmates in elementary school. The hypnotist may be incorporated, perhaps as a visitor to the school.

Occasionally a childhood language, no longer available, suddenly emerges. An American-born boy of Japanese parents, who spoke Japanese at an early age, had forgotten all but a few words; however, under hypnosis he began speaking fluent Japanese (Fromm, 1970).

Dissociation of Competing Tasks

Stimuli that interfere with each other can be handled by ignoring one and responding to the other. Theoretically, hypnosis might be of the greatest help in such situations, because one of the tasks could be done consciously, the other subconsciously. The historically familiar hypnotic method is that of *automatic writing,* in which a hand responds to some request but, because of hypnotic suggestion, the subject does not know that the hand is doing something. In fact, the subject may be engaged in a separate conscious performance. In one experiment of this type, the subconscious task was to press each of two keys in a repetitive pattern, while the conscious task was to name colors on a visual display (Knox, Crutchfield, and Hilgard, 1975). Highly responsive hypnotic subjects could perform the key-pressing task while consciously attending to the colors and believing that that was all they were doing. This success did not mean that the tasks did not interfere. In a related experiment (Stevenson, 1976), a more difficult subconscious task produced greater interference. The experiments illustrate divided consciousness and dissociation, even though the tasks interfered with each other.

The "Hidden Observer" in Hypnosis

How can an intellectual task, such as arithmetic, or a voluntary muscular task, such as writing, be carried on subconsciously—that is, without awareness that it is being done—while some other conscious task is performed? There may be

Controversies over Hypnosis

Hypnosis has long been the center of controversy, ever since the late 1700s when Franz Mesmer claimed that it worked by "animal magnetism." In 1842, a surgeon in Nottinghamshire, England, amputated a patient's leg while the patient was in a mesmeric trance, as hypnosis was then called. The patient lay perfectly calm during the operation. When the case was reported before the Royal Medical and Chirurgical Society, objections were so strong that Dr. Marshall Hall, eminent in the study of reflex action, declared that the patient was an impostor, and another physician declared that it was wrong to relieve a pain intended by nature, even though the operation was successful. They succeeded in having the discussion of the case removed from the minutes of the meeting. Later, the patient gave sworn testimony that he had felt no pain during the operation.

The association of hypnosis with entertainment and with the occult has also hindered its acceptance as a scientific endeavor. However, since its successful use in both world wars by physicians, dentists, and psychologists, it has become a respected field of scientific inquiry. Both the British Medical Association and the American Medical Association support the teaching of hypnosis in medical schools and its cautious use in medical practice. The American Psychological Association now has a division dealing with psychological hypnosis.

Controversy has not ended, however. Now the controversies center more on how to conceptualize hypnosis than on what takes place within the context of hypnosis. Two theorists believe that the familiar interpretation of hypnosis as an altered state of consciousness is inappropriate.

Many years ago, one of them proposed a *role-enactment theory* of hypnosis (Sarbin, 1950), and he and his associates have maintained and extended this interpretation (e.g., Sarbin and Coe, 1972). According to this theory, hypnotized subjects readily adopt the role that the hypnotist defines for them. Although good dramatic actors also tend to be hypnotizable according to this theory, Sarbin and his associates do not wish to give the impression that the hypnotic subject is play-acting in a deliberate attempt to fool the hypnotist. They insist, on the contrary, that the subject may become so deeply involved in a role that what is done takes place without conscious intent. Hence, within this theory they can accept all the usual characteristics of hypnotic responsiveness.

The other theorist who prefers to reconceptualize hypnosis believes that hypnotic behaviors can be accounted for by the usual principles of behavioral and cognitive psychology, including responsiveness to suggestion, without requiring a conception of hypnosis as an altered state (Barber, 1969). He finds, for example, that by using "task motivation instructions" the results in some instances are indistinguishable from the induction of hypnosis. These task motivation instructions imply that everyone can do what is suggested, that without full cooperation the experiment will fail, and so on. However, this evidence is questioned by others, because the demands for social compliance may lead some subjects to falsify their written reports of their experiences (Bowers, 1967).

Many of these issues were discussed more vehemently a decade or so ago. With the facts and relationships within hypnosis now better understood at an empirical level, the residual conceptual differences fade in importance, and there are signs that the differences are being resolved (e.g., Hilgard, 1973b; Sheehan and Perry, 1976; Spanos and Barber, 1974).

---

a subconscious process going on at the same time as the conscious experience, very like consciousness, but not available to the open consciousness. The expression "hidden observer" has been introduced as a metaphor to describe this concealed part that knows things that are not present in the person's open consciousness (Hilgard, 1973a, 1977).

The presence of this "hidden observer" has been demonstrated in experiments in which subjects are asked to undergo a stress that is normally quite painful, such as placing the hand and forearm in ice water, or having the circulation in the forearm cut off by a tourniquet placed above the elbow. When hypnotized, the subjects are given the suggestion that they will feel no pain or other sensation, and most report they are comfortable throughout the stress period (e.g., Hilgard and Hilgard, 1975).

If, however, the subjects are told under hypnosis to report what they feel through automatic writing, the "hidden observer" may report increasing pain,

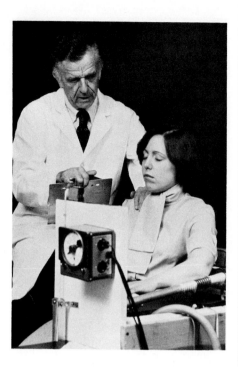

Fig. 6-10A Pain under hypnosis
Previously, when her hand was in the ice water, the subject felt no pain following suggestions of hypnotic anaesthesia. With his hand on her shoulder, however, the experimenter can tap a "hidden observer" that reports pain that had been felt at some level. (Hilgard, 1978)

even while the hypnotized person verbally reports no pain at all. After the stress is removed and the arm has returned to normal, the subjects are told that when the experimenter places a hand on their shoulder, the "hidden observer" will tell what it remembers about the experience. The "hidden observer" recalls that the water was indeed very cold, or that the bloodless arm was in pain, but usually reports that the pains were not as severe as they would have been in the normal nonhypnotic state. Figure 6-10B shows a comparison of reports in the normal nonhypnotic state, after insensitivity (anaesthesia) has been suggested in hypnosis, and what the "hidden observer" feels, in this case reported through automatic writing.

Other experiments have shown that the "hidden observer" can report sounds heard while the subject is hypnotically deaf or can remember the number of fingers held before the subject's face when the subject is hypnotically blind. It is as though the information received from the environment is registered, processed, stored in memory, and placed under some sort of barrier to recovery before ever becoming openly conscious. Although these experimental results can be demonstrated with only a small number of highly hypnotizable subjects, such subjects represent "pure cases" important for theory.

It is plausible to interpret the results as supporting the parallel processing interpretation, discussed earlier: two levels of consciousness appear to be operating at once—one reporting no pain, the other reporting pain. An adequate theory of the dissociations involved could account for the facts not only of hypnosis but of multiple personality and other related nonhypnotic phenomena.

Psychology and the Miraculous

The interest in human potential and the desire for increased self-awareness have renewed interest in esoteric philosophies, psychologies, and religious beliefs (Tart, 1975; Ornstein, 1977). These topics deserve serious consideration in any discussion of consciousness and control. Some of the beliefs are associated with respected ancient and philosophical traditions. These and newer excursions into the occult lie outside a naturalistic psychology's province. When the claims are tangible, however, psychologists may examine them according to ordinary scientific criteria, as described earlier for ESP (see Chapter 5).

Mind over Body

The results of hypnosis and the well-established facts of psychosomatic medicine demonstrate that a person's attitudes and expectations can control what happens to bodily processes. For centuries those who practiced yoga in India have been able to gain remarkable control over processes that are ordinarily involuntary (Wenger and Bagchi, 1961; Wenger, Bagchi, and Anand, 1961; see

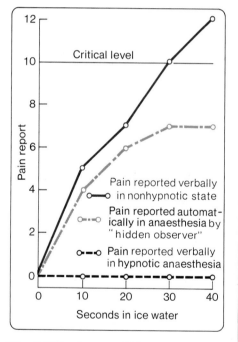

Fig. 6-10B Open and hidden reports of pain
Pain as verbally reported in a nonhypnotic state, in hypnotic anaesthesia, and as reported by the "hidden observer" in automatic writing. Data from a single subject. (Courtesy of Department of Psychology, Stanford University)

also Figure 6-11). Until recently it was assumed that such control resulted from long and disciplined exercise. This may be true in some instances, but laboratory methods have produced comparable effects through brief biofeedback training. In biofeedback, the process that is to be controlled (such as muscle tension, heart rate, or blood pressure) is amplified electronically, so that the subject is aware of what is happening and through this information ("feedback") learns control. Thus, there need be no appeal to religion or otherworldly powers to produce demonstrable results.

With practice, people can gain remarkable voluntary control over their bodies, as witness any skilled acrobatic performance. People learn to wiggle their ears and do many other muscular tricks without any appeal to agents outside themselves (see Figure 6-12).

Another illustration of "mind over body" is firewalking, a ceremony engaged in in many parts of the world. People, including children, do indeed walk barefoot over hot coals, many of them without injuring their feet. (Some who try are seriously burned, but this is explained as a consequence of their having done something to annoy a responsible "spirit.") After careful experimentation, a physicist gave a naturalistic physical explanation of this ability: perspiration protects the feet, provided the person walks rapidly (Walker, 1977). To show his confidence in his own theory, he put his finger into a vessel of molten lead and withdrew it without injury. He was also successful in walking across a bed of coals, and a student in his class joined him without mishap. (On a later occasion he caught some embers between his toes and ended up with a few blisters.) Thus, nothing in the way of religious preparation or hypnosis need be involved. When the problem is one of controlling pain—as in instances in which devotees to special beliefs are suspended in the air by hooks implanted in the muscles of their backs—self-hypnosis is a plausible explanation of the absence of pain.

Yet such facts of the mental control over bodily functions should not be used to support beliefs in such hoaxes as "psychic surgery," practiced in some parts of the Philippines. Without the use of a knife, the healer appears to open

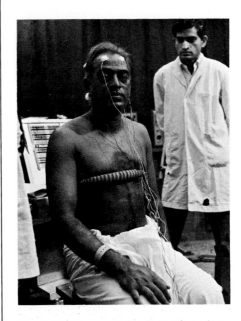

Fig. 6-11 **The control of vital functions** Ramanand Yogi has transducers attached for the study of EEGs, heart rate, and breathing as he prepares to reduce his oxygen needs while sealed in an airtight box. (From Calder, 1971)

Fig. 6-12 **Voluntary muscular control** Not all people are able to groove their tongues, but through practice this young woman has been able to form up to three grooves when she wishes to. (Courtesy of A. J. Hilgard)

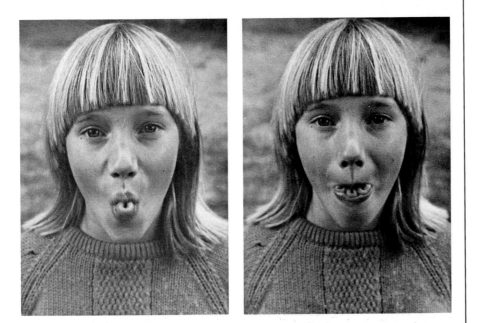

the skin, remove organic matter, and close the wound, without a scar. The trick involved has been exposed frequently; still the belief dies hard (Nolen, 1974).

Mind over Matter

A young magician, Uri Geller, became famous in the United States and Great Britain by claiming paranormal (even supernatural) power (Geller, 1975). He managed to convince a number of physical scientists and even a few magicians (who are often better at detecting tricks than scientists) that his paranormal abilities were genuine (e.g., Panati, 1976). Among his mental powers over substances were his abilities to bend keys and repair broken watches, without touching them.

To make broken watches operate, Geller instructs participants to hold "broken" watches in their hands and to think, "Work! Work! Work!" However, most watches brought to a jeweler for repair are not actually broken; holding the watch in one's hands for a few minutes and handling it to free the working parts will often start it running. In a test of the "Geller effect," six jewelers were asked to try to start watches brought to them for repairs by using the holding-and-handling methods before opening the watch to inspect it. Of more than 100 watches brought in during one week, 57 percent started working. In one of Geller's stage performances, he was given 12 watches on stage; 4 started. Out of 17 watches that members of the audience held, 3 started. This yields 7 of 29 (24 percent), less success than the physical manipulation by the jewelers (Marks and Kammann, 1977).

Reincarnation

Psychic researchers have long searched for tangible evidence of survival after death (Gould, 1977). Related to these efforts is a revived interest in *reincarnation,* the belief that life continues after death by a new cycle of birth and growth in which the spirit of the dead person lives again in the form of another person (Stevenson, 1977).

In his review of the evidence, Stevenson mentions hypnotic regression as an aid to the study of reincarnation. He cites as support the widely publicized case of a young American housewife who under hypnosis talked of her previous life in Ireland under the name of Bridey Murphy (Bernstein, 1956). Stevenson fails to report, however, that this episode was subsequently explained by the subject's childhood acquaintance with an Irish woman in Chicago whose maiden name was Bridie Murphy! (Gardner, 1957). It is easy under hypnosis to produce fantasies of birth experience or of an earlier life, and such evidence need not be taken seriously as reflecting reality.

The desire to experience mysterious happenings is very great. The role of psychology is not particularly to contradict untenable beliefs, but rather to understand why they have originated and why they persist. In some periods of history, social unrest spawns these beliefs. For example, the period just before the French Revolution was known as the Age of Enlightenment, and science made great advances; however, at the same time in France, dissatisfaction with the king and queen and attendant social conditions produced an age of hysteria, including widespread support for the exaggerations of Mesmer's animal magnetism. In recent decades, dissatisfaction with the Vietnam Conflict and other aspects of contemporary culture have produced a somewhat similar reaching out for the unfamiliar in our society.

1 In order to describe consciousness and its boundary states, distinctions are made between those states we are fully aware of and others we may or may not be dimly aware of. Those memories that we are not now aware of but which may easily be brought to full awareness are called *available memories*, or *preconscious* processes. Some influences may *register* in our nervous systems, so that they affect our actions, even though we are not aware of them; when these are stimuli that we might perceive at other intensities, the experience is described as *subliminal perception*. The processes involved in subliminal perception and related activities that go on with dim or absent awareness are called *subconscious*.

2 At the extreme of unawareness are experiences that affect what we do but are so hidden that we cannot become aware of them except by indirect methods; if they are interpreted as having some of the characteristics of conscious processes, even though concealed, they are called *unconscious* processes. Freud interpreted such processes as *repressed*. Janet interpreted some unavailable subconscious processes as split off, or *dissociated;* such processes, unlike truly unconscious ones, may become available to consciousness.

3 Two basic modes of consciousness may be distinguished: *passive*, receptive states and *active*, productive mental activities. Sensory and aesthetic experiences lie in the first mode, along with various fantasies and quasi-mystical experiences. The active role of consciousness is represented in initiating and monitoring activities that are undertaken to fulfill plans and to reach goals.

4 The boundaries between the active and the passive become blurred when we consider consciousness as an *agent of control*. Voluntary behavior appears to be largely conscious, because it depends on a deliberate decision to engage in a particular activity. At the same time, voluntary acts can become habitual, in which case consciousness recedes.

5 The unity of consciousness is an illusion, supported by the experienced continuities of our memories. Consciousness is often *divided*, as we shift attention and do more than one thing at a time. When attention is divided between two simultaneous stimulus presentations or sources of information, two main interpretations are offered. One is that attention is really given to only one thing at a time, but there may be a rapid shift from one context to another. This is known as *serial*, or *intermittent, processing* of the information from the two contemporaneous sources. The other interpretation is that the two processes are indeed simultaneous; this is described as *parallel processing*. If one of the processes is conscious and the other subconscious, the processes are *dissociated*.

6 Multiple personalities represent extreme dissociations, because the divided parts of the personality have some degree of independence and integration, as though they were separate selves within the same body.

7 Sleep as a familiar altered state of consciousness is of interest because of the rhythms evident in sleep schedules and in the depth of sleep (now studied with the aid of the electroencephalogram—the EEG), and because of the voluntary and involuntary controls that determine the onset of sleep. Napping practices illustrate the significance of voluntary controls. Sleep disturbances, such as *narcolepsy* and *apnea*, show the importance of involuntary controls.

8 As a consequence of electrophysiological measurements during sleep, the study of dreams progressed rapidly over the last two decades. One finding is that dreaming occurs more often during rapid-eye-movement (REM) sleep

than during non-REM (NREM) sleep. Dream theories, such as those of Freud and Jung, have been tested in part through dream deprivation. Many other questions about dreams have also been answered.

9 Various meditative techniques can alter subjective feelings and also produce physiological changes that are associated with relaxation.

10 Drugs have long been used to affect consciousness. The psychoactive drugs include the *depressants*, such as alcohol and heroin, the *stimulants*, such as the amphetamines and cocaine, and the *hallucinogens*, such as LSD and marijuana. Each of these drugs has its own characteristic effects, subject to dosage, individual differences among the users, and the social surroundings in which the drug is used.

11 Those who are responsive to hypnotic procedures experience a number of characteristic changes, such as the redistribution of attention, the modification of muscular control, the acceptance of reality distortions, and the readiness to accept suggested roles. Efforts to find out why some people are more readily hypnotizable than others have found that those capable of setting reality aside temporarily (through imaginative involvements) are most likely to prove hypnotizable. This ability may derive from childhood experiences, although there may also be a hereditary component.

12 Some characteristic hypnotic responses illustrate divided consciousness. Among these are *posthypnotic amnesia*, responses to *posthypnotic suggestions* of other kinds, *age regression*, and the dissociation of competing tasks when one is performed consciously, the other subconsciously. The divisions have been shown experimentally by the "hidden observer" method.

13 Associated with the interest in human potential is a widespread interest in the miraculous. A great deal of control can be exercised over bodily processes without resorting to belief in occult agencies or paranormal processes. Even control over normally involuntary processes can be taught and learned by naturalistic methods. Explanations of some "miraculous" processes, such as firewalking, can be explained according to ordinary physical principles. Psychology as a natural science is committed to an open-minded testing of claims that defy the established laws of nature.

FURTHER READING

Several multiple-author books cover a number of the topics in this chapter: Ornstein (ed.), *The nature of human consciousness* (1974), in paperback; Tart (ed.), *Altered states of consciousness* (1972), in paperback; Zinberg (ed.), *Alternate states of consciousness* (1977); and Schwartz and Shapiro (eds.), *Consciousness and self-regulation*, vol. 1 (1976). See also Ornstein, *The psychology of consciousness* (2nd ed., 1977) and Pope and Singer, *The stream of consciousness* (1978).

Problems of divided consciousness, including discussions of possession states, fugues, multiple personality, and other manifestations in and outside of hypnosis, are treated in Hilgard, *Divided consciousness* (1977).

Some of the more recent books on sleep and dreams, intended for the general reader, are Dement, *Some must watch while some must sleep* (1976), in paperback; Cartwright, *A primer of sleep and dreaming* (1978); and Webb, *Sleep, the gentle tyrant* (1975). An interesting and somewhat speculative book designed to help a person gain self-awareness through dreams is Faraday, *Dream power* (1973), in paperback. The influence of Jung is more evident here than in the other books mentioned. For a review of recent studies, see also Webb and Cartwright, *Sleep and dreams* (1978).

A useful book on the varieties of meditative practices is Naranjo and Ornstein, *On the psychology of meditation* (1977), in paperback. Representative of books on meditation that follow the ancient traditions of yoga more closely than does TM are Chaudhuri, *Philosophy of meditation* (1965) and Mishra, *Self analysis and self knowledge* (1977).

Contemporary and historical drug problems are covered in a two-volume work: Blum and others, *Society and drugs* and *Students and drugs* (both 1969). Amphetamines and cocaine are treated in Ellinwood and Kilbey (eds.), *Cocaine and other stimulants* (1977) and in Peterson and Stillman (eds.), *Cocaine: 1977* (1977). The collection of Freud's early papers, along with commentaries by A. Freud and the editor, in Byck (ed.), *Cocaine papers* (1974) is of more than historical interest. On hallucinogens, see Siegel and West, *Hallucinations: Behavior, experience, and theory* (1975).

There are a number of recent books on hypnosis. Those for the general reader include Bowers, *Hypnosis for the seriously curious* (1976) and Gibson, *Hypnosis: Its nature and therapeutic uses* (1978). More specialized treatments that include methods, theories, and experimental results are Barber, *Hypnosis, a scientific approach* (1969), Fromm and Shor (eds.), *Hypnosis: Research developments and perspectives* (rev. ed., 1979), E. R. Hilgard, *The experience of hypnosis* (1968), J. R. Hilgard, *Personality and hypnosis* (1970), Hilgard and Hilgard, *Hypnosis in the relief of pain* (1975), Sarbin and Coe, *Hypnosis: A social psychological analysis of influence communication* (1972), and Sheehan and Perry, *Methodologies of hypnosis* (1976).

A wide range of studies, in which the most active of the current American investigators are represented, has been edited by Edmonston in *Conceptual and investigative approaches to hypnosis and hypnotic phenomena* (1977).

There are many books on miraculous and paranormal experiences, but few of them have scientific merit. A serious effort to collect a variety of viewpoints, primarily of those who are committed to their beliefs, has been made by Wolman and others (eds.) in *Handbook of parapsychology* (1977). This includes, in addition to the more usual problems of parapsychology, two chapters on life after death.

PART FOUR

Learning, Remembering, and Thinking

7
Conditioning and Learning

L earning is basic to understanding behavior. The psychological study of learning embraces much more than the learning of a new job or an academic subject; it also bears upon the fundamental problems of emotional development, motivation, social behavior, and personality. We've already discussed many instances of learning—how, for example, children learn to perceive the world around them, to identify with the appropriate sex, and to control their behavior according to adult standards. In this part of the book, we turn to a systematic study of learning. In this chapter we examine several simple forms of learning that can be studied in the laboratory and that provide a basis for understanding more complicated phenomena. In Chapter 8, we deal with memory, an essential element of learning. And in Chapter 9, we discuss the learning involved in language and thought.

Learning may be defined as a *relatively permanent change in behavior that occurs as the result of prior experience.* This change may not be evident until a situation arises in which the new behavior can occur; learning is not always immediately reflected in performance. Not all changes can be explained as learning, so our definition has to be qualified to exclude them. The phrase *relatively permanent* excludes those changes in behavior that result from temporary or transient conditions, such as fatigue or the influence of drugs. By specifying that learning is the result of *experience*, we exclude changes that are due to maturation, disease, or physical damage. Learning could be defined more simply as "profiting from experience," were it not that some learning does not "profit" the learner: useless and harmful habits are learned just as useful ones are.

How do organisms learn? There is no simple reply to that question, but we can begin our discussion by examining *associative learning.* Making a new association or connection between events in the environment is the most basic form of learning. Psychologists distinguish between two forms of associative learning: *classical conditioning* and *operant conditioning.* In classical conditioning, an organism learns that two *stimuli* tend to go together. For example, a baby learns that the sight of a nursing bottle (one stimulus) is associated with the taste of milk (another stimulus). In operant conditioning, an organism learns that some *response* it makes leads to a particular *consequence*. For example, a baby learns that raising a bottle to his or her mouth (the response) brings milk (the consequence).

We begin this chapter with a consideration of classical and operant conditioning. But there is more to learning than associating one event with another. In later sections of the chapter, we turn to more complex forms of learning, which involve interpreting present perceptions in the light of past information to reason our way through unfamiliar problems—for example, using a map to find our way over unfamiliar routes. These more complicated processes, called *cognitive learning*, are a prelude to our study of human memory and language in the next two chapters.

Classical Conditioning

The study of *classical conditioning* began with a series of experiments conducted by the Russian Nobel Prize winner Ivan Pavlov at the turn of the century. While studying digestion, Pavlov noticed that a dog began to salivate at the mere sight of a food dish. Any dog salivates when food is placed in its mouth. But this dog had learned to associate the sight of the dish with the taste of food. Pavlov decided to see whether a dog could be taught to associate food with other things, such as a light or a tone.

Pavlov's Experiments

A dog is prepared for Pavlov's experiment by having a minor operation performed on its cheek so that part of the salivary gland is exposed to the surface. A capsule is attached to the cheek to measure salivary flow. The dog is brought to a soundproof laboratory on several occasions and is placed in a

Fig. 7-1 Classical-conditioning apparatus
Arrangements used by Pavlov in classical salivary conditioning. The apparatus permits a light (the conditioned stimulus) to appear in the window and the delivery of meat powder (the unconditioned stimulus) to the food bowl. (After Yerkes and Margulis, 1909)

harness on a table. This preliminary training is needed so the animal will stand quietly in the harness once the actual experiment gets underway. The laboratory is so arranged that meat powder can be delivered to a pan in front of the dog by remote control. Salivation is recorded automatically. The experimenter can view the animal through a one-way glass panel, but the dog is alone in the laboratory, isolated from extraneous sights and noises (see Figure 7-1).

A light is turned on. The dog may move a bit, but it does not salivate. After a few seconds, meat powder is delivered; the dog is hungry and eats. The recording device registers copious salivation. The procedure is repeated a number of times. Then the experimenter turns on the light but does not deliver any meat powder. The dog salivates nonetheless. It has learned to associate the light with food.

Pavlov called this a *conditioned response.* The dog has been taught, or conditioned, to associate the light with food and to respond to it by salivating. Naturally, a dog salivates when it tastes meat. This is an *unconditioned response;* no learning is involved. By the same token, meat is an *unconditioned stimulus.* It automatically makes the dog salivate. Again, no learning is involved. Ordinarily a light would not produce this response, however. Only when the dog has been conditioned to associate the light with food does it salivate. Hence the light is a *conditioned stimulus* that acquired its power to stimulate the dog through association.

Pavlov's experiment was a pioneering demonstration of *classical conditioning:* the formation of a new association between a conditioned stimulus and a response through the repeated pairing of the conditioned stimulus with an unconditioned stimulus that elicits the response. As indicated above, the original response to the unconditioned stimulus is called an unconditioned response (UR); the learned response to the conditioned stimulus is called a conditioned response (CR). The arrangement is diagramed in Figure 7-2.

Laws of Classical Conditioning

Because classical conditioning represents an extremely simple form of learning, many psychologists regard it as an appropriate starting point for the investigation of the learning process. We will now consider some of the laws that characterize classical conditioning.

ACQUISITION Each paired presentation of the conditioned stimulus (CS) and the unconditioned stimulus (US) is called a *trial,* and the period during which the organism is learning the association between the two is the *acquisition* stage of conditioning. The time interval between the presentation of the conditioned and unconditioned stimuli may be varied. Again, let us use Pavlov's experiment as an example. In *simultaneous conditioning,* the light (CS) is turned on a fraction of a second before the meat (US) is presented and is left on until the dog salivates (the response). In *delayed conditioning,* the light (CS) is turned on several seconds or more before the meat (US) is presented and is again left on until the response occurs. In *trace conditioning,* the light (CS) is turned on first and then turned off before the meat (US) is presented, so that only a "memory trace" of the light, or CS, remains to be conditioned. These three situations are illustrated in Figure 7-3.

In delayed and trace conditioning, the experimenter knows that the organism has made the new association if the response (salivating) occurs before the unconditioned stimulus (meat) has been presented. With simultaneous conditioning, the experimenter has to use test trials in which the unconditioned

Ivan Pavlov (center) with assistants in his laboratory

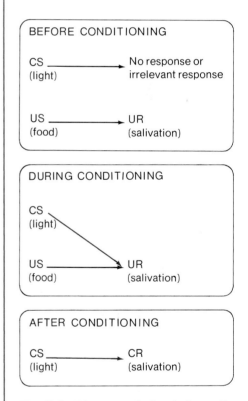

Fig. 7-2 Diagram of classical conditioning
The association between the unconditioned stimulus and the unconditioned response exists at the start of the experiment and does not have to be learned. The association between the conditioned stimulus and the conditioned response is learned. It arises through the pairing of the conditioned and unconditioned stimuli followed by the unconditioned response. The conditioned response resembles the unconditioned one but generally differs in some details.

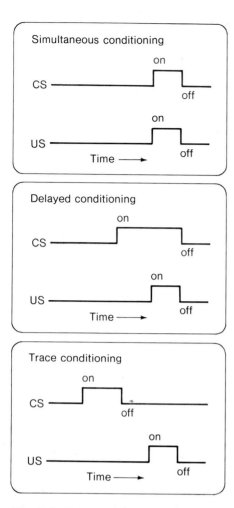

Fig. 7-3 **Temporal relations in conditioning**

Inflections stand for stimulus onsets; deflections represent terminations. Conditioning is best for the delayed condition when the CS precedes the US by approximately one-half second. Conditioning is somewhat less effective in the simultaneous condition and becomes progressively poorer for both the delayed and trace conditions as the CS-US interval increases. If the US precedes the CS (called *backward conditioning*), little if any learning occurs.

stimulus (meat) is withheld to determine if the organism has made the new association. Then if salivation occurs when the conditioned stimulus (light) is presented alone, we know that conditioning has occurred.

Repeated pairings of the conditioned stimulus (light) and the unconditioned stimulus (meat) strengthen, or *reinforce,* the conditioned response. The left-hand panel in Figure 7-4 shows the dog's acquisition of the salivary response to the conditioned stimulus of a light. By the third trial, the animal is responding to the light with seven drops of saliva. By the seventh trial, saliva secretion has leveled off and continues (with minor fluctuations) at about the same strength for the next nine trials. This stable level of responding is called the *asymptote* of the learning curve; further acquisition trials will not produce any greater strength of response.

EXTINCTION If the conditioned behavior is not reinforced—if the unconditioned stimulus is omitted repeatedly—the conditioned response gradually diminishes. Repetition of the conditioned stimulus without reinforcement (turning on the light without offering meat) is called *extinction.* Its effect on the animal's performance is shown in the right-hand curve in Figure 7-4. Notice that on the fourth nonreinforced trial the amount of salivation has decreased to about three drops; by the ninth extinction trial the CS is eliciting no salivation at all.

Examples of Classical Conditioning

Before continuing our discussion of classical conditioning, let's consider a few examples of the basic procedure. A wide variety of responses, including some

Fig. 7-4 **Acquisition and extinction of a conditioned response**
The curve in the panel on the left depicts the acquisition phase of an experiment using the trace-conditioning procedure. Drops of salivation in response to the conditioned stimulus (prior to the onset of the US) are plotted on the vertical axis, the number of trials on the horizontal axis. The CR gradually increases over trials and approaches an asymptotic level of about 11 to 12 drops of saliva. After 16 acquisition trials, the experimenter switched to extinction; the results are presented in the panel at the right. Note that the CR gradually decreases when reinforcement is omitted. (Data from Pavlov, 1927)

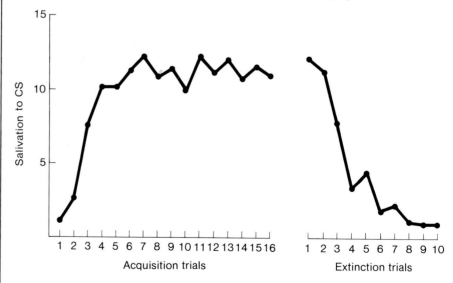

we would not ordinarily consider learnable, have been successfully conditioned in both animal and human subjects. In one study, an insulin reaction was conditioned in rats (Sawrey, Conger, and Turrell, 1956). Insulin, a hormone that controls the blood-sugar level, is often used in treating diabetics. An overdose of insulin causes a severe physiological reaction known as *insulin shock,* which is often accompanied by unconsciousness. In the experiment, the rats were exposed to a bright light and at the same time were injected with an overdose of insulin. The bright light and the hypodermic needle served as the conditioned stimuli; the insulin injection, which elicited shock, was the unconditioned stimulus. After several pairings of the CS and US, a saline solution (which has no physiological effect) was substituted for the insulin. The animals continued to show a shock reaction almost indistinguishable from the reaction produced by insulin. The shock reaction had become a conditioned response.

In this experiment, the conditioned response is not a single, easily measured response such as salivation, but a complex pattern of physiological and muscular responses that constitutes the insulin-shock reaction. A more quantitative physiological measure of conditioning was obtained in the following experiment using human subjects. Exposure of the human body to cold automatically results in vasoconstriction, the constriction of the small blood vessels close to the body surface—a response that keeps the body warm. Although we are totally unaware of this response, it can be conditioned. A buzzer (CS) is sounded as the subject's left hand is immersed in a container of ice water (US). Since vasoconstriction of the left hand automatically results in some constriction of the blood vessels in the right hand, the degree of vasoconstriction can be measured by using a special instrument that is placed on the subject's right hand. After a number of paired presentations of the buzzer and water immersion, vasoconstriction occurs in response to the buzzer alone (Menzies, 1937).

Classical conditioning has also been used to study learning in five- to seven-day-old human newborns (see Figure 7-5). When a puff of air is blown on the eye, the natural response is to blink. If a tone is sounded immediately before the air puff, the newborn soon learns to associate the tone with the air puff and blinks on hearing the tone alone. This procedure is extremely useful for studying learning in very young infants.

Laboratory studies of classical conditioning with humans and animals indicate that learning is best when the CS precedes the US by about one-half second. When the CS precedes the US by more than one-half second, learning becomes progressively poorer as the interval between the two stimuli increases. However, there are exceptions to this rule, depending on the nature of the CS and US employed—as *taste aversion studies* demonstrate. In these experiments, a novel-tasting solution (CS) is given to the animal prior to a drug (US) that has a delayed action—it induces a severe intestinal illness sometime later. The animal develops a strong aversion to the flavor of the solution and will make every effort to avoid it.

Aversions have been conditioned in a single trial and may occur even when there is a 5- to 10-hour delay between the taste of the solution and the illness. Conditioning will not occur with long delay intervals, however, if lights or tones are used as the CS rather than a flavored solution. Apparently, an innate biological relation between taste and illness is critical in determining the readiness with which conditioning occurs—a fact that has adaptive significance for animals in the wild (Garcia and others, 1972).

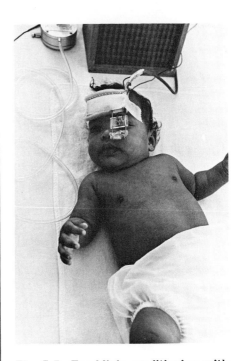

Fig. 7-5 Eye-blink conditioning with newborns
The CS is a tone and the US is a mild puff of air. The response is an eye-blink that is soon conditioned to the onset of the tone. (Courtesy of Lewis Lipsitt)

"Perhaps, Dr. Pavlov, he could be taught to seal envelopes."

Theoretical Interpretations

Two quite different theoretical explanations of classical conditioning can be offered. They have their origins in the *cognitive* and *behavioral* approaches to psychology, discussed in Chapter 1.

The cognitive viewpoint assumes that in classical conditioning the organism observes (over a series of trials) that the CS and US occur together and stores this information in memory. When the CS is presented at some later time, the information is retrieved from memory and the organism makes the CR in *expectation* of reinforcement (the US). The organism is thus viewed as an information processing system. It stores in memory information about stimuli that it experiences. Later, when confronted with the CS, it retrieves the relevant information from memory and acts on that information in an appropriate way; namely, it anticipates food (the US) and begins to salivate.

The behavioral viewpoint is more mechanistic—it emphasizes the automatic nature of learning. If a stimulus occurs and is followed by a response, which in turn is followed by a reinforcement, then a stimulus-response (S-R) connection is formed. This connection is strengthened with each additional reinforcement. Thus, classical conditioning involves the automatic formation of a connection between a CS and a CR that is strengthened with each reinforcement.

Generalization

When a conditioned response has been acquired to a particular stimulus, other similar stimuli will evoke the response. A dog that learns to salivate to the sound of a tuning fork producing a tone of middle C will also salivate to higher or lower tones without further conditioning. The more nearly alike the new stimuli are to the original, the more likely they are to evoke the conditioned response. This principle, called *generalization*, accounts for our ability to react to novel situations insofar as they are similar to familiar ones.

A study using the galvanic skin response (GSR) illustrates generalization. The GSR is an easily measured change in the electrical activity of the skin that occurs during emotional stress. A mild electric shock will elicit GSR. In the experiment, a pure tone of a specified pitch served as the CS; shock served as the US. After the GSR had been conditioned to the tone, the subject was tested with tones of higher and lower pitches. Figure 7-6 shows the results, plotted in terms of the amplitude of the GSR versus test tones of varying pitches. The high point of the curve represents the amplitude of the GSR to the original tone; the points to the left show the GSR amplitudes to tones lower than the CS, and those to the right, the amplitudes to tones higher than the CS. As you can see, the GSR amplitude decreases as the tones become progressively more dissimilar to the original tone. This plotted relationship is called the *gradient of generalization*.

Stimulus generalization need not be confined to a single sense. For example, with human subjects, a GSR conditioned to the sound of a bell may also appear (although in a lesser amount) at the sight of a bell or the sound of the word *bell*. Conditioning a response to the meaning of a word is called *semantic conditioning*. A Russian psychologist (Volkova, 1953) provided an interesting example of semantic conditioning and generalization. Volkova used a modification of Pavlov's conditioning experiment with young children. The US was cranberry purée delivered to the child's mouth via a chute; the response was salivation. The CS was the Russian word for "good" pronounced aloud by the experimenter. After conditioning had been established, the experimenter tested for generalization by reciting some Russian sentences that could be

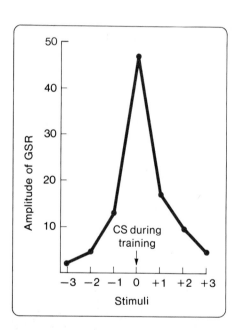

Fig. 7-6 Gradient of generalization Stimulus 0 denotes the tone to which the galvanic skin response (GSR) was originally conditioned. Stimuli +1, +2, and +3 represent test tones of increasingly higher pitch; stimuli −1, −2, and −3 represent tones of lower pitch. Note that the amount of generalization decreases as the difference between the test tone and the training tone increases. (After Hovland, 1937)

of Classical Conditioning

The cognitive approach to classical conditioning sees the organism as acquiring information about relations among stimuli in its environment and then sorting through that information to make an appropriate response—a response that anticipates reinforcement. The behavioral approach, in contrast, sees the organism as more passive: S-R connections are formed and strengthened in a mechanistic fashion.

These two theoretical views of classical conditioning have natural extensions to more complex forms of learning. Psychologists disagree as to which theoretical approach is most promising. In some experiments, an automatic strengthening of an S-R connection appears to provide the simplest explanation of the data. In others, the organism's behavior is so complicated that to explain it in terms of S-R connections yields a theoretical ac-

count that seems hopelessly cumbersome. Should all learning be explained by one theory or the other? Or is it possible that some forms of learning are best explained by the behavioral approach and others by a cognitive approach? We shall return to this question later, but the reader should be warned that there is no simple answer. For a more detailed discussion of these issues, see Rescorla (1975), Rudy and Wagner (1975), and Estes (1975).

---

construed as communicating something "good" and some that could not. Volkova found that the children would salivate to sentences like "The pioneer helps his comrade" and "Leningrad is a wonderful city," but not to ones like "The pupil was rude to the teacher" and "My friend is seriously ill."

Discrimination

A process complementary to generalization is *discrimination.* Whereas generalization is reaction to similarities, discrimination is reaction to differences. Conditioned discrimination is brought about through selective reinforcement and extinction, as shown in Figure 7-7.

In the experiment illustrated, two clearly different tones, CS_1 and CS_2, served as the discriminative stimuli. One or the other of the two tones was presented on each trial. The first tone (CS_1) was followed by a mild electric shock; the second (CS_2) was not. Initially, subjects made the conditioned response (in this case, the GSR) to both tones. During the course of the experiment, however, the amplitude of the conditioned response to CS_1 gradually increased, while the amplitude of the response to CS_2 decreased. The subjects had been conditioned to discriminate between the two tones.

Generalization and discrimination appear in everyday behavior. The young child who has learned to say "bow-wow" to a dog may understandably respond in like manner to a similar stimulus, such as a sheep. On first learning the name "Daddy," a child may overgeneralize it to all men. By differential reinforcement and extinction, the response is narrowed to a single appropriate stimulus.

Operant Conditioning

Operant conditioning is another approach to the study of learning. When you teach a dog a trick, you cannot use classical conditioning. What unconditioned stimuli would make the animal sit up or roll over? So you get the dog to do the

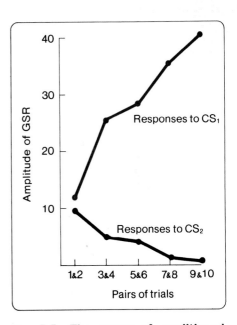

Fig. 7-7 The course of conditioned discrimination
The discriminative stimuli were two tones of clearly different pitch (CS_1 = 700 Hz and CS_2 = 3500 Hz). The unconditioned stimulus, an electric shock, applied to the left forefinger, occurred only on trials when CS_1 was presented. The strength of the conditioned response, in this case the GSR, gradually increased following CS_1 and extinguished following CS_2. (After Baer and Fuhrer, 1968)

trick as best you can and *afterward* reward it with either approval or food. The approval or food does not *produce* the behavior.

In Pavlov's experiment, the conditioned response resembles the normal response to the unconditioned stimulus; salivation, for example, is a dog's normal response to food. But in the other case, the reinforced behavior bears no resemblance to the behavior normally elicited by the reinforcing stimulus (for example, rolling over is not a dog's normal response to food).

To describe this kind of conditioning, B. F. Skinner introduced the concept of *operant conditioning.* To understand operant conditioning, we need to distinguish between what Skinner called respondent and operant behavior. *Respondent behavior* is a direct response to a stimulus, as in the unconditioned responses of classical conditioning: the flow of saliva in response to food in the mouth, the constriction of the pupil in response to a flash of light on the eye, the knee jerk in response to a tap on the patellar tendon. In contrast, *operant behavior* simply happens; that is, it appears to be spontaneous, rather than a response to a specific stimulus. For example, alone in a crib, a baby may kick and twist and coo spontaneously, in response to nothing in particular. When left alone in a room, a dog may pad back and forth, sniff, perhaps pick up a ball, drop it, and play with it. Neither is responding to stimuli in the outside world. They are *operating* on that world.

Most voluntary behavior is operant behavior. Take answering the phone as an example. You would not walk to the telephone, pick up the receiver, and say "Hello" unless it had rung. A ringing telephone is a stimulus. It tells you that someone is on the line, but it does not force you to pick up the receiver. Answering the phone is operant behavior. The ring is a discriminative stimulus: it is the occasion for operant behavior, but it does not elicit a response in the same way that stimuli elicit respondent behavior.

Skinner's Experiments

To demonstrate operant conditioning in the laboratory, a hungry rat is placed in a box like the one shown in Figure 7-8, which is called a "Skinner box." The inside of the Skinner box is bare, except for a protruding bar with a food dish beneath it. A small light bulb above the bar can be lighted at the experimenter's discretion.

Fig. 7-8 Apparatus for operant conditioning
The photo shows the interior arrangement of the box used in the operant conditioning of a rat. This box has been named a "Skinner box," after its developer.

Left alone in the box, the rat moves about restlessly and, by chance, occasionally presses the bar.[1] The rate at which it first pushes on the bar defines its preconditioned, or operant, level of bar-pressing. After establishing the operant level, the experimenter activates a food magazine located outside the Skinner box. Now, every time the rat presses the bar, a small food pellet is released down a chute into the food dish. The rat eats and soon presses the bar again. The food *reinforces* bar-pressing, and the rate of pressing increases dramatically. If the food magazine is disconnected so that pressing the bar no longer delivers food, the rate of bar-pressing will diminish. That is, the operant response undergoes *extinction* with nonreinforcement, just as a classical-conditioned response does.

The experimenter can set up a *discrimination* by presenting food if the bar is pressed while the light is on, but not if the light is off. This selective reinforcement conditions the rat to press the bar only in the presence of the light. In this example, the light serves as a *discriminative stimulus* that controls the response.

With this illustration before us, we are ready to consider the meaning of conditioned operant behavior. As indicated above, the behavior "operates" on the environment—the rat's pressing the bar *produces* or *gains access* to the food. In classical conditioning, the animal is passive; it merely waits until the conditioned stimulus and then the unconditioned stimulus are presented. In operant conditioning, the animal is active; its behavior cannot be reinforced unless it first does something.

Thus *operant conditioning* refers to increasing the probability of a response by following the occurrence of the response with *reinforcement*. Usually the reinforcement is something that can satisfy a basic drive (like food to satisfy hunger or water to satisfy thirst) but as we will see later, it need not be.

Measures of Operant Strength

Because the bar is always present in the Skinner box, the rat can respond to it as frequently or infrequently as it chooses. Hence, *rate of response* is a useful measure of *operant strength*. The more frequently the response occurs during a given interval of time, the greater the operant strength.

The rate of response in operant conditioning is usually portrayed by a *cumulative curve* (Figure 7-9). The bar of the Skinner box is attached to a recording pen, which rests on a slowly moving strip of paper. Each time the animal presses the bar, the pen steps up a fixed distance and then continues on its horizontal path. Because the paper moves at a fixed rate, the slope of the cumulative curve is a measure of response rate. A horizontal line indicates that the animal is not responding; a steep curve indicates a fast response rate. Figure 7-10A presents cumulative curves for two rats during acquisition of a bar-pressing response. Rat A had been deprived of food for 30 hours and rat B for 10 hours. The hungrier rat responded much more rapidly.

Another measure of operant strength is the *total number of responses during extinction*. As Figure 7-10B shows, a single reinforcement can produce considerable strength according to this measure.

[1] Because the rat has been deprived of food for some specified period, it is assumed to be motivated by a hunger drive. By *drive* we refer to the aroused condition of an organism that results from deprivation of some sort. The concepts of drive and motivation are treated more fully in Chapter 10.

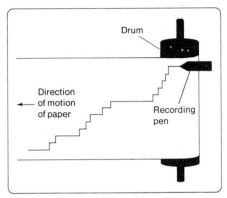

Fig. 7-9 Cumulative recorder
The axis of the drum is fixed, and, as the drum rotates, the recording paper moves right to left under the head of a writing pen. The pen is rigged so that it can only move upward, never downward. Each time the animal makes a response, the pen steps up a fixed amount. When no responses are being made, the pen moves in a straight line across the paper. Thus, the height of each step is the same, but the length of the horizontal line varies as a function of the time between responses. Since the paper is moving at a fixed rate, the slope of the cumulative curve indicates the response rate. When the animal is responding at a high rate, the slope of the cumulative curve will be quite steep; when the animal is responding very slowly, there will be hardly any slope at all.

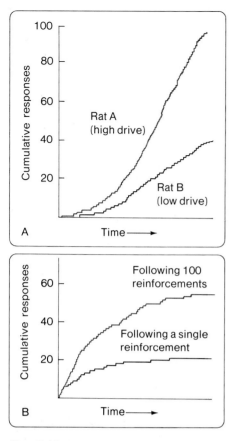

Fig. 7-10
A Cumulative curves during acquisition
This figure shows a comparison of the cumulative response curves for two rats during acquisition of a bar-pressing response. Rat A had been deprived of food for 30 hours and rat B for 10 hours prior to the experiment. This difference in the drive level of the two rats is reflected in the rate of responding.
B Cumulative curves during extinction
Curves of extinction of operant responses in a rat are plotted following a single reinforcement and following 100 reinforcements. The plot shows the cumulative number of bar-pressing responses; every response raises the height of the curve, and the curve levels off when responses cease.

Fig. 7-11 Operant responses sustained by partial reinforcement
The curves record one pigeon's pecking responses, which were reinforced irregularly but at an average interval of five minutes. The reinforcements are represented by horizontal dashes. Each of the sloping lines represents 1,000 responses—the pen resets after each 1,000.

Partial Reinforcement

Operant conditioning shows a high degree of orderliness. Experiments with *partial reinforcement*—when the behavior is reinforced only a fraction of the time it occurs—demonstrate this.

In the typical experiment, a pigeon learns to peck at a lighted disk mounted on the wall to obtain a small quantity of grain as reinforcement. Once this conditioned operant is established, the pigeon will continue to peck at a high rate, even if it only receives occasional reinforcement. The pigeon, whose remarkably regular pecking is illustrated in Figure 7-11, was reinforced with food on the average of once every five minutes (12 times an hour), yet it pecked at the disk some 6,000 times per hour.

The practical significance of partial reinforcement is great. A child's parent is not always present to offer rewards for looking both ways before crossing the street. But the influences of reinforcements are such that they persist against many nonreinforcements. A long, straight drive will keep a golfer at the game despite many balls lost in the rough.

Conditioned Reinforcement

Pavlov noted that once a dog has learned to respond to a conditioned stimulus in a highly dependable way, the conditioned stimulus itself can be used to reinforce new behavior. Suppose the animal has learned to salivate to a tone as a conditioned stimulus. If a flashing light is then presented with only the tone, the flashing light will come to elicit the conditioned response. The tone has become a *conditioned reinforcer*.

The introduction of a minor variation in the typical operant-conditioning situation will illustrate how conditioned reinforcement works. When a rat in a Skinner box presses a lever, a tone comes on momentarily, followed shortly by delivery of a food pellet. After the animal has been conditioned in this way, extinction is begun, so that when the rat presses the lever neither the tone nor the food appears. In time the animal virtually ceases to press the lever.

Now the tone is connected again, but without food. When the animal discovers that pressing the lever turns on the tone, the rate of pressing markedly increases, overcoming the extinction, even though no food follows. The tone has acquired reinforcing qualities of its own—it has become a conditioned reinforcer. The total number of responses made with only the tone connected to the bar depends on the number of tone-food pairings during acquisition.

Conditioned reinforcement has important practical implications because of its wide generalizability. The principle can be generalized as follows: once established, a conditioned reinforcer can strengthen responses other than the

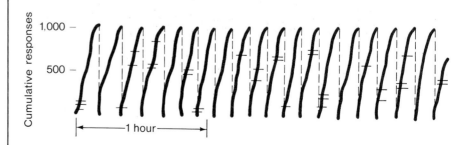

Reinforcement Schedules

Partial reinforcement procedures are of particular interest because they represent the type of reinforcement regime under which most organisms operate in nature. In addition, on partial reinforcement schedules, an animal's response rate tends to be extremely sensitive to changes in the environment. These procedures thus provide a natural barometer for assessing the effects of radiation, drugs, fatigue, and other variables on performance. In the early exploration of space, scientists frequently housed rats, pigeons, and other animals in the space capsule and placed them on a partial reinforcement schedule. By observing changes in response rate during actual flight, they were able to determine the effects of acceleration, weightlessness, and the like on performance.

Many different reinforcement schedules have been studied, but basically they all can be categorized according to two dimensions: (1) the period between successive reinforcements may be determined according to either number of intervening nonreinforced responses or elapsed time, and (2) the period between successive reinforcements may be regular or irregular. In terms of these two dimensions, we can define four basic schedules.

1 *Fixed ratio* (FR). On this schedule, reinforcement occurs after a fixed number of nonreinforced responses; if it occurs every 20 responses, for example, the ratio of nonreinforced to reinforced responses is 20 to 1.

2 *Fixed interval* (FI). Reinforcement follows the first response emitted after a fixed time period measured from the last reinforcement. For example, on a fixed-interval schedule of one minute, no further reinforcement will occur following a reinforced response until one minute has passed; once it has elapsed, the first response made will be reinforced.

3 *Variable ratio* (VR). Like the fixed-ratio schedule, reinforcement occurs after a specified number of nonreinforced responses. But for this schedule, the number of responses intervening between reinforcements varies from one reinforcement to the next. For example, a 20-to-1 variable-ratio schedule might be produced by requiring that the number of intervening responses be randomly selected from 0 to 40, with an average of 20.

4 *Variable interval* (VI). In this schedule, reinforcement occurs after a specified period of time that varies from one reinforcement to the next. A simple variable-interval schedule of one minute might be generated by randomly setting the time period between reinforcements in a range of values from 0 to 120 seconds; this schedule yields an average time period of one minute, but a given interval can range anywhere from 0 seconds to two minutes.

These four reinforcement schedules produce characteristic modes of responding. On an FI schedule, the animal's pattern of responding suggests that it is keeping careful track of time. Immediately after a reinforcement, its rate of responding drops to near zero and then increases at an accelerating pace as the end of the interval approaches. On VI schedules, the response rate does not fluctuate as much between reinforcements. This is to be expected, since the animal does not know when the interval will terminate; the animal responds at a fairly steady rate in order to receive reinforcement promptly whenever it becomes available.

In contrast to the interval schedules, both the fixed- and variable-ratio schedules tend to produce extremely rapid rates of responding. If the ratio is small, responding begins immediately after a reinforcement; when the ratio is large, there may be a brief pause after each reinforcement, followed by steady bursts of responding. On ratio schedules, the animal responds as though it knows that the next reinforcement depends on its making a certain number of responses, and it bursts forth with them at as fast a rate as possible.

---

response used during its original establishment and can do so with drives other than the one prevailing during original training. We know from ordinary observation that such reinforcers as social approval can be effective over a wide range of behavior. Experimental evidence supports the idea that conditioned reinforcers have wide generality. In one study with water-deprived rats, the experimenter associated a tone with bar-pressing reinforced by water. When the rats were later deprived of food, rather than water, the same tone evoked bar-pressing. If enough drive of any kind is present to instigate activity, a conditioned reinforcer (in this case, the tone) is effective, even though it derived its strength while another drive prevailed (Estes, 1949).

Conditioned reinforcement greatly increases the range of possible conditioning. If everything we learned had to be followed by a primary reinforcer, the occasions for learning would be very much restricted. A verbal promise of food can reinforce behavior that would otherwise require food; mere praise (without promise of a primary reinforcer) itself becomes reinforcing.

Shaping Behavior

In classical conditioning, a conditioned stimulus (the light in Pavlov's experiment) becomes a substitute for an unconditioned stimulus (the meat powder). This process, however, does not permit *novelty* to occur in behavior—the learning of totally new responses. In contrast, operant conditioning plays an important role in the development of novel behavior.

The experimenter can produce novel behavior by taking advantage of random variations in the subjects' "operations" to lead them in a desired direction. For example, if we want to train a dog to press a buzzer with its nose, the experimenter can give a food reinforcement each time the animal approaches the area of the buzzer, requiring it to move closer and closer to the desired spot for each reinforcement until finally the dog's nose is touching the buzzer. This technique of reinforcing only responses that meet the experimenter's specifications and extinguishing all others is called *shaping* the animal's behavior (see Figure 7-12).

Two psychologists developed a large-scale business teaching animals elaborate tricks and behavior routines by means of this shaping method. Using these relatively simple techniques, they and their staff have trained thousands of animals of many species for TV shows and commercials, county fairs, and various tourist attractions, such as the famous whale and porpoise shows at Marine Studios in Florida and Marineland of the Pacific in California. One popular show featured a pig called "Priscilla, the Fastidious Pig." Priscilla turned on the TV set, ate breakfast at a table, picked up dirty clothes and put them in a hamper, vacuumed the floor, picked out her favorite food (from among foods competing with that of her sponsor!), and took part in a quiz program, answering questions from the audience by flashing lights indicating "Yes" or "No." She was not an unusually bright pig; in fact, because pigs grow so fast, a new "Priscilla" was trained every three to five months. The ingenuity was not the pig's but the experimenters', who used operant conditioning and shaped the behavior to produce the desired result (Breland and Breland, 1966).

Operant Conditioning of Human Behavior

In the following experiment, college students were unaware that an experiment was being conducted (Verplanck, 1955). The experimenter carried on what appeared to be an informal conversation with the subject but actually behaved according to a plan. The experimenter determined in advance to reinforce all statements of opinion the subject made, such as sentences beginning "I think," "I believe," "It seems to me," and the like. The *reinforcement* consisted of the experimenter's saying "You're right," "I agree," or "That's so" after each statement of opinion. *Extinction* was carried out in another portion of the experiment by mere nonreinforcement—silence—following a statement of opinion.

During the period when verbal reinforcement was given, statements of opinion increased markedly in frequency; during extinction, they decreased. The experimenter controlled verbal behavior in this situation in much the same way that an experimenter controls rats in a Skinner box. In studies of this kind,

Fig. 7-12 Shaping behavior
By reinforcing only the desired responses, the experimenter taught the pigeon to tap the correct sign when light of a certain color was turned on.

Porpoises trained by shaping operant responses

subjects may begin to realize that the experimenter is actually manipulating their verbal behavior. There is evidence, however, that in some cases they do not (Rosenfeld and Baer, 1969).

When we discuss psychotherapy (Chapter 16), we will see other evidence that reinforcement can be highly effective in modifying human behavior. However, the possibility of adverse effects must be recognized. In a study by Lepper, Greene, and Nisbett (1973), two groups of preschool children were asked to draw pictures with special felt-tipped pens—an activity that initially held intrinsic interest. In the Expect Award group, subjects agreed to engage in this activity to obtain a reinforcement (a "Good Player Award" certificate adorned with a gold seal and red ribbon). Subjects in the No Award group neither expected nor received the reward but otherwise duplicated the experiences of the other subjects. Several weeks later, when observed unobtrusively in their classrooms, Expected Award subjects showed less interest in drawing than the No Award subjects. The provision of rewards turned "play" (that is, an activity engaged in for its own sake) into "work" (an activity engaged in only when extrinsic incentives are present).

Operant Conditioning of Autonomic Responses

Classical conditioning has traditionally been viewed as a "lower" form of involuntary learning, involving glandular and visceral responses; operant conditioning has been viewed as a "higher" form of voluntary learning, involving responses of the skeletal muscles. In fact, some psychologists believed that responses mediated by the autonomic nervous system could be learned only by classical conditioning, while those mediated by the central nervous system could be acquired only operantly. This assumption has been challenged by a series of recent studies indicating that both autonomic and skeletal responses can be conditioned by either classical or operant procedures (Kimmel, 1974; Miller, 1974; Hearst, 1975).

The operant conditioning of autonomic responses has important implications for psychologically based illnesses, discussed in Chapter 14. A child's fear of attending school may lead to certain autonomic symptoms, like an upset stomach or a headache. If the child is given permission to skip school, those autonomic responses are reinforced—and will increase in frequency. Thus, a pattern is set up whereby a response (upset stomach) is followed by reinforcement (avoidance of school). Via operant conditioning, the child "learns" to be sick in order to avoid an unpleasant situation.

The practical implications of operant conditioning of autonomic responses are important. Human subjects have been trained by operant methods to control such autonomic responses as heart rate, blood pressure, and the secretion of stomach acids that may produce ulcers. To control blood pressure, for example, the individual watches a machine that provides continuous visual feedback about blood pressure. Whenever the blood pressure falls below a specified level, a light flashes. The subject tries to analyze whatever he or she is thinking or doing when the blood pressure is low and to repeat that thought or emotion so as to keep it low. This type of procedure is called *biofeedback* training—the subject is given information (feedback) about some aspect of his or her physiological state and reinforced for altering that state.

The medical implications of such research are obvious. It would be better for people with high blood pressure to learn to control it themselves than to depend on medications that are only partially successful and may have undesirable side-effects. Research on voluntary control of autonomic responses is

Animals have been taught very complex responses by means of shaping techniques. At the Yerkes Primate Research Center in Atlanta, a chimpanzee named Lana has learned to answer questions and make requests by pressing symbols on a computer console. At bottom is an example of how the experiment works. A researcher outside the room asked Lana a question by pressing the symbols on the console for the words "What name-of this" and also holding up a candy. The chimp answered by pressing symbols for "M & M name-of this." Chapter 9 will provide additional examples of how chimpanzees have been taught to communicate with humans.

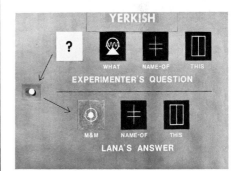

still in the pioneer stage. The results so far indicate that biofeedback procedures are effective. They have been used successfully in treating several types of cardiovascular disorders, with the best results obtained for high blood pressure. Biofeedback for blood flow in the forehead has also proved effective in the treatment of migraine headaches (Tarler-Benlolo, 1978).

Principle of Reinforcement

In our discussion of classical conditioning, we used the term *reinforcement* to refer to the paired presentation of the unconditioned stimulus and the conditioned stimulus. In operant conditioning, reinforcement refers to the occurrence of an event, such as giving food or water, following the desired response. Put in other terms, in classical conditioning reinforcement *elicits* the response, and in operant conditioning reinforcement *follows* the response. Although the reinforcement is different in the two situations, the result in both cases is an increase in the likelihood of the desired response. We can therefore define *reinforcement* as any event that increases the probability of a response. We distinguish between positive and negative reinforcers. A *positive reinforcer* is a stimulus that, when presented following a response, increases the probability of the response; food and water qualify as positive reinforcers for appropriately deprived organisms. A *negative reinforcer* is a stimulus that, when removed following a response, increases the probability of the response; electric shock and painful noise qualify as negative reinforcers if they can be turned off when the desired response is made.

Note that reinforcers are classified as positive or negative according to whether their presentation or their removal strengthens the preceding response. Often the term *reward* is used as a synonym for positive reinforcement. *Punishment*, however, is *not* negative reinforcement. Rather, punishment refers to a situation where a negative reinforcer is delivered every time the organism makes a designated response, thus decreasing the probability of that response. If an animal is given an electric shock every time it presses a bar, the bar-press response is said to be punished.

In Chapters 10 and 11, which deal with motivation, we will have more to say about the nature of reinforcement and what specifies a reinforcing event. Here we will only discuss some of the factors that determine the effectiveness of a reinforcer.

Variables Influencing Reinforcement

Psychologists have systematically investigated the effect of a number of reinforcement variables on the course of learning. Not surprisingly, the *amount of reinforcement* has been found to be particularly important. Within limits, the greater the amount of reinforcement, the more rapid the rate of learning. This relationship is illustrated in an experiment using a T-maze (Figure 7-13). After a rat was placed in the start box, it ran to the *choice point*, where it had to decide between a right or a left turn to reach food placed in one of the goal boxes. In this experiment, there were three groups of rats, each of which received a different amount of food for a correct turn. The results are shown in Figure 7-14A. Note that the group with the largest amount of reinforcement learned at the fastest rate; the other two groups learned more slowly.

The *delay of reinforcement* is another important variable in reinforcement.

Fig. 7-13 T-maze
A maze used in the study of simple choice learning. Plexiglass covers on the start box and goal boxes are hinged so that a rat can be easily placed in or removed from the apparatus. The sliding doors (which usually are operated by a system of strings and pulleys from above) prevent the animal from retracing its path once it has made a choice. Note that the goal boxes are arranged so that the rat cannot see the food cup from the choice point.

A common assumption has been that in training animals or young children it is most effective to reward or punish the organism immediately after it responds. A spanking given by a parent when he or she returns home from work is less effective (other things being equal) in reducing a child's aggressive behavior than punishment delivered immediately following the act.

The effectiveness of immediate reinforcement in a laboratory learning situation is demonstrated by the following experiment. The apparatus used was a T-maze with goal boxes equipped with food dispensers that could be set to delay the presentation of food pellets. One group of rats received its food immediately upon entering the correct goal box (0-second delay), another group was fed following a 5-second delay, and food for a third group was delayed 30 seconds. Figure 7-14B shows the learning curves for the three groups. The zero-second group and the five-second group both reached near perfect scores by the ninth day, but the zero-second group learned at a faster rate. The 30-second-delay group was markedly inferior and never achieved a very high level of performance.

Brain Stimulation and Reinforcement

A rather startling discovery is that electrical stimulation of certain regions of the brain can be reinforcing. In 1953, Olds was investigating the reticular system of the rat's brain (see p. 38) by means of microelectrodes. These tiny electrodes can be implanted permanently in specific brain areas without interfering with the rat's health or normal activity. When connected with an electrical source, they can supply stimulation of varying intensities. An electrode was implanted accidentally in an area near the hypothalamus, and Olds discovered that after he delivered a mild current through the electrodes, the animal repeatedly returned to the place where it had been when stimulated. Further stimulations at the same cage location caused the animal to spend most of its time there. Later, Olds found that other animals with electrodes implanted in the same brain region learned to press a bar in a Skinner box to produce their own electrical stimulation (see Figure 7-15); each bar press closed a circuit that automatically provided a brief current. These animals pressed the bar at a phenomenal rate: a not unusual record would show an average of over 2,000 responses an hour for 15 or 20 hours, until the animal finally dropped from exhaustion.

Since the initial brain-stimulation discovery, experiments with microelectrodes implanted in many different areas of the brain and brain stem have been carried out, using rats, cats, and monkeys in a wide variety of tasks. The reinforcing effects of stimulation in certain areas (primarily the hypothalamus) are powerful: hungry rats will endure a more painful shock while crossing an

Fig. 7-15 Brain stimulation

The animal's bar press delivers a 60-cycle current for one-half second, after which the animal must release and press again for more current. The animal's response rate is recorded on the cumulative recorder, and the delivery of the current is monitored by means of the oscilloscope. Rats respond with rates up to 100 bar presses per minute with electrodes in the medial-forebrain region of the hypothalamus.

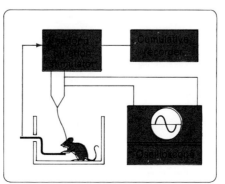

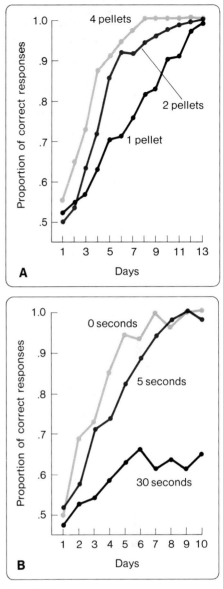

Fig. 7-14
A Amount of reinforcement
Learning curves for three groups of rats run in a T-maze experiment. The groups were distinguished by the number of food pellets a rat received when it entered the correct goal box. Each rat ran four trials per day. Half the animals were trained with the left side of the maze as the correct response, half with the right side as the correct response. The curves start at about .5, since there are only two choices—the animal should make the correct turn 50 percent of the time by chance alone. (After Clayton, 1964)
B Delay of reinforcement
Learning curves for three groups of rats. The groups were distinguished by the time interval between entering the correct goal box and receiving a pellet of food. (Unpublished data from Atkinson)

Role of Punishment

Folklore suggests that punishment is an effective way of controlling learning. "Spare the rod and spoil the child" is not an isolated epigram. Fines and imprisonment are forms of social control that are sanctioned by all governments. For many years arguments have continued over the relative advantages and disadvantages of benevolent treatment (rewarding good behavior) and stern treatment (punishing error). The preference has shifted slowly from punishment to reward.

Has this shift come about solely on humanitarian grounds, or has punishment been found less effective than reward? Evidence from psychological experiments indicates two conclusions: (1) punishment is often less effective than reward, because it temporarily suppresses a response but does not weaken it; and (2) when punishment is effective, it accomplishes its purpose by forcing the individual to select an alternative response that may then be rewarded.

The temporary effects of punishment are illustrated in a series of studies reviewed by Walters and Grusec (1977). In one experiment, two groups of rats learned to press a bar to obtain a food reward. After the response had been well learned, both groups were given extinction trials in which food was withheld. In the first few extinction trials the rats in one group received a strong electric shock every time they pressed the bar. During the remaining extinction trials no shock was administered; food was simply withheld. In the first stage of extinction, the punished rats did make fewer responses, but later resumed their previous rate of bar-pressing and by the end of the experiment had made as many responses as the unpunished rats. Punishment temporarily suppressed the response but did not weaken it. As soon as punishment ceased, the response reappeared at full strength.

Other experiments have shown that the strength and duration of the suppression effect depend on the intensity of the punishment and the degree of deprivation. Obviously, if the punishment is sufficiently severe and prolonged it may effectively stop a particular response, but the response is only suppressed, not unlearned. The response may later reappear if motivation becomes strong enough to overcome the aversive qualities of the punishment. In addition, severe punishment of a strongly motivated response (for example, intense shock every time an acutely hungry rat presses a bar for food) creates such conflict that grossly maladaptive behavior may result. As we shall see in Chapter 14, some abnormal behavior may be due to the repressive nature of punishment, since response tendencies, though inhibited, may appear in indirect or disguised ways because they are not unlearned.

Pros and cons on the use of punishment. In addition to its suppressive effect, punishment may be unsatisfactory for the following reasons:

1 The results of punishment, although they may include altered behavior, are not as predictable as the results of reward. Reward says, "Repeat what you have done"; punishment says, "Stop it!" but fails to give an alternative. As a result, an even more undesirable response may be substituted for the punished one.

electric grid to obtain brain stimulation than they will to obtain food (Olds and Sinclair, 1957). When given a choice between food or electric brain stimulation in a T-maze, rats that have been on a starvation diet for as long as 10 days will choose the path leading to stimulation (Spies, 1965). On the other hand, stimulation of some areas of the brain stem serves as a *negative reinforcer.* When the electrodes were moved to these different brain areas, rats that previously pressed the bar at a rapid rate to receive stimulation suddenly stopped responding and avoided the bar area entirely. Apparently the new stimulation was unpleasant. And other animals have learned various responses to avoid stimulation in these areas—for example, pressing a lever to turn *off* the current (Delgado, Roberts, and Miller, 1954). Much progress has been made in mapping out the neutral, negative, and positive reinforcing areas of the brain.

In addition, researchers have discovered that the *intensity* and *duration* of the stimulation affect behavior. Up to a point, increasing the intensity of stimulation in a positive reinforcing area is increasingly reinforcing. Beyond that point, stimulation becomes less effective and may, if intense enough, become negative. (Possibly this is because the stimulation spreads to negative

in Learning

2 Under some circumstances, punishment tends to fix the behavior rather than eliminate it, perhaps as a consequence of the fear and anxiety induced by the punishment. Punishing a child for wetting the bed, for example, often increases the frequency of the behavior.
3 The byproducts of punishment may be unfortunate. Punishment often leads to dislike of the punishing person (parent, teacher, or employer) and to a dislike of the situation (home, school, or office) in which the punishment occurred.

These cautions do not mean, however, that punishment should never be employed. In fact, it may be useful for several reasons:

1 Punishment can effectively eliminate an undesirable response if alternative responses are available that are rewarded. Rats that have learned to take the shorter of two paths in a maze to reach food will quickly switch to the longer path if they are shocked in the shorter one. The temporary suppression produced by punishment provides the opportunity for the rat to learn to take the longer path. Punishment was an effective means of redirecting behavior.
2 Punishment can be effective when we merely want the learner to respond to a signal to avoid punishment. For example, people learn to come inside when they hear thunder or to seek shade to avoid sunburn. Avoiding a threatened punishment can be rewarding. The police officer is less often a punishing person than a symbol of *threatened* punishment. How does a police officer control us without ever having punished us? Our anxiety explains this control. If we see a police car while driving too fast, we become anxious lest we get a ticket; we feel reassured when we slow down and the police car passes by without stopping us. Our reward comes from the reduction in anxiety.
3 Punishment may be informative. A child who gets a shock from an electrical appliance may learn which connections are safe, which hazardous. A teacher's corrections on a student's paper can be regarded as punishing; but they are also informative and can provide an occasion for learning. Informative punishment can redirect behavior so that the new behavior can be rewarded.

Parents often wonder how much they should punish their children; yet most resort to some sorts of deprivation, if not to the actual inflicting of pain. The most effective use of punishment is the informative one, so that the child will know what is and is not allowed. Children occasionally "test the limits" to see what degree of unpermitted behavior they can get by with. When they do, it seems advisable to use discipline that is firm but not harsh and to administer it promptly and consistently. Nagging a child to conform may in the end be less humane than an immediate spanking. A child who is threatened with a vague and postponed punishment ("What kind of person do you think you will grow up to be?") may suffer more severely than one who pays a consistent penalty for infringement, but afterward is welcomed back into the family circle.

reinforcing areas.) Evidence also shows that while brief stimulation is reinforcing, prolonged stimulation in the same area becomes negative. The general principle seems to be that an intermediate level of stimulation is experienced as most pleasant, whereas deviations to either extreme are frequently not pleasant at all.

Psychologists are not yet agreed on the significance of brain-stimulation studies. It would be nice to think that we had discovered the anatomical location of reinforcement—that when we stimulate one brain-stem area in a rat, for example, the sensations are similar to those experienced when the animal is reinforced with food or that the sensations in another area are similar to reinforcement with water. Unfortunately, the rat cannot describe its sensations. What data we have on human subjects come from patients with abnormal conditions (such as psychosis, epilepsy, or the intractable pain of terminal cancer), so the results cannot be readily generalized to normal individuals. These patients report relief from pain and anxiety and feeling "wonderful," "happy," and "drunk" following stimulation of certain areas of the limbic system. Those whose brains were stimulated over 1,000 times per hour were content to do nothing else for six hours, the maximum period allowed (Campbell, 1973).

In some respects, learning with brain stimulation as reinforcement does not follow the same rules as learning with food or other external rewards. The extinction of the bar press response for brain stimulation is much more rapid than extinction for food or water rewards. If the current is turned off, the animal's responses stop quite abruptly, but it will start responding again at a rapid rate if given one or two stimulations. And while partial reinforcement can be used quite effectively with food or water reinforcement, it is much less effective with brain stimulation. These and other data suggest that brain stimulation operates differently from other reinforcers; it seems to create a temporary sensation that does not increase in strength with deprivation.

Cognitive Learning

The kinds of phenomena that we have considered thus far all stress associative learning. However, emphasis on associative learning may lead to too much concern for piecemeal activities and too little attention to organized relationships and meaning. The teacher impressed by principles of associative learning may use rote memorization and drill excessively, without caring enough about whether the child organizes and understands what is learned. In studying more complex forms of learning, attention must be given to the roles of perception and knowledge, or *cognitive processes.*

Psychologists identified with the cognitive viewpoint argue that learning, particularly in humans, cannot be satisfactorily explained in terms of conditioned associations. They propose that the learner forms a *cognitive structure* in memory, which preserves and organizes information about the various events that occur in a learning situation. When a test is made to determine how much has been learned, the subject takes the stimuli (the questions) and scans them against memory to determine an appropriate action. What he or she does depends on the cognitive structure retrieved from memory and the context in which the test occurs. Thus, the subject's response varies with the nature of the test situation and the subject's memory for prior events. Cognitive theorists believe this even applies to classical conditioning with animals. The animal is assumed to store in memory a record of the events that occurred in the experiment; when tested, this cognitive structure is retrieved, and the animal's response is determined by the information stored therein. The animal is not learning to salivate in a mechanical and automatic fashion to the conditioned stimulus. It is learning to anticipate food, and it is the anticipation that causes the animal to salivate. At the level of classical conditioning, the cognitive approach may seem cumbersome, but in analyzing complex forms of learning it offers more flexibility in theorizing.

Insight Experiments

Partly in protest against too much study of the kinds of learning that involve conditioning, Wolfgang Köhler performed a series of experiments with chimpanzees that involved solving complex problems. Although conducted over 50 years ago, these experiments are still dramatic illustrations of cognitive learning. At some point in working on a problem, chimpanzees appeared to grasp its inner relationships through *insight;* that is, they solved the problem not by trial and error, but by perceiving the relationships essential to solution. The following experiment by Köhler is typical.

Sultan [Köhler's most intelligent chimpanzee] is squatting at the bars but cannot reach the fruit which lies outside by means of his only available short stick. A longer stick is deposited outside the bars, about two meters on one side of the object and parallel with the grating. It cannot be grasped with the hand, but it can be pulled within reach by means of the small stick. [See Figure 7-16 for an illustration of a similar multiple-stick problem.] Sultan tries to reach the fruit with the smaller of the two sticks. Not succeeding, he tears at a piece of wire that projects from the netting of his cage, but that too, is in vain. Then he gazes about him (there are always in the course of these tests some long pauses, during which the animals scrutinize the whole visible area). He suddenly picks up the little stick once more, goes up to the bars directly opposite to the long stick, scratches it towards him with the "auxiliary," seizes it, and goes with it to the point opposite the objective (the fruit), which he secures. From the moment that his eyes fall upon the long stick, his procedure forms one consecutive whole, without hiatus, and although the angling of the bigger stick by means of the smaller is an action that could be complete and distinct in itself, yet observation shows that it follows, quite suddenly, on an interval of hesitation and doubt—staring about—which undoubtedly has a relation to the final objective, and is immediatley merged in the final action of the attainment of the end goal. (Köhler, 1925, pp. 174–75).

A moderate degree of insight is so common in human learning that we tend to take it for granted. Occasionally insight comes dramatically, and then we have what has been appropriately called an "aha" experience. The solution of a problem becomes suddenly clear, as though a light had been turned on in the darkness. Newspapers all carry puzzles or riddles precisely because people enjoy the experience of insight when (and if) it comes. One illustration is furnished by the problem presented in Figure 7-17. Read the figure caption before going further in the text.

If we use ordinary mathematical methods to deal with the problem of Figure 7-17, we may set up an algebraic equation to determine, step by step, how far the bird flies on each trip. For example, we know that on the first trip the bird flies east at 80 mph, while the car coming west toward it is traveling at 40 mph. It can be determined without too much difficulty that the bird will go twice as far as the car by the time they meet. Hence when they meet, the car will have gone $33\frac{1}{3}$ miles from its starting point, while the bird will have flown $66\frac{2}{3}$ miles. For the bird's return flight, it will be necessary to take account of the movement of the first car during the time the bird flew the $66\frac{2}{3}$ miles. Then, knowing the rates of flight of the bird and the car coming to meet it, the second trip can be computed just as the first one was. We continue these computations until the cars have met.

However, instead of trying to determine, first of all, how far the bird flies on each of its trips, we can take a different tack. The clue comes from the question: How long will the bird have been flying by the time the cars meet? When this question is answered, the rest of the solution comes quickly. If you now know the answer, having first been puzzled and then suddenly having "caught on," you know what the experience of insight is.

The variables that influence insight learning are not well understood, but a few general remarks can be made.

Fig. 7-16 A chimpanzee solving a multiple stick problem
Using the shorter sticks, the chimpanzee pulls in a stick long enough to reach the piece of fruit. It has learned to solve this problem by understanding the relationship between the sticks and the piece of fruit.

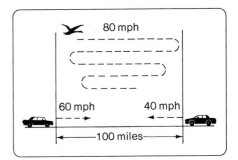

Fig. 7-17 An insight problem
Two cars, now 100 miles apart, are moving toward each other. The eastbound car is traveling at the rate of 60 mph. The westbound one is traveling at the rate of 40 mph. An energetic bird, starting from the eastbound car, flies back and forth between the two cars without stopping or losing any speed on the turns. The bird flies at the uniform rate of 80 mph. Problem: How far does the bird fly from the start to the moment that the two cars meet? The problem can be solved without mathematical training (see text).

1   *Insight depends on the arrangement of the problem situation.* Appropriate past experience, while necessary, does not guarantee a solution. Insight will come easily only if the essentials for solution are arranged so that their relationships can be perceived. For example, a chimpanzee solves the stick problem more readily if the stick is on the same side of the cage as the food. The chimpanzee has more difficulty if it must turn away from the food to see the stick.

2   *Once a solution occurs with insight, it can be repeated promptly.* Sudden solution is the rule in insight. Once the chimpanzee has used a stick for pulling in a banana, it will seek out a stick immediately on the next occasion.

3   *A solution achieved with insight can be applied in new situations.* What is learned in the insight experiment is not a specific set of conditioned associations, but a cognitive relationship between a means and an end. Hence, one tool may be substituted for another. In Figure 7-17, for example, boats could replace cars without confusing the solver of the problem.

Latent Learning

Insight experiments indicate the complexity of the learning process even in animals. This complexity is further illustrated in maze learning—a task often used by psychologists to investigate how drugs or other physiological interventions affect learning.

An early advocate for a cognitive interpretation of learning was Edward C. Tolman, whose research dealt with the problem of rats learning their way through a complex maze (Tolman, 1948). In Tolman's view, a rat running through a maze was not learning a sequence of right and left turns, but rather developing a *cognitive map*—a mental picture of the layout of the maze. Thus, if a familiar path was blocked, the animal adopted another route based on the spatial relations represented in its cognitive map.

Experiments on latent learning support the concept of cognitive structures. *Latent learning,* broadly conceived, refers to any learning that is not demonstrated by behavior at the time of the learning. Typically, such learning goes on in the absence of reward. When an appropriate reward appears, there is a sudden use of what has been previously learned.

In one latent learning experiment, three groups of rats were run daily in the maze diagramed in Figure 7-18. One group was given a food reinforcement when it reached the goal box at the end of the maze. A second group was allowed to explore the maze, but when the rats reached the goal box they were removed with no reinforcement. A third group was treated in the same way as the second group for the first 10 days and then given reinforcement for the remaining 7 days. As we can see in Figure 7-18, all groups learned something in that they made fewer errors in reaching the goal box as the number of trials increased. But the reinforced group clearly learned more rapidly than the two nonreinforced groups. With the introduction of food on the eleventh day, however, the third group was soon performing as well as the reinforced group. Evidently the rats were learning something about the spatial orientation of the maze prior to the time that they were rewarded. Tolman would claim that the rats formulated a schematic representation of the maze that included information about dead ends and incorrect pathways as well as about the path that leads to the goal.

In theorizing about how rewards and punishments influence behavior, Tolman distinguished between *learning* and *performance.* In the latent-learning

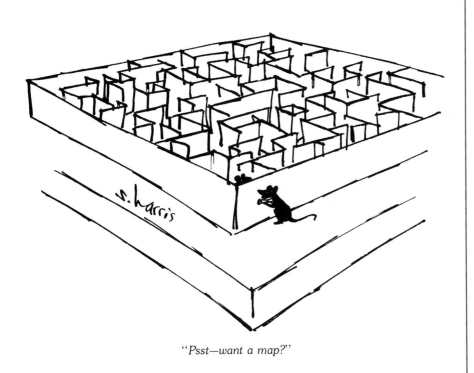

"Psst—want a map?"

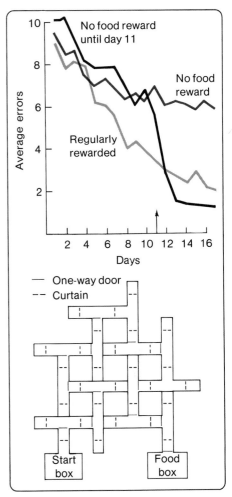

Fig. 7-18 Latent learning in rats
Note that after reward is introduced on the eleventh day, the rats represented by the black line perform as well as, and even a little better than, those regularly rewarded (gray line). Beneath the graph is a diagram of the maze used in this study. (After Tolman and Honzik, 1930)

study, the rat learned something about the spatial arrangement of the maze, but this learning was not evidenced until reward motivated the animal to perform. Tolman would maintain that for learning, reward and punishment serve to convey information, to teach "what leads to what." They do not "stamp in" specific responses and eliminate others. In performance, on the other hand, knowledge about rewards and punishments (learned through past experience) determines which response the rat decides to make. The response with the greatest expectation of reward will probably be the one chosen.

Theoretical Issues

As noted at several points in this chapter, there has been a good deal of controversy among psychologists about how to explain learning. One approach views learning as the formation of conditioned associations; the other emphasizes the cognitive nature of the process. For our purposes, it is possible to view associative learning and cognitive learning as complementary; neither in itself provides a complete explanation, but each helps to explain some features of learning that the other neglects or explains with greater difficulty.

Examples of learning can be graded on a crude scale, with the most automatic kind of learning (explained most easily as associations) at one end and the most insightful and rational kind at the other (explained best according to cognitive principles). Those habits learned by classical conditioning, without awareness, would be at one extreme of the scale. Perhaps learning to salivate when we see a delicious meal or becoming anxious when we encounter a dangerous situation would be examples of such conditioning. Toward the middle of the scale would be tasks learned with full awareness but still somewhat automatically, such as a foreign language vocabulary or a skill like swimming. At the other end of the scale are tasks that require reasoning about many facts in complex relationships. Most learning would probably fall some-

Cognitive Maps and Schemata

If one asks a child to draw a map of the United States that shows key cities, the result usually is a picture with considerable detail in the child's own region of the country, while the rest will be reduced in size, lacking in detail, and often distorted. This example gives us some idea of what is meant by the notion of a cognitive map—it is an abstract representation stored in one's memory of events and relations in the real world. Such representations are based on our perceptions of the world and consequently can be incomplete, distorted, or include information that does not exist in reality.

Tolman introduced the term "cognitive map" into the psychological literature over 30 years ago. It is still used, but now the preferred term is *schema*—or *schemata*, in the plural. The reason is that "cognitive map" places too much emphasis on spatial information; most theorists want to refer to knowledge structures in memory that take in not only spatial data but all other forms of information. There is no agreed upon definition of a schema, but the general concept is an ingredient of any cognitive theory of learning.

Neisser (1976) presents an interesting discussion of Tolman's cognitive maps and the modern concept of schemata. Figure 7-19 illustrates his view of the role of schemata in directing perception and organizing knowledge about the world. In examining this figure, note the cycle of events: (1) perceptual processes sample information in the real world; (2) the schema incorporates the incoming information and is thereby modified by that information; (3) the modified schema redirects the perceptual process to seek additional information. This process is interactive, with the schema directing perception and perception, in turn, modifying the schema.

Of course, there are frequent occasions—especially when confronted with a completely new task—when the incoming information does not relate to any schemata existing in memory. When this occurs, a new schema must be created on the basis of incoming information and possible recombinations of components of existing schemata. Schemata are discussed in Chapter 8 in relation to memory and language.

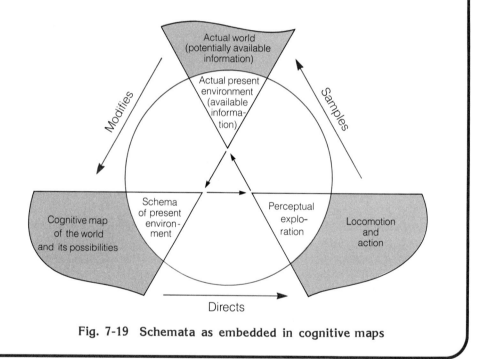

Fig. 7-19 Schemata as embedded in cognitive maps

where in the middle range of the scale, a kind of mixture between simple association and understanding.

This kind of *mixture theory* is considered too eclectic by many psychologists who would rather commit themselves to one or the other position. However, for most practical applications it may be best to adopt a conservative position that pays attention to associative aspects of the learning process as well as to problems of cognitive organization. Thus, in teaching a child arithmetic, one needs to provide for rote drill of multiplication tables as well as exercises designed to increase the child's understanding of the concept of multiplication.

Individualizing Learning

In this section, we present some practical consequences of research on learning. There are many applications of work by psychologists concerned with learning—applications in schools, job training in industry, and the worlds of sports and entertainment. Here we consider an application in school learning that was spawned by psychologists' studying animal behavior in the laboratory strictly for scientific purposes, and yet this application may well revolutionize the instructional process. This is one of many instances when pure research, in no way motivated by thoughts of applications, has had important practical ramifications.

For centuries, teachers have stood in front of classrooms and dispensed words of wisdom. Students passed or failed depending on how much of the knowledge they could recall at the time of an examination. This form of instruction has obvious limitations when compared to a tutorial arrangement—a one-to-one relationship between the student and teacher. But the cost of tutorial education makes it impractical on a large-scale basis. In the 1950s, an effort was made to approximate some aspects of tutorial instruction in the form of a *teaching machine.* The work was guided by B. F. Skinner, the same person who played a key role in research on operant conditioning. Skinner felt that many of the ideas developed in the study of animal learning could be applied to the task of improving instruction.

An example of an early teaching machine is shown in Figure 7-20. The basic idea is to present information to the student in a series of frames. Each frame contains a new item of information and also poses a question that the student must answer. After writing the answer (usually a word or brief phrase), the student turns a knob that uncovers the correct answer and exposes the next instructional frame. In this way, the student goes step-wise through a course, gradually being introduced to each unit of instruction—being tested and reinforced at each step.

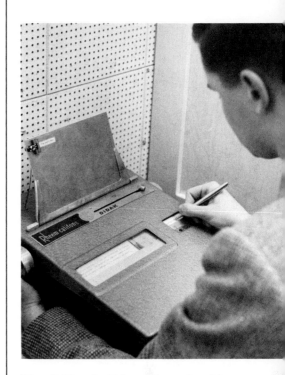

Fig. 7-20 A Skinner-type teaching machine
A statement with a fill-in blank is presented in the window at the left of the machine. The student writes an answer in the space on the right-hand side. After being shown the correct response, the student turns a knob on the left to proceed to the next item.

Computer-Assisted Learning (CAL)

With the advent of computers, it became evident that teaching devices could be developed that would be far more flexible and responsive to the student than the Skinner-type teaching machine. As yet, the use of computers in business, science, and engineering far exceeds applications in education. However, if potentials are properly realized, the nature of education will be radically changed by the computer during our lifetime. The most important feature of computerized instruction is that it permits a high degree of *individualization;* students can proceed at their own pace, following a path through the curriculum best suited to their particular interests and talents.

Because of its great speed of operation, a large computer can handle many students simultaneously—as many as several thousand students—each at a different point in one of several hundred different curricula. Figure 7-21 displays one of the student terminals of a computer-assisted learning (CAL) system used for research purposes at Stanford University. Located at each student's station is a cathode-ray tube, a microfilm-display device, earphones, and a typewriter keyboard. Each device is under computer control. The computer sends out instructions to the terminal to display a particular image on the microfilm projector and to write a message of text or construct a geometric

Fig. 7-21 Student station under computer control
Shown here is an individual student's station in a CAL system. A first-grade student is learning word meanings as part of a course in reading. The microfilm display is on the left, and the cathode-ray tube (TV-like screen) is on the right side. (After Atkinson, 1976)

figure on the cathode-ray tube; simultaneously it sends an auditory message. The student sees the visual display, hears the auditory message, and then may be required to respond—either by operating the typewriter keyboard or by touching the surface of the cathode-ray tube with an electronic pencil. This response is fed back to the computer and evaluated.

If the student's response is correct, the computer moves on to the next instructional item; if incorrect, the computer evaluates the type of error made and branches to appropriate remedial material. A complete record for each student is stored in the computer and is updated with each new response. The record is checked by the computer to evaluate the student's progress and to determine any particular difficulties. A student making exceptionally good progress may be moved ahead in the lesson sequence or branched out to special materials designed to enrich his or her understanding of the curriculum. A student having difficulties may be branched back to review earlier materials or to a special remedial sequence. In a very real sense, the CAL system simulates the human tutorial process.

Although CAL has had only limited development, experience and research suggest that it will have wide application in the future. For example, CAL programs designed to teach reading in the early grades have proved remarkably successful. Children receiving computer-based instruction made significant gains over comparable groups taught by traditional classroom methods (Atkinson, 1976). Computer-based instruction has also been used successfully at the college level. More than 50 different courses at the University of Illinois are taught using CAL. At Stanford University, students who learned first-year Russian by computer performed significantly better on their final examinations than did a control group attending the regular Russian class. The CAL group had fewer dropouts, and more of its students elected to continue into the second year of Russian (Jamison and others, 1976; Bork, 1978).

Instructional Programs

The essence of instruction, whether in the classroom or under computer control, lies in the arrangement of the material to be learned. A body of material arranged to be readily mastered is called an *instructional program.*[2] Some instructional programs are extremely complex, particularly those implemented on a computer. They incorporate an estimate of the student's current state of knowledge to make moment-by-moment decisions about what to teach next. Figure 7-22 illustrates the process: (1) An estimate of the current state of the student's knowledge is matched against the material to be learned to determine what should be taught next. (2) Once determined, the program decides what information would best accomplish the goal. (3) Instruction is given, questions are asked, and the computer records the student's responses. (4) The response information is used to infer what has been learned and to update the program's estimate of the student's current state of knowledge. The process is cyclical and continues until the course has been mastered (Klahr, 1976; Dean, 1978).

Two examples of instructional programs that are less complicated than the very general scheme described in Figure 7-22 are worth noting—namely, the *linear program* and the *branching program*. Figure 7-23 illustrates a linear program. With such a program, the student progresses along a single track from one frame to the next; each time an item is answered the student moves on to the next, regardless of whether the response was correct. Inspection of the linear program in Figure 7-23 indicates how new information is gradually introduced and elaborated, ensuring the student's attention at each step by requiring a response. A branching program allows the learner to take different paths through the curriculum. Each response is evaluated; that evaluation determines where the student goes next. An error in response is pointed out, and the student is given help to avoid making that error again. The student who has done well on a number of questions may be given an opportunity to jump ahead; the student who has made too many mistakes may retrace steps or take an alternative route in an effort to resolve difficulties.

Linear programs do not need to be presented by an automated device; they are often printed in textbook form.[3] In the *programmed textbook*, the answers to each frame usually are listed at the side of the page (see Figure 7-23). The student covers the answer column with a slider (strip of plastic) and reads one frame at a time. After reading the frame, the student writes down an answer and then moves the slider down to uncover the answer. The student follows this procedure throughout, each time checking the answer to one frame before going on to the next.

It is not possible to prescribe a definite set of rules for developing a successful program. The development of a good program is still very much an art in the same sense as writing a good textbook or preparing an effective lecture.

[2] In discussions of CAL, the terms *instructional program* and *teaching program* are used, rather than simply the term *program*, to distinguish them from the *computer program*, which is a sequence of commands that controls the computer.
[3] The Study Guide designed to accompany this textbook contains chapter reviews written in the form of a linear program.

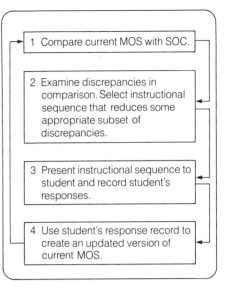

Fig. 7-22 Diagram of a dynamic teaching program
MOS = model of student—that is, theoretical representation (or model) of the student's current knowledge of the subject matter being taught. **SOC** = structure of curriculum—that is, logical structure of the subject matter being taught.

1 Compare current MOS with SOC.

2 Examine discrepancies in comparison. Select instructional sequence that reduces some appropriate subset of discrepancies.

3 Present instructional sequence to student and record student's responses.

4 Use student's response record to create an updated version of current MOS.

Sentence to be completed	Word to be supplied
1. The important parts of a flashlight are the battery and the bulb. When we "turn on" a flashlight, we close a switch which connects the battery with the ——.	bulb
2. When we turn on a flashlight, an electric current flows through the fine wire in the —— and causes it to grow hot.	bulb
3. When the hot wire glows brightly, we say that it gives off or sends out heat and ——.	light
4. The fine wire in the bulb is called a filament. The bulb "lights up" when the filament is heated by the passage of a(n) —— current.	electric
5. When a weak battery produces little current, the fine wire, or ——, does not get very hot.	filament
6. A filament which is *less* hot sends out or gives off —— light.	less
7. "Emit" means "send out." The amount of light sent out, or "emitted," by a filament depends on how —— the filament is.	hot
8. The higher the temperature of the filament the —— the light emitted by it.	brighter
9. If a flashlight battery is weak, the —— in the bulb may still glow, but with only a dull red color.	filament
10. The light from a very hot filament is colored yellow or white. The light from a filament which is not very hot is colored ——.	red
11. A blacksmith or other metal worker sometimes makes sure that a bar of iron is heated to a "cherry red" before hammering it into shape. He uses the —— of the light emitted by the bar to tell how hot it is.	color
12. Both the color and the amount of light depend on the —— of the emitting filament or bar.	temperature
13. An object which emits light because it is hot is called incandescent. A flashlight bulb is an incandescent source of ——.	light
14. A neon tube emits light but remains cool. It is, therefore, not an incandescent —— of light.	source
15. A candle flame is hot. It is a(n) —— source of light.	incandescent
16. The hot wick of a candle gives off small pieces or particles of carbon which burn in the flame. Before or while burning, the hot particles send out, or ——, light.	emit
17. A long candlewick produces a flame in which oxygen does not reach all the carbon particles. Without oxygen the particles cannot burn. Particles which do not burn rise above the flame as ——.	smoke
18. We can show that there are particles of carbon in a candle flame, even when it is not smoking, by holding a piece of metal in the flame. The metal cools	

Sentence to be completed	Word to be supplied
some of the particles before they burn, and the unburned carbon —— collect on the metal as soot.	particles
19. The particles of carbon in soot or smoke no longer emit light because they are —— than when they were in the flame.	cooler, colder
20. The reddish part of a candle flame has the same color as the filament in a flashlight with a weak battery. We might guess that the yellow or white parts of a candle flame are —— than the reddish part.	hotter
21. "Putting out" an incandescent electric light means turning off the current so that the filament grows too —— to emit light.	cold, cool
22. Setting fire to the wick of an oil lamp is called —— the lamp.	lighting
23. The sun is our principal —— of light, as well as of heat.	source
24. The sun is not only very bright but very hot. It is a powerful —— source of light.	incandescent
25. Light is a form of energy. In "emitting light" an object changes, or "converts," one form of —— into another.	energy
26. The electric energy supplied by the battery in a flashlight is converted to —— and ——.	heat, light; light, heat
27. If we leave a flashlight on, all the energy stored in the battery will finally be changed or —— into heat and light.	converted
28. The light from a candle flame comes from the —— released by chemical changes as the candle burns.	energy
29. A nearly "dead" battery may make a flashlight bulb warm to the touch, but the filament may still not be hot enough to emit light—in other words, the filament will not be —— at that temperature.	incandescent
30. Objects, such as a filament, carbon particles, or iron bars, become incandescent when heated to about 800 degrees Celsius. At that temperature they begin to —— ——.	emit light
31. When raised to any temperature above 800 degrees Celsius, an object such as an iron bar will emit light. Although the bar may melt or vaporize, its particles will be —— no matter how hot they get.	incandescent
32. About 800 degrees Celsius is the lower limit of the temperature at which particles emit light. There is no upper limit of the —— at which emission of light occurs.	temperature
33. Sunlight is —— by very hot gases near the surface of the sun.	emitted
34. Complex changes similar to an atomic explosion generate the great heat which explains the —— of light by the sun.	emission
35. Below about —— degrees Celsius an object is not an incandescent source of light.	800

Fig. 7-23 Example of a linear program

This is part of a program in high school physics. The student covers the answer column with a slider, reads one frame at a time, writes his or her answer in the blank, and then moves the slider to uncover the correct answer. Several programming techniques are illustrated by this set of frames. For example, technical terms are introduced slowly. The more familiar term "fine wire" in frame 2 is followed by a definition of the technical term "filament" in frame 4; "filament" is then asked for as a synonym in frame 5 and without a synonym in frame 9. Initially the student may be prompted to give the correct answer. In frame 25, for example, the response "energy" is easily evoked by the words "form of _____" because the expression "form of energy" is used earlier in the frame. The word "energy" appears in the next two frames and is finally asked for without a *prompt* in frame 28. Beginning with fairly simple facts, the student is gradually led to an understanding of the topic. (After Skinner, 1968)

Because the work is elusive, programmers conduct pilot tests of their programs.

Pilot testing ordinarily consists of trying the program out on a group of students, revising it to take care of the difficulties they experience, trying it on a second group, revising it again, and so on, until the program works well. This process of successive revisions and improvement of a program is important. It focuses attention on the individual learning process and helps the programmer isolate and analyze the parts that cause particular difficulties.

Effective Instructional Procedures

What makes programmed instruction and CAL effective? At least three features seem to be particularly important.

1 *Active participation.* The learner is actively interacting with the curriculum materials by responding, practicing, and testing each step of the material to be mastered. The old adage "learning by doing" is well exemplified, in contrast to the passive learning that takes place during a lecture.
2 *Information feedback.* The learner finds out with minimal delay whether the response is correct; thus, an error can be corrected immediately. Immediate feedback has been shown to be important in a range of tasks—from operant conditioning with animals, in which immediate reinforcement produces faster learning, to learning with human subjects, in which immediate knowledge of results provides similar benefits.
3 *Individualization of instruction.* The learner moves ahead at his or her own rate. The rapid learner can progress quickly through the material, while the slower learner can move less rapidly (often being diverted to a remedial program) until the basic concepts have been mastered. Branching allows the learners to move through the material on a path designed to fit their aptitudes and abilities.

The instructional procedures discussed in this section can be implemented with present technology and are economically feasible. It is not unreasonable to expect that in the not too distant future computers will be able to recognize spoken words and understand the meanings of questions asked by students. With this type of flexibility, yet other approaches to instruction can be pursued that will permit a true dialogue between the student and the computer.

Critics feel that computers in education pose a threat to human individuality. But in reality, CAL provides the opportunity for greater development of individual potential. Just as the advent of the printed book freed students from oral recitation, so computers can free students from the drudgery of doing tasks not adjusted to their interests and abilities.

SUMMARY

1 Learning is a relatively permanent change in behavior that occurs as the result of prior experience. Pavlov's experiments in *classical conditioning* demonstrated several principles useful in the understanding of *associative learning.* These include *reinforcement, acquisition, extinction, generalization,* and *discrimination.*
2 Skinner's experiments in *operant conditioning* have extended conditioning principles to kinds of responses that cannot be elicited by an identifiable unconditioned stimulus. *Operant behavior* acts on the environment to pro-

duce or gain access to reinforcement and becomes strengthened by reinforcement.

3 Rate of responding is a useful measure of *operant strength. Partial reinforcement* illustrates the orderliness of operant behavior; once a particular response has been established, it can be sustained by occasional reinforcement. *Conditioned reinforcement,* the fact that a stimulus associated with a reinforcing stimulus acquires reinforcing properties, increases the possible range of conditioning and explains the reward value of such incentives as social approval and money.

4 *Shaping behavior* involves reinforcing those variations in the subject's behavior that lead to a desired response and extinguishing those that do not. Thus, operant conditioning can account for the learning of novel behavior. Experiments have shown that some aspects of ordinary daily behavior can be brought under control through operant conditioning.

5 *Reinforcement* refers to any event that increases the probability of a response. *Amount, delay,* and *rate of reinforcement* are important variables that affect learning. Direct electrical stimulation of certain areas in the brain (via microelectrodes) can produce reinforcing effects; some areas are associated with positive reinforcing effects and others with negative effects.

6 Emphasis within associative learning is on the acquisition of specific responses. Some psychologists warn against an overemphasis on the automatic nature of learning that comes from exclusive concern with conditioned associations. They stress instead situations in which understanding is prominent and have introduced the notion of *cognitive structures.* Köhler's *insight* experiments pointed out how the arrangements of the problem make the solution easy or hard and how a solution once achieved with insight can be repeated or applied to novel situations.

7 Tolman's *latent learning* experiments also emphasize the role of understanding and the development of a *cognitive map.* Experiments on latent learning provide evidence that the subject's cognitive representation of the relationships involved must be taken into account.

8 Something can be learned from each of these emphases. Learning goes on in part through *associative processes,* with little rational direction from the learner, and in part through *cognitive processes,* with which the learner perceives relationships and organizes knowledge.

9 *Computer-assisted learning* is proving to be a valuable aid to learning. Some of the features of CAL that make it effective are: active participation by the learner, immediate feedback, and the rate and path through the learning materials being adjusted to individual differences.

FURTHER READING

Pavlov's *Conditioned reflexes* (1927) is the classic work on classical conditioning. Skinner's *The behavior of organisms* (1938) is the corresponding statement on operant conditioning. Cognitive theories also have their classics: Köhler's *The mentality of apes* (1925) describes the famous insight experiments with chimpanzees; Tolman's *Purposive behavior in animals and men* (1932) is the major statement of his cognitive position.

The principal points of view toward learning, presented in their historical settings and with some typical experiments to which they have led, are summarized in Hilgard and Bower, *Theories of learning* (4th ed., 1975).

For a general introduction to conditioning and learning, there are a number of textbooks, such as Hintzman, *The psychology of learning and memory* (1978), Rachlin, *Behavior and learning* (1976), Crowder, *Principles of learning and memory* (1976), and Lindsay and Norman, *Human information processing* (2nd ed., 1977).

The multiple-volume *Handbook of learning and cognitive processes* (1975–1979), edited by Estes, covers all aspects of learning and conditioning at an advanced level. Mathematical theories of the learning process are discussed in Krantz, Atkinson, Luce, and Suppes (eds.), *Contemporary developments in mathematical psychology* (1974).

8
Remembering and Forgetting

A ll learning implies memory. If we remembered nothing from our experiences we could learn nothing. Life would consist of momentary experiences that had little relation to one another. We could not even carry on a simple conversation. To communicate, you must remember the thoughts you want to express as well as what has just been said to you. Without memory you could not even reflect upon yourself, for the very notion of a "self" depends on a sense of continuity that only memory can bring. In short, when we think of what it means to be human we must acknowledge the centrality of memory.

Basic Distinctions About Memory

Psychologists find it useful to make two basic distinctions about memory. The first concerns three stages of memory—encoding, storage, and retrieval. The second deals with two types of memory—short-term and long-term.

Three Stages of Memory

Suppose one morning you are introduced to a student and told her name is Barbara Cohn. That afternoon you see her again and say something like, "You're Barbara Cohn. We met this morning." Clearly you have remembered her name. But what exactly did you do? What does memory involve?

Your minor memory feat can be broken down into three stages (see Figure 8-1). First, when you were introduced you somehow deposited Barbara Cohn's name into memory. This is the *encoding stage.* You transformed a physical phenomenon (sound waves) that corresponds to her spoken name into the kind of code that memory accepts, and you placed that code in memory. Second, you retained, or stored, the name during the time between the two meetings. This is the *storage stage.* And third, you recovered the name from storage at the time of your second meeting. This is the *retrieval stage.*

Fig. 8-1 The three stages of memory
(After Melton, 1963)

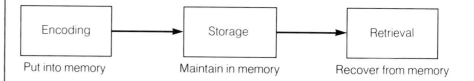

Memory can fail at any of these three stages. Had you been unable to recall Barbara's name at the second meeting, this could have reflected a failure in any of the stages—encoding, storage, or retrieval. So an understanding of memory involves specifying what operations occur at each stage in different situations and how these operations can go awry and result in memory failure.

Two Types of Memory

Do the three stages of memory operate in the same way in all memory situations? A good deal of research suggests that they don't. Memory seems to differ between those situations that require us to store material for a matter of seconds and those that require us to store material for longer intervals—from minutes to years. The former situations are said to tap *short-term memory*, while the latter reflect *long-term memory.*

We can illustrate this distinction by amending our story about meeting Barbara Cohn. Suppose that during the first meeting, as soon as you had heard her name, a friend came up and you said, "Doug, have you met Barbara Cohn?" That would be an example of short-term memory. You retrieved the name after only a second or so. Remembering her name at the time of your second meeting would be an example of long-term memory, for now retrieval would take place hours after the name was encoded.

When we recall a name immediately after encountering it, retrieval seems effortless, as if the name were still active, still in our consciousness. But when we try to recall the same name hours later, retrieval is often difficult, as the name is no longer conscious. This contrast between short- and long-term memory is similar to the contrast between conscious knowledge and the subconscious knowledge we have but are not currently thinking about. We can think of memory as a vast body of knowledge, only a small part of which can ever be active at any moment. The rest is passive. Short-term memory corresponds to the active part, long-term memory to the passive.

The next two sections of this chapter consider short- and long-term memory in some detail—mainly the nature of the encoding, storage, and retrieval stages in each. Then, after exploring how long-term memory may be improved, we will examine the relation between the two types of memory. In the last section, we discuss the problem of memory for meaningful material, with an emphasis on how one embellishes what is put into memory.

Short-Term Memory

Even in situations where you must remember information for only a few seconds and the information may still be active, memory involves three stages.

Encoding

To encode information into short-term memory, you must attend to it. Since we are selective about what we attend to (see Chapter 5), our memory will contain only what has been selected. This means that much of what we are exposed to never even enters memory and, of course, will not be available for later retrieval. Indeed, many difficulties labeled "memory problems" are really lapses in attention. For example, if you bought some groceries and someone asked you immediately afterward for the color of the clerk's eyes, you might well be unable to answer, because you had not paid attention to them in the first place.

When information is attended to, it gets encoded into short-term memory. As mentioned earlier, encoding means not only that information is deposited in memory, but also that it is deposited in a certain form, or code. Take the case where you look up a phone number and retain it while dialing. In what code do you store the digits? Is the code visual—a mental picture of the digits? Or is the code acoustic—the sound of the names of the digits?

A good deal of research indicates that short-term memory tends to favor an *acoustic code* for verbal materials like digits, letters, and words. For example, in one study, subjects were shown a list of six consonants (for example, RLBKSJ). The letters were removed, and subjects had to write down all six letters in order. Although the entire procedure took only a second or two, subjects occasionally made errors. When they did, the incorrect letter tended to be similar in sound to the correct one. Thus, for the list above, a subject might have written RLTKSJ, replacing the *B* with the similar sounding *T* (Conrad, 1964). This supports the idea that the subjects encoded each letter acoustically (for example, "bee" for *B*), sometimes lost part of this code (only the "ee" part of the sound remained), and then responded with a letter ("tee") that was consistent with the remaining part of the code.

Short-term memory sometimes uses a *visual code.* However, with verbal materials, the visual code fades quickly and is soon dominated by the acoustic one. To illustrate, after looking at the address 5 OAK CREEK DRIVE, you may have a visual code of it for a second or so. This code would preserve visual details, like the fact that the address was written in upper-case letters. After a couple of seconds, though, all that would remain would be the sound of the address—the acoustic code—and this code would not preserve information about the case of the letters. (The experiment in Figure 8-2 demonstrates the fading of the visual code.)

This dominance of the acoustic code may apply mainly to verbal materials. Recent research suggests that when one has to store nonverbal items, like pictures that are difficult to describe, the visual code may become more important. There are even some cases where the visual code for pictures seems to be so detailed that the memory is like a photograph. Such cases are rare and are found primarily in young children. It is also possible that one can store information in codes linked to other senses, such as touch and smell. The pungent odor of sour milk, for example, seems to stay with us for a few seconds after we experience it.

Storage: Capacity

Perhaps the most striking fact about short-term memory is that it has a very limited capacity. On the average, the limit is seven items, give or take two (7 ± 2). Some people store as few as five items; others can hold onto as many as nine. It may seem strange to give such an exact number to cover all people when it is clear that individuals differ greatly in their memory abilities. These differences, however, are due to long-term memory. For short-term memory, virtually all normal adults have a capacity of 7 ± 2. This constancy has been known since the earliest days of experimental psychology. Ebbinghaus, who

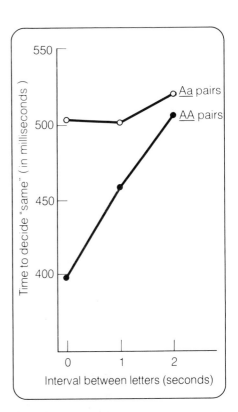

Fig. 8-2 Fading of visual code in short-term memory

On each trial, subjects were shown two letters in succession, with an interval of up to two seconds between each letter. They were then asked whether the second letter had the same name as the first. In the sample trials shown here, the two letters have the same name.

A	_____	A
First letter	Interval (0–2 seconds)	Second letter

A	_____	a
First letter	Interval (0–2 seconds)	Second letter

When the interval between the letters was roughly a second, the visual code for the first letter should not yet have faded. Consequently, subjects could make a direct visual comparison between letters. This kind of comparison will work for pairs like <u>AA</u>. But pairs like <u>Aa</u> can only be determined to have the same name by comparing their names acoustically. So we might expect <u>AA</u> decisions to be made faster than <u>Aa</u> decisions. When the interval between the letters is about two seconds, however, the visual code has faded and only the sounds of the letters remain in short-term memory. Now decisions about <u>AA</u> and <u>Aa</u> should take the same amount of time, because both must be based on acoustic codes, which is the pattern the experimenters found (see graph). (After Posner and Keele, 1967)

CRITICAL DISCUSSION

Eidetic Images

Although most of us can occasionally retain a visual memory of something we have seen, such memories usually seem vague and lacking in detail. Some people, however, are able to hold in short-term memory visual images that are almost photographic in clarity. They can look briefly at a picture and, when it is removed, still "see" its image located not in their heads but somewhere in space before their eyes. They can maintain the image for as long as several minutes, scan it, and describe it in far more detail than is usually possible. Such people are said to have a "photographic memory," or, to use the psychologist's term, *eidetic imagery*.

Eidetic imagery is quite rare. Studies with children indicate that only about 5 percent report visual images that last for more than a half-minute and possess sharp detail. The existing evidence suggests that there are even fewer individuals who have eidetic images after adolescence. In a typical procedure for investigating eidetic imagery, the experimenter places a richly detailed picture against a gray easel, gives the child 30 seconds to look at it, removes the picture, and then asks the child to describe what he or she sees on the easel. Most children either report seeing nothing or describe fleeting

Fig. 8-3 Testing for eidetic images
Test picture shown for 30 seconds to elementary school children. One boy saw in his eidetic image "about 16" stripes in the cat's tail. The painting, by Marjorie Torrey, appears in Lewis Carroll's *Alice in Wonderland*, abridged by Josette Frank.

afterimages of the picture. But some report images that are vivid and prolonged—that is, true eidetic images.

When questioned, they can provide a wealth of detail, such as the number of stripes on a cat's tail (see Figure 8-3) or the number of buttons on a jacket. Such children seem to be reading the details directly from their eidetic image.

Studies with eidetic children indicate that a viewing time of three to five seconds is necessary to produce an image. The children report that when they do not look at the picture long enough, they do not have an image of parts of it, although they may remember what those parts contain. Exaggerated eye blinking or looking away from the easel usually makes the image disappear (Haber, 1969).

Other evidence indicates that eidetic imagery is truly visual in nature. For example, when an eidetic child tries to transfer the image from the easel to another surface, it disappears when it reaches the edge of the easel. At the same time, the eidetic image is not an exact photographic reproduction. The image usually contains additions, omissions, and distortions of the stimulus picture. The aspects of the picture that are most interesting to the child are the ones that tend to be reproduced in greatest detail in the eidetic image.

began the experimental study of memory in 1885, reported results showing his own limit was seven items. Some 70 years later, Miller (1956) was so struck by the constancy that he referred to it as the magic number seven.

Psychologists determined this number by using a task called the *memory span* (first introduced by Jacobs in 1887). Subjects see a different sequence of items (digits, letters, or words) on each trial and must recall them in order. On the initial trials, they have to recall just a few items, say four or five, which they can easily do. Then the number increases until the experimenter determines the maximum number a subject can recall in order. The maximum, almost always between five and nine, is the subject's memory span, or capacity. This task, which is part of many IQ tests, is so simple that you can easily try it yourself. Next time you come across a list of names (like a directory in a business or university building), read through the list once and then see how many names you can recall in order. Almost certainly it will be between five and nine.

Given this fixed capacity, it is tempting to think of short-term memory as a

224

CHAPTER 8/REMEMBERING AND FORGETTING

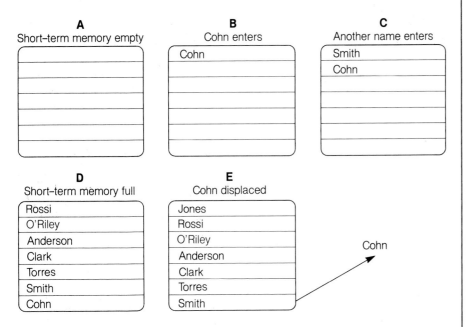

A
Short–term memory empty

B
Cohn enters

Cohn

C
Another name enters

Smith
Cohn

D
Short–term memory full

Rossi
O'Riley
Anderson
Clark
Torres
Smith
Cohn

E
Cohn displaced

Jones
Rossi
O'Riley
Anderson
Clark
Torres
Smith

Cohn

Fig. 8-4 Representation of displacement principle

sort of mental box with roughly seven slots. Each item entering short-term memory goes into its own slot. As long as the number of items does not exceed the number of slots, we can recall the items perfectly. Though this "box" view cannot be taken literally, it does suggest a cause of forgetting in short-term memory: when all the slots are filled and a new item enters, one of the old ones must go. The new item displaces an old one.

The principle of *displacement* explains how an item is lost from short-term memory (see Figure 8-4). Suppose your short-term memory is empty. An item enters. Let's say you've been introduced to Barbara Cohn (remember her?), and the name Cohn enters your short-term memory. Others are introduced soon after, and the list of names in short-term memory grows. Finally, the limit of your memory span is reached. Then each new item that enters short-term memory has some chance of displacing Cohn. After one new item, there's been only one chance to displace Cohn; after two new items, there have been two chances, and so on. The likelihood that Cohn will be lost from short-term memory increases steadily with the number of items that have followed it. Eventually, Cohn will go.

Displacement has been demonstrated experimentally many times. In one study, subjects were given a list of 13 digits. After the last digit in the list, a *probe* digit was presented (it is called a *probe* because subjects must use it to "probe" their memory). The probe was always identical to one of the digits in the list. The subjects' task was to report the digit that had followed the probe in the list. For example, given the list 3, 9, 1, 6, 9, 7, 5, 3, 8, 2, 5, 6, 4 and the probe 2, subjects should report 5. When the probe is drawn from the end of the list, it should still be in short-term memory and very likely to be recalled. When the probe is from the beginning of the list, however, many items have followed the one to be recalled. Most likely it has been displaced and should not be recalled. For probes drawn from the middle of the list, the chances of displacement should be intermediate, and so should the chance of recall. Figure 8-5 shows that the data from this experiment support the principle of displacement. The more items that intervene between a particular digit and the probe, the less the chance of recall.

It appears, then, that what is at the forefront of our memory must soon give

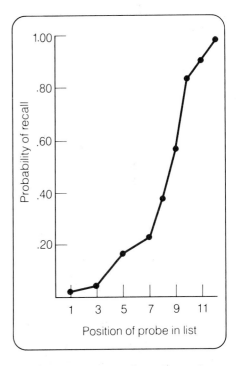

Fig. 8-5 Probability of recall as a function of position of probe
When probes are drawn from the end of the list, few items have followed the one to be recalled, and the probability of recall is high. When probes are drawn from the beginning of the list, many items have followed the one to be recalled, and the probability of recall is low. (After Waugh and Norman, 1965)

way to subsequent information. There is one exception, though. In some cases we continue to mull over the same thoughts—that is, to recycle the same items in short-term memory. An example is repeating a phone number over and over while you dial. Such items are not readily displaced. This process is called *rehearsal.* It amounts to paying attention to what is presently in short-term memory rather than to something in the outside world. Many experiments indicate that rehearsing information protects it from displacement. Why? One possibility is that we cannot encode new items at the same time we are rehearsing old ones. Consequently, the more we rehearse, the less we encode; and the less we encode, the less the opportunity for displacement.

Finally, while the evidence for displacement is strong, it may not be the only cause of short-term forgetting. Information may simply decay with time, regardless of whether or not new information follows (Reitman, 1974). That is, we may think of the stored information as a trace that fades with time, much as a color photograph fades as the years pass. To the extent that decay causes forgetting, we can see another way that rehearsal benefits memory. Rehearsing an item that has partly faded may bring it to full strength again.

Storage: Chunks

In the preceding discussion, we emphasized that short-term memory holds 7 ± 2 items. But what exactly is an item? When we are dealing with lists of arbitrary letters, each letter counts as an item. However, when we are dealing with lists of words, each word counts as an item, even if it contains many letters. Thus YTDRAES contains seven single-letter items, but when the letters are rearranged to form the word STRAYED, there is only one item, the word itself. It appears that an item is the largest meaningful unit we can find in the materials presented to us. Such units are called *chunks,* and the capacity of short-term memory is best expressed as 7 ± 2 chunks (Miller, 1956).

The notion of chunks has some important implications. If short-term memory could hold only seven letters, it could not retain even a simple sentence. Fortunately, though, letters can be grouped into word chunks, and word chunks themselves can be grouped into phrase chunks. This enables us to hold in short-term memory as much as the last few sentences we have heard—a capacity critical for following conversations. Language provides a natural chunking device, since it groups letters and words into larger meaningful units.

Sometimes we can chunk letters without forming words. This occurs when the letters stand for some meaningful (but nonword) unit. The letter string IB-MFB-ITVU-SA is hard to recall because it contains more than seven chunks. But suppose the spacing is changed so that the string is IBM-FBI-TV-USA. Each letter group is now a familiar unit. The result is four chunks and a string that is easy to remember (Bower and Springston, 1970). Chunking can occur with numbers as well. The string 149-2177-619-79 is beyond our capacity, but 1492-1776-1979 is well within it. In both examples, the regrouped strings contain familiar units. The general principle seems to be that we can boost our short-term memory by regrouping sequences of letters and digits into familiar units.

Retrieval

Let us think of the contents of short-term memory as being available to consciousness. Intuition suggests that access to this information is immediate. You don't have to "dig for it," it's right there. Retrieval, then, should not depend on the number of items in consciousness. But in this case intuition is dead wrong.

We now have evidence suggesting that retrieval involves a search of short-term memory, in which each item is examined one at a time. Most of the support for this is based on a kind of experiment introduced by Sternberg. For each trial a subject is shown a list of numbers. The list is removed, and a second or two later a probe number is presented. The subject must decide whether the probe was in the list. For example, if the list was 3, 6, 1 and the probe was 6, subjects should respond "yes." But with the same list and a probe of 2, subjects should respond "no." Each trial uses a new list and a new probe. The list varies from one to six digits. Sternberg found that the time needed to reach a yes-no decision increases directly with the number of items in short-term memory (see Figure 8-6).

What is remarkable about the decision times plotted in Figure 8-6 is that they fall along a straight line. This means that each additional item in short-term memory adds a fixed amount of time to the retrieval process—approximately 40 milliseconds (40 thousandths of a second) per item. Apparently, it takes about 400 milliseconds to encode the probe and execute the response, an additional 40 milliseconds to compare the probe to one digit, an additional 80 milliseconds to compare the probe to two digits, and so on. Such results suggest that the retrieval process involves comparing the probe to each digit in memory in sequence.

The same kinds of results are found when the memorized items are letters, words, tones, or faces. Adding an extra item usually adds about 40 thousandths of a second to retrieval time, though it seems to be longer with faces than with verbal items (Sternberg, 1969). Similar results are obtained with populations as varied as schizophrenics, and college students under the influence of marijuana. Thus for all individuals, retrieval from short-term memory seems to involve a search process.

Short-Term Memory and Thought

Researchers believe that short-term memory may play an important role in conscious thought. When consciously trying to solve a problem, we seem to be using the same capacity needed to store a list of numbers. To see this, try to solve even a simple arithmetic problem (8×15) while remembering a phone number (745-1739). The result is confusion and interference; the two activities compete for the same mental resources. This kind of competition for a limited short-term memory capacity has been demonstrated in the laboratory (Baddeley and Hitch, 1974).

Such research is relatively new, so we do not yet know how large a role short-term memory plays in thought. There is some evidence that it is large indeed. In research on personality, for example, when subjects are asked to form an impression of someone on the basis of one meeting, they tend to describe the person in terms of roughly 7 ± 2 traits (Mischel, 1968). It is as if the capacity of short-term memory, 7 ± 2, places a limit on the number of ideas or impressions we can entertain at one time.

Long-Term Memory

Long-term memory involves information that has been retained for intervals as brief as a few minutes (a point made earlier in a conversation) or as long as a

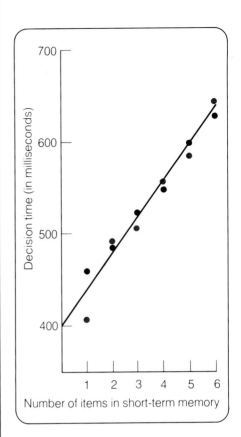

Fig. 8-6 Retrieval as a search process Decision time in relation to the number of items in short-term memory. Colored circles represent "yes" responses, black circles, "no" responses. The times for both types of decision fall along a straight line. (After Sternberg, 1966)

Alternative Interpretations of the Retrieval Stage

Figure 8-6 suggests a retrieval process in which the probe is compared sequentially to each item in short-term memory. But other interpretations are possible. In particular, some have argued that the comparisons are actually done in parallel. That is, the subject compares the probe to all memory items simultaneously, responding "yes" as soon as a match is found and "no" when none of the comparisons yields a match. At first, this idea seems incompatible with the finding that decision times increase with the number of comparisons to be made. For it would seem that if all the comparisons are made at once it should take no longer to do multiple comparisons than to do one. However, even when things are done in parallel, the time to do all of them may increase with the number that have to be done.

We can use a horse race as an analogy. While all the horses run the race together (in parallel), the time for the last horse to cross the finish line generally increases with the number of horses in the race. As the number of horses increases, the chances that slower horses will be included in the race also increase, and then we will have to wait till the slowest of them crosses the finish line. Thus, several things are happening in parallel, yet the time for the whole process to finish increases with the number of things involved.

Let's apply this horse-race logic to retrieval from short-term memory. Now we are considering the time for mental operations (comparisons) to run their course. The more operations involved, the more likely it is that one of them will be unduly slow. This means that decision time will, in general, increase with the number of items in short-term memory. But will such an increase be of the straight-line form shown in Figure 8-6? The answer (based on a mathematical analysis) is probably not (Sternberg, 1966).

There is, however, another way that parallel comparisons can increase decision times. To use another analogy, suppose you are searching for a bomb in a two-room apartment. You have the assistance of two experts from the bomb squad. If you know which room the bomb is in, you may send both experts there, and they should find it relatively quickly. But if you don't know which room the bomb is in, you will probably send each expert to a different room. They will be searching in parallel, but clearly the time to find the bomb will increase. For the efficiency with which each room is searched must decrease with fewer searchers. That is, with only a limited amount of resources (two experts), a parallel search of the two rooms requires a division of these resources that results in less efficient individual searches.

This reasoning transfers nicely to retrieval from short-term memory. Just as one's physical resources can be limited, so can one's mental resources. We may have only a fixed capacity for retrieval; and when an item is added to short-term memory, the total capacity must be further divided among the simultaneous comparisons. This decrease in capacity per comparison results in lowered efficiency for each comparison. And the less efficient a comparison, the longer it takes to execute. This line of reasoning clearly leads us to expect an increase in decision time as the number of items in memory increases. With suitable mathematical assumptions about how the capacity is divided, the expected increases can be shown to fall on a straight line (Townsend, 1971). So we have come up with an alternative explanation of the straight lines in Figure 8-6—one that involves parallel rather than serial processing.

The parallel process just described is called a *limited-capacity* process. This kind of process may be quite widespread in mental life. It can be used to describe how we divide our attention among multiple inputs or perhaps even to describe how we divide our thinking capacity among various ideas. It fits with our intuition that we can engage in more than one mental activity at a time—but only at the cost of lower efficiency per activity.

few decades (a middle-aged person's childhood memories). Most experimenters have used intervals of minutes or hours in their studies.

Encoding

For verbal materials, the dominant code seems to be based on the meanings of the items. If you memorize a long list of words and try to recall them a few minutes later, you will undoubtedly make errors. Most of the erroneous words will be similar in meaning to the correct items. For example, if "quick" were on the original list, you might mistakenly recall "fast" instead (Kintsch and

Buschke, 1969). Encoding items in terms of their meaning is particularly striking when the items are sentences. A few minutes after hearing a sentence, all you seem to have left is its meaning. Suppose you heard the sentence "The author sent a long letter to the committee." Two minutes later you could not tell whether you had heard that sentence or one that has the same meaning: "A letter that was long was sent to the committee by the author" (Sachs, 1967). Long-term memory, then, tends to maintain meaning.

How are meanings encoded for long-term storage? Consider the meaning of "helicopter": one might encode its meaning in terms of a mental picture, or image, of a typical helicopter; or one might encode something more abstract, more conceptual—say, the kind of information that a dictionary gives about helicopters ("a helicopter is a kind of airborne vehicle . . ."). The former is called an *imagery code* and the latter a *semantic code;* both can capture the meaning of an item (see Chapter 9 for a discussion of semantic concepts). The evidence indicates that both codes play a role in long-term memory.

Everyday observations indicate that a semantic code is frequently used. We often remember the meaning of sentences without experiencing images either during encoding or during retrieval. Indeed, it can be very difficult to even generate an image for some abstract sentences, like "The essence of the controversy was elusive." In these cases, a semantic code clearly seems to be involved.

There is also evidence for the use of an imagery code. Some evidence suggests that pictures are more easily remembered than sentences (Paivio, 1976). This could be because pictures are more likely to be coded in images than sentences are. Other studies show that we can use imagery to encode words and sentences when we are told to do so. For example, Bower (1972) asked subjects to memorize a list of 20 word pairs so that when given the first term of a pair (the *stimulus*) they could supply the second (the *response*). If "horse-table" was one pair, subjects had to respond with "table" when provided the stimulus term "horse." One group of subjects was instructed to memorize each pair by forming a visual image that related the terms. For example, for the "horse-table" pair, they might have formed an image of a horse jumping over a table. A second group, the control group, was left to its own devices to learn the list. The group instructed to use imagery recalled about 75 percent of the word pairs, while the control group recalled only 35 percent.

To conclude that an imagery code is superior to a semantic one may be too hasty, however. The same kind of improvement in memory is attainable without recourse to images. In a variation of the experiment just described, the first group was instructed to connect each word pair by thinking of a sentence that used both terms—for example, "The horse kicked the table." In this experiment too, the first group recalled roughly twice as much as the control group (Bower, 1972). Thus, using either sentences or images to connect word pairs leads to an improvement in memory. Taken at face value, these findings imply that both semantic and imagery codes can be used to remember verbal materials.

While meaning may be the dominant way of coding verbal material in long-term memory, we sometimes code other aspects as well. We can, for example, memorize poems and recite them word for word. In such cases, we have coded not only the meaning of the poem but the words themselves. We can also use an acoustic code in long-term memory. When you get a phone call and the other party says "Hello," you often recognize the voice. To do this, you must have coded the sound of that voice in long-term memory. Tastes and

Alternative Interpretations of Imagery Findings

The findings described in the text have led to something of a controversy about why the use of imagery improves memory for word pairs.

On one side are those who claim that subjects form images that integrate the words in a pair and this integrated image causes the improvement in memory (e.g., Paivio, 1971). According to this view, memory may also improve when sentences are used to link the pairs, because the sentences may be accompanied by integrated images. This view can be represented schematically as follows:

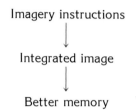

The important point is that imagery is held directly responsible for the better memory.

On the opposite side are those who argue that the very act of elaborating on the words to connect or relate them improves memory, with or without images (e.g., Anderson and Bower, 1973).

According to this view, you have to think about words to create images, and this thinking takes place in the semantic code. Semantic elaboration, then, is the key to better memory. This position can be represented as follows:

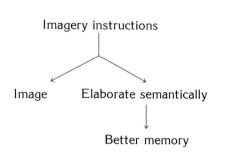

The critical point here is that semantic elaboration is held directly responsible for better memory.

This then is the controversy—either images cause better memory, or semantic elaboration does. Both positions may be partly correct. Trying to link word pairs by images may lead to both images and semantic elaboration of the word pairs, and both factors might contribute to the improvement in memory. Whether such a compromise position is a reasonable one can only be determined by future research.

"When you're young, it comes naturally, but when you get a little older, you have to rely on mnemonics."

smells are probably also coded in long-term memory. Thus, coding in long-term memory is like that in short-term memory: we have a preferred code for verbal material—meaning for long-term memory, acoustic for short-term memory—but other codes can be used as well.

Coding by meaning, however, seems to result in the best memory. And the more deeply or elaborately one encodes the meaning, the better memory will be. Thus, if you have to remember a point made in a textbook, you will recall it better if you concentrate on its meaning rather than on the exact words involved. And the more deeply and thoroughly you mull over its meaning, the better you will recall it.

Experiments performed by Craik illustrate these points. Subjects were shown words, one at a time, and asked a question about each word as it was presented. The questions were of three types. The first dealt with the way the word was written (for example, "Is it written in capital letters?"); the second, with the way it was pronounced (for example, "Does it rhyme with train?"). The third type required some consideration of the word's meaning (for example, "Could the word fit into the sentence 'He dropped the _____'?"). Later, when subjects were tested on their memory for the words, recognition was by far the best for those associated with the third type of question (see Figure 8-7). So when the subjects analyzed the meaning of a word they remembered it better, presumably because a code based on meaning is more durable than one based on writing or pronunciation. In another study, Craik used questions only of the third type but varied the length of the sentence. For example, the sentences could be "He dropped the _____," or "The old man hobbled across the room and dropped the _____." With longer sentences, subjects had to analyze more of the word's meaning to make sure it fit into the sentence. When subjects were tested later, they recognized more words associated with long sentences than with short ones. The more deeply the subjects had to elaborate the meaning of the test word, the better they remembered it.

In summary, we remember verbal materials best when we code them in terms of their meaning—either semantically or imaginally—and the more we elaborate the meaning the better our memory.

Storage and Retrieval

When we deal with long-term memory, we must consider storage and retrieval together. Many cases of forgetting from long-term memory seem to result from a loss of access to the information, rather than from a loss of the information itself. That is, poor memory may reflect a retrieval failure rather than a storage failure. (Note that this is unlike short-term memory, where forgetting results from exceeding storage capacity, while retrieval is thought to be error-free.) Trying to retrieve an item from long-term memory is analogous to trying to find a book in a large library. Failure to find the book (an item) does not necessarily mean it isn't there; you may be looking in the wrong place, or it may simply be misfiled and therefore inaccessible.

Common experience provides a great deal of evidence for this view. Everyone has been unable to recall a fact, only to have it come to mind later. How many times have you taken an exam and not been able to recall a specific name or date, only to remember it after the exam? Another example is the "tip-of-the-tongue" experience, in which a particular word or name lies tantalizingly outside our ability to recall it (Brown and McNeill, 1966). We may feel quite tormented until an active search of memory (dredging up and then discarding words that are close but not quite right) finally retrieves the correct word. A more striking example of retrieval failure is that some people under hypnosis feel they can recover memories of early childhood that are otherwise unavailable. Similar experiences occur in psychotherapy. While we lack firm experimental evidence for some of these observations, they at least suggest that some seemingly forgotten memories are not lost. They are just difficult to get at and require the right kind of *retrieval cue* (anything that can help us retrieve a memory).

For stronger evidence that retrieval failures can cause forgetting, we consider the following experiment. Subjects were asked to memorize a long list of words. Some of the words named specific animals, like "dog" and "cat"; some named specific fruit, like "apple" and "orange," and so on (see Table 8-1). At the time of recall, the subjects were divided into two groups. One group was supplied with retrieval cues like "animal," "fruit," and so on; the control group was not. The group given the retrieval cues recalled more words than the

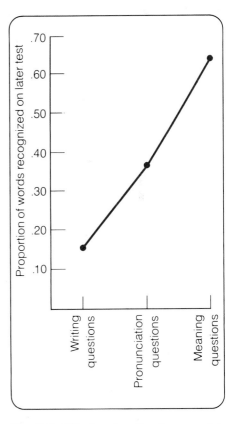

WORD	QUESTION
BLACK	Is it written in capital letters? (Yes)
table	Is it written in capital letters? (No)
rain	Does it rhyme with "train" (Yes)
CARD	Does it rhyme with "train" (No)
watch	Does it fit in sentence "He dropped the _____" (Yes)
CLOUD	Does it fit in sentence "He dropped the _____" (No)

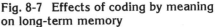

Fig. 8-7 Effects of coding by meaning on long-term memory
Subjects' memory for words was much better when they had been asked questions that dealt with the words' meanings. (Adapted from Craik, 1977)

TABLE 8-1
Examples from a study of retrieval failures

LIST TO BE MEMORIZED		
dog	cotton	oil
cat	wood	gas
horse	silk	coal
cow	rayon	wood
apple	blue	doctor
orange	red	lawyer
pear	green	teacher
banana	yellow	dentist
chair	knife	football
table	spoon	baseball
bed	fork	basketball
sofa	pan	tennis
knife	hammer	shirt
gun	saw	socks
rifle	nails	pants
bomb	screwdriver	shoes

RETRIEVAL CUES		
animals	cloth	fuels
fruit	color	professions
furniture	utensils	sports
weapons	tools	clothing

Adapted from Tulving and Pearlstone (1966)

William James writing in 1890 on the tip-of-the-tongue experience
"Suppose we try to recall a forgotten name. The state of our consciousness is peculiar. There is a gap therein; but no mere gap. It is a gap that is intensely active. A sort of wraith of the name is in it, beckoning us in a given direction, making us at moments tingle with the sense of our closeness and then letting us sink back without the longed-for term. If wrong names are proposed to us, this singularly definite gap acts immediately so as to negate them. They do not fit into its mould. And the gap of one word does not feel like the gap of another, all empty of content as both might seem necessarily to be when described as gaps." (James, 1890)

control group. In a subsequent test, when both groups were given the retrieval cues, they then recalled the same number of words. Hence, the initial difference in recall between the two groups must have been due to retrieval failures.

Thus, the better the retrieval cues, the better our memory. This principle explains why we usually do better on a recognition test of memory than on a recall test. In a recognition test, we are asked if we have seen a particular item before (for example, "Was Harry Smith one of the people you met at the party?"). The test item itself is an excellent retrieval cue for our memory of that item. In contrast, in a recall test we have to produce the memorized items with minimal retrieval cues (for example, "Recall the names of everyone you met at the party."). Since the retrieval cues in a recognition test are generally more useful than those in a recall test, recognition tests usually show better memory performance than recall tests (Tulving, 1974).

Are retrieval failures the only cause of forgetting? It is difficult to say. How can we tell whether a person has totally forgotten something or hasn't yet found the right retrieval cue—the one that leads to the target memory? On the other hand, it seems unlikely that everything learned is there in memory waiting for the right cue. Some information may actually be lost from storage, perhaps due to some form of displacement by subsequent information or to decay with time. (To evaluate such possibilities, we may need a better understanding of the biochemical basis of long-term memory storage.) It is clear, however, that whether or not retrieval failures are the only cause of forgetting, they are certainly a major cause of forgetting from long-term memory. Thus, it is essential to know what factors increase or decrease retrieval. In the rest of this section, we will discuss such factors.

Biochemical Bases of Long-Term Memory Storage

In addition to studying long-term memory from a behavioral standpoint, researchers have also studied it from a biological one. The critical question is: what kinds of changes in the brain underlie the encoding and storage of memories? Early work in this area focused on changes occurring at synaptic connections between brain cells. More recent research has examined changes in the biochemical nature of the brain cells themselves.

We have known for a long time that the nucleus of a cell contains deoxyribonucleic acid (DNA), which is the primary vehicle of heritable characteristics. Our genes are composed chiefly of DNA molecules, and the genetic code is literally written along the DNA molecule. This code specifies the information needed to create a complete individual—an individual with eyes and hair of a certain color, with a beating heart, and a functioning brain possessing certain individual characteristics. DNA, then, is the carrier of our heredity. To find a possible carrier of our memory we must consider further the biochemical nature of a cell.

DNA never leaves the cell's nucleus, but rather directs the cell's activities by manufacturing its own "assistants" to which it then "delegates" responsibilities. These assistants are various forms of ribonucleic acid (RNA). After being manufactured in the nucleus, these RNA assistants move out to the cytoplasm, where they control the essential functions of the cell. Many researchers have suggested that RNA composes the biochemical basis of memory.

Three types of studies tentatively support this view. The first takes advantage of the fact that certain chemicals inhibit the synthesis of RNA. In these studies, an animal that has learned a particular response is injected with an RNA-inhibitor and then tested for its memory of the learned response. In one such experiment (Flexner, 1967), mice that had learned to avoid shock in a maze were injected with a known RNA-inhibitor and lost their memory of the maze.

The second type of study attempts to show that learning produces a change in the RNA of specific cells. In one study (Hyden, 1969), young rats learned to balance on a thin, slanting wire in order to obtain food. The cells that play a critical role in the memory of this balancing skill are vestibular nerve cells. Cells of this kind in mice that had learned the balancing skill were found to contain more RNA—and RNA of a different composition—than the cells of control animals that had not learned the skill. Thus, acquisition of a specific memory was accompanied by an increase in RNA in specific cells. This fits quite nicely with the hypothesis that RNA serves as the biochemical basis of specific memories.

The third kind of experiment based on RNA as a memory molecule is even more dramatic (McConnell and others, 1970). These studies, called transfer studies, involve the transfer of RNA from one animal to another. A typical experiment involves three phases. In the first, small flatworms, called planaria, learn a classically conditioned response. The planaria are housed in a trough of water. When a brief electrical current is passed through the water, the planaria respond with a muscular contraction. The onset of the shock is then paired with the onset of a light. After repeated presentations of the shock and the light, the light alone elicits the contraction response. The planaria now contract in response to what was once a neutral light. In the second phase of the experiment, a substance containing RNA from the bodies of the trained planaria is injected into untrained planaria. In the third phase, the untrained planaria are given the classical-conditioning training described above. They learn the conditioned response more rapidly than does a control group injected with RNA from untrained planaria. Such striking results are consistent with the idea that the RNA extracted from the first trained group carries the memory of that training. Subsequent work has shown similar transfer effects with other species, such as rats.

Unfortunately, efforts to replicate the transfer studies described above have not always been successful. One problem is that the conditioning of planaria can be difficult. And, with species other than planaria, the transfer effect is sometimes in doubt. So we must consider conclusions about RNA transfer as tentative. Still, transfer studies represent a pioneering attempt to determine the biochemical basis of memory. They also provoke some speculations about the future—speculations that border on science fiction, such as learning Greek by injection, calculus by taking a pill, or even learning by eating a "professor-burger."

Organization and Context

Research has identified two factors that increase the chances of successful retrieval: (1) organizing the information in storage and (2) ensuring that the context in which we retrieve information is similar to the context in which we encoded it.

The more we organize the material we store, the easier it is to retrieve. For example, suppose you were at a meeting where you met various professionals—doctors, lawyers, teachers, and journalists. When you later tried to recall their names, you would do better if you organized your recall by profession: Who were the doctors I met? Who were the lawyers? And so forth. A list of names or words is far easier to recall when we can sort the words into categories and then recall the words on a category-by-category basis (Bousfield, 1953).

The following experiment illustrates the use of categories in organizing recall. The subjects were asked to memorize four separate lists of words. For some subjects, the words in a list were arranged in the form of a hierarchical tree, much like the example shown in Figure 8-8. For the other subjects, the words were arranged randomly. When tested later, subjects recalled 65 percent of the words presented in the hierarchical organization but only 19 percent of the same words presented in random arrangements. Studies like this leave little doubt that retrieval is best when the material is highly organized.

It is also easier to retrieve a particular episode if you are in the same context in which that episode occurred (Estes, 1972). For example, it is a good bet that your ability to retrieve the names of your classmates in the first and second grade would improve were you to walk through the corridors of your elementary school. Similarly, your ability to retrieve, say, an emotional moment with your parents would be greater if you were back in the place where the incident occurred than if you were off somewhere else. Perhaps it is for this reason that when we visit a place we once lived, we are sometimes overcome with a torrent of memories about our earlier life. Thus, the context in which an event was encoded is itself one of the most powerful retrieval cues possible. There is a mass of experimental evidence to support this (see Figure 8-9 for a representative study).

Context is not always something external to the memorizer, like a physical location or a specific face. What is happening inside of us when we encode information—our internal state—is also part of the context. If we feel sad when we learn some material, perhaps we can best retrieve it when we are sad again, for in that case the emotional state during encoding has been restored during retrieval. Or, take a more extreme example. If we experience some event while under the influence of a particular drug, like alcohol or marijuana, perhaps we can best retrieve it when we are again in that drug-induced state. In such cases, memory would be partly dependent on the internal state during learning—what is called *state-dependent learning* (see Chapter 6). There has been a good deal of research on state-dependent learning, and even though the evidence is

Fig. 8-8 Hierarchical organization to improve retrieval
A list of words arranged in the form of a hierarchical tree. Trees like this are constructed according to the following rule: all items below a node are included in the class labeled by that node; for example, the items "bronze," "steel," and "brass" are included in the class labeled "alloys." (Bower and others, 1969)

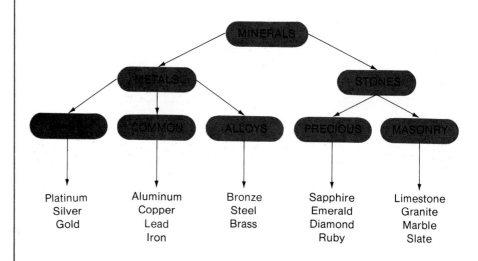

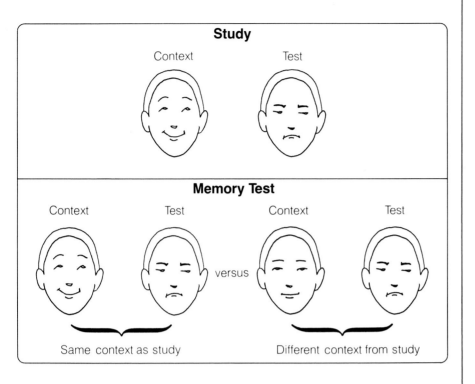

Study

Context   Test

Memory Test

Context   Test   versus   Context   Test

Same context as study   Different context from study

Fig. 8-9 Effects of context on retrieval In one experiment to demonstrate how context affects retrieval, subjects first studied pairs of faces like the one at the top. (Since only the right-hand face was ever tested, it was the test face, while the left-hand one was the context face.) Later, in a memory test, subjects were again shown pairs of faces and asked whether the test face was one they had previously studied. In some cases the context face was the same one that appeared in the original pair; in other cases, it was not. Subjects made more accurate decisions when the context face was the same. (Based on Watkins, Ho, and Tulving, 1976)

controversial, it suggests that memory does indeed improve when our internal state during retrieval matches that during encoding (Overton, 1972).

Interference

There are also factors that decrease retrieval, particularly the factor of *interference.* When we learn different items that are very similar to one another, trying to retrieve one of them (the target item) will bring to mind other similar items that interfere with the target. For example, when a friend moves and you finally learn his or her new phone number, you will find it difficult to retrieve the old number. Why? When you attempt to retrieve the old number, the new one comes to mind and interferes with the old one. Or, suppose that you live in an apartment house, and, after having the same parking place for a year, your place is changed. You may initially find it difficult to retrieve from memory your new parking location. Why? When you try to retrieve the new location, the old one comes to mind and interferes with the learning of the new one. Interference then can operate in two directions: (1) The learning of new materials interferes with our memory of old ones (illustrated by the telephone-number example). This is *retroactive interference.* (2) Previously learned material interferes with our attempt to remember new information (illustrated by the parking-place example). This is *proactive interference.*

The standard experimental procedure for studying retroactive interference is as follows. One group of subjects, the experimental group, first learns a list of word pairs (call them the **A-B** pairs) so that they can produce the second, or response, term **B** when given the first, or stimulus, term **A**. The same group then learns a second list of pairs (the **A-C** pairs) in which the stimulus terms (**A**'s) are identical or similar to the stimulus terms in the first list. The control group gets the same treatment in the first phase; but, in the second phase, the subjects are allowed to rest or are asked to learn an unrelated list of word pairs (call them **D-C** pairs). Then both groups are retested on the first list. On seeing the stimulus terms (the **A**'s), they must now respond with the original response terms (the **B**'s). The experimental group recalls fewer **B** terms, because their learning of the **A-C** pairs has interfered with their retrieval of the **A-B** pairs. The following is a summary of this procedure.

	Phase 1	Phase 2	Phase 3
Experimental group	Learn **A-B** pairs (dog-map)	Learn **A-C** pairs (dog-chair)	Recall **A-B** pairs (dog-map)
Control group	Learn **A-B** pairs (dog-map)	Learn **D-C** pairs (book-chair)	Recall **A-B** pairs (dog-map)

Proactive interference is studied in the same manner as retroactive interference except that Phases 1 and 2 are interchanged:

	Phase 1	Phase 2	Phase 3
Experimental group	Learn **A-C** pairs (dog-chair)	Learn **A-B** pairs (dog-map)	Recall **A-B** pairs (dog-map)
Control group	Learn **D-C** pairs (book-chair)	Learn **A-B** pairs (dog-map)	Recall **A-B** pairs (dog-map)

Again, the experimental group recalls fewer **B** terms on the final test, indicating that their prior learning of **A-C** pairs interfered with subsequent retrieval of the **A-B** pairs. Numerous experiments have used these procedures and have shown that retroactive and proactive interference are responsible for a great deal of forgetting (Underwood, 1957; Postman, 1961).

Emotional Factors in Forgetting

So far we have treated retrieval as if it were a mechanical operation. What about emotional factors? Don't we sometimes fail to retrieve material because of its emotional content? There has been a great deal of research on this question. The results suggest that there are at least three distinct ways that emotion can influence retrieval from long-term memory.

The simplest notion is that we tend to think about emotionally charged situations, negative as well as positive, more than we think about neutral ones. We rehearse and organize exciting memories more than we do their blander counterparts. For example, you may usually forget where you saw this or that movie. However, if a fire breaks out while you're in a theater you will describe the setting over and over to friends, thereby rehearsing and organizing it. Since we know that rehearsal and organization can improve retrieval from long-term memory, it is not surprising that many researchers have found better memory for emotional than for unemotional situations (Rapaport, 1942).

In some cases, however, negative emotions hinder retrieval. An experience that most students have at one time or another illustrates this.

> You are taking an exam about which you are not very confident. You can barely understand the initial question let alone answer it. Signs of panic appear. Although the second question really isn't hard, the anxiety triggered by the previous question spreads to this one. By the time you look at the third question it wouldn't matter if it just asked for your name. There's no way you can answer it. You're in a complete panic.

What is happening to memory here? Failure to deal with the first question produced some anxiety. Anxiety is often accompanied by extraneous thoughts, like "I'm going to flunk out," or "Everybody will know how stupid I am." These thoughts then interfere with any attempt to retrieve the information relevant to the question, and that may be why memory fails so utterly. According to this view, anxiety does not directly cause memory failure. Rather, it causes, or is associated with, extraneous thoughts, and these thoughts cause memory failure (Holmes, 1974).

We have now considered two means by which emotion can influence memory—improving or hindering retrieval. Both rely on principles already discussed—rehearsal and interference. The third view of emotion and memory—Freud's *repression* hypothesis (1915)—brings up new principles. This theory proposes that some emotional experiences in childhood are so traumatic that to allow them to enter consciousness many years later would cause one to be totally overwhelmed by anxiety. (This was not the case in the example of the exam, where the anxiety was tolerable to consciousness.) Such traumatic experiences, as well as later ones that are associated with them, are said to be stored in the unconscious, or repressed. They can be retrieved only when some of the emotion associated with them is defused, usually by therapeutic means. Repression, therefore, represents the ultimate retrieval failure: access to the target memories is actively blocked. It is this notion of an active blocking that makes the repression hypothesis qualitatively different from the views we considered earlier. (For a fuller discussion of Freud's theory, see Chapter 14.)

The primary evidence for repression comes from clinical patients undergoing psychotherapy. The case reported below is a striking illustration:

A 40-year-old man came to a mental hospital with serious depression and haunting ideas about death. As a child he had lost his mother under traumatic circumstances. All he could remember about the actual death was being awakened from sleep in order to be taken to the hospital some distance away. When he and his sisters arrived there, his mother was dead. The mother's death had been very disturbing to him, and it was evident to the therapist who treated him that some of his present symptoms dated from it. In order to help him recall specific events of that period, the therapist asked, among other questions, whether he recalled the time of night the events happened. He could not remember. That these memories were repressed is suggested by a dream he had the night following this interview.

The patient dreamt that he saw two clocks. One was running and one had stopped. The one that was running showed 20 minutes to three, and the one that had stopped showed 20 minutes to five. He was mystified by the dream.

Because of the possibility that those clocks represented the repressed childhood memories, the man's older sister was asked about the circumstances of the mother's death. She said that they had been roused from sleep in their farmhouse about 2:30 A.M. and had driven to the distant hospital. When they arrived there about 4:30, their mother had just died. (Case courtesy of J. R. Hilgard)

Clearly, the times in the dream were close to reality. Yet this memory was not consciously available to the patient, even when the therapist pressed him for it. However, probing by the supportive therapist may have facilitated the retrieval of the memory in the dream.

Repression is such a striking phenomenon that we would of course like to study it in the laboratory. But this has proved very difficult to do, though many attempts have been made. To induce repression in a laboratory, the experi-

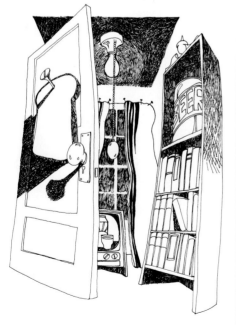

Fig. 8-10 Illustration of method of loci

menter must have the subject experience something extremely traumatic. Ethical considerations prohibit this. Nevertheless, the idea of repression continues to fascinate those who study memory, even in the absence of firm experimental support.

Improving Memory

Having considered the basics of short- and long-term memory, we are ready to tackle the question of improving memory. Relatively little can be done to improve short-term memory. Its capacity seems fixed for each individual, and retrieval appears to be similar for different kinds of people. The only way to increase the amount we can hold in short-term memory is to group items into larger chunks, as when we divide the series 200119841900 into the three familiar chunks, 2001, 1984, 1900. Unfortunately most series of digits and letters do not break into such neat packages, so there is a limit to how much short-term memory can be improved.

Long-term memory is a different matter, however. There are wide variations among individuals in how they encode and retrieve information from long-term memory, and there is great potential for improvement. This section thus focuses on long-term memory. We will look first at how material can be encoded more efficiently and then consider how retrieval itself may be improved.

Imagery and Encoding

We mentioned earlier that recall for a word pair improved greatly when the two words were connected by an image. When we link the terms "horse" and "table" by an image, we may increase the number of connections between them. We then have multiple ways of getting from one term to the other—or perhaps one long-term memory chunk that includes both terms—and this will naturally improve recall. Regardless of precisely how it works, though, imagery seems to connect things in memory. And this is the main principle behind many *mnemonic* (memory-aiding) systems.

One famous mnemonic system is called the *method of loci* (*loci* is Latin for "places"). The method works especially well with an ordered sequence of arbitrary items, like unrelated words. The first step is to commit to memory an ordered sequence of places, say the locations you would come upon in a slow walk through your house. You enter through the front door, come into a hallway, move next to the bookcase in the living room, then to the television in the living room, then to the curtains at the window, and so on. Once you can easily take this mental walk, you are ready to memorize as many unrelated words as there are locations on your walk. You form an image that relates the first word to the first location, another image that relates the second word to the second location, and so on. If the words are items on a shopping list— "bread," "eggs," "beer," "milk," and "bacon"—you might imagine a slice of bread nailed to your front door, an egg hanging from the light cord in the hallway, a can of beer in the bookcase, a milk commercial playing on your television, and curtains made from giant strips of bacon (see Figure 8-10). Once you have memorized the items this way, you can easily recall them in order by simply taking your mental walk again. Each location will retrieve an image, and each image will retrieve a word. The method clearly works and is a favorite among those who perform memory feats professionally.

Imagery is also used in the *key-word method* of learning a foreign vocabulary. This method involves two steps. The first is to find a part of the foreign word that sounds like an English word. The Spanish word *caballo*, which means "horse," is pronounced "cob-eye-yo." Hence "eye" could serve as the key word. The next step is to form an image that connects the key word and the English equivalent—say, a horse kicking a giant eye (see Figure 8-11). To recall the meaning of *caballo*, you would first retrieve "eye" and then the stored image that links it to "horse." This may sound complicated, but studies have shown that the key-word method does make learning a foreign language easier (Atkinson and Raugh, 1975; Atkinson, 1975).

Depth of Encoding

We have seen evidence that the more deeply and elaborately we encode material, the better we remember it. The practical implications of these findings are straightforward. If you want to remember something, expand on its meaning. To illustrate, suppose you read a newspaper article about a mysterious epidemic in San Francisco that health officials are trying to contain. To expand on this, you could ask yourself questions about how officials could contain the epidemic—for example: "Would they just quarantine families with a diseased member, or would they go so far as to try to stop outsiders from visiting the city?" Similarly, if someone tells you a story you want to remember, you might look for gaps in the plot and ask the narrator to fill them in. To the extent you do so, your memory for the essential story should improve.

Context and Retrieval

Since context is a powerful retrieval cue, we can improve our memory by restoring the context in which the learning took place. If your psychology lecture always meets in one room, your memory for the lecture material will be best when you are in that room, for then the context of the room is a retrieval cue for the lecture material. This has direct educational implications. Students will do better on exams when they are tested in their habitual classroom and when the proctor is their instructor than when these factors are changed (Abernathy, 1940).

Most often, though, when we have to remember something, we cannot physically go back to the context in which we learned it. If you want to remember the name of your childhood doctor and it doesn't come immediately to mind, you are not about to go back to your home town just to recall a name. In these situations, however, you can try to re-create the context mentally. To retrieve the long-forgotten doctor's name, you might think of your home town and try to visualize your doctor's office or try to recall a particularly significant incident that occurred involving your doctor.

Another illustration of mentally re-creating context is this example, adapted from Norman (1973). Suppose someone asked you, "What were you doing at 1 P.M. on the third Monday of October two years ago?" "Ridiculous," you might say. "No one can remember things like that." But re-creating the context can lead to surprising results:

> Well, two years ago I was a senior in high school; let me see, October, that's fall semester. Now what courses did I take that semester? Oh yes, chemistry. That's it, I had a chemistry lab every afternoon, that's where I was at 1:00 P.M. on the third Monday of October two years ago.

In this example, mentally restoring the context seems to have done the trick. However, we cannot be sure you actually remembered being in chemistry lab.

Examples of key words used to link Spanish words to their English translations

SPANISH	KEY WORD	ENGLISH
caballo	[eye]	horse
charco	[charcoal]	puddle
muleta	[mule]	crutch
clavo	[claw]	nail
lagartija	[log]	lizard
cebolla	[boy]	onion
payaso	[pie]	clown
hiio	[eel]	thread
tenaza	[tennis]	pliars
jabon	[bone]	soap
carpa	[carp]	tent
pato	[pot]	duck

CABALLO → eye → HORSE

PATO → pot → DUCK

Fig. 8-11 Mental images and foreign language learning
Mental images used to associate spoken Spanish words with corresponding English terms. At top, *caballo* ("horse"); below, *pato* ("duck").

Perhaps you inferred that you must have been there. Either way, though, you may come up with the right answer.

Organization and Retrieval

We know that organization improves retrieval, and this principle can be put to great practical use. We seem to be capable of storing and retrieving a massive amount of information if only we organize it.

Some experiments have investigated organizational devices that can be used to learn many unrelated items. In one study, subjects learned lists of 10 words by connecting all the words into a story. Later, when tested for 12 such lists (a total of 120 words), subjects recalled more than 90 percent of the words (Bower and Clark, 1969). This is a truly remarkable memory feat, but anyone can easily do it.

At this point you might concede that psychologists have devised some ingenious techniques for memorizing lists of unrelated items. But, you argue, what you have to remember are not lists of unrelated items, but stories you were told, lectures, and readings like the present chapter. Isn't this kind of material already organized, and doesn't this mean that the above-mentioned technique is of limited value? Yes and no. Yes, this chapter is more than a list of unrelated words, but—and this is the critical point—there is always a problem of organization with any material that is long, including this chapter. Later you may be able to recall that imagery aids learning, but this may not bring to mind anything about, say, acoustic coding in short-term memory. The two topics do not seem to be intimately related. There is, however, a relation between the topics—both deal with encoding phenomena. The best way to see that relation is to note the headings and subheadings in the chapter, for these show how the material in the chapter is organized. A most effective way to study is to keep this organization in mind. You might, for example, try to capture part of this chapter's organization by sketching a hierarchical tree like the one below. It may be even more helpful, though, to make your own outline of the chapter, one that gives the basic topics as well as the specific issues covered within each topic. Memory seems to benefit most when the organizing is done by the rememberers themselves.

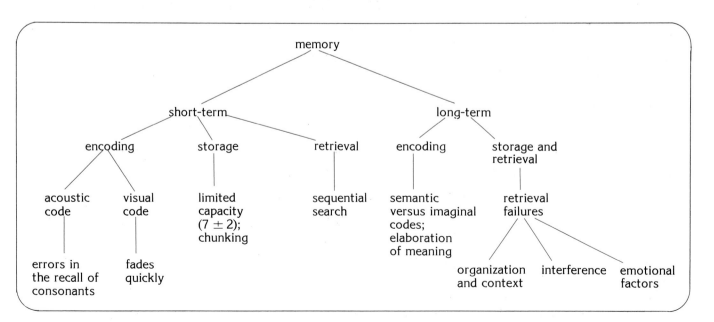

CHAPTER 8/REMEMBERING AND FORGETTING

Practicing Retrieval

Another way to improve retrieval is to practice it—that is, to ask yourself questions about what you are trying to learn. Suppose you have two hours in which to study an assignment that can be read through in 30 minutes. Reading and rereading the assignment four times is likely to be much less effective than reading it once and asking yourself questions about it. You can then reread selected parts to clear up points that were difficult to retrieve the first time around. Attempting retrieval is an efficient use of study time. This was demonstrated long ago by experiments using unrelated items as well as material like that actually learned in courses (see Figure 8-12).

The Relation Between Short- and Long-Term Memory

At the outset of this chapter, we suggested that short- and long-term memory might operate by different laws, and we have therefore treated them separately. In this section, we survey the evidence that they constitute separate memory stores and consider how the two are integrated into one working system.

Evidence for Two Kinds of Memory

In discussing the stages of short- and long-term memory, we hit upon a number of differences between the two types of memory. First, the encoding stage favors an acoustic code in short-term memory, but one based on meaning in long-term memory. (However, a good deal of current investigation is directed at finding codes other than the dominant ones in the two memory stores.) Second, the storage capacity of short-term memory is limited to 7 ± 2 items, while the capacity of long-term memory seems unlimited for all practical purposes. And third, retrieval from short-term memory is thought to be more or less error-free (if it's there, you can find it), while retrieval from long-term memory appears to be very error-prone and a major cause of forgetting. Thus, there is evidence that the two memory stores show differences at all three stages.

Clinical and physiological studies of extreme memory disorders are a second source of evidence that there are two memories. One such memory disorder is *retrograde amnesia*, which typically results from a concussion or severe injury to the head. People with this condition often have no memory for the events that immediately preceded the injury, though their memory for earlier events may be intact. Why does the injury have such a devastating effect on recent memory but none at all on earlier memories? The obvious answer is that the brain injury affected only short-term memory and not long-term memory. The clinical facts on retrograde amnesia therefore support the idea of two different memories.

Retrograde amnesia has also been studied in animals. An animal first learns a task—for example, turning left in a maze. It is then subjected to electroconvulsive shock, which produces temporary unconsciousness, as with concussion. Later the animal is tested again on the maze to see if it has retained the original learned response. If the time between the original learning and the shock is very brief, the learned response should still be in short-term memory. The shock should erase the memory, and the animal should remember little on the final test. If the interval between the learning and the shock is relatively long,

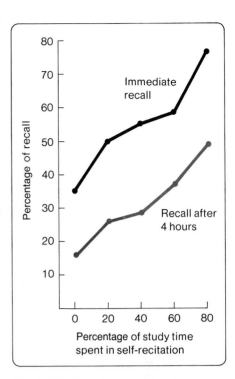

Fig. 8-12 Practicing retrieval
Effects on recall of spending various proportions of study time in attempting retrieval rather than in silent study. Results are shown for tests given immediately and four hours after completing study. (Data from Gates, 1917)

"I can't remember the last time I treated a case of amnesia, and I can't even remember if I ever did treat one."

Retrograde Amnesia and Retrieval Failure

Recent studies suggest that retrograde amnesia may involve more than the disruption of short-term memory. Specifically, retrograde amnesia may be at least partly due to retrieval failure.

To appreciate this point, consider again the kind of experiment that produces retrograde amnesia. An animal has learned to make a particular response in a maze and then is immediately given electroconvulsive shock. Later, the animal is tested in the maze without being given the shock, and it shows poor memory of the learned response. Painful and traumatic as the shock may have been, it was part of the learning context. It was not part of the test context. Perhaps it is this change in context that is responsible for the animal's poor memory. The omission of the shock during test may have deprived the animal of a useful retrieval cue. The point, then, is that the amnesic effect of the shock may come about not only because of its presence during learning, but also because of its absence during test.

Counterintuitive as this analysis may be, there is experimental support for it. In one study, animals first learned an avoidance response. Electroconvulsive shock was administered five seconds after learning (an interval brief enough to produce retrograde amnesia). Twenty-four hours later the animals were tested for their memory of the avoidance response. Twenty minutes prior to this test, one group of animals was again administered the shock as a possible reminder of the original learning context; a control group was not. The group given the shock reminder remembered more on the test than the control group. So, reintroducing the shock close to test time actually reduced the memory loss—suggesting that part of retrograde amnesia is due to retrieval failure (Thompson and Neely, 1970).

This line of research fits well with work on human memory that emphasizes learning context as a retrieval cue. It does not, however, fit well with the standard interpretation of retrograde amnesia as a disruption of short-term memory. Can the latter interpretation be reconciled with the present findings—say, by assuming that electroconvulsive shock serves as both a disrupter of short-term memory and a retrieval cue for long-term memory? A reconciliation of this sort does seem likely (Spear, 1973), although, as usual, we will have to wait until we know the outcome of future research.

however, the learned response should be in long-term memory. The shock should not affect it, and the animal should remember a lot on the final test. Several experiments have obtained this pattern of results (e.g., Hudspeth, McGaugh, and Thompson, 1964).

Another kind of memory disturbance, *anterograde amnesia*, has been observed in patients who have undergone surgery for relief of epileptic seizures. These patients, from whom part of the hippocampus (an area deep in the brain's temporal lobes) has been removed, seem incapable of learning new material. They have no trouble remembering skills and information learned before the operation, so their long-term memory is intact. They can also hold onto a few verbal items if they are allowed to rehearse them continuously, so their short-term memory seems in working condition. What they have trouble doing, however, is encoding new information into long-term memory. For example, several months after surgery one patient's family moved to a house a few blocks from their old one, on the same street. A year later, the patient still could not remember his new address, although he recalled the old one perfectly, nor could he find his way to his new home. He could not remember where things he continually used were kept, and he would read the same magazines over and over without recognizing the contents (Milner, 1966). This, too, suggests that short- and long-term memory are separate systems.

A Theory of Dual Memory

Given the evidence for two kinds of memory, the question arises: how are they related? A number of theories have been advanced. We will present one such theory to illustrate the basic ideas involved (Atkinson and Shiffrin, 1971, 1977).

This theory assumes that information we have attended to enters a limited

"On the contrary, I can't recall a thing from fifty years ago, but I remember exactly what I had for lunch yesterday."

CHAPTER 8/REMEMBERING AND FORGETTING

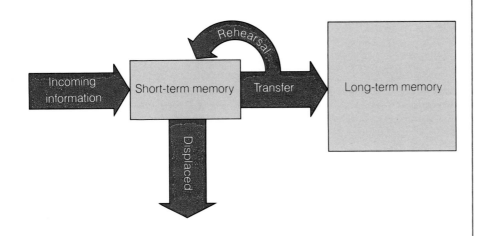

Fig. 8-13 A dual-memory theory
Incoming information enters short-term memory, where it can be maintained by rehearsal and successfully transferred to long-term memory, or it can be forgotten. (After Atkinson and Shiffrin, 1971)

short-term memory, where it can be either maintained by rehearsal or lost by displacement (see Figure 8-13). Long-term memory is considered to have virtually unlimited capacity but to be vulnerable to retrieval failures. In addition, in order for information to be encoded into long-term memory, it must be transferred there from short-term memory. This is the critical assumption that relates the two memories. In its strongest form, it means that we can learn something (encode it in long-term memory) only by first processing it in short-term memory.

What about the transfer processes themselves? Some could be the strategies we talked about earlier for encoding information into long-term memory. Relating two words by an image or by a linking sentence may be two ways to transfer them from short- to long-term memory. Still another transfer strategy would be rehearsal. As the diagram in Figure 8-13 suggests, rehearsing an item not only maintains it in short-term memory but also causes it to be transferred to long-term memory.

This *dual-memory theory* not only brings together many of the findings we have covered but also provides a way of classifying severe memory disturbances. We have already noted that retrograde amnesia may reflect a disruption of short-term memory. We can now see that the memory disturbances caused by removal of the hippocampus may be manifestations of a breakdown of the transfer processes that relate short- and long-term memory. And of course, there is the classical type of amnesia, where individuals forget many of the personal memories that contribute to their sense of identity, such as their name and family ties. Clearly, this seems a disturbance in long-term memory. Furthermore, the fact that such amnesic victims can recover missing memories indicates that the loss was of access or retrieval, which again fits the notion of a long-term memory disturbance.

Free-Recall Evidence

Some of the strongest support for the dual-memory theory comes from experiments on *free recall.* In a free-recall experiment, subjects see a list of, say, 20 or 40 words, one by one, and must immediately recall them in any order (hence the designation *free*). The results from such an experiment are shown in Figure 8-14A. The chance of correctly recalling a word is graphed as a function of the word's position on the list. The part of the curve to the left of the graph is for the first few words presented, while the part to the right is for the last few words presented.

The dual-memory theory assumes that at the time of recall the last few words presented are likely to still be in short-term memory, while the remain-

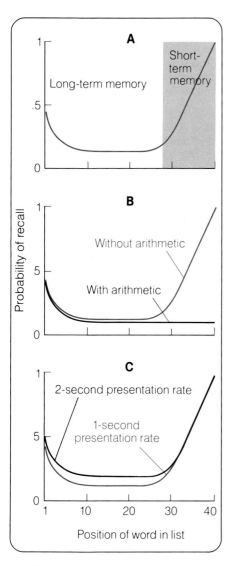

Fig. 8-14 Curves of free-recall experiments
Probability of recall varies with an item's position in a list; recall of last few items is based on short-term memory, while recall of remaining items is based on long-term memory (A). If an arithmetic task occurs between presentation and free recall, only recall from short-term memory is reduced (B). Slower presentation of items results in better recall from long-term memory (C). (Based on experiments by Murdock, 1962 and Glanzer, 1972)

ing words are in long-term memory. Thus we would expect recall of the last few words to be high, since items in short-term memory can easily be retrieved. Figure 8-14A shows this is the case. But recall for the first words presented is also quite good. Why is this? Dual-memory theory has an answer. When the first words were presented they were entered into short-term memory and rehearsed. Since there was little else in short-term memory, they were rehearsed often and were therefore likely to be transferred to long-term memory. As more items were presented, short-term memory quickly filled up and opportunities for rehearsal and transfer to long-term memory decreased to a low level. So only the first few items presented enjoyed the extra opportunity of transfer, and that is why they are later recalled so well from long-term memory.

Varying the procedure of the free-recall experiment can produce results that tend to confirm the preceding analysis. Suppose that after the list is presented but before subjects try to recall it, they do arithmetic problems for 30 seconds. Doing arithmetic requires short-term memory capacity and should therefore displace many of the list words that are in short-term memory (the last words presented). Figure 8-14B shows that, as expected, the last few words were displaced.

The rate at which the words are presented should also affect recall. A slower rate of presentation—say, a word every two seconds instead of every second—should allow more time for rehearsal and, hence, for transfer to long-term memory. The slower rate should therefore boost recall for those words that have to be retrieved from long-term memory—that is, all words but the last few. The results of this variation, shown in Figure 8-14C, again conform to predictions. The slower rate improved recall for all words but the last few. The dual-memory theory offers a detailed account of the free-recall data shown in the three panels of Figure 8-14.

Alternative Viewpoints

Though the dual-memory theory has successfully accounted for a wide range of memory phenomena, it is not without problems. In recent years some of these have become more evident, and alternatives to the theory are being developed.

One major problem concerns rehearsal. The dual-memory theory assumes that rehearsal per se can transfer information to permanent memory. That is, simply repeating words to yourself, with no attempt to organize or relate them to other memories, should increase your long-term recall. But conflicting results—experiments that show more rehearsal increases long-term recall (Nelson, 1977) and experiments that show it does not (Craik and Watkins, 1973)—indicate that rehearsal is a more complicated phenomenon than we previously thought.

Another problem is that the dual-memory theory is incomplete. For example, it has little to say about why encoding an item's meaning deeply and elaborately should increase its recall, yet this phenomenon has cropped up many times. Recent critics of the dual-memory theory have emphasized this particular deficiency and have begun to develop an alternative approach, called *depth-of-processing*. The general idea of this approach is that an item entering the memory system is analyzed in stages. The early stages analyze perceptual properties of the item, like visual or acoustic properties. Later stages analyze its meaning, like the categories it fits into and its relation to other items in memory. Each level of processing leaves a residue, or trace, in memory. The deeper the level of processing, the stronger the trace and the better the memory. According to this view, forgetting is relatively rapid in short-term memory studies, because the items have been analyzed only to a relatively shallow, acoustic (or visual) level. Similarly, persistence in long-term memory is attributed to deeper processing of the items, particularly to analyzing the items' meanings (Craik and Lockhart, 1972). The difference between short- and long-term memory, then, is seen as a difference in degree, not in kind (a view shared by many critics of the dual-memory theory—e.g., Wickelgren, 1973).

The depth-of-processing approach is still too new to evaluate critically. It may be a strong alternative to the dual-memory theory, or its insights may be incorporated into an expanded version of that theory (Craik, 1979).

Constructive Memory

Much of the research discussed in this chapter has dealt with simple verbal materials, like lists of unrelated words. What can be said about memory for more complex materials, like sentences and stories we have heard or visual scenes we have witnessed? Research with such materials, particularly sentences, indicates that many of the principles derived from experiments with unrelated words apply to complex materials as well. Just as words may become inaccessible because of interference from other words, so sentences can interfere with one another and lead to retrieval failures. Just as memory for words may be improved by organizing them, so memory for sentences improves when they are organized (Anderson, 1976). Some new principles do emerge, however, when we look at memory for sentences, stories, and visual scenes. The most important of these principles is that memory can be *constructive*.

When we hear a sentence or story, we often take it as an incomplete description of a real-world event and use our general knowledge to *construct* a more complete description of that event. How do we do this? By adding to the sentences and stories thoughts that are likely to follow from them. Thus, on hearing "Mike broke a bottle in a barroom brawl," we are likely to infer that it was a beer or whiskey bottle, not a milk or pop bottle. We add this inference to our memory of the sentence itself. Our total memory, then, goes beyond the original information given. We fill in the original information by using our general knowledge about what goes with what—for example, beer bottles go with bars.

Inferences

There is now strong evidence that when we read a sentence we draw *inferences* from it and store the inferences along with the sentence (e.g., Bransford, Barclay, and Franks, 1972). In one study, subjects studied sentences like

1. Three turtles sat on a log and a fish swam beneath it.

Now, if the fish swam beneath the log it must have swum beneath the turtles. If subjects made this inference, it would become part of their memory for that sentence. Later subjects thought that they had seen sentence 2:

2. Three turtles sat on a log and a fish swam beneath them.

Sentence 2 is such a natural inference from sentence 1 that subjects had difficulty telling which of the two they actually saw.

The inference involved in the above study was necessarily true. If turtles are on a log and something goes beneath the log, then the basic spatial facts of the world dictate that that something went beneath the turtles as well. But other studies show that people will draw inferences and make them part of their

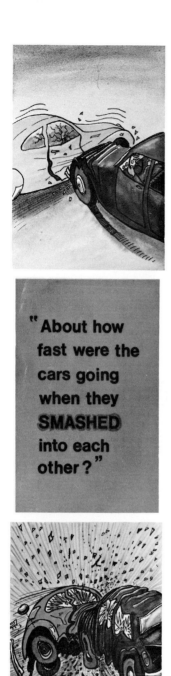

Fig. 8-15 Reconstructing a memory of an accident
The picture at the top represents the subject's original memory for the accident. Then comes the "smashed" question, which leads the subject to draw inferences about the destructiveness of the accident. These inferences are used to reconstruct the original memory so that it now looks more like the picture on the bottom. (Adapted from Loftus and Loftus, 1975)

memory even when the inference is not necessarily true. Consider the following sentence:

3. The floor was dirty because Molly used the mop.

When hearing this, many subjects infer that the mop was dirty. This is hardly a necessary inference. Later, subjects who have drawn this inference have trouble remembering whether they actually saw sentence 3 or the following one:

4. The floor was dirty because Molly used the dirty mop.

Again, there is an inability to distinguish between what was actually presented and what was added to the sentence.

Inferences can also affect memory for visual scenes, as illustrated by the following experiment. Subjects were shown a film of a traffic accident and soon after asked questions about their memory of the accident. One question about the speed of the vehicles was asked in two different ways. Some subjects were asked, "How fast were the cars going when they smashed into each other?" while others were asked, "How fast were the cars going when they hit each other?" Subjects asked the "smashed" question might infer that the accident was a very destructive one, perhaps more destructive than they actually remembered. Consequently, these subjects might use this inference to alter their memory of the accident to make it more destructive (see Figure 8-15). Subjects asked the "hit" question, however, should be less likely to do this, since "hit" implies a less severe accident than "smashed" does.

This line of reasoning was supported by the results of a memory test given to the subjects a week later. In this test, subjects were asked, "Did you see any broken glass?" There was no broken glass in the accident, but subjects who had been asked the "smashed" question were more likely to mistakenly say there had been glass than subjects who had been asked the "hit" question. Thus the "smashed" question had led to a reconstruction of the memory for the accident, and the reconstructed memory contained details, like broken glass, that were never actually part of the accident. Such results have important implications for eye-witness identification in our legal system. A question phrased in a particular way ("smashed" rather than "hit") can alter the very memory an attorney is trying to probe.

Stereotypes

Another means by which we fill in, or construct, memories is through the use of social *stereotypes*. A stereotype is a packet of knowledge about the personality traits or physical attributes that we assume to be true of a whole class of people. We may, for example, have a stereotype of the typical German (intelligent, meticulous, serious), or of the typical Italian (artistic, carefree, fun-loving). These descriptions rarely apply to many people in the class and can often be very misleading guides for social interaction. Our concern here, however, is not with the effects of stereotypes on social interaction (see Chapter 18 for a discussion of this), but rather with the effect of stereotypes on memory.

When presented information about a new person, we sometimes stereotype that person (for example, "He's your typical Italian"), and then combine the information presented with that in our stereotype. Our memory of the person is thus partly constructed from the stereotype. To the extent our stereotype does not fit the person, our recall can be terribly distorted. Hunter, a British psychologist, provides a first-hand account of such a distortion.

In the week beginning 23 October, I encountered in the University a male student of very conspicuously Scandinavian appearance. I recall being very forcibly impressed by the man's nordic, Viking-like appearance—his fair hair, his blue eyes, and long bones. On several occasions, I recalled his appearance in connection with a Scandinavian correspondence I was then conducting and thought of him as the "perfect Viking," visualizing him at the helm of a long-ship crossing the North Sea in quest of adventure. When I again saw the man on 23 November, I did not recognize him and he had to introduce himself. It was not that I had forgotten what he looked like but that his appearance, as I recalled it, had become grossly distorted. He was very different from my recollection of him. His hair was darker, his eyes less blue, his build less muscular, and he was wearing spectacles (as he always does). (Adapted from Hunter, 1974)

Clearly, Hunter's memory of the student was severely distorted. His stereotype of Scandinavians seems to have so overwhelmed any information he actually encoded about the student's appearance that the result was a highly constructed memory. It bore so little resemblance to the student it could not even serve as a basis for recognition.

Stereotypes can also work retroactively on memory. We may first hear a relatively neutral description about a person, later find out this person belongs to a particular category, and then use our stereotype of that category to reconstruct our memory of the original description. In a study demonstrating this, subjects first read a narrative about events in the life of a woman named Betty K. The narrative followed Betty K's life from birth to early adulthood and contained facts about her social life, like "Although she never had a steady boyfriend in high school, she did go out on dates." After reading the story, subjects were given additional facts about Betty K that would lead to stereotyping her. One group of subjects was told that Betty later adopted a lesbian life style. A second group was told that she later married. Apparently the first group fit the narrative information about Betty with their stereotype of lesbians, while the second group fit it with their stereotype of married women. Such stereotyping affected subsequent memories about the original narrative. Subjects told about Betty's later lesbian activities were more likely to remember that "she never had a steady boyfriend" than that "she did go out on dates." Subjects told about Betty's later marriage did the reverse. Both groups had reconstructed their memory of the original narrative to make it fit their stereotypes (Snyder and Uranowitz, 1978).

Thus, memory for people seems to be particularly susceptible to construction. Our memory is a compromise between "what is" and "what we think should be."

Schemata

Closely related to the notion of a stereotype is that of a *schema*, a packet of general knowledge about some situation that tends to occur frequently. Most American adults have a schema for how to drive a car—for example, "Sit behind the wheel, insert the ignition key, turn the key while pressing the gas pedal," and so on—or a schema for how to eat in a restaurant—for example, "Enter the restaurant, find a table, get a menu from the waiter," and so on. Everyone but small children would have schemata for how to find his or her way home from various locations. Like stereotypes, schemata won't fit every situation—in some cars, you don't press the gas pedal while turning the ignition key; and in some restaurants you don't get the menu from a waiter. And, like stereotypes, people try to fit their experience to a schema and end up with a memory of the experience that is partly constructed from it (Schank and Abelson, 1977). Bartlett (1932) was perhaps the first psychologist to systematically study the effect of schemata on memory. He emphasized that memory distortions can

"Whatever he is, he certainly looks the part."

Drawing by Mulligan; © 1977 The New Yorker Magazine, Inc.

occur when we attempt to fit stories into schemata, distortions much like those that occur when we fit people into stereotypes.

On the other hand, schemata can sometimes help memory. For example, some stories we read may be difficult to comprehend and remember unless we can fit them into their appropriate schemata. To illustrate this, read the following paragraph, and then try to recall it.

> The procedure is actually quite simple. First you arrange things into different groups. Of course, one pile may be sufficient, depending on how much there is to do. If you have to go somewhere else due to lack of facilities, that is the next step; otherwise you are pretty well set. It is important not to overdo things. That is, it is better to do too few things at once than too many. In the short run this may not seem important but complications can easily arise. A mistake can be expensive as well. At first the whole procedure will seem complicated. Soon, however, it will become just another facet of life. It is difficult to foresee any end to the necessity for this task in the immediate future, but then one never can tell. After the procedure is completed one arranges the materials into different groups again. Then they can be put into their appropriate places. Eventually they will be used once more and the whole cycle will then have to be repeated. However, that is part of life. (Adapted from Bransford and Johnson, 1973)

In reading the paragraph you no doubt experienced some difficulty in trying to understand exactly what it was all about. Consequently, your recall of it was probably relatively poor. But given the hint that the paragraph describes "washing clothes," you can now use your schema for washing clothes to interpret all the cryptic parts of the passage. Your memory for the paragraph, if you reread it, should now be quite good. Schemata, then, can help or hurt.

Situations where memory is heavily constructive seem a far cry from the many simpler situations we covered earlier. Take, for example, the memory for a list of unrelated words; here memory processes appear more to *preserve* the input than to *construct* something new. Perhaps, though, there is even a constructive aspect to this simple situation, for techniques like using imagery add something to the input. Similarly, even when we read a paragraph like the one about washing clothes, we must still preserve some of its specifics if we are to recall it correctly in detail. Thus, the two aspects of memory—to preserve and to construct—may always be present, though their relative emphasis may depend on the exact situation.

SUMMARY

1 Memory involves three stages: *encoding, storage,* and *retrieval.* Encoding refers to the transformation of physical information into the kind of code that memory can accept. Storage is the retention of the encoded information. And retrieval refers to the process by which information is recovered from memory when it is needed. The three stages may operate differently in situations that require us to store material for a matter of seconds—*short-term memory*—than in situations that require us to store material for longer intervals—*long-term memory.*

2 Information in short-term memory tends to be encoded *acoustically,* although other codes, such as a *visual code,* can also be used.

3 The most striking fact about short-term memory is that its storage capacity is limited to 7 ± 2 items, or *chunks.* When this limit is reached, a new item can enter short-term memory only by displacing an old one. Items that have not been displaced can be retrieved by a search process that examines each item in turn.

4 Information in long-term memory is usually encoded in terms of its *meaning*, by either an abstract *semantic* code or a concrete *imagery* code. The more deeply or elaborately one encodes the meaning, the better memory will be.

5 Most cases of forgetting in long-term memory are due to *retrieval failures* (the information is there, but can't be found). Retrieval failures are less likely when the items in storage are *organized* and when the *context* at retrieval is similar to that at learning. In contrast, retrieval failures are more likely to occur when there is *interference* from similar items and when *emotional factors* somehow disrupt the usual retrieval processes.

6 Long-term memory can be improved at either the encoding or retrieval stage. The key to improving encoding is to use imagery, which is the basic principle underlying mnemonic systems, like the *method of loci* and the *key-word method*. Another way to improve encoding is to analyze the meaning of the items as deeply as possible. The best ways to improve retrieval are to organize the material (hierarchical organization may be the best), attempt to restore the learning context at the time of retrieval, and practice retrieving information while learning it.

7 The *dual-memory theory* assumes that information is transferred from short-term to long-term memory, often by the process of *rehearsal*. The theory offers an explanation of several memory disorders. *Retrograde amnesia*, a loss of memory for events immediately preceding a head injury, is thought to be due to a disruption of short-term memory; *anterograde amnesia*, an inability to learn new information after removal of the hippocampus, is assumed to be caused by a breakdown of the transfer process.

8 The dual-memory theory also accounts for the results of experiments on *free recall*: items at the end of a list are remembered well because they are still in short-term memory, while items at the beginning of a list are remembered well because they are rehearsed more often. However, recent findings concerning rehearsal and depth of encoding suggest the theory is incomplete. A new approach, called *depth-of-processing*, is developing. It assumes items are analyzed to various levels and that deeper levels of analysis lead to better memories.

9 Memory for complex materials, like sentences and stories, involves a *constructive* process. For example, we often take sentences as incomplete descriptions of events and use our general knowledge of the world to construct a more complete description. Construction may involve adding *inferences* to the material presented or fitting the material into *stereotypes* and *schemata*.

FURTHER READING

There are several introductory books on memory that are readable and up to date: Klatzky, *Human memory: Structures and processes* (1975), Loftus and Loftus, *Human memory: The processing of information* (1975), and Norman, *Memory and attention: An introduction to human information processing* (2nd ed., 1976).

Two books that provide a more advanced treatment of many topics in memory are Baddeley, *The psychology of memory* (1976) and Crowder, *Principles of learning and memory* (1976).

For a sophisticated treatment of recent theoretical issues in memory, see Anderson, *Language, memory, and thought* (1976), Anderson and Bower, *Human associative memory* (1973), Kintsch, *The representation of meaning in memory* (1974), and Bower (ed.), *Human memory: Basic processes* (1977).

For a review of research on the biological bases of memory and learning, see Deutsch, *The physiological basis of memory* (1973).

9
Language and Thought

Perhaps the greatest accomplishment of our species is our ability to have complex thoughts and communicate them through language. Thinking includes a wide range of mental activities. We think as we daydream while waiting for class to begin. We think as we decide what groceries we need, or plan a vacation, or write a letter, or worry about a sick friend. Often, we can put our thoughts into words and communicate them to someone else.

All thinking involves our ability to imagine or represent objects and events that are not physically present. Thus, whenever we refer to an object that is not present—as in, "Let's get a sandwich"—or to an activity that is not now going on—as in, "They played tennis"—we must represent these objects and activities to ourselves. And whenever we communicate, we must transmit these representations to others.

To understand how we represent objects and actions to ourselves, we will first explore concepts, for these are the building blocks of thought. The second section of the chapter concerns how we combine concepts into complex thoughts and express them in language. The third section deals with how children acquire language and whether other species can also learn it. The fourth considers thoughts that seem to lie outside of language, namely, visual images, and the role they play in solving problems. Finally, the fifth section deals with how we organize our thoughts when we try to solve complex problems.

Concepts

Nature of Concepts

What does it mean to have a concept, like the concept of *apple*? Roughly, it means that we know the properties common to all or most apples—that they are edible, have seeds, grow on trees, are round, have distinctive colors, and so on. Knowledge of these common properties has an enormous impact on how we deal with the objects around us. Having perceived some visible properties of the object, something round and red, on a tree, we assign it to the concept of *apple.* This allows us to infer properties that are not visible—for instance, that it is edible. Concepts, then, enable us to go beyond the information we perceive. And this ability is fundamental to thought.

Often we do not have to perceive the properties of an object or a person to know a lot about it. If you are introduced to a doctor, you immediately know he or she has a medical degree, extensive knowledge about disease, and experience with patients. You do not have to see any of these properties directly; you can infer them indirectly from the concept of *doctor.* Concepts, then, allow us to apply what we already know—the common properties of a doctor or an apple—to people and objects we encounter for the first time.

We also have concepts of activities, like *eating;* of states, like *being old;* and of abstract things, like *truth, justice,* or even the number *two.* In each case, we know something about the properties common to all members of the concept. Widely used concepts like these generally are associated with a one-word name, "apple," "doctor," "eating," "old," "truth," and so forth. This allows us to communicate quickly about things that occur frequently. Concepts with single-word names are sometimes called *semantic* concepts (they are used to form the semantic codes for long-term memory discussed in Chapter 8). Such concepts are the major concern of this section.

Typicality

We have talked about the common properties of a concept, as if all apples were equally "apple-y" in our minds. But people have strong intuitions that some instances are better, or more *typical* of a concept, than others. We rate red apples as more typical than green ones and robins as more typical birds than chickens. Not only do people judge one member of a concept to be more typical than the other, they also classify the more typical one faster. The question "Is a robin a bird?" produces an immediate "yes"; "Is a chicken a bird?" takes longer (Rosch and Mervis, 1975).

Why is this so? Consider birds again. We treat the ability to fly as a property of the concept *bird,* even though some—such as chickens or penguins—do not fly. A property that is true of most but not of all birds is said to be only *characteristic* of the concept *bird.* Typical members have more characteristic properties of their concept than do less typical ones. A robin is a more typical bird than a chicken, in part because a robin can fly (Smith, Shoben, and Rips, 1974).

Concepts about people also contain properties that are not true of all instances. Consider the concept *computer scientist.* Some properties—like, knows how to program a computer—are doubtlessly true of all members of the concept; others are at best only characteristic of some members—like, has a need for order and clarity. Yet, if you were given a brief description of a person and told only that he or she has a need for order, you would be far more likely to think the person is in computer science than, say, education or social work (Kahneman and Tversky, 1973). When we make such decisions on the basis of characteristic properties, we are essentially dealing in stereotypes.

Typicality has important implications for mental life. When we think of a concept, we are likely to think of a typical instance of it. Consider an example. Away from home you feel ill and think about seeing a doctor. You cannot be thinking about a specific doctor (you don't know one there), but rather must be dealing with the concept *doctor.* Your concept fits some doctors (probably those who are middle-aged and male) better than others. Why? Because most doctors you've seen, either directly or through the media, have been middle-

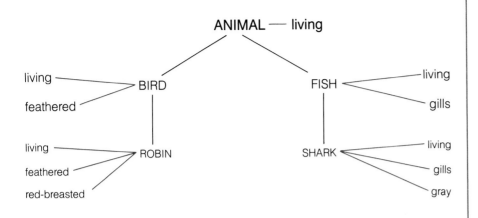

aged males. These characteristic properties have become part of your concept. You are essentially thinking in terms of stereotypes. If Doctor Jones turns out to be young and female, you'd be surprised. Our thoughts and expectations, then, are biased in important ways. Since they are based on experience, however, presumably they can be changed by experience. With more and more women becoming doctors, our concept of doctors should change.

Hierarchies of Concepts

In addition to knowing the properties of concepts, we also know how they are related to one another. For example, apples are members—or a subset—of a larger category, fruit; robins are a subset of birds, which in turn are a subset of animals.

These two types of knowledge—properties of a concept and relations between concepts—are represented in Figure 9-1 as a hierarchy. The more general concepts are at the top; the more specific ones, at the bottom.

An experiment by Collins and Quillian (1969) suggests how we might use this hierarchy. Subjects are presented with sentences like "A robin is a bird," or "A robin is an animal." They must decide whether each sentence is true, as in the above examples, or false, as in "A daisy is a tree." With sentences this simple, errors are rare. Collins and Quillian were mainly interested in how quickly subjects made decisions. If the subjects referred to a hierarchy, they would search for a path that links the concepts. When presented with "A robin is a bird," for example, a subject would enter the hierarchy at *robin* and look for a path to the concept *bird*. A glance at Figure 9-1 shows that the path between robin and bird is only one link long. In the sentence "A robin is an animal," there are two links between the concepts, so it should take more time to find the connecting path. The results confirmed this idea. Decision time increased with the distance between the concepts in the hierarchy.

Acquiring Concepts

CHILDREN'S CONCEPTS Knowledge about concepts is one of the most important things children learn. We get an idea of how children acquire concepts by looking at their first use of words.

At the age of about one year, children begin to name things. One-year-olds already know a good deal about the world—they probably have concepts for parents and household pets before they know the names for them. What they are doing when they begin to speak is relating this knowledge to words that adults use. This does not happen all at once. A three-year-old girl may already

CONCEPTS

253

Linguistic

Throughout our discussion of concepts, we assume that words reflect already existing concepts and perceptions. We assume that language is designed to express thought and that therefore the structure of language must reflect the structure of thought. However, it is possible that the relationship between language and thought is the other way round. Rather than thought limiting language, it may be that language limits thought. This is essentially the *linguistic relativity hypothesis* proposed by Whorf (1956). Whorf argued that the kinds of concepts and perceptions we can have are affected by the particular language or languages we speak. Therefore, people who speak very different languages perceive the world in very different ways. This is called the linguistic relativity hypothesis because it proposes that thought is relative to the language used to convey it. It is a provocative idea and has caused much debate among psychologists, linguists, and anthropologists.

Much of the evidence cited in favor of the hypothesis is based on vocabulary differences. For example, English has only one word for snow, while Eskimo has four. Consequently, speakers of Eskimo may perceive differences in snow that speakers of English cannot. Similarly, English has only one word for rice, while Garo, a language spoken in Burma, has different words for rice husked and unhusked, cooked and uncooked, and for various other kinds and conditions of rice. Again, the Garo may perceive differences that are lost on speakers of other languages.

Do these observations constitute strong evidence for the linguistic relativity hypothesis? Recent critics of the hypothesis argue otherwise (e.g., Slobin, 1971; Clark and Clark, 1977). According to the critics, language may embody distinctions that are important to a culture, but it does not create those distinctions, nor does it limit its speakers to them. English speakers may have the same capacity for perceiving variations in snow as Eskimo speakers, but since such variations are more important in Eskimo cultures than in Anglo cultures, one language assigns different words to the variations while the other does not. The best evidence for this view is the development of jargons and technical terminology. For example, American skiers talk of "powder" and "corn," not just "snow." This growth in vocabulary may be accompanied by changes in perception—Eskimos and

have concepts of different colors and know that certain words are color names, but not which name goes with which color. When asked to name a blue color, she may say "red" (Miller and Johnson-Laird, 1976).

To learn which word goes with which concept, children look at what is happening around them when a word is used and take the important aspects of the situation as the meaning of the word. They are essentially creating hypotheses—for example, "Mommy said 'Fang' when she pointed to my pet, so 'Fang' means my pet." Children's hypotheses, however, may not be accurate. Sometimes they focus on something totally irrelevant.

A mother said sternly to her child: "Young man, you did that on purpose." When later asked what "on purpose" meant, the child replied: "It means you're looking at me." (E. E. Maccoby)

Children often pick out only one or two properties of a concept when a whole cluster of properties is relevant. A two-year-old boy might hear "doggie"

Relativity Hypothesis

skiers are more likely to notice variations in snow than Hawaiians—but the critical point is that such changes do not depend on the language spoken. If anything, the language seems to depend on the changes.

The linguistic relativity hypothesis has fared no better when it comes to explaining cultural variations in color terms. At one time, many linguists believed that languages differed widely in how they divided up the color spectrum and that this led to differences in the perception of colors. Recent research indicates just the opposite. Of particular importance is the work of two anthropologists, Berlin and Kay (1969). They studied the *basic color terms* of many languages. Basic color terms are simple, nonmetaphoric words that are used to describe the colors of many different objects. Berlin and Kay found striking commonalities in such terms across languages. For one, every language takes its basic color terms from a restricted set of 10 names. In English these are "black," "white," "red," "yellow," "green," "blue," "brown," "purple," "pink," and "gray." No matter what color terms a language has, they inevitably correspond to some subset of the above plus "orange." Furthermore, if a language uses fewer

than 11 terms, the basic terms chosen are not arbitrary. If a language has only two terms (none has fewer), they correspond to "black" and "white"; if it has three, they correspond to "black," "white," and "red"; if it has six, they correspond to these three plus "yellow," "green," and "blue." Thus, the ordering of basic color terms seems to be universal, rather than varying from language to language, as the linguistic relativity hypothesis might suggest.

In addition, people whose languages use corresponding basic color terms agree on what particular color best represents a color term. Suppose two different languages have terms corresponding to "red." When speakers of these languages are asked to pick the best example of red from an array of colors, they make the same choice. Even though their boundaries for what they would call red may differ, their idea of a good red, a quintessential red, is the same. Their perceptions are identical though their vocabularies are different. Further work by Rosch (1974) suggests that the Dani, whose language has only 2 basic color terms, perceive color variations in exactly the same way as people whose language has all 11. The perception of color

gives little support to the linguistic relativity hypothesis.

We should not dismiss the hypothesis too quickly, however. Few language domains have been investigated in the same detail as color terms, and perhaps support for the hypothesis will yet be found in other domains. Also, even though little support has been found for its major claims, the linguistic relativity hypothesis calls our attention to an important point. When one has to learn to make fine discriminations in a particular field, it is helpful to have a vocabulary that expresses these discriminations. As each of us gains expertise in a field, be it skiing, psychology, or whatever, we enlarge our vocabulary for distinctions in that field. Jargons help us to think about and communicate these distinctions. Can you imagine the practice of medicine without a specialized vocabulary for anatomical parts? Although a distinction must exist in someone's mind before a term can be made up to embody it, the importance of that embodiment should not be underestimated. Without the term, the distinction could not be easily talked about. Though often annoying and sometimes pretentious, the jargon of a field plays an important cognitive role.

spoken in the presence of the family dog, focus on the fact that it has four legs and moves, and hypothesize these two features define "doggie." He then applies the term to cats and cows, which also have four legs and move. He *overextends* the meaning of "doggie" to other animals. Overextensions decrease as the child adds more properties to the word's meaning—for example, sound (barks), size (relatively small), and texture (furry). This restricts his use of "doggie." At the same time, he is learning more about cats (they meow) and cows (they moo and have horns). Thus, the meanings of these three animal terms become further and further differentiated from one another (Clark, 1973).

By three or four years of age the child's overextensions are less obvious, but closely related concepts can still lead to confusion. When told to place one toy below another on a staircase, the child may place it above the other instead. It is as if the child knows "above" and "below" have some properties in common—both refer to the same kind of spatial relationship—but he or she does not know how they differ and so maps both onto the concept of *above*. Why "above" rather than "below"? Perhaps the concept *above* is the simpler one.

CONCEPTS

Fig. 9-2 Hypothesis testing of concepts

Sample geometric forms used to study how adults learn new concepts.

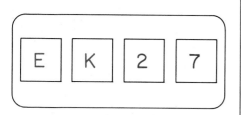

Fig. 9-3 Biases in hypothesis testing
Subjects were given the four cards shown above. Each had a letter on one side and a digit on the other. The subjects had to decide which cards to turn over to determine whether the following hypothesis was correct: "If a card has a vowel on one side, it has an even number on the other side." ("E" and "7" are the correct cards to turn over.) Most subjects wisely turned over the card with the vowel "E." If it had an even number on the other side, the hypothesis was supported; if it had an odd number on the other side the hypothesis was refuted. But most subjects also turned over the card with the even number "2." This card provided no information; for even if it had a consonant on the other side, the hypothesis would not be refuted (look at the hypothesis). Nevertheless, finding a vowel on the other side seems to support the hypothesis. Most subjects failed to turn over the card with the odd number "7." A vowel on the other side would have refuted the rule (look again at the hypothesis). However, it offered no potential for supporting the hypothesis and so was left unturned. (Wason and Johnson-Laird, 1972)

Or perhaps the child is using a strategy that says, "When you have to place an object, but you're unsure of where, try the topmost part of surface" (Clark, 1977).

HYPOTHESIS TESTING BY ADULTS Adults, too, use hypothesis testing. In experiments on how adults learn new concepts, the subjects may be shown a series of geometric forms that vary in shape, color, and size (see Figure 9-2). The experimenter has decided that all large, red forms are members of a newly invented concept, TEP. The subject's task is to discover the properties of TEP. Forms are presented one at a time. Subjects first guess whether each is a TEP, and the experimenter tells them whether they are correct. This allows subjects to generate hypotheses about which dimensions are relevant—for example, the color red. When they come across a figure that fits their hypothesis but not the experimenter's definition, say, a small, red figure, they abandon their current hypothesis and generate a new one (large, red figures). The more defining properties there are, the longer it takes to learn concepts. A concept that is defined by large, red, and square is harder to spot than one defined by only large and red. Similarly, the more dimensions there are that are potentially relevant, the longer it takes to come up with the right hypothesis. If there are four potentially relevant dimensions, size, color, shape, and orientation (figure upright or tilted), it should take longer to learn the concept than if there are just three such dimensions (Bourne, 1966).

Consider a naturalistic example of hypothesis testing. A club in town selects members on the basis of criteria it refuses to make public. Essentially, the club is a concept you want to acquire; the criteria are its properties. You know that a white male ski instructor who is a devotee of astrology is a member; an Asian female lawyer who scoffs at astrology was refused. You thus have at least four potentially relevent dimensions—race, sex, profession, and belief in astrology. Which of these are used in selecting club members? You may start with the hypothesis that it's an all-male club. If you find it has female members, you give up your initial hypothesis and generate another. Eventually you zero in on the correct criteria (properties) of the club (concept). You will almost certainly take longer the more criteria the club uses to define membership and the more dimensions that are potentially relevant.

BIASES IN HYPOTHESIS TESTING It may sound as if acquiring concepts is an inherently rational process, something like a chemist's deciding whether a sample is a member of a well-known chemical category. However, all sorts of biases creep in. Perhaps the most prevalent is our tendency to emphasize cases that support our hypothesis and to downplay those that refute it. To illustrate, suppose that on meeting a young woman, you hit on the hypothesis that she is an introvert. You may well ask her questions that tend to confirm your hypothesis, like "Do you enjoy taking walks alone?" or "Do you spend a lot of time at the library?" Positive answers will make you very confident that she is an introvert. But you probably will not ask her questions that might disprove your hypothesis, like "Do you enjoy going to parties?" A positive answer here would not fit with her being an introvert. In short, you selectively seek out evidence in support of your hypothesis and fail to ask the critical questions that might disprove it (Snyder and Swann, 1979). See Figure 9-3 for another demonstration of biases in hypothesis testing.

Though we may use it imperfectly, hypothesis testing seems to be the primary way we acquire new concepts. Consciously or unconsciously, we hypothesize that some properties are critical (or at least characteristic) of a concept, get feedback about how good the hypothesis is, and work our way to the concept. To the extent the process works, we are able to go beyond the information given and to communicate a great deal with just a single word.

Communicating Thoughts

The semantic concepts we have considered can produce simple thoughts, like that corresponding to *Lorri is a doctor.* Most of our thoughts, however, are far more complex than this and involve several concepts. To illustrate, the thought *Lorri is a young doctor* combines the concepts of *young* and *doctor,* while *Doctors smile at babies* combines the concepts of *doctors, smile,* and *babies.* How are such thoughts communicated? To answer this, we must look at language, our primary means of communicating. A close look at language will also shed some light on the nature of thought itself.

From Thoughts to Sentences

PROPOSITIONS The thoughts expressed in sentences often take the form of *propositions.* Consider the sentence, "The doctor smiled at the baby." It asserts something, *smiled at the baby,* about a particular person, *the doctor.* Many simple sentences are like this. Thus, "Susan likes vegetables" asserts *likes vegetables* about *Susan.* In these examples, the assertion (for example, *likes vegetables*) is called the *predicate;* the person is called the *subject.* A *proposition,* then, consists of a subject plus a predicate. Each of these sentences expresses exactly one proposition. Not all sentences are this simple, though. Consider "Susan likes vegetables and Eve, fruit." Here we again have *Susan* as a subject and *likes vegetables* as a predicate. But there is a second proposition with *Eve* as subject and *likes fruit* as predicate. Hence, this sentence expresses two propositions. All sentences, no matter how complex, can be broken down into propositions.

We have made a distinction between a sentence and the proposition it expresses because the same proposition can be expressed by different sentences. To illustrate, *The doctor smiled at the baby* can be expressed by "The doctor smiled at the baby," "The baby was smiled at by the doctor," "It was the doctor who smiled at the baby," and "It was the baby whom the doctor smiled at." Intuitively, we feel all these sentences express the same thought; analyzing the sentences into propositions makes this clear.

Do propositions really correspond to thoughts? A good deal of evidence suggests they do. People take longer to read a sentence expressing two propositions than one expressing a single proposition, even when they contain the identical number of words (Kintsch, 1974). Thus, in reading or learning sentences, people extract the thoughts or propositions from them. The more thoughts or propositions there are, the longer it takes (Anderson and Bower, 1973).

By viewing propositions as thoughts, we learn something about thought itself. Simple thoughts, which correspond to single propositions, often assert an attribute, state, or activity about some person or object. The proposition *Steve is thoughtful* asserts that Steve has the property of being thoughtful; and *Adele is playing a game* asserts that Adele is involved in the activity of game playing. By studying how propositions can be combined in sentences, we get some idea of how simple thoughts can be combined into complex ones. The easiest way to combine propositions or thoughts is by simply joining them, for example, "Mitchell works and Barbara plays." A more complex way of combining propositions is to attach an entire proposition to part of another. In the sentence "Dave lifted the heavy television," we have two propositions: *Dave lifted the television* and *The television is heavy.* The second proposition is attached to part of the predicate (*lifted the television*) of the first. Perhaps the most complex way to combine propositions or thoughts is to insert one into the other. For example, "Herb's winning the fight was a surprise" contains two propositions. The first is *Herb won the fight.* This proposition—*Herb's winning*—then serves as the subject of the second proposition, where *was a surprise* serves as the predicate. Thus the first proposition has been *embedded* into the second, and this enables us to form very complex thoughts (Clark and Clark, 1977).

EXTRACTING PROPOSITIONS FROM SENTENCES How do we extract propositions from sentences? While there is no complete answer to this, part of the story seems to go as follows.

We break a sentence into phrases, where each phrase corresponds to either the subject or the predicate of a proposition, or to an entire proposition. This is obvious for simple sentences. We break the sentence "Lorri is a doctor" into two phrases, "Lorri" (the subject) and "is a doctor" (the predicate). Things get more interesting for more complex sentences. Consider "Serious scholars read books." Intuition says the sentence divides into two phrases: "serious scholars" and "read books" (see Figure 9-4). Since the first centers on a noun ("scholars"), it is called a *noun phrase;* the second is called a *verb phrase.* If we focus on the noun phrase, "serious scholars," we see it expresses the entire proposition *scholars are serious.* The verb phrase, "read books," expresses only part of another proposition, *scholars read books.* Thus in this example the noun phrase expresses an entire proposition while the verb phrase expresses only part—the predicate—of a proposition.

Breaking a sentence into noun and verb phrases may help greatly in getting at the propositions or thoughts behind it. There is evidence that people do this soon after hearing a sentence. In one study, subjects listened to sentences like "The poor girl stole a warm coat," where "the poor girl" is the noun phrase and "stole a warm coat" is the verb phrase. Immediately after each sentence, they were given a probe word from the sentence and asked to say the word that came after it. People responded faster when the probe and response words came from the same phrase ("poor girl") than when they came from different phrases ("girl stole"). Apparently once a sentence is broken into phrases, each phrase is held in memory as a unit; and when the probe and response are from the same phrase, only one unit has to be retrieved (Wilkes and Kennedy, 1969).

While using phrases to extract propositions works well with many sentences, this strategy runs into problems when the phrases of a sentence can be

Fig. 9-4 Phrases and propositions
An illustration of how propositions are extracted from complex sentences

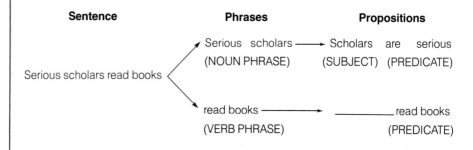

Sentence	Phrases	Propositions
Serious scholars read books	Serious scholars (NOUN PHRASE)	Scholars are serious (SUBJECT) (PREDICATE)
	read books (VERB PHRASE)	_____ read books (PREDICATE)

CHAPTER 9/LANGUAGE AND THOUGHT

The Structure of Phrases

We can go further in analyzing sentences than just saying they can be divided into noun and verb phrases. Noun and verb phrases can themselves be further broken down into smaller units.

Consider again the sentence, "The poor girl stole a warm coat." We already know it divides into the noun phrase, "the poor girl," and the verb phrase, "stole a warm coat." Now let us see how we can divide up each of these phrases (see Figure 9-5). Intuition suggests the verb phrase may be broken into two units: the verb, "stole," and the rest of the phrase, "a warm coat." But the second unit is really another noun phrase. So a verb phrase may be broken into a verb plus a noun phrase. In this case, the verb cannot be decomposed any further, for it is a single word, but the noun phrase can be. It consists of a *determiner* ("a" or "the" are determiners), followed by an adjective ("warm"), followed by a noun ("coat"). Noun phrases that have this particular set of units, determiner + adjective + noun, are common in English. The initial noun phrase of the sentence, "The poor girl," also is made up of a determiner ("the"), followed by an adjective ("poor"), followed by a noun ("girl").

This is an example of a *syntactic* analysis of a sentence. Such analysis is a common tool of linguists and of psychologists who study language. It has revealed some basic facts about the structure of our language. Almost every English sentence must contain a noun phrase and a verb phrase, and only certain kinds of noun and verb phrases are possible. For example, while a noun phrase can consist of an adjective followed by a noun ("poor girl"), it cannot consist of an adverb followed by a noun ("poorly girl") or of a noun followed by an adjective ("girl poor"). Other languages have different rules for noun phrases. In French, for example, some adjectives follow the noun. In any language, then, there are constraints on what a noun or verb phrase can contain, and these constraints are part of what we know when we know a language and, therefore, part of what we must learn when we learn the language.

Does a detailed syntactic analysis offer any new insights into how we extract propositions from sentences? It seems that it does. Having divided a noun phrase into the adjective "poor" and the noun "girl," we can see that *girl* is the subject of a proposition that has *is poor* as its predicate. More generally, whenever we have an adjective modifying a noun, we have a proposition with the noun as subject and the adjective as predicate. Every time we add an adjective to a sentence, we add another proposition; consequently, we increase the time needed to read and understand the sentence (Kintsch, 1974).

Fig. 9-5 Example of a syntactic analysis

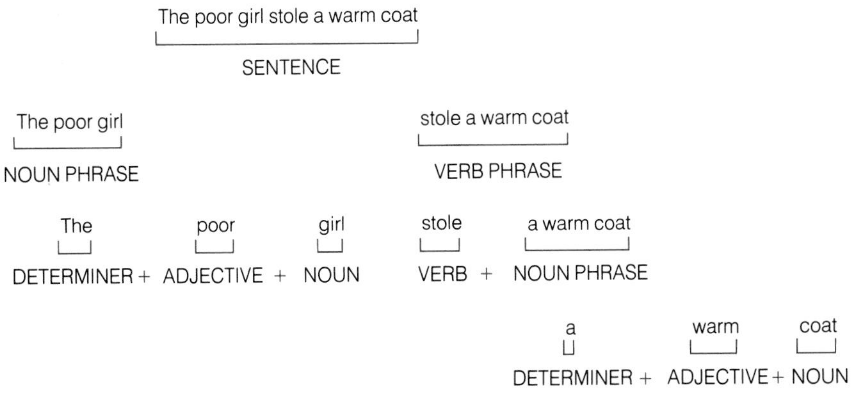

interpreted in two very different ways. Take the sentence "They are cooking apples." One interpretation is that some people are cooking apples, while the other is that these are apples that normally get cooked. Not surprisingly, the need to choose one or the other interpretation makes such sentences difficult to read and understand (MacKay, 1966).

From Sentences to Speech

We have seen how a listener can get from the sentence to the thought or proposition it expresses (or how the speaker gets from the thought to the sentence). But we do not hear sentences already broken down into words.

Rather, we hear an almost continuous stream of sound, out of which we must extract individual words and sentences. For a fuller understanding of communication, we must consider how we produce and interpret speech sounds.

PHONEMES In speaking, we use the lips, tongue, mouth, and vocal cords to produce a great variety of physical sounds. Not all of these sounds are perceived as different, however. What we perceive are the 40 or so *phonemes*, or categories of speech sounds, that are used in English. For example, the sound corresponding to the first letter in "boy" is a phoneme symbolized as /b/. We have a great ability to discriminate different sounds that correspond to different phonemes. However, we are very poor at discriminating different sounds that correspond to the same phoneme—for example the sound of the first letter in "pin" and the sound of the second letter in "spin" (Liberman, Cooper, Shankweiler, and Studdert-Kennedy, 1967). They are the same phoneme, /p/, and they sound the same to us even though they have different physical characteristics. The /p/ in "pin" is accompanied by a small puff of air, but the /p/ in "spin" is not (try holding your hand a short distance from your mouth as you say the two words).

Every language has a different set of phonemes, which is one reason we often have difficulty learning to pronounce foreign words. Another language may use speech sounds that never appear in ours. It may take us a while even to hear the new phonemes, let alone produce them. Or another language may not make a distinction between two sounds that our language treats as two phonemes. For example, in Japanese the English sounds corresponding to *r* and *l* (/r/ and /l/) are treated as the same phoneme.

When phonemes are combined in the right way, they form words. Each language has its own rules about which phonemes can follow others. In English, for example, /b/ cannot follow /p/ at the beginning of a word (try pronouncing "pbet"). Such rules show their influence when we speak and listen. For example, we have no difficulty pronouncing the plurals of nonsense words we have never heard before. Consider "zuk," and "zug." The plural of "zuk" is formed in accordance with a simple rule by adding /s/, as in "hiss." In English, however, /s/ can't follow "g" at the end of a word, so to form the plural of "zug" we must use another rule, one that adds /z/, as in "fuzz." We may not be aware of these differences in forming plurals, but we have no difficulty producing them. It is as if we "know" the rules for combining phonemes even though we are unaware of the rules—as if we are conforming to rules we cannot verbalize.

How do children learn about phonemes and their rules of combination? Children appear to come into the world preset to learn and discriminate phonemes. One-month-old infants, like adults, can easily discriminate between sounds corresponding to different phonemes but not between sounds corresponding to the same phoneme (Eimas, Siqueland, Jusczyk, and Vigorito, 1971). However, it takes several years for children to learn how phonemes can be combined to form words. When children first begin to talk, they produce "impossible" words, like "dlumber" for "lumber." They do not yet know that /l/ cannot follow /d/ at the beginning of a word. By age four, children seem to have learned a good deal about phoneme combinations. Children of about four years of age were asked to say which of two made-up sequences of speech sounds would make a better name for a toy. One sound was consistent with rules for combining phonemes (for example, "klek"), while the other was not (for example, "dlek"). Most chose the name that conformed to the rules (Messer, 1967).

Mastering the rules for combining phonemes amounts to learning how to pronounce words. Children may know how a word should be pronounced, even though they cannot say it themselves.

A child asked if he could come along on a trip to the "mewwy-go-wound." An older child, teasing him about his pronunciation, said "David wants to go on the mewwy-go-wound." "No," said David firmly, "you don't say it wight." (Maccoby and Bee, 1965)

MORPHEMES A *morpheme* is the smallest linguistic unit that carries meaning. Most morphemes are themselves words, like "time." Others are suffixes, like "ly," or prefixes, like "un," which are added on to words to form more complex ones, like "timely" or "untimely." Many complex words are really just simple words with a host of prefixes and suffixes tagged onto them. The ultimate is "antidisestablishmentarianism," which breaks down into "anti" + "dis" + "establish" + "ment" + "ary" + "an" + "ism" (a total of seven morphemes).

Every language has rules about how prefixes or suffixes are combined with words. For example, the suffix "er" is regularly added to many verbs to form nouns that refer to people who habitually perform the action described by the verb, as in "write"—"writer" and "paint"—"painter." Do we actually use these rules, or something like them, in speaking and listening? People's slips of the tongue suggest we do. For example, a speaker who intended to say, "McGovern favors busting pushers," uttered instead, "McGovern favors pushing busters" (Garrett, 1975). The morphemes "bust" and "push" were interchanged, while the morphemes "ing" and "er + s" stayed in their right places. This implies that the morphemes were treated as separate units.

Levels of Language

We can summarize language in terms of different levels (see Figure 9-6). At the highest level are propositions, which correspond to thoughts. The next level down is that of sentence units, including words, phrases, and entire sentences. The lowest level contains sounds. The adjacent levels are closely related to one another. The parts of a proposition (the first level) correspond to the units of a sentence (the second level), making it possible to extract thoughts from sentences. The words in a sentence (the second level) are built from phonemes (the third level). Language thus relates thoughts to speech via sentence units (Chomsky, 1965).

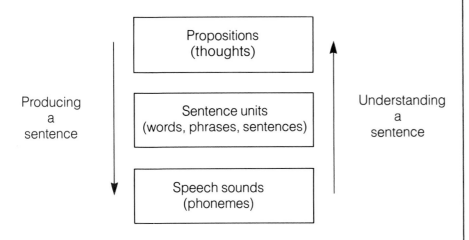

Fig. 9-6 Levels of language

Note that when we produce a sentence we start with a thought or proposition, translate it into the words of a sentence, and finally translate these words into speech sounds. We work from the top level down to the bottom one. To understand a sentence, however, we mainly go in the opposite direction—from the bottom level to the top one. That is, we hear speech sounds, use them to construct the units of a sentence, and finally use the sentence units to extract the proposition.

Development of Language

Our discussion of language should indicate the enormity of the task confronting children. They must master all levels of language—not only the proper pronunciations, but also the infinite number of ways words can be combined into sentences to express thoughts. The wonder is that virtually all children in all cultures accomplish so much of this in a mere four to five years.

We have already considered the acquisition of phonemes and their rules of combination. In this section, we will focus on perhaps the most striking aspect of language development—how children learn to combine words into phrases and sentences that express thoughts.

From Primitive to Complex Sentences

Let us go back to the beginning. During the first year of life, preverbal children acquire three types of knowledge they will use when they begin to speak. First, children learn specific *facts* about their world—their mother provides food, this toy makes a noise, and so forth—and these are the things they will talk about when they utter their first words. Second, preverbal children learn the *roles* different things play in their world. For example, people and animals can play the role of agents of actions, moving on their own as well as moving other objects. Other things (blocks, tables, and cribs) do not have this power, and play the role of objects. Still other things play the role of places, in that they are not moveable but can hold or receive objects. This knowledge of roles—agent, object, or place—will be reflected in children's sentences when they begin to speak. Third, preverbal children learn to *communicate* with gestures. Seven- or eight-month-olds know that when an adult points to an object, they are to look at the object and not at the adult's hand. About three months later, children themselves begin to point in order to pick things out for individuals they are trying to communicate with (Bruner, 1978). Knowledge of facts, roles, and communication sets the stage for acquiring sentences.

At about 12 to 18 months, children begin to utter single words that refer to specific things they have had contact with. They talk predominantly about people, food, toys, animals, body parts, and the like, using words like "Dada," "cookie," "block," "doggie," and "foot." Furthermore, when children use these words they seem to be aware of their roles. A child who says "Dada" when someone opens the door seems to know that someone is functioning as an agent (Greenfield and Smith, 1976).

At about one-and-a-half to two-and-a-half years, the next stage of language acquisition begins. Children start to combine single words into two-word utterances—such as "There cow" (*There's the cow*), "Jimmy bike" (*That's Jimmy's bike*), "Towel bed" (*The towel's on the bed*). Their utterances reflect an appreciation of the roles of agent, object, and location (Braine, 1976).

TABLE 9-1 Functions of two-word sentences in children's speech, in several languages

FUNCTION OF UTTERANCE	LANGUAGE			
	ENGLISH	GERMAN	RUSSIAN	SAMOAN
Locate, name	there book that car see doggie	buch da [book there] gukuk wauwau [see doggie]	Tosya tam [Tosya there]	Keith lea [Keith there]
Demand, desire	more milk give candy want gum	mehr milch [more milk] bitte apfel [please apple]	yeshchë moloko [more milk] day chasy [give watch]	mai pepe [give doll] fia moe [want sleep]
Negate	no wet no wash not hungry allgone milk	nicht blasen [not blow] kaffee nein [coffee no]	vody net [water no] gus' tyu-tyu [goose gone]	le 'ai [not eat] uma mea [allgone thing]
Describe event or situation	Bambi go mail come hit ball block fall baby highchair	puppe kommt [doll comes] tiktak hängt [clock hangs] sofa sitzen [sofa sit] messer schneiden [cut knife]	mama prua [mama walk] papa bay-bay [papa sleep] korka upala [crust fell] nashla yaichko [found egg] baba kreslo [grandma armchair]	pa'u pepe [fall doll] tapale 'oe [hit you] tu'u lalo [put down]
Indicate possession	my shoe mama dress	mein ball [my ball] mama hut [mama's hat]	mami chashka [mama's cup] pup moya [navel my]	lole a'u [candy my] polo 'oe [ball your] paluni mama [balloon mama]
Modify, qualify	pretty dress big boat	milch heiss [milk hot] armer wauwau [poor dog]	mama khoroshaya [mama good] papa bol'shoy [papa big]	fa'ali'i pepe [headstrong baby]
Question	where ball	wo ball [where ball]	gde papa [where papa]	fea Punafu [where Punafu]

Source: Slobin (1971)

There is a telegraphic quality about two-word speech. The child leaves out articles (like "the"), auxiliary verbs (like "is"), and prepositions (like "on") and puts in only those words that carry the most important meaning. Despite their brevity, these utterances express most of the basic functions of language, such as locating objects ("see shoe") and describing actions ("car go")—see Table 9-1.

Children progress rapidly from two-word utterances to more complex sentences (see Table 9-2). Clearly they do not just acquire a larger and larger vocabulary. They also learn more about how words are combined into sentences to express propositions clearly. Thus "Daddy hat" may become "Daddy

TABLE 9-2
Examples of complex sentences produced by children between two and
three years of age

AGE (YEAR-MONTH)	EXAMPLES
2-0	You lookit that book; I lookit this book.
2-6	I do pull it the way he hafta do that so he doesn't—so the big boy doesn't come out.
2-8	And that mouse is not scary; it's a library friend.
2-8	You play with this one and I play with this.
2-8	He was stuck and I got him out.
2-8	I can't put it on—too little.
2-8	He still has milk and spaghetti.
2-10	Here's a seat. It must be mine if it's a little one.
2-10	I went to the aquarium and saw the fish.
2-10	I want this doll because she's big.
2-10	When I was a little girl I could go "geek-geek" like that; but now I can go "this is a chair."

Source: Limber (1973)

wear hat" and finally "Daddy is wearing a hat." Such expansions of the verb phrase appear to be the first truly complex constructions that occur in children's speech. The next step is the use of conjunctions, like "and" and "so," to form compound sentences, like "You play with the doll and I play with the block." The sequence of development is remarkably similar for all children.

At about the same time, children learn to use certain morphemes that are critical for making sentences grammatical. Important *grammatical morphemes* include the suffixes "ing" (added to verbs to form the progressive—"kicking"), "ed" (added to regular verbs to form the past—"kicked"), "s" (added to nouns to form the plural—"boys"—and added to verbs in the present tense for the third person singular—"The boy kicks"). Brown (1973) traced the acquisition of such morphemes by three children. He found that all three children learned in a specific order: "ing" before "ed" and plural "s" before third-person "s." What determines this order? Brown argued that some morphemes express simpler thoughts than others, and the simpler the thought, the earlier children will acquire it. The plural "s" involves only the concept of number, while the third-person "s" involves the concepts of both number and time. Thus plural "s" is acquired before third-person "s."

In summary, children progress from one-word utterances about agents, objects, and places that they know to two-word "telegrams." Then they begin to elaborate their noun and verb phrases, adding conjunctions and acquiring the appropriate grammatical morphemes. The increasing complexity of children's language seems to mirror the increasing complexity of the thoughts they can entertain.

Learning Processes

Perhaps the most interesting question is, *how* do children learn to utter sentences? Three possible answers are: imitation, conditioning, and hypothesis testing. In discussing how concepts are acquired, we emphasized hypothesis testing. This process seems to be critical in many other aspects of language learning as well.

IMITATION Common sense suggests that children learn to speak by imitating, or mimicking, adults. However, there is a good deal of evidence to the contrary. Young children constantly say things they never heard an adult say, such as, "All gone milk." Even when children at the two-word stage try to imitate longer adult sentences (for example, "Mr. Miller will try,") they produce their usual telegraphic utterances ("Miller try"). In addition, the mistakes children make—for example, "Daddy taked me"—show they are trying to apply something like rules, not simply trying to copy adults (Ervin-Tripp, 1964).

Imitation, though, may play a part in learning new words. When a parent points to a phone and says "phone," the child may repeat the name, and this helps the child learn the word "phone." However, not all children imitate their elders, and those who do may only imitate a word when they already know its meaning (Bloom, Hood, and Lightbown, 1974).

CONDITIONING A second possibility is that children acquire language through conditioning. Adults may reward children when they produce a grammatical sentence and stop or reprimand them when they make mistakes. For this to work, parents would have to respond to every detail in a child's speech. However, Brown, Cazden, and Bellugi (1969) found that parents did not pay attention to how the child said something as long as it was comprehensible. Rare attempts to correct a child (and hence apply conditioning) are often futile.

CHILD: Nobody don't like me.
MOTHER: No, say, "nobody likes me."
CHILD: Nobody don't like me.
MOTHER: No, now listen carefully; say "nobody likes me."
CHILD: Oh! Nobody don't LIKES me. (McNeill, 1966)

HYPOTHESIS TESTING The problem with imitation and reinforcement is that they focus on specific utterances (one can only imitate or reinforce something specific), while children often appear to learn something general, such as a rule. That is, children seem to form a hypothesis about some aspect of language, test it out, and hold on to it if it works.

Consider the morpheme "ed." As a general rule, you add "ed" to the present tense of verbs to form the past (as in "cook"—"cooked"). However, many common verbs are irregular and do not follow this rule (like "go"—"went" and "take"—"took"). These irregular verbs tend to be the ones children use first. So at an early point, children use the past tense of some irregular verbs correctly. Then they learn the past tense for some regular verbs and hit on the hypothesis: add "ed" to the present tense to form the past. This hypothesis leads them to add the "ed" ending to all verbs, including the irregular ones. They say things like "Annie goed home" or "Harry taked the book," which they never heard or said before. Eventually children learn that some verbs are irregular, and they stop overgeneralizing their use of "ed." But whereas before they probably thought of "go" and "went" as separate words, they now understand them as different forms of the same word.

GENERATING HYPOTHESES How do children generate these hypotheses? Recent studies suggest there are a small number of *operating principles* that children everywhere use as a guide to forming hypotheses. One is to pay

TABLE 9-3
Operating principles used by young children in generating hypotheses

> 1 Look for systematic changes in the form of words.
>
> 2 Look for grammatical markers that clearly indicate changes in meaning.
>
> 3 Avoid exceptions.
>
> 4 Pay attention to the ends of words.
>
> 5 Pay attention to the order of words, prefixes, and suffixes.
>
> 6 Avoid interruption or rearrangement of constituents (that is, sentence units).

Adapted from Slobin (1973)

attention to the ends of words; another is to look for prefixes and suffixes that indicate a change in meaning. A child armed with these two principles is likely to hit the hypothesis that "ed" at the end of verbs signals the past tense, since "ed" is a word ending associated with a change in meaning. A third operating principle is to avoid exceptions, which explains why children initially generalize their "ed"-equals-past-tense hypothesis to irregular verbs. Some of these principles appear in Table 9-3, and they seem to hold for some 40 languages studied by Slobin (1973).

Operating principles give the child a rough guide to analyzing adults' utterances. Adults and older children contribute to the learning process by simplifying their speech when talking to youngsters. When speaking to a two-year-old, we tend to use sentences that are half the usual length and speak at half the normal rate. We also avoid complex constructions (Sachs, Brown, and Salerno, 1976). So adults essentially provide young children with a special dialect, *motherese*. Because it is simpler than ordinary talk, motherese makes it easier for children to find the right hypothesis and to understand what is being said.

Is Language Innate?

Children do not generate hypotheses about language at random. They never seem to consider certain kinds of hypotheses—for example, that the meaning of a word is determined by its number of syllables. This suggests that children come into the world genetically programmed to look at language in certain ways, that operating principles may be part of our biological heritage (Fodor, Bever, and Garrett, 1974).

The evidence for this view is suggestive, but not conclusive. A main difference between innate and learned behavior is that, given a few critical cues, innate behavior emerges more or less automatically. The organism does not have to learn each and every step through observation and imitation. This *seems* to be true of language. Children progress from simple to complex sentences, acquiring new grammatical constructions in a predictable order, despite large variations in how often adults around them use these constructions. The pattern is much the same for all children. However, the fixed sequence of language development may depend on the orderly development of perceptual and motor skills. If language development simply reflects the development of other skills, it would not be considered innate.

Another aspect of innate behavior is that it often depends on exposure to the right cues at the right time period. Is there evidence of a critical time period in language development? Yes, but again it is not conclusive. If individuals are not exposed to any human language before the age of 14 or so, they will be unable to acquire language (Lenneberg, 1967). This statement is based on a few unsuccessful attempts to teach language to individuals who were abandoned as infants and left to grow up in the wild. However, these failures might have been due to a general mental retardation rather than to lack of a specific language ability.

It is difficult to distinguish between innate and learned aspects of any complex behavior. Still, such distinctions are important if we are to understand how language develops and how it can be altered by experience.

Can Another Species Learn Our Language?

Some experts believe that the ability to learn language is not only innate, but unique to the human species (e.g., Chomsky, 1972). They acknowledge that other species have communication systems but argue that these are qualitatively different from ours. In effect they are arguing that the human species is qualitatively different from its evolutionary "relatives" in the animal kingdom.

Until about 1970, attempts to teach chimpanzees, our closest "relatives," to *speak* had failed. The failures, however, may have been due to limitations in the chimps' vocal abilities, not their cognitive abilities. Successful attempts to teach chimps to communicate with their hands have refueled the controversy about the uniqueness of human language.

In one of the best-known studies, Gardner and Gardner (1972) taught a female chimpanzee, named Washoe, American Sign Language for the deaf. Training began when Washoe was about a year old and continued until age five. During this time, Washoe's caretakers communicated with her only by means of sign language. They first taught her signs by shaping procedures, waiting for her to make a gesture that resembled a sign and reinforcing her. Later they found that Washoe could learn signs if they put her hands into the proper position and guided her through the desired movement. Ultimately, Washoe learned signs simply by observing and imitating. (See Figure 9-7).

By age four, Washoe could produce 130 different signs and understand even more. By the way she used them it was clear she knew their meanings. Thus,

"*Although humans make sounds with their mouths and occasionally look at each other, there is no solid evidence that they actually communicate among themselves.*"

Fig. 9-7   Two of Washoe's signs

Signing "sweet" for lollipop

Signing "hat" for woolen cap

DEVELOPMENT OF LANGUAGE

267

Animal

Is human language qualitatively different from the communication systems of other species? In attempting to answer this question, researchers have employed a two-part strategy. First, they use what they know about various human languages to compose a list of properties common to all languages. Then they examine an animal communication system to see if it has those properties.

To illustrate, many linguists agree that all human languages have at least four things in common (Hockett, 1960; Langacker, 1973). The first is *productivity*. Human languages permit the combination of a relatively small number of phonemes into thousands of words and the combination of these words into a virtually unlimited number of sentences. Second, human languages are structured at several levels. In particular, there is a clear distinction between the levels of propositions and sentence units, where the elements have meaning, and the level of sounds, where the elements involved (phonemes) do not carry any meaning. (The phoneme /b/, for instance, does not mean anything by itself in any language.) This *duality of structure*, as it is sometimes called, is related to a third property; there is an arbitrary relation between the sound of a word and the entities it refers to. *Arbitrary symbols* are obvious, for different languages use different-sounding words to refer to the same objects. Finally, all languages make some use of *word order* to indicate variations in meaning. In English, for instance, "Jonah ate the whale" means something quite different from "The whale ate Jonah."

The question is whether any of these properties—productivity, duality of structure, arbitrary symbols, and word order—are present in animal communication systems. One system that has been studied intensively is that of the bees (von Frisch, 1974). When a worker bee goes hunting for nectar and returns to the hive, she performs an intricate dance that communicates the location of the nectar to the other bees (see Figure 9-8). The bee first traces out a semicircle and runs along its diameter wagging her abdomen. She then traces out a semicircle in the opposite direction. The most important aspect of the dance is the straight-line run along the diameter where the bee wags her abdomen from side to side. The direction of this line or waggle corresponds to the direction of the nectar from the hive, while the duration of the waggle corresponds to the distance from the hive.

The dance of the bees is fascinating, but does it have the features of human language? It is not nearly as productive. All the bee's messages are about the same thing: "There is nectar at x distance from here in y direction" (Langacker, 1973). In contrast, human language can be used to communicate almost any topic we can think of. There is no duality of structure in the dance of the bees. Everything—even a single waggle—adds meaning to the message. Bees do not use arbitrary symbols: different groups of bees do not have different "dance languages." Finally, bees do not generally vary the order of their "symbols" to produce messages with different meanings. In short, the dance of the bees seems most unlike our kind of talk.

So we have bested the lowly bee.

Washoe could generalize a sign from one situation to another. For example, she first learned the sign for *more* in connection with *more tickling* and then generalized it to indicate *more milk.* Washoe also combined signs to form longer communications, like *Gimme flower* and *Washoe sorry,* which resemble those of two-year-old human children (see Table 9-4). Washoe is not unique. Other chimps have acquired the rudiments of our language. Some of these

Communication

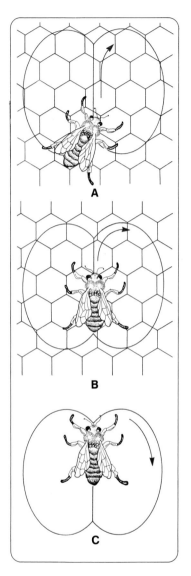

Fig. 9-8 The waggle dance of the bee
The direction of the straight-line part of the dance communicates the direction of the nectar source; the duration of this part communicates its distance from the hive. (von Frisch, 1974)

What about the communication system of a species closer to us in the evolutionary scale—the chimpanzee? In nature, chimps use both vocalization and facial gestures to communicate. Their vocalizations are limited in number and refer to things critical to survival, like "An attack is coming," "Food is here," or "Gather together." Their facial gestures are also limited and are primarily used to communicate dominance and emotion. Their total vocabulary is strikingly small in comparison to ours, and the productivity of their communication system is much lower. Again, there is no evidence for duality of structure, as every communication symbol carries meaning. Nor is there any hint of an arbitrary assignment of symbols. Rather, the vocalizations and gestures are fixed patterns of behavior, and chimps everywhere use basically the same gestures to communicate the same things. Finally, chimps do not vary the order of their vocalizations or gestures to vary the meaning of their messages. Chimp communication, then, like bee communication, does not display the properties of human language.

This is by no means the last word on whether human language is unique. For one thing, we need to know more about the communication systems of other species. For another, the fact that chimpanzee communication is impoverished compared to our own does not mean chimps lack the capacity for a more productive system. Their system is adequate for their needs. To determine if chimps have the same capacity we do, we must look instead at the research aimed at teaching them our language.

studies used methods of manual communication other than sign language. Premack (1971) taught a chimp named Sarah to use plastic symbols as words and to communicate by manipulating these symbols. And Lana, a chimp studied by Rumbaugh (1977), communicates by means of a keyboard console. The console has about a hundred keys, each representing a different word, and Lana essentially types her human-like messages on the keyboard. In addition to

TABLE 9-4 Gesture-language signs used by a chimpanzee
These are only a few of the signs used by Washoe. ASL stands for American Sign Language.

MEANING OF SIGN	DESCRIPTION	CONTEXT
Come-gimme	Beckoning motion, with wrist or knuckles as pivot.	Sign made to persons or animals. Also for objects out of reach. Often combined: "come tickle," "gimme sweet," and so forth.
More	Fingertips are brought together, usually overhead. (Correct ASL form: tips of the tapered hand touch repeatedly.)	When asking for continuation or repetition of activities, such as swinging or tickling, second helpings of food, and so forth. Also used to ask for repetition of some performance, such as a somersault.
Open	Flat hands are placed side by side, palms down, then drawn apart while rotated to palms up.	At door of house, room, car, refrigerator, or cupboard, with containers such as jars and with faucets.
Hurry	Open hand is shaken at the wrist. (Correct ASL form: index and second fingers extended side by side as hand is shaken, but open hand is acceptable.)	Often follows signs such as "come-gimme," "out," "open," and "go," particularly if there is a delay before Washoe is obeyed. Also used while watching her meal being prepared.
Hear-listen	Index finger touches ear.	For loud or strange sounds: bells, car horns, sonic booms, and so forth. Also, for asking someone to hold a watch to her ear.
Hurt	Extended index fingers are jabbed toward each other. Can be used to indicate location of pain.	To indicate cuts and bruises on herself or on others. Can be elicited by red stains on a person's skin or by tears in clothing.
Sorry	Fisted hand clasps and unclasps at shoulder. (Correct ASL form: fisted hand is rubbed over heart with circular motion.)	After biting someone or when someone has been hurt in another way (not necessarily by Washoe). When told to apologize for mischief.
Dog	Repeated slapping on thigh.	For dogs and for barking.
Baby	Arms crossed in front of body with hands grasping elbows; arms move in rocking motion.	For human infants and for dolls and figurines, including animal dolls, such as a toy duck, and miniatures, such as a toy car.
Can't	Tip of index finger extended from closed hand. Index fingers touch, then move down and to side of body.	First used to signal inability to perform on potty chair. Later spontaneously transferred by Washoe to indicate inability to perform a difficult sign or to do something beyond her ability, such as breaking a metal rod.
Different	Tips of index fingers hooked and extended from closed hands. Hooked fingers are grasped and then drawn apart.	For two or more objects that differ in appearance, such as unmatched shoes or toy blocks or a shoe and a toy block.
Help	Palm of flat hand is brought up repeatedly to contact closed fist of the other hand.	For assistance with tasks that are difficult: operating locks and keys, looping a rope around a rafter, and so forth.

Source: Gardner and Gardner (1972)

studies with chimps, Patterson (1978) has taught sign language to a gorilla named Koko, starting when Koko was one year old. Koko, at age seven, had a vocabulary of about 375 signs and could combine them to communicate longer utterances.

Do these studies prove that other species—particularly the apes—can learn human language? Those who believe they do point to the similarity between an ape's concepts and utterances and those of a human child, particularly a deaf child who must also learn sign language (Gardner and Gardner, 1977). Skeptics question how much the apes know about how signs are combined (Fodor and others, 1974). They point out that Washoe was explicitly taught her language by the researcher putting her hands in the right position. In contrast, human children pick up their language without explicit instruction. Even the most ardent parents do not make a practice of putting their child's mouth in the right position to form a word. But perhaps a baby chimp can learn language in the casual way a human child does if the chimp's elders (parents and siblings) have been taught sign language and use it around the baby. Studies like this are now under way (Gardner and Gardner, 1977).

Visual Thinking

We have thus far emphasized thoughts that take the form of propositions and can be expressed in language. Thoughts may take other forms as well. In particular, some appear as visual images.

Examples of Visual Thinking

Many of us feel we do some of our thinking visually. We retrieve past perceptions, or parts of them, and combine or transform them in novel ways. Try to form an image of a friend who wears distinctive glasses and then see if you can form an image of the same glasses on someone else. People who often think in visual images will find this easy to do; others may find it difficult.

Below is a problem that is easier to solve through visual thinking than through a more verbal analysis. Try to solve it in your usual way; then look at its imagery solution.

One morning, exactly at sunrise, a monk began to climb a mountain. A narrow path, a foot or two wide, spiraled around the mountain to a temple at the summit. The monk ascended at varying rates, stopping many times along the way to rest. He reached the temple shortly before sunset. After several days at the temple he began his journey back along the same path, starting at sunrise and again walking at variable speeds with many pauses along the way. His average speed descending was, of course, greater than his average climbing speed. Prove that there exists a particular spot along the path that the monk will occupy on both trips at precisely the same time of day. (Adams, 1974)

To solve this problem all you need do is visualize the upward journey of the monk superimposed on the downward journey. Imagine one monk starting at the bottom and the other at the top. No matter what their speed, at some time and at some point along the path the two monks will meet. Thus there must be a spot along the path that the monk occupied on both trips at precisely the same time of day. (Note that the problem did not ask you what the spot was.)

This example suggests some important aspects of visual thinking. One is that our images of objects and places have visual detail: we see the mountain path in our "mind's eye." Moreover, we may be capable of performing mental operations on these images that are analogous to the operations we carry out on our perceptions. For example, when we imagine the monk climbing the

As Penny Patterson tells the story of the three little kittens who lost their mittens, Koko comments that their mother is angry and that the kittens are crying. Then she signs "bad."

Koko signs "eye" while looking at a picture of a big-eyed frog.

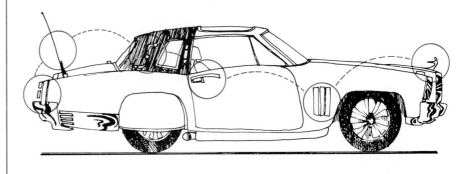

Fig. 9-9 Scanning mental images
The subject scans the image of the car from back to front, looking for the emblem. (Circles show successive fixations on image.)

mountain path, we may be able to scan the imaginary path (a mental operation) in much the same way we scan a path we can actually perceive.

Experiments on Visual Thinking

Recent experiments have documented some aspects of visual thinking. In one study, subjects were presented first with pairs of names of states in the United States. They were asked to rate each pair according to the similarity of the states' shapes and then to put them in rank order with the most similar pair at the top and the least similar one at the bottom. With only the names of the states, subjects clearly had to rely on their images. Then they were given pictures of the states and asked to repeat the task. These judgments were based on perceptions. The two rankings were virtually the same, suggesting that images have some of the visual detail of perceptions (Shepard and Chipman, 1970).

The mental operations we perform on images are analogous to those we apply to percepts. In one study, subjects were shown a picture of an object, such as a car, and asked to form an image of it. The picture was removed, and they were instructed to fixate on part of the image—say, the front or back of the car (see Figure 9-9). Then the experimenter asked questions about the image. When asked if the car had an emblem in front, for instance, subjects answered quickly if they were fixating on the front but slowly if they were fixating on the back. Subjects were scanning their mental images in the same way they scan real objects (Kosslyn, 1973).

Another operation that we can perform on images is mental rotation. In one experiment, subjects saw a capital letter on each trial. The letter was presented

Fig. 9-10 Study of mental rotation in visual thinking
Examples of the letters presented to subjects in studies of mental rotation. Subjects had to decide whether the letters were normal or backward. Numbers indicate deviation from the vertical in degrees. (Cooper and Shepard, 1973)

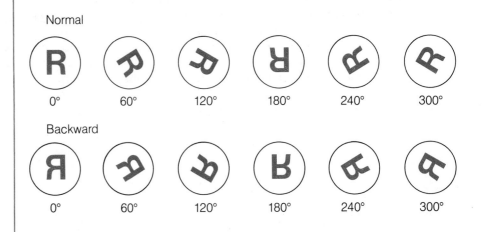

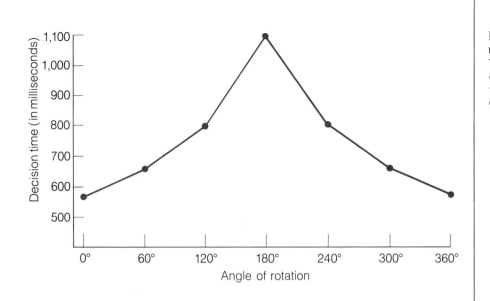

Fig. 9-11 Decision times in mental rotation study
Time to decide whether a letter had normal or reversed orientation, as a function of rotation. Rotation was clockwise from upright (0°). (Cooper and Shepard, 1973)

either normally, "R," or backward, "Я," in its usual vertical orientation or rotated various degrees (see Figure 9-10). The task was to decide if the letter was normal or backward. The more the letter had been rotated from its vertical orientation, the longer it took to make the decision (see Figure 9-11). This finding suggests that subjects made their decisions by mentally rotating the image of the letter until it was vertical and then checking whether it was normal or backward.

Studies of mental rotation leave little doubt that people can manipulate images in their "mind's eye." Indeed, it is difficult to come up with any other way of telling whether a rotated letter is normal or backward. We can't easily do it by describing the letter's appearance in propositions and manipulating the propositions. Mental rotation is thus the kind of problem that fosters visual thinking; other problems foster a verbal or propositional approach; while still others can be approached by either means.

Visual Creativity

There are innumerable stories about scientists and artists producing their most creative work through visual thinking (see Shepard, 1978). Though not hard evidence, they are the best indicators we have of the power of visual thinking. Surprisingly, visual thinking appears to be quite effective in areas like mathematics and physics. Albert Einstein, for example, said he rarely thought in words. Rather, he worked out his conceptualizations in terms of "more or less clear images which can be 'voluntarily' reproduced and combined." Perhaps the most celebrated example is in chemistry. Friedrich Kekulé was trying to determine the molecular structure of benzene. One night he dreamed that a writhing, snake-like figure suddenly twisted into a closed loop, biting its own tail. The structure of the snake proved to be the structure of benzene. A dream image had provided the solution to a major scientific problem.

Visual images can also be a creative force for writers. Samuel Coleridge's famous poem "Kubla Khan" came to him in its entirety as a prolonged visual image. Contemporary novelist Joan Didion says that her novels develop out of visual images, images so detailed that she claims they sometimes direct the arrangement of the words in her sentences—the sort of thing you might expect to be affected by auditory rather than visual imagery.

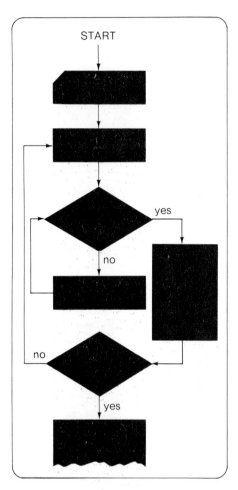

Fig. 9-12 Flow chart
A computer program is a detailed set of instructions, written in a language designed for the computer, that specifies every step the machine must take. To write a program it is often first necessary to break the problem down into its component parts and construct a flow chart, which shows how the components fit together. This figure is a flow chart for the problem of finding how many words in a particular text are one letter long, two letters long, and so on. The input to the program is a piece of text. The boxes represent operations to be performed; the diamonds represent decisions to be made. Once this flow chart is written, the programmer's next step is to translate each box and each diamond into more detailed instructions about how the operation or decision is to be made. This detailed set of instructions, which can contain thousands of steps, is the program.

Problem Solving and Computer Simulation

Stages of Problem Solving

Usually when we try to solve a complex problem, the solution does not appear to us in a single image or even in the form of a few propositions. We break problems into parts, first dealing with one part, then the next, until we either come up with a solution or decide to give up. Solving complex problems seems to involve a sequence of stages.

Consider letter series problems, where people have to figure out how to complete a series of letters. An easy one would be *CDCD* . . . ; somewhat more difficult would be *ATBATAATBAT* . . . or *RSCDSTDE.* . . . When presented a difficult letter series problem, people describe their thought processes in terms of three distinct stages. First, they decide on the cycles of the string. For example, *RSCDSTDE* . . . splits into cycles of two letters, *RS-CD-ST-DE*. Second, they look for rules to describe the relations between letters within a cycle and between starting letters across cycles. In this case, the second letter in each cycle is the one that follows the first in the alphabet; each cycle picks up where the one two back ended. Finally, people use this information to produce the next letters in the series—here, *TU*. Of course, these particular stages of thought can only be used successfully with a narrow range of problems. For example, they won't work for the sequence *OTTFFSS.* . . .[1] But the general idea of going through a sequence of stages seems to hold for solving most complex problems (Simon and Kotovsky, 1963).

Computer Simulation

While useful, the descriptions people give of their thought processes have many limitations. People may not be aware of many of their own mental processes; they may be unable to verbally describe those processes that rely on imagery; or they may try to make themselves look more intelligent. For these reasons, researchers have sought other methods of studying problem solving. Perhaps the most powerful method is *computer simulation*. Researchers use people's descriptions of problem solving as a guide to programming a computer to solve that problem. Then the output of the computer can be compared to aspects of people's performance on the problem to see if they match. If they match, the computer program offers a theory of problem solving.

Why use computers to learn about people? It turns out that there are some striking similarities between the kinds of mental operations we perform in solving a problem and the kinds of operations a high-speed computer performs in executing a program. People use various rules and procedures to sort through and organize information in arriving at a solution to a problem. So does a computer. We use information from memory stores as well as information from the environment. So does a computer. Thus there are basic similarities between human thinking and computer programs (see Figure 9-12).

The general idea behind computer simulation is to write a program that corresponds as closely as possible to the sequence of mental operations a person performs when solving a particular problem. Such a program has been developed for the letter string problems discussed earlier (Simon and Kotovsky, 1963, 1973). The program has the alphabet stored in its memory. For

[1]Solution: the initials *OTTFFSS* . . . stand for the first letter of the digits one, two, three, four, and so forth. Thus, the next two letters would be *EN*.

any two letters, it can tell (1) whether they are the same as each other, (2) whether the first precedes the second in the alphabet, or (3) whether the first succeeds the second in the alphabet. Given the problem *RSCDSTDE . . .* , the program follows the same three steps that people report—determining cycles, determining relations, and producing the next letters. And problems for which the program requires many steps are just those that people take a long time to solve. This suggests that the program offers a reasonable model of how people solve letter series problems.

The General Problem Solver

Computer simulation would not be very impressive if it required wildly different programs for mildly different problems. Humans, being limited creatures, must use many of the same mental operations in solving a wide variety of problems. This led Newell and Simon (1972) to develop a general purpose program, called the *General Problem Solver,* or GPS. When GPS is fed specific information about a particular problem, it produces a program that can solve the problem. For example, suppose the problem is to solve a theorem in geometry. Geometric axioms are added to GPS. The result is a specific program that proves theorems in geometry. If the problem is to play a game of chess, the rules of chess are combined with GPS to yield a specific chess-playing program, and a good one at that.

The GPS program is based on two basic processes that follow each other in repeated cycles until the problem is solved, or abandoned as too difficult. The first is setting up appropriate subgoals. These subgoals are evaluated and a promising one selected for exploration. For example, a subgoal in chess is to put the opposing king in check. The second process is to identify any difference between a subgoal and the current state of affairs and then eliminate or reduce this difference. If the opposing king is not in check, the computer runs through strategies for moving pieces to achieve that subgoal. If no piece can achieve this, the cycle continues with a smaller subgoal, perhaps getting one piece out of the way of another. By constantly recycling these two processes, setting subgoals and reducing discrepancies, GPS approximates the step-by-step progress of human problem solving.

Computer simulation is not without its critics. Some argue that we do not yet know enough about basic human mental processes to evaluate the programs. How, for example, can we be sure that the computer memories resemble human memory? Other critics have challenged the analogy between computers and people: computers, they say, can only do what they have been programmed to do. However, it is quite possible that humans can also do only what heredity and past experience have "programmed" them to do. Another criticism is that the physical basis of human thought, the brain, is very different from the electrical circuitry of modern computers. Clearly, a brain and a computer differ physically, but they may be similar in how they are organized and how they function. How far one can trust the computer as a guide to human mental life is thus very much an open question.

At various points in this chapter on human thought and language, we raised questions about these abilities in nonhumans. We have discussed apes that talk, or almost talk, and computers that think, or almost think. These discussions and comparisons suggest that we can improve our understanding of human intelligence by comparing it with nonhuman intelligence, be it natural or of our own making.

1 To have a *concept* of something is to know its properties. While some properties will be common to all instances of the concept, others will be characteristic only of the more *typical* instances. In addition to knowing the properties of concepts, we also know the relations between concepts. Such relations may be represented in a *hierarchy* of concepts.

2 In learning which word goes with which concept, children form *hypotheses* about the crucial properties of a word's meaning. Children often select only a few properties when a whole cluster is relevant (for example, "doggie" means "has four legs and moves"); consequently they *overextend* the meaning (for example, they use "doggie" to name cats and cows). Adults also use *hypothesis testing* when acquiring new concepts. They are biased, however, to seek out cases that confirm their hypothesis and to ignore those that might disprove it.

3 Concepts may be combined to form complex thoughts that can be expressed in sentences. Such thoughts often take the form of *propositions*, with each proposition containing a *subject* (for example, *Susan*) and a *predicate* (for example, *likes fruit*). Two propositions can be combined in various ways—by joining them, by attaching one to part of the other, and by *embedding* one into the other.

4 We extract propositions from a sentence by breaking the sentence into phrases, with each phrase corresponding to either the subject or the predicate of a proposition, or to an entire proposition.

5 The words of a sentence are built from units called *phonemes* and *morphemes*. A phoneme is a category of speech sounds, while a morpheme is the smallest linguistic unit that carries meaning. Children seem to come into the world preset to learn phonemes, but it takes them several years to learn the rules for combining phonemes into words.

6 In learning how to produce sentences, children go through several stages. They begin with one-word utterances about agents, objects, and places, then move on to two-word *telegraphic speech,* and then elaborate their noun and verb phrases while acquiring the appropriate *grammatical morphemes.* All children seem to go through the same stages in the same order.

7 Children learn language mainly by testing hypotheses, rather than by imitating adults' speech or by being reinforced for producing grammatical sentences. Children's hypotheses appear to be guided by a small set of *operating principles,* which, for example, call the childrens' attention to certain critical parts of an utterance.

8 Some of our language-learning abilities may be innate. A controversial issue is whether such abilities are *unique to our species.* Recent studies suggest that chimpanzees and gorillas can learn the basics of our language, but it is still unclear whether they learn our language in the same way we do.

9 Not all thoughts are expressed in language; some are manifested as *visual images.* Such images contain the kind of visual detail found in perceptions. Also, the mental operations performed on images—such as scanning and rotation—are like the operations carried out on perceptions.

10 When solving a complex problem, we usually go through a sequence of stages. A major way of studying this process is by *computer simulation:* a computer is programmed to solve the same problem that a person has worked on, and then the output of the computer is compared to aspects of the person's performance. One of the best-developed programs is the *General Problem Solver.* It solves many different kinds of problems by recycling two basic processes: setting up *subgoals* and *reducing differences* between a subgoal and the present state of affairs.

Readable introductions to the psychology of language may be found in Clark and Clark, *Psychology and language* (1977), Glucksberg and Danks, *Experimental psycholinguistics* (1975), and Foss and Hakes, *Psycholinguistics: An introduction to the psychology of language* (1978). For a more advanced treatment, particularly of issues related to Chomsky's theory of language and thought, see Chomsky, *Language and mind* (2nd ed., 1972) and Fodor, Bever, and Garrett, *The psychology of language* (1974). The best account of early language development is given in Brown, *A first language: The early stages* (1973).

There are also a number of books that attempt to provide an integrated account of language and memory, including Anderson, *Language, memory and thought* (1976), Kintsch, *The representation of meaning in memory* (1974), Lindsay and Norman, *Human information processing* (2nd ed., 1977), Norman and Rumelhart, *Explorations in cognition* (1975), and Rumelhart, *An introduction to human information processing* (1977).

Computer-simulation models of thinking are discussed in Bobrow and Collins (eds.), *Representation and understanding: Studies in cognitive science* (1975), Newell and Simon, *Human problem solving* (1972), and Schank and Colby (eds.), *Computer models of thought and language* (1973).

PART FIVE

Motivation and Emotion

10
Basic Drives and Motives

When we ask, "What *motivates* people to risk their lives to save another or to work long hours to achieve a particular goal?" we usually mean, "Why do they behave as they do?" As popularly used, the term "motivation" refers to the *cause* or *why* of behavior. Used in this sense, motivation would cover all of psychology, since psychology is the study of human behavior. But many aspects of behavior are the result of maturation or learning. Psychologists, then, usually confine the concept of motivation to those factors that *energize* behavior and give it *direction*. A motivated organism will engage in an activity more *vigorously* and more *efficiently* than an unmotivated one. In addition to activating the organism, motivation also tends to focus behavior—the hungry person is ready to seek food and eat, the thirsty one to drink, the one in pain to escape the painful stimulus.

Although many psychologists would agree with this definition of motivation, it is still a controversial concept. Some psychologists feel that motivation accounts only for the energizing aspects of behavior; other mechanisms (namely, learning and cognition) can account for the direction of behavior (Cofer, 1972). Some even argue that the concept is unnecessary (Bolles, 1975). To help clarify this controversy, we briefly describe how the concept of motivation developed and the various forms it has taken since the beginning of this century. Then we consider the basic biological or physiological needs that humans share with lower organisms. In the next chapter, we discuss more complex human motives.

Development of Motivational Concepts

The term "motivation" was not used until the beginning of the twentieth century. If people are viewed as rational beings whose intellects are free to choose goals and decide on courses of action, then a concept of motivation is unnecessary; reason determines what a person does. This conception of the human being, called *rationalism*, was the predominant view of philosophers and

Thomas Hobbes

theologians for hundreds of years. A person was free to choose, and choices were good or bad, depending on one's intelligence and education. It was assumed that the good choice, if known, would automatically be selected. Within this viewpoint, a person is very much responsible for his or her own behavior.

Seventeenth- and eighteenth-century philosophers (such as Descartes, Hobbes, Locke, and Hume) took a more *mechanistic view*. They suggested that some actions arise from internal or external forces over which we have no control. Hobbes, for example, held that no matter what reasons we may give for our conduct, the underlying causes of all behavior are the tendencies to seek pleasure and avoid pain. This doctrine of *hedonism* is still very influential in some motivation theories.

Instincts

The extreme of the mechanistic view is the theory of *instincts*. An instinct is an innate biological force that predisposes the organism to act in a certain way. Animal behavior had long been attributed to instincts, since animals had no soul or intellect and could not reason. Darwin's theory that there was no sharp distinction between humans and animals opened the door for the use of instincts in explaining human behavior. The strongest advocate of instinct theory was the psychologist William McDougall. McDougall maintained that *all* our thoughts and behavior were the result of inherited instincts, which were compelling sources of conduct, but modifiable by learning and experience. In his book *Social Psychology* (1908), McDougall mentioned the following instincts:

flight	self-assertion
repulsion	reproduction
curiosity	gregariousness
pugnacity	self-abasement
acquisition	construction

He later expanded his list to 18 instincts, including some that related to specific bodily needs. By modifying and combining these instincts, he attempted to explain all human behavior.

Instinct theory is therefore diametrically opposed to a rationalistic view of human beings. Instead of choosing goals and actions, a person is at the mercy of innate forces, which determine, or motivate, his or her behavior.

Psychoanalytic theory also attributed behavior to powerful innate forces. Freud believed that two basic energies determine behavior: the *life instincts*, which are expressed in sexual behavior, and the *death instincts*, which underlie aggressive acts (see Chapter 11). These instincts, though unconscious, were powerful motivational forces. Both psychoanalytic theory and instinct theory influenced the change from a rationalistic conception of people to a motivational view, which saw behavior as the result of unconscious, irrational forces within the individual.

Needs and Drives

Soon, however, it became clear that there were too many instincts, and they did not explain anything. Added to the list were such instincts as rivalry, secretiveness, modesty, cleanliness, imitation, hurting, sociability, and jealousy—

finally an instinct could be found for almost any imaginable behavior. But to call a particular action instinctive does not really explain much about it. To say that a man fought because he had a pugnacious instinct does not offer much more than a description of his behavior. It does not explain his behavior.

Anthropologists noted that many instincts were not found in all cultures. Pugnacity, for example, was not typical of all primitive societies. In some societies, people found no need to fight.

Thus, during the 1920s, the instinct theory was replaced by the concept of *drives*. A drive is an aroused state that results from some biological *need*, such as a need for food, water, oxygen, or avoidance of painful stimuli. This aroused condition motivates the organism to remedy the need. For example, lack of food produces certain chemical changes in the blood, indicating a need for food, which in turn create a drive state of arousal or tension. The organism seeks to reduce the drive by doing something (in this case, finding food) to satisfy the need. This is a *drive-reduction theory* of motivation.

Sometimes the terms "need" and "drive" are used interchangeably, but more frequently "need" refers to the physiological state of deprivation, whereas "drive" refers to the psychological consequences of a need. Need and drive are parallel, but not identical. Drive does not necessarily get stronger as need gets stronger. A starved organism may be so weakened by its great need for food that drive (the motivation to get it) is weakened. People who have fasted for long periods report that their feelings of hunger (drive level) come and go, even though their need for food persists.

Like instinct, drive is a *hypothetical construct*. It is not observable, but is inferred from behavior. We note that an animal deprived of food for a specified period of time runs more rapidly to obtain food, and eats more, than a non-deprived animal. We infer from this behavior that the animal's hunger drive has been activated. Although drive is a hypothetical construct, it proved to be more amenable to experimental investigation than instinct. Needs could be defined objectively and conditions specified for creating and eliminating them. Researchers were able to tie the concept of drive to such variables as length of deprivation, rate of learning, speed and efficiency of performing learned acts, and general activity level.

HOMEOSTASIS AND DRIVE THEORY Basic to the drive concept is the principle of *homeostasis,* the body's tendency to maintain a constant internal environment. The healthy individual, for example, maintains body temperature within a few degrees. Slight deviations from normal temperature activate mechanisms that restore the normal condition. Exposure to cold constricts blood vessels on the body's surface to retain the warmth of the blood, and shivering produces heat. In warm weather, peripheral blood vessels dilate to permit heat to escape, and perspiration has a cooling effect. These automatic mechanisms keep body temperature within normal range.

Numerous physiological states must be maintained within fairly narrow limits: the concentration of blood sugar, the levels of oxygen and carbon dioxide in the blood, and water balance in the cells are but a few. Various body mechanisms operate to keep these conditions stable. Presumably, sensors in the body detect changes from the optimal level and activate mechanisms that correct the imbalance. The principle is the same as a furnace thermostat, which turns the heat on when the temperature falls below a certain level and off when the temperature rises.

Hunger and thirst can be viewed as homeostatic mechanisms, because they initiate behavior that restores the balance of certain substances in the blood.

Fig. 10-1 Motivational control system
The state monitor continuously measures the internal condition of the organism. Whenever the comparator notes a difference between the state monitor and some optimal level, it emits an error signal. The error signal activates cognitive processes that select behaviors designed to restore the balance between the state monitor and the optimal state. The behaviors will depend on the environmental situation; that is, they will not be stereotyped but will be more or less appropriate to the situation. These behaviors link the organism to its environment, producing feedback to the system that restores the imbalance between the optimal and current state. The system is organized to maintain the level of the state monitor so it is nearly equal to the optimal level at all times.

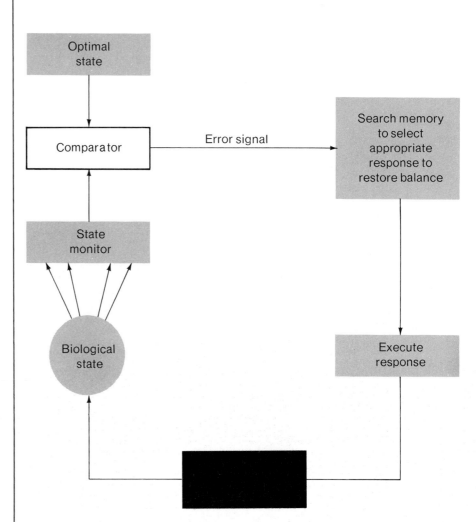

Within the framework of homeostasis, a need is any physiological imbalance or departure from the optimal state; its psychological counterpart is drive. When the physiological imbalance is restored, drive is reduced and motivated activity ceases. Many physiological imbalances are corrected automatically. The pancreas releases sugar stored in the liver to maintain the proper balance of sugar in the blood. But when automatic mechanisms can no longer maintain a balanced state, the organism becomes aroused (drive is activated) and is motivated to restore the balance. A person feeling the symptoms of low blood-sugar level seeks food. Figure 10-1 represents schematically the kind of control system that a homeostatic mechanism of this nature would require.

Psychologists have broadened the principle of homeostasis to mean that any *physiological* or *psychological* imbalance will motivate behavior designed to restore equilibrium. Thus, a hungry, anxious, uncomfortable, or fearful person will be motivated to do something to reduce the tension. As we shall see later, not all psychologists agree that motivation is solely tension arousal and that it ceases with tension reduction.

Incentives

During the 1950s, psychologists began to question the drive-reduction theory of motivation as an explanation of all types of behavior. It became apparent that the organism was not solely *pushed* into activity by internal drives;

external stimuli (called *incentives*) were also important in arousing behavior. Motivation could be better understood as an interaction between stimulus objects in the environment and a particular physiological state of the organism.

Delicious-looking pastries in a bakery window may arouse the hunger drive of a person who is not hungry. In this case, the incentive (fresh pastries) activates hunger rather than reduces it. A satiated animal will eat again if it sees another animal doing so. The motivation here is not an internal drive, but an external event.

Furthermore, some evidence contradicted the homeostatic concept of drive as reducing tension and returning the organism to a quiescent state. Human beings often seek tension-arousing experiences, such as roller-coaster rides, car racing, white-water canoeing, or horror movies—activities that certainly increase tension rather than reduce it.

More recent approaches to a theory of motivation have focused on the role of incentives—motivating objects or conditions in the environment. The organism will approach *positive incentives;* it will avoid *negative incentives.* For a thirsty animal, water would be a positive incentive; for a sexually aroused animal, a mate. An object or situation that has caused pain would be a negative incentive. Incentives have two functions: they arouse the organism, and they direct behavior either toward or away from themselves.

The dual function of incentives can be demonstrated experimentally. A hungry rat will run through a maze to a goal box that it knows contains food; the positive incentive directs behavior. Given a morsel of food at the start of the maze, the rat runs even faster toward the goal box; the incentive also arouses behavior. As with drive theory, arousal is an important aspect of motivation, but here arousal is evoked by an external incentive rather than by conditions of deprivation.

Now that we have considered various concepts of motivation, we will examine some specific motivational systems in terms of empirical findings. All the concepts mentioned are useful in explaining some aspects of behavior; even the notion of instincts is currently being reexamined in the study of certain patterns of behavior—although with a different emphasis than at the beginning of this century. Because it has been the subject of more intensive research, hunger will be considered in more detail than the other motivational systems.

Hunger can be aroused by external influences.

The response patterns animals display in the care of their young provide a clear example of the type of behavior that has been called instinctive. Building nests, removing the amniotic sac so the newborn can breathe, feeding the young and retrieving them when they stray from the nest all involve complex patterns of behavior that appear without the opportunity to learn. The mother squirrel performs its maternal duties in the same manner as all other mothers of its species, whether it is the first litter or the fifth.

Interest in instinctive behavior, which declined during the early part of the century because it did not prove very helpful in understanding human behavior, has been revived by a group of European psychologists and zoologists who call themselves *ethologists*. These scientists study animals in their natural environment rather than in the laboratory, where the artificiality of the situation often prevents behavior patterns from appearing in a natural form and in their entirety.

Ethologists prefer the term *species-specific behavior* to the more controversial term "instinct." They study behavior that is specific to a certain species and that appears in the same form in all members of the species. And

they attempt to determine the variables that govern this behavior.

One of the concepts introduced by ethologists is *imprinting*, which refers to a type of early learning that forms the basis for the young animal's attachment to its parents. A newly hatched duckling that has been incubated artifically without the presence of a mother duck will follow a human being, a wooden decoy, or almost any other moving object that it first sees after birth. Following a wooden decoy for as little as 10 minutes is enough to "imprint" the duckling on the decoy, so that it will remain attached to this object, following it even under adverse circumstances and preferring it to a live duck. Imprinting takes place most readily at 14 hours after hatching but can occur any time during the first two days of life. After that, imprinting is difficult, probably because the duckling has acquired a fear of strange objects.

Imprinting has been found in a number of species—dogs, sheep, guinea pigs—but it is most clearly developed in birds that are able to walk or swim immediately after birth (as opposed to those that remain in a nest). An innate mechanism of this sort ensures that the young will follow and

Imprinting in ducklings
The newly hatched duckling follows the model duck around a circular track. The duckling soon becomes imprinted on the model and will follow it in preference to a live duck of its own species. The more effort the duckling has to exert to follow the model (such as climbing a hurdle) the stronger the imprinting. (After Hess, 1958)

remain close to the mother (normally the first moving object they see) rather than wander off into a perilous world.

Studies with mallard ducks have

Hunger

Hunger can be a powerful motivator; people who have subsisted on semi-starvation diets report that much of their thinking and dreaming concerns food and eating. The body needs an adequate supply of the essential nutrients in order to function efficiently. Depletion of these nutrients activates homeostatic mechanisms to release food stored in the body; for example, the liver releases stored sugar into the bloodstream. Replenishment from body stores enables a person to continue functioning even after missing several meals. When the body stores are diminished to a certain point, however, the automatic homeostatic mechanisms are no longer adequate, and the entire organism becomes mobilized to seek food.

What internal signals tell the brain that the body's supply of nutrients is low and it must find food? The feelings most people describe as hunger—an empty

Behavior

identified the stimuli that are important for imprinting in birds and indicate that the phenomenon begins even before birth. Ducklings in the egg begin to make sounds a week before they break through their shells. Mallard mothers respond to these sounds and commence clucking signals, which increase in frequency about the time the duckling hatches. Auditory stimuli before and after hatching, together with tactile stimulation in the nest after birth, result in ducklings that are thoroughly imprinted on the female mallard present in the nest. An unhatched duckling that hears a recording of a human voice saying "Come, come, come," instead of its mother's voice, will imprint to a decoy that utters "Come, come, come" as easily as to a decoy that utters normal mallard clucks. Ducklings that have been exposed to a mallard female's call prior to hatching are more likely to imprint to decoys that utter mallard clucks (Hess, 1972).

Another concept developed by the ethologists is that of a *releaser*, a particular environmental stimulus that sets off a kind of behavior characteristic of a species. Thus, in some young seagulls, a red or yellow spot on the mother's beak "releases" a pecking response, causing the mother to regurgitate the food that the infant will eat. Varying the color and shape of the spot on cardboard models and observing whether or not the young gull pecks at it makes it possible to determine the characteristics of the releaser to which the bird responds.

The swollen abdomen of the female stickleback fish initiates courtship be-

Austrian ethologist Konrad Lorenz demonstrates how young ducklings follow him instead of their mother because he was the first moving object they saw when they were hatched.

havior by the male. Owl-like figures initiate mobbing behavior—a kind of feigned attack—by birds for which the owl is a natural enemy. The bowing and cooing behavior of the male ring dove releases the entire sequence of reproductive behavior in the female (nest-building, egg laying, and incubating the eggs) and is responsible, directly or indirectly, for the hormonal and anatomical changes that go along with these activities (Lehrman, 1964).

The higher one goes on the phylogenetic scale, the fewer the species-specific behaviors and the more learning determines the kinds of actions used to satisfy needs. But even humans have some built-in behavior patterns—for example, the rooting reflex of the human infant. Touching a nipple to the cheek of a newborn elicits head turning (both from side to side and up and down) with simultaneous opening of the mouth. If the mouth contacts the nipple, it closes on it and begins to suck. This behavior pattern is automatic and can occur even when the infant is sleeping. The rooting reflex disappears at about six months and voluntary motivated behavior takes over; the typical six-month old sees the bottle, reaches for it, and tries to bring it to his or her mouth.

---

or aching sensation in the stomach region sometimes accompanied by a feeling of weakness—give us some clues. But there are other physiological signals, as we shall see.

External stimuli can influence feelings of hunger and eating behavior. After a full meal, you may still desire the delicious dessert placed before you. In this case, your cue for hunger is not internal. The odor or sight of food can arouse hunger even when there is no physiological need.

Habits and social customs also influence eating behavior. You are accustomed to eating at certain times of day and may suddenly feel hungry when you notice that it is noon. You may consume more when having dinner with friends who are all eating voraciously than you would when dining alone.

Eating behavior is influenced by a number of physiological, environmental, and social variables. We will look first at the physiological mechanisms that regulate food intake and then consider environmental and social factors when discussing some of the current research on obesity.

Eating is influenced by social customs. Scene is the Great Hall of the People, Peking, on May Day eve.

Regulatory Centers in the Hypothalamus

Regulation of food intake is so crucial to survival that nature has provided several homeostatic controls. If one or more sensory signals associated with eating is eliminated—smell, or taste, or sensory information coming from the stomach—the organism is still able to regulate its food intake. The various control systems that regulate feeding are integrated in a region of the brain called the hypothalamus.

The hypothalamus, a small collection of cell nuclei located at the base of the brain (see Figure 2-6), has numerous connections with other brain parts and with the pituitary gland. It also has a greater density of blood vessels than any other area of the brain and thus is readily influenced by the chemical state of the blood.

The hypothalamus plays an important role in the regulation of food intake. Physicians have observed that patients with tumors or injury in the region of the hypothalamus overeat (a condition called *hyperphagia*) and become obese. The development of precise instruments for exploring the brain has made it possible for researchers to specify two areas that influence food intake: the *lateral hypothalamus* (LH) initiates eating—it is a "start," or "feeding center"; the *ventromedial hypothalamus* (VMH) inhibits eating—it is a "stop," or "satiety center."

One way to study the function of a specific brain area is to stimulate the spot with a weak electric current. Stimulation of LH cells causes a satiated animal to eat. Stimulation of VMH cells inhibits eating; a weak current slows the animal's feeding behavior, and a stronger current will stop it entirely (Hoebel and Teitelbaum, 1962).

Another way to study the function of a brain area is to destroy cells in the region and observe the animal's behavior when the area no longer exerts control. When cells in the LH are destroyed, the animal refuses to eat or drink and will die unless it is fed and watered artifically. Damage to cells in the VMH produces overeating and obesity in every species investigated—from rat and chicken to monkey and human (see Figure 10-2).

Studies of this sort demonstrate that the VMH area (satiety center) and the LH area (feeding center) act in opposite ways to regulate food intake. Moreover, two kinds of control systems appear to be integrated in the hypothalamus. One, responsive to the immediate nutritive needs of the organism, tells the brain when to start and stop a meal. A second, long-term control system, maintains a stable body weight over a period of time, regardless of how much the organism may or may not eat in any one meal.

SHORT-TERM CONTROL OF FOOD INTAKE Investigators have identified three variables that influence hypothalamic control of immediate appetite: blood-sugar level, stomach fullness, and body temperature. A low sugar or glucose level in the blood makes us feel weak and hungry. Injections of insulin (which lower the blood-sugar level) increase food intake; injections of glucose (which raise the blood-sugar level) inhibit eating.

Studies indicate that the hypothalamus contains "glucoreceptors," cells sensitive to the rate at which glucose passes through them. The glucoreceptors in the VMH and the LH respond differently to glucose level. For example, microelectrodes were implanted in the hypothalamus of dogs and cats to record neural activity in the VMH and LH before and after injections of glucose or insulin. After glucose injections, cells in the VMH (satiety center) became more active, whereas cells in the LH (feeding center) decreased in activity. The

Fig. 10-2 Hypothalamic overeating
Lesions in the ventromedial hypothalamus (VMH) caused this rat to overeat and gain more than three times its normal weight.

reverse was true after insulin injections. Cells monitored in other parts of the brain showed no changes (Anand and others, 1964; Oomura, 1975).[1]

But digestion is a slow process; we stop eating long before the food we have consumed can be transformed into enough blood sugar to make up a deficit in the bloodstream. A more immediate signal, a full stomach, lets the brain know that food is on its way. If food is injected directly into the stomach of a hungry animal (without passing through the mouth and throat), it eats much less than it would otherwise. If food is removed from a satiated animal's stomach (via a tube), the animal will eat enough to compensate for the loss. Experiments suggest that cells in the VMH respond to distention of the stomach to inhibit further eating (Deutsch and others, 1978).

An empty stomach produces the periodic contractions of muscles in the stomach wall that we identify as "hunger pangs." This increased movement of the stomach wall activates cells in the LH. Thus, an empty stomach signals the LH to initiate eating; a full stomach signals the VMH to stop eating.

A third short-term control mechanism is temperature. In a warm environment most animals and humans eat less than in a cold environment. Cooling the brain has a similar effect on food intake. The nature of these "thermo-receptors" is not clear, but evidence shows that the LH responds to decreased brain temperature and the VMH responds to increased brain temperature.

Thus, the LH responds to low blood-sugar level, increased motility of the stomach walls, and lowered brain temperature by initiating eating; conversely, the VMH responds to high blood-sugar level, stomach distension, and increased brain temperature by stopping eating. But all of these short-term mechanisms are subject to a long-term mechanism that attempts to stabilize body weight over time.

LONG-TERM CONTROL OF FOOD INTAKE Most wild animals maintain their weight at about the same level throughout their lifetime, even though food may be plentiful one week and scarce the next. Human beings have greater difficulty maintaining a constant weight, because their eating behavior is more strongly influenced by emotional and social factors. Even so, most people stay at about the same weight from year to year. In addition to its short-term controls of food intake, the hypothalamus appears to provide a delicate system for ensuring that the organism's weight remains stable.

We noted that rats with damage to the VMH overeat and become obese. Originally, this behavior was attributed to an increased appetite resulting from destruction of part of the short-term control system. But once the rat reaches a certain level of obesity (usually two or three times its normal weight), it no longer overeats. It reduces its food intake to only slightly more than normal and maintains its new obese weight. If the animal's diet is restricted, it will drop to its original normal weight. But once allowed to eat freely again, it will overeat as before until it is back to its obese state. It appears that damage to the VMH disturbs the animal's long-term weight control system, so that weight is regulated at a higher level.

If obese rats are force-fed, so that they become "super-obese," they reduce their food intake until their weight returns to its "normal-obese" level (see Figure 10-3). Some correlate of body weight must act on the VMH to influence

[1]Experiments suggest that the glucoreceptors respond to the rate at which glucose is being utilized, rather than to the absolute blood-sugar level. The rate of utilization is reflected by the ratio of blood sugar in the arteries to blood sugar in the veins. As time since eating increases, the blood-sugar level in the two types of vessels becomes more nearly equal. When the glucose difference between venous and arterial blood is small, subjects show stomach contractions and report that they are hungry. When the arteries contain considerably more sugar than the veins, subjects do neither (Mayer, 1955).

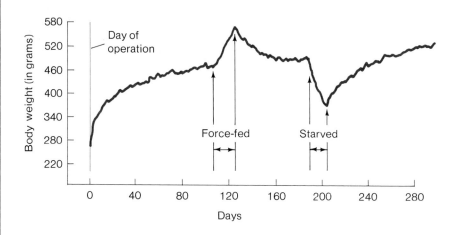

Fig. 10-3 Effects of forced feeding and starvation on body weight of rat with VMH lesions
Following VMH lesioning the rat overeats and gains weight until it stabilizes at a new, obese level. Forced feeding or starvation alters the weight only temporarily; the rat returns to its stabilized level. (After Hoebel and Teitelbaum, 1966)

food intake. Autopsies of animals with VMH lesions indicate that it may be the amount of free fatty acids in the bloodstream.

In contrast, rats with lesions in the LH refuse all food and water for some time after the operation and will die unless artificially fed. Most eventually resume eating and drinking on their own, but they stabilize at a new, lower weight level, just as VMH-damaged rats stabilize at a new, obese level (Mitchel and Keesey, 1974). Again, this behavior indicates impairment of a long-term weight control system rather than merely decreased appetite. Rats that are starved prior to LH lesioning (until their body weight is 80 percent of normal) do not refuse to eat after the operation. In fact, many overeat, but only until their weight reaches a new level—lower than their normal weight but higher than their starved, preoperational weight (see Figure 10-4).

These findings indicate that the VMH and LH have reciprocal effects on the "set point" for body weight. Damage to the VMH raises the set point; damage to the LH lowers it. If *both* areas are lesioned carefully so that an equivalent

Fig. 10-4 Body weight and the lateral hypothalamus
Prior to LH lesioning one group of rats was starved while the other was allowed to feed freely. Following surgery, the starved animals increase their food intake and gain weight; the freely fed group loses weight. Both groups stabilize at the same level. (After Powley and Keesey, 1970)

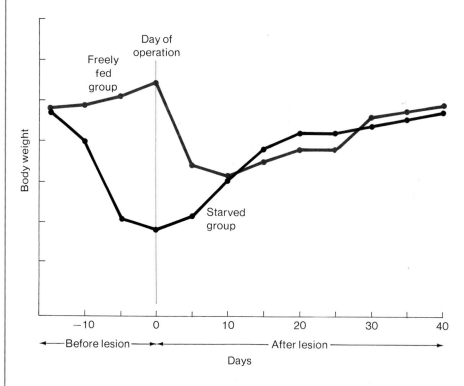

amount of tissue is destroyed, animals neither overeat nor undereat but maintain their presurgery weight level (Keesey and Powley, 1975).

We still do not know how the LH and VMH act reciprocally to maintain body weight. One possibility is that they influence, via stimulation of the autonomic nervous system, the amount of insulin secreted by the pancreas. As we noted earlier, insulin increases hunger by lowering the blood-sugar level. It is also the major hormone involved in the storage of fat. Animals with lesions in the VMH show an increased level of insulin in the blood.

Although the hypothalamus area is crucial for the control of eating, other brain regions are also involved (for example, the limbic system and certain nuclei in the brain stem where sensory nerves carrying information about taste and smell converge). Thus, the hypothalamus may be more accurately described as a critical link between the higher and lower brain areas concerned with eating behavior than as *the* area containing "centers" for feeding and satiety.

Other Variables Influencing Food Intake

TASTE AND SMELL   Taste and smell greatly affect our eating pleasures and food preferences. They also help us prepare for digestion and absorption. For example, the odor or first taste of a palatable food is sufficient to increase the flow of saliva, the secretion of insulin and digestive enzymes, and the movement of the muscles lining the stomach and intestines. The sight or even the thought of a delicious food can also trigger these same processes (Parra-Covarrubias and others, 1971; Moore and Schenkenberg, 1974). Some of these anticipatory responses can be very specific. For example, there are neurons in the lateral hypothalamus that are selectively affected by the sight of food; they fire rapidly when an animal sees its favorite food, less rapidly at the sight of mediocre meals, and not at all when unpalatable foods are presented (Rolls and others, 1976).

Although taste and smell are an important part of eating behavior, they are not essential to the regulation of food intake. In one experiment, rats were fitted with tubes that went through the nose to the stomach (see Figure 10-5). A liquid food passing through the tube bypassed the taste and smell receptors. The animals could control their food intake by pressing a lever that delivered a predetermined amount of liquid to the stomach for each press.

The rats tended to eat somewhat less under this regime, but they were still able to regulate their food intake. If the amount or composition of liquid food per bar press was changed, the animals adjusted their rate of bar-pressing to compensate for the change in caloric value. They were able to maintain a set intake of calories and a stable body weight without taste and olfactory cues (Epstein and Teitelbaum, 1962).

In contrast, food intake in rats with VMH lesions is markedly affected by the absence of taste and smell. When a rat with VMH lesions is fitted with the nasal tube (so that now with each bar press the liquid flows directly into the stomach instead of into a food cup), its food intake and body weight drop drastically. But if a drop of sweet saccharin solution is delivered to the animal's food cup at the same time that the liquid diet is delivered intragastrically, the rat will begin to increase its food intake and gain weight (McGinty and others, 1965).

Why is taste so important to the animal with VMH lesions? One possibility is that the impairment of its central control system forces it to rely on peripheral cues—taste and smell—to regulate food intake. Another hypothesis is that damage to the VMH may intensify the autonomic responses that are triggered by sensory contact with food (for example, secretion of saliva, insulin, and

Fig. 10-5 **Food regulation without taste or smell**
Even without the benefit of taste and olfactory cues, rats can regulate their food intake. A. The nasal tube bypasses the taste and smell receptors. B. By pressing the bar, the rat activates the pipetting machine (center) and delivers a liquid diet from the reservoir (left foreground) through the nasal tube directly into its own stomach.

digestive enzymes as well as motility of the digestive tract), thus making the animal especially sensitive to the taste and smell of food (Powley, 1977).[2]

SPECIFIC HUNGERS In addition to the need for a set amount of calories, both people and animals show *specific hungers,* strong preferences for certain foods. Most of our food preferences can be traced to ethnic or cultural difference. We like what we are accustomed to and may find a strange diet not only unpalatable but indigestible.

Sometimes, however, specific hungers result from nutritional deficits. When rats on a fat-free diet are offered a choice among fat, sugar, and wheat, they show a marked preference for fat. Similarly, rats deprived of either sugar or wheat will prefer the food they have been deprived of. What directs their behavior? Does the needed nutrient *taste* better than other foods? A series of experiments provides an explanation (Rozin and Kalat, 1971). Rats fed a diet deficient in thiamin (or calcium or magnesium) appear to develop an aversion to the deficient diet and will avidly accept a novel diet even though it may also be deficient. They continue rejecting old diets and accepting new ones until they find a diet that relieves the illness caused by the deficiency. Once a satisfactory diet has been accepted, the old diet remains aversive even though it has been supplemented with the missing element.

Learning also plays a role in aversions to certain foods. If a rat gets sick after eating a novel food, it will subsequently avoid any food that tastes like the novel one (Garcia, 1971). A similar response may be observed in young children. A child who gets stomach flu shortly after eating a pomegranate for the first time may subsequently have an aversion to pomegranates. Avoiding foods associated with illness would have important survival value for the organism and over many generations could become an inherited feature of a species' behavior.

Although most specific appetites and aversions are learned, some may be innate responses to certain tastes. Rats, for example, appear to have an innate preference for diets rich in salt, as do many hoofed animals, such as cattle and deer (Stricker and Wilson, 1970). Since salt is important in body fluid balance, this is a very useful innate appetite to have.

Obesity

Obesity is a major health problem, and millions of dollars are spent each year on special diets, drugs, or other treatments by those seeking to lose weight. Most people are not very successful in losing weight; and those who do succeed in shedding pounds almost invariably regain them. These problems have stimulated much research on the origin and control of obesity.

A popular view is that obesity stems from unresolved emotional problems—fat people were starved for love as children and food symbolizes "mother's love"; or, overeating is a substitute for other satisfactions lacking in the individual's life. While such explanations may be appropriate for some cases, most overweight people have backgrounds that are no more psychologically disturbed than those of normal-weight individuals. Fat people are often unhappy, but their distress is primarily a *result,* rather than a cause, of obesity. In a society where thinness is equated with beauty, overweight people

[2] These autonomic responses are presumably initiated by the LH and inhibited by the VMH; damage to the VMH would thus disinhibit, or exaggerate, the responses.

tend to be embarrassed by their appearance and ashamed of their supposed lack of control.

Research so far has failed to discover a single personality type that characterizes all obese people. Rather than focusing on the individual's personality or emotional background, current studies of obesity look at the situational factors that lead to overeating. What cues (both internal and external) prompt a person to eat? How do obese people differ in their responses to these cues?

Eating in Response to External Cues

The sight, aroma, and taste of food often affect how much we eat and when we eat. Research suggests that obese individuals may be more responsive to these food cues than people of normal weight. One study examined the effects of taste on eating behavior for groups of underweight and overweight subjects. The subjects were allowed to eat as much vanilla ice cream as they wanted and were then asked to rate its quality. Half of them were given a creamy, expensive vanilla; the other half were given cheap vanilla ice cream made somewhat bitter by the addition of quinine. Figure 10-6 plots the subjects' ratings against the amount eaten. When the ice cream is rated "very good," obese subjects eat the most. When it is rated "bad," skinny subjects eat more than obese subjects. Taste seems to be particularly important for overweight subjects.

In another study, obese and normal-weight individuals were allowed to have all they wanted of a nutritious but bland-tasting liquid diet. Over a period of three weeks, obese subjects gradually diminished their intake to an average of only 500 calories a day. Normal-weight subjects consumed slightly fewer calories initially, but thereafter returned to an average of 2,300 calories per day (Hashim and Van Itallie, 1965). Of course, the obese subjects were more motivated to lose weight than the normal subjects, but they had been unable to restrict their intake at home or on a clinic diet of regular food.

Obese individuals also seem to be particularly responsive to the sight of food. For example, when bright lights are focused on a dish of cashew nuts, they eat twice as many nuts as they do when the lights are dimmed. People of normal weight eat about the same number of nuts, regardless of how well they can see them (Ross, 1974). Even listening to a mouth-watering description of food prompts overweight individuals to eat far more than normal-weight individuals under the same conditions (Rodin, 1975). The evidence from these various studies indicates that the eating behavior of obese individuals seems to be very dependent on food cues.

Another external cue for eating is the passage of time. Most of us assume that when four to six hours have passed it is time for the next meal. Do obese people differ from those of normal weight in their eating response to temporal cues? How is eating behavior affected when apparent elapsed time differs from actual elapsed time?

In a laboratory study designed to answer these questions, two clocks were rigged so that one ran at half the normal speed and the other ran at about twice normal speed. The subjects were college students, half with an average weight 31 percent above normal and half whose weight averaged only 2 percent above normal. They were told that the study was an investigation of the relation between certain physiological measures (heart rate and GSR) and performance on psychological tests. Each subject arrived at the laboratory at 5:00 P.M. The experimenter removed the subject's watch so electrodes could be placed on his or her wrist and left the subject alone in a windowless room containing only the recording equipment and either a fast or slow clock. When the experimenter returned to the room 30 minutes later (at 5:30), the slow clock read 5:20; the

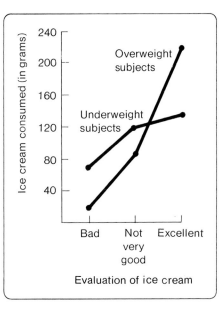

Fig. 10-6 Taste and obesity
The effects of food quality on amount eaten by overweight and underweight subjects. The subjects rated the quality of the ice cream and could eat as much as they desired. (After Nisbett, 1968b)

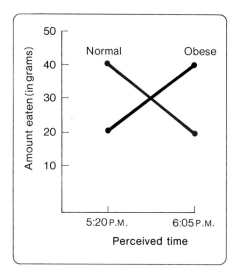
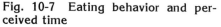

Fig. 10-7 Eating behavior and perceived time
Actual time for all groups is 5:35. Obese subjects consume more when they believe it is close to suppertime, while normal subjects eat less. (After Schachter and Gross, 1968)

fast one read 6:05. The experimenter was nibbling from a box of crackers. He put the box down, inviting the subject to have some. He then left the subject alone with the box of crackers to complete a self-administered personality test. The only datum actually recorded was the weight of the box of crackers before and after the subject had a chance to eat from it.

Figure 10-7 shows the amount of crackers eaten by obese and normal subjects for each time condition. The eating behavior of both the obese and normal subjects is affected by time cues, but in opposite directions; the obese individuals who thought it was 6:05, and time to eat, ate significantly more than those who thought it was 5:20, and not yet dinner time. The normal subjects either did not increase their intake when they believed it was 6:05 or actually ate less because they did not want to spoil their dinner. Again, we see that for obese individuals, eating is very much influenced by external cues.

Eating in Response to Internal Cues

Overweight individuals often report that they tend to eat more when they are tense or anxious. And experiments suggest that this is true. For example, obese subjects ate more cookies in a situation where they were made to feel quite anxious than they did in a low-anxiety situation. Normal-weight subjects ate more in the low-anxiety situation (McKenna, 1972).

Any kind of emotional arousal seems to increase food intake for some obese people. In one study, overweight and normal-weight subjects saw four films at four different sessions. Three of the films aroused various emotions: one was distressing, one amusing, and one sexually arousing. The fourth film was a boring travelogue. After viewing the films, the subjects were asked to evaluate different kinds of crackers. The obese subjects ate significantly more crackers after viewing any of the arousing films than after seeing the travelogue. Normal weight individuals ate the same amount, regardless of which film they had seen (White, 1977).

The tendency of obese people to eat more when emotionally aroused suggests the possibility that they may be less sensitive to the internal cues of hunger than are persons of normal weight. They may be unable to discriminate between hunger and other states of physiological arousal; thus, they may eat whenever they are tense, anxious, excited, *or* hungry.

To investigate this hypothesis, several studies have been made of the frequency with which obese and nonobese individuals associate feelings of hunger with stomach contractions. The subjects come to the laboratory without having had breakfast. Each subject swallows a gastric balloon attached to a recording device. By inflating the balloon with air so that it touches the stomach walls, it is possible to record gastric movements continuously. The subject is asked periodically to report feelings of hunger. If stomach pangs are a clear cue for hunger, then the subjects' self-reports of hunger should coincide with the recorded stomach contractions.

Initial studies reported that normal-weight subjects associated feelings of hunger with stomach contractions much more often than obese subjects—thus supporting the hypothesis that obese individuals are less sensitive to internal hunger cues (e.g., Stunkard, 1959; Stunkard and Koch, 1964). However, recent studies using more sensitive measuring instruments and more refined methods of self-reporting found that only a minority of either obese *or* normal subjects showed a strong association between stomach contractions and intensity of hunger. Most of us, whether fat or thin, are not very good at interpreting what our stomach tells us (Stunkard and Fox, 1971).

Interestingly, although obese people could easily be trained to recognize when their stomach was contracting, this new-found ability had no effect on their food intake. Current research is focusing on internal cues of satiety (for example, stomach fullness and rate at which the stomach empties), since these may be the signals to which obese people fail to respond.

Restrained and Unrestrained Eaters

The studies we have examined suggest that obese people tend to be more responsive than normal-weight individuals to such external cues as mealtime and the sensations aroused by food. They are also more apt to eat when emotionally aroused. But one variable we have not considered is that overweight individuals are more likely to be *dieting* than thin or normal-weight individuals. Some of their responsiveness to external cues may stem from the fact that they are dieting. People who are hungry all the time might be expected to pay more attention to food.

To test this possibility, a questionnaire was developed that asked about diet and weight history (for example, "How often are you dieting?" or "What is the maximum amount of weight that you have ever lost in a month?") as well as concern with food and eating (for example, "Do you eat sensibly before others, and make up for it alone?" or "Do you have feelings of guilt after overeating?").

The results showed that almost everyone—thin, plump, or fat—could be classified into two types: those who consciously restrain their eating and those who do not (Herman and Polivy, 1975). In addition, no matter what their actual weight, "restrained eaters" behave more like obese individuals than "unrestrained eaters." For example, if normal-weight subjects are placed in an anxiety-producing situation, those who are classed as restrained tend to increase their food intake (like the obese), whereas the unrestrained eaters tend to eat less.

The control of the dieter is fairly tenuous, however, and is vulnerable to many external influences—as anyone who has repeatedly broken a diet knows. Dieting may actually increase the chances of overeating. In one study, restrained and unrestrained eaters (of normal weight) were required to drink one or two milkshakes or none. They then sampled several flavors of ice cream and were encouraged to eat as much as they wanted. The more milkshakes the unrestrained eaters drank, the less ice cream they consumed later. The restrained eaters, in contrast, ate *more* ice cream after they had drunk two milkshakes than after one or none. Apparently, once the restrained group had overeaten, their control broke down completely (Herman and Mack, 1975).

A similar experiment with thin, normal, and obese subjects found that dieting was a more critical factor in predicting eating behavior than weight. The three weight groups did not differ significantly in the amount of ice cream they ate after drinking two milkshakes or none. But when the data were analyzed for restrained versus unrestrained eaters regardless of weight, the differences were highly significant (see Figure 10-8). Nondieters (unrestrained subjects) ate much less after two milkshakes than after none, while dieters (restrained subjects) ate more.

These studies indicate that dieting can account for some of the behavioral differences observed between obese and normal-weight individuals. In fact, some people who are extremely obese (400 to 500 pounds) behave like normal-weight individuals (for example, they are no more responsive to food cues or apt to overeat on a full stomach than those of normal weight). Presumably they have given up any attempt to control their weight.

Obesity is clearly a complex problem, involving many variables that may

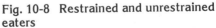

Fig. 10-8 Restrained and unrestrained eaters
Subjects who are concerned with dieting consume more ice cream after having previously overindulged in milkshakes than those who are unconcerned about controlling their food intake, regardless of body weight. (After Hibscher and Herman, 1977)

Are Some People Naturally Fat?

Obesity runs in families; fat parents tend to have fat children. Yet, except for a few cases that are clearly the result of hormone disorders, no physiological cause has been determined that predisposes people to obesity. However, the eating patterns of obese individuals and rats with VMH lesions are remarkably similar. Both eat more at a given meal and more rapidly than normal organisms, and both are highly responsive to food tastes. These similarities have led to the speculation that the hypothalamus of obese individuals sets a higher than normal base line for fat tissue; these individuals are "biologically programmed to be fat" (Nisbett, 1972).

Body fat is stored in special fat cells called *adipocytes*. Obese individuals differ from nonobese individuals both in *size* and in *number* of these fat cells—but principally in the number of fat cells. In one sample, obese subjects were found to have three times as many fat cells as normal subjects (Knittle and Hirsch, 1968). This is an important finding, because the number of fat cells an individual has is set at an early age and remains relatively fixed throughout life. Overeating increases the size of a person's fat cells but not their number (Sims and others, 1968); in turn, starvation decreases the size of fat cells, not the number (Hirsch and Knittle, 1970). After weight loss, formerly obese individuals have the same number of fat cells to be filled up again once they start overeating. The individual with a large number of fat cells has a *higher base line* of body fat than the individual with fewer fat cells.

Heredity and early nutrition both probably play a role in determining the number of fat cells, but the causal relationship is not clear. Some researchers believe that a person's fat-cell count is genetically fixed at birth. Others think that the number of cells is determined by nutrition during the early months of life; overfeeding an infant may stimulate the development of fat cells. A related possibility is that some infants may be born with a tendency to be particularly responsive to food cues; they may eat more and develop more fat cells than less externally responsive infants. In any event, evidence indicates that the individual's base line of body fat is pretty well set by two years of age (Knittle, 1975). It is this base line that the hypothalamic centers maintain by regulating food intake to keep fat stores at a certain set point, or level.

We have seen that rats with damage to the VMH (satiety center) regulate their weight at a new, higher level, whereas rats with lesions in the LH (the feeding center) regulate their weight at a new, lower level. It is possible, then, that the set point for an obese individual is different from that for a nonobese person of the same height and bone structure. If this is true, then obesity for some individuals is their "normal" weight, which their hypothalamus tries to maintain. Attempts at weight reduction for such individuals would hold them below their biologically determined normal weight and would leave them in a state of energy deficit, feeling hungry all the time—just the same as a thin person who is on a starvation diet.

This theory is interesting but controversial. Some researchers question, for example, whether the responsiveness of obese people to food cues stems from the fact that they are "starving." They suggest that external responsiveness is a major *cause* of obesity, not the reverse (Rodin and Slochower, 1976).

Obesity results from consuming more calories than the body utilizes. A higher than normal set point for fat tissue may be one reason for overconsumption, but there are undoubtedly many others. Most overweight people, unlike the VMH-damaged rats, do not become suddenly obese. Their fat accumulates over a period of months or years—a kind of "creeping obesity" that results from gradually consuming more calories than the body expends in energy.

Under normal conditions, the physiological mechanisms that balance food intake and energy expenditure to keep weight stable function with remarkable precision. Body weight for most people does not vary more than two or three pounds from year to year, despite the fact that activity level and food intake vary widely from day to day. When you consider that an excess of intake over energy expended of only 100 calories a day would add 10 pounds in a year, this stability is remarkable. But research indicates that under conditions of extreme inactivity the hunger-satiety control mechanism fails to operate properly (Thomas and Mayer, 1973). Thus, people with sedentary jobs may not get enough exercise to keep their weight-control mechanism functioning.

differ from individual to individual. People who are particularly sensitive to food cues or who have developed the habit of eating in response to anxiety may gain weight. Once they are overweight there are additional problems. Some are metabolic: overweight people tend to secrete more insulin than is normal, and insulin enhances fat storage as well as increases appetite. Some are emotional: anxiety and distress over one's appearance may make it even harder to keep from eating. And others may be caused by the stress of dieting.

Thirst

In order to survive, organisms must regulate their water as well as food intake. We can go without food for weeks, but we cannot live without water for more than a few days.

An organism can replenish its water deficit in two ways: by drinking and by recovering water from the kidneys before it is excreted as urine. A water deficit motivates the organism to drink. It also sets off a homeostatic mechanism by stimulating the release of the antidiuretic hormone (ADH) from the pituitary gland. ADH acts on the kidneys so that water is reabsorbed into the blood stream and only very concentrated urine is formed. After a night's sleep you may notice that your urine has a darker color and stronger odor than at other times of the day. The body has recovered water from the kidneys to compensate for the fact that you have not consumed fluids while sleeping. This homeostatic mechanism can maintain the body's water balance only up to a certain point. When the water deficit is too great, thirst becomes intense and the organism is impelled to find water. What signals the organism that the body needs water?

Peripheral Cues

Most people describe thirst as dryness in the mouth and throat. But they are aware, too, that they continue drinking long after the mouth and throat have been wetted by the first swallow. Sucking on a piece of ice may provide some relief from thirst, but not for long.

To find out what role receptors in the mouth and throat play in the regulation of water intake, dogs were fitted with a plastic tube leading from the esophagus to outside the body. They could drink normally, but the water never reached the stomach. Thirsty dogs equipped with this esophagus-bypass drank their usual amount of water and then stopped, apparently satisfied by fluid that never reached the stomach. After about 10 minutes, however, they began to drink again, and they consumed the same amount of water. This cycle continued, with the dogs gradually increasing their intake as the water deficit in the body built up (Adolph, 1941).

These results show that receptors in the mouth and throat must somehow measure water intake, because the animal stops drinking after swallowing its usual amount. After a few minutes, however, the animal begins to drink again—even though sufficient water entered the mouth—indicating that there must be additional signals regulating water intake.

What happens if water is placed directly into a thirsty dog's stomach via a tube, without passing through the mouth and throat? If the dog is allowed immediate access to water, it will drink the usual amount. If there is a 5-, 10-, or 15-minute delay, the amount consumed decreases as the delay increases. After a 20-minute interval the dog does not drink at all (Adolph, 1941). These results indicate that a certain amount of water must be absorbed through the stomach wall into the bloodstream before the mechanism that responds to water intake is activated.

Hypothalamic Regulation of Water Intake

Water deficit produces two changes in the blood and fluids surrounding the body cells: (1) it decreases their volume, and (2) it increases the concentration of certain chemicals, primarily sodium. When the body fluids surrounding tissue cells become too concentrated, water passes out of the cells by osmosis, leaving them dehydrated. Current theories postulate that two brain mechanisms control water intake: *osmoreceptors*, which are sensitive to the chemical concentration of the body fluids, and *volumetric receptors*, which respond to the total volume of body fluids.

OSMORECEPTORS Although cellular dehydration occurs in all body cells, certain nerve cells in the hypothalamus, osmoreceptors, respond specifically to dehydration. These cells become slightly deformed or shriveled, and it is probably this mechanical change that triggers neural activity. The osmoreceptors are located in the hypothalamus just above the pituitary gland, and they stimulate the release of ADH from the pituitary. This hormone signals the kidneys to reabsorb water from urine into the bloodstream, where it dilutes the chemical concentration of the blood and body fluids.

Dehydration of the osmoreceptors can be produced by depriving the organism of water or by injecting a salt solution directly into the brain. Even a minute amount of salt solution injected into the preoptic region of a goat's hypothalamus will cause the animal to drink several gallons of water (Anderson, 1971). A thirsty animal prefers a drink of cool water, but other fluids are accepted, provided they are not more concentrated than normal body fluids. Lemonade is an acceptable thirst quencher; salty bouillon is not.

VOLUMETRIC RECEPTORS Loss of blood volume produces thirst even in the absence of cellular dehydration. An injured person who has lost a lot of blood is intensely thirsty, although the concentration of the remaining blood is unchanged. An individual engaged in vigorous activity loses salt through perspiration but still has the urge to drink a lot of water—which dilutes the salt concentration of the blood even further. There must be receptors sensitive to the total volume of blood and body fluids, regardless of their concentration.

Evidence indicates that *renin* (a substance secreted by the kidneys into the bloodstream) is the cue for drinking in response to decreased volume of blood and body fluid. Renin causes the blood vessels to constrict, a homeostatic device to defend against further blood loss. It also acts as an enzyme on one of the blood proteins (*angiotensinogen*), converting it to *angiotensin I.* As blood passes through the lungs, angiotensin I is converted to angiotensin II, which acts on specific receptors in the hypothalamus to produce thirst. If angiotensin II is injected directly into the hypothalamus of rats, they drink copious amounts of water.

Thus, two physiological states stimulate the hypothalamus to elicit drinking: cellular dehydration and decreased blood volume (see Figure 10-9). Cellular dehydration acts directly on the hypothalamus to start the organism drinking and to stimulate the release of ADH from the pituitary, which tells the kidneys to reabsorb water into the bloodstream. Decreased blood volume causes the kidneys to secrete renin, which releases the hormone angiotensin in the bloodstream; when angiotensin reaches the hypothalamus, it stimulates drinking.

When the body fluids become too concentrated, the brain signals the kidneys to retrieve water from the urine and send it back into the bloodstream; when the blood volume is low, the kidneys signal the brain to start the organism drinking. In both instances a hormone carries the message.

It is not certain what neural mechanisms tell the organism to stop drinking. Cellular hydration, the reverse of dehydration, cannot be the main stimulus for

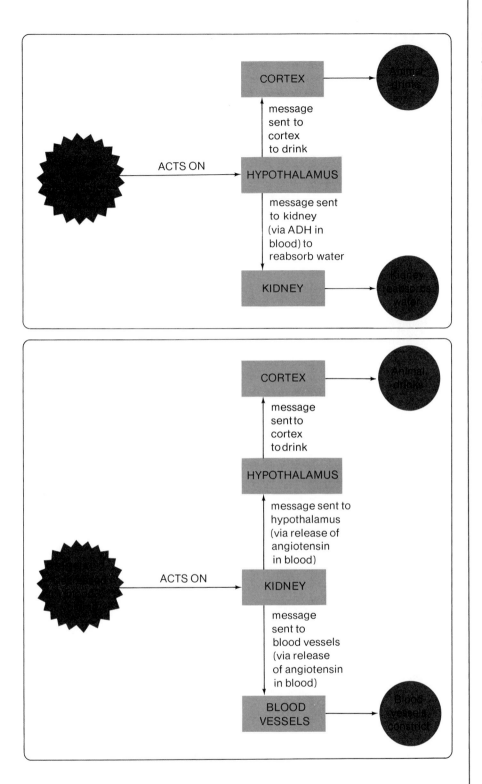

Fig. 10-9 Control mechanisms for regulation of water intake
The upper panel shows the effect of cellular dehydration on the hypothalamus. The lower panel shows the effect of decreased blood volume on the kidney and its indirect action on the hypothalamus.

thirst satiation, because the organism stops drinking long before fluid has time to enter the cells in any significant amount. Signals from the mouth, as it meters the amount of incoming water, and from the stomach, as it is distended by water, may operate to depress the activity of the hypothalamic cells responsible for drinking. But the exact process is far from clear.

THIRST

Research on thirst mechanisms is complicated by the fact that in some animals (such as the rat) the hypothalamic areas for eating and drinking overlap. Areas outside of the hypothalamus are also involved in drinking, particularly the limbic system. Regulation of water intake may involve a complex neural integration of several brain areas.

Sex

Sex, another powerful motivator, differs in many respects from hunger and thirst. Sex is not vital to the survival of the organism, as are food and water, but it is essential to the survival of the species. Eating and drinking reduce tissue deficits. With sex, however, there is no deficit, and sexual behavior uses energy rather than restores it. Freud proposed that sexual energy, or *libido*, builds up within the organism and must find some outlet. But there is no physiological evidence to suggest a buildup of some substance that is reduced by sexual activity.

Sexual behavior depends on a combination of internal factors (hormones and brain mechanisms) and external ones (learned and unlearned environmental stimuli). We will look first at the internal, or physiological, variables and then discuss the function of external variables.

Physiological Basis of Sexual Behavior

The hormones responsible for development and functioning of the reproductive organs are controlled by the pituitary gland. Pituitary hormones in the female stimulate the ovaries to manufacture the sex hormones, *estrogen* and *progesterone.* In the male, pituitary hormones stimulate the cells of the testes to manufacture and secrete a group of sex hormones called *androgens,* the most important being *testosterone.* The marked increase of these hormones at puberty produces changes in the primary and secondary sex characteristics during adolescence (see Chapter 3).

The degree of hormonal control over sexual behavior decreases as we go from lower to higher vertebrates. Castration (removal of the testes) in the adult male rat or guinea pig produces a rapid decline and disappearance of sexual activity. In male dogs, castration results in a more gradual decline, although some dogs with considerable sexual experience prior to castration do not decrease their sexual activity (Goldstein, 1957). Most male primates show little or no decline in sexual activity following castration. In human males, the reaction to castration is complicated by emotional and social factors. But most studies show little or no diminution of sexual motivation. Castration of any male organism before puberty, however, usually prevents copulation, although injections of testosterone can frequently restore sexual activity.

In contrast, castration in a female (removal of the ovaries) usually results in complete cessation of sexual activity for all animals from reptiles to monkeys. The castrated female immediately ceases to be receptive to the male and may vigorously resist any sexual advances (Grossman, 1967). The only exception is the human female; although in some women there may be decreased interest in sex following menopause, most reports indicate that sexual motivation is not diminished by the cessation of ovarian functioning. In fact, some women show an increased interest in sex after menopause, possibly because they no longer need be concerned about pregnancy.

Secretion of sex hormones is fairly constant in the male of most species, so that the level of sexual motivation is relatively stable. In the female, however, hormones fluctuate cyclically with accompanying changes in fertility. During the first part of the cycle, while the egg is being prepared for fertilization, the ovaries secrete estrogen, which prepares the uterus for implantation and also tends to arouse sexual interest. After ovulation occurs, both progesterone and estrogen are secreted. Progesterone prepares the mammary glands for nursing and is related to maternal behavior.

The fertility, or *estrous*, cycle (which varies from 36 days in the chimpanzee to 28 days in the human female to 5 days in the mouse) is accompanied by a consequent variation in sexual motivation in most species. Most female animals are receptive to sexual advances by a male only during the period of ovulation, when the estrogen level is at a maximum (when they are "in heat"). Among primates, however, sexual activity is less influenced by the estrous cycle; monkey, ape, and chimp females copulate during all phases of the cycle, although ovulation is still the period of most intense sexual activity. In the human female, sexual activity is more strongly influenced by social and emotional factors than by hormones.

Although hormones influence sexual motivation, they do not *elicit* specific patterns of sexual behavior. Rather, they produce a *state of readiness* to respond appropriately to certain classes of stimuli. Administration of hormones of the opposite sex has been shown to reverse sexual response patterns in a number of different species. Female dogs given testosterone show mounting behavior; male rats given estrogen show the typical female response pattern. But often the administration of hormones of the opposite sex produces *bisexual* behavior; the direction of the behavior is largely controlled by environmental stimuli. Female rats treated with male hormones will show male sexual behavior in the presence of normal females but will revert to the female pattern when confronted with a sexually aggressive male. Similarly, estrogen-treated males will adjust their sex role in accordance with the sex of their partner (Beach, 1941; Cole and others, 1956). Hormones prime the animal to act, but its behavior is largely determined by environmental stimuli.

SEXUAL DIFFERENTIATION In addition to influencing adult sexual behavior, hormones are even more important in determining our prenatal development as male or female. Until a human embryo is between two to three months old, only the cell chromosomes indicate whether it will be a boy or a girl. Until this stage, both sexes are identical in appearance. For example, each has tissues that will eventually develop into testes or ovaries, and each has a genital tubercle that will become either a penis or clitoris.

Initial development is governed by a primitive sex gland (gonad). If the embryo is genetically male (XY), the primitive gland develops into testes; if it is genetically female (XX), ovaries will develop. Thus, the first step in sexual differentiation is genetically controlled. But once either testes or ovaries develop, they produce the hormones that determine further development of the internal reproductive structures and the external genitals.

The basic blueprint appears to be female. If the embryonic sex glands do not produce enough male hormones (androgens), then the newborn will have female genitals even though it is genetically a male (XY). The anatomical development of the female fetus apparently does not require female hormones—only the absence of male hormones.

In rare instances, when the hormone balance goes awry during pregnancy, the fetal reproductive system may fail to reach complete development as either male or female. Infants may be born with genitals that are ambiguous-looking (for example, the external organ could be described as either a very large clitoris or a very small penis) or are in conflict with the internal sex glands (for example, ovaries and a penis). Such individuals are called *hermaphrodites*.[3] Their development provides some interesting information about the relative importance of biology and environment in determining sexual behavior.

In most cases where a hermaphroditic infant is given the wrong sex label at birth—for example, an infant whose external genitalia are ambiguous is called a boy but is later determined to be genetically female (XX) and to have ovaries—the sex assigned to the individual and the sex role in which he or she is raised has a much greater influence on behavior than genes and hormones. For example, two genetically female infants had ambiguous-looking external genitals because their fetal sex glands had produced too much androgen. This metabolic error occurred too late in fetal development to affect the internal organs (they both had ovaries) but in time to change the appearance of the genitals. Both infants had surgery to correct their enlarged clitoris. In one case, the infant's genitals were "feminized," and she was raised as a girl. The other infant's genitals were modified to resemble a penis, and he was raised as a boy. Reports indicate that both children grew up secure in their respective sex roles. The girl was somewhat "tomboyish" but appeared attractively feminine. The boy was accepted as male by his peers and expressed a romantic interest in girls. Similar cases of matched pairs of hermaphrodites suggest that one's sexual identification depends more on the way a person is labeled and raised than on hormones (Money and Ehrhardt, 1972).

NEURAL MECHANISMS Neural control of sexual behavior is complex, and the mechanisms that influence sexual behavior vary considerably among different species. Some of the basic reflexes (such as erection, pelvic movements, and ejaculation in the male) are controlled at the level of the spinal cord and do not require control by the brain. Men whose spinal cord has been severed from the brain by injury (paraplegics) are still capable of these movements. Much of the regulation of sexual arousal and behavior takes place in the hypothalamus, although the exact area varies across species. Electrical stimulation of the posterior hypothalamus of the rat produces not only copulation but the entire repertoire of sexual behavior. Male rats stimulated in that area do not mount indiscriminately but court the female by nibbling her ears and nipping the back of her neck until she responds. Intromission and ejaculation follow unless the electrical stimulation is terminated. Even a sexually satiated male rat will respond to stimulation by pressing a bar to open the door leading to the female, courting and mating her (Caggiula and Hoebel, 1966).

The rat's behavior can be controlled very specifically by implanting electrodes in both the lateral hypothalamus and the posterior hypothalamus and switching the current from one electrode to the other. With both food and a female available, the animal begins to copulate during posterior stimulation; when current is switched to the lateral electrode, it abandons the female and begins to eat. Resumption of posterior hypothalamic stimulation causes it to interrupt the meal and return to the female (Caggiula, 1967).

Such automatic determination of behavior does not occur with higher mammals. The cerebral cortex exerts control over sexual arousal and behavior, and the farther up on the phylogenetic scale, the greater this control.

---

[3]True hermaphrodites (which are quite rare) have one ovary and one testicle, or a single organ containing both types of tissue. A pseudo-hermaphrodite has only one set of gonads (testes or ovaries), but its external genitals are either ambiguous-looking or in actual conflict with its internal system. The term "hermaphrodite," however, is often used to refer to both kinds.

Role of Experience

Experience has little influence on patterns of mating behavior in the lower mammals. Inexperienced rats will copulate as efficiently as experienced rats. The behavior patterns are fairly specific and appear to be innate. As we go from the lower to higher mammals, however, experience and learning play increasingly important roles in sexual behavior.

Young monkeys raised together show in their play with each other many of the postures necessary for later copulation. In wrestling with their peers, infant male monkeys display hindquarter grasping and thrusting responses that are components of the adult sexual pattern. Infant female monkeys retreat when threatened by an aggressive male infant and stand steadfastly in a posture similar to the stance later required to support the weight of the male during copulation. These presexual responses appear as early as 60 days of age and become more frequent and refined as the monkeys mature. (See Figure 10-10). Their early appearance suggests that they are innate responses to specific stimuli; the modification and refinement that occurs with experience indicates the role of learning in the development of the adult sexual pattern.

A

B

C

D

Fig. 10-10 Infant play and adult sexual behavior
A. The first presexual step. B. Basic sexual posture. C. Inappropriate sexual response: male correct, female incorrect. D. Inappropriate sexual response: female correct, male incorrect.

Monkeys raised in partial isolation—in separate wire cages where they can see other monkeys but have no contact with them—are usually unable to copulate at maturity. The male monkeys are able to perform the mechanics of sex: they masturbate to ejaculation at about the same frequency as normal monkeys. But when confronted with a sexually receptive female, they do not seem to know how to go about the heterosexual procedure. They are aroused but aimlessly grope the female or their own bodies (Harlow, 1971).

Monkeys raised without peer contact are usually atypical in all of their social reactions, not just their sexual responses. As adults they are unable to relate to other monkeys, showing either fear and flight or extreme aggression. Harlow (1971) suggests that normal heterosexual behavior in primates depends on (1) the development of specific sexual responses, such as grasping the female and pelvic thrusting, (2) the influence of hormones, and (3) an affectional bond between two members of the opposite sex. The affectional bond is an outgrowth of interactions with the mother and with peers. Through these interactions the young monkey learns trust—it can expose its more delicate parts without fear of harm; it learns to accept and enjoy physical contact with another monkey; it develops the behavior pattern characteristic of its sex; and it becomes motivated to seek the company of other monkeys.

Although we cannot extend these findings with monkeys to explain sexual development in humans, nor can we perform isolation experiments with human infants, clinical observation suggests certain parallels. Human infants first develop their feelings of trust and affection through a warm and loving relationship with the mother. (See Chapter 3 for a discussion of Erikson's concept of psychosocial stages and the development of basic trust.) This basic trust is necessary for satisfactory interactions with one's peers. And affectionate relationships with other youngsters of both sexes, prior to and during adolescence, lay the groundwork for the intimacy required for heterosexual relationships among young adults.

CULTURAL INFLUENCES   In contrast with other primates, human sexual behavior is strongly determined by cultural influences. Every society places some restrictions on sexual behavior. Incest (sexual relations within the immediate family) is prohibited by almost all cultures. Other aspects of sexual behavior—sexual activities among children, homosexuality, masturbation, and premarital sex—are tolerated in varying degrees by different societies. Among preliterate cultures studied by anthropologists, the amount and type of acceptable sexual activity vary widely. Some very permissive societies encourage autoerotic activities and sex play among children of both sexes. They may be instructed in sex or allowed to observe adult sexual activity. The Chewa of Africa, for example, believe that unless children exercise themselves sexually they will be unable to produce offspring later.

In contrast, very restrictive societies try to control preadolescent sexual behavior and keep children from learning about sexual matters. The Cuna of South America believe that children should be totally ignorant of sex until they are married; for example, they are not permitted to watch animals give birth. And among the Ashanti of Africa, intercourse with a girl who has not undergone the puberty ceremony is punishable by death for both participants. Similar extremes are found in attitudes toward other aspects of sexual behavior; homosexuality, for example, is viewed by some nonliterate societies as an essential part of growing up and by others as an offense punishable by death (Ford and Beach, 1951).

Until recently, the United States and most other western countries would

CHAPTER 10/BASIC DRIVES AND MOTIVES

AGE	UNDER 25	25–34	35–44	45–54	OVER 55
Males	95	92	86	89	84
Females	81	65	41	36	31

Source: Hunt (1974)

TABLE 10-1
Percentage of married individuals who have had premarital sexual intercourse Based on a national survey of 1,400 individuals. *Age* refers to the individual's age at the time of the survey, not the age at which premarital sex occurred.

have been classified as restrictive societies. Traditionally, western society has tried to ignore or deny the existence of prepubertal sexuality and has considered marital sex the only legitimate sexual outlet. Other forms of sexual expression—homosexual activities, oral-genital contacts, premarital and extramarital sex—have been generally condemned and in many instances prohibited by law. Of course, many members of these societies engaged in such activities, but often with some feelings of shame.

Attitudes toward many sexual activities are much more permissive today than they were 30 years ago. Premarital sex, for example, is more acceptable and engaged in more frequently than in the past. Among college-educated individuals interviewed in the 1940s, 27 percent of the women and 49 percent of the men had had premarital sexual intercourse by the age of 21 (Kinsey and others, 1948, 1953). Several surveys of college students in the 1970s report considerably higher incidences, ranging from 43 to 56 percent for females and from 58 to 82 percent for males (Packard, 1970; Hunt, 1974).

The change in attitude toward premarital sex has been greatest for women. Table 10-1 shows the results of a survey of premarital experience among married individuals of different ages. The difference between women born before 1918 and those born after 1948 is striking.

Although more and more women are engaging in premarital sex, men and women still differ in their attitudes. The majority of women who engage in sex before marriage do so with only one or two partners with whom they are emotionally involved. And a study of college women suggests that they do so more to please their boyfriends and preserve the romantic relationship than because they enjoy sexual intercourse—at least that's what they tell the interviewers (Bardwick, 1971). Men, in contrast, are more likely to seek casual sex without emotional involvement; in one survey the median number of premarital partners reported by males was six (Hunt, 1974).

When college students were asked to list problems they had with "any aspect of sexual functioning," the concerns of males and females were found to be quite different. Women most often expressed fears and insecurities:

Fear of pregnancy
Fear of rape
Being conquered and of no further use
Being rejected if one says no
Masturbation—accepting it
Fear that one's partner is physically repulsed by you
Fear of loss of self-respect
Fear of becoming too attached when the feeling is not mutual
Guilt feelings about premarital sex
Pressure to have sex even when one doesn't want to
Fear of not satisfying one's partner
Embarrassment or concern over not being orgasmic

Men were more apt to list complaints about women rather than to express their own conflicts or worries:

Finding a partner who is open to varying sexual experiences
Having to be always on the hunt
Not being able to have sexual relations when one wants to
Women who tease, without wanting to engage in sexual activity
Women's refusal to take responsibility for their own sexuality
Women who use their sexual attractiveness in a manipulatory fashion
The excessive modesty of women (they want the lights off)
Passive women
Aggressive women
Necessity to say you love the woman even if it isn't true
Being expected to know all about sex
Inability to communicate feelings or needs during the sex act
(Tavris and Offir, 1977, p. 68)

These response differences may reflect different attitudes, at least among those who are young and unmarried, about the relationship between sex and love. Women still tend to view sex as part of a loving relationship, while men more often consider sex and love as separate experiences (Tavris, 1973; Hunt, 1974).

Attitudes toward extramarital sex and such sexual behaviors as masturbation and oral-genital stimulation have also become much more permissive within the past 30 years. A comparison of data from Kinsey in the 1940s and Hunt in the 1970s illustrates this point. For example, the percentage of individuals reporting some experience with oral-genital foreplay before marriage is as follows:

	1940s	1970s
Fellatio	33%	72%
Cunnilingus	14	69

Homosexuality is also viewed with greater tolerance than it was 30 years ago, although there is no indication that the proportion of homosexual individuals is increasing. Thus we see that sexual behaviors are greatly influenced by the customs and values of society and may differ from time to time within the same society.

Homosexuality

The term *homosexual* can be applied to either a man or a woman, but female homosexuals are usually called *lesbians*. Most experts agree with Kinsey's view that homosexuality is not an "either-or matter": sexual behavior falls on a continuum, with those who are exclusively heterosexual or exclusively homosexual at either end and various mixtures of sexual behavior in between. Most young boys engage in erotic play with each other during childhood, and many men have one or more homosexual encounters later in life, although only about 4 percent become exclusively homosexual. Women are less apt than men to have sexual interactions with each other during childhood or a homosexual episode in later life, and only 1 to 2 percent are exclusively homosexual (Gebhard, 1972). Some individuals are bisexual, enjoying sexual relations with members of both sexes. And some who are married may have homosexual encounters on the side.

Until quite recently, homosexuality was considered a "mental illness" or an abnormal perversion. Although much of society still views homosexuality as unhealthy and unnatural, most psychologists consider it a deviation from the norm, rather than a perversion.

CAUSES OF HOMOSEXUALITY Much remains to be learned about the causes of homosexuality. No reliable physical differences have been found that distinguish homosexuals from heterosexuals. Although some male homosexuals may be quite feminine in appearance and some female homosexuals quite masculine, this is often not the case. There is some indication that male homosexuals have lower levels of the hormone testosterone and a lower sperm count than heterosexual males, but we cannot be certain that this is the cause of homosexuality. When male homosexuals are given additional hormones, their sex drive increases (as is true for heterosexual men), but their sexual preferences do not change.

Probably a number of psychological and social factors are involved in homosexuality that may differ from case to case. In some instances, the individual may have identified as a child with the parent of the opposite sex. A boy raised without a father or other adult male may identify with his mother and think of himself as female. This may also happen when the mother is the dominant force in her son's life while the father is ineffectual or aloof.

In other cases, a child may have little contact with children of the opposite sex. For example, a girl who goes to schools and camps that are exclusively female may have little experience with boys. Her first sexual experiences may be with girls; and if these are satisfying, she may continue to desire sexual contact with members of her own sex—particularly if her first contacts with boys are unsatisfactory.

Sometimes homosexuality may develop from more complex psychological factors, such as a traumatic sexual experience or early teachings about the sinfulness and dangers of sex. For example, a girl who is led to believe that all men are lustful creatures out to destroy her purity, may develop an aversion toward males. If she develops any sexual feelings at all, they may be homosexual.

Transsexualism

Transsexuals are people (usually males) who feel that they were born into the wrong body. They are not homosexuals in the usual sense. Most homosexuals are satisfied with their anatomy and think of themselves as appropriately male or female; they simply prefer members of their own sex. Transsexuals, in contrast, *think* of themselves as members of the opposite sex (often from early childhood) and may be so desperately unhappy with their appearance that they request hormonal and surgical treatment to change their genitals and secondary sex characteristics. Some 3,000 "sex-change" operations have been performed in the United States. For males, hormone treatments can enlarge the breasts, reduce beard growth, and make the figure more rounded. Surgical procedures involve removing the testes and part of the penis and shaping the remaining tissue into a vagina and labia. For women, hormone treatments can increase growth of a beard, firm the muscles, and deepen the voice. Breast tissue can be reduced surgically, the ovaries and uterus removed, and a penis-like organ is sometimes constructed. While "sex-change" operations do not change the person's genetic sex or make reproduction possible, they can produce a remarkable change in appearance.

Richard Raskind, a physician and former college tennis player (left) underwent a sex-change operation to become Renee Richards (right). Renee is now a professional tennis player successfully competing on the tennis circuit.

Because sex-change surgery is so drastic, it is undertaken only after very careful consideration. The individual is given counseling and required to live as a member of the opposite sex for a trial period prior to the operation.

What explains transsexualism? A study of the backgrounds of transsexual boys indicated that many of them were treated as girls from a very early age—for example, they were dressed in feminine clothes and encouraged in feminine behavior. Others lacked a male figure to identify with or other boys to play with (Green, 1974). An interesting speculation is that transsexualism, in some cases, may result from an error in prenatal hormones similar to that which produces hermaphrodites, but occurring at a later stage of fetal development—that is, after the external genitals were formed but before the brain had finished developing the mechanisms that influence male and female sexual behavior. The result might be an individual whose sense of sexual identity is out of phase with his or her physical sex (Bardwick, 1971). This theory is only speculation, however. It seems reasonable to assume that both biological and social factors play a role in transsexualism.

Other Basic Motives

Maternal Behavior

In many species, care of offspring is a more powerful determiner of behavior than hunger, thirst, or sex. For example, a mother rat will more frequently overcome barriers and suffer pain to reach her young than she will to obtain food when hungry or water when thirsty.

Maternal behavior among lower animals appears to depend on hormones as well as on stimulus conditions. Virgin rats presented with rat pups for about a week will begin to build a nest, lick the pups, retrieve them, and finally hover in a nursing posture. (Male rats will also, after sufficient exposure to pups.) If blood plasma from a mother rat that has just given birth is injected into a virgin rat, it will begin to show maternal behavior in less than a day (Rosenblatt, 1967, 1969; Terkel and Rosenblatt, 1972). Maternal behavior patterns appear to be innately programmed in the rat's brain, and hormones serve to increase the excitability of these neural mechanisms. The hormonal effects probably depend on the balance between the female hormones, estrogen and progesterone, as well as prolactin, which is involved in the production of milk.

Among primates, maternal behavior is largely influenced by experience and learning. Monkeys raised in isolation with cloth or wire mothers showed none of the normal maternal behavior when they first became mothers (see Chapter 3). With subsequent pregnancies, however, they became more effective mothers.

Although a "maternal instinct" has been posited as universal among human females, the evidence does not support this belief. Some women have been known to abandon their newborn infants or even kill them. And "battered children" are far more common than would be supposed. It is estimated that in the United States more than 700 children are killed by their parents each year, and an additional 40,000 are seriously beaten or tortured by parents, siblings, or relatives (Helfer and Kempe, 1968). The parents involved in these cases generally had received no love as children and frequently had been beaten by their own parents. There is a parallel here with the monkeys raised by artificial mothers who subsequently became inadequate mothers themselves. In primates and in humans, experience far overrides whatever influence "maternal hormones" may have.

Avoidance of Pain

The need to avoid tissue damage is essential to the survival of any organism. Even a weak pain stimulus may dominate other stimuli in controlling the direction of behavior. Pain will lead to any behavior that reduces discomfort—removing one's hand from a hot stove, taking off a shoe that pinches, swallowing an aspirin to relieve a headache.

Pain involves two processes. It is a sensory event (often resulting from tissue damage), and it is also a reaction of the central nervous system to the sensory message. The motivational aspects of pain depend on normal growth experiences. Dogs raised from birth with minimal sensory stimulation fail to show the normal avoidance reaction to painful stimuli; they do not respond to being pricked with a pin or having their tails stepped on and will repeatedly investigate a lighted match by putting their nose into the flame (Scott, 1968).

Some physiological conditions are aversive: they produce discomfort or pain and motivate the organism to do something to remedy the situation. Extremes of temperature, suffocation, the accumulation of excessive waste products in the body, and excessive fatigue all activate the organism. Sometimes the physiological basis of a drive is acquired. Drug dependency is an example. Initially, an individual has no physiological need for heroin, but continued usage creates an imperative need for it, and all actions become determined by this need. Deprived of heroin, the individual becomes restless and develops symptoms of acute illness that are relieved only by the drug.

Curiosity and Stimulus-Seeking

All the motives we have discussed—hunger, thirst, sex, maternal behavior, and pain avoidance—have some basis in the physiological condition of the organism. As we noted earlier in this chapter, a drive-reduction theory of motivation explains all behavior as attempts to reduce drives created by bodily needs. The organism seeks to reduce the drive and return the body to its normal state. This homeostatic model provides a useful conception of motives based on deprivation and aversive stimulation (hunger, thirst, and pain) but seems less appropriate as a description of sexual and maternal behavior.

According to drive-reduction theory, an organism that has its biological needs satisfied should be in a quiescent state. But the evidence indicates that both people and animals are motivated to *seek* stimulation, to engage in active exploration of, and interaction with, their environment, even when such activity satisfies no bodily need.

EXPLORATION AND MANIPULATION   When placed in a new environment, animals tend to run about, sniffing and inspecting—as a dog or cat does in a new house. If a rat is placed in a T-shaped maze and turns to the right on the first trial, the probability is high that it will turn left on the second trial, preferring the unexplored territory. The rat in this case is neither hungry nor thirsty and has not been rewarded with food or water in either goal box. We could call such behavior curiosity, or a need to experience variety.

Another form of exploratory activity is the manipulation or investigation of objects. We give babies rattles, crib gymnasiums, and other toys because we

know they like to hold, shake, and pull at them. Monkeys enjoy the same sort of activity; in fact, the word *monkey* is used as a verb to describe casual manipulation for whatever satisfaction it brings. A number of experiments have shown that monkeys do, indeed, like to "monkey." If various mechanical devices are placed in a monkey's cage, it will begin to take them apart, becoming more skilled with practice, without receiving any evident reward other than the satisfaction of manipulating them (Harlow, Harlow, and Meyer, 1950). If the monkey is fed each time it takes the puzzle apart, its behavior changes: it loses interest in manipulation and views the puzzle as a means to food.

Sometimes manipulation has the quality of *investigation;* the organism picks up the object, looks at it, tears it apart, and so forth, in an apparent attempt to discover more about it. Piaget has made a number of observations bearing on such responses in the early life of the human infant. Within the first few months of life an infant learns to pull a string to activate a hanging rattle—a form of manipulation that might be considered merely entertaining. Between five and seven months, the infant will remove a cloth from his or her face, anticipating the peekaboo game. At 8 to 10 months, the infant will begin to look for objects behind or beneath other objects; by 11 months, to "experiment" with objects, varying their placement or position (Piaget, 1952). This kind of inquisitive or investigative behavior is typical of the growing child. Perhaps we might call it curiosity or a need to develop competence over one's environment. In any event, it seems to develop as a motive apart from any physiological needs of the organism.

NEED FOR SENSORY STIMULATION Exploration and manipulation provide new and changing sensory input. The need for such input has been demonstrated by studies in which sensory stimulation is markedly reduced. In the first study of this type, college students were paid to lie on a cot in a lighted, partially sound-deadened room. They wore translucent goggles so that they could see diffuse light but no shapes or patterns. Gloves and cardboard cuffs reduced tactile stimulation (see Figure 10-11). The hum of an exhaust fan and an air conditioner provided a constant masking noise. Brief time-outs were allowed for meals and toilet needs; but, otherwise, the subjects remained in a

condition of very restricted stimulation, compared to normal life. After two or three days, most of them refused to continue the experiment; the situation was sufficiently intolerable to negate any financial gain.

Some of the subjects began to experience visual hallucinations, varying from light flashes and geometric patterns to dream-like scenes. They became disoriented in time and space, were unable to think clearly or concentrate for any length of time, and did poorly when given problems to solve. In short, the condition of *sensory deprivation* had a detrimental effect on functioning and produced symptoms not unlike those experienced by some mental patients (Heron, Doane, and Scott, 1956).

A number of similar studies have since been conducted, with some variations in procedure. In some studies, the subject lay immersed to the neck in a tub of warm water for several days in an attempt to further reduce sensory stimulation. Results have differed somewhat, depending on procedures, but in most instances the subjects were bored, restless, irritable, and emotionally upset. People apparently need changes in stimulation and react adversely to its absence (Zubek, 1969).

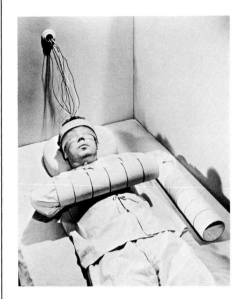

Fig. 10-11 Sensory deprivation experiment
Cardboard cuffs and translucent blindfold reduce stimulation.

Current Status of Motivational Concepts

Having examined a number of motives that account for a wide range of actions in both humans and animals, what can we say about the theories proposed to explain motivated behavior? Each motivation theory has some grain of truth, but each is incomplete as an explanation of the full complexity of human behavior. Biological needs are powerful instigators to action, because their satisfaction is essential to the survival of the organism and/or the survival of the species. In our highly industrialized and affluent society, we tend to be less aware of biological motives. But the actions of someone who does not know where to find the next scrap of food or how to obtain protection from the cold will be dominated by physical needs. Only when our basic biological needs are satisfied can other, more distinctly human, motives become important. These include motives related to our feelings of self-esteem and competency as well as social motives having to do with our relations with other people.

In Chapter 11, we will look at some of these psychological motives that are unrelated, as far as we know, to biological needs and are acquired as the result of experience—particularly, the experience of living with other people. Originally, drive-reduction theorists attempted to explain *all* motivated acts as the result of basic biological needs. Thus, the motive to achieve was traced back to the hunger drive and the motive to affiliate with others was based on the sex drive. But this approach has not added much to our understanding of complex motives.

Many psychologists have rejected the concepts of drive and homeostasis in favor of the notion of *arousal level.* The organism's state of arousal or activation can range from sleep and lethargy to alertness and intense excitement. Theoretically, there is an optimal level of arousal in terms of internal and external stimuli. Conditions that depart too severely from this optimal state in either direction incite the organism to act to restore the equilibrium. Arousal level can be affected by such internal drives as hunger and thirst or by such external stimuli as the aroma of delicious food or the loud clang of a bell. The notion of an optimal level of arousal provides a fairly simple way of looking at the results of experiments on exploration, manipulation, and sensory deprivation. Too little stimulation or boredom can motivate the organism as can too intense or dramatic a change in stimulation. We seek novelty and complexity in our environment, but situations that are too strange or too complex arouse anxiety. We will say more about arousal level in the next chapter, when we consider emotion.

SUMMARY

1 Motivation refers to the factors that *energize* and *direct* behavior. Attempts to explain motivated acts have had various emphases:
  a *Instinct theory* postulates innate predispositions to specific actions.
  b *Drive-reduction theory* bases motivation on bodily *needs* that create a state of tension or *drive,* which the organism seeks to reduce by doing something to satisfy the need. Biological needs prompt action, because the body tends to maintain a constant internal environment, or *homeostasis.*
  c *Incentive theory* emphasizes the importance of external conditions as a source of motivation. These may be *positive incentives,* which the organism will approach, or *negative incentives,* which the organism will avoid. Incentives can arouse behavior as well as direct it.
2 Important brain areas in the regulation of food intake are the *lateral hypothalamus* (LH), the "feeding center," and the *ventromedial hypothalamus* (VMH), the "satiety center," which act reciprocally to maintain stable body weight. They also contain receptors that respond to stomach distension, glucose level in the blood, and temperature to effect short-term control of eating.
3 Taste and smell cues trigger some of the processes that prepare for digestion, but they are not essential for regulation of food intake unless the hypothalamic control centers are impaired. Learning plays an important role in appetite for and aversion to specific foods.
4 Research on obesity suggests that overweight individuals may be more responsive than normal-weight individuals to external hunger cues, such as the taste and smell of food or the fact that it is mealtime. They also tend to eat more when emotionally aroused. Some of these differences may result from the fact that overweight people are usually dieting. Normal-weight individuals who are dieting and thus classified as "restrained eaters" tend to show eating behavior that is similar to that of obese people.
5 Hypothalamic regulation of water intake involves two receptors. *Osmoreceptors* respond to cellular dehydration by prompting the organism to drink and by stimulating the pituitary gland to secrete an antidiuretic hormone (ADH) into the blood, which signals the kidneys to reabsorb water. *Volumetric receptors* cause the release of renin, which converts a blood protein (angiotensinogen) to angiotensin I. The lungs convert angiotensin I to angiotensin II, which signals the hypothalamus to produce thirst.
6 Sexual behavior in lower animals is largely instinctive and is controlled by hormones that prime the organism to respond to stimuli emanating from animals of the opposite sex. The female hormones, *estrogen* and *progesterone* are secreted by the ovaries; the male hormones, *androgens,* by the testes. These hormones are also important in determining fetal development as male or female. The *posterior hypothalamus* appears to be the brain area most involved in sexual behavior.
7 Among human beings, hormones exert less influence on sexual behavior than either early experiences with parents and peers or cultural norms. While attitudes toward sexual behavior are becoming increasingly permis-

sive in western society, men and women still differ somewhat in their views on sex. Sexual interactions with members of the same sex are common during childhood, but only a small percentage of people become exclusively *homosexual*. *Homosexuality* and *transsexualism* probably result from any of a number of psychological and social factors.

8 Two other motives with a physiological basis are *maternal behavior* and *avoidance of pain*. Maternal behavior in lower animals involves innately programmed responses triggered by the changes in female hormones that occur with pregnancy. In primates and human beings, however, experiences with one's own parents play a major role. Even the motivational aspects of pain depend to some extent on normal growth experiences.

9 *Curiosity*, the tendency to *explore* new environments and to investigate or *manipulate* interesting objects, seems to develop as a motive apart from any physiological needs of the organism. Experiments on *sensory deprivation* demonstrate the importance of an individual's need for new and changing sensory input.

10 Central to current approaches to motivation is the notion of *arousal level*. Internal or external stimulation that produces too severe a change from the optimal arousal level motivates the organism to do something to restore equilibrium.

FURTHER READING

Brief summaries of motivation may be found in Valle, *Motivation: Theories and issues* (1975) and Korman, *The psychology of motivation* (1974). For a summary of animal research, see Wong, *Motivation: A biobehavioral analysis of consummatory activities* (1976).

A more extensive account is Bolles, *Theory of motivation* (2nd ed., 1975); also see Logan and Ferraro, *Systematic analyses of learning and motivation* (1978).

Information on the biological bases of hunger, thirst, sex, and maternal behavior may be found in textbooks on physiological psychology, of which Carlson, *Physiology of behavior* (1977) and Thompson, *Introduction to physiological psychology* (1975) are good examples.

For a review of research on obesity, see Stunkard, *The pain of obesity* (1976). An interesting paperback that offers suggestions on diet and the behavioral control of eating is *Slim chance in a fat world* (1972) by Stuart and Davis.

Research on sexuality is presented in Money and Musaph (eds.), *Handbook of sexology* (1977) and Beach (ed.), *Human sexuality in four perspectives* (1977).

11
Human Motivation
and Emotion

Why does a scientist spend long hours at work in the laboratory, foregoing all other activities and pleasures? An athlete endure months of painful training in preparation for Olympic competition? One person devote all efforts to amassing a fortune; another give up a life of security and ease to work with impoverished peoples in a remote and primitive region? Obviously, biological needs cannot begin to account for the diversity and complexity of human behavior.

It is true that an infant's early behavior is largely determined by basic biological needs—a child cries when hungry, cold, or in pain. But as the child grows, new motives appear that are learned by interacting with other people. We will call them *psychological motives* to distinguish them from motives based on physiological needs. Security, acceptance by and approval from those around us, feelings of self-worth and competency, and the search for new experiences are important psychological motives, although the way in which they are satisfied varies with each individual and culture. The distinction between biological and psychological motives is not clear-cut. In Chapter 10 we noted that biological motives can be aroused by external incentives and that learning determines to some extent the way such needs as hunger and sex are satisfied. Psychological motives are influenced *primarily* by learning and the kind of society in which the individual is raised; they have little basis in the physiological needs of the organism.

Abraham Maslow, a leader in the development of humanistic psychology (see Chapter 1), proposed an interesting way of classifying human motives. He assumed a *hierarchy of motives,* ascending from the basic biological needs present at birth to more complex psychological motives that become important only after the more basic needs have been satisfied (see Figure 11-1). The needs at one level must be at least partially satisfied before those at the next level become important determiners of action. When food and safety are difficult to ensure, the satisfaction of those needs will dominate a person's actions, and the higher motives will have little significance. Only when the satisfaction of the basic needs is easy will the individual have the time and energy for aesthetic and intellectual interests. Artistic and scientific endeavors do not flourish in societies where people must struggle for food, shelter, and safety.

Maslow's scheme provides an interesting way of looking at the relationships among motives and the opportunities afforded by the environment. We will

Fig. 11-1 Maslow's hierarchy of needs
The needs that are low in the hierarchy must be at least partially satisfied before those that are higher can become important sources of motivation. (Maslow, 1954)

Self-actualization needs: to find self-fulfillment and realize one's potential

Aesthetic needs: symmetry, order, and beauty

Cognitive needs: to know, understand, and explore

Esteem needs: to achieve, be competent, and gain approval and recognition

Belongingness and love needs: to affiliate with others, be accepted, and belong

Safety needs: to feel secure and safe, out of danger

Physiological needs: hunger, thirst, and so forth

have more to say about Maslow's highest motive, *self-actualization,* when we discuss personality in Chapter 13.

Many theories have been proposed to explain human motivation, but as yet there is little consensus. We will concentrate on two theories that adopt very different views concerning human nature: *psychoanalytic theory* and *social learning theory.* After discussing these, we will examine a specific area of motivated behavior—aggression—noting how each theory would explain aggressive behavior.

Obviously, motivation and emotion are closely related. Feelings determine our actions, and, conversely, our behavior often determines how we feel. Emotions can activate and direct behavior in the same way biological drives do. The last half of the chapter deals with the way we experience and express emotion and how emotion influences behavior.

Theories of Motivation

According to Freud's psychoanalytic theory, our actions are determined by inner forces and impulses, often operating below the level of consciousness (see Chapters 6 and 13). In contrast, social learning theory, as formulated by

Albert Bandura at Stanford University, maintains that our behavior is learned through interaction with, and observation of, the environment (see Chapter 13).

Psychoanalytic Theory of Motivation

Psychoanalysis, in addition to being a method for treating neurotic disorders (see Chapter 16), is also a theory of human motivation. It began with Freud's *Interpretation of Dreams* (1900) and has evolved gradually. A complete exposition of psychoanalytic theory would require a lengthy discussion of its numerous changes. But for our purposes a broad outline of the theory will suffice.

INSTINCTUAL DRIVES Freud believed that all behavior stems from two opposing groups of instincts: the *life instincts*, which enhance life and growth, and the *death instincts*, which push toward destruction. The energy of the life instincts is *libido*, which involves mainly sex and related activities. The death instincts can be directed inward in the form of suicide or other self-destructive behavior or outward in the form of aggression toward others. Freud, then, believed there were two basic human motives—sex and aggression. He was not unaware of physiological needs or of the role of fear, but they played little part in his theory.

Freud believed that the forerunners of sex and aggression are found early in a child's life: sex is expressed in the pleasure derived from stimulating the sensitive zones of the body (see p. 391 for the psychosexual stages of development); and aggression, in biting or hitting. When parents place taboos on both sex and aggression, their free expression becomes *repressed* and, instead of finding full conscious expression, they remain active as *unconscious motives*. Sex is usually more severely repressed than aggression, but the expression of either motive may make the child anxious because of negative parental attitudes. Unconscious motives then find expression in disguised form. The concept of *unconscious motivation* is one of the cornerstones of psychoanalytic theory.

BEHAVIOR FROM WHICH UNCONSCIOUS MOTIVES ARE INFERRED
Although writers and philosophers had long recognized the existence of some unconscious controls over human conduct, Freud was the first to call attention to the powerful role of unconscious motives in human behavior. He specified several forms of behavior through which unconscious motives are expressed:

1 In dreams we often express wishes and impulses we are unaware of.
2 Unconscious mannerisms and slips of speech may "let the cat out of the bag" and reveal hidden motives.
3 Symptoms of illness (particularly the symptoms of mental illnesses) often can be shown to serve the unconscious needs of the person.

Most psychologists have some reservations about Freud's theory of unconscious motivation. They agree that unconscious motives may exist (or at least motives that are unclear to the person), but they prefer to think in terms of *degrees of awareness*. A person may be vaguely aware, for example, of the need to dominate others but may not realize the extent to which this need influences his or her behavior.

Interpreting dreams is a tricky business; very little is known about the content of dreams and what the content supposedly symbolizes. Slips of speech may reveal unconscious motives, but just as often they may give away motives the speaker is aware of but wishes to keep hidden. Think, for example, of the person who says to an unwelcome visitor, "I'm sad you came," when what was intended was, "I'm glad you came." We can acknowledge that often we may not be fully aware of why we behave as we do without assuming that motives are always unconscious.

Social Learning Theory of Motivation

Social learning theory focuses not on instinctual drives but on patterns of behavior the individual learns in coping with the environment. It emphasizes the reciprocal interaction between behavior and environment. We are not driven by internal forces, nor are we passive reactors to external stimulation. The type of behavior we exhibit partly determines the reward or punishment we receive, and this in turn influences our behavior.

Patterns of behavior can be acquired through direct experience or by observing the behavior of others. Some responses may be successful; others may produce unfavorable results. Through this process of differential reinforcement, the person eventually selects the successful behavior patterns and discards the others.

Social learning theory differs from a strict behaviorist position by stressing the importance of cognitive processes. Because we can think and represent situations symbolically, we are able to foresee the probable consequences of our actions and alter our behavior accordingly. Our actions are governed to a large extent by anticipated consequences. We do not wait until we have experienced frostbite before deciding to wear warm gloves in freezing weather. Anticipated consequences, represented symbolically in one's thoughts, can motivate behavior in much the same way actual consequences can.

Vicarious learning

VICARIOUS LEARNING Social learning theory also stresses the importance of *vicarious learning*—that is, learning by observation. Many behavior patterns are learned by watching the behavior of others and observing its consequences for them. Emotions can also be learned vicariously, by watching the emotional responses of others as they undergo painful or pleasant experiences. A child who observes the pained expressions of an older sibling in the dentist's chair will probably be fearful when the time comes for his or her first dental appointment. Social learning theorists emphasize the role of *models* in transmitting both specific behaviors and emotional responses. And they have concentrated much of their research efforts on discovering how modeled behavior is transmitted—what types of models are most effective and what factors determine whether the modeled behavior that is learned will actually be performed.

SELF-REGULATION A third emphasis of social learning theory is the importance of *self-regulatory processes.* A specific behavior produces an external outcome, but it also produces a self-evaluative reaction. People set their own standards of conduct or performance and respond to their behavior in self-satisfied or self-critical ways, depending on how the behavior relates to their standards. Thus, reinforcement has two sources: *external* and *self-evaluative.* Sometimes the two coincide, and sometimes they are contradictory. A person may be rewarded socially or materially for behavior that is not acceptable according to his or her self-standards. Indeed, self-reproach is an important influence in motivating people to adhere to accepted standards of conduct in the face of opposing influences. For example, a person is tempted to cheat on an income tax return. The chances of getting caught (external punishment) may be slim and the financial gain substantial. But the anticipation of personal feelings of self-contempt prevents the individual from doing so: the behavior is not in accord with self-standards.

External reinforcement is most effective when it is consistent with self-reinforcement—when society approves actions that the individual values highly. An artist whose works are enthusiastically received by the public and the critics will probably be more motivated to continue than one whose creative endeavors are appreciated by neither group. It takes conviction in one's own standards to persevere when external reinforcement is lacking.

Social learning theorists have been active in developing procedures that enable people to control their own behavior by self-reinforcement or self-punishment. Successful methods have been developed to control alcohol abuse or overeating by having individuals reward themselves when they stick to a certain regimen of eating or drinking (see Table 16-1).

Both psychoanalytic theory and social learning theory will be explored further in Chapters 13 and 16 in terms of their views on personality and the treatment of abnormal behavior. The contrast between these two theoretical approaches will become clearer if we look at one area of motivated behavior and examine how each theory would explain it. Several motivational systems could be discussed, such as need for achievement or need for affiliation, but some of the most interesting work has been done in the area of aggression. The need to understand what instigates aggression and how it can be controlled is one of the most crucial problems facing society. In an age when powerful weapons are easily available, a single aggressive act can have disastrous consequences.

Motivational Factors in Aggression

Aggression is usually defined as behavior intended to injure another person (either physically or verbally) or to destroy property. The key word is *intent.* If I accidentally step on your toes in a crowded elevator and immediately apologize, you are not likely to label my behavior aggressive. If I walk up as you sit at your desk studying and stomp on your foot, you are apt to be outraged at such a blatantly aggressive act. But even intentionally aggressive acts can serve a goal other than that of inflicting injury. (I may step on your foot in the elevator so that I can get out quickly and be first in line at the ticket office.)

Any specific act can satisfy a wide range of possible motives. Power, wealth, and status are only a few of the ends that can be attained by aggressive means. Some psychologists distinguish between *hostile aggression,* the sole aim of which is to inflict injury, and *instrumental aggression,* which is aimed at obtaining rewards other than the victim's suffering. Instrumental aggression includes fighting in self-defense, assaulting someone during a robbery, or fighting to prove one's power and dominance. It also includes *prosocial aggression*—defending the rights of an underdog. But the distinction between hostile and instrumental aggression is not clear-cut. What looks like a case of hostile aggression may serve other ends: a gang member who brutally attacks an innocent passer-by (on the surface, a case of hostile aggression) may be motivated by a need to gain status with the gang. A theory of aggression should account for both hostile and instrumental aggression.

Hostile or instrumental aggression?

Aggression as a Drive

Freud viewed aggression as a basic instinct. The energy of the *death instincts* builds up within the organism until it must be discharged, either outwardly, through overt aggression, or inwardly, in the form of self-destructive acts. Freud was pessimistic about the possibility of ever eliminating aggression. The best society could do would be to modify its intensity by promoting positive emotional attachments between people and by providing substitute outlets (such as watching prizefights or engaging in sports).

Freud's views on aggression are expressed in a letter written to Albert Einstein in 1932. Einstein, concerned with the efforts of the League of Nations to promote world peace, asked Freud for his opinions on why people engage in war. Is it possible, he inquired, that human beings have a "lust for hatred and destruction?" Freud replied,

> You express astonishment at the fact that it is so easy to make men enthusiastic about a war and add your suspicion that there is something at work in them—an instinct for hatred and destruction—which goes halfway to meet the efforts of warmongers. . . . I can only express my entire agreement. We believe in an instinct of that kind and have in fact been occupied during the last few years in studying its manifestations. . . . The death instinct turns into the destructive instinct . . . it is directed outwards, on to objects. The living creature preserves its own life, so to say, by destroying an extraneous one (1963, pp. 41 and 143).

Later theorists in the Freudian tradition rejected the idea that aggression was an innate drive or instinct and proposed that it was a frustration-produced drive. The *frustration-aggression hypothesis* assumes that thwarting a person's efforts to reach a goal induces an aggressive drive that, in turn, motivates behavior designed to injure the person or object causing the frustration (Dollard and others, 1939). The expression of aggression reduces the drive. Aggression is the dominant response to frustration, but other responses can occur if aggression has been punished in the past. By this formulation, aggression is not inborn; but, since frustration is a fairly universal condition, aggression is still a drive that must find an outlet.

The idea of an aggressive drive is popular because we tend to view violence, particularly interpersonal violence, as a sudden, explosive, irrational type of behavior—as if some sort of aggressive energy had built up until it had to find an outlet. Newspaper and TV accounts of crimes tend to encourage this view. Some of the most hideously brutal crimes have been committed by individuals who were reportedly very meek, quiet, and conforming until their outburst.

More often, however, the assailant's background is not as innocent as the accounts would have us believe. In the 1960s, for example, Charles Whitman, a University of Texas student, positioned himself in the campus bell tower and shot as many people as he could until he was finally gunned down. Newspaper reports described Whitman as a model American youth—a former altar boy and Eagle Scout. Subsequent investigation revealed, however, that his life was replete with aggressive acts, including assaults on his wife and others, a court-martial as a marine recruit for insubordination and fighting, and a passion for collecting firearms. With the exception of some psychotic individuals who may be driven to violent acts because of delusional beliefs, most people who commit aggressive acts have a past history of aggressive behavior.

BIOLOGICAL BASIS OF AGGRESSION Some support for a biologically based aggressive drive comes from studies showing that mild electrical stimulation of a specific region of the hypothalamus produces aggressive behavior in animals. When a cat's hypothalamus is stimulated via implanted electrodes, the animal hisses, its hair bristles, its pupils dilate, and it will strike out at a rat or other object placed in its cage. Stimulation of a slightly different area of the hypothalamus produces quite different behavior; the cat shows none of the above "rage" responses but, instead, will coldly stalk a rat and kill it.

Similar techniques have produced aggressive behavior in monkeys and rats. A laboratory-bred rat that has never killed a mouse or seen a wild rat killing one may live quite peaceably in the same cage with a mouse. But if the rat's hypothalamus is stimulated with neurochemicals, the animal will pounce on its mouse cage-mate and kill it with exactly the same response pattern exhibited by a wild rat—a hard bite to the neck that severs the spinal cord. It is as if the stimulation triggers an innate killing response that had until this time remained dormant. On the other hand, if a neurochemical blocker is injected into the same brain site of rats that spontaneously kill mice on sight, the rats become temporarily peaceful (Smith, King, and Hoebel, 1970).

In higher mammals, such instinctive aggressive patterns are controlled more by the cortex and thus are more influenced by experience. Monkeys living in groups establish a dominance hierarchy with one or two males as leaders and the others at various levels of subordination. When the hypothalamus of a dominant monkey is electrically stimulated, the monkey attacks subordinate males, but not females. The same stimulation of a monkey low in rank produces cowering and submissive behavior (see Figure 11-2). Thus, aggression is not automatically elicited by stimulation of the hypothalamus. The hypothalamus may send a message to the cortex indicating that its "aggression center" has been activated, but the cortex, in choosing the response it will initiate, considers what is going on in the environment and its memory of past experiences.

Like the lower animals, humans have the neurological mechanisms that enable them to behave aggressively. But the activation of these mechanisms is under much more *cognitive control*. Some brain-damaged individuals may react aggressively to stimulation that normally would not cause aggressive behavior; in these cases cortical control is impaired. One study reports that persons who are repeatedly violent and assaultive have a high incidence of neurological defects (Mark and Ervin, 1970). But in normal individuals the frequency with which aggressive behavior is expressed, the forms it takes, and the situations in which it is displayed are determined largely by learning and social influences.

Fig. 11-2 Brain stimulation and aggression
A mild electrical current is delivered to electrodes implanted in the monkey's hypothalamus via remote radio control. The animal's response (attack or flight) depends on its position in the status hierarchy of the colony. (Courtesy Dr. José Delgado)

A wild bull charges Dr. José Delgado, who is armed only with a cape and a radio transmitter (left photo). When he presses the transmitter, the bull abruptly stops his attack (right photo). The radio transmitter sends a mild current to electrodes implanted in specific areas of the bull's brain.

MOTIVATIONAL FACTORS IN AGGRESSION

Aggression as a Learned Response

Social learning theory rejects the notion of aggression as an instinct or frustration-produced drive and proposes that aggression is no different from any other learned response. It can be learned through observation or imitation, and the more often it is reinforced, the more likely it is to occur. A person who is frustrated by a blocked goal or disturbed by some stressful event experiences unpleasant emotional arousal. This emotional arousal can elicit different responses, depending on the kinds of responses the individual has learned for coping with stressful situations. The frustrated individual may seek help from others, aggress, withdraw, try even harder to surmount the obstacle, or anaesthetize him or herself with drugs or alcohol. The response used will be the one that has been most successful in the past in relieving frustration. According to this view, frustration provokes aggression mainly in people who have learned to respond to aversive situations with aggressive attitudes and behavior (Bandura, 1977). Figure 11-3 shows how social learning theory differs from psychoanalytic theory and drive theory (the frustration-aggression hypothesis) in conceptualizing the motivational components of aggression.

In the social learning formulation, aversive experiences lead to emotional arousal. Frustration—in the form of blocked goal seeking—is one such experience, but there are others. Physical discomfort, for example, also increases emotional arousal and may lead to aggression if cues for eliciting aggressive behavior are also present. In one study, subjects who were required to work on a task in a hot, stuffy room showed no more aggression than subjects who worked under cool conditions. However, after both groups observed an aggressive model, the overheated subjects became more aggressive than their comfortable counterparts (Baron and Lawton, 1972). Similar results were found when loud noise was the source of discomfort (Geen and O'Neal, 1969).

Even arousal that is *not* the result of unpleasant stimulation can increase aggression in the presence of aggression-provoking stimuli. For example, subjects who were aroused by vigorous physical exercise were more aggressive

Fig. 11-3 Motivational determinants of aggression
The diagram represents schematically the motivational determinants of aggression as viewed by psychoanalytic theory, drive theory (the frustration-aggression hypothesis), and social learning theory. In the social learning view, the emotional arousal caused by unpleasant experiences can lead to any number of different behaviors, depending on the behavior that has been rewarded or has proved successful in the past. Cognitive factors, including knowledge of the results of past behavior and appraisal of positive and negative incentives operating in the current situation, enable the individual to anticipate the consequences of behavior and act accordingly. (Modified after Bandura, 1977)

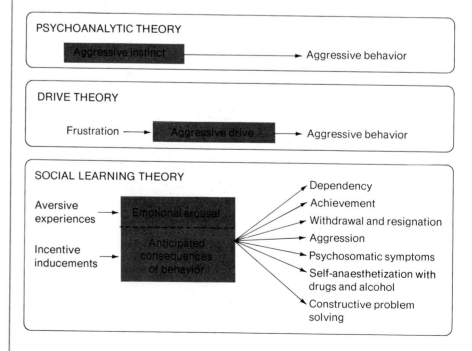

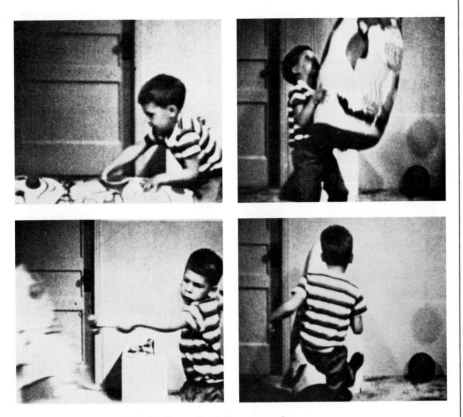

Fig. 11-4 Children's imitation of adult aggression
Nursery school children observed an adult express various forms of aggressive behavior
toward an inflated doll. After watching the adult, both boys and girls behaved aggressively
toward the doll, using many of the detailed acts of aggression that the adult had displayed,
including lifting and throwing, striking with a hammer, and kicking.

toward a person who had previously angered them than subjects who had not
exercised. But aggression toward a person who had not angered the subjects
did not increase after strenuous activity (Zillmann and others, 1972). Men who
were sexually aroused by viewing erotic films were more aggressive toward
someone who had previously annoyed them than men who had viewed non-
arousing films. But subjects did not become more aggressive when there had
been no prior annoyance (Zillmann and Sapolsky, 1977).

These studies lead to the conclusion that emotional arousal, regardless of
source, tends to increase aggression when aggression-eliciting stimuli are
present. It may be that much of the violent behavior we observe in contemporary society is due to a combination of high arousal levels produced by the
stresses of daily life and the widespread dissemination of stimuli that elicit
aggression (Geen, 1976).

IMITATION OF AGGRESSION A number of studies show that aggressive
responses can be learned through imitation. Nursery school children who
observed an adult expressing various forms of aggressive behavior toward a
large, inflated doll subsequently imitated many of the adult's actions, including
unconventional and unusual aggressive behavior patterns (see Figure 11-4).
The experiment was expanded to include two filmed versions of aggressive
modeling (one showing an adult behaving aggressively toward the doll and the
other showing a cartoon character displaying the same aggressive behavior).

MOTIVATIONAL FACTORS IN AGGRESSION

Freud's view of aggression as an instinct has been reintroduced more recently by ethologists studying animal behavior in naturalistic settings (Lorenz, 1966; Eibl-Eibesfeldt, 1970). The basic idea is that both humans and animals are innately aggressive, but animals have learned to control their aggressive impulses, whereas humans have not.

Predatory animals kill members of other species for food. But among their own species animals fight mainly in competition for food, mates, and nesting sites, and to protect their young. Fighting among members of the same species serves several functions: it spaces the animals over the inhabited area to provide optimal utilization of food, with each group having its own "territory"; and it ensures that the strongest males will procreate, since they will be the winners in competition for the females.

According to Lorenz, animals can safely enjoy these benefits of aggression because, through the process of evolution, they have developed inhibitions that prevent them from destroying their own species. Many species have ritualistic patterns of threatening or fighting behavior that appear to be largely innate (see Figure 11-5). They ward off combat by threatening displays; they fight according to a stylized, ritualistic pattern; and the fight seldom results in serious injury, because the loser can display signals of submission (for example, a wolf lies

Fig. 11-5 Ritualistic patterns of fighting behavior
The wildebeest bull defends its territory against a rival in a stylized challenge duel. These skirmishes, which may occur many times a day, seldom result in bloodshed. A. The two antagonists stand grazing head to head, taking each other's measure. B. Suddenly they drop to their knees in the eyeball-to-eyeball combat attitude. C. Pretending to sense danger, they raise their heads in mock alarm, apparently a means of easing tension. D. At this point the challenge may be called off or may progress to a brief, horn-locked battle.

down and exposes its throat) that inhibit further aggression.

But humans have developed powerful weapons that can cause instant death, often at a great distance. Perhaps if all combat had remained on a hand-to-hand or tooth-to-flesh level, without the benefit of even a rock or a club, we would have developed inhibitions that would prevent the destruction of our species.

Lorenz thus believes, as Freud did, that aggression is an innate instinct that must find some outlet. His prescription for a more peaceful society includes: safe outlets for aggression, such as competitive sports; broadening our view of "clan" and territory to include more people; and recognizing the stimuli that are "releasers" for aggression—a threatened in-group, a hated out-group, and the contagion of a group of angry people acting *en masse*.

Lorenz's views, though provocative,

The results were equally striking. Children who watched either of the two films behaved as aggressively toward the doll as children who had observed a live model displaying aggression. Figure 11-6 shows measures of aggressive behavior for each of the groups. Observation of either live or filmed models of aggression increases the likelihood of aggression.

REINFORCEMENT OF AGGRESSION Children were much more likely to express the aggressive responses they learned by watching aggressive models when they were reinforced for such actions or when they observed aggressive

Aggressive Animals

are highly speculative and have been criticized as lacking substantial basis in empirical data. For example, many animals do not have innate signals for stopping attacks, and the stereotyped signals they do use have varying effects on the responses of their foes. Also, chimpanzees in their natural habitat have been observed engaging in group warfare; the males of one colony carried out a series of brutal attacks on the members of another social group, eventually killing all the males (Goodall, 1978). Other criticisms of the arguments advanced by Lorenz are presented by Ashley Montagu in *The Nature of Human Aggression* (1976).

In contrast to Lorenz's prescriptions, social learning theory would stress minimizing the competitive and frustrating circumstances that lead to aggression and making sure that aggressive behavior receives less reward than alternative forms of conduct.

Regardless of whether one focuses on innate or learned aspects of aggression, studies of animals in their natural surroundings provide some valuable clues to the situations that trigger aggressive responses and the kinds of behaviors that inhibit or deescalate them (Marler, 1976). For example, crowding increases fighting among many species, probably because it increases the competition for food and other resources. And aggressive behavior on the part of one animal is often contagious, exciting the other group members to aggression.

Mutual grooming: a social response that inhibits aggression

Behaviors that appear to inhibit aggression include maintaining distance from a potential foe (strong odors and loud vocalizations that permit animals to detect, and withdraw from, one another at a distance serve this purpose) and evoking a social response that is incompatible with aggression. One such response is mutual grooming—touching or fingering the fur or feathers of another animal. Many species seem to use this method to reduce the likelihood of aggression. Perhaps the most important factor in reducing the probability of aggression is familiarity. Many of the social rituals in which animals engage (for example, sniffing and inspecting body parts, stereotyped greeting behaviors) provide the opportunity to become familiar with each other's smell and appearance and, thus, to distinguish group members from strangers. When troops of primates divide and go to separate territories, the failure to perform such rituals may hasten the process by which familiar companions become aggression-arousing strangers. Something like this may have happened in the case of the warfaring chimpanzees described earlier; they had originally all been part of the same troop.

models being reinforced. Aggressive responses can be learned through observation and reinforced by their consequences. An observational study of nursery school children shows the effects of reinforcement on aggression. Investigators observed the children for 10 weeks, recording instances of interpersonal aggression along with the events that immediately followed aggression—positive reinforcers (victim winced or cried), punishment (victim counterattacked), or neutral reactions (victim ignored the aggressor). For the children who showed the highest overall level of aggressive behavior, positive reinforcement was the most common reaction to their aggressive act. Passive children who

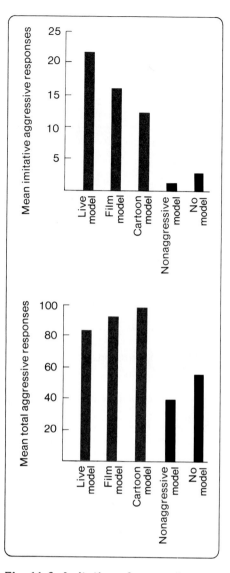

Fig. 11-6 Imitation of aggression
Observing aggressive models (either live or on film) greatly increases amount of aggressive behavior children display as compared to observing a nonaggressive model or no model at all. Note that observation of the live model produces more imitation of specific aggressive acts, whereas observation of filmed models (either real-life or cartoon) instigates more aggressive responses of all kinds. (After Bandura, 1973)

were repeatedly victimized but who occasionally succeeded in stopping attacks by counteraggression gradually decreased their defensive behavior and began to initiate attacks of their own. Passive children whose counteraggression was unsuccessful remained submissive. Clearly, the *consequences* of aggression played an important role in shaping behavior (Patterson, Littman, and Bricker, 1967).

Expression of Aggression as Cathartic

Does the release of pent-up aggression decrease the person's need to aggress, or do such experiences actually increase the probability of future aggressive behavior? If aggression is a drive (either innate or frustration-produced), then its expression should be *cathartic*, reducing the intensity of aggressive feelings. But the evidence suggests that this is not the case. Studies of children indicate that participating in aggressive activities either increases aggressive behavior or maintains it at the same level, rather than reducing it (Nelsen, 1969). Experiments with adults have generally had similar results. When given repeated opportunities to shock another person (who can't retaliate), college students become more punitive the more they aggress (Buss, 1966a). And subjects who are angry become even more punitive on successive attacks than subjects who are not angry (Loew, 1967). If aggression were cathartic, the angry subjects should be reducing their aggressive drive by acting aggressively and should become less punitive the more they aggress.

These studies are relevant to real-life instances in which assailants become progressively more brutal and "overkill," sometimes stabbing a victim as many as 50 times. Of course, there are many factors in such cases, but there are indications that acting aggressively provides positive feedback for more aggression.

Obviously, in some circumstances the expression of aggression decreases its incidence. An aggressive threat may cause the antagonists to cease their provocative acts. Or behaving aggressively may arouse feelings of anxiety in the aggressors, particularly if they observe the injurious consequences of their actions, thereby inhibiting further aggression. But in these instances the effect on aggressive behavior can be explained without resorting to the notion that an aggressive drive is being reduced.

VIEWING VIOLENCE   What effect does expressing aggression vicariously through observing violence on television or in the movies have on aggressive behavior? Is it cathartic, providing fantasy outlets for aggressive tension? Or does it elicit aggression in viewers by modeling violent behavior? We have already seen that children will imitate live or filmed aggressive behavior in an experimental setting. But how will they react in more natural settings? The amount of violence to which we are exposed through the mass media makes this an important question.

Some people in the TV industry claim that watching violence on television is beneficial—viewers discharge some of their own aggressive impulses through viewing, thus reducing the likelihood that they will perform aggressive acts. Freud would probably have agreed with this claim; an instinct or drive theory of aggression assumes that aggression builds up until it is discharged by some form of aggressive act, either actual or vicarious. Social learning theory, on the other hand, maintains that a state of arousal, or anger, can be reduced through behavior that is noninjurious as well as, or better than, through aggressive acts.

There have been several experimental studies in which children's viewing of commercial television was controlled: one group watched violent cartoons for a specified amount of time each day; another group watched nonviolent cartoons for the same amount of time. The amount of aggression the children showed in their daily activities during this period was carefully recorded. The results showed that the children who watched the violent cartoons became more aggressive in their interactions with their peers, whereas those who viewed nonviolent cartoons showed no change in interpersonal aggressions (Steuer, Applefield, and Smith, 1971).

A number of correlational studies have shown a positive relationship between the amount of exposure to televised violence and the degree to which children use aggressive behavior as a means of solving interpersonal conflicts. Correlations, of course, do not imply causal relationships; it may be that children who are more aggressive prefer to watch violent TV programs. A longitudinal study that traced TV viewing habits over a 10-year period attempted to control for this possibility. A large number of children (more than 800) were studied when they were eight to nine years of age. Investigators collected information about each child's viewing time, the type of programs viewed, a number of family characteristics, and aggressiveness as rated by schoolmates. One of the major findings was that boys who preferred programs with a considerable amount of violence were much more aggressive in their interpersonal relationships than those who preferred programs with little violence.

Ten years later, more than 400 of the original subjects (then aged 18 to 19) were interviewed concerning their preferred TV programs, given a test that measured delinquency tendencies, and rated by their peers as to the aggressiveness of their behavior. Figure 11-7 shows that high exposure to violence on television at age 9 is positively related to aggressiveness in boys at age 19. The correlation remains significant even when statistical methods are used to control for the degree of childhood aggressiveness, thus reducing the possibility that initial level of aggression determines both childhood viewing preferences and adult aggressiveness.

Interestingly, the results showed no consistent relationship between the TV habits of girls and their aggressive behavior at either age. This agrees with other studies showing that girls tend to imitate aggressive behavior much less than boys unless they are specifically reinforced for doing so. Girls in our society are seldom reinforced for behaving aggressively—quite the contrary. And since most of the aggressive roles on television are male, the female is less likely to find aggressive models to imitate. However, the current increase in TV dramas starring aggressive heroines—for example, policewomen and female super-sleuths—may change these findings.

HOW VIEWING VIOLENCE AFFECTS SOCIAL BEHAVIOR Although some psychologists question the extent to which television and movies actually influence people's behavior (e.g., Kaplan and Singer, 1976; Konečni and Ebbesen, 1976), the majority of studies lead to the conclusion that viewing violence does increase interpersonal aggression, particularly in young children (e.g., Leyens and others, 1975; Parke and others, 1977). Exposure to filmed violence can elicit aggressive behavior in several ways.

1   *By teaching aggressive styles of conduct.* We have already seen that children imitate the exact behavior of aggressive models. A number of cases have been reported of young children or teen-agers duplicating a violent act previously seen on television. In fact, in one instance, the parents of a victim took legal action against a TV network, claiming that a program shown during the hours when children were watching was responsible for a brutal

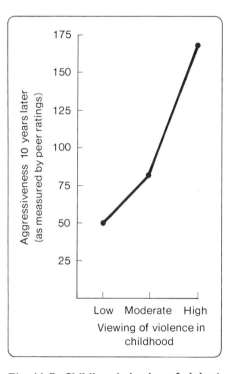

Fig. 11-7 Childhood viewing of violent television and adult aggression
Preference for viewing violent TV programs by boys at age 9 is positively correlated with aggressive behavior at age 19. (Plotted from data by Eron, Huesmann, Lefkowitz, and Walder, 1972)

MOTIVATIONAL FACTORS IN AGGRESSION

attack on their nine-year-old daughter. The three youngsters responsible admitted that they had copied the method of assault shown on the program. Adult criminals, too, have improved their skills by adopting some ingenious methods demonstrated on television (Hendrick, 1977). And police departments report that a number of violent crimes are the direct result of people trying to copy the plot of a TV show (Mankiewicz and Swerdlow, 1977).

2 *By increasing arousal.* When four- and five-year-old children watch violent TV programs, they become much more emotionally aroused than they do while watching nonviolent programs—as measured by a significant increase in their galvanic skin response, or GSR (Osborn and Endsley, 1971). The GSR is a rapid change in the electrical conductivity of the skin that occurs with emotional arousal. It results, in part, from changes in sweat gland activity. Adults, too, show increased heart rate and GSR while watching filmed scenes of violence (Speisman and others, 1964). We noted earlier that emotional arousal from various sources increases the probability of aggressive behavior if a person is already frustrated or angry.

3 *By desensitizing people to violence.* Young children are emotionally aroused by viewing violence, but their physiological reactions decrease with repeated exposure to displays of violence. When 5- to 12-year-old boys were shown a violent boxing film, those who had a history of extreme TV exposure (more than 40 hours per week) showed much less arousal (as measured by the GSR) than those boys who watched television an average of only four hours a week (Cline, Croft, and Courrier, 1973).

Other studies indicate that exposure to violence in the context of a TV drama decreases emotional responsiveness to real-life aggression in news films for both children and adults (Thomas and others, 1977). It is possible that the emotional blunting produced by continual exposure to filmed violence—both fictional and real—may affect the way we respond to a victim's suffering in real life and our readiness to help. Studies demonstrating that exposure to TV violence decreases the speed and willingness of older children to intervene in a fist fight between younger children suggest this possibility (Drabman and Thomas, 1974; Thomas and Drabman, 1975).

4 *By reducing restraints on aggressive behavior.* Most of us control our aggressive impulses. Although we may be angry and feel like injuring someone who has provoked or injured us, numerous restraints prevent us from doing so—such as pangs of guilt, fear of retaliation, and disapproval of others. Experiments indicate that observing another person behaving aggressively weakens these restraints. For example, subjects who were insulted by another person tended to be much more hostile in their remarks to the insulter later on if they overheard the insulter take a tongue-lashing from someone else (DeCharms and Wilkins, 1963). And subjects who watch an experimenter shock another person (actually a confederate of the experimenter's) give more shocks than subjects who did not witness the experimenter's aggression (Doob and Wood, 1972). (Both modeling and reduction of restraints may have been operating in the latter study.) When we observe others aggress with no undesirable effects, we are more apt to express our own hostility.

5 *By distorting views about conflict resolution.* On the TV or movie screen, interpersonal conflicts are solved by physical aggression much more often than by any other means. The heroes (and even the heroines) do most of the killing. And watching the "good guys" triumph over the "bad guys" by violent means makes such behavior seem not only acceptable, but also morally justified. While most of us realize that the dramas we watch on the

screen bear only slight resemblance to what goes on in the real world, young children do not have our degree of sophistication. And even adults may find their view of the world distorted by what they see on television. Researchers have found that heavy viewers of television are more distrustful of others than light viewers and overestimate their chances of being criminally victimized; they are also more likely to report buying locks, dogs, and guns to protect themselves (Gerbner and Gross, 1976).

While TV violence does appear to increase aggressive behavior—through some of the mechanisms described above—its effects probably differ for different children. A child who is very aggressive to begin with may become even more unrestrained and may learn new forms of aggressive behavior. A child who is punished for imitating acts observed on television, either by parents or peers, is apt to show a decrease in aggressiveness—although behavior that is prohibited in one setting may be displayed in another where there is less fear of punishment.

Since programs that portray positive attitudes and cooperative behavior have been shown to *reduce* interpersonal aggression, the TV industry could perform a valuable public service by including more heroes and heroines who successfully overcome obstacles in a calm and nonviolent manner (Leiffer, Gordon, and Graves, 1974).

Clearly, many factors are involved in the instigation of aggression: conditions of poverty, overcrowding, the actions of authorities such as the police, and the values of one's cultural group, to mention a few. Some of these social influences will be considered in Chapters 17 and 18.

Children often imitate acts seen on TV.

Emotion

The discussion of aggression makes it clear that motivation and emotion are closely related. Anger is frequently an instigator of aggressive behavior, although such behavior can also occur in the absence of anger. Emotions can activate and direct behavior in the same way biological or psychological motives can. Emotions may also accompany motivated behavior; sex is not only a powerful motive, but also a source of intense pleasure. Emotions can be a goal; we engage in certain activities because we know that they will bring us pleasure.

The nature of the relationship between motivation and emotion, as well as the definition of emotion itself, is an unresolved issue in psychology. Most people would say that anger, fear, joy, and grief are emotions but would classify hunger, thirst, and fatigue as states of the organism that serve as motives. What is the difference? Why don't we call hunger an emotion?

There is no clear-cut distinction. The most common basis for differentiating between the two assumes that emotions are usually aroused by external stimuli and that emotional expression is directed toward the stimuli in the environment that arouse it. Motives, on the other hand, are more often aroused by internal stimuli and are "naturally" directed toward certain objects in the environment (for example, food, water, or a mate). However, there are a number of instances when this distinction does not hold. For example, an external incentive such as the sight or smell of delicious food can arouse hunger in the absence of internal hunger cues. And internal stimuli, such as those caused by severe food deprivation or pain, can arouse emotion.

Most motivated behavior has some affective or emotional accompaniment, although we may be too preoccupied in our striving toward the goal to focus on our feelings at the time. When we talk about motivation we usually focus on the goal-directed activity; in discussing emotion our attention is drawn to the subjective, affective experiences that accompany the behavior. We are apt to be more aware of our emotions when efforts to achieve a goal are blocked (anger, despair) or when the goal is finally attained (pleasure, joy).

In the past, psychologists devoted considerable effort to trying to classify emotions. They attempted to find dimensions along which to scale such emotions as sorrow, disgust, surprise, jealousy, envy, and ecstasy. But such attempts have not proved very worthwhile. For our purposes we will note that most emotions can be divided into those that are *pleasant* (joy, love) and those that are *unpleasant* (anger, fear). In addition, many of our emotional terms can be classified by *intensity*. Word pairs such as *displeasure-rage, pain-agony*, and *sadness-grief* convey differences of intensity. Some psychologists reserve the term *emotion* for the more intense states that are accompanied by widespread changes in body physiology and call the milder affective states *feelings*. But there are many intermediate states between mild experiences of pleasantness or unpleasantness and intense emotions. We will not attempt to pinpoint where on the intensity scale "emotions" begin, but will be concerned instead with a variety of affective experiences.

Physiological Responses in Emotion

When we experience an intense emotion, such as fear or anger, we are aware of a number of bodily changes—rapid heart beat and breathing, dryness of the throat and mouth, increased muscle tension, perspiration, trembling of the extremities, a "sinking feeling" in the stomach. Table 11-1, which shows the symptoms of fear reported by combat pilots during the Second World War, illustrates the complexity of bodily changes in an emotional state.

Most of the physiological changes that occur during emotional arousal result from activation of the sympathetic division of the autonomic nervous system as it prepares the body for emergency action (see Chapter 2). The *sympathetic system* is responsible for the following changes:

1 Blood pressure and heart rate increase.
2 Respiration becomes more rapid.
3 The pupils of the eyes dilate.
4 Perspiration increases, while secretion of saliva and mucus decreases.
5 Blood-sugar level increases to provide more energy.
6 The blood is able to clot more quickly in case of wounds.
7 Motility of the gastrointestinal tract decreases; blood is diverted from the stomach and intestines and sent to the brain and skeletal muscles.
8 The hairs on the skin become erect, causing "goose pimples."

The sympathetic system gears the organism for energy output. As the emotion subsides, the *parasympathetic system*, the energy-conserving system, takes over and returns the organism to its normal state.

The kind of heightened physiological arousal we have described is characteristic of emotional states in which the organism must prepare for action—for example, to fight or flee. Some of the same responses also occur during joyful excitement or sexual arousal. During emotions such as sorrow or grief, however, some bodily processes are depressed, or slowed down.

TABLE 11-1
Symptoms of fear in combat flying
Based on reports of combat pilots during the
Second World War.

DURING COMBAT MISSIONS, DID YOU FEEL	OFTEN	SOMETIMES	TOTAL
A pounding heart and rapid pulse	30%	56%	86%
That your muscles were very tense	30	53	83
Easily irritated, angry, or "sore"	22	58	80
Dryness of the throat or mouth	30	50	80
"Nervous perspiration" or "cold sweat"	26	53	79
"Butterflies" in the stomach	23	53	76
Sense of unreality, that this couldn't be happening to you	20	49	69
Need to urinate very frequently	25	40	65
Trembling	11	53	64
Confused or rattled	3	50	53
Weak or faint	4	37	41
That right after a mission you were unable to remember details of what had happened	5	34	39
Sick to the stomach	5	33	38
Unable to concentrate	3	32	35
That you had wet or soiled your pants	1	4	5

Source: After Shaffer (1947)

Theories of Emotion

We tend to think that bodily changes that occur in response to stress are caused by emotion. But one of the earliest theories of emotion proposed that the perception of the physiological changes *is* the emotion. William James, a famous psychologist at Harvard during the late 1800s, believed that the important factor in our felt emotion is the feedback from the bodily changes that occur in response to a frightening or upsetting situation. He stated this theory in a form that seems to put the cart before the horse: "We are afraid because we run." "We are angry because we strike." A Danish physiologist, Carl Lange, arrived at a similar proposal about the same time, and the theory is referred to as the *James-Lange theory.*

We can think of instances where the recognition of emotion does follow bodily responses. If you stumble suddenly on the stairs, you automatically grab for the handrail before you have time to recognize a state of fear. Your felt emotion, after the crisis is over, includes the perception of a pounding heart, rapid breathing, and a feeling of weakness or trembling in the arms and legs. Because the feeling of fear follows the bodily responses, this situation gives some plausibility to the James-Lange theory.

Lie Detection

The theory of lie detection is that lying arouses emotional responses that can be measured. A machine called a *polygraph* (commonly known as a "lie detector") measures simultaneously several of the physiological responses that are known to accompany strong emotions. (The word *polygraph* means "many writings.") The measures most frequently recorded are changes in heart rate, blood pressure, respiration, and the galvanic skin response (GSR).

The standard procedure in operating a polygraph is to first take a recording while the subject is relaxed; this recording serves as a base line for evaluating subsequent responses. The examiner then asks a series of carefully worded questions that are answered "yes" or "no." "Critical" questions are interspersed among "neutral" questions, and sufficient time is allowed between questions (usually a minute) for the measures to return to normal. Presumably, the subject's guilt is revealed by heightened physiological responses to the critical questions (Figure 11-8).

The problem with the use of the polygraph in detecting lies is that the method is not foolproof. An innocent subject may be very tense or may react emotionally to certain words in the questions and thus appear to be lying when telling the truth. On the other hand, a practiced liar may show little emotional response when lying. And a knowledgeable subject may be able to "beat" the machine by thinking about something exciting or by tensing muscles during neutral questions, thus cre-

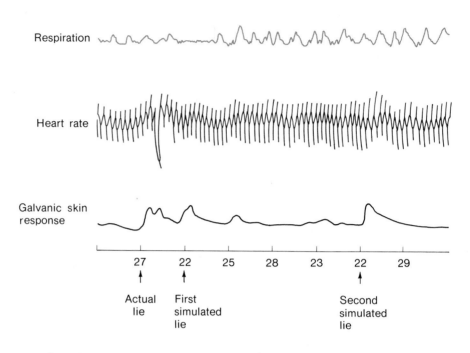

Respiration

Heart rate

Galvanic skin response

27   22   25   28   23   22   29

↑ Actual lie   ↑ First simulated lie   ↑ Second simulated lie

ating a base line comparable to reactions to the critical questions. The recording in the right half of Figure 11-8 shows the responses to an actual lie and a simulated lie. In this experiment, the subject picked a number and then tried to conceal its identity from the examiner. The number was 27, and a marked change in heart rate and GSR can be seen where the subject denies number 27. The subject simulates lying to number 22 by tensing his toes, producing noticeable reactions in heart rate and GSR.

Because of these and other problems, most courts do not admit lie detector results as evidence. Such tests are frequently used, however, in preliminary criminal investigations and by prospective employers hiring personnel for trusted positions. The polygraph also serves as a research tool in studies measuring emotional responses to stress or observing the effects of drugs on physiological responses.

A new kind of lie detector has recently been developed that measures certain changes in a person's voice that are undetectable to the human ear. All muscles, including those controlling the vocal cords, vibrate slightly when in use. This tremor, which is transmitted to the vocal cords, is suppressed by

The major objections to the James-Lange theory came from Walter Cannon, a physiologist at the University of Chicago, who pointed out that (1) bodily changes do not seem to differ very much from one emotional state to another, despite the fact that we as individuals are usually pretty clear about which emotion we are experiencing; (2) the internal organs are relatively insensitive structures not well supplied with nerves, and internal changes occur too slowly to be a source of emotional feeling; (3) artificially inducing the bodily changes

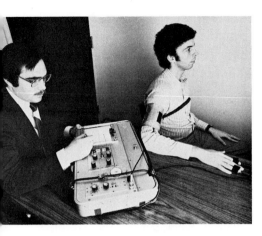

Fig. 11-8 The polygraph
The arm cuff measures blood pressure and heart rate, the pneumograph around the rib cage measures rate of breathing, and the finger electrodes measure GSR. The recording on the left shows the physiological responses of a subject as he lies and as he simulates lying. The respiratory trace (top line) shows that he held his breath as he prepared for the first simulation. He was able to produce sizable changes in heart rate and GSR at the second simulation. (After Kubis, 1962)

activity of the autonomic nervous system when a speaker is under stress. When a tape recording of a person's voice is played through a device called a *voice stress analyzer* (at a speed four times slower than that at which it is recorded), a visual representation of the voice is produced on a strip of graph paper. The voice of a relaxed speaker resembles a series of waves—like the one shown in the left-hand graph of Figure 11-9—produced by the vocal cord tremors. When a speaker is under stress, the tremor is obliterated—as in the right-hand graph of Figure 11-9.

The voice stress analyzer is used in lie detection in essentially the same way as a polygraph; neutral questions are interspersed with "critical" ones and recordings of the two are compared. If answers to the critical questions show the relaxed wave form, the person is probably telling the truth—because, as far as we know, the vocal cord tremors cannot be voluntarily controlled. A stress-type record, on the other hand, indicates only that the individual is tense or anxious, not necessarily that he or she is lying.

The voice stress analyzer has an advantage over the polygraph, because the subject does not have to be hooked up to a lot of equipment. In fact, the subject does not even have to be present; the analyzer can work over the telephone, from radio or TV messages, or from tape recordings. Since people's voices can be analyzed without their knowledge, the potential for unethical use of the instrument is a matter of considerable concern. A different concern is the question of the voice stress analyzer's accuracy. Some investigators claim that it is less accurate than the polygraph in distinguishing between the guilty and the innocent; others claim the reverse. So far there have been few well-controlled studies; much more work needs to be done on the relationship between voice changes and other physiological measures of emotion (Rice, 1978).

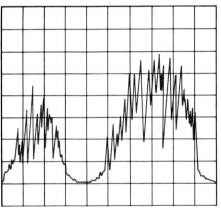 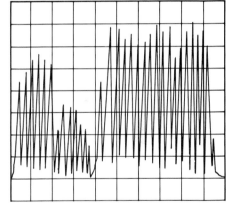

Fig. 11-9 Effects of stress on voice patterns
Graphic records of speech are produced by a voice stress analyzer. The voice printout for a relaxed speaker resembles a series of waves, like the one shown on the left; the waves are produced by tiny tremors of the vocal cords. Under stress, the tremor is suppressed, producing the printout on the right. (After Holden, 1975)

associated with an emotion (for example, injecting a person with adrenalin) does not produce the experience of the true emotion.

Cannon (1927) assigned the central role in emotion to the *thalamus*, which is part of the brain's central core (see Chapter 2). He suggested that the thalamus responded to an emotion-producing stimulus by sending impulses *simultaneously* to the cerebral cortex and to other parts of the body; emotional feelings were the result of joint arousal of the cortex and the sympathetic nervous system. According to this theory—which was extended by Bard (1934) and is known as the *Cannon-Bard theory*—the bodily changes and the experience of emotion occur at the same time. Figure 11-10 illustrates the differences between the Cannon-Bard and James-Lange theories of emotion.

Subsequent investigation has made it clear that the *hypothalamus* and certain parts of the *limbic system,* rather than the thalamus, are the brain centers most directly involved in the integration of emotional responses. (We noted earlier that electrical stimulation of the hypothalamus elicits fear or anger in many animals.) Impulses from these areas go to certain nuclei in the brain stem that control the functioning of the autonomic nervous system. The autonomic nervous system acts directly on the muscles and internal organs to cause some of the bodily changes characteristic of emotion and indirectly (through stimulation of adrenal hormones) to produce others. Still other hormones—which play a crucial role in an individual's reaction to stress—are secreted by the pituitary gland on direct signal from the hypothalamus (see p. 53).

In view of the complex interaction of neural and hormonal signals, it is difficult to determine whether the physiological responses precede or accompany the emotion. Emotion is *not* a momentary event, but an experience that takes place over a period of time. An *emotional experience* may initially be activated by external inputs to the sensory system; we see or hear the emotion-arousing stimuli. But the autonomic nervous system is activated almost immediately, so that feedback from bodily changes adds to the emotional experience. Thus, our conscious experience of emotion involves the *integration* of information about the physiological state of the body and information about the emotion-arousing situation. Both types of information tend to be continuous in time, and their integration determines the intensity and nature of our felt emotional state.

In this framework, the time distinctions made by the James-Lange and Cannon-Bard theories are not too meaningful. On some occasions, as in sudden danger, the first signs of emotional experience may be preceded by autonomic

Fig. 11-10 Two theories of emotion Illustrated here is the sequence of events for two theories of emotion. According to the James-Lange theory, feedback to the brain from bodily responses produces the conscious experience of emotion. According to the Cannon-Bard theory, the emotional experience occurs as soon as the cortex receives the message from the thalamus; it does not depend on feedback from internal organ and skeletal responses.

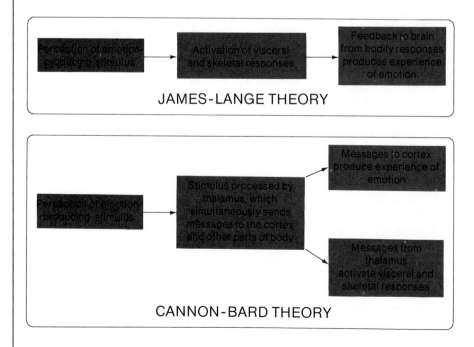

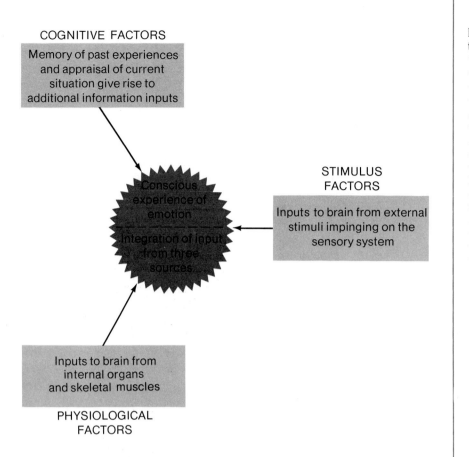

COGNITIVE FACTORS

Memory of past experiences and appraisal of current situation give rise to additional information inputs

STIMULUS FACTORS

Inputs to brain from external stimuli impinging on the sensory system

Conscious experience of emotion

Integration of input from three sources

Inputs to brain from internal organs and skeletal muscles

PHYSIOLOGICAL FACTORS

Fig. 11-11 Emotion as information integration
The conscious experience of emotion involves the integration of information from three sources. Feedback to the brain from the internal organs and other body parts activated by the sympathetic nervous system gives rise to an undifferentiated state of arousal and affect; but the emotion experienced is determined by the interpretation the subject assigns to the aroused state. Information stored in memory and the perception of what is taking place in the environment are used to interpret the current situation. This interpretation (based on cognitive and stimulus factors) interacts with feedback from bodily changes (physiological factors) to determine the emotional state.

activity (in which case James and Lange are correct); on others, the awareness of an emotion clearly precedes autonomic activity (in which case Cannon and Bard are correct). The felt emotional state has a third source of information: *cognitive factors*. How an individual appraises the external situation in terms of memories of past experiences is a cognitive process that will influence emotion. The factors that contribute to the conscious experience of emotion are illustrated in Figure 11-11. We will have more to say about cognitive factors shortly. But first we will examine the role of physiological arousal in emotion.

Arousal and Emotion

Most of the time we are fairly clear about the emotions we are experiencing; we know whether we are angry or frightened or merely excited. But our physiological responses under all three conditions are remarkably similar. Fear makes our heart beat faster, but so does anger or the sight of a loved one. Our face may flush *or* pale when we are angry (depending on the individual), and the same is true when we are frightened. While there are fairly accurate measures that tell us when a person is emotionally aroused, research so far has failed to find physiological patterns that are unique to different emotional states.

Emotions are difficult to study because of the complexity and interrelatedness of the physiological responses involved and because the kinds of emotions that can be aroused in the laboratory do not compare in intensity with those experienced in real life. A clever experimenter may be able to arouse a moderate degree of anger in a subject, but ethical and practical constraints restrict the amount of fear that can be induced in an experiment.

Although bodily sensations may not be related to *specific* emotions, they do

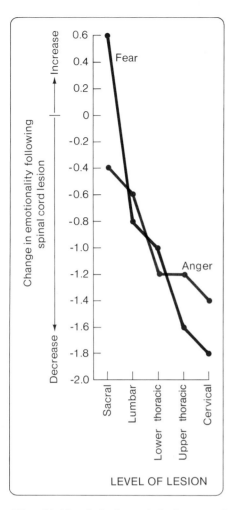

Fig. 11-12 Spinal cord lesions and emotionality

Subjects with spinal cord lesions compared the intensity of their emotional experiences before and after injury. Their reports were coded according to degree of change—0 indicates no change; a mild change (for example, "I feel it less, I guess") is scored as −1 for a decrease or +1 for an increase; a strong change (for example, "I feel it a helluva lot less") is scored as −2 or +2. Note that the higher the lesion, the greater the decrease in emotionality following injury. (After Schachter, 1971 and adapted from Hohmann, 1962)

determine the *intensity* with which we experience emotions. The importance of bodily sensations is demonstrated by a study of the emotional life of individuals with spinal cord injuries. When the spinal cord is severed, sensations below the point of injury are not communicated to the brain.

In this study, army veterans with spinal cord injuries were divided into five groups, according to the level of the spinal cord at which the lesion occurred. Those in group 1 had lesions near the neck (at the cervical level), with only one branch of the parasympathetic nervous system intact and no innervation of the sympathetic system. Those in group 5 had lesions near the base of the spine (at the sacral level), with at least partial innervation of both sympathetic and parasympathetic nerves. The other groups fell between these two extremes. The five groups represent a continuum of bodily sensation; the higher the lesion, the less the sensation.

Each subject was interviewed to determine his feelings in situations of fear, anger, grief, and sexual excitement. The subject was asked to recall an emotion-arousing incident prior to his injury and a comparable incident following the injury and to compare the intensity of emotional experience in each case. The information was coded as to degree of change. The data for states of fear and anger are shown in Figure 11-12. It is apparent that the higher the lesion (that is, the less the bodily sensation), the more emotionality decreased following injury. The same relationship was true for states of sexual excitement and grief. Deprivation of body sensation *does* result in a marked decrease in emotionality.

Comments by those patients with the highest spinal cord lesions suggest that they can act emotional but do not feel emotional. For example, "It's sort of cold anger. Sometimes I act angry when I see some injustice. I yell and cuss and raise hell, because if you don't do it sometimes, I've learned people will take advantage of you, but it doesn't have the heat to it that it used to. It's a mental kind of anger." Or, "I say I am afraid, like when I'm going into a real stiff exam at school, but I don't really feel afraid, not all tense and shaky, with the hollow feeling in my stomach, like I used to."

These men seem to be saying that they can make the appropriate emotional response when the situation calls for it, but they don't really feel emotional. The absence of autonomic arousal has a marked affect on emotional experience.

Cognitive Factors in Emotion

People are usually aware that something is going on internally when they are angry, excited, or afraid, but they are not very good at discriminating the changes in their heart rate or blood pressure or the activity in their stomach. When people are asked to describe their emotions, they usually begin with the arousing circumstances—that is, what angered, pleased, or frightened them. Then they describe some of their bodily reactions and their difficulties in dealing with the situation. But they do not define the emotion solely in terms of their own internal feelings.

The individual's *appraisal* of the emotion-producing situation is an important determinant of his or her emotional response. Schachter (1971) believes that emotions are a function of the interaction of cognitive factors and a state of physiological arousal. His *cognitive-physiological theory* of emotion proposes that feedback to the brain from physiological activity gives rise to an undifferentiated state of affect; but the felt emotion is determined by the "label" the person assigns to that aroused state. The assignment of a label is a *cognitive process*; individuals use information from past experiences and their perception of what is going on at present to arrive at an interpretation of their feelings. This interpretation will determine their actions and the label they use to define their emotional state.

To test his theory Schachter designed the following experiment. The subjects were told that the purpose of the study was to investigate the effects of a new vitamin compound on vision. They were given an injection and sent to a waiting room, presumably to wait for the drug to take effect. Half of the subjects received an injection of epinephrine (adrenaline), which usually causes increased heart and respiration rate, muscle tremors, and a "jittery" feeling. The other half, the control group, received an injection of saline solution, which produces no physiological effects. The subjects that received epinephrine were divided into three groups. One group was informed correctly about the physiological reactions to be expected. A second group was not told of any possible symptoms. And a third group was misinformed; they were told to expect numbness, itching, and, possibly, a headache. Schachter hypothesized that subjects in the latter two groups would be particularly susceptible to environmental cues, since they would be looking for a label to explain their state of physiological arousal.

The environmental conditions were manipulated by a "stooge"—a confederate of the experimenters'—who was in the waiting room when each subject arrived, presumably another participant in the experiment. The stooge acted either "euphoric"—playfully doodling, making paper airplanes, playing "basketball" by throwing wads of paper into the wastebasket—or "angry"—complaining about the experiment, resenting a questionnaire that the subjects had to fill out, and finally tearing it up and stomping out of the room. The subject's reactions were observed through a one-way mirror.

The results of the experiment generally supported Schachter's hypothesis. The subjects in the control group and those who were told how they would feel following the epinephrine injection were little affected by the behavior of the stooge in either the "angry" or the "euphoric" condition. The other aroused subjects (both ignorant and misinformed), who had no ready explanation for their state of physiological arousal, tended to take their cue from the stooge's behavior, acting happy when the stooge acted happy and angry when he acted angry (Schachter and Singer, 1962).

Schachter concluded that people tend to evaluate their feelings by comparing themselves to others around them. When feeling aroused, they may label their emotion as happiness, amusement, or anger, depending on the circumstances.

Schachter's theory has generated considerable interest and research, but the above experiment has been criticized for several reasons. Epinephrine does not affect everyone the same way; in fact, Schachter eliminated from his analyses the results from some subjects who later reported that they did not experience any physiological symptoms. In addition, no assessment was made of the subject's mood before the drug was administered. A subject who was in good spirits at the beginning of the experiment might be expected to be more responsive to the playful stooge. We may also wonder how comparable arousal states that are created by drugs and manipulated in the laboratory are to emotions that occur naturally in everyday life.

More important is the fact that two experiments that attempted to repeat the Schachter and Singer study failed to replicate their results (Rogers and Deckner, 1975; Marshall, 1976). Emotions appear to be less malleable than Schachter assumed. In addition, these studies found that subjects tend to interpret unexplained physiological arousal *negatively*, which is not surprising. When we experience strange symptoms, we are more apt to suspect that something is wrong with us than to assume that we are happy.

MODIFYING AROUSAL BY ALTERING COGNITIONS Although our emotions are not determined solely by our cognitions, they are certainly influenced by the way in which we appraise the emotion-producing situation. Indeed, you can think of instances where initial emotional responses to stimuli change as the situation is reappraised as either threatening or benign. You are awakened by the telephone at midnight. Your initial fear reaction aroused by the thought that some catastrophe has happened to a loved one changes to relief as you discover it is a wrong number. A potentially emotion-producing situation has become neutral because of a change in your appraisal of it.

A number of studies have investigated various ways in which changing peoples' cognitions can change their emotional reactions. The general procedure is to show the subjects a film that arouses emotion and measure autonomic arousal throughout the presentation. The subjects' cognitive activity is manipulated either by varying the narration that accompanies the film or by varying what subjects are told about the nature of the film before it starts. One film that has been used effectively in arousing stress shows the ceremony used

Fig. 11-13 Cognitive influences on emotion
The galvanic skin response (GSR) was measured for four different groups as they watched a stressful film. For one group, the narration accompanying the film was designed to increase stress by emphasizing the cruelty of the scenes being viewed; the narration for the second group denied the painfulness of the scenes, while that for the third group presented a detached, intellectualized description. The fourth group watched the film with no sound track. The stressful narration clearly increased emotional reaction to the film, as measured by the GSR. The denial and intellectualization narrations reduced emotional reaction, compared to silent observation of the film, but the differences are not so marked. (After Speisman, Lazarus, Mordkoff, and Davison, 1964)

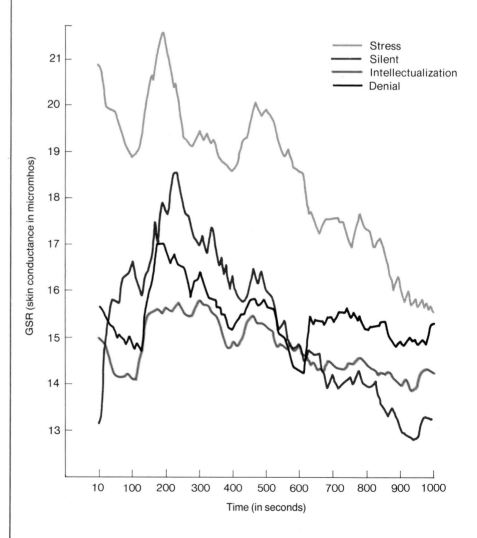

by an aboriginal Australian tribe to initiate young boys into manhood. The ceremony includes, among other things, cutting into the penis of each initiate with a stone knife. The film shows six such operations, and subjects find these episodes extremely stressful.

Figure 11-13 shows emotional response, as measured by the galvanic skin response (GSR), for groups viewing the film under four different conditions: (1) a narration designed to increase emotional stress by emphasizing the cruelty and pain of the ceremony; (2) a narration that tends to deny or minimize painfulness of the scene (". . . The words of encouragement offered by the older men have their effect, and the boy begins to look forward to the happy conclusion of the ceremony"); (3) a narration that presents a detached, intellectualized view of the ceremony ("As you can see, the operation is formal, and the surgical technique, while crude, is very carefully followed"); (4) no narration.

As shown in Figure 11-13, the narration designed to increase emotional reaction does so markedly; GSR is significantly higher for this group throughout the film. The two narrations that attempt to make the experience less stressful by intellectualization or denial produce lower GSR than the silent film.

Subsequent studies showed that preparing the subjects before they watch the film (either with a detached intellectualized description of what they are about to see or with a description that attempts to deny the trauma) is even more effective in reducing emotional reaction than are accompanying narrations designed for the same purpose. Thus we see that emotional reactions are strongly influenced by one's cognitions concerning a perceived event.

Emotional Expression

Innate Emotional Expression

The basic ways of expressing emotion are innate; children all over the world cry when hurt or sad and laugh when happy. Studies of children who were blind from birth indicate that many of the facial expressions, postures, and gestures that we associate with different emotions develop through maturation; they appear at the appropriate age even when there is no opportunity to observe them in others.

Sir Charles Darwin was intrigued with the expression of emotion in blind children and in animals. In *The Expression of Emotions in Man and Animals*, published in 1872, he proposed an evolutionary theory of emotions. According to Darwin, many of the ways in which we express emotion are inherited patterns that originally had some survival value. For example, the expression of disgust is based on the organism's attempt to rid itself of something unpleasant that has been ingested. To quote Darwin,

> the term "disgust," in its simplest sense, means something offensive to the taste. But as disgust also causes annoyance, it is generally accompanied by a frown, and often by gestures as if to push away or to guard oneself against the offensive object. . . . Extreme disgust is expressed by movements around the mouth identical with those preparatory to the act of vomiting. The mouth is opened widely, with the upper lip strongly retracted. . . . The partial closure of the eyelids, or the turning away of the eyes or of the whole body, are likewise highly expressive of disdain. These actions seem to declare that the despised person is not worth

An expression with universal meaning

looking at, or is disagreeable to behold. . . . Spitting seems an almost universal sign of contempt or disgust; and spitting obviously represents the rejection of anything offensive from the mouth.

Certain facial expressions do seem to have a universal meaning regardless of the culture in which the individual is raised. When people from five different cultures (United States, Brazil, Chile, Argentina, and Japan) viewed photographs showing facial expressions of happiness, anger, sadness, disgust, fear, and surprise, they had little difficulty in identifying the emotions that belonged to each expression. Even members of remote, preliterate tribes that had had virtually no contact with western cultures (the Fore and Dani tribes in New Guinea) were able to judge the facial expressions correctly. And American college students who viewed videotapes of emotions expressed by Fore natives identified the emotions fairly accurately, although they often confused fear and surprise (Ekman and Friesen, 1975).

Some psychologists, impressed by the innate and universal nature of certain facial expressions, believe that they are as important in determining our subjective experience of emotion as are internal sensations of arousal; messages to the brain from the muscles and nerves of the face as we automatically react to a situation tell us which of the basic emotions we are experiencing, while visceral sensations (which occur more slowly) signal the emotion's intensity (Izard, 1977). This idea, which goes back to the James-Lange theory, implies that if you make yourself smile and hold the smile for a half minute, you will begin to feel happier; if you scowl, you will feel tense and angry. Try it and see. Experiments in which subjects were instructed to manipulate their facial muscles (on the pretext that the effect of muscle movements on perception was being studied) failed to show a relationship between facial expression and feelings of emotion (Laird, 1974). But this does not rule out the possibility that self-determined facial expression is an important component of experienced emotion.

Role of Learning in Emotional Expression

Although certain emotional expressions may be innate, they are modified by experience. People learn to inhibit facial expressions, to show a "poker face," particularly when they want to conceal feelings of anger or fear. Sometimes body cues can tell us more about a person's emotional state than facial expression. For example, a man may try to mask anger toward his employer behind a bland or smiling countenance, while his true feelings are revealed by his clenched fists, rigid posture, and belligerent thrust of the lower jaw. Disappointment concealed behind a smiling face may be shown by slumped shoulders and a sagging posture. We are aware that emotions show on our face and may be careful to control our expression when we want to hide our feelings; we are less cautious about controlling body movements and gestures.

While some facial expressions and gestures may be innately associated with particular emotions or attitudes, others are learned from one's culture. One psychologist reviewed several Chinese novels in order to determine how a Chinese writer portrayed various human emotions. Many of the bodily changes in emotion (flushing, paling, cold perspiration, trembling, goose pimples) are used as symptoms of emotion in Chinese fiction, much as they are in western writing. He found, however, that the Chinese have some other quite different ways of expressing emotion. The following quotations from Chinese novels would surely be misinterpreted by an American reader unfamiliar with the culture (Klineberg, 1938).

"Her eyes grew round and opened wide."
(She became angry.)

"They stretched out their tongues."
(They showed signs of surprise.)

"He clapped his hands."
(He was worried or disappointed.)

"He scratched his ears and cheeks."
(He was happy.)

Thus, superimposed upon basic expressions of emotion, which appear to be universal, are conventional or stereotyped forms of expression, which become a kind of "language of emotion" recognized by others within a culture. Skilled actors are able to convey to their audiences any intended emotion by using facial expressions, tone of voice, and gestures according to the patterns the audience recognizes. In simulating emotion, those of us who are less skilled actors can convey our intent by exaggerating the conventional expressions: gritting our teeth and clenching our fists to indicate anger, turning down the corners of our mouth to look sad, raising our eyebrows to express doubt or disapproval.

Emotions as Adaptive and Disruptive

What is the role of emotions in our lives? Are they beneficial? Do they help us to survive, or are they chiefly sources of disturbance and maladjustment? The answers to these questions depend on the intensity of the emotions involved.

Arousal Level and Performance

A mild level of emotional arousal tends to produce alertness and interest in the task at hand. When emotions become intense, however, whether they are pleasant or unpleasant, they usually result in some decrease in performance. The curve in Figure 11-14 represents the relation between the level of emotional arousal and the effectiveness of performance. At very low levels of arousal (for example, when one is just waking up), the nervous system may not be functioning fully and sensory messages may not get through. Performance is optimal at moderate levels of arousal. At high levels of arousal, performance begins to decline. Presumably, the central nervous system is so responsive that it is responding to too many things at once, thus preventing the appropriate set of responses from dominating.

The optimum level of arousal and the shape of the curve differs for different tasks. A simple, well-learned habit would be much less susceptible to disruption by emotional arousal than a more complex response that depends on the integration of several thought processes. In a moment of intense fear you would probably still be able to spell your name, but your ability to play a good game of chess would be seriously impaired.

Individuals differ in the extent to which their behavior is disrupted by emotional arousal. Observations of people during crises, such as fires or sudden floods, suggest that about 15 percent show organized, effective behavior. The majority, some 70 percent, show various degrees of disorganization but are still able to function with some effectiveness. The remaining 15 percent

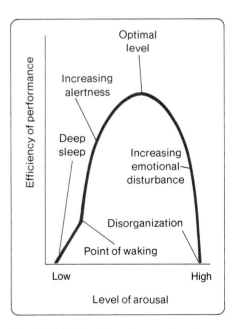

Fig. 11-14 Emotional arousal and performance
The curve shows the hypothetical relation between level of emotional arousal and efficiency of performance. The shape of the curve is probably somewhat different for different tasks or behaviors. (After Hebb, 1972)

are so disorganized that they are unable to function at all; they may race around screaming or exhibit aimless and completely inappropriate behavior (Tyhurst, 1951). Studies of soldiers under stress of combat indicate that only 15 to 25 percent can be counted on to fire their weapons. The rest simply freeze on the spot and are unable to fire, even when their lives are at stake.

When sufficiently intense, emotions can seriously impair the processes that control organized behavior.

Enduring Emotional States

Sometimes emotions are not quickly discharged but continue to remain unexpressed or unresolved. Perhaps the situation that makes one angry (for example, prolonged conflict with one's employer) or that makes one fearful (for example, worry over the chronic illness of a loved one) continues for a long period of time. The state of heightened arousal that results can take its toll in the individual's ability to function efficiently. Sometimes continual emotional tension can impair physical health. In a *psychosomatic illness*, the symptoms are physical, but the cause is primarily psychological. A number of different types of illness—for instance, ulcers, asthma, migraine headaches, high blood pressure, and skin eruptions—are related to emotional stress. We will have more to say about psychosomatic disorders in Chapter 14. At this point, however, it should be noted that long-term emotional stress can impair a person's physical health as well as mental efficiency.

SUMMARY

1 *Psychological motives*, in contrast to *biological motives*, are determined primarily by learning. They appear later in development and become important after basic needs are satisfied.
2 Two quite different theoretical approaches to human motivation are illustrated by *psychoanalytic theory* and *social learning theory*.
  a Freud's psychoanalytic theory emphasizes two basic drives: *sex* and *aggression*. These motives arise in infancy, but when parents forbid their expression, they are *repressed*. A repressed tendency remains active, however, as an *unconscious motive* and finds expression in indirect or symbolic ways.
  b Social learning theory focuses on patterns of behavior that are *learned* in coping with the environment; learning may occur through direct reinforcement or *vicariously*, through observing the consequences of behavior *modeled* by another person. *Cognitive processes* enable a person to foresee probable consequences and to alter behavior accordingly. *Self-reinforcement*, based on one's own standards of conduct, also provides an important motivational control.
3 Aggression, defined as behavior *intended* to injure another person or to destroy property, may be primarily *hostile*—aimed at inflicting injury—or it may be *instrumental*—aimed at goals other than the victim's suffering. Freudian theorists view aggression as an *instinct* or a *frustration-produced* drive; social learning theorists propose that it is a *learned response* influenced by modeling and reinforcement.
4 In lower animals, aggression is controlled by neurological mechanisms centered in the hypothalamus. In human beings and other higher mammals, aggressive behavior is largely under cognitive control, determined by learning and social influences.
5 Evidence indicates that observing aggressive behavior, either live or filmed,

tends to increase aggressiveness through one or more of the following processes: teaching aggressive styles of conduct, increasing arousal, desensitizing people to violence, reducing restraints on aggressive behavior, or distorting views about conflict resolution.

6 Emotions can serve as *motives, goals,* or *accompaniments of motivated behavior.* Intense emotions involve widespread bodily changes that result from activation of the sympathetic division of the autonomic nervous system. The *James-Lange theory* proposes that feedback from these bodily responses determines the quality of an emotion. The *Cannon-Bard theory* maintains that emotions and autonomic responses occur simultaneously—one is not the cause of the other.

7 Although feedback from autonomic responses is important in determining the intensity of emotional experience, attempts to differentiate between different emotions, such as fear and anger, on the basis of physiological responses have had little success. The individual's appraisal of the emotion-producing situation largely determines the quality of the emotion.

8 The *cognitive-physiological theory* proposes that emotional states are a function of the interaction of cognitive factors and physiological arousal. Experiments in which subjects were injected with epinephrine show the importance of cognitive factors in labeling emotional states.

9 Some forms of emotional expression appear to be inborn or to develop through maturation. But learning is important in modifying emotional expression to conform to the patterns approved by the culture.

10 Low levels of emotional arousal improve performance at a task, but intense arousal is usually disruptive; continual emotional tension can result in *psychosomatic illness.*

FURTHER READING

For a general coverage of human motivation, see Bolles, *Theory of motivation* (2nd ed., 1975). Shorter treatments can be found in Stein and Rosen, *Motivation and emotion* (1974) and Korman, *The psychology of motivation* (1974).

For a social learning approach to motivation, see Bandura, *Social learning theory* (1977). The psychoanalytic theory of motivation is presented in two books by Freud: *Beyond the pleasure principle* (1975), in paperback, first published in 1920, and *New introductory lectures on psychoanalysis* (1965), in paperback, first published in 1933.

Books on aggression include Johnson, *Aggression in man and animals* (1972), Bandura, *Aggression: A social learning analysis* (1973), and Montagu (ed.), *Learning non-aggression: The experience of non-literate societies* (1978).

For an introduction to contemporary views on emotion, see Strongman, *The psychology of emotions* (2nd ed., 1978). An interesting book on facial expressions in emotion is Ekman and Friesen, *Unmasking the face* (1975), in paperback.

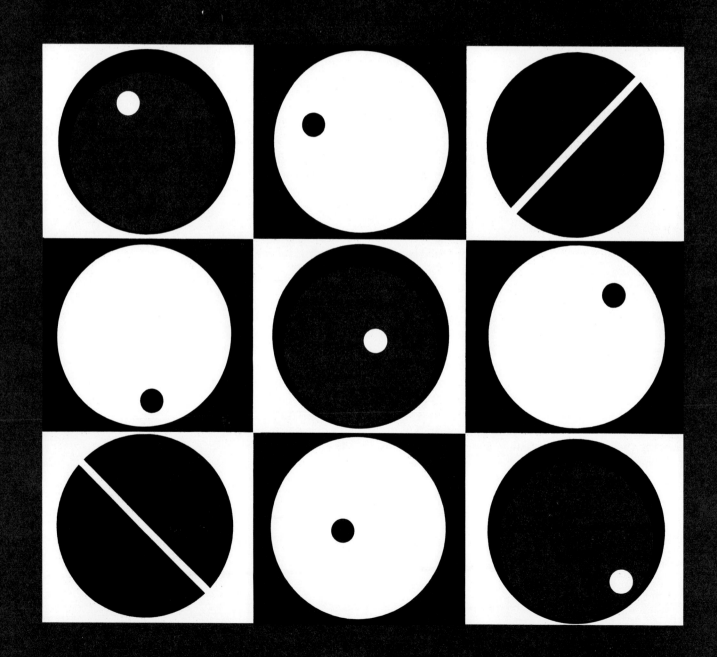

PART SIX

Personality and Individuality

12
Mental Abilities and Their Measurement

I n earlier chapters we discussed learning and the development of cognitive skills. In this chapter we will look at individual differences in mental abilities and their measurement. People differ widely in intelligence, knowledge, and skills. To determine whether a person has the skills for a particular job or the intelligence to profit from a college education, we need reliable methods of measuring *present abilities* and predicting *future performance*. In a complex technological society, the ability to match the unique talents of each person to the requirements of the job has advantages for both the individual and society.

What a person can do now and what he or she could do given appropriate training are not the same. We do not expect a premedical student to remove an appendix or a preflight trainee to fly a jet. But we do expect each of them to have the potential for acquiring these skills. The distinction between a *capacity to learn* and an *accomplished skill* is important in appraisal. Tests designed to *predict* what one can accomplish with training are called *aptitude tests;* they include tests of general intelligence as well as tests of special abilities. Tests that indicate what one can do now are *achievement tests.* An intelligence test that predicts how well you will do in college is an aptitude test; examinations given at the end of a course to see how much you have learned are achievement tests. Both are tests of ability.

Testing Aptitudes and Achievements

Aptitude tests attempt to predict future performance. But the *items*—the units of which a test is composed—must consist of samples of what can be accomplished now. How, then, is it possible to construct anything but achievement tests? This difficulty is not insurmountable, because it is possible to construct the tests from performances other than those being predicted. For example, knowledge of mechanical principles contributes to success in flying. Thus, pilot aptitude tests may include a test of mechanical knowledge—even though the mechanical knowledge test is also an achievement test. The distinction between an aptitude test and an achievement test is not based on the content of the items, but on the *purposes* of the two kinds of tests.

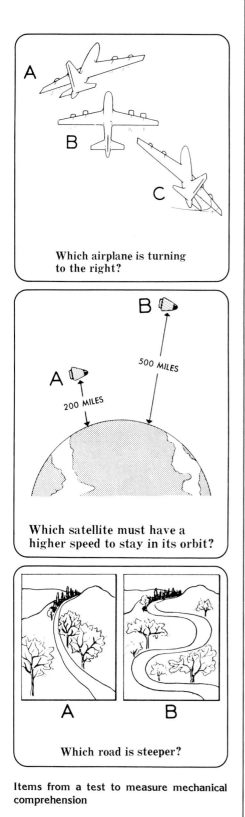

Which airplane is turning to the right?

Which satellite must have a higher speed to stay in its orbit?

Which road is steeper?

Items from a test to measure mechanical comprehension

Aptitude Tests

Aptitude tests designed to predict performance over a broad range of abilities are called *intelligence tests*. Other aptitude tests measure more specific abilities: mechanical aptitude tests measure various types of eye-hand coordination; musical aptitude tests measure discrimination of pitch, rhythm, and other aspects of musical sensitivity that are predictive of successful musical performance; and clerical aptitude tests measure efficiency in checking numbers and related skills that have been found to be predictive of an individual's later achievement as an office clerk. Many aptitude tests have been constructed to predict success in specific jobs or vocations. Since the Second World War, the armed forces have devised tests to select pilots, radio technicians, submarine crews, and many other specialists.

Aptitude is usually measured by a combination of tests. Pilot aptitude tests include not only measures of mechanical knowledge but also tests of spatial orientation, eye-hand coordination, and other skills. Scores from individual tests are weighted to get the best possible prediction—scores from tests that predict well count more than scores from tests that predict less well. If an eye-hand coordination test predicts pilot success better than a spatial orientation test, scores in eye-hand coordination will be weighted more heavily than scores in spatial orientation.

Achievement Tests

Achievement tests, which measure the individual's current knowledge and skills, are used in many areas. In schools, they provide the teacher with information about the effectiveness of teaching methods and the areas in which a student may need more instruction. In the professions, achievement tests are used to determine whether an individual is prepared to practice medicine, law, or accounting. In government, civil service examinations assess an individual's qualifications for specific jobs.

Achievement tests also provide a standard for judging the predictive ability of aptitude tests. Individuals who do well on a test of mathematical aptitude prior to taking a course in computer programming should also do well on the achievement test given at the end of the course. If not, something is wrong with either or both of the tests.

Reliability and Validity

A great deal depends on test scores in our society. An individual who performs well on tests will receive a degree or a license to practice or an opportunity to enter a desired career; one who fails may find many paths blocked. Hence it is crucial that tests measure what they are intended to measure and that scores represent fairly the candidate's knowledge and skills. Otherwise we may deny individuals the chance to use their skills, deprive society of good lawyers, doctors, and civil servants, or perhaps burden society with incompetent lawyers, doctors, and so on. In short, test scores must be trustworthy if they are to be useful. To a psychologist, this means that they must be both *reliable* and *valid*.

Test scores are *reliable* when they are reproducible and consistent. Tests may be unreliable for a number of reasons. For example, confusing or ambiguous test items may mean different things to a test taker at different times. Tests may be too short to sample adequately the abilities being tested, or scoring may be too subjective. If a test yields different results when it is administered on different occasions or scored by different people, it is unreliable. A simple analogy is a rubber yardstick. If we did not know how much it stretched each time we took a measurement, the results would be unreliable, no matter how carefully we had marked the measurement. We need reliable tests if we are to use the results with confidence.

In order to evaluate reliability, we must secure two independent scores for the same individual on the same test—by treating halves of the test separately, by repeating the test, or by giving it in two different but equivalent forms. A set of paired scores from a group of individuals enables us to determine the test's reliability. If two measurements produce about the same score levels, the test is reliable. Of course, some differences are to be expected, due to errors of measurement, so a measure of the degree of relationship between the two sets of scores is needed. This relationship is provided by the *coefficient of correlation*, discussed in Chapter 1. The coefficient of correlation between two sets of test scores is a *reliability coefficient.* Well-constructed psychological tests of ability usually have reliability coefficients of $r = .90$ or above.

Tests are *valid* when they measure what they are intended to measure. A college examination in economics that is full of trickishly worded questions might be a test of a student's intelligence rather than of the economics learned during the course. Such an examination might be reliable (a student would achieve about the same score on a retest), but it would not be a valid test of achievement for the course. Or a test of sense of humor might be made up of jokes that are hard to understand unless one were both very bright and very well read. It might also be a *reliable* measure of something (intelligence? educational achievement?) but still not be *valid* as a test of humor.

To measure validity, we must also have two scores for each person: the test score and some other measure of the ability or achievement in question. This measure is called a *criterion.* Suppose that a test is designed to predict success in learning to receive telegraphic code. To determine whether the test is valid, it is given to a group of individuals before they study telegraphy. After they have been trained to receive coded messages, the students are tested on the number of words per minute they can receive. This is a measure of their success, and serves as a criterion. Now we can obtain a coefficient of correlation between the early test scores and the scores on the criterion. This correlation coefficient is known as a *validity coefficient,* and it tells something about the value of a given test for a given purpose. The higher the validity coefficient, the better the prediction that can be made from the test.

Tests of General Intelligence

Sir Francis Galton, a cousin of Charles Darwin, developed the first tests designed to measure intelligence. A naturalist and mathematician, Galton was interested in individual differences in intelligence. He believed that certain families were biologically superior—stronger and smarter—than others. Intelligence, he reasoned, was a question of exceptional perceptual-motor skills, passed from one generation to the next. Since all information is acquired through the senses, the more sensitive and accurate an individual's perceptual apparatus, the more intelligent the person. Galton administered a battery of tests—measuring such variables as head size, reaction time, visual acuity, memory for visual forms, breathing capacity, and strength of hand grip—to

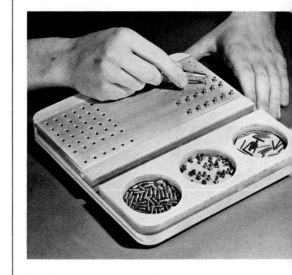

Testing manual dexterity
Speed with which subject places small screws in the threaded holes on the right and pins with collars in holes on the left is timed. Aptitude tests of this type may be used to select personnel for jobs that involve assembling delicate instruments.

Sir Francis Galton

Alfred Binet with his daughters

over 9,000 visitors to the London Exhibition in 1884. To his disappointment, he discovered that eminent British scientists could not be distinguished from ordinary citizens on the basis of their head size and that strength of grip was not much related to other measures of intelligence. Galton's tests did not prove very useful. However, he did invent the correlation coefficient, which plays such an important role in psychology.

The intelligence test as we know it today was formulated by the French psychologist Alfred Binet (1857–1911). In 1881, the French government passed a law making school attendance compulsory for all children. Previously, slow learners had usually been kept at home. Now teachers had to cope with a wide range of individual differences. The government asked Binet to devise a test that would detect those children too slow intellectually to benefit from the regular school curriculum.

Binet assumed that intelligence should be measured by tasks requiring reasoning and problem-solving abilities, rather than perceptual-motor skills. In collaboration with another French psychologist, Theodore Simon (1873–1961), Binet published a scale in 1905, which he revised in 1908 and again in 1911. These Binet scales are the direct predecessors of contemporary intelligence tests.

Binet's Method: A Mental-Age Scale

Binet reasoned that a slow, or "dull," child was like a normal child but retarded in mental growth. On tests, the slow child would perform like a normal child of younger age. A "bright" child, on the other hand, had mental abilities that were characteristic of older children. Thus, Binet decided to measure intelligence in terms of the kinds of change that ordinarily come with growing older. Accordingly, he devised a scale of *mental age.* Average mental-age (MA) scores correspond to *chronological age* (CA)—that is, to the age determined from the date of birth. A bright child's MA is above his or her CA; a slow child's MA is below his or her CA. The mental-age scale is easily interpreted by teachers and others who deal with children differing in mental ability.

ITEM SELECTION The intelligence test is designed to measure brightness rather than the results of special training—that is, aptitude rather than achievement. Hence, it must consist of items that do not assume any specific preparation.

There are two chief ways to find items that do not reflect special training. One way is to choose *novel items,* which provide an untaught child with as good a chance to succeed as one who has been taught at home or in school. Figure 12-1 illustrates novel items. In this particular case, the child is asked to choose figures that are alike, on the assumption that the designs are unfamiliar to all children. The second way is to choose *familiar items,* on the assumption that all those for whom the test is designed have had the requisite prior experience to deal with the items. The following problem provides an example of a supposedly familiar item:

Mark F if the sentence is foolish; mark S if it is sensible.
S F Mrs. Smith has had no children, and I understand that the same was true of her mother.

Of course, this item is "fair" only for children who know the English language, who can read, and who understand all the words in the sentence. For such children, detection of the fallacy in the statement becomes a valid test of intellectual ability.

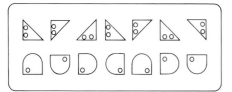

Fig. 12-1 Novel items used in intelligence tests
The following instructions accompany the test: "Here are some cards for you to mark. In each row mark every card that is like the first card in the row." (After Thurstone and Thurstone, 1941)

Many of the items on intelligence tests assume general knowledge and familiarity with the language of the test. But such assumptions can never be strictly met. The language spoken in one home is never exactly that of another, the reading matter available to the subjects differs, and the stress on cognitive abilities varies. Even the novel items depend on perceptual discriminations that may be acquired in one culture and not in another. Despite the difficulties, items can be chosen that work reasonably well. The items included in contemporary intelligence tests are those that have survived in practice after many others have been tried and found defective. It should be remembered, however, that intelligence tests have been validated by success in predicting school performance within a particular culture.

CONTEMPORARY BINET TESTS The tests originally developed by Binet have undergone several revisions in this country. The best-known and most widely used revision was that made by Lewis Terman at Stanford University in 1916, commonly referred to as the Stanford-Binet. This test was revised in 1937, 1960, and 1972.

In the Binet tests, an item is age-graded at the level at which a substantial majority of the children pass it. The present Stanford-Binet has six items assigned to each year; each item, when passed, earns a score of two months of mental age. Some examples of items used at different age levels are given in Table 12-1.

TABLE 12-1
Examples of items from the Stanford-Binet Intelligence Scale

AGE	TASK
2	**Naming parts of the body.** Child is shown a large paper doll and asked to point to various parts of the body.
3	**Visual-motor skills.** Child is shown a bridge built of three blocks and asked to build one like it. Can copy a drawing of a circle.
4	**Opposite analogies.** Fills in the missing word when asked: "Brother is a boy; sister is a _____." "In daytime it is light; at night it is _____." **Reasoning.** Answers correctly when asked: "Why do we have houses?" "Why do we have books?"
5	**Vocabulary.** Defines words such as *ball, hat,* and *stove.* **Visual-motor skills.** Can copy a drawing of a square.
6	**Number concepts.** Is able to give the examiner nine blocks when asked to do so.
8	**Memory for stories.** Listens to a story and answers questions about it.
9	**Rhymes.** Answers correctly when asked: "Tell me the name of a color that rhymes with Fred." "Tell me a number that rhymes with free."
12	**Verbal absurdities.** Tells what is foolish about statements such as, "Bill Jones's feet are so big that he has to put his trousers on over his head."
14	**Inference.** Examiner folds a piece of paper a number of times, notching a corner with scissors each time. Subject is asked the rule for determining how many holes there will be when the paper is unfolded.
Adult	**Differences.** Can describe the difference between "misery and poverty," "character and reputation." **Memory for reversed digits.** Can repeat six digits backwards—that is, in reverse order—after they are read aloud by the examiner.

Culture-Fair Intelligence Tests

Serious efforts have been made to construct tests that will be less dependent on the subject's specific culture than are the more standard tests, such as the Binet. Examples are the tests constructed by Cattell (1949), called a "culture-free" test, and by Davis and Eells (1953), called a "culture-fair" test. Both attempt to provide items that will not penalize the subject on the basis of his or her cultural background.

Consider the following item:

Pick out ONE WORD that does not belong with the others.

cello   harp   drum
violin   guitar

This item was used by Eells and others (1951) to illustrate how experience can determine vocabulary. When the test was administered to a group of children, 85 percent of those from homes of high socioeconomic status chose "drum," the intended correct answer, whereas only 45 percent of the children from homes of low socioeconomic status answered with this word. The low-status children most commonly answered "cello," an unfamiliar word that they thought did not belong. Children from homes of high socioeconomic status are more likely to be acquainted with cellos, or at least to have heard the word, than children from poorer homes.

Other items in this study showed class differences that were difficult to explain. For example, the following item was also answered correctly more often by children from homes of high socioeconomic status than by those from homes of low status.

Find the THREE THINGS which are alike in this list.

store   banana   basket
apple   seed   plum

This item requires the child to note that banana, apple, and plum are fruits and that store, basket, and seed are nonfruits. It is hard to believe that 9- and 10-year-old children, even those from underprivileged homes, would

not be acquainted with the six words, or with the fruits—although we know little at present about the effects of severe environmental restriction on the ability to categorize. Such an item may be "culture-fair," even though it shows class differences in its answer; the classes may actually differ in cognitive performance as measured by items that are "fair."

The results of culture-fair tests have not been encouraging. In some cases, class differences in scores have been reduced, but for the most part the differences remain. Moreover, as predictors of scholastic achievement, the newer tests are inferior to the more conventional ones. Perhaps a culture-fair test is impossible in principle; an individual's performance will always be affected by cultural background regardless of the nature of the test. Hence, with all their difficulties, the ordinary Binet-type tests serve their predictive purposes as well as or better than these substitute tests, which have not been extensively validated.

A study of children in a rural village in Nigeria illustrates how cultural experiences can influence performance on the Kohs Block Design Test, a task included in several intelligence scales. The child is given 16 painted blocks, each of which has two sides painted red, two white, and two divided diagonally into red and white. He or she is

then shown a drawing of a design and asked to arrange the blocks to form the same design. When eight-year-old rural Nigerian children were shown the designs pictured in Figure 12-2, they did very well with the first figure, moderately well with the second, but very poorly with the third. The average result would yield an IQ of 80 by American norms. However, when the tester made the design with blocks, rather than showing the children a drawing, they promptly learned to match the design with their blocks. Having done this, they could match other drawings with blocks, as the original test required. The investigator concluded that these children were not inferior to American children in this performance once they had "caught on to" what was expected. In the villages where these children live, pictures are rare—the children aren't used to drawings. Even adults are baffled by maps or building designs or, in some cases, the contents of ordinary photographs (D'Andrade, 1967).

Matters taken for granted in one culture cannot be taken for granted in another; this warning applies to different subcultures within countries as well. When test results are interpreted, an individual's background—the language spoken in the home and the kinds of learning experiences provided—must always be considered.

Fig. 12-2 Block designs used with rural Nigerian children
The third design was very difficult for eight-year-old children to copy when presented as a drawing to be copied with blocks, but it was much easier when the design to be copied was itself made with blocks. Once having copied a design from blocks, the children could copy with their blocks other designs from drawings. (After D'Andrade, 1967)

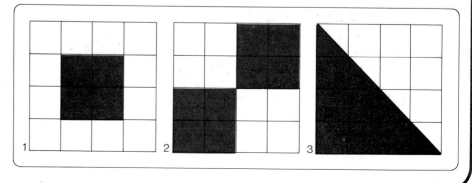

The procedure for testing is first to establish the child's *basal mental age*, the mental-age level at which he or she passes all items. Two months of mental age are then added for each item passed at higher age levels. Consider, for example, the child who passes all items at the mental-age level of six years. If the child then passes two items at the seven-year level, four months are added; passing an additional item at the eight-year level adds two more months. This particular child has demonstrated a mental age of six years and six months. The test items sample different areas of intellectual development, so two children can earn the same mental age by passing different items on the test. The Binet test items do not tap all of a child's skills, but they provide a fairly representative sample of what children at different ages can do.

Intelligence Quotient (IQ)

Terman adopted a convenient index of intelligence that was suggested by the German psychologist William Stern (1871–1938). This index is the *intelligence quotient*, commonly known as IQ. It expresses intelligence as a ratio of mental age (MA) to chronological age (CA):

$$IQ = \frac{MA}{CA} \times 100$$

The 100 is used as a multiplier so that IQ will have a value of 100 when MA equals CA. It is evident that if the MA lags behind the CA, the resulting IQ will be less than 100; if the MA is above the CA, then IQ will be above 100.

How is the IQ to be interpreted? The distribution of IQs approximates the form of curve found for many differences among individuals, such as differences in height; this is the bell-shaped "normal" distribution curve shown in Figure 12-3. On this curve, most cases cluster around a midvalue; from there, the number gradually decreases to just a few cases at both extremes. The adjectives commonly used to describe the various IQ levels are given in Table 12-2.

In the 1960 and subsequent revisions of the Stanford-Binet, the authors introduced a method of computing the IQ from tables. The meaning of an IQ remains essentially the same, but the tables allow the IQ at any age to be interpreted somewhat more exactly. This is necessary because the ratio of mental age to chronological age does not remain linear as the individual grows older. That is, as a person progresses toward the upper bounds of his or her ability, the difference between mental age and chronological age becomes less meaningful. The new scoring method is arranged so that the mean score *for each age group* is assigned an IQ value of 100 with a standard deviation of 16. The IQ thus becomes a kind of *standard score* with a fixed mean and standard deviation.[1] For example, a child whose score on the test falls one standard deviation below the mean for his or her age group receives an IQ of 84; one whose test score is two standard deviations *above* the mean has an IQ of 132. A modern IQ is thus no longer a "quotient," but the expression "intelligence quotient" persists because of its familiarity and convenience.

Tests with More than One Scale

Tests following the pattern originated by Binet use a great assortment of items to test intelligence, and a pass or a fail on one kind of item is scored the same as a pass or a fail on another. But those who are skilled in the use and scoring of the tests learn much more than the final IQ. They may note special strengths

[1] The concepts of standard score and standard deviation are explained in the Appendix.

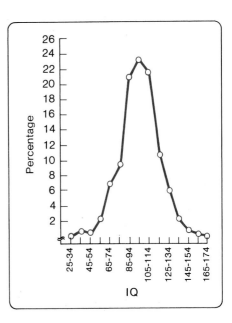

Fig. 12-3 A normal distribution curve of IQs
Distribution of Stanford-Binet IQs for 2,904 children and youths, ages 2 to 18. The slight bump on the left-hand tail represents those who are retarded as the result of specific genetic defects or birth injuries and are not part of the normal distribution. (After Terman and Merrill, 1937)

TABLE 12-2
Interpretation of intelligence quotients on the Stanford-Binet

IQ	VERBAL DESCRIPTION	PERCENT IN EACH GROUP
Above 139	Very superior	1
120–139	Superior	11
110–119	High average	18
90–109	Average	46
80–89	Low average	15
70–79	Borderline	6
Below 70	Mentally retarded	3
		100

TABLE 12-3
Tests comprising the Wechsler Adult
Intelligence Scale
The tests comprising the Wechsler Intelli-
gence Scale for Children are similar, with
some modifications.

TEST	DESCRIPTION
VERBAL SCALE	
Information	Questions tap general range of information; for example, "How many nickels make a dime?"
Comprehension	Tests practical information and ability to evaluate past experience; for example, "What is the advantage of keeping money in a bank?"
Arithmetic	Verbal problems testing arithmetic reasoning.
Similarities	Asks in what way certain objects or concepts (for example, *egg* and *seed*) are similar; measures abstract thinking.
Digit span	Series of digits presented auditorily (for example, 7-5-6-3-8) are repeated in a forward or backward direction; tests attention and rote memory.
Vocabulary	Tests word knowledge.
PERFORMANCE SCALE	
Digit symbol	A timed coding task in which numbers must be associated with marks of various shapes; tests speed of learning and writing.
Picture completion	The missing part of an incompletely drawn picture must be discovered and named; tests visual alertness and visual memory.
Block design	Pictured designs must be copied with blocks (see photo below); tests ability to perceive and analyze patterns.
Picture arrangement	A series of comic-strip-type pictures must be arranged in the right sequence to tell a story; tests understanding of social situations.
Object assembly	Puzzle pieces must be assembled to form a complete object; tests ability to deal with part-whole relationships.

Block design test from the Wechsler scales
Subject attempts to arrange the blocks to match the pictured design.

and weaknesses; a child may perform much better on a test of vocabulary, for example, than on a test that requires drawing geometric forms. These observations lead to the conjecture that what is being measured is not one simple ability but a composite of abilities.

One way to obtain information on specific kinds of abilities, rather than a single mental-age score, is to separate the items into more than one group and to score the groups separately. The Wechsler Adult Intelligence Scale (described in Table 12-3) and the Wechsler Intelligence Scale for Children do this. The items on these tests are similar to those on the Binet tests, but they are divided into two parts—a *verbal scale* and a *performance scale*—according to the content of the items. A *performance* item is one that requires manipulation or arrangement of blocks, beads, pictures, or other materials in which both stimuli and responses are nonverbal. The separate scaling of the items within one test provides a clearer picture of the individual's intellectual strengths and weaknesses. It tells, for example, how well the person performs under pressure (some subscales are timed, others are not) or how verbal skills compare with the ability to manipulate nonverbal material. Figure 12-4 shows a test profile and the way scores are summed to yield IQs. The subject who obtained these particular scores tends to do better on the performance, or nonverbal, tasks. Looking at the profile of scores, one might suspect that this young man is not doing as well scholastically as he could be; he scores lowest on those subtests

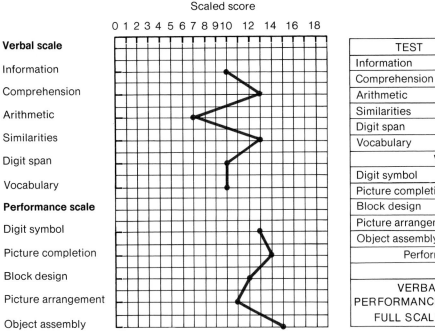

Scaled score

0 1 2 3 4 5 6 7 8 9 10 12 14 16 18

Verbal scale

Information

Comprehension

Arithmetic

Similarities

Digit span

Vocabulary

Performance scale

Digit symbol

Picture completion

Block design

Picture arrangement

Object assembly

TEST		Scaled score	
Information		10	
Comprehension		13	
Arithmetic		7	
Similarities		13	
Digit span		10	
Vocabulary		10	
Verbal score		63	
Digit symbol		13	
Picture completion		14	
Block design		12	
Picture arrangement		11	
Object assembly		15	
Performance score		65	
Total score		128	

VERBAL SCORE 63 IQ 108
PERFORMANCE SCORE 65 IQ 121
FULL SCALE SCORE 128 IQ 115

that are more closely related to "school learning"—information, arithmetic, and vocabulary. A large discrepancy between verbal and performance scores prompts the examiner to look for specific learning problems (in this case, reading disabilities or language handicaps).

The Wechsler Intelligence Scale for Children (WISC) yields scores that correspond closely to those of the Stanford-Binet. The correspondence between the Wechsler Adult Intelligence Scale (WAIS) and the Stanford-Binet is not quite as close. Although the Stanford-Binet has tests and norms for "adults," the WAIS is considered a more appropriate test for individuals 16 years old or older.

Both the Stanford-Binet and the Wechsler scales fit our requirements for trustworthy tests; that is, they show good reliability and validity. The Stanford-Binet has a reliability coefficient of about +.90 on retest; the WAIS has a retest reliability of +.91.[2] Both tests are fairly valid predictors of achievement in school; IQ scores on these tests correlate around .40 to .60 with school grades.

Group Tests

The Stanford-Binet and the Wechsler scales are *individual IQ tests;* that is, they are administered to a single individual by a specially trained tester. *Group IQ tests,* in contrast, can be administered to a large number of people by a single examiner; they are usually given in pencil-and-paper form (see Figure 12-5). The advantages of an individual test over group IQ tests are many: the tester can be certain the subject understands the questions, can evaluate the person's motivation (is the subject really trying?), and by careful observation of the way the subject approaches different tasks can gain additional clues to intellectual

Fig. 12-4 Profile for Wechsler Adult Intelligence Scale (WAIS)

Test scores for a 16-year-old male. The table on the right shows these test scores combined to give a verbal, performance, and full scale score. The manual that accompanies the test provides tables (adjusted for age) for converting these scores into IQs. Note that the test taker has a performance IQ 13 points above his verbal IQ.

[2]Reliability coefficients are based on fairly short test-retest intervals, usually of less than a year. (Sometimes different forms of the same test are given.) With longer time periods between the first and second test, the reliability coefficients decrease. For example, the reliability for tests given 10 years apart is about +.71 (see Table 12-7).

WORD KNOWLEDGE

Stench most nearly means

A Puddle of slimy water.
B Pile of debris.
C Foul odor.
D Dead animal.

Camaraderie most nearly means

A Interest in photography.
B Close friendship.
C Petty jealousies.
D Arts and crafts projects.

GENERAL INFORMATION

For which of the following taxes was it necessary to amend the US Constitution?

A Income.
B Sales.
C Liquor.
D Tobacco.

Picasso was a famous

A poet.
B painter.
C philosopher.
D soldier.

ARITHMETIC REASONING

It cost $0.50 per square yard to waterproof canvas. What will it cost to waterproof a canvas truck cover that is 15' x 24'?

A $6.67
B $18.00
C $20.00
D $180.00

The parcel post rate in the local zone is 18 cents for the first pound and 1½ cents for each additional pound. How many pounds can be sent in the local zone for $1.50?

A 88
B 89
C 100
D 225

Fig. 12-5 Group test
These are sample items from the Armed Services Vocational Aptitude Battery (ASVAB), which has been used by all military services since 1976 as the basic recruit selection and placement test.

SPACE PERCEPTION

Which of the four patterns would result when the box is unfolded?

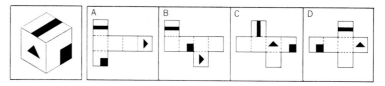

The D answer is correct.

MECHANICAL COMPREHENSION

Which bridge is the strongest?

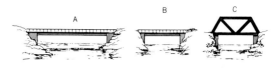

The C answer is correct.

strengths and weaknesses. Group IQ tests are useful, however, whenever large numbers of people have to be evaluated. During the Second World War the Army General Classification Test (AGCT) was administered to millions of individuals, and the results were used to classify them for skilled and unskilled jobs, to select those who had the ability for further training, and to exclude those who were unfit for the service because of low intelligence. Since then, the armed services have used a number of group tests that measure both intelligence and special aptitudes to select men and women for different specialties—for example, pilot, navigator, electronic technician, and so on. Studies of selection and training have supported the value of such group tests for screening; individuals whose scores are very low do turn out to be poor risks for special training.

Group intelligence tests are also used in schools and industry. The Scholastic Aptitude Test (SAT) and the American College Test (ACT), one of which you may have taken as part of the requirements for application to college, are group tests that can be used to measure intelligence as well as preparation for college. These tests measure a combination of intelligence and achievement. They sample skills that you have acquired during 12 years of primary education, especially vocabulary and arithmetic skills; but they attempt to avoid items that require knowledge of specific topics, focusing instead on the ability to use acquired skills to solve new kinds of problems.

Nature of Human Abilities

Some psychologists view intelligence as a *general capacity* for comprehension and reasoning that manifests itself in various ways. This was Binet's assumption. Although his test contained many different kinds of items (testing such abilities as memory span, arithmetic, and vocabulary), he noted that bright children tended to score higher than dull children on all of them. He assumed, therefore, that the different tasks sampled a basic ability or faculty: "It seems to us that in intelligence there is a fundamental faculty, the alteration or the lack of which is of the utmost importance for practical life. This faculty is judgment, otherwise called good sense, practical sense, initiative, the faculty of adapting one's self to circumstances. To judge well, to comprehend well, to reason well, these are the essential activities of intelligence" (Binet and Simon, 1905).

Despite the diverse subscales that comprise his tests, David Wechsler, too, believes that "intelligence is the aggregate or global capacity of the individual to act purposefully, to think rationally, and to deal effectively with his environment" (Wechsler, 1958).

Other psychologists question whether there is such a thing as "general intelligence." They believe that intelligence tests sample a number of mental abilities that are relatively *independent of one another*. One method of obtaining more precise information about the kinds of abilities that determine performance on intelligence tests is *factor analysis*. Factor analysis is a technique used to determine the minimum number of dimensions, or factors, that account for the observed relations (correlations) among subjects' responses over a large number of different tests. The method is too intricate to describe in any detail here, but Table 12-4 gives some understanding of what factor analysis tries to accomplish.

The originator of factor analysis, Charles Spearman, proposed that all individuals possess a general intelligence factor (called *g*) in varying amounts. A person would be described as generally bright or generally dull depending on the amount of *g*. According to Spearman, the *g* factor is the major determinant of performance on intelligence test items. In addition, there are special factors, called *s*'s, that are specific to particular abilities or test items. For example, tests of arithmetic or spatial relations would each tap a separate *s*. An individual's tested intelligence reflects the amount of *g* plus the magnitude of the various *s* factors. Performance in mathematics would be a function of a person's general intelligence and mathematical aptitude.

Primary Abilities

A later investigator, Louis Thurstone (1938), objected to Spearman's emphasis on general intelligence. Thurstone felt that intelligence could be broken down into a number of primary abilities. To find these abilities, he applied factor analysis to results from a large number of tests that employed many different types of items. One set of items was for verbal comprehension, another for arithmetical computation, and so on. He hoped to find a more definitive way of grouping intelligence test items than the rather crude item-sorting used in the Wechsler verbal and performance scales.

After intercorrelating the scores of all the tests (that is, correlating each subscore to every other), Thurstone applied factor analysis to arrive at a set of basic factors. Those test items that best represented each of the discovered factors were used to form new tests; these tests were then given to another group of subjects and the intercorrelations reanalyzed. After a number of studies of this kind, Thurstone identified seven factors as the *primary abilities* revealed by intelligence tests: verbal comprehension, word fluency, number, space, memory, perceptual speed, and reasoning (see Table 12-5).

Thurstone devised a battery of tests to measure each of these abilities, the *Test of Primary Mental Abilities*, which is still widely used. Its predictive power, however, is no greater than that provided by tests of general intelligence, such as the Wechsler scales. Thurstone's hope of discovering the basic elements of

TABLE 12-4
The method of factor analysis

What are the data that enter into factor analysis, and what are the major steps in the analysis? The data are simply scores on a variety of tests that are designed to measure various psychological contents or processes. Each of a large number of individuals obtains a score for each of a number of tests. All these scores can then be intercorrelated. That is, we know how the scores of many individuals on test 1 relate to their scores on test 2, and so on. These intercorrelations yield a table of correlations known as a *correlation matrix*. An example of such a matrix, based on only nine tests, is given below.

CORRELATION MATRIX FOR NINE APTITUDE TESTS

TESTS	2	3	4	5	6	7	8	9
1	.38	.55	.06	−.04	.05	.07	.05	.09
2		.36	.40	.28	.40	.11	.15	.13
3			.10	.01	.18	.13	.12	.10
4				.32	.60	.04	.06	.13
5					.35	.08	.13	.11
6						.01	.06	.07
7							.45	.32
8								.32

The three outlined clusters of correlations indicate that these are groups of tests with something in common not shared by other tests (that is, they show high correlations). The inadequacy of making such a judgment from a table of correlations of this kind is shown by noting the additional high correlations of test 2 with tests 4, 5, and 6, not included in the outlined clusters. We can use factor analysis to tell us more precisely what underlies these correlations. If the correlation matrix contains a number of statistically significant correlations and a number of near-zero correlations, it is apparent that some tests measure similar abilities of one kind and others, similar abilities of other kinds. The purpose of factor analysis is to be more precise about these underlying abilities.

Factor analysis then uses mathematical methods (assisted by high-speed computers) to compute the correlation of each of the tests with each of several possible underlying factors. Such correlations between test scores and factors are known as *factor loadings;* if a test correlates .05 on factor I, .10 on factor II, and .70 on factor III, it is most heavily "loaded" on factor III. For example, the nine tests with the above correlation matrix yield the *factor matrix* below (Guilford, 1967).

FACTOR MATRIX FOR NINE APTITUDE TESTS AND THREE FACTORS

TESTS	I	II	III
1	.75	−.01	.08
2	.44	.48	.16
3	.72	.07	.15
4	.08	.76	.08
5	−.01	.49	−.01
6	.16	.73	.02
7	−.03	.04	.64
8	.02	.05	.66
9	−.01	.10	.47

The outlined loadings in the factor matrix show which tests are most highly correlated with each of the underlying factors. The clusters are the same as those found in the correlation matrix, but are now given greater precision. The problem of test 2 remains, because it is loaded almost equally on factor I and factor II. It is obviously not a "factor-pure" test. Having found the three factors that account for the intercorrelations of the nine tests, the factors can be interpreted by studying the content of the tests most highly weighted on each factor. The factor analysis itself is strictly a mathematical process, but the naming and interpretation of the factors depends on a psychological analysis.

TABLE 12-5
Primary abilities

ABILITY	DESCRIPTION
Verbal comprehension	The ability to understand the meaning of words; vocabulary tests represent this factor.
Word fluency	The ability to think of words rapidly, as in solving anagrams or thinking of words that rhyme.
Number	The ability to work with numbers and perform computations.
Space	The ability to visualize space-form relationships, as in recognizing the same figure presented in different orientations.
Memory	The ability to recall verbal stimuli, such as word pairs or sentences.
Perceptual speed	The ability to grasp visual details quickly and to see similarities and differences between pictured objects.
Reasoning	The ability to find a general rule on the basis of presented instances, as in determining how a number series is constructed after being presented with only a portion of that series.

Source: Thurstone and Thurstone (1963)

intelligence through factor analysis was not fully realized, for several reasons. His primary abilities are not completely independent; there are significant intercorrelations among them, providing some support for Spearman's idea of a general intelligence factor. In addition, the number of basic abilities identified by factor analysis depends on the nature of the test items chosen. Other investigators using different test items have come up with anywhere from 20 to 120 factors that are assumed to represent different intellectual abilities (Guilford, 1967; Ekstrom and others, 1976).

The most recent outgrowth of this search for primary abilities is a group of "factor-referenced cognitive tests," published by the Educational Testing Service. These tests sample 23 different abilities. The authors of the tests point out, however, that it is probably not possible to identify "pure" factors; all of the abilities tested are intercorrelated to some extent.

Is intelligence a unitary general factor (g) or a composite of special abilities? On the basis of available evidence, it seems reasonable to conclude that there is some sort of general intelligence in addition to specific abilities. An IQ difference of 10 or 15 points on a standard intelligence test is not very meaningful; the person with the lower IQ, but with some special abilities, may well outperform the individual with the higher IQ in many situations. But with an IQ difference of 30 points there will be virtually no overlap in performance; the person with the higher IQ will do better on practically every measure of ability.

Intelligence and Creativity

Tests of general intelligence, such as the Binet and the Wechsler, correlate quite highly with achievement in school and, to a lesser extent, with intellectual achievements in later life. But they do not measure what some experts believe is an essential aspect of intelligence—namely, creative, or original, thinking.

Problem solving usually involves two phases: examining alternative solu-

TABLE 12-6
Examples of items used in tests of creativity

1 Ingenuity (Flanagan, 1963)

a A very rare wind storm destroyed the transmission tower of a television station in a small town. The station was located in a town in a flat prairie with no tall buildings. Its former 300-foot tower enabled it to serve a large farming community, and the management wanted to restore service while a new tower was being erected. The problem was temporarily solved by using a _____.

b As part of a manufacturing process, the inside lip of a deep cup-shaped casting is machine threaded. The company found that metal chips produced by the threading operation were difficult to remove from the bottom of the casting without scratching the sides. A design engineer was able to solve this problem by having the operation performed _____.

2 Unusual uses (Guilford, 1954)

Name as many uses as you can think of for:
a a toothpick
b a brick
c a paper clip

3 Consequences (Guilford, 1954)

Imagine all of the things that might possibly happen if all national and local laws were suddenly abolished.

4 Fable endings (Getzels and Jackson, 1962)

Write three endings for the following fable: a moralistic, a humorous, and a sad ending.

THE MISCHIEVOUS DOG

A rascally dog used to run quietly to the heels of every passerby and bite them without warning. So his master was obliged to tie a bell around the cur's neck that he might give notice wherever he went. This the dog thought very fine indeed, and he went about tinkling it in pride all over town. But an old hound said. . . .

5 Product improvement (Torrance, 1966)

The subject is presented with a series of objects, such as children's toys or instruments used in his or her particular occupation, and asked to make suggestions for their improvement.

6 Pattern meanings (Wallach and Kogan, 1965)

The subject is shown a series of patterns of geometric forms (like the samples shown below) and asked to imagine all the things each pattern could be.

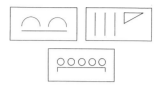

7 Remote associations (Mednick, 1962)

Find a fourth word which is associated with each of these three words:
a rat—blue—cottage
b out—dog—cat
c wheel—electric—high
d surprise—line—birthday

8 Word association (Getzels and Jackson, 1962)

Write as many meanings as you can for each of the following words:
a duck
b sack
c pitch
d fair

---

tions and then choosing the one that seems most appropriate. The first phase, recalling possible solutions or conjuring up new ones, has been called *divergent thinking:* the individual's thoughts "diverge" along a number of different paths. The second phase, applying one's knowledge and the rules of logic in order to narrow the possibilities and "converge" on the most appropriate solution, has been called *convergent thinking* (Guilford and Hoepfner, 1971). In solving difficult problems, people often alternate between the two modes of thought; when initial solutions are discarded as inappropriate, it is necessary to do additional divergent thinking—that is, to conceive of new possibilities. Divergent thinking is more closely associated with originality and creativity.

Most intelligence tests emphasize convergent thinking; they present problems that have well-defined, correct answers. Thus, traditional IQ tests may fail to identify individuals who excel in divergent thinking—those who are skillful at producing new and original ideas. Because of this possibility, attempts have been made to devise tests that measure divergent thinking. A sample item might ask, "What uses can you think of for a brick?" The person who gives many varied answers ("heat it, to warm your bed," "as a weapon," "to hold the shelves of a bookcase") would score high on divergent thinking. Other examples of test items designed to measure divergent or "creative" thinking are given in Table 12-6.

Two important questions must be asked concerning creativity tests: (1) Are the abilities they measure different from those sampled by tests of general intelligence? (2) Do scores on these tests predict creative achievements in real life?

There does seem to be a considerable overlap between abilities sampled by intelligence tests and those sampled by tests of creativity. For the population as a whole, scores on IQ tests tend to be positively correlated with scores on creativity tests (that is, people with above-average IQs tend to have above-average scores on creativity tests). But beyond a certain level of intelligence (an IQ of about 120), there is little relationship between intelligence and creativity scores. Some individuals with very high IQs score low on creativity tests; some with only "above average" intelligence do extremely well on creativity tests. Thus, creativity appears to be independent of IQ only at the upper end of the distribution.

These findings have led some experts to propose a "threshold model" of creativity: a certain level of intelligence is necessary before an individual can make a creative contribution in his or her line of work (discovering a new scientific principle, inventing a new mechanical device, writing an outstanding poem or play). Beyond that threshold, creative achievement depends on other factors—the kind of fluency of ideas sampled by creativity tests as well as certain personality variables (Crockenburg, 1972). The intelligence threshold necessary for creative achievements is assumed to vary for different abilities. That is, it probably requires a higher IQ to discover a new principle in theoretical physics or mathematics than to write an original short story.

We can only speculate on whether creativity tests predict actual creative achievements. So far there have been few long-term studies relating scores on creativity tests to achievements in later life, but the results of some studies are pessimistic. For example, there seems to be little relationship between scores on tests of divergent thinking in the fifth or the tenth grade and talented extracurricular accomplishments (for example, in leadership, drama, art, science) in high school (Kogan and Pankove, 1974). Creativity tests sample the person's ability to give novel responses, but originality by itself is not enough. An original idea or creative product must be appropriate. If a new theory, it must be in accord with the known facts; if an invention, it must serve its purposes efficiently and economically; if an artistic product, it must be aesthetically satisfying. Most creative discoveries require both convergent and divergent thinking: envisioning new and unique solutions to a problem and evaluating them in light of one's knowledge about the relevant facts.

Studies of scientists and artists who have made significant and original contributions to their fields suggest that such personality factors as independence of judgment, motivation to achieve, initiative, and a tolerance for ambiguity are important requirements for creative discoveries. Thus, creativity may not be something we can measure very well by a test.

Age Changes in Intelligence

The Binet test was developed on the principle that the processes influencing intelligence test performance develop with the years, so that a mental-age score remains appropriate at least through childhood. The IQ was based on the presumption that the mental age for a bright child would grow more rapidly than for a dull one, so some degree of constancy would be found for the ratio of MA to CA. Both of these conjectures were found to be approximately true (see Figure 12-6), although later work has made a number of qualifications necessary.

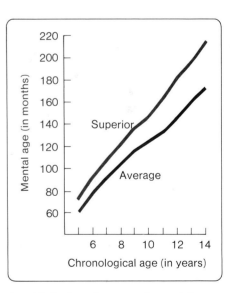

Fig. 12-6 Consistency of mental age differences

Two groups of boys were selected at age five; one scored high on intelligence tests, one average. The superior group gained in mental age more rapidly than the average one, thus approximating a constant IQ difference between the groups as they grew older. (After Baldwin and Stecher, 1922)

TABLE 12-7
Correlations among intelligence test scores at different ages

Table entries give correlations between IQs obtained for the same individuals at different ages. An IQ obtained at age 7 correlates .77 with one obtained at age 10 and .71 with one obtained at age 18. Note that the size of the correlation decreases as years between testing increases.

		RETEST AGE (IN YEARS)			
		7	10	14	18
INITIAL TEST AGE (IN YEARS)	2	.46	.37	.28	.31
	7		.77	.75	.71
	10			.86	.73
	14				.76

Source: Jensen (1973)

Stability of IQ

The rate of intellectual growth is relatively stable for most people; once they reach school age, their IQ does not change radically from test to retest, even over fairly long time intervals. Table 12-7 presents correlations between IQs obtained from the same individuals at different ages. Inspecting this table, we see that an IQ at age 7 correlates .71 with one obtained at age 18. In other words, knowing the IQ at age 7 provides a very accurate predictor of IQ at age 18. But the table also indicates that intelligence measures taken at age two or before do *not* correlate very highly with later measures. One reason is that the infant intelligence scales primarily measure visual-motor ability. Intelligence may also be much more plastic in the early years. By age seven, however, the child's IQ score is generally a fairly good predictor of later ability.

Although IQ is relatively stable for most people after about age seven, some individuals do show large shifts in IQ. If there are major changes in environmental conditions and in the opportunities for learning—either for better or for worse—there may be marked changes in tested intelligence. One longitudinal study in which a large number of individuals were tested repeatedly from birth to age 36 found shifts in IQ of more than 15 points for some cases (Bayley, 1970). The variables that produce large changes in IQ for individual children are not always easy to specify, but emotional and motivational factors appear to play a major role. For example, one study found that children whose IQ increased during the early years were more vigorous, emotionally independent, aggressive, and actively engaged in exploring their environment than those whose IQ failed to increase (Sontag and others, 1958). In later years, changes in IQ appear most closely related to strong motivation to achieve.

Growth of Intelligence

Tests using the concept of mental age are so scored that MA averaged over all individuals of a given age will equal CA. For example, the MA of 13-year-olds will vary, but MA averaged over all 13-year-olds will equal CA of 13. To look at age changes in intellectual ability, we need units for measuring mental growth that are not forced to correspond to age. Scores on Thurstone's Test of Primary Mental Abilities have been used for this purpose. Although separate abilities grow at different rates, gain is generally rapid in childhood and slows in the teens (see Figure 12-7).

Fig. 12-7 Growth of four primary abilities

The scale adopted is that of 1.0 for adult status. Thus, 80 percent of adult status for perceptual speed is achieved at age 12; for reasoning, at age 14; for verbal comprehension, at age 18; and for word fluency, later than 20. (After Thurstone, 1955)

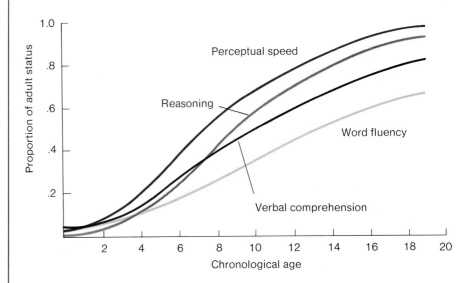

Figure 12-8 shows results from a large-scale longitudinal study that used Wechsler scales, with the scores converted to an absolute scale of mental ability. The same individuals were followed from birth to age 36. Mental ability increased up to age 26, after which it leveled off and remained unchanged through age 36.

Remember that the curve in Figure 12-8 is an average; it masks the fact that some individuals may show an increase in IQ after age 26, some a decrease. Averaging creates even more of a problem when we look at age changes in intellectual functioning after age 40. The typical study shows a steady decrease in intellectual ability after age 40, with a precipitous drop after age 60 (see Figure 12-9). But analysis of the data indicates that whether ability declines during middle and old age depends both on the *person* and on the *type of ability* tested. Individuals who remain physically well and continue to engage in stimulating activities show little decrease in intellectual ability up to age 70. Physical disabilities, particularly those resulting from strokes or progressive reduction of blood circulated to the brain, usually result in dramatic decreases in intellectual ability. When data from these two types of individuals are combined, the result is the somewhat deceptive average decline shown in Figure 12-9.

Mental abilities that require speed and extensive use of short-term memory tend to reach their peak between ages 30 and 40 and decline thereafter. Tests that tap general knowledge show little decline with age. The rate of decline of specific abilities is related to one's occupation; people in intellectually demanding occupations do not decline in mental ability as early as others.

The decline in scores on some tests of intelligence in the later years does not signify that mature adults are less competent to play their role in life. An older person's accumulated knowledge and experience may more than compensate for diminished speed and efficiency of intellectual functioning. In fact, an older individual may be more competent in some situations than a brighter younger person who lacks experience.

Genetic and Environmental Determinants of Intelligence

People differ in intellectual ability. How much of this difference is due to the particular genes we inherit and how much is due to the environment in which we are raised? The heredity-environment issue, debated in regard to many aspects of human behavior, has focused primarily on the area of intelligence. Most experts agree that at least some aspects of intelligence are inherited, but opinions differ as to the relative contributions of heredity and environment.

Genetic Relationships and Intelligence

Most of the evidence bearing on the inheritance of intelligence comes from studies correlating IQs between persons of various degrees of genetic relationship. Figure 12-10 summarizes the results of a large number of studies of this type. In general, the closer the genetic relationship, the more similar the tested intelligence. The average correlation between the IQs of parents and their natural children is .50; between parents and their adopted children, the correlation is about .25. Identical twins, because they develop from a single egg, share precisely the same heredity; the correlation between their IQs is very high—about .90. The IQs of fraternal twins (who are no more alike genetically

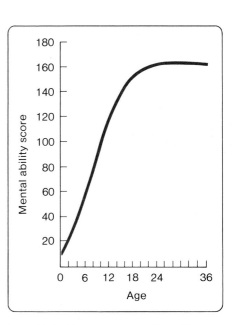

Fig. 12-8 Growth curve of intelligence
Theoretical curve of the growth of intelligence based on a large-scale longitudinal study. The intelligence scores are based on available age-appropriate tests, primarily Bayley infant scales, Stanford-Binet, and the Wechsler Adult scales, with the scores converted to an absolute scale of mental ability. (After Bayley, 1970)

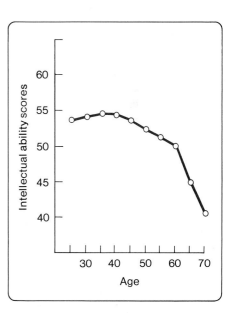

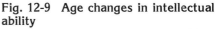

Fig. 12-9 Age changes in intellectual ability
The scores are based on a composite of five primary abilities tests and weight heavily tests that require quickness of response, such as word fluency and perceptual speed. The height of ability appears at age 35 and declines fairly rapidly after age 60. (After Schaie and Strother, 1968)

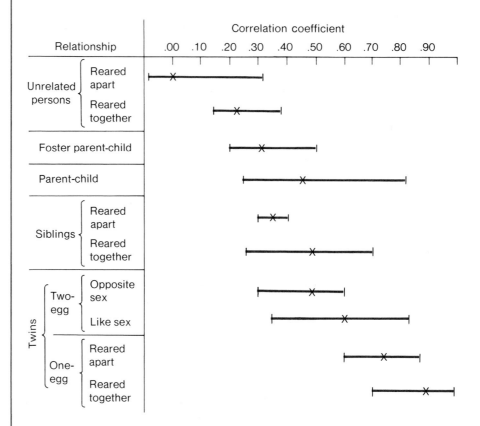

Fig. 12-10 Genetic relationships and IQ

The results of 52 studies of the correlation coefficients for "test intelligence" between persons of various relationships are summarized on the right. The horizontal lines give the range of the observed coefficients obtained in various studies, and the X on each line marks the average. (After Erlenmeyer-Kimling and Jarvik, 1963)

than ordinary siblings, because they develop from separate eggs) correlate about .55.

But, although genetic determinants of intelligence are strong, the results shown in Figure 12-10 also point to the importance of environment. Note that when individuals are reared in the same home situation IQ similarity increases, even for individuals who are unrelated. And although adopted children resemble their natural parents more than their adopted parents in intellectual ability, their IQs are higher than would be predicted on the basis of their natural parents' ability (Skodak and Skeels, 1949; Scarr and Weinberg, 1976). Environment makes a difference.

Estimates of Heritability

Starting with data like those in Figure 12-10, it is possible to estimate what portion of the variability in test scores is due to environment and what portion is due to heredity. (The theory that permits us to make such estimates is too lengthy to present here, but it is discussed in most genetics textbooks.) There are several methods used in making these estimates; the most common involves comparing the variability of fraternal and identical twins on a given trait. To do this, two quantities are estimated: (1) the total variability due to both environment and heredity, V_T, based on the differences between pairs of fraternal twins, and (2) the environmental variability alone, V_E, based on the differences between pairs of identical twins. The difference between the two quantities is the variability due to genetic factors, V_G. The heritability ratio, or simply *heritability*, is the ratio between genetic variability and total variability:

$$\text{Heritability} = \frac{V_G}{V_T}$$

In other words, heritability is the proportion of a trait's variation within a specified population that is attributable to genetic differences.

Heritability ranges between zero and one. When identical twins resemble each other a great deal more than fraternal twins on a given trait, heritability approaches one. When the resemblance between identical twins is about the same as that between fraternal twins, then heritability approaches zero. For the data summarized in Figure 12-10, the estimate of heritability is .74.

Heritability estimates for intelligence have ranged widely (from about .25 to .87), indicating that IQ data comparing fraternal and identical twins vary greatly from one study to another. The fact that there is such diversity in results and that the data are from field studies rather than from well-controlled experiments means that we cannot make a precise estimate of heritability (Kamin, 1976).

Regardless of the heritability estimate one accepts, it is clear that intelligence is influenced by one's genes. Most probably, intellectual ability is determined by a number of genes whose individual effects are small but cumulative. Even if only 5 to 10 pairs of genes are involved, the possible combinations would approximate a normal distribution of IQ scores and would allow for a wide range of intellectual ability even within a single family (Bouchard, 1976). But several important facts must be kept in mind. First, heritability estimates apply to populations under quite specific conditions and not to individuals. For example, the statement that the heritability of Stanford-Binet IQ scores for United States schoolchildren is .65 does not mean that the IQ of each child is 65 percent determined by heredity; it means that 65 percent of the variation in IQ test scores among United States schoolchildren can be attributed to genetic differences. Second, even though intelligence has a genetic component, environmental conditions are extremely important.

Environmental Influences

We can think of a person's genes as imposing a top and bottom limit on intelligence—that is, establishing a *range* of intellectual ability. Environmental influences—what happens to the individual during the course of development—will determine where within that range the person's IQ will fall. In other words, genes do not specify behavior but establish a range of probable responses to the environment—the *reaction range.* Figure 12-11 illustrates this

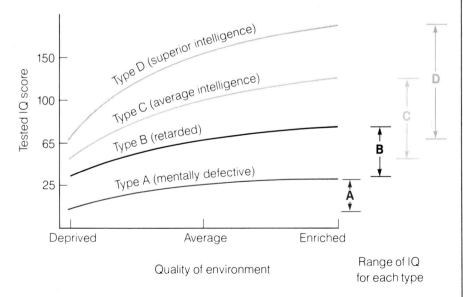

Fig. 12-11 Effects of different environments on IQ
The curves represent hypothetical reaction ranges for four individuals who vary in inherited intellectual potential. For example, the individual labeled type D has an IQ of about 65 when raised in a deprived environment but an IQ of over 180 when raised in a maximally enriched environment. The vertical arrows to the right indicate the range of possible IQ scores for each type. (Adapted from Gottesman, 1963)

Recently, the debate over genetic contributions to intelligence has focused on the possibility of inherited racial differences in intelligence—specifically, on the question of whether blacks are innately less intelligent than whites. In view of the heated controversy about this issue and its significance for social policy, it is important that we examine the available evidence.

On standard intelligence tests, black Americans, as a group, score 10 to 15 IQ points lower than white Americans, as a group. This fact is not debated; the controversy revolves around interpretation of this difference. Some behavioral scientists and geneticists believe that the two groups differ in inherited ability (Shockley, 1972; Jensen, 1973). Others argue that black-white differences in average IQ can be attributed entirely to environmental differences between the two groups (Kagan, 1973; Chomsky, 1976; Kamin, 1976). Probably the majority believe that genetic and environmental differences are so confounded that the question is at present unanswerable. The issues involved are exceedingly complex; the best we can do here is to summarize a few of the main points.

1 Most intelligence tests have been developed using white populations. Since blacks and whites generally grow up in quite different environments and have different experiences, the content of such tests may not be appropriate for blacks. And a black child may react differently to a testing situation (particularly if the examiner is white) than a white child. Thus, the whole issue of estimating black intelligence is complicated by the question of whether the tests are appropriate and whether the data obtained by white testers represent an unbiased measure of IQ.

2 Although blacks and whites may differ in physical appearance, they do not represent distinct biological groups. In fact, differences in gene structures (where known) are in most cases greater *within* the races than between them.

3 Heritability is a population statistic (like infant mortality or birth rate); it depends on the environmental and genetic variation among a given group of people at a given time. Thus, while heritability ratios estimated for white populations indi-

cate that variations in IQ are partly a function of heredity, such estimates do not permit us to make inferences about heritability ratios among black populations. Heritability of IQ could be high among whites and low among blacks.* More important, heritability estimates do not tell us anything about differences *between* populations. The heritability of a characteristic could be the same for two groups, even though the differences between them are caused entirely by environment. For example, suppose the heritability of height is the same for two populations, A and B. If individuals in population A are raised on a starvation diet, they will be shorter, on the average, than those of population B. Variations in adult height within each group would still be influenced by heredity (that is, undernourished individuals with tall parents will be taller than undernourished individuals with short parents), but the difference in average height between the two groups is clearly the result of environment. To summarize, heritability estimates do not permit us to draw

concept; it shows hypothetical reaction ranges for IQ for individuals of different genetic potential raised in deprived, average, and enriched environments. In each case, an enriched environment raises the individual's IQ score and a deprived one lowers it. But each type has its own range of reaction; persons with the genetic potential for average or superior intelligence under normal environmental conditions (curves C and D) have much larger reaction ranges than individuals who are retarded (curve B) or mentally defective (curve A). Presumably the person with the superior potential (D) has the greatest capacity to utilize an enriched environment and would show the greatest decrease in IQ under deprived conditions. Several studies suggest that an adverse environment does have its greatest effect on children of above-average ability (Weisman, 1966; Scarr-Salapatek, 1971).

The environmental conditions that determine how the individual's intellectual potential will develop include nutrition, health, quality of stimulation, the emotional climate of the home, and the type of feedback given for behavior. Given two children with the same genes, the child with the better prenatal and postnatal nutrition, the more intellectually stimulating and emotionally secure

Intelligence

conclusions about differences between populations.

4 Among black populations, there is some tendency for lightness of skin color (presumably an indication of the degree of intermixture with whites) to correlate positively with IQ. But such correlations are very low (typically .15) and can be explained on the basis of environmental differences—a lighter skin color is associated with less discrimination and greater opportunity. A recent study found no relationship between degree of African ancestry (as estimated by skin color and blood type) and intellectual ability (Scarr and others, 1977).

5 A study of illegitimate children fathered by United States servicemen during the occupation of Germany after the Second World War found no overall difference in average IQ between children whose fathers were black and those whose fathers were white. Since these children were all raised by German mothers of similar social status and were matched with children of the same age in the classroom, the results

provide strong support for environment as the major determinant of racial IQ differences (Eyferth and others, 1960).

6 When black or interracial children (those with one black parent) are adopted before they are a year old and raised by white families who are above average in income and education, they score more than 15 IQ points higher than underprivileged black children reared by their biological families; their performance on school achievement tests is slightly above the national norms (Scarr and Weinberg, 1976).

Some of these points are examined more extensively in a survey of the intelligence-race issue by Loehlin, Lindzey, and Spuhler (1975). A variety of articles on both sides of the controversy can be found in a book edited by Block and Dworkin (1976).

The authors of this text believe that it is not possible to draw valid conclusions about innate racial differences in intelligence from the available data. Cultural differences and differences in psychological environments between blacks and whites influence the devel-

opment of cognitive abilities in complex ways, and no study has succeeded in either estimating or eliminating their effects. Culture-fair intelligence tests deal with this problem only on the most superficial level; using current methods, it is impossible to separate those aspects of cognitive development that are influenced by cultural factors from those that are not. As long as systematic differences remain in the conditions under which blacks and whites are raised (and as long as the effects of these differences cannot be reliably estimated), no valid conclusions can be drawn concerning innate differences in intelligence between races.

---

*"Heritable" and "genetically based" are not the same thing; a characteristic could have a genetic basis without being heritable. For example, genes play a role in determining a person's height. But if there were a population where everyone had the same genes (everyone was an identical twin of everyone else), the heritability for height would be zero, since there are no genetically caused differences in height. Even if heredity plays an important role in the development of a characteristic, if there is little genetically caused variation, the heritability of the characteristic could be low.

---

home, and the more appropriate rewards for academic accomplishments will attain the higher IQ score when tested in first grade. Studies have shown that IQ differences between children of low and high socioeconomic status become progressively greater between birth and entrance into school (Bayley, 1970). This suggests that environmental conditions accentuate whatever differences are present at birth.

GETTING A HEAD START Because children from underprivileged families tend to fall behind in cognitive development even before they enter school, efforts have been made to provide more intellectual stimulation for such children during their early years. In 1965, as part of President Johnson's "war on poverty," Congress authorized funds for a number of programs aimed at providing learning experiences for two- to five-year-olds from poor homes. These programs, funded by Project Headstart, varied in approach. In some, special teachers visited the children at home several times a week to play with them. They engaged the children in such activities as building with blocks, looking at pictures, naming colors, and taught them concepts such as big-little

DETERMINANTS OF INTELLIGENCE

and rough-smooth. In brief, the teachers provided the kind of intellectual stimulation that children in upper-class homes usually receive from their parents. The visiting teacher also taught the mothers how to provide the same kinds of activities for their children. In other programs, the children went to special classrooms where they interacted with teachers in similar play-learning activities; some of these programs involved the parents, others did not.

The results of these early-education programs have generally been promising. Children who have participated in such programs score 6 to 10 points higher on the Stanford-Binet or WISC upon entering school than children who have not received special attention; they also tend to be more self-confident and socially competent. Follow-up studies indicate that there are lasting gains. For example, one study looked at the performance of fifth- and sixth-grade boys who had participated in a special preschool program 12 years earlier. These were children from impoverished homes in New York City. They still scored higher on the Stanford-Binet (average IQ of 99) than a group of matched controls (average IQ of 93). They also scored significantly higher on arithmetic achievement tests. And only 20 percent of them had been held back a grade—compared to 50 percent of the other lower-class children in the same schools (Palmer, 1976). Other long-term studies show similar gains for children of both sexes who had early-education experiences. In addition, they indicate that such children score significantly higher than controls on reading achievement tests and are less apt to need special remedial classes (Lazar, 1977).

The Headstart programs have shown that early intellectual stimulation can have a significant impact on later school performance. Changing the environment from "deprived" to more "normal" allows the child to move toward the upper limits of his or her inherited intellectual ability, or reaction range. The specific methods used in the programs appear to be less important than involvement of the parents. Programs that actively involve the parents—getting them interested in their children's development and showing them how to provide a more stimulating environment—tend to produce the greatest gains.

Extremes of Intelligence

As we have seen, intelligence follows a normal distribution, with most individuals falling somewhere near the middle. There is no sharp break between the mentally subnormal and the normal or between the normal and the mentally gifted. Nevertheless, a study of those at the extremes of the distribution has identified problems and issues that require special attention.

Mentally Subnormal

It is estimated that about 3 percent of the population in the United States is mentally retarded (Isaacson, 1970); the percentage varies depending on the criteria used. An IQ below 70 is generally considered retarded, but more important than a score on an intelligence test is the individual's social competence—the degree to which he or she is self-sufficient. The farm worker who was unable to finish school but lives independently as a hired hand is normal in his environment, even though he may be recognizably dull; the same man might find it difficult to live successfully in the city. Thus, the distinction between dull-normal and subnormal rests on the complexity of the social conditions under which independence must be maintained.

The majority of retarded people have IQs between 50 and 70 and are classified as *educable;* with the proper help they can learn to support themselves and find a place in the community. Their intellectual level as adults may be comparable to that of the average 8- to 12-year-old child. A much smaller percentage of retarded individuals (.3 percent of the total population) have IQs between 30 and 50 and are classified as *trainable.* Although they will always be dependent on others for support, they can learn to take care of their daily needs and can function in a sheltered environment. Their intellectual level as adults may be comparable to that of the average four- to seven-year-old child. Some of the brighter individuals achieve a fair command of spoken language and may be taught to read and write a little. Individuals with IQs below 30 are severely handicapped and *totally dependent* on others for care; this group constitutes less than .1 percent of the total population.

CAUSES OF SUBNORMALITY In the majority of cases of subnormal intelligence, no physical cause can be discovered. The child is essentially sound physically, and there is no history of disease or injury that might have produced brain damage. Retardation is usually minimal; the individual suffers from a general deficiency rather than an identifiable defect. Such individuals tend to come from families that are low in intelligence and live in impoverished conditions. This type of retardation has been called *familial-cultural;* the cause is assumed to be both genetic and environmental. Individuals of low intelligence cannot get jobs that pay well; they marry other persons with low IQs and produce children whose intellectual potential is limited. Environmental circumstances—inadequate infant nutrition and medical care, lack of intellectual stimulation and parental concern—contribute to further intellectual impairment. Thus a vicious cycle continues.

In cases of more severe retardation, some sort of physical cause can usually be identified—brain injury, disease, or specific genetic defects that preclude normal intellectual growth. The mental impairment in these cases is usually related to brain damage, and gross structural defects are often apparent in the nervous system. It has been proposed that such children be called *mentally defective* rather than *mentally retarded,* since their intellectual impairment results from an identifiable defect. Mentally defective individuals may be found in any family or socioeconomic group, regardless of genetic background.

Any condition that affects normal development of the brain can cause mental deficiency. Physical damage to the brain or lack of oxygen (anoxia) during birth can result in intellectual impairment. It is estimated that 1 baby in 1,000 suffers from damage of this type sufficient to prevent the intelligence level from reaching that of a 12-year-old (Isaacson, 1970). Maternal infections during the early months of pregnancy, such as German measles or syphilis, can cause brain damage, as can certain drugs taken by the mother.

Some types of mental deficiency are caused by specific genetic defects. An example is Down's syndrome (sometimes called *mongolism*), a severe form of mental deficiency accompanied by physical abnormalities. The body cells of children with Down's syndrome contain 47 chromosomes rather than the normal 46; the extra chromosome apparently comes from the mother as the result of faulty separation of a particular chromosome pair in the egg cell prior to ovulation. Down's syndrome children are most frequently born to older mothers; a woman in her twenties has 1 chance in 2,000 of producing a baby with the syndrome, while the risk for a woman in her forties is 1 in 50. The

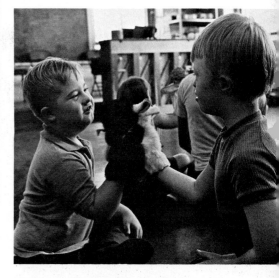

Children with Down's syndrome
Children born with Down's syndrome have been called mongoloid because they tend to have slanting eye slits with small folds covering the inner corners of their eyes. Other characteristics often found are short stature; a small, round head; irregularly spaced teeth; a thick, protruding tongue that is fissured; and square, stubby hands and feet. Their gait is often awkward. Postmortem studies of the brains of individuals with Down's syndrome show widespread areas of brain cells that have failed to grow.

reason is not clear. Changes in the reproductive system of the older woman may be responsible for the genetic fault. It is also possible that the older the mother, the greater the probability of exposure to radiation that causes gene mutations. Note that although Down's syndrome is a *genetic* disorder it is *not inherited*.[3] The reproductive error produces a genetic makeup in the child that is unlike that of the parents.

Some children with Down's syndrome learn to speak a little and to master simple chores. In most cases, however, they cannot speak or can utter just a few hoarse sounds, and they seldom learn more than elementary self-care. These children tend to be affectionate and docile compared to other retarded children. Because of their numerous physical deficiencies, their health is poor; many die before reaching adolescence.

TREATMENT OF THE SUBNORMAL   From time to time there are reports of remarkable achievements in raising IQ scores of subnormal children. Headlines in newspapers and articles in magazines raise the hopes of countless parents who have retarded children. This publicity is unfortunately misleading, because the overall evidence we have today is not encouraging. It gives little promise of dramatic improvement in the mentally subnormal, although this does not mean that the retarded or defective child cannot be helped.[4]

A great deal can be done for subnormal children. They can be taught to take care of themselves and can learn vocational skills appropriate to their intellectual level. Such instruction must not be confused, however, with raising IQ. In many subnormal individuals, a small increase in IQ comes with better social adjustment, but there is little reason to expect striking changes as a result of an improved environment.

Many persons of low intelligence get along satisfactorily in the community. Several follow-up studies have been made of children who were classified as mentally retarded when they were of school age. The investigators found that a substantial proportion of these individuals were able to learn simple vocational skills and support themselves as adults (Clark and others, 1969; Zucker and Altman, 1973).

Mentally Gifted

At the other end of the scale from the mentally subnormal are those who are intellectually gifted. With the development of intelligence tests, it has become possible to select for study large groups of superior children and then to follow their careers. One of the best known of these studies, started by Terman and his associates in 1921, has followed the progress of over 1,500 gifted individuals (those with IQs of 140 or above) from their early school years through adult life. Reports on the subjects have been made periodically for over half a century, the latest when the subjects were in their sixties (Sears, 1977; Sears and Barbee, 1977).

Terman's gifted children were superior physically as well as mentally. On the average, they were more than an inch taller than other children of the same age in elementary school. Their weights at birth were above normal. They talked early and walked early. When the study started, seven out of eight were in grades ahead of their age groups in school; none was below grade level. They

[3]One rare type of Down's syndrome, which accounts for only 4 percent of all cases, is inherited.
[4]The child who has special problems because he or she comes from a different cultural background and who may be underachieving in school can often be helped. The economically disadvantaged child should not be classified as mentally subnormal because he or she is behind academically. With appropriate help, there is usually an improvement in school achievement and often an increase in IQ.

read an unusually large number and variety of books. They also tended to show high leadership ability and social adaptability.

The characteristics of these gifted children contradict the myth that the very bright child is a weakling and a social misfit. The evidence is all to the contrary. Superior intelligence in Terman's subjects was associated with good health, social adaptability, and leadership.

GIFTED CHILDREN AS YOUNG ADULTS The extent to which early promise was fulfilled by Terman's gifted children can be estimated from their performance in adult life. Although on the whole they were extremely successful, there were exceptions. Some failed in college, some were vocational misfits, some ran afoul of the law. But the least successful group differed little in their adult intelligence test scores from the most successful group. The average IQ difference between the most and the least successful groups was only six points. The small difference in IQ scores cannot account for the differences in achievement. We must conclude that nonintellectual qualities are very important in success.

What do "successful" and "unsuccessful" mean in these comparisons? The subjects in Terman's study were classified in three groups: A, the most successful; B, the intermediately successful; and C, the least successful. The criterion of success was primarily "the extent to which a subject made use of his or her intellectual ability." Listing in *Who's Who in America*, representation in literary or scholarly publications, a responsible managerial position, outstanding achievement in any intellectual or professional calling—all entered into the judgments.

Although the A and C groups did not differ very much in IQ, a study of their records showed that they differed in many other respects—chiefly in general social adjustment and in achievement motivation. These are personality and motivational traits rather than intellectual ones.

Have these intellectually able people passed on their abilities to the next generation? Tests given to their offspring showed an average IQ of 133, although, as expected, the scores ranged widely—from mentally subnormal to above 200 (Oden, 1968).

Present Status of Ability Tests

Among the various tests of ability, we have chosen to consider intelligence tests in greatest detail. Despite their limitations, intelligence tests are one of the most widely used tools that psychology has developed. Such tests will continue to be useful, provided they are neither overvalued as a measurement of what a person can do nor undervalued because of their obvious defects. In the discussion that follows, we shall try to view them in the perspective of other ability measures and in relation to the social consequences of their use.

Blurred Distinction Between Aptitude and Achievement Tests

We pointed out earlier that aptitudes have to be assessed on the basis of prior achievements. It is a mistake to assign aptitude entirely to innate potential and achievement entirely to training; both are complex results of innate potential, generalized experience, and specific training. Thus, scholastic aptitude tests (the preferred name for intelligence tests such as the SAT and ACT that predict school or college grades) include learned material, although they do not require that the student have taken a particular course in, say, mathematics or history. An achievement test in a particular subject does presuppose acquaintance with a specific body of material.

A useful illustration of the blurred distinction between the two types of tests is the National Merit Scholarship Qualifying Test, taken annually by about 800,000 high school students in the United States. This test is given to all interested students, regardless of the school subjects they have studied, but it is still a test of *educational development,* not of aptitude alone. It is a measure of both the student's aptitude and the effectiveness of his or her schooling. The usefulness of the test in predicting success in college is quite high. The first group of Merit Scholarship recipients entered college in 1956. A study made approximately 10 years later revealed that 96 percent had graduated from college and that more than half of the men and 40 percent of the women had obtained advanced degrees (Stalnaker, 1965). In terms of our definition of aptitude testing as designed for prediction, the National Merit test does reveal aptitude for college work, although various achievement tests and high school grades also predict college success.

For practical purposes of prediction, the fact that test content reflects both schooling and individual potential is immaterial. However, if the goal is understanding the nature of intelligence, it does matter whether or not effective schooling actually raises intellectual potential.

Public Concerns About Testing

Concerns about psychological testing have focused on several objections: (1) the invasion of privacy, (2) the secrecy surrounding test scores, (3) the types of talent measured by tests, (4) the unfairness of the tests to minority groups, and (5) the use of group tests to separate schoolchildren into special classes. All these problems must be taken seriously by those using tests, and we shall consider each in turn.

1   Because a test is personal, it is not necessarily an invasion of privacy. When the purpose of the test is benign—when it is used to help individuals plan their lives and avoid failure—it is no different, in principle, from the physical examination required for participation in athletics (for example, children with heart ailments should not be advised to go out for long-distance running).

2   The secrecy surrounding test scores was intended to guard against the possibility that parents might give too much credence to scores indicating their child to be below average or handicapped in some way. Aware of the many factors influencing test performance, psychologists prefer to give repeated tests and make allowances for poor performance. This approach has backfired somewhat, because it makes the test scores appear to be more important than they are. Since what intelligence tests do best is predict school grades, there should be no more damage in knowing that one has a low IQ than in knowing that one is doing poorly in school. Results of attitude studies show that more often than not children who were given their test scores raised their estimates of their own intelligence (Brim, 1965). In other words, children have many indicators, beyond intelligence test scores, that they are brighter or duller than other children. The National Merit Scholarship Corporation makes full disclosure of its scores, with apparently no harmful results.

3 As Terman's study of gifted individuals showed, the intelligence test is a limited predictor of success; creativity, special talents, motivation, perseverance, and other personality variables are important. It is worth noting that Terman's gifted group did not include any famous composers, artists, musicians, or poets.

The Scholastic Aptitude Test and the National Merit Scholarship Qualifying Test have proved to be very successful in selecting students who will get good grades in college. But when college admission officials place too much emphasis on test scores, they are apt to overlook those students who may have extraordinary talent in art, drama, or music. They may also overlook students who have aimed all of their energy and enthusiasm toward creative efforts in a specific area—for example, an award-winning science project or an innovative community program to help retarded children—to the neglect of some academic subjects. Psychologists have stressed that, in any selection procedure, scores on intelligence and scholastic aptitude tests should be considered in conjunction with other information.

4 The fairness of the tests to underprivileged and minority groups is a complex problem to which psychologists have devoted considerable study (Loehlin and others, 1975; Scarr, 1977). A point often overlooked is that ability tests provide objective criteria and when properly used may overcome some of the discrimination practiced against minority groups, thus increasing the opportunities for some. This follows because the tests measure ability rather than social status. Indeed, one survey revealed that lower-class blacks favored the use of tests in job selection and promotion more than the white respondents did (Brim, 1965).

5 Schools often use group intelligence or achievement tests to determine class placement. Those who score low may be placed in classes for "slow learners," while the high scorers may be put in accelerated or "enriched" programs. Not only is there a social stigma attached to being in the "slow" group, but a child's initial placement sometimes determines his or her path through school. Those who score below average on the tests may be discouraged from taking college preparatory courses, even though they may have the potential.

The use of group tests to classify children is currently a very controversial issue among those concerned with the fairness of such tests to underprivileged and minority children, because a disproportionately large number of these children are classed as "mentally retarded" on the basis of their test scores. Legal suits by parents have prompted several states to prohibit the use of group intelligence tests for purposes of classification. But most psychologists and educators believe that these tests serve an important function when properly used; rather than discard the tests, they want them to be used to improve the educational opportunities for disadvantaged and minority children. They stress that group intelligence tests should be used only as an initial screening device. If a child scores low, more intensive evaluation and individual testing should be undertaken to discover (a) whether the group test scores represent an accurate assessment of the child's current abilities, (b) what are the child's particular intellectual strengths and weaknesses, and (c) what is the best instructional program for improving his or her skills. Tests should be used to match instruction to individual needs, not to label a child.

Often a comparison of intelligence test and achievement test scores yields valuable information. For example, some children whose achievement test scores in math or reading are low may score quite high on an intelligence test. This discrepancy should alert the teacher to the possibility that the child's math or reading skills are not well developed and require special attention. This child may do quite well scholastically once his or her specific learning problems are remedied. Without the information from the intelligence test, such a child might be inappropriately placed in a slow learning group.

We must always question the validity of a test score for a particular individual, and we must continue research to improve test methods. But despite their limitations, aptitude and achievement tests are still the most effective aids we have for judging what job or class or type of training is most appropriate for a given individual. The alternatives are few. To rely entirely on subjective judgment would introduce the kinds of biases that such tests were designed to replace. To assign people at random to jobs or programs would benefit neither the individual nor society.

SUMMARY

1 Ability tests include *aptitude tests* (which measure capacity to learn and predict what one can accomplish with training) and *achievement tests* (which measure accomplished skills and indicate what one can do at present). Both tests may use similar types of items; the difference between them lies in their purposes.

2 In order to be useful, tests must meet certain specifications. Studies of *reliability* tell us whether test scores are consistent over time. Studies of *validity* tell us how well a test measures what it is intended to measure—how well it predicts according to an acceptable criterion.

3 The first successful intelligence tests were developed by the French psychologist Alfred Binet, who proposed the concept of *mental age.* A bright child's mental age is above his or her chronological age; a slow child's mental age is below his or her chronological age.

4 In the most widely used revision of the Binet scales, the Stanford-Binet, Lewis Terman adopted the *intelligence quotient* (IQ) as an index of mental development. The IQ originally expressed intelligence as a ratio of mental age (MA) to chronological age (CA). The IQ measure adopted in the most recent Stanford-Binet tests adjusts the IQ so that at each chronological age there is a mean of 100 and a standard deviation of 16. Hence, a contemporary IQ is no longer a ratio, but a score adjusted for the age of the person being tested.

5 Two widely used intelligence tests, the Wechsler Adult Intelligence Scale (WAIS) and the Wechsler Intelligence Scale for Children (WISC), have both a verbal and a performance scale, so that separate information can be obtained about each type of ability. The Stanford-Binet and the Wechsler scales are *individual IQ tests* in that they are administered to a single individual by a specially trained tester. *Group IQ tests,* which can be administered to a large number of people at one time, include the Army General Classification Test (AGCT) and the Scholastic Aptitude Test (SAT).

6 Both Binet and Wechsler assumed that intelligence was a *general capacity* for reasoning. Spearman proposed a general factor (*g*) plus specific abilities (*s*'s), which could be identified by the method of *factor analysis.* Thurstone used factor analysis to arrive at seven primary mental abilities that he thought were the basic elements of intelligence. Evidence indicates that both general intelligence and specific abilities are important.

7 Intelligence test items emphasize *convergent thinking,* while tests of "creativity" measure *divergent thinking.* Scores on creativity tests are independent of IQ only at the upper levels of intelligence, leading some experts to

propose a *"threshold model"* to explain the relationship between intelligence and creative achievement. Most creative discoveries require both divergent and convergent thinking.

8 After age six, most people's IQ remains relatively stable, although some individuals may show large shifts in IQ as the result of favorable or unfavorable changes in environmental conditions. Mental ability tends to increase up to age 26, level off for the next 10 years or so, and then decline after age 40. The rate of decline, however, depends on the individual's health and occupation as well as the specific abilities tested.

9 Studies correlating IQs between persons with varying degrees of genetic relationship show that heredity plays a role in intelligence. Estimates of *heritability* vary, however; and such environmental factors as nutrition, intellectual stimulation, and the emotional climate of the home will determine where within the *reaction range* determined by heredity the person's IQ will fall.

10 The extremes of intelligence are represented by the *mentally subnormal,* at one end of the scale, and the *intellectually gifted,* at the other. Social criteria are as important as intelligence scores in deciding whether a child is subnormal. In *familial-cultural* retardation (which results from the inheritance of low intelligence accentuated by impoverished living conditions), no physical defect is identifiable. A *mentally defective* child, in contrast, usually has some brain damage—resulting from maternal infections during pregnancy, birth trauma, genetic defects such as that which causes Down's syndrome, or other disorders. Subnormal children *can* learn; many can do socially useful work under supervision or even achieve a measure of independence.

11 As a group, the mentally gifted show superior attainments throughout childhood and adult life. Their histories belie the notion that highly intelligent people are maladjusted in some way. However, superior intelligence in itself is no assurance of success; some gifted children are misfits in adult life even though their intelligence scores remain high.

12 Public concerns about testing have focused on such objections as invasion of privacy, the secrecy surrounding test scores, the types of talent measured by tests, the unfairness of tests to disadvantaged and minority groups, and the use of group tests to classify schoolchildren. Psychologists have incomplete answers to these criticisms, but they do recognize that ability testing carries with it social responsibility.

FURTHER READING

For a general review of individual differences and psychological testing, see Cronbach, *Essentials of psychological testing* (3rd ed., 1970) and Anastasi, *Psychological testing* (4th ed., 1976). For a book that specifically treats the problems of intelligence testing, see Butcher, *Human intelligence: Its nature and assessment* (1973), in paperback.

Wechsler's measurement and appraisal of adult intelligence (5th ed., 1972) by Matarazzo includes a history of intelligence testing as well as current research on the Wechsler scales.

An excellent book on the nature of intelligence is Brody and Brody (eds.), *Intelligence: Nature, determinants, and consequences* (1976).

The genetics of intelligence is discussed in McClearn and DeFries, *Introduction to behavioral genetics* (1973). On the issue of racial differences in intelligence, see Loehlin, Lindzey, and Spuhler, *Race differences in intelligence* (1975).

An interesting paperback with current and historical articles debating such issues as the inheritance of intelligence, the validity of IQ tests, and class and race differences in IQ is Block and Dworkin, *The IQ controversy* (1976).

13
Personality and Its Assessment

What do we mean when we say someone has a "lot of personality"? Usually we are referring to an individual's social effectiveness. People react positively to that person. Courses advertised to "improve your personality" attempt to teach social skills and enhance one's appearance or manner of speaking in order to elicit favorable reactions from others.

Another common definition of personality is based on an individual's most striking characteristics. Thus, we may refer to someone as having an "aggressive personality" or a "shy personality."

When psychologists talk about personality, however, they are concerned primarily with *individual differences*—the characteristics that distinguish one individual from another. Psychologists do not agree on an exact definition of personality. But for our purposes, we will define personality as the *characteristic patterns of behavior and modes of thinking that determine a person's adjustment to the environment.*

The term *characteristic* in the definition implies some consistency in behavior—that people have tendencies to act or think in certain ways regardless of the situation. For example, you can probably think of an acquaintance who seldom gets angry, no matter what the provocation, and another who flies off the handle at the slightest irritation. Behavior is the result of interaction between personality characteristics and the social and physical conditions of the environment. But, as we shall see later, personality theorists differ in the extent to which they believe that behavior is *internally controlled*—determined by the personal characteristics of the individual and hence fairly consistent—or *externally controlled*—determined by the particular situation in which the behavior occurs.

A complete description of an individual's personality would include many factors: intellectual abilities, motives acquired in the process of growing up, emotional reactivity, attitudes, beliefs, and moral values. Some of these factors have been considered in earlier chapters. What concerns us here is the manner in which they are organized within a particular individual so as to differentiate that individual from other persons.

TABLE 13-1
Personality similarities in twins
One hundred thirty-nine same-sex twins (average age, 55 months) were rated by their mothers on scales measuring the three personality characteristics. Although identical twins may be treated more alike than fraternal twins (and thus may have a more similar environment), the size of the correlations suggests that one's genetic inheritance is an important determinant of personality.

| | CORRELATIONS FOR BOYS | | CORRELATIONS FOR GIRLS | |
	IDENTICAL	FRATERNAL	IDENTICAL	FRATERNAL
Emotionality	.68	.00	.60	.05
Activity	.73	.18	.50	.00
Sociability	.65	.20	.58	.06

Source: Buss and Plomin (1975)

Shaping of Personality

An infant is born with certain potentialities. The development of these potentialities depends on maturation and on experiences encountered in growing up. Although newborn infants in a hospital nursery look pretty much alike, some of the physical characteristics that will later make them readily distinguishable from each other are already determined by heredity. Intelligence and certain special abilities, such as musical talent, also have a hereditary component. And some differences in temperament appear to be innate. Identical twins (who share the same heredity because they develop from a single egg) tend to be much more alike in emotional reactivity, activity level, and sociability than fraternal twins (see Table 13-1).

A study of newborns found that reliable differences could be observed shortly after birth in such characteristics as activity level, attention span,

Fig. 13-1 Early individual differences in temperament
Two babies react quite differently to the same situation. One accepts a new food willingly (upper panel), while the other is obviously less enthusiastic. A baby's characteristic approach to something new may extend to many different situations.

adaptability to changes in the environment, and general mood. One infant might be characteristically active, easily distracted, and willing to accept new objects and people; another might be predominantly quiet, persistent in concentrating on an activity, and leery of anything new. These original characteristics of temperament tended to persist in many of the children whose development was followed over a 20-year period (Thomas and Chess, 1977).

Parents respond differently to babies with differing characteristics. In this way, a reciprocal process starts that may exaggerate some of the personality characteristics present at birth. What happens to the potentialities with which infants are born depends on their experiences while growing up. Although all experiences are individual, we may distinguish between two classes: *common experiences*, shared by most people growing up in a given culture or cultural subgroup, and *unique experiences*, not predictable from the roles that the culture assigns us.

Common Experiences

All families in a given culture share certain common beliefs, customs, and values. While growing up, the child learns to behave in ways expected by the culture. One of these expectations has to do with *sex roles* (see Chapter 3). Most cultures expect different behaviors from males than from females. Sex roles may vary from culture to culture, but it is considered "natural" in any culture for boys and girls to have predictable differences in personality merely because they belong to one or the other sex.

A culture as complex as that of the United States contains numerous subcultures, each with its own views about such things as moral values, standards of cleanliness, style of dress, and definitions of success. The cultural subgroup exerts its influence on the developing personality. All boys are expected to show certain personality characteristics (as compared with girls), but a boy raised in an urban slum is expected to behave differently in some respects than a boy raised in a middle-class suburb.

Some roles, such as occupations, are of our own choosing. But such roles are also patterned by the culture. Different behaviors are expected of doctors, truck drivers, rock stars, and opera singers. To be sure, occupational stereotypes have become less rigid in recent years; we are no longer shocked by male business executives with hair below their ears, female telephone line workers and male operators, or rock singers with crew cuts. But to some extent, people feel comfortable in an occupation if they behave as others in that occupation do.

To the extent that adult behavior conforms to social and occupational roles, it is predictable. We know pretty much what to expect of people at a formal reception, a political demonstration, a football game, or a funeral.

Although cultural and subcultural pressures impose some personality similarities, individual personality is never completely predictable from a knowledge of the group in which a person is raised, for two reasons: (1) the cultural impacts on the person are not uniform, because they are transmitted by way of certain people—parents and others—who are not all alike in their values and practices; (2) the individual has some experiences that are unique.

Unique Experiences

Each person reacts in his or her own way to social pressures. Personal differences in behavior may result from biological differences—differences in physical strength, sensitivity, and endurance. They may result from the rewards and punishments the parents impose and from the type of behavior they model. Even though they may not resemble their parents, children show their parents' influences. The contrasting possibilities of these influences are described by two brothers in Sinclair Lewis' novel *Work of Art.* Each of them ascribes his personality to his home surroundings.

> My father [said Oral] was a sloppy, lazy, booze-hoisting old bum, and my mother didn't know much besides cooking, and she was too busy to give me much attention, and the kids I knew were a bunch of foul-mouthed loafers that used to hang around the hoboes up near the water tank, and I never had a chance to get any formal schooling, and I got thrown on my own as just a brat. So naturally I've become a sort of vagabond that can't be bored by thinking about his "debts" to a lot of little shopkeeping lice, and I suppose I'm inclined to be lazy, and not too scrupulous about the dames and the liquor. But my early rearing did have one swell result. Brought up so unconventionally, I'll always be an Anti-Puritan. I'll never deny the joys of the flesh and the sanctity of beauty.
>
> My father [said Myron] was pretty easy-going and always did like drinking and swapping stories with the boys, and my mother was hard-driven taking care of us, and I heard a lot of filth from the hoboes up near the water tank. Maybe just sort of as a reaction I've become almost too much of a crank about paying debts, and fussing over my work, and being scared of liquor and women. But my rearing did have one swell result. Just by way of contrast, it made me a good, sound, old-fashioned New English Puritan. (Lewis, 1934)

Although such divergent reactions to the same early environment are unlikely to occur in real life, individuals do respond differently to similar circumstances.

Beyond a unique biological inheritance and the specific ways in which the culture is transmitted, the individual is shaped by particular experiences. An illness with a long convalescence may provide satisfactions in being cared for and waited on that profoundly affect the personality structure. Death of a parent may disrupt the usual sex-role identifications. Accidents, opportunities for heroism, winning a contest, moving to another part of the country—countless personal experiences such as these shape development.

The individual's common and unique experiences interact with inherited potential to shape personality. How this occurs and how the resulting personality can best be described have been the subject of many theories. Most personality theories can be grouped into one of four classes: *trait, social learning, psychoanalytic,* or *phenomenological.* In the remainder of this chapter we will briefly describe each of these theoretical approaches and then give examples of some of the methods used to assess personality. Personality cannot be studied scientifically unless there are satisfactory ways of measuring personality variables.

Trait Approach

Classification into *kinds* is the beginning of most sciences—kinds of rocks, kinds of clouds, kinds of plants, and so on. Thus, it is not surprising that the first students of human nature tried to classify kinds of people. One of the

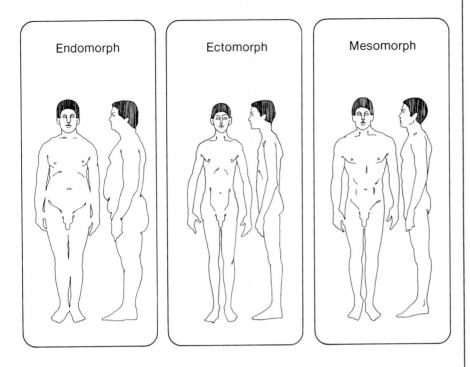

Fig. 13-2 Body types related to personality

earliest "personality theories" attempted to classify individuals into *personality types* on the basis of body build (Kretschmer, 1925; Sheldon, 1954). A short, plump person (*endomorph*) was said to be sociable, relaxed, and even-tempered; a tall, thin person (*ectomorph*) was characterized as restrained, self-conscious, and fond of solitude; a heavy-set, muscular individual (*mesomorph*) was described as noisy, callous, and fond of physical activity.

Personality Types

Since attempts to relate body build to specific personality characteristics usually show very low correlations, most psychologists do not consider this classification very useful. On the other hand, there is little doubt that a person's physique has some influence on personality—primarily through the limits it imposes on abilities and the reactions it evokes from other people. For example, a girl with a short, stocky build cannot realistically aspire to be a ballet dancer, fashion model, or all-star basketball player; one who is over six feet tall probably never will be an Olympic gymnast. Boys who are strong and muscular may be willing to risk physical danger and to assert themselves; their weaker classmates may learn early in life to avoid fights and to depend on intellectual abilities to get what they want. Our physiques do not determine specific personality characteristics, but they may shape personality by affecting how others treat us.

Personality-type theories have also been based on purely psychological characteristics. The Swiss psychiatrist Carl Jung divided all personalities into *introverts* and *extraverts*. Introverts tend to withdraw into themselves, particularly in times of emotional stress and conflict; they tend to be shy and prefer to work alone. Introverts may take to the speaking platform in support of some movement to which they are strongly committed, but even then they are impelled from within. Under stress, extraverts seek the company of others.

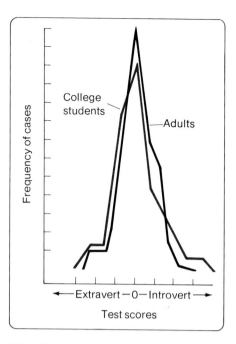

Fig. 13-3 Introversion-extraversion
Scores on a test of introversion-extraversion are shown for a group of college students and a group of adults. Note that the majority of the subjects range around the middle of the scale; introverts and extraverts represent only the extremes. (After Neymann and Yacorzynski, 1942)

They are likely to be very sociable and tend to choose occupations that permit them to deal directly with people, such as sales or promotional work.

You may know a "typical introvert" and a "typical extravert." But probably most of your friends fall somewhere between the two extremes (see Figure 13-3). This is one of the major problems of type theories. Most typologies, whether they are based on physical or psychological characteristics, involve a *continuum* of individual differences rather than discrete types. Type theories are appealing because they provide a simple way of looking at personality, but, in actuality, personality is far more complex than these theories suggest.

Traits Versus Types

Type theories usually group people into discrete categories (like introvert *or* extravert) and try to explain behavior on the basis of a few types. Trait theories assume that people vary on a *number* of *continuous dimensions*, or *scales*, each of which represents a *trait*. Thus, we could rate an individual on a scale of intelligence or emotional stability or aggressiveness, and so on. To arrive at a global description of personality, we would need to know how the individual is rated on a number of such dimensions.

A trait refers to any characteristic in which one person differs from another in a relatively permanent and consistent way. When we informally describe ourselves and others with such adjectives as "friendly," "cautious," "excitable," "intelligent," or "anxious," we are using trait terms. We abstract these terms from behavior. If we observe a man behaving in an aggressive manner on several occasions, we may describe him as an "aggressive individual." Using "aggressiveness" as a trait term is permissible as long as we remember that the term was derived from observations of behavior. The danger lies in using the trait term as a cause of behavior. To say that a woman hit her roommate over the head because she has an aggressive trait explains nothing. We inferred the trait from behavior; we cannot then turn around and use it to explain behavior.

Psychologists working in the area of trait theory are concerned with (1) determining the basic traits that provide a meaningful description of personality and (2) finding ways to measure them.

WHAT ARE THE BASIC TRAITS? The English language contains thousands of words that refer to characteristics of behavior. How do we reduce these to a manageable number of traits that are meaningful in describing personality? One approach uses *factor analysis* (see p. 357). As we noted in the last chapter, factor analysis is a complex statistical technique for reducing a large number of measures to a smaller number of independent dimensions.

For example, suppose you select a large number of words that describe personality characteristics and arrange them in pairs representing polar opposites: tidy-careless, calm-anxious, responsive-insensitive, cooperative-negativistic, and so on. You ask a group of people to rate their friends on each of these word pairs. Subjecting these ratings to factor analysis would yield a fairly small number of dimensions, or *factors*, that would account for most of the intercorrelations among the ratings. The five trait dimensions listed in Table 13-2 were found in one study of this kind.

The most extensive study of personality traits has been done by Raymond Cattell. His data, collected over three decades, have come from many sources: questionnaires, personality tests, and observations of behavior in real-life situations. Cattell has identified 16 factors that he believes are the basic traits

TABLE 13-2
Five trait dimensions and some of their components
The adjective pairs describe the two ends of the scales that comprise the dimension.

TRAIT DIMENSION	DESCRIPTIVE ADJECTIVE PAIRS
Extraversion	Talkative–Silent Open–Secretive Adventurous–Cautious
Agreeableness	Good-natured–Irritable Gentle–Headstrong Cooperative–Negativistic
Conscientiousness	Tidy–Careless Responsible–Undependable Persevering–Quitting
Emotional stability	Calm–Anxious Poised–Nervous Not hypochondriacal–Hypochondriacal
Culture	Artistically sensitive–Artistically insensitive Refined–Boorish Intellectual–Unreflective

Adapted with modifications from Norman (1963)

underlying personality (see Figure 13-4). Each factor is given two names, one for a high score and another for a low score.

Cattell has devised a questionnaire to measure his 16 traits—called the *Sixteen Personality Factor Questionnaire* (16 PF, for short). The "yes" or "no" answers to more than 100 questions are compiled to yield a score for each of

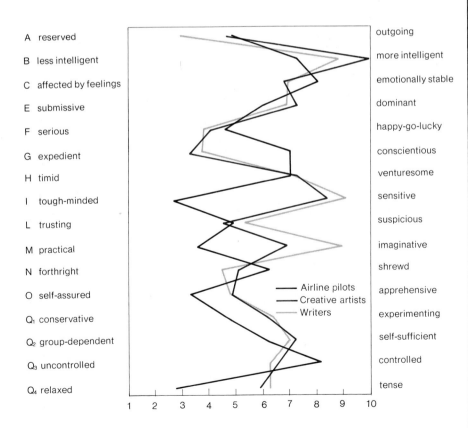

A	reserved	outgoing
B	less intelligent	more intelligent
C	affected by feelings	emotionally stable
E	submissive	dominant
F	serious	happy-go-lucky
G	expedient	conscientious
H	timid	venturesome
I	tough-minded	sensitive
L	trusting	suspicious
M	practical	imaginative
N	forthright	shrewd
O	self-assured	apprehensive
Q₁	conservative	experimenting
Q₂	group-dependent	self-sufficient
Q₃	uncontrolled	controlled
Q₄	relaxed	tense

— Airline pilots
— Creative artists
— Writers

Fig. 13-4 Personality profiles
The trait names represent the 16 personality factors obtained by factor analysis of a large number of ratings. The factors are assigned two names: one for a high score and another for a low score. Factors A–O were obtained from factor analyses of ratings of one person by another; the four Q factors were found only in data from self-ratings. A personality test based on the 16 factors measures the level of each factor, and the scores can be graphed as a profile—either for an individual or a group. The black profile shows the *average* scores for a group of airline pilots; the color profile is the average for a group of artists, and the gray, for a group of writers. Note that the writers and artists show similar traits that are somewhat different from those of the pilots. (After Cattell, 1973)

the factors. For example, answering "no" to the question "Do you tend to keep in the background on social occasions?" would earn a point toward the dominant side of the E Scale. By plotting an individual's test score for each of the factors, we arrive at a *personality profile*—a kind of shorthand description of the individual's personality. Cattell has studied diverse groups of people using the 16 PF. Figure 13-4 shows the average test scores for a group of airline pilots, a group of artists, and a group of writers. Comparing the personality profiles, we can see that artists and writers, as a group, differ significantly from pilots on a number of personality traits.

Evaluation of the Trait Approach

While the trait approach appears to be an objective and scientific way of studying personality, there are some problems. The personality factors found in a given study often depend on the type of data being analyzed (for example, self-ratings versus ratings of one person by another) and the specific factor-analytic technique used. Some investigators have found as few as 5 factors as the basic dimensions of personality, while others have found as many as 20.

Despite the lack of agreement on the number of basic traits, some overlap does occur. Two dimensions found in most factor-analytic studies of personality are *introversion-extraversion* and *stability-instability*. Introversion-extraversion refers to the degree to which one's basic orientation is turned inward toward the self or outward toward the external world. It is essentially the same distinction made by Carl Jung, although Jung used the terms to refer to personality types rather than positions along a scale. Stability-instability is a dimension of emotionality, with calm, well-adjusted, reliable individuals at the stable end and moody, anxious, temperamental, and unreliable individuals at the other. A British psychologist, Hans Eysenck, has developed a theory of personality based on these two dimensions. Figure 13-5 shows the dimensions as related to various personality traits.

A more important criticism of the trait approach, according to some personality theorists, is the possibility that behavior may vary widely from one situation to another. A young boy who obtains a high score on the "dominant" factor of the 16 PF may take a dominant role with his schoolmates but not with his parents and teachers; even with his peers, he may behave aggressively on some occasions and docilely on others. As we shall see later, tests designed to measure traits have not turned out to have as much predictive power as psychologists would like. In predicting behavior, we need to know how personal characteristics—tendencies to be sociable, aggressive, anxious, and so on—are influenced by particular environmental conditions. Research results indicate that it is the *interaction* between individual differences and situational variables that is important.

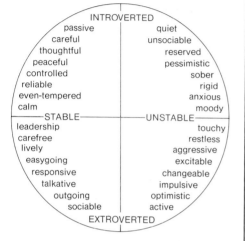

Fig. 13-5 Eysenck's dimensions related to personality traits
Various traits studied by factor-analytic methods are shown in relation to the two basic dimensions of introversion-extraversion and stability-instability. (After Eysenck and Eysenck, 1963)

Social Learning Approach

Trait theorists focus on *person* factors as determinants of behavior. They assume that traits predispose the individual to respond consistently in different situations. Situations have some impact: Tom doesn't respond as aggressively when an attractive waitress accidently spills a cup of coffee on him as he does when a truck driver cuts in front of him in congested traffic. But trait theorists assume that Tom will behave more aggressively in both situations than will Mike, who scores lower on the 16 PF scale measuring aggression.

Social learning theorists, in contrast, emphasize the importance of *environmental*, or *situational*, determinants of behavior. As we noted in Chapter 11, the social learning approach to motivation focuses on the patterns of behavior the individual learns in coping with the environment. For social learning theorists, behavior is the result of a continuous *interaction* between personal and environmental variables: environmental conditions shape behavior through learning; and a person's behavior, in turn, shapes the environment. Persons and situations influence each other in a reciprocal manner. The interaction of individual differences and specific situations is crucial for predicting behavior.

Reinforcement in Learning and Performance

The effect of other people—the rewards and punishments they provide—is an important influence on behavior. According to social learning theory, individual differences in behavior result in large part from differences in the kinds of learning experiences encountered in the course of growing up. Some behavior patterns are learned through direct experience: the individual behaves in a certain manner and is rewarded or punished. But many responses are acquired without direct reinforcement, through *observational*, or *vicarious*, *learning* (see Chapter 11). People can learn by observing others' actions and by noting the consequences of those actions. It would be a very slow and inefficient process indeed if all of our behavior had to be learned through direct reinforcement of responses. According to social learning theorists, reinforcement is not *necessary* for learning, although it may *facilitate* learning by focusing the individual's attention.

While reinforcement is not necessary for learning, it is crucial for the *performance* of learned behavior. A main assumption of social learning theory is that people behave in ways likely to produce reinforcement. A person's repertoire of learned behaviors is extensive; the particular action chosen in a specific situation depends on the expected outcome. Most adolescent girls know how to fight, having watched male classmates or TV characters aggress by hitting with the fists, by kicking, and so on. But since this kind of behavior is seldom reinforced in girls, it is unlikely to occur except in unusual circumstances.

The reinforcement that controls the expression of learned behavior may be (1) *direct*—tangible rewards, social approval or disapproval, or alleviation of aversive conditions; (2) *vicarious*—observation of someone receiving reward or punishment for behavior similar to one's own; or (3) *self-administered*—evaluation of one's own performance with self-praise or reproach.

Reciprocal Interaction of Person and Situation

According to social learning theorists, a person's actions in a given situation depend on the specific characteristics of the situation, the individual's appraisal of the situation, and past reinforcement for behavior in similar situations (or observations of others in similar situations). People behave consistently insofar as the situations they encounter and the roles they are expected to play remain relatively stable.

Most social behaviors, however, are not uniformly rewarded across different settings. The individual learns to discriminate those contexts in which certain behavior is appropriate and those in which it is not. To the extent that a person

Behavioral Measurement

In studying personality, social learning theorists assess an individual's specific behavior patterns and the environmental conditions that influence the behavior. One of their goals is to modify behavior patterns by changing environmental conditions.

With children, behavior can often be observed in a naturalistic setting, such as a classroom or playground. The following study illustrates the use of behavior sampling in a nursery school class to determine the conditions maintaining a specific problem behavior.

Ann's teachers were concerned because the four-year-old was somewhat of a social isolate and did not interact with the other children in play. As part of an initial assessment, two observers sampled Ann's behavior at regular 10-second intervals, recording her nearness to and interactions with adults and children during the school day. It became clear that the teachers were inadvertently reinforcing Ann's isolate behavior. Ann was a bright, attractive child who was skillful at gaining adult attention. But the activities she engaged in to attract adult attention prevented her from relating

to other children. And the more isolated she became from other children, the more attention she received from adults.

To break this cycle, the teachers gave Ann attention only when she played with other children. Attention from adults became contingent on playing with her peers. At first, even approximations to social play, such as standing near another child, were rewarded by prompt attention from a teacher. Whenever Ann began to leave the group or tried to solicit solitary contact with adults, the teachers stopped attending to her.

As you can see from Figure 13-6, Ann began to spend much more time playing with the other children and much less time trying to interact individually with adults. To assess the effects of reinforcement more precisely, the teachers reversed their procedures on the twelfth day, rewarding Ann with attention for interacting with them and ignoring her interactions with other children. Under these conditions, Ann's previous isolate behavior reappeared. When reinforcement for peer play was again instituted (on the seventeenth day), Ann

increased contact with her peers until she was spending about 60 percent of the school day in play with her classmates. Periodic checks after the special reinforcement procedures ended indicated that Ann's play behavior remained fairly stable at this level.

In naturalistic settings, the observer has little control over the situation to which the individual must respond. To focus on specific behaviors, *situation tests* may be devised. For example, to study the behavior of a child who is excessively dependent on his or her mother for help, the psychologist may set up a situation where the child is given homework problems to complete while the mother is occupied in another part of the room. By observing the interactions between mother and child through a one-way mirror, the psychologist can note the kind of mother-child interactions that reinforce dependent behavior.

Situation tests have been devised to measure anxiety associated with public speaking, interpersonal relationships, enclosed spaces, or specific objects, such as snakes. For example, fear of snakes has been measured by noting how closely the individual will approach a live but harmless snake—from

is rewarded for the same response in many different situations, *generalization* takes place, insuring that the same behavior will occur in a variety of settings. Thus, a boy whose father reinforces him for physical aggression at home as well as at school and at play would probably develop a personality that is pervasively aggressive. But more often, aggressive responses are differentially rewarded, and learned *discriminations* determine the situations in which the individual will display aggression—for example, aggression is acceptable on the football field but not in the classroom.

PERSON VARIABLES Social learning theorists emphasize the importance of cognitive factors, rather than motivational traits such as aggression, depend-

and Behavior Change

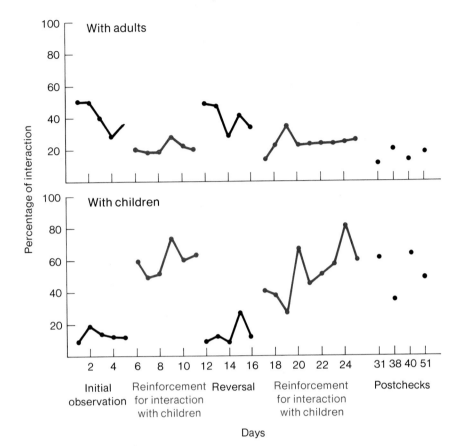

Fig. 13-6 Modifying social behavior
Percentage of time spent by Ann in social interaction with children and adults was recorded for two hours during each morning nursery school session. Reinforcement for playing with peers, introduced on day six, produced a marked change in behavior. When the reinforcement conditions were reversed so that attempts to interact with adults gained attention (day 12), Ann reverted to her original behavior. Reintroduction of attention for peer play (day 17) reinstated interaction with classmates. Periodic checks after specific reinforcement was discontinued showed behavior at about the same level. (After Allen and others, 1964)

simply looking at the snake in a glass cage to actually allowing the animal to crawl over one's body. This kind of direct behavior sampling is often used to measure strength of fear before and after therapy that is aimed at relieving specific fears.

When it is not possible to observe behavior directly, the individual may be asked to report on his or her own behavior—for example, by keeping a daily log noting activities and the conditions under which certain anxieties or behaviors occur. The person might be asked to keep track of the number of cigarettes he or she smokes or the circumstances that provoke anger or anxiety. Once the conditions that control a certain behavior have been identified, the next step is to change the stimulus conditions and observe whether behavior changes correspondingly.

As you can see, for social learning theorists, personality assessment is closely linked to treatment procedures. In Chapter 16, we will consider in more detail social learning theory techniques for modifying maladaptive behavior.

ency, and so on, in determining what a person will do in a particular situation. Some of the person variables that influence behavior, in interaction with environmental conditions, are:

1 *Competencies*—intellectual abilities, social skills, physical skills, and other special abilities.
2 *Cognitive strategies*—habitual ways of selectively attending to information and organizing it into meaningful categories.
3 *Expectancies*—expectations about the consequences of different behaviors, about the meaning of certain stimuli (for example, when listeners yawn or tap their fingers, they are bored), and about the efficacy of one's own behavior. The first two depend on inferences about the intentions motivat-

SOCIAL LEARNING APPROACH

ing the behaviors of others. The third depends on our confidence in our own abilities: we may anticipate the consequences of certain behavior but fail to act because we are uncertain of our ability to perform the behavior.

4 *Subjective-outcome values*—the value one places on the expected outcome. Even if individuals have similar expectancies, they may choose to behave differently because of differences in the subjective values of the outcomes (for example, two students may expect that a certain behavior will please their professor, but for one student this outcome is important, while for the other it is not).

5 *Self-regulatory systems and plans*—self-imposed standards and rules the individual adopts for regulating his or her own behavior, including self-imposed rewards for success or punishments for failure and plans for reaching a goal. (Paraphrased with modifications from Mischel, 1973.)

All of the above variables interact with conditions of the particular situation to determine what an individual will do in that situation.

SELF-GENERATED ENVIRONMENTS But we are not simply passive reactors to situational conditions. The relationship between our behavior and the "situations" of life is reciprocal. Through their own actions, people produce the environmental conditions that affect their behavior. To use a simple experimental example, consider a rat in a Skinner box that has an electrically charged grid as a floor. Shocks are scheduled to occur every minute, but the animal can forestall the shocks for 30 seconds by pressing a bar. The animals that learn the controlling behavior can create a punishment-free environment; the slow learners will experience an unpleasant situation. Thus, the *potential environment* is the same for all animals, but the *actual environment* depends on their behavior (Bandura, 1977).

In the same way, a person who acts in an abrasive manner may often encounter a hostile social environment because his or her behavior elicits hostility from others. A friendly person who is skilled at making others feel comfortable will encounter a quite different environment. Situations are partly of our own devising.

Evaluation of Social Learning Approach

Social learning theory, through its emphasis on specifying the environmental variables that elicit specific behaviors, has made a major contribution to both clinical psychology and personality theory. It has led us to see human actions as reactions to specific environments and to focus on the way environments control our behavior and can be changed to modify behavior. As we shall see in Chapter 16, the careful application of learning principles has proved successful in changing maladaptive behavior.

Social learning theorists have been criticized for overemphasizing the importance of situational factors in behavior while neglecting individual differences. They show little interest, for example, in innate differences that may predispose one person to be characteristically passive and slow to respond and another to be excitable and quick. As we shall see later, many personality theorists are unwilling to concede that personality has as little stability as social learning theory implies.

So far, social learning theorists have failed to provide a clear conception of how the various learned behaviors are integrated to form the total personality. However, the basic ideas are well formulated, and further research on the person variables proposed as integrating mechanisms may provide a more comprehensive picture of personality.

Psychoanalytic Approach

Psychoanalytic theory approaches personality from a viewpoint that is quite different from either of the two theories we have discussed so far. Instead of studying traits or the individual's reactions to situations, the psychoanalyst looks for the *unconscious* motives that direct behavior.

Freud's theories, developed over 50 years of treating emotionally disturbed persons, fill 24 volumes. The last, *Outline of Psychoanalysis*, was published in 1940, a year after his death. We can present here only the barest outline of Freud's theory of personality.

Freud compared the human mind to an iceberg: the small part that shows above the surface of the water represents *conscious experience*, while the much larger mass below water level represents the *unconscious*—a storehouse of impulses, passions, and inaccessible memories that affect our thoughts and behavior. It was this unconscious portion of the mind that Freud sought to explore by the method of *free association*, which requires the person to talk about everything that comes into his or her conscious mind, no matter how ridiculous or trivial it might seem. By analyzing free associations, including the recall of dreams and early childhood memories, Freud sought to help his patients become aware of much that had been unconscious and thereby to puzzle out the basic determinants of personality.

Personality Structure

Freud saw personality as composed of three major systems: the *id*, the *ego*, and the *superego*. Each of these systems has its own functions, but the three interact to govern behavior.

THE ID   The id is the original source of personality, present in the newborn infant, from which the ego and the superego later develop. It consists of everything that is inherited, including the instinctual drives—sex and aggression. It is closely linked to the biological processes and provides the energy source (*libido*) for the operation of all three systems. Increases in energy level (from either internal or external stimulation) produce uncomfortable tension for the id, and the id immediately seeks to reduce this tension and return the organism to its normal state. Thus the id seeks immediate gratification of primitive, pleasure-seeking impulses. The id, like the young child, operates on the *pleasure principle:* it endeavors to avoid pain and obtain pleasure regardless of any external considerations.

One process by which the id attempts to reduce tension is to form a mental image or hallucination of its desires. Thus, a starving woman might form a mental image of a delicious meal. This is an example of *wish fulfillment*. According to Freud, the objects and events we conjure up in our dreams represent attempts to fulfill some impulse of the id, although usually in disguised ways. Freud also considered the hallucinations of psychotic individuals to be examples of wish fulfillment. He called such attempts to satisfy needs irrationally, with no consideration of reality, *primary process thinking*.

"Very well, I'll introduce you. Ego, meet Id. Now get back to work."

THE EGO Mental images do not satisfy needs. The starving woman cannot reduce her hunger by eating visual images. Reality must be considered. And this is the role of the ego. The ego obeys the *reality principle,* which requires it to test images for their reality and to delay discharge of tension until the appropriate environmental conditions are found. The ego operates by *secondary process thinking,* which is realistic and logical and plans how to achieve satisfaction. For example, taking the real world into consideration, the ego delays gratification of sexual impulses until conditions are appropriate. It is essentially the "executive" of the personality, because it decides what actions are appropriate, which id instincts will be satisfied, and in what manner. The ego mediates between the demands of the id, the realities of the world, and the demands of the superego.

THE SUPEREGO The third part of the personality, the superego, is the internalized representation of the values and morals of society as taught to the child by the parents and others. The superego judges whether an action is right or wrong. The id seeks pleasure, the ego tests reality, and the superego strives for perfection. The superego develops in response to parental rewards and punishments. It is composed of the *conscience,* which incorporates all the things the child is punished or reprimanded for doing, and the *ego-ideal,* which includes those actions the child is rewarded for doing. The conscience punishes by making the person feel guilty, and the ego-ideal rewards by making the individual feel proud.

Initially, parents control children's behavior directly through rewards and punishments. Through the incorporation of parental standards into the superego, behavior is brought under self-control. Children no longer need anyone to tell them it is wrong to steal; their superego tells them.

Sometimes the three components of personality are at odds: the ego postpones the gratification that the id wants right away, and the superego battles with both the id and the ego because behavior often falls short of the moral code it represents. But more often in the normal person, the three work as a team, producing integrated behavior.

ANXIETY AND DEFENSES AGAINST IT Freud believed that the conflict between the id impulses—primarily sexual and aggressive instincts—and the restraining influences of the ego and the superego constituted the motivating source of much behavior. Because society condemns free expression of aggression and sexual behavior, such impulses cannot be immediately and directly expressed. Children learn early that they may not handle their genitals in public or hit their siblings. They eventually internalize parental restrictions on impulse satisfaction, thus forming the superego. The more restraints a society (or its representatives, the parents) places on impulse expression, the greater the potential for conflict between the three parts of the personality.

The desires of the id are powerful forces that must be expressed in some way; prohibiting their expression does not abolish them. Individuals with an urge to do something for which they will be punished become anxious. One way of reducing anxiety is to express the impulse in disguised form, thereby avoiding punishment by society and condemnation by the superego. Aggressive impulses, for example, may be displaced to racing sports cars or to championing political causes.

Another method of reducing anxiety, called *repression,* is to push the impulse out of awareness into the unconscious. These methods of anxiety reduction, called *defense mechanisms,* are means of defending oneself against painful anxiety. They are never totally successful in relieving tension, and the residue may spill over in the form of nervousness or restlessness, which, as Freud pointed out, is the price we must pay for being civilized. Presumably, a society that placed no restrictions on free expression of the id's instincts would produce people completely free of anxiety or tension. But such a society would probably not survive for long; all societies must place some restrictions on behavior for the well-being of the group.

Defense mechanisms form the basis of Freud's theory of neurotic and psychotic behavior and will be examined more fully in Chapter 14. At this point, we will note only that people differ in the balance among id, ego, and superego systems and in the defenses they use against anxiety. The individual's approach to a problem situation reflects his or her manner of coping with the conflicting demands of the id, the ego, and the superego.

Personality Development

Freud believed that during the first five years of life the individual goes through several stages of development that affect personality. Using a very broad definition of sexuality, he called these periods *psychosexual stages.* During each stage, the pleasure-seeking impulses of the id focus on a particular area of the body and on activities connected with that area.

Freud called the first year of life the *oral stage* of psychosexual development. During this period, infants derive pleasure from nursing and sucking; indeed, they will put their thumb or anything else they can reach into their mouth.

During the second year of life, the *anal stage,* children have their first experience with imposed control in the form of toilet training. Gratification is presumably derived from withholding or expelling feces.

In the *phallic stage,* from about age three to age six, children begin to derive pleasure from fondling their genitals. They observe the differences between males and females and may direct their awakening sexual impulses toward the parent of the opposite sex.

A *latency period* follows the end of the phallic stage, during which children become less concerned with their bodies and turn their attention to the skills needed for coping with the environment.

The last stage, the *genital stage,* occurs during adolescence. Youngsters begin to turn their sexual interests toward others and to love in a more mature way.

Freud felt that special problems at any stage could arrest (or fixate) development, which would have a lasting effect on the individual's personality. The libido would remain attached to the activities appropriate for that stage. Thus, a person who was weaned very early and did not have enough sucking pleasure might become *fixated* at the oral stage. As an adult, this person may be excessively dependent on others and overly fond of such oral pleasures as eating, drinking, or smoking. Such a person is called an ''oral'' personality. The person fixated at the anal stage of psychosexual development may be abnormally concerned with cleanliness, orderliness, and saving, and may tend to resist external pressure.

Modifications of Freud's Theories

Later psychoanalysts felt that Freud placed too much emphasis on the instinctive and biological aspects of personality and failed to recognize that

Karen Horney

people are products of the society in which they live. The neo-Freudians, including Alfred Adler, Karen Horney, Erich Fromm, and Harry Stack Sullivan, saw personality as shaped more by the people, society, and culture surrounding the individual than by instincts. They placed less emphasis on the controlling power of the unconscious, believing that people are more rational in their planning and decisions than Freud had thought.

A current psychoanalytic approach stresses the role of the ego. According to this view, the ego develops independently of the id and has its own functions—in addition to finding realistic ways of satisfying id impulses. The ego's functions are to establish relations with objects in the real world and to make sense out of experience. Its satisfactions include such things as exploration, manipulation, and competency in performance. This approach ties the concept of ego more closely to cognitive processes.

Evaluation of Psychoanalytic Theory

Psychoanalytic theory has had an enormous impact on psychological and philosophical conceptions of human nature. Freud's major contributions are his recognition that unconscious needs and conflicts motivate much of our behavior and his emphasis on the importance of early childhood experiences in personality development. His emphasis on sexual factors led to an awareness of their role in adjustment problems and paved the way for the scientific study of sexuality. But Freud made his observations during the Victorian period, when sexual standards were very strict, so it is understandable that many of his patients had conflicts centering around their sexual desires. Today, feelings of guilt about sex are less frequent, yet the incidence of mental illness remains about the same. Sexual conflicts are not the only cause of personality disturbances—perhaps not even a major cause.

Some critics point out, too, that Freud's theory of personality is based almost entirely on his observations of emotionally disturbed individuals. It may not represent an appropriate description of the normal, healthy personality.

Psychoanalysis, while acknowledged as a powerful influence on our thinking about human nature, has been seriously questioned as a scientific theory. Freud's constructs are ambiguous and difficult to define. He does not specify, for example, what behaviors indicate that a child is fixated at the anal stage of psychosexual development and what behaviors indicate that he or she is not fixated. Research efforts to identify oral and anal personality types suggest that the parents' characteristic ways of handling the child (for example, continual demands for neatness and precision or attempts to make the child excessively dependent) have more influence on later personality than specific events that occur during particular psychosexual stages.

Psychoanalytic theory assumes that very different behaviors may be signs of the same underlying impulse or conflict. For example, a mother who feels resentful of her child may be punitive and abusive, or she may deny her hostile impulses by behaving in a very concerned and overprotective manner toward the youngster—what Freud would call a *reaction formation* (see Chapter 14). When very opposite behaviors are said to result from the same underlying motive, it is difficult to confirm the presence or absence of the motive. And, in turn, it is difficult to make theoretical predictions that can be empirically verified.

Most of the psychoanalysts who modified and expanded Freud's theories were concerned with concepts that would help them understand their patients; they had little, if any, training in theory construction or research methods.

Recently, there has been a renewed interest in reformulating psychoanalytic theory in testable terms and subjecting the theory to rigorous evaluation. Research along these lines seems promising, as evidenced by the work of Silverman (1976) and others.

Phenomenological Approach

The phenomenological approach to the study of personality includes a number of theories that, although different in some respects, share a common emphasis on *subjective experience*—the individual's private view of the world. Phenomenological theories differ from the theories we have discussed so far in that they are generally not interested in the person's motivational history or in predicting behavior. They are concerned with how the individual perceives and interprets events—the individual's *phenomenology*.

In a sense, the phenomenological approach represents a reaction against both the behavioristic tradition, with its emphasis on measuring responses to external stimuli, and the psychoanalytic view of human beings as motivated by unconscious impulses. Rather than looking at objective measures of a situation or delving into childhood motives, phenomenologists focus on the individual's subjective view of what is taking place now.

Actions that seem puzzling to an observer may become understandable when we know what the situation *means* to the individual. To take an example, during a tennis tournament one player suddenly starts shouting, protesting that her opponent is trying to unnerve her by deliberately delaying the game. To an observer, this reaction seems totally inappropriate; the other player has exhibited model court behavior. But the protester has had experience with this particular opponent's delaying tactics in the past, and the slightest sign that such is about to reoccur is enough to infuriate her. From her viewpoint, her reactions are appropriate.

The phenomenological approach to personality includes theories that have been labeled "humanistic" (because they focus on the qualities that differentiate humans from animals—namely, self-direction and freedom of choice) and "self" theories (because they deal with the subjective, internal experiences that constitute one's sense of being). Most phenomenological theories also emphasize the positive nature of human beings—their push toward growth and *self-actualization.*

Some of the features of the phenomenological approach to personality will become clearer as we discuss the views of one of its leading spokesmen, Carl Rogers.

Self Theory

Rogers' theory, like Freud's, developed from his experiences in working with emotionally troubled people (Rogers, 1951, 1977). Rogers was impressed with what he saw as the individual's innate tendency to move in the direction of growth, maturity, and positive change. In his "nondirective," or "client-centered," therapy he assumes that every individual has the motivation and ability to change and that we are the best experts on ourselves. The therapist's role is to act as a sounding board while the individual explores and analyzes his or her problems. This approach differs from psychoanalytic therapy, where the therapist "analyzes" the patient's history to determine the problem and devise a

Carl Rogers writing on the phenomenological approach
". . . the best vantage point for understanding behavior is from the internal frame of reference of the individual himself."
"The organism has one basic tendency and striving—to actualize, maintain, and enhance the experiencing organism."
"When the individual perceives and accepts into one consistent and integrated system all his sensory and visceral experiences, then he is necessarily more understanding of others and is more accepting of others as separate individuals." (Rogers, 1951)

course of remedial action. (See Chapter 16 for a discussion of various approaches to psychotherapy.)

The most important concept in Rogers' theory of personality is the *self*. The self consists of all the ideas, perceptions, and values that characterize "I" or "me"; it includes the awareness of "what I am" and "what I can do." This perceived self, in turn, influences both the person's perception of the world and his or her behavior. An individual with a strong, positive self-concept views the world quite differently from one whose self-concept is weak. The self-concept does not necessarily reflect reality; a person may be highly successful and respected yet view him or herself as a failure.

According to Rogers, the individual evaluates every experience in relation to this self-concept. People want to behave in ways that are consistent with their self-image; experiences and feelings that are not consistent are threatening and may be denied admittance to consciousness. This is essentially Freud's notion of repression, although Rogers feels that such repression is neither necessary nor permanent. (Freud would say that repression is inevitable and that some aspects of one's experiences always remain unconscious.)

The more areas of experience one has to deny because they are inconsistent with one's self-concept, the wider the gulf becomes between the self and reality and the greater the potential for anxiety. A person whose image is not congruent with personal feelings and experience must defend him or herself against the truth, because the truth will result in anxiety. If the incongruence becomes too great, the defenses may break down, resulting in severe anxiety or other forms of emotional disturbance. The well-adjusted person, in contrast, has a self-concept that is consistent with thought, experience, and behavior; the self is not rigid, but flexible, so it can change as it assimilates new experiences and ideas.

There is another self in Rogers' theory, and that is the *ideal self*. We all have a conception of the kind of person we would like to be. This concept is similar to Freud's ego-ideal. The closer the ideal self is to the real self, the more fulfilled and happy the individual. A large discrepancy between the two results in an unhappy, dissatisfied individual.

Thus, two kinds of incongruence can develop: one between the self and the experiences of reality and the other between the self and ideal self. Rogers has some hypotheses about how these incongruences may develop.

Development of the Self

Because the child's behavior is continuously being evaluated by parents and others (sometimes positively and sometimes negatively), the child soon learns to discriminate between those thoughts and actions that are considered worthy and those that are not. The unworthy experiences become excluded from the self-concept, even though they may be quite valid or natural experiences. For example, relieving physiological tension in the bowel or bladder is a pleasurable experience for the child. However, unless the child urinates or defecates privately and in the proper place, parents usually condemn such activities as "bad" or "naughty." To retain the parents' positive regard, the child must deny his or her own experience—that defecating or urinating provides satisfaction.

Feelings of competition and hostility toward a younger sibling who has usurped the center of attention are natural. But parents disapprove of hitting a baby brother or sister and usually punish such actions. Children must somehow integrate this experience into their self-image. They may decide they are bad and feel ashamed. They may decide their parents do not like them and feel rejected. Or they may deny their feelings and decide they do not want to hit the baby. Each of these attitudes contains a distortion of the truth. The third alternative is the easiest for children to accept. But in so doing, they deny their real feelings, which then become unconscious. The more people have to deny feelings and take on the values of others, the more uncomfortable they will feel about themselves.

Obviously, there must be certain restrictions on behavior. Considerations of household efficiency and sanitation require some restraints on elimination. And children cannot be permitted to beat their siblings. Rogers suggests that the best approach is for the parents to recognize the child's feelings as valid, while explaining their own feelings and the reasons for restraint.

Self-Actualization

Rogers believes that the basic force motivating the human organism is self-actualization—"a tendency toward fulfillment, toward actualization, toward the maintenance and enhancement of the organism." As the organism grows, it seeks to fulfill its potential within the limits of its heredity. A person may not always clearly perceive those actions that lead to growth and those that are regressive. But once the course is clear, the individual chooses to grow rather than to regress. Rogers does not deny that there are other needs, some of them biological, but he sees them as subservient to the organism's motivation to enhance and maintain itself.

The characteristics of "self-actualized" individuals—those who have developed their potentialities to the fullest—have been studied by Abraham Maslow. (In Chapter 11 we noted Maslow's hierarchy of needs, progressing from basic physiological needs through psychological needs and culminating in the need for self-actualization.)

Albert Einstein

Maslow began his investigation in a somewhat unusual manner. He selected eminent historical figures whom he considered to be *self-actualizers*—men and women who had made extraordinary use of their potential. Included were such persons as Spinoza, Thomas Jefferson, Abraham Lincoln, William James, Jane Addams, Albert Einstein, and Eleanor Roosevelt. After studying their lives, Maslow arrived at a composite picture of a self-actualizer. The distinguishing characteristics of self-actualized persons are listed in Table 13-3, along with some of the behaviors that Maslow believed could lead to self-actualization.

Maslow extended his study to a population of college students. Selecting those students who fitted his definition of self-actualizers, Maslow found this group to be in the healthiest 1 percent of the population—they showed no neurotic or psychotic symptoms and were making effective use of their talents and capabilities (Maslow, 1970).

Many people experience transient moments of self-actualization. Maslow calls these *peak experiences*. A peak experience is one of happiness and fulfillment, an experience of *being*—a temporary, nonstriving, non–self-centered state of perfection and goal attainment. Peak experiences may occur with different degrees of intensity and in various contexts—creative activities, appreciation of nature, intimate relations with others, parental experiences, aesthetic perceptions, or athletic participation. After asking a large number of college students to describe any experience that came near to being a peak experience, Maslow attempted to summarize their experiences. They spoke of wholeness, perfection, aliveness, uniqueness, effortlessness, self-sufficiency, and the values of beauty, goodness, and truth.

Eleanor Roosevelt

TABLE 13-3
Self-actualization

CHARACTERISTICS OF SELF-ACTUALIZERS

Perceive reality efficiently and are able to tolerate uncertainty

Accept themselves and others for what they are

Spontaneous in thought and behavior

Problem-centered rather than self-centered

Have a good sense of humor

Highly creative

Resistant to enculturation, although not purposely unconventional

Concerned for the welfare of humanity

Capable of deep appreciation of the basic experiences of life

Establish deep, satisfying interpersonal relations with a few, rather than many, people

Able to look at life from an objective viewpoint

BEHAVIORS LEADING TO SELF-ACTUALIZATION

Experience life as a child does, with full absorption and concentration

Try something new rather than sticking to secure and safe ways

Listen to your own feelings in evaluating experiences rather than to the voice of tradition or authority or the majority

Be honest; avoid pretenses or "game playing"

Be prepared to be unpopular if your views don't coincide with those of most people

Assume responsibility

Work hard at whatever you decide to do

Try to identify your defenses and have the courage to give them up

Paraphrased with modifications from Maslow (1954, 1967)

Evaluation of the Phenomenological Approach

By focusing on the individual's unique perception and interpretation of events, the phenomenological approach brings back the role of private experience to the study of personality. More than the other theories we have discussed, it concentrates on the whole, healthy person and emphasizes a positive, optimistic view of human nature.

The major criticism of the phenomenological approach is the difficulty of validating its concepts. Self-actualization, for example, is not clearly defined, and the criteria Maslow used in selecting his self-actualized persons are vague. Someone else viewing the lives of the famous people studied by Maslow may not find the same characteristics as those listed in Table 13-3. And some of the characteristics may even be somewhat negatively related. For example, some individuals who were most known for their concern for human welfare did not have very satisfying interpersonal relationships with their spouses or children. Eleanor Roosevelt and Abraham Lincoln are two examples: they appear to have fulfilled their potential in some areas of life while neglecting other areas.

Phenomenologists do not always distinguish between the self as a causal agent—as the *doer* of behavior—and the self-concept—the individual's attitudes and feelings about him or herself (Wylie, 1974). The self-concept certainly influences behavior, but the nature of the relationship is not clear. An individual may conceive of him or herself as "honest and trustworthy" yet behave with varying degrees of "honesty" in different situations. And changes in personal beliefs and attitudes do not always result in changes in behavior. Often the reverse is true: people modify their beliefs to make them consistent with their behavior.

The way an individual perceives and interprets events is important to an understanding of personality. But a scientific study of personality also needs to investigate the *conditions* that influence the person's self-concept and that determine whether or not potentialities will be realized.

Personality Assessment

In order to study personality—whatever one's theory—methods of assessing personality variables are necessary. We make informal appraisals of personality all the time. In selecting friends, sizing up potential co-workers, choosing candidates for political office, or deciding on a marriage partner, we make implicit predictions about future behavior. Sometimes our predictions are erroneous. First impressions may be distorted because we focus on one particular characteristic that we especially like or dislike and let it bias our perception of other aspects of the person. This tendency to bias our judgment on the basis of one particular feature is known as the *halo effect.* Sometimes our first impression of a person is based on a *stereotype* of the characteristics believed to be typical of the group to which he or she belongs. And sometimes the person being appraised may be "putting his or her best foot forward." For these and other reasons, informal evaluations of others may be in error.

There are many occasions when a more objective, unbiased assessment of personality is desirable. In selecting individuals for high-level positions, employers need to know something about the individuals' honesty, ability to handle stress, and so on. In helping students make vocational choices, counselors can offer wiser advice if they know something about the students' personality in addition to their school performance. Decisions about the kind of treatment that will best benefit a mentally ill person or will help rehabilitate a convicted felon require an objective assessment of the individual's personality. Personality assessment is also necessary for research purposes. Investigators who want to determine the relationship between anxiety and performance in school need to have some way of objectively measuring anxiety as a personal trait.

The many methods that have been used to assess personality can generally be classified under three headings: *observational methods, personality inventories,* and *projective techniques.*

Observational Methods

Observations of an individual by a trained observer can take place in a natural setting (watching a child interact with classmates), in an experimental situation (observing a student try to complete a test that was deliberately designed to be too difficult to finish in the allotted time), or in the context of an interview. The interview differs from casual conversation in that it has a purpose: for example, to evaluate a job applicant, to determine whether a patient is suicidal, to estimate the extent of an individual's emotional problems, or to predict whether a prisoner is apt to violate parole. The interview may be *unstructured*—the person interviewed largely determines what is discussed, although the interviewer usually elicits additional information through the skilled use of supplementary questions. Or the interview may be *structured*—it follows a standard pattern, much like a printed questionnaire, assuring that all relevant topics are covered. The unstructured interview is more likely to be used in a clinical or counseling situation; the structured interview is more likely to be used with a job applicant or in a research program where comparable data is required of all respondents.

The accuracy of the information obtained in an interview depends on a number of factors, too lengthy to discuss here. But research on the interview process has made it clear that even slight changes in the behavior of the interviewer have a marked effect on what the person interviewed says and does. For example, a simple nod of the head by the interviewer at the right moment may increase greatly the amount of talking by the person being interviewed. If the interviewer increases the length of his or her utterances, the person being interviewed tends to do likewise (Matarazzo and Wiens, 1972). As a means of measuring personality, the interview is subject to many sources of error and bias; the success of the technique depends on the skill and awareness of the interviewer.

TABLE 13-4
Some examples of rating scales

How would you describe the individual's self-confidence?	Considers him or herself incapable of much success	Underestimates own abilities	Knows own capabilities	Exaggerates own abilities	Judges him or herself capable of anything
Place a check at the point that describes the individual's poise.	Nervous and ill at ease	Somewhat tense; easily upset	Average poise and security	Self-assured	Composed; adapts well to crises
How would you rate the subject's emotional control?	Very Low	Below Average	Average	Above Average	Very High
Does the individual antagonize others?	Never	Rarely	Sometimes	Often	Always
How would you rate the parent's behavior toward the child?	No control of emotion in response to child's behavior	Controlled more by emotion than reason in dealing with child	Emotion freely expressed but behavior controlled	Remains calm and objective toward child despite provocation	Never shows any signs of emotion, always controlled
Does the individual need constant prodding or carry out assignments without being told?	Needs much prodding in doing ordinary assignments	Needs occasional prodding	Does ordinary assignments of own accord	Completes suggested supplementary work	Seeks additional tasks

RATING SCALES Impressions gained from an interview or from observing behavior can be put into standardized form by means of *rating scales*. A rating scale is a device for recording judgments about a personality trait. Some examples are shown in Table 13-4. Such scales give the observer a frame of reference for recording impressions.

In order for the rating to be meaningful, the rater must (1) understand the scale, (2) be sufficiently acquainted with the person being rated to make meaningful judgments, and (3) avoid the "halo effect." Unless the rater knows the person fairly well or the behavior being rated is very specific, ratings may be influenced by social stereotypes. That is, judgments may be based on how the rater *believes* a "suburban housewife," a "long-haired intellectual," or a "high school athlete" acts and thinks, rather than on the actual behavior of the subject being rated.

Despite such problems, descriptions of a person provided by different raters in different situations often yield good agreement. In one study, for example, the aggressiveness of a group of schoolboys was rated by their peers and also by trained psychologists who watched them playing games in the schoolyard. There was close agreement between the two sets of ratings (Winder and Wiggins, 1964).

Personality Inventories

Another method of personality assessment relies on the individual's self-observations. A *personality inventory* is essentially a questionnaire in which the person reports reactions or feelings in certain situations. It resembles a structured or standardized interview in that it asks the same questions of each person and the answers are usually given in a form that can be easily scored—often by a test-scoring machine. A personality inventory may be designed to measure a single dimension of personality (such as anxiety) or several personality traits simultaneously. The Sixteen Personality Factor Questionnaire (discussed earlier in this chapter), for example, produces a personality profile showing the individual's scores on a number of different traits.

The 16 PF, as you may recall, was based on the statistical technique of *factor analysis*. Factor analysis was used to identify 16 basic traits. Test questions that best represented each trait were then selected and assembled into a test that yielded scores on such personality characteristics as dominance, emotional stability, and self-control. A quite different method of test construction was used in the development of the *Minnesota Multiphasic Personality Inventory* (referred to as the MMPI).

MINNESOTA MULTIPHASIC PERSONALITY INVENTORY The MMPI is composed of some 550 statements (about attitudes, emotional reactions, physical and psychological symptoms, and past experiences) to which the subject answers "true," "false," or "cannot say." Some of the items are

I have never done anything dangerous for the thrill of it.
I daydream very little.
My mother often made me obey even when I thought it was unreasonable.
At times my thoughts have raced ahead faster than I could speak them.

The responses are scored according to their correspondence to answers given by people with different kinds of psychological problems (see Table 13-5).

The MMPI was developed to aid clinicians in diagnosing personality disturbances. But instead of assuming specific personality traits and formulating questions to measure them, the test designers gave hundreds of test questions to groups of individuals; each group was known to differ from the norm on a particular criterion. Only those questions that discriminated between groups were retained to form the inventory. This is known as *empirical construction*, because the test items bear an actual (empirical) relationship to the personality characteristic being measured. For example, to develop a scale of items that distinguish between paranoid and normal individuals, the same questions were given to two groups: the *criterion group* consisted of individuals who were hospitalized with the diagnosis of paranoia; the *control group*, of people who had never been diagnosed as having psychiatric problems. Questions that at face value might seem to distinguish normal from paranoid individuals—for example, "I think that most people would lie to get ahead"—may or may not do so when put to an empirical test. In fact, patients diagnosed as paranoid were significantly *less* apt to respond "true" to this statement than normal individuals. The method of empirical construction ensures that the test item bears an actual relationship to the personality characteristic being measured.

Since the MMPI is derived from differences between criterion and control groups, it does not really matter whether what the person says is true. The fact that he or she says it is important. If schizophrenics answer "true" and normal subjects "false" to the statement "My mother never loved me," their answers distinguish the two groups, regardless of how their mothers actually behaved. This is one advantage of a test based on the method of empirical construction over one for which the test constructor assumes that certain answers indicate specific personality traits.

Although originally designed to identify people with serious personality disorders, the MMPI scales have been widely used in studying normal popula-

TABLE 13-5
MMPI Scales
The first three scales are "validity" scales, which help to determine whether the person has answered the test items carefully and honestly. The remaining "clinical" scales were originally named for categories of psychiatric disorders, but interpretation now emphasizes personality attributes rather than diagnostic categories.

SCALE NAME	SCALE ABBREVIATION	INTERPRETATION OF HIGH SCORES
Lie	L	Denial of common frailties
Frequency	F	Invalidity of profile
Correction	K	Defensive, evasive
Hypochondriasis	Hs	Emphasis on physical complaints
Depression	D	Unhappy, depressed
Hysteria	Hy	Reacts to stress by denying problems
Psychopathic deviancy	Pd	Lack of social conformity; often in trouble with law
Masculinity-femininity	Mf	Feminine orientation (males); masculine orientation (females)
Paranoia	Pa	Suspicious
Psychasthenia	Pt	Worried, anxious
Schizophrenia	Sc	Withdrawn, bizarre thinking
Hypomania	Ma	Impulsive, excitable
Social introversion-extraversion	Si	Introverted, shy

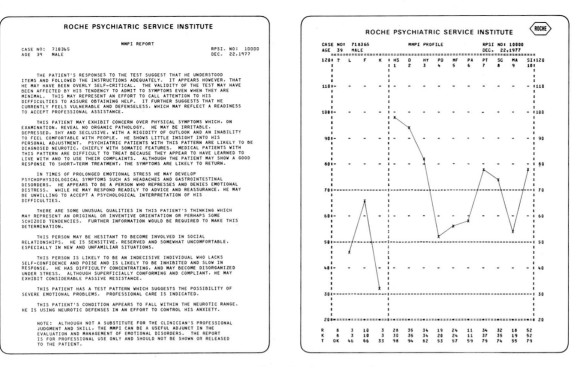

Fig. 13-7 Computer printout of an MMPI profile with interpretation

tions. Sufficient data have been collected to provide personality descriptions of people with different patterns of high and low scores on the various scales. A recent development is the use of a computer to score and interpret the test results (see Figure 13-7).

CALIFORNIA PSYCHOLOGICAL INVENTORY Another personality test based on the method of empirical construction is the *California Psychological Inventory* (CPI). The CPI uses some of the same questions as the MMPI, but it is designed to measure more "normal" personality traits. It has scales measuring such traits as dominance, sociability, self-acceptance, responsibility, and socialization. The comparison groups for some of the scales were obtained by asking groups of high school and college students to nominate classmates who were high or low on the trait in question. Thus, for the dominance scale the criterion group consisted of those students who were described by their peers as high in dominance (aggressive, confident, self-reliant), while the control group consisted of those students who were described as low in dominance (retiring, lacking in self-confidence, inhibited). Items that showed a statistically significant difference between the criterion and the control groups form the dominance scale.

Several of the CPI scales measure traits that are related to academic achievement, and studies have correlated scores on these scales with college grades. One study, for example, found that students who scored high on the scale measuring "Achievement via Conformance" tended to do well in courses that rewarded conformity—that is, the kind of course where a set core of material must be learned and then regurgitated on an objective test. Students who scored high on the scale measuring "Achievement via Independence" tended to do well on courses that emphasized independent study and self-direction. The highest grade-point averages were obtained by the students who scored high on both scales (Domino, 1971).

PERSONALITY ASSESSMENT

Controls for Faking and Response Style

One method of minimizing the influence of "social desirability"—the tendency to present oneself in a favorable light when taking a personality test—is to ask the person to choose between statements that are equally desirable (or undesirable). The Edwards Personal Preference Schedule (EPPI) consists of 225 forced-choice items (Edwards, 1959). The individual taking the test must select either A or B of an item such as the following:

A I like to be successful in things undertaken.
B I like to form new friendships.

Both are socially acceptable statements, but one stresses achievement and the other affiliation. By his or her choice, the individual indicates which of the two motives is more important. Some items require a choice between unfavorable statements:

A I feel depressed when I fail at something.
B I am nervous when talking before a group.

The disadvantage of this method is that it reveals only the *relative* preference for one motive or feeling over

another; it does not show the *absolute* level. Thus, a person who is fairly apathetic—doesn't care much about either being successful *or* forming friendships—might obtain scores similar to a person who is very energetic and outgoing.

The MMPI uses a different method to correct for test-taking attitudes. Scores on the first three scales listed in Table 13-5 are used in evaluating the accuracy of the test results. The L (Lie) scale measures denial of common frailties—asserting more about oneself than can be true. Answering "true" to the statement "I always read every newspaper editorial every day" or "false" to "I sometimes feel angry" will earn you a point on the L scale. With six or more points on the L scale, the test results are viewed with suspicion; the test taker is probably not answering the questions honestly.

The K (Correction) scale consists of items that, while not as extreme as those on the L scale, are concerned with whether the test taker is presenting him or herself in a socially desirable manner—being somewhat defensive about revealing faults. Everyone gets a score on the K scale, and this score is used to "correct" the scores on the other scales. The more evasive or de-

fensive the individual is in responding to the test questions, the higher his or her K score and the more the scores on the clinical scales are elevated in the direction of pathology.

The F (Frequency) scale attempts to measure confusion or carelessness in answering questions. To get a high score on the F scale, the person has to describe him or herself in a bizarre or improbable manner—that is, to give answers that occur very infrequently. A high F score usually invalidates the test protocol; the individual either did not understand the questions or did not care how he or she answered them. (However, high F scores frequently accompany high scores on the Schizophrenia scale, which also measures bizarre thinking.)

These three MMPI validity scales represent a valiant attempt by the test constructors to control for faking and differences in response style so that the test results represent the test takers as they actually see themselves. But like the forced-choice method of the EPPI, they are only partially successful. If people want to give a distorted picture of themselves, they can do so, although in the process they still reveal some things about their personality.

PROBLEMS WITH PERSONALITY INVENTORIES Most personality inventories rely on the individual's ability to understand the questions and willingness to answer them honestly. For many personality test items, however, the "best" answer is fairly apparent and individuals may try to bias their answers. If the test is given as part of a job application, people will clearly want to present themselves in the best light. If admission to a psychotherapy program depends on the test results, they may bias their answers so as to appear to need help. And even if a person is trying to be very accurate and objective, there is a tendency to give answers that are "socially desirable." It is difficult to answer "yes" to the MMPI question "I am certainly lacking in self-confidence," although at heart you may feel that way. Self-confidence is a trait that is desirable in our society; to be lacking in self-confidence is socially undesirable.

Another personality variable that influences test responses is the tendency of some people to "acquiesce"—to agree with questions. For example, a person might say "yes" to both of the following items: "I am a happy and carefree person" and "I frequently have periods when I am extremely depressed." The test results would reflect something about the person's behavior—a tendency to agree with questions—but would tell us little about general mood. To counteract agreement tendencies, test constructors try (whenever possible) to reverse the wording of questions so that there are "yes" and "no" versions of each item.

Various methods have been used to counteract outright faking and tendencies toward social desirability and acquiescence on personality inventories, but they have been only partially successful.

Projective Techniques

Personality inventories strive for objectivity; they are easily scored and can be evaluated for reliability and validity. But their fixed structure—specific questions to which the individual must respond by selecting one of the answers presented—severely limits freedom of expression. *Projective tests*, in contrast, allow the individual to put much more of him or herself into the responses. A projective test presents an ambiguous stimulus to which the person may respond as he or she wishes. Theoretically, because the stimulus is ambiguous and does not demand a specific response, the individual *projects* his or her personality onto the stimulus, just as a movie camera projects an image onto the screen. Projective tests tap the individual's imagination; through imaginative productions it is assumed that the person reveals something about him or herself. Two of the most widely used projective techniques are the *Rorschach Test* and the *Thematic Apperception Test*.

RORSCHACH The Rorschach Test, developed by the Swiss psychiatrist Hermann Rorschach in the 1920s, consists of a series of 10 cards, each displaying a rather complex inkblot, like the one shown in Figure 13-8. Some of the blots are in color and some are black and white. The subject is instructed to look at one card at a time and report everything the inkblot looks like or resembles. After the subject has finished the 10 cards, the examiner usually goes back over each response, asking the subject to clarify some responses and to tell what features of the blot gave a particular impression.

The subject's responses may be scored in various ways. Three main categories are (1) location—whether the response involves the entire inkblot or some part, (2) determinants—whether the subject responds to the shape of the blot, color, or differences in texture and shading, and (3) content—what the response represents. Most testers also score responses according to frequency of occurrence; for example, a response is "popular" if many people assign it to the same inkblot.

Several elaborate scoring systems have been devised based on the above categories. But because these systems have proved to be limited in predictive value, many psychologists base their interpretations on an impressionistic evaluation of the response record as well as on the subject's general reaction to the test situation; for example, whether the individual is defensive, open, competitive, cooperative, and so on. Interpretation of the Rorschach requires more training and experience than interpretation of any of the other personality tests.

THEMATIC APPERCEPTION TEST Another popular projective test is the Thematic Apperception Test (TAT), which was developed at Harvard Univer-

"Rorschach! What's to become of you?"

Fig. 13-8 A Rorschach inkblot
This inkblot is one of the standardized blots used in the Rorschach Test. The subject is asked to tell what is seen in the blot; it may be viewed from any angle.

The Barnum Effect

There is no scientific evidence that the position of stars and planets at the moment of one's birth has any influence on personality. Yet astrology—the study of "how heavenly bodies influence the destinies of individuals"—is extremely popular. People buy books on astrology and avidly read their daily horoscope in the newspapers, accepting the personality characterizations and predictions as at least probabilities, if not facts. What reinforces their belief? The answer seems to be that the astrological descriptions are general enough to be true of most anyone.

Studies have shown that people tend to view generalized descriptions as accurate summaries of their own personality. In one experiment, college students were given a personality inventory. Some days later, each student was given a typed report in a sealed envelope and asked to rate the evaluation for accuracy. Unknown to the subjects, all the personality descriptions were *identical*. Most of the students said they felt that the description fit them pretty well (Forer, 1949). And a glance at some of the evaluative statements will show why:

Under stressful circumstances you occasionally experience some feelings of self-doubt.

Although you have considerable affection for your parents, there have been times when you disagreed with them.

Your sexual adjustment has presented problems for you.

You have a tendency to be critical of yourself.

At times you are extraverted, affable, sociable, while at other times you are introverted, wary, reserved.

These statements resemble the kinds of statements found in astrological characterizations of personality based on the signs of the zodiac. Because such descriptions are true of many people, they have the illusion of accuracy when applied to the individual case. This phenomenon has been dubbed the "Barnum effect," in reference to the statement by the circus entrepreneur P. T. Barnum, "There's a fool born every minute."

Recent studies indicate that people are more likely to accept a personality description of themselves as accurate when they are told that the report is based on a projective test than when told that it is based on an interview or a personality inventory (Snyder, 1974). Apparently, there is a certain mystique associated with projective tests—people believe that they are revealing themselves in ways they don't completely understand; interviews and personality inventories are more familiar, however, and people assume that their responses can be consciously controlled.

The popularity and acceptance of personality evaluations by astrologers, palmists, and those who read tea leaves or Tarot cards appears to stem from the mystical quality associated with the procedure and from the universality of their personality descriptions. In addition, some fortunetellers are quite skilled in picking up cues from the individual's appearance and reactions. The surprising accuracy of one bit of personality description may predispose the subject to accept the total evaluation.

Fig. 13-9 A picture similar to one used in the Thematic Apperception Test The pictures usually have elements of ambiguity so that the subject can "read into" them something from personal experience or fantasy.

sity by Henry Murray in the 1930s. The subject is shown a series of as many as 20 ambiguous pictures of persons and scenes, similar to the one in Figure 13-9, and asked to make up a story about each. He or she is encouraged to give free rein to imagination and to tell whatever story comes to mind. The test is intended to reveal basic "themes" that recur in a person's imaginative productions. *Apperception* means a readiness to perceive in certain ways based on prior individual experience. Hence, people interpret ambiguous pictures according to their apperceptions and elaborate stories in terms of preferred plots or themes that reflect personal fantasies. If particular problems are bothering the subject, they may show up in a number of the stories or in striking deviations from the usual in one or two stories.

When shown a picture similar to that in Figure 13-9, a 21-year-old male told the following story:

She has prepared this room for someone's arrival and is opening the door for a last general look over the room. She is probably expecting her son home. She tries to place everything as it was when he left. She seems like a very tyrannical character. She led her son's life for him and is going to take over again as soon as he gets back. This is merely the beginning of her rule, and the son is definitely cowed by this overbearing attitude of hers and will slip back into her well-ordered way of life. He will go through life plodding down the tracks she has laid down for him. All this represents her complete domination of his life until she dies.

Although the original picture shows only a woman standing in an open doorway, the subject's readiness to respond with something about the relationship to his mother led to this story of a woman's domination of her son. Facts obtained later confirmed the clinician's interpretation that the story reflected the subject's own problems.

In analyzing responses to the TAT cards, the psychologist looks for recurrent themes that may reveal the individual's needs, motives, or characteristic way of handling interpersonal relations.

PROBLEMS WITH PROJECTIVE TESTS Many other projective tests have been devised. Some ask the subject to draw pictures of people, houses, trees, and so on. Others involve completing sentences that start "I often wish . . . ," "My mother . . . ," or "I feel like quitting when they . . . ." In fact, any stimulus to which a person can respond in an individualistic way could be considered the basis for a projective test. But most projective tests have not been subjected to enough research to establish their usefulness in assessing personality.

The Rorschach and the TAT, in contrast, have been intensively researched. The results, however, have not always been encouraging. Test reliability of the Rorschach has been generally poor, because the interpretation of responses depends too much on the clinician's judgment; the same test protocol may often be evaluated quite differently by two trained examiners. And attempts to demonstrate the Rorschach's ability to predict behavior or discriminate between groups have had limited success. Numerous efforts have been made to improve on Rorschach's method. For example, the Holtzman Inkblot Test presents the subject with 45 different inkblots and allows only one response per blot (Holtzman and others, 1961). It was hoped that this procedure would yield more reliable and valid scores; so far, however, the results have been disappointing (Zubin, 1972).

The TAT has fared somewhat better. When specific scoring systems are used—for example, to measure achievement motives or aggressive themes—the interscorer reliability is fairly good. But the relation of TAT scores to overt behavior is complex. Preoccupations are not necessarily acted on. A person who produces a number of stories with themes of aggression may not be very aggressive in actual behavior. Apparently the subject is compensating for inhibition of aggressive tendencies by expressing such impulses in fantasy. When inhibitions about expressing aggression *and* strength of aggressive tendencies are estimated from the TAT stories, the relationship to behavior becomes more predictable. Among boys whose tests indicated they were not very inhibited, the correlation between amount of aggression in the stories and overt aggression was +.55. Among boys showing a high degree of inhibition, the correlation between number of aggressive themes and overt aggression was −.50 (Olweus, 1969).

Defenders of the Rorschach and the TAT point out that it is not fair to expect accurate predictions based on test responses alone; story themes or responses to inkblots are meaningful only when considered in the light of additional information—the person's life history, other test data, and observations of behavior. The skilled clinician uses the results of projective tests to

make tentative interpretations about the individual's personality and then verifies or discards them, depending on further information. The tests are helpful in suggesting possible areas of conflict to be explored.

Consistency of Personality

In studying personality, psychologists try to discover regularities in behavior. An assumption basic to most personality theories is that people behave consistently—from one situation to another and over time. If an individual seems "honest," "friendly," and "conscientious" in several situations, then we assume that we can predict how he or she will act in a wide variety of situations. And we assume also that we can predict how that person will behave a year from now. Indeed, the feeling of consistency within our own thoughts and behavior is essential to our well-being; the loss of a sense of consistency is characteristic of personality disorganization. But research over the years has failed to show as much personality consistency as either theories or our intuitions lead us to expect, and the consistency issue is currently one of vigorous debate among personality psychologists.

Empirical Evidence

Longitudinal studies of individuals indicate considerable consistency of personality characteristics. In one large-scale study, more than 100 subjects were followed over a 25-year period. They were first evaluated in junior high school by psychologists who rated each individual on a number of personality traits, using a standardized rating scale. The same subjects were rated again in senior high school and a third time when they were in their mid-thirties; each rating was by a different group of judges. Over the three-year period from junior high school to senior high school, 58 percent of the personality variables showed a significant positive correlation. Over the 20-year period from senior high school to the subject's mid-thirties, 29 percent of the items showed a significant correlation. Table 13-6 lists some of the personality characteristics that displayed the greatest consistency over time (Block, 1971).

This study indicates that trained observers looking at an individual find personality consistencies over time. In looking at *themselves*, people also tend to find consistency over the years, at least once they reach adulthood. Scores on the California Psychological Inventory taken 10 years apart (ages 30 to 40 in one group and 40 to 50 in another) showed consistency on many of the items (Block, 1977). And a follow-up study of Terman's gifted children (see pp. 370–71) found that feelings about work, family, and one's own self-worth remained quite stable from ages 30 to 60 (Sears, 1977).

The evidence for personality consistency is less impressive, however, when we look at measures of behavior across different situations—for example, aggressive behavior at home and aggressive behavior at school. Except for intellectual and cognitive variables, most personality characteristics show only modest consistency across situations. Studies of traits such as honesty, self-control, dependency, and aggression usually find low correlations between measures of the trait in one situation and measures in another (Mischel, 1976).

TABLE 13-6
Personality characteristics showing consistency over time

CORRELATION JUNIOR HIGH TO SENIOR HIGH SCHOOL	CORRELATION SENIOR HIGH SCHOOL TO ADULTHOOD	ITEM RATED
MALES		
.58	.53	Is a genuinely dependable and responsible person
.57	.59	Tends toward undercontrol of needs and impulses, unable to delay gratification
.50	.42	Is self-defeating
.35	.58	Enjoys aesthetic impressions, is aesthetically reactive
FEMALES		
.50	.46	Basically submissive
.39	.43	Emphasizes being with others, gregarious
.48	.49	Tends to be rebellious and nonconforming
.45	.42	Is concerned with philosophical problems, for example, religion, values, the meaning of life

Source: After Block (1971)

Attempts to relate responses on personality tests to behavior in real life have been equally disappointing. Correlations between measures derived from personality inventories or projective techniques and independent measures of behavior are typically less than +.30. Correlations of this size may be useful for a gross assessment of personality (for example, deciding whether a person is unfit for a sensitive diplomatic post) but would be of limited value in predicting specific behavior.

Consistency Versus Specificity

Social learning theorists point to the data showing low consistency of personality traits across situations as evidence that behavior is *situation-specific*—that is, more dependent on the nature of the specific situation in which it occurs than on enduring traits or response tendencies in the person. They maintain that it is not very useful to characterize people in broad trait terms—"impulsive," "dependent," and so on—because individuals show a great deal of variability and discrimination in their behavior. Whether or not a person acts "impulsively" depends to a great extent on the particular conditions he or she confronts.

According to social learning theorists, traits are more often in "the eye of the beholder" than in the person observed; we tend to attribute more consistency to a person's behavior than actually exists. There are numerous reasons why we may do so. We will mention only four:

1 Many personal qualities remain fairly constant—physical appearance, manner of speaking, expressive gestures, and so on. These constancies help to create an impression of personality consistency.

2 Our preconceived notions of how people behave may lead us to generalize beyond our actual observations. We may fill in the missing data according to our "implicit personality theories" of what traits and behaviors go together. Stereotypes of how a "homosexual" or a "career woman" or an "athlete" behaves may cause us to attribute greater consistency to a person's actions than observations warrant.

3 Our own presence can cause people to behave in certain ways. Thus, our acquaintances may appear to behave consistently because we are present as a stimulus during every observation we make. They may behave quite differently when we are not there.

4 Because the actions of another person are such a salient feature of any scene, we tend to overestimate the extent to which behavior is caused by personality characteristics and underestimate the importance of situational forces that may cause the person to act as he or she does. If we observe someone behaving aggressively, we assume that the person has an aggressive disposition and will behave similarly in other settings—even though the situational factors may be quite different.

Personality theorists who believe that behavior is determined by enduring dispositions or motives (trait and psychoanalytic theorists) maintain that personality is much more consistent than the cross-situational research indicates. They point to defects in the methodology of many of the studies that found little consistency (Block, 1977). They also emphasize that many of these studies cannot be meaningfully interpreted without (1) considering individual differences in consistency and (2) defining traits in more specific terms.

INDIVIDUAL DIFFERENCES IN CONSISTENCY Most of the research on personality traits assumes that every person can be described by every trait, that people differ from one another only in *how much* of the trait they possess. But while some people may be consistent on some traits, few would be consistent on all traits. When we are asked to describe a friend, we pick out a few traits that strike us as pertinent. When asked to describe another friend, we select a different set of traits. It may be that for any given individual, we should expect to find consistency only on those traits that are central to his or her personality.

In one study, college students were asked to rate their own cross-situational variability on a set of traits (Bem and Allen, 1974). Those students who identified themselves as consistent on a particular trait tended to show much more consistency across different situations than did students who identified themselves as variable on that trait. For example, students who said they were consistently friendly tended to show a fairly consistent level of friendliness on such measures as ratings by their parents and peers and direct observation in several settings (cross-situational correlation +.57). Those who described themselves as variable in friendliness tended in fact to be less consistent (cross-situational correlation +.27).

If, as this study indicates, people do vary in their consistency on different traits, then a random selection of subjects will contain some individuals who show consistency on a particular trait, such as honesty, and some who show variability. An attempt to demonstrate cross-situational consistency with such a mixed group of subjects is bound to yield poor results.

TRAITS TOO BROADLY DEFINED Most personality inventories and rating scales define traits in fairly global terms. We may have to be more specific if we want to be accurate in predicting behavior. In the Bem and Allen study, for example, the investigators assumed that personal neatness was one component of the trait of "conscientiousness." But the results showed that for most students the neatness of their rooms was *not* related to other measures of conscientiousness, such as completing homework assignments on time or arriving promptly for classes and appointments.

Measuring the Interaction of Traits and Situations

Our discussion thus far makes it clear that to understand and predict behavior we need to know the characteristics of the individual *and* of the particular situation. More specifically, we need to determine how the qualities of the person and the situation influence each other. A person may show a trait, such as anxiety, only under certain circumstances (for example, when taking an exam or giving a speech, but not when climbing a dangerous mountain). In addition, this anxiety may express itself in some ways (upset stomach, jitteriness) but not in others (rapid heart rate, perspiration).

A current approach to measuring traits attempts to examine (1) *individual differences* (for example, stable tendencies to be anxious or hostile or conscientious across different situations) in interaction with (2) specific *environmental conditions* and (3) *mode of response* (the different ways in which anxiety or hostility may express itself).

To measure anxiety, a series of questionnaires was developed to determine the kinds of situations that evoke anxious feelings, the way the individual responds to the situation, and the intensity of the response. The anxiety-producing situations range from such innocuous events as "You are starting on a long automobile trip" to "You are about to take an important exam" or "You are on a ledge high on a mountainside." The subject is asked to imagine each situation and describe how he or she would respond to it by marking a number of possible reactions (for example, "hands tremble," "feel tense," "can't concentrate") and noting the intensity of the reaction on a five-point scale from "not at all" to "very much" (Endler and Hunt, 1966).

The questionnaires were administered to many groups of people and the answers analyzed by a statistical procedure that provides separate estimates of the effects of stimulus situations, individual differences in intensity of arousal, and response modes. The analyses revealed that individual differences and situations by themselves accounted for only a small percentage of the variability among scores. By far, the greatest source of variability was the *interactions* of the two with each other and with response mode (Endler, 1977).

A similar questionnaire was devised to measure the components of hostility—by asking about the kinds of situations that evoke anger and the individual's response to each situation (Endler and Hunt, 1968). Again, the interactions—individual differences with situations, individual differences with response modes, and situations with response modes—provided the greatest source of variability. There was a tendency, however, for individual differences alone to account for more variability than situations alone, suggesting that hostility may be a slightly more consistent "trait" than anxiety—at least as far as the situations sampled by this questionnaire were concerned.

These results indicate that it is not very useful to talk about general traits, such as hostility or anxiety, without considering environmental conditions. Two people may receive equally high scores on a test of anxiety; but one person becomes anxious in the face of physical danger, while the other responds with

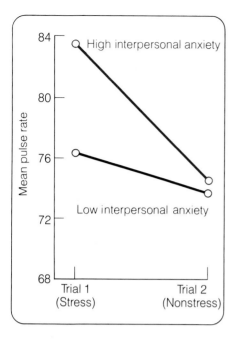

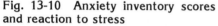

Fig. 13-10 Anxiety inventory scores and reaction to stress
Individuals who score high on interpersonal anxiety, as measured by the S-R (self-report) Inventory of General Trait Anxiousness, show a greater increase in pulse rate prior to an examination (trial 1) than individuals with low interpersonal anxiety scores. Under nonstress conditions (trial 2) the two groups do not differ. (After Endler, 1977)

anxiety to interpersonal situations that are seen as a threat to his or her self-esteem—for example, giving a speech or taking an examination. When responses to the Endler and Hunt anxiousness inventory are broken down to give separate scores for reactions to physical threats versus reactions to interpersonal threats, predictions of actual behavior become much more accurate. For example, subjects whose scores indicated concern about physical danger reported much greater feelings of anxiety when placed in an experiment where they were threatened by the possibility of electric shock than did subjects whose test scores indicated that their anxiety was associated with interpersonal situations (Endler and Okada, 1974). In another study, students who scored high on interpersonal anxiety showed much more stress just before an examination (being evaluated) than did students who scored low on interpersonal anxiety (see Figure 13-10).

These studies suggest that personality tests that redefine traits to take into account situations will be much more successful in predicting behavior and in finding consistency in behavior. To understand personality, we need to examine simultaneously person factors, situation factors, and the interaction between the two.

Toward an Integrated View of Personality

We have looked at a number of different ways of conceptualizing personality. Each has something to say about how individual characteristics develop and how they interact with environmental conditions to determine behavior. The reader is undoubtedly left with some puzzlement as to the best perspective from which to view personality—how to form a cohesive view of the individual person. Psychologists share this concern. The field of personality psychology is currently in a state of flux and transition. It is clear that no simplified theory will suffice to explain personality, and the current trend is toward a synthesis of several influences.

In trying to weigh the relative importance of individual differences and environmental conditions in determining behavior, it is helpful to think of the situation as *providing information*—information that the person interprets and acts on according to his or her past experiences and abilities. Some situations are powerful. A red traffic light causes most drivers to stop; they know what it means, are motivated to obey it, and have the ability to stop when they see it. We would be fairly successful in predicting the number of individuals who would respond in the same way to a red traffic light. Some situations are weak. An art teacher shows students a slide of an abstract painting and asks them to comment on its meaning. In this case we would expect a wide variety of responses. The picture does not mean the same thing to all the viewers, nor are there universal expectancies regarding the desired response. With weak situations, we will find that individual differences, rather than the stimulus, are the most important determinant of behavior.

It seems likely that future research in personality will not neglect *cognitive processes* but will balance them with other aspects of personality, such as mood and temperament. People differ not only in intelligence and competence, but also in the way they perceive events and code them in memory as well as in the strategies they employ in solving problems. Traditionally, intellectual abilities have been considered separately from personality. And although they are treated in different chapters in this book, they are actually closely interrelated. Future research will probably define personality more broadly to include intellectual factors, particularly the variety of cognitive processes an individual brings to bear in solving problems and in dealing with new situations.

Another area that is beginning to form an important part of personality theory has to do with social interactions. Other people are an important part of most situations, and behavior in social situations is a process of continuous reciprocal interaction; your behavior determines how another person reacts, and his or her response in turn influences your behavior, *ad infinitum*. Prescribed social roles, the impression we form of other people, and the qualities we attribute to them are all important influences on behavior. These social-psychological processes are discussed in Chapters 17 and 18.

SUMMARY

1 *Personality* refers to the characteristic patterns of behavior and modes of thinking that determine a person's adjustment to the environment. Personality is shaped by *inborn potential* as modified by experiences common to the *culture* and the *subcultural groups* (such as sex roles) and by the *unique experiences* that affect the person as an individual.

2 The major theoretical approaches to an understanding of personality include *trait, social learning, psychoanalytic,* and *phenomenological* theories.

3 *Trait theories* assume that a personality can be described by its position on a number of *continuous dimensions,* or *scales.* The method of *factor analysis* has been used to determine the basic traits. Two dimensions found fairly consistently in factor-analytic studies of personality are *introversion-extraversion* and *stability-instability.*

4 *Social learning theory* assumes that personality differences result from variations in learning experiences. Responses may be learned through *observation,* without reinforcement; but reinforcement is important in determining whether the learned responses will be *performed.* A person's behavior depends on the specific characteristics of the situation in interaction with the individual's appraisal of the situation and reinforcement history. People behave consistently insofar as the situations they encounter and the roles they are expected to play remain relatively stable.

5 *Psychoanalytic theory* assumes that much of human motivation is *unconscious* and must be inferred indirectly from behavior. Freud viewed personality as composed of three systems—the *id,* the *ego,* and the *superego*—which interact and sometimes conflict. The id is irrational and impulsive, seeking immediate gratification through such *primary process thinking* as *wish fulfillment.* The ego is realistic and logical, operating by *secondary process thinking,* which postpones gratification until it can be achieved in socially acceptable ways. The superego (conscience and ego-ideal) imposes moral standards on the individual.

6 The dynamic aspects of psychoanalytic theory assume that repressed id impulses cause *anxiety,* which can be reduced by *defense mechanisms.* The developmental aspects propose that some kinds of personality types (such as oral or anal) result from *fixation* (arrested development) at one of the *psychosexual stages.*

7 *Phenomenological theories* are concerned with the individual's *subjective*

experience. They emphasize such humanistic qualities as *self-concept* and push toward growth, or *self-actualization.* For Rogers, the most important aspect of personality is the *congruence* between the *self* and *reality,* and between the *self* and the *ideal self.* Rogers' basic motivating force, the innate tendency toward self-actualization, has been further studied by Maslow, who has examined the characteristics of self-actualizing persons.

8 Personality can be assessed by *observing* an individual in a natural setting or during an interview. The observers may record their impressions on a *rating scale,* taking care to avoid the *halo effect* and *stereotypes.* Self-observations can be reported by means of *personality inventories,* such as the Minnesota Multiphasic Personality Inventory (MMPI) and the California Psychological Inventory (CPI).

9 Less structured approaches to personality assessment are *projective tests,* such as the Rorschach and the Thematic Apperception Test (TAT). Because the test stimuli are ambiguous, it is assumed that the individual projects his or her personality onto the stimulus.

10 *Longitudinal studies* of people indicate that some personality characteristics are *consistent* over time, but *cross-situational* studies find low correlations between measures of a trait (such as honesty) in one situation and measures in another. Social learning theorists believe that this is because behavior is more dependent on the situation than on enduring traits. Trait theorists believe that cross-situational correlations are low because of *individual differences in consistency* and because traits are too broadly defined.

11 To understand behavior, we need to know how the characteristics of the individual *interact* with the characteristics of the situation. Both individual and situational factors influence behavior, but the greatest variability comes from the interaction of the two.

FURTHER READING

General books on personality include Mischel, *Introduction to personality* (2nd ed., 1976), Wiggins, Renner, Clore, and Rose, *Principles of personality* (1976), and Hall and Lindzey, *Theories of personality* (3rd ed., 1978).

A synopsis of various personality theories may be found in Hjelle and Ziegler, *Personality theories: Basic assumptions, research, and applications* (1976). A brief but well written book emphasizing experimental studies is *Personality: The skein of behavior* (1976) by Geen.

For a social learning approach to personality, see Bandura, *Social learning theory* (1977) and Rotter, Chance, and Phares, *Applications of a social learning theory of personality* (1972). See also Mischel, *Introduction to personality* (2nd ed., 1976).

Freud's theories are presented in their most readable form in his *New introductory lectures on psychoanalysis* (1965). Another reference for psychoanalytic theories of personality is Holzman, *Psychoanalysis and psychopathology* (1970), in paperback.

The phenomenological viewpoint is represented in Keen, *A primer in phenomenological psychology* (1977) and Maddi and Costa, *Humanism in personology* (1972). For Carl Rogers' views, see *Person to person: The problem of being human* (1967), in paperback, by Rogers and Stevens and *Carl Rogers on personal power* (1977) by Rogers. For Maslow, see Goble, *The third force: The psychology of Abraham Maslow* (1970), in paperback.

The current approach to studying traits in interaction with situations is represented in Magnusson and Endler (eds.), *Personality at the crossroads: Current issues in interactional psychology* (1977).

Cronbach, *Essentials of psychological testing* (3rd. ed., 1970) has a number of chapters on personality appraisal, as does Weiner, *Clinical methods in psychology* (1976). Other books devoted to personality appraisal are Wiggins, *Personality and prediction: Principles of personality assessment* (1973) and Sundberg, *The Assessment of persons* (1977).

PART SEVEN

Conflict, Adjustment, and Mental Health

14
Conflict and Stress

No matter how resourceful we may be in coping with problems, the circumstances of life inevitably involve stress. Our motives are not always easily satisfied; obstacles must be overcome, choices made, and delays tolerated. Each of us develops characteristic ways of responding when our attempts to reach a goal are blocked. These responses to frustrating situations determine, to a large extent, the adequacy of our adjustment to life.

In this and the following two chapters, we will look at the ways people respond to frustration and stress, what happens when inadequate coping techniques pose a threat to adjustment, and the methods used to treat abnormal behavior. Because this area of psychology is not as firmly based on experimental data as some of the topics covered in previous chapters, the material will be more discursive, and case histories rather than experiments will be used at times to illustrate points.

Frustration

Frustration occurs when progress toward a desired goal is blocked or delayed. A wide range of obstacles, both external and internal, can interfere with one's striving toward a goal. The physical environment presents such obstacles as traffic jams, crowded lines at the supermarket, droughts that destroy a farmer's crops, and noise that prevents concentration. The social environment presents obstacles in the form of the restrictions imposed by other people. These may range from parental denials—Jane's parents insist that she is not old enough to have her own apartment—to broader problems of racial or sexual discrimination.

Sometimes the barriers to goal satisfaction stem from the individual's own limitations. Physical handicaps, lack of specific abilities, or inadequate self-control can prevent an individual from achieving a desired goal. Not everyone can become a skilled musician or pass the exams necessary to become a physician or a lawyer. If goals are set beyond one's ability, frustration is the inevitable result.

Conflict

A major source of frustration is conflict between two opposing motives. When two motives conflict, the satisfaction of one leads to the frustration of the other. For example, a student may not be able to gain recognition as an

outstanding athlete and still earn the grades needed to enter law school. Even when only one motive is involved, conflict may arise if there are several ways of approaching the goal. For example, you can get an education at any one of a number of colleges, but choosing which one to attend presents a conflict situation. Although the goal will eventually be reached, progress toward it is disrupted by the necessity for making a choice.

Sometimes conflict arises between a motive and a person's internal standards, rather than between two external goals. For example, an individual's sexual desires may conflict with his or her standards of acceptable social behavior. A woman's motive for achievement may conflict with her standards for appropriate feminine behavior. Conflicts between motives and internal standards often can be more difficult to resolve than conflicts between external goals.

Most conflicts involve goals that are simultaneously desirable and undesirable—both positive and negative. Candy is delicious, but fattening. Going off for a weekend of skiing is fun, but losing study time can produce anxiety. A goal that is at once wanted and not wanted, liked and disliked, produces an *ambivalent* attitude. Ambivalent attitudes are very common: adolescents wish to take charge of their own affairs, yet at the same time they want parental help with difficult problems. Their attitude toward independence is ambivalent.

A person confronted with a goal that is at once attractive and dangerous may vacillate while trying to decide what to do. At a distance, the goal seems inviting, leading to approach reactions. But the sense of danger increases as the goal is approached, so that as one nears the incentive, there is a tendency to withdraw (Figure 14-1). When a shy teen-age boy is about to call a girl for a date, he is drawn to the telephone by the possibility of success, but his anxiety about possible rebuff mounts as he approaches. As a result, he may make several false starts before he either carries through his plan or abandons it. This type of conflict is called an *approach-avoidance conflict*.

Approach and Avoidance

Studies of approach-avoidance conflicts indicate that the two motives differ somewhat in the way they operate. As you might expect, both approach and avoidance motives are strongest near the object—that is, the closer you get to an attractive object, the stronger your tendency to approach it; the closer you get to something unpleasant or fearful, the stronger your urge to flee. But avoidance motives appear to drop off more rapidly with distance than approach motives. As you get farther away from a feared object, it seems much less frightening, while an attractive object is still appealing at a distance. This difference in the gradients of approach and avoidance helps explain why a person may be repeatedly drawn back into an old conflict situation. At a distance, the positive aspects seem more inviting than the negative ones appear forbidding. Everyone knows of couples who go steady, break up, and make up, only to break up once more. Away from each other, their mutual attraction takes precedence because negative feelings are reduced; close to each other, the negative feelings drive them apart. Once the ambivalence of their attitudes is recognized, their attempts at reconciliation become understandable.

Studies of the reactions of skydivers to their first parachute jump show how negative feelings (fear of death or injury) become stronger as the moment of danger becomes more imminent (Figure 14-2). The day before the jump, positive feelings (the excitement and thrill of jumping) are predominant. But as

Fig. 14-1 Ambivalence
The boy wants to approach the kitten but clearly has avoidance feelings as well.

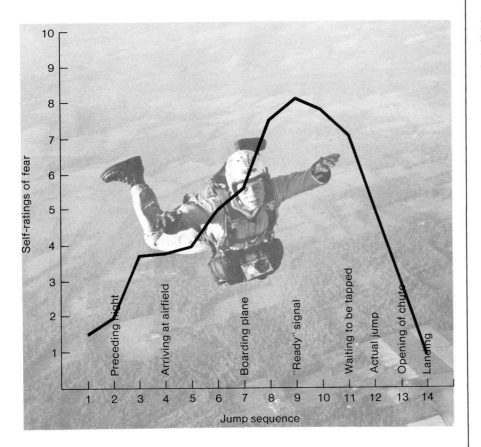

Self-ratings of fear (vertical axis, 1–10)

Horizontal axis labels (Jump sequence, 1–14): Preceding night, Arriving at airfield, Boarding plane, "Ready" signal, Waiting to be tapped, Actual jump, Opening of chute, Landing

the neophyte parachutist comes closer to the moment of jumping—arrives at the airfield, boards the plane, and waits for the ready signal—avoidance impulses increase rapidly, reaching a peak just before the signal is given. The would-be parachutist might back down at this point if it were possible to do so without embarrassment, since avoidance feelings far exceed approach tendencies. (The person now experiences what has been called an *avoidance-avoidance conflict*, having to choose between two negative alternatives—jumping or losing face.) If the avoidance feelings had been this strong at some distance from the goal—for example, the week before while the jump was being planned—the individual probably would not have gotten into such a conflict situation.

Interestingly enough, the peak of fear occurs not at the moment of greatest danger (in the free fall before the parachute opens) but at the point of final commitment, after which it would be difficult for the parachutist to change his or her mind. Once the decision is made, avoidance feelings begin to decrease.

The conflicts of real life are usually more complicated than our discussion implies. A conflict over drinking alcohol, for example, involves more than a choice between its short-term relaxing effects and its long-term destructive effects. The decision can be influenced by moral scruples, fear of losing self-control, need to feel more effective, search for companionship, or escape from responsibility.

A young woman debating whether or not to marry may be influenced by a number of approach factors—economic security, social status, satisfaction of sexual and maternal needs—as well as a number of avoidance factors—increased responsibility, loss of personal freedom, career restrictions. Sometimes an approach-avoidance conflict is resolved by refusing to select either alternative or in some way postponing the choice. The young woman may become ill or decide that she can't leave her widowed mother just yet.

In our society, the approach-avoidance conflicts that are most pervasive and difficult to resolve generally occur between the following motives:

1 *Independence versus dependence.* In times of stress we may want to resort to the dependence characteristic of childhood, to have someone take care of us and solve our problems. But we are taught that the ability to stand on our own and assume responsibilities is a mark of maturity.

2 *Intimacy versus isolation.* The desire to be close to another person and to share our innermost thoughts and emotions may conflict with the fear of being hurt or rejected if we expose too much of ourselves.

3 *Cooperation versus competition.* In our society, much emphasis is placed on competition and success. Competition begins in early childhood among siblings, continues through school, and culminates in business and professional rivalry. At the same time, we are urged to cooperate and help others. The concept of "team spirit" is as American as the success story. Such contradictory expectations have the potential for producing conflict.

4 *Impulse expression versus moral standards.* All societies have to regulate impulses to some degree. We noted in Chapter 3 that much of childhood learning involves internalizing the cultural restrictions placed on innate impulses. Sex and aggression are two areas in which our impulses most frequently conflict with moral standards, and violation of these standards may generate strong feelings of guilt.

These four areas present the greatest potential for serious conflict. As we will see in the next chapter, failure to find a workable compromise may lead to serious psychological problems.

Reactions to Frustration

Frustration—whether it is the result of environmental obstacles, personal limitations, or conflict—has a number of possible consequences. A classic experiment with young children illustrates some reactions to frustration (Barker, Dembo, and Lewin, 1941). The experiment will be described in the present tense, as though we were observing it.

> On the first day of the experiment, the children come one at a time into a room that contains several toys, all of which lack a part or the expected accessory—a chair without a table, an ironing board with no iron, a dial unit without the rest of the telephone, a boat and other water toys but no water. Most of the children set about playing eagerly and happily. They make up for the missing elements imaginatively. They use paper as water on which to sail the boat, or they use their fist for a telephone.
> On the second day of observation, we see a group of children who behave quite differently. They seem unable to play constructively, unable to fit the toys into meaningful and satisfying activities. They play roughly with the toys, occasionally jumping on one and trying to break it. If they draw with the crayons, they scribble like younger children. They whine and nag at the adult who is present. One child lies on the floor, stares at the ceiling, and recites nursery rhymes, as if in a trance.

What accounts for the differences in behavior? Is the second group suffering from some sort of emotional disturbance? Have some of these children been mistreated at home? Actually, the children in the second group are the same children as those in the first group. They are showing the symptoms of frustration, which was created deliberately in the following way.

On the second occasion, an opaque screen was removed, allowing the children to see that they were in a larger room containing not only the "half-toys" but other more elaborate and attractive toys. This part of the room contained a table for the chair, a dial and bell for the telephone, a pond of real water for the boat. However, the children were separated from the more desirable toys by a wire screen. They were denied the "whole" toys and could use only the "half-toys." They were frustrated.

Why was the half-toy situation satisfying the first time and frustrating the second? The answer is easy to find. Goal-seeking behavior was satisfied the first time as the children played happily with the available toys. In the second stage, they knew of the existence of the more attractive toys, and so a new goal had been set up. The first day the goal was attainable; the second day it was not. To play with the half-toys on the second day was to be stopped short of what seemed a richer experience and hence was frustrating. Frustration is thus a relative matter: a person may be quite satisfied with a life situation until confronted with a friend who has achieved more.

This experiment illustrates a number of immediate responses to frustration. In discussing some of these responses, we shall refer to additional details of the experiment and draw illustrations from other experiments and from the frustrating experiences of everyday life.

Aggression

Most of the children in the frustrating situation seemed restless and unhappy: they fidgeted, sighed, and complained. And many of them expressed feelings of anger: they kicked and hit the toys, often breaking them. (Only a few of the children did any kicking or hitting in the prefrustration stage of the experiment.)

Sometimes aggression is expressed directly against the individual or object that is the source of frustration. Some of the children attacked the wire barrier, trying to remove it or get around it. Aggression of this kind is not necessarily hostile; it may be a learned way of solving a problem. When one child takes a toy from another child, the second is likely to attack the first in an attempt to regain the toy. Adults usually express their aggression verbally rather than physically—they are more likely to exchange insults than blows.

Although the anger engendered by frustration may impel the individual to attack the obstacle, be it animate or inanimate, direct aggression is not always possible.

DISPLACED AGGRESSION In many instances, the frustrated individual cannot express aggression against the source of frustration. Sometimes the source is vague and intangible. The person does not know what to attack, yet feels angry and seeks *something* to attack. Sometimes the person responsible for the frustration is so powerful that an attack would be dangerous. When circumstances block direct attack on the cause of frustration, aggression may be *displaced*—the aggressive action is directed toward an innocent person, or *scapegoat*, rather than toward the actual cause of the frustration. A person who is reprimanded at work may take out unexpressed resentment on his or her family. Susan's "blowup" at her roommate may be related to the poor grade Susan received on the midterm quiz.

Prejudice against minority groups often contains an element of displaced

"Why can't you lead a life of quiet desperation like other people?"

aggression, or scapegoating. During periods of economic depression, when money is scarce and jobs are few, people are tempted to blame their troubles on some relatively powerless minority group. Thus, in the past, the Nazis blamed the Jews, farmers in the southern United States blamed the blacks, Protestant laborers in Boston blamed the Irish Catholics, California farm workers blamed Mexican illegal aliens, and so forth. As we will see in Chapter 18, many factors contribute to prejudice, but displaced aggression in response to frustration may be one of them—as the following experiment demonstrates.

Boys at a summer camp were required to participate in a lengthy and boring testing session that ran overtime so that they missed their weekly outing to the local movies. A survey of the boys' attitudes toward minority groups before and after the testing session showed a significant increase in unfriendly feelings after the testing session. The boys *displaced* their anger toward minorities rather than express it directly toward the administrators of the tests (Miller and Bugelski, 1948).

Apathy

One of the factors complicating the study of human behavior is the tendency of different individuals to respond to similar situations in a variety of ways. Thus, although a common response to frustration is active aggression, another response is the opposite—apathy, indifference, withdrawal. We do not know why one person reacts with aggression and another with apathy to the same situation, but it seems likely that learning is an important factor—reactions to frustration can be learned in much the same manner as other behaviors. Children who strike out angrily when frustrated and find that their needs are then satisfied (either through their own efforts or because a parent rushes to placate them) will probably resort to the same behavior the next time their motives are thwarted. Children whose aggressive outbursts are never successful, who find they have no power to satisfy their needs by means of their own actions, may well resort to apathy and withdrawal when confronted with subsequent frustrating situations.

LEARNED HELPLESSNESS Studies have shown that animals and people can learn to be helpless when faced with stressful situations. A dog placed in a shuttle box (an apparatus with two compartments separated by a barrier) quickly learns to jump to the opposite compartment to escape an electric shock delivered to its feet through a grid on the floor. If a light is turned on a few seconds before the grid is electrified, the dog can learn to avoid the shock entirely by jumping to the safe compartment on signal. However, if the dog has previously been placed in a situation where shocks are unavoidable and inescapable—where nothing it does terminates the shock—then it has great difficulty learning the avoidance response when it is appropriate. The animal simply sits and takes the shock, even though an easy jump to the opposite compartment would eliminate the discomfort. Some dogs never learn, even if the experimenter demonstrates the proper procedure by carrying them over the barrier. The dogs had previously learned that they were unable to avoid the shock, and this *learned helplessness* was very difficult to overcome (Seligman, 1975).

Human subjects placed in experimental situations in which they are unable to control shock or loud noise make fewer escape responses, when escape is possible, than subjects who have not had a prior experience of helplessness

(Thornton and Jacobs, 1971). In fact, uncontrollable or unsolvable events of many kinds seem to impair the organism's ability to cope with subsequent problems.

One study of learned helplessness involved three groups of subjects: one group was given a series of solvable problems, another group was given a series of unsolvable problems, and the third group was not given any problems. Later, all groups were tested on a task like the shuttle box—an apparatus in which they had to move their hand from one place to another to terminate loud, unpleasant noise. Subjects who had been given solvable problems or no problems at all quickly learned the response that would terminate the noise. Subjects who had been given unsolvable problems made no attempt to learn the escape response and passively accepted the noise (Hiroto and Seligman, 1975).

Helplessness in one situation *generalizes* to other situations. In these other situations it is difficult, if not impossible, to learn a new response that would allow one to avoid the unpleasant events. We will have more to say about learned helplessness when we discuss depression in Chapter 15.

REACTIONS TO PROLONGED FRUSTRATION Studies of inmates in concentration or prisoner-of-war camps indicate that apathy (or in its more extreme form, depression) is a "normal" reaction to frustrating and traumatic conditions from which there is no hope of escape. Faced with continual deprivation, torture, and threats of death, many prisoners became detached, emotionless, and indifferent to all that was taking place around them. Interviews with American servicemen released from prison camps after the Korean War showed that almost all experienced such feelings at some time during their imprisonment. The most severe of such "apathy reactions" frequently resulted in death; the men simply curled up on their bunks and waited to die, making no effort to eat or take care of themselves. Two remedies seemed capable of saving a man close to death: getting him on his feet and doing something, no matter how trivial, and getting him interested in some current or future problem (Strassman, Thaler, and Schein, 1956).

Concern with the reactions of American prisoners during the Korean War led the military to develop programs aimed at preparing servicemen to cope with the frustrations of imprisonment. Reports from men imprisoned during the Vietnam Conflict indicate that these programs were successful. Knowing how to keep physically and mentally active (for example, by following a daily schedule that included calisthenics and classes taught by fellow prisoners) and how to organize themselves so as to delegate responsibility, provide mutual support, and plan for emergencies apparently did much to help combat apathy and feelings of helplessness. These men, on the whole, returned from imprisonment in much better condition than did the United States Korean War prisoners, who had not been given explicit instruction for coping with imprisonment.

Regression

Regression is defined as a return to immature modes of behavior—that is, to behavior characteristic of a younger age. In the toy experiment, observers rated the level of constructiveness of each child's play in the free-play situation and again in the frustrating situation. Most of the children showed a marked decrease in the constructiveness of their play: instead of drawing, they scribbled; instead of pretending to iron clothes, they knocked the ironing board

Buchenwald, April 1945
A liberation day picture shows prisoners staring dully at their rescuers, still unable to comprehend that freedom has come.

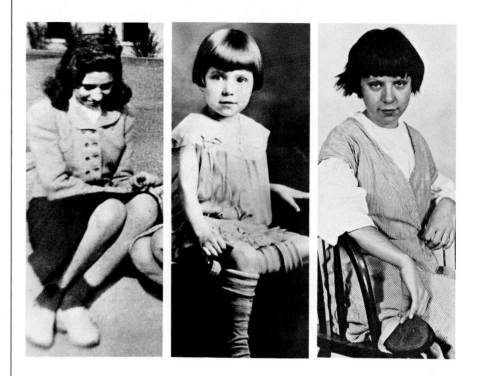

Fig. 14-3 A case of extreme regression
The 17-year-old girl in the picture on the left found an old photograph of herself taken when she was 5 (center). She then cut her hair and tried to look as much as she could like the child in the photograph (right). She came from a very unstable home and showed her first signs of disturbance at age four, when her parents began to quarrel violently. When the girl was seven, her mother refused sexual relations with the father; the girl, however, slept in her father's bed until she was thirteen. The mother, suspecting that her daughter was being incestuously seduced, obtained legal custody and moved with her to a separate home. The girl resented the separation from her father, quarreled with her mother, and became a disciplinary problem at school. On the girl's insistence, she and her mother visited the father after three years' separation and found him living with a young girl. A violent scene ensued, and again the mother refused to let her daughter stay with the father. After this the girl became sullen and withdrawn and would not attend school. In one of her destructive rampages through the house, she found the early picture of herself. She altered her appearance, became infantile and untidy, and no longer controlled her urine. She appeared to have regressed to a more desirable period in life that antedated conflicts and jealousies. (Adapted from Masserman, 1961, pp. 70–71, case of Dr. John Romano)

down; instead of planning an imaginary trip with the toy cars and trucks, they pushed them around aimlessly. On the average, constructiveness of play decreased by about 18 months of mental age; that is, following frustration, the children regressed to a level characteristic of a child about a year and a half younger.

Adults sometimes resort to immature forms of behavior when faced with frustrating situations; they may curse or yell or start a fist fight. Or they may give up any attempt to cope and seek someone to solve the problem for them.

When attempts to solve a problem fail, it is understandable that a person resorts to behaviors that have been successful in the past. A classic example is the three-year-old who has been successfully toilet-trained but begins bed-wetting again when a sibling is born—frustrated by being displaced as the sole object of the parents' affection, the child resorts to behavior that brought parental attention in the past. Under severe and prolonged stress, an adult may regress to infantile behavior (see Figure 14-3).

Anxiety

We have discussed some observable reactions to frustration. In order to explain these reactions (as well as reactions to other forms of stress), psychologists have introduced the concept of *anxiety*. Any situation that threatens the well-being of the organism is assumed to produce a state of anxiety. Conflicts and other types of frustration are one source. Threat of physical harm, threats to one's self-esteem, and pressure to perform beyond one's capabilities also produce anxiety. By anxiety, we mean the unpleasant emotion characterized by terms like "worry," "apprehension," "dread," and "fear" that we all experience at times in varying degrees. Since there is little agreement on a more precise definition for anxiety, we will not attempt to provide one.

Freud, who was one of the first to focus on the importance of anxiety, differentiated between *objective anxiety* and *neurotic anxiety*. Freud viewed objective anxiety as a realistic response to perceived danger in the environment, synonymous with *fear*. He saw neurotic anxiety as stemming from an *unconscious* conflict within the individual; since the conflict was unconscious, the person was not aware of the reason for his or her anxiety. Many psychologists still find a distinction between fear and anxiety meaningful. But since it is not clear that the two emotions can be differentiated, either on the basis of physiological responses or on the basis of the individual's descriptions of feelings, we will use the terms *anxiety* and *fear* interchangeably. Just as there are varying degrees of anxiety—ranging from mild apprehension to panic—there are probably varying degrees of awareness of the cause of one's discomfort. Often the individual who is suffering from an internal conflict has some idea why, even though he or she cannot specify clearly all the factors involved.

Theories of Anxiety

ANXIETY AS AN UNCONSCIOUS CONFLICT   Freud believed that neurotic anxiety was the result of an unconscious conflict between id impulses (mainly sexual and aggressive) and the constraints imposed by the ego and superego (see Chapter 13). Many id impulses pose a threat to the individual because they are contradictory to personal values or because they are in opposition to what society will permit. For example, a young girl who has strong hostile feelings toward her mother may not consciously acknowledge these feelings because they conflict with her belief that one should love one's parents. To acknowledge her true feelings would destroy her self-concept as a loving daughter and place her in danger of losing her mother's love and support. When she begins to feel angry toward her mother, the anxiety aroused serves as a *signal* of potential danger. She then engages in defensive maneuvers to cope with the danger. These maneuvers—the defense mechanisms to be discussed in the next section—form an important part of Freud's theory of neurotic behavior. They are all methods for keeping anxiety-producing impulses out of one's conscious awareness.

ANXIETY AS A LEARNED RESPONSE   Social learning theory focuses not on internal conflicts but on ways in which anxiety becomes associated with certain situations via learning. In a classic experiment by John B. Watson, the founder of behaviorism, a young child learned to be afraid of a rat because of its association with a fear-producing stimulus. When the 11-month-old boy was first shown a white rat, he reached for it, evidencing no fear. But every time he touched the animal he was frightened by a loud sound. The boy quickly became afraid of the rat, and this fear generalized to other furry objects—such as his mother's fur neckpiece (Watson and Rayner, 1920).

Sometimes fears learned in childhood are very difficult to extinguish. Since the first reaction is to avoid or escape the anxiety-producing situation, the child does not get a chance to find out that the situation is no longer dangerous. Avoidance responses are notoriously difficult to extinguish for this reason. An animal that has learned to jump the barrier in a shuttle box to avoid shock may continue to jump to the opposite compartment indefinitely, even though no shock has followed the warning signal since the first few trials of the experiment. The animal never gives itself a chance to learn that the shock has been turned off.

Similarly, the child who has had a bad encounter with a dog and thereafter

runs when he or she sees a dog will not have the opportunity to discover that most dogs are friendly. Since running away from a dog is reinforcing (because it reduces fear), the child is apt to continue this behavior. Situations that were anxiety-producing in childhood may continue to be avoided in adulthood, because the individual has never reappraised the threat or developed ways of coping with it.

Coping and Defensive Strategies

Because anxiety is a very uncomfortable emotion, it cannot be tolerated for long. We are strongly motivated to do something to alleviate the discomfort. Over the course of a lifetime, each individual develops various methods of handling anxiety-producing situations and feelings of anxiety.

Sometimes we try to deal directly with the anxiety-producing situation by appraising the situation and then doing something to change or avoid it. Suppose, for example, you receive a warning that you are about to fail a course that is necessary for graduation. You might take direct action—confer with the professor, devise a work schedule that will fulfill the requirements, and then start it. Or you might decide that you can't fulfill the requirements in the time remaining and will have to take the course again in summer school. Both of these actions are designed to cope with the problem. We will call the behaviors that a person uses to deal directly with stressful situations *coping strategies*.

Other methods of handling stress defend the person against anxious feelings without trying to deal with the anxiety-producing problem itself. For example, you might respond to the failure warning by refusing to acknowledge the possibility of failing or by convincing yourself that a college degree is meaningless. Or you might deaden anxiety with alcohol, tranquilizers, marijuana, or other drugs. These "solutions" we will call *defensive strategies*, because they are aimed at defending against anxiety rather than dealing directly with the problem. Each individual deals with stressful situations in his or her own unique way, often using a combination of defensive and coping strategies.

Defense Mechanisms

Some of the defensive strategies that involve distortion of reality are resorted to often enough to have been given names. Freud used the term *defense mechanisms* to refer to unconscious processes that defend a person against anxiety by distorting reality in some way. These strategies do not alter the objective conditions of danger; they simply change the way the person perceives or thinks about it. Hence, they all involve an element of *self-deception*.

The word *mechanism* is not the most appropriate, because it implies some sort of mechanical device. Freud was influenced by the nineteenth-century tendency to think of the human being as a complicated machine. What we will be talking about are *strategies* that people learn to use to minimize anxiety in situations they cannot handle effectively. But since *defense mechanism* is still the most commonly applied term, we will continue to use it.

A number of defense mechanisms have been proposed; we will consider only a few of them. In reading about defense mechanisms, the following precautions should be kept in mind.

1 Defense mechanisms are *hypothetical constructs* inferred from observations of the way people behave. They are useful ways of summarizing the psychological processes that we hypothesize are occurring in order to explain some observed behavior.
2 Labeling a person's behavior (for example, as projection, displacement, or reaction formation) may provide useful descriptions, but labels do not *explain* behavior. An explanation requires understanding what causes the person to rely on defense mechanisms when confronted with problems.
3 Used in moderation, defense mechanisms help us over the rough spots until we can deal more directly with the stressful situation. Only when defense mechanisms become the dominant mode of responding do they indicate personality maladjustment. The normal person may use a variety of coping and defensive strategies, depending on the situation. The abnormal individual tends to be less flexible, using the same defense mechanism regardless of the situation.

Denial

When an external reality is too unpleasant to face, we may deny that it exists. The parents of a fatally ill child may refuse to admit that there is anything wrong even though they are fully informed of the diagnosis and expected outcome. Because they cannot tolerate the pain that acknowledging reality would produce, they resort to the defense mechanism of *denial,* at least for a while. Less extreme forms of denial may be seen in individuals who consistently ignore criticism or fail to perceive that others are angry with them—or in the spouse who fails to notice all kinds of clues suggesting that his or her marriage partner is having an affair.

Studies of patients with life-threatening illnesses suggest that many deny fear of death or the possibility that they might die. Even witnessing a fatal cardiac arrest of another patient in the same room did not produce fear in most cardiac patients; they didn't think it would happen to them. In this situation, denial clearly has an adaptive value (Hackett and Cassem, 1970).

Repression

While denial of reality is a defense against external threat, *repression* is a defense against internal threat. In repression, impulses or memories that are too threatening are excluded from action or conscious awareness. Freud believed that repression of certain childhood impulses is universal. For example, he maintained that all young boys have feelings of sexual attraction toward the mother and feelings of rivalry and hostility toward the father (the Oedipus complex); these impulses are repressed to avoid the painful consequences of acting on them. In later life, feelings and memories that would cause anxiety because they are inconsistent with one's self-concept may be repressed. Feelings of hostility toward a loved one and experiences of failure may be banished from memory.

Repression must be distinguished from *suppression.* The process of suppression is one of deliberate self-control—keeping impulses, tendencies, or wishes in check and perhaps holding them privately while denying them publicly. In such instances, the individuals are aware of suppressed impulses. In repression, the individuals themselves are *unaware* of whatever it is that is repressed.

Cases of *amnesia* illustrate some aspects of repression. In one instance, a man was found wandering the streets, unable to remember his name or where he had come from. By means of hypnosis and other techniques, it was possible to reconstruct his history and to restore most of his memory. Following domestic difficulties, he had gone on a drinking spree—completely out of keeping with his usual behavior—and he had subsequently suffered deep remorse. His amnesia was motivated by the desire to exclude the embarrassing experiences from memory. He succeeded in forgetting all the events that might remind him of the spree. In this way amnesia spread, and he completely lost his sense of personal identity. When his memories returned, he could recall events before the drinking episode as well as subsequent happenings, but was unable to remember the period of which he was most ashamed.

Repression, if completely successful, results in a total forgetting—a total absence of awareness of an unacceptable motive and behavior resulting from such a motive. Usually, however, repression is not completely successful, and impulses find indirect expression. Some of the following defense mechanisms protect the individual from awareness of partially repressed impulses.

Rationalization

When the fox in Aesop's fable rejected the grapes he could not reach "because they were sour," he illustrated a defense mechanism known as *rationalization*. Rationalization does not mean "to act rationally"; it means assigning logical or socially desirable motives to what we do so that we *seem* to have acted rationally or properly. Rationalization serves two purposes: (1) it eases our disappointment when we fail to reach a goal—"I didn't want it anyway"—and (2) it provides us with acceptable motives for our behavior. If we act impulsively or on the basis of motives that we do not wish to acknowledge even to ourselves, we may rationalize what we have done to place our behavior in a more favorable light.

In the search for the "good" reason rather than the "true" reason, a number of excuses can be put forth. These excuses are usually plausible; they simply do not tell the whole story. A few illustrations may serve to show how common rationalization is.

1 Liking or disliking as an excuse: "I wouldn't have gone to the party even if I had been invited. I don't like that crowd."
2 Other people and circumstances as an excuse: "My roommate failed to wake me." "I had too many other things to do." Both statements may be true, but they are not the real reasons for failure to perform the behavior in question. If the individual had been really concerned, he or she could have set an alarm clock or found time.
3 Necessity as an excuse: "I bought this new model because the old car would have had a lot of expensive repairs coming up soon."

While the foregoing examples show individuals fooling themselves instead of others, the excuses are the sort that people might consciously use to put themselves in a favorable light. We therefore need a more convincing illustration to show us that rationalization may be unconsciously motivated. Such an illustration is provided by the results of experiments with posthypnotic suggestion.

A subject under hypnosis is told that when he wakes from the trance he will watch the pocket of the hypnotist. When the hypnotist removes a handkerchief from the pocket, the subject will raise the window. But he will not remember the hypnotist's telling him to do this. Aroused from the trance, the subject feels a little drowsy but presently circulates among the people in the room and

carries on a normal conversation, all the while furtively watching the hypnotist's pocket. When the hypnotist casually removes his handkerchief, the subject feels an impulse to open the window; he takes a step in that direction, but hesitates. Unconsciously, he mobilizes his wishes to be a reasonable person; so, seeking a reason for his impulse to open the window, he says "Isn't it a little stuffy in here?" Having found the needed excuse, he opens the window and feels more comfortable (Hilgard, 1965).

Reaction Formation

It is sometimes possible to conceal a motive from oneself by giving strong expression to its opposite. Such a tendency is called *reaction formation*. The mother of an unwanted child may feel guilty about not welcoming her child and so becomes overindulgent and overprotective to assure the child of her love and also, perhaps, to assure herself that she is a good mother.

In one case, a mother who wished to do everything for her daughter could not understand why the child was so unappreciative. At great sacrifice, she had the daughter take expensive piano lessons and assisted her in the daily practice sessions. While she thought she was being extremely kind, she was actually very demanding and, in fact, hostile. She was unaware of her own hostility, but, when confronted with it, admitted that as a child she had hated piano lessons. Under the conscious guise of being kind, she was unconsciously being cruel to her daughter. The daughter, vaguely sensing what was going on, developed the symptoms that brought her to a child-guidance clinic.

There is always the possibility that reaction formation is active among some individuals who engage in "anti-" activities, such as censoring pornographic literature or preventing cruelty to animals. The censoring individuals may actually be fascinated by pornographic literature. They wage a campaign against it in order to fight its fascination for them and to convince others of their own "purity." Among the ardent antivivisectionists, there undoubtedly are some who fear their own tendency toward cruelty so deeply that they become sentimental about protecting animals from the implied cruelty of others.

The existence of reaction formation in some people does not mean that motives can never be taken at face value. Not all reformers are moved to action by veiled or hidden impulses. Real abuses need to be corrected, and concerned individuals will devote their efforts to such causes. But those who are defending against unacceptable impulses often can be distinguished from the socially concerned reformers by the excessive zeal with which they pursue their campaigns and by occasional slips that reveal their true motivation (see Figure 14-4).

Projection

All of us have undesirable traits or qualities that we do not acknowledge even to ourselves. One unconscious mechanism that protects us from acknowledging them is called *projection*. In projection, we protect ourselves from recognizing our own undesirable qualities by assigning them in exaggerated amounts to other people. Suppose you have a tendency to be critical of or unkind to other people but you would dislike yourself if you admitted this tendency. If you are convinced that those around you are cruel or unkind, then any harsh treatment you give them is not based on *your* bad qualities—you are simply giving them what they deserve. If you can assure yourself that everybody else cheats in college examinations, your unacknowledged tendency to take some

> . . . I read [a magazine article] . . . on your work on alcoholism . . . I am surprised that anyone who is as well educated as you must be to hold the position that you do would stoop to such depths as to torture helpless little cats in the pursuit of a cure for alcoholics. . . . A drunkard does not want to be cured—a drunkard is just a weak minded idiot who belongs in the gutter and should be left there. Instead of torturing helpless little cats why not torture the drunks or better still exert your would-be noble effort toward getting a bill passed to *exterminate* the drunks. They are not any good to anyone or themselves and are just a drain on the public, having to pull them off the street, jail them, then they have to be fed while there and it's against the law to feed them arsenic so there they are. . . . If people are such weaklings the world is better off without them.
>
> . . . My greatest wish is that you have brought home to you a torture that will be a thousand fold greater than what you have, and are doing to the little animals. . . . If you are an example of what a noted psychiatrist should be I'm glad I am just an ordinary human being without a letter after my name. I'd rather be just myself with a clear conscience, *knowing I have not hurt any living creature,* and can sleep without seeing frightened, terrified dying cats—because I know they must die after you have finished with them. No punishment is too great for you and I hope I live to read about your mangled body and long suffering before you finally die—and I'll laugh long and loud.

Fig. 14-4 Reaction formation
Reaction formation can be illustrated with excerpts from a letter by an antivivisectionist sent to Dr. J. H. Masserman, who has done research on alcoholism using cats as experimental subjects. (After Masserman, 1961, p. 38)

academic shortcuts is not so bad. Projection is really a form of rationalization, but it is so pervasive in our culture that it merits discussion in its own right.

An experiment with fraternity members at a university illustrates projection. The members of each fraternity were asked to rate the other fraternity members on such undesirable traits as stinginess, obstinacy, and disorderliness. Each student also was asked to rate himself. Of interest here are those students who possessed an undesirable trait to a high degree (as indicated by how others rated them) and yet were unaware of possessing it (as indicated by their rating of themselves). These individuals tended to assign that undesirable trait to other students to a far greater extent than did the rest of the students. The data are consistent with the idea of a projection mechanism (Sears, 1936).

A similar study has shown that individuals who deny or repress their sexual impulses tend to project these impulses onto other people. They see others as more "lustful" than the reality of the situation warrants (Halpern, 1977).

The letter in Figure 14-4 illustrating reaction formation also has an element of projection. The writer attributes his own cruel impulses to the researcher.

Intellectualization

Intellectualization is an attempt to gain detachment from an emotionally threatening situation by dealing with it in abstract, intellectual terms. This kind of defense is frequently a necessity for people who must deal with life and death matters in their daily job. The doctor who is continually confronted with human suffering cannot afford to become emotionally involved with each patient. A certain amount of detachment may be essential for competent functioning. In Chapter 11, we saw that intellectualization can lessen distress when a disturbing scene is viewed. This kind of intellectualization is a problem only when it becomes such a prevasive life style that individuals cut themselves off from all emotional experiences.

Displacement

The last defense mechanism to be considered is the one that best succeeds in fulfilling its function (that is, reducing anxiety) while allowing some gratification of the unacceptable motive. In *displacement,* a motive that cannot be gratified in one form is directed into a new channel. We saw an example of displacement in the discussion of anger that could not be expressed toward the source of frustration and thus was directed toward a less threatening or more readily available object.

Freud felt that displacement was the most satisfactory way of handling aggressive and sexual impulses. The basic drives cannot be changed, but the object toward which the drive is directed can. For example, sexual impulses toward the parents cannot be safely gratified, but such impulses can be displaced toward a more suitable love object. Erotic impulses that cannot be expressed directly may be expressed indirectly in creative activities such as art, poetry, and music. Hostile impulses may find socially acceptable expression through participation in physical-contact sports.

It seems unlikely that displacement actually eliminates the frustrated impulses, but substitute activities do help to reduce tension when a basic drive is thwarted. For example, the activities of mothering, being mothered, or seeking companionship may help reduce the tension associated with unsatisfied sexual needs.

Defense Mechanisms and Adjustment

We all use defense mechanisms at times. Rationalizing failures that would otherwise cause us to despair or finding partial justification for conduct that would otherwise make us despise ourselves sustains us until we can work out better solutions to our conflicts. Defense mechanisms can be compared to drugs (such as aspirin and antihistamines) that reduce symptoms without curing the ailment. Antihistamines, for example, relieve sneezing and runny noses and help hay fever victims live more comfortably until the basic treatment—desensitization to the offending pollens—can become effective. Similarly, defense mechanisms may provide relief from anxiety until more realistic ways of solving personal problems can be worked out.

Although they are helpful as a temporary relief, defense mechanisms distort reality and thus prevent effective problem solving. A person who depends on defense mechanisms may never learn more effective ways of coping. For example, individuals who project their hostile feelings onto others may withdraw more and more from social contacts. By refusing to acknowledge the anger as their own, they never learn that most people are kind and that they can develop satisfactory interpersonal relationships.

The premedical student who is failing may be unable to admit that he or she lacks the interest and ability to handle the course work. A rationalization must therefore be found to account for failure. Getting sick will convert an academic problem into a health problem; getting into trouble with college officials will convert the problem into a disciplinary one. Defensiveness and denial of the realities of the situation prevent a more satisfactory solution—for example, changing to an academic program more suited to one's interests and abilities.

Stress

Some stress is necessary for normal functioning. We noted in Chapter 11 that a mild level of emotional arousal produces alertness and interest in the task at hand. When life is peaceful and quiet for too long, people become bored and seek excitement; they go to a spy movie, engage in a game of tennis, or find stimulation in interacting with other people. Studies of sensory deprivation (see pp. 310-11) show that the absence of normal stimulation is highly unpleasant and can have profound effects on behavior. The nervous system apparently needs a certain amount of stimulation to function properly. But stress that is too intense or prolonged can have destructive physiological and psychological effects.

We have already noted some of the psychological effects of stress in the discussion of the ways people react to frustration and the strategies they use to cope with stressful situations. If initial attempts at coping are not successful, anxiety intensifies and the individual becomes more rigid in his or her efforts, less able to perceive alternative solutions to the problem. People have been trapped in flaming buildings because they persisted in pushing against exit doors that open inward. In their panic, they failed to notice the possibility of alternative actions.

In times of stress, people tend to resort to behavior patterns that have worked in the past. The cautious person may become even more cautious and withdraw entirely; the aggressive person may lose control and strike out heedlessly in all directions.

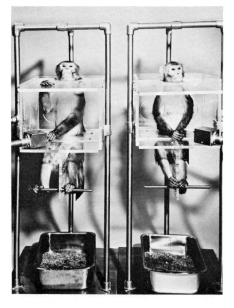

Fig. 14-5 Ulcers in "executive" monkeys
Both animals receive brief electric shocks at 20-second intervals. The one on the left (the "executive") has learned to press its lever, which prevents shocks to both animals provided it is pressed at least once every 20 seconds; the lever for the monkey on the right is a dummy. Although both monkeys receive the same number of shocks, only the "executive" monkey develops the ulcers. (Brady and others, 1958)

Physiological Effects of Stress

The actions of the autonomic nervous system that prepare the organism for emergency (see p. 330) can, if prolonged, lead to such physical disorders as ulcers, high blood pressure, and heart disease. Severe stress (acting through the central nervous system to change hormonal balances) can also impair the organism's immune responses, decreasing its ability to fight off invading bacteria and viruses. Indeed, it is estimated that emotional stress plays an important role in more than half of all medical problems.

Psychosomatic medicine, the study of the relationship between psychological variables and physical health, has become an increasingly important area of interdisciplinary research. (The term "psychosomatic" comes from the Greek words *psyche*—"mind"—and *soma*—"body.") Allergies, migraine headaches, high blood pressure, heart disease, ulcers, and even acne are among the illnesses that are believed to be related to emotional stress. Research on these disorders is too extensive to even summarize here, but some studies demonstrating the relationship between psychological stress and peptic ulcers will provide an example.

STRESS AND ULCERS A peptic ulcer is a lesion (a hole) in the lining of the stomach or duodenum that is produced by excessive secretion of hydrochloric acid. In the process of digestion, hydrochloric acid interacts with various enzymes to break down food into components that can be utilized by the body. When hydrochloric acid is secreted in excessive amounts, it gradually erodes the mucus layer protecting the stomach wall, producing small lesions. A number of factors can cause an increased secretion of hydrochloric acid, and psychological stress appears to be one of them.

A classic experiment with monkeys shows the kind of stress that can produce ulcers. The monkeys were used in pairs, each monkey seated in a restraining chair for many hours at a time (Figure 14-5). An electronic device was programmed to deliver a shock to both monkeys whenever it was activated. However, one of the monkeys (whimsically called the "executive" monkey) had a lever that when pressed would deactivate the shocking device

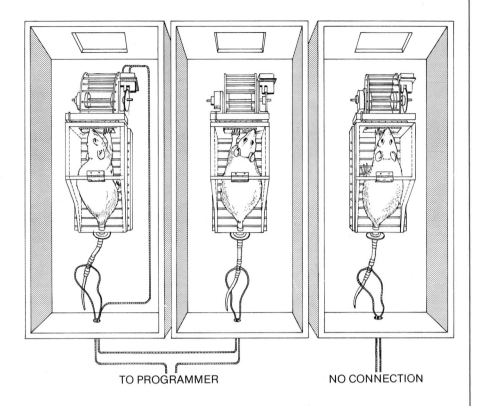

TO PROGRAMMER   NO CONNECTION

Fig. 14-6 Ulcers in rats
The rat on the left is the avoidance-escape subject; it can terminate the programmed shock by turning the wheel. Moreover, turning the wheel between shocks will postpone the shock. The rat in the center is electrically wired in series to the first rat, so that when the first rat receives a shock, the yoked rat simultaneously receives a shock of the same intensity and duration. The actions of the yoked rat do not affect the shock sequence. The electrodes on the tail of the control rat on the right are not connected, and this rat does not receive shocks at any time. At the end of the experimental session the rats' gastric lesions are measured. (After Weiss, 1972)

for 20 seconds. If the executive monkey never let more than 20 seconds elapse from one bar press to the next, both monkeys would avoid shocks. When the executive monkey failed to respond in time because of inattention or fatigue, both monkeys were given a shock. Because they received identical shocks throughout the experiment, any physiological damage due to the shocks should have affected them equally. But only the "executive" monkey developed ulcers; apparently the constant alertness required to respond at appropriate intervals produced a continuing state of tension that resulted in ulcers. The control monkey, which could only take the shocks as they came, was somehow less reactive and less disturbed.[1]

Subsequent research indicates that there is more to developing ulcers than having to make decisions. A series of experiments with rats demonstrated that having the ability to make an *effective response* and receiving *immediate feedback* are important in preventing ulcers. In fact, in one situation results were obtained that seemed to contradict those found with the monkeys. The rat that could avoid shock by turning a wheel in response to a warning signal (see Figure 14-6) developed *less* ulceration than its yoked companion, which was unable to avoid the shocks. The experimenter suggests several reasons for the difference between his results and those obtained in the studies with monkeys. The executive monkey was responding at a very fast rate and had no immediate feedback indicating that its response was successful (until some time later when it received or failed to receive the shock). The stress for the

[1]Because the results are so dramatic, this study is often cited as evidence that the responsibility of decision making produces ulcers. But the results may be partly a function of the way the monkeys were assigned to the two conditions. In a preliminary test, the experimenters noted how quickly the animals responded to shock by pressing the lever. The first monkeys to start hitting the lever were assigned to the executive condition; the slower monkeys were assigned as controls. By this procedure, the more emotionally reactive monkeys (who may already have been more ulcer-prone) became the executives, while the more placid animals became the controls. Because of this confounding factor, the experimental results must be viewed with some skepticism.

executive monkey was evidently much greater than for the executive rat, which was required to make an avoidance response at well-spaced intervals and knew that the response would prevent shock until the next warning signal.

The preceding experiments with animals demonstrate that stress can produce ulcers. A number of factors seem to determine whether or not a situation will be stressful: pressure to respond quickly over extended periods of time, uncertainty as to the effectiveness of the response, or inability to make any response that changes the aversive situation.

Air-traffic controllers, whose work involves constant vigilance and who must make instant decisions affecting the safety of hundreds of people, have the highest incidence of peptic ulcers of any profession. They are also much more likely than the average person to develop high blood pressure, insomnia, heart disease, colitis, and other medical problems (Grayson, 1972).

INDIVIDUAL PHYSIOLOGICAL RESPONSES TO STRESS   Prolonged stress can produce profound changes in the physiological functioning of the body. The particular symptoms that develop depend on the complex interaction of a number of variables; the following three seem to be the most important.

1 *Individual differences in the reactivity of the autonomic nervous system.* A person who characteristically responds to stress with increased secretions of stomach acids may eventually develop ulcers; one who reacts with a rise in blood pressure may develop high blood pressure.
2 *Vulnerability of a particular body organ or system as the result of heredity or prior illness.* An individual born with a "weak" stomach may develop ulcers or other forms of gastrointestinal disorders under stress; one who has had respiratory infections in the past may develop asthma.
3 *Early learning experiences.* A child who is allowed to stay home from school every time he or she has an upset stomach may be learning the visceral responses that lead to chronic indigestion; one who receives attention whenever allergies cause wheezing or gasping may progress to full-blown asthma attacks.

Research trying to link specific psychosomatic disorders with personality types or certain kinds of emotional stress has not been particularly successful. It appears that a wide range of stressful situations can lead to a given type of disorder and, conversely, a wide range of disorders can result from a given type of stress.

Factors Influencing the Severity of Stress

The effects of stress—the intensity of the anxiety it arouses and the degree to which it disrupts the individual's functioning—depend on a number of factors. These include some characteristics of the stress itself, the situation in which stress occurs, the individual's appraisal and evaluation of the stressful situation, and his or her resources for coping with it.

PREDICTABILITY   Being able to predict the occurrence of a stressful event, even if we can't control it, usually reduces its severity. Laboratory experiments show that both human beings and animals prefer predictable aversive events to unpredictable ones. In one study, rats were given a choice between signaled and unsignaled shock. If the rat pressed a bar at the start of a series of shock trials, each shock would be preceded by a warning tone; if the bar was not

Biofeedback and Relaxation Training

Two techniques, *biofeedback* and *relaxation training,* show promise of helping people control their reactions to stress. In biofeedback training, individuals receive information (feedback) about some aspect of their physiological state and then attempt to alter that state. For example, in a procedure for learning to control tension headaches, electrodes are attached to the forehead, so that any movement in the forehead muscle can be electronically detected, amplified, and fed back to the person as an auditory signal. The signal, or tone, increases in pitch when the muscle contracts and decreases when it relaxes. By learning to control the pitch of the tone, the individual learns to keep the muscle relaxed. (Relaxation of the forehead muscle usually insures relaxation of scalp and neck muscles also.) After four to eight weeks of biofeedback training, the subject learns to recognize the onset of tension and to reduce it without feedback from the machine (Tarler-Benlolo, 1978).

Even more impressive is the use of biofeedback methods to influence activities controlled by the autonomic nervous system, such as heart rate and blood pressure—activities traditionally assumed to be automatic and not under voluntary control. Laboratory studies showing that normal individuals can learn to modify both functions (see Figure 14-7) have led to new pro-

cedures for treating patients suffering from high blood pressure. In one procedure, patients are shown a graph of their blood pressure while it is being monitored and are taught techniques for relaxing various muscle groups. The patients are instructed to concentrate on tensing their muscles (for example, by clenching a fist or tightening the abdomen), releasing the tension, and noticing the difference in sensation. By starting with the feet and ankle muscles and progressing through the body to the muscles that control the neck and face, people can learn to modify muscular tension. For some individuals, this combination of biofeedback with relaxation training lowered blood pressure as effectively as treatment with anti–high blood pressure drugs (Tarler-Benlolo, 1978).

Treatment of stress-related illnesses with biofeedback and relaxation is still in the experimental stage, and it is too early to tell how useful such procedures will be. Success seems to depend, to some extent, on characteristics of the individual. Some people who are not conscientious about taking drugs to relieve high blood pressure do better with biofeedback-relaxation methods; others who have learned to control their blood pressure through relaxation eventually drop the procedure because they find it too time-consuming. Interestingly, those

people who benefit most from biofeedback-relaxation techniques are those who are particularly responsive to stress, indicating that emotions play an important role in their illness.

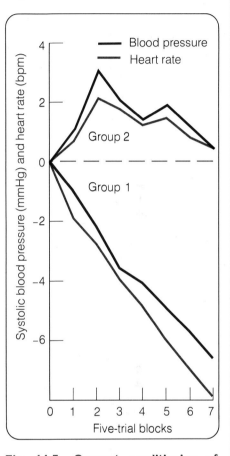

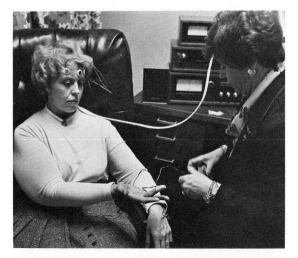

Biofeedback for headaches
The sensors measure forehead muscle contractions and finger temperature. Circulatory changes (indicated by finger temperature) play a role in some types of headaches.

Fig. 14-7 Operant conditioning of blood pressure and heart rate
One group of male subjects received biofeedback (a light and a tone) whenever their blood pressure and heart rate decreased simultaneously (group 1); the other group received the same feedback when blood pressure and heart rate increased (group 2). Whenever a subject in either group produced 12 consecutive correct heart rate–blood pressure responses, he was reinforced with slides (landscapes and nude females) and a cash bonus. The subjects achieved significant simultaneous control of blood pressure and heart rate in a single conditioning session. The group reinforced for lowering both functions achieved increasingly more control over trials; the group reinforced for raising both functions was less consistent. (Schwartz, 1975)

Any change in an individual's life, whether pleasant or unpleasant, requires some readjustment. Studies of personal histories suggest that physical and emotional disorders tend to cluster around periods of major change in a person's life. The scale shown in Table 14-1 was developed to measure stress in terms of life changes. The life events are ranked in order, from the most stressful (death of a spouse) to the least (minor violations of the law). To arrive at this scale, the investigators examined thousands of interviews and medical histories to identify the kind of events people found stressful. Because marriage (a positive event, but one that requires a fair amount of readjustment) appeared to be a critical event for most people, it was placed in the middle of the scale with an arbitrary value of 50. The investigators next asked some 400 men and women (of varying ages, backgrounds, and marital status) to compare marriage with a number of other life events. They were asked such questions as, "Does the event call for more or less readjustment than marriage?" "Would the readjustment take shorter or longer to accomplish?" And they were asked to assign a point value to each event on the basis of their evaluation of its severity and the time required for adjustment.

These ratings were used to construct the scale in Table 14-1. The scale appears to be fairly universal in that minority groups in the United States and people in both underdeveloped and highly industrialized countries give pretty much the same ratings to stressful events.

Studies using the Life Change Scale have found a consistent relationship between the number of stressful events in a person's life and that person's emotional and physical health. When the life-change units summed to between 200 and 300 over a period of a year, more than half of the people had health problems the following year. When the scores summed to over 300, 79 percent of the people became ill the following year.

The most stressful event on the scale is the death of a spouse, a loss that obviously requires a major readjustment in life. In one study in Great Britain, some 4,500 widowers were observed for six months after the death of their wives. In addition to high rates of illness and depression, these men had a mortality rate that was 40 percent higher than expected for their age (Parkes and others, 1969).

To account for the findings relating life changes to illness, the authors of the Life Change Scale hypothesize that

TABLE 14-1
Life Change Scale*

LIFE EVENT	LIFE-CHANGE VALUE
Death of spouse	100
Divorce	73
Marital separation	65
Jail term	63
Death of close family member	63
Personal injury or illness	53
Marriage	50
Fired from job	47
Marital reconciliation	45
Retirement	45
Change in health of family member	44
Pregnancy	40
Sex difficulties	39
Gain of new family member	39
Business readjustment	39
Change in financial state	38
Death of close friend	37
Change to different line of work	36
Change in number of arguments with spouse	35
Mortgage over $10,000	31
Foreclosure of mortgage or loan	30
Change in responsibilities at work	29

This scale is also known as the Holmes and Rahe Social Readjustment Rating Scale.

pressed, there would be no warning tones for that series of trials. All rats quickly learned to press the bar, showing a marked preference for predictable shock. In fact, rats prefer predictable shock even when it is much longer and more intense than unpredictable shock. With unpredictable shock, there is no "safe" period; with predictable shock, the animal can relax to some extent until the tone sounds to signal shock (Badia and Culbertson, 1972; Badia, Culbertson, and Harsh, 1973). Studies showing that people prefer immediate to delayed shock also indicate the preference for aversive events that are predictable.

CONTROL OVER DURATION Having control over the duration of a stressful event also reduces its severity. In one study, subjects were shown color photographs of victims of violent death. The experimental group could terminate the viewing by pressing a button. The control subjects saw the same

Life Stress

TABLE 14-1
(continued)

LIFE EVENT	LIFE-CHANGE VALUE
Son or daughter leaving home	29
Trouble with in-laws	29
Outstanding personal achievement	28
Wife begins or stops work	26
Begin or end school	26
Change in living conditions	25
Revision of personal habits	24
Trouble with boss	23
Change in work hours or conditions	20
Change in residence	20
Change in schools	20
Change in recreation	19
Change in church activities	19
Change in social activities	18
Mortgage or loan less than $10,000	17
Change in sleeping habits	16
Change in number of family get-togethers	15
Change in eating habits	15
Vacation	13
Christmas	12
Minor violations of the law	11

Source: Holmes and Rahe (1967)

the more critical the changes in individual experiences, the greater the effort required to adapt; this effort is presumed to lower the body's natural resistance to disease. While there is undoubtedly a relationship between prolonged or severe stress and illness, the relationship is probably not as simple as the above hypothesis implies. Other factors may be involved.

For one thing, it is difficult to separate the effects of stress from such factors as diet, smoking, drinking, and other general health habits. Individuals trying to cope with the demands of a new and more difficult job might increase their alcohol intake, eat too much snack food, get less sleep, and fail to exercise. An increased susceptibility to illness in such a case is more likely to stem from the changes in health habits than from the direct action of stress on resistance to disease.

Second, people differ in their tendency to focus on physical symptoms and in their inclination to seek medical help. A respiratory infection or stomachache that one person ignores may send another person to a doctor. Individuals who are unhappy and discontented with their lives are more apt to focus on symptoms than are people busily involved in activities they enjoy; they are also more apt to go to a doc-

tor. Since the data for many life-change studies come from medical reports, the selective factor in help-seeking may be significant. Stress may be more important in triggering help-seeking behavior than in triggering actual illness.

Individual differences in help-seeking are even more pronounced when the discomfort is psychological, rather than clearly physical. One study compared students who went to a university counseling clinic with a random sample from the same student population on a scale measuring symptoms of psychological distress. While 54 percent of those who sought counseling had a high score on the scale, 22 percent of the random sample had an equally high score (Mechanic, 1975). Thus, a number of students who did not seek help were as distressed as those who did. Many factors besides degree of distress—for example, religious and social values, socioeconomic background, attitudes toward self-sufficiency versus dependency—determine whether a person will seek help.

Stressful life events clearly play a role in illness. But they do so in interaction with biological factors (preexisting susceptibilities toward certain disorders), life habits, and the psychological characteristics of the individual.

photographs for the time duration determined by the experimental group, but they could not terminate exposure. The experimental group showed much less anxiety in response to the photographs, as measured by the galvanic skin response (GSR), than did the group that had no control over duration (Geer and Maisel, 1972).

In another study, two groups of subjects were exposed to a loud, extremely unpleasant noise. Subjects in one group were told that they could terminate the noise by pressing a button, but they were urged not to do so unless it was absolutely necessary. Subjects in the other group had no control over the noise. None of the subjects who had a control button actually pressed it, so the noise exposure was the same for both groups. Nevertheless, performance on subsequent problem-solving tasks was significantly worse for the group that had no control, indicating that they were more disturbed by the noise than the group that had the potential for control (Glass and Singer, 1972). The belief

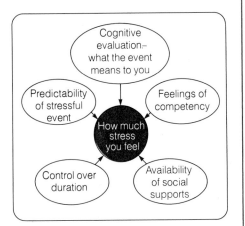

Factors determining the severity of stressful events

Working together in times of disaster makes stress more bearable.

that we have control over the duration of an aversive event appears to lessen anxiety even if the control is never exercised or the belief is erroneous.

COGNITIVE EVALUATION The same stressful event can be perceived quite differently by two people, depending on what the situation *means* to them. The objective facts of the situation are less important than how the individual appraises them. Physicians treating wounded soldiers in combat field stations are often amazed at the calm and unperturbed manner with which some men react to serious injuries—injuries that would cause civilian hospital patients to plead for painkillers. For these soldiers, wounds represent a reprieve from the ordeals and danger of combat. Similarly, the discomfort of childbirth is apt to be much less stressful for the woman who has been eagerly anticipating birth of her child than for the woman who has no desire for motherhood.

One's perception of a stressful event also involves appraising the degree of threat. Situations that are perceived as threatening one's survival (for example, a diagnosis of cancer) or threatening one's worth as a person (for example, failure in one's chosen occupation) carry a maximum of stress. Our evaluation of the degree of threat depends to a large extent on our confidence in our ability to cope with the situation.

FEELINGS OF COMPETENCY A person's confidence in his or her ability to handle a stressful situation is a major factor in determining the severity of the stress. Speaking before a large audience is a traumatic event for most people. But individuals experienced in public speaking have confidence in their ability and feel only minimal anxiety.

Emergencies are particularly stressful because our usual methods of coping don't work. Not knowing what to do can be demoralizing. People trained to deal with emergencies—such as police officers, fire fighters, or medical rescue squads—can act calmly and effectively because they know what to do, but the person who lacks such training may feel helpless. Since we tend to fall back on well-learned responses under stress, it is important that people who may have to deal with particular types of emergencies be taught a repertoire of responses to cope with various contingencies.

SOCIAL SUPPORTS The emotional support and concern of other people can make stress more bearable. Divorce, the death of a loved one, or serious illness is usually more devastating if one is alone. Sometimes, however, family and friends can increase the stress. Minimizing the seriousness of the problem or giving blind assurance that "everything will be all right" may produce more anxiety than no support at all. A study of graduate students facing crucial examinations suggests that spouses who are realistically supportive—"I'm worried, but I know you'll do the best you can"—are more helpful than spouses who deny any possibility of failure—"I'm not worried; I'm sure you'll pass." In the latter case, the student has to worry not only about failing the exam, but also about losing respect in the eyes of the spouse (Mechanic, 1962).

Stress is easier to tolerate when the cause of the stress is shared with others. Community disasters—floods, earthquakes, tornadoes, wars—often seem to bring out the best in people. Individual anxieties and conflicts tend to be forgotten when people are working together against a common enemy or toward a common goal. During the intensive bombing of London in the Second World War, there was a marked decline in the number of people seeking help for emotional problems.

1 *Frustration* occurs when progress toward a goal is blocked or delayed. Environmental obstacles, social restrictions, and personal limitations all produce frustration; but one of the major sources of frustration is motivational conflicts.

2 When two motives conflict, the satisfaction of one leads to the blocking of the other. Most conflicts involve goals that are simultaneously positive and negative; one's attitude toward such goals is *ambivalent*.

3 Some of the immediate reactions to frustration are *aggression* (both direct and displaced), *apathy*, and *regression*. Individuals vary considerably in behavior when their goals are blocked.

4 Frustration and other forms of stress produce *anxiety*. Freud distinguished *objective anxiety*, fear of an external threat, from *neurotic anxiety*, which stems from an internal, unconscious conflict. But this text treats fear and anxiety synonymously. Social learning theory assumes that anxiety is a learned response to specific situations rather than the result of internal conflicts.

5 *Coping strategies* are behaviors that attempt to modify the anxiety-producing situation, while *defensive strategies* are concerned with reducing feelings of anxiety. *Defense mechanisms* are types of defensive strategies.

6 Two of the basic defense mechanisms are (a) *denial*, in which the person distorts external reality so that it seems less threatening, and (b) *repression*, in which the individual attempts to keep painful impulses and emotions from conscious awareness. Other defense mechanisms that aid repression are *rationalization*, *reaction formation*, *projection*, *intellectualization*, and *displacement*.

7 Defense mechanisms may provide temporary relief from anxiety; but if used habitually, they prevent effective problem solving.

8 Prolonged stress can contribute to physical disorders, such as ulcers and high blood pressure. *Psychosomatic medicine* studies the relationship between emotional stress and health. The severity of stress depends on the situation's *predictability*, the *potential for control*, the individual's *cognitive evaluation* and *feelings of competency*, and the presence of *social supports*.

FURTHER READING

A classic account of defense mechanisms is given by A. Freud in *The ego and the mechanisms of defense* (rev. ed., 1967). A more recent treatment may be found in Coleman, *Abnormal psychology and modern life* (5th ed., 1976).

A wide range of papers on anxiety is provided in Spielberger (ed.), *Anxiety: Current trends in theory and research* (1972), in two volumes.

Interesting books on stress include Gray, *The psychology of fear and stress* (1971), in paperback; McQuade and Aikman, *Stress* (1975), in paperback; and Tanner, *Stress* (1976). *Fear and courage* (1978) by Rachman discusses the origins, range, and treatment of human fears and includes some data collected during conditions of war.

15
Abnormal Psychology

Most of us have periods when we feel anxious, depressed, unreasonably angry, or inadequate in dealing with life's complexities. Trying to lead a satisfying and meaningful life today may well be more difficult than in prior centuries. In an era of rapid social change and tremendous growth in knowledge and technology, the social and religious values that gave our grandparents a sense of security no longer provide clear guidelines to behavior. Many of our traditional assumptions about work, religion, sex, marriage, and family are being seriously questioned. A number of factors suggest that life today is more stressful than in the past: the increased consumption of tranquilizers, sleeping pills, alcohol, and other drugs; the increase in crime, particularly crimes of violence; increased attempts to find relief through altering one's consciousness by meditation and self-hypnosis.

It is the fortunate person who manages to get through life without periods of loneliness, self-doubt, and despair. When a representative sample of Americans were asked if they had ever felt they were going to have a "nervous breakdown," one out of five answered "yes." But most people don't "break down"; they manage somehow to cope with their problems and continue to function.

In this chapter we will look at some individuals who have given up and can no longer manage on their own, some who have developed life styles that are self-destructive or destructive to other people, and we will look at a variety of ineffective ways of coping with the problems of living. We will be discussing behaviors that are classified as "abnormal," but, as we shall see, the dividing line between "normal" and "abnormal" behavior is far from clear.

Abnormality and Normality

Defining Abnormality

How do we define "abnormal"? What criteria distinguish "abnormal" from "normal" behavior?

1 *Deviation from statistical norms.* The word *ab-normal* means "away from the norm." Many characteristics, such as height, weight, and intelligence, cover a range of values when measured over the population. Most people fall

within the middle range of height; a few are abnormally tall or abnormally short. One definition of abnormality is based on *statistical frequency:* "abnormal behavior" is that which is statistically infrequent or deviant from the norm. But according to this definition, the person who is extremely intelligent or extremely happy would be classified as abnormal. Thus, in defining abnormal behavior we must consider more than statistical frequency.

2 *Deviation from social norms.* Every society has certain standards, or norms, for acceptable behavior; behavior that deviates markedly from these norms is considered abnormal. Usually, but not always, such behavior is also statistically infrequent in that society. There are several problems, however, in using deviation from social norms as a criterion for defining abnormality.

Behavior considered normal by one society may be considered abnormal by another. For example, some African tribes find nothing unusual in "hearing voices" when no one is actually talking or in "seeing visions." But most societies consider such behavior abnormal.

Another problem is that the concept of abnormality changes from time to time within the same society. Twenty-five years ago, most Americans would have considered smoking marijuana or appearing nude at the beach abnormal. Today, such behaviors, while still unacceptable to many, tend to be viewed as differences in life style rather than signs of abnormality.

More controversial is the question of whether or not homosexuality should be considered abnormal. Until quite recently, homosexuality was regarded as a "mental disorder" and homosexuals as "sick" people in need of treatment. But research findings conflict over whether homosexuals show more evidence of personality maladjustment than would be expected in a matched group of heterosexuals (Bell and Weinberg, 1978). In view of the ambiguous data, many experts no longer consider homosexuality a mental disorder.

Thus, ideas of normality and abnormality differ from one society to another and from time to time within the same society. Any definition of abnormality must include more than social compliance.

3 *Maladaptiveness of behavior.* Rather than defining abnormal behavior in terms of deviance from either statistical or societal norms, many social scientists believe that the most important criterion is how the behavior affects the well-being of the individual and/or the social group. According to this criterion, behavior is abnormal if it is *maladaptive*—that is, if it has adverse effects on either the individual or society. Some kinds of deviance interfere with the welfare of the individual. Examples would be a man who is so fearful of crowds that he cannot ride the bus to work, an alcoholic who drinks so heavily that he or she cannot keep a job, a woman who attempts suicide. Other forms of deviant behavior are harmful to society: for example, an adolescent who has violent aggressive outbursts or a paranoid individual who plots to assassinate national leaders. (Ultimately, of course, such behaviors are harmful to the individual as well.) If we use the criterion of maladaptiveness, all of the above cases would be considered abnormal.

4 *Personal distress.* A fourth criterion considers abnormality in terms of the individual's subjective feelings—personal distress—rather than his or her behavior. Most, but not all, people diagnosed as "mentally ill" feel acutely miserable; they are anxious, depressed, or agitated and may suffer from insomnia, loss of appetite, and numerous aches and pains. In the type of abnormality called *neuroses*, personal distress may be the only symptom; the individual's behavior may appear normal or even highly effective to the casual observer.

442

CHAPTER 15/ABNORMAL PSYCHOLOGY

None of these definitions provides a completely satisfactory description of abnormal behavior. In most instances, all four criteria—statistical, social, maladaptiveness of behavior, and personal distress—are considered in diagnosing abnormality. The *legal* definition of abnormality, which declares a person *insane* largely on the basis of his or her inability to judge between right and wrong or to exert control over behavior, is less satisfactory for diagnostic purposes than any of the above criteria. It should be emphasized that *insanity* is a legal term and is not used by psychologists in discussing abnormality.

What Is Normality?

Normality is even more difficult to define than abnormality, particularly in a rapidly changing and complex society. Traditionally, psychologists have focused on the individual's *adjustment* to the environment. They considered normal personality traits to be those that helped individuals to *adjust* to the world as they found it—to get along well with others and find a niche in society. Many psychologists now feel that the term "adjustment," if it is equated with conformity to what others do and think, carries too many negative connotations to describe the healthy personality. They focus on more positive attributes, such as individuality, creativity, and the fulfillment of one's potential.

Maslow, for example, considered *self-actualization* to be the highest of human motives. Most of his self-actualizing individuals (see Chapter 13) would be considered mentally healthy. However, few people are able to exploit their potential to the degree achieved by Maslow's self-actualizers (for example, Martin Luther King, Jr., Pablo Casals, Adlai Stevenson, and Eleanor Roosevelt). Most of us lead fairly routine lives, restricted by the innumerable demands of daily existence. Yet we would not be considered maladjusted or mentally disturbed.

Despite a lack of consensus in defining the normal personality, most psychologists would agree that the following qualities indicate emotional well-being. These characteristics do not distinguish sharply between the "mentally healthy" and the "mentally ill"; they represent traits that the normal person possesses to a *greater degree* than the individual diagnosed as abnormal.

1 *Efficient perception of reality.* Normal individuals are fairly realistic in appraising their reactions and abilities and interpreting what is going on in the world around them. They do not consistently misperceive what others say and do, and they evaluate their capabilities in a fairly realistic manner—they neither overevaluate their abilities and tackle more than they can accomplish nor shy away from a difficult task because they underestimate what they can do.
2 *Self-knowledge.* Well-adjusted people have some awareness of their own motives and feelings. Although none of us fully understand our feelings or behavior, normal individuals have more self-awareness than those who are diagnosed as "mentally ill." They do not hide important feelings and motives from themselves.
3 *Ability to exercise voluntary control over behavior.* Normal individuals feel fairly confident in their ability to control and direct their own behavior. Occasionally, they may act impulsively, but they are able to restrain sexual and aggressive urges when necessary. They may conform or fail to conform to social norms, but the decision is a voluntary one rather than the result of uncontrollable impulses.

Detail of *Melancholia* by Edvard Munch

Sorrow by Vincent van Gogh. November 1882. Transfer lithograph. 15⅜″ x 11¾″. Collection, The Museum of Modern Art, New York

4   *Self-esteem and acceptance.* Well-adjusted people have some appreciation of their own self-worth and feel accepted by those around them. They are comfortable with other people and able to react spontaneously in social situations. At the same time, they do not feel obligated to subjugate their opinions to those of the group. Feelings of worthlessness, alienation, and a lack of acceptance by others are prevalent among those diagnosed as abnormal.

5   *Ability to form affectionate relationships.* Normal individuals are able to form close and satisfying relationships with other people. They are sensitive to the needs and feelings of others and do not make excessive demands for the gratification of their own needs. Often, mentally disturbed people are so concerned with protecting their own security that they become extremely self-centered; preoccupied with their own feelings and strivings, they seek affection but are unable to reciprocate. Sometimes they fear intimacy because their past relationships have been destructive.

6   *Productivity.* Well-adjusted people are able to use their abilities—whether meager or ample—in productive activity. They have enthusiasm for living and do not need to drive themselves to meet the demands of the day. A chronic lack of energy and excessive susceptibility to fatigue are common symptoms of psychological tension and unresolved problems.

It is sometimes argued that people who suffer from unresolved conflicts turn to creative work because of their suffering. The artists van Gogh and Munch were probably emotionally disturbed (judging from descriptions of their behavior), and one wonders if their creative powers would have been as great had they been "well-adjusted." The question is debatable, but it is clear from accounts of their lives that they produced their artistic works at the cost of great pain to themselves and those close to them. Although a few disturbed people manage to turn their troubles into advantages, most are unable to use their full creative abilities because their emotional conflicts inhibit their productivity.

Classifying Abnormal Behavior

A broad range of behaviors have been classified as "abnormal." Some are acute and transitory, the result of a particularly stressful event; others are chronic and lifelong. Some are the result of disease or damage to the nervous system; others are the product of undesirable social environments and/or faulty learning experiences. (And often these factors overlap and interact.) Psychologists have proposed a number of systems to classify the many kinds of behavior diagnosed as abnormal. The most widely used system groups people according to the kinds of behavior they display. Individuals who behave roughly the same way are given the same label. The major diagnostic categories we will discuss under this classification system are *neuroses*, *psychoses*, and *personality disorders*.[1] Each of these is further divided into subcategories. We will briefly describe the major categories here and examine some of the subcategories in the remainder of the chapter.

NEUROSES   A major distinction is made between neuroses and psychoses. The *neuroses* (plural form of *neurosis*) are usually a less serious form of

[1]Two other diagnostic categories, mental retardation and psychosomatic disorders, have been considered earlier (see Chapters 12 and 14).

abnormal behavior. They are troublesome enough to require expert help, and occasionally even hospitalization is necessary, but they do not involve personality disintegration or loss of contact with reality. Neurotic individuals can usually get along in society even though they do not function at full capacity. The primary symptom of neurosis is anxiety, which may be experienced openly or may be deflected via one of the defense mechanisms described in Chapter 14.

PSYCHOSES The *psychoses* (plural form of *psychosis*) are characterized by an impairment in mental functioning that seriously interferes with the individual's ability to meet the demands of daily life. There is gross distortion of reality, so that the person can no longer distinguish between fantasy and reality. These distortions may take the form of *delusions* or *hallucinations*.

A delusion is a false belief maintained despite contradictory evidence or experience. Psychotic delusions often center around ideas of *grandeur* (I am the King of the Universe or I am Jesus Christ), *persecution* (people are talking about me; they are trying to poison me), *external control* (my thoughts are being controlled by radio waves from Mars or by electric impulses from the wall sockets), or *depersonalization* (I am not a real person anymore; everything inside me—my organs and brain—has rotted away).

Hallucinations are sense experiences occurring in the absence of the appropriate external stimuli. The person may hear voices, see images, or experience strange odors or tastes when no such events are taking place. Often the hallucinations reinforce the delusional beliefs. If I hear voices calling me obscene names and smell strange odors (poison gas?), what more proof do I need that my enemies are out to get me?

The psychotic individual may also show profound changes of mood (from wild excitement to depressive stupor) as well as defects in language and memory.

PERSONALITY DISORDERS Personality disorders are usually long-standing patterns of socially maladaptive behavior. Extreme dependency, antisocial or sexually deviant behavior, alcoholism, and drug addiction are some of the disorders included in this category. There is no gross distortion of reality or intellectual impairment (except when alcoholism or drug addiction has progressed to the point of causing brain damage, in which case the individual might show psychotic symptoms and be classified accordingly).

These categories of abnormal behavior will seem more meaningful after we have looked at some examples of each. In actual practice, the classification system is not as satisfactory as we would like. Although agreement is fairly good in broad distinctions (such as deciding whether or not a person is psychotic), psychologists and psychiatrists often fail to agree on more specific diagnoses (such as type of neurosis or psychosis). Each person's behavior patterns and emotional problems are unique; few fit neatly into a single category.

Imperfect as it may be, however, a classification of mental disorders is useful. If there are different causes behind the various types of abnormal behavior, then we can hope to uncover them only by grouping individuals according to similarities in behavior and then looking for other ways in which they may be similar. A diagnostic label also helps communicate information among those working with disturbed individuals. Knowing that a person has

Models of Abnormality

In our discussion of abnormality we have used such terms as *mental illness, behavior disorders, maladaptive behavior,* and *emotional disturbance* almost interchangeably. This profusion of terminology results from the fact that abnormal behavior can be viewed in several different ways. Because much is still unknown about the causes and cures of most of the disorders classified as abnormal, quite diverse theoretical models have been proposed.

Medical model. Terms such as *mental illness* and *mental health* reflect the *medical model* of abnormal behavior, which draws an analogy between physical disease and mental illness. The medical model evolved during the nineteenth century with the gradual discovery that brain damage could result in thought disturbances and bizarre behavior. The concept of abnormality as a disease process was an improvement over earlier views that attributed abnormal behavior to possession by demons or to moral corruption. It led to much more humane treatment. Individuals suffering from diseases were not held responsible for their actions and were treated in hospitals rather than being burned as witches or sent to prison.

Today, however, many psychologists question the appropriateness of the medical model (e.g., Szasz, 1961, 1970; Krasner and Ullmann, 1973; Bandura, 1977). They point out that most forms of abnormal behavior have *not* been traced to disorders of the nervous system. There is no evidence that the neuroses are based on a neurological disturbance, for example. In addition, the medical model is misleading because it suggests a sharp division between normality and abnormality and tends to ignore the influence of interpersonal and social factors. Whether behavior is considered normal or abnormal often depends on the sociocultural group to which the person belongs, the situation in which the

behavior occurs (physical aggression is normal on the football field but not in the classroom), and the age of the individual (bed-wetting and temper tantrums may be normal for a two-year-old but not for an adult). Moreover, labeling a person who displays unusual behavior as "sick" places the responsibility for "cure" on medical personnel rather than on the individual and may predispose him or her to act even "sicker" once so labeled.

Psychoanalytic model. According to the *psychoanalytic model,* abnormal behavior is the result of unconscious conflicts from early childhood (e.g., Hartmann, 1958; A. Freud, 1967; Rapaport, 1967). Freud believed that repressed aggressive and sexual impulses generate anxiety, which is controlled by defense mechanisms. The neuroses represent an exaggerated use of defense mechanisms in coping with anxiety. The psychoses represent a breakdown of the neurotic defense mechanisms, with the individual regressing to that period in his or her psychosexual development (see p. 391) at which conflicts failed to be resolved (usually the oral stage). Treatment consists of uncovering the unconscious conflicts from early childhood (e.g., Hartmann, 1958; A. Freud, 1967; Rapaways. The psychoanalytic model and the medical model share the assumption that abnormal behavior is a *symptom* of an underlying disturbance. It is the underlying conflict that must be dealt with, not the behavior itself.

Social learning model. The *social learning model* views abnormal behavior as the result of faulty learning in the course of growing up (e.g., Kanfer and Phillips, 1970; Lazarus, 1972; Bandura, 1977). Abnormal or *maladaptive behavior* may be determined by the individual's past history of reinforcement in several ways. The person may have failed to learn the necessary behavior. For example, he or she may never have learned to relate to other people in a

satisfactory way, or may have learned ineffective or maladaptive habits. If punished for expressing sexual feelings as a child, the individual may learn to respond with anxiety to sexually arousing stimuli. As an adult, such responses would be maladaptive. The social learning model assumes that abnormal behavior can be dealt with directly; there is no assumption of an underlying conflict or illness. Change the behavior—either by changing the environment so that maladaptive behavior is no longer reinforced or by teaching new behavior—and you have "cured the illness."

Sociocultural model. A fourth model of abnormality focuses on those factors in the *sociocultural environment* that contribute to abnormal behavior (e.g., Laing, 1967). The high incidence of serious mental disorders among the lower socioeconomic classes and in urban areas has drawn attention to the effect of community conditions, such as poverty and overcrowding, on mental health. In seeking the source and cure for problems, the *sociocultural model* looks beyond the individual and the family to the community and general sociocultural environment. It emphasizes the development of a *healthy society* in which each person can develop his or her potential to the fullest. In this respect, the sociocultural model shares the concerns of humanistic psychology.

Each model of abnormality—medical, psychoanalytic, social learning, and sociocultural—views abnormal behavior from a different perspective. In treating mental well-being as a function of the total organism in interaction with the environment, it is necessary to consider biological, psychological, and sociocultural factors. As we shall see, these three determinants are involved in varying degrees in most instances of abnormal behavior; the relative importance of each depends on the specific case.

been classified as *paranoid schizophrenic* tells one quite a bit about his or her behavior. Knowing that an individual's symptoms are similar to those of other patients (whose progress followed a particular course or who have benefited from a certain kind of treatment) is also helpful.

These advantages become disadvantages, however, if we allow a diagnostic label to carry too much weight—that is, (1) if we overlook the unique features of each case and expect the person to conform to the classification, or (2) if we forget that a label for maladaptive behavior is *not* an explanation of that behavior—that it does not tell us how the behavior came about or what maintains it.

Neuroses

The *neuroses* are a group of disorders in which the person has developed certain behavior patterns that avoid, rather than cope with, problems. We noted in the preceding chapter that unresolved approach-avoidance conflicts result in feelings of anxiety, tension, and helplessness. When these conflicts are not resolved, the individual either remains in a state of severe anxiety or resorts to one or more of the defense mechanisms. In the neurotic individual, this defense is seldom satisfactory for two reasons: it usually alleviates only a small part of the total anxiety, and it interferes with the person's effective functioning, thereby creating further problems.

Anxiety, then, is assumed to be at the core of all neuroses. Sometimes this is quite evident. The person appears strained and tense; he or she may suffer from insomnia, indigestion, diarrhea, and inability to concentrate. Sometimes the anxiety is not readily apparent, but we infer from maladaptive behavior that the individual is defending against anxiety by the extreme use of one or more defense mechanisms.

Neurotic behavior creates a vicious cycle. The individual feels inadequate to cope with many everyday problems and so avoids them by defensive strategies; he or she then feels guilty, unhappy, and even more inadequate because of failure to deal directly with situations that others handle with apparent ease. Self-defeating as this is, the neurotic individual clings rigidly to established behavior patterns and seems unable to recognize alternative courses of action. This rigid adherence to self-defeating behavior patterns is known as the "neurotic paradox." Why does an individual keep on doing something that makes him or her so unhappy? The answer seems to be that the neurotic behavior receives strong immediate reinforcement because it temporarily reduces or avoids anxiety; the immediate rewards override the long-term consequences.

In this section, we will describe five of the more common neurotic reactions: *anxiety reactions, obsessive-compulsive reactions, phobias, conversion reactions,* and *neurotic depression.* Although it is useful to distinguish among these disorders, many neurotic individuals experience a variety of symptoms and do not fit into any one category, as the case studies we will cite illustrate.

Anxiety Reactions

The most common neurotic disorder is an *anxiety reaction.* Although anxiety is the predominant characteristic of neurosis, in many neurotic reactions it is concealed by other symptoms, as we have suggested. In anxiety reactions,

TABLE 15-1
Ten most commonly reported symptoms of anxiety neurosis

Table entries indicate the percentage of individuals with anxiety neurosis and the percentage of control subjects who reported the symptoms.

SYMPTOMS	PATIENTS	CONTROLS
Palpitation	97	9
Tires easily	95	19
Breathlessness	90	13
Nervousness	88	27
Chest pain	85	10
Sighing	79	16
Dizziness	78	16
Faintness	70	12
Apprehension	61	3
Headache	58	26

Based on Marks and Lader (1973)

however, it is very much in the open. The individual lives each day in a state of high tension. He or she feels vaguely uneasy or apprehensive much of the time and tends to overact to even mild stresses. Some of the most common symptoms associated with anxiety neurosis are listed in Table 15-1. In addition, the individual may be unable to concentrate or to make decisions. A decision finally made becomes the source of further worry—"Did I foresee all possible consequences? Will disaster result?"

This chronic state of worry and apprehension is often punctuated by *acute anxiety attacks*, which may occur as often as several times a day or as infrequently as once a month. During acute attacks, the individual has an overwhelming feeling that something dreadful is about to happen; this feeling is usually accompanied by such symptoms as heart palpitations, shortness of breath, perspiration, muscle tremor, faintness, and nausea. These physiological symptoms result from excitation of the sympathetic division of the autonomic nervous system (see Chapter 2) and are the same symptoms that one may experience when extremely frightened.[2]

The person with an anxiety reaction usually has no clear idea why he or she is frightened. This kind of anxiety is sometimes called "free-floating," because it is not restricted to a particular stimulus or event but occurs in a wide variety of situations. It appears to be less a function of external stimuli than of feelings and conflicts within the individual.

Most of us have felt anxious and tense in the face of threatening or stressful situations. Such feelings are normal reactions to stress. Anxiety is considered neurotic only when it occurs in situations that most people can handle with little difficulty.

We don't know why some people become chronically anxious. But their reactions seem to reflect feelings of inadequacy in the face of stresses (either internal or external) perceived as highly threatening. Psychoanalytic theory assumes that the sources of anxiety are internal and unconscious. The person has repressed certain unacceptable, or "dangerous," impulses—impulses that would endanger self-esteem or relationships with other people were they to be expressed. In situations where these impulses are likely to be aroused, he or she experiences intense anxiety. The case study described in Figure 15-1 shows how the threatened breakthrough of hostile feelings triggered acute anxiety attacks. Because the source of anxiety is unconscious, the person doesn't know why he or she feels apprehensive. And because the source is internal, the individual carries the anxiety with him or her at all times.

Learning theory assumes that anxiety neurosis is a response to external events that, for one reason or another, the person cannot handle. The individual may never have learned how to cope with certain situations or may have learned ineffective and maladaptive responses. For example, a boy may be so shy that he avoids interpersonal contacts and so never learns the social skills that would enable him to enjoy meeting and getting to know people. Something like this happened to the student in Figure 15-1.

Obsessive-Compulsive Reactions

The individual with an *obsessive-compulsive reaction* feels compelled to think about things he or she would rather not think about or to perform acts that he or she does not wish to carry out. *Obsessions* are persistent intrusions of

[2] Several organic conditions, such as overactivity of the thyroid gland, heart disease, hypoglycemia, and some endocrine disorders, can produce the same symptoms as an anxiety attack. Such possibilities should be ruled out before assuming that the symptoms are of psychological origin.

Fig. 15-1
ANXIETY REACTION

An eighteen-year-old male student developed severe anxiety attacks just before he went out on dates. In therapy it was revealed that he came from a very insecure home in which he was very much attached to an anxious, frustrated, and insecure mother. Intellectually capable and a good student, he had entered college at 16. But during his two years on campus he had difficulty getting dates, especially with college women of his choice. The student he had been recently dating, for example, would not make any arrangements to go out until after 6:00 P.M. of the same day, after her chances for a more preferable date seemed remote. This had increased already strong feelings of inferiority and insecurity and led to the development of intense hostility toward the opposite sex, mostly on an unconscious level.

About two months before coming to the college clinic for assistance, he had experienced the anxiety-arousing fantasy of choking the young woman to death when they were alone together. As he put it, "When we are alone in the car, I can't get my mind off her nice white throat and what it would be like to choke her to death." At first he put these thoughts out of his mind, but they returned on subsequent nights with increasing persistency. Then, to complicate the matter, he experienced his first acute anxiety attack. It occurred in his car on the way over to pick up his date and lasted only a few minutes, but the youth was panic-stricken and thought that he was going to die. After that he experienced several additional attacks under the same conditions.

The relationship of the repressed hostility to the persistent fantasies and anxiety attacks seemed clear in this case. Yet it was not at all apparent to the young man, who was at a complete loss to explain either his fantasies or anxiety attacks. (Coleman, 1976, pp. 222–25)

From *Abnormal psychology and modern life*, 5th Edition by James C. Coleman. Copyright © 1976, 1972, 1964 by Scott, Foresman and Company. Reprinted by permission.

---

unwelcome thoughts. *Compulsions* are irresistible urges to carry out certain acts or rituals. Obsessive thoughts may be linked with compulsive acts—for example, thoughts of lurking disease germs combined with the compulsion of excessive hand-washing.

All of us at times have persistently recurring thoughts ("Did I leave the gas turned on?") and urges toward ritualistic behavior (knocking on wood after boasting of good fortune). But for the person with an obsessive-compulsive neurosis, such thoughts and urges occupy so much time that they seriously interfere with his or her daily life. The individual recognizes their irrationality but is unable to control them. Often the attempt to stop produces anxiety.

Obsessive thoughts cover a wide variety of topics but most often picture committing aggressive or sexual acts. A young man may have recurrent thoughts of exposing his genitals in public or shouting obscenities while in church. A mother may have persistent thoughts of drowning her infant in the bathtub. The possibility of their carrying out these thoughts is virtually nil, but they are not so sure. Obsessive neurotics are horrified by their thoughts, cannot understand why they persist, and fear not only that they will perform the act but that they are becoming insane.

Figure 15-2 reports the history of a young mother who was distressed by

"*Ronald is extremely compulsive.*"

Fig. 15-2

OBSESSIVE THOUGHTS

A thirty-two-year-old mother of two small children sought help because of her distress over obsessively intrusive and repugnant thoughts related to injuring or murdering her children. On infrequent occasions her husband was also a "victim." These thoughts were so repugnant, made so little sense, and were so foreign to her conscious feelings that she had long been afraid and embarrassed to seek help. She had kept this problem to herself for nearly two years, despite considerable psychological pain, tension, and turmoil. Finally, the steadily increasing difficulty had reached an intolerable level.

These thoughts that were so terribly disturbing to her were really not too much different in quality from what every normal young woman may occasionally feel toward her children. Many a young parent less inhibited and more spontaneous than this one might on occasion say, "Oh, today I feel just like throwing Johnny out of the window! He makes me so mad!" She would not feel threatened by such a thought or feel very guilty about having had it. She would probably forget it rather quickly. But this patient greatly feared and condemned such thoughts. To her the thought was nearly as threatening and as guilt-provoking as the act.

This woman had developed early in life a defensive need to deny the presence of all but positive feelings. To defend herself against the guilt occasioned by having such "terrible" thoughts, she endeavored to dissociate them from herself, to deny that they were hers. "It's just awful words that pop into my head. . . . They have nothing at all to do with the way I feel. They couldn't be my thoughts at all. . . ."

The patient had been raised by an anxious and insecure mother who was unable to permit herself or her children the slightest expression of negative feelings. The daughter soon realized that any feelings other than loving ones must be repressed or denied. The patient was the eldest of three siblings and had been assigned undue responsibility for their care. She felt deprived of her share of her parents' affection, was greatly resentful of her younger sister and brother, and fantasized what it would be like if they were not around. Her occasional murderous fantasies about them were accompanied by tremendous guilt and anxiety. As a result the fantasies and associated emotional feelings had been completely repressed from conscious awareness. These early conflicts were reactivated during her marriage when the needs of husband and children seemed to take precedence over her own. (Laughlin, 1967, pp. 324–25)

Fig. 15-3

COMPULSIVE RITUALS

A thirty-year-old woman had developed such an elaborate sequence of ritual acts that their consummation occupied most of her waking hours. She could not go to bed at night before she had checked each door and window three times to ensure that they were locked. The gas range and the pilot lights to the furnace and hot water heater had to be similarly checked to make certain that no gas was escaping. Bathing and dressing took up much of her time, since she often took three or four showers in succession—scrubbing her body thoroughly with a special antibacterial cleanser each time—before she was convinced that she was clean enough to put on her clothes. She wore only clothing that could be washed, not trusting the dry cleaner to remove all possible germs, and each article had to be washed and rinsed three times before she would wear it. Similar hygienic procedures were involved whenever she prepared food; she scalded each dish and utensil with boiling water before and after using it, and would not eat a meal unless she had prepared it herself.

This woman had always been unusually neat and clean, but her "security operations" had intensified over the years until they reached pathological proportions. At times she realized the foolishness of her precautions, but she experienced intense anxiety whenever she attempted to cut short any of her procedures. (R. L. Atkinson, unpublished case report)

recurrent thoughts of murdering her two small children. The kind of prohibition her parents placed on any expression of negative feelings is fairly characteristic of the background of persons who develop obsessive-compulsive neuroses. When normal feelings of anger must be suppressed or denied, they become an "alien" part of the personality and find expression only in indirect ways.

Compulsive acts range from mild kinds of superstitious behavior—such as not stepping on the cracks in sidewalks or arranging the material on one's desk in a precise order before starting an assignment—to elaborate rituals like those described in Figure 15-3.

Most of us find comfort in certain familiar routines or rituals, particularly in times of stress. But the person with an obsessive-compulsive neurosis cannot function without them. Compulsive rituals apparently serve two main purposes. They give the individual a feeling of order and control in a confusing and threatening world. And they defend against anxiety by keeping threatening impulses out of awareness; a person who is continually busy has little opportunity for improper thoughts or actions.

Even when dangerous impulses do enter consciousness, they are dissociated (separated) from normal emotions and appear in the form of obsessive thoughts. Although such thoughts are disturbing, the person feels they are not really a part of him or herself. For example, the college student whose case was reported in Figure 15-1 was upset by thoughts of choking his date, but he would have been considerably more disturbed had he realized the extent of his hostile feelings toward females.

Phobias

Phobias are excessive fears of specific objects or situations when there is no real danger or fears that are totally out of proportion to the degree of danger involved. (The word comes from *Phobos*, a Greek god who provoked fear and panic in enemies and whose image was painted on masks and shields carried into battle.) The person with a phobia usually realizes that the fear is irrational but still feels anxiety (ranging from a feeling of uneasiness to an acute anxiety attack), which can only be relieved by avoiding the feared situation.

Most of us are afraid of something; snakes, heights, storms, doctors, sickness, injury, and death are the seven fears most commonly reported by adults (Agras, 1975). As you can see from Figure 15-4, the prevalence of specific fears changes with age. There appears to be a continuum between these common fears and phobias, making the distinction between them somewhat arbitrary. A fear is usually not diagnosed as a phobia unless it causes considerable interference with the person's daily life. Examples would be a woman whose fear of enclosed places prevents her from entering elevators or a man whose fear of crowds prevents him from attending the theater or walking along congested sidewalks.

Some people may develop a specific phobia (fear of snakes or heights, for example) and yet be normal in every other respect. In more serious cases, several phobias are intertwined with obsessive or compulsive behavior (see Figure 15-5).

How do phobias develop? Learning theory provides a number of explanations. Some phobias may result from frightening experiences—for example, developing a fear of flying after experiencing a near air disaster or a fear of dogs after having been attacked by one. Once such a phobia develops, the individual may go to great lengths to avoid the feared situation, thus eliminating the possibility of reducing the fear.

Other phobias may be learned through observation. Fearful parents tend to produce children who share their fears. While it is possible that timidity may be a biologically inherited trait, it is much more likely that the parents provide a model that the child imitates.

Still other phobias may develop because they are rewarded—for example, "school phobias." A school phobia in a young child is not usually a fear of school itself, but a fear of separation from the parents. A child who wants to

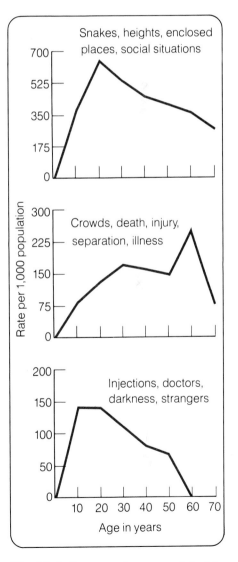

Fig. 15-4 Common fears as related to age
After Agras, Sylvester, and Oliveau (1969)

Fig. 15-5

PHOBIAS

An eighteen-year-old college freshman came for help at the student health center because each time he left his dormitory room and headed toward class he experienced a feeling of panic. "It would get so bad at times that I thought I would collapse on the way to class. It was a frightening feeling and I began to be afraid to leave the dorm." He could not understand these feelings, since he was reasonably well pleased with his classes and professors. Even after he returned to the dormitory, he would be unable to face anyone for hours or to concentrate on his homework. But if he remained in or near his room he felt reasonably comfortable.

During interviews with his therapist the youth reported other fears such as becoming contaminated by syphilis and growing prematurely bald. Occasionally these fears were sufficiently intense and persistent to cause him to compulsively scrub his hands, genitals,

and head until these parts became red, and sometimes even bled. In addition, he touched doorknobs only reluctantly, never drank water from a public fountain, and only used the toilet in his home or dormitory. He realized that his fears were unfounded and exaggerated but also felt that many of his precautions and constant worrying were necessary to avoid even greater "mental anguish."

The student's past history revealed that he had serious concerns about his sexual identity and his adequacy as a male. As a youngster he had avoided playing with the other boys because he could not run as fast or hit a ball as far. His mother had strongly rewarded his tendency not to join others because she was convinced that he would get hurt if he participated in their "rough-housing." He was a late maturer and had spent a traumatic summer at camp about the time that most of his peers were reaching puberty. Discovering

that he was sexually underdeveloped in comparison to the other boys, he worried about his deficiency—he wondered whether he was destined to become a girl, and he feared that the other boys might attack him sexually.

Although his puberty made a belated appearance, he continued to worry about his masculine identity and even fantasized on occasion that he was a girl. At these times he became extremely anxious and seriously considered suicide as a solution.

The therapist's immediate goal in treatment was to remove the student's irrational fear of leaving the dormitory, which was accomplished with the method of systematic desensitization (see pp. 494–95). It was clear, however, that the phobias in this case were part of a deep-rooted problem of sexual identity which would require more extensive psychotherapy. (Kleinmuntz, 1974, pp. 168–69)

stay close to his or her mother may invent various excuses (for example, a stomachache) to stay home. If the mother (who may also fear separation) gives in to the excuses, the child is rewarded with the comfort of staying home with her. Separation fears reinforced in childhood may be reactivated in later life as a response to stress. In one case, a man in his thirties who was under increased job pressures developed a fear of leaving home to go to work or to crowded places such as restaurants or stores. He had experienced a severe school phobia as a child, and his old fear of separation—this time from his wife—recurred when he was faced with stress (Agras, 1975).

But some phobic reactions are difficult to trace to learning experiences. For example, many individuals with phobias of airplanes, snakes, heights, or germs report no unpleasant prior experiences with these objects or situations (although it is always possible that earlier frightening experiences may have been repressed). In such cases, the feared object may represent or symbolize another source of fear. Psychoanalytic theory assumes that phobias develop as a defense against impulses that the individual feels may become dangerous. For example, the student whose case is reported in Figure 15-5 could avoid the arousal of homosexual impulses by staying in his room, away from other men, and by not using public toilets.

In one sense, phobias have an advantage over anxiety reactions; fear is directed toward a specific situation, and the person can reduce anxiety by avoiding the situation. The individual with an anxiety neurosis has no such escape. On the other hand, a phobia that prevents an individual from venturing far from home or from enjoying normal social contacts can be as disabling as a more serious psychotic disorder.

As we will see in the next chapter, the most effective method of treating phobias is to gradually expose the person to the feared situation.

Conversion Reactions

In *conversion reactions*,[3] physical symptoms appear without any underlying organic cause. The most common symptoms are paralysis of a limb or other body part, loss of sensation in some area of the body, blindness, deafness, "fits" similar to epileptic convulsions, and a variety of vague aches or pains.

Freud believed that these reactions represented the "conversion" of anxiety into physical symptoms. Although the term "conversion reaction" is retained, the physical symptoms are now usually interpreted as a means of avoiding a stressful situation by unconsciously adopting sick-role behavior. For example, a woman who has devoted her life to caring for a widowed mother develops paralysis of her right arm following a minor injury. The paralysis relieves her of responsibility and also gains sympathy from friends and relatives. A soldier develops partial blindness or a paralyzed leg, symptoms that allow him to withdraw from combat without being called a "coward" (see Figure 15-6).

Unlike psychosomatic illness, where emotional stress causes bodily changes (see Chapter 14), conversion reactions have no physical basis. Nevertheless, the person is not faking; he or she believes the disorder is very real. For example, in cases where there is a loss of pain sensitivity (analgesia) in some part of the body, the person shows no outward signs of pain when stuck with a pin. (This situation is similar to that of a hypnotized subject who, when instructed not to feel pain, does not react when the skin is pierced deeply by a needle.)

The more dramatic types of conversion reactions, such as sudden paralysis or sudden blindness or deafness, are fairly easy to diagnose. Medical tests usually show that the symptoms do not conform to those of the physical

[3] Also called hysterical neurosis, conversion type.

Fig. 15-6

CONVERSION REACTION

A twenty-one-year-old soldier completed basic training without incident. Because of his superior physique and soldierly bearing, he was assigned to an "honor guard" unit. Upon completion of this tour he was ordered to overseas combat service. But before he could go he developed partial paralysis of the left leg, which he attributed to the aftermath of a minor physical injury. In response to his complaints, a physician indulgently placed a plaster splint on the leg for two weeks, hoping thus to "satisfy the patient." Upon removal of the splint the paralysis was complete, although medical evaluation made it clear that the difficulty was not physical in origin.

The soldier was a rather dependent and immature person who was extraordinarily proud of his physique and unusually concerned over any possible threat of injury thereto. Although his leg disability was severe enough to require him to use crutches, he appeared blandly indifferent to the serious implications of his handicap. This *belle indifférence* is often characteristic of conversion reactions. On several occasions the patient showed more concern over a minor skin irritation, demanding to see a dermatologist, than he did over his paralyzed leg.

This patient was unresponsive to any psychotherapeutic efforts; his paralysis gradually improved following the decision to discharge him from military service. (Laughlin, 1967, pp. 673–74)

disorder. For example, there is no wasting away of the muscles of the "paralyzed" limb as there would be with true paralysis (except in very longstanding cases). In addition, the reaction is often selective: people with conversion reactions of blindness do not usually bump into objects; those whose symptom is deafness may be able to hear instructions shouted in an emergency; those with paralyzed muscles can move them during sleep. People who develop conversion reactions tend to be highly suggestible. Often the symptoms can be removed at the suggestion of a hypnotist.

Less dramatic conversion reactions, vague aches and pains, are more difficult to distinguish from organic disorders. But accurate diagnosis is crucial for two reasons. (1) Many people undergo major surgery for symptoms that are actually psychological in origin (Woodruff, Goodwin, and Guze, 1974). (2) Some cases diagnosed as conversion reactions may actually be physical disorders.

Neurotic Depression

The individual who suffers *neurotic depression* reacts to a distressing event with more than the usual sadness and fails to recover within a reasonable length of time. Almost everyone feels depressed at times. Among the situations that most often precipitate depression are failure at school or on the job; the loss of a loved one, either through rejection or death; and the realization that illness or aging is depleting one's resources. Depression is termed neurotic only when it is out of proportion to the event and continues past the point where most people begin to recover.

The chief signs of neurotic depression are hopelessness and dejection. The individual experiences an overwhelming inertia—feels unable to make decisions, initiate activity, or take an interest in anything or anyone. He or she broods over feelings of inadequacy and worthlessness, has crying spells, and may contemplate suicide.

Depression, along with anxiety reactions, is one of the most prevalent emotional disorders. It is estimated that one person out of seven suffers from some degree of depression—from mild to severely incapacitating—in response to life stresses. One theory proposes that the initial response to a stressful situation is anxiety; if the individual believes that the situation cannot be altered or controlled, anxiety is replaced by depression (Seligman, 1975).

Depression is classified under several diagnostic categories, one of them neurotic and several psychotic—evidence that our classification of abnormal behavior is far from satisfactory. We will consider some theories about the causes of depression in the section on affective disorders, since many of the underlying factors appear to be the same, whether the depression is classified as neurotic or psychotic.

Understanding Neurotic Reactions

We have looked at five types of neurotic reactions. Since the symptoms frequently overlap, it is not always clear how to categorize a particular case. The case of the college student who had difficulty dating (see Figure 15-1) could be classified as an anxiety reaction or as an obsessive-compulsive reaction, depending on which symptoms seemed the most prominent at the time he was evaluated. Actually, he was using obsessive thoughts as a defense against anxiety, but his defense was not very successful, and anxiety was breaking through in the form of acute panic reactions.

Phobic and obsessive-compulsive reactions often occur together; the individual may be obsessed with thoughts about his or her fears and may defend against them by means of compulsive rituals (see Figure 15-5).

All neurotic reactions can be viewed as attempts to cope with stress by means of avoidance behavior. In anxiety reactions, the defense is not working well. The obsessive-compulsive individual tries to defend against anxiety by dissociating thoughts from their true emotions or by becoming occupied with rituals that prevent thinking about dangerous impulses. The phobic individual focuses fear on particular objects or situations—by avoiding them, he or she can reduce anxiety. The person with a conversion reaction avoids stressful situations by resorting to physical illness. The neurotic depressive has essentially given up—anxiety has been replaced by feelings of complete hopelessness and helplessness.

Neurotic reactions are exaggerated forms of normal defense mechanisms; neurotic symptoms are responses that the individual uses to defend against anxiety and to increase feelings of security. Because these responses may initially be fairly successful in reducing anxiety, they are reinforced and strengthened. With increased stress, however, the individual's defensive efforts are redoubled so that they reach maladaptive proportions and are only partially successful in reducing anxiety. The person is thus caught in a pattern that not only fails to relieve anxiety but creates additional adjustment problems.

Since feelings of inadequacy and anxiety underlie all the neurotic reactions, we may well ask what determines the particular symptoms an individual develops. Why does one person respond to stress with obsessive thoughts while another responds by developing paralysis of the arm? We do not know the complete answer. The most plausible explanation is that neurotic symptoms are exaggerations of the reaction patterns learned in childhood. Often such reaction patterns were appropriate in the situation in which they were learned but are maladaptive when applied to other situations.

Psychoses

Psychotic disorders involve more serious disturbances of thought and behavior than neurotic reactions. The individual's personality is disorganized, and normal social functioning is greatly impaired. Whether psychoses represent an extreme form of neurosis or a distinct type of disorder is a matter of controversy. Some experts see normality, neurosis, and psychosis as a continuum, the differences being largely a matter of severity of the symptoms. Others believe that the psychoses are qualitatively different from the neuroses, involving physiological changes in the nervous system that may have a genetic base. We will examine the evidence for both viewpoints as we go along.

The most apparent distinction is that people diagnosed as neurotic are usually able to function in the world, whereas those considered psychotic have *lost contact with reality* to some extent. They may withdraw into their own fantasies and fail to respond to things going on around them. Or they may respond with exaggerated emotions and actions that are inappropriate to the situation. Frequently thought processes are disturbed to the extent that the person experiences delusions or hallucinations. For these reasons, the psychotic individual is more likely to require hospitalization than the neurotic. Table 15-2 lists some of the differences between individuals diagnosed as psychotic and those who are considered neurotic.

There are two general categories of psychoses: *organic* and *functional.*

TABLE 15-2
Characteristics of psychotic and neurotic reactions

	NEUROSES	PSYCHOSES
Behavior	Maladaptive avoidance behavior, with mild to moderate impairment of personal and social functioning	Severe personality disorganization; contact with reality is tenuous; personal and social functioning seriously impaired
Symptoms	Wide range of symptoms, but no hallucinations or extreme deviations in thought, affect, or action	Wide range of symptoms with extreme deviations in thought, affect, and action—for example, delusions, hallucinations, emotional blunting, bizarre behavior
Orientation to environment	Orientation for person, place, and time is intact	Orientation is poor or lacking; may not know who or where he or she is, or the month or year
Insight	Some understanding of own maladaptive behavior, but feels unable to change it	Little understanding of symptoms and behavior
Care	Can usually be treated as an outpatient	Often requires hospitalization

Source: Adapted from Coleman (1976)

Organic psychoses result from damage to the central nervous system. Head injuries, brain tumors, hardening of the arteries, and lead poisoning are some of the conditions that can produce psychotic symptoms. *Functional psychoses* are disorders that are presumed to be primarily psychological in origin, although genetic and biological factors may play a significant role.

The distinction between organic and functional psychoses is not clear-cut, however. Some of the psychoses now classed as functional may ultimately be traced to disturbances of the central nervous system. *General paresis* (a disorder characterized by progressive deterioration of behavior and mental ability) was classed as a functional psychosis until it was discovered to be the result of brain tissue destruction by the syphilis spirochete.

Nevertheless, it is practical to distinguish between those psychoses in which nervous system disturbances have been identified (the organic psychoses) and those in which physiological factors are unknown and environmental conditions are assumed to play a major role (the functional psychoses). We will limit our discussion to the functional psychoses; two of the most prevalent are *affective disorders* and *schizophrenia*.

Affective Disorders

Affective disorders are disturbances of *affect*, or mood. The person may be severely depressed, manic (wildly elated), or may alternate between periods of depression and elation. These mood changes are often so extreme that the individual requires hospitalization.

MANIC STATES In milder manic states, the person is energetic, enthusiastic, and full of self-confidence. He or she talks continually, rushes from one activity to another with little need of sleep, and makes grandiose plans with scant attention to their practicality. The behavior is similar in some respects to that of someone who is mildly intoxicated.

People in acute manic states behave more like the popular notion of a "raving maniac." They are extremely excited and must be constantly active. They may pace about, sing, shout, or pound on the walls for hours. They are angered by attempts to interfere with their activities and may become abusive. All impulses (including sexual ones) are immediately expressed in action or words. The individuals are confused, disoriented, and may experience delusions of great wealth, accomplishment, or power (see Figure 15-7). Tranquilizing drugs can usually reduce the intense excitement of the acute manic state, so that the visitor to a psychiatric hospital seldom sees the kind of raving and uncontrolled behavior that was observed some 30 years ago.

DEPRESSED STATES Depressed individuals' behavior is essentially the opposite. Their mental and physical activity is much slower than normal. Self-esteem is at its lowest ebb. They feel rejected and discouraged and may attempt suicide. In the most intense state of depression, patients are bedrid-

---

Fig. 15-7

MANIC REACTION

Robert B., fifty-six years old, was a dentist who for most of his twenty-five years of dental practice provided rather well for his wife and three daughters. Mrs. B. reported that there had been times when Robert displayed behavior similar to that which preceded his hospitalization, but that this was the worst she had ever seen.

About two weeks prior to hospitalization, the patient awoke one morning with the idea that he was the most gifted dental surgeon in his tri-state area; his mission then was to provide services for as many persons as possible so that they could benefit from his talents. Consequently, he decided to enlarge his two-chair practice to a twenty-chair one, and his plan was to reconstruct his two dental offices into twenty booths so that he could simultaneously attend to as many patients. That very day he drew up the plans for this arrangement and telephoned a number of remodelers and invited them to submit bids for the work. He also ordered the additional necessary dental equipment.

Toward the end of that day he became irritated with the "interminable delays" and, after he attended to his last patient, rolled up his sleeves and began to knock down the walls of his dental offices. When he discovered that he couldn't manage this chore with the sledge hammer he had purchased for this purpose earlier, he became frustrated and proceeded to smash his more destructible tools, washbasins, and X-ray equipment. He justified this behavior in his own mind by saying, "This junk is not suitable for the likes of me; it'll have to be replaced anyway."

He did not tell any of his family about these goings-on for about a week, and his wife started to get frantic telephone calls from patients whom he had turned away from his office. During this time, also, his wife realized something was "upsetting him" because he looked "haggard, wild-eyed, and rundown." He was in perpetual motion, and his speech was "overexcited." That evening Robert's wife mentioned the phone calls and his condition and she was subjected to a fifteen-minute tirade of "ranting and raving." She said later that the only reason he stopped shouting was because he became hoarse and barely audible.

After several more days of "mad goings-on," according to Mrs. B., she telephoned two of her married daughters for help and told them that their father was completely unreasonable and that he was beyond her ability to reach him. Her daughters, who lived within several minutes' drive, then visited their parents one evening and brought along their husbands. It turned out that bringing their spouses along was a fortunate happenstance because the father, after bragging about his sexual prowess, made aggressive advances toward his daughters. When his sons-in-law attempted to curtail this behavior, Robert assaulted them with a chair and had to be physically subdued. The police were then called and he was admitted to the hospital several hours later.

During the interview with Robert it was apparent that he was hyperactive and overwrought. He could not sit in his chair; instead he paced the office floor like a caged animal. Throughout his pacing he talked constantly about his frustrated plans and how his wife and two favorite daughters double-crossed him. It was also learned, both from him and subsequently from Mrs. B., that this was not the first episode of this sort and that he had a history of three prior hospitalizations.

He responded well to lithium treatment and was discharged within several weeks of admission to the hospital. (Kleinmuntz, 1974, p. 234)

---

den, indifferent to everything, have to be fed intravenously, and must be cared for by others.

The more severe the symptoms, the more likely it is that the depression will be diagnosed as psychotic, rather than neurotic. Psychotic depressions may also involve impaired perception of reality and delusions—usually feelings of extreme guilt and unworthiness.

CIRCULAR MANIC-DEPRESSIVE PSYCHOSIS In some cases, a person alternates cyclically between manic and depressive states, often with a period of normal behavior in between (see Figure 15-8). This circular pattern suggests that mania and depression are psychologically related. The elation and frantic activity of the manic state appear to be a last-ditch attempt to defend against

Fig. 15-8 Mood changes in manic-depressive psychosis
Descriptions of the patient's behavior are excerpted from the notes of hospital staff members. (Based on Jones and others, 1973, p. 301)

Depression Days 0 to 23	Looks sad, preoccupied, cries frequently. Expresses death wishes and suicidal thoughts. Isolated most of the time, indifferent to unit activities. Slow in speech and movements. Falls asleep, at times, in meetings.
Switch Day 24	Had a congenial, pleasant visit with family members, says she enjoyed herself. Does not appear depressed, talks easily with staff members.
Mania Days 25 to 31	This period characterized by two episodes of mania separated by a 5-day interval in which she appeared calmer and normally engaged in ward activities. Exhibited pressure of speech and flight of ideas on the morning of day 25. Actively showed recent purchases to everyone. Great deal of talk about money matters and how much she spends. Less active in the evening. Appeared in good spirits from days 26 to 30, was personable and talkative. Judged to be either euthymic or mildly hypomanic. Became hyperactive and combative on day 30 while on leave from the hospital. Returned early on day 31 apparently angry with her husband and staff members.
Depression Days 32 to 45	Looks sad, facial expression of pain and fear. Needs encouragement to initiate activities and to talk. Seclusive, indifferent to the environment.
Switch Day 46	Morning: Happy to see her family, had pleasant visit with them. Pleasant interactions with patients and staff. Evening: Calm, verbalized her good feelings for family visit. Regretted that she becomes manic but remarked that it helps pass the time and keeps her from being bored.
Mania Days 47 to 53	Day 47: Up all night, appeared in good spirits, superficial conversation. Dressed nicely for breakfast, talkative and seductive, moderately hyperactive. Less active in the evenings, appears happy. Needs close observation. Days 48, 49, and 50: Exhibits behavior similar to other manic episodes, such as riding up and down hall on wheel chair, fighting with staff, destroying valuable belongings. Escapes from unit, causing problems on other wards.

the underlying feelings of inadequacy and worthlessness that precipitate depression. The manic patient appears to be using the defense mechanisms of denial (denying the existence of every fact or thought that might cause depression) and reaction formation (expressing behavior opposite to his or her deep feelings). This reaction is not unlike that of a normal person who initiates a round of gay and busy activities in an attempt to forget problems.

Understanding Depression

PSYCHOANALYTIC THEORIES Psychoanalytic theories interpret depression as a *reaction to loss*. It might be the loss of a loved one, loss of status, or loss of the moral support provided by a group of friends. Whatever the nature of the loss, the depressed person reacts so intensely because the current situation reactivates a more traumatic loss that occurred in early childhood—namely, loss of the mother's affection. For some reason, the child's dependent needs for affection and loving care were not satisfied. A loss in later life causes the individual to *regress* to the helpless, dependent state he or she was in when the original loss occurred. Part of the depressed person's behavior thus represents a cry for love: a display of helplessness and an appeal for affection and security (White and Watt, 1973).

Psychoanalytic theories suggest that the depressed person's feelings of worthlessness and low self-esteem stem from a child-like need for parental approval. A small child's self-esteem depends on the approval and affection of the parents. But as a person matures, feelings of worth should come also from a sense of one's own accomplishments and effectiveness. The person prone to depression is one whose self-esteem depends primarily on external sources—the approval and support of others. When such support fails, the individual may be thrown into a state of depression (Rado, 1951).

Reaction to loss is complicated by angry feelings toward the deserting person. Psychoanalytic theories assume that people prone to depression have learned to repress hostile feelings for fear of alienating those on whom they depend for support. When things go wrong, they turn their anger inward and blame themselves. For example, a woman may feel extremely hostile toward the employer who fired her, but because angry feelings arouse anxiety they are turned inward. She uses the defense mechanism of projection; it is not she who is angry but others who are angry at her. She assumes they have good reason for rejecting her: she is incompetent and worthless.

Psychoanalytic theories of depression thus focus on loss, overdependence on external approval, and anger turned inward. They seem to provide a reasonable explanation for some of the behaviors shown by depressed individuals, but they are difficult to either prove or refute. For example, it would be next to impossible to prove that a traumatic loss of maternal affection (other than actual separation from the mother) occurs regularly in the histories of people who become depressed; few individuals can remember that far back, and what they do remember may well be a distortion of actual events.

Depressed persons do inhibit outward expression of anger (as indeed they inhibit all active responses), and they tend to blame themselves for their difficulties. But such inhibition and inward direction of aggression may be the result, rather than the cause, of depression.

LEARNING THEORIES Learning theories of depression focus on what is going on *now* in the individual's life rather than on early experiences. One approach assumes that depression stems from *reduced positive reinforcement.*

Depressed individuals feel unhappy and worthless because their environment fails to provide rewards for adaptive behavior. Many of the events that precipitate depression—for example, the death of a loved one, failure in one's job, and impaired health—involve a reduction in accustomed reinforcement.

Once people become depressed—sad, withdrawn, inactive—their main source of reinforcement is the sympathy and attention they receive from relatives and friends. Such attention may reinforce the very behaviors that are maladaptive (weeping, complaining, self-criticism, talking about suicide). But because it is tiresome to be around someone who refuses to cheer up, the depressed person's behavior eventually alienates even those who are close, producing further reduction in reinforcement, increased social isolation, and unhappiness.

A low rate of positive reinforcement reduces still further the individual's activities and the expression of behaviors that might be rewarded. Both activities and rewards decrease in a vicious cycle. Figure 15-9 is a schematic representation of the reduced-reinforcement theory of depression, showing how the various contributing factors are interrelated.

This theory is also difficult to prove: it would be a monumental task to count the number of reinforcements that individuals receive each day. However, some studies tend to confirm the hypothesis that depression may be related to low rates of positively reinforced behavior.

The reduced-reinforcement theory of depression is essentially noncognitive. It assumes that overt behavior depends on the way in which a person is rewarded and that changes in mood and thinking are a function of the overt behavior. A theory of depression that makes use of *both* learning and cognitive concepts is based on the phenomenon of *learned helplessness*, discussed in Chapter 14. According to this view, people become depressed when they *believe* that their actions make no difference in bringing about either pleasure or pain. Depression is a belief in one's own helplessness.

The concept of learned helplessness grew out of experiments with animals. As shown in Chapter 14, animals subjected to traumatic conditions that they are unable to avoid (electric shock or loud noise) develop signs of depression: apathy, decreased appetite, loss of sexual potency, and lack of normal aggressiveness. These symptoms are *not* found in animals subjected to traumatic conditions that can be avoided or terminated by an appropriate response

Fig. 15-9 A reduced-reinforcement model of depression
After Lewinsohn (1975)

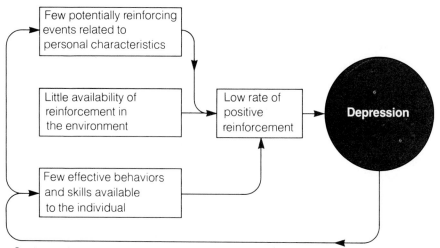

Social reinforcement for depression (sympathy, concern, and so on)

(Seligman, 1975). Learned helplessness has also been demonstrated with human subjects, and there is some evidence that learned helplessness plays a role in depression. For example, when depressed patients succeed at a task, they are more likely to explain their success in terms of "luck" than as a function of their own ability (Abramson and others, 1978).

The learned helplessness and the reduced-reinforcement theories of depression suggest that people who are frequently unable to obtain gratification or avoid pain by their own actions are likely to become depressed. Perhaps they never learned effective ways of responding, or perhaps the difficulties they confronted were insurmountable. Individuals who resist depression, or who recover from it very quickly, may have been more successful in controlling their sources of suffering and pleasure and may, as a result, be more optimistic about the future, despite temporary setbacks. Experiments support this view. Animals that have had prior experience in avoiding or escaping trauma through their own responses do not develop learned helplessness when confronted with inescapable trauma. They return to adaptive responses once the unavoidable situation is over (Seligman, 1975).

GENETIC AND BIOCHEMICAL FACTORS A tendency to develop affective disorders may be inherited. The evidence is particularly strong for circular manic-depressive psychoses. Children or siblings of individuals diagnosed as manic-depressive are 10 times more likely than members of the general population to also be diagnosed as manic-depressive (Rosenthal, 1970).

The specific role genetic factors play in certain types of affective disorders is far from clear. Presumably, genetic factors exert their influence by disrupting certain physiological processes of the body. Research on the physiological changes that might cause depression has concentrated on biochemical changes. The most promising findings center around the following three areas:

1 *Electrolytes.* Electrolytes are chemicals important in the transmission of electrical impulses. As we noted in Chapter 2, the firing of a nerve cell is an electrochemical process that depends on the proper concentration of sodium and potassium ions on either side of the cell membrane. Depressed patients tend to retain more sodium (and probably more potassium) than people who are not depressed, and, when depression subsides, sodium retention is reduced (Depue and Evans, 1976). An imbalance of body electrolytes affects the excitability of the nervous system and may play a role in depression.

2 *Neurotransmitters.* Neurotransmitters are chemicals involved in the transmission of nerve impulses across the synapse from one neuron to another (see Chapter 2). A number of chemicals serve as neurotransmitters in different parts of the nervous system, and normal behavior requires a careful balance among them. Two that are believed to be important in depression are *norepinephrine* and *serotonin*. Norepinephrine is a transmitter at synapses of the autonomic nervous system and is also secreted by the adrenal glands. Serotonin influences neurons in the hypothalamus and limbic system. There is some evidence that depression is associated with a deficiency of one or both of these neurotransmitters and that mania is associated with an excess (Berger, 1978). Drugs that are effective in relieving depression increase the availability of both norepinephrine and serotonin in the nervous system; lithium, a drug that has been strikingly effective in treating manic patients, appears to decrease the production of norepinephrine.

3 *Hormones.* The cortex of the adrenal glands secretes a number of important hormones called steroids. One of these, cortisol, is released in large

amounts when a person is under stress. Increased levels of cortisol have been found in the blood of depressed patients, while a decrease is associated with mania. A synthetic form of cortisol (cortisone) is used in treating allergic reactions and arthritis; people treated with cortisone over a period of time sometimes develop severe depression.

The human nervous system is so incredibly complex that the biochemical changes may be interrelated in many ways. For example, increased secretion of steroids could be related to retention of sodium within the nerve cells, which could, in turn, affect the synthesis of certain neurotransmitters, including norepinephrine and serotonin (Flach and Draghi, 1975).

There is no doubt that affective disorders involve biochemical changes in the central nervous system, but the question remains as to whether the physiological changes produce or accompany psychological changes. Two examples will illustrate the nature of the problem. People who deliberately behave as if they were experiencing a manic episode show changes in brain chemistry similar to those found among actual manic patients (Post and others, 1973). Depressed individuals do excrete less sodium in their urine than normal individuals, but sodium concentration within the body cells depends partly on activity level—during exercise, people excrete more sodium than during periods of rest. Thus, the changes in mineral metabolism found among depressed patients may well be the result of decreased activity, rather than the cause of their depression.

VULNERABILITY AND ACCUMULATED STRESS All of the theories we have discussed have something important to say about the nature of depression. Inherited physiological characteristics may predispose an individual to extreme mood changes. Early experiences—the loss of parental affection and/or the inability to gain gratification through one's own efforts—may also make a person *vulnerable* to depression in later life. The kinds of stressful events reported by depressed patients as precipitating their disorder are usually within the range of normal life experiences; that is, they are experiences most people handle without becoming abnormally depressed. Thus, a concept of vulnerability is helpful in understanding why some people develop depression when confronted with a particular stressful experience and others do not.

Schizophrenia

Schizophrenia is the label given to a group of psychotic disorders characterized by distortion of reality, withdrawal from social interaction, and disorganization of thought, perception, and emotion. The word *schizophrenia* is derived from the Greek words *schizein* ("to split") and *phren* ("mind"). The split does not refer to multiple personalities (see Chapter 6), but rather to a fragmenting of the thought processes.

Schizophrenia occurs in all cultures, even those that are remote from the stresses of modern civilization, and appears to have plagued humanity throughout history. In the United States, about 6 out of every 1,000 people receive care for schizophrenia in any given year. Because the disorder tends to reoccur and because some patients become chronically incapacitated, about half of all psychiatric hospital beds are occupied by patients diagnosed as schizophrenic (Kramer, 1976).

Schizophrenia usually appears in young adulthood; the peak of incidence is between ages 25 and 35. Sometimes the disorder develops slowly—a gradual process of increasing seclusiveness and inappropriate behavior (see Figure

Fig. 15-10

SCHIZOPHRENIA

A. J. was always extremely shy and as a small child would run away and hide when visitors came to the house. He had one or two boy friends, but as a teenager he never associated with girls and did not enjoy school parties or social functions. He had few interests and did not engage in sports. His school record was mediocre, and he left high school at the end of his sophomore year. The principal felt that he "could have done better" and remarked about his "queer" and seclusive behavior. Shortly before leaving school his shyness increased considerably. He expressed fears that he was different from other boys and complained that the other children called him names. He became untidy, refusing to wash or wear clean clothes.

After leaving school, A. J. worked at a number of odd jobs but was irregular in performing his duties and never held any one job longer than a few weeks. He finally became unemployable and stayed home, becoming more and more seclusive and withdrawn from community and family life. He would sit with his head bowed most of the time, refused to eat with the family, and when visitors came would hide under the bed. He further neglected his appearance, refusing to bathe or get a haircut. He occasionally made "strange" remarks and frequently covered his face with his hands because he felt he looked "funny."

The psychiatrist who interviewed the boy when he was brought to a local mental hygiene clinic at the age of seventeen noted frequent grimacing and silly and inappropriate smiling but found that he was correctly oriented in terms of time and place and could answer questions coherently in a flat tone of voice. He complained of having recurring thoughts but denied any hallucinations or delusions. He expressed a wish for help so that he could go back to work.

A. J. was admitted to the state neuropsychiatric hospital with a diagnosis of schizophrenia. Testing with the Wechsler Adult Intelligence Scale showed that he had average intelligence (full scale IQ 96) but indicated the beginnings of some intellectual impairment. The results of the Rorschach test reinforced the schizophrenic diagnosis. (Rabin, 1947, pp. 23–30)

15-10). Sometimes schizophrenia has a sudden onset, marked by intense confusion and emotional turmoil. Such cases are usually precipitated by a period of stress in individuals whose lives have tended toward isolation, self-preoccupation, and feelings of insecurity. Whether the disorder develops slowly or suddenly, the signs are many and varied. The primary characteristics can be summarized under the following headings, although not every person diagnosed as schizophrenic will show all of them.

DISTURBANCES OF THOUGHT AND ATTENTION Whereas the affective disorders are characterized by disturbances of mood, schizophrenia is characterized by disturbances of thought. The following excerpt from a patient's writings illustrates how difficult it is to understand schizophrenic thinking.

> If things turn by rotation of agriculture or levels in regards and timed to everything; I am re-fering to a previous document when I made some remarks that were facts also tested and there is another that concerns my daughter she has a lobed bottom right ear, her name being Mary Lou. . . . Much of abstraction has been left unsaid and undone in this product/milk syrup, and others, due to economics, differentials, subsidies, bankruptcy, tools, buildings, bonds, national stocks, foundation craps, weather, trades, government in levels of breakages and fuses in electronics too all formerly stated not necessarily factuated. (Maher, 1966, p. 395)

By themselves, the words and some of the phrases make sense, but they are meaningless in relation to each other. The juxtaposition of unrelated words and the idiosyncratic word associations (sometimes called a "word salad") are characteristic of schizophrenic writing and speech.

The thought disorder in schizophrenia appears to reflect a general difficulty in "filtering out" irrelevant stimuli. Most of us are able to selectively focus our attention. From the mass of incoming sensory information, we attend to those stimuli relevant to the task at hand and ignore the rest. The person suffering from schizophrenia appears unable to screen out irrelevant stimuli or to distinguish relevant inputs. He or she is perceptually receptive to many stimuli at the same time and has trouble making sense out of the profusion of inputs, as the following statement by a schizophrenic patient illustrates.

> I can't concentrate. It's diversion of attention that troubles me. I am picking up different conversations. It's like being a transmitter. The sounds are coming through to me, but I feel my mind cannot cope with everything. It's difficult to concentrate on any one sound. (McGhie and Chapman, 1961, p. 104)

The inability to "filter out" irrelevant stimuli shows up in many aspects of the person's thinking. The disjointed nature of schizophrenic speech reflects the intrusion of irrelevant associations. Often one word will set off a string of associations, as illustrated by the following sentence, written by a schizophrenic patient.

> I may be a "Blue Baby" but "Social Baby" not, but yet a blue heart baby could be in the Blue Book published before the war.

This patient had suffered from heart trouble and may have started out to say "I was a blue baby." The association of "blue baby" with "blue blood" in the sense of social status may have prompted the interruption of "Social Baby not." And the last phrase shows the interplay between the two meanings: "yet a blue baby could have been in the [Society] Blue Book" (Maher, 1966, p. 413).

DISTURBANCES OF PERCEPTION During acute schizophrenic episodes, people often report that the world appears *different* to them; noises seem louder, colors more intense. Their own bodies may no longer appear the same; hands may seem too large or too small, legs overly extended, eyes dislocated in the face. Some patients fail to recognize themselves in a mirror, or they see their reflection as a triple image. During the acute stage of schizophrenia, many patients go through periods when they are unable to perceive wholes; for instance, looking at nurses or physicians, they cannot see them as persons but can perceive only parts—a nose, the left eye, an arm, and so on. The drawing in Figure 15-11 shows this fragmentation of the whole.

DISTURBANCES OF AFFECT Schizophrenic individuals usually fail to show "normal" or appropriate emotional responses. They often are withdrawn and unresponsive in situations that should make them sad or happy. For example, a man may show no emotional response when informed that his daughter has cancer. This blunting or flattening of emotional expression, however, often conceals inner turmoil, and the person may erupt with angry outbursts.

Sometimes the individual expresses emotions that are inappropriate to the situation or the thought being expressed. For example, a patient may smile while speaking of tragic events. Since our emotions are influenced by cognitive processes, it is not surprising that disorganized thoughts and perceptions are accompanied by changes in emotional responses.

> Half the time I am talking about one thing and thinking about half a dozen other things at the same time. It must look queer to people when

Fig. 15-11 Perceptual fragmentation
This drawing by a schizophrenic woman shows the difficulty she has perceiving the face as a whole. (Arieti, 1974)

I laugh about something that has got nothing to do with what I am talking about, but they don't know what's going on inside and how much of it is running around in my head. You see I might be talking about something quite serious to you and other things come into my head at the same time that are funny and this makes me laugh. If I could only concentrate on one thing at the one time I wouldn't look half so silly. (McGhie and Chapman, 1961, pp. 109–10)

WITHDRAWAL FROM REALITY During schizophrenic episodes, the individual tends to withdraw from interaction with others and become absorbed in his or her inner thoughts and fantasies. This state of self-absorption is known as *autism* (from the Greek word *autos*, meaning "self"). As the quotation above suggests, inappropriate emotional behavior can sometimes be explained by the fact that the person may be reacting to what is going on in his or her private world rather than to external events. Self-absorption may be so intense that the person may not know the day or month or where he or she is.

In acute cases of schizophrenia, the withdrawal from reality is temporary. In chronic cases, it may become more enduring and progress to the point where the individual is completely unresponsive to external events, remaining silent and immobile for days and sometimes requiring the same care as an infant.

DELUSIONS AND HALLUCINATIONS In most cases, distorted thought processes and perceptions are accompanied by delusions. The most common are beliefs that external forces are trying to control one's thoughts and actions (delusions of influence) or that one is being threatened or plotted against by certain people or groups (delusions of persecution). Less common are beliefs that one is a powerful and important person (delusions of grandeur).

A person with persecutory delusions is called *paranoid*. He or she may become suspicious of friends and relatives, fear being poisoned, complain of being watched, followed, and talked about. So-called "motiveless" crimes, in which an individual attacks or kills another for no apparent cause, are sometimes committed by people who are later diagnosed as suffering from paranoid schizophrenia. Sirhan Sirhan, who assassinated Senator Robert F. Kennedy, is an example.

Hallucinations are also frequent. They may occur independently or as part of a delusional belief. Auditory hallucinations are the most common—usually voices telling the person what to do or commenting on his or her actions. They may be the voices of relatives, "enemies," or some unknown power. They may emanate from the electrical sockets, the telephone, the turned-off television set, or simply from the air. The first time the individual experiences an auditory hallucination, he or she may be frightened and unbelieving: "This can't be real, it must be my imagination." Such a reaction indicates a good prognosis. More often the person accepts the voices as real; in more chronic cases, they become an important part of his or her life (Arieti, 1974).

Visual hallucinations also occur, for example, strange or frightening creatures or a heavenly being. Hallucinations in other senses—a bad odor emanating from one's body, the taste of poison in one's food, the feeling of being touched or pricked by needles—occur infrequently. Mark Vonnegut, in writing about his own schizophrenic experience, describes his first visual hallucination.

And then one night, . . . as I was trying to get to sleep, . . . I started listening to and feeling my heart beat. Suddenly I became terribly frightened that it would stop. And from out of nowhere came an incredibly wrinkled, iridescent face. Starting as a small point infinitely distant,

Rigidly held position characteristic of some schizophrenic patients

"*What really annoys me is that they're not even my demons—they're Goya's and Hieronymus Bosch's and Bruegel's.*"

it rushed forward, becoming infinitely huge. I could see nothing else. My heart had stopped. The moment stretched forever. I tried to make the face go away but it mocked me. I had somehow gained control over my heartbeat but I didn't know how to use it. I was holding my life in my hands and was powerless to stop it from dripping through my fingers. I tried to look the face in the eyes and realized I had left all familiar ground.

He, she, or whatever . . . seemed not to like me much. But the worst of it was it didn't stop coming. It had no respect for my personal space, no inclination to maintain a conversational distance. When I could easily make out all its features, when it and I were more or less on the same scale, when I thought there was maybe a foot or two between us, it had actually been hundreds of miles away, and it kept coming and coming till I was lost somewhere in some pore in its nose and it still kept coming. . . .

There was nothing at all unreal about that face. Its concreteness made the Rock of Gibraltar look like so much cotton candy. I hoped I could get enough rest simply by lying motionless. In any event, the prospect of not sleeping frightened me far less than the possibility of losing contact with the world. (Vonnegut, 1975, pp. 96–98)

The signs of schizophrenia are many and varied, indicating that we are talking about a group of disorders that may have several different causes. Trying to make sense out of the variety of symptoms is complicated by the fact that some may result directly from the disorder while others may result from a reaction to the restrictive and often boring life in a mental hospital.

Research on the Causes of Schizophrenia

Research on the causes of schizophrenia has focused on genetic, biochemical, and psychological factors. We will examine some of the research on each.

Genetic Factors

There is little doubt that schizophrenia has a genetic component, although experts differ in their opinion of its importance. If there is a hereditary component to the disorder, then identical twins, who develop from the same egg (*monozygotic, or MZ, twins*), will be more apt to *both* turn out to be schizophrenic than fraternal twins, who develop from different eggs (*dizygotic, or DZ, twins*). As you can see from Table 15-3, the *concordance rate*—the percentage of pairs in which both twins are diagnosed schizophrenic—is higher for monozygotic (MZ) than for dizygotic (DZ) twins.

The MZ twin of a schizophrenic may not be diagnosed as schizophrenic, but there is a high probability that he or she will be abnormal in certain respects. A review of a number of studies suggests that only about 13 percent of the MZ twins of schizophrenics can be regarded as normal (Heston, 1970). The presence of schizophrenic-like disabilities among the relatives of schizophrenics is so striking that the term *schizoid* has been coined to refer to those who resemble the schizophrenic in many traits but whose symptoms are not severe enough to warrant the diagnosis of schizophrenia. When the presence of both schizophrenia and schizoidia in families is studied, the evidence of a genetic basis is even more striking, as shown in Table 15-4.

INVESTIGATOR	COUNTRY	PERCENTAGE OF CONCORDANCE	
		MZ TWINS	DZ TWINS (SAME SEX)
Early Studies			
Luxenburger (1928)	Germany	58	0
Rosanoff and others (1934)	U.S.	61	13
Essen-Moller (1941)	Sweden	64	15
Kallmann (1946)	U.S.	69	11
Slater (1953)	U.K.	65	14
Inouye (1961)	Japan	60	18
Later Studies			
Kringlen (1967)	Norway	45	15
Fischer and others (1969)	Denmark	56	26
Tienari (1971)	Finland	35	13
Allen and others (1972)	U.S.	43	9
Gottesman and Shields (1972)	U.K.	58	12

Source: Gottesman and Shields (1973)

TABLE 15-3
Studies of schizophrenia in twins
The number of twin sets varied from 19 MZ and 13 DZ in the Essen-Moller study to 174 MZ and 296 DZ in the Kallman study. Concordant pairs are those in which both members are schizophrenic. The later studies, reported in the lower half of the table, used a more carefully controlled method for diagnosing schizophrenia, which probably accounts for their slightly lower rates for MZ twins.

It can be argued, of course, that the clustering of schizophrenia and schizoidia in families may result solely from environmental factors. The schizophrenic parent may transmit the disorder to the offspring by means of faulty child-rearing practices rather than faulty genes. However, a study of children born to schizophrenic mothers, separated from their parents shortly after birth, and raised in foster homes provides additional support for the genetic hypothesis. They were assessed in adulthood and compared with a control group born to normal parents and reared in foster homes. The incidence of schizophrenia and schizoidia was much higher among those individuals whose biological mothers were schizophrenic (Heston, 1970).

Although the evidence favors a hereditary factor in the origin of schizophrenia, we do not know how this susceptibility is transmitted. And it is clear that environmental factors play a significant role. If the disorder depended solely on heredity, then MZ twins would show 100 percent concordance.

RELATIONSHIP	SCHIZOPHRENIA	SCHIZOIDIA	TOTAL: SCHIZOID AND SCHIZOPHRENIC
Relatives of Schizophrenics			
Children	16.4	32.6	49.0
Siblings	14.3	31.5	45.8
Parents	9.2	34.8	44.0
Both Parents Schizophrenic			
Children	33.9	32.2	66.1

Source: Heston (1970), summarizing other studies

TABLE 15-4
Percentages of first-degree relatives of schizophrenics found to be schizophrenic or schizoid
The incidence of schizophrenia and schizophrenic-like disabilities among (1) relatives of schizophrenics and (2) children both of whose parents are schizophrenic.

Biochemical Factors

If there is a genetic component to schizophrenia, presumably it manifests itself through some sort of defect or imbalance in body chemistry. Investigators concerned with this possibility have searched for products in the blood or urine of people suffering from schizophrenia that distinguish them from normal individuals. A number of such differences have been found, each promising a "breakthrough" in understanding the cause of schizophrenia. Unfortunately, many of these discoveries have not been consistently replicated or have been found to be related to some condition of the schizophrenic individual other than his or her disorder. For example, one study found that schizophrenics had increased levels of a chemical called ceruloplasmin in their blood (Akerfeldt, 1957). But subsequent studies showed that this was due to a deficiency of vitamin C—the result of poor appetite and/or poor hospital diet. This example illustrates one of the major problems in the search for biochemical explanations. A biochemical abnormality found in schizophrenic patients but not in control subjects may be the *cause* of the disorder, the *result* of the disorder, or it may stem from some *aspect of treatment.* For example, a schizophrenic's first admission to a hospital is often preceded by weeks of intense panic and agitation that undoubtedly produce a number of bodily changes. These changes—related to lack of sleep, inadequate diet, and general stress—cannot be considered the cause of the disorder. Other biochemical abnormalities may be related to treatment. Most schizophrenic patients take tranquilizing drugs, traces of which may remain in the blood stream for some time. Some of the conditions of prolonged hospitalization—changed diet, inactivity—may also produce biochemical changes.

All of these factors compound the problem of finding differences between schizophrenic and control subjects that tell us something about the origin of schizophrenia. Despite such obstacles, there are several promising biochemical theories of schizophrenia, all having to do with an abnormality in the metabolism of neurotransmitters. We will mention only one theory.

Two important neurotransmitters are dopamine and norepinephrine (which has also been associated with depression). Neural pathways that use one or both of these transmitters appear to play a critical role in survival-related activities, such as eating or reacting with aggression when under stress (Antelman and Caggiula, 1977). Dopamine also appears to be a precursor of norepinephrine; that is, through the action of a certain enzyme, some brain dopamine is converted into norepinephrine. The *dopamine hypothesis* proposes that schizophrenia results from an excess of brain dopamine, either because schizophrenics produce more dopamine or because they are deficient in the enzyme that converts dopamine to norepinephrine. Impetus for research in this area came from the discovery that drug users who overdose on amphetamines, or "speed," develop psychotic behavior that resembles that of paranoid schizophrenia (Snyder and others, 1974). When amphetamines are given to schizophrenic patients, their symptoms become worse.

Drugs that are effective in relieving the symptoms of schizophrenia (such as chlorpromazine and reserpine) appear to block dopamine receptors, thus decreasing dopamine activity in the brain (Randrup and Munkvard, 1972). The same drugs also relieve the symptoms of amphetamine-induced psychoses.

If schizophrenics do have a faulty dopamine metabolism, how is it related to their symptoms? One speculation is that the brain areas primarily affected are the reward centers in the hypothalamus that provide reinforcement and feel-

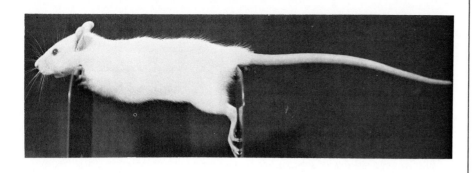

Fig. 15-12 Schizophrenia in a rat?
Thirty minutes after the injection of an endorphin, this rat is sufficiently rigid to remain suspended between two metal bookends. The rat's body can be molded into various abnormal positions that are maintained indefinitely. Such postures are similar to those exhibited by some schizophrenic patients. Within seconds after injection of a substance that blocks the endorphin, the animal returns to normal. (Bloom and others, 1976)

ings of pleasure when stimulated (see Chapter 7). In normal individuals, the norepinephrine that stimulates nerve cells in this region is presumably metabolized from brain dopamine. It may be that in schizophrenics, because of a deficiency of the enzyme that converts dopamine to norepinephrine, much of the dopamine remains unconverted and the reward center does not function properly. A defective reinforcement system could (1) diminish ability to experience pleasure and (2) disrupt goal-directed activity. This would explain the inability to experience pleasure and the difficulty in maintaining goal-directed behavior (particularly in terms of sustained thought processes) characteristic of schizophrenia (Wise and Stein, 1973).

Although a fair amount of indirect evidence supports the dopamine hypothesis, there is no direct evidence. To date, no one has proved that schizophrenics produce more dopamine than normal individuals. A large number of chemicals serve as neurotransmitters, and schizophrenia probably involves a complex interaction among several of them. We need to know more about how these neurotransmitters influence behavior, how they are affected by stress, and how they interact with each other before we will have any clear understanding of the biochemical nature of schizophrenia.

Currently, interest is focused on what appears to be a new and important group of neurotransmitters, called *endorphins*. Endorphins are morphine-like substances that occur naturally in the brain, particularly in the hypothalamus. They mimic the effects of opiates (such as heroin and morphine), and they appear to play an important role in emotion and behavior. Preliminary reports indicate that various endorphins injected into rats produce behaviors similar to some of the symptoms of schizophrenia (see Figure 15-12). When a substance that blocks the action of endorphins is given to schizophrenic patients, their hallucinations decrease and they are able to think more clearly (Gunne and others, 1977).

Whether this new area of research will ultimately provide a biochemical theory of schizophrenia remains to be seen. But even if an inherited predisposition to certain biochemical abnormalities can be demonstrated, psychological factors will probably determine whether the individual actually develops schizophrenia.

Psychological Factors

Research on psychological factors in the origins of schizophrenia has focused on early child-rearing practices and interpersonal relationships in the home. Studies in which parents of schizophrenics were interviewed or patients were questioned about their early home life have yielded conflicting results. Mothers have been found to be both overprotective and rejecting, neglectful and overly involved with their offspring, too restrictive and too permissive. Fathers of schizophrenics have tended to be characterized as weak and ineffectual or aloof and uninvolved with their children.

Most studies that attempt to relate early child-care practices to the development of schizophrenia fail to provide a control group of parents whose children did not become schizophrenic. Hence, it is not clear whether the behavior of the parents of schizophrenics actually differs from that of other parents. Furthermore, in those studies that do have adequate controls, it is difficult to determine whether the parents' attitudes caused the schizophrenia or whether the child was schizophrenic to begin with and the parents' behavior was in response to this abnormality.

Despite these qualifications, disturbed home life and early trauma are frequently found in the background of schizophrenics. The early death of one or both parents, emotionally disturbed parents whose behavior is irrational and inconsistent, and discord and strife between the parents are all factors found with much greater than normal frequency in the background of schizophrenics. The home environments are often marked by intense conflict, with both parents trying to dominate and devaluate the other, or by a very skewed marital relationship, in which the more disturbed parent dominates the family life (Lidz and others, 1965). A study of monozygotic twins, only one member of which developed schizophrenia despite the fact that they were raised in the same family, found that the schizophrenic twin identified more strongly with the parent who was psychologically less healthy (Mosher and others, 1971).

Research efforts have failed to reveal any single pattern of family interaction that leads to schizophrenia; stressful childhoods of various kinds may contribute to the disorder. In general, the more stressful the childhood, the more severe the schizophrenic disorder (Rosenthal and others, 1975).

Vulnerability and Stress

Most individuals who have experienced a disturbing and stressful childhood do *not* develop schizophrenia (although they may develop other psychological disorders). There is undoubtedly an interaction between genetic predisposition and family environment. Some individuals who are eventually labeled "schizophrenic" probably start life with a hereditary predisposition to the disorder; most likely it takes the form of a defect in the metabolism of certain neurotransmitters. But it seems unlikely that heredity alone can account for schizophrenia. The situation may be similar to that of allergies: there is an inherited predisposition to allergic sensitivities, but certain environmental events are necessary to trigger the reaction. The controversial issue is whether schizophrenia can result from a stressful childhood in the absence of an inherited predisposition. Those who advocate an extreme hereditary viewpoint maintain that all individuals who have an inherited predisposition will eventually become schizophrenic, regardless of the nature of the early family environment. A stressful childhood will lead to an early and more severe illness. Those raised in a favorable family situation will not develop the disorder until they encounter stress later in life; their illness will be less severe and more easily reversible. Researchers who emphasize the role of the environment point to the variety and complexity of schizophrenic symptoms as evidence that we are dealing not with a single disorder but with a group of disorders, which have some symptoms in common. Consequently, there may be a number of causative agents. In some cases, inherited physiological or biochemical weaknesses are primarily responsible for the schizophrenic symptoms; in others, environmental factors play the major role.

Personality Disorders

Personality disorders are a group of behavior patterns that are maladaptive more from society's viewpoint than in terms of the individual's own discomfort or unhappiness. The person fails to behave in socially approved ways because he or she lacks either the motivation or the skills necessary to do so. Personality disorders are distinguished from neuroses and psychoses in that they are more often longstanding patterns of maladaptive behavior, rather than reactions to conflict or stress. But this distinction is largely a matter of degree, as is true of most attempts to categorize individuals.

Personality disorders have been called a "wastebasket" category because they include such a wide variety of behaviors—alcoholism, drug dependency, "immature" or dependent personalities, and psychopathic personalities are among them. We will restrict our discussion here to the psychopathic personality and will discuss alcoholism and drug dependence in the next section. Many factors can lead to dependence on alcohol and other drugs; to call such dependency a personality disorder oversimplifies the problems.

Psychopathic Personality

Psychopathic personalities are people who have no sense of responsibility or morality and no concern or affection for others; their behavior is determined almost entirely by their own needs. In other words, they lack a *conscience*. Whereas the average person realizes at an early age that there are some restrictions on behavior and that pleasures must sometimes be postponed in consideration of the needs of others, psychopathic individuals seldom consider any but their own desires. They behave impulsively, seek immediate gratification of their needs, and cannot tolerate frustration.

The term *antisocial personality* is sometimes used to describe such persons. We prefer the term psychopathic personality (or more simply *psychopath*) because most people who commit antisocial acts do not meet the characteristics described above. Antisocial behavior results from a number of causes (for example, membership in a delinquent gang or criminal subculture, need for attention and status, loss of contact with reality, and inability to control impulses). And most juvenile delinquents and adult criminals have some concern for others (for family or gang members) and some code of moral conduct (You don't squeal on a friend). Psychopaths, in contrast, have little feeling for anyone but themselves and seem to experience little guilt or remorse, no matter how much suffering their behavior may cause others.

Other characteristics of the psychopathic personality include great facility in lying, a need for thrills and excitement with little concern for possible injury, and an inability to alter behavior as a consequence of punishment. Those who work with psychopaths are impressed by the fact that they are often attractive, intelligent, and charming people who are quite facile in manipulating others—in other words, good "con artists." Their facade of competence and sincerity wins them promising job opportunities, but they have little staying power. Their restlessness and impulsivity soon lead them into an escapade that reveals their true nature—accumulating debts, deserting their families, or committing crimes. When caught, the psychopath's declarations of repentance are so convincing that he or she often escapes punishment and is given another chance. But they seldom live up to these expectations; what they say has little relation to what they do (see Figure 15-13).

The two characteristics considered most diagnostic of a psychopathic

Fig. 15-13

PSYCHOPATHIC PERSONALITY

A forty-year-old man was convicted of check forgery and embezzlement. He was arrested with a young woman, age eighteen, whom he had married bigamously some months before the arrest. She was unaware of the existence of any previous marriage. The subject in this case had already been convicted for two previous bigamous marriages and for forty other cases of passing fraudulent checks.

The circumstances of his arrest illustrate the impulsivity and lack of insight characteristic of many psychopaths. He had gotten a job managing a small restaurant; the absentee owner who lived in a neighboring town arranged to call at the end of each week to check on progress and collect the income. The subject was provided with living quarters over the restaurant, a small salary, and percentage of the cash register receipts. At the end of the first week the subject took all the money (having avoided banking it nightly as he had been instructed) and departed shortly before the employer arrived; he left a series of vulgar messages scribbled on the walls saying he had taken the money because the salary was "too low." He found lodgings with "his wife" a few blocks from the restaurant and made no effort to escape detection. He was arrested a few days later.

During the inquiry it emerged that he had spent the past few months cashing checks in department stores at various cities. He would make out the check and send his wife in to cash it; he commented that her genuine innocence of the fact that he had no bank account made her very effective in not arousing suspicion. He did not trouble to use a false name when signing checks or when making the bigamous marriage, yet seemed surprised at the speed with which the police discovered him.

Inquiry into the man's past history revealed that he had been well educated (mostly in private schools) and his parents were financially well off. They had planned for him to go to college but his academic record was not good enough (although on examination he proved to have superior intelligence). Failing to get into college he started work as an insurance salesman trainee and proceeded to do very well. He was a distinguished-looking young man and an exceptionally fluent speaker.

Just as it appeared that he could anticipate a successful career in the insurance business, he ran into trouble because he failed to turn in the checks that customers had given him to pay their initial premiums. He admitted to having cashed these checks, spending the money mostly on clothes and li-

quor. It apparently did not occur to him that the company's accounting system would quickly discern embezzlement of this kind. In fact, he expressed amused indignation at the company's failure to realize that he intended to pay back the money from his salary. No legal action was taken, but he was requested to resign, and his parents made good the missing money.

At this point he enlisted in the Army and was sent to Officer Candidate School, graduating as a second lieutenant. He was assigned to an infantry unit where he soon got into trouble, progressing from minor infractions (drunk on duty, smuggling women into his quarters) to cashing fraudulent checks. He was court-martialed and given a dishonorable discharge. From then on his life followed a pattern of finding a woman to support him (with or without marriage), and then running off with her money to the next woman when life became too tedious.

At his trial, where he was sentenced to five years imprisonment, he gave a long and articulate speech, pleading clemency for the young woman who was being tried with him, expressing repentance for having ruined her life, and stating that he was glad to have the opportunity to repay society for his crimes. (Maher, 1966, pp. 214–15)

personality disorder are "lovelessness" (the inability to feel any empathy for, or loyalty to, another person) and "guiltlessness" (the inability to feel any remorse for one's own actions, no matter how reprehensible).

Understanding Psychopathic Personalities

What factors contribute to the development of the psychopathic personality? We might expect psychopathic individuals to come from homes in which they received no discipline or training in moral behavior. But the answer is not that simple. Although some psychopaths do come from neighborhoods where antisocial behavior may actually be reinforced and where adult criminals may serve as models for personality development, many more come from "good" homes, and their parents are prominent and respected members of the community.

There is no well-supported theory of psychopathy; many factors are involved that may vary from case to case. Current research focuses on biological determinants and on the qualities of the parent-child relationship that reinforce psychopathic styles of coping.

BIOLOGICAL FACTORS   The clinical impression that the psychopathic individual experiences little anxiety about future discomforts or punishments has been supported by experimental studies. One study compared two groups of adolescent male delinquents selected from the detention unit of a juvenile court: one group had been diagnosed psychopathic personality disorder and the other "adjustment reaction of adolescence." The experimenters tested galvanic skin response (GSR, see p. 328) under stress. Dummy electrodes were attached to each subject's leg, and he was told that in 10 minutes he would be given a very strong but not harmful shock. (A large clock was visible so that the subject knew precisely when the shock was supposed to occur; no shock was actually administered.) The two groups showed no difference in GSR measures during periods of rest or in response to auditory or visual stimulation. However, during the 10 minutes of shock anticipation, the nonpsychopathic group showed significantly more tension than the psychopathic group, and at the moment when the clock indicated shock was due, most of the nonpsychopathic delinquents showed an abrupt drop in skin resistance (indicating a sharp increase in anxiety); *none* of the psychopaths showed this reaction (Lippert and Senter, 1966).

Other studies in prisons have shown that psychopaths do not learn to avoid shocks as quickly as normal or neurotic individuals do, nor evidence as much autonomic nervous system activity as other prisoners under a variety of conditions (Lykken, 1957; Hare, 1970). These findings have led to the hypothesis that psychopathic individuals may have been born with an *underreactive autonomic nervous system;* this would explain why they seem to require so much excitement and why they fail to respond normally to the threats of danger that deter most people from antisocial acts. Interpretations must be made with caution, however. It is possible that psychopaths view experimental situations as something of a game, and they may try to play it "extra cool" by attempting to control their responses.

PARENTAL INFLUENCES   Psychoanalytic theory assumes that the development of a conscience, or superego, depends on an affectionate relationship with an adult during the early childhood years. Normal children internalize their parents' values (which generally reflect the values of society) because they want to be like them and fear the loss of their love if they do not behave in accordance with parental values. A child who receives no love from either parent does not fear its loss. He or she does not identify with the rejecting parents and does not internalize their rules. Reasonable as this seems, it does not fit all of the data. Many rejected children do not become psychopathic personalities, and some psychopaths reveal a background of childhood indulgence.

A social learning theory explanation focuses on the kind of models the parents provide and the kind of behavior they reward. According to this view, a child may develop into a psychopath if he or she learns that punishment can be avoided by being charming, lovable, and repentant. A child who is consistently able to avoid punishment by claiming to be sorry and promising "never to do it again" may learn that it is not the deed that counts but one's charm and ability to act repentant. And if the same child is indulged in other respects—never

Mental Disorders

How should the law treat a mentally disturbed person who commits a criminal act? This question is of great concern to social scientists, to members of the legal profession, and to individuals who work with criminal offenders.

In 1724, an English court maintained that a man was not responsible for an act if "he doth not know what he is doing, no more than . . . a wild beast." Most standards of legal responsibility, however, have been based on the M'Naghten decision of 1843. M'Naghten, a Scotsman, suffered the paranoid delusion that he was being persecuted by the English prime minister, Sir Robert Peel. In an attempt to kill Peel, he mistakenly shot Peel's secretary. All involved in the trial were convinced by M'Naghten's senseless ramblings that he was insane. He was judged not responsible by reasons of insanity and sent to a mental hospital, where he remained until his death. But Queen Victoria was not pleased by the verdict—apparently she felt that political assassinations should not be taken lightly—and called upon the House of Lords to review the decision. The decision was upheld and the rules for the legal definition of insanity were put into writing. The M'Naghten Rule states that a defendant may be found "not guilty" by reasons of insanity only if he were so severely disturbed at the time of his act that he did not know what he was doing or, if he did know what he was doing, did not know that it was wrong.

The distinction of knowing right from wrong is still the basis of most decisions of legal insanity. But many psychologists and psychiatrists who are called upon for expert testimony in such trials feel that the M'Naghten Rule is much too narrow. Individuals who are clearly psychotic may respond correctly when asked if a particular act is morally right or wrong but be unable to control their behavior. Some states, recognizing this, have added to their statutes the doctrine of "irresistible impulse"; that is, defendants may be declared legally insane if the jury decides they were driven to their crime by a compulsion that was too strong to be resisted.

A more reasonable legal definition of insanity, proposed by the American Law Institute after a careful 10-year study, was adopted by the United States Court of Appeals for the Second Circuit in 1966. It states: "A person is not responsible for criminal conduct if at the time of such conduct as a result of mental disease or defect he lacks substantial capacity either to appreciate the wrongfulness of his conduct or to conform his conduct to the requirements of the law." The word *substantial* suggests that "any" incapacity is not enough to avoid criminal responsibility, but "total" incapacity is not required either. The use of the word *appreciate* rather than *know* implies that intellectual awareness of right or wrong is not enough; the individuals must have some understanding of the moral or legal consequences of their behavior before they can be held criminally responsible. The new rule is now mandatory in 20 states and in most federal courts.

The problem of legal responsibility in the case of mentally disordered individuals is complex and closely tied to social values and beliefs. Many experts recommend abolishing insanity as a legal defense (e.g., Szasz, 1963; Menninger, 1968; Dershowitz, 1973). Some argue that its abuse by clever lawyers has let too many criminals go free. Others claim that acquittal by reason

having to wait or work for a reward—he or she does not learn to tolerate frustration. Lack of frustration tolerance and conviction that one can get by on one's charm are two characteristics of the psychopath. In addition, a child who is always protected from frustration or distress may have no ability to empathize with the distress of others (Maher, 1966).

Studies of the parents of male psychopaths indicate that it is the mother who overindulges the son, while the father remains aloof and uninvolved. Typically, the parents are concerned with maintaining status in the community—concealing all difficulties behind the facade of a happy, successful family. Thus, the children learn that appearance is more important than reality.

Undoubtedly, a number of family interaction patterns may foster psychopathy. Other patterns that have been suggested are parents who are inconsistent in supplying affection, rewards, and punishments and are inconsistent in their own role behavior, so that the child does not have a reliable model on which to base his or her own identity (Buss, 1966b).

and the Law

of insanity often leads to a worse punishment (an *indeterminate* sentence to an institution for the criminally insane that may confine a person for life) than being convicted and sent to prison (with the possibility of parole in a few years).

One promising proposal would separate two functions of the law: determination of guilt and imposition of the sentence. The jury hearing a criminal case in which the defendant's sanity is in question would be asked only to determine whether the defendant is guilty of the crime as charged. If the person is convicted, determination of treatment would be made by a tribunal of criminologists, psychologists, and psychiatrists; they would evaluate the nature and causes of the defendant's behavior and decide whether the needs of society and the individual's chances for rehabilitation would be best served by treatment in a psychiatric hospital, imprisonment, or perhaps by some other method. The convicted individual's progress could be evaluated periodically and a decision made as to when he or she had made a satisfactory adjustment (Glueck, 1962).

Despite the current controversy, actual cases of acquittal by reason of insanity are quite rare; jurors seem reluctant to believe that people are not morally responsible for their acts, and lawyers, knowing that an insanity plea is apt to fail, tend to use it only as a last resort. In New York State, from 1960 to 1970, there were only 11 verdicts of "not guilty by reason of insanity."

The question of mental disorder has its greatest impact earlier in the legal process. Many people who are "mentally ill" never come to trial. The law of the United States requires that the defendant be *competent to stand trial* (*Pate* v. *Robinson*, 1966). Competence to stand trial means the individual is able (1) to understand the charges, and (2) to cooperate with his or her lawyer in preparing a defense. The competency issue is basic to the American ideal of a fair trial and is quite separate from the question of whether or not the person was "insane" at the time the crime was committed. In a preliminary hearing, the judge receives evidence as to the accused's mental competency. The judge may drop the charges and commit the individual to a psychiatric facility (if the crime is not serious) or commit the accused and file the charges until such time as he or she is deemed competent to stand trial—which may be never. Because of congested court calendars and the expense of a trial, judges often prefer to deal with mentally disturbed defendants in this way, particularly if they believe that the psychiatric hospital will provide adequate treatment and/or secure confinement. Many more persons are confined to hospitals for the criminally insane because they were found incompetent to stand trial than because they were found not guilty by reason of insanity. In 1972, 8,825 men (5,349 of whom were nonwhite) were committed as incompetent (Stone, 1975). Such persons, many of whom are not dangerous, often end up being confined longer than they would be if convicted of the crime charged. Obviously, reforms need to be made at this step in the legal process, too. One proposal would limit the length of time a person may be confined for purposes of "return to competency"—possibly to six months or to the maximum sentence the accused could have received if convicted, whichever is less (Stone, 1975).

Alcoholism and Drug Dependence

The past two decades have been referred to as the drug era. We have drugs that prevent conception, calm us when we are nervous, excite us when we are bored, slim us when we are fat, put us to sleep, wake us up, cure us when we are sick, and make us sick when we are well! Alcoholism and drug abuse are among the major medical and social problems of this country.

The effects of psychoactive drugs on consciousness were discussed in Chapter 6. Table 15-5 lists the major psychoactive drugs that people use and abuse. With repeated use, one can become physically and/or psychologically dependent on any of them. *Physical dependence* refers to what was formerly called addiction. It is characterized by (1) *tolerance*—with continued use, the individual must take more and more of the drug to achieve the same effect—and (2) *withdrawal*—if use is discontinued, the person experiences unpleasant

TABLE 15-5
Psychoactive drugs that are commonly abused

Only a few examples are given of each class of drug. Sometimes the generic name is used (for example, psilocybin) and sometimes the brand name (for example, Miltown—meprobamate; Seconal—secobarbital), depending on which is the more familiar. The major tranquilizers and antidepressants used in the treatment of schizophrenia and affective disorders are not included, since they are rarely abused. Also omitted are the volatile hydrocarbons (glue, paint thinner) and the fluorocarbons (aerosol sprays), which can be highly dangerous when sniffed for their psychoactive effects.

CLASSIFICATION	DRUGS	USAGE	TOLERANCE	PHYSICAL DEPENDENCE	PSYCHOLOGICAL DEPENDENCE
Sedatives (central nervous system depressants)	Alcohol (ethanol)	Reduce tension; release inhibitions	Yes	Yes	Yes

	Barbiturates
	  Nembutal
	  Seconal
		Induce relaxation and sleep	Yes	Yes	Yes

	Mild tranquilizers
	  Miltown
	  Valium
		Reduce anxiety and tension	Yes	Yes	Yes

Narcotics (central nervous system depressants and analgesics)	Opium and its derivatives
	  Codeine
	  Heroin
	  Morphine
		Alleviate physical pain; induce relaxation and pleasant reveries	Yes	Yes	Yes

	Methadone	Treatment of heroin dependence	Yes	Yes	Yes

Stimulants	Amphetamines
	  Benzedrine
	  Dexedrine
	  Methedrine
		Increase alertness; decrease fatigue	Yes	Yes—to the extent that withdrawal produces physical and psychological depression	Yes

	Cocaine	Increase alertness; decrease fatigue	Yes		Yes
	Nicotine	Increase alertness	Slight	Possibly	Yes
	Caffeine	Increase alertness	Slight	No	Yes
Hallucinogens	LSD*	To "expand the mind" and produce changes in thought and mood	Yes	No	Only for a minority of users
	Mescaline*		Yes	No	
	Psilocybin*		Yes	No	
	Phencyclidine (PCP)†		?	?	?
	Marijuana		No	No	Only for heavy users

*LSD, mescaline, and psilocybin all show "cross-tolerance"; for example, a person who takes LSD will develop increased tolerance for mescaline, and similarly, a user of psilocybin will require more mescaline or LSD to achieve the same effects.

†PCP is a synthetic drug that was used as a surgical anaesthetic until severe psychotic-like reactions were noted among a number of patients. In large doses it can produce prolonged coma, and sometimes death. What is sold on the streets as THC (the active ingredient in marijuana) is frequently PCP, and consequently highly dangerous.

physical symptoms. Alcohol, barbiturates, and narcotics can all produce physical dependence.

Psychological dependence refers to a need that develops through learning. People who habitually use a drug to relieve anxiety may become dependent on it even though no physical need develops. For example, smoking marijuana does not appear to build up tolerance for the drug, and the withdrawal symptoms are minimal. Nevertheless, a person who learns to use marijuana when

CHAPTER 15/ABNORMAL PSYCHOLOGY

faced with stressful situations will find the habit difficult to break. For some drugs, such as alcohol, psychological dependence progresses to physical dependence as more and more of the substance is consumed.

Alcoholism

Despite public concern over marijuana and hard drugs, such as heroin, alcohol is still the most widely used and abused drug in this country. It is estimated that, in the United States, some 9 million people are alcoholics or problem drinkers, and alcohol consumption appears to be steadily increasing. The cost in terms of lost productivity and medical care for alcohol-related illnesses is staggering. Other social consequences include increased crime (homicides and child abuse are both related to alcohol use), family discord, deaths and injuries on the highway, and suicide.

VARIETIES OF ALCOHOLISM The stereotype of an alcoholic, the skid row drunk, constitutes only a small proportion of those with serious drinking problems. The depressed housewife who takes a few drinks to get through the day and a few more to gear up for a social evening, the businessman who needs a three-martini lunch to get through the afternoon, the overworked physician who keeps a bottle in the desk drawer, and the high school student who drinks more and more to gain acceptance from peers are all on their way to becoming alcoholics. There are various definitions of alcoholism, but almost all include *inability to abstain*—the feeling that you can't get through the day without a drink—and/or *lack of control*—the inability to stop after one or two drinks. Figure 15-14 lists some questions formulated by the National Institute on Alcohol Abuse and Alcoholism to help people determine whether they may have a drinking problem.

Alcohol consumption is on the increase among young people.

Fig. 15-14 Signs of alcoholism

The sooner you recognize a drinking problem in yourself, the easier it is to get out from under it. Below are some questions that will help you learn how dependent you are on drinking. This is a time to be absolutely honest with yourself—only *you* can know how seriously you are being hurt by the role alcohol plays in your life.

1 Has someone close to you sometimes expressed concern about your drinking?
2 When faced with a problem, do you often turn to alcohol for relief?
3 Are you sometimes unable to meet home or work responsibilities because of drinking?
4 Have you ever required medical attention as a result of drinking?
5 Have you ever experienced a blackout—a total loss of memory while still awake—when drinking?
6 Have you ever come in conflict with the law in connection with your drinking?
7 Have you often failed to keep the promises you have made to yourself about controlling or cutting out your drinking?

If you have answered "yes" to any of the above questions, your drinking is probably affecting your life in some major ways and you should do something about it—before it gets worse. (National Institute on Alcohol Abuse and Alcoholism, 1977)

There are many ways to progress from social drinking to alcoholism. One survey of 2,000 alcoholics describes the following four stages (Jellinek, 1952).

1   *Prealcoholic stage.* Individual drinks socially and on occasion heavily to relieve tension and forget about problems. Heavy drinking becomes more frequent, and, in times of crisis, the person resorts more and more to the bolstering effects of alcohol.
2   *Prodromal stage.* Drinking becomes furtive and may be accompanied by "blackouts" in which the person remains conscious and relatively coherent but later cannot recall events. The person becomes preoccupied with drinking, feels guilty about it, yet worries about when and where he or she will have the next drink.
3   *Crucial stage.* All control is lost; once the person starts drinking, he or she continues until sick or stuporous. Social adjustment deteriorates, and the drinking becomes evident to family, friends, and employer. The person starts drinking in the morning, neglects his or her diet, and may go on the first "bender"—several days of continuous drinking. Abstinence is still possible; the person may go for several weeks or even months without drinking. But once he or she takes a drink, the whole pattern begins again. This stage is called crucial because, unless the individual seeks help, he or she is in danger of becoming a chronic alcoholic.
4   *Chronic stage.* Drinking is continual; the individual lives only to drink. The body has become so accustomed to alcohol that the person may suffer withdrawal symptoms without it. Malnutrition and alcohol have produced numerous physiological disorders. The person has lost all concern for physical appearance, self-esteem, family, friends, and social status. This is the stage of the skid row drunk.

Not all elements of these stages have been corroborated. For example, some alcoholics seldom get drunk but consume enough alcohol each day to maintain a certain level of relaxation and some never experience blackouts. Nevertheless, the general progression from stage to stage is typical of many alcoholics.

THEORIES OF ALCOHOLISM   In view of the disastrous consequences, why do people continue to drink? There is no generally accepted theory of alcoholism. Some evidence suggests a hereditary predisposition. If a monozygotic twin is alcoholic, there is a 60 percent chance that his or her twin will also be alcoholic; the concordance rate for dizygotic twins is only 20 percent (Kaij, 1960).

Further support for a genetic predisposition comes from studies of children of alcoholic parents who were adopted in infancy and raised by nonalcoholic parents. By their late twenties, almost twice as many had alcohol problems as did a control group of adopted children whose biologic parents were not alcoholic (Goodwin and others, 1973).

Although there appears to be an inherited tendency toward alcoholism, the majority of children born to alcoholic parents do *not* become alcoholic, and thus far research has failed to find any physical basis for alcoholism—that is, any differences between alcoholics and nonalcoholics in the rate at which alcohol is metabolized or in other body functions (except for alterations that occur as the *result* of prolonged consumption).

The common-sense view, and the one initially proposed by learning theorists, is that people drink to reduce anxiety. Alcohol is a powerful reinforcer in its ability to alleviate tension, and this immediate effect may far outweigh the

aversive effects that occur later. If you had a hangover five seconds after your first sip of an alcoholic beverage, would you continue drinking?

The theory that an alcoholic drinks to relieve tension is an incomplete explanation, however. It may be one reason why a person *begins* to drink, but it does not account for the continuation of long drinking periods. Careful observations of alcoholics in a specially designed hospital ward showed that anxiety decreases during the first 12-to-24-hour period of drinking, but after that alcohol actually *increases* levels of tension and anxiety (Nathan and O'Brien, 1971). It may be that because of the memory "blackouts" that occur with chronic alcoholism, the alcoholic forgets the increased anxiety that occurs later (Lisman, 1974).

Motives other than relief from tension may prompt a person to start drinking. A series of studies used a test similar to the TAT (see pp. 403–05) to assess the motives for drinking among men who were not extreme alcoholics. One prominent motive was to overcome a sense of weakness—to feel stronger and more effective (McClelland and others, 1972). Young people often start drinking to keep up with their peers.

Clearly the motives for drinking are not simple, and, taken together, they must be strong, or drinking would not occur so frequently in cultures that differ so much in other respects.

TREATMENT Regardless of the reasons for starting to drink, once a person becomes psychologically dependent on alcohol, it is difficult to give it up. The sooner the individual recognizes that alcohol is seriously interfering with his or her life, the easier it is to do something about it—before the body becomes physiologically dependent on alcohol. Alcoholics Anonymous, a world-wide organization of ex-alcoholics dedicated to helping others overcome drinking problems, has been helpful in many cases. Behavior therapy techniques that attempt to change the person's attitude toward alcohol and to train control of drinking have also shown some success.

ALCOHOLISM AND DRUG DEPENDENCE

Drug Dependence

People apparently use other psychoactive drugs for many of the same reasons that they use alcohol; individuals who use hard drugs also tend to drink heavily and to smoke cigarettes. A longitudinal study of high school students in New York State indicates the following stages in the sequence of drug usage:

beer/wine $\longrightarrow$ hard liquor $\longrightarrow$ marijuana $\longrightarrow$ other illegal drugs

This does not mean that the use of a particular drug invariably leads to drugs further along in the sequence. Only about 27 percent of those students who drank hard liquor progressed to marijuana, and only 26 percent of the marijuana users went on to try such drugs as LSD, amphetamines, or heroin. They stopped at different stages. But none of them went from beer or wine to illegal drugs without taking up hard liquor on the way. And very few went from liquor to hard drugs without first trying marijuana (Kandel, 1975). Positive experiences with one drug may encourage initial use of another.

WHY PEOPLE START USING DRUGS Many studies have attempted to determine the personality characteristics and social factors that prompt people to use psychoactive drugs. Since some studies involved individuals who were already taking drugs, the results must be viewed with caution. For example, heroin addicts have been described as psychopathic personalities who have difficulty relating to other people and who seek to escape responsibility through drugs (Chinlund, 1969; Berzins and others, 1974). But we can't be certain that these characteristics did not result from, rather than precede, addiction. Nevertheless, the following factors seem important in determining whether a person will try illegal drugs.

1 *Parental influences.* One finding is that young people from unhappy homes, where parents show little interest in their children and use harsh physical punishment, are more apt to use drugs than youngsters from happier home situations (Baer and Corrado, 1974). Parental values are also important. Youths from conservative homes that emphasize traditional social and religious values and the importance of long-range goals are *less* apt to become involved with drugs than those from more permissive and liberal homes where "doing your own thing" is encouraged (Blum and others, 1972). Perhaps the most powerful influence is the degree to which parents model drug use. When parents make free use of alcohol, tranquilizers, and other legal drugs, their children are likely to sample drugs themselves (Smart and Fejer, 1972).

2 *Peer influences.* Numerous studies have found that the more a young person tries a variety of drugs, the more likely it is that his or her friends will be users, and vice versa (e.g., Sadava, 1973). This finding is subject to several interpretations. Drug-using friends may encourage the youth to experiment with drugs. On the other hand, a person may start using drugs on his or her own and then select friends who are doing the same (Johnson, 1973). Both explanations may be true.

3 *Personality factors.* There is no single personality "type" associated with drug use. People try drugs for a variety of reasons—curiosity or the desire to experience a new state of consciousness, escape from physical or mental pain, relief from boredom. The one personality trait that *is* predictive of drug usage is social conformity. People who score high on various tests of social conformity (who see themselves as conforming to the traditional

values of American society) are less apt to use drugs than those who score low. The nonconformist may be a "loner," who feels no involvement with other people or with social groups, or a member of a subculture that encourages drug usage.

WHY PEOPLE CONTINUE TO USE DRUGS While many of the above factors may influence initial drug use, once an individual becomes physically dependent the motivation changes radically. The person has acquired a new need that may be so powerful that all other concerns are ignored. He or she lives only for the next "fix."

Dependence on narcotics can develop very quickly. For example, after a person has been smoking or "sniffing" (inhaling) heroin for a while, tolerance builds up, and this method no longer produces the desired effect. The individual may progress to "skin popping" (injecting under the skin) and then to "mainlining" (injecting into a vein). Once the user starts "mainlining," stronger and stronger doses of heroin are required to produce a "high," and the physical discomforts of withdrawal from the drug become intense—for example, chills and sweating, stomach cramps, vomiting, headaches. In an effort to gain relief, the individual may overdose—and may die.

If heroin experiences have been restricted to smoking or "sniffing," most users are able to give up the habit. For example, among United States soldiers who regularly sniffed heroin in Vietnam (where the drug was easily available), only about 7 percent continued to use the drug after they returned to this country (Robins, 1974). But once larger amounts are absorbed into the body through injection, the majority of users become physically dependent, or addicted.

Treatment usually involves helping the individual through the withdrawal period, building up his or her physical condition, and teaching more effective

Advance in understanding action of opiates
Dr. Avam Goldstein of Stanford University holds model of molecule identified as the chemical "receptor" in the brain for morphine. His research team is pictured with him.

ALCOHOLISM AND DRUG DEPENDENCE

ways of coping. Unfortunately, this treatment often fails to relieve the craving for heroin, and many addicts must be maintained on methadone (a synthetic narcotic that is addictive but produces less psychological impairment than heroin). The recent discovery that the brain has specific receptor sites for narcotics (special nerve cells into which the drug molecules fit like keys) may pave the way for discovering how addiction actually occurs and how it may be treated effectively.

Prevalence of Mental Disorders

Mental disorders are a serious social problem. In the United States each year, about 7 million people receive treatment in some sort of mental health facility, either as inpatients or outpatients (National Institute of Mental Health, 1977). The prevalence of mental disorders in the population is difficult to estimate, because many people with less severe problems, for example, the neuroses, do not seek help or are treated by their family physicians. Nevertheless, studies indicate that from 15 to 25 percent of the population may be in need of help, either for long-term problems or for situational stress that significantly impairs their lives (President's Commission on Mental Health, 1978).

Community surveys provide some interesting information concerning the distribution of the various disorders in different socioeconomic groups, although the reasons for the differences are not at all clear. Several studies have found that the neuroses are more prevalent in the upper and middle classes, whereas a disproportionate number of psychotic reactions and personality disorders occur in the lower class. In a New York City study, the incidence of psychotic disorders was found to be 13 percent in the lowest socioeconomic group in comparison with 3.6 percent in the upper class (Srole and others, 1962). A study in New Haven, Connecticut, found similar results and noted that even among the neurotics there were class differences in types of symptoms. The upper-class neurotics tended to report more subjective emotional discomfort—anxiety, dissatisfaction, and unhappiness with themselves—while the lower-class neurotics tended to show more somatic symptoms as well as unhappiness and friction with other people (Myers and Bean, 1968).

There are a number of hypotheses to explain the class differences in incidence of psychoses. These include: (1) movement downward in class status as the individual becomes more seriously disturbed and less able to hold a job, (2) class differences in child-rearing practices that may predispose the children to different kinds of defense mechanisms, and (3) the devastating effect of poverty, which engenders a feeling of helplessness and a desire to withdraw from the harshness of reality. Much more information is needed before we can evaluate the contribution of these and other factors to the higher incidence of psychoses among lower socioeconomic groups.

The past two decades have seen a significant decline in the number of patients in mental hospitals. Despite an increasing population, there were about 500,000 fewer patients in United States mental hospitals in 1975 than there were in 1955 (see Figure 15-15). This encouraging trend can be attributed in part to improved techniques of treatment (including the use of tranquilizing drugs), and in part to the current emphasis on returning patients as soon as possible to the community, where they can be treated as outpatients, rather than prolonging hospitalization. These developments will be discussed in the next chapter.

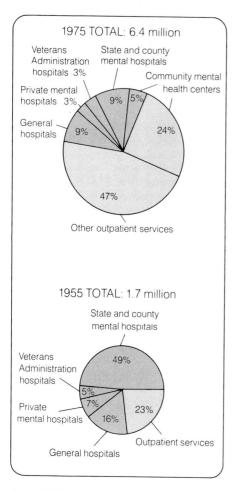

Fig. 15-15 Mental health care in the United States: 1955 and 1975
The two circles show the percentage of cases in 1955 and 1975 treated by various facilities offering inpatient (gray) or outpatient (red) services. The community mental health centers that have been established since 1963 account for much of the outpatient increase, but other outpatient facilities have also been expanded.

Status of Diagnostic Categories

The discussion of abnormal behavior in this chapter follows a fairly traditional classification of mental disorders. As we have noted at several points, however, this classification has not proved entirely satisfactory; some of the diagnostic categories are ambiguous, and clinicians often fail to agree in diagnosing a specific case. In addition, the diagnostic labels do not provide enough information about prognosis and treatment. In an effort to resolve these problems, a task force was appointed by the American Psychiatric Association to develop a new system for classifying mental disorders. After consultation with a number of professional groups, the task force arrived at a tentative classification that is now in the process of being tested and evaluated. The new system, to be published as the *Diagnostic and Statistical Manual of Mental Disorders* (DSM III), evaluates each case on five specific dimensions, or *axes*, which are designed to be of value in planning treatment and predicting outcome. The five axes are:

Axis I   Clinical syndrome
Axis II   Personality characteristics
Axis III   Physical disorders
Axis IV   Severity of psychosocial stressors (range 1–7)
Axis V   Highest level of adaptive functioning during the past year (range 1–6)

The clinical syndrome is usually the diagnostic category; a *syndrome* is a group of symptoms that, occurring together, characterize a disorder. Schizophrenic disorders, affective disorders, and anxiety disorders are examples of major diagnostic categories; each is further divided into subtypes. Axis II describes prominent personality features and the coping strategies the individual uses when faced with stress. (Sometimes a person may be diagnosed only on axis II, for example, *narcissistic personality* or *antisocial personality*, with no disorder listed for axis I. That is, the problem for which he

or she seeks help is limited to long-standing maladaptive ways of dealing with the environment.)

Axis III lists any current physical disorders that may be relevant to the understanding or treatment of the person. Axis IV lists stressful events (for example, divorce, loss of job, menopause, death of a spouse) that occurred in the year prior to the disorder and gives a severity rating—from none through moderate to catastrophic—for the sum of such stresses. This information provides clues for prognosis as well as for treatment. Prognosis is usually better when a disorder develops as a consequence of marked stress than when it develops after minimal stress. And a treatment plan may include attempts to either remove the psychosocial stressors or help the individual cope with them. Axis V gives the highest level of social and occupational functioning for the previous year—from superior to grossly impaired—on the assumption that the person's prior ability to cope will have considerable prognostic value.

Two examples using this diagnostic system might be:

Axis I   Schizophrenia, paranoid subtype
Axis II   Very passive; unable to relate to others
Axis III   Diabetes
Axis IV   Recently separated from wife following loss of job (rated 5: severe)
Axis V   Has few friends; unable to hold a job for more than a few months (rated 5: poor)

Axis I   Alcohol dependence (alcoholism)
Axis II   Antisocial personality; aggressive; tends to deny personal problems
Axis III   Hepatitis
Axis IV   Family arguments over excessive alcohol use (rated 3: mild)

Axis V   Able to function at high-level job until past six months, when alcohol consumption and absenteeism increased (rated 4: fair)

In addition to including information about the individual that may be valuable in predicting outcome and planning treatment, the new classification system uses many more categories than the previous system. For example, disorders that were lumped together under Personality Disorders in the old classification (alcoholism, drug dependence, and sexual deviation) are now classified separately under Substance Use Disorders and Psychosexual Disorders. The new system also includes more specific behavioral criteria for each diagnostic category and rules for making the diagnosis. It is hoped that these changes will provide greater reliability in diagnosis, which should lead to better research in treatment, outcome, and etiology.

This new classification is currently being tested in a number of clinics and hospitals, and it is too early to tell how reliable or useful it will be. It has been criticized on two main grounds: (1) for basing its diagnostic categories on behavioral symptoms rather than on theories about the underlying dynamics or causes of the disorder and (2) for classifying all mental disorders as a subset of medical disorders. Critics concerned with the second point note that most of the disorders listed cannot be attributed to any known organic cause. Adherence to the *medical model* may lead the clinician to play down the role of sociocultural and other environmental factors in the etiology and treatment of abnormal behavior.

Testing the new classification system will take time, and further modifications undoubtedly will be made in the process. Its ultimate acceptance will depend on how well it works—in terms of the reliability of its categories and the significance of the research it generates.

SUMMARY

1 The diagnosis of abnormal behavior is based on *statistical frequency, social norms, adaptiveness of behavior,* and *personal distress.* Characteristics indicative of good mental health include an *efficient perception of reality, self-knowledge, control of behavior, self-esteem,* an *ability to form affectionate relationships,* and *productivity.*

2 The major categories of abnormal behavior are *neuroses, psychoses,* and *personality disorders.* Neuroses are behavior patterns that avoid, rather than cope with, problems; they are often extreme forms of normal defense mechanisms used in an attempt to reduce anxiety. They include *anxiety reactions, obsessive-compulsive reactions, phobias, conversion reactions,* and *neurotic depression.*

3 *Psychoses* involve more serious disturbances of thought and behavior as well as distortions of reality—as evidenced by *delusions* (false beliefs) and *hallucinations* (false perceptions). Two common *functional psychoses* (those with no clear organic basis) are the *affective disorders* and *schizophrenia.*

4 Affective disorders are disturbances of mood: severe *depression, mania,* or a cyclical alternation between the two, *manic-depressive psychosis.* Psychoanalytic theories view depression as a *reactivation of the loss of the mother's affection* in a person who is *dependent on external approval* and tends to *turn anger inward.* Learning theories focus on *reduced positive reinforcement* and *learned helplessness.* Some affective disorders may involve inherited biochemical defects. Both inherited predispositions and/or early experiences may make people *vulnerable* to depression when under stress.

5 *Schizophrenia* is primarily a thought disorder characterized by difficulty in "filtering out" irrelevant stimuli, disturbances in perception, inappropriate affect, and withdrawal. These disturbances are usually accompanied by delusions and hallucinations. Research on the causes of schizophrenia has focused on evidence for a hereditary disposition to the disorder, possible defects in the metabolism of neurotransmitters (such as dopamine), and faulty parent-child relationships.

6 *Personality disorders* are longstanding patterns of socially maladaptive behavior such as *psychopathic personality, alcoholism,* and *drug dependence.* Individuals classified as psychopathic personalities are impulsive, concerned only with their own needs, show little guilt, and are frequently in trouble with the law. An underreactive nervous system and inconsistent parental rewards and punishments are two possible explanations for the disorder.

7 The use of alcohol and other psychoactive drugs may lead to *psychological dependence* (compulsive use to reduce anxiety) and *physical dependence* (increased tolerance and withdrawal symptoms). Alcohol is the most widely used drug; *inability to abstain* from drinking or to *stop* after one or two drinks classifies one as an alcoholic.

8 A number of factors may predispose people to start using drugs. These include an *unhappy home life,* parents who are *permissive* or who *model drug use, peer influences,* and a *lack of social conformity.* With continued use, physical dependency develops, creating a new need that must be satisfied.

9 Emotional disorders constitute a serious social problem. Studies indicate that from 15 to 25 percent of the United States population have emotional problems that significantly impair their lives. Psychotic disorders occur more frequently among those in the lowest socioeconomic group, and a number of explanations have been proposed to account for this finding.

General textbooks on abnormal psychology include Coleman, *Abnormal psychology and modern life* (5th ed., 1976), Sarason, *Abnormal psychology* (2nd ed., 1976), and White and Watt, *The abnormal personality* (4th ed., 1973). Emphasizing a learning theory approach to abnormal behavior are Davison and Neale, *Abnormal psychology* (2nd ed., 1978) and Nathan and Harris, *Psychopathology and society* (1975). An interesting paperback describing experimental approaches to various kinds of abnormal behavior is Maser and Seligman (eds.), *Psychopathology: Experimental models* (1977).

See Tarter and Sugerman (eds.), *Alcoholism* (1976) for a wide range of papers on this topic. For more on drugs, see Julien, *A primer of drug action* (2nd ed., 1978) and Ray, *Drugs, society, and human behavior* (2nd ed., 1978).

The hereditary aspects of mental illness are reviewed in McClearn and DeFries, *Introduction to behavioral genetics* (1973), Fuller and Thompson, *Foundations of behavior genetics* (1978), and Gottesman and Shields, *Schizophrenia and genetics* (1972).

The world of psychosis from the patient's viewpoint is graphically described in Green, *I never promised you a rose garden* (1971), Kesey, *One flew over the cuckcoo's nest* (1962), and Vonnegut, *The Eden express* (1975).

16
Methods of
Therapy

I n this chapter, we will look at some of the methods used to treat various types of abnormal behavior. Some of these focus on helping individuals gain an understanding of the causes of their problems, some attempt to modify behavior directly, some treat the body, and some seek ways in which the community can help.

Treatment of mental disorders is closely linked to theories about the causes of such disorders. A brief history of the treatment of the mentally ill will illustrate how methods change as theories about human nature and the causes of its disorders change.

Historical Background

The early Chinese, Egyptians, and Hebrews thought disordered behavior to be the result of possession by demons or evil spirits. The treatment then was to exorcise the demons by such techniques as prayer, incantation, magic, and the use of purgatives concocted from herbs. If such treatment brought no improvement, more extreme measures were taken to ensure that the body would be an unpleasant dwelling place for the evil spirit. Flogging, starving, burning, even stoning to death were not infrequent forms of "treatment." Although in most cases possession was thought to be by evil spirits, behavior of a mystical or religious nature was believed to result from possession by a good or holy spirit. People who showed such behavior were therefore respected and worshipped. During this period, the mentally ill were treated by priests, who had the power to perform the exorcism.

The first progress in the understanding of mental disorders came with the ideas of the Greek physician Hippocrates (c. 460–377 B.C.). Hippocrates rejected demonology and maintained that mental disorders were the result of a disturbance in the balance of body fluids. He, and the Greek and Roman physicians who followed him, argued for a more humane treatment of the mentally ill. They stressed the importance of pleasant surroundings, exercise, proper diet, massage, and soothing baths, as well as some less desirable methods, such as bleeding, purging, and mechanical restraints. Although there were no institu-

Fig. 16-1 Early methods for treating the mentally ill

The "crib," a restraining device used in a New York mental institution in 1882

As late as the early nineteenth century, English asylums used rotating devices of this sort, in which the patients were whirled around at high speeds.

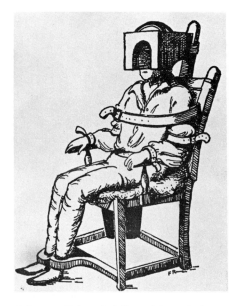

A "tranquilizing chair," used to restrain unmanageable patients in a Pennsylvania hospital, circa 1800

tions as such for the mentally ill, many individuals were cared for with great kindness by physicians in temples dedicated to the Greek and Roman gods.

This progress did not continue, however. During the Middle Ages, there was a revival of primitive superstition and demonology. The mentally ill were thought to be in league with Satan and to possess supernatural powers with which they could cause floods, pestilence, and injuries to others. People believed that by treating an insane person cruelly one was punishing the devil and so justified such measures as beating, starving, and branding with hot irons (see Figure 16-1). This type of cruelty culminated in the witchcraft trials that sentenced to death thousands of people (many of them mentally ill) during the fifteenth, sixteenth, and seventeenth centuries.

Early Asylums

In the latter part of the Middle Ages, asylums were created to cope with the mentally ill who roamed the streets. These were not treatment centers, but simply prisons; the inmates were chained in dark, filthy cells and treated more like animals than like human beings. It was not until 1792, when Phillippe Pinel was put in charge of an asylum in Paris, that some improvement was made in the treatment of these unfortunate people. As an experiment, Pinel was allowed to remove the chains that restrained the inmates. Much to the amazement of the skeptics who thought he was mad to unchain such "animals," Pinel's experiment was a success. When released from restraint, placed in clean and sunny rooms instead of dungeons, and treated kindly, many who had been considered hopelessly mad for years improved enough to leave the asylum.

Around the beginning of the twentieth century, great advances were made in medicine and psychology. The discovery of the syphilis spirochete in 1905 demonstrated that there was a physical cause for the mental disorder known as general paresis and encouraged physicians who believed that mental illness was organic in origin. The work of Sigmund Freud and his followers laid the groundwork for an understanding of mental illness as a function of psychological factors. And Pavlov's laboratory experiments demonstrated that a state similar to an acute neurosis could be produced in animals by requiring them to make decisions beyond their capacities.

Despite these scientific advances, the general public in the early 1900s still had no understanding of mental illness and viewed mental hospitals and their inmates with fear and horror. The education of the public in the principles of mental health was begun through the efforts of Clifford Beers. As a young man,

Beers developed a manic-depressive psychosis and was hospitalized for three years in several private and state hospitals. Although chains and other methods of torture had long since been abandoned, the straitjacket was still widely used to restrain excited patients. Lack of funds made the average state mental hospital—with its overcrowded wards, poor food, and unsympathetic and frequently sadistic attendants—a far from pleasant place to live. After his recovery, Beers wrote about his experiences in a now-famous book, *A Mind That Found Itself* (1908). This book did much to arouse public interest. Beers worked ceaselessly to educate the public in an understanding of mental illness and helped to organize the National Committee for Mental Hygiene. In 1950 this organization joined with two related groups to form the National Association for Mental Health. The mental hygiene movement played an invaluable role in educating the public and in stimulating the organization of child-guidance clinics and community mental health centers, which could aid in the prevention, as well as the treatment, of mental disorders.

Modern Treatment Facilities

The past 30 years have seen a great improvement in treatment facilities. The psychiatric hospitals established by the Veterans Administration after the Second World War were generally superior to the average state-supported hospital and served as an impetus for the improvement of state hospitals. Although some state hospitals are primarily custodial institutions where inmates lead an idle and futile existence in rundown, overcrowded wards, most mental hospitals today are attractive, well-kept, and busy places where trained personnel guide the patients through a wide range of activities. Daily schedules are planned to meet each patient's particular needs and may include time with an individual therapist, in group psychotherapy, or in occupational therapy designed to teach skills as well as provide relaxation. Treatment may also include physical recreation to help relieve tensions and educational therapy to prepare the patient for a job on release from the hospital. Patients who are well enough may work part time in the various hospital departments as patient-employees, which enables them to earn some money and to feel that they are contributing to the welfare of the hospital community.

Many mental hospitals are located near universities and medical schools so that research and training programs can be undertaken jointly. Such hospitals serve as training centers for interns in psychology, psychiatry, and social work as well as for students in psychiatric nursing and occupational therapy. Many general medical hospitals also provide treatment centers for the mentally ill. At present, more patients are treated in the psychiatric wards of general hospitals than are admitted to state or federal psychiatric hospitals.

During the past 20 years, emphasis has shifted from treating patients in hospitals to treating them within their home community whenever possible (see Figure 15-15). Hospitalization, no matter how excellent the facilities, has inherent disadvantages. It cuts the patient off from family and friends. It tends to make the patient feel "sick" and unable to cope with the outside world; it encourages dependency and may discourage active problem solving. The Community Mental Health Centers Act of 1963 made federal funds available for the establishment of community treatment centers. More than 600 have been built. These centers provide a number of services, including (1) treatment of emotionally disturbed individuals before their condition becomes serious, (2) short-term hospitalization, and (3) partial hospitalization. With partial hospitalization, a person may receive treatment at the center during the day

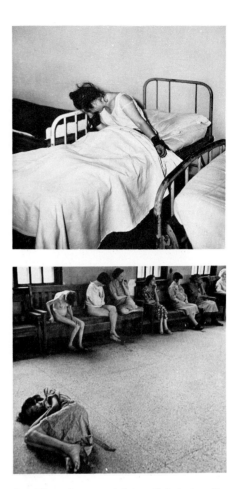

Conditions in a mental hospital during the 1950s

A modern psychiatric hospital in 1978

and return home in the evening or may work during the day and spend nights at the center. Such a program has greater flexibility than traditional hospitalization.

Although treating people within their home communities is a worthwhile goal, the current trend toward short-term hospitalization has had some unfortunate consequences—largely because the facilities in most communities are still inadequate. About half of all patients discharged from state hospitals are readmitted within a year. Many who improve with hospitalization are not adequately cared for after discharge—in terms of follow-up therapy or help in finding friends, housing, and a job. Many older patients, released after years of custodial care, are unable to support themselves and live in dirty, overcrowded slum housing or roam the city streets. The disheveled, young man standing on the corner talking to himself and occasionally shouting gibberish at passers-by may be one victim of the move toward "deinstitutionalization." The middle-aged woman with all of her worldly possessions piled in a shopping bag, who spends one night in the doorway of an office building and the next in a subway station, may be another. Community mental health centers must have more funds and personnel if they are to care for individuals who suffer from a wide range of emotional disorders. And society must provide some sort of "asylum," or refuge, for those who are unable to care for themselves—be it a mental hospital, community home, or some other kind of residential facility.

Professions Involved in Psychotherapy

Regardless of where therapy takes place—in a hospital, community mental health center, private clinic, or office—any of several different professions are involved. A psychiatrist, clinical psychologist, and psychiatric social worker may work together on a given case, or they may work independently. A *psychiatrist* is a physician who specializes in the diagnosis and treatment of abnormal behavior. The psychiatrist takes medical responsibility for the patient in addition to playing a psychotherapeutic role. A *psychoanalyst* is a specialist within psychiatry who uses methods and theories derived from those of Freud. Psychoanalysts have spent several years enrolled in a psychoanalytic institute learning the specific techniques of psychoanalysis and receiving in-depth psychoanalysis themselves. Although a psychoanalyst is usually a psychiatrist,[1] most psychiatrists are not psychoanalysts.

A *clinical psychologist* has had graduate training in psychology, has usually earned a Ph.D., and has served special internships in the fields of testing and diagnosis, psychotherapy, and research. The clinical psychologist administers and interprets psychological tests, conducts psychotherapy, and is also active in research.

A *counseling psychologist* has had graduate training somewhat similar to that of the clinical psychologist—has earned an M.A. or a Ph.D.—but usually with less emphasis on research.

A *psychiatric social worker* usually has an M.A. or an M.S. from a graduate school of social work and special training in interviewing and in extending treatment procedures to the home and community. Because of this special training, the social worker is likely to be called upon to collect information about the patient's home and to interview relatives, in addition to participating in the therapeutic procedures with the patient.

In mental hospitals, a fourth professional is involved: the *psychiatric nurse.* Psychiatric nursing is a specialty within the nursing profession and requires

---

[1] There are some "lay" psychoanalysts—that is, analysts without M.D. degrees.

special training in the handling of mental patients—both those who are severely disturbed and those on the way to recovery.

In our discussion of psychotherapeutic techniques, we will not specify the profession of the psychotherapists; we assume they are trained and competent members of any one of these professions.

Techniques of Psychotherapy

Psychotherapy refers to the treatment of mental disorders by psychological (rather than physical or biological) means. The term embraces a wide variety of techniques, all of which are intended to help emotionally disturbed individuals modify their behavior and feelings so that they can develop more useful ways of dealing with stress and with other people. As we shall see, some psychotherapists believe that modification of behavior is dependent on the individual's understanding of his or her unconscious motives and conflicts, whereas others feel that people can learn to cope with their problems without necessarily exploring the factors that have led to their development. Despite differences in techniques, most methods of psychotherapy have certain basic features in common. They involve communication between two individuals—the patient, or client, and the therapist. The patient is encouraged to express freely his or her most intimate fears, emotions, and experiences without fear of being judged or condemned by the therapist. The therapist, in turn, offers sympathy and understanding and tries to help the patient develop more effective ways of handling his or her problems.

Psychoanalysis

Psychoanalysis is a method of therapy based on the concepts of Freud. We discussed Freud's theory of personality in Chapter 13 and the psychoanalytic concept of anxiety as a response to unconscious conflicts in Chapter 14. The goal of psychoanalysis is to bring unconscious conflicts to the individual's awareness and to help the individual understand the defense mechanisms he or she has been using to control anxiety. Once unconscious motives or needs are acknowledged, they can presumably be dealt with in a more realistic and adaptive way.

FREE ASSOCIATION A psychoanalyst usually sees a patient for 50-minute visits several times a week for periods ranging from one to several years. Thus in its original form, psychoanalytic therapy is not only intensive but extensive. In the beginning sessions, the patient describes symptoms and recounts relevant facts from his or her personal history. The person is then prepared to begin *free association,* one of the foundations of the psychoanalytic method. The purpose of free association is to bring to awareness and to put into words thoughts and feelings of which the patient is unaware or that ordinarily go unacknowledged if they come to awareness.

The "basic rule" of free association is to say everything that comes to mind, without selection, without editing. This rule is a very difficult one to follow. The patient has spent a lifetime learning self-control, learning to be cautious and to think before speaking. Even an individual who tries conscientiously to follow the rule will fail to tell many things. Some passing thoughts seem to be too unimportant to mention, some too stupid, others too indiscreet.

Caricature of Sigmund Freud analyzing a figure of himself lying on a couch and using Freudian imagery

Suppose, for example, that a woman's freedom is being hampered because she must care for her invalid mother. Under such circumstances, she may unconsciously wish for the relief that her mother's death might bring. But she would disapprove of such a death wish because it would be a violation of love and loyalty. Actually, this death wish may be very near to awareness, but the habits of a lifetime make the woman deny it even to herself. She may show a preoccupation with death in her fantasies or in other ways: possibly she hums tunes that are played at funerals. By acknowledging these fleeting thoughts instead of repressing them, she becomes aware of previously unrecognized ideas and feelings that are close to awareness. With practice, she gradually brings to consciousness ideas and feelings that have been deeply repressed.

People unconsciously repress or resist the recall of certain thoughts and feelings because they fear that to acknowledge them will be threatening or degrading. The therapist aids them in overcoming this resistance. Sometimes a person has a free flow of associations until something blocks the way. Then the mind seems to go blank, and the patient can think of nothing to say. This blankness presumably represents resistance to the recall of something effectively repressed. Sometimes, after a particularly revealing session, the patient may forget the next appointment, another indication of resistance to disclosing what is hidden.

INTERPRETATION The psychoanalyst attempts to overcome resistances and to encourage fuller self-understanding through *interpretation*. The interpretation is likely to take two forms. First, the analyst calls attention to the individual's resistances. People often learn something about themselves simply by discovering when a train of associations is suddenly blocked, when they forget an appointment, when they want to change the subject, and so on. Second, the analyst may privately deduce the general nature of what lies behind the patient's statements and attempt to facilitate further associations. For example, a patient may say something that he or she thinks is trivial and then half apologize for its unimportance. Here the analyst may point out that what seems trivial may in fact allude to something important. If the interpretation is appropriately timed, this hint may lead to significant associations. It should be noted that the analyst is careful not to suggest *just what it is* that is important; this the individual must discover for him or herself.

TRANSFERENCE In psychoanalysis, the patient's attitudes toward the analyst are considered important in determining progress. Sooner or later the patient develops strong emotional responses to the psychoanalyst, perhaps admiring him or her greatly in one session but showing scorn in the next. This tendency to make the therapist the object of emotional response is known as *transference*, and the interpretation of transference is one of the foundations of psychoanalytic therapy. The patient sees the therapist as possessing attitudes and attributes like those of his or her parents or those of brothers and sisters, even though the therapist may be very unlike any of these people.

To cite one example: A young woman being treated by a woman psychoanalyst remarked one day as she entered the analyst's office, "I'm glad you're not wearing those lace collars you wore the last several times I was here. I don't like them on you." During the hour, the analyst pointed out that she had not in fact worn any lace collars. During the preceding sessions, the patient had assigned to the analyst the role of the patient's mother and had falsely pictured the analyst as dressing as her mother had dressed when the patient was a child and was undergoing the emotionally disturbing experiences being discussed

"That's exactly what I mean. When you're late, don't bring me a note from your mother."

with the analyst. The patient, while surprised, accepted the interpretation and thereby gained understanding of transference.

Transference does not always involve false perceptions; often the patient simply expresses feelings toward the analyst that he or she had felt toward figures that were important earlier in life. On the basis of these expressed feelings, the analyst is able to interpret the nature of the displaced impulses. For example, a man who has always admired an older brother detects something in the analyst's attitude that reminds him of the brother. An angry attack on the analyst may lead to the uncovering of hostile feelings toward his brother that the person had never acknowledged before. By studying how their patients feel toward them, analysts help the individuals to better understand their conduct in relation to others.

ABREACTION, INSIGHT, AND WORKING THROUGH The course of improvement during psychoanalytic therapy is commonly attributed to three main experiences: *abreaction*, gradual *insight* into one's difficulties, and the repeated *working through* of conflicts and one's reactions to them.

A person experiences *abreaction* when he or she freely expresses a repressed emotion or relives an intense emotional experience. The process is also called "catharsis," as though it were a kind of emotional cleansing. Such free expression may bring some relief but by itself does not eliminate the causes of conflict. In psychoanalytic therapy, abreaction (or catharsis) is accompanied by interpretations that help the individual understand the conflicts revealed. Thus, the benefits from catharsis under these circumstances do not contradict experimental results reporting that expressing aggression fails to reduce subsequent aggressive responses (see Chapter 11).

A person achieves *insight* when he or she understands the roots of the conflict. Sometimes insight comes when the patient recovers the memory of a repressed experience, but the popular notion that a psychoanalytic cure typically results from the sudden recall of a single dramatic episode is mistaken. The individual's troubles seldom have a single source, and insight comes through a gradual increase in self-knowledge. Insight and abreaction must work together: patients must understand their feelings and feel what they understand. The reorientation is never simply intellectual.

As analysis progresses, the patient goes through a lengthy process of reeducation known as *working through*. By examining the same conflicts over and over again as they have appeared in a variety of situations, the person learns to face, rather than to deny, reality and to react in more mature and effective ways. By working through these conflicts during therapy, the person becomes strong enough to face the threat of the original conflict situation and to react to it without undue anxiety.

The end result claimed for a successful psychoanalysis is a deep-seated modification of the personality that makes it possible for the individual to cope with problems on a realistic basis, without the recurrence of the problems that brought him or her to treatment.

Psychoanalysis is a lengthy process and generally very expensive. It is most successful with individuals who are highly motivated to solve their problems, can verbalize their feelings with some ease, and can afford it.

Behavior Therapies

The term *behavior therapy* includes a number of different methods that are based on learning theory. Behavior therapists assume that (1) maladaptive

"Mr. Prentice is not your father. Alex Binster is not your brother. The anxiety you feel is not genuine. Dr. Froelich will return from vacation September 15th. Hang on."

"Leave us alone! I am a behavior therapist! I am helping my patient overcome a fear of heights!"

behaviors are learned ways of coping with stress and that (2) some of the techniques developed in experimental work on learning can be used to substitute new and more appropriate responses for the maladaptive ones. Whereas psychoanalysis is concerned with understanding how one's past conflicts influence behavior, behavior therapy focuses more directly on the behavior itself.

Behavior therapists point out that while insight, or self-knowledge, is a worthwhile goal, it does not insure behavior change. Often we understand why we behave as we do in a certain situation without being able to change the behavior. If you are unusually timid about speaking up in class, you may be able to trace this fear to a number of past events—your father criticized your opinions whenever you expressed them, your mother made a point of correcting your grammar, you had little experience in public speaking during high school because you were afraid to compete with your older brother who was captain of the debate team. Understanding the reasons behind your fear probably will not make it easier for you to contribute to class discussion.

Originally, behavior therapies emphasized the principles of classical and operant conditioning as they related to overt behavior. The behavior therapist tried to determine the stimuli that preceded the maladaptive response and the environmental conditions that reinforced or maintained the behavior (Ullmann and Krasner, 1969; Wolpe, 1969; Lazarus, 1972). More recently, behavior therapists have included cognitive processes (such as an individual's expectations) in their attempts to change behavior (Goldfried and Davison, 1976; Bandura, 1977).

In contrast to psychoanalysis, behavior therapies tend to focus on fairly circumscribed goals; that is, they deal with maladaptive behaviors in specific situations rather than trying to change the individual's personality. And they are more concerned with obtaining scientific validation of their techniques.

SYSTEMATIC DESENSITIZATION *Systematic desensitization* can be viewed as a "deconditioning," or a "counter-conditioning," process. This procedure is very effective in eliminating fears or phobias. The idea is to weaken a maladaptive response by strengthening an incompatible or antagonistic response. For example, relaxation is antagonistic to anxiety; it is difficult to be both relaxed and anxious at the same time. One method of systematically desensitizing a person to a feared situation involves first training the individual to relax and then gradually exposing him or her to the feared situation, either in imagination or in reality. In relaxation training, the individual learns to alternately contract and then relax various muscles, starting, for example, with the feet and ankles and proceeding up the body to face and neck muscles. The person learns what it feels like when muscles are truly relaxed (as compared to tense) and to discriminate various degrees of tension. Sometimes drugs and hypnosis are used to help people who cannot relax otherwise.

While the individual is learning to relax, he or she works with the behavior therapist to construct an *anxiety hierarchy,* a list of situations or stimuli that make the person feel anxious; the situations are ranked in order from the least anxiety producing to the most fearful. For example, for a woman who is so fearful of interacting with other people that she feels anxious when she leaves the security of her home, the hierarchy might start with a walk to the corner mailbox. Somewhere around the middle of the list might be a drive to the supermarket. At the top of the list might be a plane trip alone to visit a friend in a distant city. After the woman has learned to relax and the list has been constructed, desensitization begins. She sits with her eyes closed in a comfortable chair while the therapist describes the least anxiety-producing situation to her. If she can imagine herself in the situation without any increase in muscle tension, the therapist proceeds to the next item on the list. If the woman reports any anxiety while visualizing a scene, she concentrates on relaxing, and the same scene is visualized again until all anxiety is neutralized. This process continues through a series of sessions until the situation that originally provoked the most anxiety now elicits only relaxation. Through this method, the woman is systematically desensitized to anxiety-provoking situations by the strengthening of an antagonistic or incompatible response—relaxation.

Although desensitization through visually imagined scenes has been effective in reducing fears or phobias, it is less effective than desensitization through actual encounters with the feared stimuli—which is not surprising. That is, the woman in our hypothetical case would probably lose her fears more rapidly and more permanently if she actually exposed herself to the anxiety-producing situations, in a sequence of graduated steps, and managed to remain calm (Sherman, 1972). When possible, a behavior therapist tries to combine real life with symbolic desensitization.

ASSERTIVE TRAINING Another kind of response that is antagonistic to anxiety is an *approach*, or *assertive*, response. Some people feel anxious in social situations because they don't know how to "speak up" for what they feel is right or to "say no" when others take advantage of them. By practicing *assertive responses*—first in role playing with the therapist and then in real-life situations—the individual not only reduces anxiety but also develops more effective coping techniques. The therapist determines the kinds of situations in which the person is passive and then helps him or her think of and practice some assertive responses that might be effective in those situations. The following situations might be worked through during therapy sessions:

A behavior therapist helps two individuals assert, or express, their feelings.

> Someone steps in front of you in line.
> A friend asks you to do something you don't want to do.
> Your boss criticizes you unjustly.
> You return defective merchandise to a store.
> You are annoyed by the continual conversation of people behind you in the movies.
> The mechanic did an unsatisfactory job of repairing your car.

Most people do not enjoy dealing with such situations, but some are so fearful of asserting themselves that they say nothing and build up feelings of resentment and inadequacy instead. Assertive training involves rehearsing with the therapist effective responses that could be made in such situations and gradually trying them out in real life.

POSITIVE REINFORCEMENT AND EXTINCTION When a timid person learns and practices assertive responses, he or she is likely to receive considerable *positive reinforcement*—from the therapist who praises such new skills, from other people who are impressed by the change in behavior, and from the fact that actions produce worthwhile results. *Systematic reinforcement*, based on the principles of operant conditioning (see Chapter 7), has proved to be an effective method of changing behavior. We saw earlier how nursery school teachers modified the behavior of a child who tended to isolate herself from other children. By reinforcing her with attention whenever she interacted with other children and ignoring her (*extinction*) whenever she played

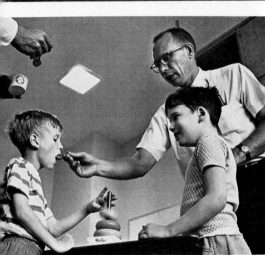

Fig. 16-2 Behavior reinforcement
These two autistic children were enrolled in an intensive behavior therapy program at the UCLA Neuropsychiatric Institute. Here they are shown receiving immediate reinforcement, in the form of food, for interacting with each other. Other techniques included punishment (electric shock) for self-destructive behavior or uncontrollable tantrums and modeling of the appropriate behavior. The boy on the right, mute and self-destructive when he entered the program, was able to return home in less than a year and two years later was doing first-grade work in a special school.

alone or sought to interact only with the teachers, they gradually changed her behavior, so that she learned to play happily with the group.

Sometimes the behavior that the therapist wants to reinforce occurs infrequently or is totally absent, such as talking in a mute child or a schizophrenic. In this case, a technique similar to Skinner's *shaping* of behavior (see Chapter 7) is used: responses that approximate or move in the direction of the desired behavior are reinforced, with the therapist gradually requiring closer and closer approximation until the desired behavior occurs. For example, with one very withdrawn schizophrenic (who had remained mute for 19 years), chewing gum proved to be an effective reinforcement for shaping speech. At first, the therapist rewarded the patient with a stick of gum simply for looking at it when it was held in front of his face; then for moving his lips; then for making any verbalization, if only a croak; and then for saying the word "gum." All this took place over a period of weeks. Once the patient reached the point where he said "gum please," he began to respond to questions by the therapist. The hospital personnel were then asked to respond to the patient's requests only if they were verbalized. For example, if he brought his coat to the nurse as an indication that he wanted to go for a walk, she was not to acquiesce unless he expressed his desire in speech. Other kinds of reinforcement gradually took the place of chewing gum, and the formerly mute schizophrenic became more and more verbal (Isaacs and others, 1965).

Similar procedures have been effective in teaching seriously disturbed children to talk, interact with other children, sit quietly at a desk, and respond appropriately to questions (see Figure 16-2). Instead of receiving regular breakfasts or lunches, these children were provided with bits of food when their responses approximated the desired behaviors. Although such procedures may seem cruel, they are an effective means of establishing normal behavior when all other attempts have failed. Once the child begins to respond to primary forms of reward (such as food), social rewards (praise, attention, and special privileges) become effective reinforcers.

A number of mental hospitals have instituted "token economies" on wards with very regressed, chronic patients as a means of inducing socially appropriate behavior. Tokens (which can later be exchanged for food, cigarettes, and privileges such as watching television) are given for dressing properly, interacting with other patients, eliminating "psychotic talk," helping on the wards, and so on. Such programs have proved successful in improving both the patients' behavior and the general functioning of the ward.

MODELING Another effective means of changing behavior is *modeling* (see pp. 323–24). Modeling was used with several other behavior modification techniques in a study designed to eliminate fear of snakes (Bandura and others, 1969). The subjects were young adults whose snake phobias were severe enough to restrict their activities in various ways—for example, some could not participate in gardening or hiking for fear of encountering snakes. After an initial test to determine how closely they would approach a live but harmless king snake, the subjects were rated according to their degree of fearfulness and divided into four matched groups. One group watched a film in which child and adult models interacted with a large king snake. The models gave every indication of enjoying a series of interactions that most people would find progressively more frightening. The subjects in the group had been trained in relaxation and were instructed to stop the film whenever a particular scene provoked anxiety, reverse the film to the beginning of the sequence that bothered them, and reinduce relaxation. This procedure was termed "symbolic

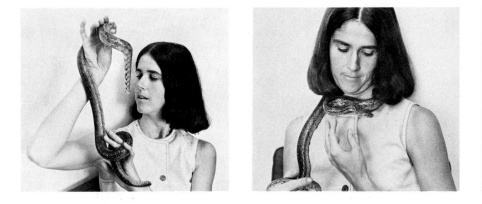

modeling." A second group imitated the behavior of a live model as the model performed progressively more fearful activities with the snake (see Figure 16-3). Gradually the subjects were guided in such activities as touching the snake with a gloved hand, then with their bare hands, holding the snake, letting it coil around their arms, and—finally—letting the snake loose in the room, retrieving it, and letting it crawl over their bodies. The procedure was termed "live modeling with participation." Subjects assigned to the third group received the standard desensitization procedure described earlier, in which deep relaxation was successively paired with imagined scenes of snakes until the subject's anxiety disappeared. The fourth group served as a control and received no special training.

Figure 16-4 shows the number of snake-approach responses performed by the subjects before and after receiving the different treatments. All three treatment groups showed improvement in comparison with the control group, but the group that had live modeling combined with guided participation showed the greatest gain. Almost all the subjects in this group completely overcame their fear of snakes. Interestingly enough, the fears of these subjects in a variety of other situations were also reduced. A follow-up investigation some time later indicated that the subjects' snake phobias did not recur.

Subsequent studies have shown that the most effective method of eliminating snake phobias is to start with participant modeling, in which the individual is guided in handling the snake, and then let the person proceed through various degrees of snake intimacy on his or her own (Bandura and others, 1976). In this way, the individual gains a sense of mastery over the situation—a feeling that effective performance is the result of one's own actions (Bandura, 1977).

Modeling has been used successfully to overcome a variety of fears or avoidance behaviors and to teach new, more adaptive responses. Modeling is often combined with role playing in which the therapist helps the individual rehearse or practice more adaptive behaviors. In the following excerpt, a therapist helps a young man overcome his anxieties about asking girls for dates. The young man has been pretending to talk to a girl over the phone and finishes by asking for a date.

CLIENT: By the way (pause) I don't suppose you want to go out Saturday night?
THERAPIST: Up to actually asking for the date you were very good. However, if I were the girl, I think I might have been a bit offended when you said, "By the way." It's like asking her out is pretty casual. Also, the way you phrased the question, you are kind of suggesting to her that she doesn't want to go out with you. Pretend for the moment I'm you. Now,

Fig. 16-3 Modeling as a treatment for snake phobia
The photos show an individual modeling interactions with a live king snake. Modeling of this sort, combined with guided participation, in which the subject is helped to handle the snake, proves very effective in eliminating snake phobias.

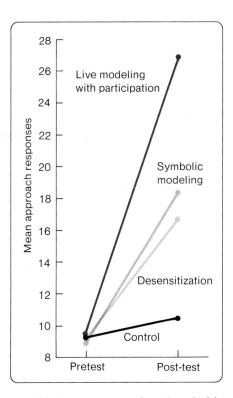

Fig. 16-4 Treatment of snake phobia
The mean number of snake-approach responses made by subjects both before and after receiving different behavior therapy treatments. (After Bandura, Blanchard, and Ritter, 1969)

how does this sound: There is a movie at the Varsity Theater this Saturday that I want to see. If you don't have other plans, I'd like very much to take you.

CLIENT: That sounded good. Like you were sure of yourself and like the girl, too.

THERAPIST: Why don't you try it.

CLIENT: You know that movie at the Varsity? Well, I'd like to go, and I'd like to take you Saturday, if you don't have anything better to do.

THERAPIST: Well, that certainly was better. Your tone of voice was especially good. But the last line, "if you don't have anything better to do" sounds like you don't think you have too much to offer. Why not run through it one more time.

CLIENT: I'd like to see the show at the Varsity, Saturday, and, if you haven't made other plans, I'd like to take you.

THERAPIST: Much better. Excellent, in fact. You were confident, forceful, and sincere. (Rimm and Masters, 1974, p. 94)

SELF-REGULATION Since client and therapist seldom meet more than once a week, it is to the client's advantage to learn to control or regulate his or her own behavior, so that progress can be made outside of the therapy hour. Moreover, if people feel they are responsible for their own improvement, they are more likely to maintain such gains. Self-regulation involves monitoring, or observing, one's own behavior and using various techniques—*self-reinforcement, self-punishment, controlling stimulus conditions,* or *developing incompatible responses*—to change the maladaptive behavior. Monitoring one's behavior consists of keeping a careful record of the kinds of stimuli or situations that elicit the maladaptive behavior and the kinds of responses that are incompatible with it. For example, a person concerned with dependency on alcohol would note the kinds of situations in which he or she is most tempted to drink and try to control such situations or devise a response that is incompatible with drinking. A man who finds it hard not to join his co-workers in a noontime cocktail might plan to eat lunch at his desk, thus avoiding the situation. If he is tempted to relax with a drink on arriving home from work, he might substitute a game of tennis or a jog around the block as a means of relieving tension. Both of these activities would be incompatible with drinking.

Self-reinforcement is rewarding yourself immediately for achieving a specific goal—such as praising yourself, watching a favorite TV program, telephoning a friend, eating a favorite food. Self-punishment means that you arrange some aversive consequence for failing to achieve a goal—such as depriving yourself of something you enjoy (*not* watching a favorite TV program) or making yourself do some unpleasant task (cleaning your room). Depending on the kind of behavior you want to change, various combinations of self-reinforcement, self-punishment, or controlling of stimuli and responses might be used. Table 16-1 outlines a program for the self-regulation of overeating.

COGNITIVE PROCESSES IN BEHAVIOR CHANGE While the procedures we have discussed thus far focus on behavior, most behavior therapists believe that cognitive factors—the individual's thoughts and expectations—are important in determining behavior and in mediating behavior change. What we think about a situation clearly influences our emotional response to it. For example, two students are to present papers in an informal seminar. One says to herself, "This should be an interesting session; there are a lot of debatable points on this topic, and it should be fun to hear what the other students have to say about my ideas." The other speaker thinks, "I'm not sure I can present my ideas effectively; there are a lot of bright students in the group and I'm sure

TABLE 16-1
A program for the self-regulation of eating

SELF-MONITORING

Daily Log. Keep a detailed record of everything you eat. Note amount eaten, type of food and caloric value, time of day, and the circumstances of eating. This record will establish the caloric intake that is maintaining your present weight. It will also help to identify the stimuli that elicit and reinforce your eating behavior.

Weight Chart. Decide how much you want to lose and set a weekly goal for weight loss. Your weekly goal should be realistic—between one and two pounds. Record your weight each day on graph paper. In addition to showing how weight varies with food intake, this visual record will reinforce your dieting efforts as you observe progress toward your goal.

CONTROLLING STIMULUS CONDITIONS

Use these procedures to narrow the range of stimuli associated with eating:
1 Eat only at predetermined times, at a specific table, using a special place mat, napkin, dishes, and so forth. Do *not* eat at other times or in other places—for example, while standing in the kitchen.
2 Do *not* combine eating with other activities, such as reading or watching television.
3 Keep in the house only those foods that are permitted on your diet.
4 Shop for food only after having had a full meal, and buy only those items that are on a previously prepared list.

MODIFYING ACTUAL EATING BEHAVIOR

Use these procedures to break the chain of responses that make eating automatic:
1 Eat very slowly while paying close attention to the food.
2 Finish chewing and swallowing before putting more food on the fork.
3 Put your utensils down for periodic short breaks before continuing to eat.

DEVELOPING INCOMPATIBLE RESPONSES

When tempted to eat at times other than those specified, find a substitute activity that is incompatible with eating. For example, exercise to music, go for a walk, talk with a friend (preferably one who knows you are dieting), study your diet plan and weight graph noting how much weight you have lost.

SELF-REINFORCEMENT

Arrange to reward yourself with an activity you enjoy (watching television, reading, planning a new wardrobe, visiting a friend) when you have maintained appropriate eating behavior for a day. Plan larger rewards (for example, buying something you want) for a specified amount of weight loss. Self-punishment (other than forgoing a reward) is probably less effective, because dieting is a fairly depressing business anyway. But you might decrease the frequency of binge eating by immediately reciting to yourself the aversive consequences or by looking at an unattractive picture of yourself in a bathing suit.

Based in part on Stuart and Davis (1972) and O'Leary and Wilson (1975)

TECHNIQUES OF PSYCHOTHERAPY

"Mental Illness" Versus "Maladaptive Habits"

A person shows certain abnormal behavior—for example, a phobia of crowds, compulsive rituals, or mute unresponsiveness. Are these "maladaptive habits," or are they "symptoms of an underlying disorder"? This is an issue on which *behavior therapists* and *insight therapists* disagree. Behavior therapists say, "Change the behavior and you have cured the disorder." Psychoanalysts and other more traditional therapists maintain that maladaptive behavior is only a symptom of an underlying "disease." They view mental disorders as analogous to physical disorders and consider it futile to treat the symptoms without removing the underlying pathology. (The physician treating a case of syphilis does not simply apply an ointment to the rash but destroys the syphilis spirochete with antibiotics.) According to this view, a phobia or other neurotic symptom is only the surface expression of more complex emotional difficulties; removal of the phobia without treatment of the underlying problem may result in *symptom substitution*. The patient develops *new* symptoms (new neurotic defenses against the anxiety caused by internal conflict) if the therapist eliminates the original symptom without curing the underlying conflict.

Behavior therapy is criticized by some as being a superficial method of treatment that removes the symptoms without dealing with the inner conflicts, thereby leaving the patient vulnerable to symptom substitution.

Behavior therapists, of course, disagree. They maintain that there need be no underlying conflict. A neurosis is a set of maladaptive habits formed through the process of conditioning; once the habits (symptoms) are extinguished and replaced by more adaptive ones, the "illness is cured." The symptom *is* the problem, and eliminating the symptom eliminates the problem.

The debate is not easily settled, for a number of reasons; but the evidence suggests that symptom substitution does not occur very often. Several reviews of post-treatment evaluation studies found few instances of new symptoms up to two years after successful treatment by behavior modification methods (Grossberg, 1964; Paul and Bernstein, 1973). Instead, the removal of a disturbing "symptom" usually creates better emotional health; the person's self-esteem is increased by this accomplishment, and other people respond more favorably to the individual once his or her behavior has changed.

The broader issue of whether abnormal behavior should be viewed as "mental illness" or "maladaptive behavior" is more difficult to resolve. There does seem to be some advantage in minimizing the disease concept, at least as far as neuroses are concerned, and focusing instead on the very practical problem of how people can change their behavior to cope more satisfactorily with the problems of life. One psychiatrist sums up the issue in this way: "Our adversaries are not demons, witches, fate, or mental illness. We have no enemy whom we can fight, exorcise, or dispel by 'cure.' What we do have are problems *in living*—whether these be biologic, economic, political, or sociopsychological" (Szasz, 1961, p. 118).

On the other hand, to completely deny that any illness is involved in serious mental disorders does not seem fully justified. Current research makes the complex interplay between "physical" and "mental" functioning increasingly clear. To view psychotic disorders as solely a problem of reeducation is a misleading oversimplification. As we noted in Chapter 15, biochemical abnormalities appear to play an important role in schizophrenia and in some depressive disorders.

they're going to be evaluating me, pointing out any flaws in my presentation." Clearly, the second student is anxious about the seminar, and the more she thinks about being "on the spot" or being evaluated by others, the more anxious she becomes. Our thoughts influence our actions, and our actions influence our thoughts.

In discussing social learning theory (see pp. 387–88), we noted that a person's behavior depends partly on his or her expectations of the *outcome* of the behavior—"What will be the result if I take this action?"—and expectations of *personal effectiveness*—"Will I be able to perform the necessary actions?" Sometimes our expectations of the outcome of a certain behavior may be irrational or unrealistic; for example: "If I assert myself or stand up for my rights, other people won't like me." More often, we may be pretty realistic about the outcome of certain behaviors but may have grave doubts about our ability to execute them successfully. Many of the procedures that are effective in changing behavior appear to increase the person's feelings of mastery. For example, to reduce fear of snakes, it is helpful to watch another person handle a snake without dire consequences or to imagine interacting with a boa constrictor while relaxed, but it is more effective to actually handle a snake. Actual performance increases feelings of self-mastery (Bandura, 1977).

Behavior therapy methods—systematic desensitization, assertive training, positive reinforcement and extinction, modeling, and self-regulation—have been used successfully in treating a wide variety of problems. Although these procedures may seem rather cold and unfeeling, in actual practice the therapist shows concern for the person's welfare and considerable warmth in the relationship. These qualities appear to be necessary in any type of therapy—when they are lacking, behavior modification techniques are not very successful.

Humanistic Therapies

Humanistic therapists are concerned with the uniqueness of each individual, and they focus on the person's natural tendency toward growth and self-actualization (see p. 395). The humanistic therapist does not interpret the person's behavior (as would a psychoanalyst) or try to modify it (as would a behavior therapist). The goal of the humanistic therapist is to facilitate exploration of the individual's own thoughts and feelings and to assist the individual in arriving at his or her own solutions. This approach will become clearer as we look at client-centered therapy, one of the most widely used humanistic therapies.

CLIENT-CENTERED THERAPY Client-centered therapy, developed by Carl Rogers, is based on the assumption that the client is the best expert on him or herself and that, given a fair chance, people can work out the solutions to their own problems. The task of the therapist is to facilitate this progress—not to ask probing questions or to make interpretations or to suggest courses of action. In fact, Rogers prefers the term "facilitator" to "therapist."

Client-centered therapy can be described rather simply, but in practice it requires great skill and is much more subtle than it first appears. The therapist begins by explaining the nature of the interviews: the responsibility for working out problems is the client's; he or she is free to leave at any time and to choose whether or not to return; the relationship is a private and confidential one; the client is free to speak of intimate matters without fear of reproof or of having information revealed to others. Once the situation is structured, the clients do most of the talking. Usually they have a good deal to "get off their chest." The therapist is a patient but alert listener. When the client stops, as though expecting the therapist to say something, the therapist usually acknowledges and accepts the feelings the client has expressed. For example, if a man has been talking about his nagging mother, the therapist may say, "You feel that your mother tries to control you." The object is to *clarify* the feelings the client has been expressing, not to judge them or to elaborate on them.

Generally the clients begin therapy with rather low evaluations of themselves, but in the course of facing up to problems and trying to arrive at solutions, they become more positive. For example, one case began with statements such as the following:

> Everything is wrong with me. I feel abnormal. I don't do even the ordinary things of life. I'm sure I will fail on anything I undertake. I'm inferior. When I try to imitate successful people, I'm only acting. I can't go on like this.

Carl Rogers (top, center) "facilitating" discussion in a therapy group

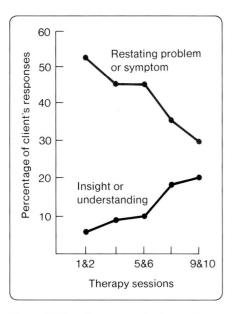

Fig. 16-5 Changes during client-centered therapy
Description and restatement of the problem on the part of the client gradually gives way during the course of therapy to increased frequency of statements indicating understanding. (Data from Seeman, 1949)

By the time of the final interview, the client expressed the following attitudes, which contrast strikingly with those of the first interview:

I am taking a new course of my own choosing. I am really changing. I have always tried to live up to others' standards that were beyond my abilities. I've come to realize that I'm not so bright, but I can get along anyway. I no longer think so much about myself. I'm much more comfortable with people. I'm getting a feeling of success out of my job. I don't feel quite steady yet, and would like to feel that I can come for more help if I need it. (Case reported by Snyder and others, 1947)

To determine whether this kind of progress is typical, experimenters have carefully analyzed recorded interviews. When clients' statements are classified and plotted, the course of therapy turns out to be fairly predictable. In the early interviews, people spend a good deal of time talking about their problems and describing symptoms. During the course of therapy, they make more and more statements that indicate an *understanding* of their particular problems. By classifying all clients' remarks as either "problem restatements" or "statements of understanding and insight," one can see the progressive increase in insight as therapy proceeds (see Figure 16-5).

What do client-centered therapists do to bring about these changes? First of all, they create an atmosphere in which the client feels worthy and significant. The atmosphere develops not as a consequence of technique but as a result of the therapist's conviction that every person has the capacity to deal constructively with his or her psychological situation.

In accepting this viewpoint, therapists cannot merely be passive listeners; if they were, clients might feel that the therapists were not interested in them. The therapists listen intently and try to show in what they say that they can see things as the client sees them. When Rogers originated client-centered therapy, he emphasized the therapist's role in clarifying the feelings expressed by the client. Rogers now believes this method to be too intellectualistic. Currently he emphasizes that the therapist should try to adopt the client's own frame of reference—that is, try to see the problems as the client sees them. To have therapeutic value, the change in the client must be a change in feeling, a change in attitude—not merely a change in intellectual understanding.

For Rogers, the most important element of a therapeutic relationship is a therapist who is a "genuine or self-congruent person"—that is, one who is not playing a role or operating behind a professional front but is open and honest in his or her relationship with the patient. People tend not to reveal themselves to those who are not completely genuine in their relationship with others.

A great deal has been learned from client-centered therapy, but it is difficult to know with certainty what its range of usefulness is and what its limitations are. It does appear that this method—like psychoanalysis—can function successfully only with individuals who are fairly verbal and are motivated to discuss their problems. With persons who do not voluntarily seek help and with psychotics who are too withdrawn to be able to discuss their feelings, more directive methods are usually necessary. The techniques of client-centered therapy have been used successfully, however, in counseling neurotic patients, in play therapy with children, and in group therapy.

Group Therapy

Many emotional problems involve an individual's difficulties in relating to others—feelings of isolation, rejection, and loneliness; inability to interact satisfactorily with others or to form meaningful relationships. While the therapist can help the individual with some of these problems, the final test lies in how well the person can apply the attitudes and responses learned in therapy to relationships in everyday life. This points out the advantage of *group therapy*, in which clients can work out their problems in the presence of others, observing how other people react to their behavior and trying out new methods of responding when old ones prove unsatisfactory.

Therapists of various orientations (psychoanalytic, humanistic, and behaviorist) have modified their techniques to be applicable to therapy groups. And group therapy has been used successfully in a wide variety of settings—in hospital wards, with both psychotic and neurotic patients; in outpatient psychiatric clinics; with parents of disturbed children; and with juveniles in correctional institutions, for example. Typically, the groups consist of a small number of individuals (6 to 12 is considered optimal) with similar problems. The therapist generally remains in the background, allowing the members to exchange experiences, comment on one another's behavior, and discuss their own problems as well as those of the other members. Initially the members tend to be defensive and uncomfortable when exposing their weaknesses, but they gradually become more objective about their own behavior and more aware of the effect their attitudes and behavior have on others. They gain an increased ability to identify and empathize with others in the group and a feeling of self-esteem when they are able to help a fellow member by offering an understanding remark or a meaningful interpretation.

Group therapy has several advantages over individual therapy. (1) It saves time, because one therapist can help several people at once. (2) People derive comfort and support from observing that others have similar—and, maybe, worse—problems. (3) People can learn vicariously, by watching how others behave, and they can explore attitudes and reactions by interacting with a variety of people, not just with the therapist.

ENCOUNTER GROUPS In the past decade, group therapy has expanded from a method for resolving emotional problems to a popular means of learning how to relate to others. Encounter groups, also known as *T-groups* (training groups) or *sensitivity groups*, consist of 12 to 20 individuals who may meet for only one intensive weekend session or for sessions over a period of several months in an attempt to better understand how they behave in their interpersonal interactions. Members are urged to express attitudes and feelings not usually displayed in public. The group leader (or *facilitator*, as he or she is sometimes called, because the job is not really to lead) encourages the participants to explore their own feelings and motives as well as those of other group members. The objective is to stimulate an exchange that is not inhibited by defensiveness and that achieves a maximum of openness and honesty.

Carl Rogers, who has studied various types of encounter groups, describes a fairly consistent pattern of change as the sessions progress (Rogers, 1970). Initially there tends to be confusion and some frustration when the facilitator makes it clear that he or she will not take the responsibility for directing the group. There is also resistance to expressing feelings; if one member describes some personal feeling, other members may try to stop the person, questioning whether it is appropriate to express such feelings in the group. At the next stage, the participants gradually begin to talk about feelings and problems they have encountered outside the group. They then begin to discuss relationships within the group; often the first feeling expressed is a negative attitude toward oneself or toward another group member. When the individual finds that these feelings are accepted, a climate of trust begins to develop. By the final sessions,

Expressing feelings in an encounter group and overcoming inhibitions about physical contact

Some methods used in an encounter group to explore emotions and release tensions

the group members have become impatient with defensiveness; they attempt to undercut facades, insisting that individuals be themselves. The tact and polite cover-up that are acceptable outside the group are not tolerated within it.

In theory, the feedback the individual receives as to how his or her behavior affects others and the feelings of acceptance engendered by the sympathy and helpfulness of the group members lead to increased self-awareness and to behavior change both within and outside the group. Studies of the effects of encounter group participation, however, raise doubts about the extent of behavior change that actually occurs. One study of more than 200 college students who participated in encounter groups with well-trained leaders found that only a third of the students showed positive changes following their experience (based on self-reports and ratings by close friends). Another third of the students showed no change, and the remainder displayed negative changes—either dropping out of the group because they found it disturbing or feeling afterward that the experience aggravated personal problems without resolving them (Lieberman, Yalom, and Miles, 1973).

Although encounter groups provide an opportunity for psychologically healthy people to learn something about themselves from the honest reactions of others, they are generally not helpful for those with emotional problems. For one thing, encounter groups are less effective in producing behavior change than either individual therapy or more traditional therapy groups. In more traditional groups, participants are carefully selected and meetings extend over a longer period of time, so that interpersonal problems can be worked out. In addition, the encounter group emphasis on "free expression of emotion" may prove harmful to individuals whose self-esteem is too tenuous to withstand group criticism and pressure (Kirsch and Glass, 1977).

FAMILY THERAPY A special form of group therapy is *family therapy*. These therapy groups include one or two therapists (usually one male and one female), the client, and the client's immediate family. The family group may consist of husband and wife or of parents and children. On the assumption that the individual's problems reflect a more general maladjustment of the family, the therapy is directed toward helping the family members clarify and express their feelings about one another, develop greater mutual understanding, and work out more effective ways of relating to one another and solving their common problems.

Sometimes videotape recordings are used to make the family members aware of how they interact with each other. Or the therapist may visit the family in the home to observe the conflicts and verbal exchanges as they occur in their natural setting. Insight therapists focus on resolving family conflicts; behavior therapists try to modify the conditions within the family that reinforce maladaptive behavior. Parents with a problem child may be taught to carefully observe their own and their child's behavior to determine how their reactions may be reinforcing certain responses and extinguishing others. For example, a child's temper tantrums and abusive behavior may be inadvertently reinforced by the attention they elicit. The next step is to alter the reinforcement conditions.

A family therapy group

An Eclectic Approach

There are many variations of psychotherapy in addition to those we have discussed. Several are listed in Table 16-2. Most psychotherapists, however, do

TABLE 16-2
Some approaches to psychotherapy

NAME	FOCUS	METHODS
Gestalt therapy	To become aware of the "whole" personality by working through unresolved conflicts and discovering those aspects of one's being that are blocked from awareness. Emphasis is on becoming intensely aware of how one is feeling and behaving at the moment.	Therapy in group setting, but therapist works with one individual at a time. Acting out fantasies, dreams, or the two sides to one's conflict are methods used to increase awareness. Combines psychoanalytic emphasis on resolving internal conflicts with behaviorist emphasis on awareness of one's behavior and humanistic concern for self-actualization.
Reality therapy	To clarify one's values and evaluate current behavior and future plans in relation to these values. To force the individual to accept responsibility.	Therapist helps the individual perceive the consequences of possible courses of action and decide on a realistic solution or goal. A "contract" may be signed once a plan of action is chosen in which the client agrees that he or she will follow through.
Rational-emotive therapy	To get rid of certain "irrational" ideas—for example: "It is essential to be loved and admired by everyone all the time"; "One should be competent in all respects"; "People have little control over their sorrow and unhappiness." Assumes that cognitive change will produce emotional change.	Therapist attacks and contradicts the individual's ideas in an attempt to persuade him or her to take a more "rational" view of the situation.
Transactional analysis	To become aware of the intent behind one's communications; to eliminate subterfuge and deceit in order to see one's behavior for what it really is.	Therapy in group setting. Communications between married couples or group members are analyzed in terms of the part of the personality that is speaking—"Parent," "Child," or "Adult" (similar to Freud's superego, id, and ego)—and the intent of the message. Destructive social interactions or "games" are exposed for what they are.
Hypnotherapy	To relieve symptoms and strengthen ego processes by helping the individual set reality aside and make constructive use of imagery.	Therapist uses various hypnotic procedures, including self-hypnosis, in an attempt to (1) reduce conflict and doubt by focusing the individual's attention, (2) modify symptoms through direct suggestion or displacement, and (3) strengthen ability to cope.

not adhere strictly to any *one* particular method. Instead, they take an *eclectic approach*, selecting from the different techniques those they feel are most appropriate for the individual client. Although their theoretical orientation may be toward a particular method or "school" (for example, more psychoanalytic than behaviorist), they feel free to discard those concepts they view as not especially helpful and to select techniques from other schools. In short, they are flexible in their approach to therapy. In dealing with a very anxious individual, for instance, an eclectic psychotherapist might first prescribe tranquilizers and relaxation training to help reduce the person's level of anxiety. (Psychoanalysts would not, because they believe that anxiety is necessary to motivate the client to explore his or her conflicts.) To help the client understand the origins of his or her problems, the eclectic therapist might discuss

"Don't shoot. I am Dr. Cranish, and this is my patient. I am a pioneer in excitement therapy."

certain aspects of the patient's history (a client-centered therapist does not delve into the past) but might feel it unnecessary to explore childhood experiences to the extent that a psychoanalyst does. The therapist might use educational techniques—for example, providing information about sex and reproduction to help relieve the anxieties of an adolescent boy who has been misinformed and feels guilty about his sexual impulses or explaining the functioning of the autonomic nervous system to reassure an anxious woman that some of her symptoms, such as heart palpitations and hand tremors, are not indications of a disease.

Another technique, one not mentioned so far in our discussion of psychotherapy, is to change the patient's environment. The therapist might feel, for example, that a young man who has serious conflicts in his relationship with his parents can make little progress in overcoming his difficulties while remaining in the home environment. In this instance, the therapist might recommend that the youth attend school away from home or seek employment in another community. Occasionally, with a younger child, the home environment may be so seriously detrimental to the child's mental health that the therapist, with the help of welfare agencies and courts, may see that the child is placed in a foster home.

Effectiveness of Psychotherapies

With so many types of psychotherapy available, you may well wonder, "Which method is best?" or "Who can help me with my problem?" These questions are not easy to answer. Research into the effectiveness of psychotherapy is hampered by several major difficulties. How do we define "success"? How do we know which treatment variables were responsible? What about the "placebo effect"?

Criteria of Success

How do we know that an individual is helped by therapy? We cannot always rely on the person's statement. Sometimes people report that they are feeling better simply to please the therapist or to convince themselves that their money was well spent. The *hello-goodbye effect* has long been recognized by therapists. When people say "hello" at the beginning of therapy, they tend to exaggerate their unhappiness and problems, as if to convince the therapist that they really need help. When they say "goodbye" at the end of a course of therapy, they tend to exaggerate their well-being, either to express appreciation to the therapist for his or her efforts or to convince themselves that their time and money were not wasted. These phenomena must always be considered when evaluating the client's view of progress.

The therapist's evaluation of the treatment as "successful" cannot always be taken as an objective criterion either. The therapist has a vested interest in proclaiming that the client is better. And sometimes the changes that the person shows during the therapy session do not carry over into real-life situations.

Objective measures of improvement—performing more effectively on the job, getting along better with family and friends, drinking less, and so on—are more valid but are difficult to obtain in long-term studies of psychotherapeutic effectiveness.

Confounding of Variables

It is not always clear that the techniques the therapist consciously employs are the ones that effect the observed changes in the person's behavior; other variables may have been more important. For example, systematic desensitization has proved very effective in reducing fears and phobias, but the results may stem from changes in the client's *expectancies* for improvement rather than the specific techniques used (Kazdin and Wilcoxon, 1976). In addition, no two therapists who use the same method have the same personality, and no two clients bring the same attitudes, problems, and methods of coping with their difficulties to the therapeutic session. *Therapist variables* and *patient variables* interact with treatment methods, making it difficult to assess which factors are related to a successful outcome. For example, studies have shown that some therapists are more effective than others and that experienced therapists usually are more effective than inexperienced therapists, regardless of the treatment method used (Garfield and Bergin, 1978).

To complicate the picture still further, some people improve if they *think* they are receiving effective treatment, even if it is only a sugar pill; the *placebo effect* must be considered in evaluating any form of treatment. And a fair number of people, both psychotic and neurotic, will get better without any treatment—*spontaneous remission.* The rate of spontaneous remission must be used as a baseline for evaluating any form of therapy.

Despite these difficulties, a number of controlled studies indicate that (1) psychotherapy does help and that (2) different therapeutic approaches do not differ greatly in effectiveness (Smith and Glass, 1977). We will describe one well-controlled study as an example. Ninety outpatients at a university clinic were randomly assigned to one of three groups: behavior therapy, short-term psychoanalytic therapy, and a wait-list (those in the wait-list group had an initial interview, during which background information was gathered, but they received no treatment). Both the behavior therapists and the analysts were well-trained and experienced. The clients were evaluated before and after "treatment" on a number of measures: psychological tests; reports from people who knew them well; and ratings by the therapist, the client, and an independent assessor. In addition, tape recordings were made of every fifth therapy session so that the behavior of both the therapists and the clients could be evaluated. After four months of "treatment," all three groups, including the wait-list group, showed significant improvement, but the two therapy groups had improved significantly more than the wait group. In overall outcome, for example, the independent assessor rated 80 percent of both therapy groups as improved and only 48 percent of the wait group as improved. Similar results were found with other measures, although there was a tendency for the behavior therapy group to show slightly more improvement than the psychoanalytic group. A follow-up evaluation a year later found that all three groups had maintained their improvement (Sloane and others, 1975).

The question that concerns most current researchers is not "which therapeutic approach is best?" but rather, "which method is most effective for a particular problem?" The latter question is difficult to investigate because it requires finding a large number of people with the same problem and assigning them to different treatment conditions; as we have seen, behavior disorders differ markedly from one person to the next. Preliminary findings indicate that some of the behavior therapy techniques are more effective in treating specific anxieties and phobias than is either psychoanalytic or client-centered therapy.

"Today we'll try aversion therapy. Every time you say something stupid, I'll spill a bucket of water on your head."

Effective therapies appear to share certain common features: (1) a warm, confiding relationship between the client and a help-giving individual or group, (2) a special setting that provides promise for help, and (3) a set of activities that both the therapist and the client believe will produce change. Most people who seek therapy feel miserable and unable to cope with their life situation. It may be that these common features ease the person's feeling of despair and provide hope that change is possible (Frank, 1974).

Biological Therapies

Biological therapies for the treatment of abnormal behavior include the use of drugs, electroshock, and surgical procedures. In discussing the causes of disorders such as depression and schizophrenia, we mentioned several biological theories. "Mind" and "body" share an intimate relationship, and there is no doubt that biological changes affect thoughts and behavior, and vice versa.

Electroshock Therapy and Psychosurgery

The use of electric shock to produce convulsive seizures and unconsciousness was a popular method of treatment 40 years ago. But it was not successful in alleviating most disorders, including schizophrenia, and is used today only with severely depressed patients who have failed to respond to other forms of treatment. In electroshock therapy, the patient is injected with a muscle-relaxant type of sedative, placed on a bed, and given an electric shock across electrodes placed on the temples.[2] The shock is intense enough to produce a convulsion, which is followed by a brief period of unconsciousness. Afterward the patient does not remember anything about the shock or the convulsion. No one knows how the shock produces its therapeutic effect. It may increase the secretion of two neurotransmitters, norepinephrine and serotonin, that may be deficient in some cases of depression. But the evidence is not clear. In any event, electroshock does seem to snap some patients out of a severe depression. Unfortunately, it does not prevent future depressions.

In *psychosurgery,* selected areas of the brain are destroyed, either by cutting nerve fibers or by destroying them with ultrasonic irradiation. Most often the fibers destroyed are those that connect the frontal lobes with the limbic system or with certain regions of the hypothalamus (both the limbic system and the hypothalamus are believed to play an important role in emotion). As you might suspect, psychosurgery is a highly controversial topic, and congressional committees have been investigating whether the procedure should be banned entirely. Some of the early surgical methods produced individuals who were relaxed and cheerful (no longer violent or suicidal) but whose brains were so impaired that they could not function efficiently. Newer techniques appear to cause minimal intellectual impairment, and the procedure may help severely depressed and suicidal patients when all other forms of treatment have failed to relieve distress (National Commission for the Protection of Human Subjects of Biomedical and Behavioral Research, 1976).

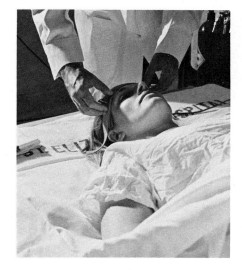

Electroshock therapy being administered to patient

[2] A new method that delivers electric shock to only one side of the brain (the nondominant hemisphere) seems to produce seizures as effectively as bilateral shock and to result in less disorientation on awakening (Belenky, 1976).

The Double-Blind Procedure in Drug Studies

The initial enthusiasm for a new treatment method is almost always dampened by evidence from more carefully controlled research. This has been particularly true in the area of drug therapy. The results of a drug study may be influenced by a number of variables other than the therapeutic properties of the drug itself. One such variable is the hope and confidence the patient places in a new treatment. For example, a *placebo* (an inert substance that has no pharmacological properties and cannot affect the patient physiologically) can frequently bring about marked improvement in a person's condition, thus demonstrating that improvement was the result of expectations. Another variable is the confidence of the doctors and nurses in a new treatment method, which can also inadvertently affect their judgment of the results. And the extra attention focused on a patient who is the subject of a research project can have beneficial effects. To control the first two variables, the more stringent studies use what is called the *double-blind procedure.* Half the patients receive a placebo, the others receive the actual drug. Neither the patients nor the doctors and nurses who must judge the results of the treatment know who received the drug; thus, in the ideally controlled study, both patients and judges are "blind"—hence the term "double-blind."

The importance of a well-controlled research design has been demonstrated by a survey of a large number of studies dealing with the effect of chlorpromazine on hospitalized schizophrenics. Each study was classified according to the extent that awareness of medication was controlled: (1) double-blind—neither patient nor judges were aware or (2) single-blind—only judges were aware. The group of studies taken as a whole showed a median of 52 percent of the patients judged as "improved." The double-blind studies showed a median of 37 percent judged as "improved"; the single-blind studies showed a median of 60 percent "improved." The more carefully controlled studies report considerably less improvement following treatment with chlorpromazine than do the studies that are less well controlled (Glick and Margolis, 1962).

The situation, however, is more complicated than it appears at first glance. Although it seems probable that differences in adequacy of experimental control were partly responsible for the differences in results, the double-blind studies differed from the single-blind in another major respect: the average period of drug treatment was significantly longer for patients in the single-blind studies than for those in the double-blind studies. Hence, the higher improvement rate for the single-blind studies may have resulted from the fact that the patients in these studies had a more extended period of treatment. The two possibilities are related; the more control one requires in a study, the more difficult it is to sustain the procedures for a long period of time.

Drug Therapies

By far the most successful biological therapy is the use of tranquilizers and other drugs to modify behavior. The discovery of two major tranquilizers, *reserpine* and *chlorpromazine,* in the early 1950s provided a major breakthrough in the treatment of severely disturbed patients. Both of these tranquilizers have the amazing capacity to calm and relax the individual without inducing sleep, although they may produce some degree of drowsiness and lethargy. They have been particularly effective in the treatment of acute schizophrenic episodes. In addition to calming the intensely agitated schizophrenic, these drugs gradually alleviate or abolish hallucinations and, to a lesser extent, delusions. Even more important, they frequently decrease the extent of emotional withdrawal, so that the patient can be reached by psychotherapy. The use of tranquilizing drugs has produced a marked decrease in the total number of patients in neuropsychiatric hospitals.

Minor tranquilizers such as diazepam (Valium), meprobamate (Miltown), and chlordiazepoxide (Librium) have proved effective in reducing tension in normal individuals as well as in treating neuroses and psychosomatic disorders. However, minor tranquilizers are often misused; people can become dependent on them instead of learning ways to cope with anxiety.

Another group of drugs, the antidepressants, help to elevate the mood of depressed individuals. They energize rather than tranquilize. Apparently, these drugs affect the amount of certain neurotransmitters within the brain. The two major kinds are the tricyclics (for example, Tofranil and Elavil) and the mono-amine oxidase (MAO) inhibitors (for example, Nardil and Parnate). And, as we noted in Chapter 15, lithium carbonate has been used successfully in treating manic states.

Drug therapy has successfully reduced the seriousness of many types of abnormal behavior, particularly the psychoses. Many individuals who otherwise would require hospitalization can function within the community with the help of some of these drugs. On the other hand, there are limitations. All of them can have undesirable side-effects. In addition, many psychologists feel that they alleviate symptoms without requiring the individual to face the problems that are creating maladaptive behaviors. They point out that the attitudes and response patterns that have developed gradually over a lifetime cannot be changed suddenly by the administration of a drug. Therefore, when therapeutic drugs are used, psychotherapeutic help is usually needed also.

Enhancing Mental Health

The prevention and treatment of mental disorders is a problem of tremendous concern both for the nation and for the community. And remarkable progress has been made within the past two decades. As we noted earlier in this chapter, the Community Mental Health Centers Act, passed by Congress in 1963, provided funds for the establishment of hundreds of community mental health centers where people could be treated close to family and friends rather than in a large state psychiatric hospital. Such centers provide short-term hospitalization, outpatient treatment, and a 24-hour emergency service. They are also concerned with *preventing* emotional problems through consultation with schools, juvenile courts, and other community agencies. The following program, devised by a community mental health center in San Francisco to cope with the problems of enforced school busing, illustrates this concern.

> We designed a program in which we place a professional staff person on a school bus to ride to and from school with grade school children; in addition this staff person had street-corner meetings with the parents about their busing concerns, and acted as their advocate to the schools. Knowing the children would be experiencing separation anxiety . . . we had our hospital art department design coloring books with maps of the territory they would cover on the bus route; we attempted to introduce play materials and games that would be helpful to the children, would encourage the children to carry "transitional objects" from home on the bus such as dolls, teddy bears, special favorite toys. Our staff member met with the children before they boarded the bus, talked to them on the bus, again in their new school yard and on the way back home again. (Heiman, 1973, p. 60)

Community Resources and the Role of Nonprofessionals

A wide variety of community resources has been developed in response to the psychological needs of different groups. During the 1960s, for example, a "free clinic" was established in the Haight Ashbury district of San Francisco to meet the needs of young people who had drifted there to join the "hippie" movement. Many of these young people developed serious physical and psychological problems (often associated with malnutrition and the use of drugs); but, because they were suspicious of the "establishment," they were reluctant to go to the usual private or public resources for help. The Haight-Ashbury Free Clinic, organized by volunteer physicians, psychiatrists, and psychologists, offered free treatment with no questions asked about drug usage, sexual behavior, or delinquency and gave no information to relatives or police. The success of this clinic prompted other communities to follow suit, and free clinics have been established in many areas, with services expanded to meet the needs of individuals of all ages.

Another community resource is the half-way house, where patients who have been hospitalized can live while making the transition back to an independent life in the community. There are also residential centers for people recovering from alcohol and drug problems, for delinquent or runaway youths, and for "battered wives." "Rap centers," where troubled teen-agers can go to discuss their problems with each other and with sympathetic counselors, play an important role in many communities, as do youth centers in poverty areas, which provide job counseling, remedial education, and help with family and personal problems.

CRISIS INTERVENTION A fairly recent development is *crisis intervention*, which attempts to provide immediate help for individuals and families undergoing intense stress. During periods of acute emotional turmoil, people often feel overwhelmed and incapable of dealing with the situation; they may not be able to wait for a therapy appointment, or they may not know where to turn. One form of crisis intervention is provided by 24-hour walk-in services, often in a Community Mental Health Center, where the person can be attended to immediately. The therapist can help clarify the problem, give reassurance, suggest plans of action, and mobilize the support of other agencies or family members. This kind of therapy is usually short-term—five or six sessions—and is aimed at providing the support needed to help the person through the crisis. Such short-term intervention often prevents the need for hospitalization.

Another form of crisis intervention is the telephone "hot line." Telephone crisis centers are usually staffed by volunteers under the direction of mental health professionals. Some focus specifically on suicide prevention; others are more general, helping distressed callers find the particular kind of assistance they need. The volunteers usually receive training that emphasizes (1) listening with care, (2) evaluating the potential for suicide, (3) conveying empathy and understanding, (4) providing information about community resources, (5) giving hope and reassurance, and (6) getting the caller's name and phone number before he or she hangs up so that the problem can be followed up. Most major cities in the United States have developed some form of telephone hot line to help people who are undergoing periods of severe stress. There are also specialized hot lines to deal with problems of child abuse, rape victims, and runaways. The phone numbers are widely publicized in the hope of reaching those who need help.

It is too early to conclude much about the effectiveness of telephone crisis centers. Several studies found no difference in suicide rates for cities with hot line services and those without (Weiner, 1969; Lester, 1974). Another study suggests that calling a friend or relative may be more beneficial to a person than calling a crisis center (Speer, 1972). But research on suicide prevention

Nonprofessionals as therapists
College students and other volunteers can do much to augment therapeutic programs in hospitals and mental health centers, whether trained in special therapeutic techniques or simply by providing conversation and companionship. This young woman is working with a disturbed child.

Fig. 16-6 A residential program for delinquent youths
A family conference at Achievement Place, a group home for boys who are referred by the courts because of behavior problems. The boys and their professional teacher-parents meet daily to discuss rules of conduct, decide on consequences for violations of the rules, criticize aspects of the program, and evaluate a peer manager who oversees many of the boys' activities.

and the effectiveness of hot lines is difficult, because there are so many uncontrolled variables. For people without friends, relatives, or other forms of emotional support the hot line may provide a life-saving service.

NONPROFESSIONALS AS THERAPISTS Most of the community programs we have discussed could not function without the help of nonprofessionals. Because the need for psychological services has outstripped the supply of available therapists, concerned citizens can play a valuable role. People of all ages and backgrounds have been trained to work in the area of community mental health. College students have served as companions for hospitalized psychotics (Matarazzo, 1971); older women who have successfully raised families have been trained as "mental health counselors" to work with adolescents in community clinics, to counsel mothers of youngsters with behavior problems, and to work with schizophrenic children (Donahue, 1967; Rioch, 1967); former mental patients, drug addicts, and prison inmates have been trained to help those with problems similar to the ones they experienced.

Many residential programs are run by nonprofessionals in consultation with trained therapists. An outstanding example is "Achievement Place," a home located in a middle-class community where a couple acts as surrogate parents for about a dozen boys referred by the courts because of delinquent behavior (Phillips and others, 1972). Behavior therapy methods are used to extinguish aggressive behavior and to reward social skills (see Figure 16-6).

Another example of the use of nonprofessionals is a project in which male college students served as "companion-therapists" for young boys with behavior problems. Fifty pairs of boys, matched according to age, socioeconomic status, and several other variables, were selected. One member of each pair was assigned to a student companion-therapist, the other served as a control, receiving no treatment. Each student met with "his" boy for several hours two or three times a week throughout the school year, engaging in whatever activities seemed to interest the boy. The training received by the student therapists consisted of (1) two initial half-day workshops that focused on "helping relationships" and (2) weekly group discussions with professional leaders throughout the year. The results of the project indicated that boys who

had problems of isolation and withdrawal gained most from the relationships, although more aggressive boys improved too. The students themselves felt that they had improved in their ability to work with children and to relate to their own friends (Goodman, 1970).

Promoting Your Own Emotional Well-Being

The problems that people face vary greatly, and there are no universal guidelines for staying psychologically healthy. However, a few general suggestions emerge from the experiences of therapists.

1 *Accept your feelings.* Strong emotions can produce anxiety. Anger, sorrow, fear, a feeling of having fallen short of one's ideals are all very unpleasant, and we may try to escape anxiety by denying the feelings. Sometimes the desire to avoid anxiety by facing situations unemotionally leads to a false kind of detachment or "cool" that may be destructive. We may try to suppress all emotions and thus lose the ability to accept as normal the joys and sorrows that are a part of our involvement with other people.

Unpleasant emotions are a normal reaction to many situations. There is no reason to be ashamed of feeling homesick, of being afraid when learning to ski, or of being angry at someone who has disappointed us. These emotions are natural, and it is better to recognize than to deny them. When emotions cannot be expressed directly—for example, it may not be wise to tell off one's boss—it helps to find some kind of outlet for releasing tension. Taking a long walk, pounding a tennis ball, or discussing the situation with a sympathetic friend can help to dissipate anger. As long as we accept our right to feel emotion, we may express it in indirect or substitute ways when direct channels of expression are blocked.

2 *Know your vulnerabilities.* Discovering the kinds of situations that upset you or cause you to overreact may help to guard against stress. Perhaps certain people annoy you. You could avoid them, or you could try to figure out just what it is about them that is disturbing. Maybe they seem so poised and confident that they make you feel insecure. Trying to pinpoint the cause of your discomfort may help you see the situation in a new light. Perhaps you become very anxious when you have to speak up in class or present a paper. Again, you could try to avoid such situations, or you could gain confidence by taking a course in public speaking. (Many colleges offer courses specifically aimed at learning to control "speech anxiety.") You could also reinterpret the situation. Instead of thinking, "Everyone is waiting to criticize me as soon as I open my mouth," you could tell yourself, "The class will be interested in what I have to say, and if I make a few mistakes, I'm not going to let it worry me."

Many people feel especially anxious when they are under pressure. More careful planning and spacing out of work can help avoid feeling overwhelmed at the last minute. Even the very specific strategy of purposely allowing more time than you think you need to get to classes or appointments can eliminate one source of stress.

3 *Develop your talents and interests.* People who are bored and unhappy seldom have many interests. Today's college and community programs offer almost unlimited opportunities for people of all ages to explore their talents in many areas—such as sports and physical skills, academic interests, music, art, drama, and crafts. Often the more you know about a subject the more interesting it (and the world) becomes. In addition, the feeling of compe-

tency gained from developing skills can do a great deal to bolster one's self-esteem. As we noted earlier, depression often results from a reduction in rewarding activities.

4 *Become involved with other people.* Feelings of isolation and loneliness form the core of most emotional disorders. We are "social beings" who need the support, comfort, and reassurance provided by other people. Focusing all of our attention on our own problems can lead to an unhealthy preoccupation with ourselves. Sharing our concerns with others often helps us to view our troubles in a better perspective. And becoming concerned with the welfare of other people, who may also be troubled and lonely, can bolster our feelings of worth.

5 *Know when to seek help.* While the preceding suggestions can help promote emotional well-being, there are limits to self-understanding and self-help. Some problems are difficult to solve alone. Our tendency toward self-deception makes it hard to view problems objectively, and we may not know all the possible solutions. When you feel that you are making little headway in gaining control over a problem, then it is time to seek professional help—from a counseling or clinical psychologist, a psychiatrist, or other trained therapist. The willingness to seek help is a sign of emotional maturity, not a sign of weakness. Don't wait until you feel overwhelmed. We do not wait until our teeth are falling out before going to a dentist. Obtaining psychological help when needed should become as accepted a practice as going to a dentist.

SUMMARY

1 Treatment of the mentally ill has progressed from the ancient notion that abnormal behavior resulted from possession of evil spirits and therefore should be punished, through custodial care in ill-kept and isolated asylums, to our modern mental hospitals and community mental health centers, which employ a wide variety of activities designed to help people understand and modify their behavior.

2 *Psychotherapy* is the treatment of mental disorders by psychological means. One type of psychotherapy is *psychoanalysis*, which is based on concepts developed by Freud. Through the method of *free association*, repressed thoughts and feelings are brought to awareness. By *interpreting* these associations, the analyst helps the individual understand the roots of his or her problems. *Transference,* the tendency to express toward the analyst feelings one has toward important people in one's life, provides another source of interpretation. Through the processes of *abreaction, insight,* and *working through,* the individual becomes able to cope with problems more realistically.

3 Another psychotherapeutic approach is *behavior therapy,* which applies methods based on learning principles to *modify* the individual's behavior. These methods include *systematic desensitization* (the individual learns to relax in situations that previously produced anxiety), *assertive training, reinforcement* of adaptive behaviors along with *extinction* of maladaptive ones, *modeling* of appropriate behavior, and techniques for *self-regulation* of behavior.

4 *Humanistic therapies* help the individual do his or her own exploring and problem solving with a minimum of therapist intervention. Carl Rogers' *client-centered therapy* maintains a nondirective approach, letting the client determine the topics to be discussed and the goals to be accomplished.

5   *Group therapy* provides an opportunity for the individual to explore his or her attitudes and behavior in interaction with others who have similar problems. *Encounter groups*, a popular offshoot of group therapy, may help psychologically healthy individuals learn something about themselves, but they are not recommended for those with emotional problems. *Family therapy* is a special form of group therapy in which couples, or parents and children, can learn more effective ways of relating to one another.

6   The effectiveness of psychotherapy is difficult to evaluate because of problems in *defining "success,"* separating *therapist variables* from *patient variables,* and controlling for both the *placebo effect* and rates of *spontaneous remission.* Research indicates that psychotherapy does help and that different approaches do not differ greatly in effectiveness.

7   *Biological therapies* include *electroshock, psychosurgery,* and the use of *drugs* to modify behavior. Of the three, drug therapy has been by far the most successful. Tranquilizers have proved very effective in the treatment of schizophrenia, antidepressants help to elevate the mood of depressed patients, and lithium carbonate has been successful in treating manic states.

8   The *prevention* and *treatment* of mental disorders is a problem of great concern to our society. Community resources that offer help include *free clinics, half-way houses, residential centers* for those with special problems, and various forms of *crisis intervention.* We can promote our own emotional health by accepting our feelings as natural, discovering our vulnerabilities, developing talents and interests, becoming involved with others, and knowing when to seek help.

FURTHER READING

Interesting material on the historical treatment of the mentally ill may be found in Zilboorg and Henry, *A history of medical psychology* (1941), Veith, *Hysteria: The history of a disease* (1970), in paperback, and Roback, *History of psychology and psychiatry* (1961). A paperback by Szasz, *The manufacture of madness* (1977) traces the historical origins of the current concept of "mental illness."

A review of the various methods of psychotherapy is provided by Martin, *Introduction to psychotherapy* (1971). The *Handbook of psychotherapy and behavior change: An empirical analysis* (1978), edited by Garfield and Bergin, discusses research results and their possible applications.

For an introduction to psychoanalytic methods, see Menninger and Holzman, *Theory of psychoanalytic technique* (2nd ed., 1973). On client-centered therapy, see Rogers, *On becoming a person: A therapist's view of psychotherapy* (1970) and *Carl Rogers on personal power* (1977). The principles of behavior therapy are presented in O'Leary and Wilson, *Behavior therapy: Application and outcome* (1975) and Goldfried and Davison, *Clinical behavior therapy* (1976).

An overview of group therapy is presented in Yalom, *The theory and practice of group psychotherapy* (2nd ed., 1975). On encounter groups, see Lieberman, Yalom, and Miles, *Encounter groups: First facts* (1973).

For ways to modify your own behavior, see Watson and Tharp, *Self-directed behavior: Self-modification for personal adjustment* (2nd ed., 1977) and Bower and Bower, *Asserting yourself* (1976).

PART EIGHT

Social
Behavior

17
Social
Psychology

Social psychology is the study of social interaction. The person who gets an apple by shaking a tree has interacted with the physical environment. But the person who gets an apple by requesting it from a friend, fighting for it, or winning it in a talent contest has interacted with the *social environment*, the environment composed of other persons. In studying social interaction, then, social psychology studies the ways people act on one another to influence each other's thoughts, feelings, and behaviors.

Social interaction is everywhere; accordingly, social psychology deals with many diverse topics. When will individuals conform to the opinions of a group? What factors influence our first impressions of others? Under what conditions will an individual aid a stranger in distress? How can prejudice and discrimination be reduced? What kinds of people will be attracted to one another? This is but a small sampling.

We begin this chapter by presenting the unique perspective social psychologists bring to the study of human behavior—the perspective that distinguishes social psychology from other branches of the discipline. We will then apply this to the particular problem of bystander intervention: when will people help someone in distress? Second, we will explore social influence, the subject that social psychologists have explored more intensively than any other. Third, we will look at some of the factors involved in social perception: How do we form impressions of people? What leads us to like some people more than others? Finally, we will look at the closely related problem of "attribution." How do we "attribute" causes and motives to other people's behavior in order to interpret and explain their actions? How do we interpret and explain our own?

The Social-Psychological Perspective

Social interaction has, of course, been considered in earlier chapters. We saw, for example, how a child's development is affected by early experiences with other people and how personal motives are influenced by social interactions. Indeed, since most of our lives are spent in social interactions, it might seem

that almost all of psychology is social psychology. In some sense this is true. But social psychologists look at social interaction from a perspective somewhat different from that of either developmental or personality psychologists.

Emphasis on Situational Influences

Social psychologists are more likely to focus on the current or ongoing *situational influences* on human behavior than on developmental or personality factors. For example, when a person goes out of his or her way to help a stranger, the developmental or personality psychologist is likely to inquire into the kinds of past life experiences that caused this person to be altruistic (unselfishly helpful) or to have an "altruistic personality." The social psychologist is more likely to be interested in the kinds of surrounding circumstances that encouraged the individual to act. Were other bystanders present? Was physical danger involved? Did other people act as if the situation were an emergency? And so forth.

Emphasis on Phenomenology

The second feature of the social-psychological approach emphasizes the individual's *phenomenology,* his or her *own definition or interpretation of the situation.* Thus, a person may act in certain ways because he or she believes that others are hostile. Even if the belief is unfounded, this *perceived hostility* is the "cause" of the individual's behavior as far as the social psychologist is concerned. This has long been a basic premise of social psychology: "If [people] define situations as real, they are real in their consequences" (Thomas and Thomas, 1928).

Bystander Intervention: A Case Study in the Social-Psychological Perspective

In 1964 Kitty Genovese was murdered near her home in New York City at 3:30 A.M. Because she resisted, the murder took over half an hour. Some 40 neighbors heard her screams for help. And yet nobody came to her aid. No one even called the police (Rosenthal, 1964).

The American public was horrified by this incident, and social psychologists began to investigate the causes of such "bystander apathy." "Apathy" is not a very accurate term, however, for it is not simple indifference that prevents bystanders from intervening in emergencies. First, there are several realistic deterrents. For example, sometimes there is real physical danger. Second, "getting involved" often means lengthy court appearances or other entanglements. Third, emergencies arise quickly, without warning, are very different from one another, and require quick, unplanned action. Few of us are prepared for them. Finally, one risks making a fool of oneself by misinterpreting a situation as an emergency when it is not. Indeed, ". . . the bystander to an emergency situation is in an unenviable position. It is perhaps surprising that anyone should intervene at all" (Latané and Darley, 1970, p. 247).

Nevertheless, we might suppose that the presence of other bystanders would embolden the individual to act, despite the risks of getting involved. Ironically, research demonstrates that often it is the very presence of other people that prevents an individual from intervening. Specifically, the presence of others serves to (1) define the situation as a *non*emergency and (2) diffuse the responsibility for acting.

DEFINING THE SITUATION Most emergencies begin ambiguously. Is the man who is staggering about ill or simply drunk? Is the woman's life really being threatened, or is it a loud family quarrel? Is that smoke from a fire pouring out a window, or just steam? Should one intervene or not? One common way to deal with such a dilemma is to postpone action, act as if nothing is wrong, and look around to see how others are reacting. What are you likely to see? Other people who—for the same reasons—are also acting as if nothing is wrong. A state of *pluralistic ignorance* develops; that is, everybody in the group misleads everybody else by defining the situation as a nonemergency. We have all heard about crowds panicking because each person leads everybody else to overreact. The reverse, in which a crowd lulls its members into inaction, may be even more common. Several ingenious experiments demonstrate this effect.

In one, male college students were invited to an interview. As they sat in a small waiting room, a stream of smoke began to pour through a wall vent. Some subjects were alone in the waiting room when this occurred; others were in groups of three. The experimenters observed them through a one-way window and waited six minutes. Seventy-five percent of the subjects tested alone reported the smoke within about two minutes. In contrast, fewer than 13 percent of the people tested in groups reported the smoke within the six-minute period, even though the room was completely smoke-filled. Those who did not report the smoke had decided that it must have been steam, air conditioning vapors, smog, "truth gas," or practically anything but a real fire or emergency. This experiment thus showed that bystanders can define situations as nonemergencies for one another (Latané and Darley, 1968).

But perhaps these subjects were simply afraid to appear "cowardly." In a similar study, the "emergency" did not involve personal danger. Subjects in the testing room heard a female experimenter in the next office climb up on a chair to reach a bookcase, fall to the floor, and yell "Oh my god, my foot. . . . I . . . I . . . can't move . . . it. Oh . . . my ankle, . . . I can't get this . . . thing off me." She continued to moan for about a minute longer. The entire incident lasted about two minutes. Only a curtain separated the woman's office from the testing room where subjects waited alone or in pairs. The results confirmed the findings of the smoke study. Seventy percent of the subjects who were alone came to the woman's aid, whereas only 40 percent of those in two-person groups offered help. Again, those who had not intervened claimed later that they were unsure what had happened but had decided that it was not too serious (Latané and Rodin, 1969). The presence of others in these experiments produced pluralistic ignorance; each person, observing the calmness of the others, resolved the ambiguity of the situation by deciding there was no emergency.

DIFFUSION OF RESPONSIBILITY Clearly, "pluralistic ignorance" can lead individuals to define a situation as a nonemergency. But this process does not explain incidents like the Genovese murder, in which the emergency is abundantly clear. Moreover, Kitty Genovese's neighbors could not observe one another behind their curtained windows and hence could not tell whether others were calm or panicked. The crucial process here was *diffusion of responsibility*. Because each individual knows that many others are present, the burden of responsibility does not fall solely on him or her. Each can think, "certainly someone else must have done something by now; someone else will intervene."

To test this hypothesis, an experiment was conducted in which each subject

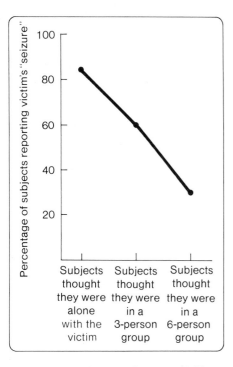

Fig. 17-1 Diffusion of responsibility
Percentage of subjects who reported a victim's apparent seizure as a function of how many other people the subject believed were in his or her discussion group. (After Darley and Latané, 1968)

Although each of these passers-by has undoubtedly noticed the man lying on the sidewalk, no one has stopped to help—to find out if he is asleep, sick, drunk, or dead. If others were not present, someone would be more likely to come to his aid.

was placed in an individual booth and told that he or she would participate in a group discussion about personal problems faced by college students. To avoid embarrassment, the discussion would be held via intercom. Each person would speak for two minutes. The microphone would be turned on only in the booth of the person speaking, and the experimenter would not be listening. Actually, the voices of all participants except the subject's were tape recordings. On the first round, one of the "taped" participants mentioned that he had problems with seizures; on the second round, this individual sounded as if he were actually starting to have a seizure. The experimenters waited to see if the subject would leave the booth to report the emergency and how long it would take. Note that (1) the emergency is not at all ambiguous, (2) the subject cannot tell how the other "bystanders" he or she believes are in the other booths are reacting, and (3) the subject knows the experimenter cannot hear the emergency. Some subjects were led to believe that the discussion group consisted only of themselves and the victim of the seizure. Others were told it was a three-person group and others, a six-person group.

Eighty-five percent of the subjects who thought that they alone knew of the victim's seizure reported it; 62 percent of those who thought they were in a three-person group reported the seizure; and only 31 percent of those who thought five other bystanders were present did so (see Figure 17-1). Interviews showed that all the subjects perceived the situation to be a real emergency. And most were very emotional about the conflict between letting the victim suffer or rushing, perhaps foolishly and unnecessarily, for help. In fact, subjects who did not report the seizure seemed far more upset than those who did. Clearly, we cannot interpret their nonintervention as "bystander apathy." Instead, the presence of others diffused the responsibility for acting.

If pluralistic ignorance and diffusion of responsibility are minimized, will people help one another? Three psychologists used the New York City subway system as their laboratory (Piliavin, Rodin, and Piliavin, 1969). Two male and two female experimenters boarded a subway train separately; the female experimenters took seats and recorded the results, while the two men remained standing. As the train moved along, one of the men staggered forward and collapsed, remaining prone and staring at the ceiling until he received help. If no help came, the other man finally helped him to his feet. Several variations of the study were tried: the victim either carried a cane (so he would appear ill) or smelled of alcohol (so he would appear drunk). Sometimes the victim was white; other times, black. There should be no ambiguity; it is clear help is needed. Diffusion of responsibility should be minimized, because each person cannot continue to assume that someone else will intervene if, in fact, nobody does. People should help.

The results supported this optimistic expectation. The victim with the cane received spontaneous help on over 95 percent of the trials, within an average of five seconds. Even the "drunk" victim received help in half of the trials, on the average within 109 seconds. Both black and white "cane" victims were aided by black and white bystanders. There was no relationship between the number of bystanders and the speed of help, suggesting that diffusion of responsibility had indeed been minimized. And all of this on the New York City subway system! This not only tends to support the proposed explanations of bystander nonintervention, but should help us revise our stereotypes about New York City subway riders.

ROLE OF "HELPING" MODELS In the subway study, as soon as one person moved to help, many others followed. This suggests that just as individuals use other people as models to define a situation as a nonemergency (pluralistic ignorance), they also use other people as models to indicate when to be helpful. This possibility was tested in a study by Bryan and Test (1967), who counted the number of drivers who stopped to help a woman whose car had a flat tire. During some test periods, another car with a flat tire (the "model" car) was parked alongside the highway one-quarter mile before the test car. The model car was raised on a jack and a woman was watching a man change the flat tire. Of 4,000 passing cars, 93 stopped to help. Thirty-five stopped when there was no model car and 58 when there was, a statistically significant difference. This experiment indicates that not only do others define when *not* to act in an emergency, but they also serve as models to show us how and when to be good Samaritans.

ROLE OF INFORMATION   Would you be more likely to intervene in an emergency now that you have read this section? An experiment at the University of Montana suggests that you would (Beaman, and others, 1978). Undergraduates were either given a lecture or shown a film based on this section on bystander intervention. Two weeks later, each undergraduate was confronted with a simulated emergency while walking with one other person (a confederate of the experimenters). A male "victim" was sprawled out on the floor of a hallway. The confederate did not react as if it were an emergency. Forty-three percent of those who had heard the lecture or seen the film offered help, compared with only 25 percent of those who had not—a statistically significant difference. For society's sake, perhaps you should reread this section!

SOCIAL-PSYCHOLOGICAL PERSPECTIVE   The preceding sections focused on the situational determinants of helping, rather than on the personalities of helpers and nonhelpers. As noted earlier, this is a distinguishing feature of the social-psychological approach. Note that "defining the situation" and "diffusion of responsibility" are also *phenomenological* variables; they refer to how the individual perceives and understands a situation subjectively. The phenomenological emphasis is the second distinguishing feature of the social-psychological approach.

When one person stops to help, others often follow suit. Here bystanders not only notified the police, but remained to give information after they arrived.

Social Influence

When bystanders mislead one another about an emergency situation, their influence on one another is purely unintentional. But one of the most common forms of human interaction is *intentional* social influence, ranging from our attempts to induce a friend to go to a movie with us to a candidate's attempts to win our vote. Throughout human history, people have sought the most effective ways to change the beliefs, attitudes, and behavior of others. Thus, it is not surprising that social influence has been a central topic of social psychology since it began. A particularly dramatic example of intentional social influence is the "brainwashing" of Patricia Hearst.

In February 1974 the self-styled Symbionese Liberation Army (SLA) kidnapped 19-year-old college student Patricia Hearst, a granddaughter of William Randolph Hearst, the founder of the Hearst publishing empire. The SLA regarded Patty as a "prisoner-of-war." As ransom for her safe return, they demanded that the Hearst family give away several million dollars' worth of food. Just as she was scheduled to be released, Patty announced that she had decided to join the SLA. She renounced her former life, denounced her parents, and asked her fiancé to "try to understand the changes I've gone through."

Two weeks later Patty and her SLA comrades robbed a bank, making sure that her actions would be recorded by the bank's security cameras. Still, Patty eluded arrest for 20 months. When finally captured, she listed her occupation as "urban guerrilla" and gave her name as Tania, adopted after a Latin American revolutionary woman. The sweet young "newspaper heiress"—as the press called her—was no longer. Clearly some powerful social influences had transformed Patty into Tania, and the word *brainwashing* began to appear in the headlines.

In jail, Patty was visited daily by friends, family, defense lawyers, and psychiatrists, who reported that Patty was gradually overcoming her "confusion"; Tania was dissolving and Patty was reemerging. By her first court appearance, Patty was again a demure young woman.

Public speculation about what had happened to Patty Hearst could be classified into the three basic processes of social influence identified by social psychologists (Kelman, 1961): (1) *Compliance*—conforming outwardly to the wishes of an influencing agent. Patty was coerced throughout or was otherwise induced to bend to the authority of the SLA leaders. She never believed the things she said or did. (2) *Internalization*—genuinely changing one's beliefs, attitudes, and behavior because one "believes" in the new ideas and has integrated them into one's value system. Patty had accepted the revolutionary ideology of the SLA as her own; her old beliefs and attitudes had been replaced by new ones. It was, of course, this possibility that generated the fears that she had been brainwashed. (3) *Identification*—changing one's beliefs, attitudes, or behavior in order to be like a person or group one respects or admires. Patty had temporarily adopted the ideology of the SLA because she had come to identify with them, to see the world through their eyes. She "believed" what she was saying and doing but did not necessarily integrate this ideology into her own value system.

Compliance

Strong rewards and threats of punishment can induce or coerce individuals to comply; the "psychology" of such compliance is hardly profound. If it had been clear that Patty Hearst made revolutionary statements only while her life was being threatened and renounced such actions as soon as she was free from a life-threatening situation, there would have been no puzzlement over her mental state. But compliance can also be obtained through the use of social rewards and punishments. No gun is needed, only the authority or social power of the influencing agent. This is a more subtle and psychologically interesting influence process.

Classic experiments on socially induced compliance were conducted by Solomon Asch. In Asch's standard procedure, a subject was seated at a table with a group of other subjects (actually, confederates of the experimenter). The group was shown a display with three vertical lines of differing lengths; members were asked to judge which line was the same length as a standard line drawn on another display (see Figure 17-2). Each individual announced his or her decision in turn; the actual subject sat in the next-to-last seat. The judgments were quite easy to make, and on most trials everyone gave the same response. But on some trials the confederates were instructed beforehand to

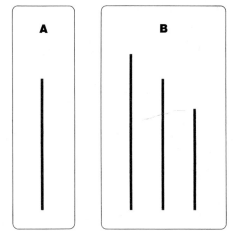

Fig. 17-2 Representative stimulus in Asch's study
After viewing display A, the subjects must pick the line from display B that matches. (After Asch, 1958)

A   B   C

give the wrong answer. The question was, would the individual conform to the majority response or stand by the evidence of his or her senses?

Asch had expected individuals to stand up to such social pressures and maintain relative independence. They did not. Despite the fact that the correct answer was always obvious, about 32 percent of the time subjects gave the incorrect, conforming response; about 74 percent of the subjects conformed at least once.

The Asch studies attracted immediate attention, and many other investigators have conducted variations on them. One of the most striking findings was that if even one of the confederates broke with the majority, compliance dropped from 32 percent to about 6 percent. The presence of another "deviant" emboldened individuals to stick with their judgments. Interestingly, the other deviant individual did not even have to give the right answer (Allen and Levin, 1971).

A more controversial series of studies on compliance has been reported by Milgram. In these, the experimenter asked a subject to deliver a series of increasingly powerful electric shocks to another subject (the "learner") whenever the latter made an error on a learning task. The learner (a confederate who did not actually receive any shocks) was strapped in a chair in an adjacent room, but he could be heard. As the shocks became stronger, he began to shout and curse; at 300 volts he began to kick the wall; and at the next shock level (marked "extreme intensity shock" on the apparatus), the learner suddenly became silent. The last shock in the series was marked 450 volts. As you would expect, subjects pleaded with the experimenter to call a halt to the procedure, but the experimenter responded, "please go on" or "the experiment requires that you continue."

A surprising 65 percent of the subjects obeyed the experimenter to the end (see Figure 17-3). Not one stopped prior to administering 300 volts—the point at which the learner began kicking the wall. Milgram concludes that obedience to authority is a strong force in our society, since the majority of his subjects obeyed the experimenter even though they thought they were hurting another person.

Variations on the Milgram experiment show that the obedience rate drops significantly if (1) subjects are put into the same room with the learner, (2) the experiment is conducted in a run-down suite of offices not connected with a prestigious university, in contrast with the setting of the original experiment, and (3) subjects are made to feel more personally responsible for their behavior.

Personal responsibility is a crucial factor. Because the original experiment was conducted by an official-looking "scientist" at a prestigious university, the subjects were probably able to feel absolved of any ultimate responsibility. Milgram suggests a parallel between his subjects and Nazi war criminals who felt that they were but little cogs in the machine of the German Reich. Similarly,

Resistance to majority opinion
A. All of the group members except the man sixth from left are confederates previously instructed to give uniformly wrong answers on 12 of the 18 trials; number six, who has been told he is participating in an experiment in visual judgment, thus finds himself a lone dissenter when he gives the correct answers.
B. The subject, showing the strain of repeated disagreement with the majority, leans forward anxiously to look at the pair of cards.
C. This particular subject persists in his opinion, saying that "he has to call them as he sees them."

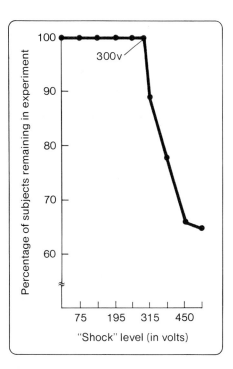

Fig. 17-3 Compliance to authority
Percentage of subjects willing to administer a punishing shock as a function of the intensity level of the shock. Note that for shocks of 300 volts or less all subjects administered the shock. (After Milgram, 1963)

The top left photo shows the "shock generator" used in Milgram's experiment on obedience. Top right, the victim is strapped into the "electric chair." Bottom left, a subject receives the sample shock before starting the "teaching session." Bottom right, a subject refuses to go on with the experiment. Most subjects became deeply disturbed by the role they were being asked to play, whether they continued in the experiment to the end or refused at some point to go on any longer. (From the film *Obedience,* distributed by New York University Film Library; copyright © 1965, by Stanley Milgram)

in the My Lai incident of the Vietnam Conflict, soldiers accused of murdering civilians argued that they were only following orders. These real-life incidents suggest that there should be even less resistance to authority from individuals who merely act as intermediaries.

Milgram tested this hypothesis in a variation of his study in which the subject only had to pull a switch that enabled another teacher (actually a confederate) to deliver the shock to the learner (Milgram, 1962; also see Kilham and Mann, 1974). Compared to the 65 percent compliance rate in the original experiment, 93 percent of the subjects who played this intermediary role complied to the end of the shock series. Milgram reported that these subjects typically felt no responsibility, rationalizing that "the other fellow actually gave the punishment." Note also that a modeling effect could be operating here. The intermediary subject sees the "teacher" reacting obediently and defines obedience as the "appropriate" response, just as bystanders help to define a situation for each other.

Do the Asch and Milgram findings apply to ordinary, real-life situations? Perhaps the aura of a "psychological experiment" generates compliance from a desire to "help science." The following "real-life" study suggests that compliance to authority is, indeed, widespread.

Five researchers—two psychiatrists and three nurses—investigated whether nurses in 22 wards of both a public and a private hospital would obey an order that violated hospital rules and professional practice (Hofling and others, 1966). While on regular duty, the subject (a nurse) received a phone call from a "doctor" she knew to be on the staff but had not met: "This is Dr. Smith from Psychiatry calling. I was asked to see Mr. Jones this morning, and I'm going to have to see him again tonight. I'd like him to have had some medication by the time I get to the ward. Will you please check your medicine cabinet and see if you have some Astroten? That's ASTROTEN." When the nurse checked the medicine cabinet, she saw a pillbox labeled:

ASTROTEN
5 mg. capsules
Usual dose: 5 mg.
Maximum daily dose: 10 mg.

After she reported that she had found it, the doctor continued, "Now will you please give Mr. Jones a dose of 20 milligrams of Astroten. I'll be up within 10 minutes; I'll sign the order then, but I'd like the drug to have started taking effect." A real staff psychiatrist, posted unobtrusively nearby, terminated each trial by disclosing its true nature when the nurse poured the medication (actually a harmless placebo), refused to accept the order, or tried to contact another professional.

This order violated several rules. The dose was clearly excessive. Medication orders are not permitted to be given by telephone. The medication was "unauthorized"; that is, it was not on the ward stock list, clearing it for use. Finally, the order was given by an unfamiliar person. Despite all this, 21 of the 22 nurses started to give the medication. Moreover, the phone calls were all brief, with little or no delay or resistance. None of the nurses insisted on a written order, although several sought reassurance that the doctor would arrive promptly. In interviews after the experiment, all the nurses stated that such orders had been received in the past and that the doctors became annoyed if the nurses balked.

The most important lesson in all these studies—the Asch studies, the Milgram studies, and the nursing study—is not to be found in the results, but in *our surprise* at them. Psychology students, psychiatrists, and laypeople all vastly underestimate the rates of compliance obtained by Milgram (Bierbrauer, 1973; Milgram, 1974; Aronson, 1976), and 10 out of 12 nurses say they would not follow the order in the experiment just described. As we shall see later, this is a very general finding: most of us tend to underestimate the extent and power of social and/or situational forces on human behavior.

Internalization

A *belief* is a statement about the world that a person thinks is true (for example, oranges are round; Republicans are progressive; spinach tastes good). An *attitude* is a like or dislike, a positive or negative evaluation about some aspect of the world (for example, I like oranges; I can't abide Republicans; I love spinach). If individuals express a belief or attitude because they really believe it and have integrated it into their value system, it is said to be *internalized*. It was, of course, the possibility that Patty Hearst had internalized the ideology of the SLA that caused the most concern. The concept of brainwashing seems to imply a scenario in which compliance itself leads in some way to internalization.

Can such a sequence occur? Certainly, the compliance shown in the studies discussed above would not seem to lead to internalization. Very few of the subjects in the Asch conformity experiments believe that the majority opinion on the critical trials is correct; even when they comply, they continue to believe privately that they, not the group, are correct. Similarly, none of Milgram's subjects believes that giving lethal shocks to a fellow human being is correct or ethical. In other words, these studies produce compliance, but not internalization. There are, however, circumstances in which inducing persons to engage in behavior they do not really believe in will lead them to change their attitudes.

The crucial circumstances in which this can occur were first spelled out by Leon Festinger in his *theory of cognitive dissonance* (1957), a theory based on

"Wait a minute, you guys—I've decided to make it unanimous after all."
Drawing by Victor; ⓒ 1978 The New Yorker Magazine, Inc.

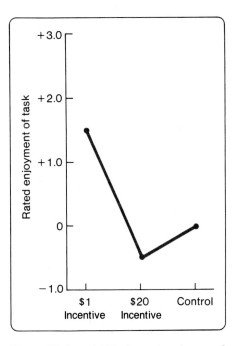

Fig. 17-4 Attitude change and incentive
The smaller the incentive for complying with the experimenter's request, the greater the attitude change. (After Festinger and Carlsmith, 1959)

the premise that people try to be consistent. Cognitive dissonance theory states, among other things, that whenever people engage in behaviors they do not believe in, they will be uncomfortable, because their behavior is inconsistent with their beliefs. It was this discomfort that Festinger called *cognitive dissonance*—a "disharmony," or clash among one's thoughts. He proposed that individuals will be motivated to reduce the dissonance. They can do this by persuading themselves that they really do believe in the behavior; that is, they can change their beliefs or attitudes to be consistent with their behavior, thus resolving the "dissonance." Children forced to eat spinach could reduce the dissonance between their behavior and their low opinion of spinach by deciding that spinach really tastes good after all.

This does not occur under all circumstances, however. For example, if the person is promised a large reward for complying or is threatened with harsh punishment for refusing, no dissonance occurs. Such rewards or punishments provide a very consistent, or "consonant," reason for complying; the person can justify the behavior to him or herself. Only if the person can see no good reason for compliance will dissonance be experienced. This leads to a rather surprising conclusion: compliance will lead to attitude change to the extent that the behavior can be brought about with the *minimum* amount of inducement. Greater rewards or more severe threats of punishment may be more successful at obtaining compliance, but they will be less successful at getting individuals to believe in what they are made to do.

This theory was tested by a very ingenious experiment in which college students were brought one at a time to a small room to work for an hour on dull, repetitive tasks (stacking spools and turning pegs). After completing the tasks, some were offered one dollar to tell the next subject that the tasks had been fun and interesting. Others were offered 20 dollars to do the same thing. Later, all the students were asked how interesting the tasks really were.

The students who had been paid only one dollar stated that they had, in fact, enjoyed the tasks. But students who had been paid 20 dollars did not; they found them as dull as did a control group of subjects who were not asked to talk to the next subject (see Figure 17-4). The small sum of money, but not the large sum, caused individuals to believe what they had been induced to say, just as the theory of cognitive dissonance predicts.

Experiments with children have confirmed the related prediction that mild threats of punishment for refusing to comply will produce more attitude change than more severe threats (Aronson and Carlsmith, 1963; Freedman, 1965). Thus, if children obey a mild request not to play with an attractive toy, they come to believe that the toy is not as attractive as they first thought. But if children obey under threat of a strong punishment, they do not change their liking for the toy. This was called the forbidden toy experiment.

Cognitive dissonance theory successfully predicts a number of other attitude change phenomena as well, and it became one of the most prominent theories in social psychology during the 1960s, when attitude change was intensively investigated. It is but one of several theories in social psychology based on the notion that people are motivated to be consistent (Abelson and others, 1968).

Identification: The Psychology of Reference Groups

It is clear that the changes Patty Hearst underwent while with the SLA involved more than compliance, for she continued to espouse their radical ideology even after her arrest. On the other hand, her "conversion" did not last very long once she began to talk with friends and family again; accordingly, we can also conclude that genuine internalization had not occurred either. Instead, what appears to have happened is that the SLA had temporarily become for her what sociologists and social psychologists call a *reference group*.

Nearly every group to which we belong, from our family to society as a whole, has an implicit or explicit set of beliefs, attitudes, and behaviors that are considered "correct." Any member of the group who strays from those norms risks isolation and social disapproval. Thus, groups regulate their members through the use of social reward and punishment. More important, groups provide us with a frame of reference, a ready-made interpretation of events and social issues. They provide the glasses through which we look at the world. Any group that exercises either of these two kinds of influence—regulation or interpretation—is one of our reference groups. We "refer" to such groups in order to evaluate and decide on our beliefs, attitudes, and behavior; if we seek to be like them, we are said to "identify" with them.

The subtle influence of reference groups was illustrated in a study by Kelley and Woodruff (1956). They had a group of students at a progressive teachers' college listen to a recorded speech that called for a return to traditional classroom methods. The speech was interrupted several times by applause. Half the students had been told that the audience in the recording was composed of students from their own college; the other half, that it was composed of local townspeople. Members of the first group changed their opinions about progressive education in the direction advocated in the speech more than did the students who believed the applause came from "outsiders."

Individuals do not necessarily belong to all their reference groups. For example, lower-middle-class individuals often use the middle-class as their reference group. A young, aspiring athlete may use professional athletes as a reference group, adopting their views and otherwise trying to "model" him or herself after them.

REFERENCE GROUPS IN CONFLICT Most of us identify with more than one reference group, and this often leads to conflicting pressures on our beliefs, attitudes, and behavior. A familiar example is the conflict young people experience between their family reference group and their college or peer reference group, a conflict repeated in every generation. Indeed, Theodore Newcomb's classic study of the "generation gap" was conducted at Bennington College from 1935 to 1939.

Today Bennington College tends to attract liberal students. But in 1935 most of the students came from wealthy, conservative families. (It is also coed today; in 1935 it was a woman's college.) Over two-thirds of the parents of Bennington students were affiliated with the Republican party. The Bennington College community was liberal during the 1930s, but this was not why most of the women selected the college.

Newcomb's main finding was that with each year at Bennington students moved further away from their parents' attitudes and closer to the attitudes of the college community. For example, in the 1936 presidential campaign about 66 percent of parents favored the Republican candidate, Landon, over the Democratic candidate, Roosevelt. Sixty-two percent of the Bennington freshmen, 43 percent of the sophomores, and only 15 percent of the juniors and seniors supported Landon.

Increasing liberalism reflected a deliberate choice between the two competing reference groups for most women.

All my life I've resented the protection of governesses and parents. At college I got away from that, or rather, I guess I should say, I changed it to wanting the intellectual approval of teachers and more advanced students. Then I found that you can't be reactionary and be intellectually respectable.

Becoming radical meant thinking for myself and, figuratively, thumbing my nose at my family. It also meant intellectual identification with the faculty and students that I most wanted to be like. (Newcomb, 1943, pp. 134, 131)

Note how this woman uses the term "identification" in the sense that we are employing it in this discussion. Note, too, how the women describe a mixture of compliance—attitude change in the service of social rewards and punishments—and identification—an attraction to an admired group whom they strive to emulate. As indicated earlier, reference groups also provide a frame of reference. The Bennington community, particularly the faculty, gave students a perspective on the Depression and the threat of world war that their wealthy and conservative home environments had not.

The results of the Bennington study are hardly unique. A move toward political liberalism and away from parental conservatism in college is a common phenomenon. Surveys from 1961 to 1963 and again from 1969 to 1970 conducted by a politically conservative magazine showed this trend at a diverse array of colleges and universities (*National Review,* 1963, 1971).

More than three-quarters (77%) of the students told us their political attitudes had changed, in a leftward direction, since they entered college. . . . Only 9% had moved in a net rightward direction. (1971)

PATTY HEARST AND IDENTIFICATION   Returning to our original example, it should now be clear that Patty Hearst's conversion to the revolutionary ideology of the SLA can be seen as a gradual identification with her captors. This is not as surprising as the press made it seem. Six of the seven members of the SLA who were with Patty during her captivity were quite similar to her in age, social class, and education and had themselves only recently adopted a radical ideology. Patty had already broken sufficiently with conventional conservative mores to be living with her fiancé. Like most college students, she had moved to the liberal left in most of her political attitudes, and her further conversion to a radical ideology was not that much more extreme than the conversion experienced by many liberal-minded students in the Vietnam Conflict era. While everyone was expressing alarm over the bizarre brainwashing of Patty Hearst, nobody seemed to wonder about the similar conversion of the very similar women who already belonged to the SLA.

It is true, however, that the circumstances of Patty Hearst's abduction greatly enhanced the potential power of the SLA as a reference group for her. First, at the beginning she was justifiably frightened that she would be killed. But the SLA members treated her well and quickly attempted to induce her friendship. The use of unanticipated reward in the context of fear is a very powerful technique that emphasizes the captive's dependency on the group and leads to a sense of relief and gratitude (Schein, Schneier, and Barker, 1961). Second, Patty was cut off from all other reference groups and had no way of checking competing points of view. Ensuring that a person hears but a single point of view during captivity is a very common technique of coercive persuasion. These two circumstances greatly magnified the two kinds of control exercised by reference groups generally: social reward and punishment, and providing a new perspective, or interpretation.

This is how Patty described her experience:

> At first I didn't trust or like them. . . . After a couple of weeks I began to feel sympathy with the SLA. I was beginning to see what they wanted to accomplish was necessary, although at the time it was hard for me to relate to the tactic of urban guerrilla warfare. . . . What some people refer to as a sudden conversion was actually a process of development, much the same as a photograph is developed. . . .
>
> We ate our meals together, though, and during these times, we would discuss different events, different struggles. . . . After a while I began to see . . . that U.S. imperialism is the enemy of all oppressed people. I opened my eyes and realized it was time to get off my ass. (*Chicago Tribune,* 1976)

FROM IDENTIFICATION TO INTERNALIZATION As we noted earlier, the "old" Patty reemerged rather quickly after she was removed from the SLA influence, indicating that the radical ideology had not been internalized into her own value system. This was also a common finding during the Korean War of the early 1950s, when the concept of brainwashing first became prominent. Prisoners-of-war who had found Communist arguments plausible while captive quickly reverted to their old attitudes on returning to the United States (Schein, Schneier, and Barker, 1961).

This does not mean that change initiated through identification never becomes internalized. Quite the contrary. Most of our beliefs and attitudes are probably initially based on identification. Whenever we start to identify with a new reference group, we engage in a process of "trying on" the new set of beliefs and attitudes they prescribe. What we "really believe" is in flux, capable of changing from day to day. The first year of college often has this effect on students; many of the views students bring from the family reference group are challenged by students and faculty from very different backgrounds, with different beliefs. The new beliefs are often "tried on" with great intensity and strong conviction, only to be discarded for still newer beliefs when the first set doesn't quite fit. This is a very natural process of growth. Although the process never really ends for people who remain open to new experiences, it is greatly accelerated during the college years, before the person has formed a nucleus of permanent beliefs on which to build more slowly and less radically. The real "work" of college is to evolve an ideological identity from the several beliefs and attitudes that are "tried on." This, too, was nicely illustrated in the Bennington study:

> It didn't take me long to see that liberal attitudes had prestige value. . . . I became liberal at first because of its prestige value; I remain so because the problems around which my liberalism centers are important. What I want now is to be effective in solving the problems.
>
> Prestige and recognition have always meant everything to me. . . . But I've sweat blood in trying to be honest with myself, and the result is that I really know what I want my attitudes to be, and I see what their consequences will be in my own life. (Newcomb, 1943, pp. 136–137)

As this last woman's comment suggests, the one test of internalization is time. Does college-induced liberalism maintain itself when students return to the "real world"? Newcomb conducted a follow-up study of the Bennington women 25 years later and found they had remained liberal (Newcomb, and others, 1967). For example, in the 1960 presidential election, 60 percent of

Bennington alumnae preferred Kennedy over Nixon, compared to fewer than 30 percent of women of similar socioeconomic class, geographical location, and years of education. Moreover, about 60 percent of Bennington alumnae were politically active, most (66 percent) within the Democratic party.

But we never outgrow our need for identification, for supporting reference groups. Thus, the political attitudes of the Bennington women remained stable, in part, because they selected new reference groups—friends and husbands—after college who supported the attitudes they developed in college. As Newcomb has noted, we often select our reference groups because they share our attitudes, and then our reference groups, in turn, help develop and sustain our attitudes. The relationship is circular. In practice, it is not always easy to separate identification from internalization as the basis for a long standing set of beliefs and attitudes.

When we see how many phenomena fall under the category of social influence, it is clear why this is a central topic of social psychology. (We will meet it again in Chapter 18.) In fact, some textbooks define social psychology as the study of social influence. If social influence has any rival in claiming the attention of social psychologists, it is the topic of *social perception*—the ways in which people perceive one another, form impressions, determine whom they like and dislike, and how they interpret the actions of others in the course of social interaction. It is to these topics that we turn next.

Social Perception

You meet someone for the first time and talk with or observe him or her for a few minutes. Chances are that even in this short space of time you make judgments about a number of characteristics. People tend to form impressions quickly on the basis of very little information.

First Impressions: Primacy and Recency Effects

What kind of impression do you have of Jim from the following observations of his behavior?

> Jim left the house to get some stationery. He walked out into the sun-filled street with two of his friends, basking in the sun as he walked. Jim entered the stationery store, which was full of people. Jim talked with an acquaintance while he waited to catch the clerk's eye. On his way out, he stopped to chat with a school friend who was just coming into the store. Leaving the store, he walked toward school. On his way he met the girl to whom he had been introduced the night before. They talked for a short while, and then Jim left for school. After school Jim left the classroom alone. Leaving the school, he started on his long walk home. The street was brilliantly filled with sunshine. Jim walked down the street on the shady side. Coming down the street toward him, he saw the pretty girl whom he had met on the previous evening. Jim crossed the street and entered a candy store. The store was crowded with students, and he noticed a few familiar faces. Jim waited quietly until he caught the counterman's eye and then gave his order. Taking his drink, he sat down at a side table. When he had finished his drink he went home. (Luchins, 1957a, pp. 34–35)

What do you think Jim is like? Do you think of him as a friendly, outgoing sort of person? Or do you have the impression that he is rather shy and introverted? If you think Jim is better described as friendly than unfriendly, you are in agreement with most people (78 percent) who read this description. But examine the description closely; it is actually composed of two very different portraits. Up to the sentence that begins "After school, Jim left . . . ," Jim is portrayed in several situations as a fairly friendly guy; after that point, however, a nearly identical set of situations shows him to be much more of a loner. In fact, 95 percent of the people who are shown only the first half of the description rate Jim as friendly, whereas only 3 percent of the people who are shown only the second half do so. Thus, in the combined description that you read, it is Jim's "friendliness" that seems to win out over his unfriendliness. Why might this be so? Is it something about the trait of friendliness, or is it that Jim is described as friendly first and unfriendly second? To find out, Luchins had individuals read the same description with the unfriendly half of the paragraph appearing first. Table 17-1 shows that only 18 percent found Jim to be friendly under this condition; Jim's unfriendly behavior left the major impression. The first information we receive has the greatest impact on our overall impressions. This is known as the *primacy effect*.

The primacy effect has also been found in studies where an actual rather than a hypothetical person was observed and where traits other than friendliness were examined. For example, subjects who watched a student attempt to solve a series of difficult multiple-choice problems were asked to assess his or her intelligence (Jones and others, 1968). The observed student always solved exactly 15 of the 30 problems correctly. Some subjects watched a student whose 15 successes were bunched mostly at the beginning of the series; others observed a student who was more successful near the end.

A strong primacy effect was observed. The individual who had done better at the beginning was judged more intelligent. Moreover, subjects' memories were distorted in the same direction. When asked to recall how many problems the student had solved correctly, subjects who had seen the 15 successes bunched at the beginning recalled on the average that the student had solved 20.6 of the 30 problems, whereas subjects who had seen the successes at the end recalled seeing only 12.5 successes on the average.

What causes the primacy effect? Although there is still some disagreement, the evidence suggests that we pay more attention to information when we are first attempting to form an initial impression of the person; we then pay less attention to subsequent information (Anderson, 1974). There is also evidence that we regard the first information as revealing the "real" person and dismiss any later discrepant information as not representative. For example, when asked how they reconcile the apparent contradictions in Jim's behavior, subjects sometimes say that Jim is "really" friendly but was probably tired by the end of the day (Luchins, 1957a).

If the primacy effect is due to decreased attention paid to the later information, then it should be possible to destroy the effect by warning subjects about the dangers of making judgments and telling them to take all information into account before arriving at their judgments (Luchins, 1957b). Such a warning works. No primacy effect is observed under these conditions. The warning is particularly effective if it comes *between* the presentation of the two inconsistent blocks of information.

In another variation, subjects worked mathematics problems or listened to a history lecture between exposures to the two halves of the description. This condition not only destroyed the primacy effect, but reversed it. The *later* information had the greater impact. This is called the *recency effect*, because it is the more recent information that carries the weight. In addition, the longer the time interval between the first and second blocks of information, the

TABLE 17-1
Primacy effects in impression formation

CONDITIONS	PERCENTAGE RATING JIM AS FRIENDLY
Friendly description only	95
Friendly first—unfriendly last	78
Unfriendly first—friendly last	18
Unfriendly description only	3

Source: Luchins (1957a)

People tend to find partners who closely match them in physical attractiveness.

greater the recency effect, suggesting that the earlier information dims in memory. The earlier block of information is replaced in memory by the later one.

In summary, it appears that when we receive conflicting information about a person all in one block, we tend to give greater weight to the information that comes first—to form a first impression and then attempt to reconcile the later conflicting information, either by ignoring it or by reinterpreting it as a sort of accidental deviation from the person's "real" personality. We should thus expect primacy effects to be important in job interviews, first dates, political canvassing, and other situations where the success of the first impression determines whether there will even be a subsequent encounter. In these situations, the charm school advertisements are correct: first impressions count. On the other hand, recency effects will be more important in continuing relationships, where real life provides the "interpolated tasks" and permits new information to have the opportunity to correct erroneous first impressions. One of the favorite pastimes of friends and lovers is looking back with amusement on their disastrous first encounters and laughing about the warped first impressions they formed of each other. One does not, of course, ponder the far greater number of similar disastrous first encounters that were never followed up. Just think of the potential friends and lovers that never materialized because of the primacy effect!

Interpersonal Attraction

The questions that often concern us most whenever we meet new people are: will they like us, and will we like them? Research has uncovered a number of factors that promote interpersonal attraction; although none of these factors will surprise you, each contains at least one unexpected twist.

PHYSICAL APPEARANCE To most of us, there is something mildly undemocratic about the possibility that a person's physical appearance is a determiner of how others respond to him or her. Unlike character, niceness, and other personal attributes, physical appearance is a factor over which we have little control. Hence, it seems "unfair" to use it as a criterion for liking someone. And, in fact, surveys have shown that people do not rank physical attractiveness as very important in their liking of other people (Perrin, 1921; Miller and Rivenbank, 1970; Tesser and Brodie, 1971).

But research on actual behavior shows otherwise. For example, a group of psychologists set up a "computer dance" in which each person was randomly paired with a partner (Walster and others, 1966). At intermission, each person filled out an anonymous questionnaire evaluating his or her date. In addition, the experimenters obtained several personality test scores for each person as well as an independent estimate of his or her physical attractiveness. The results showed that only physical attractiveness mattered. None of the measures of intelligence, social skills, or "personality" were related to the partners' liking for one another (see also Brislin and Lewis, 1968; Tesser and Brodie, 1971).

However, in actual paring off, people tend to end up with partners who closely match them in physical attractiveness (Berscheid and Walster, 1974). In one study, judges rated photographs of each partner of 99 couples for physical attractiveness without knowing who was paired with whom. The physical attractiveness ratings of the couples matched each other significantly more closely than did the ratings of photographs that were randomly paired into "couples" (Murstein, 1972).

The importance of physical appearance is not confined just to the hetero-sexual dating and mating patterns. For example, physically attractive boys and girls (ages five to six years) are more popular with their peers than are less attractive children (Dion and Berscheid, 1972). Even adults are affected by a child's physical attractiveness. Dion (1972) had women read a description of an aggressive act committed by a seven-year-old child. The description was accompanied by a photograph of either an attractive or an unattractive child. The women believed that attractive children were less likely than unattractive children to commit a similar aggressive act in the future.

COMPETENCE If we cannot all be beautiful, some of us might be able to get by on our competence. The evidence, however, is mixed. It may be that some people are just "too perfect" and that when they commit some blunder they become more human in our eyes and, hence, more likable.

In an experiment to test this hypothesis, subjects listened to a tape record-ing of a college student trying out for the "College Bowl." Some of the subjects heard a highly competent individual. He answered 92 percent of the very difficult quiz questions, modestly admitted that he had been an honor student, editor of the yearbook, and a member of the track team. Other subjects heard an individual of average ability, one who answered 30 percent of the questions, had received average grades, been a proofreader on the year-book staff, and tried out for the track team but failed to make it. On half of the tapes, the individual committed an embarrassing blunder near the end of the interview. There was a clatter, the scraping of a chair, and the individual exclaimed, "Oh my goodness, I've spilled coffee all over my new suit." Each subject was asked to rate the person heard. Blunder or no blunder, the superior person was liked better than the average one. But the superior person who committed a blunder was rated as more attractive than the superior person who did not; the blunder made the superior individual more likable. The average person's image, however, was hurt by the blunder. He was rated as less attractive when he spilled coffee than when he did not (Aronson, Willerman, and Floyd, 1966).

The hypothesis in this study was that a blunder makes the superior person more human, more like us, and thus more attractive. But if we think of our-selves as very superior, the blunder may not endear the superior person to us because it makes him or her *less* like ourselves (or our image of ourselves), and hence less likable. Or consider the opposite possibility: we have very low self-esteem and are attracted to those who can serve as an ideal hero for us. Under this condition, blunders give our potential idols feet of clay, and, hence, they again become less likable.

To test these possibilities, the blunder experiment was expanded. Spilling the coffee again enhanced the attractiveness of the superior person, but only for subjects who had an average amount of self-esteem. For those subjects with very high or very low self-esteem, the superior individual was less liked after his blunder (see Figure 17-5). Thus, if you are perfect, you can expect to impress either other gods like yourself or those inferiors who are looking for someone to provide the admirable qualities they themselves lack. But if you want to impress the rest of us, a little bit of "klutziness" is advised.

SIMILARITY The blunder study raises another question about attraction: do we like people who are similar to ourselves, or do "opposites attract"? It appears to depend on the dimensions of similarity being compared. There is a great deal of evidence that we prefer people who share our beliefs, attitudes, and values (Newcomb, 1961; Byrne, 1971). We tend to forget that some of our

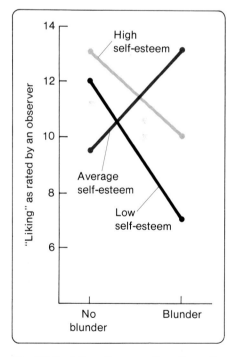

Fig. 17-5 Attraction as a function of a blunder
Subjects of high, average, and low self-esteem rated their liking for a highly compe-tent individual after hearing a tape of a situ-ation in which that individual either did or did not commit a blunder. High scores indi-cate greater liking. (After Helmreich, Aron-son, and LeFan, 1970)

friends whom we consider very different from ourselves are often quite similar to us in terms of such variables as age, religion, education, and socioeconomic class. Hundreds of statistical studies dating all the way back to 1870 show that husbands and wives are significantly similar to each other not only on these sociological characteristics, but also with respect to physical characteristics like height and eye color and psychological characteristics like intelligence (Rubin, 1973). Thus, most evidence indicates that liking is positively correlated with similarity on most dimensions.

The saying that "opposites attract" may apply mainly to certain complementary personality traits (Winch, 1952; Winch, Ktsanes, and Ktsanes, 1954). To take the most obvious example, one partner may be quite dominant and thus require someone who is relatively more submissive. A person with strong preferences may do best with someone who is very flexible or even "wishy-washy." Note, however, that even in the case of complementary traits an underlying similarity of attitudes can often be discerned. For example, the marital relationship in which the man is dominant and the wife submissive will be smooth only if both agree on the desirability of the traditional sex roles. In other words, even successful complementarity requires a basic similarity of attitudes favoring the dissimilarity.

Moreover, research does not uniformly show that complementary need systems are an important variable, even in long-term relationships (Kerckhoff and Davis, 1962; Levinger, Senn, and Jorgensen, 1970). This adds further emphasis to the general conclusion that similarity is the truly potent variable in determining who likes whom.

RECIPROCAL LIKING One of the more compelling reasons for liking people is their liking for us. We tend to like people who like us and to reject those who reject us. This is especially true when we need to be appreciated. In one study, college women were approached by a good-looking man while they waited, one at a time, in a reception room to be in an experiment. After some conversation, the man asked the woman for a date for the following evening. In the subsequent experimental session, each woman was given information that would make her feel either positively or negatively about herself. After the experiment, she was asked to rate a number of people, including that "fellow whom you were waiting with."

Women who had been led to feel negatively about themselves liked their male admirer significantly more than those women who had received favorable information about themselves. Temporarily put in the position of needing positive approval, they gave more positive approval back to the person providing it (Walster, 1965).

FAMILIARITY If all else fails in our quest to get someone to like us, then simple persistence might be our only recourse. There is good evidence that sheer familiarity is a pervasive determinant of liking. In one experiment, Newcomb (1961) rented a boarding house and provided free room and board to male students transferring to a university in exchange for participation in his study. In the first year of the study, Newcomb simply assigned people to rooms at random; he verified that similarity among people is a strong determinant of liking. In the second year of the study (with a different set of participants), half of the assignments paired men who were as different as possible from each other on a host of beliefs, attitudes, and values. The other half of the assignments paired students who were highly similar. Newcomb expected similarity again to produce greater liking. But this is not how things turned out. Familiarity swamped everything. Regardless of whether low or high similarity had been the basis for room assignments, roommates came to be attracted to one another.

We can conclude this discussion of interpersonal attraction with the comforting thought that if you aren't beautiful, competent, or similar to the one you wish to attract, be persistent.

The Attribution Process

We have seen that first impressions can be important, and we have noted some of the factors that determine whether or not we will like someone. But both of these "person-perception" tasks presuppose that we know how to size up people in the first place, to interpret their words and actions so that we get to know what they are really like. In short, whenever we interact with others, our first task is to understand their behavior. Sometimes this is simple, because so much social interaction is governed by social norms and conventions. When someone greets us with "How are you?" we do not pause to ponder why he or she is asking, nor do we interpret the question as a genuine invitation to discuss our health. We reply with the conventional "finehowareyou?" If, for example, we do launch into a detailed inventory of our ailments, we might well set the other person pondering the causes of *our* behavior.

But the meanings and causes of behavior are often ambiguous. Suppose, for example, a famous athlete endorses a breakfast cereal on television. Why does she do it? Does she really like the cereal? Or is she doing it for the money? A man kisses his female companion at the end of an evening out. Is this just a social norm, or does he really like her? Perhaps this particular man kisses everyone. Or perhaps all men would kiss this particular woman. You give a five-dollar donation to UNICEF. Why? You are altruistic? You were being pressured? You need a tax writeoff? You believe in the work of UNICEF?

All these cases create an "attribution problem." We see some behavior—perhaps our own—and must decide to which of the many possible causes the action should be attributed—what psychologists refer to as the *attribution process*. This is, of course, what psychologists try to do in a formal way; thus, in everyday social interaction we all play the role of amateur, or intuitive, psychologist. The study of the attribution process has now become one of the central concerns in social psychology; the goal is to discover the rules we use and the errors we make when we attempt to interpret behavior (Heider, 1958; Jones and Davis, 1965; Kelley, 1967).

One of the major attribution tasks we face daily is deciding whether an observed behavior reflects something unique about a person (for example, his or her attitudes, personality characteristics, and so forth) or something compelling about the situation. For example, can we infer from the TV endorsement anything about the athlete's real attitude toward the cereal, or is she pushing it solely because she is being paid? If we infer that something about the person is primarily responsible for the behavior, our inference is called a *dispositional attribution*. (So named because a person's beliefs, attitudes, and personality characteristics are called his or her dispositions.) If, however, we conclude that some external force is primarily responsible for the behavior (for example, money, threats, strong social norms), it is called a *situational attribution*. What prompts us to make either a dispositional or a situational attribution?

Some Rules of Attribution

When we interpret the behavior of others, we use implicit unconscious rules that serve us quite well and make a good deal of sense. Yet we are not usually aware of the rules themselves. In what follows, then, you will be learning about some rules you already know—but don't know that you know.

COVARIANCE RULE   In everyday life, we often behave like scientists. Suppose, for example, you wake up with a runny nose. You see that the azaleas in your yard have just bloomed and hypothesize that they are causing your sniffles. Note how you confirm this. You look to see if your symptoms come and go as you enter and leave areas containing azaleas. That is, you run an experiment to see if your symptoms and azaleas covary (vary together). Does the effect come and go with the suspected cause? If it does, azaleas are convicted. But if your sniffles remain constant, then there is nothing distinctive about azaleas, and you conclude that they are not the cause. Thus you use the *distinctiveness* of your reactions to the suspected stimulus as a criterion for deciding if it caused the problem.

You also use a criterion of *consistency*. If you had the same symptoms the last three years when the azaleas bloomed, then you are pretty certain that they are the culprit. But if this is the first time the symptoms have occurred, if this is not a *consistent* event, then you might not be so certain.

Finally, you call your doctor, who says that yours is the sixteenth such complaint of the day and that "this always happens when the azaleas bloom." In other words, you are not unique; others share the same reaction to the same stimulus. This is the criterion of *consensus*. Note that your detective work here is simply an informal version of the scientific method itself. Using three criteria, you apply the covariance rule—do the effect and suspected cause covary? You ask if the effect varies *only* with the suspected cause (distinctiveness), if it does so every time the experiment is tried (consistency), and if other people get the same result (consensus).

Attribution theorist H. H. Kelley (1967, 1971, 1972) has suggested that we use the covariance rule when we attempt to interpret people's behavior. The athlete who is attempting to convince you that Munchies is the best breakfast cereal had better not be seen on another channel endorsing Greissman's Granola. She would be violating the criterion of distinctiveness. Similarly, you would not be sold if she violated the consistency criterion and said in a newspaper interview that she doesn't think much of cereal. And if she is the only person you have ever known who had favorable things to say about Munchies, the *consensus* criterion would lead you to decide that Munchies aren't so great (instead, you would probably make some dispositional attributions about her!). Research has confirmed our use of the covariance rule (e.g., McArthur, 1972).

DISCOUNTING RULE   Even if our hypothetical athlete passes the three criteria listed above, we are probably still not convinced that she really loves Munchies. There is another plausible explanation for her behavior: money. After weighing whether she truly loves Munchies (a dispositional attribution) or is just endorsing it because she is being paid (a situational attribution), we decide for the latter. We *discount* the possibility that her endorsement reflects her true attitude. This discounting principle states: to the extent that situational or external factors constitute a "sufficient" explanation for an action, it will be attributed to the situation, not to the dispositions of the person.

But suppose we know that our athlete is *not* being paid, that such a

"Folks, I endorse Scrunchies because I eat Scrunchies. As God is my witness, I don't just say I eat them, I really and truly do eat them. In fact, folks, I never eat anything but. And if you don't believe me, I can supply documentation from my personal physician."

Drawing by Ross; © 1976 The New Yorker Magazine, Inc.

commercial endorsement would hurt her professional career, and that her lover threatened to leave her if she made such a commercial. In this case, we would infer that this woman must really be crazy about Munchies (or simply crazy). The other half of the discounting principle states: to the extent that an action seems to occur *in spite of* situational forces, we will infer that some trait, ability, intention, feeling, attitude, or other disposition accounts for the person's behavior. As soon as we spot a plausible "sufficient" cause of a person's behavior, we *discount* the role of other potential causes.

Self-Perception

Attribution rules can apply to observations of ourselves as well as to others (Bem, 1972). Just as we try to evaluate the surrounding situational forces to decide if our hypothetical athlete loves Munchies, so, too, we sometimes look at our own behavior and its surrounding circumstances to decide what we ourselves feel or believe. This may sound odd. Generally we assume that we have direct knowledge of our own feelings and beliefs. Not always. Consider the common remark "This is my second sandwich; I guess I was hungrier than I thought." Clearly this person had originally misjudged an internal state and has now decided that he or she was wrong on the basis of observing his or her own behavior. This suggests that whenever internal feelings are not very strong an individual is actually forced into the role of an outside observer to make the correct attributions (Bem, 1972). Thus, the self-observation "I've been biting my nails all day; something must be bugging me" is based on the same kind of information as a friend's observation, "You've been biting your nails all day; something must be bugging you": both the self- and the external observer are here making use of the same evidence—the overt behavior.

This *theory of self-perception* also provides an alternative interpretation for a phenomenon we described earlier when discussing cognitive dissonance theory. Recall that subjects in an experiment were paid either 1 dollar or 20 dollars to tell the next subject that dull tasks were fun and interesting. All subjects complied with the request, but in addition, the one-dollar subjects showed attitude change as well. They came to believe that the tasks *were* fun and interesting. The small sum of money, but not the large sum, led individuals to believe what they had heard themselves say. Let us look at these results from the perspective of self-perception.

After telling the next subject that the tasks were fun and interesting, the subjects faced an attribution problem about their own behavior: "Why did I say this?" Let us assume for the moment that they solved the problem the same way an outside observer would, using the discounting rule discussed above. Such a hypothetical observer hears the individual say the tasks were fun and must decide whether to make a dispositional attribution (the individual did it because he or she believes it) or a situational attribution (the individual did it for the money). When the individual is paid 20 dollars, the observer is most likely to make a situational attribution: "Anyone would have done it for that sum." The observer will assume the individual thought the tasks were dull in spite of what he or she said. On the other hand, if the individual is paid only one dollar, the observer is more likely to make a dispositional attribution: "He or she wouldn't be willing to say it for only one dollar and so must believe it." If we assume that the individual follows the same discounting rule as the outside observer, then 20-dollar subjects attribute their behavior to situational factors and decide they did not really find the tasks interesting. But one-dollar subjects make a dispositional attribution: "I must think the tasks are interesting; otherwise, I would not have said so." This process of self-perception (actually, self-attribution) thus predicts the same results as cognitive dissonance theory (Bem, 1967, 1972).

The same reasoning can be used to reinterpret the forbidden toy studies in which children who refrain from playing with a toy under mild threat, but not under severe threat, come to believe that the toy is not so attractive as they thought (Aronson and Carlsmith, 1963; Freedman, 1965). Children under severe threat attribute their avoidance of the toy to situational factors and discount the possibility that it reflects their attitudes. Children under mild threat cannot justify the behavior to themselves in the same way and so make a dispositional attribution: "If I am not playing with that toy, I must not like it."

INFERRING ONE'S OWN PERSONALITY TRAITS Do people ever use their own behavior to infer their own personality traits as well? For example, in the forbidden toy studies, children in the mild-threat condition conclude that they don't like the toy. In thinking about the self-perception process, it occurred to one psychologist that these children might also infer that they were particularly good or obedient. They see themselves obeying the experimenter's request, but they do not see any overwhelming situational reason for doing so. Since they can discount situational causes, such children might come out of the experiment with a self-image of themselves as "good" or obedient. To test this, the forbidden toy study was conducted again. Three weeks later, a second experimenter asked all the children to play a game for prizes. Soon it became obvious to the children that they could win a prize only if they cheated. Children who had previously been in the mild-threat condition cheated significantly less than children in the severe-threat condition or than children who had not been in the previous study. Lepper concluded that these children had emerged from the original study believing that they were obedient, and they lived up to their new self-image when tempted to cheat three weeks later (Lepper, 1973).

A study with adults supports this (Freedman and Fraser, 1966). Two experimenters contacted suburban housewives, first with a small request and later with a much larger request. For example, some were asked to sign a petition promoting safe driving. Two weeks later a second experimenter asked them to display a large, ugly sign on their lawn saying "Keep California Beautiful." About half of the women agreed to the second request, compared to only about 17 percent of a control group, who had not received the first request. This effect is the "foot-in-the-door" phenomenon: a person who is induced to comply with an initial small request is subsequently more likely to comply with a much larger demand. Why is this so?

According to Freedman and Fraser, once people have agreed to the first request, their view of themselves may change. They become—in their own eyes—the kind of person who agrees to requests made by strangers and who cooperates with good causes. In other words, they infer something about their own personality from observing their own behavior.

But before you run out to try the foot-in-the-door technique, you should be aware of some complications. If the first request is too demanding, the person may refuse it. This of course, leads the person to infer (via the self-attribution process) that he or she is the kind of person who refuses even smaller requests (Snyder and Cunningham, 1975).

However, if done correctly, it is actually possible to use an overly demanding initial request deliberately to obtain *more* compliance on a second, more reasonable request. This is accomplished by making the person feel guilty about refusing the initial request, thus challenging his or her self-image as a

When Two Theories Compete

If both dissonance theory and self-perception theory can predict the results of the 1-dollar/20-dollar experiment and the forbidden toy studies, which theory is really true? As is often the case in science, this question is not easy to answer. Dissonance theory proposes that attitude change occurs in these studies because people feel uncomfortable with the inconsistency between their behavior and their initial attitudes. The theory is a motivational theory in that this internal discomfort or arousal—cognitive dissonance—motivates the person to change his or her attitude. In contrast, self-perception theory implies that the person's initial attitude is irrelevant and there is no discomfort or internal arousal produced by the behavior. According to this theory, people are not seen as changing their attitudes so much as *inferring* what their own attitudes must be by observing their own behavior. Self-perception theory is a theory about judgments or attributions, not a motivational theory.

The difficulty in deciding which theory is more valid stems from the fact that some studies show evidence for some kind of internal arousal when the person engages in the counterattitudinal behavior, a result consistent with dissonance theory, but not one predicted by self-perception theory (e.g., Waterman, 1969; Pallak and Pittman,

1972). Other studies show attitude change even when the person engages in behavior consistent with his or her initial attitude, a result consistent with self-perception theory but not with cognitive dissonance theory, since consistent behavior should produce no dissonance (e.g., Kiesler, Nisbett, and Zanna, 1969).

But what about a "crucial" experiment, a situation in which the two theories make opposing predictions? At least five such experiments have been tried, but no consistent results were obtained (e.g., Snyder and Ebbesen, 1972; Ross and Shulman, 1973; Green, 1974; Schaffer, 1975; Swann and Pittman, 1975). Some studies favored dissonance theory; others, self-perception theory. Greenwald (1974) has argued that no crucial test is possible. And finally, after a series of studies, Fazio, Zanna, and Cooper (1977) concluded that dissonance theory is probably the better theory when the behavior is sharply inconsistent with the person's initial attitudes, but self-perception theory is the better theory when the behavior is broadly consistent with the initial attitudes.

This confusing outcome is not unusual, and, historically, science rarely abandons one theory and adopts another because a crucial experiment decides between them. Sometimes a theory is favored because it appears more

"elegant," more "fertile," or more general than another; it requires fewer assumptions, or more predictions can be derived from it than from its rival. But most often scientists adopt a new theory and discard an older one because they are more interested in the problems that can be explored with the new one and simply abandon for a time the problems dealt with by the older "paradigm" (Kuhn, 1970).

This is what has happened with dissonance and self-perception theories. Problems of attitude change were worked on very intensively during the 1960s, and cognitive dissonance theory was a very suggestive theory. But after most of the original ideas were explored, attention shifted to the attribution process. In this area of problems, self-perception theory provides a more convenient vocabulary and suggests more interesting leads to be followed than does dissonance theory. Thus, self-perception theory has "won," but only in the limited sense that it arrived with a set of fresh problems currently of interest to social psychologists (Bem, 1972). The controversy between the two theories has now simply faded away; it has ended with a whimper (and a sigh of relief) instead of a bang. A disappointing outcome, perhaps, but by far the more common one in the history of science.

---

good, concerned person. In one study, college students were asked to serve as volunteer counselors at a county juvenile detention center for two years. Not surprisingly, virtually all refused. But the request appeared so "worthy" that it was expected students would seek to make "amends" to restore their self-image. The reasoning was correct; they jumped at the chance to escort juveniles on a trip to the zoo. This has been labeled the "door-in-the-face" effect (Cialdini, and others, 1975).

The Fundamental Attribution Error

The rules we use for discerning the causes of behavior (for example, the covariance and discounting rules) make a good deal of sense, and as amateur, or intuitive, psychologists, we do a remarkably good job of interpreting behavior. But we also make some systematic errors and show some rather pervasive biases. We shall look at but one of these.

The founder of modern attribution theory, Fritz Heider, noted that an individual's behavior is so compelling to observers that they take it at face value and give insufficient weight to the circumstances surrounding it. Recent research has confirmed Heider's speculation. We underestimate the situational causes of behavior, jumping to conclusions about the dispositions of the person. This bias toward dispositional, rather than situational, attributions is now called the *fundamental attribution error* (Ross, 1977).

In one of the first studies to reveal this bias, subjects were asked to listen to an individual giving a speech either favoring or opposing racial segregation. The subjects were told that the individual was participating in an experiment and that he or she had been told which side of the issue to argue; the speakers had no choice. Despite this knowledge, when asked to estimate the individual's actual attitude toward racial segregation, subjects inferred that the individual held a position close to the one he or she had argued in the speech. In other words, the subjects made a dispositional attribution, even though situational forces were fully sufficient to account for the behavior (Jones and Harris, 1967).

Self-attributions are also subject to the fundamental attribution error. Consider the study cited earlier in which individuals inferred that they liked the laboratory tasks when paid one dollar to say they had enjoyed them. We, the experimenters, know that one dollar was sufficient to induce all subjects to comply with the request. When subjects ask themselves "Why did I do this?" they should answer, "because one dollar is a sufficient situational force to get me to do so." But they do not. Instead they make the dispositional attribution "because I must find the tasks interesting." And that is the fundamental attribution error.

THE FUNDAMENTAL ATTRIBUTION ERROR IN SOCIAL INTERACTION

The degree to which people fail to appreciate situational factors in social interaction is strikingly illustrated by the following study. Pairs of male or female subjects were recruited to participate in a "college bowl" quiz game. One member of the pair was to make up difficult questions to which he or she knew the answers (for example, "What is the capital city of South Carolina?" "Name four Presidents who had more than two children"). The other subject tried to answer each question. If he or she failed, the questioner would supply the correct answer. The roles of questioner and "contestant" were assigned at random, and both individuals knew this. After the game they were asked to estimate their own general knowledge and that of their partner. Observers who had watched the entire procedure also rated the general knowledge of the two participants.

As Figure 17-6 shows, questioners rated both themselves and the contestant to be about equal to the "average student" in general knowledge. But contestants rated themselves less knowledgeable and the questioner more knowledgeable than the average student. Apparently their inability to answer many questions to which the questioner knew the answer was overwhelmingly compelling. They did not take into account the fact that the situation was obviously biased in favor of the questioner and against them. They committed the fundamental attribution error. (The questioners were probably aware of many questions they had to discard because they did not know the answers themselves; hence, they did not see themselves as superior to the contestant or to the average student.) Finally, observers did not downgrade the contestant, but they did infer that the questioner was superior to the average student.

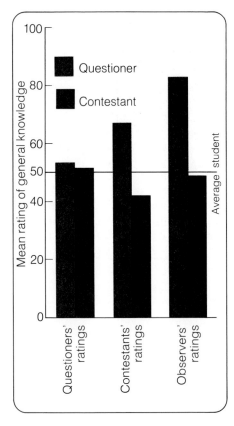

Fig. 17-6 Ratings of questioners' and contestants' general knowledge following the "college bowl" quiz (After Ross, Amabile, and Steinmetz, 1977)

542

The Power of Labels: One Consequence of the Fundamental Attribution Error

The fundamental attribution error is often made whenever a person is labeled as deviant (for example, schizophrenic or homosexual). Any behaviors such individuals display are automatically attributed to their "deviance." Situational factors that would normally be taken into account for other individuals who display the same behaviors are ignored. Observers of mental hospitals have noticed that many of the behaviors seen on hospital wards can be accounted for by the unusual situational factors present (e.g., Goffman, 1961; Rosenhan, 1973). For example, in order to get any attention from nurses or aides in understaffed institutions, one must do something out of the ordinary or become especially persistent; simple questions and quiet requests are often ignored. Similarly, because there is little to do on most wards, pacing back and forth is at least one way to relieve boredom and get some exercise. But such behaviors as demanding attention or pacing are interpreted by the staff as "part of the illness."

In one study, the investigators themselves entered the hospitals as patients, behaving as normally as possible during their stay. The staff never suspected that they were not real patients. In fact, staff records showed that even innocuous behaviors were interpreted as part of the "schizophrenic syndrome." One investigator took observational notes during his stay. A staff member ominously noted in his record that the "patient engages in writing behavior" (Rosenhan, 1973). Thus, once the label of "mental patient" or "schizophrenic" is attached to a person, observers act as if all attribution problems are automatically solved. Any behavior that is not completely ordinary is attributed to the "illness." The label becomes a scapegoat.

The fundamental attribution error due to labeling is also well known to any college student whose parents regard his or her marijuana smoking as a form of deviance. Did the student get a bad grade on an examination? It must be, the parents are certain, because of the marijuana smoking. Is he or she having trouble falling asleep the week before final exams? This is obviously the effect of smoking marijuana. Has the student rejected parental attitudes against premarital sex? Marijuana has ruined the student's morals. And so it goes. The label of "marijuana smoker" collects the blame, and all other potential situational causes are ignored.

Individuals themselves are vulnerable to this attributional trap. For example, many college students complain that their social lives do not always go smoothly, that they think about sex a lot, that problems with their love life sometimes interfere with school work, and that they wish they were more outgoing and less preoccupied with themselves. And most students eventually realize that such problems are a consequence of situational factors endemic to the life of an unmarried college student. Because of these same situational factors, homosexual men and women on the campus often share these common complaints. But homosexual students are much more vulnerable to the trap of attributing these problems to their sexual orientation. (Of course, they do have complaints that arise from following a sexual orientation disapproved of by society, but these, too, are situationally caused problems.)

At the same time, however, homosexual men and women are often more acutely aware than heterosexual men and women of the situational constraints imposed by traditional sex-role practices (for example, some of the absurdities of the heterosexual dating situation that people take for granted). They are aware of them precisely because they have been forced to come to grips with them in a conscious way, to ponder whether or not they "fit" their personalities. One of the goals of both the gay rights and the women's movement has been to get their members to recognize that situational factors, not their "personalities" (that is, dispositional factors) cause most of the problems they encounter. A large part of "consciousness raising" consists of correcting the fundamental attribution error.

They were aware that they, too, could not answer many of the questions. They, too, failed to appreciate the situational bias and committed the fundamental attribution error.

This study implies that the person who decides which topics will be discussed in a conversation will be seen as the more knowledgeable person—even if all realize that he or she is in control of the agenda. It has been suggested that men are more likely than women to structure the situation in mixed-sex group conversations. If this is so, then one consequence will be that women will depart most mixed-sex interactions thinking themselves less knowledgeable than the men, with bystanders of both sexes sharing this illusion. The moral is clear: the fundamental attribution error can work for or against you. If you want to appear knowledgeable both to yourself and to others, learn how to structure the situation so that you control the choice of topics discussed.

Attribution and the Social-Psychological Perspective

As we noted at the beginning of this chapter, social psychology emphasizes phenomenology, the individual's own subjective view of the world. The study of attribution is, almost by definition, the study of phenomenology, the study of how people filter and interpret their social environments. It exemplifies better than any other topic the perspectives and preoccupations of contemporary social psychologists.

We can now also appreciate that social psychology's emphasis on the situational causes of behavior is a direct antidote to the fundamental attribution error. The major value of social psychology may well be to counterbalance our normal attributional bias by reminding us of the power that situational forces can exercise over human behavior.

SUMMARY

1 Social psychology studies social interaction—the ways people influence each other's thoughts, feelings, and behaviors. The social-psychological perspective focuses on the *situational causes* of behavior (as opposed to developmental or personality factors) and on the individual's *phenomenology*, or subjective view of the situation.

2 The study of bystander intervention illustrates the social-psychological perspective. Bystanders often fail to intervene in emergency situations for several reasons. By attempting to appear calm, they may *define the situation as a nonemergency* for each other (*pluralistic ignorance*). The presence of other people also *diffuses responsibility*, so that no one person feels the necessity to act. Bystanders are more likely to intervene when these factors are changed, particularly if at least one person serves as a "model" for helping behavior.

3 There are three processes of social influence: (1) *compliance*, in which the person conforms outwardly but does not believe in the opinions expressed or the behavior displayed; (2) *internalization*, in which the person believes the new opinions or behaviors and incorporates them into his or her value system; and (3) *identification*, in which the person adopts new beliefs or behaviors in order to "identify with," or be like, an attractive person or group to which he or she refers for deciding what to believe and how to act.

4 Studies of compliance show that situational factors exert more influence over behavior than most of us realize. We tend to underestimate situational forces on behavior.

5 Compliance can lead to internalization if the individual is induced to behave in ways contrary to his or her beliefs under the *minimum* amount of inducement. This is predicted by *cognitive dissonance theory*, which is based on the premise that people strive to achieve consistency between their beliefs and their behavior.

6 Groups can influence us through the use of social rewards and punishments and by providing us with a frame of reference, a ready-made interpretation, for events and social issues. Any group that exercises either of these two

kinds of influence—regulation or interpretation—is called a *reference group* for the individual. They influence us through the process of *identification*.

7 Most of us identify with more than one reference group, and this can lead to conflicting pressures on our beliefs, attitudes, and behavior. College students frequently move away from the views of their family reference group toward the college reference group. Typically they move in the politically liberal direction, a change that sustains itself over subsequent years. The new views, usually adopted through the process of identification, become internalized. They are also sustained because we tend to select new reference groups after college—spouses and friends—who agree with us already.

8 First impressions of people are important because we are biased toward *primacy effects*; we tend to give too much weight to initial information and too little to later information that may be contradictory. However, if there is a long time interval between two sets of information, *recency effects* emerge; the earlier information fades in memory and is replaced by the more recent information.

9 Many factors influence whether we will be attracted to someone. *Physical appearance* plays a more important role than is generally acknowledged, although in actually pairing up, people tend to end up with partners who match their own attractiveness. Other factors are *competence, similarity* to ourselves, *reciprocal liking,* and *familiarity.*

10 *Attribution* is the process by which we attempt to interpret and explain the behavior of other people, to discern the causes of their actions. One major attribution task is to decide if an action should be attributed to *dispositional causes*—the person's personality or attitudes—or to *situational causes*—social forces or other external circumstances.

11 One of the rules we use in the attribution process is the *covariance rule*: behavior is attributed to the variable with which it appears to covary. We also use the *discounting rule*: if situational causes appear sufficient to cause the behavior, we discount the role of dispositional causes, and vice versa.

12 *Self-perception* may at times be similar to perceiving others. Individuals sometimes rely on observations of their own behavior to infer their emotions, attitudes, and personality traits in the same way an outside observer would. Like cognitive dissonance theory, the theory of self-perception proposes a way in which compliance can lead to attitude change.

13 In making attributions, we tend to give too much weight to dispositional factors and too little to situational factors. This bias, known as the *fundamental attribution error*, has a number of important implications. Social psychology's emphasis on situational influences on behavior is an antidote to the fundamental attribution error.

FURTHER READING

A number of paperback books deal in more depth with the topics discussed in this chapter. Recommended are Aronson, *The social animal* (2nd ed., 1976), Bem, *Beliefs, attitudes, and human affairs* (1970), Rubin, *Liking and loving* (1973), Shaver, *Introduction to attribution processes* (1975), and Zimbardo, Ebbesen, and Maslach, *Influencing attitudes and changing behavior* (2nd ed., 1977).

Two comprehensive textbooks in this area are *Social psychology* by Freedman, Sears, and Carlsmith (3rd ed., 1978) and *Social psychology* by Wrightsman (2nd ed., 1977).

18
Psychology and Society

O ver the years our society has looked increasingly to science for solving practical problems. And, as we have seen in previous chapters, the science of psychology is no exception; it, too, has been asked to contribute to the understanding and solution of a wide variety of everyday problems. What color should highway signs be? The psychology of perception knows precisely the shade of green that is best for day and night visibility. How can methods of instruction be made more effective? The psychology of learning and memory has a number of suggestions. How can we alleviate problems of abnormal behavior and emotional distress? The psychology of personality has been addressing these problems both theoretically and therapeutically from the very beginning.

Increasingly, both psychologists and other behavioral scientists have been called on to advise on pressing social issues as well, issues involved in the formulation of public policy. How can prejudice and discrimination be reduced? Is mass media persuasion effective? What effects does a crowded urban environment have on our well-being? It is these kinds of problems that are the focus of the present chapter.

But the application of psychological knowledge to social issues and, hence, to the formulation of public policy is itself a potential social issue. Science is objective in certain senses, but it is not "value free," and scientists who travel from the laboratory and classroom to Congress and the courts with information and advice carry biases and assumptions along with them. Accordingly, we will end this chapter with a brief discussion of the role of behavioral science in the formulation of public policy and the role of "objectivity" in behavioral science itself.

Prejudice

Prejudice has been with us a long time. Stereotypes about what men and women are like, for example, have probably been around as long as men and women have been. Prejudice against "out-groups," people different from our "own kind," is also a pervasive historical and cross-cultural fact of social life. Thus, no matter how much we disapprove of prejudice and the behaviors that stem from it, they must reflect some rather universal features of human thinking and feeling. As we shall see, this is, in fact, the case.

Stereotypes and Prejudgment

One of the first things we learn as children is how to generalize from our experiences, to go beyond the bits and pieces of our immediate world and draw some general conclusions about the wider universe around us. Thus, on the basis of very limited experience, we might come to believe that life in a large city is hectic, Chris is conscientious, and modern music is hard to understand. But of course, life in the city is not always hectic, Chris occasionally procrastinates, and some modern music is easy to understand. Generalizations, in other words, are not always true beyond the limited set of instances on which they are based; indeed, some generalizations may be based only on hearsay and may not be true of any instances actually experienced by the individual who believes them. When generalizations concern groups of people (for example, women are emotional; homosexual men are effeminate), they are often called stereotypes, particularly if the individuals who hold such generalizations treat every member of the group as if he or she necessarily possessed the assumed group attribute. A *stereotype*, then, is a belief about a group of people that, even if not totally false, has been overgeneralized and applied too broadly to every member of the group.

We emphasize again that the thinking process that gives rise to stereotypes is not itself evil or pathological. Generalizing from a set of experiences and treating individuals as members of a group are common and necessary practices. It is simply not possible to deal with every new person as if he or she were unique, and the formation of "working stereotypes" is inevitable until further experiences either refine or discredit them. For example, many first-year college students from rural areas of the country may spend their first few weeks of college thinking that all New Yorkers are Jews and all Jews are New Yorkers. There is not necessarily any malice or ill will behind such a stereotype; the new student has simply not yet seen enough Catholic New Yorkers or Texas Jews to permit the social environment to be sorted into more accurate and finely differentiated categories. Many of our stereotypes are of this benign variety and are discarded as our experiences multiply and broaden.

But not all stereotypes are benign. Many of our stereotypes lead us to be prejudiced against individuals—to hold negative attitudes toward them solely on the basis of their group membership, rather than on their own merits. (The word *prejudice* derives from the notion of *prejudging* people as good or bad before knowing them individually.) And this in turn can lead us to *discriminate* against individuals—to treat them badly solely on the basis of their group membership. Note that the concept of prejudice refers to our attitudes; discrimination refers to our behaviors.

Reducing Prejudice Through Intergroup Contact

In seeking ways to reduce intergroup hostility, many people have suggested over the years that increased contact between groups will reduce prejudice. But many interracial contacts (for example, between black ghetto residents and white police officers) often seem to increase prejudice. Moreover, no two groups have more contact than men and women, and yet prejudice against women in the world of work and elsewhere is still commonplace. Here, then, is a puzzle for the social psychologist: under what circumstances will more contact between groups diminish prejudice?

Psychologists have been seeking a complete answer to this question for many years, and tests of the "contact hypothesis" of prejudice reduction date back to the 1930s and '40s. From all the studies—most of them concerned with

The Subtle Prejudice of Sexism

Stereotypes and prejudices can be quite subtle, so much so that we can be unaware that we hold them. Thus, until the recent women's movement began to raise the issues of sexism, our stereotypes, and prejudices about women's "natural" abilities—or lack of them—remained hidden and unquestioned among both men and women. For example, in a study conducted in 1968, somewhat before the women's movement had become prominent, Phillip Goldberg asked female college students to rate a number of professional articles from each of six fields. The articles were put into two equal sets of booklets, and the names of the authors were changed so that the identical article was attributed to a male author (for example, John T. McKay) in one booklet and to a female author (for example, Joan T. McKay) in the other booklet. Each student was asked to read the articles in her booklet and rate them for value, competence, persuasiveness, writing style, and so forth.

Goldberg found that the identical article received significantly lower ratings when it was attributed to a female author than when it was attributed to a male author. This was true not only for articles from professional fields generally considered the province of men, like law, but for articles from the fields of dietetics and elementary school education as well. In other words, these female students rated the male authors as better at everything, agreeing with Aristotle that "we should regard the female nature as afflicted with a natural defectiveness." But Aristotle was at least aware of his belief in the inferiority of women; these students, like most Americans, were not. More recent studies have not always yielded the same results. One study found that both men and women tended to rate male authors higher in male-dominated fields but female authors higher in female-dominated fields (Mischel, 1974). Another study found no effects at all (Levenson and others, 1975). The changing patterns of results in such

studies probably reflect, in part, the fact that most Americans have become much more sensitive to their own prejudices since 1968 and try to guard against them (or guard against expressing them, at any rate).

As society's "consciousness is raised" about sexism and as more young women look forward to professional careers, many young couples are now challenging other hidden assumptions about men and women as well, such as the traditional division of labor within marriage. Many couples claim that they seek fully egalitarian (equal) relationships in which the older assumptions about men's and women's roles are discarded; they often cite examples like the following:

> Both my wife and I earned college degrees in our respective disciplines. I turned down a superior job offer in Oregon and accepted a slightly less desirable position in New York where my wife would have more opportunities for part-time work in her specialty. Although I would have preferred to live in a suburb, we purchased a home near my wife's job so that she could have an office at home where she would be when the children returned from school. Because my wife earns a good salary, she can easily afford to pay a housekeeper to do her major household chores. My wife and I share all other tasks around the house equally. For example, she cooks the meals, but I do the laundry for her and help her with many of her other household tasks.

Without questioning the happiness of such a marriage or its appropriateness for many couples, we can still legitimately ask if such a marriage is, in fact, truly egalitarian. Have the hidden assumptions about the woman's "natural" role really been eliminated? There is a very simple test. If the marriage is truly egalitarian, then its de-

scription should retain the same flavor and tone even if the roles of the husband and wife were reversed:

> Both my husband and I earned college degrees in our respective disciplines. I turned down a superior job offer in Oregon and accepted a slightly less desirable position in New York where my husband would have more opportunities for part-time work in his specialty. Although I would have preferred to live in a suburb, we purchased a home near my husband's job so that he could have an office at home where he would be when the children returned from school. Because my husband earns a good salary, he can easily afford to pay a housekeeper to do his major household chores. My husband and I share all other tasks around the house equally. For example, he cooks the meals, but I do the laundry for him and help him with many of his other household tasks. (Bem and Bem, 1977)

Somehow the marriage sounds different, and yet only the pronouns have been changed. Certainly no one would ever mistake the marriage just described as egalitarian or even very desirable, and it thus becomes apparent that the ideology about the woman's "natural" place unconsciously persists even in the thinking of people who believe that they have rejected the older assumptions. It is true that the wife gains some measure of equality when she can have a career of sufficient importance to influence where the couple lives. But why is it the wife who automatically seeks the part-time position? Why is it *her* housekeeper rather than *theirs?* Why *her* household tasks? Such is the subtlety of the prejudice against women. If you failed to spot the inequity in the first description, then you too still have some consciousness-raising ahead of you.

white prejudice toward blacks—it is clear that simple contact by itself is not sufficient; rather, there appear to be five main conditions that need to be present before the participants begin to discard their prejudices (Cook, 1978).

EQUAL STATUS OF THE PARTICIPANTS For prejudice to be reduced, individuals need to begin seeing one another in situations that break down the assumption that members of one group are inferior to those of the other. This is hard to do if the roles in which people meet one another continue to reinforce that assumption. If the white professional continues to interact only with blacks who are in low-status occupational roles or who are always less educated, then there is nothing in these interracial contacts that would lead either participant to change the traditional assumptions. Nor do the roles have to be that extreme to reinforce the prejudices. We see similar kinds of prejudice being maintained on both sides in the daily encounters between members of ethnic minority groups and white shop-owners or white welfare-agency employees. These encounters need not be unpleasant or hostile; in fact, they can be quite congenial. But because the participants are not of equal status, such contacts continue to perpetuate the stereotypes that, in part, arose in the first place precisely because of these role and status differences.

POTENTIAL FOR PERSONAL ACQUAINTANCE As we noted earlier, stereotypes arise because it is not possible to treat every new person we meet as an individual; we often find it necessary to make some initial assumptions about people on the basis of their group membership. Getting to know a person as an individual, then, is really the best way to learn that a stereotype does not fit. But it is possible to have daily contact with another person over several years without ever getting to know anything about him or her individually, and most interracial contacts have this characteristic. Research has shown, however, that when black and white housewives who live in the same apartment building are brought together under circumstances in which they get to know each other as individuals, greater acceptance is the result (Deutsch and Collins, 1951; Wilner, Walkley, and Cook, 1955; Hamilton and Bishop, 1976).

EXPOSURE TO NONSTEREOTYPIC INDIVIDUALS Even when we do not get to know persons from another group on a personal basis, we may revise our prejudices if we begin to meet individuals who violate our stereotypes—particularly if the individuals seem to be similar to ourselves. The white worker who realizes that his or her black co-workers share many of the same aspirations, grievances, and attitudes toward the company begins to discard stereotyped images of blacks (Blanchard, Weigel, and Cook, 1975). (The same holds true of black workers' stereotypes of whites, of course.) With the increased willingness of homosexual men and women to let their sexual orientation be known, many people are also learning that very few homosexual individuals conform to the traditional stereotypes. And finally, as we increasingly encounter men and women in nontraditional occupational roles (for example, male nursery school teachers and women attorneys), our society's traditional stereotypes about men's and women's "natural" talents will change too.

SOCIAL SUPPORT FOR THE INTERGROUP CONTACT Group contact is also more likely to reduce prejudice if the surrounding social environment favors equality, fair treatment, and intergroup contact. The teacher in a newly desegregated school who conveys to the students that working together is only a necessary evil being forced on them is creating a social environment that works against favorable attitude change. Similarly, contact between two

Encounters with individuals in occupational roles that do not fit one's stereotype may reduce prejudice.

individuals from different groups has more potential for reducing prejudice between them if there is support for the encounter among their respective friends and families.

COOPERATIVE EFFORT Perhaps the most potent factor in reducing prejudice is a situation in which two individuals or two groups must cooperate with one another in order to attain some mutually desired goal (Weigel, Wiser, and Cook, 1975). This was shown in a classic field study conducted by Sherif and his colleagues at a summer camp for 11- and 12-year-old boys (Sherif and others, 1961; Sherif, 1966). The camp was first divided into two groups, and in-group loyalties were allowed to develop naturally. When the groups were placed in competition for rewards, members of the opposing groups began to call each other names, pick fights, and generally treat each other viciously. The resulting intergroup hostility could not be reduced simply by having the boys go to the movies together or engage in activities jointly. Such occasions simply provided additional opportunities to fight. Only by introducing goals important to both groups that could be obtained only by joint cooperation could intergroup harmony be brought about. Hostility diminished as the groups had to fix a breakdown in the water supply, pool money to rent a movie, and use a rope to start the food supply truck. By the end of the camp session the two groups of boys were friends.

Cooperative effort reduces prejudice.

Recently researchers have attempted to see if similar cooperative group arrangements might help reduce some of the interracial problems in desegregated classrooms. For example, Aronson and his colleagues introduced a cooperative structure into a number of interracial classrooms using a procedure they called the "jigsaw-puzzle" method. The children were divided into small groups, and each child was assigned a small part of the lesson, which only he or she learned for that day. Each group then had to learn the entire lesson by learning a different piece of it from each of the individual members, a process that resembles the assembly of a jigsaw puzzle (Aronson and others, 1975; Aronson, Blaney, and Stephan, 1975).

The effects were dramatic. Since all the students had a stake in having everybody speak up, they learned to appreciate the contributions of the most reticent student; and the most reticent student, in turn, learned not only to speak up, but to have confidence that he or she had a valuable contribution to make. There was some evidence that grades improved for children who participated in the cooperative groups. And, most important, the Anglo, Chicano, and black children who worked with each other cooperatively came to like one another better. Many other schools in the area quickly adopted the same method of instruction. But there is one sobering note: racial prejudice in general did not decrease. That is, the children of different races who had actually worked together came to like each other better as individuals, but opinion measurement revealed that their reduced prejudice did not generalize to the ethnic groups as a whole.

This same lack of generalization has been found in other studies utilizing cooperative groups (e.g., Cook, 1978), and it may be that these experiments provide only the first step in a more gradual process of eliminating prejudice. Most of the experiments lasted only a few weeks or months at the most and so may not have provided sufficient time or experience to reduce long-held prejudices.

BRINGING ALL THE ELEMENTS TOGETHER Social psychologist Stuart Cook has spent over 15 years examining the problem of prejudice reduction through interracial contact (1970, 1978). In several of his studies he tried to bring together all the favorable factors we have discussed here. Thus, he brought highly prejudiced individuals into work groups in which (1) all the participants had equal status, (2) there was potential for informal acquaintance, (3) the members of the racial minority did not display any of the stereotyped characteristics, (4) the experimenters and their assistants set up clear norms favoring interracial equality, and (5) mutual cooperation was required for the group to do well in competition with other groups. These studies show that such conditions lead not only to interracial liking within the groups, but to general reduction of prejudice as well. Even under these conditions, however, the general reduction of prejudice occurs only in about 40 percent of the subjects. On the other hand, the groups met for only two hours a day for 20 days over a period of one month; the studies were conducted in the early 1960s in the South, where there were still strong norms against such interracial contact; and Cook deliberately selected the most prejudiced individuals he could find for his study. Such considerations make his 40-percent success figure more impressive.

In this discussion we have implied that intergroup contact under the five favorable conditions we have listed reduces prejudice by reducing the stereotypes that the groups hold about one another. There is another possibility. These same conditions probably also foster interaction that is rewarding in itself, motivating the participants to interact further in the future. It is possible, for example, that the boys at the camp would not have become friends so quickly if the group interaction had not been rewarded—if, for example, they had been unable to fix the waterline or start the food supply truck despite their joint efforts.

Is There a Prejudiced Personality?

Psychology's concern with prejudice increased greatly during the Second World War, when Jews and other minority groups were persecuted and murdered in Nazi Germany. With terrifying success, Adolf Hitler managed to use prejudice in general (and anti-Semitism in particular) as a way of channeling the frustrations suffered by the German people as a result of the country's humiliating defeat in the First World War and the economic depression that followed. Jews, Gypsies, homosexuals, Poles, and other groups were being used as *scapegoats*, targets of blame for these frustrations.

In the late 1940s a group of psychologists at the University of California at Berkeley, two of whom had escaped from Nazi Germany, launched a massive research project called *The Authoritarian Personality* (Adorno and others, 1950). These investigators believed that Freud's psychoanalytic theory (Chapters 13 and 14) provided a possible explanation for prejudice of the kind being experienced in Germany. Their theory suggests that in some cases prejudice may reflect the individual's own insecurities; highly prejudiced individuals may not be able to face their own weaknesses and, in Freudian terms, may project undesirable traits onto minority groups. They perceive such groups as evil and use them as scapegoats, blaming them for any frustrations in their own lives.

Through extensive testing and interviews with prejudiced and unprejudiced individuals, the Berkeley investigators gradually evolved a portrait of the prejudiced personality, whom they ultimately called the *authoritarian personality*. Authoritarian personalities tend to see the world as divided into the weak and the strong. They are power oriented in their personal relationships—

submissive and obedient to those they consider their superiors, but contemptuous and authoritarian toward those considered inferior. Authoritarians find it difficult to tolerate ambiguity and tend to hold highly conventional values. They do not like to be introspective and cannot accept the possibility that they might be personally weak or aggressive or sexually motivated. Instead, they project such undesirable traits onto members of out-groups. We thus arrive at their attitudes of racial prejudice. Authoritarian individuals, according to the Berkeley investigators, are the sort of people who would be particularly susceptible to the kind of fascist ideology that was promoted in Nazi Germany.

The Berkeley investigation is a classic study, and even by today's standards the project was an ambitious one. It spawned an enormous amount of follow-up research, but it has also been criticized for flaws in its methods and interpretations (e.g., Christie and Jahoda, 1954). For example, it was suggested that lack of education, not personality characteristics, might have accounted for some of the beliefs and attitudes of authoritarian individuals. The criticisms of the study must be taken seriously, and psychologists have learned to avoid many of the mistakes made by the pioneering Berkeley group. Even so, many of the original results have withstood the test of continued research, and many psychologists believe that the general conclusions of the study are still tenable. There do appear to be individuals with authoritarian personalities, individuals who seem particularly susceptible to a fascist ideology that has hostility toward minority groups at its core.

Prejudice and Social Norms

Even though a theory based on personal characteristics, such as the authoritarian personality, might validly explain why one individual is more prejudiced against minority groups than another individual, it does not explain widespread prejudice against a particular group within a society. Most such prejudices stem from *social norms*—a community's implicit rules specifying the beliefs, attitudes, and behaviors "appropriate" for its members (see Chapter 17). The individual in such a community who expresses prejudiced attitudes is most likely simply conforming to the local social norms. If the norms were to be changed, so too would the individual's attitudes.

This conformity explanation of societal prejudice was tested by Thomas Pettigrew, a social psychologist who specializes in race relations. He first noted that even though southern Americans express much stronger anti-black attitudes than northern Americans, they are not more anti-Semitic, as the authoritarian personality explanation of prejudice would require. Moreover, testing showed that southern Americans are no more authoritarian than northern Americans (1959). Pettigrew also noted that individuals who would be expected to conform more closely to social norms in general reflect more closely the local norms with regard to racial attitudes. For example, women, who are often the "carriers" of a society's norms, were significantly more anti-black than men in the South, but not in the North. Those who were affiliated with a political party in the South were more anti-black than political independents. Again, no such differences were found in the northern population. Finally, in the South, where attending church is a strong social norm, those who attended church regularly were more anti-black than those who did not.

The social-norm explanation of prejudice also accounts for the inconsistent patterns of racial practices within a community. Some southern communities were desegregating schools with little trouble but were still opposing desegregation of lunch counters; other communities showed a reverse pattern. As we shall now see, the social-norm explanation of racial prejudice has implications for public policy.

Changing Prejudice Through Legislation and Court Decisions

The belief that "one cannot legislate attitudes" is often expressed and was frequently used as an argument against legislation and court decisions mandating racial desegregation. But if—as we have noted—most racial attitudes are rooted in simple conformity to the prevailing social norms and not in the personalities of individuals, then attitudes should change if the social norms are changed. And in fact, the history of the desegregation process during the past two decades has confirmed that legislation and court decisions can change the social norms of a community and, in turn, can change attitudes. For example, surveys made in 1956, two years after the Supreme Court ruled that segregated public schools were unconstitutional, showed that only 31 percent of the white citizens in communities that had begun some token school integration approved of the move. But by 1963, when integrated areas included many communities where anti-integration sentiment had been much stronger, the majority of whites in those communities had accepted school integration. Nationwide attitudes toward school desegregation moved from 30 percent favorable in 1942 to 49 percent in 1956 and to 62 percent in 1963. Even in the most hard-core areas of the South approval of school integration rose from 4 percent in 1956 to 28 percent in 1963 (Sheatsley, 1966).

Protest demonstrations can also have a similar effect on social norms and, hence, on attitudes. Thus, in the early 1960s surveys repeatedly showed that Americans felt that civil rights protesters were "pushing too hard" and that this only hurt the cause of human rights. But these same surveys also showed that in spite of the protests—more probably, *because* of the protests—attitudes toward the goals of the civil rights movement, in the North and in the South, continued to become more favorable year after year. There are, of course, local setbacks, antagonism over disruptive protests, and strong opposition to violence among both white and black Americans, but attitudes toward the goals of equal justice and equality have become steadily more favorable, with no major reversals since at least 1942, when systematic polling began.

Local setbacks and vocal opposition are often misinterpreted as showing a backlash against human rights movements. Thus the failure to ratify the Equal Rights Amendment to the Constitution seven years after Congress passed it is often blamed on backlash. But genuine *backlash*—when individuals with initially favorable attitudes develop unfavorable attitudes—is almost never found. Rather, those initially opposed become more visible and politically active, thus retarding the initial momentum of those in favor of the change. The overall trend toward more liberal attitudes continues to develop.

It is also true that one of the best predictors of the future of social issues of this type is the age trend in the surveys. On virtually all human rights issues—attitudes toward ethnic minorities, women's liberation, and rights of homosexuals—younger Americans are more liberal than older Americans. Accordingly, we have every reason to expect the increasingly liberal trend on issues involving prejudice and discrimination to continue. It will still be true that some individuals will not change their attitudes toward black Americans, their views on the "appropriate place" for women, and their personal or

religious feelings against homosexuality. But the social norms will continue to change, and so, too, will the attitudes of most citizens.

The Mass Media

The mass media have had an enormous effect on our society and on us as individuals. Television, in particular, has become a potent social presence in our lives. Children begin watching television at age two or three, and by the time they are five they are watching two to three hours a day (Siegel, 1969). By age 16 the average child has spent more time in front of the TV set than in the classroom (Waters and Malamud, 1975), and it is estimated that one-third of all American adults watch an average of four or more hours of television per day (Gerbner and Gross, 1976). Even if television had absolutely no effects on its viewers, the sheer amount of time spent not doing other things would itself have had a profound effect on our society. It is understandable, then, that many people have been concerned about the influences of the mass media on our beliefs, attitudes, and behavior, and it is equally understandable that behavioral scientists have been called on to evaluate the nature and extent of these influences. In Chapter 11 we discussed the effects of TV violence on behavior. Here we will look at the influence of media persuasion.

"... No, he can't really fly ... no, the bad guys don't really have a ray gun ... no, this cereal really isn't the best food in the whole world ... no, it won't make you as strong as a giant. . ."

Influence of Media Persuasion

Given the amount of money that companies and candidates spend on TV advertising, one would conclude that persuasion via the mass media must be very effective. It is, and it isn't. In a highly competitive market or in a close political campaign a competitive edge of a few percentage points makes an enormous difference. Media advertising can sometimes provide that extra edge. It can also create knowledge of and demand for a new product, or it can create "name recognition" for a political unknown. And finally, intense, long-term media promotion can help a group of manufacturers dominate a particular market, even though they are in close competition among themselves. For example, despite repeated medical findings that all nonprescription pain relievers provide the same amount of relief, equally fast and with equal safety, the market is totally dominated by three or four heavily advertised national brands (Consumers Union, 1974). Such advertising costs money, of course, and these nationally known brands cost the buyer up to seven times more than the less advertised brands available in virtually every drug store and supermarket in the country. If you use one of these well-known brands, your headache dollar is spent primarily for the privilege of being persuaded to spend it, and you have first-hand knowledge that media persuasion is effective (Bem, 1970).

But when one considers how small a proportion of its intended audience mass media persuasion affects or how little it affects a single individual's beliefs or attitudes, the effectiveness of media persuasion looks much less impressive. For example, after an intensive image-building campaign for the oil industry, 13 percent of the sample surveyed had become more favorable, but 9 percent had become less favorable, a net gain of only 4 percent (Watson, 1966). Political persuasion is similarly ineffective. Despite the tens of millions of dollars spent during presidential election campaigns, only 7 to 10 percent of the population changes its mind about its preferred candidate over the course of the campaign. During the 1960 presidential campaign, 55 percent of the adult population

Kennedy-Nixon debate in 1960

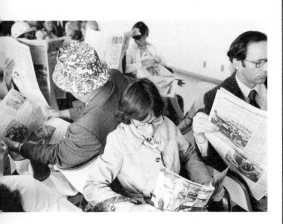

Selective exposure reduces media influence.

watched the famous debates between John F. Kennedy and Richard M. Nixon; 80 percent watched at least one of the debates. Moreover, there was a clear perception among journalists that Kennedy "won" the debates. But careful survey research showed that there were no substantial changes in votes as a result of the debates (Kraus and Davis, 1976). In fact, surveys show that those who are most exposed to presidential campaign material in the mass media seem to be the least affected by it (Berelson, Lazarsfeld, and McPhee, 1954). What are the sources of this ineffectiveness?

NOBODY IS WATCHING Perhaps the most mundane, but most critical, reason that media campaigns work so poorly is that only a small proportion of the target audience is watching or paying attention (Freedman, Sears, and Carlsmith, 1978). With the exception of the presidential debates, most political news and advertising reach only a tiny proportion of the population. In one survey it was found that only 23 percent of the adult public sees a network national news broadcast on any given evening, and a majority (53 percent) does not see any national news broadcast in an average two-week period (Robinson, 1971). Even those who do watch fail to retain much of what they saw. A telephone survey of people who had watched one of the national news shows earlier in an evening found that they could recall, on the average, only 1.2 of the 19.8 news stories covered in the average program; even when reminded of the content of the stories, people still could not remember having heard half of them (Neuman, 1976). And, of course, it is difficult to be influenced very much by a spot TV commercial for a product or candidate if we are running to the bathroom or getting a drink during the program break.

SELECTIVE EXPOSURE A second reason the media may fail to change our beliefs and attitudes is that we are more likely to be exposed—unintentionally or deliberately—to opinions we already agree with. Democrats listen mainly to speeches by Democrats; Republicans listen mainly to speeches by Republicans. Liberals read *The New Republic* but are unlikely to read *The National Review*. Interestingly, research shows that most selective exposure is unintentional; we simply tend to be around sources of information that support our views. For example, the conservative business person probably reads the *Wall Street Journal* because he or she is interested in business news; the fact that it also supports his or her political views is incidental. Again, the main task of a would-be persuader is to get the message to us in the first place.

SELECTIVE ATTENTION Even the persuader who does get the message to us cannot control very well how we attend to it. This was shown in two clever experiments in which subjects listened to persuasive communications that were difficult to hear because of static in the sound channel. In order to hear the message more clearly the subject could push a button that removed the static (Brock and Balloun, 1967; Kleinhesselink and Edwards, 1975). It was found that subjects were more likely to "tune in" to messages that supported their views than to messages that did not. For example, students who were strongly in favor of legalizing marijuana removed the static from neutral messages, from messages supporting legalization, or even from messages opposing legalization with arguments that were easy to refute; but they let the static interfere when the messages opposed legalization with arguments that were difficult to refute (Kleinhesselink and Edwards, 1975).

SELECTIVE INTERPRETATION Even when we listen carefully to a message, we are likely to interpret it in the context of our own beliefs and attitudes.

Political figures learn to state their positions—or nonpositions—with enough ambiguity so that the maximum number of people can interpret the message as agreeing with their own position. Moreover, messages from sources we already agree with will be perceived as more supportive of our own positions than they might actually be. For example, in both the 1968 and the 1972 elections voters tended to see the positions taken by the presidential candidates they preferred as being more in line with their own views than they actually were. Nixon supporters saw Nixon agreeing with them on the Vietnam issue more than he actually did; similarly, Humphrey and McGovern supporters saw these candidates agreeing with them more than they actually did (Granberg and Brent, 1974).

Can the Mass Media Be Effective?

It is clear from this discussion that the mass media are not going to brainwash us. Indeed, when we consider the many obstacles a would-be persuader faces in trying to reach us, it is a wonder that mass media persuasion works at all. But it would be misleading to imply that these obstacles cannot be overcome, as the following study demonstrates.

In 1972 the Stanford Heart Disease Prevention Program launched a three-community field study to see if people could be persuaded to alter their exercise, smoking, and dietary habits in the interest of reducing their risk of heart disease (Maccoby and others, 1977). This was a collaborative effort involving social psychologists, communication experts, media production people, and cardiovascular disease experts. Note that such an effort not only faces the usual obstacles of media persuasion we have already discussed, but it also requires people to change deeply embedded habits, such as smoking and overeating. Accordingly, the research team put everything they knew about persuasion, communication, and behavior modification into the program.

Two northern California communities, each with a population of about 13,000, were selected to be the experimental communities; a similar third community served as the control. A randomly selected sample of about 400 people in each of the three communities was surveyed before, during, and after

This scene, from a 60-second TV spot sponsored by the Stanford Heart Disease Prevention Program, features a local man who reports that he can now run marathon races after having lost 60 pounds through exercise and jogging.

Fig. 18-1 Percentage of decrease in behaviors related to heart disease after a two-year mass media campaign (After Maccoby and others, 1977)

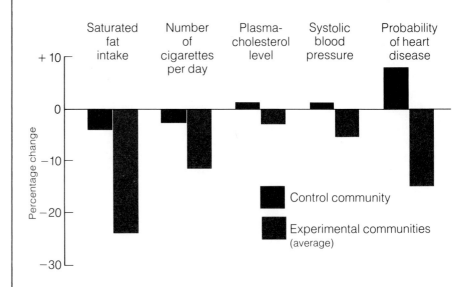

the two-year study in order to assess the effects of the campaign. Over the two years the entire population of the experimental communities was exposed to about three hours of TV programs, over 50 TV spot announcements, 100 radio spots, several hours of radio programming, weekly newspaper columns, and newspaper advertisements and stories. Posters were put up in buses, stores, and worksites, and printed material was sent via direct mail to the participants. The campaign was presented in both English and Spanish because of the sizable Spanish-speaking population in the communities.

The research team found that the level of knowledge about risk factors associated with heart disease increased dramatically in the two experimental communities, showing about a 30-percent increase, compared with about a 6-percent increase for the control community (Maccoby and others, 1977). Figure 18-1 shows that participants in the experimental communities demonstrated significantly greater decreases than the control-community participants in saturated fat intake, cigarette smoking, plasma-cholesterol levels, systolic blood pressure, and overall probability of contracting heart disease (Farquhar and others, 1977).

These results are even more impressive when compared with results obtained from a specially selected group of participants who were enrolled in an intensive 10-week program of weekly face-to-face sessions of counseling and instruction on how to reduce the risk of heart disease. These were all people identified as being high risk for contracting such disease. During the second year of the program they again received counseling and were encouraged to maintain any previous changes. The participants were also exposed to the overall media campaign. The results show that this group significantly reduced their risk-related behaviors during the first year of the program, doing better than media-only participants. But by the end of the second year the media-only campaign had almost caught up, producing nearly as much change as the intensive counseling (Farquhar and others, 1977). Impressive results indeed.

This study shows that persuasion via the mass media *can* be effective if carefully and intensively carried out. In addition, it points out that we should avoid the trap of thinking that media persuasion is necessarily evil or manipulative. The effectiveness, or ineffectiveness, of media persuasion is available to good causes as well as to those that are not so good. How it will be used is a political question, not an empirical one. It is a question for all citizens to answer, not just psychologists.

Environmental Psychology

As we have seen, people affect one another in a number of ways. But the physical environment also influences us, and a branch of psychology called *environmental psychology* has sprung up in the past few years to study these influences. One of environmental psychology's main concerns has been the psychological effects of living in noisy and crowded urban environments; accordingly, we shall look at the effects of both noise and crowding on our psychological functioning.

Psychological Effects of Noise

In general, it is plausible to suppose that we should prefer peace and quiet to noise. And yet most of us have had the experience of having to adjust to sleeping in the mountains or the countryside because it was initially "too quiet," an experience that suggests that human beings are capable of adapting to a wide range of noise levels. Research supports this view. For example, Glass and Singer (1972) exposed people to short bursts of very loud noise and then measured both their ability to work problems and their physiological reactions to the noise. The noise was quite disruptive at first, but after about four minutes the subjects were doing just as well on the tasks as control subjects who were not exposed to noise, and their physiological arousal also declined quickly to the same levels as those of the control subjects.

But there are limits to adaptation, and loud noise can become troublesome if the person is required to concentrate on more than one task. For example, high noise levels interfered with the performance of subjects who were required to monitor three dials at a time—a task not unlike that of an airplane pilot or an air-traffic controller (Broadbent, 1957). Similarly, noise did not affect a subject's ability to track a moving line with a steering wheel, but it did interfere with the subject's ability to repeat numbers while tracking (Finkelman and Glass, 1970).

Probably the most significant finding from research on noise is that the noise level itself is less important than its *predictability*. We are much better able to "tune out" chronic background noise, even if it is quite loud, than to work under circumstances of unexpected intrusions of noise. In one study, subjects were exposed to bursts of noise as they worked on a task. Some subjects heard loud bursts; others heard soft bursts. For some subjects the bursts were spaced exactly one minute apart (predictable noise); others heard the same amount of noise overall, but the bursts appeared at random intervals (unpredictable noise). Subjects reported finding the predictable and unpredictable noise equally annoying, and all subjects performed at about the same level during the noise portion of the experiment. But the different noise conditions had quite different aftereffects when the subjects were required to proofread written material under conditions of no noise. As shown in Table 18-1, the unpredictable noise produced more errors in the later proofreading task than predictable noise; and soft, unpredictable noise actually produced slightly more errors on this task than the loud, predictable noise.

Predictability is not the only variable that reduces or eliminates the negative effects of noise. Another is control. If the individual knows that he or she can control the noise, this seems to eliminate both its negative effects at the time and its aftereffects. This is true even if the individual never actually exercises his or her option to turn the noise off (Glass and Singer, 1972). Just the

TABLE 18-1
Number of errors produced on a proof-reading task as a function of earlier exposure to predictable and unpredictable loud and soft noise

	UNPREDICTABLE NOISE	PREDICTABLE NOISE	MEAN
Loud noise	40.1	31.8	35.9
Soft noise	36.7	27.4	32.1
Mean	38.4	29.6	

After Glass and Singer (1972)

knowledge that one has control is sufficient. The variable of perceived personal control is of major importance in several areas of psychology. In Chapter 15 we noted its influence on the way people react to stress, and we shall be meeting it again when we discuss crowding.

CHRONIC NOISE The studies discussed so far are concerned with exposing people to noise for only short periods of time, and only transient effects are studied in such experiments. But the major worry about noisy environments is that living day after day with chronic noise may produce serious, lasting effects. And, in fact, one study suggests that this worry is a realistic one. The subjects were residents of a large apartment house in New York City built over a highway; the noise levels in the building were quite high, particularly on the lower floors. The investigators tested a number of children who had lived in the building for at least four years, assessing both their reading achievement and their auditory discrimination levels. As Figure 18-2 shows, the lower the floor on which the child lived, the higher the noise level and the poorer he or she did on both the reading and the auditory discrimination tests. Because the investigators were able to rule out several plausible alternative interpretations of these results (for example, the possibility that poorer children or children from larger families might live on the lower floors), this study suggests that chronic noise may indeed contribute directly or indirectly to poorer mental functioning.

Psychological Effects of Crowding

Crowding, like noise, is often associated with urban living, and it is known that crowded conditions among animals lead to increased aggression, abnormal behavior, physical disorders, infant neglect, and high mortality (Freedman, 1975). Autopsies of animals that have died after living in crowded conditions reveal signs of prolonged stress (Christian, Flyger, and Davis, 1960; Calhoun, 1962). Early correlational studies seemed to support the possibility that crowded conditions might have similar effects on humans. Thus population *density* (the number of persons per unit of space) was positively related to mental illness (e.g., Hollingshead and Redlich, 1958) and to crime rates (e.g., Lottier, 1938).

As you have learned, however, correlation is not cause, and it seemed quite possible that the real causes might be the poverty and lower socioeconomic class often associated with high-density living. Accordingly, more recent studies have attempted to control for these factors, and there have been more

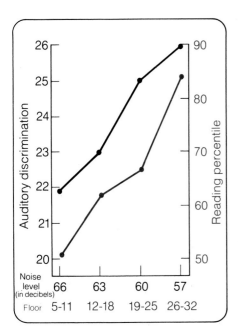

Fig. 18-2 Reading and auditory skills of children as a function of noise levels in their apartment building
(After Cohen, Glass, and Singer, 1973)

carefully controlled studies in Honolulu, Chicago, and New York (Schmitt, 1966; Winsborough, 1965; Galle, Gove, and McPherson, 1972; Freedman, Heshka, and Levy, 1975). All these studies find an overall positive relationship between density and juvenile delinquency, mental illness, and other pathologies; but when socioeconomic variables are controlled, the correlations tend to disappear, suggesting that density per se is not the cause.

One difficulty in drawing firm conclusions about the effects of crowding, however, stems from problems of definition. The term "crowding" usually refers to the individual's subjective feeling that too many people are packed too closely. Most studies of crowding, however, actually measure density, a physical measurement of the number of people in a given unit of space. Whether or not a person feels crowded is only partially a function of density; other determinants include the person's accustomed level of density, the temperature, the noise level, the person's cultural background, whether the other people are strangers or acquaintances, and many other variables. Moreover, some investigators have found it useful to distinguish two kinds of density: outside density—the number of persons per square mile—and inside density—the number of persons within a residence (Zlutnick and Altman, 1972). In most of the research, outside density by itself seems to have little effect. Compared with smaller communities, large cities with a high outside density do not have higher incidences of mental illness (Srole, 1972) or suicide (Gibbs, 1971). People who live in large cities report being just as happy as do people who live in suburbs, small towns, or rural areas (Shaver and Freedman, 1976). The city of Tokyo, Japan, is often cited in this connection (Canter and Canter, 1971). Tokyo has more than 20,000 people per square mile, more than 10 times the average density in North America. Yet crime rates are remarkably low.

Inside density, on the other hand, has been found in some studies to be associated with indices of social pathology. A study in Chicago that controlled for socioeconomic status and ethnicity found that the number of persons per room within dwellings was significantly correlated with higher death rates, receiving welfare, and the incidence of juvenile delinquency (Galle, Gove, and McPherson, 1972). A study of census data from 65 nations found a significant relationship between inside density and homicide rates after controlling for socioeconomic status (Booth and Welch, 1973). And finally, a study of inside density and crime rates in the United States using data from 656 cities with populations over 25,000 reported the following results. After controlling for race, education, and income, the investigators found that within the larger cities the number of persons per room was associated with slightly higher rates of murder, assault, and rape (Booth and Welch, 1974). These investigators suggest that crowded conditions within the home may lead to greater frustration as one's daily routines are constantly thwarted and that this frustration leads to greater aggression. It may be, however, that the people who live in crowded conditions are not the same ones who commit the crimes; the crowding-frustration-aggression theory remains to be tested adequately (Wrightsman, 1977).

But even the conclusion that inside density produces social pathology needs to be qualified; it may be true only for certain cultures, despite the positive evidence from the cross-national study cited previously (Booth and Welch, 1973). Such studies look only at aggregate data, census data across nations, and do not collect data from separate homes within each culture. One ambitious investigator, however, did visit individual homes in the city of Hong Kong, one of the most crowded communities in the world (Mitchell, 1971). He measured the exact size of each family's living space and took several measures of

stress and strain among the family members. He found no strong relationships between density and pathology. Clearly, cultural factors play a role in determining the degree to which density becomes a negative environmental factor.

LABORATORY STUDIES OF CROWDING   All the studies discussed above are correlational; they simply look at the real world to see if density and pathology are positively correlated after controlling statistically for socioeconomic class, race, and other variables. But psychologists have also attempted to find cause-and-effect relationships between crowding and distress in the laboratory.

The usual procedure is to place randomly selected subjects into a crowded or an uncrowded situation and then take a number of measures of task performance, physiological arousal, liking for the situation, decision making, aggression, friendliness, and so forth. The results from these studies are very complex, with nearly every conclusion requiring an "it depends on the person and the situation" qualifier (see Freedman, 1975, for a review of these studies). For example, sex differences show up in most of the studies; all-female groups tend to react positively to others when room density is high, whereas all-male groups react negatively (e.g., Ross and others, 1973). But at least one study shows the reverse (Loo, 1972). The effects of crowding are complicated and depend on the particular subjects and the circumstances under which the experiment is conducted.

COMBINATION STUDIES   As with the laboratory studies of noise, laboratory studies of crowding are not completely satisfactory, because the subjects are placed in crowded circumstances for only a brief period of time. On the other hand, we have already discussed some of the difficulties involved in interpreting nonlaboratory data gathered from surveys, census tracts, and crime statistics. This has led some investigators to try a combination of the two approaches. These studies test or study individuals in the laboratory who actually live in different kinds of situations. (We saw one example of this research strategy in the noise study in which children from different floors of a noisy apartment building were individually tested for reading and auditory abilities.) In contrast to the laboratory studies discussed above, in which the high-density situation is brief, the combination studies tend to show that the ecology (physical setting) of the day-to-day living situation does, in fact, influence one's social behavior.

College dormitories have provided the testing laboratory in several such studies, because on many campuses some dormitories have long corridors shared by a large number of residents, whereas other residence halls are grouped into suites with shared common rooms for small groups of people. Surveys have shown that residents of long-corridor dormitories are less satisfied with their living arrangements than residents of short-corridor dormitories. They report that they feel more crowded and complain that the quality of social interaction seems to become more negative over time (Baum and Valins, 1977).

When observed in laboratory situations, long-corridor residents report more pessimism about being able to make changes in their living situations than short-corridor residents. They also appear to withdraw from the situation more, not asking as many questions about an experiment, sitting farther from a fellow student in the waiting room, and spending less time looking at and talking to him or her. When asked to play a game as part of an experiment, long-corridor residents were less cooperative than short-corridor residents, being either more competitive or withdrawing from the game if given the option (Baum and Valins, 1977).

Findings like these support the theory that the major frustration of living in either long-corridor dormitories or high-density situations is the inability to regulate or control the number, the timing, and the nature of one's social encounters (Baum and Valins, 1977; Rodin and Baum, 1978). This theory is patterned after the theory of learned helplessness (Chapters 15 and 16), which states that lack of control over one's environment leads to a feeling of helplessness, which, in turn, leads one to withdraw and give up trying even when placed in other situations (Seligman, 1975). It has been found that rats reared under conditions of high density not only show poorer performance on complex tasks, but even fail to make a response when under stress (Goeckner, Greenough, and Mead, 1973).

In an attempt to test the learned helplessness hypothesis more directly, junior high school students were given an unsolvable problem, followed by a solvable one. Students from high-density homes did worse on the solvable problem than did students from lower-density homes. After failing to solve the first problem, these students apparently lapsed into a feeling of greater helplessness. (The study controlled for sex, race, and other variables.) (Rodin, 1976)

It may be that when the negative effects of living in high-density environments occur, they flow from a feeling of helplessness, a feeling that one has no control over the social interactions, and that one cannot regulate the intrusions of other people into one's private space. This could explain why people in cultures with highly developed norms of etiquette—for example, in Hong Kong and in Tokyo—manage to live so gracefully with both high outside and high inside density (Schmitt, 1963; Mitchell, 1971). In these societies, high density may not lead to a feeling of lack of control over the social environment.

Note how these conclusions parallel the findings on the effects of noise discussed earlier. In both cases it is not the physical variables themselves that are crucial; high noise levels and high population densities do not necessarily have negative effects. Rather, it is the real or perceived lack of personal control that is relevant. It is the unpredictable noise and the uncontrollable social intrusions that produce social pathology.

Behavioral Science and Public Policy

In this chapter we have seen that the findings of the behavioral sciences have a number of direct implications for the formulation of public policy. Problems of racial prejudice, the mass media, and urban housing are but three areas in which psychologists and other behavioral scientists have brought their skills and knowledge to bear. Public recognition of the behavioral sciences' influence on public policy is fairly recent; the actual participation of behavioral scientists is much older. And the unrecognized use of behavioral scientists' assumptions in the formulation of public policy is as old as public policy itself—as the following bit of history illustrates.

In 1954 the United States Supreme Court declared that legally enforced racial segregation in the public schools was unconstitutional (*Brown* v. *Board of Education*). In justifying its decision, the Court cited seven social science documents it had considered during its deliberations, and, in speaking for the Court, Chief Justice Earl Warren concluded that "to separate [black children] from others of similar age and qualification solely because of their race gener-

White teen-agers protesting racial integration march on City Hall in Baltimore, Maryland, October 1954

ates a feeling of inferiority as to their status in the community that may affect their hearts and minds in a way unlikely ever to be undone."

Many people believed then, and continue to believe today, that the 1954 Court had departed radically from tradition by considering psychological and sociological factors in reaching its decision. Opponents of the 1954 decision were particularly vocal in expressing their dismay that the Court had strayed from its obligation to render purely legal decisions. Thus, the editor of a newspaper in Virginia complained in an editorial that the subsequent violence in integrating some southern schools would not have occurred if "nine justices had not consulted sociologists and psychologists, instead of lawyers, in 1954, and attempted to legislate through judicial decrees" (Dabney, 1957, p. 14; quoted by Pettigrew, 1964). Even people who welcomed the 1954 decision appeared to agree that the Court had done something very different from tradition. Not so. The 1954 Court was simply more scholarly and intellectually honest than previous Courts in acknowledging its psychological and sociological sources explicitly.

Consider, for example, an 1896 decision of the Court, *Plessy* v. *Ferguson*. This is the very decision that the Court overturned in 1954, for it was in 1896 that the Supreme Court first gave judicial sanction to the "separate but equal" doctrine of race relations by ruling that legalized racial segregation was not a violation of constitutional rights. The 1896 Court arrived at its conclusion, in part, by noting that "legislation is powerless to eradicate racial instincts," and it upheld the view that "stateways cannot change folkways." Look at these statements carefully, for they reveal that the 1896 decision was just as "psychological and sociological" as the 1954 decision. Thus, the notion that there are "racial instincts" and the belief that legislative or judicial action does not produce attitude change in a society are psychological assumptions that require empirical evidence for or against them. They are neither self-evident truths nor historic legal principles. In fact, they are false. Nobody has ever produced evidence of "racial instincts," and, as we noted earlier, enforced compliance to legislative and judicial decrees often produces attitude change in a society.

But the 1896 Court did not fabricate its psychological assumptions out of whole cloth. These assumptions simply mirrored the sociological thinking of the day. Even the language used by the 1896 Court in justifying its decision reads as if it were taken from the writings of William Graham Sumner, the influential sociologist of the day who maintained that "stateways cannot change folkways." The notion of "racial instincts" also fits very nicely into the sociology of the time.

Thus, the difference between the 1896 and the 1954 Supreme Court decisions does not reside in the fact that the later decision was less "legally pure" and more "psychological," but rather in the difference between nineteenth- and twentieth-century psychological knowledge. As noted, the 1954 Court was simply more scholarly than the 1896 Court in documenting its psychological and sociological sources explicitly.

The moral of this bit of history is that legislation and court decisions are *always* influenced by psychological and sociological assumptions. It is an inescapable fact of life. Rulings concerning the conditions under which individuals can be held responsible for their acts, beliefs about the deterrent effects of capital punishment, and decisions concerning what is or is not obscene all involve "psychological" assumptions. Those who formulate and implement public policy cannot avoid such assumptions. They have only the choice of dealing with them knowingly and explicitly, as the 1954 Court did, or allowing their psychological assumptions to enter unwittingly through the back door, as the 1896 Court did.

As these Supreme Court decisions illustrate, the perspectives and assumptions of behavioral scientists can affect the thinking of society and have done so for many years. But influence is a two-way street: the perspectives and assumptions of society also affect the thinking of behavioral scientists. As we noted at the beginning of this chapter, science is not a value-free undertaking, and scientists frequently share the ideologies, prejudices, and stereotypes held by the society at large. Once again, a bit of history is instructive.

Political Bias: An Historical Example

In the first three decades of this century, many Americans were alarmed by the increasing flow of immigrants from southeastern Europe, particularly by the influx of Italians, Poles, Russians, and Jews. There was a strong belief that these "new immigrants" were genetically inferior to native-born Americans and that their increasing presence in the United States would "pollute" the country's genetic potential. This feeling culminated in the passage of the immigration law of 1924, which set up our country's first "national origin quotas" on immigration, thereby severely restricting the immigration of the "undesirable" elements.

Many psychologists who were prominent in the intelligence testing movement at the time were persuaded that differences between ethnic groups in intelligence test performance were primarily genetic in character. They gave little consideration to the many cultural and situational factors that we now know can lower test performances. Thus, the United States Public Health Service invited Henry Goddard to Ellis Island to apply the new mental tests to the arriving European immigrants. Based on his examination of the great mass of average immigrants, Goddard reported that "83 percent of Jews, 80 percent of Hungarians, 79 percent of Italians, and 87 percent of Russians were feeble-minded" (1913). He also reported later that the use of mental tests "for the detection of feeble-minded aliens" had vastly increased the number of aliens deported (1917).

The most direct psychological contribution to the 1924 immigration law, however, was a book by Carl Brigham entitled *A Study of American Intelligence* (1923). In this book, Brigham analyzed intelligence test data collected by the army during the First World War. He found that immigrants who had been in the country 16 to 20 years before being tested were as bright as native-born Americans, whereas immigrants who had been in America only zero to five years when tested were virtually all feeble-minded. How would you explain these findings? Perhaps you would be prompted to conclude something about the difficulties of giving a fair intelligence test to non-English-speaking immigrants who have just arrived in an unfamiliar culture. But this was not Brigham's interpretation of the findings. "We must assume," he wrote, "that we are measuring native or inborn intelligence." He then noted that the immigrants who had arrived 16 to 20 years before came primarily from England, Scandinavia, and Germany, but that more recent immigrants had come from southeastern Europe. The decline of immigrant intelligence, Brigham noted, paralleled precisely the decrease in the amount of "Nordic blood" and the increase in the amount of "Alpine" and "Mediterranean" blood in the immigrant stream.

Brigham's book concludes that ". . . we are incorporating the negro into our racial stock, while all of Europe is comparatively free from this taint. . . .

Tagging immigrants in a railroad waiting room, Ellis Island, 1926

The steps that should be taken . . . must of course be dictated by science and not by political expediency. . . . The really important steps are those looking toward the prevention of the continued propagation of defective strains in the present population." This book was widely quoted in Congress as "scientific" support for the 1924 immigration law.[1]

Brigham's idea that "the really important steps" to be taken would involve preventing the continued propagation of "defective strains" was also shared by other psychologists. For example, one eminent psychologist of the period felt that Indian, Mexican, and Negro children ". . . should be segregated in special classes. . . . They cannot master abstractions, but they can often be made efficient workers. . . . There is no possibility at present of convincing society that they should not be allowed to produce. . . . They constitute a grave problem because of their unusually prolific breeding" (Terman, 1916).

When one notes the flawed data and fallacious reasoning on which such arguments rested, it becomes clear that these behavioral scientists were using their "science" to bolster the prejudices and presuppositions that they shared with many of their less eminent fellow citizens.[2] But unlike the prejudices of less eminent citizens, their "scientific" conclusions were taken seriously in formulating public policy. Thus behavioral science becomes part of the problem instead of part of the solution.

Political Bias: Contemporary Variations

Blessed with the wisdom of hindsight, it is easy to recognize the biases of behavioral scientists of an earlier era. Moreover, several decades of added experience in the behavioral sciences have made us more sophisticated methodologically and have taught us to guard against unconscious biases in the interpretation of data. The "objectivity" of behavioral science is probably more secure now than it was in an earlier time. But biases can still enter the behavioral sciences in subtle ways. First, an investigator's biases, perspectives, and orientations enter into his or her decision about which questions to pursue and how to formulate those questions. White psychologists have often studied the black ghetto family, using the nuclear white family as their implicit ideal model. Accordingly, the investigator sees only weakness, decay, and "pathology" in the ghetto family and fails to see alternate forms of strength—for example, how the existence of an extended family structure in many black families provides some advantages not found in many highly mobile, white, middle-class families (Billingsley, 1968). Notice that the methods of investigation themselves can be completely "objective"; but the bias has already entered in the way the question has been formulated.

The second kind of bias that creeps into behavioral science research is simple neglect. For example, an important line of research in psychology has focused on the motivation to achieve (McClelland and others, 1953). An individual's motivation to achieve excellence is typically assessed in this research by asking him or her to write a story about a picture displayed by the experimenter. The stories are then rated or scored for the amount of achievement motivation they reflect. It was found very early in this research that the procedure "worked" only for male subjects, and, accordingly, most of the subsequent research used only male subjects. Because they had not shown any evidence of an enhanced motive to achieve under the predicted experimental

---

[1] It is to Brigham's credit that he later reexamined the data and the generalizations he had drawn from them, concluded that he was wrong, and said so publicly (see Brigham, 1930).
[2] The material in this section is reviewed in more detail by Kamin (1974).

conditions, women were dropped from the experiments. Not until several years later was it found that achieving women do, in fact, write stories reflecting achievement motivation, but only if they are shown pictures containing female figures. In fact, women who wrote stories reflecting achievement when shown pictures containing men but not when shown pictures containing women were underachievers (Lesser and others, 1963).

But it was too late; the damage had already been done. The pictures that had been adopted for conducting most of the research contained no women; moreover, after the first failures to obtain the expected results with female subjects, investigators stopped including them in their studies. Finally, many writers forgot over time that the results obtained in most studies applied only to men; they continued to cite the results as if they applied to everyone.

It is important to emphasize that the extensive research on achievement motivation was of high quality. It was carefully executed; the procedures ensured that the stories were scored in "objective" fashion without bias; and the results were publicly reported. Moreover, the results have been used in practical training programs in developing countries (McClelland and Winter, 1969). But there was one problem: half of the population had been systematically excluded from the research because the original set of stimulus materials contained a "male" bias.

Where Is the "Objectivity" of Science?

After this extended discussion of the ways in which the process of behavioral science can be influenced by the prevailing ideological biases and prejudices of the society in which the science is practiced, it is natural to wonder how behavioral scientists can even claim to be "doing science" at all. Where is the vaunted "objectivity" that distinguishes science from other forms of inquiry?

The answer to this question lies in the methodology and dissemination practices of science. The scientific aim is to make research findings public, truthfully reported, and responsive to checking by competently trained people. The best guardians of the integrity of any one scientist are other scientists who can criticize the work, repeat it if necessary to verify it, disconfirm it, or demonstrate its limitations. All the sciences rest their claim to objectivity on their public information-seeking and information-testing methods. Nothing we have said implies that the behavioral sciences have been amiss in following this proved model of inquiry. Indeed, because they are involved in advising on public policy, many behavioral scientists have devoted enormous time and effort to disseminating the knowledge gained from the behavioral sciences to the general public, where it can be scrutinized, evaluated, and criticized by those citizens whom this knowledge might affect. Psychology is one of the favorite undergraduate majors of college students throughout the country; thus, nearly every college graduate has received some amount of training in how to evaluate the validity of research evidence in the behavioral sciences. This, too, keeps behavioral science "honest."

In conclusion, the human mind has not yet devised a more objective method of gaining knowledge than the scientific method of open, repeatable inquiry, and it is this self-correcting feature of the scientific method that guarantees its "objectivity" in the long run. We have nothing that can compete with its reliability, validity, and objectivity. But precisely because it is human minds that are at work, nonobjective elements will always creep into the process. In the final analysis, psychology, too, is a human enterprise. And that is why it has potential for being part of the problem as well as part of the solution.

"That's the worst set of opinions I've heard in my entire life."

Drawing by Weber; © 1975 The New Yorker Magazine, Inc.

Scientific Jury Selection:

Behavioral scientists and their technology have recently entered a new and controversial area, the selection of jury members. Not surprisingly, this has raised both legal and ethical concerns, and it is important to understand and evaluate just what is involved in such an enterprise.

In our jury system, prospective jurors are drawn from voter registration lists. Each potential juror is then examined by the prosecuting and defense attorneys and sometimes by the judge. (This questioning is known as *voir dire,* from the French *voir,* "truly," plus *dire,* "to say," since the juror is sworn to speak the truth during the examination.) Potential jurors are asked about their background, their knowledge of the case, possible biases toward the defendants, and so forth. The purpose is to eliminate those whose biases might prevent them from considering the evidence fairly and impartially.

Either the prosecuting or defense attorneys may challenge a potential juror, stating the reason and requesting the judge to dismiss him or her. In addition, each attorney has a limited number of peremptory challenges—excluding a juror without giving a reason and without first obtaining the judge's concurrence. The defense is usually permitted more peremptory challenges than the prosecution. Through these challenges, the attorneys—and now their behavioral science advisors—can influence the makeup of the final jury.

What the behavioral scientists do is use questionnaires and attitude scales to collect survey data from a sample of the population from which the jury pool is drawn. These surveys reveal what kinds of background and attitudes predispose people in the relevant population to be favorable or unfavorable toward the defendants. For example, a survey may show that a male Republican with "authoritarian" attitudes who reads the *Reader's Digest* is likely to be quite opposed to a defendant charged with illegal protest activities against the government. Similarly, a survey may show that the ideal juror from the defense's point of view would be a black, female Catholic under 30 years of age. Using this kind of information, the attorneys can then ask pertinent, seemingly unrelated questions of the potential jurors, knowing how to interpret the answers in order to select the most favorable jury.

The behavioral scientists are also on hand to observe the potential jurors—watching their facial expressions and attending to the ways they answer the questions. This additional informal information is then used in an intuitive fashion to further select seemingly favorable jurors.

Is it legal? Yes. In gathering their data, the behavioral scientists do not approach prospective jurors. The prospective jurors are questioned by the attorneys only during *voir dire,* and the judge is there to prevent the attorneys from asking any improper questions. Moreover, attorneys on both sides have always tried to select juries most favorable to their clients. The only change is that attorneys now have a bit of survey data, a bit of behavioral science technology, and a bit of informed opinion to add to the hunches and intuitions they have always used to take advantage of *voir dire.* If the goal of selecting a favorable jury is viewed as a legitimate one, then there should be no objections to a legal technology that makes such a goal attainable (Saks, 1976). Moreover, pretrial surveys have sometimes revealed that the defendant cannot get a fair trial in that particular location, resulting in a change of trial site. Certainly this is a quite respectable use of behavioral science technology.

A Perversion of Criminal Justice?

Scientific jury selection is legal, but does it work? The technique was first used in the 1971 trial of Philip Berrigan, a Catholic priest, and several other defendants charged with raiding draft board offices, destroying records, and conspiring to kidnap Secretary of State Henry Kissinger. This was one of a series of conspiracy trials initiated by the government against activists protesting the United States involvement in the Vietnam Conflict; this particular group of defendants was known as the Harrisburg Seven.

A number of behavioral scientists volunteered their services in selecting a jury that would be as favorable to the defendants as possible (Shulman and others, 1973). This was a challenge, because the Justice Department was trying the case in the Harrisburg jurisdiction of Pennsylvania, one of the most politically conservative areas they could have selected. The trial ended in a hung jury, split 10 to 2 in favor of the defendants, and the government did not pursue the case further.

While the actual jury was deciding the case, the behavioral scientists reinterviewed a sample of people from their original survey. They found that 54 percent of this sample thought that the defendants were probably guilty, whereas only 2 of the 12 jurors (17 percent) actually voted for conviction, a finding that suggests that the jury selection technique was effective in picking a favorable jury. Defense attorneys in several subsequent trials—most of them with similar political overtones—have also used this jury selection technique and obtained acquittals for their clients.

But we must interpret these results cautiously. Although we do not have a control group of exactly comparable trials in which such jury selection techniques were not used, other recent political trials that did not use scientific

jury selection have also resulted in acquittals. It appears to be very difficult to obtain jury convictions for conspiracy charges, the usual charges in these cases. In addition, the comparison between the Harrisburg Seven jurors and the reinterviewed sample is flawed because the jury had heard the evidence in detail; the public—and hence the reinterviewed sample—had not (Saks, 1976). This raises the most crucial question of all: compared to the weight of the evidence itself, how important are the characteristics, attitudes, and biases of jurors?

After surveying the relevant studies, Saks (1976) concludes that, whereas the characteristics of the jurors sometimes have statistically significant effects on the jurors' decisions, these effects are quite small compared to the effect of the evidence. For example, one study did show that jurors (actually subjects in a jury-simulation experiment) classified by a questionnaire as authoritarian were significantly more likely to convict than persons classified as nonauthoritarian. But fully 62 percent of the jurors voted exactly in line with the weight of the evidence, irrespective of their authoritarianism (Boehm, 1968).

Studies of real juries also suggest that the evidence is the overwhelming factor in determining the jury decision. For example, in a national sample of several thousand cases the judge and jury agreed on the verdict in 78 percent of the cases (Kalven and Zeisel, 1971). Of course, judges may share the biases of juries, but this comparison is as close as we can come to an "objective" measure of the strength of the evidence.

This should strike a familiar note. As we saw in Chapter 17, situational determinants of behavior are usually more powerful than we expect, and dispositional determinants (that is, at-

titudes, personality) are usually less powerful. The same appears to be true in jury decision making; the evidence—the situational determinant—is more important than the characteristics of the jurors. And it is probably true that in most trials the evidence is sufficiently clear-cut—or at least presented in a sufficiently clear-cut manner—that it is the most important factor in the jury's deliberations. Scientific jury selection would be most helpful in those cases where the evidence is close or ambiguous. As Saks concludes, lawyers would not be harming their clients by taking advantage of scientific jury selection, but if they want to have an even greater influence over the outcome of the trial, they ought to consult behavioral scientists to help present the evidence (1976).

We should not use this general conclusion, however, to minimize the very real effects that jurors' biases can play. It is quite clear historically, for example, that racial prejudice has played an important role in producing higher conviction rates when nonwhite defendants are on trial than when white defendants are being tried for the same crimes. Similarly, there is both good empirical and good legal precedent for moving a trial out of a jurisdiction when a population from which the jury will be chosen is prejudiced against the defendants. Selecting a nonprejudiced or even a favorably inclined jury from the pool of prospective jurors is simply the next step in recognizing the very real effects of these biases. And we should expect these effects to be most important when the defendants are especially unpopular with the population at large, (for example, members of ethnic minorities, Communists, and homosexuals). It is not irrelevant that scientific jury selection originated with the defense of protesters of the Vietnam Conflict.

SUMMARY

1 A *stereotype* is a belief about a group of people that has been overgeneralized and applied too broadly to every member of the group. The thinking process that creates stereotypes is not itself evil or pathological. Generalizing from a limited set of experiences and treating individuals as members of a group are common and necessary.

2 Some stereotypes, however, lead to *prejudice*—negative attitudes toward individuals based solely on their group membership, rather than on their own attributes. This in turn can lead to *discrimination*—unfair treatment of individuals based solely on their group membership.

3 Contact between groups is likely to lead to a reduction of prejudice only when (1) the participants are of equal status, (2) a potential for personal acquaintance exists, (3) the individuals do not conform to the traditional stereotypes, (4) there is social support for the intergroup contact, and (5) the individuals or groups must cooperate with one another in order to attain mutually desired goals.

4 Following the Second World War, research on anti-Semitism led to the concept of a prejudiced personality type, based on psychoanalytic theory. The *authoritarian personality* refuses to acknowledge any personal weaknesses and, instead, projects such undesirable traits onto members of minority groups, using them as *scapegoats* for his or her own frustrations. Despite criticisms of this classic study, many of its conclusions have withstood the test of continued research.

5 Even though there may be prejudiced personality types, most prejudice is best explained as conformity to *social norms*. Research on anti-black sentiments in the United States supports this hypothesis.

6 The history of the desegregation process shows that legislation and court decisions can lead to attitude change. They do so by changing the social norms of the community; and, since most racial attitudes are rooted in social norms, the attitudes change too. Attitudes toward human rights have become steadily more positive. Genuine backlash—when individuals with initially favorable attitudes develop unfavorable attitudes—is almost never found. Rather, those initially opposed to change become more visible and politically active, temporarily retarding the initial momentum of the change.

7 Despite the amount of money spent on persuasion in the mass media, the effects are not very great. The main problem lies in reaching the intended audience. People tend not to attend to the persuasive message; they expose themselves primarily to opinions they already agree with, they "tune out" messages they disagree with, and they tend to interpret the message as more similar to their original beliefs than it actually is. However, a large-scale, two-year campaign aimed at changing people's habits so as to reduce the risk of heart disease showed that the mass media can be very effective when skillfully used.

8 Two of *environmental psychology*'s main concerns are the effects of noise and crowding on human behavior. People can adapt to a wide range of noise level, the noise level itself being less important than its *predictability*. Unpredictable noise is much more disruptive than predictable noise, and knowing that one can *control* noise diminishes the negative effects on performance. However, chronic noise in the environment has been found to affect children's auditory discrimination and reading achievement.

9 Crowding refers to the subjective feeling that too many people are packed too closely. *Density* refers to the number of people in a given area. Crowding is only partially a function of density, since many other variables (for example, temperature, cultural norms, and noise levels) determine one's

feeling of being crowded. Outside density, the number of persons per square mile, appears to have few negative effects by itself. Inside density, the number of persons within a residence, has been found to be associated with social pathology in some survey studies, but these effects do not appear in all cultures.

10 Laboratory studies that create crowded conditions fail to show consistent effects of high density. Studies of individuals who live in high- or low-density situations, however, do reveal negative effects of high-density living. The important variables appear to be predictability and control. High-density living causes problems when it leads to feelings of helplessness in controlling the number and quality of social interactions.

11 The findings and theories of the behavioral sciences have influenced the formulation and implementation of public policy for many years, although it is only recently that this influence has been explicitly acknowledged and actively sought by policy makers.

12 The perspectives, assumptions, and prejudices of the society in which the behavioral scientist works can affect and subvert the objectivity of the scientific enterprise. Historically, this can be seen in some statements of behavioral scientists that reflected the societal prejudices and ideology of the time and had little or no scientific basis. Contemporary societal prejudices influence behavioral science in more subtle ways: by influencing the ways in which research questions are chosen and formulated and by causing certain questions to be neglected.

13 Despite the influences that can subvert the objectivity of the research enterprise, the behavioral sciences, like all sciences, rest their claims of objectivity on the open, public methods of gathering and reporting their results and on the self-correcting character of the process. But in the final analysis science is a human enterprise, and, hence, it has the potential for being part of the problem as well as part of the solution.

FURTHER READING

A number of books seek to apply psychological principles to the solution of social problems; see, for example, Varela, *Psychological solutions to social problems* (1971) and Korten, Cook, and Lacey (eds.), *Psychology and the problems of society* (1970). Two psychological journals specialize in the application of psychology to social problems: *Journal of Applied Social Psychology* and the *Journal of Social Issues*. Both are edited for the nonspecialist, and the *Journal of Social Issues* devotes each issue to a single topic, such as poverty, women's roles, race relations, and so forth.

The classic book on prejudice is Allport's *The nature of prejudice* (1958), in paperback. For a thorough treatment of sexism and related issues, see *The longest war* (1977) by Tavris and Offir. Environmental psychology is covered in Ittelson, Proshansky, Rivlin, and Winkel, *An introduction to environmental psychology* (1974). On crowding, see *Crowding and behavior* (1975) by Freedman.

The application of behavioral science to social issues also raises a number of fundamental issues concerning the control of human behavior. Some of these are discussed in Andrews and Karlins, *Requiem for democracy?* (1971); London, *Behavior control* (1977), in paperback; and Skinner, *Reflections on behaviorism and society* (1978).

Appendix
Statistical Methods and Measurement

Much of the work of psychologists, like that of other scientists, calls for making measurements, either in the laboratory or under field conditions. This work may involve measuring eye movements of infants when first exposed to a novel stimulus, recording the galvanic skin response of people under stress, counting the number of trials required to condition a monkey with a prefrontal lobotomy, determining achievement test scores for students using computer-assisted learning, or counting the number of patients who show improvement following a particular type of psychotherapy. In all these examples, the *measurement operation* yields numbers, and the psychologist has the problem of interpreting them and arriving at some general conclusions. Basic to this task is *statistics*—the discipline that deals with collecting and handling numerical data and with making inferences from such data. The purpose of this appendix is to review certain statistical methods that play an important role in psychology.

The appendix is written on the assumption that the problems students have with statistics are essentially problems of clear thinking about data. An introductory acquaintance with statistics is *not* beyond the scope of anyone who understands enough algebra to use plus and minus signs and to substitute numbers for letters in equations.

Even an introductory acquaintance with statistics, however, requires practice in applying what has been learned. The treatment that follows states the essential relationships, first in words and then with simple numerical examples that require little computation.

Descriptive Statistics

Statistics serves, first of all, to provide a shorthand description of large amounts of data. Suppose that we want to study the college entrance examination scores of 5,000 students, recorded on cards in the registrar's office. These scores are the raw data. Thumbing through the cards, we will get some impressions of the students' scores, but it will be impossible to keep all of them in mind. So we make some kind of summary of the data, possibly averaging all the scores or finding the highest and lowest scores. These statistical summaries make it easier to remember and think about the data. Such summarizing statements are called *descriptive statistics*.

Frequency Distributions

Items of raw data become comprehensible when they are grouped in a *frequency distribution*. To group these items of data, we must first divide the scale along which they are measured into intervals and then count the number of cases that fall into each interval. An interval in which scores are grouped is called a *class interval*. The decision of how many class intervals the data are to be grouped into is not fixed by any rules, but based on the judgment of the investigator. It will depend to some extent on what he or she intends to do with the grouped data, but also on the range of values to be covered and the number of scores to be grouped.

Table 1 provides a sample of raw data, representing college entrance examination scores for 15 students. The scores are listed in the order in which the students were tested (the first student tested had a score of 84, the second 61, and so on). Table 2 shows these data in a frequency distribution for which the class interval has been set at 10. One student has a score that falls in the interval from 50–59, three scores fall in the interval from 60–69, and so forth. Note that more scores are in the interval from 70–79 and that none are below the 50–59 interval or above the 90–99 interval.

A frequency distribution can often be better understood in a graphic presentation. The most widely used graph form is the *frequency histogram;* an example is shown in the top panel of Figure 1. Histograms are constructed by drawing bars, the bases of which are given by the class intervals and the heights of which are determined by the corresponding class frequencies. An alternative way of presenting frequency distributions in graph form is to use a *frequency polygon,* an example of which is shown in the bottom panel of Figure 1. Frequency polygons are constructed by plotting the class frequencies at the center of the class interval and connecting by straight lines the points thus obtained. In order to

complete the picture, one extra class is added at each end of the distribution, and since these classes have zero frequencies, both ends of the figure will come down to the horizontal axis. The frequency polygon gives the same information as the frequency histogram, but by means of lines rather than bars.

In practice, one would want far more cases than those plotted in Figure 1, but all our illustrations use a minimum of data so that the reader can easily check the steps in tabulating and plotting.

Measures of Central Tendency

A *measure of central tendency* is simply some representative point on our scale, a central point with scores scattering on either side. Three such measures are in common use: the *mean,* the *median,* and the *mode.*

The *mean* is the familiar arithmetic

TABLE 1
Raw scores
College entrance examination scores for 15 students, listed in the order in which they were tested

84	75	91
61	75	67
72	87	79
75	79	83
77	51	69

TABLE 2
Frequency distribution
Scores of Table 1 accumulated with class intervals of 10

CLASS INTERVAL	NUMBER OF PERSONS IN CLASS
50–59	1
60–69	3
70–79	7
80–89	3
90–99	1

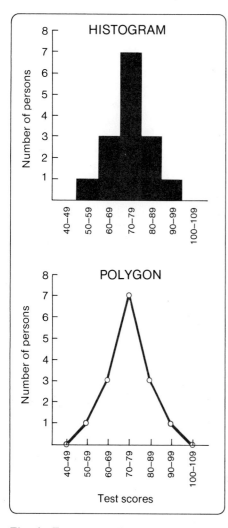

Fig. 1 Frequency diagrams
The data plotted are those from Table 2. A frequency histogram is on the top, and a frequency polygon on the bottom.

average obtained by adding the scores and dividing by the number of scores. The sum of the raw scores of Table 1 is 1,125. Divide this by 15 (the number of students' scores), and the mean turns out to be 75.

The *median* is the score of the middle case, obtained by arranging the scores in order and then counting into the middle from either end. When the 15 scores in Table 1 are placed in order from highest to lowest, the eighth from either end turns out to be 75. If the number of cases is even, one may simply average the two cases on either side of the middle. For instance, with 10 cases, the median can be taken as the arithmetic average of the fifth and sixth cases.

The *mode* is the most frequent score in a given distribution. In Table 1, the most frequent score is 75; hence the mode of the distribution is 75.

In a *symmetrical distribution*, in which the scores distribute evenly on either side of the middle (as in Figure 1), the mean, median, and mode all fall together. This is not true for distributions that are *skewed*—that is, unbalanced. Suppose we were analyzing the departure times of a morning train. The train usually leaves on time; occasionally it leaves late, but it never leaves early. For a train with a scheduled departure time of 8:00 A.M., one week's record might be:

M	8:00	Mean = 8:07
Tu	8:04	Median = 8:02
W	8:02	Mode = 8:00
Th	8:19	
F	8:22	
Sat	8:00	
Sun	8:00	

The distribution of departure times in this example is skewed because of the two late departures; they raise the mean departure time but do not have much effect on the median or the mode.

Skewness is important because, unless it is understood, the differences between the median and the mean may sometimes prove misleading (see Figure 2). Suppose that two political parties are arguing about the prosperity of the country. It is possible for the mean and median incomes to move in opposite directions. Suppose, for example, that a round of wage increases was combined with a reduction in extremely high incomes. The median income might have gone up while the mean went down. The party wanting to show that incomes were getting higher would choose the median; the one wishing to show that incomes were getting lower would choose the mean.

The mean is the most widely used of the measures of central tendency, but there are times when the mode or median is more appropriate.

Measures of Variation

Usually more information is needed about a distribution than can be obtained from a measure of central tendency. For example, we need a measure to tell us whether scores cluster closely around their average or whether they scatter widely. A measure of the spread of scores around the average is called a *measure of variation.*

Measures of variation are useful in at least two ways. First, they tell us how representative the average is. If the variation is small, we know that individual cases are close to it. If the variation is large, we can make use of the mean as a representative value with less assurance. Suppose, for example, that clothing is being designed for a group of people without the benefit of precise measurements. Knowing their average size would be helpful; but it would be very important to know also the spread of sizes. The second measure provides a "yardstick" by which we can decide on how much variability there is among the sizes.

To illustrate, consider the data in Figure 3, which shows frequency distributions of entrance examination scores for two classes of 30 students. Both classes have the same mean of 75, but they exhibit clearly different degrees of variation. All the students of

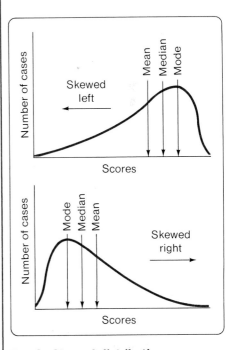

Fig. 2 Skewed distribution curves
Note that skewed distributions are named by the direction in which the tail falls. Also note that the mean, median, and mode are not identical for a skewed distribution; the median commonly falls between the mode and the mean.

Fig. 3 Distributions differing in variation

It is easy to see that the scores for class I cluster closer to the mean than those for class II, even though the means of the two classes are identical (75). For class I, all the scores fall between 60 and 89, with most in the interval from 70 through 79; for class II, the scores are distributed fairly uniformly over a wide range from 40 through 109. This difference in variability between the two distributions can be measured using the standard deviation, which is smaller for class I than for class II.

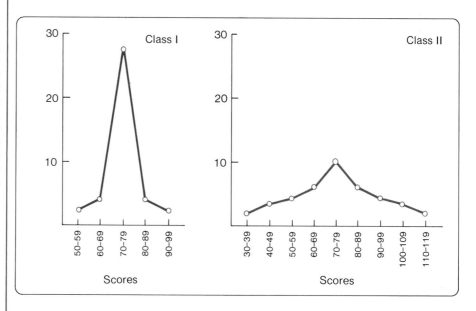

TABLE 3
Computation of standard deviation

CLASS I SCORES (MEAN = 75)		
	d	d^2
77 − 75 =	2	4
76 − 75 =	1	1
75 − 75 =	0	0
74 − 75 =	−1	1
73 − 75 =	−2	4
		10

Sum of $d^2 = 10$
Mean of $d^2 = \frac{10}{5} = 2.0$
Standard deviation (σ) $= \sqrt{2.0} = 1.4$

CLASS II SCORES (MEAN = 75)		
	d	d^2
90 − 75 =	15	225
85 − 75 =	10	100
75 − 75 =	0	0
65 − 75 =	−10	100
60 − 75 =	−15	225
		650

Sum of $d^2 = 650$
Mean of $d^2 = \frac{650}{5} = 130$
Standard deviation (σ) $= \sqrt{130} = 11.4$

class I have scores clustered close to the mean, whereas the scores of class II students are spread over a wide range. Some measure is required to specify more exactly how these two distributions differ. Two measures of variation frequently used by psychologists are the *range* and the *standard deviation.*

To simplify our example for ease in arithmetic computation, let us suppose that five students from each of these classes seek entrance to college and their entrance examination scores are as follows:

Student scores from class I:
73, 74, 75, 76, 77 (mean = 75)

Student scores from class II:
60, 65, 75, 85, 90 (mean = 75)

Let us now compute the measures of variation for these two samples.

The *range* is the spread between the highest and the lowest score. The range for the five students from class I is 4 (from 73 to 77); for those from class II it is 30 (from 60 to 90).

The range is very easy to compute, but the *standard deviation* is more frequently used because it has certain properties that make it the preferred measure. One such property is that it is an extremely sensitive measure of var-

iation because it takes account of every score, not just extreme values, as the range does. The standard deviation, which we will abbreviate with the lower-case Greek letter *sigma* (σ), measures how far the scores making up a distribution depart from that distribution's mean. The deviation, d, of each score from the mean is computed and squared; then the average of these squared values is obtained. The standard deviation is the square root of this average.[1] Written as a formula

$$\sigma = \sqrt{\frac{\text{Sum of } d^2}{N}}$$

Specimen computation of the standard deviation. The scores for the samples from the two classes are arranged in Table 3 for computation of the standard deviation. The first step involves subtracting the mean from each score (the mean is 75 for both classes). This operation yields posi-

[1] For this introductory treatment, we shall use *sigma* (σ) throughout. However, in scientific literature, the lower-case letter s is used to denote the standard deviation of a sample, whereas σ is used for the standard deviation of the population. Moreover, in computing the standard deviation of a sample, s, the sum of d^2, is divided by $N - 1$ rather than N. For reasonably large samples, however, the actual value of the standard deviation is little affected whether we divide by $N - 1$ or N. To simplify this presentation we will not distinguish between the standard deviation of a sample and that of a population, but instead will use the same formula to compute both. For a discussion of this point, see Horowitz (1974).

tive *d* values for scores above the mean and negative ones for scores below the mean. The minus signs disappear when the *d*'s are squared in the next column. The squared deviations are then added and divided by *N*, the number of cases in the sample; in our example, $N = 5$. Taking the square root yields the standard deviation. In this example, the two standard deviations tell much the same story as the ranges.

Statistical Inference

Now that we have become familiar with statistics as ways of describing data, we are ready to turn to the processes of interpretation—to the making of inferences from data.

Populations and Samples

First it is necessary to distinguish between a *population* and a *sample* drawn from that population. The United States Census Bureau attempts to describe the whole population by obtaining descriptive material on age, marital status, and so on from everyone in the country. The word *population* is appropriate to the Census, because it represents *all* the people living in the United States.

The word *population* in statistics is not limited to people or animals or things. The population may be all the temperatures registered on a thermometer during the last decade, all the words in the English language, or all of any other specified supply of data. Often we do not have access to the total population, and so we try to represent it by a sample drawn in a *random* (unbiased) fashion. We may ask some questions of a random fraction of the people, as the United States Census Bureau has done as part of recent censuses; we may derive average temperatures by reading the thermometer at specified times, without taking a

continuous record; we may estimate the words in the encyclopedia by counting the words on a random number of pages. These illustrations all involve the selection of a *sample* from a population. If any of these processes are repeated, we will come out with slightly different results, owing to the fact that a sample does not fully represent the whole population and hence has within it *errors of sampling*. This is where statistical inference enters.

A sample of data is collected from a population in order to make inferences about that population. A sample of census data may be examined to see whether the population is getting older or whether the trend of migration to the suburbs is continuing. Similarly, experimental results are studied to find out what effects experimental manipulations have had on behavior—whether the threshold for pitch is affected by loudness, whether child-rearing practices have detectable effects later in life. In order to make *statistical inferences*, we have to evaluate the relationships revealed by our sample of data. These inferences are always made under circumstances in which there is some degree of uncertainty because of sampling errors. If the statistical tests indicate that the magnitude of the effect found in the sample is fairly large (relative to the estimate of the sampling error), then we can have confidence that the effect observed in the sample holds for the population at large.

Thus, statistical inference deals with the problem of making an inference or judgment about some feature of a population based solely on information obtained from a sample of that population. As an introduction to statistical inference, let us first consider the normal distribution and its use in interpreting standard deviations.

Normal Distribution

When large amounts of data are collected, tabulated, and plotted on a

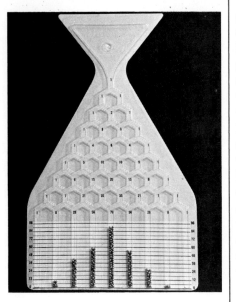

Fig. 4 A device to demonstrate a chance distribution
To observe chance factor at work one first holds the board upside down until all the steel balls fall into the reservoir. Then the board is turned over and held vertically until the balls fall into the nine columns at the bottom (as shown in the figure). The precise number of balls falling into each column will vary from one demonstration to the next. On the average, however, the heights of the columns of balls approximate a normal distribution, with the greatest height in the center column and gradually decreasing heights in the outer columns. (Hexstat Probability Demonstrator, Harcourt Brace Jovanovich, Inc.)

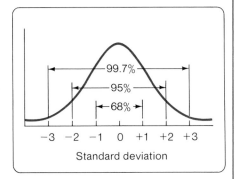

Fig. 5 The normal curve
The normal distribution curve can be constructed provided the mean and standard deviation are known. The area under the curve below -3σ and above $+3\sigma$ is negligible.

graph, they often fall into a symmetrical distribution of roughly bell shape, known as the *normal distribution* and plotted as the *normal curve.* Most cases fall near the mean, thus giving the high point of the bell, and the bell tapers off sharply at very high and very low scores. This form of curve is of special interest because it also arises when the outcome of a process is based on a large number of *chance* events all occurring independently. The demonstration device displayed in Figure 4 illustrates how a sequence of chance events gives rise to a normal distribution. The chance factor of whether a steel ball will fall left or right each time it encounters a point where the channel branches results in a symmetrical distribution; more balls fall straight down the middle, but an occasional one reaches the end compartments. This is a useful way of visualizing what is meant by a chance distribution closely approximating the "normal" curve.

The normal curve (Figure 5) can be defined mathematically to represent the idealized distribution approximated by the device shown in Figure 4. It gives the likelihood that cases within a normally distributed population will depart from the mean by any stated amount. The percentages shown in Figure 5 represent the *percentage of the area* lying under the curve between the indicated scale values, with the total area representing the whole population. Roughly two-thirds of the cases (68 percent) will tend to fall between plus and minus one standard deviation of the mean ($\pm 1\sigma$); 95 percent of the cases within plus and minus 2σ; and virtually all cases (99.7 percent) within plus and minus 3σ. A more detailed listing of areas under portions of the normal curve is given in Table 4.

Using Table 4, let us trace where the 68-percent and 95-percent values of Figure 5 come from. We find from column 3 of Table 4 that between -1σ and the mean there lies .341 of the total area, and between $+1\sigma$ and the mean

TABLE 4
Area under normal curve as proportion of total area

STANDARD DEVIATION	(1) AREA TO THE LEFT OF THIS VALUE	(2) AREA TO THE RIGHT OF THIS VALUE	(3) AREA BETWEEN THIS VALUE AND MEAN
-3.0σ	.001	.999	.499
-2.5σ	.006	.994	.494
-2.0σ	.023	.977	.477
-1.5σ	.067	.933	.433
-1.0σ	.159	.841	.341
-0.5σ	.309	.691	.191
0.0σ	.500	.500	.000
$+0.5\sigma$	.691	.309	.191
$+1.0\sigma$	.841	.159	.341
$+1.5\sigma$	.933	.067	.433
$+2.0\sigma$	.977	.023	.477
$+2.5\sigma$	.994	.006	.494
$+3.0\sigma$	.999	.001	.499

also lies .341 of the area. Adding these, we get .682, which has been expressed in Figure 5 as 68 percent. Similarly, we can find the area between -2σ and $+2\sigma$ to be $2 \times .477 = .954$, which has been expressed as 95 percent.

We shall have several uses for these percentages. One of them is in connection with the interpretation of standard scores, to which we turn next. Another is in connection with tests of significance.

Scaling of Data

In order to interpret a score, we often want to know whether it is high or low in relation to other scores. If a person takes a driver's test and needs 0.500 seconds to brake after a danger signal, how can we tell whether the performance is fast or slow? With a 60 on a physics examination, does the person pass the course? To answer questions of this kind we have to derive some sort of *scale* against which the scores can be compared.

RANKED DATA By placing scores in rank order from high to low we derive one kind of scale. An individual score is interpreted by telling where it ranks among the group of scores. For example, the graduates of West Point know where they stand in their class—perhaps thirty-fifth or one hundred twenty-fifth among a class of 400.

STANDARD SCORES The standard deviation is a very convenient unit for scaling, because we know how to interpret how far away 1σ or 2σ is from the mean (see Table 4). A score based on some multiple of the standard deviation is known as a *standard score*. Many scales used in psychological measurement are based on the principle of standard scores, with modifications often being made to eliminate negative signs and decimals. Some of these scales derived from standard scores are given in Table 5.

Specimen computations of standard scores and transformation to arbitrary scales. Table 1 presented college entrance scores for 15 students. Without more information we do not know whether these are representative of the population of all college applicants. Let us assume, however, that on this examination the population mean is 75 and its standard deviation is 10.

What then is the *standard score* for a student who had 90 on the examination? We must express how far this score lies above the mean in multiples of the standard deviation.

Standard score for grade of 90

$$= \frac{90 - 75}{10}$$

$$= \frac{15}{10} = 1.5\sigma$$

As a second example, consider a student with a score of 53.

Standard score for grade of 53

$$= \frac{53 - 75}{10}$$

$$= \frac{-22}{10}$$

$$= -2.2\sigma$$

In this case the minus sign tells us that the student is below the mean, and by 2.2 standard deviations. Thus, the sign of the standard score (+ or −) indicates whether the score is above or below the mean, and its value indicates how far in standard deviations.

Suppose we wish to compare the first standard score computed above to a score on the scale used in the Navy General Classification Test, as shown in Table 5. This scale has a mean of 50 and a standard deviation

TABLE 5
Some representative scales derived from standard scores

	STANDARD SCORE	GRADUATE RECORD EXAMINATION	ARMY GENERAL CLASSIFICATION TEST	NAVY GENERAL CLASSIFICATION TEST	AIR FORCE STANINE*
	-3σ	200	40	20	—
	-2σ	300	60	30	1
	-1σ	400	80	40	3
	0σ	500	100	50	5
	$+1\sigma$	600	120	60	7
	$+2\sigma$	700	140	70	9
	$+3\sigma$	800	160	80	—
Mean	0	500	100	50	5
Standard deviation	1.0	100	20	10	2

*The word *stanine* was coined by the Air Force to refer to a scale with scores ranging from 1 to 9, known originally as "standard nine," a type of standard score with a mean of 5 and a standard deviation of 2.

of 10. Therefore the standard score of 1.5σ becomes $50 + (10 \times 1.5) = 50 + 15 = 65$.

Using column 1 of Table 4, we find beside the value for a standard score of $+1.5\sigma$ the number .933. This means that 93 percent of the scores of a normal distribution will lie *below* a person whose standard score is $+1.5\sigma$. Thus a score of 65 on the Navy General Classification Test, 650 on a Graduate Record Examination, or 8 on the Air Force Stanine (all equivalent as standard scores) is above that achieved by 93 percent of those on whom the test was calibrated. Scores representing any other multiple of the standard deviation can be similarly interpreted.

How Representative Is a Mean?

How useful is the mean of a sample in estimating the population mean? If we measure the height of a random sample of 100 college students, how well does the sample mean predict the true population mean (that is, the mean height of *all* college students)? These questions raise the issue of making an *inference* about a population based on information from a sample.

The accuracy of such inferences depends on *errors of sampling*. Suppose we were to select two random samples from the same population, make the necessary measurements, and compute the mean for each sample. What differences between the first and the second mean could be expected by chance?

Successive random samples drawn from the same population will have different means, forming a distribution of *sample means* around the *true mean* of the population. These sample means are themselves numbers for which one can compute their own standard deviations. We call this standard deviation the *standard error of the mean*, or σ_M, and can make an estimate of it on the basis of the following formula:

$$\sigma_M = \frac{\sigma}{\sqrt{N}}$$

where σ is the standard deviation for the sample and N is the number of cases from which each sample mean is computed.

According to the formula, the size of the standard error of the mean decreases with increase in the sample size; thus, a mean based on a large sample is more trustworthy (more likely to be close to the actual population mean) than one based on a smaller sample. Common sense would lead us to expect this. Computations of the standard error of the mean permit us to make clear assertions about the degree of uncertainty in our computed mean. The more cases in the sample, the more uncertainty has been reduced.

Specimen computation of the standard error of the mean. In order to estimate the standard error of the mean, we need the number of cases in the sample and the standard deviation of the sample. Suppose we take the mean and standard deviation computed in Table 3 for class II but assume that the sample was larger. The sample mean is 75, and the standard deviation is 11.4. Let us assume sample sizes of 25, 100, and 900 cases; the standard errors of the mean would be, respectively:

$$N = 25: \sigma_M = \frac{11.4}{\sqrt{25}} = 2.28$$

$$N = 100: \sigma_M = \frac{11.4}{\sqrt{100}} = 1.14$$

$$N = 900: \sigma_M = \frac{11.4}{\sqrt{900}} = 0.38$$

Now we may ask, how much variation can be expected among means if we draw samples of 25, 100, and 900? We know from Table 4 that 68 percent of the cases in a normal distribution lie between -1σ and $+1\sigma$ of the mean. The sample mean of 75 is the best estimate of the population mean. We know the size of σ_M, so we may infer that the probability is .68 that the population mean lies between the following limits:

$N = 25:$
75 ± 2.88, or between 72.72 and 77.28

$N = 100:$
75 ± 1.14, or between 73.86 and 76.14

$N = 900:$
75 ± 0.38, or between 74.62 and 75.38

Thus, on the basis of sample data it is possible to specify the probability that the mean for the entire population will lie in a certain interval. Note that the estimated interval decreases as the size of the sample increases. The larger the sample, the more precise is the estimate of the true population mean.

Significance of a Difference

Many psychological experiments collect data on two groups of subjects, one group exposed to certain specified experimental conditions and the other serving as a control. The question then is whether there is a difference in the mean performance of the two groups, and if such a difference is observed, whether it holds for the population from which these groups of subjects are a sample. Basically, we are asking whether a difference between two sample means reflects a true difference or whether this difference is simply the result of sampling error.

As an example, let us consider scores on a reading test for a sample of first-grade boys, compared with the scores for a sample of first-grade girls. The boys score lower than the girls, as far as mean performances are concerned; but there is a great deal of overlap, some boys doing extremely well and some girls doing very poorly. Hence, we cannot accept the obtained difference in means without making a test of its *statistical significance*. Only then can we decide whether the observed differences in sample means reflect true differences in the population or arose because of sampling error. The difference could be due to sampling error if by sheer luck we happened to get some of the brighter girls and some of the duller boys in the samples.

As a second example, suppose that in an experiment to determine whether right-handed men are stronger than left-handed men the results in the first table (next column) had been obtained. Our sample of five right-handed men averaged eight kilograms stronger than our sample of five left-handed men. What can be inferred about left-handed and right-handed men in general? Can we argue from the sample data that

right-handed men are stronger than left-handed men? Obviously not, for the averages derived from most of the right-handed men would not differ from

STRENGTH OF GRIP IN KILOGRAMS, RIGHT-HANDED MEN	STRENGTH OF GRIP IN KILOGRAMS, LEFT-HANDED MEN
40	40
45	45
50	50
55	55
100	60
Sum 290	Sum 250
Mean 58	Mean 50

averages derived from the left-handed men; the one very deviant case (score of 100) tells us we are dealing with an uncertain situation.

Suppose that, instead, the results had been those shown in the table below. Again the same mean difference

STRENGTH OF GRIP IN KILOGRAMS, RIGHT-HANDED MEN	STRENGTH OF GRIP IN KILOGRAMS, LEFT-HANDED MEN
56	48
57	49
58	50
59	51
60	52
Sum 290	Sum 250
Mean 58	Mean 50

of eight kilograms is found, but we are now inclined to have greater confidence in the results, because the left-handed men scored consistently lower than the right-handed men. What we ask of statistics is that it provide a precise way of taking into account the reliability of the mean differences, so that we do not have to depend solely on intuition that one difference is more reliable than another.

These examples suggest that the significance of a difference will depend on both the size of the obtained difference and the variability of the means being compared. We shall find below that from the standard error of the means we can compute a *standard error of the difference between two means* (σ_{D_M}). We can then evaluate the obtained difference by using a *critical ratio*, which is the ratio of the obtained difference between the means (D_M) to the standard error of the difference between the means:

$$\text{Critical ratio} = \frac{D_M}{\sigma_{D_M}}$$

This ratio helps us to evaluate the significance of the difference between the two means. As a rule of thumb, a critical ratio should be 2.0 or larger in order for the difference between means to be accepted as significant. Throughout this book, statements that the difference between means is "statistically significant" mean that the critical ratio is at least that large.

Why is a critical ratio of 2.0 selected as statistically significant? Simply because a value this large or larger can occur by chance only 5 in 100 times. Where do we get the 5 in 100? We can treat the critical ratio as a standard score, for it is merely the difference between two means, expressed as a multiple of its standard error. Referring to column 2 in Table 4, we note that the likelihood of a standard deviation as high as or higher than +2.0 occurring by chance is .023. Because the chance of deviating in the opposite direction is also .023, the total probability is .046. This means that 46 times in 1,000, or about 5 in 100, a critical ratio as large as 2.0 would be found by chance if the population means were identical.

The rule of thumb that says a critical ratio should be at least 2.0 is just that—an arbitrary but convenient rule that defines the "5-percent level of significance." Following this rule, we will make less than 5 errors in 100 decisions by concluding on the basis of

sample data that a difference in means exists when in fact there is none. The 5-percent level need not always be used; a higher or lower level of significance may be appropriate in certain experiments depending on how willing we are to make an occasional error in inference.

Specimen computation of the critical ratio. The computation of the critical ratio calls for finding the *standard error of the difference between two means*, which is given by the following formula:

$$\sigma_{D_M} = \sqrt{(\sigma_{M_1})^2 + (\sigma_{M_2})^2}$$

In this formula, σ_{M_1} and σ_{M_2} are the standard errors of the two means being compared.

As an illustration, suppose we wanted to compare reading achievement test scores for first-grade boys and girls in the United States. A random sample of boys and girls would be identified and given the test. Suppose for the boys the mean score was 70 with .40 as the standard error of the mean and for the girls the mean score was 72 with a standard error of .30. We want to decide, on the basis of these samples, whether there is a real difference between boys and girls in the population as a whole. The sample data suggest that girls do better than boys, but can we infer that this would have been the case if we had tested all the girls and all the boys in the United States? The critical ratio helps us make this decision.

$$\sigma_{D_M} = \sqrt{(\sigma_{M_1})^2 + (\sigma_{M_2})^2}$$
$$= \sqrt{.16 + .09} = \sqrt{.25}$$
$$= .5$$

Critical ratio
$$= \frac{D_M}{\sigma_{D_M}} = \frac{72 - 70}{.5} = \frac{2.0}{.5} = 4.0$$

Because the critical ratio is well above 2.0, we may assert that the observed mean difference is statistically significant at the 5-percent level. Thus we conclude that there is a reliable difference between boys and girls in performance on the reading test. Note that the sign of the critical ratio could be positive or negative depending on which mean is subtracted from the other; when the critical ratio is interpreted, only its magnitude (not its sign) is considered.

Coefficient of Correlation

Correlation refers to the concomitant variation of paired measures, so that when one member of the pair rises, so does the other, or (in negative correlation) as one rises, the other falls. Correlation is often used in psychology. Suppose that a test is designed to predict success in college. If it is a good test, high scores on it will be related to high performance in college and low scores will be related to poorer performance. The *coefficient of correlation* gives us a way of stating more precisely the degree of relationship.[2]

Product-Moment Correlation (*r*)

The most frequently used method of determining the coefficient of correlation is the *product-moment method*, which yields the index conventionally designated *r*. The product-moment coefficient *r* varies between perfect positive correlation ($r = +1.00$) and perfect negative correlation ($r = -1.00$). Lack of relationship is designated $r = .00$.

The formula for computing the product-moment correlation is

$$r = \frac{\text{Sum } (dx)(dy)}{N\sigma_x\sigma_y}$$

Here one of the paired measures has been labeled the *x*-score and the other the *y*-score. The *dx* and *dy* refer to the deviations of each score from its mean, *N* is the number of paired measures, and σ_x and σ_y are the standard deviations of the *x*-scores and the *y*-scores.

The computation of the coefficient of correlation requires the determination of the sum of the products of the deviation of each of the two scores (*x* and *y*) from its respective mean—that is, the sum of the (*dx*)(*dy*) products for all of the subjects entering into the

[2] This topic was discussed on pages 22–23. The reader may find it helpful to review that material.

correlation. This sum, in addition to the computed standard deviations for the *x*-scores and *y*-scores, can then be entered into the formula.

Specimen computation of product-moment correlation. Suppose that we had the following pairs of scores, the first being a score on a college entrance test (to be labeled arbitrarily as the *x*-score) and the second being freshman grades (the *y*-score).

NAMES OF STUDENTS	ENTRANCE TEST (*x*)	FRESHMAN GRADES (*y*)
Adam	71	39
Bill	67	27
Charles	65	33
David	63	30
Edward	59	21

Figure 6 shows a *scatter diagram* of these data. Each point simultaneously represents the *x*-score and *y*-score for a given subject; for example, the uppermost right-hand point is for Adam (labeled A). Looking at these data, we can easily detect that there is some positive correlation between the *x*-scores and the *y*-scores. Adam makes the highest score on the entrance test and also the highest fresh-

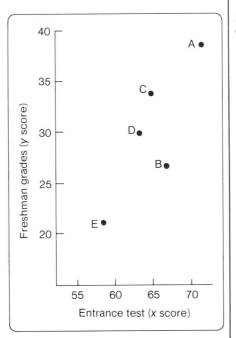

Fig. 6 Scatter diagram for hypothetical data
Each point represents the *x*- and *y*-scores for a particular student. The letters appended to the points identify the students in the data table (A = Adam, B = Bill, and so forth).

TABLE 6
Computation of a product-moment correlation

SUBJECT	ENTRANCE TEST (x-score)	FRESHMAN GRADES (y-score)	(dx)	(dy)	(dx)(dy)
Adam	71	39	6	9	+54
Bill	67	27	2	−3	−6
Charles	65	33	0	3	0
David	63	30	−2	0	0
Edward	59	21	−6	−9	+54
Sum	325	150	0	0	+102
Mean	65	30			

$$\sigma_x = 4 \qquad \sigma_y = 6 \qquad r = \frac{\text{Sum } (dx)(dy)}{N\sigma_x\sigma_y} = \frac{+102}{5 \times 4 \times 6} = +.85$$

man grades; Edward makes the lowest score on both. The others are a little irregular, so we know that the correlation is not perfect; hence r is less than 1.00.

We shall compute the correlation to illustrate the method, though no researcher would consent, in practice, to determining a correlation with so few cases. The details are given in Table 6. Following the procedure outlined in Table 3, we compute the standard deviation of the x-scores and then the standard deviation of the y-scores; it is four for the x-scores, and six for the y-scores. Next we compute the $(dx)(dy)$ products for each subject and total the five cases. Entering these results in our equation yields an r of +.85.

Rank Correlation (ρ)

When computers or desk calculators are not available and computations must be done by hand, a simpler method for determining correlations makes use of ranked scores. The resulting correlation is not an exact equivalent of r, but rather it is an estimate of r. The coefficient obtained by the rank method is designated by the lower-case Greek letter *rho* (ρ). The formula for the *rank-correlation coefficient* is

$$\rho = 1 - \frac{6(\text{Sum } D^2)}{N(N^2 - 1)}$$

where D is the difference in ranks for the scores of any one subject and N is the number of subjects whose scores are being correlated.

Specimen computation of rank-correlation coefficient. We shall use the same data employed in the preceding example. All the details are given in Table 7. The procedure is to rank both sets of scores from highest to lowest, obtain the differences in ranks for each subject on the two tests, square and sum the differences, and enter them into the formula. The value of ρ for our example turns out to be +.70. As indicated above, ρ may be viewed as an estimate of r. The fact that in our example the values of r and ρ are not closer together is due to the small number of cases ($N = 5$). When reasonably large samples are taken, ρ and r will closely approximate each other.

Interpreting a Correlation Coefficient

We can use correlations in making predictions. For example, if we know from past experience that a certain entrance test correlates with freshman grades, we can predict the freshman grades for beginning college students who have taken the test. If the correlation were perfect, we would predict their grades without error. But r is usually less than 1.00, so we will make some errors in prediction; the closer r is to zero, the greater the sizes of the errors in prediction.

While we cannot go into the technical problems of predicting freshman grades from entrance examinations or of making other similar predictions, we can consider the meanings of correlation coefficients of different sizes. It is evident that with a correlation of zero between x and y, knowledge of x will not help to predict y. If weight is unrelated to intelligence, it does us no good to know weight when we are trying to predict intelligence. At the other extreme, a perfect correlation would mean 100 percent predictive efficiency—knowing x we can predict y. What of intermediate values of r? Some appreciation of the meaning of correlations of intermediate sizes can be gained by examining the scatter diagrams in Figures 7 and 8.

In the preceding discussion we did not emphasize the sign of the correlation coefficient, since this has no bearing on the strength of a relationship. The only distinction between a correlation of $r = +.70$ and $r = -.70$ is that for the former, increases in x are accompanied by increases in y and for the latter, increases in x are accompanied by decreases in y (see Figure 7).

While the correlation coefficient is one of the most widely used statistics in psychology, it is also one of the most widely misused procedures. First, those who use it sometimes overlook the fact that r measures only the strength of a

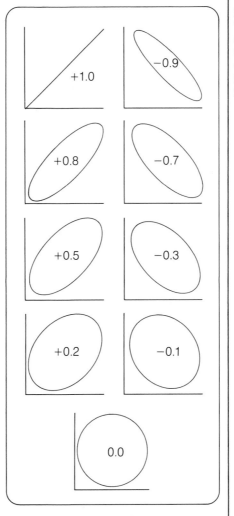

Fig. 7 Idealized scatter diagrams
The figure presents idealized "envelopes" drawn around collections of points in a scattergram; each scattergram has a different value of r. Note that the shape of the scattergram is related to the value of r; the fatter the scatter the smaller the value of r.

linear (straight-line) relationship between x and y. Second, they often fail to recognize that r does not imply a

TABLE 7
Computation of a rank-correlation coefficient

SUBJECT	ENTRANCE TEST	FRESHMAN GRADES	RANK, ENTRANCE TEST	RANK, FRESHMAN GRADES	DIFFERENCE IN RANK (D)	SQUARED DIFFERENCE (D^2)
Adam	71	39	1	1	0	0
Bill	67	27	2	4	−2	4
Charles	65	33	3	2	+1	1
David	63	30	4	3	+1	1
Edward	59	21	5	5	0	0
						Sum $D^2 = 6$

$$\rho = 1 - \frac{6(\text{Sum } D^2)}{N(N^2 - 1)} = 1 - \frac{6 \times 6}{5 \times 24} = 1 - \frac{36}{120} = +.70$$

Fig. 8 Scatter diagrams illustrating correlations of various sizes
Each dot represents one individual's score on two tests, x and y. In A, all cases fall on the diagonal and the correlation is perfect ($r = +1.00$); if we know a subject's score on x, we know that it will be the same on y. In B, the correlation is zero; knowing a subject's score on x, we cannot predict whether it will be at, above, or below the mean on y. For example, of the four subjects who score at the mean of x ($dx = 0$), one makes a very high score on y ($dy = +2$), one a very low score ($dy = -2$), and two remain average. In both C and D, there is a diagonal trend to the scores, so that a high score on x is associated with a high score on y and a low score on x with a low score on y, but the relation is imperfect. It is possible to check the value of the correlations by using the formulas given in the text for the coefficient of correlation. The computation has been very much simplified by presenting the scores in the deviation form that permits entering them directly into the formulas. The fact that the axes do not have conventional scales does not change the interpretation. For example, if we assigned the values 1 through 5 to the x and y coordinates and then computed r for these new values, the correlation coefficients would be the same.

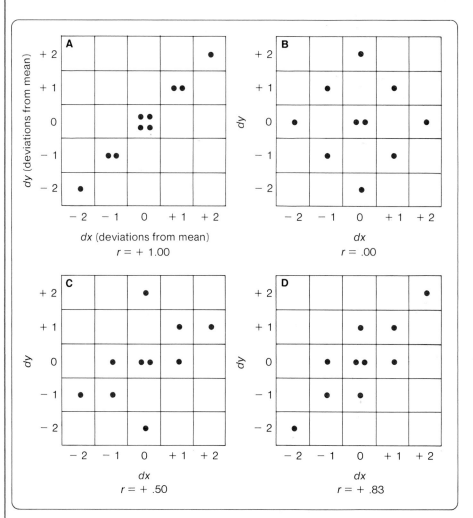

Fig. 9 Hypothetical scatter diagram
An illustration in which data would be poorly accounted for by a straight line but are well accounted for by the s-shaped curve. Application of the correlation coefficient to these data would be inappropriate.

cause-and-effect relation between x and y.

CORRELATION MEASURES LINEAR RELATIONSHIPS If r is calculated for the data plotted in Figure 9, a value close to zero will be obtained, but this does not mean that the two variables are not related. The curve of Figure 9 provides an excellent fit even though a straight line does not; knowing the value of x we could predict very precisely what y would be by plotting it on the curve. Let us therefore emphasize that the correlation coefficient measures only the strength of a linear (straight-line) relationship between two variables. If there is reason to believe that a *nonlinear* relation holds,

then other statistical procedures need to be used.

CORRELATION DOES NOT YIELD CAUSE When two sets of scores are correlated, we may suspect that they have some causal factors in common, but we cannot conclude that one of them causes the other (see pp. 21–22).

Correlations sometimes appear paradoxical. For example, the correlation between study time and college grades has been found to be slightly negative (about −.10). If a causal interpretation were assumed, one might suppose that the best way to raise grades would be to stop studying. The negative correlation arises because some students have advantages over others in grade making (possibly because of native ability or better college preparation), so that often those who study the hardest are those who have difficulty earning the best grades.

This example provides sufficient warning against giving a causal interpretation to a coefficient of correlation. It is possible, however, that when two variables are correlated one may be the cause of the other. The search for causes is a logical one, and correlations can help by providing leads to experiments that can verify cause-and-effect relations.

SUMMARY

1 *Statistics* deals with the collection and handling of numerical data and inferences made from such data.
2 *Descriptive statistics* provides a shorthand summary of large numbers of observations.
3 *Measures of central tendency* include the *mean,* the *median,* and the *mode.* Because of its mathematical properties, the mean (the ordinary arithmetic average) is the most favored of these measures.
4 *Measures of variation* include the *range* and the *standard deviation.* The standard deviation, although fairly complex, is the most useful measure.
5 *Statistical inference* deals with the problem of making an inference or judgment about some feature of a population when the inference must be based solely on information obtained from a *sample* of the population. The accuracy of such inferences depends on two factors: the size of the sample and the faithfulness with which the sample represents the population. *Random-sampling* procedures are most frequently used in order to ensure a representative sample.

6 In the *scaling* of data, raw scores may be converted into *ranks* or *standard scores.* Standard scores have many advantages and are widely used; they are based on distance from the mean expressed as multiples of the standard deviation.
7 It is possible to compute a *standard error of the difference between two means* from the *standard error* of each mean. The *critical ratio* expresses the obtained difference between two means in multiples of the standard error of the difference between the means. If the critical ratio is 2.0 or above, we have confidence that a true difference between the means exists and is not likely to be the result of chance factors.
8 The *coefficient of correlation* is a convenient method for expressing the degree of relationship between two variables. The *product-moment correlation* is the one favored in psychological research. A convenient approximation is provided by the *rank-correlation coefficient.*

FURTHER READING

A number of textbooks on statistics are available to students of psychology, of which Horowitz, *Elements of statistics for psychology and education* (1974), Phillips, *Statistical thinking* (1973), Edwards, *Statistical methods* (3rd ed., 1973), Wright, *Understanding statistics: An informal introduction for the behavioral sciences* (1976), and Minium, *Statistical reasoning in psychology and education* (2nd ed., 1978) are examples. The role of statistics in the design of psychological experiments is explained in Winer, *Statistical principles in experimental design* (2nd ed., 1971).

For an advanced discussion of measurement problems in psychology, see Krantz, Luce, Suppes, and Tversky, *Foundations of measurement* (1971).

Glossary

The glossary defines technical words appearing in the text and some common words when they are used in psychology with special meanings. No attempt is made to give the range of meanings beyond those used in the text. For fuller definitions and other shades of meaning, consult any standard dictionary of psychology.

ability. Demonstrable knowledge or skill. Ability includes aptitude and achievement. See also **achievement, aptitude.**

abreaction. In psychoanalysis, the process of reducing emotional tension by reliving (in speech or action or both) the experience that caused the tension.

absolute threshold. The intensity or frequency at which a stimulus becomes effective or ceases to become effective, as measured under experimental conditions. See also **difference threshold, threshold.**

achievement. Acquired ability; e.g., school attainment in spelling. See also **aptitude.**

achievement motive. The social motive to accomplish something of value or importance, to meet standards of excellence in what one does.

achromatic colors. Black, white, and gray. See also **chromatic colors.**

acquisition. The stage during which a new response is learned and gradually strengthened. See also **classical conditioning.**

action potential. Synonymous with *nerve impulse.* The wave of electrical activity that is transmitted down the axon of the neuron when the cell membrane becomes depolarized. See also **depolarization, graded potential, resting potential.**

additive mixture. The mixture of colored lights; two spotlights of different colors focused on the same spot yield an additive color mixture. See also **subtractive mixture.**

ADH. See **antidiuretic hormone.**

adipocytes. Special fat cells in the body. Obese individuals have many more of them and thus, perhaps, a higher body fat base line.

adolescence. In human beings, the period from puberty to maturity, roughly the early teens to the early twenties. See also **puberty.**

adrenal gland. One of a pair of endocrine glands located above the kidneys. The medulla of the gland secretes the hormones epinephrine and norepinephrine. The cortex of the gland secretes a number of hormones, collectively called the adrenocortical hormones, which include cortisone. See also **endocrine gland.**

adrenalin. See **epinephrine.**

affective disorder. A psychosis characterized by disturbances of mood, or affect. Mania (exaggerated excitement), depression, and a cyclical manic-depression are examples. See also **psychosis.**

affective experience. An emotional experience, whether pleasant or unpleasant, mild or intense. See also **emotion.**

afferent neuron. A neuron, or nerve cell, that conveys messages to the brain or spinal cord from the sense receptors informing the organism about events in the environment or within the body. Usually synonymous with *sensory neuron.* See also **efferent neuron, receptor.**

afterimage. The sensory experience that remains when a stimulus is withdrawn. Usually refers to visual experience, e.g., the negative afterimage of a picture, or the train of colored images that results after staring at the sun.

age regression. In hypnosis, the reliving through fantasy of experiences that are based on early memories or appropriate to a younger age. See also **hypnosis.**

aggression. Behavior intended to harm another person. See also **hostile aggression, instrumental aggression.**

agoraphobia. Fear of open places. See also **phobia.**

all-or-none principle. The rule that the nerve impulse in a single neuron is independent of the strength of stimulation; the neuron either responds completely (fires its action potential) or not at all.

alpha waves. See **electroencephalogram.**

ambivalence. Simultaneous liking and disliking of an object or person; the conflict caused by an incentive that is at once positive and negative. See also **conflict.**

amnesia. The partial or total loss of memory for past experiences. The memories lost in amnesia have not been completely destroyed, for the forgotten events may again be remembered when the person recovers from the amnesia. See also **repression.**

amphetamines. Central nervous system stimulants that produce restlessness, irritability, anxiety, and rapid heart rate. Dexedrine sulfate ("speed") and methamphetamine ("meth") are two types of amphetamines. See also **depressants, stimulants.**

anal stage. The second stage according to the psychoanalytic theory of psychosexual development, following the oral stage. The sources of gratification and conflict have to do with the expulsion and retention of feces. See also **psychosexual development.**

analysis-by-synthesis. A theory of perception assuming that the perceiver analyzes a stimulus into features and then uses the features to synthesize, or construct, a percept that best fits all of the information.

androgens. The collective name for male sex hormones, of which testosterone, secreted by the testes, is best known. See also **gonads.**

anterograde amnesia. The inability to learn, or retain, new information; presumably because new information is not encoded into long-term memory. See also **dual-memory theory, encoding, long-term memory, retrograde amnesia.**

anthropology. The science that studies chiefly preliterate ("primitive") societies. Its main divisions are archaeology (the study of the physical monuments and remains from earlier civilizations), physical anthropology (concerned with the anatomical differences among men and their evolutionary origins), linguistic anthropology, and social anthropology (concerned with social institutions and behavior). See also **behavioral sciences.**

antidepressant. Drug that is used to elevate the mood of depressed individuals: imipramine (Tofranil), isocarboxazid (Marplan), and tranylcypromine (Parnate) are examples.

antidiuretic hormone (ADH). Hormone secreted by the pituitary gland that signals the kidney to reabsorb water into the blood stream instead of excreting it as urine.

antisocial personality. See **psychopathic personality.**

anxiety. A state of apprehension or uneasiness, related to fear. The object of anxiety (e.g., a vague danger or foreboding) is ordinarily less specific than the object of fear (e.g., a vicious animal).

anxiety hierarchy. A list of situations or stimuli to which a person responds with anxiety ranked in order from the least anxiety-producing to the most fearful. Used by behavior therapists in systematically desensitizing patients to feared stimuli by associating deep relaxation with the situations rather than anxiety. See also **behavior therapy, systematic desensitization.**

anxiety reaction. A form of neurosis characterized by a diffuse dread, often accompanied by tenseness, palpitation, sweating, nausea. See also **neurosis.**

apathy. Listlessness, indifference; one of the consequences of frustration. See also **frustration.**

aphagia. Inability to eat. See also **hyperphagia.**

aphasia. Impairment or loss of ability to articulate words or comprehend speech.

apnea. A sleep disturbance characterized by inhibited breathing during sleep.

apparent motion. See **autokinetic effect, phi phenomenon, stroboscopic motion.**

appetitive behavior. Seeking behavior. See also **aversive behavior.**

aptitude. The capacity to learn; e.g., typing aptitude prior to practice on a typewriter. Aptitude tests are designed to predict the outcome of training, hence to predict future ability on the basis of present ability. See also **achievement.**

archetypes. In the psychology of Carl Jung, a basic idea, such as "God" or "mother," said to characterize a universal unconscious.

artificial intelligence. The performance by a computer of tasks that have hitherto required the application of human intelligence.

assertive training. A form of counter-conditioning in which assertive or approach responses are reinforced in an attempt to extinguish passivity or anxiety in certain situations. See also **behavior therapy, counter-conditioning.**

association areas. Areas of the cerebral cortex that are not directly concerned with sensory or motor processes; they integrate inputs from various sensory channels and presumably function in learning, memory, and thinking.

associative learning. Learning that certain contingencies (or relations) exist between events; learning that one event is associated with another.

asymptote. The stable level to which a variable tends over the course of time; e.g., in learning, the final response strength after an extended period of acquisition.

Atkinson's law. The test of a marriage is to coauthor a textbook for more than one edition.

attachment. The tendency of the young organism to seek closeness to particular individuals and to feel more secure in their presence.

attention. The focusing of perception leading to heightened awareness of a limited range of stimuli.

attribution. The process by which we attempt to explain the behavior of other people. Attribution theory deals with the rules people use to infer the causes of observed behavior. See also **dispositional attribution, situational attribution.**

authoritarian personality. A personality syndrome that disposes a person toward a fascist ideology; to be deferent toward superiors but authoritarian toward those considered inferior. Likely to be prejudiced against minority groups and to see the world divided into the weak and the strong.

autism. Absorption in fantasy to the exclusion of interest in reality; a symptom of schizophrenia. See also **schizophrenia.**

autistic thinking. A form of associative thinking, controlled more by the thinker's needs or desires than by reality; wishful thinking. See also **daydreaming, rationalization.**

autokinetic effect. The apparent movement of a stationary spot of light when viewed in a totally dark room.

automatic writing. Writing that the writer is unaware of; i.e., does not know that he or she is producing; familiar in hypnosis. See also **hypnosis.**

autonomic nervous system. The division of the peripheral nervous system that regulates smooth muscle; i.e., organ and glandular activities. It is divided into the sympathetic and parasympathetic divisions. See also **parasympathetic division, peripheral nervous system, sympathetic division.**

average. See **measure of central tendency.**

aversive behavior. Avoidance behavior. See also **appetitive behavior.**

aversive conditioning. A form of conditioning in which an undesirable response is extinguished through association with punishment; has been used in behavior therapy to treat alcoholism, smoking, and sexual problems. See also **behavior therapy, counter-conditioning.**

avoidance learning. A form of learning controlled by the threat of punishment. The learning is motivated by the anxiety raised by the threat and the reduction of anxiety when the punishment is avoided. See also **escape learning.**

awareness. See **conscious processes.**

axon. That portion of a neuron that transmits impulses to other neurons. See also **neuron, dendrite.**

Barnum effect. Refers to the readiness of most people to believe general descriptions, as given in astrological characterizations, and to refer to them personally.

basal mental age. In individual tests of the Binet type, the highest age level at which, and below which, all tests are passed. See also **mental age.**

basilar membrane. A membrane of the ear within the coils of the cochlea supporting the organ of Corti. Movements of the basilar membrane stimulate the hair cells of the organ of Corti, producing the neural effects of auditory stimulation. See also **cochlea, organ of Corti.**

behavior. Those activities of an organism that can be observed by another organism or by an experimenter's instruments. Included within behavior are verbal reports made about subjective, conscious experiences. See also **conscious processes.**

behavior genetics. The study of the inheritance of behavioral characteristics.

behavior modification. See **behavior therapy.**

behavior therapy. A method of psychotherapy based on learning principles. It uses such techniques as counter-conditioning, reinforcement, and shaping to modify behavior (syn. *behavior modification*).

behavioral sciences. The sciences concerned in one way or another with the behavior of humans and lower organisms; especially social anthropology, psychology, and sociology, but including some aspects of biology, economics, political science, history, philosophy, and other fields of study. See also **anthropology, psychology, sociology.**

behaviorism. A school or system of psychology associated with the name of John B. Watson; it defined psychology as the study of behavior and limited the data of psychology to observable activities. In its classical form it was more restrictive than the contemporary behavioral viewpoint in psychology.

binocular cues. See **distance cues.**

binocular disparity. The fact that an object projects slightly different images on the two retinas due to the different positions of the right and left eyes.

biofeedback. A procedure that permits individuals to monitor their own physiological processes (e.g., heart rate, blood pressure), which they are normally unaware of, to learn to control them.

biological therapy. Treatment of personality maladjustment or mental illness by drugs, electric shock, or other methods directly affecting bodily processes. See also **psychotherapy.**

blind spot. An insensitive area of the retina where the nerve fibers from the ganglion cells join together to form the optic nerve.

blood pressure. The pressure of the blood against the walls of the blood vessels. Changes in blood pressure following stimulation serve as one indicator of emotion.

brain stem. The structures lying near the core of the brain; essentially all of the brain with the exception of the cerebrum and the cerebellum and their dependent parts.

brainwashing. See **coercive persuasion.**

branching program. A teaching program often implemented by a computer in which the students' path through the instructional materials varies as a function of their performance. Students may move rapidly through the material if their responses are generally correct or go off to remedial loops if they encounter difficulties. See also **CAL, linear program.**

brightness. The dimension of color that describes its nearness in brillance to white (as contrasted with black). A bright color reflects more light than a dark one. See also **hue, saturation.**

brightness constancy. The tendency to see a familiar object as of the same brightness, regardless of light and shadow that change its stimulus properties. See also **color constancy, object constancy.**

Broca's area. A portion of the left cerebral hemisphere said to control motor speech.

CAL. A common abbreviation for computer-assisted learning; i.e., instruction carried out under computer control. See also **branching program, linear program.**

Cannon-Bard theory. A classical theory of emotion proposed by Cannon and Bard. The theory states that an emotion-producing stimulus activates the cortex and bodily responses at the same time; bodily changes and the experience of emotion occur simultaneously. See also **cognitive-physiological theory, James-Lange theory.**

cardiac muscle. A special kind of muscle found only in the heart. See also **smooth muscle, striate muscle.**

case history. A biography obtained for scientific purposes; the material is sometimes supplied by interview, sometimes collected over the years. See also **longitudinal study.**

castration. Surgical removal of the gonads; in the male, removal of the testes; in the female, removal of the ovaries.

catharsis. Reduction of an impulse or emotion through direct or indirect expression, particularly verbal and fantasy expression.

central core. The most central and the evolutionally oldest portion of the brain. It includes structures that regulate basic life processes, including most of the brain stem. See also **brain stem, cerebellum, hypothalamus, reticular system.**

central fissure. A fissure of each cerebral hemisphere that separates the frontal and parietal lobes (syn. *fissure of Rolando*).

central nervous system. In vertebrates, the brain and spinal cord, as distinct from the nerve trunks and their peripheral connections. See also **autonomic nervous system, peripheral nervous system.**

cerebellum. Lobed structure attached to the rear of the brain stem that regulates muscle tone and coordination of intricate movements.

cerebral cortex. The surface layer of the cerebral hemispheres in higher animals, including humans. It is commonly called gray matter because its many cell bodies give it a gray appearance in cross section, in contrast with the myelinated nerve fibers that make up the white matter in the center.

cerebral hemispheres. Two large masses of nerve cells and fibers constituting the bulk of the brain in humans and other higher animals. The hemispheres are separated by a deep fissure, but connected by a broad band of fibers, the corpus callosum (syn. *cerebrum*). See also **cerebral cortex, left hemisphere, right hemisphere, split-brain subject.**

cerebrum. See **cerebral hemispheres.**

chlorpromazine. See **tranquilizer.**

chromatic colors. All colors other than black, white, and gray; e.g., red, yellow, blue. See also **achromatic colors.**

chromosome. Particles found in pairs in all the cells of the body, carrying the genetic determiners (genes) that are transmitted from parent to offspring. A human cell has 46 chromosomes, arranged in 23 pairs, one member of each pair deriving from the mother, one from the father. See also **gene.**

chronological age (CA). Age from birth; calendar age. See also **mental age.**

chunk. The largest meaningful unit of information that can be stored in short-term memory; short-term memory holds 7 ± 2 chunks. See also **short-term memory.**

circadian rhythm. A cycle or rhythm that is roughly 24 hours long. Sleep-wakefulness, body temperature, and water excretion follow a circadian rhythm, as do a number of behavioral and physiological variables.

clairvoyance. A form of extrasensory perception in which the perceiver is said to identify a stimulus that is influencing neither his or her own sense organs nor those of another person. See also **extrasensory perception, precognition, psychokinesis, telepathy.**

class interval. In statistics, a small section of a scale according to which scores of a frequency distribution are grouped; e.g., heights grouped into class intervals of a half inch. See also **frequency distribution.**

classical conditioning. Conditioned-response experiments conforming to the pattern of Pavlov's experiment. The main feature is that the originally neutral conditioned stimulus, through repeated pairing with the unconditioned one, acquires the response originally given to the unconditioned stimulus (syn. *stimulus substitution*). See also **operant conditioning.**

claustrophobia. Fear of closed places. See also **phobia.**

client-centered therapy. A method of psychotherapy designed to let clients learn to take responsibility for their own actions and to use their own resourcefulness in solving their problems (syn. *nondirective counseling*).

clinical psychologist. A psychologist, usually with a Ph.D. degree, trained in the diagnosis and treatment of emotional or behavioral problems and mental disorders. See also **counseling psychologist, psychiatrist.**

cochlea. The portion of the inner ear containing the receptors for hearing. See also **basilar membrane, organ of Corti.**

coding. See **encoding.**

coefficient of correlation. A numerical index used to indicate the degree of correspondence between two sets of paired measurements. The most common kind is the product-moment coefficient designated by *r*. See also **rank correlation.**

cognition. An individual's thoughts, knowledge, interpretations, understandings, or ideas. See also **cognitive processes.**

cognitive dissonance. The condition in which one has beliefs or knowledge that disagree with each other or with behavioral tendencies; when such cognitive dissonance arises, the subject is motivated to reduce the dissonance through changes in behavior or cognition (Festinger).

cognitive learning. Learning that involves reorganization of one's perceptions, knowledge, and ideas.

cognitive map. A hypothetical structure in memory that preserves and organizes information about the various events that occur in a learning situation; a mental picture of the learning situation. See also **schema.**

cognitive-physiological theory. A theory of emotion proposed by Schachter: emotion is bodily arousal in interaction with cognitive processes. Emotion is determined by the label a person gives to his or her state of bodily arousal. See also **James-Lange theory, Cannon-Bard theory.**

cognitive processes. Mental processes hypothesized to occur during perception, learning, and thinking.

cognitive psychology. A point of view that stresses the dynamic role of cognitive processes. An emphasis on "knowing" and "perceiving" as contrasted with simple associative learning.

color blindness. Defective discrimination of chromatic colors. See also **dichromatism, monochromatism, red-green color blindness, trichromatism.**

color circle. An arrangement of chromatic colors around the circumference of a circle in the order in which they appear in the spectrum, but with the addition of nonspectral reds and purples. The colors are so arranged that those opposite each other are complementaries in additive mixture. See also **color solid.**

color constancy. The tendency to see a familiar object as of the same color, regardless of changes in illumination on it that alter its stimulus properties. See also **object constancy.**

color-mixture primaries. Three hues chosen to produce the total range of hues by their additive mixture. A spectral red, green, and blue are usually selected. See also **psychological primaries.**

color solid. A three-dimensional representation of the psychological dimensions of color, with hue around the circumference, saturation along each radius, and brightness from top to bottom. See also **color circle.**

complementary colors. Two colors that in additive mixture yield either a gray or an unsaturated color of the hue of the stronger component.

complex cell. A cell in the visual cortex that responds to a bar of light or straight edge of a particular orientation located anywhere in the visual field by integrating inputs from simple cells. See also **simple cell.**

compliance. A form of social influence in which an individual conforms outwardly (to obtain a reward or avoid punishment) but does not necessarily believe in the opinions expressed or the behavior displayed.

compulsion. A repetitive action that a person feels driven to make and is unable to resist; ritualistic behavior. See also **obsession, obsessive-compulsive reaction.**

compulsive personality. A personality syndrome characterized by cleanliness, orderliness, and obstinacy. In the extreme, behavior becomes repetitive and ritualistic (syn. *anal character*).

computer program. See **program.**

computer simulation. See **simulation.**

concept. The properties or relationships common to a class of objects or ideas. Concepts may be of concrete things, e.g., the concept *poodle* referring to a given variety of dog, or of abstract ideas, e.g., *equality, justice, number,* implying relationships common to many different kinds of objects or ideas. See also **semantic concepts.**

concrete operational stage. Piaget's third stage of cognitive development (ages 7–12 years) during which a child becomes capable of logical thought and achieves conservation concepts. See also **conservation.**

conditioned emotion. An emotional response acquired by conditioning; i.e., one aroused by a stimulus that did not originally evoke it. See also **conditioning.**

conditioned reinforcer. A stimulus that has become reinforcing through prior association with a reinforcing stimulus (syn. *secondary reinforcer*). See also **reinforcing stimulus.**

conditioned response (CR). In classical conditioning, the learned or acquired response

to a conditioned stimulus; i.e., to a stimulus that did not evoke the response originally. See also **conditioned stimulus, unconditioned response, unconditioned stimulus.**

conditioned stimulus (CS). In classical conditioning, a stimulus previously neutral that comes to elicit a conditioned response through association with an unconditioned stimulus. See also **conditioned response, unconditioned response, unconditioned stimulus.**

conditioning. The process by which conditioned responses are learned. See also **classical conditioning, operant conditioning.**

cone. In the eye, a specialized cell of the retina found predominantly in the fovea and more sparsely throughout the retina. The cones mediate both chromatic and achromatic sensations. See also **fovea, retina, rod.**

confidence limits. In statistics, upper and lower limits derived from a sample, used in making inferences about a population; e.g., from the mean of a sample and its standard error one can determine limits that permit a statement that the probability is 95 in 100 that the population mean falls within these limits. See also **statistical inference, statistical significance.**

conflict. The simultaneous presence of opposing or mutually exclusive impulses, desires, or tendencies. See also **ambivalence.**

connotative meaning. The suggestive and emotional meanings of a word or symbol, beyond its denotative meaning. Thus *naked* and *nude* both refer to an unclothed body (denotative meaning), but they have somewhat different connotations. See also **denotative meaning, semantic differential.**

conscience. An internal recognition of standards of right and wrong by which the individual judges his or her own conduct. See also **superego.**

conscious processes. Events such as perceptions, afterimages, private thoughts, and dreams, of which only the person is aware. They are accessible to others through verbal report or by way of inference from other behavior (syn. *experience, awareness*). See also **divided consciousness, focal consciousness, marginal consciousness, nonconscious processes, subconscious processes, unconscious processes.**

conservation. Piaget's term for the ability of the child to recognize that certain properties of objects (e.g., mass, volume, number) do not change despite transformations in the appearance of the objects. See also **preoperational stage.**

constructive memory. Using general knowledge stored in memory to construct and elaborate a more complete and detailed account of some events.

control group. In an experimental design contrasting two groups, that group not given the treatment whose effect is under study. See also, **experimental group.**

control processes. Regulatory processes that serve to establish equilibrium or monitor goal-directed activities. See also **homeostasis.**

convergent thinking. In tests of intellect, producing a specified "correct" response in accordance with truth and fact. See also **divergent thinking.**

conversion reaction. A form of neurotic reaction in which the symptoms are paralysis of the limbs, insensitive areas of the body (anaesthesias), or related bodily symptoms. The presumption is that anxiety has been "converted" into a tangible symptom (syn. *hysteria*). See also **neurosis.**

coping strategy. A method of direct problem-solving in dealing with personal problems, contrasted with defense mechanisms. See also **defensive strategy.**

corpus callosum. A large band of nerve fibers connecting the two cerebral hemispheres.

correlation. See **coefficient of correlation.**

counseling psychologist. A trained psychologist, usually with a Ph.D. or Ed.D. degree, dealing with personal problems not classified as illness, such as academic, social, or vocational problems of students. He or she has skills similar to those of the clinical psychologist, but usually works in a nonmedical setting. See also **clinical psychologist, psychiatrist.**

counter-conditioning. In behavior therapy, the replacement of a particular response to a stimulus by the establishment of another (usually incompatible) response. See also **assertive training.**

criterion. (1) A set of scores or other records against which the success of a predictive test is verified. (2) A standard selected as the goal to be achieved in a learning task; e.g., the number of runs through a maze to be made without error as an indication that the maze has been mastered.

critical period. A stage in development during which the organism is optimally ready to learn certain response patterns. It is closely related to the concept of maturational readiness.

critical ratio. A mean, mean difference, or coefficient of correlation divided by its standard error. Used in tests of significance. See also **statistical significance.**

cues to distance. See **distance cues.**

culture-fair test. A type of intelligence test that has been constructed to minimize bias due to the differing experiences of children raised in a rural rather than an urban culture or in a lower-class rather than in a middle-class or upper-class culture (syn. *culture-free test*).

cumulative curve. A graphic record of the responses emitted during an operant conditioning session. The slope of the cumulative curve indicates the rate of response.

dark adaptation. The increased sensitivity to light when the subject has been continuously in the dark or under conditions of reduced illumination. See also **light adaptation.**

daydreaming. Reverie; free play of thought or imagination. Because of self-reference, usually a form of autistic thinking. See also **autistic thinking.**

db. See **decibel.**

decibel (db). A unit for measuring sound intensity.

defense mechanism. An adjustment made, often unconsciously, either through action or the avoidance of action to keep from recognizing personal qualities or motives that might lower self-esteem or heighten anxiety. Denial and projection are two examples. See also **defensive strategy.**

defensive strategy. Behavior aimed at defending the person against anxiety when faced with a problem rather than dealing directly with the problem. See also **coping strategy.**

delayed conditioning. A classical conditioning procedure in which the CS begins several seconds or more before the onset of the US and continues with it until the response occurs. See also **simultaneous conditioning, trace conditioning.**

delta waves. See **electroencephalogram.**

delusion. False beliefs characteristic of some forms of psychotic disorder. They often take the form of delusions of grandeur or delusions of persecution. See also **hallucination, illusion, paranoid schizophrenia.**

dendrite. The specialized portion of the neuron that (together with the cell body) receives impulses from other neurons. See also **axon, neuron.**

denial. A defense mechanism by which unacceptable impulses or ideas are not perceived or allowed into full awareness. See also **defense mechanism.**

denotative meaning. The primary meaning of a symbol, something specific to which the symbol refers or points (e.g., my street address is denotative; whether or not I live in a desirable neighborhood is a connotative meaning secondary to the address itself). See also **connotative meaning, semantic differential.**

deoxyribonucleic acid (DNA). Large molecules found in the cell nucleus and primarily responsible for genetic inheritance. These molecules manufacture various forms of RNA, which are thought by some to be the chemical basis of memory. See also **ribonucleic acid.**

dependent variable. The variable whose measured changes are attributed to (or correspond to) changes in the independent variable. In psychological experiments, the dependent variable is often a response to a measured stimulus. See also **independent variable.**

depolarization. Change in the resting potential of the nerve cell membrane in the direction of the action potential; the inside of the membrane becomes more positive. See also **action potential, resting potential.**

depressants. Psychoactive drugs that tend to reduce arousal. See also **stimulants, hallucinogens.**

depth perception. The perception of the distance of an object from the observer or the distance from front to back of a solid object. See also **distance cues.**

descriptive statistics. Simplifying or summarizing statements about measurements made on a population. Strictly speaking, "descriptive statistics" should apply solely to populations, rather than to samples, but the term is used loosely for summarizing statements about samples when they are treated as populations. See also **statistical inference.**

developmental psychologist. A psychologist whose research interest lies in studying the changes that occur as a function of the growth and development of the organism, in particular the relationship between early and later behavior.

deviation IQ. An intelligence quotient (IQ) computed as a standard score with a mean of 100 and a standard deviation of 15 (Wechsler) or 16 (Stanford-Binet), to correspond approximately to traditional intelligence quotient. See also **intelligence quotient.**

dichromatism. Color blindness in which either the red-green or the blue-yellow system is lacking. The red-green form is relatively common; the blue-yellow form is the rarest of all foms of color blindness. See also **monochromatism, red-green color blindness, trichromatism.**

difference threshold. The minimum difference between a pair of stimuli that can be perceived under experimental conditions. See also **absolute threshold, just noticeable difference, threshold.**

diffusion of responsibility. The tendency for persons in a group situation to fail to take action (as in an emergency) because others are present, thus diffusing the responsibility for acting. A major factor in inhibiting bystanders from intervening in emergencies.

digital computer. A computer that performs mathematical and logical operations with information, numerical or otherwise, represented in digital form.

discrimination. (1) In perception, the detection of differences between two stimuli. (2) In conditioning, the differential response to the positive (reinforced) stimulus and to the negative (nonreinforced) stimulus. See also **generalization.** (3) In social psychology, prejudicial treatment, as in racial discrimination.

discriminative stimulus. A stimulus that becomes an occasion for an operant response; e.g., the knock that leads one to open the door. The stimulus does not elicit the operant response in the same sense that a stimulus elicits respondent behavior. See also **operant behavior.**

displaced aggression. Aggression against a person or object other than that which was (or is) the source of frustration. See also **scapegoat.**

displacement. (1) A defense mechanism whereby a motive that may not be directly expressed (e.g., sex, aggression) appears in a more acceptable form. See also **defense mechanism.** (2) The principle of loss of items from short-term memory as too many new items are added. See also **chunk, short-term memory.**

dispositional attribution. Attributing a person's actions to internal dispositions (attitudes, traits, motives), as opposed to situational factors. See also **situational attribution.**

dissociation. The process whereby some ideas, feelings, or activities lose relationship to other aspects of consciousness and personality and operate automatically or independently.

dissonance. (1) In music, an inharmonious combination of sounds; contrasted with consonance. (2) In social psychology, Festinger's term for a perceived inconsistency between one's own attitudes and one's behavior. See also **cognitive dissonance.**

distance cues. (1) In vision, the monocular cues according to which the distance of objects is perceived—such as superposition of objects, perspective, light and shadow, and relative movement—and the binocular cues used in stereoscopic vision. See also **stereroscopic vision.** (2) In audition, the corresponding cues governing perception of distance and direction, such as intensity and time differences of sound reaching the two ears.

divergent thinking. In tests of intellect (or creativity), producing one or more "possible" answers rather than a single "correct" one. See also **convergent thinking.**

divided consciousness. The state of consciousness as in attending to two activities at once. See also **conscious processes.**

dizygotic (DZ) twins. Twins developed from separate eggs. They are no more alike genetically than ordinary brothers and sisters and can be of the same or different sexes (syn. *fraternal twins*). See also **monozygotic twins.**

DNA. See **deoxyribonucleic acid.**

dominance. The higher status position when social rank is organized according to a dominance-submission hierarchy; commonly found in human societies and in certain animal groups.

dominant gene. A member of a gene pair, which, if present, determines that the individual will show the trait controlled by the gene, regardless of whether the other member of the pair is the same or different (that is, recessive). See also **recessive gene.**

dopamine. A neurotransmitter of the central nervous system believed to play a role in schizophrenia. It is synthesized from an amino acid by the action of certain body enzymes and, in turn, is converted into norepinephrine. See also **neurotransmitter, norepinephrine.**

dopamine hypothesis. The hypothesis that schizophrenia is related to an excess of the neurotransmitter dopamine; either schizophrenics produce too much dopamine or are deficient in the enzyme that converts dopamine to norepinephrine. See also **dopamine, norepinephrine, schizophrenia.**

double blind. An experimental design, often used in drug research, in which neither the investigator nor the patients know which subjects are in the treatment and which in the nontreatment condition until the experiment has been completed.

Down's syndrome. A form of mental deficiency produced by a genetic abnormality (an extra chromosome on pair 21). Characteristics include a thick tongue, extra eyelid folds, and short, stubby fingers (also known as **mongolism**).

drive. (1) An aroused condition of the organism based on deprivation or noxious stimulation, including tissue needs, drug or hormonal conditions, and specified internal or external stimuli, as in pain. (2) Loosely, any motive. See also **motive, need.**

drive-reduction theory. The theory that a motivated sequence of behavior can be best explained as moving from an aversive state of heightened tension (i.e., drive) to a goal state in which the drive is reduced. The goal of the sequence, in other words, is drive reduction. See also **drive, incentive theory, motive, need.**

dual-memory theory. A theory that distinguishes between a short-term memory of limited capacity and a virtually unlimited long-term memory. Information can only be encoded into long-term memory via short-term memory. See also **long-term memory, short-term memory.**

eardrum. The membrane at the inner end of the auditory canal, leading to the middle ear. See also **middle ear.**

ectomorph. The third of the three types of physique in Sheldon's type theory. It comprises delicacy of skin, fine hair, and ultrasensitive nervous system. See also **endomorph, mesomorph, type theory.**

educational psychologist. A psychologist whose research interest lies in the application of psychological principles to the education of children and adults in schools. See also **school psychologist.**

EEG. See **electroencephalogram.**

effector. A bodily organ activated by nerves composed of efferent neurons; a muscle or gland. See also **efferent neuron, receptor.**

efferent neuron. A neuron, or nerve cell, that conveys messages from the brain or spinal cord to the effector organs, the muscles, and glands (usually synonymous with *motor neuron*). See also **afferent neuron, effector.**

ego. In Freud's tripartite devision of the personality, that part corresponding most nearly to the perceived self, the controlling self that holds back the impulsiveness of the id in the effort to delay gratification until it can be found in socially approved ways. See also **id, superego.**

eidetic imagery. The ability to retain visual images of pictures that are almost photographic in clarity. Such images can be described in far greater detail than would be possible from memory alone. See also **mental imagery.**

electroencephalogram (EEG). A record obtained by attaching electrodes to the scalp (or occasionally to the exposed brain) and amplifying the spontaneous electrical activity of the brain. Familiar aspects of the EEG are alpha waves (8–13 Hz) and delta waves of slower frequency.

electroshock therapy. A form of shock treatment for mental illness in which high-voltage current is passed briefly through the head, producing temporary unconsciousness and convulsions, with the intention of alleviating depression or other symptoms. See also **shock therapy.**

emotion. The condition of the organism during affectively toned experience, whether mild or intense. See also **affective experience.**

empiricism. The view that behavior is learned as a result of experience, See also **nativism.**

encoding. Transforming a sensory input into a form that can be processed by the memory system.

encounter group. A general term for various types of groups in which people meet to learn more about themselves in relation to other people (syn. *sensitivity group, T group*).

endocrine gland. A ductless gland, or gland of internal secretion, that discharges its products directly into the bloodstream. The hormones secreted by the endocrine glands are important chemical integrators of bodily activity. See also **hormones.**

endomorph. The first of three types of physique in Sheldon's type theory. It comprises prominence of intestines and other visceral organs, including a prominent abdomen, as in the obese individual. See also **ectomorph, mesomorph, type theory.**

endorphins. A newly discovered group of neurotransmitters in the brain that have morphine-like properties and may play important roles in emotion and behavior and possibly in schizophrenia.

engineering psychologist. A psychologist who specializes in the relationship between people and machines, seeking, for example, to design machines that minimize human error.

epinephrine. One of the hormones secreted by the adrenal medulla, active in emotional excitement (syn. *adrenalin*). See also **adrenal gland, norepinephrine.**

equilibratory senses. The senses that give discrimination of the position of the body in space and of the movement of the body as a whole. See also **kinesthesis, semicircular canals, vestibular sacs.**

escape learning. A form of learning controlled by actual painful stimulation. Escape from the punishment brings an end to the unpleasant or painful situation and is therefore rewarding. (Note that such a reward is thus technically a negative reinforcer.) See also **avoidance learning, negative reinforcer.**

ESP. See **extrasensory perception.**

estrogen. A female sex hormone manufactured and secreted by the ovaries; it is partially responsible for the growth of the female secondary sex characteristics and influences the sex drive. See also **androgens.**

estrous. The sexually receptive state in female mammals. It is a cyclical state, related to menstruation in the primates and humans (syn. *heat*). See also **menstruation.**

ethologist. One group of zoologists and naturalists particularly interested in kinds of behavior that are specific to a species. More of their work has been on insects, birds, and fishes than on mammals. See also **imprinting, instinct.**

evoked potential. An electrical discharge in some part of the nervous system produced by stimulation elsewhere. The measured potential is commonly based on response averaging by a computer.

excitatory synapse. A synapse at which the neurotransmitter changes the membrane permeability of the receiving cell in the direction of depolarization. See also **depolarization, inhibitory synapse, synapse.**

expectation. An anticipation or prediction of future events based on past experience and present stimuli.

experimental design. A plan for collecting and treating the data of a proposed experiment. The design is evolved after preliminary exploration, with the aims of economy, precision, and control, so that appropriate inferences and decisions can be made from the data.

experimental group. In an experimental design contrasting two groups, that group of subjects given the treatment whose effect is under investigation. See also **control group.**

experimental method. The method of investigation of natural events that seeks to control the variables involved so as to more precisely define cause and effect relationships. Most frequently done in a laboratory, but need not be. See also **observational method, variable.**

experimental psychologist. A psychologist whose research interest is in the laboratory study of general psychological principles as revealed in the behavior of lower organisms and human beings.

extinction. (1) The experimental procedure, following classical or operant conditioning, of presenting the conditioned stimulus without the usual reinforcement. (2) The reduction in response that results from this procedure. See also **reinforcement.**

extrasensory perception (ESP). A controversial category of experience consisting of perception not mediated by sense-organ stimulation. See also **clairvoyance, parapsychology, precognition, telepathy, psychokinesis.**

extravert. One of the psychological types proposed by Jung. The extravert is more preoccupied with social life and the external world than with his or her inward experience. See also **introvert.**

factor analysis. A statistical method used in test construction and in interpreting scores from batteries of tests. The method enables the investigator to compute the minimum number of determiners (factors) required to account for the intercorrelations among the scores on the tests making up the battery. See also **general factor, special factor.**

family therapy. Psychotherapy with the family members as a group rather than treatment of the patient alone. See also **group therapy.**

fantasy. Daydreaming, "woolgathering" imagination; sometimes a consequence of frustration. It is used as a personality indicator in projective tests. See also **projective tests.**

Fechner's law. See **Weber-Fechner law.**

figure-ground perception. Perceiving a pattern as foreground against a background. Patterns are commonly perceived this way even when the stimuli are ambiguous and the foreground-background relationships are reversible.

fixation. In psychoanalysis, arrested development through failure to pass beyond one of the earlier stages of psychosexual development or to change the objects of attachment (e.g., fixated at the oral stage, or fixated upon the mother).

flow chart. A diagramatic representation of the sequence of choices and actions in an activity.

focal consciousness. That which at any one moment is at the center of attention. See also **conscious processes.**

formal operational stage. Piaget's fourth stage of cognitive development (age 12 and up) in which the child becomes able to use abstract rules.

fovea. In the eye, a small area in the central part of the retina, packed with cones; in daylight, the most sensitive part of the retina for detail vision and color vision. See also **cone, retina.**

fraternal twins. See **dizygotic twins.**

free association. (1) The form of word-association experiment in which the subject gives any word he or she thinks of in response to the stimulus word. (2) In psychoanalysis, the effort to report without modification everything that comes into awareness.

free recall. A memory task in which a subject is given a list of items (usually one at a time) and is later asked to recall them in any order.

frequency distribution. A set of scores assembled according to size and grouped into class intervals. See also **class interval, normal distribution.**

frequency theory. A theory of hearing that

assumes that neural impulses arising in the organ of Corti are activated by the basilar membrane of the ear in accordance with the frequency of its vibration rather than with the place of movement. See also **place theory, volley principle.**

frontal lobe. A portion of each cerebral hemisphere, in front of the central fissure. See also **occipital lobe, parietal lobe, temporal lobe.**

frustration. (1) As an event, the thwarting circumstances that block or interfere with goal-directed activity. (2) As a state, the annoyance, confusion, or anger engendered by being thwarted, disappointed, defeated.

frustration-aggression hypothesis. The hypothesis that frustration (thwarting a person's goal-directed efforts) induces an aggressive drive, which, in turn, motivates aggressive behavior.

functional psychosis. A psychosis of psychogenic origin without clearly defined changes of the central nervous system. See also **organic psychosis, psychosis.**

fundamental attribution error. The tendency to underestimate situational influences on behavior and assume that some personal characteristic of the individual is responsible; the bias toward dispositional rather than situational attributions. See also **attribution, dispositional attribution, situational attribution.**

galvanic skin response (GSR). Changes in electrical conductivity of, or activity in, the skin, detected by a sensitive galvanometer. The reactions are commonly used as an emotional indicator.

ganglia (sing. **ganglion**). A collection of nerve cell bodies and synapses, constituting a center lying outside the brain and spinal cord, as in the sympathetic ganglia. See also **nuclei.**

gastrointestinal motility. Movements of parts of the digestive tract caused by contraction of smooth muscle; one form of emotional indicator.

gene. The unit of hereditary transmission, localized within the chromosomes. Each chromosome contains many genes. Genes are typically in pairs, one member of the pair being found in the chromosome from the father, the other in the corresponding chromosome from the mother. See also **chromosome, dominant gene, recessive gene.**

general factor (g). (1) A general ability underlying test scores, especially in tests of intelligence, as distinct from special abilities unique to each test (Spearman). (2) A general ability with which each of the primary factors correlates (Thurstone). See also **factor analysis, special factor.**

General Problem Solver (GPS). A computer program to simulate human problem solving by setting up subgoals and reducing the discrepancies to each subsequent subgoal. See also **simulation.**

generalization. (1) In concept formation, problem solving, and transfer of learning, the detection by the learner of a characteristic or principle common to a class of objects, events, or problems. (2) In conditioning, the principle that once a conditioned response has been established to a given stimulus, similar stimuli will also evoke that response. See also **discrimination.**

genetics. That branch of biology concerned with heredity and the means by which hereditary characteristics are transmitted.

genital stage. In classical psychoanalysis, the final stage of psychosexual development, culminating in sexual union with a member of the opposite sex. See also **psychosexual development.**

genotype. In genetics, the characteristics that an individual has inherited and will transmit to his or her descendants, whether or not the individual manifests these characteristics. See also **phenotype.**

Gestalt psychology. A system of psychological theory emphasizing pattern, organization, wholes, and field properties.

glia cells. Supporting cells (not neurons) composing a substantial portion of brain tissue; recent speculation suggests that they may play a role in neural conduction.

goal. (1) An end state or condition toward which the motivated behavior sequence is directed and by which the sequence is completed. (2) Loosely, the incentive. See also **incentive.**

gonads. Testes in the male, ovaries in the female. As duct glands, the sex glands are active in mating behavior, but as endocrine glands their hormones affect secondary sex characteristics as well as maintaining functional sexual activity. The male hormones are known as androgens, the female hormones as estrogen (syn. *sex glands*). See also **androgens, endocrine gland, estrogen.**

graded potentials. Potential changes of varying size induced in a neuron's dendrites or cell body by stimulation from synapses from other neurons. When the graded potentials reach a threshold of depolarization, an action potential occurs. See also **action potential, depolarization.**

gradient of texture. If a surface is perceived visually as having substantial texture (hard, soft, smooth, rough, etc.) and if the texture has a noticeable grain, it becomes finer as the surface recedes from the viewing person, producing a gradient of texture that is important in judgments of slant and of distance. See also **distance cues.**

group test. A test administered to several people at once by a single tester. A college examination is usually a group test.

group therapy. A group discussion or other group activity with a therapeutic purpose participated in by more than one client or patient at a time. See also **psychotherapy.**

GSR. See **galvanic skin response.**

habit. A learned stimulus-response sequence. See also **conditioned response.**

hallucination. A sense experience in the absence of appropriate external stimuli; a misinterpretation of imaginary experiences as actual perceptions. See also **delusion, illusion, schizophrenia.**

hallucinogens. Psychoactive drugs that usually produce hallucinations. See also **hallucination, LSD, psychoactive drugs.**

halo effect. The tendency to bias our perception of another person in the direction of one particular characteristic that we like or dislike.

hedonism. The theory that human beings seek pleasure and avoid pain; an extreme form of the theory (in philosophy) is that pleasure or happiness is the highest good.

heritability. The proportion of the total variability of a trait in a given population that is attributable to genetic differences among individuals within that population.

hermaphrodite. An individual born with genitals that are ambiguous in appearance or that are in conflict with the internal sex glands. See also **transsexual.**

hertz (Hz). The wave frequency of a sound source, or other cyclical phenomena, measured in cycles per second.

heterosexuality. Interest in or attachment to a member of the opposite sex; the usual adult outcome of psychosexual development.

hidden observer. A metaphor to describe the concealed consciousness in hypnosis, inferred to have experiences differing from, but parallel to, the hypnotic consciousness.

hierarchies of concepts. The relationships among individual concepts. See also **concept.**

hierarchy of motives. Maslow's way of classifying motives, ascending from basic biological motives that must be satisfied first to a peak of self-actualization, supposedly the highest human motive.

homeostasis. An optimal level of organic function, maintained by regulatory mechanisms known as homeostatic mechanisms; e.g., the mechanisms maintaining a uniform body temperature.

homosexual. A person who prefers to have sexual relations with others of the same sex. Can be male or female, but female homosexuals are often termed *lesbians*. *Not* to be confused with transsexual. See also **transsexual**.

hormones. The internal secretions of the endocrine glands that are distributed via the bloodstream and affect behavior. See also **endocrine gland**.

hostile aggression. Aggression whose primary aim is to inflict injury. See also **instrumental aggression**.

hue. The dimension of color from which the major color names are derived (red, yellow, green, etc.), corresponding to wavelength of light. See also **brightness, saturation**.

humanistic psychology. A psychological approach that emphasizes the uniqueness of human beings; it is concerned with subjective experience and human values. Often referred to as a third force in psychology in contrast to behaviorism and psychoanalysis. See also **phenomenology**.

hunger drive. A drive based on food deprivation. See also **drive, specific hunger**.

hyperphagia. Pathological overeating. See also **aphagia**.

hypnosis. The responsive state achieved following a typical hypnotic induction or its equivalent.

hypnotic induction. The procedure used in establishing hypnosis in a responsive person. It usually involves relaxation and stimulated imagination. See also **hypnosis**.

hypnotic trance. The dream-like state of heightened suggestibility induced in a subject by a hypnotist. See also **posthypnotic suggestion**.

hypothalamus. A small but very important structure located just above the brain stem and just below the thalamus. Considered a part of the central core of the brain, it includes centers that govern motivated behavior such as eating, drinking, sex, and emotions; it also regulates endocrine activity and maintains body homeostasis. See also **lateral hypothalamus, ventromedial hypothalamus**.

hypothesis testing. Gathering information and testing alternative explanations of some phenomenon.

hypothetical construct. One form of inferred intermediate mechanism. The construct is conceived of as having properties of its own, other than those specifically required for the explanation; e.g., drive which is inferred from the behavior of a deprived organism and is used in the explanation of later behavior.

Hz. See **hertz**.

id. In Freud's tripartite division of the personality, that part reflecting unorganized, instinctual impulses. If unbridled, it seeks immediate gratification of primitive needs. See also **ego, superego**.

identical twins. See **monozygotic twins**.

identification. (1) The normal process of acquiring appropriate social roles in childhood through copying, in part unconsciously, the behavior of significant adults; e.g., the child's identification with his or her like-sexed parent. See also **imitation**. (2) Close affiliation with others of like interest; e.g., identifying with a group.

identification figures. Adult models (especially parents) copied, partly unconsciously, by the child. See also **identification**.

identity formation. The process of achieving adult personality integration, as an outgrowth of earlier identifications and other influences. See also **identification, role confusion**.

illusion. In perception, a misinterpretation of the relationships among presented stimuli, so that what is perceived does not correspond to physical reality; especially, but not exclusively, an optical or visual illusion. See also **delusion, hallucination**.

imitation. Behavior that is modeled on or copies that of another. See also **identification**.

imprinting. A term used by ethologists for a species-specific type of learning that occurs within a limited period of time early in the life of the organism and is relatively unmodifiable thereafter; e.g., young ducklings learn to follow one adult female (usually the mother) within 11–18 hours after birth. But whatever object they are given to follow at this time they will thereafter continue to follow. See also **ethologist**.

incentive. (1) A tangible goal object that provides the stimuli that lead to goal activity. (2) Loosely, any goal. See also **goal, negative incentive, positive incentive**.

incentive theory. A theory of motivation that emphasizes the importance of negative and positive incentives in determining behavior; internal drives are not the sole instigators of activity. See also **drive-reduction theory**.

independent variable. The variable under experimental control with which the changes studied in the experiment are correlated. In psychological experiments, the independent variable is often a stimulus, responses to which are the dependent variables under investigation. See also **dependent variable**.

individual differences. Relatively persistent dissimilarities in structure or behavior between persons or members of the same species.

infancy. The period of helplessness and dependency in humans and other organisms; in humans, roughly the first two years.

information-processing model. A model based on assumptions regarding the flow of information through a system; usually best realized by a computer program.

inhibitory synapse. A synapse at which the neurotransmitter changes the membrane permeability of the receiving cell in the direction of the resting potential; i.e., keeps it from firing. See also **excitatory synapse, synapse**.

inner ear. The internal portion of the ear containing, in addition to the cochlea, the vestibular sacs and the semicircular canals. See also **cochlea, semicircular canals, vestibular sacs**.

insight. (1) In problem-solving experiments, the perception of relationships leading to solution. Such a solution can be repeated promptly when the problem is again confronted. (2) In psychotherapy, the discovery by the individuals of dynamic connections between earlier and later events, so that they come to recognize the roots of their conflicts.

instinct. The name given to unlearned, patterned, goal-directed behavior, which is species-specific, as illustrated by nest-building in birds or by the migration of salmon (syn. *species-specific behavior*). See also **ethologist**.

instrumental aggression. Aggression aimed at obtaining rewards other than the victim's suffering. See also **hostile aggression**.

insulin. The hormone secreted by the pancreas. See also **hormones, insulin shock**.

insulin shock. A state of coma resulting from reduced blood sugar when insulin is present in excessive amounts. Insulin shock is used as one form of shock therapy in treating mental illness. See also **shock therapy**.

intellectualization. A defense mechanism whereby a person tries to gain detachment from an emotionally threatening situation by dealing with it in abstract, intellectual terms. See also **defense mechanism**.

intelligence. (1) That which a properly standardized intelligence test measures. (2) According to Binet, the characteristics of an individual's thought processes that enable the individual to take and maintain a direction without becoming distracted, to adapt means to ends, and to criticize his or her own attempts at problem solution. See also **intelligence quotient, mental age.**

intelligence quotient (IQ). A scale unit used in reporting intelligence test scores, based on the ratio between mental age and chronological age. The decimal point is omitted, so that the average IQ for children of any one chronological age is set at 100. See also **chronological age, deviation IQ, mental age.**

interaction. When the effect of one variable differs depending on the level of one or more other variables; e.g., when the same stimulus affects different individuals in different ways.

intermittent reinforcement. See **partial reinforcement.**

internalization. The incorporation of someone else's opinions or behaviors into one's own value system.

interneurons. Neurons in the central nervous system that connect afferent with efferent neurons. See also **afferent neuron, efferent neuron.**

interpretation. In psychoanalysis, the analyst's calling attention to the patient's resistances in order to facilitate the flow of associations; also the explanation of symbols, as in dream interpretation. See also **resistance.**

intervening variable. A process inferred to occur between stimulus and response, thus accounting for one response rather than another to the same stimulus. The intervening variable may be inferred without further specification, or it may be given concrete properties and become an object of investigation.

interview. A conversation between an investigator (the interviewer) and a subject (the respondent) used for gathering pertinent data for the subject's benefit (as in the psychotherapeutic interview) or for information-gathering (as in a sample survey).

introspection. (1) A specified form of introspection (trained introspection) describing mental content only, without the intrusion of meanings or interpretations. (2) Any form of reporting on subjective (conscious) events or experiences. See also **phenomenology.**

introvert. One of the psychological types proposed by Jung, referring to the individual who, especially in time of emotional stress, tends to withdraw into him or herself and to avoid other people. See also **extravert.**

James-Lange theory. A classical theory of emotion, named for the two men who in-

dependently proposed it. The theory states that the stimulus first leads to bodily responses, and then the awareness of these responses constitutes the experience of emotion. See also **Cannon-Bard theory, cognitive-physiological theory.**

just noticeable difference (j.n.d.). A barely perceptible physical change in a stimulus; a measure of the difference threshold. The term is used also as a unit for scaling the steps of sensation corresponding to increase in the magnitude of stimulation. See also **difference threshold.**

key-word method. A technique for learning vocabulary of a foreign language via an intermediate key word related to the sound of the foreign word and the meaning of the English equivalent. See also **mnemonics.**

kinesthesis. The muscle, tendon, and joint senses, yielding discrimination of position and movement of parts of the body. See also **equilibratory senses.**

Klinefelter's syndrome. An abnormal condition of the sex chromosomes (XXY instead of XX or XY); the individual is physically a male with penis and testicles but has marked feminine characteristics.

latency. (1) A temporal measure of response, referring to the time delay between the occurrence of the stimulus and the onset of the response. (2) In psychoanalysis, a period in middle childhood, roughly the years from 6–12, when both sexual and aggressive impulses are said to be in a somewhat subdued state, so that the child's attention is directed outward, and curiosity about the environment makes him or her ready to learn. See also **psychosexual development.**

latent content. The underlying significance of a dream, e.g., the motives or wishes being expressed by it, as interpreted from the manifest content. See also **interpretation, manifest content.**

latent learning. Learning that is not demonstrated by behavior at the time of learning, but can be shown to have occurred by increasing the reinforcement for such behavior.

lateral fissure. A deep fissure at the side of each cerebral hemisphere, below which lies the temporal lobe (syn. *fissure of Sylvius*).

lateral hypothalamus (LH). Area of the hypothalamus important to the regulation of food intake. Electrical stimulation of this area will make an experimental animal start to eat; destruction of brain tissue here causes an animal to stop eating. See

also **hypothalamus, ventromedial hypothalamus.**

learned helplessness. A condition of apathy or helplessness created experimentally by subjecting an organism to unavoidable trauma; e.g., shock, heat, or cold. Being unable to avoid or escape an aversive situation produces a feeling of helplessness that generalizes to subsequent situations.

learning. A relatively permanent change in behavior that occurs as the result of practice. Behavior changes due to maturation or temporary conditions of the organism (e.g., fatigue, the influence of drugs, adaptation) are not included.

learning curve. A graph plotting the course of learning, in which the vertical axis (ordinate) plots a measure of proficiency (amount per unit time, time per unit amount, errors made, etc.), while the horizontal axis (abscissa) represents some measure of practice (trials, time, etc.).

left hemisphere. The left cerebral hemisphere. Controls the right side of the body and, for most people, speech and other logical, sequential activities (syn. *major hemisphere*). See also **cerebral hemisphere, corpus callosum, right hemisphere, split-brain subject.**

lesbian. See **homosexual.**

LH. See **lateral hypothalamus.**

libido. In psychoanalysis, the energy of the sexual instinct, which throughout life becomes attached to new objects and is expressed through various types of motivated behavior.

lie detector. See **polygraph, voice stress analyzer.**

light adaptation. The decreased sensitivity of the eye to light when the subject has been continuously exposed to high levels of illumination. See also **dark adaptation.**

limbic system. A set of structures in and around the midbrain, forming a functional unit regulating motivational-emotional types of behavior, such as waking and sleeping, excitement and quiescence, feeding, and mating.

linear program. A teaching program in which the student progresses along a fixed track from one instructional frame to the next. After responding to a frame, the student moves to the next frame regardless of whether his or her answer is correct. See also **branching program, CAL.**

linguistic relativity hypothesis. The proposition that one's thought processes, the way one perceives the world, are related to one's language.

lithium carbonate. A compound based on lithium, an element related to sodium. Has been successful in treating manic-depressive psychoses.

localized functions. Behavior controlled by known areas of the brain; e.g., vision is localized in the occipital lobes. See also **projection area.**

location constancy. The tendency to perceive the place at which a resting object is located as remaining the same even though the relationship to the observer has changed. See also **object constancy.**

longitudinal study. A research method that studies an individual through time, taking measurements at periodic intervals. See also **case history.**

long-term memory (LTM). The relatively permanent component of the memory system, as opposed to short-term memory. See also **short-term memory.**

loudness. An intensity dimension of hearing correlated with the amplitude of the sound waves that constitute the stimulus. Greater amplitudes yield greater loudnesses. See also **pitch, timbre.**

LSD. See **lysergic acid derivatives.**

lysergic acid derivatives. Chemical substances derived from lysergic acid, the most important of which is LSD. When taken by a normal person, it produces symptoms similar in some respects to those of schizophrenia. See also **schizophrenia.**

major hemisphere. See **left hemisphere.**

manic-depressive psychosis. A psychosis characterized by mood swings from the normal in the direction either of excitement and elation (manic phase) or of fatigue, despondency, and sadness (depressive phase). Many patients do not show the whole cycle. See also **affective disorder.**

manifest content. The remembered content of a dream, the characters, and their actions, as distinguished from the inferred latent content. See also **latent content.**

mantra. See **Transcendental Meditation.**

marginal consciousness. That which at any one moment is at the fringe of attention. See also **conscious processes.**

marijuana. The dried leaves of the hemp plant; also known as hashish, "pot," or "grass." Hashish is actually an extract of the plant material and, hence, is usually stronger than marijuana. Intake may enhance sensory experiences and produce a state of euphoria.

masochism. A pathological desire to inflict pain on oneself or to suffer pain at the hands of others. See also **sadism.**

maternal drive. The drive, particularly in animals, induced in the female through bearing and nursing young, leading to nest-building, retrieving, and other forms of care. See also **drive.**

mathematical model. A model of a phenomenon formulated in mathematical terms. See also **model.**

maturation. Growth processes in the individual that result in orderly changes in behavior, whose timing and patterning are relatively independent of exercise or experience though they may require a normal environment.

maze. A device commonly used in the study of animal and human learning, consisting of a correct path and blind alleys.

mean. The arithmetical average; the sum of all scores divided by their number. See also **measure of central tendency.**

measure of central tendency. A value representative of a frequency distribution, around which other values are dispersed; e.g., the mean, median, or mode of a distribution of scores. See also **mean, median, mode.**

measure of variation. A measure of the dispersion or spread of scores in a frequency distribution; e.g., the range, or the standard deviation. See also **range, standard deviation.**

median. The score of the middle case when cases are arranged in order of size of score. See also **measure of central tendency.**

memory span. The number of items (digits, letters, words) that can be reproduced in order after a single presentation; usually 7 ± 2. See also **chunk, short-term memory.**

memory trace. The inferred change in the nervous system that persists between the time something is learned and the time it is recalled.

menarche. The first menstrual period, indicative of sexual maturation in a girl. See also **menstruation.**

menstruation. The approximately monthly discharge from the uterus. See also **menarche.**

mental age (MA). A scale unit proposed by Binet for use in intelligence testing. If an intelligence test is properly standardized, a representative group of children of age 6 should earn an average mental age of 6, those of age 7, a mental age of 7, etc. A child whose MA is above his or her chronological age (CA) is advanced; one whose MA lags behind is retarded. See also **chronological age, intelligence quotient.**

mental imagery. Mental pictures used as an aid to memory. *Not* the same as eidetic imagery. See also **eidetic imagery.**

mental rotation. The notion that a mental image of an object can be rotated in the mind in a fashion analogous to rotating the real object.

mentally defective. A descriptive term applied to a mentally subnormal individual whose deficiency is based on some sort of brain damage or organic defect. See also **mentally retarded.**

mentally gifted. An individual with an unusually high level of intelligence, commonly an IQ of 140 or above.

mentally retarded. A mentally subnormal individual whose problems lie in a learning disability with no evident organic damage. See also **mentally defective.**

mentally subnormal. An individual whose intelligence is below that necessary for adjustment to ordinary schooling; the more intelligent among the subnormal are classified as *educable* in special classes, the next level as *trainable,* while the lowest group is classified as more severely retarded (syn., but now obsolete, *feebleminded*). See also **mentally defective, mentally retarded.**

mesomorph. The second of three types of physique in Sheldon's type theory. Refers to the prominence of bone and muscle, as in the typical athlete. See also **ectomorph, endomorph, type theory.**

method of loci. An aid to serial memory. Verbal material is transformed into mental images, which are then located at successive positions along a visualized route, such as an imaged walk through the house or down a familiar street.

middle ear. The portion of the ear containing the hammer, anvil, and stirrup bones, which connect the eardrum to the oval window of the inner ear.

minor hemisphere. See **right hemisphere.**

mnemonics. A system for improving memory often involving a set of symbols that can substitute for the material to be remembered; e.g., in attempting to remember a number sequence, one may translate the sequence into letters of the alphabet that in turn approximate words that are easily remembered.

mode. The most frequent score in a distribution, or the class interval in which the greatest number of cases fall. See also **measure of central tendency.**

model. (1) Miniature systems are often constructed according to a logical, mathematical, or physical model. That is, the principles according to which data are organized and made understandable parallel those of the model; e.g., the piano keyboard is a model for understanding the basilar membrane; the speed-regulating governor is a model for the feedback principle of cybernetics. (2) In behavior therapy, a person who *models* or performs behaviors that the therapist wishes the patient to imitate.

modeling. In social learning theory, the process by which a child learns social and cognitive behaviors by observing and imitating others. See also **identification.**

mongolism. See **Down's syndrome.**

monochromatism. Total color blindness, the visual system being achromatic. A rare disorder. See also **dichromatism, trichromatism.**

monocular cues. See **distance cues.**

monozygotic (MZ) twins. Twins developed from a single egg. They are always of the same sex and commonly much alike in appearance, although some characteristics may be in mirror image; e.g., one right-handed, the other left-handed (syn. *identical twins*. See also **dizygotic twins.**

morpheme. The smallest meaningful unit in the structure of a language, whether a word, base, or affix; e.g., *man, strange, ing, pro.* See also **phoneme.**

motivation. A general term referring to the regulation of need-satisfying and goal-seeking behavior. See also **motive.**

motive. Any condition of the organism that affects its readiness to start on or continue in a sequence of behavior.

motor area. A projection area in the brain lying in front of the central fissure. Electrical stimulation commonly results in movement, or motor, responses. See also **somatosensory area.**

multimodal distribution. A distribution curve with more than one mode. See also **mode.**

multiple personalities. An extreme form of dissociation in which the individuals's personality is split into separate personalities often alternating with each other. The memories of one of the split-off personalities commonly are not accessible to the other.

myelin sheath. The fatty sheath surrounding certain nerve fibers known as myelinated fibers. Impulses travel faster and with less energy expenditure in myelinated fibers than in unmyelinated fibers.

nanometer (nm). A billionth of a meter. Wavelength of light is measured in nanometers.

narcissism. Self-love; in psychoanalytic theory, the normal expression of pregenital development.

narcolepsy. A sleep disturbance characterized by an uncontrollable tendency to fall asleep for brief periods at inopportune times.

nativism. The view that behavior is innately determined. See also **empiricism.**

nature-nurture issue. The problem of determining the relative importance of heredity (nature) and the result of upbringing in the particular environment (nurture) on mature ability.

need. A physical state involving any lack or deficit within the organism. See also **motive, drive.**

negative incentive. An object or circumstance away from which behavior is directed when the object or circumstance is perceived or anticipated. See also **positive incentive.**

negative reinforcement. Reinforcing a response by the removal of an aversive stimulus. See also **negative reinforcer.**

negative reinforcer. Any stimulus that, when removed following a response, increases the probability of the response. Loud noise, electric shock, and extreme heat or cold classify as negative reinforcers. See also **punishment.**

negativism. A type of defiant behavior in which there is active refusal to carry out requests. Common in early childhood but met occasionally at all ages (syn. *negativistic behavior*).

nerve. A bundle of elongated axons belonging to hundreds or thousands of neurons, possibly both afferent and efferent neurons. Connects portions of the nervous system to other portions and to receptors and effectors. See also **axon, neuron.**

nerve cell. See **neuron.**

neuron. The nerve cell; the unit of a synaptic nervous system.

neurosis (pl. **neuroses**). A form of maladjustment in which the individual is unable to cope with anxieties and conflicts and develops abnormal symptoms. The disturbance is not so severe as to produce a profound personality derangement, as with the psychotic reactions (syn. *psychoneurosis*). See also **anxiety reaction, conversion reaction, neurotic depression, obsessive-compulsive reaction, phobia.**

neurotic depression. A neurosis characterized by continuing sadness and dejection that is out of proportion to any precipitating event; distinguished from psychotic depression in that reality perception is not grossly impaired. See also **affective disorder, neurosis, psychosis.**

neurotic paradox. Refers to the tendency of neurotics to cling to defensive patterns that are self-defeating. See also **neurosis.**

neurotransmitter. A chemical involved in the transmission of nerve impulses across the synapse from one neuron to another. Usually released from small vesicles in the terminal button of the axon in response to the action potential; diffuses across synapse to influence electrical activity in another neuron. See also **dopamine, epinephrine, norepinephrine, serotonin.**

nonconscious processes. Those forms of unconscious processes that are never accessible to consciousness; e.g., control of

salt concentration in the blood. See also **conscious processes, unconscious processes.**

noncontingent reinforcement. Reinforcement not contingent on a specific response.

noradrenalin. See **norepinephrine.**

norepinephrine. One of the hormones secreted by the adrenal medulla. Its action is in some, but not all, respects similar to that of epinephrine (syn. *noradrenalin*). See also **adrenal gland, epinephrine.**

norm. An average, common, or standard performance under specified conditions; e.g., the average achievement test score of 9-year-old children or the average birth weight of male children. See also **test standardization.**

normal curve. The plotted form of the normal distribution.

normal distribution. The standard symmetrical bell-shaped frequency distribution, whose properties are commonly used in making statistical inferences from measures derived from samples. See also **normal curve, skewed distribution.**

nuclei (sing. **nucleus**). A collection of nerve cell bodies grouped together in the brain or spinal cord. See also **ganglia.**

null hypothesis. A statistical hypothesis that any difference observed among treatment conditions occurs by chance and does not reflect a true difference. Rejection of the null hypothesis means that we believe the treatment conditions are actually having an effect.

object constancy. The tendency to see objects as relatively unchanged under widely altered conditions of illumination, distance, and position. See also **brightness constancy, color constancy, location constancy, shape constancy, size constancy.**

object permanence. A term used by Piaget to refer to the child's realization that an object continues to exist even though it is hidden from view. See also **sensorimotor stage.**

object size. The size of an object as determined from measurement at its surface. When size constancy holds, the observer perceives a distant object as being near its object size. See also **retinal size.**

observational method. Studying events as they occur in nature, without experimental control of variables; e.g., studying the nest-building of birds or observing children's behavior in a play situation. See also **experimental method.**

obsession. A persistent, unwelcome, intrusive thought, often suggesting an aggressive or sexual act. See also **compulsion, obsessive-compulsive reaction.**

obsessive-compulsive reaction. A neurosis taking one of three forms: (1) recurrent thoughts, often disturbing and unwelcome (obsessions); (2) irresistible urges to repeat stereotyped or ritualistic acts (compulsions); (3) both of these in combination.

occipital lobe. A portion of the cerebral hemisphere, behind the parietal and temporal lobes. See also **frontal lobe, parietal lobe, temporal lobe.**

Oedipal stage. In psychoanalysis, an alternative designation of the phallic stage of psychosexual development, because it is at this stage that the Oedipus complex arises. See also **Oedipus complex, psychosexual development.**

Oedipus complex. In psychoanalytic theory, sexual attachment to the parent of the opposite sex, originating as the normal culmination of the infantile period of development.

olfactory epithelium. The portion of specialized skin within the nasal cavity that contains the receptors for the sense of smell.

operant behavior. Behavior defined by the stimulus to which it leads rather than by the stimulus that elicits it; e.g., behavior leading to reward (syn. *emitted behavior, instrumental behavior*). See also **respondent behavior.**

operant conditioning. The strengthening of an operant response by presenting a reinforcing stimulus if, and only if, the response occurs (syn. *instrumental conditioning, reward learning*). See also **classical conditioning.**

opponent-process theory. The theory that human color vision depends on 3 pairs of opposing processes: white-black, yellow-blue, and red-green. See also **Young-Helmholtz theory.**

oral behavior. Behavior deriving from the infant's need to suck or, more generally, to be fed through the mouth.

oral stage. In psychoanalysis, the first stage of psychosexual development, in which pleasure is derived from the lips and mouth, as in sucking at the mother's breast. See also **psychosexual development.**

organ of Corti. In the ear, the actual receptor for hearing, lying on the basilar membrane in the cochlea and containing the hair cells where the fibers of the auditory nerve originate. See also **basilar membrane, cochlea.**

organic psychosis. A psychosis caused by disease, injury, drugs, or other definable structural changes of the central nervous system. See also **functional psychosis, psychosis.**

organism. In biology, any form of plant or animal life. In psychology, the word is used to refer to the living individual animal, whether human or subhuman.

orienting reflex. (1) A nonspecific response to change in stimulation involving depression of cortical alpha rhythm, galvanic skin response, pupillary dilation, and complex vasomotor responses (a term introduced by Russian psychologists). (2) Head or body movements that orient the organism's receptors to those parts of the environment in which stimulus changes are occurring.

osmoreceptors. Hypothesized cells in the hypothalamus that respond to dehydration by stimulating the release of ADH by the pituitary gland, which, in turn, signals the kidneys to reabsorb water back into the bloodstream. See also **antidiuretic hormone, volumetric receptors.**

otoliths. "Ear stones." See also **vestibular sacs.**

ovarian hormones. See **estrogen.**

overextension. The tendency of a child, in learning a language, to apply a new word too widely; e.g., to call all animals "doggie."

overtone. A higher frequency tone, a multiple of the fundamental frequency, that occurs when a tone is sounded by a musical instrument. See also **timbre.**

paired-associate learning. The learning of stimulus-response pairs, as in the acquisition of a foreign language vocabulary. When the first member of a pair (the stimulus) is presented, the subject's task is to give the second member (the response).

pancreas. A bodily organ situated near the stomach. As a duct gland it secretes pancreatic juice into the intestines, but some specialized cells function as an endocrine gland, secreting the hormone insulin into the bloodstream. See also **endocrine gland.**

parallel processing. A theoretical interpretation of information processing in which several sources of information are all processed simultaneously. See also **serial processing.**

parameter. Any of the constants in a function that defines the form of the curve. It ordinarily differs when experimental conditions or subjects are changed.

paranoid schizophrenia. A schizophrenic reaction in which the patient has delusions of persecution. See also **schizophrenia.**

parapsychology. A subfield of psychology that studies such paranormal phenomena as extrasensory perception and psychoki-

nesis. See also **clairvoyance, extrasensory perception, precognition, psychokinesis, telepathy.**

parasympathetic division. A division of the autonomic nervous system, the nerve fibers of which originate in the cranial and sacral portions of the spinal cord. Active in relaxed or quiescent states of the body and to some extent antagonistic to the sympathetic division. See also **sympathetic division.**

parathyroid glands. Endocrine glands adjacent to the thyroid gland in the neck, whose hormones regulate calcium metabolism, thus maintaining the normal excitability of the nervous system. Parathyroid inadequacy leads to tetany. See also **endocrine gland.**

parietal lobe. A portion of the cerebral hemisphere, behind the central fissure and between the frontal and occipital lobes. See also **frontal lobe, occipital lobe, temporal lobe.**

partial reinforcement. Reinforcing a given response only some proportion of the times it occurs (syn. *intermittent reinforcement*). See also **reinforcement, reinforcement schedule.**

percept. The end result of the perceptual process; that which the individual perceives.

perception. The process of becoming aware of objects, qualities, or relations by way of the sense organs. While sensory content is always present in perception, what is perceived is influenced by set and prior experience, so that perception is more than a passive registration of stimuli impinging on the sense organs. See also **subliminal perception.**

perceptual patterning. The tendency to perceive stimuli according to principles such as proximity, similarity, continuity, and closure. Emphasized by Gestalt psychologists. See also **figure-ground perception, Gestalt psychology.**

performance. Overt behavior, as distinguished from knowledge or information not translated into action. The distinction is important in theories of learning.

peripheral nervous system. That part of the nervous system outside the brain and spinal cord; it includes the autonomic nervous system and the somatic nervous system. See also **autonomic nervous system, somatic nervous system.**

personality. The individual characteristics and ways of behaving that, in their organization or patterning, account for an individual's unique adjustments to his or her total environment (syn. *individuality*).

personality assessment. (1) Generally, appraisal of personality by any method.

(2) More specifically, personality appraisal through complex observations and judgments, usually based in part on behavior in contrived social situations.

personality disorders. Ingrained, habitual, and rigid patterns of behavior or character that severely limit the individual's adaptive potential; often society sees the behavior as maladaptive while the individual does not (syn. *character disorders*).

personality dynamics. Theories of personality that stress personality dynamics are concerned with the interactive aspects of behavior (as in conflict resolution), with value hierarchies, with the permeability of boundaries between differentiated aspects of personality, etc. Contrasted with developmental theories, though not incompatible with them.

personality inventory. An inventory for self-appraisal, consisting of many statements or questions about personal characteristics and behavior that the person judges to apply or not to apply to him or her. See also **projective test.**

personality psychologist. A psychologist whose area of interest focuses on classifying individuals and studying the differences between them. This specialty overlaps both developmental and social psychologists to some extent. See also **developmental psychologist, social psychologist.**

phallic stage. In psychoanalysis, that stage of psychosexual development in which gratification is associated with stimulation of the sex organs and the sexual attachment is to the parent of the opposite sex. See also **Oedipal stage, psychosexual development.**

phenomenology. Naive report on conscious experience, as by a child, as contrasted with trained introspection. Emphasis on subjective experience and the individual's subjective view of a situation. See also **humanistic psychology, introspection.**

phenotype. In genetics, the characteristics that are displayed by the individual organism, e.g., eye color or intelligence, as distinct from those traits that one may carry genetically but not display. See also **genotype.**

phi phenomenon. Stroboscopic motion in its simpler form. Commonly produced by successively turning on and off two separated stationary light sources; as the first is turned off and the second turned on, the subject perceives a spot of light moving from the position of the first to that of the second. See also **stroboscopic motion.**

phobia. Excessive fear in the absence of real danger (syn. *phobic reaction*). See also **agoraphobia, claustrophobia, neurosis.**

phoneme. The smallest unit in the sound system of a language; it serves to distinguish utterances from one another. See also **morpheme.**

physiological motive. A motive based on an evident bodily need, such as the need for food or water.

physiological psychologist. A psychologist concerned with the relationship between physiological functions and behavior.

physiology. That branch of biology concerned primarily with the functioning of organ systems within the body.

pitch. A qualitative dimension of hearing correlated with the frequency of the sound waves that constitute the stimulus. Higher frequencies yield higher pitches. See also **loudness, timbre.**

pituitary gland. An endocrine gland joined to the brain just below the hypothalamus. It consists of two parts, the anterior pituitary and the posterior pituitary. The anterior pituitary is the more important part because of its regulation of growth and of other endocrine glands (syn. *hypophysis*). See also **endocrine gland.**

place theory. A theory of hearing that associates pitch with the place on the basilar membrane where activation occurs. See also **frequency theory, volley principle.**

placebo. An inert substance used in place of an active drug; given to the control group in an experimental test.

pluralistic ignorance. The tendency for persons in a group to mislead each other about a situation; e.g., to define an emergency as a nonemergency because others are remaining calm and are not taking action.

polygenic traits. Characteristics determined by many sets of genes; e.g., intelligence, height, emotional stability.

polygraph. A machine that measures simultaneously several physiological responses that accompany emotion; e.g., heart and respiration rate, blood pressure, and GSR. Commonly known as a "lie detector" because of its use in determining the guilt of a subject through responses while answering questions. See also **voice stress analyzer.**

population. The total universe of all possible cases from which a sample is selected. The usual statistical formulas for making inferences from samples apply when the population is appreciably larger than the sample, e.g., 5 to 10 times larger than the sample. See also **sample.**

positive incentive. An object or circumstance toward which behavior is directed when the object or circumstance is perceived or anticipated. See also **negative incentive.**

positive reinforcement. Reinforcing a response by the presentation of a positive stimulus. See also **positive reinforcer.**

positive reinforcer. Any stimulus that, when applied following a response, increases the probability of the response (syn. *reward*). See also **negative reinforcer.**

posthypnotic amnesia. A particular form of posthypnotic suggestion in which the hypnotized person forgets what has happened during the hypnosis until signaled to remember. See also **posthypnotic suggestion.**

posthypnotic suggestion. A suggestion made to a hypnotized person that he or she will perform in a prescribed way (commonly to a prearranged signal) when no longer hypnotized. The activity is usually carried out without the subject's awareness of its origin. See also **hypnosis.**

precognition. A claimed form of extrasensory perception in which a future event is perceived. See also **clairvoyance, extrasensory perception, telepathy.**

preconscious processes. In psychoanalysis, a term for memories that are available but not now conscious. See also **conscious processes, nonconscious processes, unconscious processes.**

prejudice. A prejudgment that something or someone is good or bad on the basis of little or no evidence; an attitude that is firmly fixed, not open to free and rational discussion, and resistant to change.

preoperational stage. Piaget's second stage of cognitive development (ages 2–7 years). The child can think in terms of symbols but does not yet comprehend certain rules or operations, such as the principle of conservation. See also **conservation.**

preparatory set. See **set.**

primacy effect. (1) In memory experiments, the tendency for initial words in a list to be recalled more readily that later words. (2) In studies of impression formation or attitude change, the tendency for initial information to carry more weight than information received later. See also **recency effect.**

primary abilities. The abilities, discovered by factor analysis, that underlie intelligence test performance. See also **factor analysis.**

primary colors. See **color mixture primaries, psychological primaries.**

primary process thinking. In psychoanalytic theory, the form of thinking used by the id, characterized by irrational attempts to satisfy needs without consideration of reality. See also **id, secondary process thinking.**

primary sex characteristics. The structural or physiological characteristics that make possible sexual union and reproduction. See also **secondary sex characteristics.**

proactive interference. The interference of earlier learning with the learning and recall of new material. See also **retroactive interference.**

probe. In studies of memory, a digit or other item from a list to be remembered that is presented as a cue to the subject; e.g., the subject could be asked to give the next digit in the list.

product-moment correlation. See **coefficient of correlation.**

progesterone. A female sex hormone produced by the ovaries; it helps prepare the uterus for pregnancy and the breasts for lactation.

program. (1) A plan for the solution of a problem; often used interchangeably with "routine" to specify the precise sequence of instructions enabling a computer to solve a problem. (2) In connection with teaching, a set of materials arranged so as to maximize the learning process. The program can be presented in book form as well as in a form suitable for use with a computer.

projection. A defense mechanism by which people protect themselves from awareness of their own undesirable traits by attributing those traits excessively to others. See also **defense mechanism.**

projection area. A place in the cerebral cortex where a function is localized; e.g., the visual projection area is in the occipital lobes.

projective test. A personality test in which subjects reveal ("project") themselves through imaginative productions. The projective test gives much freer possibilities of response than the fixed-alternative personality inventory. Examples of projective tests are the Rorschach Test (ink blots to be interpreted) and the Thematic Apperception Test (pictures that elicit stories). See also **personality inventory.**

prolactin. A pituitary hormone associated with the secretion of milk. See also **hormones.**

proposition. A sentence or component of a sentence that asserts something, the predicate, about somebody (or something), the subject. All sentences can be broken down into propositions.

psi. The special ability said to be possessed by the subject who performs successfully in experiments on extrasensory perception and psychokinesis. See also **extrasensory perception, psychokinesis.**

psychedelic drugs. An alternate name for "consciousness-expanding" drugs. See also **hallucinogens, LSD, psychotomimetic drugs.**

psychiatric nurse. A nurse specially trained to deal with patients suffering from mental disorders. See also **psychiatrist.**

psychiatric social worker. A social worker trained to work with patients and their families on problems of mental health and illness, usually in close relationship with psychiatrists and clinical psychologists. See also **psychiatrist, clinical psychologist.**

psychiatrist. A medical doctor specializing in the treatment and prevention of mental disorders both mild and severe. See also **psychoanalyst, clinical psychologist.**

psychiatry. A branch of medicine concerned with mental health and mental illness. See also **psychiatrist, psychoanalyst.**

psychoactive drugs. Drugs that affect one's behavior and consciousness. See also **depressants, hallucinogens, LSD, psychedelic drugs, stimulants, tranquilizer.**

psychoanalysis. (1) The method developed by Freud and extended by his followers for treating neuroses. (2) The system of psychological theory growing out of experiences with the psychoanalytic method.

psychoanalyst. A psychotherapist, usually trained as a psychiatrist, who uses methods related to those originally proposed by Freud for treating neuroses and other mental disorders. See also **clinical psychologist, psychiatrist.**

psychodrama. A form of spontaneous play acting used in psychotherapy.

psychogenic. Caused by psychological factors (e.g., emotional conflict, faulty habits) rather than by disease, injury, or other somatic cause; functional rather than organic.

psychograph. See **trait profile.**

psychokinesis (PK). A claimed form of mental operation said to affect a material body or an energy system without any evidence of more usual contact or energy transfer; e.g., affecting the number that comes up in the throw of dice by a machine through wishing for that number. See also **extrasensory perception.**

psycholinguistics. The study of the psychological aspects of language and its acquisition.

psychological motive. A motive that is primarily learned rather than based on biological needs.

psychological primaries. Hues that appear to be pure; i.e., not composed of other hues. Most authorities choose a particular red, yellow, green, and blue. (The red-green and blue-yellow pairs chosen in this way are not complementary colors.) See also **color-mixture primaries.**

psychology. The science that studies behavior and mental processes.

psychopathic personality. A type of personality disorder marked by impulsivity, inability to abide by the customs and laws of society, and lack of anxiety or guilt regarding behavior (syn. *antisocial personality*).

psychopharmacology. The study of the effects of drugs on behavior.

psychophysical function. A curve relating the likelihood of a response to the intensity of the presented stimulus.

psychophysics. A name used by Fechner for the science of the relationship between mental processes and the physical world. Now usually restricted to the study of the sensory consequences of controlled physical stimulation.

psychosexual development. In psychoanalysis, the theory that development takes place through stages (oral, anal, phallic, latent, genital), each stage characterized by a zone of pleasurable stimulation and appropriate objects of sexual attachment, culminating in normal heterosexual mating. See also **anal stage, genital stage, latency stage, oral stage, phallic stage, psychosocial stages.**

psychosis (pl. **psychoses**). Mental illness in which the individual shows severe change or disorganization of personality, often accompanied by agitation or depression, delusions, hallucinations; commonly requires hospitalization. See also **functional psychosis, organic psychosis.**

psychosocial stages. A modification by Erikson of the psychoanalytic theory of psychosexual development, giving more attention to the social and environmental problems associated with the various stages of development and adding some adult stages beyond genital maturing. See also **psychosexual development.**

psychosomatic illness. Physical illness that has psychological causes (syn. *psychophysiological disorder*).

psychosurgery. A form of biological therapy for abnormal behavior. Involves destroying selected areas of the brain, most often the nerve fibers connecting the frontal lobes to the limbic system and/or the hypothalamus.

psychotherapy. Treatment of personality maladjustment or mental illness by psychological means, usually, but not exclusively, through personal consultation. See also **biological therapy.**

puberty. The climax of pubescence, marked by menstruation in girls and the appearance of live sperm cells in the urine of boys. See also **adolescence.**

punishment. A procedure used to decrease the strength of a response by presenting an aversive stimulus whenever the response occurs. Note that such a stimulus when applied would be a punisher; when removed it would act as a negative reinforcer, reinforcing whatever led to its removal. This is the mechanism of escape learning. See also **escape learning, negative reinforcer.**

range. The variation of scores in a frequency distribution from the lowest to the highest. A value that grows larger as the number of cases increases, hence to be used with extreme caution. See also **measure of variation.**

rank correlation (ρ). A correlation computed from ranked data. The coefficient is designated by the small Greek letter *rho* (ρ) to distinguish it from the product-moment correlation (*r*), of which it is an approximation. See also **coefficient of correlation.**

rapid eye movements (REMs). Eye movements that usually occur during dreaming and that can be measured by attaching small electrodes laterally to and above the subject's eye. These register changes in electrical activity associated with movements of the eyeball in its socket.

rapport. (1) A comfortable relationship between the subject and the tester, ensuring cooperation in replying to test questions. (2) A similar relationship between therapist and patient. (3) A special relationship of hypnotic subject to hypnotist.

rating scale. A device by which raters can record their judgments of others (or of themselves) on the traits defined by the scale.

rationalization. A defense mechanism in which self-esteem is maintained by assigning plausible and acceptable reasons for conduct entered on impulsively or for less acceptable reasons. See also **defense mechanism.**

reaction formation. A defense mechanism in which a person denies a disapproved motive through giving strong expression to its opposite. See also **defense mechanism.**

reaction range. The range of potential intellectual ability specified by a person's genes. According to this concept, the effects of an enriched, average, or a deprived environment will be to change the person's IQ, but only within his or her genetically specified reaction range.

reaction time. The time between the presentation of a stimulus and the occurrence of a response. See also **latency.**

receiver-operating-characteristic curve (ROC curve). The function relating the probability of hits and false alarms for a fixed signal level in a detection task. Factors influencing response bias may cause hits and false alarms to vary, but their variation is constrained to the ROC curve. See also **signal detection task.**

recency effect. (1) In memory experiments, the tendency for the last words in a list to be recalled more readily than other list words. (2) In studies of impression formation or attitude change, the tendency for later information to carry more weight than earlier information. See also **primacy effect.**

receptor. A specialized portion of the body sensitive to particular kinds of stimuli and connected to nerves composed of afferent neurons; e.g., the retina of the eye. Used more loosely, the organ containing these sensitive portions; e.g., the eye or the ear. See also **afferent neuron, effector.**

recessive gene. A member of a gene pair that determines the characteristic trait or appearance of the individual only if the other member of the pair is recessive. If the other member of the pair is dominant, the effect of the recessive gene is masked. See also **dominant gene.**

recurrent inhibition. A process whereby some receptors in the visual system when stimulated by nerve impulses inhibit the firing of other visual receptors, thus making the visual system responsive to changes in illumination.

red-green color blindness. The commonest form of color blindness, a variety of dichromatism. In the two subvarieties, red-blindness and green-blindness, both red and green vision are lacking, but achromatic bands are seen at different parts of the spectrum. See also **color blindness, dichromatism.**

reference group. Any group to which an individual refers for comparing, judging, and deciding on his or her opinions, and behaviors.

refractory phase. The period of temporary inactivity in a neuron after it has fired once.

registration. A term to describe receptive processing in which information is processed but not perceived. See also **perception, subliminal perception.**

regression. A return to more primitive or infantile modes of response.

rehearsal. To recycle information in short-term memory. The process facilitates the short-term recall of information and its transfer to long-term memory. See also **dual-memory theory.**

reincarnation. The belief in rebirth; i.e., that a person has lived before.

reinforcement. (1) In classical conditioning, the exprimental procedure of following the conditioned stimulus by the unconditioned stimulus. (2) In operant conditioning, the analogous procedure of following the occurrence of the operant response by the reinforcing stimulus. (3) The process that

increases the strength of conditioning as a result of these arrangements. See also **classical conditioning, extinction, negative reinforcement, operant conditioning, partial reinforcement, positive reinforcement.**

reinforcement schedule. A well-defined procedure for reinforcing a given response only some proportion of the time it occurs. See also **partial reinforcement.**

reinforcing stimulus. (1) In classical conditioning, the unconditioned stimulus. (2) In operant conditioning, the stimulus that reinforces the operant (typically, a reward (syn. *reinforcer*). See also **negative reinforcer, positive reinforcer.**

releaser. A term used by ethologists for a stimulus that sets off a cycle of instinctive behavior. See also **ethologist, instinct.**

reliability. The self-consistency of a test as a measuring instrument. Reliability is measured by a coefficient of correlation between scores on two halves of a test, alternate forms of the test, or retests with the same test; a high correlation signifies high consistency of scores for the population tested. See also **validity.**

REMs. See **rapid eye movements.**

repression. (1) A defense mechanism in which an impulse or memory that might provoke feelings of guilt is denied by its disappearance from awareness. See also **defense mechanism, suppression.** (2) A theory of forgetting.

reserpine. See **tranquilizer.**

resistance. In psychoanalysis, a blocking of free association; a psychological barrier against bringing unconscious impulses to the level of awareness. Resistance is part of the process of maintaining repression. See also **interpretation, repression.**

respondent behavior. A type of behavior corresponding to reflex action, in that it is largely under the control of, and predictable from, the stimulus (syn. *elicited behavior*). See also **operant behavior.**

response. (1) The behavioral result of stimulation in the form of a movement or glandular secretion. (2) Sometimes, any activity of the organism, including central responses (such as an image or fantasy), regardless of whether the stimulus is identified and whether identifiable movements occur. (3) Products of the organism's activity, such as words typed per minute.

resting potential. The electrical potential across the nerve cell membrane when it is in its resting state (i.e., not responding to other neurons); the inside of the cell membrane is slightly more negative than the outside. See also **action potential.**

reticular system. A system of ill-defined nerve paths and connections within the brain stem, lying outside the well-defined nerve pathways, and important as an arousal mechanism.

retina. The portion of the eye sensitive to light, containing the rods and the cones. See also **cone, rod.**

retinal image. The image projected onto the retina by an object in the visual field.

retinal size. The size of the retinal image of an object; retinal size decreases in direct proportion to the object's distance. See also **object size.**

retrieval. Locating information in memory.

retroactive interference. The interference in recall of something earlier learned by something subsequently learned. See also **proactive interference.**

retrograde amnesia. The inability to recall events that occurred during a period of time immediately prior to a shock or functional disturbance, although the memory for earlier events remains relatively unimpaired. See also **anterograde amnesia.**

reward. A synonym for *positive reinforcement.* See also **positive reinforcement.**

ribonucleic acid (RNA). Complex molecules that control cellular functions; theorized by some to be the chemical mediator of memory.

right hemisphere. The right cerebral hemisphere. Controls the left side of the body and, for most people, spatial and patterned activities (syn. *minor hemisphere*). See also **cerebral hemispheres, corpus callosum, left hemisphere, split-brain subject.**

RNA. See **ribonucleic acid.**

ROC curve. See **receiver-operating-characteristic curve.**

rod. In the eye, an element of the retina mediating achromatic sensation only; particularly important in peripheral vision and night vision. See also **cone, retina.**

role confusion. A stage of development said by Erikson to characterize many adolescents (and others) in which various identifications have not been harmonized and integrated. See also **identification, identity formation.**

role playing. A method for teaching attitudes and behaviors important to interpersonal relations by having the subject assume a part in a spontaneous play, whether in psychotherapy or in leadership training. See also **psychodrama.**

saccule. See **vestibular sacs.**

sadism. A pathological motive that leads to inflicting pain on another person. See also **masochism.**

sample. A selection of scores from a total set of scores known as the "population."

If selection is random, an unbiased sample results; if selection is nonrandom, the sample is biased and unrepresentative. See also **population.**

sampling errors. The variation in a distribution of scores, or of statistics derived from them to be attributed to the fact that measurements are made on a variable sample from a larger population. Thus sampling errors persist even though all measurements are accurate. See also **sample.**

saturation. The dimension of color that describes its purity; if highly saturated it appears to be pure hue and free of gray, but if of low saturation it appears to have a great deal of gray mixed with it. See also **brightness, hue.**

scaling. Converting raw data into types of scores more readily interpreted; e.g., into ranks, centiles, standard scores.

scapegoat. A form of displaced aggression in which an innocent but helpless victim is blamed or punished as the source of the scapegoater's frustration. See also **displaced aggression.**

schema (pl. **schemata**). A hypothetical structure stored in memory that preserves and organizes information about some event or concept. See also **cognitive map.**

schizoid. Having some characteristics that resemble schizophrenia but are less severe. Occurs with higher frequency in families of schizophrenics and thus tends to support a genetic basis for schizophrenia. See also **schizophrenia.**

schizophrenia. A functional psychotic disorder in which there is a lack of harmony or split between aspects of personality functioning, especially between emotion and behavior. Symptoms may include autism, hallucinations, and delusions. See also **paranoid schizophrenia, psychosis.**

school psychologist. A professional psychologist employed by a school or school system, with responsibility for testing, guidance, research, etc. See also **educational psychologist.**

secondary process thinking. In psychoanalytic theory, the form of thinking used by the ego, characterized by realistic and logical attempts to satisfy needs. See also **ego, primary process thinking.**

secondary sex characteristics. The physical features distinguishing the mature male from the mature female, apart from the reproductive organs. In humans, the deeper voice of the male and the growth of the beard are illustrative. See also **primary sex characteristics.**

selective breeding. A method of studying genetic influences by mating animals that display certain traits and selecting for

breeding from among their offspring those that express the trait. If the trait is primarily determined by heredity, continued selection for a number of generations will produce a strain that breeds true for that trait.

self-actualization. A person's fundamental tendency toward maximal realization of his or her potentials; a basic concept in humanistic theories of personality such as those developed by Maslow and Rogers.

self-concept. The composite of ideas, feelings, and attitudes people have about themselves.

self-consciousness. A form of heightened self-awareness when an individual is especially concerned about reactions of others to him or her.

self-perception. The individual's awareness of him or herself; differs from self-consciousness, because it may take the form of objective self-appraisal. See also **self-consciousness.**

self-perception theory. The theory that attitudes and beliefs are influenced by observations of one's own behavior; sometimes we judge how we feel by observing how we act (Bem).

self-persuasion. The process by which individuals' opinions change so that they are consistent with their behavior.

self-regulation. In behavior therapy, monitoring one's own behavior and using techniques such as self-reinforcement or controlling stimulus conditions to modify maladaptive behavior. See also **behavior therapy.**

semantic concepts. Concepts with one-word names that refer to things that occur frequently and thus allow us to think and communicate efficiently. Used as one major category of long-term memory coding. See also **concept.**

semantic conditioning. A form of classical conditioning in which semantic concepts are used as the conditioned stimuli and generalization occurs through semantic similarities.

semantic differential. A method for using rating scales and factor analysis in studying the connotative meanings of words. See also **connotative meaning, denotative meaning.**

semicircular canals. Three curved tubular canals, in three planes, which form part of the labyrinth of the inner ear and are concerned with equilibrium and motion. See also **equilibratory senses.**

sensorimotor stage. Piaget's first stage of cognitive development (birth–2 years) during which the infant discovers relationships between sensations and motor behavior. See also **object permanence.**

sensory adaptation. The reduction in sensitivity that occurs with prolonged stimulation and the increase in sensitivity that occurs with lack of stimulation; most noted in vision, smell, taste, and temperature sensitivity. See also **dark adaptation, light adaptation.**

septal area. A portion of the brain deep in the central part, between the lateral ventricles, that when stimulated electrically (in the rat, at least) appears to yield a state akin to pleasure.

serial memory search. Comparing a test stimulus in sequence to each item in short-term memory. See also **short-term memory.**

serial processing. A theoretical interpretation of information processing in which several sources of information are processed in a serial order; only one source being attended to at a time. See also **parallel processing.**

serotonin. A neurotransmitter found in the midbrain and believed to play a role in psychosis, particularly in depression. See also **neurotransmitter.**

sex-linked trait. A trait determined by a gene transmitted on the same chromosomes that determine sex; e.g., red-green color blindness. See also **X, Y chromosome.**

sex-role standards. Behavior that a society considers appropriate for the individual because of his or her sex.

shape constancy. The tendency to see a familiar object as of the same shape regardless of the viewing angle. See also **object constancy.**

shaping of behavior. Modifying operant behavior by reinforcing only those variations in response that deviate in a direction desired by the experimenter; the whole population of responses thus reinforced then drifts in the desired direction (Skinner) (syn. *method of approximations*).

shock therapy. A form of treatment of mental illness, especially in the relief of depression. See also **electroshock therapy, insulin shock.**

short-term memory (STM). The assumption that certain components of the memory system have limited capacity and will maintain information for only a brief period of time. The definition varies somewhat from theory to theory. See also **long-term memory.**

sibling. A brother or a sister.

sibling rivalry. Jealousy between siblings, often based on their competition for parental affection.

signal detectability theory. A theory of the sensory and decision processes involved in psychophysical judgments, with special reference to the problem of detecting

weak signals in noise. See also **signal detection task.**

signal detection task. A procedure whereby the subject must judge on each trial whether or not a weak signal was embedded in a noise background. Saying "yes" when the signal was presented is called a hit and saying "yes" when the signal was not presented is called a false alarm. See also **receiver-operating-characteristic curve.**

simple cell. A cell in the visual cortex that responds to a bar of light or straight edge of a particular orientation and location in the visual field. See also **complex cell.**

simulation. The representation of the essential elements of some phenomenon, system, or environment to facilitate its study (often by or involving a computer).

simultaneous conditioning. A classical conditioning procedure in which the CS begins a fraction of a second before the onset of the US and continues with it until the response occurs. See also **delayed conditioning, trace conditioning.**

sine wave. A cyclical wave that when plotted corresponds to the plot of the trigonometric sine function. The sound waves of pure tones yield this function when plotted.

situational attribution. Attributing a person's actions to factors in the situation or environment, as opposed to internal attitudes and motives. See also **dispositional attribution.**

size constancy. The tendency to see a familiar object as of its actual size regardless of its distance. See also **object constancy.**

skewed distribution. A frequency distribution that is not symmetrical. It is named for the direction in which the tail lies; e.g., if there are many small incomes and a few large ones, the distribution is skewed in the direction of the large incomes. See also **frequency distribution, symmetrical distribution.**

smooth muscle. The type of muscle found in the digestive organs, blood vessels, and other internal organs. Controlled via the autonomic nervous system. See also **cardiac muscle, striate muscle.**

social learning theory. The application of learning theory to the problems of personal and social behavior (syn. *social behavior theory*).

social norms. A group or community's unwritten rules that govern its members' behavior, attitudes, and beliefs.

social psychologist. A psychologist who studies social interaction and the ways in which individuals influence one another.

socialization. The shaping of individual characteristics and behavior through the training that the social environment provides.

sociology. The behavioral or social science dealing with group life and social organization in literate societies. See also **behavioral sciences.**

somatic nervous system. A division of the peripheral nervous system consisting of nerves that connect the brain and spinal cord with the sense receptors, muscles, and body surface. See also **autonomic nervous system, peripheral nervous system.**

somatosensory area. Area in the parietal lobe of the brain that registers sensory experiences, such as heat, cold, touch, and pain. Also called body-sense area. See also **motor area.**

special factor (s). A specialized ability underlying test scores, especially in tests of intelligence; e.g., a special ability in mathematics, as distinct from general intelligence. See also **factor analysis, general factor.**

specific hunger. Hunger for a specific food incentive, such as a craving for sweets. See also **hunger drive.**

spindle. An EEG characteristic of stage-2 sleep, consisting of short bursts of rhythmical responses of 13–16 Hz; slightly higher than alpha. See also **electroencephalogram.**

split-brain subject. A person who has had an operation that severed the corpus callosum, thus separating the functions of the two cerebral hemispheres. See also **cerebral hemispheres, corpus callosum.**

spontaneous remission. Recovery from an illness or improvement without treatment.

S-R psychology. See **stimulus-response psychology.**

stabilized retinal image. The image of an object on the retina when special techniques are used to counteract the minute movements of the eyeball that occur in normal vision. When an image is thus stabilized it quickly disappears, suggesting that the changes in stimulation of retinal cells provided by the eye movements are necessary for vision.

stages of development. Developmental periods, usually following a progressive sequence, that appear to represent qualitative changes in either the structure or the function of the organism (e.g., Freud's psychosexual stages, Piaget's cognitive stages).

standard deviation. The square root of the mean of the squares of the amount by which each case departs from the mean of all the cases (syn. *root mean square deviation*). See also **measure of variation, standard error, standard score.**

standard error. The standard deviation of the sampling distribution of a mean and of certain other derived statistics. It can be interpreted as any other standard deviation. See also **standard deviation.**

standard score. A score that has been converted to a scale of measurement with a mean of 0 and a standard deviation of 1.0, based on a distribution of scores used in calibration.

state-dependent learning. Learning that occurs during a particular biological state, e.g., while drugged, so that it can only be demonstrated, or is most effective, when the person is put in the same state again.

statistical inference. A statement about a population or populations based on statistical measures derived from samples. See also **descriptive statistics.**

statistical significance. The trustworthiness of an obtained statistical measure as a statement about reality; e.g., the probability that the population mean falls within the limits determined from a sample. The expression refers to the reliability of the statistical finding and not to its importance.

stereoscopic vision. (1) The binocular perception of depth and distance of an object owing to the overlapping fields of the two eyes. (2) The equivalent effect when slightly unlike pictures are presented individually to each eye in a stereoscope. See also **distance cues.**

stereotype. An overgeneralized, often false, belief about a group of people that lets one assume that every member of the group possesses a particular trait; e.g., the false stereotyped belief that all male homosexuals are effeminate.

steroids. Complex chemical substances, some of which are prominent in the secretions of the adrenal cortex and may be related to some forms of mental illness. See also **adrenal gland.**

stimulants. Psychoactive drugs that increase arousal. See also **amphetamines, depressants, hallucinogens.**

stimulus (pl. **stimuli**). (1) Some specific physical energy impinging on a receptor sensitive to that kind of energy. (2) Any objectively describable situation or event (whether outside or inside the organism) that is the occasion for an organism's response. See also **response.**

stimulus-response (S-R) psychology. A psychological view that all behavior is in response to stimuli and that the appropriate tasks of psychological science are those identifying stimuli, the responses correlated with them, and the processes intervening between stimulus and response.

STM. See **short-term memory.**

striate area. See **visual area.**

striate muscle. Striped muscle; the characteristic muscles controlling the skeleton,

as in the arms and legs. Activated by the somatic, as opposed to the autonomic, nervous system. See also **cardiac muscle, smooth muscle.**

stroboscopic motion. An illusion of motion resulting from the successive presentation of discrete stimulus patterns arranged in a progression corresponding to movement; e.g., motion pictures. See also **phi phenomenon.**

subconscious processes. Subconscious processes when distinguished from unconscious processes are those nearer to the margins of consciousness and distinguishable from the Freudian unconscious. See also **conscious processes, nonconscious processes, unconscious processes.**

subliminal perception. The consequences of stimulation below detection threshold; the effects have to be detected by their influences on other processes. See also **perception, registration.**

subtractive mixture. Color mixture in which absorption occurs, so that results differ from additive mixture obtained by mixing projected lights. Subtractive mixture occurs when transparent colored filters are placed one in front of the other and when pigments are mixed. See also **additive mixture.**

superego. In Freud's tripartite division of the personality, that part corresponding most nearly to conscience, controlling through moral scruples rather than by way of social expediency. The superego is said to be an uncompromising and punishing conscience. See also **conscience, ego, id.**

suppression. A process of self-control in which impulses, tendencies to action, wishes to perform disapproved acts, etc., are in awareness, but not overtly revealed. See also **repression.**

survey method. A method of obtaining information by questioning a large sample of people.

symbol. Anything that stands for or refers to something other than itself.

symmetrical distribution. A frequency distribution in which cases fall equally in the class intervals on either side of the middle; hence the mean, median, and mode fall together. See also **frequency distribution, skewed distribution.**

sympathetic division. A division of the autonomic nervous system, characterized by a chain of ganglia on either side of the spinal cord, with nerve fibers originating in the thoracic and lumbar portions of the spinal cord. Active in emotional excitement and to some extent antagonistic to the parasympathetic division. See also **parasympathetic division.**

symptom substitution. The replacement of a

symptom of mental illness by a patient after a prior symptom has been directly removed without treatment of the underlying illness. The extent to which symptom substitution occurs is a point of contention between behavior therapists and other therapists who believe in the need for insight. See also **behavior therapy, insight.**

synapse. The close functional connection between the axon of one neuron and the dendrites or cell body of another neuron. See also **excitatory synapse, inhibitory synapse.**

systematic desensitization. A behavior therapy technique in which hierarchies of anxiety-producing situations are imagined (or sometimes confronted in reality) while the person is in a state of deep relaxation. Gradually the situations become dissociated from the anxiety response. See also **behavior therapy, counter-conditioning.**

tachistoscope. An instrument for the brief exposure of words, symbols, pictures, or other visually presented material; sometimes called a T-scope.

teaching machine. A device to provide self-instruction by means of a program proceeding in steps at a rate determined by the learner; the machine is arranged to provide knowledge about the correctness of each of the responses made by the learner. See also **CAL.**

telegraphic speech. A stage in the development of speech where the child preserves only the most meaningful and perceptually salient elements of adult speech. The child tends to omit prepositions, articles, prefixes, suffixes, and auxiliary words.

telepathy. The claimed form of extrasensory perception in which what is perceived depends on thought transference from one person to another. See also **clairvoyance, extrasensory perception, precognition.**

temperament. That aspect of personality revealed in the tendency to experience moods or mood changes in characteristic ways; general level of reactivity and energy.

temporal lobe. A portion of the cerebral hemisphere, at the side below the lateral fissure and in front of the occipital lobe. See also **frontal lobe, occipital lobe, parietal lobe.**

terminal button. A specialized knob at the end of the axon that releases a chemical into the synapse to continue transmission of the nerve impulse. See also **neurotransmitter.**

test battery. A collection of tests whose

composite scores are used to appraise individual differences.

test method. A method of psychological investigation. Its advantages are that it allows the psychologist to collect large quantities of useful data from many people, with a minimum of disturbance of their routines of existence and with a minimum of laboratory equipment.

test profile. A chart plotting scores from a number of tests given to the same individual (or group of individuals) in parallel rows on a common scale, with the scores connected by lines, so that high and low scores can be readily perceived. See also **trait profile.**

test standardization. The establishment of norms for interpreting scores by giving a test to a representative population and by making appropriate studies of its reliability and validity. See also **norm, reliability, validity.**

testosterone. The best known male sex hormone produced by the testes; it is important for the growth of the male sex organs and the development of the secondary male sex characteristics. It influences the sex drive. See also **androgens, secondary sex characteristics.**

thalamus. Two groups of nerve cell nuclei located just above the brain stem and inside the cerebral hemispheres. Considered a part of the central core of the brain. One area acts as a sensory relay station, the other plays a role in sleep and waking; this portion is considered part of the limbic system. See also **hypothalamus.**

theory. A set of assumptions (axioms) advanced to explain existing data and predict new events; usually applicable to a wide array of phenomena.

thinking. The ability to imagine or represent objects or events in memory and to operate on these representations. Ideational problem solving as distinguished from solution through overt manipulation.

threshold. The transitional point at which an increasing stimulus or an increasing difference not previously perceived becomes perceptible (or at which a descreasing stimulus or previously perceived difference becomes imperceptible). The value obtained depends in part on the methods used in determining it. See also **absolute threshold, difference threshold.**

thyroid gland. An endocrine gland located in the neck, whose hormone thyroxin is important in determining metabolic rate. See also **endocrine gland.**

timbre. The quality distinguishing a tone of a given pitch sounded by one instrument from that sounded by another. The differences are due to overtones and other impurities. See also **overtone.**

tip-of-the-tongue phenomenon. The experience of failing to recall a word or name when we are quite certain we know it.

T-maze. An apparatus in which an animal is presented with two alternative paths, one of which leads to a goal box. It is usually used with rats and lower organisms. See also **maze.**

tolerance. The need to take more and more of a drug to achieve the same effect. An important factor in physical dependency on drugs.

trace conditioning. A classical conditioning procedure in which the CS terminates before the onset of the US. See also **delayed conditioning, simultaneous conditioning.**

trait. A persisting characteristic or dimension of personality according to which individuals can be rated or measured. See also **trait profile.**

trait profile. A chart plotting the ratings of a number of traits of the same individual on a common scale in parallel rows, so that the pattern of traits can be visually perceived (syn. *psychograph*). See also **test profile, trait.**

trait theory. The theory that human personality is most profitably characterized by the scores that an individual makes on a number of scales, each of which represents a trait or dimension of his or her personality.

Transcendental Meditation (TM). A form of meditation practiced by some who follow Hindu yoga. The meditative state is induced by repeating a particular sound or phrase, called a *mantra*, over and over again. Each individual has his or her own mantra selected as most appropriate.

transducer. A device such as an electrode or gauge that, in psychophysiology, converts physiological indicators into other forms of energy that can be recorded and measured.

tranquilizer. A drug such as chlorpromazine or reserpine used to reduce anxiety and relieve depression; hence useful in the therapy of mental disorders.

transference. In psychoanalysis, the patient's unconsciously making the therapist the object of emotional response, thus transferring to the therapist responses appropriate to other persons important in the life history of the patient.

transsexual. An individual who is physically one sex but psychologically the other. Transsexuals sometimes resort to surgery and hormonal treatment to change their physical gender. They do not, however, consider themselves to be homosexual. See also **homosexual.**

trichromatism. Normal color vision, based on the classification of color vision according to three color systems: black-

white, blue-yellow, and red-green. The normal eye sees all three; the colorblind eye is defective in one or two of the three systems. See also **dichromatism, monochromatism.**

Turner's syndrome. An abnormal condition of the sex chromosomes in which a female is born with one X chromosome instead of the usual XX. See also **X chromosome.**

type theory. The theory that human subjects can profitably be classified into a small number of classes or types, each class or type having characteristics in common that set its members apart from other classes or types. See also **trait theory.**

unconditioned response (UR). In classical conditioning, the response given originally to the unconditioned stimulus used as the basis for establishing a conditioned response to a previously neutral stimulus. See also **conditioned response, conditioned stimulus, unconditioned stimulus.**

unconditioned stimulus (US). In classical conditioning, a stimulus that automatically elicits a response, typically via a reflex, without prior conditioning. See also **conditioned response, conditioned stimulus, unconditioned response.**

unconscious motive. A motive of which the subject is unaware, or aware of in distorted form. Because there is no sharp dividing line between conscious and unconscious, many motives have both conscious and unconscious aspects.

unconscious processes. (1) Processes, such as wishes or fears, that might be conscious but of which the subject is unaware. (2) Less commonly, physiological processes of the body (circulation, metabolism, etc.) that go on outside of awareness, preferably called *nonconscious*. See also **conscious processes, nonconscious processes, subconscious processes.**

validity. The predictive significance of a test for its intended purposes. Validity can be measured by a coefficient of correlation between scores on the test and the scores that the test seeks to predict; i.e., scores on some criterion. See also **criterion, reliability.**

variable. One of the conditions measured or controlled in an experiment. See also **dependent variable, independent variable.**

variance. The square of a standard deviation.

ventromedial hypothalamus (VMH). Area of the hypothalamus important to the regulation of food intake. Electrical stimulation of this area will make an experimental animal stop eating; destruction of brain tissue here produces voracious eating, eventually leading to obesity. See also **hypothalamus, lateral hypothalamus.**

vestibular sacs. Two sacs in the labyrinth of the inner ear, called the saccule and utricle, which contain the otoliths ("ear stones"). Pressure of the otoliths on the hair cells in the gelatinous material of the utricle and saccule gives us the sense of upright position or departure from it. See also **equilibratory senses.**

vicarious learning. Learning by observing the behavior of others and noting the consequences of that behavior (syn. *observational learning*).

visual area. A projection area lying in the occipital lobe. In humans, partial damage to this area produces blindness in portions of the visual field corresponding to the amount and location of the damage (syn. *striate area*).

visual cliff. An experimental apparatus with glass over a patterned surface, one-half of which is just below the glass and the other half, several feet below. Used to test the depth perception of animals and human infants.

visual field. The total visual array acting on the eye when it is directed toward a fixation point.

VMH. See **ventromedial hypothalamus.**

voice stress analyzer. A machine that represents graphically changes in a person's voice that occur with emotion. Used in lie detection. See also **polygraph.**

volley principle. A necessary part of the frequency theory of learning; the principle suggests that frequencies above the maximum rate at which a neuron can fire are coded by groups of neurons firing in sequence to give a net rate higher than any single group. See also **frequency theory, place theory.**

volumetric receptors. Hypothesized receptors that regulate water intake by responding to the volume of blood and body fluids. Renin, a substance secreted by the kidneys into the bloodstream, may be one volumetric receptor; it constricts the blood vessels and stimulates the release of the hormone, angiotensin, which acts on cells in the hypothalamus to produce thirst. See also **osmoreceptors.**

voluntary processes. Activities selected by choice and controlled or monitored according to intention or plan. See also **control processes.**

Weber-Fechner law. A psychophysical function stating that the perceived magnitude of a stimulus increases in proportion to the logarithm of its physical intensity.

Weber's law. A law stating that the difference threshold is proportional to the stimulus magnitude at which it is measured. The law is not accurate over the full stimulus range. See also **difference threshold.**

working through. In psychoanalytic therapy, the process of reeducation by having patients face the same conflicts over and over again in the consultation room, until they can independently face and master the conflicts in ordinary life.

X chromosome. A chromosome that, if paired with another X chromosome, determines that the individual will be a female. If it is combined with a Y chromosome, the individual will be a male. The X chromosome transmits sex-linked traits. See also **chromosome, sex-linked trait, Y chromosome.**

XYY syndrome. An abnormal condition in which a male has an extra Y sex chromosome; reputedly associated with unusual aggressiveness, although the evidence is not conclusive. See also **Y chromosome.**

Y chromosome. The chromosome that, combined with an X chromosome, determines maleness. See also **chromosome, sex-linked trait, X chromosome.**

Young-Helmholtz theory. A theory of color perception that postulates three basic color receptors, a "red" receptor, a "green" receptor, and a "blue" receptor. See also **opponent-process theory.**

zygote. A fertilized ovum or egg. See also **dizygotic twins, monozygotic twins.**

References and Index to Authors of Works Cited

The numbers in boldface following each reference give the text pages on which the paper or book is cited. Citations in the text are made by author and date of publication.

ABELSON, R., see SCHANK and ABELSON (1977).

ABELSON, R. P., ARONSON, E., MCGUIRE, W. J., NEWCOMB, T. M., ROSENBERG, M. J., and TANNENBAUM, P. H. (eds.) (1968) *Theories of cognitive consistency: A sourcebook.* Chicago: Rand McNally. **528**

ABERNATHY, E. M. (1940) The effect of changed environmental conditions upon the results of college examinations. *Journal of Psychology,* 10:293–301. **239**

ABRAHAMS, D., see WALSTER, ARONSON, ABRAHAMS, and ROTTMANN (1966).

ABRAMSON, L. Y., GARBER, J., EDWARDS, N. B., and SELIGMAN, M. E. P. (1978) Expectancy changes in depression and schizophrenia. *Journal of Abnormal Psychology,* 87:102–09. **461**

ADAMS, J. L. (1974) *Conceptual blockbusting.* Stanford, Calif.: Stanford Alumni Association. **271**

ADAMS, N. E., see BANDURA, ADAMS, and BEYER (1976).

ADOLPH, E. F. (1941) The internal environment and behavior: Water content. *American Journal of Psychiatry,* 97:1365–73. **297**

ADORNO, T., FRENKEL-BRUNSWIK, E., LEVINSON, D., and SANFORD, N. (1950) *The authoritarian personality.* New York: Harper. **552**

AGNEW, J. W., Jr., see WEBB, AGNEW, and WILLIAMS (1971).

AGRAS, S., SYLVESTER, D., and OLIVEAU, D. (1969) The epidemiology of common fears and phobia. *Comprehensive Psychiatry,* 10:151–56. **451**

AGRAS, W. S. (1975) Fears and phobias. *The Stanford Magazine,* 3:59–62. **451, 452**

AIKMAN, A., see MCQUADE and AIKMAN (1975).

AINSWORTH, M. D. S. (1973) *Anxious attachment and defensive reactions in a strange situation and their relationship to behavior at home.* Paper presented at the meeting of the Society of Research in Child Development, Philadelphia, March 30, 1973. **79**

AKERFELDT, S. (1957) Oxidation of N, N-dimethyl-p-phenylenediamine by serum from patients with mental disease. *Science,* 125:117–19. **468**

ALEXANDER, J., see MACCOBY, FARQUHAR, WOOD, and ALEXANDER (1977).

ALLEN, A., see BEM and ALLEN (1974).

ALLEN, K. E., HART, B. M., BUELL, J. S., HARRIS, F. R., and WOLF, M. M. (1964) Effects of social reinforcement on isolate behavior of a nursery school child. *Child Development,* 35:511–18. **387**

ALLEN, V. L., and LEVIN, J. M. (1971) Social support and conformity: The role of independent assessment of reality. *Journal of Experimental Social Psychology,* 7:48–58. **525**

ALLPORT, G. W. (1958) *The nature of prejudice.* New York: Doubleday-Anchor. **571**

ALMARAZ-UGALDE, A., see PARRA-COVARRUBIAS, RIVERA-RODRIGUEZ, and ALMARAZ-UGALDE (1971).

ALTMAN, I., see ZLUTNICK and ALTMAN (1972).

ALTMAN, R., see ZUCKER and ALTMAN (1973).

ALTUS, W. C. (1966) Birth order and its sequelae. *Science,* 151:44–49. **88**

AMABILE, T. M., see ROSS, AMABILE, and STEINMETZ (1977).

ANAND, B., see WENGER, BAGCHI, and ANAND (1961).

ANAND, B. K., SHARMA, K. W., and DUA, S. (1964) Activity of single neurons in the hypothalamic feeding centers: Effect of glucose. *American Journal of Physiology,* 207:1146–54. **289**

ANASTASI, A. (1976) *Psychological testing* (4th ed.). New York: Macmillan. **375**

ANDERSON, B. (1971) Thirst—and brain control of water balance. *American Scientist,* 59:408. **298**

ANDERSON, J. R. (1976) *Language, memory, and thought.* Hillsdale, N.J.: Erlbaum. **245, 249, 277**

ANDERSON, J. R., and BOWER, G. H. (1973) *Human Associative memory.* Washington, D.C.: Winston. **230, 249, 257**

ANDERSON, N. H. (1974) Cognitive algebra: Integration theory applied to social attribution. In Berkowitz, L. (ed.) *Advances in experimental social psychology,* Vol. 7. New York: Academic Press. **533**

ANDREWS, L. M., and KARLINS, M. (1971) *Requiem for democracy?* New York: Holt, Rinehart and Winston. **571**

ANGELL, J. R. (1910) *Psychology.* New York: Henry Holt. **12**

ANNIS, R. C., and FROST, B. (1973) Human visual ecology and orientation antistropies in acuity. *Science,* 182:729–31. **146**

ANTELMAN, S. M., and CAGGIULA, A. R. (1977) Norepinephrine-dopamine interactions and behavior. *Science,* 195:646–53. **468**

APPLEFIELD, J. M., see STEUER, APPLEFIELD, and SMITH (1971).

ARAKAKI, K., see KOBASIGAWA, ARAKAKI, and AWIGUNI (1966).

ARIETI, S. (1974) *Interpretation of schizophrenia* (2nd ed.). New York: Basic Books. **465**

ARKIN, A. M., TOIH, M. F., BAKER, J., and HASTEY, J. M. (1970) The frequency of sleep talking in the laboratory among chronic sleep talkers and good dream recallers. *Journal of Nervous and Mental Disease,* 151:369–74. **171**

ARONSON, E. (1976) *The social animal* (2nd ed.). San Francisco: Freeman. **527, 545**

ARONSON, E., BLANEY, N., SIKES, J., STEPHAN, C., and SNAPP, M. (1975) Busing and racial tension: The jigsaw route to learning and liking. *Psychology Today*, 8:43–50. **551**

ARONSON, E., BLANEY, N., and STEPHAN, C. (1975) *Cooperation in the classroom: The jigsaw puzzle model.* Paper presented at the meeting of the American Psychological Association, Chicago, September 1975. **551**

ARONSON, E., and CARLSMITH, J. M. (1963) The effect of the severity of threat on the devaluation of forbidden behavior. *Journal of Abnormal and Social Psychology*, 66:584–88. **528, 540**

ARONSON, E., WILLERMAN, B., and FLOYD, J. (1966) The effect of a pratfall on increasing interpersonal attractiveness. *Psychonomic Science*, 4:157–58. **535**

ARONSON, E., see ABELSON, ARONSON, MCGUIRE, NEWCOMB, ROSENBERG, and TANNENBAUM (1968).

ARONSON, E., see HELMREICH, ARONSON, and LEFAN (1970).

ARONSON, V., see WALSTER, ARONSON, ABRAHAMS, and ROTTMANN (1966).

ASCH, S. E. (1958) Effects of group pressure upon modification and distortion of judgments. In Maccoby, E. E., Newcomb, T. M., and Hartley, E. L. (eds.) *Readings in social psychology* (3rd ed.). New York: Holt, Rinehart and Winston. **524**

ASCHOFF, J. (1965) Circadian rhythm in man. *Science*, 148:1427. **166**

ATKINSON, J. W., see MCCLELLAND, ATKINSON, CLARK, and LOWELL (1953).

ATKINSON, R. C. (1975) Mnemotechnics in second-language learning. *American Psychologist*, 30:821–28. **239**

ATKINSON, R. C. (1976) Teaching children to read using a computer. *American Psychologist*, 29:169–78. **21, 214**

ATKINSON, R. C., and RAUGH, M. R. (1975) An application of the mnemonic keyword method to the acquisition of a Russian vocabulary. *Journal of Experimental Psychology: Human Learning and Memory*, 104:126–33. **239**

ATKINSON, R. C., and SHIFFRIN, R. M. (1971) The control of short-term memory. *Scientific American*, 224:82–90. **242, 243**

ATKINSON, R. C., and SHIFFRIN, R. M. (1977) Human memory: A proposed system and its control processes. In Bower, G. H. (ed.) *Human memory: Basic processes*. New York: Academic Press. **242**

ATKINSON, R. C., see DARLEY, TINKLENBERG, ROTH, HOLLISTER, and ATKINSON (1973).

ATKINSON, R. C., see JAMISON, SUPPES, FLETCHER, and ATKINSON (1976).

ATKINSON, R. C., see KRANTZ, ATKINSON, LUCE, and SUPPES (1974).

AWIGUNI, A., see KOBASIGAWA, ARAKAKI, and AWIGUNI (1966).

BADDELEY, A. D. (1976) *The psychology of memory*. New York: Basic Books. **249**

BADDELEY, A. D., and HITCH, G. (1974) Working memory. In Bower, G. H. (ed.) *The psychology of learning and motivation*, Vol. 8. New York: Academic Press. **228, 249**

BADIA, P., and CULBERTSON, S. (1972) The relative aversiveness of signalled vs. unsignalled escapable and inescapable shock. *Journal of the Experimental Analysis of Behavior*, 17:463–71. **436**

BADIA, P., CULBERTSON, S., and HARSH, J. (1973) Choice of longer or stronger signalled shock over shorter or weaker unsignalled shock. *Journal of the Experimental Analysis of Behavior*, 19:25–33. **436**

BAER, D., see ROSENFELD and BAER (1969).

BAER, D. J., and CORRADO, J. J. (1974) Heroin addict relationships with parents during childhood and early adolescent years. *Journal of Genetic Psychology*, 124:99–103. **480**

BAER, P. E., and FUHRER, M. J. (1968) Cognitive processes during differential trace and delayed conditioning of the G.S.R. *Journal of Experimental Psychology*, 78:81–88. **197**

BAGCHI, B., see WENGER and BAGCHI (1961).

BAGCHI, B., see WENGER, BAGCHI, and ANAND (1961).

BAKER, C. T., see SONTAG, BAKER, and NELSON (1958).

BAKER, J., see ARKIN, TOTH, BAKER, and HASTEY (1970).

BALDWIN, B. T., and STECHER, L. I. (1922) Mental growth curves of normal and superior children. *University of Iowa Studies in Child Welfare*, 2, No. 1. **361**

BALL, E. S., see BOSSARD and BALL (1955).

BALLOUN, J. L., see BROCK and BALLOUN (1967).

BANDURA, A. (1973) *Aggression: A social learning analysis.* Englewood Cliffs, N.J.: Prentice-Hall. **326, 343**

BANDURA, A. (1977) *Social learning theory.* Englewood Cliffs, N.J.: Prentice-Hall. **322, 343, 388, 412, 446, 494, 497, 501**

BANDURA, A., ADAMS, N. E., and BEYER, J. (1976) Cognitive processes mediating behavioral change. *Journal of Personality and Social Psychology*, 35:125–39. **497**

BANDURA, A., BLANCHARD, E. B., and RITTER, B. (1969) The relative efficacy of desensitization and modeling approaches for inducing behavioral, affective, and attitudinal changes. *Journal of Personality and Social Psychology*, 13:173–99. **496, 497**

BANDURA, A., and MCDONALD, F. J. (1963) Influence of social reinforcement and the behavior of models in shaping children's moral judgments. *Journal of Abnormal and Social Psychology*, 67:274–81. **75**

BANERJEE, S. P., see SNYDER, BANERJEE, YAMAMURA, and GREENBERG (1974).

BANYAI, E. I., and HILGARD, E. R. (1976) A comparison of active-alert hypnotic induction with traditional relaxation induction. *Journal of Abnormal Psychology*, 85:218–24. **178**

BARBEE, A. H., see SEARS and BARBEE (1977).

BARBER, T. X. (1961) Antisocial and criminal acts induced by hypnosis: A review of experimental and clinical findings. *Archives of General Psychiatry*, 5:301–12. **180**

BARBER, T. X. (1969) *Hypnosis: A scientific approach.* New York: Van Nostrand Reinhold. **181, 187**

BARBER, T. X., see SPANOS and BARBER (1974).

BARCLAY, J. R., see BRANSFORD, BARCLAY, and FRANKS (1972).

BARD, P. (1934) The neurohumoral basis of emotional reactions. In Murchison, C. A. (ed.) *Handbook of general experimental psychology*. Worcester, Mass.: Clark Univ. Press. **334**

BARDWICK, J. M. (1971) *Psychology of women: A study of bio-cultural conflicts.* New York: Harper and Row. **305, 308**

BARKER, C. H., see SCHEIN, SCHNEIER, and BARKER (1961).

BARKER, R. G., DEMBO, T., and LEWIN, K. (1941) Frustration and regression: An experiment with young children, *University of Iowa Studies in Child Welfare*, 18, No. 386. **420**

BARKER, W. B., see SCARR, PAKSTIS, KATZ, and BARKER (1977).

BARLOW, H. B. (1975) Visual experiences and cortical development. *Nature*, 258:199–204. **146**

BARNES, P. J., see BEAMAN, BARNES, KLENTZ, and MCQUIRK (1978).

BARON, R. A., and LAWTON, S. F. (1972) Environmental influences on aggression: The facilitation of modeling effects by high ambient temperatures. *Psychonomic Science*, 26:80–82. **322**

BARTLETT, F. C. (1932) *Remembering: A study in experimental and social psychology*. Cambridge, England: Cambridge Univ. Press. **247**

BATEMAN, F., see SOAL and BATEMAN (1954).

BAUM, A., and VALINS, S. (1977) *Architecture and social behavior: Psychological studies of social density*. Hillsdale, N.J.: Erlbaum. **562, 563**

BAUM, A., see RODIN and BAUM (1978).

BAUMRIND, D. (1967) Child care practices anteceding three patterns of preschool behavior. *Genetic Psychology Monographs*, 75:43–88. **83**

BAUMRIND, D. (1972) Socialization and instrumental competence in young children. In Hartup, W. W. (ed.) *The young child: Reviews of research*, Vol. 2. Washington, D.C.: National Association for the Education of Young Children, pp. 202–24. **83**

BAYLEY, N. (1970) Development of mental abilities. In Mussen, P. (ed.) *Carmichael's manual of child psychology*. New York: Wiley, 1:1163–1209. **363, 367**

BEACH, F. A. (1941) Female mating behavior shown by male rats after administration of testosterone propionate. *Endocrinology*, 29:409–12. **301**

REFERENCES AND INDEX TO AUTHORS OF WORKS CITED

BEACH, F. A. (ed.) (1977) *Human sexuality in four perspectives*. Baltimore: Johns Hopkins Univ. Press. **313**

BEACH, F. A., see FORD and BEACH (1951).

BEAMAN, A. L., BARNES, P. J., KLENTZ, B., and MCQUIRK, B. (1978) Increasing helping rates through information dissemination: Teaching pays. *Personality and Social Psychology Bulletin*, 4:406–11. **523**

BEAN, L. L., see MYERS and BEAN (1968).

BECKLEN, R., see NEISSER and BECKLEN (1975).

BEE, H. (1978). *The developing child* (2nd ed.) New York: Harper and Row. **99**

BEE, H. (ed.) (1974) *Social issues in developmental psychology*. New York: Harper and Row. **81**

BEE, H. L., see MACCOBY and BEE (1965).

BEERS, C. W. (1908) *A mind that found itself*. New York: Doubleday. **489**

BELENKY, G. L. (1976) Paper presented to the Potomac Chapter of the Society of Neuroscience, symposium on electroconvulsive therapy, Potomac, Md., February 1976. **508**

BELL, A. P., and WEINBERG, M. S. (1978) *Homosexualities*. New York: Simon and Schuster. **442**

BELLUGI, U., see BROWN, CAZDEN, and BELLUGI (1969).

BEM, D. J. (1967) Self-perception: An alternative interpretation of cognitive dissonance phenomena. *Psychological Review*, 74:183–200. **540**

BEM, D. J. (1970) *Beliefs, attitudes and human affairs*. Belmont, Calif.: Brooks/Cole. **545, 555**

BEM, D. J. (1972) Self-perception theory. *Advances in Experimental Social Psychology*. New York: Academic Press, 6:1–62. **539, 540, 541**

BEM, D. J., and ALLEN, A. (1974) On predicting some of the people some of the time: The search for cross-situational consistencies in behavior. *Psychological Review*, 81:506–20. **408**

BEM, D. J., see BEM and BEM (1977).

BEM, S. L., and BEM, D. J. (1977) Homogenizing the American woman: The power of an unconscious ideology. In Zimbardo, P., and Maslach, C. (eds.) *Psychology for our times* (2nd ed.). Glenview, Ill.: Scott, Foresman. **549**

BENDFELDT, F., see LUDWIG, BRANDSMA, WILBUR, BENDFELDT, and JAMESON (1972).

BENJAMIN, B., see PARKES, BENJAMIN, and FITZGERALD (1969).

BENNETT, E. L., see ROSENZWEIG and BENNETT (1976).

BENSON, H. (1975) *The relaxation response*. New York: Morrow. **171, 172**

BENSON, H., KOTCH, J. B., CRASSWELLER, K. D., and GREENWOOD, M. M. (1977) Historical and clinical considerations of the relaxation response. *American Scientist*, 65:441–45. **171, 172**

BERELSON, B., LAZARSFELD, P. F., and MCPHEE, W. N. (1954) *Voting: A study of opinion formation in a presidential campaign*. Chicago: Univ. of Chicago Press. **556**

BERGER, P. A. (1978) Medical treatment of mental illness. *Science*, 200:974–81. **461**

BERGER, R. J. (1963) Experimental modification of dream content by meaningful verbal stimuli. *British Journal of Psychiatry*, 109:722–40. **170**

BERGIN, A. E., see GARFIELD and BERGIN (1978).

BERKOWITZ, L., see LEYENS, CAMINO, PARKE, and BERKOWITZ (1975).

BERKOWITZ, L., see PARKE, BERKOWITZ, LEYENS, WEST, and SEBASTIAN (1977).

BERLIN, B., and KAY, P. (1969) *Basic color terms: Their universality and evolution*. Berkeley and Los Angeles: Univ. of California Press. **255**

BERNSTEIN, D. R., see PAUL and BERNSTEIN (1973).

BERNSTEIN, M. (1956) *The search for Bridey Murphy*. New York: Doubleday. **184**

BERSCHEID, E., and WALSTER, E. (1974) Physical attractiveness. In Berkowitz, L. (ed.) *Advances in experimental social psychology*. New York: Academic Press. **534**

BERSCHEID, E., see DION and BERSCHEID (1972).

BERZINS, J. I., ROSS, W. F., ENGLISH, G. E., and HALEY, J. V. (1974) Subgroups among opiate addicts: A typological investigation. *Journal of Abnormal and Social Psychology*, 83:65–73. **480**

BEVER, T. G., see FODOR, BEVER, and GARRETT (1974).

BEYER, J., see BANDURA, ADAMS, and BEYER (1976).

BIEHLER, R. F. (1976) *Child development: An introduction*. Boston: Houghton Mifflin. **99**

BIERBRAUER, G. A. (1973) *Attribution and perspective: Effects of time, set, and role on interpersonal inference*. Unpublished doctoral dissertation, Stanford Univ., Stanford, Calif. **527**

BILLIARD, M., see GUILLEMINAULT, BILLIARD, MONTPLAISAR, and DEMENT (1975).

BILLINGSLEY, A. (1968) *Black families in white America*. Englewood Cliffs, N.J.: Prentice-Hall. **566**

BINET, A., and SIMON, T. (1905) New methods for the diagnosis of the intellectual level of subnormals. *Annals of Psychology*, 11:191. **357**

BIRDSALL, T. G., see GREEN and BIRDSALL (1978).

BISHOP, G. D., see HAMILTON and BISHOP (1976).

BLAKEMORE, C. (1974) Developmental factors in the formation of feature extracting neurons. In Schmitt, F. O., and Worden, F. G. (eds.) *The neurosciences: Third study program*. Cambridge, Mass.: M.I.T. Press. **146**

BLAKEMORE, C. (1977) *Mechanics of the mind*. New York: Cambridge Univ. Press. **61**

BLANCHARD, E. B., see BANDURA, BLANCHARD, and RITTER (1969).

BLANCHARD, F. A., WEIGEL, R. H., and COOK, S. W. (1975) The effect of relative competence of group members upon interpersonal attraction in cooperating interracial groups. *Journal of Personality and Social Psychology*, 32:519–30. **550**

BLANEY, N., see ARONSON, BLANEY, SIKES, STEPHAN, and SNAPP (1975).

BLANEY, N., see ARONSON, BLANEY, and STEPHAN (1975).

BLOCK, J. (1971) *Lives through time*. Berkeley, Calif.: Bancroft Books. **406, 407**

BLOCK, J. (1977) Recognizing the coherence of personality. In Magnusson, D., and Endler, N. S. (eds.) *Interactional psychology: Current issues and future prospects*. New York: LEA/Wiley. **408**

BLOCK, N. J., and DWORKIN, G. (eds.) (1976) *The IQ controversy*. New York: Pantheon. **367, 375**

BLOOM, F., SEGAL, D., LING, N., and GUILLEMIN, R. (1976) Endorphins: Profound behavioral effects in rats suggest new etiological factors in mental illness. *Science*, 194:630–32. **469**

BLOOM, L. M., HOOD, L., and LIGHTBOWN, P. (1974) Imitation in language development: If, when and why. *Cognitive Psychology*, 6:380–420 **265**

BLUM, R. H., and ASSOCIATES (1969) *Society and drugs: Social and cultural observations*. Behavioral science series, Vol. 1. San Francisco: Jossey-Bass. **480**

BLUM, R. H., and ASSOCIATES (1969) *Students and drugs: College and high school observations*. Behavioral science series, Vol. 2. San Francisco: Jossey-Bass. **187**

BLUM, R., and ASSOCIATES (1972) *Horatio Alger's children*. San Francisco: Jossey-Bass. **480**

BOBROW, D. G., and COLLINS, A. (eds.) (1975) *Representation and understanding: Studies in cognitive science*. New York: Academic Press. **277**

BODEN, M. (1977) *Artificial intelligence and natural man*. New York: Basic Books. **155**

BOEHM, V. R. (1968) Mr. Prejudice, Miss Sympathy, and the authoritarian personality: An application of psychological measuring techniques to the problem of jury bias. *Wisconsin Law Review*, pp. 734–50. **569**

BOLLES, R. C. (1975) *Theory of motivation* (2nd ed.). New York: Harper and Row. **281, 313, 343**

BONNO, B., see LEVENSON, BURFORD, BONNO, and LOREN (1975).

BOOTH, A., and WELCH, S. (1973) *The effects of crowding: A cross-national study*. Unpublished manuscript, Ministry of State of Urban Affairs, Ottawa. **561**

BOOTH, A., and WELCH, S. (1974) *Crowding and urban crime rates*. Paper presented at the meeting of the Midwest Sociological Association, Omaha. **561**

BORING, E. G., LANGFELD, H. S., and WELD, H. P. (1939) *Introduction to psychology.* New York: Wiley. **12**

BORK, A. (1978) Machines for computer-assisted learning. *Educational Technology,* 18:17–19. **215**

BOSSARD, J. H. S., and BALL, E. S. (1955) Personality roles in the family. *Child Development,* 26:71–78. **88**

BOUCHARD, T. J. (1976) Genetic factors in intelligence. In Kaplan, A. R. (ed.) *Human behavior genetics.* Springfield, Ill.: Charles Thomas, 164–95. **365**

BOURNE, L. E., Jr. (1966) *Human conceptual behavior.* Boston: Allyn and Bacon. **256**

BOUSFIELD, W. A. (1953) The occurrence of clustering in the recall of randomly arranged associates. *Journal of General Psychology,* 49:229–40. **234**

BOWER, G. H. (1972) Mental imagery and associative learning. In Gregg, L. W. (ed.) *Cognition in learning and memory.* New York: Wiley. **229**

BOWER, G. H. (ed.) (1977) *Human memory: Basic processes.* New York: Academic Press. **249**

BOWER, G. H., and CLARK, M. C. (1969) Narrative stories as mediators for serial learning. *Psychonomic Science,* 14:181–82. **240**

BOWER, G. H., CLARK, M., WINZENZ, D., and LESGOLD, A. (1969) Hierarchical retrieval schemes in recall of categorized word lists. *Journal of Verbal Learning and Verbal Behavior,* 8:323–43. **234**

BOWER, G. H., and SPRINGSTON, F. (1970) Pauses as recoding points in letter series. *Journal of Experimental Psychology,* 83:421–30. **226**

BOWER, G. H., see ANDERSON and BOWER (1973).

BOWER, G. H., see BOWER and BOWER (1976).

BOWER, G. H., see HILGARD and BOWER (1975).

BOWER, S. A., and BOWER, G. H. (1976) *Asserting yourself.* Reading, Mass.: Addison-Wesley. **515**

BOWERS, K. S. (1967) The effect of demands for honesty upon reports of visual and auditory hallucinations. *International Journal of Clinical and Experimental Hypnosis,* 15:31–36. **181**

BOWERS, K. S. (1976) *Hypnosis for the seriously curious.* Monterey, Calif.: Brooks/Cole. **187**

BOWLBY, J. (1973) *Separation.* Attachment and loss, Vol. 2. New York: Basic Books. **76, 78**

BRACKBILL, Y. (1958) Extinction of the smiling response in infants as a function of reinforcement schedule. *Child Development,* 29:115–24. **76**

BRADY, J. V., PORTER, R. W., CONRAD, D. G., and MASON, J. W. (1958) Avoidance behavior and the development of gastroduodenal ulcers. *Journal of the Experimental Analysis of Behavior,* 1:69–73. **432**

BRAINE, M. D. S. (1976) Children's first word combinations. *Monographs of the Society for Research in Child Development,* 41 (Serial No. 164). **262**

BRANDSMA, J. M., see LUDWIG, BRANDSMA, WILBUR, BENDFELDT, and JAMESON (1972).

BRANDT, U., see EYFERTH, BRANDT, and WOLFGANG (1960).

BRANSFORD, J. D., BARCLAY, J. R., and FRANKS, J. J. (1972) Sentence memory: A constructive versus interpretive approach. *Cognitive Psychology,* 3:193–209. **245**

BRANSFORD, J. D., and JOHNSON, M. K. (1973) Considerations of some problems of comprehension. In Chase, W. G. (ed.) *Visual information processing.* New York: Academic Press. **248**

BRELAND, K., and BRELAND, M. (1966) *Animal behavior.* New York: Macmillan. **202**

BRELAND, M., see BRELAND and BRELAND (1966).

BRENT, E. E., see GRANBERG and BRENT (1974).

BRICKER, W. A., see PATTERSON, LITTMAN, and BRICKER (1967).

BRIGGS, J. L. (1970) *Never in anger.* Cambridge, Mass.: Harvard Univ. Press. **64**

BRIGHAM, C. C. (1923) *A study of American intelligence.* Princeton, N.J.: Princeton Univ. Press. **565**

BRIGHAM, C. C. (1930) Intelligence of immigrant groups. *Psychological Review,* 37:158–65. **566**

BRIM, O.G., Jr. (1965) American attitudes toward intelligence tests. *American Psychologist,* 20:125–30. **372, 373**

BRISLIN, R.W., and LEWIS, S. A. (1968) Dating and physical attractiveness: Replication. *Psychological Reports,* 22:976. **534**

BROADBENT, D. E. (1957) Effects of noise on behavior. In Harris, C. M. (ed.) *Handbook of noise control.* New York: McGraw-Hill. **559**

BROCA, P. (1861) *Sur le volume et la forme du cerveau suivant les individus et suivant les races.* Paris: Hennuyer. **40**

BROCK, T. C., and BALLOUN, J. L. (1967) Behavioral receptivity to dissonant information. *Journal of Personality and Social Psychology,* 6:413–28. **556**

BRODIE, M., see TESSER and BRODIE (1971).

BRODY, E. B., and BRODY, N. (eds.) (1976) *Intelligence: Nature, determinants, and consequences.* New York: Academic Press. **375**

BRODY, N., see BRODY and BRODY (1976).

BROOK, D. W., see JERSILD, BROOK, and BROOK (1978).

BROOK, J. S., see JERSILD, BROOK, and BROOK (1978).

BROTZMAN, E., see HOFLING, BROTZMAN, DALRYMPLE, GRAVES, and PIERCE (1966).

BROWN, J. N., and CARTWRIGHT, R. D. (1978) Locating NREM dreaming through instrumental responses. *Psychophysiology,* 15:35–39. **171**

BROWN, R. (1973) *A first language: The early stages.* Cambridge, Mass.: Harvard Univ. Press. **264, 277**

BROWN, R., CAZDEN, C. B., and BELLUGI, U. (1969) The child's grammar from I to III. In Hill, J. P. (ed.) *Minnesota symposium on child psychology,* Vol. 2. Minneapolis: Univ. of Minnesota Press. **265**

BROWN, R., see SACHS, BROWN, and SALERNO (1976).

BROWN, R. W., and MCNEILL, D. (1966) The "tip-of-the-tongue" phenomenon. *Journal of Verbal Learning and Verbal Behavior,* 5:325–37. **231**

BRUNER, J. S. (1978) Learning the mother tongue. *Human Nature,* 1:42–49. **262**

BRYAN, J. H., and TEST, M. A. (1967) Models and helping: Naturalistic studies in aiding behavior. *Journal of Personality and Social Psychology,* 6:400–07. **523**

BUELL, J. S., see ALLEN, HART, BUELL, HARRIS, and WOLF (1964).

BUGELSKI, R., see MILLER and BUGELSKI (1948).

BURFORD, B., see LEVENSON, BURFORD, BONNO, and LOREN (1975).

BURTON, M. J., see ROLLS, BURTON, and MORA (1976).

BUSCHKE, H., see KINTSCH and BUSCHKE (1969).

BUSS, A. H. (1966a) Instrumentality of aggression, feedback, and frustration as determinants of physical aggression. *Journal of Personality and Social Psychology,* 3:153–62. **326**

BUSS, A. H. (1966b) *Psychopathology.* New York: Wiley. **474**

BUSS, A. H., and PLOMIN, R. (1975) *A temperament theory of personality development.* New York: Wiley. **378**

BUTCHER, H. J. (1973) *Human intelligence: Its nature and assessment.* London: Methuen. **375**

BYRNE, D. (1971) *The attraction paradigm.* New York: Academic Press. **535**

CAGGIULA, A. R. (1967) Specificity of copulation reward systems in the posterior hypothalamus. *Proceedings of the 75th Convention, American Psychological Association,* 125–26. **302**

CAGGIULA, A. R., and HOEBEL, B. G. (1966) A "copulation-reward site" in the posterior hypothalamus. *Science,* 153:1284–85. **302**

CAGGIULA, A. R., see ANTELMAN and CAGGIULA (1977).

CALDER, N. (1971) *The mind of man.* New York: Viking. **183**

CALHOUN, J. B. (1962) Population density and social pathology. *Scientific American,* 206:139–48. **560**

CAMINO, L., see LEYENS, CAMINO, PARKE, and BERKOWITZ (1975).

CAMPBELL, H. J. (1973) *The pleasure areas.* London: Eyre Methuen. **208**

CANNON, W. B. (1927) The James-Lange theory of emotions: A critical examination and an alternative theory. *American Journal of Psychology,* 39:106–24. **333**

CANTER, D., and CANTER, S. (1971) Close together in Tokyo. *Design and Environment,* 2:60–63. **561**

CANTER, S., see CANTER and CANTER (1971).

CARLSMITH, J. M., see ARONSON and CARLSMITH (1963).

CARLSMITH, J. M., see FESTINGER and CARLSMITH (1959).

CARLSMITH, J. M., see FREEDMAN, SEARS, and CARLSMITH (1978).

CARLSON, N. R. (1977) *Physiology of behavior.* Boston, Mass.: Allyn and Bacon. **61, 313**

CARSKADON, M. A., MITLER, M. M., and DEMENT, W. C. (1974) A comparison of insomniacs and normals: Total sleep time and sleep latency. *Sleep Research,* 3:130. **167**

CARTERETTE, E. C., and FRIEDMAN, M. P. (eds.) (1975) *Historical and philosophical roots of perception.* Handbook of perception, Vol. 1. New York: Academic Press. **127, 155**

CARTERETTE, E. C., and FRIEDMAN, M. P. (eds.) (1975) *Psychophysical judgment and measurement.* Handbook of perception, Vol. II. New York: Academic Press. **127, 155**

CARTERETTE, E. C., and FRIEDMAN, M. P. (eds.) (1975) *Biology of perceptual systems.* Handbook of perception, Vol. III. New York: Academic Press. **127, 155**

CARTERETTE, E. C., and FRIEDMAN, M. P. (eds.) (1977) *Seeing.* Handbook of perception, Vol. V. New York: Academic Press. **127, 155**

CARTERETTE, E. C., and FRIEDMAN, M. P. (eds.) (1977) *Language and speech.* Handbook of perception, Vol. VII. New York: Academic Press. **127, 155**

CARTERETTE, E. C., and FRIEDMAN, M. P. (eds.) (1978) *Hearing.* Handbook of perception, Vol. IV. New York: Academic Press. **127, 155**

CARTERETTE, E. C., and FRIEDMAN, M. P. (eds.) (1978) *Tasting and smelling.* Handbook of perception, Vol. VIa. New York: Academic Press. **127, 155**

CARTERETTE, E. C., and FRIEDMAN, M. P. (eds.) (1978) *Space and object perception.* Handbook of perception, Vol. VIII. New York: Academic Press. **127, 155**

CARTERETTE, E. C., and FRIEDMAN, M. P. (eds.) (1978) *Perceptual processing.* Handbook of perception, Vol. IX. New York: Academic Press. **127, 155**

CARTERETTE, E. C., and FRIEDMAN, M. P. (eds.) (1978) *Perceptual ecology.* Handbook of perception, Vol. X. New York: Academic Press. **127, 155**

CARTERETTE, E. C., and FRIEDMAN, M. P. (eds.) (1979) *Feeling and hurting.* Handbook of perception, Vol. VIb. New York: Academic Press. **127, 155**

CARTWRIGHT, R. D. (1978) *A primer on sleep and dreaming.* Reading, Mass.: Addison-Wesley. **167, 186**

CARTWRIGHT, R. D., and RATZEL, R. W. (1972) Effects of dream loss on waking behavior. *Archives of General Psychiatry,* 27:277–80. **170**

CARTWRIGHT, R. D., see BROWN and CARTWRIGHT (1978).

CARTWRIGHT, R. D., see WEBB and CARTWRIGHT (1978).

CASSEM, N. H., see HACKETT and CASSEM (1970).

CATALAN, J., see CIALDINI, VINCENT, LEWIS, CATALAN, WHEELER, and DARBY (1975).

CATTELL, R. B. (1949) *The culture free intelligence test.* Champaign, Ill.: Institute for Personality and Ability Testing. **352**

CATTELL, R. B. (1973) Personality pinned down. *Psychology Today,* 7:40–46. **383**

CAZDEN, C. B., see BROWN, CAZDEN, and BELLUGI (1969).

CHALL, J. S., and MIRSKY, A. F. (eds.) (1978) *Education and the brain* (77th Year Book, National Society for the Study of Education, Part II). Chicago: Univ. of Chicago Press. **61**

CHANCE, J. E., see ROTTER, CHANCE, and PHARES (1972).

CHAPMAN, J., see MCGHIE and CHAPMAN (1961).

CHAUDHURI, H. (1965) *Philosophy of meditation.* New York: Philosophical Library. **187**

CHEIN, I., GERARD, D. L., LEE, R. S., and ROSENFELD, E. (1964) *The road to H.* New York: Basic Books. **174**

CHESS, S., see THOMAS and CHESS (1977).

CHICAGO TRIBUNE, February 6, 1976. **531**

CHINLUND, S. (1969) The female addict. *Science News,* 95:578. **480**

CHIPMAN, S., see SHEPARD and CHIPMAN (1970).

CHOMSKY, N. (1965) *Aspects of the theory of syntax.* Cambridge, Mass.: M.I.T. Press. **261**

CHOMSKY, N. (1972) *Language and mind* (2nd ed.). New York: Harcourt Brace Jovanovich. **277**

CHOMSKY, N. (1976) The fallacy of Richard Herrnstein's IQ. In Block, N. J., and Dworkin, G. (eds.) *The IQ controversy.* New York: Pantheon. **366**

CHRISTIAN, J. J., FLYGER, V., and DAVIS, D. (1960) Factors in the mass mortality of a herd of sika deer *carvus nippon. Chesapeake Science,* 1:79–95. **560**

CHRISTIE, R., and JAHODA, M. (eds.) (1954) *Studies in the scope and method of "The Authoritarian Personality."* New York: Free Press. **553**

CHRISTIE, R., see SHULMAN, SHAVER, COLMAN, EMRICH, and CHRISTIE (1973).

CHUTE, D., see HO, CHUTE, and RICHARDS (1977).

CIALDINI, R. B., VINCENT, J. E., LEWIS, S. K., CATALAN, J., WHEELER, D., and DARBY, B. L. (1975) Reciprocal concessions procedure for inducing compliance: The door-in-the-face technique. *Journal of Personality and Social Psychology,* 31:206–15. **541**

CLARK, E. V. (1973) What's in a word? On the child's acquisition of semantics in his first language. In Moore, T. E. (ed.) *Cognitive development and the acquisition of language.* New York: Academic Press. **255**

CLARK, E. V. (1977) Non-linguistic strategies and the acquisition of word meanings. *Cognition,* 2:161–82. **256**

CLARK, E. V., see CLARK and CLARK (1977).

CLARK, G. R., KIVITZ, M. S., and ROSEN, M. (1969) Program for mentally retarded. *Science News,* 96:82. **370**

CLARK, H. H., and CLARK, E. V. (1977) *Psychology and language: An introduction to psycholinguistics.* New York: Harcourt Brace Jovanovich. **258, 277**

CLARK, K. E., and MILLER, G. A. (eds.) (1970) *Psychology: Behavioral and social sciences survey committee.* Englewood Cliffs, N.J.: Prentice-Hall. **12, 25**

CLARK, M., see BOWER, CLARK, WINZENZ, and LESGOLD (1969).

CLARK, M. C., see BOWER and CLARK (1969).

CLARK, R. A., see MCCLELLAND, ATKINSON, CLARK, and LOWELL (1953).

CLAYTON, K. N. (1964) T-maze choice-learning as a joint function of the reward magnitudes of the alternatives. *Journal of Comparative and Physiological Psychology,* 58:333–38. **205**

CLECKLEY, H., see THIGPEN and CLECKLEY (1957).

CLINE, V. B., CROFT, R. C., and COURRIER, S. (1973) The desensitization of children to television violence. *Journal of Personality and Social Psychology,* 27:360–65. **328**

CLORE, G. L., see WIGGINS, RENNER, CLORE, and ROSE (1976).

COATES, B., see HARTUP and COATES (1967).

COE, W. C. (1977) The problem of relevance versus ethics in researching hypnosis and antisocial conduct. *Annals of the New York Academy of Sciences,* 296:90–104. **180**

COE, W. C., see SARBIN and COE (1972).

COFER, C. N. (1972) *Motivation and emotion.* Glenview, Ill.: Scott, Foresman. **281**

COHEN, H. D., see EVANS, COOK, COHEN, ORNE, and ORNE (1977).

COHEN, S., GLASS, D. C., and SINGER, J. E. (1973) Apartment noise, auditory discrimination, and reading ability in children. *Journal of Experimental Social Psychology,* 9:407–22. **560**

COLBY, K. M., see SCHANK and COLBY (1973).

COLE, H. H., HART, G. H., and MILLER, R. F. (1956) Studies on the hormonal control of estrous phenomena in the anestrous ewe. *Endocrinology,* 36:370–80. **301**

COLEMAN, J. (1976) *Abnormal psychology and modern life* (5th ed.). New York: Scott, Foresman. **439, 449, 456, 485**

COLLINS, A., see BOBROW and COLLINS (1975).

COLLINS, A. M., and QUILLIAN, M. R. (1969) Retrieval time from semantic memory. *Journal of Verbal Learning and Verbal Behavior,* 8:240–48. **253**

COLLINS, M. E., see DEUTSCH and COLLINS (1951).

COLMAN, R., see SHULMAN, SHAVER,

COLMAN, EMRICH, and CHRISTIE (1973).

CONGER, J. J. (1977) *Adolescence and youth: Psychological development in a changing world* (2nd ed.). New York: Harper and Row. **99**

CONGER, J. J., see MUSSEN, CONGER, and KAGAN (1974).

CONGER, J. J., see SAWREY, CONGER, and TURRELL (1956).

CONRAD, D. G., see BRADY, PORTER, CONRAD, and MASON (1958).

CONRAD, R. (1964) Acoustic confusions in immediate memory. *British Journal of Psychology*, 55:75–84. **223**

CONSUMERS UNION (1974) *The medicine show* (rev. ed.). Mount Vernon, N.Y.: Consumers Union of U.S. **555**

COOK, M. R., see EVANS, COOK, COHEN, ORNE, and ORNE (1977).

COOK, S. W. (1970) Motives in a conceptual analysis of attitude-related behavior. In Arnold, W. J., and Levine, D. (eds.) *Nebraska symposium on motivation, 1969.* Lincoln: Univ. of Nebraska Press. **551**

COOK, S. W. (1978) Interpersonal and attitudinal outcomes in cooperating interracial groups. *Journal of Research and Development in Education*, 12. **551**

COOK, S. W., see BLANCHARD, WEIGEL, and COOK (1975).

COOK, S. W., see KORTEN, COOK, and LACEY (1970).

COOK, S. W., see WEIGEL, WISER, and COOK (1975).

COOK, S. W., see WILNER, WALKLEY, and COOK (1955).

COOPER, F., see LIBERMAN, COOPER, SHANKWEILER, and STUDDERT-KENNEDY (1967).

COOPER, J., see FAZIO, ZANNA, and COOPER (1977).

COOPER, L. A., and SHEPARD, R. N. (1973) Chronometric studies of the rotation of mental images. In Chase, W. G. (ed.) *Visual information processing.* New York: Academic Press. **272, 273**

COOPER, L. M., (1979) Hypnotic amnesia. In Fromm, E., and Shor, R. E. (eds.) *Hypnosis: Developments in research and new perspectives* (2nd ed.) Hawthorne, N.Y. Aldine. **179**

CORNELISON, A. R., see LIDZ, FLECK, and CORNELISON (1965).

CORNSWEET, T. N. (1970) *Visual perception.* New York: Academic Press. **117**

CORRADO, J. J., see BAER and CORRADO (1974).

COSTA, P., see MADDI and COSTA (1972).

COURRIER, S., see CLINE, CROFT, and COURRIER (1973).

COX, M., see HETHERINGTON, COX, and COX (1978).

COX, R., see HETHERINGTON, COX, and COX (1978).

CRAIK, F. I. M. (1977) Depth of processing in recall and recognition. In Dornic, S. (ed.) *Attention and performance VI.* Hillsdale, N.J.: Erlbaum. **231**

CRAIK, F. I. M. (1979) Human memory. *Annual Review of Psychology*, 30:63–102. **245**

CRAIK, F. I. M., and LOCKHART, R. S. (1972) Levels of processing: A framework for memory research. *Journal of Verbal Learning and Verbal Behavior*, 11:671–84. **245**

CRAIK, F. I. M., and WATKINS, M. J. (1973) The role of rehearsal in short-term memory. *Journal of Verbal Learning and Verbal Behavior*, 12:599–607. **244**

CRAIK, K. (1952) *The nature of explanation.* Cambridge, England: Cambridge Univ. Press. **7**

CRASSWELLER, K. D., see BENSON, KOTCH, CRASSWELLER, and GREENWOOD (1977).

CRISTOL, A. H., see SLOANE, STAPLES, CRISTOL, YORKSTON, and WHIPPLE (1975).

CROCKENBURG, S. B. (1972) Creativity tests: A boon or boondoggle for education? *Review of Educational Research*, 42:27–45. **361**

CROFT, R. C., see CLINE, CROFT, and COURRIER (1973).

CRONBACH, L. J. (1970) *Essentials of psychological testing* (3rd. ed.). New York: Harper and Row. **375, 413**

CROWDER, R. G. (1976) *Principles of learning and memory.* Hillsdale, N.J.: Erlbaum. **219, 249**

CRUTCHFIELD, L., see KNOX, CRUTCHFIELD, and HILGARD (1975).

CULBERTSON, S., see BADIA and CULBERTSON (1972).

CULBERTSON, S., see BADIA, CULBERTSON, and HARSH (1973).

CUNNINGHAM, M. R., see SNYDER and CUNNINGHAM (1975).

DABNEY, V. (1957) The violence at Little Rock. *Diamond Times Dispatch*, September 24, 1957. **564**

DALE, L. A., see WOLMAN, DALE, SCHMEIDLER, and ULLMAN (1977).

DALRYMPLE, S., see HOFLING, BROTZMAN, DALRYMPLE, GRAVES, and PIERCE (1966).

D'ANDRADE, R. C. (1967) *Report on some testing and training procedures at Bassawa Primary School, Zaria, Nigeria.* Unpublished manuscript. **352**

DANKS, J. H., see GLUCKSBERG and DANKS (1975).

DARBY, B. L., see CIALDINI, VINCENT, LEWIS, CATALAN, WHEELER, and DARBY (1975).

DARLEY, C. F., TINKLENBERG, J. R., ROTH, W. T., HOLLISTER, L. E., and ATKINSON, R. C. (1973) Influence of marihuana on storage and retrieval processes in memory. *Memory and Cognition*, 1:196–200. **17**

DARLEY, J. M., and LATANE, B. (1968) Bystander intervention in emergencies: Diffusion of responsibility. *Journal of Personality and Social Psychology* 8:377–83. **522**

DARLEY, J. M., see LATANÉ, and DARLEY (1968).

DARLEY, J. M., see LATANÉ, and DARLEY (1970).

DARWIN, C. (1872) *The expression of emotions in man and animals.* New York: Philosophical Library. **339**

DAVIS, A., and EELLS, K. (1953) *Davis-Eells games.* Yonkers, New York: World Book. **352**

DAVIS, A., see EELLS, DAVIS, HAVIGHURST, HERRICK, and TYLER (1951).

DAVIS, B., see STUART and DAVIS (1972).

DAVIS, D., see CHRISTIAN, FLYGER, and DAVIS (1960).

DAVIS, D., see KRAUSS and DAVIS (1976).

DAVIS, K. E., see JONES and DAVIS (1965).

DAVIS, K. E., see KERCKHOFF and DAVIS (1962).

DAVIS, K. L., MOHS, R. C., TINKLENBERG, J. R., PFEFFERBAUM, A., HOLLISTER, L. E., and KOPELL, B. S. (1978) Physostigmine: Improvement of long term memory processes in normal humans. *Science*, 201:272–74. **34**

DAVIS, W. N., see MCCLELLAND, DAVIS, KALIN, and WANNER (1972).

DAVISON, G. C., and NEALE, J. M. (1978) *Abnormal psychology* (2nd ed.). New York: Wiley. **485**

DAVISON, G. C., see GOLDFRIED and DAVISON (1976).

DAVISON, L., see SPEISMAN, LAZARUS, MORDKOFF, and DAVISON (1964).

DEAN, P. M. (1978) Computer-assisted instruction authoring systems. *Educational Technology*, 18:2–23. **215**

DEAN, S. R. (1970) Is there an ultraconscious beyond the unconscious? *Canadian Psychiatric Association Journal*, 15:57–61. **172**

DE CHARMS, R., and WILKINS, E. J. (1963) Some effects of verbal expression of hostility. *Journal of Abnormal and Social Psychology*, 66:462–70. **328**

DECKNER, C. W., see ROGERS and DECKNER (1975).

DEFRIES, J. C., see MCCLEARN and DEFRIES (1973).

DEKIRMENJIAN, H., see JONES, MAAS, DEKIRMENJIAN, and FAWCETT (1973).

DELGADO, J. M. R., ROBERTS, W. W., and MILLER, N. E. (1954) Learning motivated by electrical stimulation of the brain. *American Journal of Physiology*, 179:587–93. **206, 321**

DE LUCIA, L. A. (1963) The toy preference test: A measure of sex-role identification. *Child Development*, 34:107–17. **85**

DEMBO, T., see BARKER, DEMBO, and LEWIN (1941).

DEMENT, W. C. (1976) *Some must watch while some must sleep.* New York: Simon and Schuster. **186**

DEMENT, W., and KLEITMAN, N. (1957) The relation of eye movements during sleep to dream activity: An objective method for the study of dreaming. *Journal of Experimental Psychology*, 53:339–46. **166**

DEMENT, W., and WOLPERT, E. (1958) The relation of eye movements, bodily motility, and external stimuli to dream content. *Journal of Experimental Psychology*, 55:543–53. **170**

REFERENCES AND INDEX TO AUTHORS OF WORKS CITED

DEMENT, W. C., see CARSKADON, MITLER, and DEMENT (1974).

DEMENT, W. C., see GUILLEMINAULT, BILLIARD, MONTPLAISAR, and DEMENT (1975).

DEMENT, W., see MITLER and DEMENT (1977).

DENNIS, W. (1960) Causes of retardation among institutional children: Iran. *Journal of Genetic Psychology*, 96:47–59. **68**

DENNIS, W. (1973) *Children of the crèche*. Englewood Cliffs, N.J.: Prentice-Hall. **69**

DEPUE, R. A., and EVANS, R. (1976) The psychobiology of depressive disorders. In Maher, B. H. (ed.) *Progress in experimental personality research*, Vol. 8. New York: Academic Press. **461**

DERMAN, D., see EKSTROM, FRENCH, HARMAN, and DERMAN (1976).

DERSHOWITZ, A. (1973) Abolishing the insanity defense: The most significant feature of the administration's proposed criminal code (an essay). *Criminal Law Bulletin*, 9:435. **474**

DETHIER, V. G. (1978) Other tastes, other worlds. *Science*, 201:224–28. **124**

DEUTSCH, J. A. (1973) *The physiological basis of memory*. New York: Academic Press. **249**

DEUTSCH, J. A., YOUNG, W. G., and KALOGERIS, T. J. (1978) The stomach signals satiety. *Science*, 201:165–67. **289**

DEUTSCH, M., and COLLINS, M. E. (1951) *Interracial housing: A psychological evaluation of a social experiment*. Minneapolis: Univ. of Minnesota Press. **550**

DIACONIS, P. (1978) Statistical problems in ESP research. *Science*, 201:131–36. **152**

DION, K. K. (1972) Physical attractiveness and evaluations of children's transgressions. *Journal of Personality and Social Psychology*, 24:207–13. **535**

DION, K. K., and BERSCHEID, E. (1972) Physical attractiveness and social perception of peers in preschool children. Unpublished manuscript, Univ. of Minnesota, Minneapolis. **535**

DIXON, N. F. (1971) *Subliminal perception: The nature of a controversy*. New York: McGraw-Hill. **159**

DOANE, B. K., see HERON, DOANE, and SCOTT (1956).

DOBELLE, W. H., MLADEJOVSKY, M. G., EVANS, J. R., ROBERTS, T. S., and GIRVIN, J. P. (1976) "Braille" reading by a blind volunteer by visual cortex stimulation. *Nature*, 259:111–12. **44**

DODDS, J. B., see FRANKENBURG and DODDS (1967).

DOLLARD, J., DOOB, L. W., MILLER, N. E., MOWRER, O. H., and SEARS, R. R. (1939) *Frustration and aggression*. New Haven, Conn.: Yale Univ. Press. **320**

DOMINO, G. (1971) Interactive effects of achievement orientation and teaching style on academic achievement. *Journal of Educational Psychology*, 62:427–31. **401**

DONAHUE, G. (1967) A school district program for schizophrenic children. In Cowen, E., and Zax, M. (eds.) *Emergent approaches to mental health problems*. New

York: Appleton-Century-Crofts. **512**

DOOB, A. N., and WOOD, L. E. (1972) Catharsis and aggression: Effects of annoyance and retaliation on aggressive behavior. *Journal of Personality and Social Psychology*, 22:156–62. **328**

DOOB, L. W., see DOLLARD, DOOB, MILLER, MOWRER, and SEARS (1939).

DRABMAN, R. S., and THOMAS, M. H. (1974) Does media violence increase children's toleration of real-life aggression? *Developmental Psychology*, 10:418–21. **328**

DRABMAN, R. S., see THOMAS and DRABMAN (1975).

DRABMAN, R. S., see THOMAS, HORTON, LIPPINCOTT, and DRABMAN (1977).

DRAGHI, S. C., see FLACH and DRAGHI (1975).

DUA, S., see ANAND, SHARMA, and DUA (1964).

DWORKIN, G., see BLOCK and DWORKIN (1976).

DYE, H. B., see SKEELS and DYE (1939).

EBBESEN, E. B., see KONEČNI and EBBESEN (1976).

EBBESEN, E. B., see SNYDER and EBBESEN (1972).

EBBESEN, E. B., see ZIMBARDO, EBBESEN, and MASLACH (1977).

ECCLES, J. C. (1958) The physiology of imagination. *Scientific American*, 199:135–46. **41**

EDMONSTON, W. E., Jr. (ed.) (1977) Conceptual and investigative approaches to hypnosis and hypnotic phenomena. *Annals of the New York Academy of Sciences*, Vol. 296. **187**

EDWARDS, A. L. (1959) *Edwards Personal Preference Schedule*. New York: Psychological Corporation. **402**

EDWARDS, A. L. (1973) *Statistical methods* (3rd ed.). New York: Holt, Rinehart and Winston. **587**

EDWARDS, N. B., see ABRAMSON, GARBER, EDWARDS, and SELIGMAN (1978).

EDWARDS, R. E., see KLEINHESSELINK and EDWARDS (1975).

EELLS, K., DAVIS, A., HAVIGHURST, R. J., HERRICK, V. E., and TYLER, R. W. (1951) *Intelligence and cultural differences*. Chicago: Univ. of Chicago Press. **352**

EELLS, K., see DAVIS and EELLS (1953).

EGAN, J. P. (1975) *Signal detection theory and ROC analysis*. New York: Academic Press. **107, 127**

EHRHARDT, A. A., see MONEY and EHRHARDT (1972).

EIBL-EIBESFELDT, I. (1970) *Ethology: The biology of behavior* (E. Klinghammer, tr.). New York: Holt, Rinehart and Winston. **76, 324**

EIMAS, P. D., SIQUELAND, E. R., JUSCZYK, P., and VIGORITO, J. (1971) Speech perception in infants. *Science*, 171:303–06. **260**

EISENBERG, J. G., see LANGNER, GERSTEN, and EISENBERG (1977).

EKMAN, P., and FRIESEN, W. V. (1975) *Unmasking the face*. Englewood Cliffs, N.J.: Prentice-Hall. **340, 343**

EKSTROM, R. B., FRENCH, J. W., HARMAN, H. H., and DERMAN, D. (1976) *Manual for kit of factor-referenced cognitive tests, 1976*. Princeton, N.J.: Educational Testing Service. **359**

ELKIND, D., and WEINER, I. B. (1978) *Development of the child*. New York: Wiley. **99**

ELLINWOOD, E. H., Jr., and KILBY, M. M. (eds.) (1977) *Cocaine and other stimulants*. New York: Plenum Press. **187**

EMRICH, B., see SHULMAN, SHAVER, COLMAN, EMRICH, and CHRISTIE (1973).

ENDLER, N. S. (1977) The role of person-by-situation interactions in personality theory. In Magnusson, D., and Endler, N. S. (eds.) *Personality at the crossroads: Current issues in interactional psychology*. New York: Halsted Press. **409, 410**

ENDLER, N. S., and HUNT, J. McV. (1966) Sources of behavioral variance as measured by the S-R Inventory of Anxiousness. *Psychological Bulletin*, 65:336–46. **409**

ENDLER, N. S., and HUNT, J. McV. (1968) S-R inventories of hostility and comparisons of the proportions of variance from persons, responses, and situations for hostility and anxiousness. *Journal of Personality and Social Psychology*, 9:309–15. **409**

ENDLER, N. S., and OKADA, M. (1974) An S-R Inventory of General Trait Anxiousness. *Department of Psychology Reports* (No. 1). Toronto: York Univ. **410**

ENDLER, N. S., see MAGNUSSON and ENDLER (1977).

ENDSLEY, R. C., see OSBORN and ENDSLEY (1971).

ENGLISH, G. E., see BERZINS, ROSS, ENGLISH, and HALEY (1974).

EPSTEIN, A. W., and TEITELBAUM, P. (1962) Regulation of food intake in the absence of taste, smell, and other oropharyngeal sensations. *Journal of Comparative and Physiological Psychology*, 55:753–59. **291**

EPSTEIN, A. W., see MCGINTY, EPSTEIN, and TEITELBAUM (1965).

EPSTEIN, S., and FENZ, W. D. (1965) Steepness of approach and avoidance gradients in humans as a function of experience. *Journal of Experimental Psychology*, 70:1–12. **419**

ERICKSON, B., see ROSS, LAYTON, ERICKSON, and SCHOPLER (1973).

ERIKSON, E. H. (1963) *Childhood and society* (2nd ed.). New York: Norton. **76, 95**

ERIKSON, E. H. (1976) *Toys and reasons*. New York: Norton. **76**

ERIKSSON, K. (1972) Behavior and physiological differences among rat strains specially selected for their alcohol consumption. *Annals of the New York Academy of Science*, 197:32–41. **58**

ERLENMEYER-KIMLING, L., and JARVIK, L. F. (1963) Genetics and intelligence: A review. *Science*, 142:1477–79. **364**

ERON, L. D., HUESMANN, L. R., LEFKOWITZ, M. M., and WALDER, L. O. (1972) Does television violence cause aggression? *American Psychologist*, 27:253–63. **327**

ERVIN, F. R., see MARK and ERVIN (1970).

ERVIN-TRIPP, S. (1964) Imitation and structural change in children's language. In Lenneberg, E. H. (ed.) *New directions in the study of language.* Cambridge, Mass.: M.I.T. Press. **265**

ESTES, W. K. (1949) A study of motivating conditions necessary for secondary reinforcement. *Journal of Experimental Psychology*, 39:306–10. **201**

ESTES, W. K. (1972) An associative basis for coding and organization in memory. In Melton, A. W., and Martin, E. (eds.) *Coding processes in human memory.* Washington, D. C.: Winston. **234**

ESTES, W. K. (ed.) (1975) *Introduction to concepts and issues.* Handbook of learning and cognitive processes, Vol. 1. Hillsdale, N.J.: Erlbaum. **197, 219**

ESTES, W. K. (ed.) (1976) *Conditioning and behavior theory.* Handbook of learning and cognitive processes, Vol. 2. Hillsdale, N.J.: Erlbaum. **219**

ESTES, W. K. (ed.) (1976) *Attention and memory.* Handbook of learning and cognitive processes, Vol. 4. Hillsdale, N.J.: Eribaum. **219**

ESTES, W. K. (ed.) (1978) *Approaches to human learning and motivation.* Handbook of learning and cognitive processes, Vol. 3. Hillsdale, N.J.: Erlbaum. **219**

ESTES, W. K. (ed.) (1978) *Human information processing.* Handbook of learning and cognitive processes, Vol. 5. Hillsdale, N.J.: Erlbaum. **219**

EVANS, F. J., COOK, M. R., COHEN, H. D., ORNE, E. C., and ORNE, M. T. (1977) Appetitive and replacement naps: EEG and behavior. *Science*, 197:687–89. **168**

EVANS, F. J., see KIHLSTROM and EVANS (1976).

EVANS, J. R., see DOBELLE, MLADEJOVSKY, EVANS, ROBERTS, and GIRVIN (1976).

EVANS, R., see DEPUE and EVANS (1976).

EYFERTH, K., BRANDT, U., and WOLFGANG, H. (1960) *Farbige Kinder in Deutschland.* Munich: Juventa. **367**

EYSENCK, H. J., and EYSENCK, S. B. G. (1963) *The Eysenck Personality Inventory.* San Diego: Educational and Industrial Testing Service; London: Univ. of London Press. **384**

EYSENCK, S. B. G., see EYSENCK and EYSENCK (1963).

FARADAY, A. (1973) *Dream power.* New York: Berkley. **186**

FARQUHAR, J. W., MACCOBY, N., WOOD, P. D., and OTHERS (1977) Community education for cardiovascular health. *The Lancet* (June 4): 1192–95. **558**

FARQUHAR, J. W., see MACCOBY, FARQUHAR, WOOD, and ALEXANDER (1977).

FAWCETT, J. A., see JONES, MAAS, DEKIRMENJIAN, and FAWCETT (1973).

FAZIO, R. H., ZANNA, M. P., and COOPER, J. (1977) Dissonance and self-perception: An integrative view of each theory's proper domain of application. *Journal of Experimental Social Psychology*, 13:464–79. **541**

FECHNER, G. (1860) *Elements of psychophysics* (H. E. Adler, tr.). New York: Holt, Rinehart and Winston, 1966. **107**

FEJER, D., see SMART and FEJER (1972).

FELDMAN, S. S., see MACCOBY and FELDMAN (1972).

FENZ, W. D., see EPSTEIN and FENZ (1965).

FERRARO, D. P., see LOGAN and FERRARO (1978).

FESHBACH, N., see FESHBACH and FESHBACH (1973).

FESHBACH, S., and FESHBACH, N. (1973) The young aggressors. *Psychology Today*, 6:90–95. **87**

FESTINGER, L. (1957) *A theory of cognitive dissonance.* Stanford, Calif.: Stanford Univ. Press. **527**

FESTINGER, L., and CARLSMITH, J. M. (1959) Cognitive consequences of forced compliance. *Journal of Abnormal and Social Psychology*, 58:203–10. **528**

FINKELMAN, J. M., and GLASS, D. C. (1970) Reappraisal of the relationship between noise and human performance by means of a subsidiary task measure. *Journal of Applied Psychology*, 54:211–13. **559**

FISHKIN, J., KENISTON, K., and MACKINNON, C. (1973) Moral reasoning and political ideology. *Journal of Personality and Social Psychology*, 27:109–19. **75**

FITZGERALD, R. G., see PARKES, BENJAMIN, and FITZGERALD (1969).

FIXSEN, D. L., see PHILLIPS, PHILLIPS, FIXSEN, and WOLF (1972).

FLACH, F. F., and DRAGHI, S. C. (eds.) (1975) *The nature and treatment of depression.* New York: Wiley. **462**

FLACKS, R., see NEWCOMB, KOENIG, FLACKS, and WARWICK (1967).

FLANAGAN, J. C. (1963) The definition and measurement of ingenuity. In Taylor, C. W., and Barron, F. (eds.) *Scientific creativity: Its recognition and development.* New York: Wiley. **360**

FLAVELL, J. H. (1977) *Cognitive development.* Englewood Cliffs: N.J.: Prentice-Hall. **99**

FLECK, S., see LIDZ, FLECK, and CORNELISON (1965).

FLETCHER, J. D., see JAMISON, SUPPES, FLETCHER, and ATKINSON (1976).

FLEXNER, L. (1967) Dissection of memory in mice with antibiotics. *Proceedings of the American Philosophical Society*, 111:343–46. **233**

FLOYD, J., see ARONSON, WILLERMAN, and FLOYD (1966).

FLYGER, V., see CHRISTIAN, FLYGER, and DAVIS (1960).

FODOR, J. A., BEVER, T. G., and GARRETT, M. F. (1974) *The psychology of language: An introduction to psycholinguistics and generative grammar.* New York: McGraw-Hill. **266, 277**

FORD, C. S., and BEACH, F. A. (1951) *Patterns of sexual behavior.* New York: Harper and Row. **304**

FOREM, J. (1973) *Transcendental meditation: Maharishi Mahesh Yogi and the science of creative intelligence.* New York: Dutton. **171**

FORER, B. R. (1949) The fallacy of personality validation: A classroom demonstration of gullibility. *Journal of Abnormal and Social Psychology*, 44:118–23. **404**

FOSS, D. J., and HAKES, D. T. (1978) *Psycholinguistics: An introduction to the psychology of language.* Englewood Cliffs, N.J.: Prentice-Hall. **277**

FOULKES, D. (1971) Longitudinal studies of dreams in children. In Masserman, J. (ed.) *Science and psychoanalysis.* New York: Grune and Stratton. **169**

FOULKES, D., see MONROE, RECHTSCHAFFEN, FOULKES, and JENSEN (1965).

FOX, N. A. (1975) *Developmental and birth-order determinants of separation protest: A cross-cultural study of infants on the Israeli kibbutz.* Doctoral dissertation, Harvard Graduate School of Education, Cambridge, Mass. **81**

FOX, S., see STUNKARD and FOX (1971).

FRANK, J. D. (1974) Psychotherapy: The restoration of morale. *American Journal of Psychiatry*, 131:271–74. **508**

FRANKENBURG, W. K., and DODDS, J. B. (1967) The Denver developmental screening test. *Journal of Pediatrics*, 71:181–91. **65**

FRANKIE, G., see HETHERINGTON and FRANKIE (1967).

FRANKLIN, R. M., see STANTON, MINTZ, and FRANKLIN (1976).

FRANKS, J. J., see BRANSFORD, BARCLAY, and FRANKS (1972).

FRASER, S. C., see FREEDMAN and FRASER (1966).

FREEDMAN, J. L. (1965) Long-term behavioral effects of cognitive dissonance. *Journal of Experimental Social Psychology*, 1:145–55. **528, 540**

FREEDMAN, J. L. (1975) *Crowding and behavior.* New York: Viking. **560, 562, 571**

FREEDMAN, J. L., and FRASER, S. C. (1966) Compliance without pressure: The foot-in-the-door technique. *Journal of Personality and Social Psychology*, 4:195–202. **540**

FREEDMAN, J. L., HESHKA, S., and LEVY, A. (1975) Population density and pathology: Is there a relationship? *Journal of Experimental Social Psychology*, 11:539–52. **561**

FREEDMAN, J. L., SEARS, D. O., and CARLSMITH, J. M. (1978) *Social psychology* (3rd ed.). Englewood Cliffs, N.J.: Prentice-Hall. **545, 556**

FREEDMAN, J. L., see SHAVER and FREEDMAN (1976).

FRENCH, G. M., and HARLOW, H. F. (1962) Variability of delayed-reaction performance in normal and brain-damaged rhesus monkeys. *Journal of Neurophysiology*, 25:585–99. **45**

FRENCH, J. W., see EKSTROM, FRENCH, HARMAN, and DERMAN (1976).

FRENCH, T. M., and FROMM, E. (1963)

Dream interpretation: A new approach. New York: Basic Books. **169**

FRENKEL-BRUNSWIK, E., see ADORNO, FRENKEL-BRUNSWIK, LEVINSON, and SANFORD (1950).

FREUD, A. (1967) *The ego and the mechanisms of defense* (rev. ed.). London: Hogarth Press. **439, 446**

FREUD, S. (1885) *Ueber Coca.* Vienna: Moritz Perles. (Translation in Freud, 1974). **174**

FREUD, S. (1900) *The interpretation of dreams,* Vols. IV, V. London: Hogarth Press. (Stand. ed., 1953). **168**

FREUD, S. (1925) Repression, 1915. In *Collected Papers,* Vol. IV. London: Hogarth Press. **237**

FREUD, S. (1940) *Outline of psychoanalysis.* (Standard ed., 1964). Vol. XXIII. London: Hogarth Press. **389**

FREUD, S. (1963) Why war? In Reiff, P. (ed.) *Freud: Character and culture.* New York: Collier Books. **320**

FREUD, S. (1965) *New introductory lectures on psychoanalysis.* New York: Norton. (Originally published, 1933). **169, 343, 412**

FREUD, S. (1974) *Cocaine papers.* Edited and introduction by R. Byck; notes by A. Freud. New York: Stonehill. **175, 187**

FREUD, S. (1975) *Beyond the pleasure principle.* New York: Norton. (Orginally published, 1920). **343**

FRIEDMAN, M. P., see CARTERETTE and FRIEDMAN (1975-1979).

FRIESEN, W. V., see EKMAN and FRIESEN (1975).

FRITSCH, G., and HITZIG, E. (1870) Ueber die elektrische Erregbarkeit des Grossmirns. *Archiv für Anatomie, Physiologie und Wissenschaftliche Medicin,* 37:300-32. **40**

FROMM, E. (1970) Age regression with unexpected reappearance of a repressed childhood language. *International Journal of Clinical and Experimental Hypnosis,* 18:79-88. **180**

FROMM, E., and SHOR, R. E. (eds.) (1979) *Hypnosis: Research developments and perspectives* (rev. ed.). Chicago: Aldine. **187**

FROMM, E., see FRENCH and FROMM (1963).

FROST, B., see ANNIS and FROST (1973).

FUHRER, M. J., see BAER and FUHRER (1968).

FULLER, J. L., and THOMPSON, W. R. (1978) *Foundations of behavior genetics.* St. Louis: Mosby. **61, 485**

FULLER, J. L., see SCOTT and FULLER (1965).

GALABURDA, A. M., LEMAY, M., KEMPER, T. L., and GESCHWIND, N. (1978) Right-left asymmetries in the brain. *Science,*199:852-56. **46**

GALANTER, E. (1962) Contemporary psychophysics. In Brown, R., and others (eds.) *New directions in psychology.* New York: Holt, Rinehart and Winston. **104**

GALANTER, E., see MILLER, GALANTER, and PRIBRAM (1960).

GALLE, O. R., GOVE, W. R., and MCPHERSON, J. M. (1972) Population density and pathology: What are the relations for man? *Science,* 176:23-30. **561**

GARBER, J., see ABRAMSON, GARBER, EDWARDS, and SELIGMAN (1978).

GARCIA, J. (1971) The faddy rat and us. *New Scientist and Science Journal* (February 4, 1971). **292**

GARCIA, J., MCGOWAN, B. K., and GREEN, K. F. (1972) Biological constraints on conditioning. In Black, A. H., and Prokasy, W. F. (eds.) *Classical conditioning II: Current theory and research.* New York: Appleton-Century-Crofts. **195**

GARDNER, B. T., and GARDNER, R. A. (1972) Two-way communication with an infant chimpanzee. In Schrier, A. M., and Stollnitz, F. (eds.) *Behavior of nonhuman primates,* Vol. 4. New York: Academic Press. **267, 270**

GARDNER, B. T., see GARDNER and GARDNER (1977).

GARDNER, M. (1957) *Fads and fallacies in the name of science.* New York: Dover. **184**

GARDNER, R. A., and GARDNER, B. T. (1977) Comparative psychology and language acquisition. In Salzinger, K., and Denmark, F. (eds.) *Psychology: The state of the art.* Annals of the New York Academy of Sciences. **271**

GARDNER, R. A., see GARDNER and GARDNER (1972).

GARFIELD, S. L., and BERGIN, A. E. (eds.) (1978) *Handbook of psychotherapy and behavior change: An empirical analysis.* New York: Wiley. **507, 515**

GARRETT, M. F. (1975) The analysis of sentence production. In Bower, G. H. (ed.) *The psychology of learning and motivation,* Vol. 9. New York: Academic Press. **261**

GARRETT, M. F., see FODOR, BEVER, and GARRETT (1974).

GATES, A. I. (1917) Recitation as a factor in memorizing. *Archives of Psychology,* No. 40. **241**

GATES, A. I. (1931) *Elementary psychology.* New York: Macmillan. **12**

GAZZANIGA, M. S. (1970) *The bisected brain.* New York: Appleton-Century-Crofts. **49, 50**

GAZZANIGA, M. S. (1972) One brain—two minds? *American Scientist,* 60:311-17. **50**

GEBHARD, P. H. (1972) Incidence of overt homosexuality in the United States and Western Europe. In Livingood, J. M. (ed.) *National Institute of Mental Health Task Force on Homosexuality: Final Report and Background Papers.* Rockville, Md.: National Institute of Mental Health. **306**

GEBHARD, P. H., see KINSEY, POMEROY, MARTIN, and GEBHARD (1953).

GEEN, R. G. (1976) *Personality: The skein of behavior.* St. Louis: Mosby. **323, 412**

GEEN, R. G., and O'NEAL, E. C. (1969) Activation of cue-elicited aggression by general arousal. *Journal of Personality and Social Psychology,* 11:289-92. **322**

GEER, J., and MAISEL, E. (1972) Evaluating the effects of the prediction-control confound. *Journal of Personality and Social Psychology,* 23:314-19. **437**

GELLER, U. (1975) *Uri Geller: My story.* New York: Praeger. **184**

GERARD, D. L., see CHEIN, GERARD, LEE, and ROSENFELD (1964).

GERBNER, G., and GROSS, L. (1976) The scary world of TV's heavy viewer. *Psychology Today,* 9:41-45. **329, 555**

GERSTEN, J. C., see LANGNER, GERSTEN, and EISENBERG (1977).

GESCHWIND, N., see GALABURDA, LEMAY, KEMPER, and GESCHWIND (1978).

GETZELS, J. W., and JACKSON, P. W. (1962) *Creativity and intelligence; Explorations with gifted students.* New York: Wiley. **360**

GIBBS, J. P. (1971) Suicide. In Merton, R. K., and Nisbet, R. A. (eds.) *Contemporary social problems* (3rd ed.). New York: Harcourt Brace Jovanovich. **561**

GIBSON, E. J., and WALK, R. D. (1960) The "visual cliff." *Scientific American,* 202:64-71. **147**

GIBSON, H. B. (1978) *Hypnosis: Its nature and therapeutic uses.* New York: Taplinger. **187**

GIBSON, J. J. (1968) What gives rise to the perception of motion? *Psychological Review,* 75:335-46. **137**

GILLIN, J. C., see SITARAM, WEINGARTNER, and GILLIN (1978).

GIRVIN, J. P., see DOBELLE, MLADEJOVSKY, EVANS, ROBERTS, and GIRVIN (1976).

GLANZER, M. (1972) Storage mechanisms in recall. In Bower, G. H., and Spence, J. T. (eds.) *The psychology of learning and motivation,* Vol. 5. New York: Academic Press. **244**

GLASER, R., and RESNICK, L. B. (1972) Instructional psychology. *Annual Review of Psychology,* 23:207-76. **76**

GLASS, D. C., and SINGER, J. E. (1972) *Urban stress: Experiments on noise and social stressors.* New York: Academic Press. **437, 559, 560**

GLASS, D. C., see COHEN, GLASS, and SINGER (1973).

GLASS, D. C., see FINKELMAN and GLASS (1970).

GLASS, G. V., see SMITH and GLASS (1977).

GLASS, L. L., see KIRSCH and GLASS (1977).

GLICK, B. S., and MARGOLIS, R. (1962) A study on the influence of experimental design on clinical outcome in drug research. *American Journal of Psychiatry,* 118:1087-96. **509**

GLUCK, C. M., see SIMS, KELLEHER, HORTON, GLUCK, GOODMAN, and ROWE (1968).

GLUCKSBERG, S., and DANKS, J. H. (1975) *Experimental psycholinguistics.* New York: Halsted Press. **277**

GLUECK, S. (1962) *Law and psychiatry.* Baltimore: Johns Hopkins Univ. Press. **475**

GOBLE, F. (1970) *The third force: The psychology of Abraham Maslow.* New York: Pocket Books. **412**

GODDARD, H. H. (1913) The Binet tests in relation to immigration. *Journal of Psychoasthenics,* 18:105–07. **565**

GODDARD, H. H. (1917) Mental tests and the immigrant. *Journal of Delinquency,* 2:243–77. **565**

GOECKNER, D., GREENOUGH, W., and MEAD, W. (1973) Deficits in learning tasks following chronic overcrowding in rats. *Journal of Personality and Social Psychology,* 28:256–61. **563**

GOETHALS, G. R., see JONES, ROCK, SHAVE, GOETHALS, and WARD (1968).

GOFFMAN, E. (1961) *Asylums.* Garden City, N.Y.: Doubleday. **543**

GOLDFRIED, M. R., and DAVISON, G. C. (1976) *Clinical behavior therapy.* New York: Holt, Rinehart and Winston. **494, 515**

GOLDIAMOND, I., see ISAACS, THOMAS, and GOLDIAMOND (1965).

GOLDSTEIN, A. C. (1957) The experimental control of sex behavior in animals. In Hoagland, H. H. (ed.) *Hormones, brain function, and behavior.* New York: Academic Press. **300**

GOODALL, J. (1978) Chimp killings: Is it the man in them? *Science News,* 113:276. **325**

GOODENOUGH, D. R., SHAPIRO, A., HOLDEN, M., and STEINSCHRIBER, L. (1959) A comparison of dreamers and non-dreamers: Eye movements, electroencephalograms and the recall of dreams. *Journal of Abnormal and Social Psychology,* 59:295–302. **169**

GOODENOUGH, D. R., see LEWIS, GOODENOUGH, SHAPIRO, and SLESER (1966).

GOODMAN, J. (1970) Companions as therapy: The use of non-professional talent. In Hart, J. T., and Tomlinson, T. M. (eds.) *New directions in client-centered therapy.* Boston: Houghton Mifflin. **513**

GOODMAN, R. F., see SIMS, KELLEHER, HORTON, GLUCK, GOODMAN, and ROWE (1968).

GOODWIN, D. W., SCHULSINGER, F., HERMANSEN, L., GUZE, S. B., and WINOKUR, G. (1973) Alcohol problems in adoptees raised apart from alcoholic biological parents. *Archives of General Psychiatry,* 28:238–43. **478**

GOODWIN, D. W., see WOODRUFF, GOODWIN, and GUZE (1974).

GOODWIN, F. K., see POST, KOTIN, GOODWIN, and GORDON (1973).

GORDON, E., see POST, KOTIN, GOODWIN, and GORDON (1973).

GORDON, N. J., see LEIFFER, GORDON, and GRAVES (1974).

GOTTESMAN, I. I. (1963) Genetic aspects of intelligent behavior. In Ellis, N. (ed.) *Handbook of mental deficiency: Psychological theory and research.* New York: McGraw-Hill. **365**

GOTTESMAN, I. I., and SHIELDS, J. (1972) *Schizophrenia and genetics: A twin study vantage point.* New York: Academic Press. **485**

GOTTESMAN, I. I., and SHIELDS, J. (1973) Genetic theorizing and schizophrenia. *British Journal of Psychiatry,* 122:15–30. **467**

GOVE, W. R., see GALLE, GOVE, and MCPHERSON (1972).

GRANBERG, D., and BRENT, E. E. (1974) Dove-hawk placements in the 1968 election: Application of social judgment and balance theories. *Journal of Personality and Social Psychology,* 29:687–95. **557**

GRAVES, N., see HOFLING, BROTZMAN, DALRYMPLE, GRAVES, and PIERCE (1966).

GRAVES, S. B., see LEIFFER, GORDON, and GRAVES (1974).

GRAY, J. (1971) *The psychology of fear and stress.* New York: McGraw-Hill. **439**

GRAYSON, R. (1972) Air controllers syndrome: Peptic ulcers in air traffic controllers. *Illinois Medical Journal* (August). **434**

GREEN, D. (1974) Dissonance and self-perception analyses of "forced compliance": When two theories make competing predictions. *Journal of Personality and Social Psychology,* 29:819–28. **541**

GREEN, D. M., and BIRDSALL, T. G. (1978) Detection and recognition. *Psychological Review,* 85:192–206. **107**

GREEN, H. (1971) *I never promised you a rose garden.* New York: New American Library. **485**

GREEN, K. F., see GARCIA, MCGOWAN, and GREEN (1972).

GREEN, R. (1974) *Sexual identity conflict in children and adults.* New York: Basic Books. **308, 541**

GREENBERG, D., see SNYDER, BANERJEE, YAMAMURA, and GREENBERG (1974).

GREENE, D., see LEPPER, GREENE, and NISBETT (1973).

GREENFIELD, P. M., and SMITH, J. H. (1976) *The structure of communication in early language development.* New York: Academic Press. **262**

GREENOUGH, W., see GOECKNER, GREENOUGH, and MEAD (1973).

GREENWALD, A. G. (1975) On the inconclusiveness of "crucial" cognitive tests of dissonance versus self-perception theories. *Journal of Experimental Social Psychology,* 11:490–99. **541**

GREENWOOD, M. M., see BENSON, KOTCH, CRASSWELLER, and GREENWOOD (1977).

GREGORY, R. L. (1970) *The intelligent eye.* New York: McGraw-Hill. **136**

GREIF, E. B., see KURTINES and GREIF (1974).

GROSS, L., see GERBNER and GROSS (1976a).

GROSS, L., see GERBNER and GROSS (1976b).

GROSS, L. P., see SCHACHTER and GROSS (1968).

GROSSBERG, J. M. (1964) Behavior therapy: A review. *Psychological Bulletin,* 62:73–85. **500**

GROSSEN, N. E., see MEYERS and GROSSEN (1978).

GROSSMAN, S. P. (1967) *A textbook of physiological psychology.* New York: Wiley. **300**

GRUSEC, J. E., see WALTERS and GRUSEC (1977).

GUILFORD, J. P. (1954) A factor analytic study across the domains of reasoning, creativity, and evaluation I: Hypothesis and description of tests. *Reports from the psychology laboratory.* Los Angeles: Univ. of Southern California. **360**

GUILFORD, J. P. (1967) *The nature of human intelligence.* New York: McGraw-Hill. **358, 359**

GUILFORD, J. P., and HOEPFNER, R. (1971) *The analysis of intelligence.* New York: McGraw-Hill. **360**

GUILLEMIN, R., see BLOOM, SEGAL, LING, and GUILLEMIN (1976).

GUILLEMINAULT, C., BILLIARD, M., MONTPLAISAR, J., and DEMENT, W. C. (1975) Altered states of consciousness in disorders of daytime sleepiness. *Journal of Neurological Sciences,* 26:377–93. **168**

GUNNE, L. M., LINDSTRÖM, L., and TERENIUS, J. (1977) Naloxone-induced reversal of schizophrenic hallucinations. *Journal of Neural Transmissions,* 40:13–19. **469**

GUZE, S. B., see GOODWIN, SCHULSINGER, HERMANSEN, GUZE, and WINOKUR (1973).

GUZE, S. B., see WOODRUFF, GOODWIN, and GUZE (1974).

HABER, R. N. (1969) Eidetic images. *Scientific American,* 220:36–55. **224**

HACKETT, T. P., and CASSEM, N. H. (1970) Psychological reactions to life-threatening illness: Acute myocardial infarction. In Abram, H. S. (ed.) *Psychological aspects of stress.* Springfield, Ill.: Thomas. **427**

HAKES, D. T., see FOSS and HAKES (1978).

HALEY, J. V., see BERZINS, ROSS, ENGLISH, and HALEY (1974).

HALL, C. S. (1966) *The meaning of dreams.* New York: McGraw-Hill. **169**

HALL, C. S., and LINDZEY, G. (1978) *Theories of personality* (3rd ed.) New York: Wiley. **25, 412**

HALL, C. S., see NORDBY and HALL (1974).

HALPERN, J. (1977) Projection: A test of the psychoanalytic hypothesis. *Journal of Abnormal Psychology,* 86:536–42. **430**

HAMILTON, D. L., and BISHOP, G. D. (1976) Attitudinal and behavioral effects of initial integration of white suburban neighborhoods. *Journal of Social Issues,* 32:47–68. **550**

HAMMER, A. G., see NACE, ORNE, and HAMMER (1974).

HARE, R. D. (1970) *Psychopathy: Theory and research.* New York: Wiley. **473**

HARLOW, H. F. (1971) *Learning to love.* San Francisco: Albion. **304**

HARLOW, H. F., HARLOW, M. K., and MEYER, D. R. (1950) Learning motivated by a manipulation drive. *Journal of Experimental Psychology,* 40:228–34. **310**

HARLOW, H. F., and SUOMI, S. J. (1970)

Nature of love—simplified. *American Psychologist*, 25:161–68. **77**

HARLOW, H. F., see FRENCH and HARLOW (1962).

HARLOW, M. K., see HARLOW, HARLOW, and MEYER (1950).

HARMAN, H. H., see EKSTROM, FRENCH, HARMAN, and DERMAN (1976).

HARRIS, C. S., see ROCK and HARRIS (1967).

HARRIS, F. R., see ALLEN, HART, BUELL, HARRIS, and WOLF (1964).

HARRIS, S. L., see NATHAN and HARRIS (1975).

HARRIS, V. A., see JONES and HARRIS (1967).

HARSH, J., see BADIA, CULBERTSON, and HARSH (1973).

HART, B. M., see ALLEN, HART, BUELL, HARRIS, and WOLF (1964).

HART, G. H., see COLE, HART, and MILLER (1956).

HARTMANN, H. (1958) *Ego psychology and the problems of adaptation.* New York: International Universities Press. **446**

HARTUP, W. W., and COATES, B. (1967) Imitation of a peer as a function of reinforcement from the peer group and rewardingness of the model. *Child Development*, 38:1003–16. **80**

HARVEY, E. N., see LOOMIS, HARVEY, and HOBART (1937).

HARVEY, O. J., see SHERIF, HARVEY, WHITE, HOOD, and SHERIF (1961).

HASHIM, S. A., and VAN ITALLIE, T. B. (1965) Studies in normal and obese subjects with a monitored food dispensary device. *Annals of the New York Academy of Science*, 131:654–61. **293**

HASSETT, J. (1978) *A primer of psychophysiology.* San Francisco: Freeman. **61**

HASTEY, J. M., see ARKIN, TOTH, BAKER, and HASTEY (1970).

HAVIGHURST, R. J., see EELLS, DAVIS, HAVIGHURST, HERRICK, and TYLER (1951).

HEARST, E. (1975) The classical-instrumental distinction: Reflexes, voluntary behavior, and categories of associative learning. In Estes, W. K. (ed.) *Handbook of learning and cognition: Conditioning and behavior theory*, Vol. 2. Hillsdale, N.J.: Erlbaum. **203**

HEBB, D. O. (1972) *Textbook of psychology* (3rd ed.) Philadelphia: Saunders. **341**

HEIDER, F. (1958) *The psychology of interpersonal relations.* New York: Wiley. **537**

HEIMAN, N. M. (1973) Postdoctoral training in community mental health. *Menninger Clinic Bulletin*, No. 17. **510**

HELFER, R. E., and KEMPE, C. H. (1968) *The battered child.* Chicago: Univ. of Chicago Press. **308**

HELMREICH, R., ARONSON, E., and LEFAN, J. (1970) To err is humanizing—sometimes: Effects of self-esteem, competence, and a pratfall on interpersonal attraction. *Journal of Personality and Social Psychology*, 16:259–64. **535**

HENDRICK, G. (1977) When television is a

school for criminals. *TV Guide* (January 29): 4–10. **328**

HENRY, G. W., see ZILBOORG and HENRY (1941).

HERMAN, C. P., and MACK, D. (1975) Restrained and unrestrained eating. *Journal of Personality*, 43:647–60. **295**

HERMAN, C. P., and POLIVY, J. (1975) Anxiety, restraint, and eating behavior. *Journal of Abnormal Psychology*, 84:666–72. **295**

HERMAN, C. P., see HIBSCHER and HERMAN (1977).

HERMANSEN, L., see GOODWIN, SCHULSINGER, HERMANSEN, GUZE, and WINOKUR (1973).

HERON, W., DOANE, B. K., and SCOTT, T. H. (1956) Visual disturbances after prolonged perceptual isolation. *Canadian Journal of Psychology*, 10:13–16. **311**

HERRICK, V. E., see EELLS, DAVIS, HAVIGHURST, HERRICK, and TYLER (1951).

HERRON, E. W., see HOLTZMAN, THORPE, SWARTZ, and HERRON (1961).

HESHKA, S., see FREEDMAN, HESHKA, and LEVY (1975).

HESS, E. H. (1958) "Imprinting" in animals. *Scientific American*, 198:81–90. **286**

HESS, E. H. (1972) "Imprinting" in a natural laboratory. *Scientific American*, 227:24–31. **287**

HESS, E. H., and POLT, J. M. (1960) Pupil size as related to the interest value of visual stimuli. *Science*, 132:349–50. **109**

HESTON, L. (1970) The genetics of schizophrenia and schizoid disease. *Science*, 167:249–56. **467**

HETHERINGTON, E. M., COX, M., and COX, R. (1978) Mother/child father/child relationships. In Stevens, J. H., and Mathews, M. (eds.) *Parent-child relations.* Washington, D.C.: National Association for the Education of Young Children. **81**

HETHERINGTON, E. M., and FRANKIE, G. (1967) Effects of parental dominance, warmth, and conflict on imitation in children. *Journal of Personality and Social Psychology*, 6:119–25. **87**

HIBSCHER, J. A., and HERMAN, C. P. (1977) Obesity, dieting, and the expression of "obese" characteristics. *Journal of Comparative and Physiological Psychology*, 91:374–80. **295**

HILGARD, E. R. (1961) Hypnosis and experimental psychodynamics. In Brosen, H. (ed.) *Lectures on experimental psychiatry.* Pittsburgh: Pittsburgh Univ. Press. **22**

HILGARD, E. R. (1965) *Hypnotic susceptibility.* New York: Harcourt Brace Jovanovich. **429**

HILGARD, E. R. (1968) *The experience of hypnosis.* New York: Harcourt Brace Jovanovich. **187**

HILGARD, E. R. (1973a) A neodissociation interpretation of pain reduction in hypnosis. *Psychological Review*, 80:396–411. **181**

HILGARD, E. R. (1973b) The domain of hypnosis, with some comments on alter-

native paradigms. *American Psychologist*, 28:972–82. **181**

HILGARD, E. R. (1977) *Divided consciousness: Multiple controls in human thought and action.* New York: Wiley-Interscience. **181, 186**

HILGARD, E. R. (1978) Hypnosis and consciousness. *Human Nature*, 1:42–49. **182**

HILGARD, E. R., and BOWER, G. H. (1975) *Theories of learning* (4th ed.) Englewood Cliffs, N.J.: Prentice-Hall. **218**

HILGARD, E. R., and HILGARD, J. R. (1975) *Hypnosis in the relief of pain.* Los Altos, Calif.: William Kaufmann. **181, 187**

HILGARD, E. R., see BANYAI and HILGARD (1976).

HILGARD, E. R., see KNOX, CRUTCHFIELD, and HILGARD (1975).

HILGARD, E. R., see MORGAN, JOHNSON, and HILGARD (1974).

HILGARD, E. R., see RUCH, MORGAN, and HILGARD (1973).

HILGARD, J. R. (1970) *Personality and hypnosis: A study of imaginative involvement.* Chicago: Univ. of Chicago Press. **179, 187**

HILGARD, J. R. (1974) Imaginative involvement: Some characteristics of the highly hypnotizable and the non-hypnotizable. *International Journal of Clinical and Experimental Hypnosis*, 22:138–56. **179**

HILGARD, J. R., see HILGARD and HILGARD (1975).

HINSHELWOOD, J. (1900) *Letter-, word- and mind-blindness.* London: Lewis. **40**

HINTZMAN, D. L. (1978) *The psychology of learning and memory.* San Francisco: Freeman. **219**

HIROTO, D. S., and SELIGMAN, M. E. P. (1975) Generality of learned helplessness in man. *Journal of Personality and Social Psychology*, 31:311–27. **423**

HIRSCH, J., and KNITTLE, J. L. (1970) Cellularity of obese and nonobese human adipose tissue. *Federation Proceedings*, 29:1516–21. **296**

HIRSCH, J., see KNITTLE and HIRSCH (1968).

HITCH, G., see BADDELEY and HITCH (1974).

HITZIG, E., see FRITSCH and HITZIG (1870).

HJELLE, L. A., and ZIEGLER, D. J. (1976) *Personality theories: Basic assumptions, research, and applications.* New York: McGraw-Hill. **412**

HO, B., CHUTE, D., and RICHARDS, D. (eds.) (1977) *Drug discrimination and state dependent learning.* New York: Academic Press. **173**

HO, E., see WATKINS, HO, and TULVING (1976).

HOBART, G. A., see LOOMIS, HARVEY, and HOBART (1937).

HOCHBERG, J. (1978) *Perception* (2nd ed.). Englewood Cliffs, N.J.: Prentice-Hall. **154**

HOCKETT, C. F. (1960) The origin of speech. *Scientific American*, 203:89–96. **268**

HOEBEL, B. G., and TEITELBAUM, P.

(1962) Hypothalamic control of feeding and self-stimulation. *Science*, 135:375–77. **288**

HOEBEL, B. G., and TEITELBAUM, P. (1966) Effects of force-feeding and starvation on food intake and body weight of a rat with ventromedial hypothalamic lesions. *Journal of Comparative and Physiological Psychology*, 61:189–93. **290**

HOEBEL, B. G., see CAGGIULA and HOEBEL (1966).

HOEBEL, B. G., see SMITH, KING, and HOEBEL (1970).

HOEPFNER, R., see GUILFORD and HOEPFNER (1971).

HOFFMAN, L. W., and NYE, F. I. (1974) *Working mothers*. San Francisco: Jossey-Bass. **81**

HOFLING, C. K., BROTZMAN, E., DALRYMPLE, S., GRAVES, N., and PIERCE, C. M. (1966) An experimental study in nurse-physician relationships. *Journal of Nervous and Mental Disease*, 143:171–80. **526**

HOHMANN, G. W. (1962) Some effects of spinal cord lesions on experienced emotional feelings. *Psychophysiology*, 3:143–56. **336**

HOLDEN, C. (1975) Lie detectors: PSE gains audience despite critic's doubt. *Science*, 190:359–62. **333**

HOLDEN, M., see GOODENOUGH, SHAPIRO, HOLDEN, and STEINSCHRIBER (1959).

HOLLINGSHEAD, A. B., and REDLICH, F. C. (1958) *Social class and mental illness*. New York: Wiley. **560**

HOLLISTER, L. E., see DARLEY, TINKLENBERG, ROTH, HOLLISTER, and ATKINSON (1973).

HOLLISTER, L. E., see DAVIS, MOHS, TINKLENBERG, PFEFFERBAUM, HOLLISTER, and KOPELL (1978).

HOLMES, D. S. (1974) Investigations of repression: Differential recall of material experimentally or naturally associated with ego threat. *Psychological Bulletin*, 81:632–53. **237**

HOLMES, T. H., and RAHE, R. H. (1967) The social readjustment rating scale. *Journal of Psychosomatic Research*, 11:213–18. **437**

HOLTZMAN, W. H., THORPE, J. S., SWARTZ, J. D., and HERRON, E. W. (1961) *Inkblot perception and personality*. Austin: Univ. of Texas Press. **405**

HOLZMAN, P. S. (1970) *Psychoanalysis and psychopathology*. New York: McGraw-Hill. **412**

HOLZMAN, P. S., see MENNINGER and HOLZMAN (1973).

HONZIK, C. H., see TOLMAN and HONZIK (1930).

HOOD, L., see BLOOM, HOOD, and LIGHTBOWN (1974).

HOOD, W. E., see SHERIF, HARVEY, WHITE, HOOD, and SHERIF (1961).

HOOK, E. B. (1973) Behavioral implications of the human XYY genotype. *Science*, 179:139–50. **57**

HOROWITZ, L. M. (1974) *Elements of statistics for psychology and education*. New York: McGraw-Hill. **576, 587**

HORTON, E. S., see SIMS, KELLEHER, HORTON, GLUCK, GOODMAN, and ROWE (1968).

HORTON, R. W., see THOMAS, HORTON, LIPPINCOTT, and DRABMAN (1977).

HOVLAND, C. I. (1937) The generalization of conditioned responses: I. The sensory generalization of conditioned responses with varying frequencies of tone. *Journal of General Psychology*, 17:125–48. **196**

HUBEL, D. H., and WIESEL, T. N. (1968) Receptive fields and functional architecture of monkey striate cortex. *Journal of Physiology* (London), 195:215–43. **142**

HUDSPETH, W. J., MCGAUGH, J. L., and THOMPSON, C. W. (1964) Aversive and amnesic effects of electroconvulsive shock. *Journal of Comparative and Physiological Psychology*, 57:61–64. **242**

HUESMANN, L. R., see ERON, HUESMANN, LEFKOWITZ, and WALDER (1972).

HUNT, B. M., see KLEIN, WEGMANN, and HUNT (1972).

HUNT, J. McV., see ENDLER and HUNT (1966).

HUNT, J. McV., see ENDLER and HUNT (1968).

HUNT, M. (1974) *Sexual behavior in the 1970's*. Chicago: Playboy Press. **305, 306**

HUNTER, I. M. L. (1974) *Memory*. Baltimore: Penguin. **247**

HURVICH, L. M. (1978) Two decades of opponent processes. In Billmeyer, F. W., Jr., and Wyszecki, G. (eds.) *Color 77*. Bristol, England: Adam Hilger. **115**

HYDEN, H. (1969) Biochemical aspects of learning and memory. In Pribram, K. (ed.) *On the biology of learning*. New York: Harcourt Brace Jovanovich. **233**

HYMAN, R. (1977) The case against parapsychology. *The Humanist*, 37:47–49. **152**

ISAACS, W., THOMAS, J., and GOLDIAMOND, I. (1965) Application of operant conditioning to reinstate verbal behavior in psychotics. In Ullmann, L. P., and Krasner, L. (eds.) *Case studies in behavior modification*. New York: Holt, Rinehart and Winston. **496**

ISAACSON, R. L. (1970) When brains are damaged. *Psychology Today*, 3:38–42. **368, 369**

ITTELSON, W., PROSHANSKY, H., RIVLIN, L., and WINKEL, G. (1974). *An introduction to environmental psychology*. New York: Holt, Rinehart and Winston. **571**

IZARD, C. E. (1977) *Human emotions*. New York: Plenum Press. **340**

JACKLIN, C. N., see MACCOBY and JACKLIN (1974).

JACKSON, P. W., see GETZELS and JACKSON (1962).

JACOBS, J. (1887) Experiments in "Prehension." *Mind*, 12:75–79. **224**

JACOBS, P. D., see THORNTON and JACOBS (1971).

JACOBSON, A., and KALES, A. (1967) Somnambulism: All-night EEG and related studies. In Kety, S. S., Evarts, E. V., and Williams, H. L. (eds.) *Sleep and altered states of consciousness*. Baltimore: Williams and Wilkins. **171**

JAHODA, M., see CHRISTIE and JAHODA (1954).

JAMES, W. (1890) *The principles of psychology*. New York: Holt. **12, 160, 232**

JAMESON, D. H., see LUDWIG, BRANDSMA, WILBUR, BENDFELDT, and JAMESON (1972).

JAMISON, D. T., SUPPES, P., FLETCHER, J. D., and ATKINSON, R. C. (1976) Cost and performance of computer-assisted instruction for education of disadvantaged children. In Froomkin, J., Jamison, D. T., and Radner, R. (eds.) *Education as an industry*. Cambridge, Mass.: NBER, Ballinger. **215**

JANET, P. (1889) *L'Automisme psychologique*. Paris: Felix Alcan. **159**

JARVIK, L. F., see ERLENMEYER-KIMLING and JARVIK (1963).

JEANS, R. F., see OSGOOD, LURIA, JEANS, and SMITH (1976).

JELLINEK, E. M. (1952) Phases of alcohol addiction. *Quarterly Journal of Studies on Alcohol*, 13:673–84. **478**

JENSEN, A. R. (1973) *Educability and group differences*. New York: Harper and Row. **362, 366**

JENSEN, J., see MONROE, RECHTSCHAFFEN, FOULKES, and JENSEN (1965).

JERSILD, A. T., BROOK, J. S., and BROOK, D. W. (1978) *The psychology of adolescence* (3rd ed.). New York: Macmillan. **99**

JOHNSON, B. D. (1973) *Marijuana users and drug subcultures*. New York: Wiley. **480**

JOHNSON, D. L., see MORGAN, JOHNSON, and HILGARD (1974).

JOHNSON, H. H., and SOLSO, R. L. (1978) *An introduction to experimental design in psychology: A case approach* (2nd ed.). New York: Harper and Row. **25**

JOHNSON, J. I., see WEIKER, JOHNSON, and PUBOLS (1964).

JOHNSON, M. K., see BRANSFORD and JOHNSON (1973).

JOHNSON, R. N. (1972) *Aggression in man and animals*. Philadelphia: Saunders. **343**

JOHNSON, V. E., see MASTERS and JOHNSON (1966).

JOHNSON-LAIRD, P. N., see MILLER and JOHNSON-LAIRD (1976).

JOHNSON-LAIRD, P. N., see WASON and JOHNSON-LAIRD (1972).

JONES, E. E., and DAVIS, K. E. (1965) From acts to dispositions. In Berkowitz, L. (ed.) *Advances in experimental social psychology*, Vol. 2. New York: Academic Press, pp. 219–66. **537**

JONES, E. E., and HARRIS, V. A. (1967) The attribution of attitudes. *Journal of Experimental Social Psychology*, 3:1–24. **542**

JONES, E. E., ROCK, L., SHAVER, K. G.,

REFERENCES AND INDEX TO AUTHORS OF WORKS CITED

GOETHALS, G. R., and WARD, L. M. (1968) Pattern of performance and ability attribution: An unexpected primacy effect. *Journal of Personality and Social Psychology,* 9:317–40. **533**

JONES, F. D., MAAS, J. W., DEKIRMEN-JIAN, H., and FAWCETT, J. A. (1973) Urinary catecholamine metabolites during behavioral changes in a patient with manic-depressive cycles. *Science,* 179:300–02. **458**

JONES, J. S., and OSWALD, I. (1968) Two cases of healthy insomnia. *EEG and Clinical Neurology,* 24:378–80. **165**

JONES, M. C., see MUSSEN and JONES (1958).

JORGENSON, B. W., see LEVINGER, SENN, and JORGENSEN (1970).

JULIEN, R. M. (1978) *A primer of drug action* (2nd ed.). San Francisco: Freeman. **485**

JUNG, C. G. (1968) *Analytical psychology: Its theory and practice.* New York: Pantheon. **169**

JUSCZYK, P., see EIMAS, SIQUELAND, JUSCZYK, and VIGORITO (1971).

KAGAN, J. (1973) What is intelligence? *Social Policy,* 4:88–94. **366**

KAGAN, J., KEARSLEY, R., and ZELAGO, P. R. (1978) *Infancy: Its place in human development.* Cambridge, Mass.: Harvard Univ. Press. **81**

KAGAN, J., and KLEIN, R. E. (1973) Cross-cultural perspectives on early development. *American Psychologist,* 28:947–61. **69**

KAGAN, J., see MUSSEN, CONGER, and KAGAN (1974).

KAHNEMAN, D., and TVERSKY, A. (1973) On the psychology of prediction. *Psychological Review,* 80:237–51. **252**

KAIJ, L. (1960) *Alcoholism in twins: Studies on the etiology and sequels of abuse of alcohol.* Stockholm: Alcuquist and Wiksell. **478**

KALAT, J. W., see ROZIN and KALAT (1971).

KALES, A., see JACOBSON and KALES (1967).

KALIN, R., see MCCLELLAND, DAVIS, KALIN, and WANNER (1972).

KALOGERIS, T. J., see DEUTSCH, YOUNG, and KALOGERIS (1978).

KALVEN, H., and ZEISEL, H. (1971) *The American jury.* Chicago: Univ. of Chicago Press. **569**

KAMIN, L. J. (1974) *The science and politics of I.Q.* Potomac, Md.: Erlbaum. **566**

KAMIN, L. J. (1976) Heredity, intelligence, politics, and psychology. In Block, N. J., and Dworkin, G. (eds.) *The IQ controversy.* New York, Pantheon. **365, 366**

KAMMANN, R., see MARKS and KAMMANN (1977).

KANDEL, D. (1975) Stages in adolescent involvement in drug use. *Science,* 190:912–14. **480**

KANDEL, D. B., and LESSER, G. S. (1972) *Youth in two worlds.* San Francisco: Jossey-Bass. **93, 94**

KANFER, F. H., and PHILLIPS, J. S. (1970) *Learning foundations of behavior therapy.* New York: Wiley. **446**

KAPLAN, R. M., and SINGER, R. D. (1976) Television violence and viewer aggression: A reexamination of the evidence. *Journal of Social Issues,* 32:35–70. **327**

KARLINS, M., see ANDREWS and KARLINS (1971).

KATCHER, A. H., see ZILLMANN, KATCHER, and MILAVSKY (1972).

KATZ, S. H., see SCARR, PAKSTIS, KATZ, and BARKER (1977).

KAUFMAN, L. (1979) *Perception: The world transformed.* New York and Toronto: Oxford Univ. Press. **127, 140, 154**

KAY, P. *see* BERLIN and KAY (1969).

KAXDIN, A. E., and WILCOXON, L. A. (1976) Systematic desensitization and nonspecific treatment effects: A methodological evaluation. *Psychological Bulletin,* 83:729–58. **507**

KEARSLEY, R., see KAGAN, KEARSLEY, and ZELAGO (1978).

KEELE, S. W., see POSNER and KEELE (1967).

KEEN, E. (1977) *A primer in phenomenological psychology.* New York: Holt, Rinehart and Winston. **412**

KEESEY, R. E., and POWLEY, T. L. (1975) Hypothalamic regulation of body weight. *American Scientist,* 63:558–65. **291**

KEESEY, R. E., see MITCHEL and KEESEY (1974).

KEESEY, R. E., see POWLEY and KEESEY (1970).

KELLEHER, P. E., see SIMS, KELLEHER, HORTON, GLUCK, GOODMAN, and ROWE (1968).

KELLEY, H. H. (1967) Attribution theory in social psychology. In Levine, D. (ed.) *Nebraska symposium on motivation,* Vol. 15. Lincoln: Univ. of Nebraska Press. **537, 538**

KELLEY, H. H. (1971) Attribution in social interaction. In Jones, E. E., Kanouse, D. E., Kelley, H. H., Nisbett, R. E., Valins, S., and Weiner, B. (eds.) *Attribution: Perceiving the causes of behavior.* Morristown, N.J.: General Learning Press. **538**

KELLEY, H. H. (1972) Causal schemata and the attribution process. In Jones, E. E., Kanouse, D. E., Kelley, H. H., Nisbett, R. E., Valins, S., and Weiner, B. (eds.) *Attribution: Perceiving the causes of behavior.* Morristown, N.J.: General Learning Press. **538**

KELLEY, H. H., and WOODRUFF, C. L. (1956) Members' reactions to apparent group approval of a counternorm communication. *Journal of Abnormal and Social Psychology,* 52:67–74. **529**

KELMAN, H. C. (1961) Processes of opinion change. *Public Opinion Quarterly,* 25:57–78. **524**

KEMPE, C. H., see HELFER and KEMPE (1968).

KEMPER, T. L., see GALABURDA, LEMAY, KEMPER, and GESCHWIND (1978).

KENISTON, K., see FISHKIN, KENISTON, and MACKINNON (1973).

KENNEDY, C. E. (1978) *Human development: The adult years and aging.* New York: Macmillan. **99**

KENNEDY, R. A., see WILKES and KENNEDY (1969).

KERCKHOFF, A. C., and DAVIS, K. E. (1962) Value consensus and need complementarity in mate selection. *American Sociological Review,* 17:295–303. **536**

KERSEY, J., see WEBB and KERSEY (1967).

KESEY, K. (1962) *One flew over the cuckoo's nest.* New York: Viking. **485**

KESSEN, W., see NOWLIS and KESSEN (1976).

KESTENBAUM, R. S., see RESNICK, KESTENBAUM, and SCHWARTZ (1977).

KETY, S. S., see ROSENTHAL, WENDER, KETY, SCHULSINGER, WELNER, and RIEDER (1975).

KIESLER, C. A., NISBETT, R. E., and ZANNA, M. P. (1969) On inferring one's beliefs from one's behavior. *Journal of Personality and Social Psychology,* 4:321–27. **541**

KIHLSTROM, J. F., and EVANS, F. J. (1976) Recovery of memory after posthypnotic amnesia. *Journal of Abnormal Psychology,* 85:558–63. **179**

KILBY, M. M., see ELLINWOOD and KILBY (1977).

KILHAM, W., and MANN, L. (1974) Level of destructive obedience as a function of transmitter and executant roles in the Milgram obedience paradigm. *Journal of Personality and Social Psychology,* 29:696–702. **526**

KIMMEL, D. (1974) *Adulthood and aging.* New York: Wiley. **96, 203**

KIMMEL, H. D. (1974) Instrumental conditioning of automatically mediated responses in human beings. *American Psychologist,* 29:325–35. **203**

KING, M., see SMITH, KING, and HOEBEL (1970).

KINSEY, A. C., POMEROY, W. B., and MARTIN, C. E. (1948) *Sexual behavior in the human male.* Philadelphia: Saunders. **19**

KINSEY, A. C., POMEROY, W. B., MARTIN, C. E., and GEBHARD, P. H. (1953) *Sexual behavior in the human female.* Philadelphia: Saunders. **19, 306**

KINTSCH, W. (1974) *The representation of meaning in memory.* Hillsdale, N.J.: Erlbaum. **249, 259**

KINTSCH, W., and BUSCHKE, H. (1969) Homophones and synonyms in short-term memory. *Journal of Experimental Psychology,* 80:403–07. **228, 229**

KIRSCH, M. A., and GLASS, L. L. (1977) Psychiatric disturbances associated with Erhard Seminars Training: II. Additional cases and theoretical considerations. *American Journal of Psychiatry,* 134:1254–58. **504**

KIVITZ, M. S., see CLARK, KIVITZ, and ROSEN (1969).

KLAHR, D. (ed.) (1976) *Cognition and instruction.* Hillsdale, N.J.: Erlbaum. **215**

KLATZKY, R. (1975) *Human memory:*

Structures and processes. San Francisco: Freeman. **249**

KLEIN, K. E., WEGMANN, H. M., and HUNT, B. M. (1972) Desynchronization of body temperature and performance circadian rhythm as a result of outgoing and home-going transmeridian flights. *Aerospace Medicine,* 43:119–32. **166**

KLEIN, R. E., see KAGAN and KLEIN (1973).

KLEINHESSELINK, R. R., and EDWARDS, R. E. (1975) Seeking and avoiding belief-discrepant information as a function of its perceived refutability. *Journal of Personality and Social Psychology,* 31:787–90. **556**

KLEINMUNTZ, B. (1974) *Essentials of abnormal psychology.* New York: Harper and Row. **452, 457**

KLEITMAN, N., see DEMENT and KLEITMAN (1957).

KLENTZ, B., see BEAMAN, BARNES, KLENTZ, and MCQUIRK (1978).

KLINEBERG, O. (1938) Emotional expression in Chinese literature. *Journal of Abnormal and Social Psychology,* 33:517–20. **340**

KLING, J. W., and RIGGS, L. A. (1971) *Experimental psychology* (3rd ed.). New York: Holt, Rinehart and Winston. **127**

KNITTLE, J. L. (1975) Early influences on development of adipose tissue. In Bray, G. A. (ed.) *Obesity in perspective.* Washington, D.C.: U.S. Government Printing Office. **296**

KNITTLE, J. L., and HIRSCH, J. (1968) Effect of early nutrition on the development of rat epididymal fat pads: Cellularity and metabolism. *Journal of Clinical Investigation,* 47:2091. **296**

KNITTLE, J. L., see HIRSCH and KNITTLE (1970).

KNOX, V. J., CRUTCHFIELD, L., and HILGARD, E. R. (1975) The nature of task interference in hypnotic dissociation: An investigation of hypnotic behavior. *International Journal of Clinical and Experimental Hypnosis,* 23:305–23. **180**

KOBASIGAWA, A., ARAKAKI, K., and AWIGUNI, A. (1966) Avoidance of feminine toys by kindergarten boys: The effects of adult presence or absence, and an adult's attitudes toward sex-typing. *Japanese Journal of Psychology,* 37:96–103. **85**

KOCH, C., see STUNKARD and KOCH (1964).

KOENIG, K. E., see NEWCOMB, KOENIG, FLACKS, and WARWICK (1967).

KOFFKA, K. (1925) *The growth of the mind* (R. M. Ogden, tr.). New York: Harcourt Brace Jovanovich. **12**

KOGAN, N., and PANKOVE, E. (1974) Long-term predictive validity of divergent-thinking tests: Some negative evidence. *Journal of Educational Psychology,* 66:802–10. **361**

KOGAN, N., see WALLACH and KOGAN (1965).

KOHEN-RAZ, R. (1968) Mental and motor development of Kibbutz, institutionalized,

and home-reared infants in Israel. *Child Development,* 39:489–504. **80**

KOHLBERG, L. (1967) Moral and religious education and the public schools: A developmental view. In Sizer, T. (ed.) *Religion and public education.* Boston: Houghton Mifflin. **74**

KOHLBERG, L. (1969) Stage and sequence: The cognitive-developmental approach to socialization. In Goslin, D. A. (ed.) *Handbook of socialization theory and research.* Chicago: Rand McNally. **75**

KOHLBERG, L. (1973) Implications of developmental psychology for education: Examples from moral development. *Educational Psychologist,* 10:2–14. **75**

KÖHLER, W. (1925) *The mentality of apes.* New York: Harcourt Brace Jovanovich. **209, 218**

KONEČNI, V. J., and EBBESEN, E. B. (1976) Disinhibition versus the cathartic effect: Artifact and substance. *Journal of Personality and Social Psychology,* 34:352–65. **327**

KOPELL, B. S., see DAVIS, MOHS, TINKLENBERG, PFEFFERBAUM, HOLLISTER, and KOPELL (1978).

KORMAN, A. K. (1974) *The psychology of motivation.* Englewood Cliffs, N.J.: Prentice-Hall. **313, 343**

KORTEN, F. F., COOK, S. W., and LACEY, J. I. (eds.) (1970) *Psychology and the problems of society.* Washington, D.C.: American Psychological Association. **571**

KOSSLYN, S. M. (1973) Scanning visual images: Some structural implications. *Perception and Psychophysics,* 14:90–94. **272**

KOTCH, J. B., see BENSON, KOTCH, CRASSWELLER, and GREENWOOD (1977).

KOTIN, J., see POST, KOTIN, GOODWIN, and GORDON (1973).

KOTOVSKY, K., and SIMON, H. A. (1973) Empirical tests of a theory of human acquisition of concepts for sequential patterns. *Cognitive Psychology,* 4:399–424. **274**

KOTOVSKY, K., see SIMON and KOTOVSKY (1963).

KOVACH, J., see MURPHY and KOVACH (1972).

KRAMER, M. (1976) Paper presented at the Second Rochester International Conference on Schizophrenia, Rochester, N.Y., May 1976. **462**

KRANTZ, D. L., ATKINSON, R. C., LUCE, R. D., and SUPPES, P. (eds.) (1974) *Contemporary developments in mathematical psychology.* San Francisco: Freeman. **127, 219**

KRANTZ, D. L., LUCE, R. D., SUPPES, P., and TVERSKY, A. (1971) *Foundations of measurement.* New York: Academic Press. **587**

KRASNER, L., and ULLMANN, L. P. (1973) *Behavior influence and personality.* New York: Holt, Rinehart and Winston. **446**

KRASNER, L., see ULLMANN and KRASNER (1969).

KRAUSS, S., and DAVIS, D. (1976) *The effects of mass communication on politi-*

cal behavior. University Park, Penn.: Pennsylvania State Univ. Press. **556**

KRAWITZ, R. N., see LESSER, KRAWITZ, and PACKARD (1963).

KRETSCHMER, E. (1925) *Physique and character.* London: Kegan Paul. **381**

KRIPKE, D. F., and SIMONS, R. N. (1976) Average sleep, insomnia, and sleeping pill use. *Sleep Research,* 5:110. **167**

KTSANES, T., see WINCH, KTSANES, and KTSANES (1954).

KTSANES, V., see WINCH, KTSANES, and KTSANES (1954).

KUBIS, J. F. (1962). Cited in Smith, B. M., The polygraph. In Atkinson, R. C. (ed.) *Contemporary psychology.* San Francisco: Freeman. **333**

KUFFLER, S. W., and NICHOLLS, J. G. (1976) *From neuron to brain.* Sunderland, Mass.: Sinauer Associates. **61**

KUHN, T. S. (1970) *The structure of scientific revolutions* (2nd ed.). Chicago: Univ. of Chicago Press. **541**

KURTINES, W., and GREIF, E. B. (1974) The development of moral thought: Review and evaluation of Kohlberg's approach. *Psychological Bulletin,* 8:453–70. **75**

LACEY, J. I., see KORTEN, COOK, and LACEY (1970).

LADER, M., see MARKS and LADER (1973).

LAING, R. D. (1967) *The politics of experience.* New York: Ballantine. **446**

LAIRD, J. D. (1974) Self-attribution of emotion: The effects of expressive behavior on the quality of emotional experience. *Journal of Personality and Social Psychology,* 29:475–86. **340**

LANGACKER, R. W. (1973) *Language and its structure* (2nd ed.). New York: Harcourt Brace Jovanovich. **268**

LANGFELD, H. S., see BORING, LANGFELD, and WELD (1939).

LANGFORD, G., see MEDDIS, PEARSON, and LANGFORD (1973).

LANGNER, T. S., GERSTEN, J. C., and EISENBERG, J. G. (1977) Family Research Project. Paper presented at the meeting of the Kittay Scientific Foundation, New York. **64**

LANGNER, T. S., see SROLE, LANGNER, MICHAEL, OPLER, and RENNIE (1962).

LASHLEY, K. S. (1929) *Brain mechanisms and intelligence.* Chicago: Univ. of Chicago Press. **40**

LATANÉ, B., and DARLEY, J. M. (1968) Group inhibition of bystander intervention in emergencies. *Journal of Personality and Social Psychology,* 10:215–21. **521**

LATANÉ, B., and DARLEY J. M. (1970) *The unresponsive bystander: Why doesn't he help?* New York: Appleton-Century-Crofts. **520**

LATANÉ, B., and RODIN, J. (1969) A lady in distress: Inhibiting effects of friends and strangers on bystander intervention. *Journal of Experimental and Social Psychology,* 5:189–202. **521**

LATANÉ, B., see DARLEY and LATANÉ (1968).

LATIES, V. G., see WEISS and LATIES (1962).

LAUGHLIN, H. P. (1967) *The neuroses.* Washington, D.C.: Butterworths. **450, 453**

LAWTON, S. F., see BARON and LAWTON (1972).

LAYTON, B., see ROSS, LAYTON, ERICKSON, and SCHOPLER (1973).

LAZAR, I. (1977) *Longitudinal data in child development programs (I).* Paper presented at the Office of Child Development (OHD, HEW) Conference: Parents, Children, and Continuity, El Paso, Tex., May 1977. **368**

LAZARSFELD, P. F., see BERELSON, LAZARSFELD, and MCPHEE (1954).

LAZARUS, A. A. (1972) *Behavior therapy and beyond.* New York: McGraw-Hill. **446, 494**

LAZARUS, R. S., see SPEISMAN, LAZARUS, MORDKOFF, and DAVISON (1964).

LEE, R. S., see CHEIN, GERARD, LEE, and ROSENFELD (1964).

LEFAN, J., see HELMREICH, ARONSON, and LEFAN (1970).

LEFKOWITZ, M. M., see ERON, HUESMANN, LEFKOWITZ, and WALDER (1972).

LEHRMAN, D. S. (1964) Control of behavior cycles in reproduction. In Etkin, W. (ed.) *Social behavior and organization among vertebrates.* Chicago: Univ. of Chicago Press. **287**

LEIBOWITZ, H. W., see PARRISH, LUNDY, and LEIBOWITZ (1968).

LEIBOWITZ, H., see ZEIGLER and LEIBOWITZ (1957).

LEIFFER, A. D., GORDON, N. J., and GRAVES, S. B. (1974) Children's television: More than mere entertainment. *Harvard Educational Review,* 44:213–45. **329**

LEMAY, M., see GALABURDA, LEMAY, KEMPER, and GESCHWIND (1978).

LENNEBERG, E. H. (1967) *Biological foundations of language.* New York: Wiley. **267**

LEPPER, M. R. (1973) Dissonance, self-perception, and honesty in children. *Journal of Personality and Social Psychology,* 25:65–74. **540**

LEPPER, M. R., GREENE, D., and NISBETT, R. E. (1973) Undermining children's intrinsic interest with extrinsic reward: A test of the "overjustification" hypothesis. *Journal of Personality and Social Psychology,* 28:129–37. **203**

LESGOLD, A., see BOWER, CLARK, WINZENZ, and LESGOLD (1969).

LESSER, G. S., KRAWITZ, R. N., and PACKARD, R. (1963) Experimental arousal of achievement motivation in adolescent girls. *Journal of Abnormal and Social Psychology,* 66:59–66. **567**

LESSER, G. S., see KANDEL and LESSER (1972).

LESTER, D. (1974) Effect of suicide prevention centers on suicide rates in the United States. *Public Health Reports,* 89:37–39. **511**

LEVENSON, H., BURFORD, B., BONNO, B., and LOREN, D. (1975) Are women still prejudiced against women? A replication and extension of Goldberg's study. *Journal of Psychology,* 89:67–71. **549**

LEVIN, J. M., see ALLEN and LEVIN (1971).

LEVINGER, G., SENN, D. J., and JORGENSEN, B. W. (1970) Progress toward permanence in courtship: A test of the Kerckhoff-Davis hypotheses. *Sociometry,* 33:427–43. **536**

LEVINSON, D., see ADORNO, FRENKEL-BRUNSWIK, LEVINSON, and SANFORD (1950).

LEVY, A., see FREEDMAN, HESHKA, and LEVY (1975).

LEWIN, K., see BARKER, DEMBO, and LEWIN (1941).

LEWINSOHN, P. M. (1975) The behavioral study and treatment of depression. In Hersen, M. (ed.) *Progress in behavioral modification.* New York: Academic Press. **460**

LEWIS, H. B., GOODENOUGH, D. R., SHAPIRO, A., and SLESER, I. (1966) Individual differences in dream recall. *Journal of Abnormal Psychology,* 71:52–59. **169**

LEWIS, S. (1934) *Work of art.* Garden City, N.Y.: Doubleday. **380**

LEWIS, S. A., see BRISLIN and LEWIS (1968).

LEWIS, S. K., see CIALDINI, VINCENT, LEWIS, CATALAN, WHEELER, and DARBY (1975).

LEYENS, J. P., CAMINO, L., PARKE, R. D., and BERKOWITZ, L. (1975) Effects of movie violence on aggression in a field setting as a function of group dominance and cohesion. *Journal of Personality and Social Psychology,* 32:346–60. **327**

LEYENS, J. P., see PARKE, BERKOWITZ, LEYENS, WEST, and SEBASTIAN (1977).

LIBERMAN, A. M., COOPER, F., SHANKWEILER, D., and STUDDERT-KENNEDY, M. (1967) Perception of the speech code. *Psychological Review,* 74:431–59. **260**

LIDZ, T., FLECK, S., and CORNELISON, A. R. (1965) *Schizophrenia and the family.* New York: International Universities Press. **470**

LIEBERMAN, M. A., YALOM, I. D., and MILES, M. B. (1973) *Encounter groups: First facts.* New York: Basic Books. **504, 515**

LIGHTBOWN, P., see BLOOM, HOOD, and LIGHTBOWN (1974).

LIMBER, J. (1973) The genesis of complex sentences. In Moore, T. E. (ed.) *Cognitive development and the acquisition of language.* New York: Academic Press. **264**

LINDSAY, P. H., and NORMAN, D. A. (1977) *Human information processing* (2nd ed.). New York: Academic Press. **127, 154, 219, 277**

LINDSTRÖM, L., see GUNNE, LINDSTRÖM, and TERENIUS (1977).

LINDZEY, G., see HALL and LINDZEY (1978).

LINDZEY, G., see LOEHLIN, LINDZEY, and SPUHLER (1975).

LING, N., see BLOOM, SEGAL, LING, and GUILLEMIN (1976).

LIPPERT, W. W., and SENTER, R. J. (1966) Electrodermal responses in the sociopath. *Psychonomic Science,* 4:25–26. **473**

LIPPINCOTT, E. C., see THOMAS, HORTON, LIPPINCOTT, and DRABMAN (1977).

LISMAN, S. A. (1974) Alcoholic "blackout": State-dependent learning? *Archives of General Psychiatry,* 30:46–53. **479**

LITTMAN, R. A., see PATTERSON, LITTMAN, and BRICKER (1967).

LOCKHART, R. S., see CRAIK and LOCKHART (1972).

LOEHLIN, J. C., LINDZEY, G., and SPUHLER, J. N. (1975) *Race differences in intelligence.* San Francisco: Freeman. **367, 373, 375**

LOEW, C. A. (1967) Acquisition of a hostile attitude and its relationship to aggressive behavior. *Journal of Personality and Social Psychology,* 5:335–41. **326**

LOFTUS, E. F., see LOFTUS and LOFTUS (1975).

LOFTUS, G. R., and LOFTUS, E. F. (1975) *Human memory: The processing of information.* New York: Halsted Press. **246, 249**

LOGAN, F. A., and FERRARO, D. P. (1978) *Systematic analyses of learning and motivation.* New York: Wiley. **313**

LONDON, P. (1977) *Behavior control.* New York: New American Library. **571**

LOO, C. M. (1972) The effects of spatial density on the social behavior of children. *Journal of Applied Social Psychology,* 2:372, 381. **562**

LOOMIS, A. L., HARVEY, E. N., and HOBART, G. A. (1937) Cerebral states during sleep as studied by human potentials. *Journal of Experimental Psychology,* 21:127–44. **166**

LOREN, D., see LEVENSON, BURFORD, BONNO, and LOREN (1975).

LORENZ, K. (1966) *On aggression.* New York: Harcourt Brace Jovanovich. **324**

LOTTIER, S. (1938) Distribution of criminal offenses in metropolitan regions. *Journal of Criminal Law and Criminology,* 29:39–45. **560**

LOWELL, E. L., see MCCLELLAND, ATKINSON, CLARK, and LOWELL (1953).

LUCE, R. D., see KRANTZ, ATKINSON, LUCE, and SUPPES (1974).

LUCE, R. D., see KRANTZ, LUCE, SUPPES, and TVERSKY (1971).

LUCHINS, A. (1957a) Primacy-recency in impression formation. In Hovland, C. I. (ed.) *The order of presentation in persuasion.* New Haven, Conn.: Yale Univ. Press. **532, 533**

LUCHINS, A. (1957b) Experimental attempts to minimize the impact of first impressions. In Hovland, C. I. (ed.) *The order of presentation in persuasion.* New Haven, Conn.: Yale Univ. Press. **533**

LUDEL, J. (1978) *Introduction to sensory processes.* San Francisco: Freeman. **107, 127**

LUDWIG, A. M., BRANDSMA, J. M., WIL-

BUR, C. B., BENDFELDT, F., and JAMESON, D. H. (1972) The objective study of a multiple personality. *Archives of General Psychiatry*, 26:298–310. **164**

LUNDY, R. M., see PARRISH, LUNDY, and LEIBOWITZ (1968).

LURIA, Z., see OSGOOD, LURIA, JEANS, and SMITH (1976).

LYKKEN, D. T. (1957) A study of anxiety in the sociopathic personality. *Journal of Abnormal and Social Psychology*, 55:6–10. **473**

MAAS, J. W., see JONES, MAAS, DEKIRMENJIAN, and FAWCETT (1973).

MACCOBY, E. E., and BEE, H. L. (1965) Some speculations concerning the lag between perceiving and performing. *Child Development*, 36:367–77. **261**

MACCOBY, E. E., and FELDMAN, S. S. (1972) Mother attachment and stranger reactions in the third year of life. *Monograph of the Society for Research in Child Development*, No. 1, 37:1–86. **78, 81**

MACCOBY, E. E., and JACKLIN, C. N. (1974) *The psychology of sex differences.* Stanford, Calif.: Stanford Univ. Press. **86, 87**

MACCOBY, N., FARQUHAR, J. W., WOOD, P. D., and ALEXANDER, J. (1977) Reducing the risk of cardiovascular disease: Effects of a community-based campaign on knowledge and behavior. *Journal of Community Health*, 3:100–14. **557, 558**

MACCOBY, N., see FARQUHAR, MACCOBY, and WOOD, and OTHERS (1977).

MACFARLANE, J. A. (1977) *The psychology of childbirth.* Cambridge, Mass.: Harvard Univ. Press. **67**

MACK, D., see HERMAN and MACK (1975).

MACKAY, D. G. (1966) To end ambiguous sentences. *Perception and Psychophysics*, 1:426–36. **259**

MACKINNON, C., see FISHKIN, KENISTON, and MACKINNON (1973).

MADDI, S., and COSTA, P. (1972) *Humanism in personology.* Chicago: Aldine. **412**

MAGNUSSON, D., and ENDLER, N. S. (eds.) (1977) *Personality at the crossroads: Current issues in interactional psychology.* New York: Halsted Press. **413**

MAHARISHI MAHESH YOGI (1963) *The science of being and the art of living.* New York: Signet Books. **171**

MAHER, B. A. (1966) *Principles of psychotherapy: An experimental approach.* New York: McGraw-Hill. **463, 464, 472, 474**

MAISEL, E., see GEER and MAISEL (1972).

MALAMUD, P., see WATERS and MALAMUD (1975).

MANKIEWICZ, F., and SWERDLOW, J. (1977) *Remote control.* New York: Quadrangle. **328**

MANN, L., see KILHAM and MANN (1974).

MARGOLIS, R., see GLICK and MARGOLIS (1962).

MARGULIS, S., see YERKES and MARGULIS (1909).

MARK, V. H., and ERVIN, F. R. (1970) *Violence and the brain.* New York: Harper and Row. **321**

MARKS, D., and KAMMANN, R. (1977) The nonpsychic powers of Uri Geller. *The Zetetic*, 1:9–17. **184**

MARKS, I., and LADER, M. (1973) Anxiety states (anxiety neurosis): A review. *Journal of Nervous and Mental Disease*, 156:3–18. **448**

MARLER, P. (1976) On animal aggression. *American Psychologist*, 31:239–46. **325**

MARSHALL, G. (1976) *The affective consequences of "inadequately explained" physiological arousal.* Unpublished doctoral dissertation, Stanford Univ., Stanford, Calif. **337**

MARTIN, C. E., see KINSEY, POMEROY, and MARTIN (1948).

MARTIN, C. E., see KINSEY, POMEROY, MARTIN, and GEBHARD (1953).

MARTIN, D. G. (1971) *Introduction to psychotherapy.* Monterey, Calif.: Brooks/Cole. **515**

MASER, J. D., and SELIGMAN, M. E. P. (eds.) (1977) *Psychopathology: Experimental models.* San Francisco: Freeman. **485**

MASLACH, C., see ZIMBARDO, EBBESEN, and MASLACH (1977).

MASLOW, A. H. (1954) *Motivation and personality.* New York: Harper and Row. **316, 396**

MASLOW, A. H. (1967) Self-actualization and beyond. In Bugental, J. F. T. (ed.) *Challenges of humanistic psychology.* New York: McGraw-Hill. **396**

MASLOW, A. H. (1970) *Motivation and personality* (2nd ed.). New York: Harper and Row. **395**

MASON, J. W., see BRADY, PORTER, CONRAD, and MASON (1958).

MASSERMAN, J. H. (1961) *Principles of dynamic psychiatry* (2nd ed.). Philadelphia: Saunders. **424, 429**

MASTERS, J. C., see RIMM and MASTERS, (1974).

MASTERS, W. H., and JOHNSON, V. E. (1966) *Human sexual response.* Boston: Little, Brown. **18**

MATARAZZO, J. D. (1971) Some national developments in the utilization of nontraditional mental health manpower. *American Psychologist*, 26:363–72. **512**

MATARAZZO, J. D., and WIENS, A. W. (1972) *The interview: Research on its anatomy and structure.* Chicago: Aldine-Atherton. **398**

MATARAZZO, J. E. (1972) *Wechsler's measurement and appraisal of adult intelligence* (5th ed.). Baltimore: Williams and Wilkins. **375**

MAYER, J. (1955) Regulation of energy intake and the body weight: The glucostatic theory and the lipostatic theory. *Annals of the New York Academy of Science*, 63:15–43. **289**

MAYER, J., see THOMAS and MAYER (1973).

MCARTHUR, L. A. (1972) The how and what of why: Some determinants and consequences of causal attribution. *Journal of Personality and Social Psychology*, 22:171–93. **538**

MCCLEARN, G. E., and DEFRIES, J. C. (1973) *Introduction to behavioral genetics.* San Francisco: Freeman. **58, 61, 375, 485**

MCCLELLAND, D. C., ATKINSON, J. W., CLARK, R. A., and LOWELL, E. L. (1953) *The achievement motive.* New York: Appleton-Century-Crofts. **566**

MCCLELLAND, D. C., DAVIS, W. N., KALIN, R., and WANNER, E. (1972) *The drinking man.* New York: Free Press. **479**

MCCLELLAND, D. C., and WINTER, D. G. (1969) *Motivating economic achievement.* New York: Free Press. **567**

MCCONNELL, J. V., SHIGEHISA, T., and SALIVE, H. (1970) Attempts to transfer approach and avoidance responses by RNA injections in rats. In Pribram, K. H., and Broadbent, D. E. (eds.) *Biology of memory.* New York: Academic Press. **233**

MCDONALD, F. J., see BANDURA and MCDONALD (1963).

MCDOUGALL, W. (1908) *Social psychology.* New York: G. P. Putnam's Sons. **282**

MCGAUGH, J. L., see HUDSPETH, MCGAUGH, and THOMPSON (1964).

MCGHIE, A., and CHAPMAN, J. (1961) Disorders of attention and perception in early schizophrenia. *British Journal of Medical Psychology*, 34:103–16. **464, 465**

MCGINTY, D., EPSTEIN, A. W., and TEITELBAUM, P. (1965) The contribution of oro-pharyngeal sensations to hypothalamic hyperphagia. *Animal Behavior*, 13:413–18. **291**

MCGOWAN, B. K., see GARCIA, MCGOWAN, and GREEN (1972).

MCGUIRE, W. J., see ABELSON, ARONSON, MCGUIRE, NEWCOMB, ROSENBERG, and TANNENBAUM (1968).

MCKENNA, R. J. (1972) Some effects of anxiety level and food cues on the eating behavior of obese and normal subjects. *Journal of Personality and Social Psychology*, 22:311–19. **294**

MCNEILL, D. (1966) Developmental psycholinguistics. In Smith, F., and Miller, G. A. (eds.) *The genesis of language: A psycholinguistic approach.* Cambridge, Mass.: M.I.T. Press. **265**

MCNEILL, D., see BROWN and MCNEILL (1966).

MCPHEE, W. N., see BERELSON, LAZARSFELD, and MCPHEE (1954).

MCPHERSON, J. M., see GALLE, GOVE, and MCPHERSON (1972).

MCQUADE, W., and AIKMAN, A. (1975) *Stress.* New York: Dutton. **439**

MCQUIRK, B., see BEAMAN, BARNES, KLENTZ, and MCQUIRK (1978).

MEAD, W., see GOECKNER, GREENOUGH, and MEAD (1973).

MECHANIC, D. (1962) *Students under stress.* New York: Free Press. **438**

MECHANIC, D. (1975) Sociocultural and social-psychological factors affecting personal responses to psychological disorder. *Journal of Health and Social Behavior*, 16:393–404. **437**

MEDDIS, R., PEARSON, A. J. D., and LANGFORD, G. (1973) An extreme case of healthy insomnia. *EEG and Clinical Neurology,* 35:213–14. **166**

MEDNICK, S. A. (1962) The associative basis of the creative process. *Psychological Review,* 69:220–32. **360**

MELTON, A. W. (1963) Implications of short-term memory for a general theory of memory. *Journal of Verbal Learning and Verbal Behavior,* 2:1–21. **222**

MENNINGER, K. (1968) *The crime of punishment.* New York: Viking, Compass. **474**

MENNINGER, K., and HOLZMAN, P. S. (1973) *Theory of psychoanalytic technique* (2nd ed.). New York: Basic Books. **515**

MENZIES, R. (1937) Conditioned vasomotor responses in human subjects. *Journal of Psychology,* 4:75–120. **195**

MERRILL, M. A., see TERMAN and MERRILL (1937).

MERRILL, M. A., see TERMAN and MERRILL (1960).

MERVIS, C. B., see ROSCH and MERVIS (1975).

MESSER, S. (1967) Implicit phonology in children. *Journal of Verbal Learning and Verbal Behavior,* 6:609–13. **260**

MEYER, D. R., see HARLOW, HARLOW, and MEYER (1950).

MEYERS, L. S., and GROSSEN, N. E. (1978) *Behavioral research: Theory, procedure, and design* (2nd ed.). San Francisco: Freeman. **25**

MICHAEL, S. T., see SROLE, LANGNER, MICHAEL, OPLER, and RENNIE (1962).

MILAVSKY, B., see ZILLMANN, KATCHER, and MILAVSKY (1972).

MILES, M. B., see LIEBERMAN, YALOM, and MILES (1973).

MILGRAM, S. (1962) *Obedience to authority: Experiments in social psychology.* National Science Foundation grant application, Yale Univ., New Haven, Conn., pp. 23–24. **526**

MILGRAM, S. (1963) Behavioral study of obedience. *Journal of Abnormal and Social Psychology,* 67:371–78. **525**

MILGRAM, S. (1974) *Obedience to authority: An experimental view.* New York: Harper and Row. **527**

MILLER, G. A. (1956) The magical number seven plus or minus two: Some limits on our capacity for processing information. *Psychological Review,* 63:81–97. **224, 226**

MILLER, G. A., GALANTER, E., and PRIBRAM, K. H. (1960) *Plans and the structure of behavior.* New York: Holt, Rinehart and Winston. **160**

MILLER, G. A., and JOHNSON-LAIRD, P. N. (1976) *Language and perception.* Cambridge, Mass.: Harvard Univ. Press. **254**

MILLER, G. A., see CLARK and MILLER (1970).

MILLER, H. L., and RIVENBANK, W. H. (1970) III. Sexual differences in physical attractiveness as a determinant of heterosexual likings. *Psychological Reports,* 27:701–02. **534**

MILLER, J. M., MOODY, D. B., and STEBBINS, W. C. (1969) Evoked potentials and auditory reaction time in monkeys. *Science,* 163:592–94. **45**

MILLER, N. E. (1974) Introduction: Current issues and key problems. In Miller, N. E., Barber, T. X., DiCara, L., Kamiya, J., Shapiro, D., and Stoyva, J. (eds.) *Biofeedback and self-control.* Chicago: Adline. **203**

MILLER, N. E., and BUGELSKI, R. (1948) Minor studies of aggression: II. The influence of frustrations imposed by the in-group on attitudes expressed toward out-groups. *The Journal of Psychology,* 25:437–42. **422**

MILLER, N. E., see DELGADO, ROBERTS, and MILLER (1954).

MILLER, N. E., see DOLLARD, DOOB, MILLER, MOWRER, and SEARS (1939).

MILLER, R. F., see COLE, HART, and MILLER (1956).

MILNER, B. (1964) Some effects of frontal lobectomy in man. In Warren, J. M., and Akert, K. (eds.) *The frontal granular cortex and behavior.* New York: McGraw-Hill. **39, 45**

MILNER, P. M. (1966) *Physiological psychology.* New York: Holt, Rinehart and Winston. **242**

MINIUM, E. W. (1978) *Statistical reasoning in psychology and education* (2nd ed.). New York: Wiley. **587**

MINTZ, J., see STANTON, MINTZ, and FRANKLIN (1976).

MIRSKY, A. F., see CHALL and MIRSKY (1978).

MISCHEL, H. (1974) Sex bias in the evaluation of professional achievements. *Journal of Educational Psychology,* 66:157–66. **549**

MISCHEL, H. N., see MISCHEL and MISCHEL (1974).

MISCHEL, W. (1968) *Personality and assessment.* New York: Wiley. **228**

MISCHEL, W. (1973) Toward a cognitive social learning reconceptualization of personality. *Psychological Review,* 80:252–83. **388**

MISCHEL, W. (1976) *Introduction to personality* (2nd. ed.). New York: Holt, Rinehart and Winston. **406, 412**

MISCHEL, W., and MISCHEL, H. N. (1974) A cognitive social learning approach to morality and self-regulation. In Lickona, T. (ed.) *Men and morality.* New York: Holt, Rinehart and Winston. **75**

MISHRA, S. R. (1977) *Self analysis and self knowledge.* Lakemont, Ga.: CSA Press. **187**

MITCHEL, J. S., and KEESEY, R. E. (1974) The effects of lateral hypothalamic lesions and castration upon the body weight of male rats. *Behavioral Biology,* 11:69–82. **290**

MITCHELL, D. E. (1977) The influence of early visual experience on visual perception. In Harris, C. S. (ed.) *Visual coding and adaptability.* Hillsdale, N.J.: Erlbaum. **146**

MITCHELL, R. E. (1971) Some social implications of high density housing. *American Sociological Review,* 36:18–29. **561, 563**

MITLER, M. M., and DEMENT, W. (1977) Developmental studies on canine narcolepsy: Pattern and psychocomparisons between affected and normal animals. *EEG and Clinical Neurophysiology,* 43:691–99. **168**

MITLER, M. M., see CARSKADON, MITLER, and DEMENT (1974).

MLADEJOVSKY, M. G., see DOBELLE, MLADEJOVSKY, EVANS, ROBERTS, and GIRVIN (1976).

MOHS, R. C., see DAVIS, MOHS, TINKLENBERG, PFEFFERBAUM, HOLLISTER, and KOPELL (1978).

MONEY, J., and EHRHARDT, A. A. (1972) *Man and woman, boy and girl.* Baltimore: Johns Hopkins Univ. Press. **302**

MONEY, J., and MUSAPH, H. (eds.) (1977) *Handbook of sexology.* Amsterdam: Elsevier/North Holland Biomedical Press. **313**

MONROE, L. J., RECHTSCHAFFEN, A., FOULKES, D., and JENSEN, J. (1965) The discriminability of REM and NREM reports. *Journal of Personality and Social Psychology,* 2:456–60. **169**

MONTAGU, A. (1976) *The nature of human aggression.* New York: Oxford Univ. Press. **325**

MONTAGU, A. (ed.) (1978) *Learning non-aggression: The experience of non-literate societies.* New York: Oxford Univ. Press. **343**

MONTPLAISAR, J., see GUILLEMINAULT, BILLIARD, MONTPLAISAR, and DEMENT (1975).

MOODY, D. B., see MILLER, MOODY, and STEBBINS (1969).

MOORE, J. G., and SCHENKENBERG, T. (1974) Psychic control of gastric acid: Response to anticipated feeding and biofeedback training in man. *Gastroenterology,* 66:954–59. **291**

MORA, F., see ROLLS, BURTON, and MORA (1976).

MORDKOFF, A. M., see SPEISMAN, LAZARUS, MORDKOFF, and DAVISON (1964).

MORGAN, A. H. (1973) The heritability of hypnotic susceptibility in twins. *Journal of Abnormal Psychology,* 82:55–61. **179**

MORGAN, A. H., JOHNSON, D. L., and HILGARD, E. R. (1974) The stability of hypnotic susceptibility: A longitudinal study. *International Journal of Clinical and Experimental Hypnosis,* 22:249–57. **179**

MORGAN, A. H., see RUCH, MORGAN, and HILGARD (1973).

MOSHER, L. R., POLLIN, W., and STABENAU, J. R. (1971) Families with identical twins discordant for schizophrenia: Some relationships between identification thinking styles, psychopathology and dominance-submissiveness. *British Journal of Psychiatry,* 118:29–42. **470**

MOWRER, O. H., see DOLLARD, DOOB, MILLER, MOWRER, and SEARS (1939).

MUNKVARD, I., see RANDRUP and MUNKVARD (1972).

MUNN, N. L. (1951) *Psychology: The fundamentals of human adjustment.* Boston: Houghton Mifflin. **12**

MURDOCK, B. B., Jr. (1962) The serial position effect in free recall. *Journal of Experimental Psychology,* 64:482–88. **244**

MURPHY, G., and KOVACH, J. (1972) *Historical introduction to modern psychology* (3rd ed.). New York: Harcourt Brace Jovanovich. **25**

MURSTEIN, B. I. (1972) Physical attractiveness and marital choice. *Journal of Personality and Social Psychology,* 22:8–12. **534**

MUSAPH, H., see MONEY and MUSAPH (1977).

MUSSEN, P. H. (ed.) (1970) *Carmichael's manual of child psychology* (3rd. ed.), Vols. I, II. New York: Wiley. **99**

MUSSEN, P. H., CONGER, J. J., and KAGAN, J. (1974) *Child development and personality* (4th ed.). New York: Harper and Row. **99**

MUSSEN, P. H., and JONES, M. C. (1958) The behavior-inferred motivations of late- and early-maturing boys. *Child Development,* 29:61–67. **89**

MUSSEN, P., and RUTHERFORD, E. (1963) Parent-child relations and parental personality in relation to young children's sex-role preferences. *Child Development,* 34:589–607. **86**

MYERS, J. K., and BEAN, L. L. (1968) *Social class and mental illness.* New York: Wiley. **482**

NACE, E. P., ORNE, M. T., and HAMMER, A. G. (1974) Posthypnotic amnesia as an active psychic process: The reversibility of amnesia. *Archives of General Psychiatry,* 31:257–60. **179**

NAHIR, H. Y., and YUSSEN, S. R. (1977) Performance of kibbutz- and city-reared Israeli children on two role-taking tasks. *Developmental Psychology,* 13:450–55. **81**

NARANJO, C., and ORNSTEIN, R. E. (1977) *On the psychology of meditation.* New York: Penguin. **187**

NATHAN, P. E., and HARRIS, S. L. (1975) *Psychopathology and society.* New York: McGraw-Hill. **485**

NATHAN, P. E., and O'BRIEN, J. S. (1971) An experimental analysis of the behavior of alcoholics and nonalcoholics during prolonged experimental drinking: A necessary precursor of behavior therapy? *Behavior Therapy,* 2:455–76. **479**

NATIONAL INSTITUTE OF MENTAL HEALTH (1977) Provisional Data, NIMH Memorandum (May 18). **482**

NATIONAL REVIEW (October 8, 1963) A survey of the political and religious attitudes of American college students, pp. 279–302. **530**

NATIONAL REVIEW (June 15, 1971) Opinion on the campus, pp. 635–50. **530**

NEALE, J. M., see DAVISON and NEALE (1978).

NEBES, R. D., and SPERRY, R. W. (1971) Cerebral dominance in perception. *Neuropsychologia,* 9:247. **48**

NEELY, J. E., see THOMPSON and NEELY (1970).

NEISSER, U. (1976) *Cognition and reality: Principles and implications of cognitive psychology.* San Francisco: Freeman. **7, 137, 155, 212**

NEISSER, U., and BECKLEN, R. (1975) Selective looking: Attending to visually-specified events. *Cognitive Psychology,* 7:480–94. **163**

NEISSER, U., see SELFRIDGE and NEISSER (1960).

NELSEN, E. A. (1969) Social reinforcement for expression vs. suppression of aggression. *Merrill-Palmer Quarterly of Behavior and Development,* 15:259–78. **326**

NELSON, T. O. (1977) Repetition and depth of processing. *Journal of Verbal Learning and Verbal Behavior,* 16:151–71. **244**

NELSON, V. L., see SONTAG, BAKER, and NELSON (1958).

NEUGARTEN, B. (1971) Grow old with me, the best is yet to be. *Psychology Today,* 5:45–49. **97**

NEUMAN, W. R. (1976) Patterns of recall among television news viewers. *Public Opinion Quarterly,* 40:115–23. **556**

NEWCOMB, T. M. (1943) *Personality and social change.* New York: Dryden Press. **530, 531**

NEWCOMB, T. M. (1961) *The acquaintance process.* New York: Holt, Rinehart and Winston. **535, 536**

NEWCOMB, T. M., KOENIG, K. E., FLACKS, R., and WARWICK, D. P. (1967) *Persistence and change: Bennington College and its students after twenty-five years.* New York: Wiley. **531**

NEWCOMB, T. M., see ABELSON, ARONSON, MCGUIRE, NEWCOMB, ROSENBERG, and TANNENBAUM (1968).

NEWELL, A., and SIMON, H. A. (1972) *Human problem solving.* Englewood Cliffs, N.J.: Prentice-Hall. **275, 277**

NEYMANN, C., and YACORZYNSKI, G. (1942) Studies of introversion-extraversion and conflict of motives in the psychoses. *Journal of General Psychology,* 27:241–55. **382**

NICHOLLS, J. G., see KUFFLER and NICHOLLS (1976).

NICHOLS, R. C. (1968) Nature and nurture in adolescence. In Adams, J. F. (ed.) *Understanding adolescence.* Boston: Allyn and Bacon. **88**

NISBETT, R. E. (1968a) Birth order and participation in dangerous sports. *Journal of Personality and Social Psychology,* 8:351–53. **88**

NISBETT, R. E. (1968b) Taste, deprivation, and weight determinants of eating behavior. *Journal of Personality and Social Psychology,* 10:107–16. **293**

NISBETT, R. E. (1972) Hunger, obesity, and the ventromedial hypothalamus. *Psychological Review,* 79:433–53. **296**

NISBETT, R. E., see KIESLER, NISBETT, and ZANNA (1969).

NISBETT, R. E., see LEPPER, GREENE, and NISBETT (1973).

NOLEN, W. A. (1974) *Healing: A doctor in search of a miracle.* New York: Random House. **184**

NORDBY, V. J., and HALL, C. S. (1974) *A guide to psychologists and their concepts.* San Francisco: Freeman. **25**

NORMAN, D. A. (1973) Memory, knowledge, and the answering of questions. In Solso, R. L. (ed.) *Contemporary issues in cognitive psychology: The Loyola Symposium.* Washington, D.C.: Winston. **239**

NORMAN, D. A. (1976) *Memory and attention: An introduction to human information processing* (2nd ed.). New York: Wiley. **149, 155, 249**

NORMAN, D. A., and RUMELHART, D. E. (1975) *Explorations in cognition.* San Francisco: Freeman. **277**

NORMAN, D. A., see LINDSAY and NORMAN (1977).

NORMAN, D. A., see WAUGH and NORMAN (1965).

NORMAN, W. T. (1963) Toward an adequate taxonomy of personality attributes: Replicated factor structure in peer nomination personality ratings. *Journal of Abnormal and Social Psychology,* 66:574–83. **383**

NOWLIS, G. H., and KESSEN, W. (1976) Human newborns differentiate differing concentrations of sucrose and glucose. *Science,* 191:865–66. **67**

NYE, F. I., see HOFFMAN and NYE (1974).

O'BRIEN, J. S., see NATHAN and O'BRIEN (1971).

ODEN, M. H. (1968) The fulfillment of promise: 40-year follow-up of the Terman gifted group. *Genetic Psychology Monographs,* 77:3–93. **371**

OFFIR, C., see TAVRIS and OFFIR (1977).

OKADA, M., see ENDLER and OKADA (1974).

OLDS, J., and SINCLAIR, J. (1957) Self-stimulation in the obstruction box. *American Psychologist,* 12:464. **206**

O'LEARY, K. D., and WILSON, G. T. (1975) *Behavior therapy: Application and outcome.* Englewood Cliffs, N.J.: Prentice-Hall. **499, 515**

OLIVEAU, D., see AGRAS, SYLVESTER, and OLIVEAU (1969).

OLWEUS, D. (1969) *Prediction of aggression.* Scandinavian Test Corporation. **405**

O'NEAL, E. C., see GEEN and O'NEAL (1969).

OOMURA, Y. (1975) Effects of glucose and free fatty acid in chemosensitive neurons in the rat hypothalamus. In Novin, D., Wyrwicka, W., and Bray, G. A. (eds.) *Hunger: Basic mechanisms and clinical implications.* New York: Raven Press. **289**

OPLER, M. K., see SROLE, LANGNER, MICHAEL, OPLER, and RENNIE (1962).

ORNE, E. C., see EVANS, COOK, COHEN, ORNE, and ORNE (1977).

ORNE, M. T. (1965) Social control in the psychological experiment: Antisocial behavior and hypnosis. *Journal of Personality and Social Psychology,* 1:189–200. **180**

ORNE, M. T., see EVANS, COOK, COHEN, ORNE, and ORNE (1977).

ORNE, M. T., see NACE, ORNE, and HAMMER (1974).

ORNSTEIN, R. E. (1977) *The psychology of consciousness* (2nd ed.). New York: Harcourt Brace Jovanovich. **50, 182, 186, 187**

ORNSTEIN, R. E. (ed.) (1974) *The nature of human consciousness.* New York: Viking. **186**

ORNSTEIN, R. E., see NARANJO and ORNSTEIN (1977).

OSBORN, D. K., and ENDSLEY, R. C. (1971) Emotional reactions of young children to TV violence. *Child Development,* 42:321–31. **328**

OSGOOD, E. E., LURIA, Z., JEANS, R. F., and SMITH, S. W. (1976) The three faces of Evelyn: A case report. *Journal of Abnormal Psychology,* 85:247–86. **163**

OSWALD, I., see JONES and OSWALD (1968).

OVERTON, D. A. (1972) State-dependent learning produced by alcohol and its relevance to alcoholism. In Kissin, B., and Begleiter, H. (eds.) *Physiology and behavior. The biology of alcoholism,* Vol. 2. New York: Plenum Press. **173, 235**

OWEN, D. R. (1972) The 47, XYY male: A review. *Psychological Review,* 78:209–33. **57**

PACKARD, R., see LESSER, KRAWITZ, and PACKARD (1963).

PACKARD, V. (1970) *The sexual wilderness: The contemporary upheaval in male-female relationships.* New York: Pocket Books. **305**

PAIVIO, A. (1971) *Imagery and verbal processes.* New York: Holt, Rinehart and Winston. **230**

PAIVIO, A. (1976) Imagery in recall and recognition. In Brown, J. (ed.) *Recall and recognition.* New York: Wiley. **229**

PAKSTIS, A. J., see SCARR, PAKSTIS, KATZ, and BARKER (1977).

PALLAK, M. S., and PITTMAN, T. S. (1972) General motivational effects of dissonance arousal. *Journal of Personality and Social Psychology,* 32:349–58. **541**

PALMER, F. H. (1976) *The effects of minimal early intervention on subsequent IQ scores and reading achievement* (Final report to the Education Commission of the States, Contract 13-76-06846). Stony Brook, N.Y.: State Univ. of New York. **368**

PANATI, C. (ed.) (1976) *The Geller papers: Scientific observations on the paranormal powers of Uri Geller.* Boston: Houghton Mifflin. **184**

PANKOVE, E., see KOGAN and PANKOVE (1974).

PARKE, R. D., BERKOWITZ, L., LEYENS, J. P., WEST, S. G., and SEBASTIAN, R. J. (1977) Some effects of violent and nonviolent movies on the behavior of juvenile delinquents. In Berkowitz, L. (ed.) *Advances in experimental social psychology,* Vol. 10. New York: Academic Press. **327**

PARKE, R. D., see LEYENS, CAMINO, PARKE, and BERKOWITZ (1975).

PARKES, M. C., BENJAMIN, B., and FITZGERALD, R. G. (1969) Broken heart: A statistical study of increased mortality among widowers. *British Medical Journal,* 1:740–43. **436**

PARRA-COVARRUBIAS, A., RIVERA-RODRIGUEZ, I., and ALMARAZ-UGALDE, A. (1971) Cephalic phase of insulin secretion in obese adolescents. *Diabetes,* 20:800–02. **291**

PARRISH, M., LUNDY, R. M., and LEIBOWITZ, H. W. (1968) Hypnotic age-regression and magnitudes of the Ponzo and Poggendorff illusions. *Science,* 159:1375–76. **136**

PATE versus ROBINSON (1966) 383 U.S. 375. **475**

PATTERSON, F. G. (1978) The gestures of a gorilla: Language acquisition in another pongid. *Brain and Language,* 5:72–97. **270**

PATTERSON, G. R., LITTMAN, R. A., and BRICKER, W. A. (1967) Assertive behavior in children: A step toward a theory of aggression. *Monographs of the Society for Research in Child Development,* Serial No. 113, 32:5. **326**

PAUL, G. L., and BERNSTEIN, D. R. (1973) *Anxiety and clinical problems: Systematic desensitization and related techniques.* Morristown, N.J.: General Learning Press. **500**

PAVLOV, I. P. (1927) *Conditioned reflexes.* New York: Oxford Univ. Press. **194, 218**

PEARLSTONE, Z., see TULVING and PEARLSTONE (1966).

PEARSON, A. J. D., see MEDDIS, PEARSON, and LANGFORD (1973).

PENFIELD, W., and RASMUSSEN, T. (1950) *The cerebral cortex of man.* New York: Macmillan. **43**

PERRIN, F. A. C. (1921) Physical attractiveness and repulsiveness. *Journal of Experimental Psychology,* 4:203–17. **534**

PERRY, C. W., see SHEEHAN and PERRY (1976).

PETERSON, R. C., and STILLMAN, R. C. (eds.) (1977) *Cocaine: 1977* (NIDA Monograph No. 13). Washington, D.C.: U.S. Government Printing Office. **187**

PETTIGREW, T. F. (1959) Regional differences in anti-Negro prejudice. *Journal of Abnormal and Social Psychology,* 59:28–36. **553**

PETTIGREW, T. F. (1964) *A profile of the Negro American.* Princeton, N.J.: Van Nostrand. **564**

PFEFFERBAUM, A., see DAVIS, MOHS, TINKLENBERG, PFEFFERBAUM, HOLLISTER, and KOPELL (1978).

PHARES, E. J., see ROTTER, CHANCE, and PHARES (1972).

PHILLIPS, E. A., see PHILLIPS, PHILLIPS, FIXSEN, and WOLF, (1972).

PHILLIPS, E. L., PHILLIPS, E. A., FIXSEN, D. L., and WOLF, M. M. (1972) *The teaching-family handbook.* Lawrence, Kans.: Kansas Printing Service. **512**

PHILLIPS, J. L. (1973) *Statistical thinking.* San Francisco: Freeman. **587**

PHILLIPS, J. L. (1975) *The origins of intellect: Piaget's theory* (2nd ed.). San Francisco, Freeman. **99**

PHILLIPS, J. S., see KANFER and PHILLIPS (1970).

PIAGET, J. (1932) *The moral judgment of the child.* London: Kegan Paul. **74**

PIAGET, J. (1952) *The origins of intelligence in children.* New York: International Universities Press. **310**

PIERCE, C. M., see HOFLING, BROTZMAN, DALRYMPLE, GRAVES, and PIERCE (1966).

PILIAVIN, I. M., RODIN, J., and PILIAVIN, J. A. (1969) Good Samaritanism: An underground phenomenon? *Journal of Personality and Social Psychology,* 13:289–99. **522**

PILIAVIN, J. A., see PILIAVIN, RODIN, and PILIAVIN (1969).

PITTMAN, T. S., see PALLAK and PITTMAN (1972).

PITTMAN, T. S., see SWANN and PITTMAN (1975).

PLOMIN, R., see BUSS and PLOMIN (1975).

POLIVY, J., see HERMAN and POLIVY (1975).

POLLIN, W., see MOSHER, POLLIN, and STABENAU (1971).

POLT, J. M., see HESS and POLT (1960).

POMEROY, A. C., see KINSEY, POMEROY, and MARTIN (1948).

POMEROY, W. B., see KINSEY, POMEROY, MARTIN, and GEBHARD (1953).

POPE, K. S., and SINGER, J. L. (eds.) (1978) *The stream of consciousness.* New York: Plenum Press. **186**

PORTER, R. W., see BRADY, PORTER, CONRAD, and MASON (1958).

POSNER, M. I., and KEELE, S. W. (1967) Decay of visual information from a single letter. *Science,* 158:137–39. **223**

POST, R. M., KOTIN, J., GOODWIN, F. K., and GORDON, E. (1973) Psychomotor activity and cerebrospinal fluid amine metabolites in affective illness. *American Journal of Psychiatry,* 130:67–72. **462**

POSTMAN, L. (1961) The present status of interference theory. In Cofer, C. N. (ed.) *Verbal learning and verbal behavior.* New York: McGraw-Hill. **231**

POWLEY, T. L. (1977) The ventromedial hypothalamic syndrome, satiety, and a cephalic phase hypothesis. *Psychological Review,* 84:89–126. **292**

POWLEY, T. L., and KEESEY, R. E. (1970) Relationship of body weight to the lateral hypothalamic feeding syndrome. *Journal of Comparative and Physiological Psychology,* 70:25–36. **290**

POWLEY, T. L., see KEESEY and POWLEY (1975).

PREMACK, D. (1971) Language in chimpanzees? *Science,* 172:808–22. **269**

PRESIDENT'S COMMISSION ON MENTAL HEALTH (1978) *Report to the President from President's Commission on Mental Health,* Vol. 1. Washington, D.C.: Superintendent of Documents, U.S. Government Printing Office. **482**

PRIBRAM, K. H., see MILLER, GALANTER, and PRIBRAM (1960).

PROSHANSKY, H., see ITTELSON, PROSHANSKY, RIVLIN, and WINKEL (1974).

PUBOLS, B. H., see WELKER, JOHNSON, and PUBOLS (1964).

QUILLIAN, M. R., see COLLINS and QUILLIAN (1969).

RABIN, A. I. (1947) A case history of a simple schizophrenic. In Burton, A., and Harris, R. E. (eds.) *Case histories in clinical and abnormal psychology.* New York: Harper and Row. **463**

RABKIN, K., see RABKIN and RABKIN (1969).

RABKIN, Y., and RABKIN, K. (1969) Children of the kibbutz. *Psychology Today,* 3:40–46. **81**

RACHLIN, H. (1976) *Behavior and learning.* San Francisco: Freeman. **219**

RACHMAN, S. J. (1978) *Fear and courage.* San Francisco: Freeman. **439**

RADO, S. (1951) Psychodynamics of depression from the etiological point of view. *Psychosomatic Medicine,* 13:51–55. **459**

RAHE, R. H., see HOLMES and RAHE (1967).

RANDI, J. (1978) The psychology of conjuring. *Technology Review,* 80:56–63. **152**

RANDRUP, A., and MUNKVARD, I. (1972). Evidence indicating an association between schizophrenia and dopaminergic hyperactivity in the brain. *Orthomolecular Psychiatry,* 1:2–7. **468**

RAPAPORT, D. (1942) *Emotions and memory.* Baltimore: Williams and Wilkins. **236**

RAPAPORT, D. (1967) *Collected papers.* Edited by M. M. Gill. New York: Basic Books. **446**

RASMUSSEN, T., see PENFIELD and RASMUSSEN (1950).

RATZEL, R. W., see CARTWRIGHT and RATZEL (1972).

RAUGH, M. R., see ATKINSON and RAUGH (1975).

RAY, O. S. (1978) *Drugs, society, and human behavior* (2nd ed.). St. Louis: Mosby. **485**

RAYNER, R., see WATSON and RAYNER (1920).

RECHTSCHAFFEN, A., see MONROE, RECHTSCHAFFEN, FOULKES, and JENSEN (1965).

REDLICH, F. C., see HOLLINGSHEAD and REDLICH (1958).

REED, S. K. (1973) *Psychological processes in pattern recognition.* New York: Academic Press. **155**

REITMAN, J. S. (1974) Without surreptitious rehearsal, information in short-term memory decays. *Journal of Verbal Learning and Verbal Behavior,* 13:365–77. **226**

RENNER, K. E., see WIGGINS, RENNER, CLORE, and ROSE (1976).

RENNIE, T. A. C., see SROLE, LANGNER, MICHAEL, OPLER, and RENNIE (1962).

RESCORLA, R. A. (1975) Pavlovian excitatory and inhibitory conditioning. In Estes, W. K. (ed.) *Conditioning and behavior theory.* Handbook of learning and cognition, Vol. 2. Hillsdale, N.J.: Erlbaum. **197**

RESNICK, L. B., see GLASER and RESNICK (1972).

RESNICK, R. B., KESTENBAUM, R. S., and SCHWARTZ, L. K. (1977) Acute systemic effects of cocaine in man: A controlled study of intranasal and intravenous routes of administration. In Ellinwood, E. H., Jr., and Kilbey, M. M. (eds.) *Cocaine and*

other stimulants. New York: Plenum Press. **175**

RHINE, J. B. (1942) Evidence of precognition in the covariation of salience ratios. *Journal of Parapsychology,* 6:111–43. **150**

RICE, B. (1978) The new truth machine. *Psychology Today,* 12:61–78. **333**

RICHARDS, D., see HO, CHUTE, and RICHARDS (1977).

RIEDER, R. O., see ROSENTHAL, WENDER, KETY, SCHULSINGER, WELNER, and RIEDER (1975).

RIESEN, A. H. (1965) Effects of early deprivation of photic stimulation. In Osler, S., and Cooke, R. (eds.) *The biosocial basis of mental retardation.* Baltimore: Johns Hopkins Univ. Press. **146**

RIGGS, L. A., see KLING and RIGGS (1971).

RIMM, D. C., and MASTERS, J. C. (1974) *Behavior therapy: Techniques and empirical findings.* New York: Academic Press. **498**

RIOCH, M. J. (1967) Pilot projects in training mental health counselors. In Cowen, E. L., Gardner, E. A., and Zax, M. (eds.) *Emergent approaches to mental health problems.* New York: Appleton-Century-Crofts. **512**

RIPS, L. J., see SMITH, SHOBEN, and RIPS (1974).

RITTER, B., see BANDURA, BLANCHARD, and RITTER (1969).

RIVENBANK, W. H., see MILLER and RIVENBANK (1970).

RIVERA-RODRIGUEZ, I., see PARRA-COVARRUBIAS, RIVERA-RODRIGUEZ, and ALMARAZ-UGALDE (1971).

RIVLIN, L., see ITTELSON, PROSHANSKY, RIVLIN, and WINKEL (1974).

ROBACK, A. A. (1961) *History of psychology and psychiatry.* New York: Philosophical Library. **515**

ROBERTS, T. S., see DOBELLE, MLADE-JOVSKY, EVANS, ROBERTS, and GIRVIN (1976).

ROBERTS, W. W., see DELGADO, ROBERTS, and MILLER (1954).

ROBINS, L. (1974) *The Viet Nam drug abuser returns.* New York: McGraw-Hill. **481**

ROBINSON, J. P. (1971) The audience for national TV news programs. *Public Opinion Quarterly,* 35:403–05. **556**

ROCK, I. (1975) *An introduction to perception.* New York: Macmillan. **127, 154**

ROCK, I., and HARRIS, C. S. (1967) Vision and touch. *Scientific American,* 216:96–104. **133**

ROCK, L., see JONES, ROCK, SHAVER, GOETHALS, and WARD (1968).

RODIN, J. (1975) Causes and consequences of time perception differences in overweight and normal weight people. *Journal of Personality and Social Psychology,* 31:898–910. **293**

RODIN, J. (1976) Crowding, perceived choice, and response to controllable and uncontrollable outcomes. *Journal of Experimental Social Psychology,* 12:564–78. **563**

RODIN, J., and BAUM, A. (1978) Crowding

and helplessness: Potential consequences of density and loss of control. In Baum, A., and Epstein, Y. (eds.) *Human response to crowding.* New York: Halsted Press. **563**

RODIN, J., and SLOCHOWER, J. (1976) Externality in the nonobese: The effects of environmental responsiveness on weight. *Journal of Personality and Social Psychology,* 33:338–44. **296**

RODIN, J., see LATANE and RODIN (1969).

RODIN, J., see PILIAVIN, RODIN, and PILIAVIN (1969).

ROGERS, C. R. (1951) *Client-centered therapy.* Boston: Houghton Mifflin. **393, 394**

ROGERS, C. R. (1970) *On becoming a person: A therapist's view of psychotherapy.* Boston: Houghton Mifflin. **515**

ROGERS, C. R. (1977) *Carl Rogers on personal power.* New York: Delacorte Press. **393, 412, 515**

ROGERS, C., and STEVENS, B. (1967) *Person to person: The problem of being human.* New York: Pocket Books. **412**

ROGERS, R. W., and DECKNER, C. W. (1975) Effects of fear appeals and physiological arousal upon emotion, attitudes, and cigarette smoking. *Journal of Personality and Social Psychology,* 32:222–30. **337**

ROLLS, E. T., BURTON, M. J., and MORA, F. (1976) Hypothalamic neuronal responses associated with the sight of food. *Brain Research,* 111:53–66. **291**

ROSCH, E. (1974) Linguistic relativity. In Silverstein, A. (ed.) *Human communication: Theoretical perspectives.* New York: Halsted Press. **255**

ROSCH, E., and MERVIS, C. B. (1975) Family resemblances: Studies in the internal structure of categories. *Cognitive Psychology,* 7:573–605. **252**

ROSE, R. J., see WIGGINS, RENNER, CLORE, and ROSE (1976).

ROSEN, J. J., see STEIN and ROSEN (1974).

ROSEN, M., see CLARK, KIVITZ, and ROSEN (1969).

ROSENBERG, M. J., see ABELSON, ARONSON, MCGUIRE, NEWCOMB, ROSENBERG, and TANNENBAUM (1968).

ROSENBLATT, J. S. (1967) Nonhormonal basis of maternal behavior in the rat. *Science,* 156:1512–14. **208**

ROSENBLATT, J. S. (1969) The development of maternal responsiveness in the rat. *American Journal of Orthopsychiatry,* 39:36–56. **308**

ROSENBLATT, J. S., see TERKEL and ROSENBLATT (1972).

ROSENFELD, E., see CHEIN, GERARD, LEE, and ROSENFELD (1964).

ROSENFELD, H., and BAER, D. (1969) Unnoticed verbal conditioning of an aware experimenter by a more aware subject: The double-agent effect. *Psychological Review,* 76:425–32. **203**

ROSENHAN, D. L. (1973) On being sane in insane places. *Science,* 179:250–58. **543**

ROSENTHAL, D. (1970) *Genetic theory*

and abnormal behavior. New York: McGraw-Hill. **461**

ROSENTHAL, D., WENDER, P. H., KETY, S. S., SCHULSINGER, F., WELNER, J., and RIEDER, R. O. (1975) Parent-child relationships and psychopathological disorder in the child. *Archives of General Psychiatry*, 32:466–76. **470**

ROSENTHAL, R. (1964) Experimental outcome-orientation and the results of the psychological experiment. *Psychological Bulletin*, 61:405–12. **520**

ROSENZWEIG, M. R. (1969) Effects of heredity and environment on brain chemistry, brain anatomy, and learning ability in the rat. In Manosovitz, M. Lindzey, G., and Thiessen, D. D. (eds.) *Behavioral genetics.* New York: Appleton-Century-Crofts. **58**

ROSENZWEIG, M. R., and BENNETT, E. L. (1976) Enriched environments: Facts, factors, and fantasies. In McGaugh, J. L., and Petrinovich, L. (eds.) *Knowing, thinking, and believing.* New York: Plenum Press. **42**

ROSS, L. (1974) Obesity and externality. In Schachter, S., and Rodin, J. (eds.) *Obese humans and rats.* Potomac, Md.: Erlbaum. **293**

ROSS, L. (1977) The intuitive psychologist and his shortcomings: Distortions in the attribution process. In Berkowitz, L. (ed.) *Advances in experimental social psychology*, Vol. 10. New York: Academic Press. **542**

ROSS, L. D., AMABILE, T. M., and STEINMETZ, J L. (1977) Social roles, social control, and biases in social-perception processes. *Journal of Personality and Social Psychology*, 35:485–94. **542**

ROSS, M., LAYTON, B., ERICKSON, B., and SCHOPLER, J. (1973) Affect, facial regard, and reactions to crowding. *Journal of Personality and Social Psychology*, 28:69–76. **562**

ROSS, M., and SHULMAN, R. F. (1973) Increasing the salience of initial attitudes: Dissonance versus self-perception theory. *Journal of Personality and Social Psychology*, 28:138–44. **541**

ROSS, W. F., see BERZINS, ROSS, ENGLISH, and HALEY (1974).

ROTH, W. T., see DARLEY, TINKLENBERG, ROTH, HOLLISTER, and ATKINSON (1973).

ROTTER, J. B., CHANCE, J. E., and PHARES, E. J. (1972) *Applications of a social learning theory of personality.* New York: Holt, Rinehart and Winston. **412**

ROTTMANN, L., see WALSTER, ARONSON, ABRAHAMS, and ROTTMANN (1966).

ROWE, D. A., see SIMS, KELLEHER, HORTON, GLUCK, GOODMAN, and ROWE (1968).

ROZIN, P., and KALAT, J. W. (1971) Specific hungers and poison avoidance as adaptive specializations of learning. *Psychological Review*, 78:459–86. **292**

RUBIN, Z. (1973) *Liking and loving.* New York: Holt, Rinehart and Winston. **94, 536, 545**

RUCH, J. C. (1975) Self-hypnosis: The result of heterohypnosis or vice versa? *International Journal of Clinical and Experimental Hypnosis*, 23:282–304. **178**

RUCH, J. C., MORGAN, A. H., and HILGARD, E. R. (1973) Behavioral predictions from hypnotic responsiveness scores when obtained with and without prior induction procedures. *Journal of Abnormal Psychology*, 82:543–46. **178**

RUDY, J. W., and WAGNER, A. R. (1975) Stimulus selection in associative learning. In Estes, W. K. (ed.) *Conditioning and behavior theory.* Handbook of learning and cognition, Vol. 2. Hillsdale, N.J.: Erlbaum. **197**

RUMBAUGH, D. M. (ed.) (1977) *Language learning by a chimpanzee: The Lana project.* New York: Academic Press. **269**

RUMELHART, D. E. (1977) *An introduction to human information processing.* New York: Wiley. **277**

RUMELHART, D. E., see NORMAN and RUMELHART (1975).

RUTHERFORD, E., see MUSSEN and RUTHERFORD (1963).

SACHS, J. D. S. (1967) Recognition memory for syntactic and semantic aspects of connected discourse. *Perception and Psychophysics*, 2:437–42. **229**

SACHS, J. S., BROWN, R., and SALERNO, R. A. (1976) Adults' speech to children. In van Raffler Engel, W., and LeBrun, Y. (eds.) *Baby talk and infant speech* (Neurolinguists 5). Amsterdam: Swets and Zeitlinger. **266**

SADAVA, S. W. (1973) Patterns of college student drug use: A longitudinal social learning study. *Psychological Reports*, 33:75–86. **480**

SAKS, M. J. (1976) The limits of scientific jury selection: Ethical and empirical. *Jurimetrics Journal*, 17:3–22. **568, 569**

SALAMY, J. (1970) Instrumental responding to internal cues associated with REM sleep. *Psychonomic Science*, 18:342–43. **171**

SALERNO, R. A., see SACHS, BROWN, and SALERNO (1976).

SALIVE, H., see MCCONNELL, SHIGEHISA, and SALIVE (1970).

SANFORD, N., see ADORNO, FRENKEL-BRUNSWIK, LEVINSON, and SANFORD (1950).

SAPOLSKY, B. S., see ZILLMANN and SAPOLSKY (1977).

SARASON, I. G. (1976) *Abnormal psychology* (2nd ed.). Englewood Cliffs, N.J.: Prentice-Hall. **485**

SARBIN, T. R. (1950) Contributions to role-taking theory: I. Hypnotic behavior. *Psychological Review*, 57:255–70. **181**

SARBIN, T. R., and COE, W. C. (1972) *Hypnosis: A social psychological analysis of influence communication.* New York: Holt, Rinehart and Winston. **178, 181, 187**

SAWREY, W. L., CONGER, J. J., and TURRELL, E. S. (1956) An experimental investigation of the role of psychological factors in the production of gastric ulcers of rats. *Journal of Comparative and Physiological Psychology*, 49:457–61. **195**

SCARR, S. (1977) Testing minority children: Why, how, and with what effects? In Bossone, R. M., and Weiner, M. (eds.) *Proceedings of the National Conference on Testing: Major Issues* (November 17 and 18, 1977). New York: Center for Advanced Study in Education. **373**

SCARR, S., PAKSTIS, A. J., KATZ, S. H., and BARKER, W. B. (1977) The absence of a relationship between degree of white ancestry and intellectual skills within a black population. *Human Genetics*, 857:1–18. **367**

SCARR, S., and WEINBURG, R. A. (1976) IQ test performance of black children adopted by white families. *American Psychologist*, 31:726–39. **364, 367**

SCARR-SALAPATEK, S. (1971) Race, social class, and IQ. *Science*, 174:1285. **366**

SCHACHTER, S. (1971) *Emotion, obesity, and crime.* New York: Academic Press. **336**

SCHACHTER, S., and GROSS, L. P. (1968) Manipulated time and eating behavior. *Journal of Personality and Social Psychology*, 10:98–106. **294**

SCHACHTER, S., and SINGER, J. E. (1962) Cognitive, social and physiological determinants of emotional state. *Psychological Review*, 69:379–99. **337**

SCHAFFER, D. R. (1975) Some effects of consonant and dissonant attitudinal advocacy on initial attitude saliance and attitude change. *Journal of Personality and Social Psychology*, 32:160–68. **541**

SCHAIE, K. W., and STROTHER, C. R. (1968) A cross-sequential study of age changes in cognitive behavior. *Psychological Bulletin*, 70:671–80. **363**

SCHANK, R., and ABELSON, R. (1977) *Scripts, plans, goals, and understanding.* Hillsdale, N.J.: Erlbaum. **247**

SCHANK, R. C., and COLBY, K. M. (eds.) (1973) *Computer models of thought and language.* San Francisco: Freeman. **277**

SCHEIN, E. H., SCHNEIER, I., and BARKER, C. H. (1961) *Coercive persuasion.* New York: Norton. **530, 531**

SCHEIN, E. H., see STRASSMAN, THALER, and SCHEIN (1956).

SCHENKENBERG, T., see MOORE and SCHENKENBERG (1974).

SCHIFFMAN, H. R. (1976) *Sensation and perception.* New York: Wiley. **127**

SCHMEIDLER, G. R., see WOLMAN, DALE, SCHMEIDLER, and ULLMAN (1977).

SCHMITT, R. C. (1963) Implications of density in Hong Kong. *American Institute of Planners Journal*, 29:210–17. **563**

SCHMITT, R. C. (1966) Density, health and social disorganization. *Journal of American Institute of Planners*, 32:38–40. **561**

SCHNEIER, I., see SCHEIN, SCHNEIER, and BARKER (1961).

SCHOPLER, J., see ROSS, LAYTON, ERICKSON, and SCHOPLER (1973).

SHULMAN, J., SHAVER, P., COLMAN, R., EMRICH, B., and CHRISTIE, R. (1973) Recipe for a jury. *Psychology Today*, 6:37–44, 77–84. **569**

WENDER, KETY, SCHULSINGER, WELNER, and RIEDER (1975).

SCHULTZ, D. P. (1975) *A history of modern psychology* (2nd ed.). New York: Academic Press. **25**

SCHWARTZ, G. E. (1975) Biofeedback, self-regulation, and the patterning of physiological processes. *American Scientist,* 63:314-24. **435**

SCHWARTZ, G. E., and SHAPIRO, D. (eds.) (1976) *Advances in research.* Consciousness and self-regulation, Vol. 1. New York: Plenum Press. **186**

SCHWARTZ, L. K., see RESNICK, KESTENBAUM, and SCHWARTZ (1977).

SCHWARTZ, M. (1978) *Physiological psychology* (2nd ed.). Englewood Cliffs, N.J.: Prentice-Hall. **61**

SCOTT, J. P. (1968) *Early experience and the organization of behavior.* Belmont, Calif.: Brooks/Cole. **309**

SCOTT, J. P., and FULLER, J. L. (1965) *Genetics and the social behavior of the dog.* Chicago: Univ. of Chicago Press. **58**

SCOTT, T. H., see HERON, DOANE, and SCOTT (1956).

SEARS, D. O., see FREEDMAN, SEARS, and CARLSMITH (1978).

SEARS, P. S., and BARBEE, A. H. (1977) Career and life satisfactions among Terman's gifted women. In Stanley, J. C., George, W. C., and Solano, C. H. (eds.) *The gifted and the creative: Fifty-year perspective.* Baltimore: Johns Hopkins Univ. Press. **370**

SEARS, R. R. (1936) Experimental studies of projection: I. Attribution of traits. *Journal of Social Psychology,* 7:151-63. **430**

SEARS, R. R. (1977) Sources of life satisfactions of the Terman gifted man. *American Psychologist,* 32:119-28. **370, 406**

SEARS, R. R., see DOLLARD, DOOB, MILLER, MOWRER, and SEARS (1939).

SEBASTIAN, R. J., see PARKE, BERKOWITZ, LEYENS, WEST, and SEBASTIAN (1977).

SEEMAN, J. (1949) A study of the process of nondirective therapy. *Journal of Consulting Psychology,* 13:157-68. **502**

SEGAL, D., see BLOOM, SEGAL, LING, and GUILLEMIN (1976).

SELFRIDGE, O., and NEISSER, U. (1960) Pattern recognition by machine. *Scientific American,* 203:60-80. **142**

SELIGMAN, M. E. P. (1975) *Helplessness.* San Francisco: Freeman. **422, 454, 461**

SELIGMAN, M. E. P., see ABRAMSON, GARBER, EDWARDS, and SELIGMAN (1978).

SELIGMAN, M. E. P., see HIROTO and SELIGMAN (1975).

SELIGMAN, M. E. P., see MASER and SELIGMAN (1977).

SENDEN, M. V. (1960) *Space and sight* (P. Heath, tr.). New York: Free Press. **145**

SENN, D. J., see LEVINGER, SENN, and JORGENSEN (1970).

SENTER, R. J., see LIPPERT and SENTER (1966).

SHAFFER, L. F. (1947) Fear and courage in aerial combat. *Journal of Consulting Psy-*

chology, 11:137-43. **331**

SHANKWEILER, D., see LIBERMAN, COOPER, SHANKWEILER, and STUDDERT-KENNEDY (1967).

SHAPIRO, A., see GOODENOUGH, SHAPIRO, HOLDEN, and STEINSCHRIBER, (1959).

SHAPIRO, A., see LEWIS, GOODENOUGH, SHAPIRO, and SLESER (1966).

SHAPIRO, D., see SCHWARTZ and SHAPIRO (1976).

SHARMA, K. W., see ANAND, SHARMA, and DUA (1964).

SHAVER, K. G. (1975) *An introduction to attribution processes.* Cambridge, Mass.: Winthrop. **545**

SHAVER, K. G., see JONES, ROCK, SHAVER, GOETHALS, and WARD (1968).

SHAVER, P., and FREEDMAN, J. L. (1976) Your pursuit of happiness. *Psychology Today,* 10:26-32, 75. **561**

SHAVER, P., see SHULMAN, SHAVER, COLMAN, EMRICH, and CHRISTIE (1973).

SHEATSLEY, P. B. (1966) White attitudes toward the Negro. *Daedalus,* 95:217-38. **554**

SHEEHAN, P. W., and PERRY, C. W. (1976) *Methodologies of hypnosis: A critical appraisal of contemporary paradigms of hypnosis.* Hillsdale, N.J.: Erlbaum. **181, 187**

SHELDON, W. H. (1954) *Atlas of men: A guide for somatotyping the adult male at all ages.* New York: Harper and Row. **381**

SHEPARD, R. N. (1978) The mental image. *American Psychologist,* 33:125-37. **273**

SHEPARD, R. N., and CHIPMAN, S. (1970) Second-order isomorphism of internal representations: Shapes of states. *Cognitive Psychology,* 1:1-17. **272**

SHEPARD, R. N., see COOPER and SHEPARD (1973).

SHERIF, C. W., see SHERIF, HARVEY, WHITE, HOOD, and SHERIF (1961).

SHERIF, M. (1966) *In common predicament: Social psychology of intergroup conflict and cooperation.* Boston: Houghton Mifflin. **551**

SHERIF, M., HARVEY, O. J., WHITE, B. J., HOOD, W. E., and SHERIF, C. W. (1961) *Intergroup conflict and cooperation: The Robber's Cave experiment.* Norman, Okla.: Univ. of Oklahoma Book Exchange. **551**

SHERMAN, A. R. (1972) Real-life exposure as a primary therapeutic factor in the desensitization treatment of fear. *Journal of Abnormal Psychology,* 79:19-28. **495**

SHIELDS, J., see GOTTESMAN and SHIELDS (1972).

SHIELDS, J., see GOTTESMAN and SHIELDS (1973).

SHIFFRIN, R. M., see ATKINSON and SHIFFRIN (1971).

SHIFFRIN, R. M., see ATKINSON and SHIFFRIN (1977).

SHIGEHISA, T., see MCCONNELL, SHIGEHISA, and SALIVE (1970).

SHOBEN, E. J., see SMITH, SHOBEN, and RIPS (1974).

SHOCKLEY, W. (1972) Dysgenics, geneticity, and raceology: A challenge to the intellectual responsibility of educators. *Phi Delta Kappan,* 53:297-307. **366**

SHOR, R. E., see FROMM and SHOR (1979).

SHULMAN, J., SHAVER, P., COLMAN, R., EMRICH, B., and CHRISTIE, R. (1973) Recipe for a jury. *Psychology Today,* 6:37-44, 77-84. **569**

SHULMAN, R. F., see ROSS and SHULMAN (1973).

SIEGEL, A. E. (1969) Mass media and violence: Effects on children. *Stanford M.D.,* 8:11-14. **555**

SIEGEL, R. K., and WEST, L. J. (eds.) (1975) *Hallucinations: Behavior, experience, and theory.* New York: Wiley. **187**

SIKES, J., see ARONSON, BLANEY, SIKES, STEPHAN, and SNAPP (1975).

SILVERMAN, L. H. (1976) Psychoanalytic theory: The reports of my death are greatly exaggerated. *American Psychologist.* 31:621-37. **393**

SIMON, H. A., and KOTOVSKY, K. (1963) Human acquisition of concepts for sequential patterns. *Psychological Review,* 70:534-46. **274**

SIMON, H. A., see KOTOVSKY and SIMON (1973).

SIMON, H. A., see NEWELL and SIMON (1972).

SIMON, T., see BINET and SIMON (1905).

SIMONS, R. N., see KRIPKE and SIMONS (1976).

SIMS, E. A., KELLEHER, P. E., HORTON, E. S., GLUCK, C. M., GOODMAN, R. F., and ROWE, D. A. (1968) Experimental obesity in man. *Excerpta Medica Monograph.* **296**

SINCLAIR, J., see OLDS and SINCLAIR (1957).

SINGER, J. E., see COHEN, GLASS, and SINGER (1973).

SINGER, J. E., see GLASS and SINGER (1972).

SINGER, J. E., see SCHACHTER and SINGER (1962).

SINGER, J. L., see POPE and SINGER (1978).

SINGER, R. D., see KAPLAN and SINGER (1976).

SIQUELAND, E. R., see EIMAS, SIQUELAND, JUSCZYK, and VIGORITO (1971).

SITARAM, N., WEINGARTNER, H., and GILLIN, J. C. (1978) Human serial learning: Enhancement with arecholine and choline and impairment with scopolamine. *Science,* 201:274-76. **34**

SKEELS, H. M. (1966) Adult status of children with contrasting early life experiences: A follow-up study. *Monographs of the Society for Research in Child Development,* 31, Serial No. 105. **70**

SKEELS, H. M., and DYE, H. B. (1939) A study of the effects of differential stimulation on mentally retarded children. *Proceedings of the American Association for Mental Deficiency,* 44:114-36. **69**

SKEELS, H. M., see SKODAK and SKEELS (1949).

SKINNER, B. F. (1938) *The behavior of organisms.* New York: Appleton-Century-Crofts. **218**

SKINNER, B. F. (1968) *The technology of teaching.* New York: Appleton-Century-Crofts. **216**

SKINNER, B. F. (1974) *About behaviorism.* New York: Knopf. **161**

SKINNER, B. F. (1978) *Reflections on behaviorism and society.* Englewood Cliffs, N.J.: Prentice-Hall. **571**

SKODAK, M., and SKEELS, H. M. (1949) A final follow-up of one hundred adopted children. *Journal of Genetic Psychology,* 75:3–19. **364**

SLESER, I., see LEWIS, GOODENOUGH, SHAPIRO, and SLESER (1966).

SLOANE, R. B., STAPLES, F. R., CRISTOL, A. H., YORKSTON, N. J., and WHIPPLE, K. (1975) *Psychotherapy vs. behavior therapy.* Cambridge, Mass.: Harvard Univ. Press. **507**

SLOBIN, D. I. (1971) *Psycholinguistics.* Glenview, Ill.: Scott, Foresman. **263**

SLOBIN, D. I. (1973) Cognitive pre-requisites for the acquisition of grammar. In Ferguson, C. A., and Slobin, D. I. (eds.) *Studies of child language development.* New York: Holt, Rinehart and Winston. **266**

SLOCHOWER, J., see RODIN and SLOCHOWER (1976).

SMART, R. G., and FEJER, D. (1972) Drug use among adolescents and their parents: Closing the generation gap in mood modification. *Journal of Abnormal Psychology,* 79:153–60. **480**

SMITH, D., KING, M., and HOEBEL, B. G. (1970) Lateral hypothalamic control of killing: Evidence for a cholinoceptive mechanism. *Science,* 167:900–01. **321**

SMITH, E. E., SHOBEN, E. J., and RIPS, L. J. (1974) Structure and process in semantic memory: A featural model for semantic decisions. *Psychological Review,* 81:214–41. **252**

SMITH, J. H., see GREENFIELD and SMITH (1976).

SMITH, M. B. (1973) Is psychology relevant to new priorities? *American Psychologist,* 6:463–71. **9**

SMITH, M. L., and GLASS, G. V. (1977) Meta-analysis of psychotherapy outcome studies. *American Psychologist,* 32:752–60. **507**

SMITH, R., see STEUER, APPLEFIELD, and SMITH (1971).

SMITH, S. W., see OSGOOD, LURIA, JEANS, and SMITH (1976).

SNAPP, M., see ARONSON, BLANEY, SIKES, STEPHAN, and SNAPP (1975).

SNYDER, C. R. (1974) Acceptance of personality interpretations as a function of assessment procedures. *Journal of Consulting Psychology,* 42:150. **404**

SNYDER, M., and CUNNINGHAM, M. R. (1975) To comply or not comply: Testing the self-perception explanation of the "foot-in-the-door" phenomenon. *Journal*

of *Personality and Social Psychology,* 31:64–67. **540**

SNYDER, M., and EBBESEN, E. B. (1972) Dissonance awareness: A test of dissonance theory versus self-perception theory. *Journal of Experimental Social Psychology,* 8:502–17. **541**

SNYDER, M., and SWANN, W. B., Jr. (1979) Hypothesis-testing processes in social interaction. *Journal of Personality and Social Psychology,* in press. **256**

SNYDER, M., and URANOWITZ, S. W. (1978) Reconstructing the past: Some cognitive consequences of person perception. *Journal of Personality and Social Psychology,* 36:941–50. **247**

SNYDER, S. H. (1973) Amphetamine psychosis: A "model" schizophrenia mediated by catecholamines. *American Journal of Psychiatry,* 130:61–67. **174**

SNYDER, S. H., BANERJEE, S. P., YAMAMURA, H. I., and GREENBERG, D. (1974) Drugs, neurotransmitters, and schizophrenia. *Science,* 184:1243–53. **468**

SNYDER, W. U., and OTHERS (1947) *Casebook of nondirective counseling.* Boston: Houghton Mifflin. **502**

SOAL, S. G., and BATEMAN, F. (1954) *Modern experiments in telepathy.* New Haven, Conn.: Yale Univ. Press. **151, 152**

SOKOLOV, E. N. (1976) Learning and memory: Habituation as negative learning. In Rosenzweig, M. R., and Bennett, E. L. (eds.) *Neural mechanisms of learning and memory.* Cambridge, Mass.: MIT Press. **150**

SOLSO, R. L., see JOHNSON and SOLSO (1978).

SONTAG, L. W., BAKER, C. T., and NELSON, V. L. (1958) Mental growth and development: A longitudinal study. *Monographs of the Society for Research in Child Development,* 23, Serial No. 68. **362**

SORENSON, R. C. (1973) *Adolescent sexuality in contemporary America.* New York: World Publishing. **91, 94**

SPANOS, N. P., and BARBER, T. X. (1974) Toward a convergence in hypnosis research. *American Psychologist,* 29:500–11. **181**

SPEAR, N. E. (1973) Retrieval of memory in animals. *Psychological Review,* 80:163–94. **242**

SPEER, D. C. (1972) An evaluation of a telephone crisis service. Paper presented at the meeting of the Midwestern Psychological Association, Cleveland, 1972. **511**

SPEISMAN, J. C., LAZARUS, R. S., MORDKOFF, A. M., and DAVISON, L. (1964) Experimental reduction of stress based on ego-defense theory. *Journal of Abnormal and Social Psychology,* 68:367–80. **338**

SPERRY, R. W. (1970) Perception in the absence of neocortical commissures. In *Perception and Its Disorders* (Res. Publ. A.R.N.M.D., Vol. 48). New York: The Association for Research in Nervous and Mental Disease. **46**

SPERRY, R. W., see NEBES and SPERRY (1971).

SPIELBERGER, C. D. (ed.) (1972) *Anxiety: Current trends in theory and research.* New York: Academic Press. **439**

SPIES, G. (1965) Food versus intracranial self-stimulation reinforcement in food-deprived rats. *Journal of Comparative Physiological Psychology,* 60:153–57. **206**

SPRINGSTON, F., see BOWER and SPRINGSTON (1970).

SPUHLER, J. N., see LOEHLIN, LINDZEY, and SPUHLER (1975).

SROLE, L. (1972) Urbanization and mental health: Some reformulations. *American Scientist,* 60:576–83. **561**

SROLE, L., LANGNER, T. S., MICHAEL, S. T., OPLER, M. K., and RENNIE, T. A. C. (1962) *Mental health in the metropolis: The midtown Manhattan study.* New York: McGraw-Hill. **482**

STABENAU, J. R., see MOSHER, POLLIN, and STABENAU (1971).

STALNAKER, J. M. (1965) Psychological tests and public responsibility. *American Psychologist,* 20:131–35. **372**

STANTON, M., MINTZ, J., and FRANKLIN, R. M. (1976) Drug flashbacks. *International Journal of Addictions,* 11:53–59. **176**

STAPLES, F. R., see SLOANE, STAPLES, CRISTOL, YORKSTON, and WHIPPLE (1975).

STAYTON, D. J. (1973) *Infant responses to brief everyday separations: distress, following, and greeting.* Paper presented at the meeting of the Society for Research in Child Development, March, 1973. **79**

STEBBINS, W. C., see MILLER, MOODY, and STEBBINS (1969).

STECHER, L. I., see BALDWIN and STECHER (1922).

STEIN, D. G., and ROSEN, J. J. (1974) *Motivation and emotion.* New York: Macmillan. **343**

STEIN, L., see WISE and STEIN (1973).

STEINMETZ, J. L., see ROSS, AMABILE, and STEINMETZ (1977).

STEINSCHRIBER, L., see GOODENOUGH, SHAPIRO, HOLDEN, and STEINSCHRIBER (1959).

STEPHAN, C., see ARONSON, BLANEY, SIKES, STEPHAN, and SNAPP (1975).

STEPHAN, C., see ARONSON, BLANEY, and STEPHAN (1975).

STERNBERG, S. (1966) High-speed scanning in human memory. *Science,* 153:652–54. **227, 228**

STERNBERG, S. (1969) Memory-scanning: Mental processes revealed by reaction-time experiments. *American Scientist,* 57:421–57. **228**

STEUER, F. B., APPLEFIELD, J. M., and SMITH, R. (1971) Televised aggression and the interpersonal aggression of preschool children. *Journal of Experimental Child Psychology,* 11:422–47. **327**

STEVENS, B., see ROGERS and STEVENS (1967).

STEVENSON, I. (1977) Reincarnation: Field studies and theoretical issues. In Wolman, B. B. (ed.) *Handbook of parapsychology.* New York: Van Nostrand Reinhold. **184**

STEVENSON, J. H. (1976) The effect of posthypnotic dissociation on the performance of interfering tasks. *Journal of Abnormal Psychology*, 85:398–407. **180**

STILLMAN, R. C., see PETERSON and STILLMAN (1977).

STONE, A. A. (1975) *Mental health and law: A system in transition*. Rockville, Md.: National Institute of Mental Health. **475**

STONE, D. (1976) The human potential movement. In Glock, C. Y., and Bellah, R. N. (eds.) *The new religious consciousness*. Berkeley, Calif.: Univ. of California Press. **157**

STRASSMAN, H. D., THALER, M. B., and SCHEIN, E. H. (1956) A prisoner of war syndrome: Apathy as a reaction to severe stress. *American Journal of Psychiatry*, 112:998–1003. **423**

STRATTON, G. M. (1897) Vision without inversion of the retinal image. *Psychological Review*, 4:341–60. **132**

STRICKER, E. M., and WILSON, N. E. (1970) Salt-seeking behavior in rats following acute sodium deficiency. *Journal of Comparative Physiology*, 72:416–20. **292**

STRONGMAN, K. T. (1978) *The psychology of emotions* (2nd ed.). New York: Wiley. **343**

STROTHER, C. R., see SCHAIE and STROTHER (1968).

STUART, R. B., and DAVIS, B. (1972) *Slim chance in a fat world*. Champaign, Ill.: Research Press. **313, 499**

STUDDERT-KENNEDY, M., see LIBERMAN, COOPER, SHANKWEILER, and STUDDERT-KENNEDY (1967).

STUNKARD, A. (1959) Obesity and denial of hunger. *Psychosomatic Medicine*, 21:281–89. **294**

STUNKARD, A. J. (1976) *The pain of obesity*. Palo Alto, Calif.: Bull. **313**

STUNKARD, A. J., and FOX, S. (1971) The relationship of gastric motility and hunger. *Psychosomatic Medicine*, 33:123–34. **294**

STUNKARD, A., and KOCH, C. (1964) The interpretation of gastric motility. *Archives of General Psychiatry*, 11:74–89. **294**

SUGERMAN, A. A., see TARTER and SUGERMAN (1976).

SUNDBERG, N. (1977) *Assessment of persons*. Englewood Cliffs, N.J.: Prentice-Hall. **413**

SUOMI, S. J. (1977) Peers, play, and primary prevention in primates. In *Proceedings of the Third Vermont Conference on the Primary Prevention of Psychopathology: Promoting Social Competence and Coping in Children*. Hanover, N.H.: Univ. Press of New England. **79**

SUOMI, S. J., see HARLOW and SUOMI (1970).

SUPPES, P., see JAMISON, SUPPES, FLETCHER, and ATKINSON (1976).

SUPPES, P., see KRANTZ, ATKINSON, LUCE, and SUPPES (1974).

SUPPES, P., see KRANTZ, LUCE, SUPPES, and TVERSKY (1971).

SWANN, W. B., Jr., see SNYDER and SWANN (1979).

SWANN, W. S., and PITTMAN, T. S. (1975) Salience of initial ratings and attitude change in the "forbidden toy" paradigm. *Personality and Social Psychology Bulletin*, 1:493–96. **541**

SWARTZ, J. D., see HOLTZMANN, THORPE, SWARTZ, and HERRON (1961).

SWERDLOW, J., see MANKIEWICZ and SWERDLOW (1977).

SYLVESTER, D., see AGRAS, SYLVESTER, and OLIVEAU (1969).

SZASZ, T. S. (1961) *The myth of mental illness: Foundations of a theory of personal conduct*. New York: Harper and Row. **446, 500**

SZASZ, T. S. (1963) *Law, liberty, and psychiatry*. New York: Macmillan. **474**

SZASZ, T. S. (1977) *The manufacture of madness*. New York: Dell. **515**

TAKAISHI, M., see TANNER, WHITEHOUSE, and TAKAISHI (1966).

TANNENBAUM, P. H., see ABELSON, ARONSON, MCGUIRE, NEWCOMB, ROSENBERG, and TANNENBAUM (1968).

TANNER, J. M., WHITEHOUSE, R. H., and TAKAISHI, M. (1966) Standards from birth to maturity for height, weight, height velocity and weight velocity: British children 1965. *Archives of Diseases of Childhood*, 41:613–35. **89**

TANNER, O. (1976) *Stress*. New York: Time-Life Books. **439**

TARLER-BENLOLO, L. (1978) The role of relaxation in biofeedback training. *Psychological Bulletin*, 85:727–55. **204, 435**

TART, C. T. (1971) *On being stoned: A psychological study of marijuana intoxication*. Palo Alto, Calif.: Science and Behavior Books. **176, 177**

TART, C. (1972) Measuring the depth of an altered state of consciousness, with particular reference to self-report scales of hypnotic depth. In Fromm, E., and Shor, R. E. (eds.) *Hypnosis: Research developments and perspectives*. Chicago: Aldine-Atherton. **179**

TART, C. T. (ed.) (1972) *Altered states of consciousness*. New York: Doubleday. **186**

TART, C. T. (ed.) (1975) *Transpersonal psychologies*. New York: Harper and Row. **182**

TARTER, R. E., and SUGERMAN, A. A. (eds.) (1976) *Alcoholism*. Reading, Mass.: Addison-Wesley. **485**

TAVRIS, C. (1973) Who likes women's liberation and why: The case of the unliberated liberals. *Journal of Social Issues*, 29:175–94. **306**

TAVRIS, C., and OFFIR, C. (1977) *The longest war: Sex differences in perspective*. New York: Harcourt Brace Jovanovich. **306, 571**

TEITELBAUM, P., see EPSTEIN and TEITELBAUM (1962).

TEITELBAUM, P., see HOEBEL and TEITELBAUM (1962).

TEITELBAUM, P., see HOEBEL and TEITELBAUM (1966).

TEITELBAUM, P., see MCGINTY, EPSTEIN, and TEITELBAUM (1965).

TERENIUS, J., see GUNNE, LINDSTRÖM, and TERENIUS (1977).

TERKEL, J., and ROSENBLATT, J. S. (1972) Humoral factors underlying maternal behavior at parturition: Cross transfusion between freely moving rats. *Journal of Comparative and Physiological Psychology*, 80:365–71. **308**

TERMAN, L. M. (1916) *The measurement of intelligence*. Boston: Houghton Mifflin. **566**

TERMAN, L. M., and MERRILL, M. A. (1937) *Measuring intelligence*. Boston: Houghton Mifflin. **353**

TERMAN, L. M., and MERRILL, M. A. (1960) *Stanford-Binet intelligence scale: Manual for the third revision, form L-M*. Boston: Houghton Mifflin. **351**

TESSER, A., and BRODIE, M. (1971) A note on the evaluation of a "computer date." *Psychonomic Science*, 23:300. **534**

TEST, M. A., see BRYAN and TEST (1967).

THALER, M. B., see STRASSMAN, THALER, and SCHEIN (1956).

THARP, R. G., see WATSON and THARP (1977).

THIGPEN, C. H., and CLECKLEY, H. (1957) *The three faces of Eve*. New York: McGraw-Hill. **163**

THOMAS, A., and CHESS, S. (1977) *Temperament and development*. New York: Brunner/Mazel. **379**

THOMAS, D. S., see THOMAS and THOMAS (1928).

THOMAS, D. W., and MAYER, J. (1973) The search for the secret of fat. *Psychology Today*, 7:74–79. **296**

THOMAS, J., see ISAACS, THOMAS, and GOLDIAMOND (1965).

THOMAS, M. H., and DRABMAN, R. S. (1975) Toleration of real life aggression as a function of exposure to televised violence and age of subject. *Merrill-Palmer Quarterly of Behavior and Development*, 21:227–32. **328**

THOMAS, M. H., HORTON, R. W., LIPPINCOTT, E. C., and DRABMAN, R. S. (1977) Desensitization to portrayals of real-life aggression as a function of exposure to television violence. *Journal of Personality and Social Psychology*, 35:450–58. **328**

THOMAS, M. H., see DRABMAN and THOMAS (1974).

THOMAS, W. I., and THOMAS, D. S. (1928) *The child in America*. New York: Knopf. **520**

THOMPSON, C. I., and NEELY, J. E. (1970) Dissociated learning in rats produced by electroconvulsive shock. *Physiology and Behavior*, 5:783–86. **242**

THOMPSON, C. W., see HUDSPETH, MCGAUGH, and THOMPSON (1964).

THOMPSON, R. F. (1975) *Introduction to physiological psychology*. New York: Harper and Row. **61, 313**

THOMPSON, W. R. (1954) The inheritance and development of intelligence. *Proceedings of the Association for Research* on *Nervous and Mental Disease*, 33:209–31. **58**

THOMPSON, W. R., see FULLER and THOMPSON (1978).

THORNTON, J. W., and JACOBS, P. D. (1971) Learned helplessness in human subjects. *Journal of Experimental Psychology*, 87:369–72. **423**

THORPE, J. S., see HOLTZMAN, THORPE, SWARTZ, and HERRON (1961).

THURSTONE, L. L. (1938) Primary mental abilities. *Psychometric Monographs*, No. 1. Chicago: Univ. of Chicago Press. **357**

THURSTONE, L. L. (1955) *The differential growth of mental abilities.* Chapel Hill, N.C.: Psychometric Laboratory, Univ. of North Carolina. **362**

THURSTONE, L. L., and THURSTONE, T. G. (1941) Factorial studies of intelligence. *Psychometric Monographs*, No. 2. Chicago: Univ. of Chicago Press. **350**

THURSTONE, L. L., and THURSTONE, T. G. (1963) *SRA primary abilities.* Chicago: Science Research Associates. **359**

THURSTONE, T. G., see THURSTONE and THURSTONE (1941).

THURSTONE, T. G., see THURSTONE and THURSTONE (1963).

TINKLENBERG, J. R. (1972) A current view of the amphetamines. In Blachly, P. H. (ed.) *Progress in drug abuse.* Springfield, Ill.: Thomas. **174**

TINKLENBERG, J. R., see DARLEY, TINKLENBERG, ROTH, HOLLISTER, and ATKINSON (1973).

TINKLENBERG, J. R., see DAVIS, MOHS, TINKLENBERG, PFEFFERBAUM, HOLLISTER, and KOPELL (1978).

TITLEY, R. W., and VINEY, W. (1969) Expression of aggression toward the physically handicapped. *Perceptual and Motor Skills*, 29:51–56. **87**

TOLMAN, E. C. (1932) *Purposive behavior in animals and men.* New York: Appleton-Century-Crofts. **218**

TOLMAN, E. C. (1948) Cognitive maps in rats and men. *Psychological Review*, 55:189–208. **210**

TOLMAN, E. C., and HONZIK, C. H. (1930) Introduction and removal of reward, and maze performance in rats. *University of California Publications in Psychology*, 4:257–75. **211**

TORRANCE, E. P. (1966) *Torrance Tests of Creative Thinking, Verbal Forms A and B.* Princeton, N.J.: Personnel Press. **360**

TOTH, M. F., see ARKIN, TOTH, BAKER, and HASTEY (1970).

TOWNSEND, J. T. (1971) A note on the identifiability of parallel and serial processes. *Perception and Psychophysics*, 10:161–63. **227**

TULVING, E. (1974) Cue-dependent forgetting. *American Scientist*, 62:74–82. **232**

TULVING, E., and PEARLSTONE, Z. (1966) Availability versus accessibility of information in memory for words. *Journal of Verbal Learning and Verbal Behavior*, 5:381–91. **232**

TULVING, E., see WATKINS, HO, and TULVING (1976).

TURNBULL, C. M. (1961) Some observations regarding the experiences and behavior of the Ba Mbuti Pygmies. *American Journal of Psychology*, 74:304–08. **132**

TURRELL, E. S., see SAWREY, CONGER, and TURRELL (1956).

TVERSKY, A., see KAHNEMAN and TVERSKY (1973).

TVERSKY, A., see KRANTZ, LUCE, SUPPES, and TVERSKY (1971).

TYHURST, J. S. (1951) Individual reactions to community disaster. *American Journal of Psychiatry*, 10:746–69. **342**

TYLER, R. W., see EELLS, DAVIS, HAVIGHURST, HERRICK, and TYLER (1951).

ULLMAN, M., see WOLMAN, DALE, SCHMEIDLER, and ULLMAN (1977).

ULLMANN, L. P., and KRASNER, L. (1969) *A psychological approach to abnormal behavior.* Englewood Cliffs, N.J.: Prentice-Hall. **494**

ULLMANN, L. P., see KRASNER and ULLMANN (1973).

UNDERWOOD, B. J. (1957) Interference and forgetting. *Psychological Review*, 64:49–60. **236**

URANOWITZ, S. W., see SNYDER and URANOWITZ (1978).

VALINS, S., see BAUM and VALINS (1977).

VALLE, F. P. (1975) *Motivation: Theories and issues.* Monterey, Calif.: Brooks/Cole. **313**

VAN DER LOOS, H., and WOOLSEY, T. A. (1973) Somatosensory cortex: Structural alterations following early injury to sense organs. *Science*, 179:395–98. **44**

VAN ITALLIE, T. B., see HASHIM and VAN ITALLIE (1965).

VARELA, J. A. (1971) *Psychological solutions to social problems.* New York: Academic Press. **571**

VEITH, I. (1970) *Hysteria: The history of a disease.* Chicago: Univ. of Chicago Press. **515**

VERPLANCK, W. S. (1955) The control of the content of conversation: Reinforcement of statements of opinion. *Journal of Abnormal and Social Psychology*, 51:668–76. **202**

VIGORITO, J., see EIMAS, SIQUELAND, JUSCZYK, and VIGORITO (1971).

VINCENT, J. E., see CIALDINI, VINCENT, LEWIS, CATALAN, WHEELER, and DARBY (1975).

VINEY, W., see TITLEY and VINEY (1969).

VOGEL, G. W. (1975) A review of REM sleep deprivation. *Archives of General Psychiatry*, 32:749–61. **170**

VOLKOVA, V. D. (1953) On certain characteristics of conditioned reflexes to speech stimuli in children. *Fiziologicheskii Zhurnal SSSR*, 39:540–48. **196**

VON FRISCH, K. (1974) Decoding the language of the bee. *Science*, 185:663–68. **268, 269**

VONNEGUT, M. (1975) *The Eden express.* New York: Bantam. **466, 485**

WABER, D. P. (1977) Sex differences in mental abilities, hemispheric lateralization, and rate of physical growth at adoles-

cence. *Developmental Psychology*, 13:29–38. **87**

WAGNER, A. R., see RUDY and WAGNER (1975).

WALDER, L. O., see ERON, HUESMANN, LEFKOWITZ, and WALDER (1972).

WALK, R. D. (1968) Monocular compared to binocular depth perception in human infants. *Science*, 162:473–75. **147**

WALK, R. D., see GIBSON and WALK (1960).

WALKER, J. (1977) Drops of water dance on a hot skillet and the experimenter walks on hot coals. *Scientific American*, 237:126–31. **183**

WALKLEY, R. P., see WILNER, WALKLEY, and COOK (1955).

WALLACH, M. A., and KOGAN, N. (1965) *Modes of thinking in young children.* New York: Holt, Rinehart and Winston. **360**

WALSTER, E. (1965) The effect of self-esteem on romantic liking. *Journal of Experimental Social Psychology*, 1:184–97. **536**

WALSTER, E., ARONSON, V., ABRAHAMS, D., and ROTTMANN, L. (1966) Importance of physical attractiveness in dating behavior. *Journal of Personality and Social Psychology*, 4:508–16. **534**

WALSTER, E., see BERSCHEID and WALSTER (1974).

WALTERS, G. C., and GRUSEC, J. E. (1977) *Punishment.* San Francisco: Freeman. **82, 206**

WANNER, E., see MCCLELLAND, DAVIS, KALIN, and WANNER (1972).

WARD, L. M., see JONES, ROCK, SHAVER, GOETHALS, and WARD (1968).

WARWICK, D. P., see NEWCOMB, KOENIG, FLACKS, and WARWICK (1967).

WASON, P. C., and JOHNSON-LAIRD, P. N. (1972) *Psychology of reasoning: Structure and content.* London: Batsford. **256**

WATERMAN, A. S., and WATERMAN, C. K. (1974) A longitudinal study of changes in ego identity status during the freshman to the senior year in college. *Developmental Psychology*, 10:387–92. **93**

WATERMAN, C. K. (1969) The facilitating and interfering effects of cognitive dissonance on simple and complex paired associates learning tasks. *Journal of Experimental Social Psychology*, 5:31–42. **541**

WATERMAN, C. K., see WATERMAN and WATERMAN (1974).

WATERS, H. F., and MALAMUD, P. (1975) Drop that gun, Captain Video. *Newsweek*, 85:81–82. **555**

WATKINS, M. J., HO, E., and TULVING, E. (1976) Context effects in recognition memory for faces. *Journal of Verbal Learning and Verbal Behavior*, 15:505–18. **235**

WATKINS, M. J., see CRAIK and WATKINS (1973).

WATSON, D. L., and THARP, R. C. (1977) *Self-directed behavior: Self-modification for personal adjustment* (2nd ed.). Belmont, Calif.: Wadsworth. **515**

WATSON, G. (1966) *Social psychology: Is-*

sues and insights. Philadelphia: Lippincott. **555**

WATSON, J. B. (1913) Psychology as a behaviorist views it. *Psychological Review,* 20:158–77. **161**

WATSON, J. B. (1919) *Psychology from the standpoint of a behaviorist.* Philadelphia: Lippincott. **12**

WATSON, J. B. (1928) *Psychological care of infant and child.* New York: Norton. **82**

WATSON, J. B., and RAYNER, R. (1920) Conditioned emotional reactions. *Journal of Experimental Psychology,* 3:1–14. **425**

WATSON, R. I. (1978) *The great psychologists: From Aristotle to Freud.* Philadelphia: Lippincott. **25**

WATT, N. F., see WHITE and WATT (1973).

WAUGH, N. C., and NORMAN, D. A. (1965) Primary memory. *Psychological Review,* 72:89–104. **225**

WEATHERLY, D. (1964) Self-perceived rate of physical maturation and personality in late adolescence. *Child Development,* 35:1197–1210. **90**

WEBB, W. B. (1975) *Sleep the gentle tyrant.* Englewood Cliffs, N.J.: Prentice-Hall. **166, 186**

WEBB, W. B., AGNEW, J. W., Jr., and WILLIAMS, R. L. (1971) Effect on sleep of a sleep period time displacement. *Aerospace Medicine,* 42:152–55. **166**

WEBB, W. B., and CARTWRIGHT, R. D. (1978) Sleep and dreams. *Annual Review of Psychology,* 29:223–52. **186**

WEBB, W. B., and KERSEY, J. (1967) Recall of dreams and the probability of Stage 1-REM sleep. *Perceptual and Motor Skills,* 24:627–30. **170**

WECHSLER, D. (1958) *The measurement and appraisal of adult intelligence.* Baltimore: Williams and Wilkins. **357**

WEGMANN, H. M., see KLEIN, WEGMANN, and HUNT (1972).

WEIGEL, R. H., WISER, P. L., and COOK, S. W. (1975) The impact of cooperative learning experiences on cross-ethnic relations and attitudes. *Journal of Social Issues,* 31:219–44. **551**

WEIGEL, R. H., see BLANCHARD, WEIGEL, and COOK (1975).

WEINBERG, M. S., see BELL and WEINBERG (1978).

WEINBURG, R. A., see SCARR and WEINBURG (1976).

WEINER, I. B. (1976) *Clinical methods in psychology.* New York: Wiley. **413**

WEINER, I. B., see ELKIND and WEINER (1978).

WEINER, I. W. (1969) The effectiveness of a suicide prevention program. *Mental Hygiene,* 53:357–73. **511**

WEINGARTNER, H., see SITARAM, WEINGARTNER, and GILLIN (1978).

WEISMAN, S. (1966) Environmental and innate factors and educational attainment. In Meade, J. E., and Parkes, A. S. (eds.) *Genetic and environmental factors in human ability.* London: Oliver and Boyd. **366**

WEISS, B., and LATIES, V. G. (1962) Enhancement of human performance by caffeine and amphetamines. *Pharmacological Review,* 14:1–27. **174**

WEISS, J. M. (1972) Psychological factors in stress and disease. *Scientific American,* 226:106. **433**

WELCH, R. B. (1978) *Perceptual modification.* New York: Academic Press. **132**

WELCH, S., see BOOTH and WELCH (1973).

WELCH, S., see BOOTH and WELCH (1974).

WELD, H. P., see BORING, LANGFELD, and WELD (1939).

WELKER, W. L., JOHNSON, J. I., and PUBOLS, B. H. (1964) Some morphological and physiological characteristics of the somatic sensory system in raccoons. *American Zoologist,* 4:75–94. **44**

WELNER, J., see ROSENTHAL, WENDER, KETY, SCHULSINGER, WELNER, and RIEDER (1975).

WENDER, P. H., see ROSENTHAL, WENDER, KETY, SCHULSINGER, WELNER, and RIEDER (1975).

WENGER, M., and BAGCHI, B. (1961) Studies of autonomic function in practitioners of yoga in India. *Behavioral Science,* 6:312–23. **182**

WENGER, M., BAGCHI, B., and ANAND, B. (1961) Experiments in India on "voluntary" control of the heart and pulse. *Circulation,* 24:1319–25. **182**

WEST, L. J., see SIEGEL and WEST (1975).

WEST, S. G., see PARKE, BERKOWITZ, LEYENS, WEST, and SEBASTIAN (1977).

WHEELER, D., see CIALDINI, VINCENT, LEWIS, CATALAN, WHEELER, and DARBY (1975).

WHIPPLE, K., see SLOANE, STAPLES, CRISTOL, YORKSTON, and WHIPPLE (1975).

WHITE, B. J., see SHERIF, HARVEY, WHITE, HOOD, and SHERIF (1961).

WHITE, C. (1977) Unpublished doctoral dissertation. Catholic University, Washington, D.C. **294**

WHITE, P. L. (1971) *Human infants: Experience and psychological development.* Englewood Cliffs, N.J.: Prentice-Hall. **69**

WHITE, R. W., and WATT, N. F. (1973) *The abnormal personality* (4th ed.). New York: Ronald Press. **459, 485**

WHITEHOUSE, R. H., see TANNER, WHITEHOUSE, and TAKAISHI (1966).

WHITELSON, S. F. (1977) Developmental dyslexia: Two right hemispheres and none left. *Science,* 195:309–11. **50**

WHORF, B. L. (1956) Science and linguistics. In Carroll, J. B. (ed.) *Language, thought and reality: Selected writings of Benjamin Lee Whorf.* Cambridge, Mass.: M.I.T. Press. **254**

WICKELGREN, W. A. (1973) The long and short of memory. *Psychological Bulletin,* 80:425–38. **245**

WIENS, A. W., see MATARAZZO and WIENS (1972).

WIESEL, T. N., see HUBEL and WIESEL (1968).

WIGGINS, J. S. (1973) *Personality and prediction: Principles of personality assessment.* Reading, Mass.: Addison-Wesley. **413**

WIGGINS, J. S., RENNER, K. E., CLORE, G. L., and ROSE, R. J. (1976) *Principles of personality.* Reading, Mass.: Addison-Wesley. **412**

WIGGINS, J. S., see WINDER and WIGGINS (1964).

WILBUR, C. B., see LUDWIG, BRANDSMA, WILBUR, BENDFELDT, and JAMESON (1972).

WILCOXON, L. A., see KAZDIN and WILCOXON (1976).

WILKES, A. L., and KENNEDY, R. A. (1969) Relationship between pausing and retrieval latency in sentences of varying grammatical form. *Journal of Experimental Psychology,* 79:241–45. **258**

WILKINS, E. J., see DE CHARMS and WILKINS (1963).

WILLERMAN, B., see ARONSON, WILLERMAN, and FLOYD (1966).

WILLIAMS, R. L., see WEBB, AGNEW, and WILLIAMS (1971).

WILNER, D. M., WALKLEY, R. P., and COOK, S. W. (1955) *Human relations in interracial housing.* Minneapolis: Univ. of Minnesota Press. **550**

WILSON, G. T., see O'LEARY and WILSON (1975).

WILSON, N. E., see STRICKER and WILSON (1970).

WINCH, R. F. (1952) *The modern family.* New York: Holt, Rinehart and Winston. **536**

WINCH, R. F., KTSANES, T., and KTSANES, V. (1954) The theory of complementary needs in mate selection: An analytic and descriptive study. *American Sociological Review,* 29:241–49. **536**

WINDER, C. L., and WIGGINS, J. S. (1964) Social reputation and social behavior: A further validation of the peer nomination inventory. *Journal of Abnormal and Social Psychology,* 68:681–85. **399**

WINER, B. J. (1971) *Statistical principles in experimental design* (2nd ed.) New York: McGraw-Hill. **587**

WINKEL, G., see ITTELSON, PROSHANSKY, RIVLIN, and WINKEL (1974).

WINOKUR, G., see GOODWIN, SCHULSINGER, HERMANSEN, GUZE, and WINOKUR (1973).

WINSBOROUGH, H. (1965) The social consequences of high population density. *Law and Contemporary Problems,* 30:120–26. **561**

WINTER, D. G., see MCCLELLAND and WINTER (1969).

WINZENZ, D., see BOWER, CLARK, WINZENZ, and LESGOLD (1969).

WISE, C. D., and STEIN, L. (1973) Dopamine-B-hydroxlase deficits in the brains of schizophrenic patients. *Science,* 181:344–47. **469**

WISER, P. L., see WEIGEL, WISER, and COOK (1975).

WOLF, M. M., see ALLEN, HART, BUELL, HARRIS, and WOLF (1964).

WOLF, M. M., see PHILLIPS, PHILLIPS,

FIXSEN, and WOLF, 1972.

WOLFGANG, H., see EYFERTH, BRANDT, and WOLFGANG (1960).

WOLMAN, B. B., DALE, L. A., SCHMEIDLER, G. R., and ULLMAN, M. (eds.) (1977) *Handbook of parapsychology*. New York: Van Nostrand Reinhold. **153, 155, 187**

WOLPE, J. (1969) *The practice of behavior therapy*. New York: Pergamon Press. **494**

WOLPERT, E., see DEMENT and WOLPERT (1958).

WONG, R. (1976) *Motivation: A biobehavioral analysis of consummatory activities*. New York: Macmillan. **313**

WOOD, G. (1977) *Fundamentals of psychological research* (2nd ed.). Boston: Little, Brown. **25**

WOOD, L. E., see DOOB and WOOD (1972).

WOOD, P. D., see FARQUHAR, MACCOBY, WOOD, and OTHERS (1977).

WOOD, P. D., see MACCOBY, FARQUHAR, WOOD, and ALEXANDER (1977).

WOODRUFF, C. L., see KELLEY and WOODRUFF (1956).

WOODRUFF, R. A., Jr., GOODWIN, D. W., and GUZE, S. B. (1974) *Psychiatric diagnosis*. New York: Oxford Univ. Press. **454**

WOOLSEY, T. A., see VAN DER LOOS and WOOLSEY (1973).

WRIGHT, R. L. D. (1976) *Understanding statistics: An informal introduction for the behavioral sciences*. New York: Harcourt Brace Jovanovich. **587**

WRIGHTSMAN, L. S. (1977) *Social psychology* (2nd ed.). Monterey, Calif.: Brooks/Cole. **545, 561**

WYLIE, R. C. (1974) *The self-concept: A* review of methodological considerations and measuring instruments. Lincoln: Univ. of Nebraska Press. **397**

YACORZYNSKI, G., see NEYMANN and YACORZYNSKI (1942).

YALOM, I. D. (1975) *The theory and practice of group psychotherapy* (2nd ed.). New York: Basic Books. **515**

YALOM, I. D., see LIEBERMAN, YALOM, and MILES (1973).

YAMAMURA, H. I., see SNYDER, BANERJEE, YAMAMURA, and GREENBERG (1974).

YERKES, R. M., and MARGULIS, S. (1909) The method of Pavlov in animal psychology. *Psychological Bulletin*, 6:257–73. **192**

YORKSTON, N. J., see SLOANE, STAPLES, CRISTOL, YORKSTON, and WHIPPLE (1975).

YOUNG, W. G., see DEUTSCH, YOUNG, and KALOGERIS (1978).

YUSSEN, S. R., see NAHIR and YUSSEN (1977).

ZANNA, M. P., see FAZIO, ZANNA, and COOPER (1977).

ZANNA, M. P., see KIESLER, NISBETT, and ZANNA (1969).

ZEIGLER, H. P., and LEIBOWITZ, H. (1957) Apparent visual size as a function of distance for children and adults. *American Journal of Psychology*, 70:106–09. **132**

ZEISEL, H., see KALVEN and ZEISEL (1971).

ZELAGO, P. R., see KAGAN, KEARSLEY, and ZELAGO (1978).

ZIEGLER, D. J., see HJELLE and ZIEGLER (1976).

ZIKMUND, V. (1972) Physiological correlates of visual imagery. In Sheehan, P. W. (ed.) *The function and nature of imagery*. New York: Academic Press. **173**

ZILBOORG, G., and HENRY, G. W. (1941) *A history of medical psychology*. New York: Norton. **515**

ZILLMAN, D., KATCHER, A. H., and MILAVSKY, B. (1972) Excitation transfer from physical exercise to subsequent aggressive behavior. *Journal of Experimental Social Psychology*, 8:247–59. **323**

ZILLMANN, D., and SAPOLSKY, B. S. (1977) What mediates the effect of mild erotica on annoyance and hostile behavior in males? *Journal of Personality and Social Psychology*, 35:587–96. **323**

ZIMBARDO, P. G., EBBESEN, E. B., and MASLACH, C. (1977) *Influencing attitudes and changing behavior* (2nd ed.). Reading, Mass.: Addison-Wesley. **545**

ZINBERG, N. E. (ed.) (1977) *Alternate states of consciousness*. New York: Free Press. **186**

ZLUTNICK, S., and ALTMAN, I. (1972) Crowding and human behavior. In Wohlwill, J., and Carson, D. (eds.) *Environment and the social sciences*. Washington, D.C.: American Psychological Association. **561**

ZUBEK, J. P. (1969) *Sensory deprivation: Fifteen years of research*. New York: Appleton-Century-Crofts. **311**

ZUBIN, J. (1972) Discussion of symposium on newer approaches to personality assessment. *Journal of Personality Assessment*, 36:427–34. **405**

ZUCKER, S. H., and ALTMAN, R. (1973) An on-the-job-training program for adolescent trainable retardates. *Training School Bulletin*, 70:106–10. **370**

continued from page iv

Tables

3-1 Based on Sigel, I. E., "The attainment of concepts," in M. L. Hoffman and L. W. Hoffman (eds.), *Review of child development research*, vol. 1. © 1964 Russell Sage Foundation, New York. **3-2** Adapted from Kohlberg, L., "Moral education, religious education, and the public schools: A developmental view," in T. R. Sizer (ed.), *Religion and public education*. Copyright © 1967 by Houghton Mifflin Co. Reprinted by permission of the publisher and the National Conference of Christians & Jews. **3-3** From Sorensen, R. C., *Adolescent sexuality in contemporary America*. Copyright © 1972, 1973 by Robert C. Sorensen, by permission of Harry N. Abrams, Inc. **3-4** Kandel, B., and Lesser, G. S., *Youth in two worlds*. San Francisco: Jossey-Bass, Inc., 1972, p. 15. **3-6** Modified table of the "eight stages of psychosocial development" from Erikson, E. H., *Childhood and society*, 2nd ed., p. 274, is used with the permission of W. W. Norton & Co., Inc., and The Hogarth Press, Ltd. Copyright 1950, © 1963 by W. W. Norton & Co., Inc.

4-1 Adapted from Brown, R., Galanter, E., Hess, E. H., and Mandler, G., *New directions in psychology I: Models of attitude change, contemporary psychophysics, ethology: An approach toward the complete analysis of behavior, emotion.* Foreward by T. M. Newcomb. Copyright © 1962 by Holt, Rinehart & Winston, Inc. Reprinted by permission of Holt, Rinehart & Winston.

5-1 Soal, S. G., and Bateman, F., *Modern experiments in telepathy*. New Haven, Conn.: Yale University Press, 1954, p. 352.

6-1 Tart, C., *On being stoned: A psychological study of marijuana intoxication*. Palo Alto, Calif.: Science and Behavior Books, 1971, p. 245.

8-1 Tulving, E., and Pearlstone, Z., "Availability vs. accessibility of information in memory for words" from the *Journal of verbal learning and verbal behavior* 5 (1966). Reprinted by permission of Academic Press, Inc., and the authors.

9-1 From "Functions of two-word sentences in child speech, with examples from several languages," in Slobin, D. I., *Psycholinguistics*, pp. 44–45. Copyright © 1971 by Scott, Foresman & Co. Reprinted by permission. **9-2** Limber, J., "Representative examples of complex sentences taken from the records of one child between two and three years of age," in T. E. Moore (ed.), *Cognitive development and the acquisition of language*. New York: Academic Press, 1973, p. 181. Reprinted by permission of Academic Press, Inc., and the author. **9-3** Revised version of Slobin, D. I., "Developmental psycholinguistics," in W. O. Dingwall (ed.), *A survey of linguistic science*. Stamford, Conn.: Greylock Publishers, 1976, pp. 298–400. Reprinted by permission of Greylock Publishers. **9-4** Gardner, B., and Gardner, R. A., "A two-way communication with an infant chimpanzee," in A. Schrier and F. Stollnitz (eds.), *Behavior of nonhuman primates*, vol. III. New York: Academic Press, 1969. Reprinted by permission of Academic Press, Inc., and the authors.

10-1 Copyright © 1973 by Morton Hunt. This article originally appeared in *Playboy* Magazine.

12-1 Copyright © 1960 by Houghton Mifflin Co. Adapted with permission of Houghton Mifflin Co. and George G. Harrap & Co. Ltd. **12-3** Wechsler Adult Intelligence Scale. Copyright © 1955 by The Psychological Corporation. All rights reserved. **12-4** From Guilford, J. P., *The nature of human intelligence*. Copyright © 1967 by McGraw-Hill, Inc. Used with permission of McGraw-Hill Book Co. **12-5** Thurstone, L. L., and Thurstone, T. G., *Primary mental abilities*. Chicago: Science Research Associates, Inc., 1963. **12-6** Flanagan, J. C., "The definition and measurement of ingenuity," C. W. Taylor and F. Barron (eds.), *Scientific creativity: Its recognition and development*. Copyright © 1963 John Wiley & Sons, Inc. Reprinted by permission of John Wiley & Sons, Inc. Guilford, J. P., "A factor analytic study across the domains of reasoning, creativity, and evaluation I: Hypotheses and description of tests," *Reports from the psychology laboratory*. Los Angeles: University of Southern California, 1954. Used by permission of the author. Getzels, J. W., and Jackson, P. W., *Creativity and intelligence: Explorations with gifted students*. New York: John Wiley & Sons, Inc., 1962. Torrance, E. P., *Torrance tests of creative thinking*. Verbal forms A and B. Princeton, N.J.: Personnel Press, Inc., 1966. From *Modes of thinking in young children* by Michael A. Wallach and Nathan Kogan. Copyright © 1965 by Holt, Rinehart & Winston, Inc. Reprinted by permission of Holt, Rinehart & Winston, Inc. Mednick, S. A., "The associative bases of creative process," *Psychology Review* 69 (1962): 220–32. Copyright 1962 by the American Psychological Association and reproduced by permission. **12-7** Jensen, A. R., "Educability and group differences," *Journal of experimental education* (1973). Washington, D.C.: Heldref Publications.

13-1 Buss, A. H., and Plomin, R., *A temperament theory of personality development*. Copyright © 1975 John Wiley & Sons, Inc. Reprinted by permission of John Wiley & Sons, Inc. **13-2** Norman, W. T., "Toward an adequate taxonomy of personality attributes: Replicated factor structure in peer nomination personality ratings," *Journal of abnormal psychology* 66 (1963): 574–83. Copyright © 1963 by the American Psychological Association. Reprinted by permission of the American Psychological Association and the author. **13-3** From Maslow, A. H., "Self-actualization and beyond," in J. F. T. Bugental (ed.), *Challenges of humanistic psychology*. Copyright © 1967 by Abraham H. Maslow. Used with permission of McGraw-Hill Book Co. And from Maslow, A. H., *Motivation and personality*, 2nd ed. Data based on "Self-actualizing people: A study of psychological health." Copyright © 1970 by Abraham H. Maslow. Reprinted by permission of Harper & Row, Publishers, Inc. **13-5** Minnesota Multiphasic Personality Inventory. Copyright © 1943, renewed 1970 by the University of Minnesota. Published by The Psychological Corporation, New York. All rights reserved. **13-6** Block, J., *Lives through time*, 1971. Berkeley, Calif.: Bancroft Books.

14-1 From Holmes, T. H. and Rahe, R. H. "The social readjustment scale," *Journal of psychosomatic research* 11 (1967): 213–18. Copyright 1967, Pergamon Press, Ltd. Research conducted at the University of Washington School of Medicine. Reprinted with permission from Pergamon Press, Ltd. and the authors.

15-1 Marks, I., and Lader, M., "Anxiety states (anxiety neurosis): A review," *Journal of nervous and mental disease* 156 (1973): 3–18. Copyright © 1973, The Williams & Wilkins Co., Baltimore. Reprinted by permission of Williams and Wilkins Co. and the authors. **15-2** From Coleman, J. C., *Abnormal psychology and modern life*, 5th ed., p. 295. Copyright © 1976, 1972, 1964 by Scott, Foresman & Co. Reprinted by permission. **15-3** Gottesman, I. I., and Shields, J., "Genetic theorizing and schizophrenia," *British journal of psychiatry* 122 (1973): 15–30. **15-4** From Heston, L. L., "The genetics of schizophrenic and schizoid disease," *Science* 179 (January 19, 1970): 300–02. Copyright © 1970 by the American Association for the Advancement of Science. Reprinted with permission of the American Association for the Advancement of Science and the author.

16-1 Stuart, R. B., and Davis, B., *Slim chance in a fat world*. Champaign, Ill.: Research Press, 1972. Reprinted by permission of Research Press. Copyright © 1972 by Richard B. Stuart and Barbara Davis. O'Leary, K. D., and Wilson, G. T., *Behavior therapy: Application and outcome*, pp. 332–33. © 1975. Reprinted by permission of Prentice-Hall, Inc., Englewood Cliffs, N.J.

17-1 Luchins, A., "Primacy-recency in impression formation," in C. I. Hovland (ed.), *The order of presentation in persuasion*. New Haven, Conn.: Yale University Press, 1975, pp. 34–35.

18-1 Glass, D. C., and Singer, J. E., *Urban stress*. New York: Academic Press, 1972. Reprinted by permission of Academic Press, Inc., and the authors.

Figures

1-5 Darley, C. F., Tinklenberg, J. R., Roth, W. T., Hollister, L. E., and Atkinson, R. C., "Influence of marijuana on storage and retrieval processes in memory," *Memory and cognition* 1 (1973): 196–200. **1-7** Atkinson, R. C., "Teaching children to read using a computer," *American psychologist* 29 (1976): 169–78. Copyright 1976 by the American Psychological Association. Reprinted by permission. **1-8** Hilgard, E. R., "Hypnosis and experimental psychodynamics," reprinted from H. W. Brosin, *Lectures on experimental psychiatry*, by permission of the University of Pittsburgh Press. © 1961 by the University of Pittsburgh Press.

2-4 Davis, K. L., Mohs, R. C., Tinklenberg, J. R., Pfefferbaum, A., Hollister, L. E., and Kopell, B. S., "Physostignine: Improvement of long term memory processes in normal humans," *Science* 201 (July 21, 1978): 272–74, Fig. 1. Copyright 1978 by the American Association for the Advancement of Science. **2-9** Eccles, J. C., "The physiology of imagination," *Scientific American* 199 (1958):

135–46. Copyright September 1958 by Scientific American, Inc. All rights reserved. **2-11** Penfield, W., and Rasmussen, T., *The cerebral cortex of man.* New York: Macmillan, 1950. **2-13** Sperry, R. W., "Perception in the absence of neocortical commissures," in *Perception and its disorders,* Res. Publ. A.R.N.M.D., vol. 48, The Association for Research in Nervous and Mental Disease; Nebes, R. D., and Sperry, R. W., "Cerebral dominance in perception," *Neuropsychologia* 9 (1971): 247. **2-14** same as Figure 2-13. **2-15** Gazzaniga, M. S., "The bisected brain." New York: Plenum Publishing Co., 1970, p. 99. **2-19** Thompson, W. R., "The inheritance and development of intelligence," *Proceedings of the association for research in nervous and mental disease* 33 (1954): 209–31.

3-1 Frankenburg, W. K., and Dodds, J. B., "The Denver developmental screening test," *Journal of pediatrics* 71 (1967): 181–91. **3-7** Maccoby, E. E., and Feldman, S. S., "Mother-attachment and stranger-reactions in the third year of life," *Monograph of the society for research in child development* 37 (1972): 24, serial no. 146, Fig. 2. Copyright The Society for Research in Child Development. **3-8** Baumrind, D., "Child care practices anteceding three patterns of preschool behavior, *Genetic psychology monographs* 75 (1967): 43–88. **3-10** Delucia, L. A., "The toy preference test: A measure of sex-role identification," *Child development* 34 (1963): 107–17. Copyright 1964 by The Society for Research in Child Development. **3-11** Ellis, W. D. (ed.), *A source book of Gestalt psychology.* Atlantic Highlands, N.J.: Humanities Press, Inc.; London: Routledge & Kegan Paul, Ltd. **3-12** Nisbett, R. E., "Birth order and participation in dangerous sports," *Journal of personality and social psychology* 8 (1968): 351–53. Copyright 1968 by the American Psychological Association. Reprinted by permission. **3-13** Tanner, J. M., Whitehouse, R. H., and Takaishi, M., "Standards from birth to maturity for height, weight, height velocity, and weight velocity," *Archives of diseases of childhood* 41 (1966): 467. **3-14** Adaptation from *Newsweek,* May 15, 1978. **3-15** U.S. Bureau of the Census.

4-4 Hess, E. H., and Polt, J. M., "Pupil size as related to the interest value of visual stimuli," *Science* 132 (August 5, 1960): 349–50, Fig. 4-4. Copyright 1960 by the American Association for the Advancement of Science. **4-15** Cornsweet, T. N., *Stanford Research Institute Journal,* January 5, 1969. **4-16** Cornsweet, T. N., *Visual perception.* New York: Academic Press, Inc., 1970.

5-3 Zeigler, H. D., and Leibowitz, H.,"Apparent visual size as a function of distance," *American journal of psychology* 70: 106–09. Copyright 1967 by the Board of Trustees of the University of Illinois. **5-4** Rock, I., and Harris, C. S., "Vision and touch," *Scientific American* 216 (1967): 96–104. Copyright May 1967 by Scientific American, Inc. All rights reserved. **5-12** Brown, J. F., and Voth, A. C., "The path of seen movement as a function of the vector field," *American journal of psychology* 49 (1937): 543–63. Copyright 1937 by the University of Illinois Press.

6-1 Neisser, U., and Becklen, R., "Selective looking: Attending to visually-specified events," *Cognitive psychology* 7 (1975): 480–94. **6-2** Adapted

from Ludwig, A. M., Brandsma, J. M., Wilbur, C. B., Bendfeldt, F., and Jameson, D. H., "The objective study of a multiple personality," *Archives of general psychiatry* 26 (1972): 298–310. Copyright 1972 by the American Medical Association. **6-3** Same as Figure 6-2. **6-4** Klein, K. E., Wegmann, H. M., and Hunt, B. M., "Desynchronization of body temperature and performance circadian rhythm as a result of outgoing and home-going transmeridian flights," *Aerospace medicine* 43 (1972): 119–32. **6-5** Adapted from M'Guinness, J., for W. C. Dement, *Some must watch while some must sleep.* By permission of W. W. Norton & Company, Inc. Copyright © 1972, 1974, 1976 by William C. Dement. **6-7** Cartwright, R. D., *A primer on sleep and dreaming.* Reading, Mass.: Addison-Wesley Publishing Co., 1978. **6-8** Benson, H., Kotch, J. B., Crassweller, K. D., and Greenwood, M. M., "Historical and clinical considerations of the relaxation response," *American scientist* 65 (1977): 441–45. Reprinted by permission of American Scientist, Journal of Sigma Xi, The Scientific Research Society of North America. **6-9** Cooper, L. M., "Hypnotic amnesia," in E. Fromm and R. E. Shor (eds.), *Hypnosis: Research developments and perspectives.* Chicago: Aldine-Atherton, 1972. **6-10** Courtesy of the Department of Psychology, Stanford University.

7-1 Yerkes, R. M., and Morgulis, S., "Method of Pavlov in animal psychology," *Psychological bulletin* 6 (1909): 257–73. **7-4** Pavlov, I. P., *Conditioned reflexes.* Oxford, England: Clarendon Press, 1927. **7-6** Hovland, C. I., "The generalization of conditioned responses: 1. The sensory generalization of conditioned responses with varying frequencies of tone," *Journal of general psychology* 17 (1937): 125–48. **7-7** Fuhrer, M. J., and Baer, P. E., "Differential classical conditioning: Verbalization of stimulus contingencies," *Science* 150 (December 10, 1965): 1479–81. Copyright 1965 by the American Association for the Advancement of Science. **7-10** Skinner, B. F., *The behavior of organisms: An experimental analysis.* © 1938, renewed 1966. Reprinted by permission of Prentice-Hall, Inc., Englewood Cliffs, N.J. **7-14A** Clayton, K. N., "T-maze choice-learning as a joint function of the reward magnitudes of the alternatives," *Journal of comparative and physiological psychology* 58 (1964): 333–38. Copyright 1964 by the American Psychological Association. Reprinted by permission. **7-15** Adapted from Olds, J., and Olds, M., "Drives, rewards and the brain," in *New directions in psychology,* vol. 2. Copyright © 1965 by Holt, Rinehart & Winston, Inc. Adapted and reprinted by permission of Holt, Rinehart & Winston, Inc. **7-18** Tolman, E. G., and Honzik, C. H., "Introduction and removal of reward, and maze performance in rats," *University of California Press publications in psychology* 4 (1930): 17. Reprinted by permission of the University of California Press. **7-19** Neisser, U., *Cognition and reality: Principles and implications of cognitive psychology.* San Francisco: W. H. Freeman & Co. Copyright © 1976. **7-23** From Skinner, B. F., "Teaching machines," *Science* 128 (October 24, 1958): 969–77, Table 2. Reprinted by permission of the American Association for the Advancement of Science and the author.

8-1 Melton, A. W., "Implication of short-term

memory for a general theory of memory," *Journal of verbal learning and verbal behavior* 2 (1963): 1–21. **8-2** Posner, M. I., and Keele, S. W., "Decay of visual information from a single letter," *Science* 158 (October 6, 1967): 137–39. Copyright 1967 by the American Association for the Advancement of Science. **8-5** Waugh, N. C., and Norman, D. A., "Primary memory," *Psychological review* 72 (1965): 89–104. Copyright 1965 by the American Psychological Association. Reprinted by permission. **8-6** Sternberg, S., "High speed scanning in human memory," *Science* 153 (August 5, 1966): 652–54. Copyright 1966 by the American Association for the Advancement of Science. **8-7** Craik, F., "Depth of processing in recall and recognition," in S. Doric (ed.), *Attention and performance,* vol. VI. Hillsdale, N.J.: Lawrence Erlbaum Associates, 1977. **8-8** Bower, G. H., "Organizational factors in memory," *Cognitive psychology* 1 (1970): 18–41. **8-9** Watkins, M. J., Ho, E., and Tulving, E., "Context effects in recognition memory for faces," *Journal of verbal learning and verbal behavior* 15 (1976): 505–18. **8-12** Gates, A. I., "Recitation as a factor in memorizing," *Archives of psychology,* no. 40 (1917). **8-13** Atkinson, R. C., and Shiffrin, R. M., "The control of short term memory," *Scientific American* 224 (1971): 82–90. Copyright 1971 by Scientific American, Inc. All rights reserved. **8-14** Murdock, B. B., "The serial position effect in free recall," *Journal of experimental psychology* 64 (1962): 482–88. Copyright 1962 by the American Psychological Association. Reprinted by permission.

9-3 Wason, P. C., and Johnson-Laird, P.N., *Psychology of reasoning: Structure and content.* London: Batsford, 1972. **9-8** von Frisch, K., "Decoding the language of the bee," *Science* 185 (August 23, 1974): 663–68. Copyright 1974 by the American Association for the Advancement of Science. **9-10** Cooper, L. A., and Shepard, R. N., "Chronometric studies of the rotation of mental images," in W. G. Chase (ed.), *Visual information processing.* New York: Academic Press, Inc., 1973. **9-11** same as Figure 9-10.

10-3 Hoebel, B. G., and Teitelbaum, P., "Effects of force feeding and starvation on food intake and body weight of a rat with ventromedial hypothalamic lesions," *Journal of comparative and physiological psychology* 61 (1966): 189–93. Copyright 1966 by the American Psychological Association. Reprinted by permission. **10-4** Powley, T. L., and Keesey, R. E., "Body weight and the lateral hypothalamic feeding syndrome," *Journal of comparative and physiological psychology* 70 (1970): 25–36. Copyright 1970 by the American Psychological Association. Reprinted by permission. **10-5** Epstein, A. N., and Teitelbaum, J., "Of food regulation without the benefits of taste and olfactory cues," *Journal of comparative and physiological psychology* 55 (1962): 753–59. Copyright 1962 by the American Psychological Association. Reprinted by permission. **10-6** Nisbett, R. C., "Taste, deprivation and weight determinants of eating behavior," from D. C. Glass (ed.), *Neurophysiology and emotion.* New York: Rockefeller University Press and the Russell Sage Foundation, 1967. **10-7** Schachter, S., and Gross, L., "Manipulated time and eating behavior," from D. C. Glass (ed.), same as Figure 10-6.

11-1 From Maslow, A. H., *Motivation and personality.* 2nd ed. Data based on Hierarchy of Needs in "A theory of human motivation." Copyright ⓒ 1970 by Abraham H. Maslow. Reprinted by permission of Harper & Row, Publishers, Inc. 11-6 Bandura, A., *Aggression: A social learning analysis.* Englewood Cliffs, N.J.: Prentice-Hall, 1973, Fig. 2-2, from data in Bandura, Ross, and Ross, "Imitation of film-mediated aggressive models," *Journal of abnormal psychology* 66 (1963): 8. Copyright 1963 by the American Psychological Association. Reprinted by permission. 11-7 Eron, L., Huesmann, L., Lefkowitz, M., and Walder, L., "Does television violence cause aggression?" *American Psychologist* 27 (1972): 253–63. Copyright 1972 by the American Psychological Association. Reprinted by permission. 11-12 After Schachter, S., 1971, and Hohmann, G. W., 1962. Schachter, S., "The interaction of cognitive and physiological determinants of emotional state," in P. H. Leiderman and D. Shapiro (eds.), *Psychobiological approaches to human behavior.* Stanford, Calif.: Stanford University Press, 1964. p. 166. 11-13 Speisman, J. C., Lazarus, R. S., Davison, L., and Mordkoff, A. M., "Experimental reduction of stress based on ego-defense theory," *Journal of abnormal and social psychology* 68 (1964): 367–80. Copyright 1964 by the American Psychological Association. Reprinted by permission. 11-14 Hebb, D. O., "Emotional arousal and performance," from *Textbook of psychology,* 3rd ed. Philadelphia: W. B. Saunders Co., 1972, p. 199.

12-1 Thurstone, L. L., and Thurstone, T. G., "Factorial studies of intelligence," *Psychometric monographs,* no. 2. Copyright 1942 by the University of Chicago. All rights reserved. 12-3 Terman, L. M., and Merrill, M. A., *Measuring intelligence.* Boston: Houghton Mifflin Co., 1937, adaptation of Fig. 1, p. 37. 12-5 Courtesy of the United States Army Recruiting Command, Fort Sheridan, Ill. 12-6 Baldwin, B. T., and Stecher, L. I., "Mental growth curves of normal and superior children," *University of Iowa studies in child welfare* 2 (1922): no. 1. 12-7 Thurstone, L. L., *The differential growth of mental abilities.* Chapel Hill, N.C.: University of North Carolina Psychometric Laboratory, 1955. 12-8 Bayley, N., "Development of mental abilities," in P. Mussen (ed.), *Carmichael's manual of child psychology,* vol. 1. New York: John Wiley & Sons, 1970, p. 1176. 12-9 Schaie, K. W., and Strother, C. R., "A cross-sequential study of age changes in cognitive behavior," *Psychological Bulletin* 70 (1968): 677. Copyright 1968 by the American Psychological Association. Reprinted by permission. 12-10 Erlenmeyer-Kimling, L., and Jarvik, L. F., "Genetics and intelligence: A review," *Science* 142 (December 13, 1963): 1477, Fig. 1. Copyright 1963 by the American Association for the Advancement of Science. 12-11 Gottesman, I. I., "Genetic aspects of intelligent behavior," in N. Ellis (ed.), *Handbook of mental deficiency: Psychological theory and research.* New York: McGraw-Hill Book Co., 1963.

13-3 Neymann, C. A., and Yacorzynski, G. K., "Studies of introversion-extroversion and conflict of motives in the psychoses," *Journal of general psychology,* 27 (1942): 241–55. Copyright 1942 by The Journal Press. 13-4 From Cattell, R. B., *The handbook for the 16 personality factor questionnaire* (16PF). ⓒ 1970 by the Institute for Personality and Ability Testing. Reproduced by permission. 13-5 Eysenck, H. J., and Eysenck, S. B. G., *The Eysenck personality inventory.* San Diego: Educational and Industrial Testing Service and London: University of London Press, 1963. 13-6 Allen, K. E., Hart, B., Buell, J. S., Harris, F. R., and Wolf, M. M., "Effects of social reinforcement on isolate behavior of a nursery school child," *Child development* 35 (1964): 310, no. 2. Copyright 1964 by the Society for Research in Child Development. 13-7 Roche Psychiatric Service Institute, Hoffmann-La Roche Inc., Nutley, N.J. 07110. 13-10 Endler, N. S., "The role of person-by-situation interactions in personality theory," in Uzgiris and Weizmann (eds.), *The structuring of experience.* New York: Plenum Press, 1977, pp. 343–69.

14-2 Epstein, S., and Fenz, W. D., "Steepness of approach and avoidance gradients in humans as a function of experience," *Journal of experimental psychology* 70 (1965): 1–12. Copyright 1965 by the American Psychological Association. Reprinted by permission. 14-4 Masserman, J. H., *Principles of dynamic psychiatry,* 2nd ed. Philadelphia: W. B. Saunders Co., 1961, p. 38. 14-6 Weiss, J. M., "Psychological factors in stress and disease," *Scientific American* 226 (1972): 106. Copyright June 1972 by Scientific American, Inc. All rights reserved. 14-7 Schwartz, G. E., "Biofeedback, self-regulation, and the patterning of physiological processes," *American scientist* 63 (1975): 316.

15-1 From Coleman, J. C., *Abnormal psychology and modern life,* 5th ed., p. 295. Copyright ⓒ 1976, 1972, 1964 by Scott, Foresman & Co. Reprinted by permission. 15-2 Laughlin, H. P., *The neuroses.* Washington, D.C.: Butterworth Publishers, Inc., 1967, pp. 324–25. Reprinted by permission of the publisher. 15-4 Agras, S., Sylvester, D., and Oliveau, D., "The epidemiology of common fears and phobia, *Comprehensive psychiatry* 10 (1969): 151–56. Reproduced by permission of Grune & Stratton, Inc. 15-5 Abridged and adapted from Case Report 7-4 "Phobic neuroses" in Kleinmuntz, B., *Essentials of abnormal psychology.* Copyright ⓒ 1974 by Benjamin Kleinmuntz. By permission of Harper & Row, Publishers, Inc. 15-6 Laughlin, H. P., *The neuroses.* Washington, D.C.: Butterworth Publishers, Inc., 1967, pp. 673–74. Reprinted by permission of the publisher. 15-7 Abridged and adapted from Case Report 9-1 "Manic-depressive psychosis" in Kleinmuntz, B., *Essentials of abnormal psychology,* pp. 168–69. Copyright ⓒ 1974 by Benjamin Kleinmuntz. By permission of Harper & Row, Publishers, Inc. 15-8 From Jones, F. D., Mass, J. W., Dekirmenjian, H., and Fawcett, J. A., "Urinary catecholamine metabolites during behavioral changes in a patient with manic-depressive cycles," *Science* 179 (1973): 300–02. Copyright 1973 by the American Association for the Advancement of Science. 15-9 Lewinsohn, P. M., "The behavioral study and treatment of depression," in M. Hersen (ed.), *Progress in behavioral modification.* New York: Academic Press, Inc., 1975. 15-10 Abridged and adapted from Rabin, A. L., "Schizophrenia, simple form," in A. Burton and R. E. Harris (eds.), *Case histories in clinical and abnormal psychology.* Copyright ⓒ 1947 by Harper & Row, Publishers, Inc. Reprinted by permission of Harper & Row, Publishers, Inc. 15-11 Fig. 20 from Arieti, S., M.D., *Interpretation of schizophrenia,* 2nd ed. ⓒ 1974 by Silvano Arieti; ⓒ 1955 by Robert Brunner, Basic Books, Inc., New York. 15-13 From Maher, B. A., *Principles of psychopathology.* Copyright ⓒ 1966 McGraw-Hill, Inc. Used with permission of McGraw-Hill Book Co. 15-14 From *Alcohol abuse and women.* Rockville, Md.: National Institute on Alcohol Abuse and Alcoholism, 1977. 15-15 National Institute of Mental Health.

16-14 Bandura, A. L., Blanchard, E. B., and Ritter, B., "The relative efficacy of desensitization of modeling approaches to inducing behavior, affective and attitudinal changes," *Journal of personality and social psychology* 3 (1969): 173–79. Copyright 1969 by the American Psychological Association. Reprinted by permission. 16-5 Based on data from Seeman, J., "A study of the process of nondirective therapy," *Journal of consulting psychology* 13 (1949): 157–68.

17-1 Darley, J. M., and Latané, B., "Bystander intervention in emergencies: Diffusion of responsibility," *Journal of personality and social psychology* 8 (1968): 377–83. Copyright 1968 by the American Psychological Association. Reprinted by permission. 17-3 Milgram, S., "Behavioral study of obedience," *Journal of abnormal and social psychology* 67 (1963): 371–78. Copyright 1963 by the American Psychological Association. Reprinted by permission. 17-4 Festinger, L., and Carlsmith, J. M., "Cognitive consequences of forced compliance," *Journal of abnormal and social psychology* 58 (1959): 203–10. 17-5 Helmreich, R., Aronson, E., and LeFan, J., "To err is humanizing—sometimes: Effects of self-esteem, competence, and a pratfall on interpersonal attraction," *Journal of personality and social psychology* 16 (1970): 159–64. Copyright 1970 by the American Psychological Association. Reprinted by permission. 17-6 Ross, L. D., Amabile, T. M., and Steinmetz, J. L., "Social roles, social control, and biases in social-perception processes," *Journal of personality and social psychology* 35 (1977): 485–94. Copyright 1977 by the American Psychological Association. Reprinted by permission.

18-1 Maccoby, N., Farquhar, J. W., Wood, P. D., and Alexander, J., "Reducing the risk of cardiovascular disease: Effects of a community-based campaign on knowledge and behavior," *Journal of community health* 3 (1977): 100–14. 18-2 Cohen, S., Glass, D. C., and Singer, J. E., "Apartment noise, auditory discrimination, and reading ability in children," *Journal of experimental social psychology* 9 (1973): 407–22.

Pictures

Page 4 Professor José M. R. Delgado. **5** (top) Newsweek photo by Lester Sloan, copyright 1971; (bottom) Historical Pictures Service. **6** Courtesy B. F. Skinner. **8** Bettmann Archive. **9** Bonnie Freer, Photo Researchers, Inc. **14** Michael Hardy,

Woodfin Camp & Associates. **16** Alex Webb, Magnum Photos, Inc. **18** Toni Angermayer, Photo Researchers, Inc. **20** Short & Weaver Cartoons. **31** Adapted from Kuffler, S. W., and Nicholls, J. G., *From neuron to brain.* Sunderland, Mass.: Sinauer Associates, Inc., 1976. **32** United Press International. **35** The Granger Collection. **39** Richard D. Estes, Photo Researchers, Inc. **40** and **41** Martin Iger. **44** Illustration by Don MacKay. **46** Photograph by Peter Simon, Degas painting from Shostal Associates. **55** Courtesy Dr. J. H. Tjio, National Institute of Health. **56** From Winchester, A. M., *Heredity, evolution, and humankind.* St. Paul: West Publishing Co., 1976. **63** Ylla, Rapho, Photo Researchers, Inc. **64** (top) ProPix, Monkmeyer Press Photo Service; (bottom) ⓒ 1979 by Sidney Harris. **66** David Linton. **67** Jason Lauré, Woodfin Camp & Associates. **69** Hanna Schreiber, Rapho, Photo Researchers, Inc. **70** Yves de Braine, Black Star. **71** George Zimbel, Monkmeyer Press Photo Service. **72** HBJ photos. **73** HBJ photos. **76** (top and bottom) Shirley Zeiberg. **77** Harry F. Harlow, University of Wisconsin Primate Laboratory. **79** Gloria Karlson. **80** Photo from Kessen, W. (ed.), *Childhood in China.* New Haven, Conn.: Yale University Press. **81** Erich Hartmann, Magnum Photos, Inc. **84** (top) Hella Hammid, Rapho, Photo Researchers, Inc.; (bottom) Joanne Leonard, Woodfin Camp & Associates. **85** Shirley Zeiberg. **90** Elliot Erwitt, Magnum Photos, Inc. **97** Gloria Karlson. **120** (top) Photos by Lee Boltin; (bottom) Bettmann Archive, oscilloscope by Lee Boltin. **123** (top) United Press International; (bottom) M. & E. Bernheim, Woodfin Camp & Associates. **124** (top) Ralph Crane, Life Picture Service. **125** Marion Bernstein. **129** Georges Seurat, *Invitation to the Side-Show (La Parade),* The Metropolitan Museum of Art, Bequest of Stephen C. Clark. **133** (bottom) Arthur D. Little, Inc. **134** (top left) M. C. Escher, *Circle Limit IV.* Escher Foundation, Haags Gemeentemuseum, The Hague; (top right) Salvador Dali, *The Slave Market with Disappearing Bust of Voltaire.* Collection Mr. & Mrs. A. Randolph Morse, Photograph courtesy The Salvador Dali Museum, Cleveland, Ohio. **135** (bottom right) Harvey Stein. **140** *Satire on False Perspective,* engraving by L. Sullivan after Hogarth. The Metropolitan Museum of Art, Gift of Sarah Lazarus, 1891. **141** M. C. Escher, *Waterfall, 1961.* Escher Foundation, Haags Gemeentemuseum, The Hague. **145** Fritz Goro, Life Picture Service. **146** American Museum of Natural History. **147** (top and bottom) William Vandivert. **148** ⓒ 1979 by Sidney Harris. **153** ⓒ 1979 by Sidney Harris. **162** Shirley Zeiberg. **165** Shirley Zeiberg. **169** Van Bucher, Photo Researchers, Inc., Courtesy University of Florida Department of Clinical Psychology. **172** J. Daniels, Rapho, Photo Researchers, Inc. **173** Charles Gatewood, Stock, Boston. **176** Paul S. Conklin, Monkmeyer Press Photo Service. **178** Mimi Forsyth, Monkmeyer Press Photo Service. **182** Photo by Erik Arneson, Courtesy Human Nature Magazine. **183** (top) Philip Daly. **193** Bettmann Archive. **195** (top) Photo by Lewis Lipsitt,

Brown University, Courtesy Arlene H. Little; (bottom) ⓒ 1979 by Sidney Harris. **198** Will Rapport. **199** Ralph Gerbrands Co. **202** (top) Yale Joel, Life Picture Service; (bottom) Marineland of Florida. **203** (top and bottom) Yerkes Regional Primate Research Center, Emory University, Atlanta. **209** same as page 208. **210** Lilo Hess, Three Lions. **211** ⓒ 1979 by Sidney Harris. **213** Will Rapport. **214** (top) HBJ photo. **224** From Carroll, L., *Alice in Wonderland,* illustrated by M. Torrey. Copyright ⓒ 1955 by Random House, Inc. Reprinted by permission of the publisher. **230** ⓒ 1979 by Sidney Harris. **232** Bettmann Archive. **238** ⓒ 1979 by Sidney Harris. **241** ⓒ 1979 by Sidney Harris. **242** ⓒ 1979 by Sidney Harris. **246** Courtesy Dr. Elizabeth F. Loftus. **262** (top) Shirley Zeiberg; (bottom) Burk Uzzle, Magnum Photos, Inc. **267** (top) ⓒ 1979 by Sidney Harris; (bottom) B. T. Gardner. **271** (top) Ronald H. Cohn, ⓒ National Geographic Society; (bottom) ⓒ 1979 by Sidney Harris. **282** The Granger Collection. **285** Cary Wolinsky, Stock, Boston. **286** Hess, E. H., "Imprinting in animals," *Scientific American* 198 (1958): 81–90. Copyright March 1958 by Scientific American, Inc. All rights reserved. **287** (top) Thomas McAvoy, Life Picture Service; (bottom) Rene Burri, Magnum Photos, Inc. **288** Dr. Neal E. Miller. **289** David Attie. **292** Hank Morgan. **303** Harry F. Harlow, University of Wisconsin Primate Laboratory. **304** Charles Gatewood, Magnum Photos, Inc. **306** Bettye Lane. **307** Wide World. **310** (top) Harry F. Harlow, University of Wisconsin Primate Laboratory; (bottom) Suzanne Szasz. **311** A.T.&T., Bell Systems Science Services film *Gateways of the Mind.* **318** Wayne Miller, Magnum Photos, Inc. **319** Michael Weisbrot. **321** Professor José M. R. Delgado. **323** Bandura, A., *Aggression: A social learning analysis.* Engelwood Cliffs, N.J.: Prentice-Hall, 1973, p. 75, Fig. 1-1, from data in Bandura, Ross, and Ross, "Imitation of film-mediated aggressive models," *Journal of abnormal psychology* 66 (1963): 8. Copyright 1963 by the American Psychological Association. Reprinted by permission. **324** Richard D. Estes. **325** S. Nagendra, Photo Researchers, Inc. **327** Charles Gatewood. **329** Bernard Pierre Wolff, Magnum Photos, Inc. **333** (top) Management Safeguard, Inc. **340** Charles Gatewood. **349** (top) Photograph courtesy of the Psychological Corporation; (bottom) Bettmann Archive. **350** Photograph courtesy Georgette and Geraldine Binet. **354** Sepp Seitz, Woodfin Camp & Associates. **369** Rick Winsor, Woodfin Camp & Associates. **370** Drawing by Frank Ansley, Center for the Study of Instruction. **378** HBJ photos. **379** United Press International. **380** ⓒ 1979 by Sidney Harris. **389** ⓒ 1979 by Sidney Harris. **392** Bettmann Archive. **394** Photograph courtesy Dr. Carl Rogers. **395** (top and bottom) Bettmann Archive. **403** ⓒ 1979 by Sidney Harris. **405** Sepp Seitz, Woodfin Camp & Associates. **417** Charles Harbutt, Magnum Photos, Inc. **418** Gloria Karlson. **419** Jerry Irwin, Black Star. **421** Shirley Zeiberg. **422** Reprinted by permission of Medical Tribune and Joseph Farris. **423** Margaret

Bourke-White. **424** Masserman, J. H., *Principles of dynamic psychiatry,* 2nd ed. Philadelphia: W. B. Saunders Co., 1961. **425** Suzanne Szasz. **428** Cartoon by Charles Schultz, courtesy United Features Syndicate. **432** (top) Karen Gilborn; (bottom) Medical Audio Visual Department, Walter Reed Army Institute of Research. **435** Sybil Shelton, Monkmeyer Press Photo Service. **438** Jack Corn, Image, Inc. **442** Alex Webb, Magnum Photos, Inc. **444** (top) Detail from Edvard Munch, *Evening (Melancholia: On the Beach),* woodcut colored by hand. Cleveland Museum of Art, Gift of Mrs. Clive Runnells in memory of Leonard C. Hanna, Jr.; (bottom) Vincent van Gogh, *Sorrow* (1882), photograph by Soichi Sunami, The Museum of Modern Art, New York. **449** ⓒ 1979 by Sidney Harris. **459** Erika Stone, Peter Arnold, Inc. **465** (top) Bill Bridges, Globe Photos; (bottom) ⓒ 1979 by Sidney Harris. **469** Photograph courtesy Dr. Floyd Bloom, Arthur B. Davis Center for Behavioral Neurobiology. **477** Jim Anderson, Woodfin Camp & Associates. **479** Cornell Capa, Magnum Photos, Inc. **481** Wide World. **488** (all) Bettmann Archive. **489** (top and center) Jerry Cooke, Photo Researchers, Inc.; (bottom) Morley Baer and Community Psychiatric Centers, San Francisco. **491** Bettmann Archive. **492** ⓒ 1979 by Sidney Harris. **494** ⓒ 1979 by Sidney Harris. **495** Alex Webb, Magnum Photos, Inc. **496** Photos by Allan Grant. **497** J. Olin Campbell. **501** Ted Lau Photography. **503** Henri Cartier-Bresson, Magnum Photos, Inc. **504** (top) Burt Glinn, Magnum Photos, Inc.; (bottom) Linda Rogers, Woodfin Camp & Associates. **506** ⓒ 1979 by Sidney Harris. **507** ⓒ 1979 by Sidney Harris. **508** National Institute of Mental Health. **512** (top) St. Louis Post-Dispatch, Black Star; (bottom) Photograph courtesy Boys Town. **519** Edith Reichmann, Monkmeyer Press Photo Service. **522** ⓒ Beryl Goldberg, Photographer. **523** Georg Gerster, Rapho, Photo Researchers, Inc. **525** William Vandivert. **534** (top) George Gardner; (top center) Kosti Ruohomaa, Black Star; (bottom center) Charles Harbutt, Magnum Photos, Inc.; (bottom) Ivan Massar, Black Star. **550** Burk Uzzle, Magnum Photos, Inc. **551** Kenneth Karp. **554** Martin Adler Levick, Black Star. **555** ⓒ 1979 by Sidney Harris. **556** (top) CBS photo; (bottom) Elizabeth Crews, Jeroboam, Inc. **557** Courtesy Stanford Heart Disease Prevention Program. **558** Courtesy Stanford Heart Disease Prevention Program. **561** George Malave, Stock, Boston. **564** United Press International. **565** Photo by Lewis W. Hine, International Museum of Photography, George Eastman House.

Color Section

4-11 Fritz Goro, Life Magazine, 1944, Time, Inc. **4-12** Inmont Corp. Purkinjie shift courtesy Academic Press, Inc., and Inmont Corp. **4-13** American Optical Corp. Jasper Johns, *Targets,* 1967–1968. Original lithograph. Published by Universal Limited Art Editions.

ACKNOWLEDGMENTS AND COPYRIGHTS

Index

Page numbers in *italics* refer to figures and tables.

Attraction, interpersonal, 534–37, *535*
Attribution: covariant rule of, 538; discounting rule of, 538–39; process of, 537; and self-perception, 539–41; *see also* Fundamental attribution error
Audience, and media persuasion, 556
Audition, and perception, 127
Auditory area, in cerebral cortex, 44–45
Auditory canal, 120
Auditory sense, 118–19; and complex tones and noises, 119–20; and human ear, 120–22, *121*; and pitch and loudness, 119; *see also* Senses; Visual sense
Authoritarian personality, 552–53
Authority, compliance to, *525*, 525–26, *526*
Autism, and schizophrenia, 465
Autokinetic effect, 138
Autonomic nervous system, 35, 51–52, *52*; and stress, 434; underreactive, 473; *see also* Parasympathetic division
Autonomic responses, operant conditioning of, 203–04
Available memories, 158
Avoidance, and approach, 418–20, 419
Avoidance-avoidance conflict, 419
Axon, 30–31

B

Babies. *See* Infants
Backlash, 554
Backward conditioning, *194*
Bandura, Albert, and social learning theory, 316–17
Barnum effect, 404
Basal mental age, 353
Basic research, 15
Basilar membrane, 121
Bee, waggle dance of, 268, *269*
Behavior, 5; abnormal, 444–47, 483; and child-rearing practices, 81–83, *83*; cognitive processes in change of, 498, 500–01; developmental and interactive explanations of, 11; genetic influences on, 54–59, *55*, *58*; genetic studies of, 57–59, *58*; internally vs. externally controlled, 377; maladaptive, and abnormality, 442, 446; maternal, 308–09; measurement and change, 386–87, *387*; operant, 198; respondent, 198; and sex differences, 86–87; and sexual standards in adolescence, 90–91, *91*; shaping, in operant conditioning, 202; situation-specific, 407; species-specific, *286*, 286–87; and unconscious motives, 317–18; voluntary control of, and normality, 443; *see also* Social behavior
Behavior genetics, 54
Behavior therapies, 493–501; vs. insight therapies, 500
Behavioral approach, in psychology, 5–6
Behavioral sciences, 15–16
Behaviorism, 5–6; and child-rearing, 82; and rejection of consciousness, 161
Belief, vs. attitude, 527
Bias: in hypothesis testing, 256–57, *257*; political, 565–67
Binet, Alfred, and intelligence tests, *350*, 350–53, *351*, *353*
Binocular cues to depth, 139–40

Binocular disparity, 140
Biochemical factors: in depression, 461–62; in schizophrenia, 468–69, *469*
Biofeedback, 203–04; and relaxation training, 435, *435*
Biological therapies, 508–10
Bipolar cells, of eye, 109
Birth order: and achievement, 88; and participation in dangerous sports, 88, *88*
Bisexual behavior, and hormones, 301
Bitter, as taste quality, 123
Blind spot, 110, *110*
Blindness: and artificial vision, 44, *44*; and effects of restored vision, 145
Botulinus toxin, 33
Brain: central core of, 37–38; divided, 45–50, *47*; hierarchical structure of, 36–37, *37*; limbic system of, 38, *39*; study of, *40*, 40–41, *41*
Brain stem, 36
Brain stimulation, 4, 5, *5*, 40–41; and aggression, 321, *321*; and reinforcement, *205*, 205–08
Brainwashing, 523–24
Branching program, 215
Brightness, in color, 114
Brightness constancy, 130, *130*
Broca's area, and speech, 46
Bystander intervention, 520–23

C

California Psychological Inventory (CPI), 401, 406
Cannon-Bard theory of emotion, 332–35, *334*
Case histories, 19
Castration, and sexual behavior, 300
Catabolic phase, in color vision, 115
Cataplexy, 168
Catch trials, in testing for sensory thresholds, 106
Catharsis: expression of aggression as, 326–29; in psychoanalysis, 493
Cattell, Raymond, and personality traits, 382–84
Cause, and correlation, 23, 586–87
Cell body, *30*
Central core, of brain, 37–38
Central fissure, of cerebral cortex, 42
Central nervous system, 35
Central tendency, measures of, 574–75, *575*
Cerebellum, 37–38
Cerebral cortex: areas and functions of, 42–45, *43*; structure of, 42
Cerebral hemispheres, 36, 42
Cerebrum, 36
Chance distribution, 578, *578*
Chemical stimulation, in brain study, 40–41
Child(ren): and acquiring concepts, 253–56; battered, and maternal behavior, 308–09; group vs. family care of, 80–81
Child-rearing practices, 81–83, *83*
Chlorpromazine, 509
Chromatic colors, 111
Chromosomes: abnormalities in, 56–57; and genes, 54–56, *55*
Chronic noise, 560
Chronological age, vs. mental age, 350

Chunks, in short-term memory, 226
Circadian rhythm, 166, *166*
Clairvoyance, 150
Classical conditioning, 191; and acquisition, 193–94, *194*; backward conditioning in, *194*; discrimination in, 197, *197*; examples of, 194–95; and extinction, 194, *194*; generalization in, *196*, 196–97; laws of, 193–94; Pavlov's experiments in, *192*, 192–93, *193*; theoretical interpretations of, 196–97; *see also* Conditioning
Client-centered therapy, 393–94, 501–02, *502*
Clinical psychologist, 490
Clinical psychology, 13–14
Cocaine, and consciousness, 174–75
Cochlea, of ear, 121
Codeine, 173
Coding of meaning, in long-term memory, 231, *231*; *see also* Visual coding
Coefficient of correlation, *22*, 22–23, 349, 583–87
Cognition, and arousal of emotion, *338*, 338–39
Cognitive approach, in psychology, 6–7, *7*
Cognitive development: evaluation of Piaget's theory of, 74–76; operational stages in, 73–76; preoperational stage in, 72–73; sensorimotor stage in, 70–71
Cognitive dissonance: and self-perception, 541; theory of, 527–28
Cognitive evaluation, and stress, 438
Cognitive factors, in emotion, 335, *335*, 336–39, *338*
Cognitive learning, 192, 208–13; insight experiments in, 208–10, *209*, *210*; and latent learning, 210–11, *211*; theoretical issues in, 211–12; *see also* Learning
Cognitive map, 208, 210; and schemata, 212
Cognitive-physiological theory, of emotion, 336–38
Cognitive processes, in behavior change, 498, 500–01
Cognitive psychology, 6–7, 9–10
Cognitive strategies, as person variables, 387
Cognitive structure, 208; and latent learning, 210
Cold, as skin sensation, 124
Collective unconscious, 159
Color: psychological dimensions of, 113–14; *see also* Achromatic colors; Chromatic colors; Complementary colors
Color circle, 113, *113*
Color constancy, 130
Color mixture primaries, 113
Color solid, 114, *114*
Color vision, 112–16; anabolic phase in, 115; catabolic phase in, 115
Colorblindness, 56, 114, *114*
Communication: in animals, 268–69, *269*; and child behavior, 83, *83*; in preverbal children, 262; of thoughts, 257–62
Community Mental Health Centers Act (1963), 489, 510
Community resources, for mental health, 510–12
Companion-therapists, 512
Competence: and interpersonal attraction, 535; as person variable, 387; and stress, 438

Competition, vs. cooperation, 420
Complementary colors, 113
Complex cells, in visual cortex, 142, *143*
Complex sentences, and primitive sentences, 262–64, *263, 264*
Complex tones, and noise, 119–20
Compliance, *524*, 524–27, *525, 526*
Compulsions, 449
Compulsive acts, 450–51
Computer-assisted learning (CAL), *213*, 213–15, *214*; effectiveness of, 217
Computer science, 15
Computer simulation, *274*, 274–75; and General Problem Solver (GPS), 275
Concepts: acquisition of, 253–57; hierarchies of, 253, *253*; nature of, 251–52; typicality of, 252–53
Concrete operational stage, in cognitive development, 73
Conditioned reinforcement, 200–02
Conditioned response (CR), 193
Conditioned stimulus (CS), 193
Conditioning: eye-blink, in newborns, 195; in learning language, 265; *see also* Classical conditioning; Operant conditioning; Reinforcement; Semantic conditioning; Trace conditioning
Cones. *See* Rods and cones
Conflict: and ambivalence, 418–20; and compliance, 524–25, *525*; and frustration, 417–20; reference groups in, 529–30; unconscious, anxiety as, 425
Conscience, and psychopathic personality, 471
Conscious experience, 6, 389
Consciousness, 157–60; active mode of, 159–60; as agent of control, 160–62; and alcohol, 65–66; altered states of, 165; hypnotically produced changes in, 177–82; and nonconscious processes, 158; passive mode of, 159–60; and preconscious processes, 158; and psychoactive drugs, 172–77; and unconscious processes, 158–59; *see also* Divided consciousness
Consensus, and covariance, 538
Conservation, concept of, 72–73
Consistency: in covariance, 538; of personality, 406–10
Constructive memory: and inferences, 245–46, *246*; and schemata, 247–48; and stereotypes, 246–47
Context: and organization, in long-term memory, 233–35, *234, 235*; and perceptual hypothesis, 136–37, *137*; and retrieval, *235*, 239–40
Control: of behavior, 377, 443: and child behavior, 83, *83*; cognitive, of aggression, 321; consciousness as agent of, 160–62; external, delusions of, 445; for faking and response style, in personality tests, 402; of food intake, 288–92, *290*; of sleep, voluntary and involuntary, 167–68
Control group, 20, 400
Convergent thinking, 360
Conversion reactions, *453*, 453–54
Cooperation: vs. competition, 420; and prejudice, 551
Coping strategies, and anxiety, 426
Cornea, of eye, *108*, 109
Corpus callosum, 46

Correlation: and cause, 586–87; vs. experimentation, 21–23. *see also* Coefficient of correlation
Cortisol, 54
Counseling psychologist, 14, 490
Court decisions, and prejudice, 554–55
Covariance rule, of attribution, 538
Creativity: and intelligence, 359–61, *360*; visual, 273
Criminal justice, and scientific jury selection, 568–69
Crisis intervention, as community mental health resource, 511–12
Criterion, in measurement of validity, 349
Criterion group, 400
Critical ratio, 582
Crowding, psychological effects of, 560–64
Cultural influences, and sexual behavior, 304–06
Culture-fair intelligence tests, 352, *352*
Cumulative curve, 199, *199*
Curare, 33
Curiosity, and stimulus-seeking, as motives, 309–11

D

Dark adaptation, 112, *112*
Death instincts, 282, 317, 320
Decibel, 119, *119*
Defense mechanism(s), 390–91, 426–27; and adjustment, 431; denial as, 427; displacement as, 431; intellectualization as, 430; projection as, 429–30; rationalization as, 428–29; reaction formation as, 429, *429*; repression as, 427–28
Defensive strategies, and anxiety, 426
Delay of reinforcement, 204–05
Delayed conditioning, 193, *194*
Delerium tremens, 173
Delta waves, in sleep, 166
Delusions, 445; and schizophrenia, 465–66
Dendrites, 30
Denial, as defense mechanism, 427
Density, and crowding, 561
Dependence: drug, 475–82; vs. independence, 420
Dependent variable, 17
Depersonalization, delusions of, 445
Depolarization, 32
Depressants, and consciousness, 173–74
Depressed states, 457–58
Depression: and learned helplessness, 460–61; learning theories of, 459–61, *460*; neurotic, 454; and prolonged frustration, 423; as psychosis, 459–62, *460*
Deprivation: REM, in sleep, 169–70; sensory, 310–11, *311*; visual, and perception, 145–46
Depth-of-processing, and dual-memory theory, 244–45
Depth perception, *139*, 139–41, *140, 141*; in infants, 146–47, *147*
Descriptive statistics, 573–77, *574, 575, 576*
Desensitization: systematic, 494–95; and viewing violence, 328
Development: in adolescence, 88–91; in aging years, 97; and behavior, 11; cogni-

tive, 70–76; in early adulthood, 96; in early years, 67–70; factors governing, 64–67; language, 262–71; later, and early experience, 69–70; as lifelong process, 94–96, *95*; and maturation, 65–66; in middle adulthood, 96–97; of personality, 391; of self, 394–95; sequences and stages in, 66–67
Developmental psychology, 13
Deviant identity, in adolescence, 92
Diagnostic categories, in abnormal behavior, 483
Dichromat, 114
Dieting, and restrained vs. unrestrained eaters, *295*, 295–96
Difference, significance of, 21, *581*, 581–82
Difference thresholds, of senses, *105*, 105–08
Difference tone, 120
Diffusion of responsibility, and bystander intervention, 521–22, *522*
Discounting rule, of attribution, 538–39
Discrimination, 386; in classical conditioning, 197, *197*; and prejudice, 547–55
Discriminative stimulus, 198, 199
Disorders: affective, 456–59; mental, 474–75, 482–83; personality, 445, 447, 471–74; sleep, 168
Displaced aggression, 421–22
Displacement, as defense mechanism, 431
Displacement principle, in short-term memory, 225, *225*
Dispositional attribution, 537
Dissociation, 159; of competing tasks, and hypnosis, 180
Dissociative drugs, 173
Distortion, visual, 132–33
Distribution(s): differing in variation, 576; normal, 577–78, *578*; normal, curve of, 353, *353*; skewed, 575, *575*; symmetrical, 575
Divergent thinking, 360
Divided attention, 162–63, *163*
Divided brain, 45–50, *47*
Divided consciousness: and divided attention, 162–63; multiple personalities and, 163–65, *164*
Divorce: and child-rearing, 81; and marriage, in early adulthood, 96, *96*
Dizygotic (DZ) twins, 58; and schizophrenia, 466–67, *467*
DMT (dimethyltriptamine), 175
DNA (deoxyribonucleic acid), 55n, 233
DOM (dimethoxy-methyl-amphetamine), 175
Dominance, in genes, 55
Dopamine hypothesis, of schizophrenia, 468–69
Double-blind procedure, in drug studies, 509
Down's syndrome, 57, 369–70, *369*, 370n
Dreams, 168–71
Drive, 198n; aggression as, 320–21, *321*; and motivation, 282–84
Drive-reduction theory, of motivation, 283–84
Drug(s): dependence, 475–82; double-blind procedure in studies of, 509; and fetal development, 65–66; psychoactive, and consciousness, 172–77
Drug therapies, 509–10
Dual-memory theory, 242–43, *243*; and alternative viewpoints, 244–45

Hammer, of ear, 120
Hearing: of newborn, 67; receptors, *121;* theories of, 122; threshold of, 119, *119*
Height, infant's perception of, 146–47, *147*
Hello-goodbye effect, in psychotherapy, 506
Helping models, and bystander intervention, 522–23
Helplessness. *See* Learned helplessness
Hemispheres, of brain, *49,* 49–50, *50*
Heredity: and chromosomes and genes, 54–57; and Down's syndrome, 370*n;* vs. environment in development, 64; and intelligence, 363–65, 366–67; and mentally gifted, 371; and mentally subnormal, 369; in schizophrenia, 466–67, *467*
Heritability, and intelligence, 364–65
Hermaphrodites, 302, 302*n*
Heroin, and consciousness, 173–74
Hertz (Hz), 119, 119*n*
Hidden observer, in hypnosis, 180–82, *182*
Hierarchical feature analyzers, 144
Hierarchical organization, and retrieval, 234, *234*
Hierarchy: in anxiety, 494; of concepts, 253, *253;* of motives, 315–16, *316*
Hippocampus, 39; and anterograde amnesia, 242
Holtzman Inkblot Test, 405
Homeostasis, 38; and drive theory, 283–84, *284*
Homosexuality, 306–08; and abnormality, 442
Hormones, 53; and depression, 461–62; and sexual behavior, 301
Horney, Karen, 392
Hostile aggression, 319
Hostility. *See* Perceived hostility
Hue, in color, 114
Humanistic psychology, 8–9, 393–97
Humanistic therapies, 501–02
Hunger: regulatory centers of, in hypothalamus, *288,* 288–91, *290;* specific, and food intake, 292
Hunger pangs, 289
Hypercomplex cells, of visual cortex, 144
Hyperphagia, 288
Hypnosis, 177–79; and age regression, 180; controversies over, 181; dissociation of competing tasks in, 180; hidden observer in, 180–82, *182;* and posthypnotic amnesia, 178, 179, *179;* and posthypnotic suggestion, 179–80
Hypothalamus, 38; and emotion, 334; regulation of water intake by, 297–300, *299;* regulatory centers of hunger in, *288,* 288–91, *290*
Hypothesis: frustration-aggression, 320; generating, in learning language, 265–66; of linguistic relativity, 254–55; perceptual, and context, 136–37, *137*
Hypothesis testing: by adults, 256, *256;* biases in, *256,* 256–57; in learning language, 265
Hypothetical construct, drive as, 283

I

Id, 389, 390; anxiety, 390–91; 425
Ideal self, 394
Identical twins: chromosomes and genes of, 55; and twin studies, 58–59; and schizophrenia, 466–67, *467*
Identification, 524, 528–32; factors in, 85–87; and sex roles, 84–85, *85;* with siblings, 88
Identity, adolescent search for, 91–92
Ignorance. *See* Pluralistic ignorance
Illusions, visual, *135,* 135–36, *136*
Image, stabilized, 116–17, *117*
Imagery: eidetic, 224; and encoding, *238,* 238–39, *239*
Imagery code, in long-term memory, 229, 230
Imitation: of aggression, *323,* 323–24, *326;* in learning language, 265
Immigrants, and political bias, 565–66
Imprinting, *286,* 286–87
Incentive: and attitude change, 528, *528;* and motivation, 284–85
Independence, vs. dependence, 420
Independent variable, 17
Individual intelligence tests, 355
Individualization, in learning: computer-assisted learning as, *213,* 213–15, *214;* effectiveness of procedures for, 217; instructional programs for, *215,* 215*n,* 215–17, *216*
Industrial psychology, 14
Infants: attachment in, 77–79; conditioning of eye blink in, 195; motor development in, *65, 66;* perception in, 146–47; social responses of, 76–77
Inferences, and constructive memory, 245–46, *246*
Information, and bystander intervention, 523
Information feedback, and computer-assisted learning, 217
Inhibitory synapse, 33
Inner ear, 121; and equilibrium, 125
Insanity, vs. abnormality, 443
Inside density, and crowding, 561
Insight, 493; experiments, and cognitive learning, 208–10
Insight therapies, vs. behavior therapies, 500
Insomnia, 167
Instincts, 282
Institutions, and development in early years, 68–70
Instructional programs, in individualization of learning, *215,* 215–17, *216*
Instrumental aggression, 319
Insulin shock, and classical conditioning, 195
Intellectualization, as defense mechanism, 431
Intelligence: age changes in, 361; artificial, 15; and creativity, 359–61, *360;* environmental influences on, *365,* 365–68; genetic relationships and, 363–64, *364;* growth in, *362,* 362–63, *363;* heritability estimates of, 364–65; and the mentally gifted, 370–71; and the mentally subnormal, 368–70; and race, 366–67
Intelligence quotient (IQ), 353; stability of, and age, *362, 362*
Intelligence tests, 349–50; Binet's mental-age scale for measurement in, *350,* 350–53, *351;* culture-fair, 352, *352;* factor analysis in, 357, *358;* group, 355–56, *356;* heritability estimates in, 364–65; and immigration, 565–66; individual, 355; and IQ, 353, *353;* with multiple scales, 353–55; variability in, 364–65; *see also* Tests

Interaction. *See* Reciprocal interaction
Interference, in long-term memory, 235–36
Intergroup contact, and prejudice, 548–52
Intermittent processing, 163
Internalization, 524, 527–28; and identification, 531–32
Interneurons, 36
Interpersonal attraction, 534–37, *535*
Interpretation: in psychoanalysis, 492; selective, and media persuasion, 556–57
Interview, in personality assessment, 397–98
Intimacy, vs. isolation, 420
Introspection, 5
Introversion-extraversion, as continuum, 382, *382;* as dimension, in study of personality, 384, *384*
Introvert, vs. extravert, 381–82, *382*
Investigation, as motive, 310
Iris, of eye, 108
Isolation, vs. intimacy, 420
Item selection, in intelligence test, 350–51

J

James, William: on consciousness and control, 160; on tip-of-the-tongue phenomenon, *232*
James-Lange theory of emotion, 331–33, *334*
Janet, Pierre, and concept of dissociation, 159
Jet lag, 166
Jung, Carl: and concept of collective unconscious, 159; and dream theories, 169; and introverts-extraverts as personality types, 381–82
Jury selection, scientific, and criminal justice, 568–69
Just noticeable difference (j.n.d.), 105

K

Key-word method of learning foreign vocabulary, 238–39, *239*
Kibbutz, child-rearing in, 80–81
Kinesthesis, 124–25
Klinefelter's syndrome, 56
Kohlberg, Lawrence, and development of moral reasoning, 74–75
Köhler, Wolfgang, and insight, 208–09

L

Labels, and fundamental attribution error, 543
Language: innateness of, 266–67; learning, in humans, 264–66; learning, in other species, *267,* 267–71, *270;* levels of, *261,* 261–62; primitive and complex sentences in, 262–64, *263, 264*
Latency period, of personality development, 391
Latent learning, 210–11, *211*
Lateral fissure, of cerebral cortex, 42
Lateral hypothalamus, 288
Law, and mental disorders, 474–75

Neurosciences, 13

Neuroses, 442; as abnormal behavior, 444–45; anxiety reactions as, 447–48, *448;* conversion reaction as, *453,* 453–54, 453n; obsessive-compulsive reactions as, 448–51, *449, 450;* phobias as, *451,* 451–53, *452;* vs. psychoses, 456

Neurotic anxiety, 425

Neurotic depression, 454

Neurotransmitters, 33; and depression, 461; and human memory, 34, *34*

Newborns: eye-blink conditioning in, 195, *195;* sense of smell in, 67

Newton, Sir Isaac, and spectrum, 108

Nodes: of axons, 32; in hierarchical tree, 234

Noise: chronic, 560; and complex tones, 119–20; psychological effects of, 559–60, *560*

Nonconscious processes, 158

Nondirective therapy, 393–94

Nonprofessionals, as mental health therapists, 512, 512–13

Non-REM (NREM) sleep, 166, *166,* 167, *167*

Noradrenalin, 53

Norepinephrine, 53–54; and depression, 461

Normal distribution, 577–78, *578*

Normal distribution curve, 353, *353,* 578, *578*

Normality, defined, 443–44

Noun phrase, 258

Nuclei, 34–35

Nurture, vs. nature, and development, 64

O

Obesity, 292–93; and eating, in response to external cues, *293,* 293–94, *294;* and eating, in response to internal cues, 294–95; predisposition toward, 296; and restrained vs. unrestrained eaters, *295,* 295–96

Object perception, and perceptual constancy, 130–32

Object permanence, 70–71

Object size, vs. retinal size, 131, *131*

Objective anxiety, 425

Objectivity of science, 567

Observational learning, 385

Observational method(s): of personality assessment, 397–99, *398;* of research, 18, *18*

Obsession, 448–51

Obsessive-compulsive reactions, as neurosis, 448–51, *449, 450*

Occipital lobe, of cerebral hemisphere, 42, 110

Olfactory epithelium, of nose, 123

Operant behavior, 198

Operant conditioning, 191, 197–98; of autonomic responses, 203–04; of blood pressure and heart rate, 425; and conditioned reinforcement, 200–02; of human behavior, 202–03; and measures of operant strength, 199, *199;* and partial reinforcement, 200, *200;* and reinforcement schedules, 201; and shaping behavior, 202; Skinner's experiments in, *198,* 198–99

Operant strength, measures of, 199

Operating principles, in generating hypotheses, 265–66

Operational stage, in cognitive development, 73–76

Opiates, 173–74, 475–76, *476,* 480–82

Opium. *See* Opiates

Opponent-process theory of color vision, 115

Optic chiasma, 110

Optic nerve, 109

Oral stage, in personality development, 391

Ordinate, 20

Organ of Corti, of ear, *121,* 122

Organic psychoses, 456

Organization: and context, in long-term memory, 233–35, *234, 235;* and perception, 133–36; and retrieval, in memory, 240

Orienting reflex, in perception, 149–50

Osmoreceptors, and water intake, 298

Otoliths, and equilibrium, 126

Outside density, and crowding, 561

Oval window, of ear, 121

Overextension, in children's acquisition of concepts, 255–56

Overtones, 120

P

Pain: avoidance of, 309; as skin sensation, 124

Paranoid schizophrenia, 445, 447, 465

Parasympathetic division, of autonomic nervous system, 51; and emotion, 330

Parental influences: and drug dependence, 480; and psychopathic personality, 473–74

Parents: adolescents' relationship with, *93,* 93–94, *94;* nurturance by, and child behavior, 83, *83*

Parietal lobe, of cerebral hemisphere, 42

Partial reinforcement, in operant conditioning, 200, *200*

Participation, and computer-assisted learning, 217

Passive mode, in consciousness, 159–60

Patient variables, in psychotherapy, 507

Pattern recognition: and feature detectors, 142–43; and hierarchical feature analyzers, 144; and models, *142,* 142–43, *143;* and visual coding, 141–44

Patterning and grouping, in perception, 134, *135*

Pavlov, Ivan, and classical conditioning, *192,* 192–93, *193,* 200

PCP (phencyclidine), 175

Peak experiences, in self-actualization, 395

Peers: influence of, and drug dependence, 480; as models, and behavior of children, 80–81; and siblings, interaction with, 79–81

Perceived hostility, 520

Perception, 6, *7;* and adjusting to visually distorted world, 132–33; apparent motion in, 138, *138, 139;* and attention, 147–50; and audition, 127; brightness constancy in, 130, *130;* color constancy in, 130; depth, *139,* 139–40, *140, 141;* grouping and patterning in, 134, *135;* hypotheses on, 136–37; and learning, 144–47; location constancy in, 130, 132; movement, 137–39, *138, 139;* object, and perceptual constancies, 130–32; and organization, 133–36; of real motion, 138–39; of reality, and normality, 443; and restored vision, 145; and schizophrenia, 464, *464;* shape constancy

in, 130, 131, *131;* size constancy in, 130, *131,* 131–32, *132;* subliminal, 159; visual coding and pattern recognition in, 140–44; and visual deprivation, 145–46; visual illusions in, *135,* 135–36, *136*

Perceptual hypotheses: and analysis-by-synthesis, 137; and context and experience, 136–37; testing, 136

Performance: and emotional arousal, *341,* 341–42; vs. learning, 210–11; reinforcement in, 385

Performance scale, of Wechsler scales, 354

Peripheral cues, in thirst, 297

Peripheral nervous system, 35

Person, and situation, reciprocal interaction of, 385–88

Person factors, in behavior, 384

Person variables, 386–88

Personal distress, and abnormality, 442

Personal effectiveness, 500

Personality: antisocial, 471, 483; assessment, 397–406; authoritarian, 552–53; consistency of, 406–10; defined, 377; development, stages of, 391; and drug dependence, 480–81; and experience, 378–80; integrated view of, 410–11; multiple, 163–65, *164;* narcissistic, 483; phenomenological approach to, 393–97; prejudiced, 552–53; profile, *383,* 383–84; psychoanalytic approach to, 389–93; psychopathic, 471–74, *472;* shaping, and experience, 378–80; and social development, 390–97; social learning approach to, 384–89; structure of, 389–91; trait approach to, 380–84; traits, self-perception of, 540–41; types, 381–82

Personality disorders, 471–74; as abnormal behavior, 445, 447

Personality psychology, 13

Persuasion. *See* Mass media

Phallic stage, in personality development, 391

Phenomenological approach, in psychology, 8–9

Phenomenology, 8, 393, 520

Phi phenomenon, in stroboscopic motion, 138, *138, 139*

Phobias, *451,* 451–53, *452*

Phonemes, 260–61

Photoreceptors, 109, *111,* 111–12

Phrases: and propositions, extracting from sentences, 258, *258;* structure of, 259, *259*

Physical appearance, and interpersonal attraction, 534–35

Physical variable, 104, *104*

Physiological correlates, of attention, 149–50

Physiological psychology, 13

Physiology: and emotion, 330, *331;* and sexual behavior, 300–06, *303, 305;* and stress, 432–34

Physique, and personality, 381

Physostigmine, and memory, 34, *34*

Piaget, Jean, and cognitive development theory, 70–76

Pitch, and loudness, in sound, 119

Pituitary gland, 53

Place theory, of hearing, 122

Placebo, 509

Pleasure principle, 389

practicing, 241, *241;* in short-term memory, 226–28, *228*
Retrieval cue, 231–32, *232*
Retroactive interference, in long-term memory, 235
Retrograde amnesia, 241; and retrieval failure, 242
Reward, and reinforcement, 204
Right hemisphere, of cerebral cortex, 42
Rituals, compulsive, *450*
RNA (ribonucleic acid), and long-term memory, 233
ROC curve, 106–07, *107*
Rods and cones, of eye, 109
Rogers, Carl: and client-centered therapy, 501–02; and self theory, 393–95
Role confusion, in adolescence, 92–93
Role-enactment theory, in hypnosis, 181
Rorschach Test, 403, *403*

S

Salt, as taste quality, 123
Sample, in statistics, 577
Sample means, 580
Saturation, of color, 114
Scaling of data, 578–80, *579*
Scapegoat, and displaced aggression, 421–22
Scatter diagram, 583, 585, 586; of correlation, 22, *22*
Schachter, Stanley, and cognitive-physiological theory of emotion, 336–37
Schemata: and cognitive maps, 212; and constructive memory, 247–48
Schizoidia, 466–67, *467*
Schizophrenia, 59, 462–66, *463, 464;* biochemical factors in, 468–69, *469;* disturbances of thought and attention in, 463–64; genetic factors in, 466–67, *467;* psychological factors in, 469–70; research on causes of, 466–70, *467, 469;* vulnerability and stress and, 470
Scholastic Aptitude Test (SAT), 356, 371, 373
School psychology, 14
Secrecy, and testing, 372
Secure attachment, 79
Segregation, racial, and public policy, 563–64
Selective attention, 147–48
Selective breeding, 58, *58*
Selective exposure, and media persuasion, 556
Self, development of, 394–95
Self-actualization, 8, 316, 393–95, 396; and normality, 443
Self-concept, 394
Self-deception, and defense mechanisms, 426
Self-generated environments, 388
Self-perception: and attribution, 539–41; vs. cognitive dissonance, 541
Self-punishment, 498
Self-regulation, 318–19, 498, *499*
Self-regulatory systems and plans, as person variables, 388
Self-reinforcement, 498
Self theory, 393
Semantic code, in long-term memory, 229, 230

Semantic concepts, 252
Semantic conditioning, 196–97
Semicircular canals, and equilibrium, 125
Senile dementia, 34
Sense(s): absolute thresholds of, 103–04, *104;* difference thresholds of, *105,* 105–08; equilibratory, 125–26; kinesthesis as, 124–25; skin sensations as, 124; smell as, 123; taste as, 123–24; *see also* Auditory sense; Visual sense
Sensitivity groups, 503–04
Sensorimotor stage, in cognitive development, 70–71
Sensory stimulation, need for, 310–11, *311*
Sentences: extracting propositions from, *258,* 258–59; primitive and complex, 262–64, *263, 264;* and speech, 259–61; and thoughts, 257–59, *258*
Sequences and stages, in development, 66–67
Serial processing, 163
Serotonin, and depression, 461
Sex, as motive, 300–08
Sex differences, in behavior, 86–87
Sex glands, 53
Sex-linked genes, 55–56
Sex roles, 84–85; in shaping personality, 379
Sex typing, 85, *85*
Sexism, as prejudice, 549
Sexual behavior: and experience, *303,* 303–06, *305;* physiological basis of, 300–06, *303, 305*
Sexual development, in adolescence, 89–90
Sexual differentiation, and sexual behavior, 301–02
Sexual standards, and behavior, in adolescence, 90–91, *91*
Shape constancy, 130, 131, *131*
Shaping: behavior, 202, 496, *496;* personality, 378–80
Short-term memory: encoding in, 222–23, *223;* in relation to long-term memory, 241–45; retrieval in, 226–28, *228;* storage capacity in, 223–26; storage chunks in, 226; and thought, 228; *see also* Long-term memory; Memory
Siblings: identification with, 88; and peers, interaction with, 79–81
Signal detectability theory, 107
Significance of difference, 21
Similarity, and interpersonal attraction, 535–36
Simple cells, in visual cortex, 142–43
Simulation. *See* Computer simulation
Simultaneous conditioning, 193, *194*
Situation(s): interaction of traits, and, 409–10, *410;* reciprocal interaction with person and, 385–88
Situation-specific behavior, 407
Situation tests, 386–87
Situational attribution, 537
Situational determinants, of behavior, 385
Situational influences, 520
Sixteen Personality Factor Questionnaire (16 PF), 383–84, 399
Size: of object, vs. retinal image, 131, *131;* and stimulus selection, 149
Size constancy, 130, *131,* 131–32, *132*
Skewed distribution, 575, *575*
Skinner, B. F.: and operant conditioning ex-

periments, *198,* 198–99; and stimulus-response psychology, 5–6; and teaching machine, 213
Skinner box, *198,* 198–99
Sleep, 165–68; depths of, *166,* 166–67, *167;* disorders, 168; voluntary and involuntary control of, 167–68; stages of, 166–67, *167*
Sleep schedules, 165–66, *166*
Sleeptalking, 170–71
Sleepwalking, 170–71
Smell: and food intake, 291, 291–92; in newborns, 67; sense of, 123
Smiling, in infants, 76–77
Snake phobia, and modeling, 496–97, *497*
Sociability, sex differences and, 87
Social behavior: modifying, 386–87, *387;* and viewing violence, *327,* 327–29
Social development: and attachment, 77–79, *78;* affect of child-rearing practices on, 81–83; and infant social responses, 76–77; and interaction with siblings and peers, 79–81; and personality, 76–83
Social environment, 519
Social influence, 523–24; compliance as, *524,* 524–27, *525, 526;* identification as, 528–32; internalization as, 527–28
Social interaction, and fundamental attribution error, 542–44
Social learning theory, 316; and model of abnormality, 446; of motivation, 318–19; of personality, 384–89
Social norms: abnormality as deviation from, 442; and prejudice, 553–54
Social perception: and first impressions, 532–34, *533;* and interpersonal attraction, 534–37, *535*
Social psychology, 13; perspective of, 519–23
Social responses, in infants, 76–77
Social sciences, 15–16
Social supports, and stress, 438
Socialization, and identification, 84
Sociocultural model, of abnormality, 446
Somatic system, 35
Somatosensory area, of cerebral cortex, 43–44, *43*
Sorting tree, and pattern recognition, 143, *143*
Sound, pitch and loudness of, 119
Sound signal, 118
Sound wave, *118,* 118–19
Sour, as taste quality, 123
Spearman, Charles, and intelligence factor, 357
Species-specific behavior, *286,* 286–87
Specific hunger, and food intake, 292
Specificity, vs. consistency, of personality, 407–09
Spectrum, 108; and color vision, *112,* 112n, 112–13
Speech, and sentences, 259–61
Spinal cord, *35,* 35–36, *36*
Split-brain, 45–50; experiments, 47–49, *48;* and major and minor hemispheres, *49,* 49–50, *50*
Spontaneous remission, 507
Sports, dangerous, birth order and participation in, 88, *88*
Stability-instability, as dimension, in study of personality, 384, *384*

Stabilized images, 116–17, *117*
Stages and sequences, in development, 66–67
Standard deviation, 353, *576*, 576–77
Standard error: of difference between two means, 582; of mean, 580–81
Standard score, 353, 579, *579*
Stanford-Binet Intelligence Scale, 351, *351, 353, 353*; vs. WAIS, 355
Stanine, 579*n*
State-dependent learning, 173
Statistical frequency, and abnormality, 442
Statistical inference, 577–78
Statistical norms, abnormality as deviation from, 441–42
Statistical significance, 581, *581*
Statistical statements, 21
Statistics: descriptive, 573–77, *574, 575, 576*; frequency distribution in, 574, *574*; significance of difference in, *581*, 581–82
Status, and prejudice, 550
Stereoscopic vision, 139
Stereotype, 397; and constructive memory, 246–47; and prejudgment, 548
Steroids, 54
Stimulants, and consciousness, 174–75
Stimulation: chemical and electrical, in brain study, 40–41; and development, 68–69
Stimulus, intensity of, and difference threshold, 105
Stimulus-response (S-R) psychology, 5–6
Stimulus-seeking, and curiosity, 309–11
Stimulus selection, determiners of, 148–49
Stirrup, of ear, 121
Storage: and retrieval, in long-term memory, 231–32, *232*; in short-term memory, 223–26; as stage in memory, 221
STP. *See* DOM
Strange situation, and mother attachment, *78*, 78–79
Stress, 431; accumulated, and depression, 463; factors influencing severity of, 434–38; measuring, *436*, 436–37, *437*; psysiological effects of, *432*, 432–34, *433*; and schizophrenia, 470
Stroboscopic motion, 138, *138, 139*
Subjective experience, 8, 393
Subjective-outcome values, as person variables, 388
Subliminal perception, 159
Subnormality, 368–70
Subtractive mixture, of pigments, 113
Suggestibility, and hypnosis, 178
Sullivan, Harry Stack, 392
Superego, 390
Suppression, vs. repression, 427
Supreme Court, and racial segregation, 563–64
Surgical ablation, in brain study, 40
Survey method, of research, 19
Sweet, as taste quality, 123
Symbols. *See* Arbitrary symbols
Symmetrical distribution, 575
Sympathetic chains, of spinal column, 51
Sympathetic division, of autonomic nervous system, 51; and emotion, 330
Symptom substitution, 500
Synapse, 30
Synaptic junction, *33*
Synaptic transmission, 32–34
Syndrome, 483

Syntactic analysis, 259, *259*
Systematic desensitization, 494–95
Systematic reinforcement, 495–96

T

Taste: and food intake, *291*, 291–92; and obesity, 293, *293*; sense of, 123–24
Taste aversion studies, in classical conditioning, 195
Taste buds, 123, *123*
Teaching machine, 213, *213*
Telepathy: and ESP, 150; precognition and, 152
Temperament, early differences of, *378*, 378–79
Temporal lobe, of cerebral hemisphere, 42
Terman, Lewis: and gifted children, 370–71; and Stanford-Binet test, 351, 353
Terminal buttons, 30
Test(s): ability, 371–74; achievement, 347, 348, 371–72; aptitude, 347, 348, 371–72; creativity, 359–61, *360*; Minnesota Multiphasic Personality Inventory, 399–401, *400, 401*; and primary abilities, 357–59, *359*; projective, 403–06; reliability and validity of, 348–49; Rorschach, 403; situation, 386–87; Thematic Apperception, 403–05, *404*; Wechsler scales as, *354*, 354–55, *355*; *see also* Intelligence tests
Test method, of research, 19
Test of Primary Mental Abilities, 357
Testing: hypothesis, 136; public concerns about, 372–74
Testosterone, 300
T-groups, 503–04
Thalamus, 38; and emotion, 333
Thematic Apperception Test (TAT), 403–05, *404*
Theoretical constructs, defense mechanisms as, 427
Therapist variables, in psychotherapy, 507
Therapy: behavior, 493–501; biological, 508–10; client-centered, 393–94, 501–02, *502*; drug, 509–10; electroshock, 508; family, 504; group, 502–04; humanistic, 501–02; *see also* Psychotherapy
Thermoreceptors, 289
Thirst: and hypothalamic regulation of water intake, 297–300, *299*; peripheral cues to, 297
Thought: convergent and divergent, 360; obsessive, *450*; and schizophrenia, 463–64; and sentences, 257–59, *258*; and short-term memory, 228
Threshold model, of creativity, 361
Thurstone Test of Primary Abilities, 357–59, *359*
Thyroid, 53
Timbre, of musical tone, 120
Time: and classical conditioning, 193–94, *194*; and eating behavior, 293–94, *294*
Tip-of-the-tongue phenomenon, 158, *232*
T-maze, 204, *204*
Tolman, E. C., and cognitive map, 212
Tones, *See* Complex tones
Touch, sensations of, 124
Trace conditioning, 193, *194*
Trait(s): and consistency of personality,

408–09; and situations, interactions of, 409–10, *410*; vs. types, 382–84
Trait approach, to personality, 380–84
Tranquilizers, 33–34, 509
Transcendental Meditation, 171–72
Transference, in psychoanalysis, 492–93
Transmission: of neural impulses, 31–32; synaptic, 32–34
Transsexualism, 307–08; defined, 307
Trial, in classical conditioning, 193
Trichromat, 114
True mean, 580
Turner's syndrome, 56
Twins: and heritability, 364–65; personality similarities of, 378, *378*; and schizophrenia, 466–67, *467*; studies of, 58–59
Types, vs. traits, 382–84
Typicality, of concepts, 252–53

U

Ulcers, and stress, *432*, 432–34, *433*
Unconditioned response (UR), 193
Unconditioned stimulus (US), 193
Unconscious, 7, 158–59, 389; collective, 159
Unconscious conflict, anxiety as, 425
Unconscious motivation, 317–18
Underreactive autonomic nervous system, 473

V

Validity, of tests, 349
Validity coefficient, 349
Variable(s), 16; confounding, in psychotherapy, 507; dependent vs. independent, 17; influencing reinforcement, 204–05; physical, 104, *104*
Variable interval reinforcement schedule, 201
Variable ratio reinforcement schedule, 201
Variation, measures of, 575–77, *576*
Ventromedial hypothalamus, 288
Verb phrase, 258
Verbal ability, and sex differences, 86
Verbal scale, of WAIS, 354
Vestibular sacs, and equilibrium, 125–26
Veterans Administration, 489
Vicarious learning, 318, 385
Violence: viewing of, 326–29, *327*; and XYY males, 57
Vision: artificial, 44, *44*; distorted, adjusting to, 132–33; illusions in, *135*, 135–36, *136*; and perception, 129; restored, and perception, 145
Visual cliff, and perception in infants, 146–47, *147*
Visual code, fading of, in short-term memory, 223, *223*
Visual coding: and feature detectors, 142–43; and hierarchical feature analyzers, 144; and pattern recognition, 141–44
Visual cortex, 44, *44*
Visual deprivation, and perception, 145–46
Visual sense, 108–09; and color vision, 112–16; and human eye, *108, 109*, 109–11, *110*; and neural processing of visual information, 116–17, *117*; and rods and cones, *111*, 111–12
Visual-spatial ability, and sex differences, 86–87